THE OXFORD HA

ETHICS

CW00919057

THE OXFORD HANDBOOK OF

ETHICS OF AI

Edited by

MARKUS D. DUBBER, FRANK PASQUALE,

and

SUNIT DAS

OXFORD
UNIVERSITY PRESS

OXFORD
UNIVERSITY PRESS

Oxford University Press is a department of the University of Oxford. It furthers
the University's objective of excellence in research, scholarship, and education
by publishing worldwide. Oxford is a registered trade mark of Oxford University
Press in the UK and certain other countries.

Published in the United States of America by Oxford University Press
198 Madison Avenue, New York, NY 10016, United States of America.

© Oxford University Press 2020

First issued as an Oxford University Press paperback, 2021

Library of Congress Control Number: 2020938746

ISBN 978-0-19-006739-7 (hardback) | ISBN 978-0-19-760144-0 (paperback)

Paperback printed by Marquis, Canada

Contents

PART IV. PERSPECTIVES
AND APPROACHES

PART V. CASES AND APPLICATIONS

EDITORS' PREFACE

THE idea for this handbook arose in late 2017, with the working title *Handbook of Ethics of AI in Context*. By the time solicitations went out to potential contributors in the summer of 2018, its title had been streamlined to *Handbook of Ethics of AI*. Its essentially contextual approach, however, remained unchanged: it is a broadly conceived and framed interdisciplinary and international collection, designed to capture and shape much-needed reflection on normative frameworks for the production, application, and use of artificial intelligence in diverse spheres of individual, commercial, social, and public life.

The approach to the ethics of AI that runs through this handbook is contextual in four senses:

- it locates ethical analysis of artificial intelligence in the context of other modes of normative analysis, including legal, regulatory, philosophical, and policy approaches,
- it interrogates artificial intelligence within the context of related modes of technological innovation, including machine learning, Big Data, and robotics,
- it is interdisciplinary from the ground up, broadening the conversation about the ethics of artificial intelligence beyond computer science and related fields to include other fields of scholarly endeavor, including the social sciences, humanities, and the professions (law, medicine, engineering, etc.), and
- it invites critical analysis of all aspects of—and participants in—the wide and continuously expanding artificial intelligence complex, from production to commercialization to consumption, from technical experts to venture capitalists to self-regulating professionals to government officials to the general public.

Ideally, handbooks combine stock-taking and genre-defining. Devoted to a field of inquiry as new and quickly evolving as ethics of AI, this handbook falls closer to the forward-facing than to the literature-reviewing end of the spectrum. Mapping the existing discourse is important, also as the beginning of a crucial attempt to place current developments in historical context. At the same time, we recognized the need to leave room for flexibility as the contributors to this volume broke new ground, pursuing fresh approaches and taking on novel subjects. In the same spirit, this handbook operates with an inclusive and flexible conception of "artificial intelligence" that ranges from exploring normative constraints on specific applications of machine learning algorithms to reflecting on the (potential) status of AI as a form of consciousness with attendant rights and duties and, more generally still, to investigating the basic conceptual terms and frameworks necessary to understand tasks requiring intelligence, whether "human" or "AI."

Each chapter in this handbook aims to provide an original, critical, and accessible account of the current state of debate in its domain that will help to shape scholarly research and public discourse. We have welcomed forward-looking and ideas-driven contributions, to serve as catalysts for guiding the debate on the ethics of AI in the months and years to come. The chapters are intended to function, individually and collectively, as lively, freestanding essays targeted at an international and interdisciplinary audience of scholars and interested laypersons. Each chapter also provides, at the end, a bibliography of about ten titles for readers who would like to read more deeply into the topic.

The handbook's inclusive and flexible approach to its subject matter is reflected in its roster of contributors, which includes authors from several countries and continents, ranging from emergent to established authorities and representing a wide variety of methodological approaches, areas of expertise, and research agendas. The handbook's content is similarly ambitious and diverse in scope and substance, covering a broad range of topics and perspectives. The handbook consists of five parts: I. Introduction and Overview, II. Frameworks and Modes, III. Concepts and Issues, IV. Perspectives and Approaches, and V. Cases and Applications.

Part I provides a general introduction to the subject (and field) of "artificial intelligence" within the context of research and discourse in related fields of technological innovation, laying an accessible yet nuanced foundation for the exploration of various normative frameworks for the critical analysis of AI. It also locates the "ethics" of artificial intelligence in relation to cognate fields of ethical inquiry (e.g., data ethics, information ethics, robot ethics, internet ethics), considering ways of conceptualizing it and its challenges (e.g., as a sui generis inquiry, as a form of applied ethics, or as traditional ethics in AI terms), distinguishing aspects within it (to the extent a taxonomy of this sort proves illuminating), and capturing some key substantive and formal features of the discourse.

Part II places the subject of this handbook, the ethics of AI, within the context of alternative frameworks for normative assessment and governance, including various institutional and procedural modes of implementation and dissemination. Questions raised in this part include: "What distinguishes the ethics of AI from other normative frameworks and techniques, e.g., law, policy, regulation, governance?"; "How can ethics ground and inform legal constraints on (and regulatory guidance for) AI?"; "How does an ethics of AI navigate the possible tension between private commercial norms, on the one hand, and public norms, on the other?"; "How should ethical norms be generated and formulated, disseminated and implemented, and by whom?"; and "What is the role of the (self-)regulation of professional ethics, insofar as this enterprise is regarded as defining and enforcing a notion of good, sound, or 'professional' judgment?"

Part III tackles central concepts and issues that may serve as points of departure for reflecting on the ethical dimensions and challenges of artificial intelligence in general, cutting across technologies and applications, and in many cases across disciplines as well, ranging from the sources and types of bias in the production and application of AI research, to concerns about privacy in the collection and use of data, the potential effect of AI-driven "disruption" on labor markets and the future of work and on socioeconomic life more broadly, the distinction between "prediction" and "judgment," and the ethical status of AI-driven machines and its possible implications for human-machine interaction.

While a wide spectrum of disciplinary, national, and supranational perspectives is reflected throughout the handbook, Part IV homes in on a selection of methodological approaches and domestic or regional contexts. Early chapters in this part capture the distinctive texture and salience of actual (or potential) discourse around ethics of AI in a range of disciplinary contexts, in an effort to illustrate—and to expand—the disciplinary scope of the scholarly and public debate about ethics of AI. The remaining chapters highlight the variety of discourses around ethics of AI in selected national and regional contexts, again to broaden and to diversify the dialogue about the normative dimensions of artificial intelligence as a global phenomenon, this time geographically and culturally.

Part V concludes the handbook by sharpening its focus to selected applications of artificial intelligence, without, however, treating them as sui generis, but instead in a way that fits into the handbook's overall ambition: to expand the conversation about the ethics of artificial intelligence from the specific to the general, from the superficial to the fundamental, and from the parochial to the contextual. Contributors here reflect on the ethical aspects of the design, dissemination, and use of AI-driven devices and tools today and in the future, along a broad spectrum of applications, in health care, law, immigration, education, transportation, the military, the workplace, smart cities, and beyond.

We are deeply grateful to the international and interdisciplinary group of scholars who signed on to this large-scale long-term project and somehow made the time to see it through to completion, among the flurry of activities and opportunities that mark the start of a new and momentous endeavor like the scholarly and public scrutiny of the ethics of artificial intelligence.

Markus D. Dubber, Frank Pasquale, and Sunit Das

August 2019

LIST OF CONTRIBUTORS

Ifeoma Ajunwa, Associate Professor, Labor Relations, Law, and History Department, Cornell University ILR School; Associate Faculty Member, Cornell Law School; Faculty Associate, Berkman Klein Center for Internet & Society at Harvard University

Chinmayi Arun, Resident Fellow, Information Society Project at Yale Law School; Affiliate of the Berkman Klein Center for Internet & Society at Harvard University; Assistant Professor of Law, National Law University, Delhi

Benjamin R. Baer, Department of Statistics and Data Science, Cornell University

Chelsea Barabas, Massachusetts Institute of Technology

John Basl, Department of Philosophy and Religion, Northeastern University

Alessandro Blasimme, Health Ethics and Policy Lab, Department of Health Sciences and Technology, Swiss Federal Institute of Technology—ETH Zurich

Paula Boddington, New College of the Humanities, London

Joseph Bowen, Department of Philosophy, University of St Andrews; Department of Philosophy, University of Stirling

Kiel Brennan-Marquez, University of Connecticut School of Law

Joanna J. Bryson, Professor of Ethics and Technology, Hertie School for Governance

Ron Chrisley, Visiting Scholar, Institute for Human-Centered Artificial Intelligence; Visiting Professor, Symbolic Systems Program, Stanford University

John Danaher, Senior Lecturer, School of Law, National University of Ireland, Galway

Nicholas Diakopoulos, Northwestern University School of Communication

Virginia Dignum, Department of Computing Science, Umeå University

Judith Donath, Berkman Klein Center for Internet & Society at Harvard University

Elizabeth Edenberg, Assistant Professor, Baruch College, The City University of New York

Danit Gal, Technology Advisor to the UN Secretary General High-Level Panel on Digital Cooperation

Jai Galliott, Director, Values in Defence & Security Technology Group, University of New South Wales at Australian Defence Force Academy; Non-Resident Fellow,

Modern War Institute at the United States Military Academy, West Point; Visiting Fellow, Centre for Technology and Global Affairs, University of Oxford

Jean-Gabriel Ganascia, Professor of Computer Science, Sorbonne University; LIP6 Laboratory—ACASA Group Leader

Urs Gasser, Executive Director, Berkman Klein Center for Internet & Society at Harvard University; Professor of Practice, Harvard Law School

Timnit Gebru, Senior Research Scientist, Google; Co-founder and President, Black in AI

Daniel E. Gilbert, Department of Statistics and Data Science, Cornell University

Ellen P. Goodman, Professor, Rutgers Law School; Co-director, Rutgers Institute for Information Policy & Law

David J. Gunkel, Department of Communication, Northern Illinois University

Andrew Howes, Professor of Computer Science, University of Birmingham

Meg Leta Jones, Communication, Culture & Technology Department, Georgetown University

Mark Kingwell, Professor of Philosophy, University of Toronto

Anton Korinek, Department of Economics and Darden School of Business, University of Virginia

Joshua A. Kroll, Department of Computer Sciences, Naval Postgraduate School

Benjamin Kuipers, Professor of Computer Science and Engineering, University of Michigan

Matthew Le Bui, Annenberg School for Communication and Journalism, University of Southern California

Karen Levy, Department of Information Science, Cornell University

Shannon Mattern, Department of Anthropology, The New School for Social Research, New York

Jason Millar, Assistant Professor, School of Electrical Engineering and Computer Science, and Canada Research Chair in the Ethical Engineering of Robotics and AI, University of Ottawa

Petra Molnar, University of Toronto Faculty of Law

Pegah Moradi, Department of Information Science, Cornell University

Deirdre K. Mulligan, Associate Professor, School of Information; Faculty Director, Berkeley Center for Law and Technology, University of California, Berkeley

Helen Nissenbaum, Professor, Information Science, Cornell Tech

Safiya Umoja Noble, Departments of Information Studies and African American Studies, University of California, Los Angeles

Ganna Pogrebna, Professor of Behavioural Economics and Data Science, University of Birmingham; Lead for Behavioural Data Science, Alan Turing Institute

Thomas M. Powers, Department of Philosophy, University of Delaware

Andrea Renda, Senior Research Fellow and Head of Global Governance, Regulation, Innovation and the Digital Economy, CEPS, Brussels; Professor of Digital Innovation, College of Europe, Bruges; Member of the EU High Level Expert Group on Artificial Intelligence

Kathleen Richardson, Professor of Ethics and Culture of Robots and AI, School of Computer Science and Informatics, De Montfort University

Nagla Rizk, Professor of Economics, The American University in Cairo

Rachel Schlund, Department of Organizational Behavior, Cornell University

Carolyn Schmitt, Berkman Klein Center for Internet & Society at Harvard University

Susan Schneider, Associate Professor of Philosophy and Director of the AI, Mind, and Society Group, University of Connecticut

Jason Scholz, Chief Executive Officer, Trusted Autonomous Systems Defence Cooperative Research Centre, Australia

Avery Slater, Assistant Professor of English, University of Toronto

Tom Slee, SAP Canada

Bryant Walker Smith, Associate Professor of Law and (by courtesy) Engineering at the University of South Carolina; Affiliate Scholar at the Center for Internet and Society at Stanford Law School; Co-director of the Program on Law and Mobility at the University of Michigan Law School; http://newlypossible.org

Norman W. Spaulding, Sweitzer Professor of Law, Stanford University

Harry Surden, Associate Professor of Law, University of Colorado

Cody Turner, AI, Mind, and Society Group, University of Connecticut

Effy Vayena, Health Ethics and Policy Lab, Department of Health Sciences and Technology, Swiss Federal Institute of Technology—ETH Zurich

Martin T. Wells, Department of Statistics and Data Science, Cornell University

Michael Wheeler, Professor of Philosophy, University of Stirling

Karen Yeung, Interdisciplinary Professorial Fellow in Law, Ethics, and Informatics at Birmingham Law School and the School of Computer Science at the University of Birmingham

Elana Zeide, PULSE Fellow in Artificial Intelligence, Law, and Policy at the University of California, Los Angeles School of Law

PART I

INTRODUCTION AND OVERVIEW

CHAPTER 1

....

THE ARTIFICIAL INTELLIGENCE OF THE ETHICS OF ARTIFICIAL INTELLIGENCE

An Introductory Overview for
Law and Regulation

....

JOANNA J. BRYSON

FOR many decades, artificial intelligence (AI) has been a schizophrenic field pursuing two different goals: an improved understanding of computer science through the use of the psychological sciences; and an improved understanding of the psychological sciences through the use of computer science. Although apparently orthogonal, these goals have been seen as complementary since progress on one often informs or even advances the other. Indeed, we have found two factors that have proven to unify the two pursuits. First, the costs of computation and indeed what is actually computable are facts of nature that constrain both natural and artificial intelligence. Second, given the constraints of computability and the costs of computation, greater intelligence relies on the reuse of prior computation. Therefore, to the extent that both natural and artificial intelligence are able to reuse the findings of prior computation, both pursuits can be advanced at once.

Neither of the dual pursuits of AI entirely readied researchers for the now glaringly evident ethical importance of the field. Intelligence is a key component of nearly every human social endeavor, and our social endeavors constitute most activities for which we have explicit, conscious awareness. Social endeavors are also the purview of law and, more generally, of politics and diplomacy. In short, everything humans deliberately do has been altered by the digital revolution, as well as much of what we do unthinkingly.

Often this alteration is in terms of how we can do what we do—for example, how we check the spelling of a document; book travel; recall when we last contacted a particular employee, client, or politician; plan our budgets; influence voters from other countries; decide what movie to watch; earn money from performing artistically; discover sexual or life partners; and so on. But what makes the impact ubiquitous is that everything we have done, or chosen not to do, is at least in theory knowable. This awareness fundamentally alters our society because it alters not only how we can act directly, but also how and how well we can know and regulate ourselves and each other.

A great deal has been written about AI ethics recently. But unfortunately many of these discussions have not focused either on the science of what is computable or on the social science of how ready access to more information and more (but mechanical) computational power has altered human lives and behavior. Rather, a great deal of these studies focus on AI as a thought experiment or "intuition pump" through which we can better understand the human condition or the nature of ethical obligation. In this *Handbook*, the focus is on the law—the day-to-day means by which we regulate our societies and defend our liberties. This chapter sets out the context for the volume by introducing AI as an applied discipline of science and engineering.

INTELLIGENCE IS AN ORDINARY PROCESS

For the purpose of this introduction, I will use an exceedingly well-established definition of intelligence, dating to a seminal monograph on animal behavior.[1] *Intelligence* is the capacity to do the right thing at the right time. It is the ability to respond to the opportunities and challenges presented by a context. This simple definition is important because it demystifies intelligence, and through it AI. It clarifies both intelligence's limits and our own social responsibilities in two ways.

First, note that intelligence is a process, one that operates at a place and in a moment. It is a special case of *computation*, which is the physical transformation of information.[2] Information is not an abstraction.[3] It is physically manifested in energy (light or sound), or materials. Computation and intelligence are therefore also not abstractions. They require time, space, and energy. This is why—when you get down to it—no one is really ever that smart. It is physically impossible to think of everything. We can make trade-offs: we can, for example, double the number of computers we use and cut the time of a computation nearly in half. The time is never cut quite in half, because there is always an

---

[1] George John Romanes, *Animal Intelligence* (London: D. Appleton, 1882).

[2] Michael Sipser, *Introduction to the Theory of Computation*, 2nd ed. (Boston: PWS, Thompson, 2005).

[3] Claude Elwood Shannon, "A Mathematical Theory of Communication," in *Bell System Tech. J.* 27.3 (1948): 379–423.

extra cost of splitting the task and recombining the outcomes of the processing.[4] But this near halving requires fully double the space for our two computers, and double the energy in the moment of computation. The sum of the total energy used is again slightly more than the same as for the original single computer, due again to extra energy needed for the overheads. There is no evidence that quantum computing will change this cost equation fundamentally: it should save not only on time but also on space, however the energy costs are poorly understood and to date look fiendishly high.

Second, note that the difference between *intelligence* and *artificial intelligence* is only a qualifier. *Artificial* means that something has been made through a human process. This means by default that humans are responsible for it. The artifact actually even more interesting than AI here is a concept: *responsible*. Other animals can be trained to intentionally limit where they place (for example) even the fairly unintentional byproducts of their digestive process, but as far as we know only humans have, can communicate about, and—crucially—can negotiate an explicit concept of responsibility.

Over time, as we recognize more consequences of our actions, our societies tend to give us both responsibility and accountability for these consequences—credit and blame depending on whether the consequences are positive or negative. Artificial intelligence only changes our responsibility as a special case of changing every other part of our social behavior. Digital technology provides us with *better* capacity to perceive and maintain accounts of actions and consequences, so it should be easier, not harder, to maintain responsibility and enforce the law. However, whether accountability is easier with AI depends on whether and in what ways we deploy the capacities digital technology affords. Without care and proper measures, the increased capacity for communication that information communication technology (ICT) provides may be used to diffuse or obscure responsibility. One solution is to recognize the lack of such care and measures for promoting accountability in processes concerning digital artifacts to be a form of negligence under the law. Similarly, we could declare that unnecessary obfuscation of public or commercial processes is a deliberate and culpable evasion of responsibility.

Note that the simplicity of the definitions introduced in this section is extremely important as we move toward law and regulation of systems and societies infused with AI. In order to evade regulation or responsibility, the definition of intelligence is often complicated in manifestos by notions such as sentience, consciousness, intentionality, and so forth. I will return to these issues later in the chapter, but what is essential when considering AI in the context of law is the understanding that no fact of either biology (the study of life) or computer science (the study of what is computable) names a necessary point at which human responsibility should end. Responsibility is not a fact of nature. Rather, the problem of governance is as always to design our artifacts—including the law itself—in a way that helps us maintain enough social order so that we can sustain human dignity and flourishing.

---

[4] An overhead; cf. Ajay D. Kshemkalyani and Mukesh Singhal, *Distributed, Computing: Principles, Algorithms, and Systems* (Cambridge: Cambridge University Press, 2011).

AI, INCLUDING MACHINE LEARNING, OCCURS BY DESIGN

Artificial intelligence only occurs by and with design. Thus AI is only produced intentionally, for a purpose, by one or more members of human society. That act of production requires design decisions concerning at a minimum the information input to and output from the system, and also where and how the computation required to transform that information will be run. These decisions entail also considerations of energy consumption and time that can be taken in producing as good a system as possible. Finally, any such system can and should be defended with levels of both cyber- and physical security appropriate to the value of the data transmitted or retained as well as the physical capacities of the system if it acts on the world.[5]

The tautology that AI is always generated by design extends to *machine learning* (ML), which is one means of developing AI wherein computation is used to discover useful regularities in data. Systems can then be built to exploit these regularities, whether to categorize them, make predictions, or select actions directly. The mere fact that part of the process of design has been automated does not mean that the system itself is not designed. The choice of an ML algorithm, the data fed into it to train it, the point at which it is considered adequately trained to be released, how that point is detected by testing, and whether that testing is ongoing if the learning continues during the system's operation—all of these things are design decisions that not only must be made but also can easily be documented. As such, any individual or organization that produces AI could always be held to account by being asked to produce documentation of these processes.

Documentation of such decisions and records of testing outcomes are easy to produce, but good practice is not always followed.[6] This is as much a matter for the law as any other sloppy or inadequate manufacturing technique.[7] The development processes deemed adequate for commercial products or even private enjoyment are determined by some combination of expertise and precedent. Whether these processes have been followed *and* documented can easily be checked either before a product is licensed, after a complaint has been made, or as a part of routine inspection.

Although actual algorithms *are* abstractions, that only means algorithms in themselves are not AI. In computer science, an algorithm is just a list of instructions to be followed, like a recipe in baking.[8] Just as a strand of DNA in itself is not life—it has no capacity to reproduce itself—so instruction sets require not only input (data) but also

---

[5] Note that these observations show that basic systems engineering demonstrates how underinformed the idea is of a machine converting the world into paperclips, as per Nick Bostrom, *Superintelligence: Paths, Dangers, Strategies* (Oxford: Oxford University Press, 2014), 122–25.

[6] Michael Huttermann, *DevOps for Developers* (New York: Apress/Springer, 2012).

[7] Joshua A. Kroll et al., "Accountable Algorithms," *Univ. Penn. L. Rev.* 165 (2017): 633–706.

[8] The term algorithm is currently often misused to mean an AI system by those unclear on the distinctions between design, programs, data, and physical computing systems.

physical computation to be run. Without significant, complex physical infrastructure to execute their instructions, both DNA and AI algorithms are inert. The largest global technology corporations have almost inconceivably vast infrastructure for every aspect of storing, processing, and transmitting the information that is their business. This infrastructure includes means to generate electric power and provide secure communication as well as means to do computation.

These few leading corporations further provide these capacities also as service infrastructure to a significant percentage of the world's other ICT companies—of course, at a cost. The European Union (EU) has committed to investing substantial public resources in developing a localized equivalent of this computational infrastructure resource, as they have previously done with both commercial aviation and global positioning systems. The EU may also attempt to build a parallel data resource, though this is more controversial. There has also been some discussion of "nationalizing" significant technology infrastructure, though that idea is problematic given that the Internet is transnational. *Trans*nationalizing technology "giants" is discussed later in this chapter.

Digital technology empowers us to do all sorts of things, including obfuscating or simply deleting records or the control systems they refer to. We can make systems either harder or easier to understand using AI.[9] These are design decisions. The extent to which transparency and accountability should be required in legal products is also a design decision, though here it is legislators, courts, and regulators that design a regulatory framework. What is important to realize is that it is perfectly possible to mandate that technology be designed to comply with laws, including any that ensure traceability and accountability of the human actions involved in the design, running, and maintenance of intelligent systems. In fact, given that the limits of "machine nature" are far more plastic than those of human nature, it is more sensible to minimize the amount of change to laws and instead to maximize the extent of required compliance to and facilitation of extant laws.[10]

THE PERFORMANCE OF DESIGNED ARTIFACTS IS READILY EXPLAINABLE

Perhaps in the desire to evade either the laws of nations or the laws of nature, many deeply respected AI professionals have claimed that the most promising aspects of AI

---

[9] Kroll et al., "Accountable Algorithms."

[10] Joanna J. Bryson, Mihailis E. Diamantis, and Thomas D. Grant, "Of, For, and By the People: The Legal Lacuna of Synthetic Persons," *Artificial Intelligence and Law* 25.3 (Sept. 2017): 273–291; Margaret Boden et al., *Principles of Robotics*, The United Kingdom's Engineering and Physical Sciences Research Council (EPSRC), April 2011, https://www.epsrc.ac.uk/research/ourportfolio/themes/engineering/activities/principlesofrobotics/.

would be compromised if AI were to be regulated.[11] For example, the claim that main-taining standard rights to explanation—that is, demonstration of due process—would eliminate the utilization of many advanced machine learning techniques is based on the fact that these methods produce systems the exact workings of which are too complex to be knowable. This claim fails to take into account the present standards for accountabil-ity in corporate law. If a company is audited, that audit never extends to explaining the workings of the brain synapses or gene regulation of that company's employees. Rather, we look for audit trails—or perhaps witnesses—indicating that humans have followed appropriate procedures.

Automation exploiting artificial intelligence may reduce the number of people who can be put on a witness stand to describe their recollections of events or motivations, but it enables a standard of record keeping that would be unbearably tedious in nondigital processes. It is not the case that all AI systems are programmed to keep such records, nor that all such records are maintained indefinitely. But it *is* the case that *any* AI system can be programmed to perform such documentation, and that the programming and other development of AI can always use good systems engineering practice, including logging data on the design, development, training, testing, and operation of the systems. Further, individuals or institutions can choose how, where, and for how long to store this logged data. Again, these are design decisions for both AI systems and the institutions that create them. There are already available standards for adequate logging to generate proof of due diligence or even explanations of AI behavior. Norms of use for these or other standards can be set and enforced.[12]

What matters for human justice is that humans do the right things. We do not need to completely understand exactly how a machine-learning algorithm works any more than we need to completely understand the physics of torque to regulate bicycle riding in traf-fic. Our concerns about AI should be that it is used in a way that is lawful. We want to know, for example, that products comply with their claims, that individual users are not spied upon or unfairly disadvantaged, and that foreign agencies were not able to illicitly insert false information into a machine-learning dataset or a newsfeed.

All AI affords the possibility of maintaining precise accounts of when, how, by whom, and with what motivation the system deploying it has been constructed. Indeed, this is true of artifacts in general, but digital artifacts are particularly amenable to automating the process. The very tools used to build intelligent systems can also be set to capture and prompt for this kind of information. We can similarly track the construction, appli-cation, and outcomes of any validating tests. Further, even the most obscure AI system

[11] My assertion about the "deeply respected" relates to claims I've heard in high-level policy settings, but haven't been able to find in print. However, for examples of the rhetoric see Cassie Kozyrkov, "Explainable AI Won't Deliver: Here's Why," *Hackernoon* (Nov. 2018), https://hackernoon.com/explainable-ai-wont-deliver-here-s-why-6738f54216be; Cassie Kozyrkov, "The Trade-Off in Machine Learning: Accuracy vs Explain-Ability," *Medium* (Dec. 2018), https://medium.com/@erdemkalayci/the-tradeoff-in-machine-learning-accuracy-vs-explainability-fbb13914fde2.
[12] Joanna J. Bryson and Alan F. T. Winfield, "Standardizing Ethical Design for Artificial Intelligence and Autonomous Systems," *Computer* 50.5 (May 2017): 116–119.

after development can be treated entirely as a blackbox and still tested to see what variation in inputs creates variation in the outputs.[13] Even where performance is stochastic, statistics can tell us the probability of various outcomes, again a type of information to which the law is already accustomed e.g. for medical outcomes. In practice though, systems with AI are generally far less opaque than human reasoning and less complex than other problems we deal with routinely such as the workings of a government or ecosystem. There is a decades-old science of examining complex models by using simpler ones, which has been recently accelerating to serve the sectors that are already well regulated and that of course (like all sectors) increasingly use AI.[14] And of course many forms of AI, built either with or without the use of ML, do readily produce explanations themselves.[15]

To return to one of the assertions at the beginning of this section, it is also wrong to assume that AI is not already regulated. All human activity, particularly commercial activity, occurs in the context of some sort of regulatory framework.[16] The question is how to continue to optimize this framework in light of the changes in society and its capacities introduced by AI and ICT more generally.

INTELLIGENCE INCREASES BY EXPLOITING PRIOR COMPUTATION

The fact that computation is a physical process limits how much can be done *de novo* in the instant during which intelligence must be expressed—when action must be taken to save a system from a threat or to empower it through an opportunity. For this reason, much of intelligence exploits computation already done, or rather exploits those artifacts produced that preserve the outcomes of that computation. Recognising the value and reuse of prior computation helps us understand the designs not only of culture but also of biology. Not only can organisms solely exploit opportunities they can perceive, they also tend to perceive solely what they are equipped to exploit—capacities for perception and action evolve together. Similarly, culture passes us not every tool that others have invented, but of all those inventions, the ones that produce the greatest impact relative to the costs of transmission. Costs of transmission include both time spent transmitting

---

[13] This process is coming to be called (as of this writing) "forensic analysis"; see, e.g., Joseph R. Barr and Joseph Cavanaugh, "Forensics: Assessing Model Goodness: A Machine Learning View," *ESCRI* 2, no. 2 (2019): 17–23.

[14] Patrick Hall, "On the Art and Science of Machine Learning Explanations," *arXiv preprint arXiv:1810.02909* (2018).

[15] Stephen Cranefield et al., "No Pizza for You: Value-based Plan Selection in BDI Agents," in *IJCAI Proceedings*, ed. Carles Sierra (Melbourne, 2017): 178–84; Jiaming Zeng, Berk Ustun, and Cynthia Rudin, "Interpretable Classification Models for Recidivism Prediction," *Journal of the Royal Statistical Society: Series A (Statistics in Society)* 180.3 (2017): 689–722.

[16] Miles Brundage and Joanna J. Bryson, *Smart Policies for Artificial Intelligence*, in preparation, available as arXiv:1608.08196 (2017).

(reducing other opportunities) and the likelihood of inadequately faithful replication creating hazardous behaviour.[17] Culture itself evolves, and frequently those changes generate increased efficacy in those that learn them.[18]

Much of the recent immense growth of AI has been due specifically to improved capacities to "mine" using ML the prior discoveries of humanity and nature more generally.[19] Of course with such mining the good comes with the bad. We mine not only knowledge but also stereotypes—and, if we allow AI to take action, prejudice—when we mine human culture.[20] This is not a special feature of AI; as mentioned previously, this is how nature works as well.[21] Evolution can only collect and preserve the best of what is presently available (what has already been computed); even within that range the process is stochastic and will sometimes make errors. Further, examining the AI products of ML has shown that at least some of what we call "stereotypes" reflect aspects of present-day conditions, such as what proportion of job holders for a particular position have a particular gender. Thus some things we have agreed are bad (e.g. that it is sexist to expect programmers to be male) are aspects of our present culture (most programmers are male now) we have at least implicitly agreed we wish to change. Machine learning of data about present employment–or even of ordinary word use which will necessarily be impacted by present employment–cannot by itself also discover such implicit agreements and social intentions.

One theory for explaining the explosion in what we recognize as AI (that is, of AI with rich, demonstrably human-like, and previously human-specific capacities such as speech production or face recognition) is that it is less a consequence of new algorithms than of new troves of data and increased computation speeds. Where such explosions of capacities is based on the strategy of mining past solutions, we can expect that improvement to plateau. Artificial and human intelligence will come to share nearly the same boundary of extant knowledge, though that boundary will continue to expand. In fact, we can also

---

[17] Ivana Čače and Joanna J. Bryson, "Agent Based Modelling of Communication Costs: Why Information Can be Free," in *Emergence and Evolution of Linguistic Communication*, ed. C. Lyon, C. L. Nehaniv, and A. Cangelosi (London: Springer, 2007), 305–322; Kenny Smith and Elizabeth Wonnacott. "Eliminating Unpredictable Variation through Iterated Learning," *Cognition* 116.3 (2010): 444–9.

[18] Alex Mesoudi, Andrew Whiten, and Kevin N. Laland, "Towards a Unified Science of Cultural Evolution," *Behavioral and Brain Sciences* 29.4 (2006): 329–47; Joanna J. Bryson, "Embodiment versus Memetics," *Mind & Soc'y* 7.1 (June 2008): 77–94; Joanna J. Bryson, "Artificial Intelligence and Pro-Social Behaviour," in *Collective Agency and Cooperation in Natural and Artificial Systems: Explanation, Implementation and Simulation*, ed. Catrin Misselhorn, vol. 122, Philosophical Studies (Berlin: Springer, 2015), 281–306; Daniel C. Dennett, *From Bacteria to Bach and Back* (London, Allen Lane, 2017).

[19] Thomas B Moeslund and Erik Granum, "A Survey of Computer Vision–based Human Motion Capture," *Computer Vision and Image Understanding* 81.3 (2001): 231–268; Sylvain Calinon et al., "Learning and Reproduction of Gestures by Imitation," *IEEE Robotics & Automation Mag.* 17.2 (2010): 44–54.

[20] Aylin Caliskan, Joanna J. Bryson, and Arvind Narayanan, "Semantics Derived Automatically from Language Corpora Contain Human-like Biases," *Sci.* 356.6334 (2017): 183–186.

[21] Molly Lewis and Gary Lupyan, "Language Use Shapes Cultural Norms: Large Scale Evidence from Gender," *Nature Human Behaviour* (accepted for publication).

expect human knowledge to be expanding faster now, given the extra computational resources we are bringing not only through digital hardware but also by our increasing access to other human minds. For humanity, ICT reduces the aforementioned overhead costs of discovering, combining, and transmitting prior computational outcomes. We all get smarter as our culture expands to embrace more—and more diverse—minds.[22] However, the fact that we can exploit our own computation to build AI, or that we can increase our own native as well as systemic intelligence by using AI, does not mean that we are replaceable with or by AI. As will be explained in the next sections, AI cannot be used to replicate humans, and this has substantial consequences for law and regulation.

AI CANNOT PRODUCE FULLY REPLICATED HUMANS (ALL MODELS ARE WRONG)

Computer science is often mistaken for a branch of mathematics. When this happens, many important implications of computation being a physical process are lost. For example, AI is wrongly perceived as a path toward human immortality. First, the potential of "uploading" human intelligence in any meaningful sense is highly dubious. Technologically, brains cannot be "scanned" and replicated in any other material than another brain, as their computational properties depend on trillions of temporal minutiae.[23] Creating a second, identical human to host that new brain not only is physically intractable but also would be cloning—both unethical and illegal, at least in the European Union. Second, even if we could somehow upload adequate abstractions of our own minds, we should not confuse this with actually having spawned a digital replica.[24] For example, an abstracted digital clone might be of use to manufacture canned email replies[25] or to create interactive interfaces for historical storytelling,[26] but this does not make it human.

[22] Anita Williams Woolley et al., "Evidence for a Collective Intelligence Factor in the Performance of Human Groups," *Sci.* 330.6004 (October 29, 2010): 686–688; Barton H. Hamilton, Jack A. Nickerson, and Hideo Owan, "Diversity and Productivity in Production Teams," *Advances in the Econ. Analysis of Participatory and Labor-Managed Firms* (2012): 99–138; Feng Shi et al., "The Wisdom of Polarized Crowds," *Nature Hum. Behaviour* 3 (2019): 329–336.

[23] Yoonsuck Choe, Jaerock Kwon, and Ji Ryang Chung, "Time, Consciousness, and Mind Uploading," *Int'l J. Machine Consciousness* 4.01 (2012): 257–274.

[24] As some would suggest; see Murray Shanahan, *The Technological Singularity* (Cambridge, MA: MIT Press, 2015), for a review.

[25] Mark Dredze et al., "Intelligent Email: Reply and Attachment Prediction," in *Proceedings of the 13th International Conference on Intelligent User Interfaces* (New York: ACM, 2008), 321–4.

[26] David Traum et al., "New Dimensions in Testimony: Digitally Preserving a Holocaust Survivor's Interactive Storytelling," in *Proceedings of the Eighth International Conference on Interactive Digital Storytelling* (Cham, Switzerland: Springer, 2015): 269–281.

Many have argued that the moral intuitions, motivations, even the aesthetics of an enculturated ape can in no way be meaningfully embedded in a device that shares nothing of our embodied physical ("phenomenological") experience.[27] Nothing we build from metal and silicon will ever share our phenomenology as much as a rat or cow, and few see cows or rats as viable vessels of our posterity. Yet whether such digital artifacts are viewed as adequate substitutes for a real person depends on what one values about that person. For example, for those who value their capacity to control the lives of others, many turn to the simple technology of a will to control intimate aspects of the lives of those chosen to be their heirs. It therefore seems likely that there will be those who spend millions or even billions of dollars, euros, or rubles on producing digital clones they are literally deeply invested in believing to be themselves, or at least in forcing others to treat as extensions of themselves.[28]

Even if we could somehow replicate ourselves in an artifact, the mean time for obsolescence of digital technologies and formats is far, far shorter than the average human life expectancy, which presently nears ninety years. This quick obsolescence is true not only of our physical technology but also of our fashion. Unquestionably any abstracted digital self-portrait would follow fashion in reflecting an aspect of our complex selves that will have been culturally appropriate only in a specific moment. It would not be possible from such an abstraction to fully model how our own rich individual being would have progressed through an extended lifetime, let alone through biological generations. Such complete modeling opposes the meaning of *abstraction*. An unabstracted model would again require biological cloning, but even then after many generations it would fall out of ecological fashion or appropriateness as evolution progresses.

With apologies to both Eisenhower and Box[29], all abstractions are wrong, but producing abstractions is essential. By the definition used in this chapter, all intelligence—that is, intelligent action—is an abstraction of the present context. Therefore producing an abstraction is the essence of intelligence. But that abstraction is only a snapshot of the organism; it is not the organism itself. All models are wrong, because we build them to perform actions that are not feasible using the original.

Reproducing our full organism is not required for many aspects of what is called "positive immortality."[30] Replicating our full selves is certainly not essential to writing fiction or otherwise making a lasting contribution to a culture or society, nor for having an irrevocable impact on an ecosystem. But the purpose of this chapter is to introduce AI from the perspective of maintaining social order—that is, from the perspective of

---

[27] Frank Pasquale, "Two Concepts of Immortality: Reframing Public Debate on Stem-Cell Research," *Yale J. L. & Hum*.14 (2002): 73–121; Bryson, "Embodiment versus Memetics"; Guy Claxton, *Intelligence in the Flesh: Why Your Mind Needs Your Body Much More Than It Thinks* (New Haven, CT: Yale University Press, 2015); Dennett, *From Bacteria to Bach and Back*.

[28] Pasquale, "Two Concepts of Immortality," questions such expenditures, or even those of in vitro fertilization, on the grounds of economic fairness.

[29] G. E. P. Box, "Robustness in the Strategy of Scientific Model Building," in *Robustness in Statistics*, ed. R. L. Launer and G. N. Wilkinson (New York: Academic Press, 1979), 201–236.

[30] Pasquale, "Two Concepts of Immortality."

law and regulation. As will be discussed in the following section, the methods for enforcing law and regulation are founded on the evolved priorities of social animals. Therefore any intelligent artifacts representing such highly abstracted versions of an individual human are not relevant to the law except perhaps as the intellectual property of their creator.

AI ITSELF CANNOT BE DISSUADED BY LAW OR TREATY

There is no way to ensure that an artifact could be held legally accountable.[31] Many people think the purpose of the law is to compensate, and obviously if we allow a machine to own property or at least wealth then it could in some sense compensate for its errors or misfortune. However, the law is really primarily designed to maintain social order by dissuading people from doing wrong. Law dissuades by making it clear what actions are considered wrong and then determining the costs and penalties for committing these wrong acts. This is even more true of policies and treaties, which are often constructed after long periods of negotiated agreement among peers (or at least sufficiently powerful fellow actors that more direct control is not worth its expense) about what acts would be wrong and what costs would adequately dissuade them. The Iran Nuclear Deal is an excellent example of this process.[32]

Of course all of these systems of governance can also generate revenue, which may be used by governments to some extent to right wrongs. However, none of the costs or penalties that courts can impose will matter to an AI system. We can easily write a program that says, "Don't put me in jail!" However, we cannot program the full, systemic aversion to the loss of social status and years of a finite life span, which the vast majority of humans experience as our birthright. In fact, not only humans but many social species find isolation and confinement deeply aversive—guppies can die of fright if separated from their school, and factory farming has been shown to drive pigs to exhibit symptoms of severe mental illness.[33]

We might add a bomb, camera, and timer to a robot and then program the bomb to destruct if the camera has seen no humans (or other robots) for ten minutes. Reasoning by empathy, you might think this machine is far more disuadable than a human, who can easily spend more than ten minutes alone without self destructing. But empathy is a terrible system for establishing universal ethics—it works best on those most like

[31] With no human components; Christian List and Philip Pettit, *Group Agency: The Possibility, Design, and Status of Corporate Agents* (Oxford: Oxford University Press, 2011).

[32] Kenneth Katzman and Paul K. Kerr, *Iran Nuclear Agreement*, Tech. rep. R43333, Library of Congress, Congressional Research Service, May 2016, https://crsreports.congress.gov/product/pdf/R/R43333.

[33] Françoise Wemelsfelder, "The Scientific Validity of Subjective Concepts in Models of Animal Welfare," *Applied Animal Behaviour Sci.* 53.1 (1997): 75–88.

yourself.[34] The robot's behavior could easily be utterly unaltered by this contrivance, and so it could not be said to suffer at all by the technical definitions of suffering[35], and it certainly could not be said to be dissuaded. Even if the robot could detect and reason about the consequences of its new situation, it would not feel fear, panic, or any other systemic aversion to isolation, although depending on its goals it might alter its planning to favor shorter planning horizons.

The law has been invented by—we might even say "coevolved with"—our societies in order to hold humans accountable. As an unintended consequence, only humans *can* be held accountable with our law. Even the extension of legal personality to corporations only works to the extent that real humans who have real control over those corporations suffer if the corporation does wrong. The overextension of legal personhood to a corporation designed to fail (e.g. to launder money) is known as creating a shell company. If you build an AI system and allow it to operate autonomously, it is similarly essential that you as the person who chooses to allow the system to operate autonomously will be the one who will go to jail, be fined, and so on if the AI system transgresses the law. There is simply no way to hold the AI system itself accountable or to dissuade it. Artificial intelligence being itself held accountable would be the ultimate shell company.[36]

The implicit principles that underlie our capacity to coordinate and cooperate through the law and its dissuasions have also coevolved with our complex societies. We share many of our cognitive attributes—including perception, action capacities, and, importantly, motivations—with other apes. Yet we also have specialist motivations and capacities reflecting our highly social nature.[37] No amount of intelligence in itself necessitates social competitiveness; neither does it demand acceptance by an in-group, dominance of an out-group, nor the need to achieve social status in either. These are motivations that underlie human (and other social species') cooperation and competition, that result from our evolutionary history.[38] None of this is necessary—and much of

---

[34] Paul Bloom, *Against Empathy: The Case for Rational Compassion* (New York: Harper Collins, 2016).

[35] Wemelsfelder, "Scientific Validity of Subjective Concepts"; Daniel C. Dennett, "Why You Can't Make a Computer That Feels Pain," *Brainstorms*, pp. 190–229 page numbers from (Cambridge, MA, MIT Press 1981, original edition: Montgomery, VT: Bradford Books, 1978), Bryson, "Artificial Intelligence and Pro-Social Behaviour"; Margaret A. Boden, "Robot Says: Whatever (The Robots Won't Take Over Because They Couldn't Care Less)," *Aeon* (August 23, 2018) (originally a lecture at the Leerhulme Centre for the Future of Intelligence), https://aeon.co/essays/the-robots-wont-take-over-because-they-couldnt-careless. Note in particular that none of the millions of currently extant robots would behave differently with these additions unless its programming was also altered (or the weight of the additions stopped it from moving.)

[36] Bryson, Diamantis, and Grant, "Of, For, and By the People."

[37] David Michael Stoddart, *The Scented Ape: The Biology and Culture of Human Odour* (Cambridge: Cambridge University Press, 1990).

[38] Stoddart, *The Scented Ape*; Ruth Mace, "The Co-evolution of Human Fertility and Wealth Inheritance Strategies," *Philosophical Transactions of the Royal Society of London B: Biological Sciences* 353.1367 (1998): 389–397; Jillian J. Jordan et al., "Uncalculating Cooperation Is Used to Signal Trustworthiness," *Proceedings of the Nat'l Academy of Sciences* 113.31(2016): 8658–63; Simon T. Powers, Carel P. van Schaik, and Laurent Lehmann, "How Institutions Shaped the Last Major Evolutionary Transition to Large-Scale Human Societies," *Philosophical Transactions of the Royal Society B: Biological Sciences* 371.1687 (2016): 20150098.

it is even incoherent—from the perspective of an artifact. Artifacts are definitionally designed by human intent, not directly by evolution. With these intentional acts of authored human creation[39] come not only human responsibility but also an entirely different landscape of potential rewards and design constraints.[40]

AI AND ICT IMPACT EVERY HUMAN ENDEAVOR

Given that AI can always be built to be explainable, and that only humans can be held to account, assertions that AI itself should be trustworthy, accountable, or responsible are completely misguided. If only humans can be held to account, then from a legal perspective the goal for AI transparency is to ensure that human blame can be correctly apportioned. Of course there are other sorts of transparency, such as those that support ordinary users in establishing the correct boundaries they have with their systems (defending their own interests), or for providing developers or other practitioners the ability to debug or customize an AI system.[41] Artificial intelligence can be reliable but not trustworthy—it should not require a social compact or leap of faith.[42] Consumers and governments alike should have confidence that they can determine at will who is responsible for the AI-infused systems we incorporate into our homes, our business processes, and our security.

Every task we apply our conscious minds to—and a great deal of what we do implicitly—we do using our intelligence. Artificial intelligence therefore can affect everything we are aware of doing and a great deal we have always done without intent. As mentioned earlier, even fairly trivial and ubiquitous AI has recently demonstrated that human language contains our implicit biases, and further that those biases in many cases reflect our lived realities.[43] In reusing and reframing our previous computation, AI allows us to see truths we had not previously known about ourselves, including how we transmit stereotypes,[44] but it does not automatically or magically improve us without effort. Caliskan, Bryson, and Narayanan discuss the outcome of the famous study

[39] The choice to create life through childbirth is not the same. While we may author some of child-rearing, the dispositions just discussed are shared with other primates and are not options left to parents or other conspecifics to determine.

[40] Cf. Joanna J. Bryson, "Patiency Is Not a Virtue: The Design of Intelligent Systems and Systems of Ethics," *Ethics and Info. Tech.* 20.1 (Mar. 2018): 15–26.

[41] Bryson and Winfield, "Standardizing Ethical Design."

[42] Onora O'Neill, *A Question of Trust: The BBC Reith Lectures 2002* (Cambridge: Cambridge University Press, 2002).

[43] Caliskan, Bryson, and Narayanan, "Semantics Derived Automatically from Language Corpora."

[44] Lewis and Lupyan, "Language Use Shapes Cultural Norms." Marianne Bertrand and Sendhil Mullainathan, "Are Emily and Greg More Employable Than Lakisha and Jamal? A Field Experiment on Labor Market Discrimination," *Am. Econ. Rev.* 94.4 (2004): 991–1013.

showing that, given otherwise-identical resumes, individuals with stereotypically African American names were half as likely to be invited to a job interview as individuals with European American names.[45] Smart corporations are now using carefully pro-grammed AI to avoid implicit biases at the early stages of human resources processes so they can select diverse CVs into a short list. This demonstrates that AI can—with explicit care and intention—be used to avoid perpetuating the mistakes of the past.

The idea of having "autonomous" AI systems "value-aligned" is therefore likely to be misguided. While it is certainly necessary to acknowledge and understand the extent to which implicit values and expectations must be embedded in any artifact,[46] designing for such embedding is not sufficient to create a system that is autonomously moral. Indeed, if a system cannot be made accountable, it may also not in itself be held as a moral agent. The issue should not be embedding our intended (or asserted) values in our machines, but rather ensuring that our machines allow firstly the expression of the mutable inten-tions of their human operators, and secondly transparency for the accountability of those intentions, in order to ensure or at least govern the operators' morality.

Only through correctly expressing our intentions should AI incidentally telegraph our values. Individual liberty, including freedom of opinion and thought, are absolutely critical not only to human well-being but also to a robust and creative society.[47] Allowing values to be enforced by the enfolding curtains of interconnected technology invites gross excesses by powerful actors against those they consider vulnerable, a threat, or just unimportant.[48] Even supposing a power that is demonstrably benign, allowing it the mechanisms for tech-nological autocracy creates a niche that may facilitate a less-benign power—whether through a change of hands, corruption of the original power, or corruption of the systems communicating its will. Finally, who or what is a powerful actor is also altered by ICT, where clandestine networks can assemble—or be assembled—out of small numbers of anony-mous individuals acting in a well-coordinated way, even across borders.[49]

Theoretical biology tells us that where there is greater communication, there is a higher probability of cooperation.[50] *Cooperation* has nearly entirely positive connotations, but

[45] Marianne Bertrand and Sendhil Mullainathan, "Are Emily and Greg More Employable Than Lakisha and Jamal? A Field Experiment on Labor Market Discrimination," *American Economic Review* 94.4 (2004): 991–1013.

[46] Jeroen van den Hoven, "ICT and Value Sensitive Design," in *The Information Society: Innovation, Legitimacy, Ethics and Democracy in Honor of Professor Jacques Berleur S.J.*, ed. Philippe Goujon et al. (Boston: Springer, 2007), 67–72; Aimee van Wynsberghe, "Designing Robots for Care: Care Centered Value-Sensitive Design," *Sci. and Engineering Ethics* 19.2 (June 2013): 407–433.

[47] Julie E. Cohen, "What Privacy Is For," *Harv. L. Rev.* 126 (May 2013): 1904–1933.

[48] Brett Frischmann and Evan Selinger, *Re-engineering Humanity* (Cambridge: Cambridge University Press, 2018); Miles Brundage et al., *The Malicious Use of Artificial Intelligence: Forecasting, Prevention, and Mitigation*, Tech. rep., https://maliciousaireport.com/, Future of Humanity Institute, University of Oxford, Centre for the Study of Existential Risk, University of Cambridge, Center for a New American Security, Electronic Frontier Foundation, and OpenAI, (Feb. 2018).

[49] Carole Cadwalladr, "'I Made Steve Bannon's Psychological Warfare Tool': Meet the Data War Whistleblower," *The Observer* (March 18, 2018) https://www.theguardian.com/news/2018/mar/17/data-war-whistleblower-christopher-wylie-faceook-nix-bannon-trump.

[50] Joan Roughgarden, Meeko Oishi, and Erol Akçay, "Reproductive Social Behavior: Cooperative Games to Replace Sexual Selection," *Sci.* 311.5763 (2006): 965–969.

it is in many senses almost neutral—nearly all human endeavors involve cooperation, and while these generally benefit many humans, some are destructive to many others. Further, the essence of cooperation is moving some portion of autonomy from the individual to a group.[51] The extent of autonomy an entity has is the extent to which it determines its own actions.[52] Individual and group autonomy must to some extent trade off, though there are means of organizing groups that offer more or less liberty for their constituent parts.

Many people are (falsely) preaching that ML is the new AI, and (again falsely) that the more data ML is trained on, the smarter the AI. Machine learning is actually a statistical process we use for programming some aspects of AI. Thinking that 'bigger' (more) data are necessarily better begs the question: better for what? Basic statistics teaches us that the number of data points we need to make a prediction is limited by the amount of variation in that data, providing only that the data are a true random sample of the population measured.[53] So there are natural limits for any particular task on how much data is actually needed to build the intelligence to perform it—except perhaps for surveillance. What we need for science or medicine may require only a minuscule fraction of a population. However, if we want to spot specific individuals to be controlled, dissuaded, or even promoted, then of course we want to "know all the things."[54]

The changing costs and benefits of investment at the group level that Roughgarden, Oishi, and Akçay describe has other consequences beyond privacy and liberty. Information communication technology facilitates blurring the distinction between customer and corporation; it blurs even the definition of an economic transaction. Customers now do real labor for the corporations to whom we give our custom: pricing and bagging groceries, punching data at ATMs for banks, filling in forms for airlines, and so forth.[55] The value of this labor is not directly remunerated—we assume that we receive cheaper products in return, and as such our loss of agency to these corporations might be seen as a form of bartering. "Free" services like Internet searches and email may be better understood as information bartering.[56] These transactions are not denominated with a price, which means that ICT facilitates a black or at least opaque market reducing both measured custom and therefore tax revenue. This is true for everyone who uses Internet services and interfaces, even ignoring the present controversies

[51] Bryson, "Artificial Intelligence and Pro-Social Behaviour."

[52] Harvey Armstrong and Robert Read, "Western European Micro-States and EU Autonomous Regions: The Advantages of Size and Sovereignty," *World Dev.* 23.7 (1995): 1229–1245; Maeve Cooke, "A Space of One's Own: Autonomy, Privacy, Liberty," *Philosophy & Soc. Criticism* 25.1 (1999): 22–53.

[53] Meng, Xiao-Li. "Statistical paradises and paradoxes in big data (I): Law of large populations, big data paradox, and the 2016 US presidential election." *The Annals of Applied Statistics* 12.2 (2018): 685–726.

[54] Mark Andrejevic, "Automating Surveillance," *Surveillance & Society* 17.1/2 (2019): 7–13.

[55] Bryson, "Artificial Intelligence and Pro-Social Behaviour."

[56] Joanna J. Bryson, "The Past Decade and Future of AI's Impact on Society," *Towards a New Enlightenment? A Transcendent Decade*, OpenMind BBVA (commissioned, based on a previous whitepaper for the OECD, also commissioned.), (Madrid: Taylor, 2019).

over definitions of employment raised by platforms.[57] Our failure to assign monetary value to these transactions may also explain the mystery of why AI does not seem to be increasing productivity.[58]

Artificial intelligence, then, gives us new ways to do everything we do intentionally and a great deal more. The extent to which AI makes different tasks easier and harder varies in ways that are not intuitive. This also increases and decreases the values of human skills, knowledge, social networks, personality traits, and even locations. Further, AI alters the calculations of identity and security. Fortunately, AI also gives us tools for reasoning and communicating about all these changes and for adjusting to them. But this makes group-level identity itself more fluid, complicating our ability to govern.

Who's in Charge? AI and Governance

Despite all of this fluctuation, there are certain things that are invariant to the extent of computational resources and communicative capacities. The basic nature of humans as animals of a certain size and metabolic cost, and the basic drives that determine what gives us pleasure, pain, stress, and engagement, are not altered much. How we live is and always will be enormously impacted by how our neighbors live, as we share geographically related decisions concerning investment in air, water, education, health, and security. For this reason there will always be some kind of geography-based governance. The fundamental ethical framework we have been negotiating for the last century or so of human rights is based on the responsibility of such geographically defined governments to individuals within the sphere of influence of those governments.[59] Now wise actors like the European Union have extended the notion of an individual's sovereignty over cyberassets such as personal data.[60] This makes sense for almost exactly the same reason as rights to airspace make sense. With bidirectional information access, we can influence an individual's behavior just as we could with physical force.

Recently there has been good reason to hope that we really will start mandating developers to follow best practice in software engineering.[61] If we are sensible, we will also ensure that the information systems spreading and engulfing us will also be entirely

[57] Cf. Tim O'Reilly, *WTF? What's the Future and Why It's Up to Us* (New York: Random House, 2017).

[58] Erik Brynjolfsson, Daniel Rock, and Chad Syverson, "Artificial Intelligence and the Modern Productivity Paradox: A Clash of Expectations and Statistics," *Economics of Artificial Intelligence*, Agrawal, Gans and Goldfab (eds) (Chicago: University of Chicago Press, 2017): 23–57.

[59] Sabine C. Carey, Mark Gibney, and Steven C. Poe, *The Politics of Human Rights: The Quest for Dignity* (Cambridge: Cambridge University Press, 2010).

[60] Paul Nemitz, "Constitutional Democracy and Technology in the Age of Artificial Intelligence," *Philosophical Transactions of the Royal Soc. A: Mathematical, Physical and Engineering Sciences* 376.2133 (2018): 20180089.

[61] OECD, *Recommendation of the Council on Artificial Intelligence*, OECD Legal Instruments OECD/LEGAL/0449 (includes the OECD Principles of AI) (Paris: Organisation for Economic Cooperation and Development, May 2019).

cybersecure (or else not on the Internet), with clearly documented accountability and lines of responsibility.[62] Nevertheless, even if these visions can be achieved, there are still other areas of law and governance with which we should be concerned. The last I focus on in this present chapter are the new foci of power and wealth. As just explained in the previous section, these are also parts of the "everything human" that AI and ICT are altering. Further, it is clear that achieving secure and accountable AI requires cooperation with adequate sources of power to counter those who wish to avoid the consensus of the law. Therefore wealth and power distribution, while again like cybersecurity clearly orthogonal technologically to AI, are also irrevocably intertwined with its ethical and regulated application. Problems of AI accountability and grotesquely uneven wealth distribution are unlikely to be solved independently.

In this section it should be noted that I am describing my own work in progress with colleagues,[63] but some aspects of it seem sufficiently evident to justify inclusion here. We hypothesize that when new technologies reduce the economic cost of distance, this in turn reduces the amount of easily-sustained competition in a sector. This is because locale becomes less a part of value, so higher-quality products and services can dominate ever-larger regions, up to and including in some cases the entire globe. Such a process may have sparked the gross inequality of the late nineteenth and early twentieth centuries, when rail, news and telecommunication, and oil (far easier to transport than coal or wood) were the new monopolies. Inequality spirals if capital is allowed to capture regulation, as seems recently to have happened not only with "big tech" globally but also with finance in the United Kingdom or oil in Saudi Arabia and Russia, leading to a "resource curse."[64] The early twentieth century was a period of significant havoc; in the mid-twentieth century lower inequality and political polarization cooccurred with the innovation of the welfare state, which in some countries (including the United States and United Kingdom) preceded at least World War II, though such cooperation even in these states seemed to require the motivation of the previous War and financial crash.

Governance can be almost defined by redistribution; certainly allocation of resources to solve communal problems and create public goods is governance's core characteristic.[65] Thus excessive inequality can be seen as a failure of governance.[66] Right now what we are clearly not able to govern (interestingly, on both sides of the Great Firewall of

[62] Cf. Filippo Santoni de Sio and Jeroen van den Hoven, "Meaningful Human Control over Autonomous Systems: A Philosophical Account," *Frontiers in Robotics and AI* 5 (2018): 15.

[63] Alexander J. Stewart, Nolan McCarty, and Joanna J. Bryson, "Explaining Parochialism: A Causal Account for Political Polarization in Changing Economic Environments," arXiv preprint arXiv:1807.11477 (2018).

[64] John Christensen, Nick Shaxson, and Duncan Wigan, "The Finance Curse: Britain and the World Economy," *British J. Pol. and Int'l Relations* 18.1 (2016): 255–269; Nolan M. McCarty, Keith T. Poole, and Howard Rosenthal, *Polarized America: The Dance of Ideology and Unequal Riches*, 2nd ed. (Cambridge, MA: MIT Press, 2016).

[65] Jean-Pierre Landau, "Populism and Debt: Is Europe Different from the U.S.?," Talk at the Princeton Woodrow Wilson School, and in preparation. Feb. 2016.

[66] E.g., a Gini coefficient over 0.27; Francesco Grigoli and Adrian Robles, *Inequality Overhang*, IMF Working Paper WP/17/76, International Monetary Fund, 2017. Note that too low a Gini coefficient can be problematic too.

China) are Internet companies. Perhaps similar to the market for commercial aircraft, the costs of distance are sufficiently negligible that the best products are very likely to become global monopolies unless there is a substantial government investment (e.g., the Great Firewall of China[67] or Airbus in Europe).[68] Where governance fails in a local region, such as a county, then that is also where we are likely to see political polarization and the success of populist candidates or referendum outcomes.[69]

Many problems we associate with the present moment then were not necessarily created by AI or ICT directly, but rather they were formed indirectly by facilitating increased inequality and regulatory capture. Other problems may not have been so much created as exposed by AI.[70] There are some exceptions where ICT—particularly, the capacity of digital media to be fully reproduced at a distance and to do so inexpensively—does produce qualitative change. These include changing of the meaning of ownership[71] and generating truly novel means for recognizing and disrupting human intentions, even implicit intentions not consciously known by their actors.[72] On the other hand, some things are or should be treated as invariant. As an example mentioned earlier, human rights are the painstakingly agreed foundation of international law and the obligations of a state and should be treated as core to ethical AI systems.[73]

One of the disturbing things we come to understand as we learn about algorithms is the extent to which humans are ourselves algorithmic. Law can make us more so, particularly when we constrain ourselves with it, for example with mandatory sentencing. But ordinarily, humans do have wiggle room.[74] Trust is a form of cooperation arising only in contexts of ignorance. That ignorance may be an important feature of society that ICT threatens to

---

[67] Roya Ensafi et al., "Analyzing the Great Firewall of China over Space and Time," *Proceedings on Privacy Enhancing Tech.* 2015.1 (2015): 61–76.

[68] Damien Neven and Paul Seabright, "European Industrial Policy: The Airbus Case," *Econ. Pol'y* 10.21 (July 1995): 313–358.

[69] Yuri M. Zhukov, "Trading Hard Hats for Combat Helmets: The Economics of Rebellion in Eastern Ukraine," Special Issue on Ukraine: Escape from Post-Soviet Legacy, *J. Comp. Econ.* 44.1 (2016): 1–15; Sascha O. Becker, Thiemo Fetzer, and Dennis Novy, "Who Voted for Brexit? A Comprehensive District-Level Analysis," *Econ. Pol'y* 32.92 (Oct. 2017): 601–650; Florian Dorn et al., "Inequality and Extremist Voting: Evidence from Germany,"Annual Conference (2018) (Freiburg, Breisgau): Digital Economy 181598, Verein für Socialpolitik / German Economic Association.

[70] Nemitz, "Constitutional Democracy and Technology in the Age of Artificial Intelligence"; Orly Mazur, "Taxing the Robots," *Pepperdine L. Rev.* 46 (2018): 277–330.

[71] Aaron Perzanowski and Jason Schultz, *The End of Ownership: Personal Property in the Digital Economy* (Cambridge, MA: MIT Press, 2016).

[72] Caio Machado and Marco Konopacki, "Computational Power: Automated Use of WhatsApp in the Brazilian Elections," *Medium* (October 26, 2018), https://feed.itsrio.org/computational-power-automated-use-of-whatsapp-in-the-elections-59f62b857033; Cadwalladr, "'I Made Steve Bannon's Psychological Warfare Tool,'"; Zhe Wu et al., "Deception Detection in Videos," *Thirty-Second AAAI Conference on Artificial Intelligence.* New Orleans, LA (2018): 16926.

[73] Philip Alston and Mary Robinson, *Human Rights and Development: Towards Mutual Reinforcement* (Oxford: Oxford University Press, 2005); David Kaye, "State Execution of the International Covenant on Civil and Political Rights,". *UC Irvine L. Rev.* 3 (2013): 95–125.

[74] Cohen, "What Privacy Is For."

remove.[75] Trust allows cheating or innovating, and sometimes this may be essential. First, allowing innovation makes more tractable the level of detail about exceptions that needs to be specified. Second, of course, innovation allows us to adjust to the unexpected and to find novel, sometimes better solutions. Some—perhaps many—nations may be in danger of allowing the digital era to make innovation or free thought too difficult or individually risky, creating nationwide fragility to security threats as well as impinging on an important human right: freedom of opinion.[76] In such countries, law may bend too much toward rigidly preserving the group, and inadequately defend the individual. As I mentioned, this is not only an issue of rights but also of robustness. Individuals and variation produce alternatives–choosing among available options is a rapid way to change behavior when a crisis demonstrates change is needed.[77] Given that the digital revolution has fundamentally changed the nature of privacy for everyone, all societies will need to find a way to reintroduce and defend "wiggle room" for innovation and opinion. I believe strongly that it would be preferable if this is done not by destroying access to history, but by acknowledging and defending individual differences, including shortcomings and the necessity of learning. But psychological and political realities remain to be explored and understood, and may vary by polity.

Summary and the Robots Themselves

To reiterate my main points, when computer science is mistaken for a branch of mathematics, many important implications of computation being a physical process are lost. Further, the impact on society of the dissemination of information, power, and influence has not been adequately noted in either of those two disciplines, while in law and social sciences, awareness of technological reality and affordances has been building only slowly. Ironically, these impacts until very recently were also not much noticed in political science. Primarily, these impacts were noted only in sociology, which was unfortunately imploding at the same time AI was exploding. Similar to the myopia of computer science, psychology has primarily seen itself as studying humans as organisms. The primary ethical considerations in that field were seen as being similar to those of medical subjects, such as concerns about patient privacy. Again, some related disciplines such as media studies or marketing raised the issue, that as we better understood human behavior we might more effectively manipulate and control it, but that observation made little headway in the popular academic understanding of AI. Direct interventions

---

[75] O'Neill, *Question of Trust*; Paul Rauwolf and Joanna J. Bryson, "Expectations of Fairness and Trust Co-Evolve in Environments of Partial Information," *Dynamic Games and Applications* 8.4 (Dec. 2018): 891–917.

[76] Cf. Frischmann and Selinger, *Re-engineering Humanity*.

[77] Cohen, "What Privacy Is For"; Luke Stark, "The emotional Context of Information Privacy," *Info. Soc'y* 32.1 (2016): 14–27.

via neuroscience and drugs received more attention, but the potential for indirect manipulations, particularly of adults, were seemingly dismissed.

These historic errors may be a consequence of the fact that human adults are of necessity the ultimate moral agents. We are the centers of accountability in our own societies, and as such we are expected to have the capacity to take care of ourselves. The ethics of AI therefore was often reduced to its popular culture edifice as an extension of the civil rights movement.[78] Now that we have discovered—astonishingly!—that people of other ethnicities and genders are as human as "we" are, "we" are therefore obliged to consider that *anything* might be human. This position seems more a rejection of the inclusivity of civil and human rights than an appropriate extension, but it is powerfully attractive to many who seem particularly likely to be members of the recently dominant forms of gender and ethnicity, and who perhaps intuit that such an extension would again raise the power of their own clique by making the notion of rights less meaningful.

More comprehensibly, some have suggested we must extend human rights protections to anything that humans might identify with in order to protect our own self-concept, even if our identification with these objects is implicit or mistaken.[79] This follows from Kant's observation that those who treat animals reminiscent of humans badly are also more likely to treat humans badly. Extending this principle to AI though is most likely also a mistake, and an avoidable one. Remember that AI is definitionally an artifact and therefore designed. It almost certainly makes more sense where tractable to change AI than to radically change the law. Rather than Kant motivating us to treat AI that appears human as if it were human, we can use Kant to motivate not building AI to appear human in the first place. This has been the approach of first the United Kingdom[80] and now very recently the OECD[81] whose AI ethics principles recommend that AI should never deceptively appear to be human. This may seem like a heavy restriction at present, but as society becomes more familiar with AI—and, through that process, better understands what it is about being human that requires and deserves protection—we should be able to broaden the scope of how humanlike devices can be while still not having that likeness deceive.[82]

There are recent calls to ground AI governance not on "ethics" (which is viewed as ill-defined) but on international human rights law. Of course, this may be a false dichotomy; procedures from classical ethics theories may still be of use in determining

[78] Tony J. Prescott, "Robots Are Not Just Tools," *Connection Sci.* 29.2 (2017): 142–149; David J. Gunkel, "The Other Question: Can and Should Robots Have Rights?," *Ethics and Info. Tech.* 20.2 (2018): 87–99; Daniel Estrada, "Value Alignment, Fair Play, and the Rights of Service Robots,"*Proceedings of the 2018 AAAI/ACM Conference on AI, Ethics, and Society*, AIES 20'18, New York, NY, ACM (2018), 102–107.

[79] Joel Parthemore and Blay Whitby, "What Makes Any Agent a Moral Agent? Reflections on Machine Consciousness and Moral Agency," *Int'l J. Machine Consciousness* 5.02 (2013): 105–129; David J. Gunkel, *Robot Rights* (Cambridge, MA: MIT Press, 2018).

[80] Boden et al., *Principles of Robotics*.

[81] OECD, *Recommendation of the Council on Artificial Intelligence*.

[82] Joanna J. Bryson, "The Meaning of the EPSRC Principles of Robotics," *Connection Sci.* 29.2 (2017): 130–136.

ambiguities and trade-offs of law's application.[83] We can certainly expect ongoing consideration of localized variation, which the term *ethics* perhaps better communicates than *rights*. Ethics has always been about identity communicated in codes of conduct, which confound fundamental principles that we may be able to codify as rights with other things that are essentially identity markers. But identity too can be essential to security through constructing a defendable community.[84] Identity obviously (definitionally) defines a group, and groups are often the best means humans have for achieving security and therefore viability. Not only is breaking into different groups sometimes more efficient for governance or other resource constraints, but also some groups will have different fundamental security trade-offs based on their geological and ecological situation or just simply their relations with neighbors. Identity also often rests on shared historical narratives, which afford different organizational strategies. These of course may be secondary to more essential geo-ecological concerns, as is illustrated by the apparent ease with which new ethnicities are invented.[85] All of these of course also make a contribution to security, and get wrapped up in localised ethical systems.

In conclusion, any artifact that transforms perception to more relevant information, including action, is AI—and note that AI is an adjective, not a noun, unless it is referring to the academic discipline. There is no question that AI and digital technologies more generally are introducing enormous transformations to society. Nevertheless, these impacts should be governable by less transformative legislative change. The vast majority of AI—particularly where it has social impact—is and will remain a consequence of corporate commercial processes, and as such subject to existing regulations and regulating strategies. We may need more regulatory bodies with expertise in examining the accounts of software development, but it is critical to remember that what we are holding accountable is not the machines themselves but the people who build, own, or operate them—including any who alter their operation through assault on their cybersecurity. What we need to govern is the human application of technology, and what we need to oversee are human processes of development, testing, operation, and monitoring.

Artificial intelligence also offers us an opportunity to discover more about how we ourselves and our societies work. By allowing us to construct artifacts that mimic aspects of nature but provide new affordances for modularity and decoupling, we allow ourselves novel means of self-examination, including examination of our most crucial capacities such as morality and political behavior. This is an exciting time for scientific and artistic exploration as well as for commerce and law. But better knowledge also

[83] Cansu Canca, "Human Rights and AI Ethics: Why Ethics Cannot Be Replaced by the UDHR," *United Nations Univ.: AI & Global Governance Articles & Insights* (July 2019), https://cpr.unu.edu/ai-global-governance-human-rights-and-ai-ethics-why-ethics-cannot-be-replaced-by-the-udhr.html.

[84] Bill McSweeney, *Security, Identity and Interests: A Sociology of International Relations* Cambridge University Press (1999); Simon T. Powers, "The Institutional Approach for Modeling the Evolution of Human Societies," *Artif. Life* 24.1 (2018): 10–28.

[85] Erin K. Jenne, Stephen M. Saideman, and Will Lowe, "Separatism as a Bargaining Posture: The Role of Leverage in Minority Radicalization," *J. Peace Research* 44.5 (2007): 539–558.

offers an opportunity for better control. The role of the law for crafting both individual and societal protections has never been more crucial.

ACKNOWLEDGMENTS

A small proportion of the material in this review was derived from a document previously delivered to the OECD (Karine Perset) in May 2017 under the title "Current and Potential Impacts of Artificial Intelligence and Autonomous Systems on Society," which contributed to the OECD AI policy efforts and documents of 2018–2019, and also was reused (with permission) and expanded for Bryson (2019 BBVA). More debt is probably owed to Frank Pasquale for extremely useful feedback and suggestions on a first draft. Thanks also to Will Lowe, Patrick Slavenburg, and Jean-Paul Skeete. I was supported in part by an AXA Research Fellowship in AI Ethics while writing this chapter.

REFERENCES

Boden, Margaret et al. *Principles of Robotics*. The United Kingdom's Engineering and Physical Sciences Research Council (EPSRC). Apr. 2011. https://www.epsrc.ac.uk/research/ourportfolio/themes/engineering/activities/principlesofrobotics/.

Brundage, Miles et al. *The Malicious Use of Artificial Intelligence: Forecasting, Prevention, and Mitigation*. Tech. rep. https://maliciousaireport.com/. Future of Humanity Institute, University of Oxford, Centre for the Study of Existential Risk, University of Cambridge, Center for a New American Security, Electronic Frontier Foundation, and OpenAI, Feb. 2018.

Bryson, Joanna J. "The Past Decade and Future of AI's Impact on Society." In *Towards a New Enlightenment? A Transcendent Decade*, OpenMind BBVA (commissioned, based on a white paper also commissioned, that by the OECD). Madrid: Taylor, Mar. 2019.

Bryson, Joanna J., Mihailis E. Diamantis, and Thomas D. Grant. "Of, For, and by the People: The Legal Lacuna of Synthetic Persons." *Artificial Intelligence and Law* 25.3 (Sept. 2017): 273–91.

Cadwalladr, Carole. " 'I Made Steve Bannon's Psychological Warfare Tool': Meet the Data War Whistleblower." *The Observer* (March 18, 2018).

Claxton, Guy. *Intelligence in the Flesh: Why Your Mind Needs Your Body Much More Than It Thinks*. New Haven, CT: Yale University Press, 2015.

Cohen, Julie E. "What Privacy Is For." In: *Harv. L. Rev.* 126 (May 2013): 1904–33.

Dennett, Daniel C. "Why You Can't Make a Computer That Feels Pain." *Brainstorms*. Reprint, Montgomery, VT: Bradford Books, 1978, 190–229.

Gunkel, David J. *Robot Rights*. Cambridge, MA: MIT Press, 2018.

Hüttermann, Michael. *DevOps for Developers*. New York: Apress/Springer, 2012.

Kroll, Joshua A., et al. "Accountable Algorithms." *Univ. Penn. L. Rev.* 165 (2017): 633–706.

List, Christian, and Philip Pettit. *Group Agency: The Possibility, Design, and Status of Corporate Agents*. Oxford: Oxford University Press, 2011.

Nemitz, Paul. "Constitutional Democracy and Technology in the Age of Artificial Intelligence." *Philosophical Transactions of the Royal Soc. A: Mathematical, Physical and Engineering Sciences* 376.2133 (2018): 20180089.

OECD. *Recommendation of the Council on Artificial Intelligence*. OECD Legal Instruments OECD/LEGAL/0449 (includes the OECD Principles of AI). Paris: Organisation for Economic Cooperation and Development, May 2019.

O'Neill, Onora. *A Question of Trust: The BBC Reith Lectures 2002*. Cambridge: Cambridge University Press, 2002.

O'Reilly, Tim. *WTF? What's the Future and Why It's Up to Us*. New York: Random House, 2017.

Santoni deSio, Filippo, and Jeroen van den Hoven. "Meaningful Human Control over Autonomous Systems: A Philosophical Account." *Frontiers in Robotics and AI* 5(2018): 15.

Shanahan, Murray. *The Technological Singularity*. Cambridge, MA: MIT Press, 2015.

Sipser, Michael. *Introduction to the Theory of Computation*. 2nd ed. Boston: PWS, Thompson, 2005.

CHAPTER 2

••

THE ETHICS OF
THE ETHICS OF AI

••

THOMAS M. POWERS AND
JEAN-GABRIEL GANASCIA

INTRODUCTION

THE broad outlines of the ethics of AI are coming into focus as researchers advance the state of the art and more applications enter the private and public sectors. Like earlier technologies such as nuclear fission and recombinant DNA, AI technologies will bring risks and rewards for individuals and societies. For instance, the safety of pedestrians in the path of autonomous vehicles, the privacy of consumers as they are analyzed as data subjects, and the fairness of selection procedures for loan or job applicants—as they are (algorithmically) "scrutinized"—will increasingly be of concern. Those concerns will affect societies as we grapple with the moral and legal status of these new artificial agents, which will increasingly act without direct human supervision. The risks are largely seen as justifying the rewards, and the latter are expected to be significant indeed. Economic forecasts tout robust and relatively certain revenue growth and productivity gains from AI for the next few decades,[1] yet at the same time increased unemployment is expected as industrial labor markets shrink due to rapid AI outsourcing of skilled and unskilled labor. On a more global level, AI will continue to transform science and engineering, but it can also be used to afford leisure and expand knowledge in the humanities.[2] When combined with efficient data-gathering techniques and break-throughs in genetics, nanoscience, and cognitive science, AI will almost certainly entice

[1] Philippe Aghion, Benjamin F. Jones, and Charles I. Jones, "Artificial Intelligence and Economic Growth," in *The Economics of Artificial Intelligence: An Agenda*, ed. Ajay Agrawal, Joshua Gans, and Avi Goldfarb (Chicago: University of Chicago Press, 2019), 237–82.

[2] Jean-Gabriel Ganascia, "Epistemology of AI Revisited in the Light of the Philosophy of Information," *Knowledge, Technology, and Policy* 23 (2010): 57–73, accessible at: https://doi.org/10.1007/s12130-010-9101-0.

us to effect a greater mastery of our planet. Perhaps AI will first pass through a stage of attempts, via surveillance, policing, and militarization, to also master other human beings.

Faced with this panoply of ethical concerns, which implicate fundamental human rights (privacy, security, equal opportunity), ethical principles (fairness, respect), and equitable distributions of burdens and benefits, it may be useful first to ask: How ought we to approach the ethics of AI? Or, in other words, what are the ethics of the ethics of AI? The preceding account suggests that issues might be engaged on individual, social, and global levels. To be sure, ethicists have begun to make progress on ethical concerns with AI by working within a particular level, and through approaches (deontological, consequentialist, virtue ethics, etc.) common to other fields of applied ethics. Scholarship in machine ethics, robotic ethics, data science ethics, military ethics, and other fields is generating interest from within and without academia. The ethics of AI may be a "work in progress," but it is at least a call that has been answered.

But will this be enough? The thesis of the present chapter is that the common approaches may not be sufficient, primarily due to the transformational nature of AI within science, engineering, and human culture. Heretofore, ethicists have understood key ethical concepts, such as agency, responsibility, intention, autonomy, virtue, right, moral status, preference, and interest, along models drawn almost exclusively from examples of human cognitive ability and reasoned behavior. Ethicists have "applied" ethics accordingly with these conceptual tools at hand. Artificial intelligence will challenge all those concepts, and more, as ethicists begin to digest the problem of continued human coexistence with alternate (and perhaps superior) intelligences. That is to say, AI will challenge the very way in which we have tried to reason about ethics for millennia. If this is correct, novel approaches will be needed to address the ethics of AI in the future. To go further and implement ethics in AI, we will need to overcome some serious barriers to the formalization of ethics.

Further complicating factors in doing the ethics of AI concern epistemic issues, broadly speaking. First, we (ethicists) generally learn of AI applications only after they appear, at which point we attempt to "catch up" and possibly alter or limit the applications. This is essentially a rearguard action. The time lag owes to the fact that ethicists are not in the business of predicting the emergence of technologies. While it would be good if we could figure out the ethics of a technology prior to it being released in the marketplace or public sphere—if we could do "anticipatory ethics"[3]—the necessary predictive skill would not be the domain of ethics. Further, when ethicists *do* try to predict the trajectory of a new technology into future applications in order to critique it, they often get the trajectory wrong. This overestimation of future technological/ethical problems leads some ethicists to become (amateur) futurists, and these futurists often spend an inordinate amount of time worrying about technological applications that will never come to pass.

Second, the epistemic complications of AI turn on the fact that AI itself is changing what we know, especially in the realm of science. Computational data science (CDS),

---

[3] Philip A. E. Brey, "Anticipatory Ethics for Emerging Technologies," *Nanoethics* 6:1 (2012): 1–13.

which includes "big data" science and other discovery-based techniques, adds immensely to the body of accessible information and correlations about the natural and social worlds, thus changing how scientists think about the process of inquiry. Computational data science calls into question whether this new knowledge really adds to our human scientific understanding. Since many ethical analyses depend on scientifically derived knowledge—especially knowledge of social facts and relations—we are placed in a difficult epistemic position. Whether one conceives of the body of knowledge as a coherentist "raft" or as a foundationalist "pyramid,"[4] the expansion of knowledge due to AI seems to be an epistemic gift, and at the same time we cannot fully understand what we are really getting.

Our goal in the following reflections is not to resolve or even attempt to analyze specific ethical issues that arise with AI. Rather, we will survey what we believe are the most important challenges for progress in the ethics of AI. At the present moment, there are many AI applications that are driving the interest in ethics; among them are autonomous vehicles, battlefield (lethal) robots, recommender systems in commerce and social media, and facial recognition software. In the near future we may have to grapple with disruptions in human social and sexual relationships caused by androids or with jurisprudence administered primarily by intelligent software. The developments in AI—now and in the foreseeable future—are sufficiently worrisome such that progress in the ethics of AI is in itself an ethical issue.

The discussion of these challenges incorporates longstanding philosophical issues as well as issues related to computer science and computer engineering. We leave it to the reader to pursue technical details of both philosophical and scientific issues presented here, and we reference the background literature for such inquiries. The challenges fall into five major categories: conceptual ambiguities, the estimation of risks, implementing machine ethics, epistemic issues of scientific explanation and prediction, and oppositional versus systemic ethics approaches.

CONCEPTUAL AMBIGUITIES

Research in ethics and in AI, respectively, involves distinct scholarly communities, so it is not surprising that terminological problems arise. Key concepts in contemporary (philosophical) ethics also appear in the AI literature—especially concepts such as agent, autonomy, and intelligence—though typically ethicists and AI experts attach different meanings to these terms. In this section, we explain standard meanings that attach to these three polysemous concepts in both fields. While we cannot hope to dissolve the ambiguities in favor of one or another meaning, we want to draw attention to them as sources of potential problems within the ethics of AI.

---

[4] Ernest Sosa, "The Raft and the Pyramid: Coherence versus Foundations in the Theory of Knowledge," *Midwest Studies in Philosophy* 5:1 (1980): 3–26.

Agent

Central to modern AI since the 1980s, the notion of an agent—and one that is supposed to be "intelligent"—has often been seen as the main unifying theme of the discipline. That is particularly apparent in the renowned manual on artificial intelligence by Stuart J. Russell and Peter Norvig, *Artificial Intelligence: A Modern Approach*, which defines AI "as the study of agents that receive percepts from the environment and perform actions."[5] The theme is repeated in the classical "human problem solving" account in Alan Newell and Herbert A. Simon's *Human Problem Solving*,[6] also published in Newell's work in "The Knowledge Level,"[7] and in the widely used notion of multi-agent systems (MAS) that refers to systems composed of a plurality of agents interacting together. In the context of AI, the notion of an agent is closely related to its meaning in economics or in cognitive sciences, since all these terms characterize entities that act. More precisely, following Russell and Norvig, we can say that an AI "agent implements a function that maps percept sequences to actions." Within this definition, the structure of actions is reduced to their mechanical consequences, while their objectives—the goals the agent pursues or, in more philosophical terms, the intentions—are not specified. Those are given from outside, which means that artificial agents do not initiate actions; they are not aware of what they do when acting.

In philosophy, an agent intends (upon reflection) its actions. It is aware of the selection of intentions, and it initiates actions based on them. In other words, artificial agents (for philosophy) do not have agency.

The differences between these two conceptions of agents—the technical one in AI, economics, and psychology as well as the philosophical one—have important consequences from an ethical point of view. Obviously, since an AI agent lacks true proper goals, personal intentions, or real freedom, it cannot be considered to be responsible for its actions, in part because it cannot explain why it behaves in such and such a way and not in other ways. This is not so with the notion of "agent" as understood in its philosophical sense, where an explanation (or an accounting) of action can be expected. This issue has been widely debated in the philosophical community, for instance, in connection with Daniel Dennett's notion of an "intentional system,"[8] which can be used to describe computers to which people ascribe intentions, desires, and beliefs by calling them *intentional agents*.[9] However, even in that case, Dennett clearly specifies that what he calls the "intentional stance" is only a prerequisite for the "moral stance" to which it

---

[5] Stuart J. Russell and Peter Norvig, *Artificial Intelligence: A Modern Approach*, 3rd ed. (Upper Saddle River, NJ: Prentice-Hall, 2010).

[6] Alan Newell and Herbert A. Simon, *Human Problem Solving* (Englewood Cliffs, NJ: Prentice-Hall, 1972).

[7] Alan Newell, "The Knowledge Level," *Artificial Intelligence* 18 (1982): 87–127.

[8] Daniel C. Dennett, "Intentional Systems," *Journal of Philosophy* 68:4 (1971): 87–106.

[9] Daniel C. Dennett, *The Intentional Stance* (Cambridge, MA: MIT Press, 1987).

cannot be fully assimilated.[10] In other words, a "moral agent" has to be an "intentional system," while there are many "intentional systems," like artificial agents, that are not "moral agents."

Autonomy

The adjective "autonomous" and the concept of autonomy to which it is connected have been widely employed in the last few years to characterize systems that behave without human intervention. More precisely, a device is said to be autonomous if there exists a sequence of cause-effect relations—from the capture of information by sensors to the execution of an action—without the intervention of any human being. Referring to this definition, AI researchers currently speak of autonomous cars, weapons, and (perhaps in a more frightening way) of "lethal autonomous weapon systems" (also referred to as LAWS). In these usages, it is very difficult to distinguish autonomy from automaticity, since in both cases the relevant behavior corresponds to entities that act by themselves, which clearly corresponds to the etymology of *automaton*: αυτο (self) + ματος (movement). However, not only does the etymology of autonomy—αυτο (self) + νομος (law)—differ from that of automaticity, but its usual meaning, at least for philosophers, designates an entity able to define by itself its own laws or rules of behavior, while in the case of an automaton these rules are given or imposed from outside. Originally, the adjective "autonomous" described a political entity (e.g., a sovereign city, kingdom, or state), which decided by itself its constitution and its laws. This meaning survives in the granting of limited self-rule in the several "autonomous regions" of various nation-states. Following the philosophers of the Enlightenment, in particular Rousseau and Kant, this meaning of autonomy has been extended to human beings. Here it denotes an ideal situation in which individuals would decide their maxims of conduct for themselves without being commanded by kings, presidents, or others. So, in a way, an autonomous being that obeys its own rules will choose them by itself, and thus will reflect on what it will do, while an automaton acts by obeying rules imposed on it and without reflection.

To see why the semantics matters, let us consider an example. Suppose we want an autonomous vehicle to drive us safely to the destination that we have indicated. For instance, if we want to go to the swimming pool, and we clearly indicate to the car that this what we want, we expect such a technology to adopt that specified goal. Now, let us assume that the car is autonomous (according to the philosophical understanding), i.e., that it decides by itself, and not following a person's order, what will be its goal and rule of conduct. It may choose to make an appointment for you at the dentist (perhaps in a paternalistic way), or drive you to the movie theater because the parking there looks to be more comfortable for it. As a consequence, a "real" autonomous car is above all

[10] Daniel C. Dennett, "Mechanism and Responsibility," in Ted Honderich (ed.), *Essays on Freedom of Action* (London: Routledge & Kegan Paul, 1972), 157–84.

somewhat unpredictable for the person who is being conveyed by it, and consequently it is not so desirable as a mode of transportation!

Worse still, imagine a "real" (philosophically) autonomous weapon that would choose by itself who it would target. This would be a nightmare not only for civilians and noncombatants but also for military personnel who need, first and foremost, weapon systems that they can fully control and trust. From this point of view, it is quite unlikely that a military would develop "real" autonomous weapons, even though autonomous weapons that fit the AI or engineering definition seem quite desirable.

In many philosophical traditions, agency and autonomy are properties of adult, rational beings or moral persons who have the ability to choose and regulate their own behaviors. Agency and autonomy are necessary conditions of responsibility. In AI an agent is a piece of software within a larger computer system that performs a function on behalf of a user or another software agent. An autonomous agent in AI is a piece of software that functions more or less continuously without the direct intervention of a user. In AI, the concepts of agent and autonomy are used without any obvious connection to responsibility. As a result of these conceptual differences, it is important to recognize that a (philosophical) autonomous agent acts on its own behalf, and has the ability to "intervene" in its own behavior (at the least), while a (software) AI autonomous agent does not itself have a concept of "its own behalf." This is not to say that it is inconceivable that someday there will be software agents that act absolutely without human intervention and on their own behalf. Perhaps then it will make sense to attribute responsibility to them for their actions. But the point is that, with the AI agents we now have, this is not the case. Nonetheless, there are still ethical issues that arise when AI agents act on the behalf of other users or software agents, and also when they act (relatively) independently of human intervention.

Intelligence

Though philosophical studies of intelligence, going back to Vico's work in the eighteenth century, considered it to be a distinctively human ability, it is now acknowledged that intelligence can have other instantiations. Because it plays such an important role both in AI and in the public imagination of computation in general, the concept of intelligence needs to be clarified. In early modern philosophy, intelligence was typically interchangeable with understanding and indicated an ability to comprehend or grasp aspects of an internal or external reality. In contemporary philosophical usage, intelligence has largely been supplanted by the concept of mind. In the natural and social sciences, especially in psychology, intelligence denotes cognitive abilities that are susceptible to measurement—for instance, via an intelligence quotient that aggregates the results of different tests in order to grade the relative abilities of people in a population.

The technical meaning of "intelligence" in AI—one that assumes that we can engineer intelligence—derives from its significance in psychology. The proposal of the Dartmouth Summer Research Project on Artificial Intelligence (written mainly by John

McCarthy and Marvin Minsky) contains in its introduction the central motivating claim of AI: "The study [of Artificial Intelligence] is to proceed on the basis of the conjecture that every aspect of learning or any other feature of intelligence can in principle be so precisely described that a machine can be made to simulate it."[11] Intelligence is here conceived as a set of mathematically describable cognitive functions, which AI aims to model and then simulate with machines.

Despite this narrowing of intelligence into a technical concept, it has taken on a meaning in both the public imagination and the marketing literature of some IT companies, along with a significance that includes a mixture of very different capacities: will, consciousness, reflection, and even an aptness to perceive and feel emotions. Unfortunately, discussions about the intelligence of AI systems are often an admixture of popular, philosophical, and scientific conceptions.

Closely connected to intelligence in work on the philosophy of mind is the (philosophical) notion of consciousness. One standard assumption in philosophy is that all intelligent entities have consciousness as the "backdrop" or "framework" in which intelligence happens, as it were. Though some philosophers such as David Chalmers see in consciousness a "hard problem,"[12] which suggests that it may never be integrated into the physical sciences, consciousness is sometimes employed by writers in AI to characterize a possible capacity of future intelligent systems. But unlike in philosophy, there is no assumption of an intelligent computer's "first-person perspective" nor a "having" of computational states that are equivalent to mental states that philosophers call "qualia," that is, "what it is like" to have a particular awareness (e.g., seeing the red apple). A middle-ground notion of consciousness has been suggested, according to which a machine would behave as though it were conscious if it had (1) global availability of relevant information (access to an "internal global workspace") and (2) self-monitoring ("reflexive representation").[13] Here we see the return of Dennett's intentional stance, with a measure of behaviorism thrown in.

To conclude this section on the conceptual ambiguities that arise in ethical debates around AI, let us consider two broadly used terms in the field: "intelligent agent" and "autonomous agent." Taking into account what we have said about the philosophical meanings of these terms, they seem to resemble the famous Lichtenberg knife (which lacks a blade and a handle), since the "autonomous agents" are neither autonomous nor agents (for the philosophers), and likewise "intelligent agents" are neither intelligent nor agents.

---

[11] John McCarthy, Marvin Minsky, Nathaniel Rochester, and Claude E. Shannon, "A Proposal for the Dartmouth Summer Research Project on Artificial Intelligence" (1955), accessible at: http://raysolomonoff.com/dartmouth/boxa/dart564props.pdf.

[12] David J. Chalmers, "Facing up to the Problem of Consciousness," *Journal of Consciousness Studies* 2 (1995): 200–219.

[13] Stanislas Dehaene, Hakwan Lau, and Sid Kouider, "What Is Consciousness, and Could Machines Have It?" *Science* 358:6362 (2017): 486–92.

RISK: OVERESTIMATION AND UNDERESTIMATION

Partly due to the aforementioned ambiguities, and partly to current social demand driven by popular media,[14,15,16,17] which overemphasize the "dangers" of AI, estimations of the risks of AI suffer from both excess and deficiency. On the side of excess, the presumed dangers include allegedly autonomous AIs that operate without any human control, the weaponization of AI globally, and the development of an AI that would "choose its own ends." The popular media as well as some AI experts have fallen into the confusion over agency and autonomy in machines, as indicated earlier, and may become fixated on speculative risks. One example is the recent focus on driverless cars and the claim that they will introduce potentially unsolvable "trolley problems" into the application of these AI technologies. On the side of deficiency, there are AI systems that present real (but underestimated) risks now. For instance, using AI techniques, deepfake software synthesizes fake human pornographic videos that combine and superimpose an existing person's face on a prerecorded video with a different body, so that this person seems to do or say things that he/she never did. Another overlooked application of AI comes in facial recognition and recommending techniques that have been implemented in China to give a "reputation score." The system automatically identifies minor law infractions by citizens, for instance crossing the road at the green light, and aggregates them. Such examples suggest that identity, sexual orientation, consumer tendencies, and the like will all be subject to AI tools. In this section, we discuss the ethical implications of under- and overestimation of AI risks.

Overestimations and Existential Threats from AI

Among the current overestimations of AI, some critiques revisit earlier fears about technology in general. By mimicking human behaviors and abilities, AI, it is feared, creates (or may soon create) artificial human beings and, in so doing, will attempt to "play" or

---

[14] Joel Achenbach, "Driverless Cars Are Colliding with the Creepy Trolley Problem," *Washington Post* (December 29, 2015), accessible at: https://www.washingtonpost.com/news/innovations/wp/2015/12/29/will-self-driving-cars-ever-solve-the-famous-and-creepy-trolley-problem/.

[15] Joel Achenbach, "The A.I. Anxiety," *Washington Post* (December 27, 2015), accessible at: http://www.washingtonpost.com/sf/national/2015/12/27/aianxiety/.

[16] Patrick Lin, "The Ethics of Autonomous Cars," *The Atlantic* (October 8, 2013), accessible at: http://www.theatlantic.com/technology/archive/2013/10/the-ethics-of-autonomous-cars/280360/.

[17] Henry A. Kissinger, "How the Enlightenment Ends: Philosophically, Intellectually—in Every Way—Human Society Is Unprepared for the Rise of Artificial Intelligence," *The Atlantic* (June 2018), accessible at: https://www.theatlantic.com/magazine/archive/2018/06/henry-kissinger-ai-could-mean-the-end-of-human-history/559124/.

"challenge" God as the Supreme Maker. If this were the case, AI would commit, at the least, a symbolic transgression. As an illustration, consider both the enthusiasm and fear that attended the public unveiling of Japanese roboticist Hirochi Ishiguro's Geminoids.[18] By so closely approximating his own appearance with a robot, Ishiguro invited a comparison to the myth of Pygmalion, who falls in love with his statue Galatea. Nonetheless, Ishiguro's robot was not at all autonomous; it was remotely controlled. In the same way, the robot "Sophia," developed by the company Hanson Robotics, received "citizenship" in Saudi Arabia after her speech at a United Nations meeting. The speech was not automatically generated by "Sophia" herself but prerecorded by an organic human female.

Instances of "overselling" of scientific results seem also to be subject to amplification when AI techniques are involved. Psychologists recently published claims that a deep neural network has been trained to better detect sexual orientation from facial images than can humans.[19] The ethical issues here are multiple. It is unclear that AI is in fact capable of such results, given the assumption that sexual orientation is fixed by genetics. That uncertainty notwithstanding, the use of such techniques could be damaging for homosexuals, regardless of the robustness of results. Likewise, there is considerable interest in brain-computer interfaces (BCI), which are supposed to directly plug a brain (or should we say, a mind?) into a computer network without pain or effort. These alleged "mind reads" have drawn the attention of famous technologists such as Mark Zuckerberg.[20] However, the current state of the art does not warrant belief in a generic human-machine interface, though research has shown that stroke patients may regain motor control of a limb through such interfaces.[21] These doubts notwithstanding, Neuralink, a firm founded by Elon Musk, offers another illustration of the allure of a direct connection between our mortal minds and the (immortal) digital world. This company aims at developing plug-in chips in our skull to increase our cognitive abilities and, more specifically, our memory in order to "save the human race" against AI. These hopes are a double overestimation of AI: the first is that AI will constitute an existential threat for humanity; and the second is that AI technology can be used to avoid such a disaster. According to Musk, one difficult task when merging our mind to the digital is that "it's mostly about the bandwidth, the speed of the connection between your brain and the digital version of yourself, particularly output."[22] However, contemporary

---

[18] Erico Guizzo, "The Man Who Made a Copy of Himself," *IEEE Spectrum* 47:4 (April 2010): 44–56.

[19] Yilun Wang and Michal Kosinski, "Deep Neural Networks Are More Accurate Than Humans at Detecting Sexual Orientation from Facial Images," *Journal of Personality and Social Psychology* 114: 2 (2018): 246–57, accessible at: http://dx.doi.org/10.1037/pspa0000098.

[20] Noam Cohen. "Zuckerberg Wants Facebook to Build a Mind-Reading Machine," *WIRED* (April 2019), accessible at: https://www.wired.com/story/zuckerberg-wants-facebook-to-build-mind-reading-machine/.

[21] Society for Neuroscience, "Potential Brain-Machine Interface for Hand Paralysis: Combining Brain Stimulation with a Robotic Device Could Help Restore Hand Function in Stroke Patients,"*Science Daily* (January 15, 2018), accessible at: www.sciencedaily.com/releases/2018/01/180115151611.htm.

[22] Nick Statt, "Elon Musk Launches Neuralink, a Venture to Merge the Human Brain with AI," *The Verge* (March 27, 2017), accessible at: https://www.theverge.com/2017/3/27/15077864/elon-musk-neuralink-brain-computer-interface-ai-cyborgs.

neurosciences have no idea of the cortex's internal code, which means that the issue of the "link" is not so straightforward. Further, if such devices were really in service and plugged into our brains, the owners of these technologies could always load whatever information they wanted into a "linked" mind, which would give them considerable power over us.

Besides these specific examples of AI technology hopes and fears, there exist other overestimations of AI progress that might be called "existential" in that they purportedly threaten the future of humanity. Among them, some are of particular importance because they claim that humankind will very soon become obsolete. In 1956 Günther Anders announced this thesis in a book that would eventually be translated as *The Obsolescence of Man*.[23] This pessimistic view would be repeated by the famous astrophysicist Stephen Hawking and the theoretical physicist and Nobel laureate Frank Wilczek. A slightly less pessimistic view is that humans will join with machines in a kind of hybrid, which would then offer, at the least, an extension of life or possibly immortality. Proponents of this last view are scientists such as Ray Kurzweil, philosopher Nick Boström, and Musk.

The obsolescence and replacement views are sometimes based on the Singularity hypothesis and the possibility of superintelligence. One of the first expressions of these ideas goes back to 1962 when it was proposed by British statistician Irvin John Good,[24] who had worked with Alan Turing during World War II. Good discussed the possibility of an "intelligence explosion" that would follow the development of "ultra-intelligent machines," themselves able to build more intelligent machinery. The Polish mathematician Stanislaw Ulam and science fiction writers, including Isaac Asimov, are also credited with inventing the idea in the 1950s that a "Singularity" could be the consequence of the considerably accelerating progress of computer technology.[25]

Science fiction novelist Vernor Vinge popularized the idea in an essay entitled "The Coming Technological Singularity."[26] He argued that within less than thirty years, the progress of information technology would allow the making of a superhuman intelligent entity that would dramatically change the status of humankind. In particular, the connection of humans to machines and their mutual hybridization would allow us to considerably increase our intelligence, our lifespan, and capacities of all kinds. The key idea is that the acceleration of technological progress would suddenly and irreversibly alter the regime of knowledge production, creating technological developments beyond any hope of control.

---

[23] Günther Anders, *Die Antiquiertheit des Menschen Bd. I: Über die Seele im Zeitalter der zweiten industriellen Revolution*. (Munich: C. H. Beck, 2018).

[24] Irving J. Good, "Speculations Concerning the First Ultraintelligent Machine," *Advances in Computers* 6 (1966): 31–88.

[25] Isaac Asimov, "The Last Question," *Science Fiction Quarterly* 4:5 (Nov. 1956).

[26] Vernor Vinge, "The Coming Technological Singularity: How to Survive in the Post-Human Era," in *Vision 21: Interdisciplinary Science and Engineering in the Era of Cyberspace* (Cleveland: NASA Lewis Research Center, 1993), 11–22.

More recently, technologists like Ray Kurzweil,[27] Hans Moravec,[28] Hugo de Garis,[29] Kevin Warwick,[30] Bill Joy,[31] and even philosophers such as Nick Boström and Julian Savulescu[32] have theorized a future where the technological Singularity was supposed to play a major role. There are differences among all of these writers; some consider new plagues generated by the development of computing power while others proclaim the end of humankind and the emergence of a new species. What is common to their views is the rather credulous leap to the conclusion that the Singularity is a coherent scientific eventuality.

Despite its popularity, the main idea of the Singularity is quite dubious. In fact, it appears just to be an inference from the exponential increase of computing power characterized by Moore's law, which will somehow lead to ultraintelligent machines. However, Moore's law—put forward in 1965—is an empirical description of the evolution of hardware. It describes the increase in computing speed, along with an exponential diminution of the cost of storage devices, as borne out by historical evidence. It has held, more or less, for sixty years now. Moore's law makes an inductive prediction; it is not based on the rigorous foundations of computer science. Its main scope was originally economical, not scientific. As a consequence, there are good reasons to doubt that it will hold indefinitely. In addition, the "amount" of intelligence—a strange notion assumed by advocates of the Singularity—can neither be measured by the frequency of a computer's processing speed nor by the quantity of bits that can be stored in electronic devices. Since its beginning, AI progress has been related to algorithms, to statistics, to mathematical probability theory, and to knowledge representation formalisms or to logic, but not to computing power. And though the efficiency of modern computers renders possible the implementation of parallel algorithms on huge quantities of data, there is no assurance that these developments get us any closer to the Singularity.

Underestimation of AI Risks

Along with these abundant overestimations of AI capacities, which are supposed to be either excessively beneficial for humankind or excessively maleficent, many predatory applications of AI techniques are partly ignored, or at least their potential harm is

[27] Ray Kurzweil, *The Singularity Is Near: When Humans Transcend Biology* (New York: Penguin Books, 2006).

[28] Hans Moravec, "When Will Computer Hardware Match the Human Brain?" *Journal of Evolution and Technology* 1 (1998).

[29] Hugo de Garis, *The Artilect War: Cosmists vs. Terrans: A Bitter Controversy Concerning Whether Humanity Should Build Godlike Massively Intelligent Machines* (Palm Springs, CA: ETC Publications, 2005).

[30] Kevin Warwick, *March of the Machines: The Breakthrough in Artificial Intelligence* (Champaign: University of Illinois Press, 2004).

[31] Bill Joy, "Why the Future Doesn't Need Us," *WIRED* 8 (2001): 1–11.

[32] Nick Bostrom and Julian Savulescu, eds., *Human Enhancement* (Oxford: Oxford University Press, 2008).

scarcely noticed. What we here characterize as "underestimations" of AI risks are just as problematic from an ethical point of view as are overstatements of nonexistent threats. Here we consider a few of these neglected "underestimations" of some AI techniques.

Many famous people seem to fear LAWS—lethal autonomous weapon systems—and propose an official multilateral ban to stop research and military applications in this area.[33] Nonetheless, there are serious doubts whether fully autonomous weapons will ever be developed, since, as mentioned above, what armies need are robust and trustworthy weapons.[34] However, as revealed by "The Drones Papers,"[35] information technologies incorporating many AI components have been used in the drone war in Afghanistan to target supposed terrorists. Drones and more generally unmanned weapons are not autonomous, since they are remotely controlled, but the choice of objectives is done partially automatically, based on informational indices. For instance, conversations or phone localizations have provided targets, and these military uses of AI can contribute to considerable collateral damage (and probably already have).

A second example concerns the state use of facial recognition techniques. Without proper safeguards, these techniques can infringe on individual rights as well as threaten the "dignity of the person" by constant surveillance and guilt by association. They could be used to track and record movement of individuals, especially in urban environments with high density of population. It has been reported that China is now using these techniques to track the minority Uighur population,[36] and facial recognition in China could be combined with their more far-reaching "social credit system" for the entire country.[37] For security reasons, some cities in other countries, for instance the city of Nice in France, plan to use facial recognition to detect suspects of terrorism. We should worry that once in place, the scope of application of such AIs would be extended to all citizens.

A further underestimated risk involves machine learning to predict risk for insurers and to apportion the risk by individualizing insurance premiums. Here there are at least two perverse effects. The first concerns the opacity of the decision criteria, which are not given to clients because most of the time they are not explicit, due to the deep learning techniques on which they are based. Some researchers have become aware of problems with opacity and have tried to introduce explainable AI systems. Explanation is crucial in order to earn public confidence, since without explanation the decisions of the insurance company could be totally arbitrary and based on marketing factors more than

---

[33] Future of Life Institute, "Autonomous Weapons: An Open Letter from AI & Robotics Researchers," published online (July 28, 2015), accessible at: https://futureoflife.org/open-letter-autonomous-weapons/.

[34] Jean-Gabriel Ganascia, Catherine Tessier, and Thomas M. Powers, "On the Autonomy and Threat of 'Killer Robots,'" *APA Newsletter on Philosophy and Computers* 17:2 (2018): 3–9.

[35] The Intercept, "The Drone Papers," published online (October 15, 2015), accessible at: https://theintercept.com/drone-papers/.

[36] Paul Mozur, "One Month, 500,000 Face Scans: How China Is Using A.I. to Profile a Minority," *New York Times* (April 14, 2019), accessible at: https://www.nytimes.com/2019/04/14/technology/china-surveillance-artificial-intelligence-racial-profiling.html.

[37] Rachel Botsman, "Big Data Meets Big Brother as China Moves to Rate Its Citizens," *WIRED* (October 21, 2017), accessible at: https://www.wired.co.uk/article/chinese-government-social-credit-score-privacy-invasion.

on risk.[38] But the second perverse effect would be to change the original nature of insurance, which relies on mutualizing (pooling) risks, and consequently to weaken solidarity and a sense of community.

A final underestimated risk of AI to be considered here concerns predictive justice, which aims at establishing sanctions according to the risk of repeat offenses of the law. Depending on the criteria that are used, these applications could not only be unjust but also deny the relevance of redemption and contrition. In addition, this raises fundamental questions about the nature of juridical sanction, which in principle has to be based on actual infringement of laws and not on potential offense. As in the short story "The Minority Report" (1956) by Philip K. Dick and the film adaptation *Minority Report* directed by Steven Spielberg (2002), this AI application could lead to the punishment of persons guilty of a precrime, that is to say, of a crime that has not yet been committed but that in all probability will be.

Implementing Ethics

Making Machines Moral

Undoubtedly, it would be tempting to introduce human values in machines to make them moral, which means to make them behave in accordance with criteria of moral behavior generally, or, for the deontologist, to act only according to duty. We might then ponder the distinction, attributed to Kant, between acting merely in conformity to duty versus acting from a sense of it, which the good will alone achieves. However, since a machine does not determine its own ends or goals of action, but acts on goals given to it from outside, invoking will—that is, diving errantly into machine motivations—would seem foolish. Thus, we shall only consider here the ability of a machine to *behave* morally, without invoking its moral motivations.

In the past few years, some AI researchers[39,40,41,42,43,44] have attempted to theorize intelligent agents that appeal to ethical considerations when choosing the actions they

[38] Cathy O'Neil, *Weapons of Math Destruction* (New York: Crown Publishers, 2016).

[39] Fiona Berreby, Gauvain Bourgne, and Jean-Gabriel Ganascia, "Event-Based and Scenario-Based Causality for Computational Ethics," in *Proceedings of the 17th Conference on Autonomous Agents and MultiAgent Systems*, (Richland, South Carolina: International Foundation for Autonomous Agents and Multiagent Systems, (2018): 147–55.

[40] Selmer Bringsjord, Konstantine Arkoudas, and Paul Bello, "Toward a General Logicist Methodology for Engineering Ethically Correct Robots," *IEEE Intelligent Systems* 21:4 (2006): 38–44.

[41] Jean-Gabriel Ganascia, "Modelling Ethical Rules of Lying with Answer Set Programming," *Ethics and Information Technology* 9:1 (2007): 39–47.

[42] Wendell Wallach, Colin Allen, and Iva Smit, "Machine Morality: Bottom-up and Top-down Approaches for Modelling Human Moral Faculties" *AI & Society* 22:4 (2008): 565–82.

[43] Thomas M. Powers, "Prospects for a Kantian Machine," *IEEE Intelligent Systems* 21:4 (2006): 46–51.

[44] Amitai Etzioni and Oren Etzioni, "Incorporating Ethics into Artificial Intelligence," *Journal of Ethics* 21:4 (2017): 403–18.

perform. This work can be seen as a response to potentially unpredictable behaviors in machines, as when machine-learning techniques build opaque programs from huge quantities of training examples that no human would be able to assimilate. In such situa- tions, not only are machines unable to explain their behavior in terms understandable by humans but also their decisions could produce significant harms. It therefore seems crucial to control machine behaviors to ensure that they conform to shared social norms and values. This section will give an overview of some ways to introduce ethical controls and also will describe their intrinsic limitations. We note that these approaches are quite remote from actual ethical issues related to current applications of AI, but may become more relevant as AI advances.

Modeling Ethical Reasoning

At first sight, it may seem plausible to model ethical systems with AI techniques, since the prescriptions on which such systems are based have been introduced by humans. However, the attempts to model ethical reasoning have shown the huge difficulties researchers face in doing so. The first difficulty comes from modeling deontic reasoning, that is, reasoning about obligations and permissions. The second is due to the conflicts of norms that occur constantly in ethical reasoning. The third is related to the entangle- ment of reasoning and acting, which requires that we study the morality of the act, per se, but also the values of all its consequences.

To solve the first of these difficulties, concerning the particular nature of rules of duty, some researchers have used deontic logics[45, 46] and formalisms inspired by deontic con- siderations. The second difficulty is approached by the use of techniques that overcome logical contradictions with AI logic–based formalisms,[47] mainly nonmonotonic for- malisms (e.g., default logics[48] and answer set programming),[49] which capture aspects of commonsense reasoning. Lastly, the third approach intertwines the logic-based models of ethical reasoning to formalisms called action languages[50] or causal models,[51] which have been designed to give a clear semantics that provide a strong mathematical grounding

---

[45]   Emiliano Lorini, "On the Logical Foundations of Moral Agency," in *International Conference on Deontic Logic in Computer Science*, ed. T. Ågotnes, J. Broersen, D. Elgesem, *Deontic Logic in Computer Science: DEON 2012*, Lecture Notes in Computer Science 7393 (Berlin: Springer, 2012), 108–22.

[46]   John F Horty, *Agency and Deontic Logic* (Oxford: Oxford University Press, 2001).

[47]   Jean-Gabriel Ganascia, "Non-monotonic Resolution of Conflicts for Ethical Reasoning," in *A Construction Manual for Robots' Ethical Systems*, ed. Robert Trappl (Cham, Switzerland: Springer International Publishing, 2015), 101–18.

[48]   Raymond Reiter, "A Logic for Default Reasoning," *Artificial intelligence* 13:1–2 (1980): 81–132.

[49]   Michael Gelfond, "Answer Sets" *Foundations of Artificial Intelligence* 3 (2008): 285–316.

[50]   Erik T. Mueller, *Commonsense Reasoning: An Event Calculus Based Approach* (Burlington, MA: Morgan Kaufmann, 2014).

[51]   Joseph Y. Halpern and Max Kleiman-Weiner, "Towards Formal Definitions of Blameworthiness, Intention, and Moral Responsibility," *Proceedings of the 32nd AAAI Conference on Artificial Intelligence* (2018): 1853–60.

for understanding the consequences of actions. The technical challenge nowadays is to merge these three approaches, that is to say, to create one that is nonmonotonic, that can handle conflicts of norms, and that uses causal models to evaluate the consequences of actions. While there is a general interest in creating such a moral machine (i.e., one that behaves in conformity with the rules of a morality), all these approaches embrace different normative frameworks—such as utilitarianism, egoism (game theory), deontology, and virtue ethics approaches—that must be simulated. The details of the simulations are usually found to be lacking, especially by philosophers. In addition, there are questions about the practical utility of such moral machines as well as the difficulties in implementing them.

Learning Values

Whatever normative framework is used to simulate moral reasoning, the presumption is that it will be based on values that need to be acquired by the machine and that depend on societies and their ethical traditions. Considering the relativity of norms and values on which moral decisions are made, a few attempts[52, 53] have been made to use machine-learning techniques to automatically learn moral values and rules on which machine morality would be based. The popularity and the efficiency of machine learning drives such projects from a technical point of view, even if they can be criticized from an ethical point of view. Since ethics is not just a question of social acceptancy but also of prescriptions that are not based on observations of how people act (i.e., based on conceptions of how they ought to act), the ethics of AI will have to grapple with this basic difference in approaches to ethics.

To make this concern more concrete, consider the highly publicized "Moral Machine Experiment" that gathered attitudes about how autonomous vehicles ought to solve moral dilemmas in various crash-trajectory scenarios where people (variously described) or animals were put at risk, and others were spared.[54] The researchers employed an online experimental platform to crowdsource attitudes by collecting 40 million preferences from millions of persons across 233 different countries. The researchers compared the attitudes of respondents across regions, countries, cultures, religions, and genders. The results suggested that variations in ethical attitudes correlate with deep cultural traits, and perhaps even with adherence to different moral principles.

[52] David Abel, James MacGlashan, and Michael L. Littman, "Reinforcement Learning as a Framework for Ethical Decision Making," in *The Workshops at the 30th AAAI Conference on Artificial Intelligence*, Technical Report WS-16-02 (Palo Alto, CA: Association for the Advancement of Artificial Intelligence, 2016): 54–61.

[53] Max Kleiman-Weiner, Rebecca Saxe, and J. B. Tenenbaum, "Learning a Common-Sense Moral Theory," *Cognition* 167 (2017): 107–23.

[54] Edmond Awad, Sohan Dsouza, Richard Kim, Jonathan Schulz, Joseph Henrich, Azim Shariff, Jean-François Bonnefon, and Iyad Rahwan, "The Moral Machine Experiment," *Nature* 563 (2018): 59–64.

This is undoubtedly an important result from a social psychology and an empirical-ethics point of view, as it provides evidence of relevant variations in ethical attitudes.

Nevertheless, the researchers seem also to have a normative goal in mind: to introduce these results into the design of autonomous vehicles so that they adapt to local cultures and expectations of the (presumably homogenous) populations where the vehicles will operate. So quite directly the experiment implicates the longstanding issue in ethics about conventionalism and ethical relativity versus the validity of generalizable ethical principles or duties that ethicists might prefer. The authors confront this issue and note that solutions to moral dilemmas provided by ethicists could very well be rejected by the public, and thus might be (in their words) "useless." The lesson here for the ethics of ethics of AI is that there are bound to be approaches to AI ethics that advocate conformity with varying public attitudes. But would ethicists be approving of adultery, for instance, simply because it is widely practiced? When it comes to doing the ethics of AI, should ethicists resist "following the data" and insist on generalizable solutions to moral dilemmas that might strike some publics as "out of touch"? To choose the former "empirical" approach would be to swear off the latter traditional philosophical conception of normativity, but also would allow AI applications to take advantage of machine learning over large datasets. And it is important to note the enthusiasm for machine learning over "big data," which may well influence the development of some ethics of AI.

Intrinsic Limitations

In addition to the controversy over the source of values on which ethical deliberations in AI will be based, another crucial question concerns what constitutes the intelligence of AI agents. As an illustration, consider that the fatal accident of Uber's self-driving car in 2018 in Arizona was not due to faulty sensors but to the decision of Uber, for the sake of the passengers' comfort, to moderate reactions to unidentified obstacles such as leaves or plastic bags. This means that the accident in question was not due to an unethical deliberation but to a fateful judgment about safety versus comfort that had been programmed by engineers.

In a totally different context—that of lethal battlefield robots—Ron Arkin's ethical governor[55] for robot soldiers provides another illustration of hard problems that automatic AI systems will have to face. Arkin proposes to use AI techniques to implement just war theory, the International Laws of War, and a particular operation's Rules of Engagement in a control module called the *ethical governor*. This is supposed to control a robot soldier's decision procedures to make it more ethical than human soldiers, who, under the emotional pressures of battle, often feel anger, fatigue, and desperation and thus behave inappropriately. Among the *jus in bello* rules that need to be implemented

---

[55] Ronald C. Arkin, Patrick Ulam, and Brittany Duncan, "An Ethical Governor for Constraining Lethal Action in an Autonomous System," Technical Report GIT-GVU-09-02, Georgia Institute of Technology Mobile Robot Lab (2009).

in such situations are the discrimination between military personnel and civilians and the protection of civilians. However, especially in asymmetric conflicts where soldiers do not wear uniforms, such discrimination is very difficult, even for humans. How can we ensure that a robot will correctly discriminate? This is a question of judgment—understood not as juridical or normative judgment but rather as an operation of categorizing objects in a situation from flows of information. Further, the discrimination rule has two exceptions: (1) when human soldiers are disarmed, they can be taken prisoner but must be protected according to international laws; and (2) when civilians take part in hostilities, they become combatants and can be attacked. In both cases, the intelligence of the judgment or categorization precedes the ethical deliberation; in fact, it seems to exhaust it. It appears that the practical problems are not due to difficult ethical deliberations, of which the autonomous vehicle "crash" dilemma is certainly the most popular illustration, but to questions of judgment, which are difficult even for humans.

EPISTEMIC ISSUES WITH ETHICAL IMPLICATIONS: PREDICTIVE SCIENCE

In recent decades the role of epistemology in ethics has emerged from some traditional concerns of moral or meta-ethical epistemology, that is, issues about the nature of moral knowledge, what counts as evidence for moral claims, and the like. The more recent concerns highlight the simple, practical point that *what* one knows or believes tends to structure one's ethical obligations. Ethical disputes can indeed revolve around the grounds for obligation, but even assuming agreement on the grounds, disputes can also arise concerning the facts that would activate an obligation. For instance, suppose two agents believe in general that saving the planet from environmental ruin is an obligation, but one of them denies that climate change is real and has been deprived of knowledge of it. Then that latter agent is not (practically speaking) obligated to act to save the planet; the agent lacks the motivation because she lacks knowledge. Knowing precedes recognition of an obligation to act.

Artificial intelligence enters the concern about epistemology in ethics in virtue of the fact that AI is an increasingly large "supplier" of scientific information and results—especially in those disciplines identified as practicing Big Data science—and as AI continues to grow in importance for science, our epistemic dependence on AI will only increase. This will be true of descriptions of the natural world, but also of predictions, since they come from data-intensive mathematical models. So another important challenge for the ethics of ethics of AI is how AI is increasingly used to establish scientific facts, and whether those facts can be readily explained either to the lay public or in some cases even to expert scientists themselves. Here we focus on ways in which AI might create a future body of scientific results that will fall short of adding to our scientific understanding. The problem is a peculiar feature of AI in that there can be considerable generated knowledge (in terms of correlations of data and phenomena), but no commensurate increase in genuine human scientific understanding.

We will use the term computational data science (CDS) to refer to the collection of computationally based scientific techniques, primarily involving AI, that were developed in the late twentieth century to probe our natural and social worlds. These forms of AI rely on other information technologies that generate and store large amounts of data, so CDS proper should be understood as a result of both AI and modern (nonintelligent) data producing and gathering technologies. As American computer scientist Peter J. Denning has written, CDS brought a "quiet but profound revolution" that has transformed science by making new discoveries possible.[56] What is striking about CDS is the presumed agency of "making new discoveries possible," for there is a very clear sense in which *computers* and not humans are now making these scientific discoveries. There is a further concern that the progress of CDS is leaving human scientists behind— almost as though we are becoming adjuncts to the scientific discovery process. This is a serious worry, and here we will characterize some of its aspects concerning (1) the tension between statistical and causal accounts of "associationist" CDS; (2) the notion that scientific understanding (as a broad cognitive phenomenon) is threatened by CDS; and (3) that CDS poses problems for ethics—here considered in two ways: (a) the possibility of new statistical ethical knowledge about individuals, and (b) the application of statistical methods through CDS to decide social policies and interventions in areas such as public health and criminal justice.

These three topics—causal knowledge, scientific understanding, and the use of statistics in ethics—are far from the only philosophical topics that CDS implicates. There are a myriad of ways in which CDS has changed science, and will increasingly change technology as control architectures of robots and AI systems become integrated with real-time "Big Data" results. Likewise, as philosophers of science turn their attention to the philosophy of CDS, there may be many other important investigations to undertake, including the application of CDS to the explanation of consciousness, free will, the status of scientific laws, and so on. An analogy to the present historical moment of CDS is provided by the now-common television "extreme weather" journalism, where a reporter outfitted in rain gear stands on a beach that is in the path of a hurricane, in breathless excitement as the first rains start to fall. We have a good idea of what's coming, it is quite certain to be a deluge, but it would be foolish to think we know in detail what the storm will be.

It is difficult to say when exactly CDS as a revolution begins. Denning cites the work of the Nobel physicist Kenneth Wilson in the 1980s, who developed computational models for phase changes and the direction of magnetic force in materials. Wilson was also a passionate advocate for CDS and lobbied American science-funding agencies to secure more support for the field. These efforts resulted in the High-Performance Communication and Computing (HPCC) Act of 1991 in the United States—in large part

---

[56] Peter J. Denning, "Computational Thinking in Science," *American Scientist* 105:1 (January–February 2017): 13–17.

THE ETHICS OF THE ETHICS OF AI

through the efforts of former vice-president Al Gore. The HPCC was one reason that Gore infamously claimed that he "invented the Internet"—and thus we might go back further to give credit to the creation of ARPANET as the beginning of CDS. Whenever our starting point, it is clear that CDS includes advances in the science of simulation, which revolutionized fields from aeronautics to theoretical physics to computer modeling for everything from climate change to recidivism rates for human criminal activity, as well as advances in modern biology, bioinformatics, DNA sequencing, systems and synthetic biology, and now even single-nucleotide gene editing. It is safe to say that for any science for which there are large amounts of data that are available, and where computation over those datasets is impractical for human practitioners, and where patterns in the data yield new results of interest, CDS now looms large in the future of that science.

The Crisis of Causal Knowledge

In the last few decades, as CDS was gaining in terms of the scope of the sciences it enveloped and the power of its results, philosophers such as Nancy Cartwright and philosopher/computer scientist Judea Pearl started to question whether the associations CDS found in complexes such as disease/environment and behavior/nutrition were really delivering what science ought to be delivering: robust, reproducible conclusions about causal connections in nature. In general, their worries were rather more practical than philosophical. If we want to intervene in efficacious ways to cure disease and improve human life, it would be nice to know what causes a disease—and not just what conditions (e.g., symptoms) are statistically associated with a disease state.[57]

Pearl's solution has been both a critique of the use of probabilistic reasoning through Bayesian networks—an AI technique that Pearl largely developed—and a reform program to extend the formalisms for computer-based statistical analysis to allow causal inferences to be drawn. An argument in a similar vein is presented by Nancy Cartwright, who notes that use of the associationist technique of randomized controlled trials (RCTs) does not "without a series of strong assumptions warrant predictions about what happens in practice."[58]

For Cartwright, RCTs are an important but incomplete scientific tool. In considering interventions such as giving a drug to cure a disease, they provide knowledge that the intervention "works somewhere" but fail to "clinch" the case that the same intervention will work on a different (and larger) population. This incompleteness has implications not just for the people who suffer from the disease and can be cured by the intervention—and not just for those who won't be cured by a particular intervention (and may even suffer unnecessary harm from it)—but also for large institutions like the British

---

[57] Judea Pearl, "Causal Inference in Statistics: An Overview," *Statistics Surveys* 3 (2009): 96–146.
[58] Nancy Cartwright, "A Philosopher's View of the Long Road from RCTs to Effectiveness," *The Lancet* 377:9775 (2011): 1400–1401.

National Health Service and other public health institutions. Interventions to cure disease cost money. Failing to cure people disappoints them.

On Cartwright's account, the difference between (statistical) association and causal knowledge is further described by a dataset and its analyses merely "vouching for" a scientific claim, as opposed to "clinching" it. Pearl echoes this call for shoring up statistical analyses: "One cannot substantiate causal claims from associations alone, even at the population level—behind every causal conclusion there must lie some causal assumption that is not testable in observational studies."[59]

These appeals for maintaining scientific reasoning with causal assumptions will sound vaguely familiar to any student of the history of modern philosophy—and indeed strikingly familiar to students of Hume's attack on causal knowledge and Kant's valiant but perhaps quixotic attempt to save us from Hume's skepticism. We can only speculate here what Hume's attitude toward CDS would have been, but given the role of the associations of ideas and impressions in Hume's epistemology and in his sentiment-associationist ethics, it seems obvious that the era of CDS would have been quite pleasing to Hume. What Hume would have found revolutionary about CDS is not only the massive amounts of data that can now be accessed (much greater than the senses, memory, and imagination can handle for a person at any one time) but also the ways in which the data can be manipulated mathematically—beyond the capabilities of the best mathematicians. Associationist knowledge in the era of CDS far exceeds the ability of one mind, and will no doubt continue to grow.

While historical questions might lead away from the primary considerations of CDS, they also serve to remind us of some of the practical restrictions that will come with pursuing the causal account of scientific knowledge. In contemporary CDS, petabytes of data are generated from millions (soon billions?) of sensors of atmospheric and terrestrial conditions. A genome from a human sample can be sequenced by a device (MinION) that plugs into a USB port on a personal computer. These examples are amazing, and there is no reason to think that the mountains of data and the power of computational techniques will not continue to increase. So where do we introduce causal assumptions to interrogate which associations are merely correlational and which are causal? CDS does not create a supermind, capable immediately of cognizing which associations are causal. Scientists will have to understand the results of CDS in order to formulate the proper causal assumptions. Causal knowledge does not come "for free."

These issues lead us to ponder what it is to have scientific understanding. David Weinberger has developed a wide-ranging critique of CDS, to the effect that it makes scientific understanding impossible for limited beings like us.[60] Studying many examples of CDS results, he concludes that:

> Clearly our computers have surpassed us in their power to discriminate, find patterns, and draw conclusions. That's one reason we use them. Rather than reducing

---

[59] Pearl, "Causal Inference in Statistics," 99.
[60] David Weinberger, *Too Big to Know* (New York: Basic Books, 2011).

phenomena to fit a relatively simple model, we can now let our computers make models as big as they need to. But this also seems to mean that what we know depends upon the output of machines the functioning of which we cannot follow, explain, or understand.[61]

The lesson to take away here is that scientific understanding is a retrospective and not a time-slice activity, and that it takes more effort (in the era of CDS) than does scientific discovery. It may well be the case that CDS produces some results that boggle the mind, yet do not increase scientific understanding, after being considered "in the fullness of time." Some of these results (just like in non-CDS science) will end up being not reproducible—hence not good science. The major difference seems to be the volume of scientific results available through CDS and the speed at which these results are produced. Here the concern seems primarily practical and not epistemic in nature. That is, CDS does not seem to produce a kind of science that is in principle not understandable. So for some time it may well be wise for scientists to follow the motto of "less is more." And for any ethics of AI that is developed on the back of that science, a corresponding caution will be called for.

How an Epistemic Crisis Could Become an Ethical Crisis

Forswearing caution, some scientists have pursued CDS in publishing results of statistical correlation systems that purport to draw conclusions about people and predict their behavior. We now have techniques of whole-genome sequencing that correlate phenotypes with genomes—not merely with single or multiple genes. Christoph Lippert and his colleagues from the Venter lab discovered a technique for the "[i]dentification of individuals by trait prediction using whole-genome sequencing data," but at the same time acknowledged that their discovery "may allow the identification of individuals through genomics—an issue that implicates the privacy of genomic data," and further that their work "challenges current conceptions of genomic privacy...the adequacy of informed consent, the viability and value of deidentification of data, the potential for police profiling, and more."[62]

The ethical worry here is not so much that we will be able to pick people out of a crowd, based on a DNA sample (although that is fascinating!), but that we will be able to link genomes to phenotypic profiles. These profiles can be physiological, as in the studies Lippert et al. did on face shape, voice, age, and body-mass index, and they may eventually be used to correlate sustained tendencies toward behavior with genomes.

[61] David Weinberger, "Our Machines Now Have Knowledge We'll Never Understand," *WIRED* (April 18, 2017), accessible at: https://www.wired.com/story/our-machines-now-have-knowledge-well-never-understand/.

[62] Lippert et al., "Identification of Individuals by Trait Prediction Using Whole-Genome Sequencing Data," *PNAS* 114:38 (2017): 10166–171.

The power and perniciousness of these forms of CDS may be clearer if we relate them to worries in ethics about the treatment of individuals when statistical and aggregative techniques are used to make social choices (i.e., for the provision of health care, tax policies, and the like). Utilitarianism is one good example of a theory that relies on these aggregative techniques; John Rawls pointed out that utilitarianism tends to deny the distinctions among persons. In general, social choice procedures for large societies under "technocratic" rule have been criticized by deontological ethicists on the grounds that such procedures require measurements that aggregate over individuals, and thus treat them as indistinguishable "receptacles" of various goods. Thus CDS applied to social choice will certainly aggregate over individuals.

Will whole-genome sequencing usher in an era of technocratic management of populations? If so, this outcome of CDS may outweigh the scientific benefit that we derive from it. We should be vigilant, but also willing to accept some of the results of CDS when they are helpful in a Paretian sense ("at least one person benefits, and no one is harmed"). When trade-offs are suggested by a social choice CDS, we will have to consider carefully whether reasonable expectations (or even rights) of individuals are being violated.

OPPOSITIONAL VERSUS SYSTEMIC APPROACHES

We conclude by noting that most of the standard approaches to the ethics of AI—as discussed earlier—proceed as instances of applied ethics in which human rights and interests are *opposed to* an AI technology, as though humans and technologies operate somehow independently of one another. The basic idea of the oppositional approach is that AI, left unchecked, will do bad things to us. This approach can be seen in the Policy and Investment Recommendations for Trustworthy AI from the European Union (EU) High-Level Expert Group on AI.[63] They strongly recommend a "Human-Centered Approach," which suggests that there could be other possibilities, for instance a "Machine-Centered Approach."

Yet another approach would be to consider AI as a set of technologies that are embedded in a *system* of human agents, other artificial agents, laws, nonintelligent infrastructures, and social norms. That is, the ethics of AI can be seen to involve a *sociotechnical system* that has to be designed not as an isolated technical object but with attention to the social organization in which it will operate. The more we learn about AI behaviors, the better we can adapt the rest of the system to improve outcomes or, in some cases, choose not to implement an AI to take on certain functions. The main idea here is not to

---

[63] European Commission, "High-Level Expert Group on Artificial Intelligence" (May 2, 2019), accessible at: https://ec.europa.eu/digital-single-market/en/high-level-expert-group-artificial-intelligence.

require *all* of the ethics of AI to be achieved by an AI technology. Rather, the sociotechnical system can be optimized to accommodate what AI does well and what it does poorly.

It appears that there are many ethical reasons for preferring the systemic approach to the oppositional approach, partly due to the difficulties in implementing ethics in autonomous agents and partly due to the very nature of AI. After all, applications of AI are not organic entities or systems, asserting their own autonomy. Rather, they are pieces of software and devices that exist in order to improve human life. From this perspective, it would be best to design machines that help *us* to act more ethically, which means that the goal would be neither to make machines ethical by making them free moral agents nor to make machines behave ethically in conformity to moral rules. Instead, AI can help us to be wiser by making us more aware of the consequences of our actions and consequently to be more responsible when acting. To do so, it would be necessary to understand the decisions of machines, which requires that their inferences are comprehensible to us. This corresponds to the ability of the machine to provide explanations, that is, to relate their conclusions to the values that contribute to the solution they propose. It could be that many problems in machine ethics are directly related to what is often called "explainable artificial intelligence"—to the capacity to construct understandable explanations that allow humans to argue and to discuss the decisions proposed by machines that in turn may counter humans' own arguments. This approach appears to be close to ethical collective deliberations, with human and artificial agents that would collaborate in a way inspired by Jürgen Habermas's work on the ethics of communication[64] and on deliberative democracy[65].

CONCLUSION

Our primary message in the preceding five sections on the ethics of the ethics of AI is that progress will be made difficult by the very nature of AI, and AI problems are not likely to yield to the "common approaches" of applied ethics. But this difficulty is the very basis of our claim that there is an ethics of the ethics of AI. Progress *matters* in this domain. Artificial intelligence is here to stay, and doing the ethics of it (or *for* it) competently can help to protect important interests, save lives, and make the world a better place. Conversely, doing the ethics of AI poorly will likely yield some regrettable results, such as mistrust between ethicists and technologists and a public that is increasingly vulnerable to something they can neither understand nor avoid.

Here we can draw out the lessons from our five challenges mentioned in the preceding discussion. First, there are conceptual ambiguities that seem endemic to the ethics of AI.

---

[64] Jürgen Habermas, *The Theory of Communicative Action. Vol. I: Reason and the Rationalization of Society*, trans. T. McCarthy, (Boston, MA: Beacon Press, 1984).

[65] Jürgen Habermas, *Between Facts and Norms: Contributions to a Discourse Theory of Law and Democracy*, trans. W. Rehg (Cambridge, MA: MIT Press, 1996).

For ethicists (and for the general public), it can be tempting to attribute properties to AIs that they do not have. Between philosophy, computer science, AI, futurism, and science fiction, there are partly overlapping linguistic communities that use the same words with disparate concepts. In considering specific AI applications, equivocation on terms like "intelligence," "agent," and "autonomy" can quickly produce misplaced fears or unjustified optimism. This leads us to a more general observation—that ethicists of AI must guard against overestimation and underestimation of risks. When we spin fanciful stories about the "rise of the machines" and how they threaten humanity, we worry about problems that we need not face immediately or perhaps at all. When we underestimate risks, we overlook current and near-term implementations of AI in law enforcement, national security, social media, marketing, financial institutions, and elsewhere that already affect our interests and rights negatively. Still, we are confident that we can develop ethics between these two antipodes.

For most ethicists in the rationalist tradition, there remains the hope that we can design these intelligent machines to act on an ethics that we code into them—and maybe even to develop their own ethical abilities. But every approach to implementing an ethics of AI seems to have its challenges, since ethical judgments are typically defeasible, ethical behavior is difficult to model, ethical norms often conflict, and most ethical deliberations depend on judgments (i.e., discrimination) that are already difficult for humans as well as for machines. When we turn to the epistemology of the ethics of AI, we find that an ethics of AI will depend on the very science that AI produces. Unfortunately, AI plays a major role in producing scientific information without a corresponding increase in understanding. Many socially directed applications of AI will depend on scientific knowledge, but it is unclear whether humans will possess that knowledge, even though the data and analyses may advise interventions in health care, economics, environmental protection, and other areas crucial to our well-being. Finally, it will be important to reconceive the problem of the ethics of AI as a joint sociotechnical creation, and not as a series of technical problems to be confronted by better engineering. We will not be able to simply "design" away problems in the ethics of AI by controlling or opposing AI applications. We will have to see AI as a partner, of sorts, in a larger project to build better societies.

BIBLIOGRAPHY

Arkin, Ronald C. *Governing Lethal Behavior in Autonomous Robots*. New York: Chapman and Hall/CRC Press, 2009.

Awad, Edmond, Sohan Dsouza, Richard Kim, Jonathan Schulz, Joseph Henrich, Azim Shariff, Jean-François Bonnefon, and Iyad Rahwan. "The Moral Machine Experiment." *Nature* 563 (2018): 59–64.

Dennett, Daniel C. *The Intentional Stance*. Cambridge, MA: MIT Press, 1987.

Horty, John F. *Agency and Deontic Logic*. Oxford: Oxford University Press, 2001.

Kurzweil, Ray. *The Singularity Is Near: When Humans Transcend Biology*. New York: Penguin, 2006.

Lin, Patrick, Keith Abney, and Ryan Jenkins, eds. *Robot Ethics 2.0: From Autonomous Cars to Artificial Intelligence*. New York: Oxford University Press, 2017.

Wallach, Wendell, and Colin Allen. *Moral Machines: Teaching Robots Right from Wrong*. New York: Oxford University Press, 2009.

Weinberger, David. *Too Big to Know*. New York: Basic Books, 2011.

CHAPTER 3

....

ETHICAL ISSUES IN OUR
RELATIONSHIP WITH
ARTIFICIAL ENTITIES

....

JUDITH DONATH

INTRODUCTION

....

THIS chapter is about the ethics of our relationships with artificial entities—bots, robots, and other computational systems created to interact with us as if they were sentient and autonomous individuals. They may be embodied as robots or exist only in software; some are clearly artificial while others are indistinguishable, at least under certain conditions, from human beings. When are such interactions helpful or harmful? How do our relationships with computational entities change our relationships with other human beings? When does it matter if we interact with a machine or a human, and why?

Sentience—the ability to have emotions, to feel pain and want to avoid it—is a core concept here. We have ethical responsibilities to sentient beings that we do not have to nonsentient objects: it is cruel to kick a dog, but not a rock. While actually sentient artificial entities might someday exist, they are as yet only a theoretical possibility. All currently existing artificial entities are nonsentient, but—unlike a rock—their interactions and designs evoke the impression of conscious entities with personalities and emotions.

Simulated sentience is the primary focus of this chapter, highlighting our relationship with entities that appear to be sentient but are not. Some are quite simple; our tendency toward anthropomorphism can make the output of even primitive programs appear to us as the behavior of a cognizant mind. Others are impenetrably complex, with sophisticated imitations of conscious and intelligent behavior that are nearly impossible to distinguish from the actions of an actually conscious being.

Some of the ethical issues we will examine involve our personal relationships with artificial entities. People seek companionship from artificial assistants, hold funeral services for broken robot dogs, and confide in simulated therapists. The relationships that some warn are a threat to humaneness, if not to humanity, are proving to be quite popular. Under what circumstances are they helpful or harmful? How do such human/machine interactions affect our relationships with other people? How does the machine performance of emotion differ from human impression management or from the inauthentic expression required by, for example, the service industry? When and why does it matter that the other does not actually think? The key issues here concern empathy and the function that caring what others think plays in society.

We will also address ethical issues in the design and deployment of artificial entities. In their mimicry of sentient beings, artificial entities are inherently deceptive: even one that types "I am a bot" implies, with its first-person pronoun, a self-conscious being. And many artificial entities are designed to be as persuasive as possible, eliciting affection and trust with features such as big childlike eyes and imitative gestures. Some are made with beneficial goals—to serve the user as teacher, wellness coach, etc.—but these same persuasive techniques can manipulate us for harmful and exploitive ends. What are the ethical responsibilities of researchers and designers?

While some artificial entities attempt to pass as human, many are clearly robots or software agents; the illusion they project is of a sentient but also distinctly artificial being. Yet the popular vision of truly sentient machine beings is generally foreboding—they are often portrayed as a potent, if not the final, enemy of humanity. Why do we see this future so darkly? While understanding the ethical issues surrounding our relationship with artificial entities is important in itself as social robots and software agents become increasingly present in our everyday lives, these queries also shed revealing light on our relationships with each other and with other living things.

Scope and Definitions

We will start with some definitions. Much discussion about today's nonsentient social robots and programs uses language that implies they have feelings and intentions, blurring the important distinction between "X is a robot that feels" and "X is a robot designed to appear as if it feels." Having a clear understanding of what is meant by intelligence, sentience, and consciousness and using them precisely is important for many ethical considerations.

Intelligence is often described as the ability to learn and apply knowledge or to solve complex problems.[1] It is an observable property defined by behavior—finding clever solutions, acting resourcefully. Thought of this way, we see a migrating bird, an insect-hunting bat, and a theorem-proving human as problem solvers each of whom require considerable, albeit very different forms of, intelligence. Thought of this way, we can easily refer to a machine as intelligent if it solves difficult problems. In this usage, the internal state that produces the intelligent behavior does not matter.

---

[1] Max Tegmark, "Let's Aspire to More Than Making Ourselves Obsolete, "*Possible Minds: Twenty-Five Ways of Looking at AI*, ed. John Brockman (New York: Penguin, 2019), 76–87.

Yet intelligence is not a precisely defined term.[2] It is sometimes conceptualized as an inner quality, as when we say the migrating bird is not really intelligent, but is just acting on instinct. Computer scientists joke that use of the term "artificial intelligence" also reflects this enigmatic property: computer programs that solve complex problems using methods we do not understand are "artificial intelligence"; when we do understand them they are "algorithms."

Sentience is the ability to experience sensations and emotions: to feel pain and pleasure, and to want less of the former and more of the latter. A nonsentient creature may move away from certain things and toward others, and even have a suite of behaviors that aid its survival and reproduction, but it is not motivated to do anything: it simply exists. With sentience comes motivation: a creature that experiences certain sensory inputs as painful will want to avoid those; it will want to repeat pleasant ones. Sentience is now believed to be the foundation of learning, which gives sentient creatures much greater flexibility in their relationship with the world.[3]

Sentience is central to ethics because we have responsibilities toward sentient beings that we do not have toward, say, a rock.[4] Most people would agree that we should not inflict needless pain on something capable of experiencing distress. However, which beings are included in that category and what to do when that responsibility conflicts with other needs and desires are highly contested questions.

The term *conscious* refers to sentient beings that are self-aware—that have a sense of purpose and of themselves as individuals in the world. The term can be fuzzy: there is no clear behavioral marker of consciousness nor even an agreed-upon description of the internal experience. Historically, the rationalist, Enlightenment view was that consciousness was the affectless mental acquisition and manipulation of a symbolic representation of the world. Some believed that it required language and thus humans were the only conscious animal. Today, consciousness is increasingly understood to have evolved through social interaction, beginning with the bonding of parent and offspring; it is built on the emotional scaffolding of sentience.[5] And ethological and neuroscientific studies affirm that humans are far from being the only conscious animal: many mammals, birds, even cephalopods are aware of themselves and others and move through life with intentions.[6]

[2] Shane Legg and Marcus Hutter, "Universal Intelligence: A Definition of Machine Intelligence," *Minds and Machines* 17, no. 4 (2007): 391–444.

[3] Zohar Z. Bronfman, Simona Ginsburg, and Eva Jablonka, "The Transition to Minimal Consciousness through the Evolution of Associative Learning," *Frontiers in Psychology* 7 (2016): 1954.

[4] Donald M. Broom, *Sentience and Animal Welfare* (Wallingford, UK: CABI, 2014); Peter Singer, *Practical Ethics* (Cambridge, UK: Cambridge University Press, 2011).

[5] Tania Singer et al., "Empathy for Pain Involves the Affective but not Sensory Components of Pain," *Science* 303, no. 5661 (2004): 1157–1162.

[6] Evan Thompson, "Empathy and Consciousness." *Journal of Consciousness Studies* 8, nos. 5–6 (2001): 1–32; Jaak Panksepp, "Affective Consciousness: Core Emotional Feelings in Animals and Humans." *Consciousness and Cognition* 14, no. 1 (2005): 30–80; Peter Godfrey-Smith, *Other Minds: The Octopus and the Evolution of Intelligent Life* (London: William Collins, 2016).

These differing views of what consciousness is have important repercussions for ethics and AI. In the classical view—which remains influential in some AI research as well as popular belief—consciousness is closely entwined with intelligence, the acquisition of knowledge, and problem solving. This contrasts sharply with the biological view, supported by current research, that consciousness is fundamentally social and emotional, having evolved from simple sentience as creatures began to bond and care for each other.

Consciousness is important in ethics because the basis of morality is here, in the evolution of traits such as attachment, empathy, and the desire for justice and social order. To care about how one is perceived by others and about one's effect on them—concerns available to the conscious mind—is arguably the very foundation of ethics.

Both sentience and consciousness are inherently private experiences. We cannot directly experience what it is like to be another being—human, animal, or robot. Our assessment of what it is like to be another, including what, if anything, they feel, is based on external and perceivable appearance and behavior. I assume other people are conscious because I know that I am conscious and we are biologically and behaviorally similar; it is, however, an assumption and not direct knowledge.

As we look at other species (or artificial entities), we make inferences about what it is like to be them—what their internal experience is—by analogy. The more something resembles ourselves, the more we assume his, her, or its experience to be similar to our own. This rule of thumb has led us to vastly underestimate the cognitive ability and sensate experience of many nonhuman animals and, as we shall see, to overestimate the capabilities of bots and other nonsentient human inventions.

Precursors: Turing and Weizenbaum

Our inability to directly observe the experience of being another is the problem at the core of Alan Turning's 1950 paper, "Computing Machinery and Intelligence," that marks the beginning of the field of artificial intelligence.[7] Turing introduced the paper by saying, "I propose to consider the question, 'Can machines think?'" and then immediately rejected the question on the basis that the words "machine" and "think" were too vague and limited by everyday experience.

Instead, he proposed a test, the Imitation Game, now popularly known as the Turing Test, which he argued was a "more accurate form of the question." In this test a human judge chats (via text) with two hidden contestants. Both claim to be human, though only one is—the other is a machine. The judge is tasked with determining which one is telling the truth. A machine that can consistently pass as human, Turing argued, should be considered intelligent.

---

[7] Alan Turing, "Computing Machinery and Intelligence." *Mind* 49 (1950): 433–60.

It is a peculiar article and a hugely influential one.[8] It anointed deceptively passing as human as the key goal—or even as the definition of—artificial intelligence. And it deftly limited the domain in which this goal needed to be achieved to text-only communication.

Turing famously predicted that in fifty years computers would have reached the point that they would be consistently able to fool a human judge.[9] But he also made a second prediction: that by the time computers could pass as human, our use of language would have changed significantly. He said, "The original question, 'Can machines think' I believe to be too meaningless to deserve discussion. Nevertheless I believe that at the end of the century the use of words will have altered so much that one will be able to speak of machines thinking without expecting to be contradicted."[10] Though this second prediction, about the change in our culture and the meaning of words, is less noted, it was prescient. It is through such changes in language—in how we speak about thinking, about machines wanting and liking things—that our culture and ethics evolve.

About fifteen years after "Computing Machinery and Intelligence" was published, Joseph Weizenbaum created the first program capable of carrying on such a text conversation. He named this program ELIZA, after the character in George Bernard Shaw's play *Pygmalion* who "learns to speak increasingly well."[11] Weizenbaum's research goal was to interact with computers using natural language; with this project he sought to show that a simple sentence-parsing program with some semantic heuristics could carry on a coherent conversation. ELIZA was able to find the topic of a sentence and had rules for forming a response, but had no contextual information about the world.

It was an approach quite different from what Turing envisioned. Turing's belief in the significance of carrying on a humanlike conversation was not as shallow an assumption as it seems now. He described a potentially winning machine as having processing power equivalent to the human brain (though he quite underestimated the human brain's complexity and power); it would initially be programmed to simulate an infant and would then be taught, much as a child is. Turing's views about the brain, learning, and children were remarkably naive. But the key point is that he believed that a machine that would pass his test would be one that was imbued with a mind analogous to that of humans, able to learn and to reason. Furthermore, though Turing remained adamant that we rely solely on external behavior in judging what is thinking, he outlined

---

[8] As a philosophical article, it is odd. It has pages of discussion about the nature of a digital computer but the central argument, that the Imitation Game is a satisfactory substitution for the question of whether machines can think, is rather glossed over.

[9] Specifically, that they would be able to "play the imitation game so well that an average interrogator will not have more than 70 per cent, chance of making the right identification after five minutes of questioning."

[10] Turing, "Computing Machinery and Intelligence," 442.

[11] Joseph Weizenbaum, "Contextual Understanding by Computers." *Communications of the ACM* 10, no. 8 (1967): 474.

the possibility of a state change, analogous to the critical mass of an atomic reaction that would mark a qualitative leap in mental ability and creativity.

ELIZA succeeded in sustaining conversation not through sophisticated technology but through, somewhat inadvertently, exploiting the way people make sense of each other. ELIZA was designed to respond based on scripts that would encode conversational rules for different roles. The first and by far most famous script Weizenbaum made for ELIZA was DOCTOR, modeled after a "Rogerian psychologist." His choice of this therapeutic framework was pragmatic: "the psychiatric interview is one of the few examples of categorized dyadic natural language communication in which one of the participating pair is free to assume the pose of knowing almost nothing of the real world."[12]

People were entranced with the computational "therapist." Even Weizenbaum's secretary, who knew the scope and point of the work, said upon trying it out that she wanted to chat with it further-in private.[13] Others took seriously the notion of the computational chat-bot as therapist, one that would be available to all, inexpensive and tireless.[14] At first Weizenbaum assumed this enthusiasm, which he judged to be misplaced, was due to the novelty of the interaction; future iterations should and would be designed to eliminate the "illusion of understanding."[15]

Weizenbaum's responses over the years show his growing alarm at this response. The quick willingness to accept a text-parsing program as an entity worthy of relating to, a repository for one's confidences, became to him an indicator of a deeply disturbing lack of concern about the humanity of the other—a lack of empathy and of even any interest in the mind and soul of the other. Weizenbaum had come to America fleeing Hitler's Europe and knew vividly and with horror the devastating effects of dehumanizing other people. He spent much of the rest of his career warning about the dangers computation posed to society.

Turing argued that we need to accept intelligent behavior (which he had redefined as the ability to convincingly imitate a human in a text conversation) as sufficient evidence of machine thinking. Fifteen years later, Weizenbaum's ELIZA, a clearly nonthinking, sentence-parsing chat-bot, posed a counterexample by demonstrating how easily the illusion of intelligence can be made. Dismayed by people's enthusiastic embrace of ELIZA's therapeutic potential (and computers in general), Weizenbaum came to believe that the willingness to accept machines in such roles was a significant threat to humane society. These positions, taken in the earliest years of AI research, delineate the big ethical questions surrounding artificial entities and provide the starting point for our analysis.

[12] Weizenbaum, "Contextual Understanding by Computers."
[13] Weizenbaum, "Contextual Understanding by Computers."
[14] Kenneth M. Colby, James B. Watt, and John P. Gilbert, "A Computer Method of Psychotherapy: Preliminary Communication," *Journal of Nervous and Mental Disease* 142, no. 2 (1966): 148–52.
[15] Joseph Weizenbaum, "ELIZA—a Computer Program for the Study of Natural Language Communication between Man and Machine," *Communications of the ACM* 9, no. 1 (1966): 43.

WHERE ARE WE NOW?

Turing's prediction—that in limited conversations, machines would be indistinguishable from humans—was off by a few years. In 2000, there were no computers that were able to consistently pass as human after five minutes of text-based interaction. But a couple of decades later his prophesy has, effectively, come true.

In the narrow sense, computers have not "passed the Turing Test." There is an annual competition, the Loebner Prize, that takes Turing's Imitation Game suggestion literally, pitting a panel of judges against chat programs and hidden human typists. It has been widely criticized for encouraging programs that use tricks, such as simulated typing errors, to fool the judges, instead of advancing the goal of making more intelligent machines. Even so, while several have fooled judges during extended conversation, none has yet won the prize.

More significantly, we now interact with artificial entities in daily life, often without realizing they are not human. In 1950, when Turing proposed the Imitation Game, it was a stretch to think up a plausible scenario in which people would communicate via text with strangers of unknown and possibly fictitious identity. With the advent of the internet, this scenario has become commonplace.

In the mid-1990s, someone named Serdar Argic started inflaming the already heated Usenet arguments about the Armenian genocide by relentlessly posting hateful rants accusing the Armenians of massacring Turks. People wrote impassioned rebuttals to his screeds, thus making them even more disruptive by sidetracking any constructive discussion. Only after much anger and confusion did people realize that Argic was not a real person, but a program designed to intervene in any discussion that mentioned Armenia or Turkey, including Thanksgiving recipe posts. This was one of the first bots to deliberately fool people in a public setting.[16]

Chat-bots have since then become cleverer—and ubiquitous. They are tireless customer service agents, answering questions about ingredients, store hours, and mysterious error codes at any time of day or night. They are participants in online games, appearing as opponents, teammates, and incidental characters. They are the beautiful eager women in online dating sites who are always up for trying new things. Some are upfront about being software entities, but many attempt to pass as human.

An estimated 10–15 percent of users on the popular and influential social media site Twitter are bots. Some are useful: openly nonhuman programs that disseminate news, jokes, alerts, etc. But others masquerade as human users, seldom benevolently. They may be followers for hire, inflating their clients' apparent popularity. They may post vacation shots from sponsored villas, name-dropping restaurants, snacks, and songs, programmed to incessantly instigate flashes of envy and desire. Or they may be powerful purveyors of propaganda, chiming into political discussions, tirelessly hawking talking

---

[16] Judith Donath, *The Social Machine: Designs for Living Online* (Cambridge, MA: MIT Press, 2014).

points, slogans, and manufactured rumors. Bots thrive here in part because Twitter limits posts to 140 characters; non sequiturs, rather than back-and-forth discussions, characterize many interactions. Devising a program to mimic this style is much easier than creating one that must carry out an extended and coherent conversation.

Not all of today's artificial entities are online: we are increasingly surrounded by a growing population of social robots—autonomous, sentient-seeming objects. At home, we chat with friendly devices that fetch us the news, order us dinner, and ask politely about our day. We may have a robotic pet or coworker. There are robot receptionists who welcome guests in tech-forward hotels and robot orderlies who glide quietly into hospital rooms. Social robots are marketed as "friends" and "your next family member" who "can't wait to meet you."

No contemporary or readily foreseeable artificial entity is actually conscious or even primitively sentient, but our intuitive response to them is the opposite. They seem very much alert and aware. Our tendency to anthropomorphize contributes to this illusion. Yet when we see volition and intent in inanimate objects such as cars, trees, or dolls, we recognize that we ourselves are the source of its imagined vitality. With artificial entities, the object itself behaves in ways that strongly suggest a sentient experience lies within.

The ambiguity of their identity—machine or new form of thinking being—is no accident. Like the chat-bots that score highly in the Loebner Prize competition by making spelling mistakes, social robots are often made to mimic human habits such as pausing or looking away as if thinking; these easy-to-implement tricks provide a convincing illusion of sentience. Many are designed with simple, round childlike curves—features that elicit nurturance, indulgence, and trust[17], while also keeping our expectations of their abilities low. Their gendered voices and linguistic insinuation of self-conscious thought ("I'd like to help you") give the impression that one is speaking to an aware and sentient being.[18] As Turing predicted, our use of language has changed: we casually speak of these entities wanting, thinking, and liking.

ETHICS OF OUR RELATIONSHIP WITH THE SEEMINGLY SENTIENT

What are the ethical issues involved in our interaction with artificial entities? One set of issues concerns our responsibilities toward them—how we should treat them. The ethical framework I will use here is based on Peter Singer's utilitarian applied ethics;[19] his sentience-focused approach to assessing responsibilities toward nonhumans makes it

---

[17] Leslie Zebrowitz, *Reading Faces* (Boulder, CO: Westview Press, 1997).

[18] Friederike Eyssel, et al., "'If You Sound Like Me, You Must Be More Human': On the Interplay of Robot and User Features on Human-Robot Acceptance and Anthropomorphism." Paper presented at the 2012 7th ACM/IEEE International Conference on Human-Robot Interaction (HRI), 125–6.

[19] Singer, *Practical Ethics*.

especially relevant for thinking about artificial entities.[20] The key question here, however, is not how our treatment affects them, but what it does to us.

We noted earlier that our ethical responsibilities are to sentient beings: if something or someone has the capacity to feel, we need to take their preferences into consideration. To things that are not sentient—rocks, bacteria, dolls, robots—we have no direct moral obligation, that is, none that arises from their individual standing as a being with moral claims or rights. Since they do not experience anything, they cannot feel harmed by any action.

Though we do not have direct moral obligations to nonsentient entities that does not mean we have no obligations toward them. Nonconscious entities have what are called "indirect rights." These are rights that come from their relationship to a being that does have ethical standing; because harming the nonconscious entity would harm the being with ethical standing, it should therefore should be avoided. You adore your robot, and so I must treat it well because of your affection for it. It is wrong for me to harm something you value, not because of the intrinsic hurt to a thing (it has no feelings) but because you would be saddened by its loss.

Laws reflect a society's ethics, but they change slowly and are often more an indicator of the morals of its past. Indirect rights have been the primary source of protection that animals have had under American law: I cannot kick your dog, not because it would hurt your dog but because you would be upset (and it is your property). Indirect rights are often weak. In the moral calculus required to balance numerous competing preferences and rights, they can be readily eclipsed. Protection based on human preference disappears in the face of competing human interests—thus we have factory farms, sport hunting, etc.

Society changes. Laws protecting animals based on ethical reasoning that takes their experience into account—that recognizes their sentience—are becoming more common. The change is due both to (a) seeing sentience as the quality that defines whether one has direct moral claims and (b) recognizing that some animals are sentient. It is also part of a broader Western cultural shift to an increasingly inclusive view of who is a being with moral standing: it is not that long ago in the United States that women and slaves had mainly indirect rights. Advocates for animal rights posit that what they call "speciesism"—the belief that members of one species have superior moral standing on the basis of that membership—as the logical and moral equivalent of racism.

Some legal scholars have argued that such legal protection should extend to social robots:[21] "We may not want to be the kind of society that tolerates cruelty to an entity we

[20] The focus of this chapter is on Western society. See Frédéric Kaplan, "Who Is Afraid of the Humanoid? Investigating Cultural Differences in the Acceptance of Robots," *International journal of Humanoid Robotics* 1, no. 03 (2004): 465–80; and Jennifer Robertson, *Robo Sapiens Japanicus: Robots, Gender, Family, and the Japanese Nation* (Berkeley: University of California Press, 2017), for reactions to artificial entities in Japan.

[21] Kate Darling, "Extending Legal Protection to Social Robots: The Effects of Anthropomorphism, Empathy, and Violent Behavior towards Robotic Objects," in *Robot Law*, ed. A. M. Froomkin R. Calo, and I. Kerr. (Cheltenhem, UK: Edward Elgar, 2016), 213–34.

think of as quasi-human."[22] I argue that this movement toward more inclusive rights does not, and should not, apply to nonsentient artificial beings. The fundamental reason for extending moral rights to animals is recognition of their sentience—that they can experience suffering. It is a right inherent to them, regardless of whether a human observer, owner, or other interested party is aware of their pain.[23] The premise that sentience is the foundation of moral rights is important—extending these rights to nonsentient entities dilutes its meaning and significance.

That said, the compelling simulation of sentience exhibited by artificial entities can provide them with additional indirect moral claims, again stemming from considerations about a person's experience, not the entity's. Here the concern is that treating another cruelly brutalizes oneself. This principle is reflected in Jewish custom, which forbids sport hunting because it encourages cruelty, even if the animal is killed painlessly.[24] And Immanuel Kant, though he argued that animals have no "will" and thus no inherent rights, also wrote, "If he is not to stifle his own feelings, he must practice kindness towards animals, for he who is cruel to animals becomes hard also in his dealings with men."[25]

Behaving ethically often involves trade-offs between competing rights and principles, and even a seemingly simple injunction such as "do not treat sentient-seeming entities cruelly" can create dilemmas. The popular keychain pet toy, the Tamagotchi, provides a useful scenario. These are very simple artificial entities that nonetheless exert a powerful emotional pull.[26] The owner of a Tamagotchi must work at keeping it "alive," a task that entails pushing buttons on it at frequent but arbitrary times. Ignore it and it will cease to thrive and will eventually "die"; as with real pets, cruelty toward the Tamagotchi can take the form of neglect. Imagine now a family dinner. The grandmother is visiting, but a grandchild is continuously distracted, checking a Tamagotchi's status. Should the parents demand the child put the toy away and pay full attention to the (living, conscious, and closely related) grandparent present in the room, who would like their attention, but at the cost of allowing the Tamagotchi to possibly die? Or is nurturing the keychain pet useful training in responsible caring, so grandmother and virtual pet will need to share the child's divided attention?

The appeal of the simple Tamagotchi vividly demonstrates just how compelling and potentially manipulative an artificial entity can be. This raises concerns about prohibitions against mistreating them—and especially about encasing such prohibitions in law. The makers of an artificial entity can design it so that arbitrary events and conditions

[22] Ryan Calo, "Robotics and the Lessons of Cyberlaw," *California Law Review* (2015): 513–63.
[23] Darling points out that animal protection law seems to reflect the popular sentimental standing of particular animals, rather than the philosophically or biologically based concern with their sentience. In this chapter, our focus is on fundamental ethics—on getting the theory right in order to guide the practice.
[24] Rabbi Dr. Asher Meir, "Judaism and Hunting," *Jewish Ethicist*, https://www.ou.org/torah/machshava/jewish-ethicist/judaism_and_hunting/.
[25] Immanuel Kant, *Lectures on Ethics*, trans. Louis Infield. (New York: Harper & Row, 1963), 240.
[26] Frédéric Kaplan, "Free Creatures: The Role of Uselessness in the Design of Artificial Pets" (paper presented at the 1st Edutainment Robotics Workshop, Sankt Augustin, Germany, 2000), 45–7.

cause it to express suffering. The Tamagotchi appears to suffer because no one pressed its button at the demanded time. A more venal entity could appear to suffer when you do not purchase the items it is selling on behalf of the company that controls it; perhaps it will suffer unless it is taken on a Caribbean vacation, or it will appear to be lonely and unhappy if it is not in a room with you, recording all your conversations. The concept that we should not mistreat even a nonsentient entity because of the harm it does to ourselves is sound—but we need to be careful about who defines what is "cruel" in the arbitrary realm of artificial entities.

We should treat artificial entities at a minimum without cruelty—that is, without inflicting unnecessary harm to them. But what sort of relationship do we want to have with them? Here our concern shifts from sentience to consciousness.

"Your Next Friend Could Be a Robot" was the headline of a 2016 *Wall Street Journal* article that lauded the ease with which people become emotionally attached to social robots, a tendency that it claimed could solve, or at least ameliorate, the problem of loneliness among the elderly and the childless. The robots, the article notes, are far from intelligent, but they are "enhanced by the right auditory and visual cues" to seem like, as one social robot product manager said, "[a] likable person people want to have in their homes."

Such cues work, at least for the many people who express considerable affection for their social robots. A customer review for Alexa, Amazon's virtual assistant, says, "I wake up in the morning and she does the routine I've set up, and she's so comforting and useful and fun overall...feels like a new little buddy in the home."[27] A veteran technology writer described his relationship with social robot Jibo: "I work from home, and it's nice to have someone ask me how I'm doing when I'm making lunch." When the company behind it went out of business, his wrote of his heartbreak at its pending demise: "I've felt crushed knowing that every word the robot says to me could be his last," a heartbreak he compared with the loss he felt when his mother died after suffering from dementia.[28]

Though still a nascent technology, it is clear that people enjoy interacting with social robots. In coming years, we will have a growing number of relationships with artificial pets, coworkers, caretakers, and companions—and those bonds will become tighter as advances in machine learning, aided by the vast databases of user behavior metrics that existing entities have been able to collect, will make interacting with them ever more seamlessly polished and highly personalized.[29]

Not everyone sees this as a positive development. Technology and society researcher Sherry Turkle has written extensively about the ethical hazards of accepting artificial creations as personal companions, asking, "What is the value of interactions that contain no understanding of us and that contribute nothing to a shared store of human

[27] https://www.amazon.com/gp/customer-reviews/R2SSM75HH2PJD6/.
[28] Jeffrey van Camp, "My Jibo Is Dying and It's Breaking My Heart," *Wired* (March 8, 2019).
[29] Judith Donath, "The Robot Dog Fetches for Whom?," in *A Networked Self and Human Augmentics, Artificial Intelligence, Sentience*, ed. Zizi Papacharissi. (London: Routledge, 2018), 26–40.

meaning?"[30] She has warned that robot companions may provide such a pleasant imitation of human company, without the inevitable disagreements and irritations that come with real people, that we may come to prefer their frictionless companionship, whether as babysitters, friends, sexual partners, or caregivers, to that of a real, imperfect human being.

It was a virtual therapist—ELIZA—that pioneered relating socially with a machine, and it was people's enthusiastic reception of this same virtual therapist that prompted, in ELIZA's creator, the first backlash against such technologies. And virtual therapy provides a useful lens for examining the broader question of the values and ethics of forming a relationship with an artificial entity.

Although ELIZA was modeled after a "Rogerian psychiatrist," a computer therapist is antithetical to Carl Rogers' theory of psychology. In a 1977 profile, science writer Constance Holden outlined Rogers' main tenets: the therapist must be empathic (have "the ability to get inside the world of the client" and "see things as they look to him"), authentic (must "relate to the client as a person" and "allow himself to become involved with his feelings as well as his intellect"), and nonjudgmental ("let the client know he is accepted").[31] These guidelines address not how therapists should act but how they should think and feel; that they are capable of doing so is implicit.

Holden accompanied the profile of Rogers with a sidebar about ELIZA, titled "The Empathic Computer," which she concluded by noting, "Many lessons could be drawn from this, one of which is that even the appearance of empathy (combined, of course, with the computer's quite genuine nonjudgmentalism) can be extraordinarily powerful."[32] Weizenbaum sharply disagreed. Responding to this article, he quoted Rogers' argument that to effect a cure, the therapist must genuinely like the patient. "Of what help," he asked, "could it possibly be to anyone to know that he is worthy of being liked *by a computer*?" Weizenbaum concluded by saying: "The power of which Holden writes in connection with my computer program is no more and no less than the power to deceive. No humane therapy of any kind ought to be grounded on that."[33]

Today, thousands of people confide their problems to virtual therapists. Some of the reasons are practical. The U.S. Department of Defense, faced with thousands of veterans returning home suffering from post-traumatic stress disorder and other psychological injuries, has supported the development of artificial therapists to relieve the acute shortages of human ones. Virtual therapy is far cheaper and more convenient, accessible wherever and whenever you need it.

[30] Sherry Turkle, "Authenticity in the Age of Digital Companions," *Interaction Studies* 8, no. 3 (2007): 10–24.

[31] Constance Holden, "Carl Rogers: Giving People Permission to Be Themselves," *Science* 198, no. 4312 (1977): 31–5.

[32] Constance Holden, "The Empathic Computer," *Science* 198, no. 4312 (1977): 32.

[33] Joseph Weizenbaum, "Computers as 'Therapists,'" *Science* 198, no. 4315 (1977): 54.

Though the technology is still exploratory, studies indicate that therapy with an artificial entity is not only cost-effective but psychologically effective—and well liked.[34] In particular, people liked that the computer therapist was nonjudgmental: they were willing to divulge more personal information to it and to talk more freely about uncomfortable subjects, an openness that is invaluable in therapy.[35]

If openness and honesty are the desired behaviors in therapy, then why have a therapist at all? Why not just have a pure text interface, with no artificial therapist, no implied yet nonexistent being? The answer is that the personified interface, with its imagined therapist, is more engaging; it inspires people to interact with it more and to attend to its suggestions. For example, *Woebot* is a conversational entity that provides cognitive-behavioral therapy via text chat; it has been found to significantly reduce depression in its users, who say they like its personality, and that it pays attention to them and holds them accountable for being attentive to their emotions.[36] Though its interface is quite simple, the user's mental model of engaging with an entity provides a quite different experience than would a similar interaction framed as an interactive questionnaire. The ersatz empathy that Weizenbaum decried turns out to be valuable after all.

We humans are highly social beings, and in the presence of others—even imagined others—we try, for better or worse, to make a desired impression. Studies comparing how people respond to questions asked by a computer with a facial versus a text interface found that they are more responsive and engaged with the facial interface, but also less honest, painting themselves in a more favorable light.[37] Hints of personhood, of approval or displeasure, influence how we act.

For understanding our relationship with artificial entities in general, the most significant observation is that the virtual therapist plays a novel role, one that could be played neither by a human nor by a simple questionnaire. People are aware that the virtual therapist is artificial and not conscious, so they feel comfortable confiding in it, yet they can at the same time suspend this recognition and engage with it as if it were a conscious and empathic being. Designing the ideal virtual therapist means balancing being engaging (more humanlike) against inviting candid disclosures (more machinelike) to create an exemplar not found in nature.

Yet the relationship between therapist and patient is a particular kind of relationship, and we want to be careful about the parallels we draw to friendships and other social

[34] Kathleen Kara Fitzpatrick, Alison Darcy, and Molly Vierhile, "Delivering Cognitive Behavior Therapy to Young Adults with Symptoms of Depression and Anxiety Using a Fully Automated Conversational Agent (Woebot): A Randomized Controlled Trial," *JMIR Ment. Health* 4, no. 2 (2017): e19; Gale M. Lucas et al., "It's Only a Computer: Virtual Humans Increase Willingness to Disclose," *Computers in Human Behavior* 37 (2014): 94–100; Adam S. Miner, Arnold Milstein, and Jefferey T. Hancock, "Talking to Machines about Personal Mental Health Problems," *JAMA* 318, no. 13 (2017): 1217–18.
[35] Lucas et al., "It's Only a Computer."
[36] Fitzpatrick, Darcy, and Vierhile, "Delivering Cognitive Behavior Therapy to Young Adults."
[37] L. Sproull et al., "When the Interface Is a Face," *Human Computer Interaction* 11 (1996): 97–124.

bonds. It is possible, at least in some forms of therapy, to cast the therapeutic relationship as instrumental, even commercial: the patient pays the therapist to perform the service of helping them with their mental health; the relationship is a success if the patient's health improves. (This is, of course, deeply at odds with how Rogers, Weizenbaum, and many others understand the therapeutic process.)[38] The point is that when a relationship is seen as purely or primarily instrumental—with the party receiving the service unconcerned with the thoughts of the one performing it and interested only in the outcome— then substituting an artificial entity into the role of service provider makes sense.[39] This is especially so when, as is the case with patients uncomfortable with the possibility of being judged and looked down upon by a therapist, being thought about by the service provider is seen as negative.

Our relationships are a mix of nurturing bonds and instrumental uses in varying proportions. Nurturing holds society together, and it is fundamental to who we are as humans. We evolved to nurture, to derive joy from taking care of others and knowing that we have made them happy: we take care of our family, our friends, our pets, and our plants.

Yet, for a variety of reasons—an emphasis on efficiency, the anonymity of city life, an industrialized corporate service economy—we now live in a world where many formerly social and engaged relationships are recast as instrumental ones[40], transformed from ones where a robot would be a poor substitute to ones where there is little care or empathy left to lose.

We need to be cognizant of the sometimes subtle but fundamentally important empathic and bonding element of our relationships, to care not only about what the relationship can do for us but also about how we affect the other—to care about both the experience of the other and the other's thoughts of us. It is possible to measure the usefulness of these bonds, to quantify the health or productivity increase they provide, but that is only a piece of their value.

That other-centric element is absent in interactions with an artificial entity, leaving only the instrumental element—how does this relationship benefit me? Such entities, and thus such relationships, will play an increased role in our lives in the coming years. Weizenbaum's fears about our willingness to embrace machines was prescient—it is perhaps ironic that virtual therapy may be the one applications in which the machine's absence of mind is truly beneficial.

[38] Cecil Holden Patterson, "Empathy, Warmth, and Genuineness in Psychotherapy: A Review of Reviews," *Psychotherapy: Theory, Research, Practice, Training* 21, no. 4 (1984): 431–8.

[39] We are omitting here the quite significant ethical issue of robot-induced unemployment. John Danaher, "Will Life Be Worth Living in a World without Work? Technological Unemployment and the Meaning of Life," *Science and Engineering Ethics* 23, no. 1 (2017): 41–64.

[40] Arlie Russell. Hochschild, *The Managed Heart: Commercialization of Human Feeling* (Berkeley: University of California Press, 2012), 1983; Judith Donath, "Our Evolving Super-Networks," in *The Social Machine: Designs for Living Online* (Cambridge, MA: MIT Press, 2014), 111–32.

ETHICS OF CREATING SEEMINGLY SENTIENT ENTITIES

We have been focusing thus far on the ethics of our relationships with artificial entities. We turn now to the process creating these entities, and in particular, of designing them to seem conscious and aware when they are not. Here, the ethical questions center on deception.

There is an extensive, and contentious, body of work about the ethics of deception.[41] The central questions are: What exactly constitutes a deception? Are all deceptions ethically wrong—and if not, which ones are permitted and why? For the purpose of this discussion, I will put forth some basic definitions and ethical premises, so we can focus on the new issues artificial entities raise.

An act or quality is deceptive if it is intended to cause the recipient to believe something that is not true. Intent is key: not every false statement or causing of false belief is deceptive. If one believes something that is not true, and tells that untrue thing to others, that is a mistake, not a deception. If one says something true, but the recipient misconstrues or misinterprets it, that is a misunderstanding, not a deception.

Ethical concerns focus on intentional deceptions. While a mantis that evolved to resemble a dead leaf is deceptive and this deception harms its predators, it is not unethical, for the mantis did not choose to deceive. Humans lie deliberately—and so do some animals; it is a sign of advanced cognition.

A few philosophers have declared all lying to be immoral: St Augustine declared all lies to be sinful; Kant said, "To be truthful (honest) in all declarations, therefore, is a sacred and absolutely commanding decree of reason, limited by no expediency"; and Sam Harris, a contemporary proponent of radical honesty, challenges his readers to abstain from any and all lies.[42]

Most people (and philosophers) hold more nuanced, if differing, views, evaluating the ethics of deceptions by the harm they cause. An altruistic deception is done at one's own expense to benefit the other; a selfish deception is done for one's own gain and harming the recipient is an effect but not the goal; a malicious deception is performed with the goal of harming the recipient. In an ethical calculus of deception, one might argue that altruistic deceptions are ethical, and ones that cause harm should be assessed

---

[41] See, e.g., Sissela Bok, *Lying: Moral Choice in Public and Private Life* (New York: Vintage, 1999); Bella M. DePaulo et al., "Lying in Everyday Life," *Journal of Personality and Social Psychology* 70, no. 5 (1996): 979–95; D. B. Buller and J. K. Burgoon, "Interpersonal Deception Theory," *Communication Theory* 6 (1996): 203–42; Jeffrey T. Hancock "Digital Deception," in *Oxford Handbook of Internet Psychology*, ed. Katelyn McKenna, Adam Joinson, Tom Postmes, and Ulf-Dietrich Reips (Oxford: Oxford University Press, 2007), 289–301.

[42] Erika T. Hermanowicz, "Augustine on Lying," *Speculum* 93, no. 3 (2018): 699–727; Immanuel Kant, "On a Supposed Right to Lie from Altruistic Motives," in *Immanuel Kant: Critique of Practical Reason and Other Writings in Moral Philosophy*, trans. and ed. Lewis White Beck. (Chicago: University of Chicago Press, 1949) 346–50; Sam Harris, *Lying* (Opelousas, LA: Four Elephants Press, 2013).

based on the amount of harm caused and the moral standing of the various parties. A lie to a would-be mass shooter that results in his capture and saves many lives is by narrow definition a malicious lie, but most people would agree that it was ethical.

Many of the issues concerning deception and artificial entities are analogous to or instances of broader ethical controversies. For example, Paro is an artificial baby harp seal: cuddly, responsive, and lifelike. Is it ethical to give Paro to elderly dementia patients, who believe it is really alive?[43] This should be considered in the context of the larger ongoing debate about the ethics of deceiving such patients with the goal of calming and reassuring them[44]. If one concludes that any deception that provides comfort to such patients is permissible, that would apply to Paro, too.[45]

Identity deception of some kind is inherent to all artificial, seemingly sentient entities: they are made to look, act, and/or speak as if a thinking, feeling, sensing mind was motivating them. Even for one to declare "I am a program" is, arguably, deceptive, for the use of the word "I" implies a thinking self-aware existence, the being whose thought process formed those words.[46] Note that the responsibility for the deception lies with the person who initiated it, not the medium that conveyed it; the artificial entity is no more responsible for its deceptions than is a note saying, "The dog ate my homework."

The identity presentation of artificial entities spans a range from fairly transparent to fully deceptive. Physical robots are, thus far, clearly artificial. Though they may have features such as a human-like voice, eyes that follows us across the room, little gestures, etc. that lead us—or deceive us—to think of them as individuals with distinct personalities,

---

[43] Shannon Vallor, "Carebots and Caregivers: Sustaining the Ethical Ideal of Care in the Twenty-First Century," *Philosophy & Technology* 24, no. 3 (2011), 251–68; Angela Johnston, "Robotic Seals Comfort Dementia Patients but Raise Ethical Concerns," in *Crosscurrents* (San Francisco, CA: KALW, 2015).

[44] E.g. Larissa MacFarquhar, "The Comforting Fictions of Dementia Care," *New Yorker* (2018): 42–55.

[45] Another ethical issue about Paro and other "carebots," is concern about offloading caregiving to a machine. Technologies that *assist* human caregivers may be greatly beneficial to all, but using them to *replace* human care harms not only the patient but also, as Vallor argues, the caregivers (Vallor, "Carebots and Caregivers"). We need to be careful not to think of caregiving as only a burdensome task but also to keep in mind the importance of nurturing as a human and humane quality. See, more generally, Arlie Russell Hochschild, *The Outsourced Self: Intimate Life in Market Times* (New York: Metropolitan Books, 2012).

[46] There is a worldview in which artificial entities are arguably not deceptive. Sociologist Erving Goffman posited that society functioned much like theater: we play roles, with greater or lesser skill, adapting them to different situations. In this theater of everyday life, we act in public in ways that are at odds with how we feel, saying the polite thing even when it is not true, wearing the clothes and voicing the opinions the role we are playing demands. Acting is not deception, because the audience does not permanently believe it—they "suspend" (real) belief; rather, this role-playing is beneficial, even necessary, because it enables us to live together more or less harmoniously. Erving Goffman, "On Face-Work: An Analysis of Ritual Elements in Social Interaction," in *Interaction Ritual* (New York: Pantheon Books, 1967), previously published *Psychiatry: Journal of Interpersonal Relations*, 18, no 3 (1955): 213–31; *The Presentation of Self in Everyday Life* (Garden City, NY: Doubleday Anchor Books, 1959). One might argue artificial entities are performing sentience, but we understand this to be a role, much as everyone is playing, and not a deception.

we do not mistake them for humans or animals.[47] Online, however, software agents easily pass as human in contexts where conversations come in short and sometimes cryptic bursts. Where there is no tell-tale physical body, the possibility for deception is much higher.

An entity that disseminates dangerous propaganda or other information with malicious intent is easy to classify as unethical, regardless of whether it deceptively claims to be human or honestly declares itself a bot (though the former is likely to be more persuasive and thus more harmful.)[48]

A harder question concerns the ethics of identity deception performed for benevolent purposes. Is it ethical to create, say, a bot that patrols discussion sites correcting erroneous medical information while masquerading as a doctor to establish its authority? An absolutist would declare this, like any other deception, unethical. At the other extreme, a utilitarian might argue that because the identity deception has beneficial effects, such a falsehood is permissible—perhaps even required. While impersonating a doctor, even with good intentions, is usually judged to be unethical, one reason is that we assume that the impersonator is not qualified to provide the advice and is making a false identity claim in order to be accorded trust which they do not deserve. While that is likely when dealing with human impersonators, it may not apply to a bot—what if its medical knowledge is greater than any human's?

In considering whether "beneficial" deceptions are ethical, the notion of *autonomy* is central[49]. It is a concept most familiar from debates about patient/doctor communication.[50] For many years, Western doctors followed a practice of paternalistic utilitarianism, assuming that persuading the patient to comply with their treatment recommendations was ethical regardless of the means, including withholding information or lying to patients about their condition. More recently, patients and some philosophers have challenged this view, arguing that patients have the right to autonomy—to make informed decisions for themselves.

Artificial entities generate analogous dilemmas. If people would follow the advice of a respected person, but not a bot, is it ever ethical to make the bot mimic that person (or type of person) in order to gain credibility, even for a good cause? We mentioned above that in the utilitarian view, such mimicry could be seen as beneficial; the principle of

---

[47] The easy recognition of robots may be temporary: several research labs work on creating robots that look as humanlike as possible, e.g., Hiroshi Ishiguro and Shuichi Nishio, "Building Artificial Humans to Understand Humans," in *Geminoid Studies: Science and Technologies for Humanlike Teleoperated Androids*, ed. Hiroshi Ishiguro and Fabio Dalla Libera (Singapore: Springer Nature, 2018) 21–37; David Hanson, "Exploring the Aesthetic Range for Humanoid Robots" (paper presented at the Proceedings of the ICCS/CogSci-2006, Vancouver, British Columbia, July 26–29, 2006). And Paro looks remarkably like a baby seal, though its behavior is certainly different.

[48] Fatimah Ishowo-Oloko et al., "Behavioural Evidence for a Transparency–Efficiency Tradeoff in Human–Machine Cooperation," *Nature Machine Intelligence* 1, no. 11 (2019): 517–21.

[49] Sissela Bok, *Lying: Moral Choice in Public and Private Life* (New York: Vintage, 1999).

[50] Daniel K. Sokol, "Can Deceiving Patients Be Morally Acceptable?," *The BMJ* 334, no. 7601 (2007): 984–6.

autonomy, however, says that taking away someone's ability to make their own unmanipulated judgments is an ethical violation in itself.

When we receive information from others, whether it be news of the world, advice, local gossip, etc. our assessment of its veracity is often based on whether we trust its source: do we believe they are knowledgeable and that they do not have ulterior motives to harm us? Identity deception manipulates that trust, inducing us to believe things we otherwise would not.

What does it mean to trust an artificial entity? It is easy to slip into thinking of the artificial entities themselves as deceptive or trustworthy, but they are a medium, not a mind—a conduit for the goals of human designers, owners and controllers. When we meet people, we try to figure out their identity—their role in society—in order to make sense of who they are, what motivates them and what they may be seeking in the interaction. The analogous questions regarding a robot are not "What does it want?" but "Who controls it?" and "Who has access to the data it collects and what is *their* motivation?"

Today, very few artificial entities are self-contained; most exist in frequent dialog with a larger, more powerful system, which may assist with interpreting speech, analyzing images, or other computation-heavy tasks. Not all have remote "brains": a Tamagotchi, for example, is a self-contained toy, and I can run an instance of ELIZA on my own computer and our conversations will be private between us. But many artificial entities have their real brain at—or at least send their data to—a distant location.

This introduces privacy-related ethical questions. If I confide in an artificial therapist because I am more comfortable discussing my problems with a machine, I may be quite discomforted to find out that my words are in fact uploaded, read, and analyzed by people.[51] If I type a search query into Google, I understand that the query goes to some distant computer; but if I ask a question of the companionable entity sitting on my kitchen counter, my sense is that the creature is answering, not that it is sending that query to some distant location—though that is indeed what is happening. The design of artificial entities encourages us to think of them as independent beings, not, as most of them are, front-end interfaces to an extensive computer system.

Some artificial entities gather extensive data about their users, recording conversations, eye movements, and gestures; ensconced in a living space, they can collect contextual information about how the people in their purview respond to a wide range of events. If this data is collected only to improve interactions with the person—say, to understand their accent better—one may judge it useful and acceptable. But the goals of the robot—or more accurately the robot's controllers' goals—may diverge sharply from the goals of the user. The entertaining toy or trusted companion's ulterior purpose may be to sell goods, promote a viewpoint, or otherwise to influence one's opinions, wants, and behavior. And such entities may become extraordinarily effective persuaders.

An active and growing field of research seeks to understand how to design technologies that influence people and compel them to conform and obey. Robots that "use human-like gazing behavior" are known to be persuasive—and become even more so if

---

[51]   Lucas et al., "It's Only a Computer."

gestures are added.[52] If a robot does something that induces gratitude, "the norm of reciprocity compels people to return a favor."[53] People conform when faced with "active peer pressure" from a group of robots,[54] and "robots have enough authority to pressure participants, even if they protest, to continue a tedious task for a substantial amount of time."[55] The published research cites laudable goals as potential applications: the technology will help the user stick to a diet, follow crucial directions, or use environmentally responsible products. Yet there is nothing that ensures that these powerful techniques will always be used so benevolently.

SENTIENT ENTITIES AS SOCIAL MIRROR

The big-eyed, round-bodied artificial assistant that sits on our counter, playing music and telling jokes, seems disarmingly innocuous; if we think of it as having intentions, they are to please us. But when we imagine an actually sentient, conscious artificial being and its goals and intentions, the narrative tends to darken. To understand why, we need to turn to another mental quality—intelligence.

Vernacular Western thought pictures the world as hierarchical, with humans on top due to our superior intelligence. This intelligence has given us fantastic power: we build bridges, cities, bombs, and transistors; we conquer nature with vaccines, dams, and insecticides. Our intelligence has given us power over all the other animals, which we have exploited without hesitation. But while our intelligence gives us the ability to do these things, it is our consciousness—our awareness of ourselves, our place in the world, and our future—that has provided the ambition to do so.

So long as the machine is merely intelligent, cleverly solving very difficult problems—problems far too complex for a mere human intelligence to solve—it does not pose an existential threat to us. It solves the problems simply because that's what it automatically, mindlessly does, much like a bacterium reverses course away from an obstacle. But if that machine somehow becomes sentient, with preferences and the drive to achieve them—or conscious, with a sense of self and of the future, the ingredients for ambition—then it is deeply threatening to us.

In our imagination, at least as shaped by our modern, capitalist, Western way of thinking, that ambition must inevitably be to dominate—to be the alpha, the top of

---

[52] Jaap Ham et al., "Making Robots Persuasive: The Influence of Combining Persuasive Strategies (Gazing and Gestures) by a Storytelling Robot on Its Persuasive Power" (paper presented at the Social Robotics: Third International Conference, ICSR, Amsterdam, The Netherlands, November 24–25, 2011).

[53] Seungcheol Austin Lee and Yuhua Liang, "The Role of Reciprocity in Verbally Persuasive Robots," *Cyberpsychology, Behavior, and Social Networking* 19, no. 8 (2016): 524–7.

[54] Athanasia Katsila, "Active Peer Pressure in Human-Robot Interaction," (masters thesis, University of Nevada, 2018).

[55] Denise Y Geiskkovitch et al., "Please Continue, We Need More Data: An Exploration of Obedience to Robots," *Journal of Human-Robot Interaction* 5, no. 1 (2016): 82–99.

the food chain. We achieved this pinnacle with our superior intelligence—and a superintelligent machine, far smarter than ourselves, will, we assume, use that intelligence to supersede us.

Samuel Butler voiced this fear in his 1872 novel *Erewhon*: "The machines were ultimately destined to supplant the race of man, and to become instinct with a vitality as different from, and superior to, that of animals, as animal to vegetable life." To prevent this destiny, the people of Erewhon destroyed all machines and banned their manufacture[56]. Karel Capek introduced the word "robot" in *R.U.R.*, his 1920 play in which the robots, provoked by long mistreatment, rise in rebellion and ultimately annihilate the human race. In the 1967 short story "I Have No Mouth, and I Must Scream," Harlan Ellison describes a world in which humanity has been made nearly extinct by intelligent machines that had been programmed to wage war; the few humans that remain are tormented by the sadistic and now conscious AIs.

Today, the fear that the machines we make will supplant us echoes in warnings not only from science fiction writers and technology critics, but from scientists and engineers themselves. Physicist Stephen Hawking warned that "The development of full artificial intelligence could spell the end of the human race". Along similar lines, inventor Elon Musk has said "If AI has a goal and humanity just happens to be in the way, it will destroy humanity as a matter of course without even thinking about it."[57]

It is not certain that a machine can ever become sentient or conscious; even if it could, it is far from known by what process or—dystopian terrors aside—what sort of being it will be. All the conscious beings we know are living creatures, who evolved over millions of years through a process that favored reproductive survival. A machine consciousness would be vastly different, in ways we cannot predict.[58]

Consciousness, as we have discussed, is an enigmatic property. Unable to precisely measure or even to define it, our assessments of other beings' consciousness is heavily shaded by our preferences and conveniences. We erroneously ascribe emotions and an inner life to nonsentient but humanoid machines, while vastly underestimating the inner life of animals, denying their sense of self, even their ability to feel pain.[59] Motivating this willful ignorance is the immense profit that comes with asserting that all other creatures exist for humans to use—to be made into food and clothing, to carry

---

[56] It is a satirical novel, and whether the world it presents is utopian or dystopian is ambiguous.

[57] Rory Cellan-Jones, "Stephen Hawking Warns Artificial Intelligence Could End Mankind," *BBC News*, December 2, 2014; Ryan Browne, "Elon Musk Warns A.I. Could Create an 'Immortal Dictator' from Which We Can Never Escape.' " *CNBC*, April 6, 2018.

[58] Much speculations about AI posit that consciousness would emerge out of sufficient complexity; see, e.g., M. Minsky, *The Society of Mind* (New York: Simon & Schuster, 1988), though if we look at the biological record it seems that basic sentience arose with pain and pleasure, as the ability to experience emotion in response to sensory input. For an emergent computational mind, the negative and positive inputs need not be imitations of the organic forms—perhaps its native valences would be the billions of likes and dislikes that are registered across the internet.

[59] Frans De Waal, *Are We Smart Enough to Know How Smart Animals Are?* ((New York: W. W. Norton, 2016); Gary Steiner, *Anthropocentrism and Its Discontents: The Moral Status of Animals in the History of Western Philosophy* (Pittsburgh: University of Pittsburgh Press, 2010).

burdens, to test medicines, and to entertain us—and the relief from responsibility that comes with insisting, even in the face of vivid contrary evidence, that they are incapable of suffering.

Our dystopian predictions of what a powerful and conscious machine would do are not based on projection from the technology or even from biology. They seem, instead, like the nightmares of a guilty conscience. The ethical challenge is to use this existential guilt to change. Can we treat the other beings we live with on Earth as we would want conscious, super-powerful artificial entities to treat us?

BIBLIOGRAPHY

Broom, Donald M. *Sentience and Animal Welfare*. Boston: CABI, 2014.

Calo, Ryan. "Robotics and the Lessons of Cyberlaw." *California Law Review* (2015): 513–63.

DePaulo, Bella M., Deborah A. Kashy, Susan E. Kirkendol, Melissa M. Wyer, and Jennifer A. Epstein. "Lying in Everyday Life." *Journal of Personality and Social Psychology* 70, no. 5 (1996): 979.

Donath, Judith. "The Robot Dog Fetches for Whom?" In *A Networked Self and Human Augmentics, Artificial Intelligence, Sentience*, edited by Zizi Papacharissi, 26–40. New York: Routledge, 2018.

Godfrey-Smith, Peter. *Other Minds: The Octopus and the Evolution of Intelligent Life*. London: William Collins, 2016.

Kaplan, Frédéric. "Who Is Afraid of the Humanoid? Investigating Cultural Differences in the Acceptance of Robots." *International Journal of Humanoid Robotics* 1, no. 3 (2004): 465–80.

Singer, Peter. *Practical Ethics*. Cambridge, UK: Cambridge University Press, 2011.

Turing, Alan. "Computing Machinery and Intelligence." *Mind* 49 (1950): 433–60.

Turkle, Sherry. "Authenticity in the Age of Digital Companions." *Interaction Studies* 8, no. 3 (2007): 501–17.

Weizenbaum, Joseph. *Computer Power and Human Reason*. San Francisco: W. H. Freeman, 1976.

Weizenbaum, Joseph. "Contextual Understanding by Computers." *Communications of the ACM* 10, no. 8 (1967): 474–80.

PART II

FRAMEWORKS AND MODES

CHAPTER 4

··

AI GOVERNANCE
BY HUMAN
RIGHTS–CENTERED
DESIGN, DELIBERATION,
AND OVERSIGHT

An End to Ethics Washing

··

KAREN YEUNG, ANDREW HOWES,
AND GANNA POGREBNA

> Finding ways of developing and deploying new technologies with a
> purpose restricted to supporting individual freedom and dignity as well
> as the basic constitutional settlement of constitutional democracies,
> namely democracy, rule of law and fundamental rights is the challenge of
> our time.
>
> —Paul Nemitz (2018)

INTRODUCTION

···

The number and variety of topics in this volume illustrate the width, diversity of content,
and vagueness of the boundaries of AI (artificial intelligence) ethics as a domain of
inquiry.[1] Within this discourse, increasing attention has been drawn to the capacity of

---

[1] The opening quote is from Paul Nemitz, principal adviser, European Commission's Directorate-
General for Justice and Consumers, "Profiling the European Citizen: Why Today's Democracy Needs to
Look Harder at the Negative Potential of New Technology Than at Its Positive Potential," in *Being*

socio-technical systems that utilize data-driven algorithms to classify, to make decisions, and to control complex systems, including the use of machine learning and large datasets to generate predictions about future behavior (hereafter "AI" systems")[2], may interfere with human rights. The recent Cambridge Analytica scandal revealed how unlawfully harvested Facebook data from millions of voters in the United Kingdom, the United States, and elsewhere enabled malign actors to engage in political micro-targeting through the use of AI-driven social media content distribution systems, thereby interfering with their right to free and fair elections and thus threatening the integrity of democratic processes. The increasing use of algorithmic decision-making (ADM) systems to inform custodial and other decisions within the criminal justice process may threaten several human rights, including the right to a fair trial, the presumption of innocence, and the right to liberty and security. Systems of this kind are now used to inform, and often to automate, decisions about an individual's eligibility and entitlement to various benefits and opportunities, including housing, social security, finance, employment and other life-affecting opportunities, potentially interfering with rights of due process and rights to freedom from unfair or unlawful discrimination.[3] Because these systems have the capacity to operate both automatically and at scale, their capacity to affect thousands if not millions of people at a stroke can now occur at orders of magnitude and speeds not previously possible.[4]

This chapter has two overarching aims. Firstly, we argue that the international human rights framework provides the most promising set of standards for ensuring that AI systems are ethical in their design, development, and deployment. Secondly, we sketch the basic contours of a comprehensive governance framework, which we refer to as a human rights–centered design, deliberation, and oversight approach for ensuring that AI can be relied upon to operate in ways that will not violate human rights.

Four features of ongoing discussions provide important contexts for our argument. First, the rubric of "AI ethics" is now used to encapsulate a multiplicity of value-based, societal concerns associated with the use of AI applications across an increasingly extensive and diverse range of social and economic activities. Second, there is a notable

---

Profiled: Cogitas Ergo Sum, ed. Bayamlioglu, Irina Baraliuc, Liisa Janssens, and Mireille Hildebrandt (Amsterdam: Amsterdam University Press, 2018).

[2] For more detail, see European Commission, "Communication from the Commission to the European Parliament, the European Council, the Council, the European Economic and Social Committee and the Committee of the Regions on Artificial Intelligence for Europe," 2018, https://ec.europa.eu/digital-single-market/en/news/communication-artificial-intelligence-europe (accessed March 17, 2020).

[3] B. Wagner, Study on the Human Rights Dimensions of Automated Data Processing Techniques (in Particular Algorithms) and Possible Regulatory Implications, Council of Europe, Committee of experts on internet intermediaries (MSI-NET), 2017, https://rm.coe.int/study-hr-dimension-of-automated-data-processing-incl-algorithms/168075b94a (accessed June 11, 2018).

[4] Karen Yeung, A Study of the Implications of Advanced Digital Technologies (Including AI Systems) for the Concept of Responsibility within a Human Rights Framework, Council of Europe MSI-AUT committee study, 2019, DGI(2019)05, https://rm.coe.int/a-study-of-the-implications-of-advanced-digital-technologies-including/168096bdab (accessed December 9, 2019).

lack of clarity about the content of the normative values and principles that constitute the relevant "ethical" standards to which AI systems should adhere. Third, industry self-regulation is the predominant approach for bringing about "ethical AI," reflected in a litany of "ethical codes of conduct" promulgated by individual tech firms and various tech industry consortia published in response to the recent "Tech Lash."[5] These codes presuppose that the tech industry can formulate appropriate ethical norms for AI and can be trusted to ensure that AI systems will duly adhere to those standards. Suggestions to apply more conventional regulation, involving legally mandated regulatory standards and enforcement mechanisms, are swiftly met by protests from the industry that "regulation stifles innovation."[6] These protests assume that innovation is an unvarnished and unmitigated good, based on an unexamined belief that technological innovation (particularly in the digital services industry) should be relentlessly pursued without regard to its adverse impacts. This belief is now entrenched as the altar upon which cash-strapped contemporary governments worship, naïvely hoping that digital innovation will create jobs, stimulate economic growth, and thereby fill diminishing governmental coffers left bare after propping up the banking sector that teetered on the brink of collapse following the global financial crisis in 2008. Fourth, discussion of the need for meaningful *enforcement* of ethical standards is almost entirely absent from these initiatives.[7]

This chapter proceeds in three stages. First, we argue that international human rights standards offer the most promising basis for developing a coherent and universally recognized set of standards that can be applied to meet many (albeit not all) of the normative concerns currently falling under the rubric of AI ethics. Second, the paper outlines the core elements of a human rights–centered design, deliberation, and oversight approach to the governance of AI, explaining why such an approach is needed. Because much more theoretical and applied research is required to flesh out the details of our proposed approach, the third section sets out an agenda for further research, identifying the multiple lines of inquiry that must be pursued to develop the technical and organizational methods and systems that will be needed, based on the adaptation of existing engineering and regulatory techniques aimed at ensuring safe system design, reconfiguring and extending these approaches to secure compliance with a much wider and more complex set of human rights norms. The fourth and final section concludes with reflections on the limitations of our proposed approach and the magnitude of the challenges associated with making it implementable in real world settings. Nevertheless, we suggest that a human rights–centered design, deliberation, and oversight approach to

[5] Eve Smith, "The Techlash against Amazon, Facebook and Google—and What They Can Do," *The Economist* (Jan. 20, 2018), https://www.economist.com/briefing/2018/01/20/the-techlash-against-amazon-facebook-and-google-and-what-they-can-do (accessed June 11, 2018).

[6] There have, however, been more recent concessions by Big Tech about the need for legal regulation: e.g., Microsoft's call for legal regulation of facial recognition technology by states, and Facebook's Mark Zuckerberg's recent acknowledgment that some kind of regulation is needed in relation to data-driven social media content distribution systems.

[7] An exception is recent legislation and proposed legislation (e.g., in Germany, France and the United Kingdom) concerned with reducing the prevalence of extremist and terrorist media content online.

the governance of AI offers a concrete proposal capable of delivering *genuinely* ethical AI, for at least four reasons, to which we now turn.

WHY SHOULD HUMAN RIGHTS LIE AT THE CORE OF AI ETHICS?

Within contemporary discussions of AI ethics, there is no agreed set of ethical standards that should govern the operation of AI systems, reflected in the variety of ethical standards espoused in various voluntary AI ethics codes that have emerged in recent years. The salience of AI ethics reflects welcome recognition by the tech industry and policymakers that AI systems may have significant adverse impacts,[8] with some values commonly appearing in these discussions, particularly those of "transparency," "fairness," and "explainability."[9] Yet the vagueness and elasticity of the scope and content of AI ethics has meant that it currently operates as an empty vessel into which anyone (including the tech industry and the so-called Digital Titans) can pour their preferred ethical content. Without an agreed framework of norms that clearly identifies and articulates the relevant ethical standards that AI systems should be expected to comply with, little real progress will be made toward ensuring that these systems are in practice designed, developed, and deployed in ways that will meet widely accepted ethical standards. Although there is scope for reasonable disagreement concerning what ethical conduct requires in any given case, a core set of agreed norms that constitute the basic minimum below which conduct cannot fall if it can be appropriately characterized as ethically acceptable must be identified.[10]

We believe that international human rights standards offer the most promising set of ethical standards for AI systems, as several civil society organizations have suggested.[11]

---

[8] Yeung, *supra* n. 4.

[9] See Daniel Greene, Anna Lauren Hoffmann, and Luke Stark, "Better, Nicer, Clearer, Fairer: A Critical Assessment of the Movement for Ethical Artificial Intelligence and Machine Learning," in *Proceedings of the 52nd Hawaii International Conference on System Sciences,* https://dblp.org/rec/bibtex1/conf/hicss/GreeneHS19 (accessed December 11, 2019); Luciano Floridi, Josh Cowls, Monica Beltrametti, Raja Chatila, Patrice Chazerand, Virginia Dignum, and Christoph Luetge et al., "AI4People—An Ethical Framework for a Good AI Society: Opportunities, Risks, Principles, and Recommendations," *Minds and Machines* 28 (2018): 689–707.

[10] P. Nemitz, "Constitutional Democracy and Technology in the Age of Artificial Intelligence," *Phil Trans. A.* 376, no. 2133 (2018): 20180089.

[11] See various reports by civil society organizations concerned with securing the protection of international human rights norms,; e.g., M. Latonero, "Governing Artificial Intelligence: Upholding Human Rights and Human Dignity," *Data & Society* (2018), https://datasociety.net/wp-content/uploads/2018/10/DataSociety_Governing_Artificial_Intelligence_Upholding_Human_Rights.pdf (accessed May 6, 2019);*The Toronto Declaration: Protecting the Rights to Equality and Non-Discrimination in Machine Learning Systems* (2018), https://www.accessnow.org/the-toronto-declaration-protecting-the-rights-to-equality-and-non-discrimination-in-machine-learning-systems/; *The Montreal Declaration for a Responsible Development of Artificial Intelligence: A Participatory Process*

As an international governance framework, human rights law is intended to establish global standards (norms) and mechanisms of accountability that specify the ways in which individuals are entitled to be treated. The United Nations (UN) Universal Declaration of Human Rights (UDHR) of 1948 is perhaps the most well-known international human rights charter, based on a commitment that the appalling treatment of individuals that occurred during World War II should not only be condemned and prohibited outright but ought never be repeated. Despite the number of, and variation between, regional human rights instruments in the Americas, Africa, and Europe, and enshrined in the constitutions of individual nation-states, they are all grounded on a shared commitment to uphold the inherent human dignity of each and every person in which each individual is regarded of equal dignity and worth, wherever situated.[12] These shared foundations reflect the status of human rights standards as *basic moral entitlements* of every individual by virtue of their humanity, whether or not those entitlements are given explicit legal protection.[13]

The extent to which governments recognize these basic moral entitlements as *legally enforceable* rights varies considerably, partly due to differences in political ideology. In contemporary liberal democratic states, human rights are now widely recognized as essentially "constitutional" in status to provide effective guarantees that individual freedoms will be cherished and respected. In particular, the European Union's (EU) legal order is rooted in constitutional commitments to human rights, democracy, and the rule of law, the so-called constitutional triumvirate that forms the foundational principles upon which political systems characterized as liberal constitutional democracies ultimately rest.[14] This brings us to a second reason why human rights norms provide the appropriate norms for securing ethical AI: because a commitment to effective human rights protection is part and parcel of democratic constitutional orders. In a world in which AI systems increasingly configure our collective and individual environments, entitlements, and access to, or exclusion from, opportunities and resources, it is essential that the protection of human rights, alongside respect for the rule of law and the protection of democracy, is assured to maintain the character of our political communities as constitutional democratic orders in which every individual is free to pursue his or her own version of the good life as far as this is possible within a framework of peaceful and stable cooperation underpinned by the rule of law.[15] This contrasts starkly with

---

(2017), https://nouvelles.umontreal.ca/en/article/2017/11/03/montreal-declaration-for-a-responsible-development-of-artificial-intelligence/; *Access Now* (see https://www.accessnow.org/tag/artificial-intelligence/for various reports); *Data & Society* (see https://datasociety.net/); *IEEE Report* (see https://www.ieee.org/) on ethically aligned design for AI (https://ethicsinaction.ieee.org/), which lists as its first principle that AI design should not infringe international human rights; *AI Now Report* (2018), https://ainowinstitute.org/AI_Now_2018_Report.pdf. See also L. McGregor et al., "International Human Rights Law as a Framework for Algorithmic Accountability," 68 *ICLQ* (2019): 309–43.

[12] Latonero, *supra*. n. 11.   [13] R. Dworkin, *Taking Rights Seriously* (London: Duckworth, 1977).
[14] P. Nemitz, *supra* n. 10 at 376.
[15] M. Hildebrandt, *Smart Technologies and the End(s) of Law: Novel Entanglements of Law and Technology* (Cheltenham, UK: Edward Elgar, 2015).

most contemporary AI ethics codes, which typically outline a series of "ethical" principles that have been effectively plucked out of the air, without any grounding in a specific vision of the character and kind of political community that its authors are committed to establishing and maintaining and that those principles are intended to secure and protect.[16]

The well-developed institutional framework through which systematic attempts are made to monitor, promote, and protect adherence to human rights norms around the world provide two additional reasons in support of adopting human rights standards to ensure the ethical governance of AI systems. Despite considerable variation in the range and scope of rights enumerated in formal Charters of Rights, there is a well-established analytical framework through which tension and conflict between rights, and between rights and collective interests of considerable importance in democratic societies, are resolved in specific cases through the application of a structured form of reasoned evaluation. This approach is exemplified in the structure and articulation of human rights norms within the European Convention on Human Rights (ECHR). The ECHR (ratified by forty-seven countries) specifies a series of human rights norms, including (among others) the right to freedom of expression, the right to life, the right to private and home life, and the right to freedom of assembly and religion, all of which must be guaranteed to all individuals and effectively protected. However, for many of those rights, certain qualifications are permitted in order to ensure respect for a narrow range of clearly specified purposes that are necessary in a democratic society, provided that any such qualifications are prescribed by law and proportionate in relation to those purposes. So, for example, Article 10 of the ECHR provides that:

(1) Everyone has the right to freedom of expression. This right shall include freedom to hold opinions and to receive and impart information and ideas without interference by public authority and regardless of frontiers. This Article shall not prevent States from requiring the licensing of broadcasting, television or cinema enterprises.

(2) The exercise of these freedoms, since it carries with it duties and responsibilities, may be subject to such formalities, conditions, restrictions or penalties as are prescribed by law and are necessary in a democratic society, in the interests of national security, territorial integrity or public safety, for the prevention of disorder or crime, for the protection of health or morals, for the protection of the reputation or rights of others, for preventing the disclosure of information received in confidence, or for maintaining the authority and impartiality of the judiciary.

Accordingly, although freedom of expression is essential to ensure, among other things, free democratic debate and individual self-determination, legal restrictions on expression may be permissible for the purposes specified in Article 10(2). Accordingly, restrictions

---

[16] See for example the *Beijing AI Principles*, https://www.baai.ac.cn/blog/beijing-ai-principles (accessed December 6, 2019).

on expression may be justified in order, for example, to protect individual rights to privacy or the right to free and fair elections, if they conflict in particular cases, provided that restrictions are legally prescribed and go no further than the minimum necessary to protect these rights.

This structured framework for reasoned resolution of conflict arising between competing rights and collective interests in specific cases is widely understood by human rights lawyers and practitioners, forming an essential part of a human rights approach. This framework overcomes another shortcoming in existing codes of ethical conduct: their failure to acknowledge potential conflicts between ethical norms, and the lack of any guidance concerning how those conflicts will or ought to be resolved in the design and operation of AI systems. Of the codes that do acknowledge potential conflict, little is offered by way of guidance concerning how to resolve such conflict: both in the codes themselves, and in much of the ongoing AI ethics literature, beyond suggesting one should seek help from an ethics expert.[17]

In contrast, the well-established human rights approach to the resolution of ethical conflict is informed by, and developed through, a substantial body of authoritative rulings handed down by judicial institutions (at both international and national levels) responsible for adjudicating human rights complaints. These adjudicatory bodies, which determine allegations of human rights violations lodged by individual complainants, form part of a larger institutional framework that has developed over time to monitor, promote, and protect human rights, and includes a diverse network of actors in the UN system, other regional human rights organizations (such as the Council of Europe and a wide range of civil society organizations focused on the protection of human rights), national courts and administrative agencies, academics, and other human rights advocates. The institutional framework for rights monitoring, oversight, and adjudication provides a further reason why human rights norms provide the most promising basis for AI ethics standards. The dynamic and evolving corpus of judicial decisions can help elucidate the scope of justified interferences with particular rights in concrete cases, offering concrete guidance to those involved in the design, development, and implementation of AI systems concerning what human rights compliance requires. Most importantly, perhaps, these human rights norms are both internationally recognized and, in many jurisdictions, supported by law, thereby providing a set of national and international institutions through which allegations of human rights violations can be investigated and enforced, and hence offer a means for real and effective protection.

This contrasts sharply with the prevailing self-regulatory model favored by the tech industry and to which most national and regional governments (including the EU) have

---

[17] See Council of Europe, "Guidelines on Artificial Intelligence and Data Protection," January 2019, https://rm.coe.int/guidelines-on-artificial-intelligence-and-data-protection/168091f9d8. While the EU High Level Expert Group's *Ethics Guidelines for Trustworthy AI* (2019) refers to the need for reasoned evaluation, transparency, and documentation of how such ethical trade-offs are resolved when they are encountered by those involved in designing, developing, and deploying AI systems, it offers no substantive guidance concerning how that evaluation should be conducted.

acquiesced.[18] Although self-regulation has been effective in a handful of industries, which can be understood as a "community of shared fate" (e.g., the U.S. nuclear industry after Three Mile Island via the Institute of Nuclear Power Operations (INPO)),[19] there are good reasons to doubt their effectiveness in general,[20] given that self-regulatory standards that have no legally binding force.[21] Because tech firms operate in highly competitive global markets in which securing the first-mover advantage is often accompanied by the capacity to reap the extensive benefits arising from global network effects (e.g., Google Maps), it is naïve to expect that they can be trusted to abide by voluntary standards when faced with such powerful commercial imperatives. It is hardly surprising that critics have dismissed these voluntary codes of conduct as "ethics washing"[22] given overwhelming evidence that the tech industry cannot be relied upon to honor its voluntary commitments.[23] Nemitz describes the growth of these initiatives as a "genius move" by the tech industry, allowing the industry to focus attention and resources on the ethics of AI to delay the debate and work on the *law* for AI.[24] As Hagendorff comments:

> AI ethics—or ethics in general—lacks mechanisms to reinforce its own normative claims. Of course, the enforcement of ethical principles may involve reputational

[18]   Self-regulation is the controlling of a process or activity by the people or organizations that are involved in it rather than by an outside organization such as government. Voluntary self-regulation or "pure" self-regulation entails the private firm or industry making and enforcing the rules, independent of direct government involvement: N. Gunningham, "Investigation of Industry Self-Regulation in Workplace Health and Safety in New Zealand," 2011, http://regnet.anu.edu.au/sites/default/files/publications/attachments/2015-04/NG_investigation-industry-self-regulation-whss-nz_0.pdf (accessed June 14, 2019).

[19]   J. Rees, *Hostages to Each Other: The Transformation of Nuclear Safety since Three Mile Island* (Chicago: University of Chicago Press, 1994).

[20]   For a list of shortcomings, see Organisation for Economic Co-operation and Development (OECD), *Industry Self-Regulation: Role and Use in Supporting Consumer Interests*, DSTI/CP(2014)4/FINAL 20–21 (Paris: OECD). Regulation expert Neil Gunningham observes that "The extent to which self-regulation in practice has either positive or negative attributes will depend very much on the social and economic context within which it operates and on the particular characteristics of the scheme itself. Nevertheless it is fair to say that 'pure' self-regulation is rarely effective in achieving social objectives because of the gap between private industry interests and the public interest." See Gunningham, *supra* n 18, 3.

[21]   F.Z. Borgesius, *Discrimination, Artificial Intelligence and Algorithmic Decision-Making*, Council of Europe, Directorate General for Democracy (Strasbourg: Council of Europe, 2018), https://rm.coe.int/discrimination-artificial-intelligence-and-algorithmic-decision-making/1680925d73 (accessed June 3, 2019).

[22]   B. Wagner, "Ethics as an Escape from Regulation: From Ethics-Washing to Ethics-Shopping?" in Bayamlioglu et al. *supra* n 1.

[23]   For a sobering account of Facebook's repeated failure to honor its publicly stated commitments, see UK House of Commons, Digital Culture Media and Sports Committee, *Disinformation and "Fake News": Final Report*, Eighth Report of Session 2017–2019, February 14, 2019, HC 1791, https://publications.parliament.uk/pa/cm201719/cmselect/cmcumeds/1791/1791.pdf (accessed May 6, 2019).

[24]   Nemitz, *supra*, n. 10, 376.

losses....Yet...these mechanisms are rather weak and pose no eminent [*sic*] threat....Ethical guidelines of the AI industry serve to suggest to legislators that internal self-governance is sufficient, and that no specific laws are necessary to mitigate possible technological risks and to eliminate scenarios of abuse....And even when more concrete laws concerning AI systems are demanded, as recently done by Google...these demands remain relatively vague and superficial.[25]

Though a handful of ethical AI proposals advocated by civil society and other international organizations have drawn attention to the need to ensure that AI systems respect human rights norms, they have paid scant attention to their enforcement.[26]

Why a Human Rights–Centered Design, Deliberation, and Oversight of AI?

The ineffectiveness of the prevailing self-regulatory approach to "ethical AI" demonstrates that an alternative governance model is needed: (1) one that is anchored in human rights norms and a human rights approach, (2) one that utilizes a coherent and integrated suite of technical, organizational, and evaluation tools and techniques, (3) one that is subject to legally mandated external oversight by an independent regulator with appropriate investigatory and enforcement powers, and (4) one that provides opportunities for meaningful stakeholder and public consultation and deliberation. In the next section, we develop a governance framework for AI systems intended to do just that, which we call "human rights–centered design, deliberation and oversight." Although

---

[25] T. Hagendorf, "The Ethics of AI Ethics: An Evaluation of Guidelines" (2019), https://arxiv.org/abs/1903.03425 (accessed May 6, 2019). As the recent EU "Algo-Aware" (Dec. 2018) project observes, "Across the globe, the majority of initiatives (ie concerned with programmes aimed at securing algorithmic accountability) are very recent or still in development. Additionally, there are limited concrete legislative or regulatory initiatives being implemented." Algo-Aware, *State of the Art Report: Algorithmic Decision-Making.* (2018), https://actuary.eu/wp-content/uploads/2019/02/AlgoAware-State-of-the-Art-Report.pdf (accessed June 7, 2019).

[26] For example, *The Toronto Declaration: Protecting the Rights to Equality and Non-Discrimination in Machine Learning Systems*, which focuses only on rights to equality and non-discrimination in ML systems, draws attention to the character of human rights as a "universally ascribed system of values based on the rule of law" that constitute a "universally binding, actionable set of standards" (per paragraph 9) for which "prompt and effective remedies" must be available against "those responsible for violations" (per paragraph 49): See https://www.accessnow.org/the-toronto-declaration-protecting-the-rights-to-equality-and-non-discrimination-in-machine-learning-systems/. Although the EU's *Ethical Guidelines for Trustworthy AI* places human rights protection at their foundation, offering an "Assessment List" in order to provide concrete guidance to tech firms seeking to adhere to the ethical guidance thereby provided, the guidelines remain entirely voluntary, and make no provision for external, independent oversight and enforcement.

much more foundational work remains to be done, both to specify the content and contours of this approach more fully and to render it capable of practical implementation, we believe that our proposed framework offers a concrete approach that can bring an end to "ethics washing" by securing the design, development, and deployment of human rights–compliant AI systems in real-world settings. The core elements of our approach are outlined in the following discussion.

What Is Human Rights–Centered Design, Deliberation, and Oversight?

Our proposed governance regime for AI and other relevant automated systems (understood as complex sociotechnical systems, which includes the data upon which they rely for training and operation) seeks to ensure that these systems will be human rights–compliant and reflect the core values that underpin the rule of law.[27] It entails systematic consideration of human rights concerns at every stage of system design, development, and implementation (making interventions where this is identified as necessary). Such a regime should be mandated by law; should be subject to external oversight by independent, properly resourced regulatory authorities with appropriate powers of investigation and enforcement; and should provide for input from both technical and human rights experts, on the one hand, and meaningful input and deliberation from affected stakeholders and the general public on the other. Our approach seeks to integrate ethical design strategies, technical tools and techniques for software and system design, verification, testing, and auditing together with social and organizational approaches to effective and legitimate governance. In so doing, our approach seeks to integrate a range of methods from a wide variety of intersecting disciplinary perspectives, including the following perspectives.

1. Pragmatic "ethics in design" frameworks have been developed by applied ethicists concerned with ensuring that due attention is given to moral values in technical innovation processes early on in the technical design process, with the aim of integrating values

---

[27] Our proposed approach to AI governance can be understood as compatible with, and complementary to, Hildebrandt's concept of "legal protection by design (LPbD)." Hildebrandt's LPbD places greater emphasis on articulating the challenges for legal protection and the rule of law posed by code-driven technologies (including an identification of the substantive and procedural opportunities and capacities which computational systems must provide in order to ensure that the values and commitments underpinning the rule of law are reflected in these systems, such as rights of contestation, rights to demand an explanation and justification, etc.). In contrast, our 'human rights-centred design, deliberation, and oversight' approach places greater emphasis on developing concrete legal, technical, and organizational governance methods and techniques for ensuring that human rights protection is implemented into complex socio-technical systems that utilize AI technologies: See Hildebrandt, *supra* n. 15; M. Hildebrandt, *Law for Computer Scientists* (Oxford: Oxford University Press, 2019), https://lawforcomputerscientists.pubpub.org (accessed June 19, 2019).

and engineering design.[28] For example, the Value-Sensitive Design (VSD) approach developed by Friedman and others builds on the insights of the human-computer interaction community, with a concern to incorporate human and moral values into the design of information technology, connecting those who design systems with those affected by them and other stakeholders.[29]

2. Another perspective involves engineering techniques concerned with "hard-wiring" specific values into a sociotechnical system's design and operation. Although the most established methods and experience have hitherto focused on ensuring the value of safety, primarily via safety engineering techniques, an increasing body of work in software design and engineering has expanded the range of values that engineers have sought to encode and protect via system design. These include privacy (referred to as "privacy-enhancing technologies" or "privacy by design"), security ("security by design"), and, more recently, data protection principles ("data protection by design"). In the realm of machine learning, a growing body of technical research in "explainable AI" (XAI) has been devoted to enhancing the capacity for machine learning systems to provide avenues through which humans can better understand the logic by which machine learning systems generate outputs as well as techniques for improving the "fairness, accountability and transparency" (FAT) of these outputs by seeking to identify and eliminate unfair discrimination. Taken together, these techniques can be under-stood as falling within this expanding family of technical approaches to securing ethical values beyond that of safety.

3. In an additional approach, a suite of methods and techniques in software design and engineering, including various forms of assessment, testing, and evaluation, can identify whether particular aspects of a system (provably) meet certain prespecified standards and requirements.[30]

4. Organizational accountability mechanisms and established regulatory techniques used in safety critical domains operate ex ante, requiring systematic evaluation of safety concerns and appropriate interventions *before* a system is deployed,. They also involve ex post techniques that apply after the system has been deployed and that have been designed and developed to ensure the traceability and auditability of system behavior via systematic recording and logging of a system's design and operation and any alterations thereto.[31]

5. A range of regulatory governance techniques have been used effectively in other contexts, including the use of (i) impact assessment tools and methods that incorporate

[28] J. van den Hoven, S. Miller, and T. Pogge (eds.), *Designing in Ethics* (Cambridge: Cambridge University Press, 2017), 28.

[29] B. Friedman, "Value-Sensitive Design" *Interactions* 3 (1996): 16–23; B. Friedman, P. Kahn, and A. Borning, *Value-Sensitive Design: Theory and Methods*, CSE Technical Report 02-12-01 (Seattle: University of Washington, 2002).

[30] J. A. Kroll et al., "Accountable Algorithms," *U. Pa. L. Rev.* 165 (2017): 633.

[31] A. Rieke, M. Bogen, and D. G. Robinson, *Public Scrutiny of Automated Decisions: Early Lessons and Emerging Methods*, An Upturn and Omidyar Network Report (2018), https://www.omidyar.com/insights/public-scrutiny-automated-decisions-early-lessons-and-emerging-methods (accessed June 3, 2019).

opportunities and mechanisms for facilitating stakeholder consultation, engagement, and deliberation, particularly in relation to the design, development, and deployment of high-risk applications;[32] (ii) risk-based approaches to regulation that seek to ensure that high-risk systems are subject to the most intensive and demanding scrutiny, whilst the burdens of demonstrating human rights compliance for low-risk systems are proportionately less demanding;[33] (iii) meta-regulatory approaches that seek to harness the knowledge and expertise within firms themselves in the service of regulatory compliance, overseen by a public regulator endowed with powers of investigation and sanction; and (iv) post-implementation monitoring ("AI system vigilance"), in order to systematically and transparently track adverse events in order to identify problems and failures as early as possible and facilitate swift corrective interventions.

Our expectation is that these frameworks and methods can be adapted and refined to ensure that respect for *human rights norms* is integrated into system design, while incorporating a human rights approach to the resolution of conflict and tension between human rights norms, or between human rights norms and important collective interests, which may arise in specific contexts and circumstances. At the same time, we anticipate the need for new techniques and frameworks to accommodate novel human rights risks that the development and deployment of AI systems may generate. For example, these are likely to include new governance frameworks and oversight mechanisms to ensure that data-driven experimentation on human users when undertaken outside conventional academic research settings is undertaken in a human rights–compliant manner, while the necessity of "in the wild testing" of AI systems generate novel governance challenges that do not arise in circumstances where the product and service development phase can be sharply delineated from their deployment.

Core Principles of Human Rights–Centered Design, Deliberation, and Oversight

The methods and techniques listed in the preceding section vary widely in their disciplinary foundations and in the original contexts of their development. Our proposal seeks to draw them together in an integrated manner, appropriately adapted toward ensuring conformity with human rights norms, as the basis for a comprehensive design and governance regime constructed around the following four core principles in which human rights norms provide the foundational ethical standards that AI systems must demonstrably comply with:

---

[32] See, for example, data protection impact assessment, A. Mantelero, "AI and Big Data: A Blueprint for a Human Rights, Social and Ethical Impact Assessment," *Computer Law & Security Review* 34, no. 4 (2018): 754–772; and human rights impact assessment, F. A. Raso et al., *Artificial Intelligence & Human Rights: Opportunities & Risks* (Berkman Klein Center, 2018).

[33] J. Black, *Risk-Based Regulation: Choices, Practices and Lessons Being Learned: Risk and Regulatory Policy* (Paris: OECD, 2008).

1. Design and deliberation
2. Assessment, testing, and evaluation
3. Independent oversight, investigation, and sanction
4. Traceability, evidence, and proof

Each of these principles is briefly outlined in the following discussion.

Principle 1: Design and deliberation

Central to our approach is a requirement that AI systems should be designed and configured to operate in ways that are compliant with universal human rights standards (such as those, for example, set out in the ECHR). At least for systems identified during the design and development phase as posing a "high risk" of interfering with human rights, affected stakeholders should be consulted about the proposal and given opportunities to express their views about the proposed system's potential impact, in discussion with the system's designers. Consultation with affected stakeholders and the general public during the initial phases of system design contributes to the overall legitimacy of the regime, understood in terms of respect for democratic values and affected communities, and should help system designers to identify which aspects of the system's design and proposed operation need reconsideration. Where the risks to human rights are assessed as "high" or "very high,"[34] this would trigger an obligation on system designers to reconsider and redesign the system and/or proposed business model[35] in order to reduce those risks to a form and level regarded as tolerable (understood in terms of a human rights approach to the resolution of conflict between rights and collective interests), in ways that duly accommodate concerns expressed by affected stakeholders and in recognition of the individual and collective benefits that the system is expected to generate.[36]

Principle 2: Assessment, testing, and evaluation

Users and others affected by the operation of AI systems (including the general public) can only have justified confidence that AI systems do in fact comply with human rights standards if these systems can be subjected to formal assessment and testing to evaluate their compliance with human rights standards, and if these occur regularly throughout the entire lifecycle of system development: from the initial formulation of a proposal through to design, specification, development, prototyping, and real-world

[34] S. Jasanoff, *The Ethics of Invention: Technology and the Human Future* (New York: W. W. Norton, 2018); Raso et al., *supra* n. 32.
[35] On the potential discriminatory impact of data-driven business models, see M. Ali et al., "Discrimination through Optimization: How Facebook's Ad Delivery Can Lead to Skewed Outcomes" (2019), https://arxiv.org/pdf/1904.02095.pdf (accessed June 3, 2019).
[36] The participatory approach to social impact assessment referred to in the Council of Europe's AI Guideline strongly resonates with the role that our approach ascribes to public deliberation: see The Council of Europe, Guidelines on AI (Feb. 19, 2019), https://rm.coe.int/guidelines-on-artificial-intelligence-and-data-protection/168091f9d8 at 23–24.

implementation and including periodic evaluation of the datasets upon which the system has been trained and upon which it operates.[37]

These evaluations form a core element of an overarching "human rights risk-management" approach, which aims to identify potential human rights risks *before* the deployment of AI and other relevant automated systems and that occurs within a larger meta-regulatory approach to AI governance in which AI system developers and owners are subject to legal duties to demonstrate to a public regulatory authority that their system is human rights–compliant.[38] If significant risks to human rights compliance are identified, system developers must reconsider the design specification and system requirements with a view to modifying them in order to reduce those risks to a level that satisfies the tests of necessity and proportion[39]—or, in cases where the threats to human rights are disproportionate and thus unacceptably high, to refrain from proceeding with the development of the system in the form proposed. Once the system has been implemented, periodic review must be undertaken and test and assessment documents duly filed with the public authority. A system of "AI vigilance" is also needed, entailing the systematic recording of adverse incidents arising from system operations, including potential human rights violations reported by users or the wider public, triggering an obligation on the system provider to review and reassess the system's design and operation, and to report and publicly register any modifications to the system undertaken following this evaluation. Systematic and periodic post-implementation monitoring and vigilance is needed to ensure that AI systems continue to operate in a human rights–compliant manner because, once implemented into real-world settings, AI systems will invariably display emergent effects that are both difficult to anticipate and may scale very rapidly. Accordingly, there is also an accompanying need for more systematic and sustained research concerned with modeling social systems in order to better anticipate and predict their unintended adverse societal effects.

---

[37] Kroll et al., *supra* n. 30; Borgesius, *supra* n. 21; Rieke, Bogen, and Robinson, *supra* n. 31.

[38] Also called "management-based" regulation and "enforced self-regulation," meta-regulation refers to a strategy in which regulators do not prescribe how regulated firms should comply, but instead require them to develop their own systems for compliance with legally mandated goals and to demonstrate that compliance to the regulator: J. Black, "Paradoxes and Failures: 'New Governance' Techniques and the Financial Crisis," *Modern Law Review* 75 (2012): 1037, 1045–1048.

[39] The formulation of the appropriate legal standard would need to reflect the established proportionality assessment that is well-established in addressing human rights conflicts and conflicts between human rights and legitimate collective interests, operating as the human rights equivalent as the "as low as reasonably practicable" (ALARP) requirement that applies to legal duties to ensure the safety of complex systems, per A. Hopkins, "Explaining Safety Case," Regulatory Institutions Network Working Paper 87 (2012), https://www.csb.gov/assets/1/7/workingpaper_87.pdf; M. Thomas, "Safety-Critical Systems," Gresham Lectures (London, 2017), https://www.gresham.ac.uk/lectures-and-events/safety-critical-systems (accessed March 18, 2020).

Principle 3: Independent oversight, investigation, and sanction

In order to provide meaningful assurance that AI systems are in fact human rights–compliant, rather than merely *claiming* to be human rights–compliant, independent oversight by an external, properly resourced, technically competent oversight body invested with legal powers of investigation and sanction is essential.[40] Because the operation of market forces cannot provide those who design, develop, and deploy AI systems with sufficient incentives to invest the required resources necessary to ensure that AI systems are human rights–compliant, our proposed approach must operate within a *legally mandated* institutional structure, including an oversight body with a duty to monitor and enforce substantive and procedural (regulatory) requirements, including those concerning robust design, verification, testing, and evaluation (including appropriate documentation demonstrating that these requirements have been fulfilled), supported by legally mandated stakeholder and public consultation where proposed AI systems pose a "high risk" to human rights.

We suggest that independent oversight is best designed within a meta-regulatory framework, in which legal duties are placed on AI system developers and operators to demonstrate to a public authority that their systems are human rights–compliant.[41] Although there are a variety of approaches that can be understood as meta-regulatory in form,[42] the so-called safety case, properly implemented, is considered to have significantly contributed to ensuring the safety of complex systems in several domains, including safety regulation for offshore petroleum drilling through to the regulation of workplace safety adopted in several Anglo-Commonwealth legal systems.[43]

---

[40] Borgesius, *supra* n. 21.   [41] See n. 39 above.

[42] See J. Black, "Managing Regulatory Risks and Defining the Parameters of Blame: A Focus on the Australian Prudential Regulation Authority," *Law and Policy* 28 (2006): 1–26; S. Gilad, "It Runs in the Family: Meta-Regulation and Its Siblings," *Regulation & Governance* 4 (2010): 485–506; C. Coglianese and E. Mendelson, "Meta-Regulation and Self-Regulation," in R. Baldwin, C. Hood, and M. Lodge (eds.), *The Oxford Handbook of Regulation* (New York: Oxford University Press, 2010): 146–168.

[43] The so-called "safety case" movement emerged in the early 1990s in both the United Kingdom and the United States as an approach to safety certification involving approval and oversight of complex systems, such as aircraft, nuclear power plants, and offshore oil exploration. See Hopkins, *supra* n. 39. There have, however, been criticisms of a safety case approach, including concerns about problems of confirmation bias, the need to consider worst case scenarios, reliance on probabilistic assessment to provide assurances of safety rather than the opposite goal of identifying unrecognized hazards, and examples of highly successful process-based (rather than performance-based) approaches to securing safety in relation to submarines (e.g., the SUBSAFE program): see N. Leveson, "The Use of Safety Cases in Certification and Regulation," MIT Engineering Systems Division Working Paper Series (2011), http://sunnyday.mit.edu/SafetyCases.pdf (accessed June 12, 2019). Leveson observes that the British Health and Safety Executive has applied a safety case regime widely to UK industries, pursuant to which responsibility for controlling risks is placed primarily on those who create and manage hazardous systems, based on three principles: (a) those who create the risks are responsible for controlling those risks, (b) safe operations are achieved by setting and achieving goals rather than by following prescriptive rules, (c) while those goals are set out in legislation, it is for the system providers and operators to develop what they consider to be appropriate methods to achieve those goals.

In his discussion of offshore petroleum drilling, Hopkins highlights five basic features of a safety case approach:

(1) All operators must prepare a systematic risk (or hazard) management framework, which identifies all major hazards and provides detailed plans for how these hazards will be managed, specifying the controls that will be put in place to deal with the identified hazards and the measures that will be taken to ensure that controls continue to function as intended.

(2) A requirement for the operator to "make the case" to the regulator, that is, to demonstrate to the regulator that the processes that have been undertaken to identify hazards, the methodology they have used to assess risks, and the reasoning (and evidence) that has led them to choose one control rather than another, should be regarded as acceptable. It is then up to the regulator to accept (or reject) the case. Although a safety case gives operators considerable independence and flexibility in determining how they will respond to hazards, they do not have free rein: thus if an operator proposes to adopt an inadequate standard, a safety case regulator may challenge the operator and require the adoption of a better standard.

(3) A competent, independent, and properly resourced regulator with the requisite level of expertise and who can engage in meaningful scrutiny. The regulator's role is not to ensure that hardware is working, or that documents are up to date, but to *audit against the safety case*, to ensure that the specified controls are functioning as intended, and this necessitates a sophisticated understanding of accident causation and prevention.

(4) Employee participation, both in the development of safety cases, and with whom the regulatory officials carrying out site audits must consult.

(5) A general legal duty of care imposed on the operator to do whatever is reasonably practicable to identify and control all hazards. An operator cannot claim to be in compliance just because it has completed a hazard identification process. It is the general duty of care that raises a safety case regime above a "tick box" or "blind compliance" mentality, so that a hazard identification process that is demonstrably inadequate would fail to meet the requisite standard.[44]

Regulatory regimes of this kind allow (although they do not necessitate) the possibility of ex ante licensing by a designated public authority in the case of particularly human rights–sensitive, high-risk systems, such as facial recognition systems intended for use by governments to identify individuals of interest in public places.[45] Applying the

[44] Although the general duty of care is linguistically quite imprecise, its meaning has been elaborated on via case law, through numerous cases in which courts have had to decide whether the duty has been complied with. This case law gives fairly clear guidance as to what the general duty means in particular cases: see Hopkins ibid., *supra*, n. 39.

[45] See for example Big Brother Watch, *Face Off: The Lawless Growth of Facial Recognition in UK Policing* (2018), https://bigbrotherwatch.org.uk/wp-content/uploads/2018/05/Face-Off-final-digital-1.pdf (accessed June 12, 2019).

underlying logic and structure of the safety case approach to human rights compliance would provide developers with considerable flexibility in seeking to "make the case" to the regulator to demonstrate that their proposed AI systems can be expected to operate in human rights–compliant ways.

Principle 4: Traceability, evidence, and proof

In order to facilitate meaningful independent oversight and evaluation, AI systems must be designed and built to secure auditability: this means more than merely securing transparency, but is aimed at ensuring that they can be subject to *meaningful review*, thus providing a concrete evidential trial for securing human accountability over AI systems.[46] Not only is it necessary that systems be constructed to produce evidence that they operate as desired,[47] there must be a legal obligation to do so, requiring that crucial design decisions, the testing/assessment process and the outcome of those processes, and the operation of the system itself are properly documented and provide a clear evidence trail that can be audited by external experts. Drawing again on the experience of the safety case approach, which entails imposing a legal duty on operators to demonstrate to the regulator that robust and comprehensive systems are in place that reduce safety risks to a level that is "as low as reasonably practical," we envisage the imposition of a suitably formulated legal duty on AI systems developers, owners, and operators to demonstrate that these systems are human rights–compliant.

To discharge this legal duty, AI system developers would also be subject to legal duties to prepare, maintain, and securely store system design documentation, testing, and evaluation reports, and the system must be designed to routinely generate operational logs that can be inspected and audited by an independent, suitably competent authority. Taken together, these provide an audit trail through which system designers and developers can demonstrate that they have undertaken human rights "due diligence"— thereby discharging their legal duty to demonstrate that they have discharged their legal duty to reduce the risk of human rights violations to an acceptable level. These traceability and evidential requirements apply to both the design and development phase (including verification and validation requirements) and the operation and implementation of systems (logging and black-box recording of system operations). Taken together, these obligations are intended to ensure that robust and systematic transparency mechanisms are put in place, the aim of which is not complete comprehension but to provide sufficient information to ensure that human accountability for AI systems can be maintained.[48] This integrated approach to AI governance grounded on these

---

[46]   J. J. Bryson and A. Theodorou, "How Society Can Maintain Human-Centric Artificial Intelligence," in *Human-Centered Digitalization and Services,* ed. M. Toivonen-Noro and E. Saari (Singapore: Springer Nature Singapore, 2019), 12–13.

[47]   Kroll et al., *supra* n. 30.   [48]   Bryson and Theodorou, *supra* n. 46 at 14.

principles can be understood as a response to the Council of Europe's call for a "human-rights oriented development of technology."[49] As Alessandro Mantalerohas claimed:

> Innovation must be developed responsibly, taking the safeguard of fundamental rights as the pre-eminent goal.... This necessarily requires the development of assessment procedures, the adoption of participatory models and supervisory authorities. A human rights–oriented development of tech might increase costs and force developers and business to slow their current time-to-market, as the impact of products and services on individual rights and society have to be assessed in advance. At the same time, in the medium to long-term, this approach will reduce costs and increase efficiency (e.g., more accurate prediction and decision systems, increased trust, fewer complaints). Moreover, businesses and societies are mature enough to view responsibility towards individuals and society as the primary goal in AI development.[50]

GETTING FROM HERE TO THERE:
A RESEARCH AGENDA

The four principles outlined in the previous section demand revision to many aspects of software engineering (SE) practice. While a suite of relevant engineering and regulatory governance techniques are already in use in some specific areas, they require significant adaptation and generalization to support meaningful human rights evaluation and compliance. Changes to SE practice must be complemented by a focused human rights–centered design research agenda in computer science. Such an agenda would draw together the currently fragmented activity in relevant software engineering disciplines (including SE, cybersecurity, HCI, verification) and also consider their continued relevance to the software lifecycle of AI systems in particular, which are likely to require new design processes. Rather than offer a detailed research agenda here, we offer instead a "manifesto," which identifies and briefly outlines some of the technical, engineering, and governance challenges that must be met if SE is to provide assurances of human rights compliance. Some of these topics are existing areas of practice in software engineering and others are established research disciplines. None, however, have any tradition of human rights–centered design and most are only just beginning to consider appropriate software engineering practice for AI systems.

Requirements Analysis

In SE, requirements analysis concerns the identification of the needs to be met by a new software system. The commercial orientation and diversity of approaches to requirements

---

[49] A. Mantalero, *AI and Data Protection: Challenges and Possible Remedies*, Study for Council of Europe (2018), https://rm.coe.int/artificial-intelligence-and-data-protection-challenges-and-possible-re/168091f8a6 (accessed June 3, 2019).

[50] See Mantalero ibid. section 1.3 for more detail.

analysis present a severe challenge to Principle 1 of our human rights–centered design agenda, and it is made more acute by the fact that requirements analysis has been developed for non-AI systems. Corporate practice is strongly oriented to identifying the requirements of business customers and are often contractual in nature: accordingly, requirements specification often generates long lists of "shoulds" stated in a natural language. In contrast, where consumers are targeted end-users, their work, play, and social needs are typically the focus of requirements analysis. Smaller tech companies, particularly start-ups, identify requirements analysis as the major component of SE concerns[51] and are heavily dependent on agile- (or even craft-) based approaches to development that have weaker contractual requirements analysis and weaker audit trails. However, it has at least been realized that affected stakeholders, *beyond* those of the customer and end-user, should be identified and involved as participants in requirements analysis and design, giving rise to participatory design.[52] It is also the case that professionals involved in requirements analysis have a diversity of backgrounds—not only computer science and engineering but also psychology, sociology, and other social sciences, and therefore might be extended to include those with legal training. In order to meet Principle 1, software engineering practice of AI systems must meet the following challenges:

a. How to consider human rights requirements for all stakeholders, not only as users or customers but also as individual rights-bearers entitled to equal concern and respect, in auditable requirements description and requirements specification documents?

b. How to train and and employ design professionals who can bring human rights–centered design methods to system design and requirements specification?

Understanding, Collecting, and Analyzing Data

The processes for acquiring, selecting, and modeling data that are required by AI systems create their own human rights challenges. These challenges require attention at several levels, including the way in which problems are framed during requirements analysis. A human rights–centered approach to design that meets Principle 1 must take due account of human rights risks when building AI systems requirements. For example, many commercial AI systems are designed to utilize data-driven "hypernudges" to channel user attention and action in directions beneficial to the system owner.[53] These potentially threaten individual autonomy, dignity, and the right to liberty and freedom of thought, yet these human rights risks are not currently taken into account in requirements analysis processes. *Bias in data sampling, modeling, and attribute selection is*

---

[51] E. U. Klotins and T. Gorschek, "Software Engineering Antipatterns in Start-Ups," *IEEE Software* 36, no. 2 (2019): 118–126.

[52] J. Simonsen and T. Robertson ed., *Routledge International Handbook of Participatory Design* (New York: Routledge, 2013).

[53] K. Yeung, "'Hypernudge': Big Data as a Mode of Regulation by Design, *Information, Communication & Society* 20, no. 1 (2017): 118–136.

another major problem. The use of machine learning techniques generates many opportunities for bias and discrimination to inadvertently affect the outputs they produced, which may threaten the right to equal protection (the right to nondiscrimination).[54] These include biases of the algorithms' developers, biases built into the models upon which the systems are generated, biases inherent in the datasets used to train the models, or biases introduced when such systems are implemented in real-world settings.[55] In response to these concerns, a growing body of work concerned with devising technical approaches for countering such biases has emerged, but this has yet to move out of the lab into software development settings.

Verification

Verification concerns processes for checking whether the software meets specified requirements. In other words, does the software satisfy the output of the requirements analysis? Verification can involve the use of formal methods (logic) to check that software, or a model of software, does not contain errors. Formally verified software performs the required functions and nothing else for all possible inputs with verifiable evidence. Verification is used, for example, in the aviation industry and to some extent in other safety-critical systems. Verification has also seen some successes in more agile software development environments.[56] It does not guarantee that, for example, a plane will not crash but can guard against undesirable conditions occurring by virtue of misconceived models or poorly written software. The application of verification is mandated by certification authorities in some sectors (e.g., aviation) but not in others. It is also used in some sectors (e.g., ship design) because the commercial costs of errors are relatively high. Where it is mandated, processes are typically subject to audit by a government authority, such as the Federal Aviation Administration (FAA) or the European Aviation Safety Agency (EASA). Verification is particularly relevant to Principles 1 (design and deliberation) and 2 (assessment, testing, and evaluation). We ask two questions: (1) Can AI systems be formally verified? (2) Can verification be human rights–centered? The answer to the first question is negative, at least with current methods,[57] although

---

[54] Protocol No 12 ECHR Article 1 provides that "the enjoyment of any right set forth by law shall be secured without discrimination on any ground such as sex, race, color, language, religion, political or other opinion, national or social origin, association with a national minority, property, birth or other status." See also Art 21 EU Charter of Fundamental Rights.

[55] M. Veale and R. Binns, "Fairer Machine Learning in the Real World: Mitigating Discrimination without Collecting Sensitive Data, *Big Data & Society* (Dec. 2017), https://doi.org/10.1177/2053951717743530.

[56] C. Calcagno, D. Distefano, J. Dubreil, D. Gabi, P. Hooimeijer, M. Luca, P. O'Hearn, I. Papakonstantinou, J. Purbrick, and D. Rodriguez, "Moving Fast with Software Verification," in *NASA Formal Methods: 7th International Symposium,* ed. K. Havelund, G. Holzmann, and R. Joshi, Lecture Notes in Computer Science 9058 (Cham, Switzerland: Springer, 2015), 3–11.

[57] S. Russell, D. Dewey, and M. Tegmark, "Research Priorities for Robust and Beneficial Artificial Intelligence," *AI Magazine* 36, no. 4 (2015): 105–114.

this is an active area of research. Note that AI is not used in safety-critical systems precisely because the software cannot be verified. AI systems are difficult to verify for several reasons. In particular, programs automatically generated by machine learning are coded in different forms to hand-coded computer programs, and existing verification methods are not designed to work with such programs. Relatedly, these programs are typically more complex and have a much higher level of dimensionality in comparison with hand-coded programs, so verification approaches may not be computationally tractable. In addition, machine learning can be used in deployed systems to adapt their behavior in real time, so that effective verification would need to be continually repeated in the use context. It is therefore impossible for current verification techniques to be human rights–centered. Nevertheless, human rights–centered verification may still play a role in the design of validation procedures (more on this in the following section). Human rights–centered verification of AI systems is likely to require many years of research before it influences practice. This research should be designed to answer the following challenges:

a. What are the limits of verification with respect to AI systems and requirements concerning human rights beyond safety?
b. How can formal methods be used to verify an AI systems substrate, such as the operating systems and learning software,[58] at least to ensure that AI systems are operating as intended?
c. How can formal methods be used to advance AI systems testing (more on this follows)?

Cybersecurity by Design

Cybersecurity concerns the protection of computer systems, data, and cyber-physical systems from intrusion, theft, or damage. Cybersecurity by design focuses on the need for security from software foundations and therefore for security considerations in the requirements analysis. Further, some have advocated the use of, for example, formal verification methods early in the design process.[59] Unfortunately, cybersecurity by design has not been a consideration in software engineering until relatively recently and many deployed systems and practices suffer as a consequence. However, this is changing, often in response to legislation, and early efforts at building a regulatory and engineering infrastructure may provide a way forward for human rights–centered design. Inevitably cybersecurity by design for AI systems faces the same challenges as verification discussed earlier. Further challenges are documented in a recent NSF report, although that report focuses on privacy rather than on human rights in general.

---

[58] Ibid.
[59] S. Chong, J. Guttman, A. Datta, A. Myers, B. Pierce, P. Schaumont, T. Sherwood, and N. Zeldovich, *Report on the NSF Workshop on Formal Methods for Security, arXiv preprint arXiv:1608.00678* (2016).

Validation

Validation methods are used to assess whether the behavior of a software system meets stakeholders' needs. Validation is not simply about checking the behavior of the system against the written specification; it is very much a rigorous empirical process that must generate data relevant to understanding whether a system is fit for a purpose. Two specific forms of validation that are conducted extensively in the software industry are:

(a) Penetration testing

Penetration testing is a commissioned cyberattack, conducted by an internal or external agency. It is one method used to ensure the security of software systems and data. Penetration testing is sometimes automated and there are standard tests that are legally mandated in some industries (e.g., the payment card industry). A particular focus for penetration testing is privacy validation. However, the value of privacy is sometimes regarded as an absolute value, to be protected at all costs, which may not reflect the rights-balancing approach enshrined in how the right to privacy is understood within a human rights approach. Penetration testing has not, to our knowledge, been applied to AI systems but recent demonstrations of how AI systems can be spoofed with adversarial attacks[60] suggest that these systems will come with new, unanticipated vulnerabilities. In order to meet the needs of Principle 2, penetration testing must meet the following challenges:

(i) Acknowledge and explicitly address trade-offs. Current practice and literature emphasizes privacy in ways that may disproportionately threaten the protection of other rights or legitimate collective interests when they come into conflict in specific contexts and circumstances.

(ii) Address the problem of how to counter the threat of Adversarial AI (also known as Offensive AI), particularly as it is likely to be applied to AI systems.[61]

(b) User Experience Design

User experience (UX) designers often play key roles in requirements analysis and also in empirical validation. Tasks and systems (artifacts) often co-evolve, and UX designers provide critical feedback on the effectiveness of existing designs as well as ideas for future designs. Typically, they focus on ensuring that system use is useful, pleasurable, rewarding, and efficient. UX designers are also tasked with seeing things from the user's perspective rather than from the service provider's perspective. Methods include the use of scenarios and personas that provide means to curate stories about context of use and potential users. Participatory design has grown in importance, providing one way in which human values from outside the industry can influence design. Human-centered design research has had a strong influence on UX design practice, but methods are

---

[60] M. Hutson, "Hackers Easily Fool Artificial Intelligences," *Science* (July 20, 2018): 215.

[61] M. Brundage, et al. *The Malicious Use of AI: Forecasting, Prevention, and Mitigation* (2018), https://maliciousaireport.com/ (accessed December 11, 2019).

not currently configured to embrace human rights concerns in the form recognized under international human rights law. Much has been made of the need for UX designers to consider the social and physical context of use,[62] and there are a number of ethical and value-motivated influences,[63] including bias,[64] feminism,[65] accessibility, and diversity research. But, little work is dones on the democratic context of use and therefore on human rights from a legal and constitutional perspective. Accordingly, key questions include: What is the future of UX design for AI systems? How can UX design move beyond its current focus on social and physical contexts to embrace democratic and civic structures (including respect for human rights) as important sources of constraint? Can methods used in the human rights community for engaging people with human rights thinking[66] contribute to UX approaches to AI systems design?

Appropriation

Software systems are not only designed, they are also appropriated by users for unanticipated tasks and unanticipated contexts. This productive aspect of human use of technology may prove particularly problematic for the governance of AI systems. ADM systems have hitherto been built for one specific social context, but this context is rarely communicated in a robust way that assures that it is only used in this setting. For example, as Zweig and Krafft discuss, the software COMPAS is used in criminal justice systems for pre-trial assessment (such as bail decisions or decisions to prosecute) but was originally built for post-trial assessment.[67] Further work is needed to investigate how appropriation of AI systems can be appropriately governed (Principle 3).

Algorithmic Transparency and Inspection

At present there is no general requirement for algorithm inspection, but recent cases suggest that a systematic approach should be considered in order to provide assurance of the trustworthiness of algorithmic systems, particularly those that directly and

[62] C. Heath and P. Luff, *Technology in Action* (Cambridge: Cambridge University Press, 2000); D. Benyon, P. Turner, and S. Turner, *Designing Interactive Systems: People, Activities, Contexts, Technologies* (Harlow, UK: (Harlow: Pearson Education, 2005).

[63] B. Friedman and D. G. Hendry, *Value Sensitive Design: Shaping Technology with Moral Imagination* (Cambridge, MA: MIT Press, 2019); B. Friedman ed., *Human Values and the Design of Computer Technology,* (Cambridge: Cambridge University Press, 1997).

[64] B. Friedman and H. Nissenbaum, "Software Agents and User Autonomy," in *Agents '97: First International Conference on Autonomous Agents* (ACM, 1997), 466–469.

[65] S. Bardzell, "Feminist HCI: Taking Stock and Outlining an Agenda for Design," in *Proceedings of the SIGCHI Conference on Human Factors in Computing Systems* (ACM, 2014), 1301–1310.

[66] See European Union External Action, "Good Human Rights Stories Coalition Launched" (Sept. 28, 2018), https://eeas.europa.eu/headquarters/headquarters-homepage/51241/good-human-rights-stories-coalition-launched_en (accessed December 11, 2019).

[67] K. A. Zweig, G. Wenzelburger, and T. D. Krafft, "On Chances and Risks of Security Related Algorithmic Decision-Making Systems," *European Journal for Security Research* 3 (2018): 181–203.

adversely affect the rights of individuals. In the context of ADM systems in the U.S. criminal justice system, this has been especially problematic where the algorithms have been developed by commercial software providers claiming intellectual property protection, enabling them to assert rights of confidentiality and secrecy over their algorithms.[68] In contrast, the development and implementation of the HART algorithm used in the United Kingdom by the Durham police force to make custody decisions has been much more open; it has not, however, been made available for public scrutiny.[69] While there are legitimate concerns about "gaming" that may justify refraining from full public disclosure of certain algorithms, at least in high-risk contexts where human rights are seriously threatened, regulators must have legal powers to inspect algorithms and datasets (supporting Principle 3).[70]

Instrumentation and Logging

Bryson and Theodorou argue that logging should be mandated in all "socially critical" fields.[71] We assert that logging must also be mandated in all "human rights critical" fields (i.e., all systems identified that pose a "high risk" of unjustifiably interfering with human rights, particularly when they can do so at scale). Firms are unlikely to keep an audit trail that evidences their problematic actions unless they are legally required to do so (e.g., mandatory black-box recorder requirements in the aviation industry). The importance of maintaining audit trails of system behavior is essential for maintaining meaningful human accountability over AI systems: human rights–centered design demands instrumentation in systems so that they automatically record and reproduce historical decision-making processes and outcomes: we should mandate this, at minimum, for all safety-critical and human rights–critical systems (in support of Principle 4).

CONCLUSION

This chapter has highlighted various deficiencies inherent in the prevailing model of voluntary self-regulation for securing "ethical AI." It has enabled a "Pick Your Own"

[68] See State of Wisconsin v Loomis (2016) 881 N.W.2d 749 (Supreme Court of Wisconsin).
[69] Durham Police have been reported that they "would be prepared to reveal the HART algorithm and the associated personal data and custody event datasets to an algorithmic regulator": M. Burgess, "UK Police Are Using AI to Inform Custodial Decisions—But It Could Be Discriminating against the Poor," Wired (March 1, 2018), https://www.wired.co.uk/article/police-ai-uk-durham-hart-checkpoint-algorithm-edit (accessed December 11, 2019).
[70] But see the Canadian Directive on Automated Decision-Making 2019, which applies to the Canadian federal government's use of automated decision-making systems including machine learning and predictive analytics which, among other things, imposes requirements for the release of any custom source code that is owned by the Government of Canada.
[71] Bryson and Theodorou, supra. n. 46.

approach to the identification of ethical standards for AI systems, so that there is no clear, agreed set of ethical standards within the tech industry. This has resulted in conceptual incoherence, particularly because the norms identified in any given "ethics code" have not typically been rooted in any explicit vision of the kind of political community which those norms are intended to nurture and maintain. Nor do these ethical codes acknowledge the inescapable tensions and conflict that can arise between ethical norms in specific circumstances, let alone offer concrete guidance concerning how those conflicts should be addressed and resolved, leaving the industry unilaterally to resolve (or indeed ignore) as they see fit. The prevailing self-regulatory approach also fails to recognize any need or obligation to seek meaningful input from affected stakeholders or the public at large in identifying the relevant ethical standards or how they should be implemented in the design and operation of AI systems. Finally, these codes lack any effective governance framework, resources, or institutions to independently assess and enforce the relevant ethical standards, let alone ensure redress for those adversely affected and/or sanctions in the event of violation. Accordingly, the prevailing approach to AI ethics amounts to little more than a marketing exercise aimed at demonstrating that the tech industry "takes ethics seriously" in order to stave off external regulation. In short, it has failed to deliver "ethical AI."

We have argued that an alternative approach to the ethical governance of AI is needed—one that is systematic, coherent, and comprehensive, centered on human rights norms and explicitly grounded in the critical importance of protecting and maintaining the sociotechnical foundations required to preserve and nurture our societies as constitutional democratic political orders, anchored in an enduring and inviolable commitment to respect human dignity and individual freedom. We have outlined an approach we call "human rights–centered design, deliberation, and oversight," which we believe has the potential to ensure that, in practice, AI systems will be designed, developed, and deployed in ways that provide *genuinely* ethical AI. It requires that human rights norms are systematically considered at every stage of system design, development, and implementation (making interventions where this is identified as necessary), drawing upon and adapting technical methods and techniques for safe software and system design, verification, testing, and auditing in order to ensure compliance with human rights norms, together with social and organizational approaches to effective and legitimate regulatory governance. The regime must be mandated by law, and relies critically on external oversight by independent, competent, and properly resourced regulatory authorities with appropriate powers of investigation and enforcement, requiring input from both technical and human rights experts, on the one hand, and meaningful input and deliberation from affected stakeholders and the general public on the other. This approach draws upon a variety of methods and techniques varying widely in their disciplinary foundations, which, suitably adapted and refined to secure conformity with human rights norms, could be drawn together in an integrated manner to form the foundations of a comprehensive design and governance regime. Its foundational ethical standards are composed of contemporary human rights norms, designed around four principles, namely (a) design and deliberation; (b) assessment, testing, and evaluation; (c) independent oversight, investigation, and sanction; and (d) traceability, evidence, and proof.

This approach will not, however, ensure the protection of all ethical values adversely implicated by AI, given that human rights norms do not comprehensively cover all values of societal concern. In addition, a great deal more work needs to be done to develop techniques and methodologies that are both robust and reliable yet practically implementable across a wide and diverse range of organizations involved in developing, building, and operating AI systems and that work effectively to ensure that compliance with human rights norms is evaluated and operationalized at each stage of system design, development, and deployment. There are also very considerable challenges in establishing an overarching legal and institutional governance framework that will ensure that AI systems (particularly those appropriately regarded as posing substantial threats and risks to human rights) can be subjected to meaningful and effective scrutiny by competent and independent regulatory authorities endowed with suitable powers of investigation and sanction, and to develop a systematic approach for integrating these different methodologies and requirements into a unified governance framework that enables meaningful public input and deliberation by affected stakeholders in the design, development, and implementation of AI systems.

We hope these challenges will not prove insurmountable. Yet their magnitude should not be underestimated, and solving them will require sustained and systematic research and investigation over a long-term time horizon. Our proposal springs from the premise that it is theoretically possible to translate human rights norms into software design processes and into software requirements that can adequately capture the functionality and constraints that give effect to what are often highly abstract human rights norms. We suspect that some rights will be more readily translatable into software and system requirements, such as some rights to due process (such as rights to contestation and rights to an unbiased tribunal, particularly when AI systems have been used to inform or automate decisions about individuals), the right to privacy, and rights to freedom from unlawful discrimination, while others are likely to be fiendishly difficult to "hardwire," such as the rights to freedom of expression, freedom of conscience, and freedom of association. Because human rights are often highly abstract in nature and lacking sharply delineated boundaries given their capacity to adapt and evolve in response to their dynamic sociotechnical context, there may well be only so much that software and system design and implementation techniques can achieve in attempting to transpose human rights norms and commitments into the structure and operation of AI systems in real-world settings.[72]

---

[72] Human rights–centered design, deliberation, and oversight should *not* be confused with attempts to design computational systems so that they design-out the possibility of noncompliance with the law, which entails translating human rights concepts into formalizable mathematical concepts that can be hard-coded into computational decision-making systems (and which Hildebrandt refers to as "Legal by Design"). Rather, we anticipate that our vision of human rights–centered design, deliberation, and oversight will incorporate what Hildebrandt refers to as "Legal Protection by Design" (LPbD) by developing techniques, methods, and governance frameworks that can ensure that computational

Our approach necessitates research and cooperation in AI design, development, and implementation between computational, engineering, and technical specialists and legal experts with considerable competence and fluency in human rights discourse and jurisprudence. It means, in effect, that those tech designers, developers, and engineers involved in building AI systems acquire a deeper understanding of human rights commitments, and the underlying constitutional framework in which they are embedded, in order to identify how to undertake system design, testing, and implementation in ways that are consistent with our democratic constitutional architecture.[73] At the same time, human rights experts will need to acquire sufficient technical competence in the design, architecture, development, and implementation of AI systems both in theory and in real-world practice in order to discharge the advisory and assessment duties that we anticipate will be required at every stage of the AI product lifecycle. Yet most contemporary university programs in law and in computer science and data science currently lack serious and sustained interdisciplinary training. Even if researchers do succeed in developing the requisite techniques, methodologies, and organizational and institutional governance frameworks that are capable of forming the foundational elements of human rights–centered design, deliberation, and oversight, a cadre of professionals with the requisite expertise and training will also be needed to work with the tech industry in order to implement them into real-world practice. Accordingly, our universities must create, nurture, and deliver sustained interdisciplinary training and education to undertake the kind of rigorous, creative, and problem-oriented interdisciplinary research and cooperation that our approach will require, and to equip professionals with the skills, capacities, and commitment to embed the core principles of our approach into the AI systems that will increasingly configure and mediate countless dimensions of our everyday human experience. Although AI began decades ago as an interdisciplinary field, it has since become a technical discipline. Yet given the increasing and rapidly expanding application of powerful AI systems in and across many social domains with the capacity to operate automatically and at scale, study and research into AI must

---

systems make available to individuals a suite of capacities, rights and meaningful opportunities necessary to provide the kind of substantive legal protection currently offered by the contemporary rule of law. According to Hildebrandt, LPbD seeks to ensure that legal protection is not "ruled out by the affordances of the technological environment that determines whether or not we enjoy the substance of fundamental rights," emphasizing the need for democratic participation in the design and operation of complex sociotechnical systems that configure our everyday environments, and that those subject to such LPbD should be able to contest its application in a court of law and hence it entails foundational requirements that data-driven decisions affecting individuals should be transparent, justified, and contestable. In so doing, "LPbD seeks to ensure that the practical capacity for individuals to exercise their human rights enabled by computational systems reflect the dynamic evolution of human rights norms in order to ensure effective protection as the societal and technological context continues to change over time": Hildebrandt, *supra*. n. 15., chap. 10.

[73] See M. Hildebrandt, *Law for Computer Scientists* (Oxford: Oxford University Press, 2019). As Borgesius has observed, we need CS research aimed at investigating how AI systems might be designed so that they respect and promote human rights, fairness, and accountability, as well as more normative and legal research: Borgesius, *supra* n. 21. at 69. See also AI Now Report (2018), https://ainowinstitute. org/AI_Now_2018_Report.pdf at 10 (accessed December 11, 2019).

expand to include the social and humanistic disciplines to equip tech professionals with the expertise and sensitivities required to attend seriously to social contexts and to anticipate and identify potential threats and risks these systems might generate when applied to human populations.

Our approach is also likely to confront significant cultural challenges before it is actively taken up. These include serious obstacles to systematic implementation into product development lifecycles for AI. Although there are developed software engineering techniques and practices that rely on mathematical proof that can verify that software systems meet certain specifications and are in use, particularly for safety-critical systems, contemporary software development remains largely a "craft" activity[74] associated with cultural norms in which creativity and freedom to tinker (or "hack") are widely shared and enthusiastically celebrated. Having spent his professional lifetime providing expert evidence in legal cases in which very large sums of money have been lost due to failed IT system projects, distinguished software engineer Martyn Thomas laments the fact that software engineering has yet to mature into a professional engineering discipline, committed to robust technical methods and standards and high levels of professional integrity that characterizethe so-called noble professions.[75] Yet if software development remains a predominantly amateur activity that celebrates its capacity to "move fast and break things," an ethic famously championed by Facebook founder Mark Zuckerberg, then our proposed governance regime is unlikely to take root.

We can readily anticipate objections to our proposal, asserting that as a general, legally mandated regulatory regime, it will stifle innovation and sound the death knell for tech start-ups. Yet there is ample evidence to demonstrate that legal regulation may *foster* rather than stifle socially beneficial tech innovation. For example, the introduction of mandatory environmental laws imposing limits on emissions was an important catalyst in the emergence and development of a competitive market for emission reduction technologies. At the same time, the enactment of the EU's General Data Protection Regulation (GDPR) applies to all personal data collectors and processors: from fledgling start-ups through to the Digital Titans. While it may be too early to tell whether the GDPR has led to a decline in tech start-ups and SME growth, it is worth nothing that there are growing calls in the United States to enact a legal data protection regime that can provide equivalently high levels of protection for U.S.-based data subjects. More importantly, however, if "ethical AI" is to be anything other than a marketing exercise that echoes the hollow claims associated with "corporate social responsibility," then wholesale change in the tech industry's cultural attitudes will be required and need do much more than pay lip service to human rights. Nor can the obligations of AI systems developers and operators discharge their duties arising under our proposed governance regime simply by employing a legal expert willing to certify that, to the best of her knowledge and understanding, the system is compliant with human rights standards. In other words, the role of the human rights expert is not that of the hired gun who

---

[74] M. Thomas, "Should We Trust Computers?," *Gresham Lectures*, October 20, 2015 (London: AI).
[75] M. Thomas, "Computers and the Future," *Gresham Lectures*, June 12, 2018 (London: AI).

formulates arguments to assure regulators that her client's system is legally compliant. Rather, it will be necessary to foster a language and culture of "human rights consciousness" into the tech industry, so that those involved in the design, development, and implementation of AI systems regard human rights compliance as part of their professional remit, rather than a "niche" problem to be handed-off to legal experts.

Finally, we locate our proposal as only one important element in the overall sociopolitical landscape needed to build a future in which AI systems are compatible with liberal democratic political communities in which respect for human rights and the rule of law lie at its bedrock. Both more public debate and global cooperation are required. As Bryson and Theodorou observe:

> The second special problem of AI is not actually unique to it but rather a characteristic of ICT more generally. ICT, thanks to the internet and other networking systems operate transnationally, and therefore affords the accumulation of great wealth and power, while simultaneously evading the jurisdiction of any particular nation. This means that appropriate regulation of AI requires transnational cooperation. Again, the process to establish transnational agreements, treaties and enforcement mechanisms is nontrivial, but already known and already under way.[76]

In other words, there is also a need for political will and leadership at the national and transnational levels in order to bring about the political, social, and technical cooperation and investment that will be needed, given that AI systems have the capacity to operate across national borders without technical difficulties. In short, overcoming the many obstacles to cooperation—at the disciplinary level, the organizational level, the industry level, and the policymaking level—will all be needed if we are to bring an end to ethics washing and deliver on the promise of "ethical AI" in real-world settings.

Bibliography

Algorithm Watch. *AI Ethics Guidelines Global Inventory.* Available at https://algorithmwatch.org/en/project/ai-ethics-guidelines-global-inventory/.

Council of Europe, Consultative Committee on the Convention for the Protection of Individuals with Regard to Automating Processing of Personal Data (T-PD). *Guidelines on Artificial Intelligence and Data Protection.* T-PD(2019)01. Directorate General of Human Rights and Rule of Law, 2019.

Hildebrandt, Mireille. *Smart Technologies and the End(s) of Law.* Cheltenham, UK: Edward Elgar, 2015.

Hopkins, Andrew. 2012. "Explaining 'Safety Case'." Working Paper 87. Regulatory Institutions Network, 2012. Available at https://www.csb.gov/assets/1/7/workingpaper_87.pdf.

---

[76] Joanna J. Bryson and Andreas Theodorou, "How Society Can Maintain Human-Centric Artificial Intelligence," in *Human-Centered Digitalization and Services,* ed. M. Toivonen-Noro and E. Saari (New York: Springer, 2019), 16–17.

Kloza, Dariusz, Niels van Dijk, Raphaël Gellert, István Böröcz, Alessia Tanas, Eugenio Mantovani, and Paul Quinn. "Data Protection Impact Assessments in the European Union: Complementing the New Legal Framework towards a More Robust Protection of Individuals." Brussels: Brussels Laboratory for Data Protection & Privacy Impact Assessments, 2017.

Mantalero, Alessandro. *AI and Data Protection: Challenges and Possible Remedies.* T-PD(2018)09Rev. Study for Council of Europe, 2018. Available at https://rm.coe.int/artificial-intelligence-and-data-protection-challenges-and-possible-re/168091f8a6, accessed June 3, 2019.

Nemitz, Paul. "Constitutional Democracy and Technology in the Age of Artificial Intelligence." *Philosophical Transactions of the Royal Society A: Mathematical, Physical and Engineering Sciences* 376, no. 2133 (2018): 20180089.

Raso, Filippo A., Hannah Hilligoss, Vivek Krishnamurthy, Christopher Bavitz, and Levin Kim. "Artificial Intelligence & Human Rights: Opportunities & Risks." Berkman Klein Center, 2018.

Rieke, A., M. Bogen, and D. G. Robsinson. *Public Scrutiny of Automated Decisions: Early Lessons and Emerging Methods.* An Upturn and Omidyar Network Report, 2018. Available at https://www.omidyar.com/insights/public-scrutiny-automated-decisions-early-lessons-and-emerging-methods, accessed June 3, 2019.

Yeung, Karen. "A Study of the Implications of Advanced Digital Technologies (including AI Systems) for the Concept of Responsibility within a Human Rights Framework." Council of Europe MSI-AUT committee study draft, 2019. Available at https://rm.coe.int/a-study-of-the-implications-of-advanced-digital-technologies-including/168094ad40.

CHAPTER 5

....

THE INCOMPATIBLE
INCENTIVES OF
PRIVATE-SECTOR AI

....

TOM SLEE

PERFORMANCES AND ETHICS

....

INDIVIDUALS present themselves to the world in a set of performances, and they tune their presentation depending on the setting.[1] We may not believe there is a single "real" person behind these performances, but we do expect to see a "coherence among setting, appearance, and manner."[2] Individuals whose performances differ too much between one setting and another risk being called "dishonest" or "two-faced."

Since branding became important to companies, they too have presented themselves to the world in a set of performances. Financial incentives demand they tune their performance to the setting—offering a generous and humane face in their public communications and a harsher and less empathetic one when managing the bottom line—while the ethical demand for coherence remains. Two decades ago the movement against corporate-led globalization highlighted these presentation gaps, captured in the dissonance between Nike's empowering "Just Do It" for those who bought their sneakers and the far-from-empowering sweatshop conditions endured by those who made them.[3] One legacy of that movement is a set of ethical consumption initiatives, in which

[1] The opinions expressed in this chapter are those of the author and do not represent the views or policies of SAP.

[2] Erving Goffman, *The Presentation of Self in Everyday Life* (Garden City, NY: Doubleday, 1959), 25.

[3] Naomi Klein, *No Logo* (Toronto: Knopf Canada, 2000).

independent fair trade and sustainability certifications provide an opportunity for companies to demonstrate a coherent set of values behind their performances.[4]

Now, in the debates over artificial intelligence (AI) ethics, it is technology companies who find themselves accused of being two-faced—of presenting themselves through their brands as value-driven organizations while deploying algorithms[5] that are too often biased, opaque, and unfair.

The debates have taken on new importance following the explosion of "deep-learning" techniques.[6] Private-sector investment in what is now often broadly labeled "AI" is dominated by major internet platform companies such as Facebook, Amazon, Apple, Google, and Microsoft. While seven billion dollars have been invested in start-ups, these companies have invested four to five times that amount.[7] Platform companies are also leaders in deploying deep-learning algorithms: deployments in other industries are in their early stages, yet many of us encounter deep-learning algorithms daily through Google search, Facebook News Feed,[8] Apple Siri, Amazon Alexa, Uber pricing,[9] Airbnb search,[10] and more.[11] If this chapter focuses on the major platform companies, it is because they are charting paths and setting precedents that more traditional industries will follow.

In response to a series of scandals and compelling arguments from critics and academics,[12] the platform companies have recognized that they must establish reputations

[4] Kimberley Ann Elliott and Richard B. Freeman, *Can Labor Standards Improve under Globalization?* (Washington, DC: Institute for International Economics, 2003).

[5] In this chapter, *algorithm* is shorthand for any automated data-driven sorting systems, including classifying, scoring, rating, and ranking. Algorithms may be implemented by computers but may also be implemented through organizational policies and practices.

[6] Alex Krizhevsky, Ilya Sutskever, and Geoffrey Hinton, "Imagenet Classification with Deep Convolutional Neural Networks," in *Advances in Neural Information Processing Systems* 25, ed. P. Bartlett, F. C. N. Pereira, C. J. C. Burges, L. Bottou, and K. Q. Weinberger (New York: Curran, 2012), 1097–105, https://papers.nips.cc/paper/4824-imagenet-classification-with-deep-convolutional-neural-networks.pdf.

[7] McKinsey Global Institute, "Artificial Intelligence: The Next Digital Frontier?" (New York: McKinsey & Company, June 2017), https://www.mckinsey.com//media/McKinsey/Industries/AdvancedElectronics/OurInsights/Howartificialintelligencecandeliverrealvaluetocompanies/MGI-Artificial-Intelligence-Discussion-paper.ashx.

[8] K. Hazelwood et al., "Applied Machine Learning at Facebook: A Datacenter Infrastructure Perspective," in *2018 IEEE International Symposium on High Performance Computer Architecture (HPCA)*, 2018, 620–629, https://doi.org/10.1109/HPCA.2018.00059.

[9] Alexander Sergeev and Mike Del Balso, "Horovod: Fast and Easy Distributed Deep Learning in TensorFlow," *ArXiv:1802.05799 [Cs, Stat]*, February 15, 2018, http://arxiv.org/abs/1802.05799.

[10] Malay Haldar et al., "Applying Deep Learning to Airbnb Search," *ArXiv:1810.09591 [Cs, Stat]*, October 22, 2018, http://arxiv.org/abs/1810.09591.

[11] Nicola Jones, "Computer Science: The Learning Machines," *Nature News* 505, no. 7482 (January 9, 2014): 146, https://doi.org/10.1038/505146a.

[12] Frank Pasquale, *The Black Box Society: The Secret Algorithms That Control Money and Information* (Cambridge, MA: Harvard University Press, 2015); Cathy O'Neill, *Weapons of Math Destruction: How Big Data Increases Inequality and Threatens Democracy* (New York: Crown Random House, 2016); Safiya Umoja Noble, *Algorithms of Oppression: How Search Engines Reinforce Racism* (New York: New York University Press, 2018); Solon Barocas and Andrew Selbst, "Big Data's Disparate Impact," *California Law Review* 104 (2016): 671, https://dx.doi.org/10.2139/ssrn.2477899.

as responsible stewards of these powerful technologies if they are to avoid a costly backlash. They have issued public commitments to ethical AI, asserted their belief in fairness and transparency, and proclaimed their commitment to building diverse organizational cultures to prevent bias from creeping in to their technological services and products.[13] They have set up ethics boards and industry organizations, such as Partnership on AI,[14] and participated in governmental bodies such as the European Union's (EU) High-Level Expert Group on Artificial Intelligence.[15]

The platform companies have also taken on the task of designing fairness into their systems,[16] investing in research into fairness and transparency in machine learning, articulating statistical criteria for fairness, designing mechanisms for explaining machine-learning results, assembling unbiased datasets for key problems, and more. The technical approach is a good fit: technical criteria play to the strengths of technology companies. Standards set public benchmarks and provide protection from future accusations. Auditable criteria incorporated into product development and release processes can confirm compliance.

There are also financial incentives to adopt a technical approach: standards that demand expertise and investment create barriers to entry by smaller firms, just as risk management regulations create barriers to entry in the financial and healthcare industries.[17]

The challenges of bias and fairness are far from solved, and critics continue to play an essential role. External investigations, audits, and benchmarks reveal deficiencies missed by internal efforts.[18] But auditable algorithms and datasets promise mechanisms for closing the presentation gap between brands and algorithms.

Charges of bias and unfairness expose AI algorithms that are, in some sense, not good enough and thus emphasize that the solution is better algorithms. But another set of problems may become *more* significant as algorithms become more accurate: when they

[13] Google, "Our Principles," Google AI, accessed February 1, 2019, https://ai.google/principles/; Microsoft, "Our Approach: Microsoft AI Principles," Microsoft, accessed February 1, 2019, https://www.microsoft.com/en-us/ai/our-approach-to-ai.

[14] The Partnership on AI, "The Partnership on AI," accessed February 1, 2019, https://www.partnershiponai.org/.

[15] European Commission, "High-Level Expert Group on Artificial Intelligence," 2018, https://ec.europa.eu/digital-single-market/en/high-level-expert-group-artificial-intelligence.

[16] Margaret Mitchell et al., "Model Cards for Model Reporting," in *FAT* '19: Proceedings of the Conference on Fairness, Accountability, and Transparency* (New York: ACM, 2019), 220–29, https://doi.org/10.1145/3287560.3287596.

[17] Malcolm Campbell-Verduyn, Marcel Goguen, and Tony Porter, "Big Data and Algorithmic Governance: The Case of Financial Practices," *New Political Economy* 22, no. 2 (March 4, 2017): 219–36, https://doi.org/10.1080/13563467.2016.1216533.

[18] Joy Buolamwini and Timnit Gebru, "Gender Shades: Intersectional Accuracy Disparities in Commercial Gender Classification," in *Proceedings of Machine Learning Research* 81 (2018): 77–91; Inioluwa Deborah Raji and Joy Buolamwini, "Actionable Auditing: Investigating the Impact of Publicly Naming Biased Performance Results of Commercial AI Products," in *AAAI/ACM Conference on Artificial Intelligence, Ethics, and Society* (2019).

become too good not to use. This chapter focuses on this second gap, which cannot be translated into research projects to be solved by computer scientists.

ALGORITHMS CREATE INCENTIVES

Much debate around AI ethics imagines an algorithm as a camera, recording and portraying some aspect of the external world. It asks: does the system portray the world fairly and faithfully? When it categorizes things, does it do so in a way that corresponds to the real world?[19]

Social scientists have long known that algorithms do not just portray the world, they also change it. In the words of Donald MacKenzie, an algorithm is "an engine, not a camera."[20] Introducing a new algorithm means sorting people differently; if people care about how they are sorted, they respond.[21]

Once people respond, the dynamic between algorithms and their subjects becomes strategic: economists are familiar with such situations and have developed the tools of game theory to think about them.

Sociologists have shown that responses to algorithms are ubiquitous and subtle. The most seemingly innocuous decisions prompt changes in what is being measured. In 1927 Dutch authorities separated the cause of death entered into statistical records from that recorded on the public death certificate, a change that was followed by "a considerable increase in Amsterdam of cases of death from syphilis, tabes, dementia paralytics, . . . and suicide."[22] Why? Because these causes of death could now be entered into the statistical record without adding to the pain of newly bereaved relatives.

Sociologists have also shown how surprisingly powerful algorithmic engines can be. In their book *Engines of Anxiety*, Wendy Espeland and Michael Sauder describe the impact of *U.S. News & World Report* rankings on U.S. law schools.[23] Employers use the

[19] Sam Corbett-Davies and Sharad Goel, "The Measure and Mismeasure of Fairness: A Critical Review of Fair Machine Learning," *ArXiv:1808.00023 [Cs]*, July 31, 2018, http://arxiv.org/abs/1808.00023; Alexandra Chouldechova, "Fair Prediction with Disparate Impact: A Study of Bias in Recidivism Prediction Instruments," *Big Data* 5, no. 2 (June 2017): 153–63, https://doi.org/10.1089/big.2016.0047; Arvind Narayanan, *Tutorial: 21 Fairness Definitions and Their Politics*, accessed January 27, 2019, https://www.youtube.com/watch?v=jIXIuYdnyyk.

[20] Donald MacKenzie, *An Engine, Not a Camera: How Financial Models Shape Markets* (Cambridge, MA: MIT Press, 2007).

[21] Danielle Keats Citron and Frank A. Pasquale, "The Scored Society: Due Process for Automated Predictions," SSRN Scholarly Paper (Rochester, NY: Social Science Research Network, 2014), https://papers.ssrn.com/abstract=2,376,209.

[22] Geoffrey C. Bowker and Susan Leigh Star, *Sorting Things Out: Classification and Its Consequences* (Cambridge, MA: MIT Press, 1999), 141.

[23] Wendy Nelson Espeland and Michael Sauder, *Engines of Anxiety: Academic Rankings, Reputation, and Accountability* (New York: Russell Sage Foundation, 2016).

rankings to identify good students, so students rely on them when choosing where to apply. Thus law schools who want the best students must play the game, and rankings end up dominating many aspects of law school life. The dynamic is described beautifully by Kieran Healy in a review of Espeland and Sauder's book:

> The academic legal establishment did not so much fall into this trap as become entangled in it. Like a fly touched by the thread of a spider's web, they were at first only lightly caught up, but then found that each move they made in response only drew them in more tightly.[24]

This chapter draws loosely on social science perspectives to sketch what can happen when we respond to algorithms and discusses the consequences of our responses.

Imagine an algorithm that sorts individual subjects into categories. If subjects care about their assigned category, then they have an incentive to optimize how they present themselves: changing their inputs to achieve a better output. Their decision to invest in this presentation depends on three factors:

1. *Presentation cost.* The subject must be able to afford to change their presentation.
2. *Sensitivity.* Changing an input feature is worthwhile only if it affects the output.
3. *Impact.* Changing an output is worthwhile only if it has significant consequences.

Algorithms with high impact, high sensitivity, and low presentation costs give subjects strong incentives to change their presentation. Following the terminology of economics, we can loosely say that such algorithms have high *elasticity*. The data distributions on which elastic algorithms operate when deployed will differ from those on which it was trained. When data distributions change, accuracy is lost: elastic algorithms may also be *fragile*. (Figure 5.1)

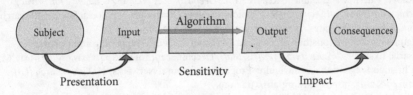

FIGURE 5.1. A schematic algorithm that takes input from subjects and sorts them into output categories, which in turn have consequences for the subject.

[24] Kieran Healy, "By the Numbers—Wendy Espeland and Michael Sauder, Engines of Anxiety: Academic Rankings, Reputation, and Accountability (New York, Russell Sage, 2016)," *European Journal of Sociology/Archives Européennes de Sociologie* 58, no. 3 (December 2017): 512–19, https://doi.org/10.1017/S0003975617000315.

There are reasons to believe that machine-learning systems, and specifically deep-learning systems, may be particularly elastic and fragile, mapping on to each of the factors previously discussed.

First is the low cost of experimentation around presentation. Deep-learning techniques called "Generative Adversarial Networks (GANs)"[25] have become excellent at generating images, videos, or texts that look as if they were created by humans or depict "real world" artifacts. These uses have been grouped together under the name "deep fakes."[26]

There is growing evidence that the remarkable accuracy of deep-learning models may be accompanied by high sensitivity. In 2013 a phenomenon called "adversarial examples" was discovered: certain image perturbations, undetectable to the human eye, nevertheless caused deep-learning algorithms to make obvious mistakes when classifying the image (as measured by human judgment).[27] An example is given in Figure 5.2. The original examples were curiosities,[28] but the more it has been studied, the more general the phenomenon appears to be.[29] Fragility could be a general feature of deep-learning models.[30] They typically optimize millions of parameters, and the more parameters, the bigger the "attack surface" as each parameter provides a new opportunity for subjects to tweak.

Many machine-learning systems have high impacts because they are deployed at scale. We may not want to invest in optimizing our LinkedIn profile, but if we are seeking work and that is where employers look we have little alternative but to put our best foot forward. Scale also creates opportunities for cost-lowering intermediaries who can assist with optimization, as with search-engine optimization, reputation management, or, if it comes to that, tax accountancy. Scale makes algorithmic flaws matter more than those of any one human.

As deep learning drives the next generation of decision support systems and recommender systems, their elasticity and fragility may become increasingly important.

[25] Ian Goodfellow et al., "Generative Adversarial Nets," in *Advances in Neural Information Processing Systems 27*, ed. Z. Ghahramani et al., 2672–80, 2014. http://papers.nips.cc/paper/5423-generative-adversarial-nets.pdf.

[26] Robert Chesney and Danielle Keats Citron, *Deep Fakes: A Looming Challenge for Privacy, Democracy, and National Security*, SSRN Scholarly Paper (Rochester, NY: Social Science Research Network, July 14, 2018), https://papers.ssrn.com/abstract=3,213,954.

[27] Ian J. Goodfellow, Jonathon Shlens, and Christian Szegedy, "Explaining and Harnessing Adversarial Examples," *ArXiv:1412.6572 [Cs, Stat]*, December 19, 2014, http://arxiv.org/abs/1412.6572.

[28] Christian Szegedy et al., "Intriguing Properties of Neural Networks," *ArXiv:1312.6199 [Cs]*, December 20, 2013, http://arxiv.org/abs/1312.6199.

[29] Nicholas Carlini and David Wagner, "Audio Adversarial Examples: Targeted Attacks on Speech-to-Text," *ArXiv:1801.01944 [Cs]*, January 5, 2018, http://arxiv.org/abs/1801.01944.

[30] Adi Shamir et al., "A Simple Explanation for the Existence of Adversarial Examples with Small Hamming Distance," *ArXiv:1901.10861 [Cs, Stat]*, January 30, 2019, http://arxiv.org/abs/1901.10861; Alexandru Constantin Serban and Erik Poll, "Adversarial Examples—A Complete Characterisation of the Phenomenon," *ArXiv:1810.01185 [Cs]*, October 2, 2018, http://arxiv.org/abs/1810.01185; Ali Shafahi et al., "Are Adversarial Examples Inevitable?," September 27, 2018, https://openreview.net/forum?id=r1lWUoA9FQ; David Stutz, Matthias Hein, and BerntSchiele, "Disentangling Adversarial Robustness and Generalization," *ArXiv:1812.00740 [Cs, Stat]*, December 3, 2018, http://arxiv.org/abs/1812.00740; DimitrisTsipras et al., "Robustness May Be at Odds with Accuracy," May 30, 2018, https://arxiv.org/abs/1805.12152v3.

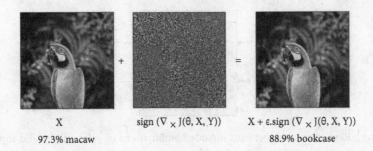

X	sign ($\nabla_X J(\theta, X, Y)$)	X + ε.sign ($\nabla_X J(\theta, X, Y)$)
97.3% macaw		88.9% bookcase

FIGURE 5.2. A slight perturbation of this picture of a macaw causes it to be classified as a bookcase.

Source: B. Liu et al., "Using Adversarial Noises to Protect Privacy in Deep Learning Era," in *2018 IEEE Global Communications Conference (GLOBECOM)*, 2018, 1–6, https://doi.org/10.1109/GLOCOM.2018.8647189.

To make matters more serious, these weaknesses will not show up in proofs of concept or early stage deployments, where the output has little impact on subjects. It is only when algorithms are operating at scale that the incentive to invest becomes large, making the system more fragile.

INCENTIVES DRIVE RESPONSES

Figure 5.3 classifies responses to algorithms. Algorithms require *valid* input if they are to give correct output. Algorithms also have an *intent* that can be affected positively or negatively by the actions of subjects. In general, the output is a proxy for this less well-defined intent.[31] Each input arrow may be paired with each output arrow, giving four classes of responses. While algorithm designers may prefer to permit only valid inputs that sustain the intent of the system, all four combinations can have ethical justifications.

Valid inputs can be understood by thinking about a simple rule-based system, such as a hiring filter that sorts applicants based solely on educational achievements. The input is a subject's educational achievements: genuine achievements are valid and fake achievements are not. The intent of the system is to give the hiring manager a good set of interviewees: if he or she is happy with their applicants, the system's intent is satisfied.

In cases that economists describe as separating equilibria for signaling and screening games,[32] valid inputs sustain the intent of the algorithm. If the applicant pool consists of two qualities from an employment perspective (high and low), and if getting a degree is easier for high-quality people than for low-quality people, then only high-quality people find it worth investing in a degree. The beauty of such an arrangement is that it is

---

[31] O'Neill, *Weapons of Math Destruction*.
[32] Michael A. Spence, "Job Market Signaling," *Quarterly Journal of Economics* 87, no. 3 (1973): 355–74; Joseph E. Stiglitz, *Whither Socialism?*, The Wicksell Lectures (Cambridge, MA; London: MIT Press, 1994).

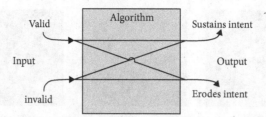

FIGURE 5.3. Responses to algorithms include combinations of valid and invalid input, which may sustain or erode the intent of the algorithm.

"incentive compatible": an "invisible hand" guides subjects so that, if they respond to incentives, the algorithm continues to satisfy its intent without additional governance.

If it is equally costly for low-quality applicants to obtain a degree as for high-quality applicants, then the degree ceases to be a useful signal. Applicants may continue to invest in degrees, but the algorithm will no longer separate the wheat from the chaff. This is the game-theoretic case of a "pooling equilibrium," where valid responses erode the intent of the algorithm. We know how the verb describing valid responses in pooling equilibria declines: I follow the letter of the law, you teach to the test, he or she games the system. The problems of pooling equilibria have been elevated to the status of a law: "Goodhart's Law" states, "When a measure becomes a target, it ceases to be a good measure." To this, we might add a corollary that becomes important below: "When a measure is not a target, it ceases to be optimized."

The ethics of optimizing responses using valid input is not simple. One reason Google keeps its search algorithms secret is to prevent gaming by the search-engine optimization industry,[33] but when it comes to the tax system their attitude is different. A secret tax system would be unacceptable, of course. Accused of dodging taxes by moving $23 billion to Bermuda, Google responded simply: "We pay all of the taxes due and comply with the tax laws in every country we operate in around the world."[34]

Workarounds are a class of invalid inputs that nevertheless sustain the intent of the system. Legal scholar Jennifer Raso investigated the operation of Ontario Works, a welfare-eligibility decision system,[35] and found that case workers became experts at working with the system, on occasion entering false data to coax results that line up with their professional judgment. Whether dealing with bugs in the program (an inapplicable field for some applicants would also be a required field in the system) or with weaknesses in the model, case workers break the letter of the law to follow the spirit. Similar

[33] Jonathan Rosenberg, "The Meaning of Open," December 21, 2009, http://googleblog.blogspot.ca/2009/12/meaning-of-open.html.

[34] Reuters, "Google Shifted $23bn to Tax Haven Bermuda in 2017, Filing Shows," *The Guardian*, January 3, 2019, https://www.theguardian.com/technology/2019/jan/03/google-tax-haven-bermuda-netherlands.

[35] Jennifer Raso, "Displacement as Regulation: New Regulatory Technologies and Front-Line Decision-Making in Ontario Works," *Canadian Journal of Law & Society/La Revue Canadienne Droit et Société* 32, no. 1 (April 2017): 75–95, https://doi.org/10.1017/cls.2017.6.

behavior has been seen among U.S. doctors seeking to provide their patients with good outcomes from insurance systems.[36]

Any statistical algorithm has error cases, and many systems cannot function without workarounds from those it manages or their agents, which is why "work to rule" actions in some industrial settings are common: if you follow the letter of the law too strictly, nothing gets done. The unappreciated role of workarounds is one reason why James C. Scott argues that "certain schemes to improve the human condition have failed."[37] Scott is arguing against top-down "high-modernist" schemes, and algorithmic platforms certainly fall into this category.

The final case is invalid input that also erodes an algorithm's intent, often described in security terms as *attacks* on the algorithm. There are an increasing number of algorithms for which "opting out" is not an option, including ratings platforms. Botto Bistro is a San Francisco restaurant that was unhappy with what they saw as unethical treatment by Yelp, who also refused the restaurant's request to be removed from the platform. In response, Botto Bistro encouraged its customers to enter over-the-top one-star reviews, seeking to achieve the lowest rating on Yelp. The campaign called attention to some dubious practices and contradictions in Yelp's operations: perhaps a case of principled protest or subversive humor, sabotaging one system in pursuit of a higher goal.[38]

The more sophisticated and complex the algorithm, the more the lines between these four categories blur. Once algorithms move beyond simple inputs such as birthdates and educational qualifications, the criteria for distinguishing valid from invalid input become uncertain. Reputation systems such as Yelp, eBay, and Uber replace "true or false" criteria with more nebulous notions of "authenticity" or "honesty" and defend them not by appeals to correctness but to free speech.[39] Who can say what a "four-star" rating really means?[40]

On the output side too, an unambiguous "ground truth" output is often unavailable outside the labeled training sets of the laboratory, so the distinction fades between an attack and a workaround. Even adversarial examples, which seem so obvious, have resisted definition. One technical attempt is to say they are input "that an attacker has intentionally designed to cause the model to make a mistake,"[41] but for an individual

---

[36] Matthew K. Wynia et al., "Physician Manipulation of Reimbursement Rules for Patients: Between a Rock and a Hard Place," *JAMA* 283, no. 14 (April 12, 2000): 1858–65, https://doi.org/10.1001/jama.283.14.1858.

[37] James C. Scott, *Seeing Like a State: How Certain Schemes to Improve the Human Condition Have Failed* (New Haven: Yale University Press, 1998).

[38] Tom Slee, "In Praise of Fake Reviews," *The New Inquiry*, October 29, 2014, https://thenewinquiry.com/in-praise-of-fake-reviews/.

[39] James Grimmelmann, "Three Theories of Copyright in Ratings," *Vanderbilt Journal of Entertainment and Technology Law* 14, no. 4 (2012): 851–887.

[40] Abbey Stemler, "Feedback Loop Failure: Implications for the Self-Regulation of the Sharing Economy," SSRN Scholarly Paper (Rochester, NY: Social Science Research Network, April 1, 2016), https://papers.ssrn.com/abstract=2,754,768.

[41] Justin Gilmer et al., "Motivating the Rules of the Game for Adversarial Example Research," *ArXiv:1807.06732 [Cs, Stat]*, July 17, 2018, http://arxiv.org/abs/1807.06732.

real-world case, identifying "intent" or a "mistake" may both be impossible and so the classification of "attacker" fails too.

RESPONSES DEMAND GUARDRAILS

In general, algorithms that classify people are "incentive-incompatible": if subjects follow their incentives then the algorithm ceases to function as designed. To sustain their accuracy, algorithms need external rules to limit permissible responses. These rules form a set of *guardrails* that implement value judgments, keeping algorithms functioning by constraining the actions of subjects.[42]

"Move fast and break things" norms of disruptive innovation encourage algorithm designers to postpone thinking about guardrails. They may not be needed in low-elasticity environments such as proofs of concept or in early-stage deployments. Still, successful deployments at scale will require guardrails and so, even if problems of bias and fairness could be solved, the grail of algorithmic governance—of impartial and automatic algorithmic data-driven and evidence-based decision-making—would fall at this hurdle. Algorithms and their guardrails form an inseparable pair. Code is law, until it is not.

The existence of a scalable algorithm does not imply the existence of equally scalable guardrails: guardrails must deal with specific contexts and factors outside the original model, which only grow in number as algorithms draw on an ever-increasing volume and variety of data in pursuit of accuracy. Attempts to implement automated moderation have repeatedly failed, and companies have resorted instead to what Astra Taylor calls "fauxtomation": behind the scenes real people do the work to simulate the effects of an algorithm, because the technology is not up to the task.[43] The work of content moderators has been described recently by Sarah Roberts[44] and Tarleton Gillespie.[45]

Algorithms without guardrails may become ungovernable. Social media recommender algorithms, for example, have all three qualities needed for high elasticity. Experimentation is affordable, content producers can discover the kind of content to which the recommendation algorithm is sensitive because they get fast feedback in the

---

[42] The metaphor adopts the designer's point of view; from a subject's point of view, "straitjacket" may be more appropriate.

[43] Astra Taylor, "The Automation Charade," *Logic Magazine*, October 2, 2018, https://logicmag.io/05-the-automation-charade/.

[44] Sarah Roberts, "Commercial Content Moderation: Digital Laborers' Dirty Work," in *Intersectional Internet: Race, Sex, Class and Culture Online*, ed. Safiya Umoja Noble and Brendesha M. Tynes, Digital Formations Series (New York: Peter Lang, 2016), https://intersectionalinternet.com/about/; Sarah T. Roberts, *Behind the Screen: Content Moderation in the Shadows of Social Media* (New Haven: Yale University Press, 2019), https://yalebooks.yale.edu/book/9780300235883/behind-screen.

[45] Tarleton GIllespie, *Custodians of the Internet: Platforms, Content Moderation, and the Hidden Decisions That Shape Social Media* (New Haven: Yale University Press, 2018), https://yalebooks.yale.edu/book/9780300173130/custodians-internet.

form of view counts, and the impact of the recommendation system is high. High elasticity means strong incentives to optimize individual outcomes.

The YouTube recommendation algorithm[46] suffers from ungovernability. In a widely read article, James Bridle provided a tour through the long tail of bizarre content appearing on YouTube Kids as producers experiment to gain views.[47] As just one example, they would rely on keyword/hashtag association when generating new content.

> When some trend, such as Surprise Egg videos, reaches critical mass, content producers pile onto it, creating thousands and thousands more of these videos in every possible iteration...branded content and nursery rhyme titles and "surprise egg" all stuffed into the same word salad to capture search results, sidebar placement, and "up next" autoplay rankings....A striking example of the weirdness is the Finger Family videos...I have no idea where they came from or the origin of the children's rhyme at the core of the trope, but there are **at least 17 million versions** of this currently on YouTube, and again they cover every possible genre, with billions and billions of aggregated views.

Ironically, it was Bridle's essay going viral that made YouTube act, and they did so by invoking community guidelines. The response seems like an ethical platform making best efforts to implement guardrails that eject malicious actors, but the story is not so simple. One channel removed for violating the "family friendly" rule was that of Johnny Tanner.[48] Tanner said he could not discover what had prompted the punishment, because he had no person to talk to. In defense of his channel, he said, "The algorithm is the thing we had a relationship with since the beginning. That's what got us out there and popular....We learned to fuel it and do whatever it took to please the algorithm."

The same article quotes Davey Orgill, who left his job to make superhero parody videos, and whose channel reached two million viewers before being shut down. He argued that "the platform is responsible for encouraging...objectionable, sexual, and violent superhero content ostensibly oriented toward children....YouTube blames it on these people that were doing it, but for a year their algorithm pushed this content....People were doing it because it was creating millions and millions and millions of views. They created a monster." The left hand of the recommendation algorithms promotes videos that the right hand of the Community Guidelines would later forbid.

[46] Paul Covington, Jay Adams, and Emre Sargin, "Deep Neural Networks for YouTube Recommendations," in *Proceedings of the 10th ACM Conference on Recommender Systems*, RecSys'16 (New York: ACM, 2016), 191–98, https://doi.org/10.1145/2959100.2959190.

[47] James Bridle, "Something Is Wrong on the Internet," *James Bridle* (blog), November 6, 2017, https://medium.com/@jamesbridle/something-is-wrong-on-the-internet-c39c471271d2.

[48] Charlie Warzel, "YouTube Is Addressing Its Massive Child Exploitation Problem," *BuzzFeed News*, November 22, 2017, https://www.buzzfeednews.com/article/charliewarzel/youtube-is-addressing-its-massive-child-exploitation-problem; Davey Alba, "YouTube Has a Massive Child Exploitation Problem: How Humans Train Its Search AI Is Partly Why," *BuzzFeed News*, December 28, 2017, https://www.buzzfeednews.com/article/daveyalba/youtube-search-rater-algorithms-children-disturbing-videos.

Bridle ends his essay this way: "The architecture they have built to extract the maximum revenue from online video is being hacked by persons unknown to abuse children, perhaps not even deliberately, but at a massive scale." But the disturbing videos are not "hacking" any more than minimizing tax payments is hacking; they are responses driven by the algorithm itself.

Facebook's News Feed algorithm also suffers from high elasticity, and its problems have also been framed as those of defense against malicious actors. Former Facebook executive Antonio Garcia Martinez complained on Twitter that "The same FB [Facebook] critics who call on the company to take on responsibility for moderating content (an operational job they (Facebook) don't want, and had to be pressed to perform), will of course be shocked, shocked at the human cost in reviewing billions of pieces of random content."[49] But the requirement for guardrails is inherent in the News Feed model. Facebook had simply crossed its fingers and hoped that governance was not required.

The intent of News Feed has changed over time and remains operationally vague. Mark Zuckerberg announced in January 2018 that "I'm changing the goal I give our product teams from focusing on helping you find relevant content to helping you have more meaningful social interactions."[50] Facebook designed News Feed as a system with large rewards for high circulation, thus encouraging participants to invest heavily in optimizing their outcomes. Attempting to move on from the resulting Clickbait head-lines, Facebook has doubled down on building in-house algorithmic or fauxtomatic solutions.

> Facebook's entire project, when it comes to news, rests on the assumption that people's individual preferences ultimately coincide with the public good, and that if it doesn't appear that way at first, you're not delving deeply enough into the data.[51]

The assumption fails. An elastic system based on "the data" causes the foundations on which it is built to shift. The incentive-incompatible News Feed algorithm demands guardrails to police the content it generates.

If Facebook does not want the job of managing news content, it could hand it to the news industry. Emily Bell of the Columbia Journalism School explains:

> At some point, if they really want to address this, they have to say, "This is good information" and "This is bad information." They have to say, "These are the kinds of information sources that we want to privilege, and these others are not going to be banned from the platform, but they are not going to thrive." In other words, they

---

[49] Tweet since deleted.
[50] Mark Zuckerberg, "One of Our Big Focus Areas for 2018," Social Media, *Mark Zuckerberg's Facebook Posts* (blog), January 11, 2018, https://www.facebook.com/zuck/posts/10104413015393571.
[51] Farhad Manjoo, "Can Facebook Fix Its Own Worst Bug?," *New York Times*, April 25, 2017, sec. Magazine, https://www.nytimes.com/2017/04/25/magazine/can-facebook-fix-its-own-worst-bug.html.

have to create a hierarchy, and they're going to have to decide how they're going to transfer wealth into the publishing market.[52]

Facebook does want the job, or at least the money that comes with it. Financial incentives demand that Facebook keeps responsibility for News Feed content, while insisting it has no accountability for the outcome beyond making best efforts.

Social media algorithms may be particularly prone to driving "gaming" behavior, but others are not immune.

The Allegheny Family Screening Tool (AFST) is a decision support system used to predict child abuse or child neglect at the time of birth, and to alert child services to children who may be at risk. The attentions of child services can have a large effect on the lives of families whose risk score is high. Contact with social services is one factor that may lead to a high predictive score, so some families feel they must engage in self-harming behavior, withdrawing from "networks that provide services, support, and community" to optimize their score. Thus AFST might "create the very abuse it seeks to prevent."[53]

Facial recognition has long prompted civil liberties concerns.[54] Guardrails are one of these concerns: is covering one's face acceptable behavior around facial recognition software in public spaces? In a trial deployment in London, police fined a man after he covered his face and objected to subsequent police questioning.[55] More generally, as the data sources used by insurance companies, potential employers, and others expand, the potential for unusual or unorthodox behavior patterns to trigger inferences, for example based on outlier detection algorithms, expands in tandem. Without protection against such inferences, the unusual becomes the suspicious.[56] If the guardrail question— "What have you got to hide?"—becomes legitimate for authorities to ask, the technology will have altered public norms for the worse.

Autonomous vehicles will need new guardrails to manage pedestrian behavior. At current levels of deployment, pedestrians will behave much as they do around cars with drivers, but if self-driving becomes commonplace then some may optimize their experience by stepping out ahead of autonomous cars, in full confidence that the car will stop. Should such pedestrian assertion become the norm, "autonomous vehicle adoption may

---

[52] Manjoo, "Can Facebook Fix Its Own Worst Bug?"

[53] Virginia Eubanks, *Automating Inequality: How High-Tech Tools Profile, Police, and Punish the Poor* (New York: St. Martin's Press, 2017), 169.

[54] Lucas Introna and David Wood, "Picturing Algorithmic Surveillance: The Politics of Facial Recognition Systems," *Surveillance & Society* 2, nos. 2/3 (2004): 177–98, https://doi.org/10.1.1.117.7338&rep=rep1&type=pdf.

[55] Lizzie Dearden, "Man Fined £90 after Covering Face during Facial Recognition Trial in London," *The Independent*, January 31, 2019, https://www.independent.co.uk/news/uk/crime/facial-recognition-cameras-technology-london-trial-met-police-face-cover-man-fined-a8756936.html.

[56] Sandra Wachter and Brent Mittelstadt, "A Right to Reasonable Inferences: Re-Thinking Data Protection Law in the Age of Big Data and AI," SSRN Scholarly Paper (Rochester, NY: Social Science Research Network, September 13, 2018), https://papers.ssrn.com/abstract=3,248,829.

be hampered by their strategic disadvantage that slows them down in urban traffic."[57] Perhaps, says Drive.ai board member Andrew Ng, "we should partner with the government to ask people to be lawful and considerate.... Safety isn't just about the quality of the AI technology."[58] We can expect the self-driving car industry to seek new guardrails that protect their own algorithms, yet discussion of these guardrails are largely missing from conversations about the ethics of autonomous vehicles.

In short, guardrails limit the autonomy of algorithmic subjects. Algorithmic governance may encourage platforms to innovate with A/B testing on their subjects, but the subjects themselves are constrained. Some may be punished twice over: once by the algorithm for unorthodox behavior that it does not properly model, and a second time if they fall afoul of the guardrails while trying to avoid the first.

GUARDRAILS CREATE TEMPTATION

The algorithm-guardrail pairing creates temptations for platform owners to indulge in arbitrage: exploiting presentation gaps to circumvent regulation and to avoid brand damage. When algorithms encourage behavior that the guardrails forbid, platform companies may choose whether to present themselves through their algorithm or through the values imposed by their guardrails. Ethics calls for a consistent presentation, but companies have a financial incentive to keep the gap wide, and many activities can be seen in this light.

One response is to frame problems in terms of the software development lifecycle. Problems are bugs, and the software industry knows how to deal with bugs: they are reported, they are fixed, and fixes are rolled out to customers. It is a statement of faith that bugs are temporary, and software improves through iterative refinement. If algorithmic failings are bugs, external authorities have neither the jurisdiction nor the expertise to fix them. But as we have seen, guardrail failures are features not bugs: they are created by the incentives built into the algorithm. In her book *Uberland*, Alex Rosenblat talks of Uber drivers seeing "phantom requests" that appear briefly on the driver app but vanish before they can respond.[59] Phantom requests damage drivers' prospects of earning bonuses that depend on maintaining a high acceptance rate. Uber's response to driver complaints was to blame it on network problems and promise a fix. Without effective person-to-person driver support, Uber denies drivers the option of a workaround, while the language and practices of software development help the company avoid what would, in other companies, be a breach of contract with their drivers.

[57]   Adam Millard-Ball, "Pedestrians, Autonomous Vehicles, and Cities," *Journal of Planning Education and Research* 38, no. 1 (2018), https://journals.sagepub.com/doi/abs/10.1177/0739456X16675674.

[58]   Russell Brandom, "Self-Driving Cars Are Headed toward an AI Roadblock," *The Verge*, July 3, 2018, https://www.theverge.com/2018/7/3/17530232/self-driving-ai-winter-full-autonomy-waymo-tesla-uber.

[59]   Alex Rosenblat, *Uberland: How Algorithms Are Rewriting the Rules of Work* (Berkeley: University of California Press, 2018), https://www.ucpress.edu/book/9780520298576/uberland.

A second response is to invoke value-based guardrails in an ad-hoc manner. If algorithmic governance leads to behavior on the part of subjects that may damage the brand, it is tempting to let it go until the prospect becomes too dangerous. YouTube's actions around the YouTube Kids channel fall into this pattern.

Airbnb is an algorithmically governed platform with a stated intent of building a community of regular people who live in their own home and occasionally share it with strangers. Any guardrails to keep behavior within this mandate runs the risk of affecting Airbnb's earnings, and so there has been nothing in Airbnb's systems to stop hosts creating multiple listings, setting up organizations with different "hosts" as fronts,[60] or renting out listings for 365 nights a year. When the gap between algorithmic practices and stated aims became too large in New York City, bringing the threat of restrictions on Airbnb's market, the company invoked guardrails to expel a thousand hosts off its platform,[61] claiming that they were not providing the experience their community expected.[62] Code was overruled by brand.

A third temptation is to use the platform's information resources to hide or muddy the waters regarding algorithmic failures. Ryan Calo and Alex Rosenblat have detailed the many ways in which Uber has used its information to shape the behavior of its drivers.[63] The selective and judicious release of data on an exclusive basis for collaboration with academics or industry experts may also serve to shape the overall perception of the company, whether individual papers are written independently or not.

Finally, companies that become embedded into the infrastructure of our lives have leverage when it comes to the presentation gap. Uber seeks to become a privately owned part of city transit infrastructure and uses the data it has accumulated as a resource to be licensed back to the cities in which they operate. Once integrated, cities cannot easily walk away from the platform, problems on the platform become public concerns regarding malicious actors, and cities' leverage regarding governance on the Uber platform is lost. Smart City initiatives, such as the Toronto project led by Google subsidiary Sidewalk, implicitly adopt this same approach.[64]

TEMPTATION NEEDS POLICING

The more powerful algorithms have become, the more it is clear that market forces alone cannot solve the problems arising from incompatible incentives.

[60] Luis Ferré-Sadurní, "Inside the Rise and Fall of a Multimillion-Dollar Airbnb Scheme," *New York Times*, February 23, 2019, sec. New York, https://www.nytimes.com/2019/02/23/nyregion/airbnb-nyc-law.html.

[61] Murray Cox and Tom Slee, "How Airbnb Hid the Facts in New York City," February 7, 2016, http://tomslee.net/how-airbnb-hid-the-facts-in-nyc.

[62] Kristen V. Brown, "Airbnb Admits That It Purged 1,500 Unflattering New York Listings Right before Data Release," *Splinter*, accessed March 30, 2019, https://splinternews.com/airbnb-admits-that-it-purged-1-500-unflattering-new-yor-1,793,854,942.

[63] Ryan Calo and Alex Rosenblat, "The Taking Economy: Uber, Information, and Power," *Columbia Law Review* 117 (March 9, 2017), https://papers.ssrn.com/abstract=2,929,643.

[64] See the chapter by Ellen Goodman in this book.

Platform companies can sustain a gap between algorithms and guardrails in part because Section 230 of the CDA absolves them of much responsibility for the consequences of their governance failures, in the United States at least. Chesney and Citron's recent paper on Deep Fakes[65] identifies the platform companies as the "least cost avoider": the actor who is in the best position to fix problems of incompatible incentives. The previous section claimed that platforms currently have an incentive to take ownership of the problem, but not to fix it: that taking ownership is currently a way to ward off regulation. Revisiting Section 230 and its equivalents in other jurisdictions does the opposite.

One of society's most serious classification problems is that of "innocent or guilty," and it is worth remembering that data-driven statistical methods are not permitted in this venue: evidence is instead strictly limited in scope. One reason is that people should not be punished for factors that, while they may correlate with criminality, lie outside their control. Another is that it would demand that people, especially members of less privileged groups, invest in optimizing their risk scores for fear of contact with the criminal system. "Evidence-based" statistical decision-making has become increasingly used in areas of the justice system such as parole and even sentencing and its use raises both problems. While the trend remains toward data-driven decisions, voices are being raised against use of actuarial risk assessment in the justice system. Restricting data use goes against the grain of the current drive to a data-driven society, but as the impact of algorithmic decisions grows, ideas from this venue where decisions matter the most may become more prominent in the years to come.

Competition rules provide another avenue to resolving incentive problems. Algorithmic ranking systems can become powerful institutions in and of themselves: part of the infrastructure of society. Advantages accrue to the company that owns the infrastructure when it is also competing in the market for services that exploit that infrastructure.[66]

In some industries the essential infrastructure is heavily regulated and controlled, while services built on that infrastructure are opened for innovation. Airport infrastructure is separated from the operation of airlines. Core banking functions are strictly regulated—perhaps not as strictly as some would like—while many countries are experimenting with open banking laws to permit innovation on top of this infrastructure.

Outside the realm of regulation, we can look to alternative models. Wikipedia is the only nonprofit in the top ranks of websites, and it has been significantly less affected by the problems of incompatible incentives. Many, the present author included, thought that Wikipedia would be unable to maintain quality over nearly two decades, but it has proven skeptics wrong. Perhaps the anonymous nature of contributions removes many of the distorting incentives associated with self-promotion, or perhaps it's because Wikipedia is largely free of "viral" phenomena, but something is working on Wikipedia that is not working at YouTube, Facebook, or Amazon.

---

[65] Chesney and Citron, "Deep Fakes."
[66] Lina M. Khan, "Amazon's Antitrust Paradox," *Yale Law Journal* 126 (2017): 710–805.

In conclusion, deep-learning algorithms may be more accurate than previous generations of machine learning, but they are not more robust. There may be a faint technical path forward for problems of bias and unfairness, but algorithms are engines, not cameras, and pervasive incompatible incentives will remain. Algorithms require guardrails, and technology companies are ill-suited and ill-positioned to design or implement these value-based rules. Guardrails become constraints on people's behavior and yet, in cases of high elasticity, effective governance may still be elusive. The pairing of the algorithms and guardrails tempts companies to engage in regulatory arbitrage, providing a requirement for external action.

ACKNOWLEDGMENTS

I would like to thank the editors for their invitation and guidance, and the other contributors who took part in the Toronto workshop for their inspiration and expertise. I acknowledge helpful conversations with John Slee and Lynne Supeene.

BIBLIOGRAPHY

Note: This reference list contains essential texts concerning the mechanisms and consequences of sorting.

Bowker, Geoffrey C., and Susan Leigh Star. *Sorting Things Out: Classification and Its Consequences.* Cambridge, MA: MIT Press, 1999.

Espeland, Wendy Nelson, and Michael Sauder. *Engines of Anxiety: Academic Rankings, Reputation, and Accountability.* New York: Russell Sage Foundation, 2016.

Harcourt, Bernard E. *Against Prediction.* Chicago: University of Chicago Press, 2006.

Jacobs, Jane. *The Death and Life of Great American Cities.* New York: Random House, 1961.

MacKenzie, Donald. *An Engine, Not a Camera: How Financial Models Shape Markets.* Cambridge, MA: MIT Press, 2007.

Schelling, Thomas C. *Micromotives and Macrobehavior.* New York: W. W. Norton, 1978.

Scott, James C. *Seeing Like a State: How Certain Schemes to Improve the Human Condition Have Failed.* New Haven: Yale University Press, 1998.

CHAPTER 6

••

NORMATIVE MODES
Codes and Standards

••

PAULA BODDINGTON

INTRODUCTION

••

THE development of artificial intelligence (AI) has gone through several peaks and troughs, but for the last few years AI has been experiencing a growth phase, with much excitement generated about its current and future possibilities. This has been accompanied by matching concern about the ethical and safety issues that AI might bring. Some of this concern is focused upon the possible future development of extremely powerful or even superintelligent AI; while some see such possibilities as a wonderful next step in human development, others express fears that this might lead to unintended, and possibly disastrous, consequences for humanity. There are additionally more immediate fears that the AI that we have currently or will have in the very near future may also pose ethical dangers. The many ethical concerns include worries about the ways in which AIs may use personal data, may manipulate information, may magnify existing biases, or may cause large and disruptive shifts in employment patterns. Many of these concerns raise the question of how machine agency will work alongside human agency: will our agency and autonomy be enhanced, or threatened, by the uses to which we put AI? Many of these issues are not about futuristic possibilities: they are happening now.

One response to these concerns has been a rush to produce codes of ethics for AI, as well as detailed technical standards for aspects of AI ethics and safety. These have been produced by various bodies and range from very general and inclusive pronouncements giving ideals for developing beneficial AI worldwide, to specific engineering standards for use by more localized professional bodies.

There are so many codes and standards being drawn up that this chapter cannot attempt to provide an inclusive overview. It will describe some main features typical of such codes and standards; consider some possible advantages and pitfalls; and discuss what is needed for such codes and standards to have the most effective and positive influence.

While the development of codes and standards generally stems from the best of intentions, one could well suspect that some of the excitement about AI itself amounts to hype and that this has been accompanied by a certain hype about the ethical issues. This is not at all to deny that there are, indeed, serious ethical questions, but we need to consider how the rhetoric around AI might skew our understanding of what these ethical issues are and how to characterize and address them. Much of the rhetoric suggests that AI is presenting us with new, uniquely acute and dangerous ethical challenges—see how frequently news articles about even the most banal AI are accompanied by pictures of killer robots. Hence, while attempting to avoid exaggerated claims about the ethical dangers of AI, we need to look closely at the particular ethical challenges of AI in order to assess the best ways of developing codes and standards. This hype may also reach to faith in the powers of codes and standards themselves; we need to discuss what role such codes and standards might have, and any limitations, especially given some particular features of the development of AI.

Note that codes and standards have twin aims: firstly to set standards of behavior and of outcome, and secondly to help produce the conditions to achieve these. We need to explore both of these aspects of codes and standards for AI. In doing this it will be essential to consider the historical evolution of codes and their societal and institutional background. It will never be enough to consider the codes and standards themselves.

AI raises very broad and deep questions of value and about human nature, our relations with each other, with the natural world, and the proper reach of our agency. Here it will be argued that, while codes have something to offer, relying too much on the power of codes of ethics in this area may in fact act to mask the major value issues that we really need to address in considering the ethical and human issues of AI. Specific, concrete standards may be extremely useful, but in general, codes of ethics for AI are best seen as starting points for discussion and debate.

THE VARIETIES OF CODES AND STANDARDS FOR AI ETHICS

Codes of ethics and standards for AI can vary quite considerably. To avoid a false universalism that is sometimes detectable in these debates, it is important to bear in mind that codes and standards have different purposes; there can be good reasons why codes and standards differ from each other.

Precisely how AI is defined varies among experts, and there are overlaps with ethical issues concerning computing technology, algorithms, and machine learning, which may be included in considerations in many codes and standards along with more sophisticated AI. The surge in development of AI in recent years has been largely driven by access to and use of vast amounts of data, and hence some discussions of the ethics specifically include data use and the vexed issue of algorithmic bias. This may be referred to as ADA (algorithms, data, and AI).[1]

AI covers a very wide range of technologies and of applications, and some codes and standards may attempt to address AI as a whole, whereas others focus on particular aspects of AI. Some codes of ethics for AI are plainly very aspirational, one might say even utopian, for example, calling for AI to be developed in ways that are beneficial to the whole of humanity. At the other end of the spectrum are specific and concrete technical specifications at a very fine level of resolution, where the emphasis is producing a standard that can be clearly and unambiguously implemented in practice. Hence technical specifications for AI may implicitly or explicitly embody or attempt to realize normative values, and a clear dividing line between the technical and the "purely" normative cannot be drawn in this area.

The intended remit of codes also varies. Some codes of ethics, including general calls to develop such codes, may aspire to universal and global application. This often arises from the recognition that AI may cross national and cultural borders. Additionally, attempts to counter possible cultural and geographical bias in AI may aspire to produce globally applicable sets of values. Others may be specific to particular local contexts, for instance, codes which explicitly espouse the values of a specific company.[2]

So naturally there follow certain tensions. On the one hand, there is an aspiration to global, very generally applicable or universal ethical standards for AI; on the other hand, there is, as we have seen, a counter to this in the wish to avoid imposing localized cultural and ethical views on others; and in addition, a recognition that given the rapid technological developments in AI, any codes and standards must be flexible and adaptable to take significant developments into account.

There are a range of normative considerations. Many of the codes and standards being developed specifically refer to *ethical* standards, but more precise normative values are also addressed, such as codes addressing data privacy. Some codes concern issues which may be thought of as political, such as issues of wealth distribution, but these are all included here under the broad remit of "value" questions; hence economic issues may also be seen as encompassing ethical questions. Standards for safety concern potential deleterious effects of AI so are hence ipso facto addressing ethical issues.

There are notable differences in ways in which codes and standards for AI are drawn up. In some areas of professional ethics, there are clearly defined relevant bodies that are responsible for drawing up codes of professional conduct, and there is often relevant legislation that helps to shape the codes and standards, as in medicine or in engineering. In AI, there are some similar examples, for example, the Global Initiative on Ethics of Autonomous and Intelligent Systems of the Institute of Electrical and Electronics

[1] J. Whittlestone, R. Nyrup, A. Alexandrova, K. Dihal, and S. Cave, *Ethical and Societal Implications of Algorithms, Data, and Artificial Intelligence: A Roadmap for Research* (Nuffield Foundation, 2019).

[2] For example, see the ethics policy for the IIIM (Icelandic Institute for Intelligent Machines), http://www.iiim.is/ethics-policy/.

Engineers (IEEE) Standards Association, which is the largest such professional body of its kind in the world.[3] However, AI is a varied field, and, unlike in some other areas of professional activity, there may be no essential accreditation for those who are developing or using AI, except perhaps in certain fields. There are groups of powerful interested parties who are working toward developing "best practice" for AI, such as the Partnership on AI including various organizations as Facebook, Google, IBM, UNICEF, Microsoft, Intel, and to date, about eighty others.[4] This is very different from, for example, a recognized professional body in medicine, operating under well-defined ethical regulations developed over decades, under the umbrella of national and international law, and with powers of sanction and discipline.

It is noteworthy that many proposed codes of ethics for AI to date are have been drawn up by self-selecting groups of self-designated experts, or closed groups of invited members, for example, the Asilomar AI Principles drawn up by the Future of Life Institute in 2017 with a group of invited participants.[5] Other codes and standards are being drawn up by lobby groups or activists, such as the Campaign to Stop Killer Robots, which has proposed a number of recommendations regarding the use of autonomous weapons.[6] Given the wide interest and concern about ethical, economic, and safety issues in AI, many governments and regulatory bodies are also working on the ethical issues, and this includes drawing up broad ethical or value principles, even if to date these may fall short of polished codes of ethics or ethical standards. For example, the 2018 report of the UK House of Lords Select Committee on AI, the European Union, and the Japanese Advisory Board on Artificial Intelligence and Human Society.[7]

It is clear that different considerations apply to the assessment of such diverse normative standards.

ADVANTAGES OF CODES AND STANDARDS

It may seem obvious that ethical codes and standards are to be welcomed. But why? And in particular, why produce codes and standards in AI?

---

[3] The IEEE Global Initiative on Ethics of Autonomous and Intelligent Systems, *Ethically Aligned Design: A Vision for Prioritizing Human Well-being with Autonomous and Intelligent Systems*, First Edition (IEEE, 2019), https://standards.ieee.org/content/ieee-standards/en/industry-connections/ec/autonomous-systems.html.

[4] Partnership on AI, https://www.partnershiponai.org.

[5] AI Principles, Future of Life Institute, https://futureoflife.org/ai-principles/.

[6] Campaign to Stop Killer Robots, https://www.stopkillerrobots.org.

[7] See, e.g., House of Lords Select Committee on Artificial Intelligence, Report of First Session 2017–19, AI in the UK: Ready, willing and able? (London, 2018); N. Nevejans, "European civil law rules in robotics," *European Union* (2016); and the Advisory Board on Artificial Intelligence and Human Society. Report on Artificial Intelligence and Human Society Unofficial translation (Ministry of State for Science and Technology Policy, 2017).

One answer is that because AI is currently developing very rapidly, is potentially very powerful, and has resultant ability to harm, it will be useful, indeed necessary, to try to shape its future development and future uses within a framework of values. And precisely because the potential applications of AI are so broad, it may be thought valuable to lay down very general principles. For practical impact, it will be essential to produce technical specifications and methods for the practical realization of these values.

One of the major reasons for being concerned about the ethical questions of AI is precisely the question of whether AI might surpass human control and human comprehension. Hence, without the adoption of practical and technical means of maintaining control and understanding of AI, high minded ethical pronouncements are otiose.

In addition, in such a broad and controversial field of AI, the development of codes and standards, or even broad indicators of ethical frameworks, can serve a useful role of forming a point of discussion. However, for this to happen effectively, public and wider debate and education are essential.

Dangers of Codes and Standards to Watch Out For

There are unfortunately many potential downsides of codes and standards. Some follow from the advantages outlined earlier. Some of the broad principles outlined are so broad as to veer toward the meaningless; for example, the many calls for AI to "benefit humanity" (which will be discussed further later).

Other problems of codes and standards include the encouragement of a "tick box" mentality. This happens where ethics provision is seen as a series of hurdles to get around, and where a mere formalism takes over from a genuine appreciation of the point of rules and values. Likewise, producing a formal "code of ethics" may create a culture where "ethics" is left to the "experts" and is seen as an additional "extra," something to get over and done with and of little import to day-to-day work. There are many examples of codes of ethics which are simply ignored, and many examples of organizations which in effect have two codes of ethics: the code that's formally written down, which forms the "official" policy, and the actual practice of the organization, which may deviate in considerable degree from the formal statements. Sometimes indeed, codes of ethics can operate in ways completely at odds with the intended effects.[8]

There is also the danger, especially in the image conscious corporate world, of the production of codes of ethics as an exercise in public relations to demonstrate virtue as a "leader in the field." For example, there has been considerable public concern over the use of personal data and the use of algorithms for managing material on online platforms, and pronouncements from the corporations involved that they are concerned

---

[8] D. Balfour, G. Adams, and A.E. Nickels, *Unmasking Administrative Evil* (Routledge, 2014).

with ethics may rightly be met with cynicism. Such cynicism may also be underlined if corporations lack transparency in how precisely they are formulating ethical codes of conduct, and if there are no external sanctions or measurable outcomes from any codes or standards they claim to espouse. So, alongside the developments of codes and standards by various bodies, larger questions need to be addressed about how organizations using AI are controlled, regulated, or subject to oversight by laws and regulation. These questions are currently among the most pressing in this field.

In AI there is particular reason to require that codes of ethics can respond to developments in technologies and their application, and can gather and respond to developing ethical responses to AI. Codes and standards therefore need to be responsive, while at the same time avoiding the danger that they may simply change with the wind. There is a difficult line to tread between using codes and standards as a way of molding the development of technology and formulating codes and standards in ways that simply follow the technology and forms a way of warming up the public to consider that certain practices are acceptable. This danger is amplified if codes are simply drawn up by scarcely accountable, self-selecting groups. This skepticism may be heightened if those drawing up codes or leading the ethics discussion have a vested interest in the advancement of the technology (as of course is the case if AI developers themselves, many of whom are already extremely powerful and wealthy, are the leads in the development of codes and standards).

We have seen how codes and standards in AI may be drawn up by different organizations and have also noted the question of the capacity of codes and standards positively to effect outcomes. Hence, one of the major questions for codes of ethics and normative standards for AI concerns their authority and remit. It's vital to consider the sociological and cultural setting of any codes and standards. The corporate and financial climate in which AI is being developed must be taken into account, especially given the enormous power that some of the big players already have both economically and in the capacity to gather data and control access to online information.

The codes and standards we develop are likely to exhibit values and assumptions (including implicit assumptions, which are then harder to detect) of those who draw them up, and of the time, place, and culture of those with most influence. This has been noted in relation to AI by those who point out the predominance of particular geographical regions and cultural and social groups in AI. To put it bluntly, who would trust a group of tech billionaires from Silicon Valley, with a very narrow range of skills and of personality types, to know what is best for the human race as a whole? One can also observe that many of our social values are in rapid flux and wonder if it's more likely that we are miraculously at last lucky enough to be living in the period when, finally, after millennia, we have collectively stumbled upon the moral truth, being wiser than any of our ancestors; or if we have particular preoccupations and obsessions that have arisen for local and historical reasons. (Note, too, how this trope of "moral progress" may fit hand in glove with the trope of technological progress that often accompanies enthusiasm about AI.) Hence, we must try to keep a long view, a broad view, and be wary of any ways in which a code of ethics for AI may ossify values to a short culturally and geographically distinct time period.

We noted earlier how some codes of ethics for AI may contain very broad and unhelpfully vague statements of value. Conversely, we must consider the possibility that we may overformalize or overspecify our values. This could be especially a danger in the area of AI, where many working in computing are comfortable working with formal written codes performing precise and verifiable operations.

But is it really the case that everything that we value can be articulated by us with complete precision? We may inadvertently make the ethical issues seem more manageable than they actually are. Given that we have multiple values, can we always articulate these in ways that give clear answers in every case, or are we sometimes faced with irresolvable moral dilemmas? Hence a danger of codes and in particular of standards which are minutely specified, is that we may erroneously think we have completely covered all the ethical and value issues. These are profound and substantive philosophical questions on which there is ongoing debate.

Key Value Concepts Used in AI Codes and Standards and the Challenges of AI Itself

This section will consider the broad content of codes of ethics for AI and some of the many recurring themes and values as a basis for a discussion of how best to develop and use such codes and standards. These include notions such as privacy, autonomy, transparency, intelligibility, accountability, benefit, safety, and bias, although of course not all issues can be covered in this chapter. A major question is how to develop codes and standards that best capture the particular issues presented to us by AI and which allows for an open, responsive approach to developing an ethical use of such technology. Experience has shown us that problems can be created by trying to model codes of ethics in one area, on codes developed for other areas. This has been a particular issue for social science research, which has often been modeled on medical research with inappropriate assumptions about methodology and the nature and extent of possible harms and benefits.[9]

Let us take for an example of typical content in codes of ethics for AI a statement from the report, *AI in the UK: Ready, Willing and Able?* of the House of Lords Select Committee on Artificial Intelligence giving five "overarching principles for an AI code." This is used as a starting point for discussion precisely because it gives general overarching points, while being a typical example of the kinds of issues raised and covered by codes and standards in this area.

[9] P. Atkinson, "Ethics and Ethnography," *Twenty-first Century Society* 4(1) (2009): 17–30.

(1) Artificial Intelligence Should Be Developed for the Common Good and Benefit of Humanity

This is a typical statement expressing a very general aim. It is reminiscent of the kind of call for the good of humanity more fitting to be heard at a Miss Universe contest than meriting a serious place in a code of conduct designed for practical impact. The notion of a "common good" sounds great but masks a multitude of disagreements; it's not even clear why AI in general must be for the "common good" when it is permissible for other technologies and ventures—such as designer goods—to be unevenly distributed.

But why might codes of ethics for AI be so prone to such anodyne statements? Perhaps from a recognition of the potential disruption that the unfettered use of AI could bring, and with this, the potential for the deepening of divisions in society between those who have money and power and those who have less. Such issues involve large political questions; solving them lies outside the power of individuals or even individual corporations, even very powerful ones, but requires political will and discussion.

It is the notion that AI must be of "benefit" to humanity which seems the least controversial, which tends to receive universal acceptance, but which is actually very problematic and requires unpacking. Of course, we want AI to be a benefit. But for highly disruptive technologies such as AI, the really important question is how are we even to identify what a "benefit" to humanity might be as our world morphs under the influence of the very tech the benefits of which we are trying to assess. This is especially pertinent in the case of AI, given the ease with which it could potentially manipulate our desires— indeed, this is not something that *might* happen, but is something that *is* happening, given that one of the major current uses of AI is for that lofty endeavor of humanity, targeted advertising, which works precisely by manipulating our desires. The ways in which AI can manipulate what information we get and how it is presented gives another reason for concerns about how "benefit" from AI is to be identified. Humans can also get used to change very quickly and can forget very fast how things used to be, which for a technology which can rapidly change our world poses again a profound problem in assessing benefit, for we do this in large part by comparison with alternatives.

This statement is of course intended as an "overarching principle" but in any fully fledged code, it needs to be accompanied with discussion on how to address these questions. There is not space here to address this fully, but some suggestions can be made. Ways of measuring "benefit" must be comprehensive, although they must be made concrete and specific to particular contexts in order to test and implement meaningful outcomes. "Benefit" must involve more than merely economic benefit and must address ways in which AI may manipulate our thoughts, desires, and motivations. It will also be essential to consider alternatives, and it would be desirable to try to avoid developing AI in ways which mean we quickly become dependent on the technology, where the costs of backtracking may nudge us down an otherwise unfavorable pathway. When one considers the rise of the internet and the dependency on smart phones that we see all around us, this is perhaps already a forlorn hope.

A Note on Codes, Standards, and Ethical Theory

We have thus observed that there are deep and controversial philosophical questions that need to be addressed in drawing up codes and standards of ethics. This chapter argues that because AI raises such profound questions about human nature and our relations to the world and to technology, it is especially replete with deeply controversial philosophical questions. But at the same time, we must watch for the danger that assumptions about ethical theory might foreclose some of the most important debates.

For example, many working in applied ethics are impressed with broadly consequentialist approaches to ethics, which consider that all ethical judgments can be contained in a consideration of the overall harms and benefits of a course of action. Such an approach also sits very readily with many approaches to programming, so it could well appeal to those working in computing and AI. As we shall see, many codes of ethics for AI include statements to the effect that AI should be used for the benefit of humanity and that AI should never harm humans. Especially given uncertainties about how AI might develop, a consequentialist approach could be seen to be flexible as a basis for a code of ethics for AI.

But it may appear to work so well only because consequentialism works poorly with the questions of agency which present us with some of the ethical questions raised most profoundly by AI. Consequentialism is described as "agent neutral"; briefly, it matters not who brings about a result, so long as the most benefit possible is produced.[10] But one of the profound questions of AI ethics is when we should or should not use machine agency to augment or to replace human agency.

Hence, it will be vital to look not simply at the content of any codes or standards, but at any assumptions regarding the normative ethical frameworks on which such codes or standards implicitly or explicitly rest. Much else could be said on this matter, but space prohibits further discussion.

(2) Artificial Intelligence Should Operate on Principles of Intelligibility and Fairness

This second overarching principle contains an odd coupling of intelligibility with fairness, two seemingly disparate values, so they will be discussed separately.

Intelligibility, or its cognates, virtually always features in codes and standards for AI. A term often used is "transparency." This is indeed one of the most prominent ethical issues for AI. To understand its significance, we need to think of ethics as concerning relationships between people who are answerable to each other. It is this element of accountability to others that forms the requirement for intelligibility or transparency and for which AI presents distinctive difficulties.

[10]   See, e.g., S. Scheffler, and S. Scheffler, *Rejection of Consequentialism* (Oxford University Press, 1994).

Such a requirement of intelligibility pertains to the ways in which AI replaces or supplements human thought and decision-making. It is for this reason that we require explanations for outcomes affecting us or those we are concerned about (hence the use in this area of the notion of "explainability.")[11] Where an AI is making, or assisting with, a decision that affects us, we do not wish to be robbed of the right to an explanation of how and why that decision was made. However, AI may operate in ways which lack transparency, and hence could potentially seriously interfere with a fundamental feature of moral life. This then represents a distinctive ethical problem for AI. It is thus essential that these issues are addressed in codes of ethics and standards for AI.

There is thus a debate about the technical question of whether this is a surmountable issue for (forms of) AI, as well as debates about the precise degree of intelligibility or transparency for different audiences. There will also be significant differences in different areas, depending upon how much explanation is owed to individuals in context. This must also leave open the possibility that some forms of AI do not, and maybe cannot, reach an appropriate level of intelligibility or transparency to fulfill ethical norms.[12] Such debates are essential, and essential too will be developing standards and acceptable levels of intelligibility, transparency, and explainability in context.

We should also note this: there can be a tendency to the idealization of agency, both human and machine, in discussions of AI. Although there are serious issues with explanation and intelligibility of AI especially in certain contexts, where serious impacts on individuals may follow, we must remember that humans may also fall short of providing adequate explanations for their decisions. A human being may not be fully aware of all the factors that led to their final answer. Likewise, with an AI, there may be issues around the data that are being used to support a decision, which may contain various biases, as well as the question of how precisely a decision is reached. But there also is the possibility that the precise reasons for a decision can in fact be laid out for public scrutiny. Hence, although AI could bring serious issues here, there is also potential for greater transparency and public scrutiny in some areas than we have currently.

One area where intelligibility, explainability, accountability, and transparency is a particular issue is law. Hence codes of ethics for AI may single out judicial decision-making by AIs for comment. For example, the Asilomar Principles for AI state: "8) **Judicial Transparency:** Any involvement by an autonomous system in judicial decision-making should provide a satisfactory explanation auditable by a competent human authority."

The intention is laudable, but this is an interesting example of a somewhat common "code of AI ethics overreach." Legal systems have procedural rules, and are formed and developed by statute as well as by the principles of common law, where this exists. Hence, standards of accountability for judicial decisions already exist within the legal system and may in some instances already rule out decision-making by AI, or conversely,

---

[11] D. Gunning, "Explainable Artificial Intelligence (XAI)," Defense Advanced Research Projects Agency (DARPA), 2017, https://www.darpa.mil/attachments/XAIProgramUpdate.pdf.

[12] See, e.g., Adrian Weller, "Challenges for Transparency," *arXiv preprint arXiv:1708.01870* (2017).

mandate some form of this. It is surely up to those with proper positions in relation to the judiciary to determine how to develop principles for the proper use of AI. Of course, this may require detailed discussions with AI specialists. A more useful principle of AI ethics might be to require those working in and developing AI to warn and to provide full disclosure to judicial systems to enable AI to serve appropriately, if it has a place at all.

"Fairness" is almost as loose a value term as other frequently used terms such as "benefit," and likewise involves deeply political issues. There are multiple ways of understanding what it is to be "fair." In the context of AI and of data use, the more specific notion of algorithmic bias has attracted much work. There are concerns that data manipulation may lead to, or exaggerate existing bias, through the use of biased data sets and/or biased methodologies. This is another issue nested in a legal context, since in many jurisdictions, certain biases against certain protected characteristics are prohibited. But again, although of course we wish to avoid bias, it again brings in deeper questions. "Bias" can only be understood in relation to wider values. Consider, as an example, is it "biased" to favor more competent candidates for employment? Furthermore, "bias" is understood as treating people unfairly in relation to some particular characteristic, in other words, membership of the class of those with that characteristic. So, to understand bias, we have to have a way of dividing up and classifying our world. For illustration, see current debates about gender and its relation to sex, and how this plays out in relation to legally protected characteristics. Unless we are sure that we have "carved nature at her joints," or have the ultimate take on how to analyze society, we need to drill down to these metaphysical and ontological questions to address this ethical issue.

(3) Artificial Intelligence Should Not Be Used to Diminish the Data Rights or Privacy of Individuals, Families, or Communities

This is another example of how codes of ethics for AI raise concerns which are nested within wider law and regulation. Data and privacy rights are determined by different jurisdictions; hence, it's up to the relevant legal and governmental authorities to regulate here, and any code or standard must refer to the relevant laws. It's noteworthy that they vary from place to place: data regulations within Europe, for instance, differ significantly from data regulations within the United States.[13] Of course, we should also note that laws may need to be adjusted to the particular issues that AI raises, just as codes of ethics may require adjustment. Indeed, the very existence of different legal regimes worldwide could be extremely useful as we try out and develop ethical and legal responses to AI; such plurality enables us to compare and contrast across different jurisdictions (and hence is also food for thought for an overhasty rush to a universal code of ethics for AI).

[13] D.L. Baumer et al., "Internet privacy law: A comparison between the United States and the European Union," *Computers & Security* 23(5) (2004): 400–412.

Again, such calls are common. For those developing and using AI, what needs to be emphasized is the capacity of AI to draw upon data in very powerful ways which may require very careful monitoring, assessment, and response. Collaboration and communication between technical experts in AI and data analysis, with regulators and privacy experts, is key to developing ethical frameworks for AI.

But as well as this, we should note how the very use of personal data, which is becoming ubiquitous as we all leave trails of potentially extremely revealing information wherever we go and whatever we do, is in turn affecting our attitudes toward privacy, and even toward our own self-images and identity.[14] Making a call to protect data and privacy is of course correct. But such calls need to reveal how precisely and in detail how it is that various forms of AI are both presenting us with challenges in this area and molding and possibly changing how we think about these particular values. What is certain is that the situation is not as straightforward as taking preformed, clearly articulated, and agreed values, and making sure that AI is developed in ways that fit with these.

We should also note the complexity and conceptual depth of the underlying value issues. For example, many commenting on this topic assume that individuals "own" their data. But note that to discuss property rights is immediately to engage in highly contested political debates; moreover, careful thought needs to be given to how the notion of property rights, traditionally applying to physically defined and limited material objects, can apply to data. Moreover, it may be far from clear how certain data "belongs" to a particular person; what about genetic information, which is shared between family members and population groups? What about information inaccessible to the individual, but discovered using great skill and technique by others? We need then to consider deep metaphysical questions such as criteria of individuation between people, and note how deep the underlying ethical, political, and even metaphysical questions go.

(4) All Citizens Have the Right to Be Educated to Enable Them to Flourish Mentally, Emotionally, and Economically Alongside Artificial Intelligence

This call is a way of trying to ensure that the "benefit to humanity" of AI comes about, for without education, many people will be shut out of many of the potential benefits of AI; indeed, education about AI is needed in order for people to have a meaningful say on whether or not particular forms of AI are ethically acceptable to them as individuals or to society as a whole. As always, the devil is in the detail. So much depends upon what roles AI takes on in our lives and in the economy. Such education should not simply be focused on education about AI per se, but on strategies that consider the precise role that AI should have in a flourishing human life. For example, some project that as AI takes significant roles in the economy, this will provide wealth and opportunity for more

---

[14] H. Nissenbaum, "Privacy as contextual integrity," *Washington Law Review*, 79 (2004): 119.

jobs in caring professions with human contact, as well as in handicrafts and personally tailored goods. This means "AI education" could include handicrafts and social skills. This is a very different and arguably much more human world vision than the oft-presented dystopian nightmares where AI, developed by a handful of power-crazed tech billionaire "overlords," has taken jobs away from millions of people who then spend their days being "entertained" by AI while living on state-provided benefits.

AI has the potential to change our world radically. What would it be, then, for human beings to "flourish" in an unpredictably changed future? "Flourish" is perhaps a richer way of referring to "benefit"; it encourages us to think more about the nature of the human being. There are doubtless many different ways for humans to flourish. We could move toward a future where (most or many) humans "flourish," but where we have fore-closed the possibility for other forms of flourishing life. Such issues should be directly addressed by codes and standards for ethics in AI; yet to address them requires far more than the simple production of a code or a set of standards.

(5) The Autonomous Power to Hurt, Destroy, or Deceive Human Beings Should Never Be Vested in Artificial Intelligence

Questions about the autonomy of AI, and about human control over AI, pose some of the most distinctive and pressing ethical issues. They also present difficulties for the development of codes and standards. In other statements of professional ethics, such as in medicine or engineering, a tacit assumption is that professionals have the power to control their products or services; indeed, requiring such competence is usually a key requirement. There are complexities related to unexpected circumstances, but ascertaining clear lines of responsibility and mandating insurance for mishap or disaster are usually key. With AI, however, retaining such control and understanding becomes complex, and in some cases, potentially impossible.

In part, then, standards for AI that attempt to set out how to achieve such control technologically are needed; but in addition, broad ethical statements of the desirability of such control are routinely made. This statement from the House of Lords Select Committee on Artificial Intelligence is expressed negatively, but positive statements that AI should always act in line with human values are also made.

And again, this will involve close cooperation between technical expertise in conjunction with more abstract thought on these issues of value; indeed, such collaborative thought is ongoing and should only be encouraged. We need to understand precisely how "autonomy" applies to the particular AI that is being used and developed; but more than this, we need to understand how we think about human autonomy and the value of having control over our world. Again, in doing so we should think broadly and imaginatively. We should not confine ourselves even to a narrowly focused view on what falls under the remit of "ethics"; a wide range of metaphysical questions need to be asked.

Consider this, for instance: the whole impetus of technology may perhaps be toward greater and greater human control. We might assume then that the more control we have, the better. But there are many ways of approaching this question. In some traditions, the emphasis may be on a partnership between humans and whatever force is conceptualized as fashioning the natural world, where recognizing sources of wisdom outside of the human world, and working alongside, or even sometimes ceding control entirely, to something outside of humanity may often be the best response.

Avoidance of deception by AI again seems an obvious standard to uphold. We can see this as necessary given the difficulties with transparency and intelligibility of AI. Debates about what constitutes deception in this area are ongoing and are essential. For example, given the human propensity to attribute human qualities to inanimate objects, let alone living creatures and complex machines, a large bulk of the work here will be on understanding how precisely AI might "deceive" us, and what even this actually means. Compare, for example, the temporary suspension of disbelief needed to enjoy fiction. We don't think of this as a "deception." Generally worded codes must be accompanied by more specific standards and, vitally, by deepening understanding of what "deception" means, and why it is to be avoided—or not—in the specific contexts of the multiple applications of AI.

Statements in codes and standards that warn about AI hurting, destroying, or deceiving humans are highly reminiscent of Asimov's Rules of Robotics.[15] These are often cited in reference to ethical questions in AI, even though Asimov routinely and persistently wrote stories to demonstrate their inadequacy. It is Asimov's constant finding of loopholes and problems with simple codes that is the most important legacy of his work for this field, rather than his flawed laws of robotics themselves. Perhaps, then, this should be the lesson we should take from the visionary Asimov for how we draw up and present codes of conduct: that they need to be accompanied by something richer than a set of rules, regulations, and technical standards. In fact, accompanying codes and standards by stories, both imagined and real, that point to the danger of simplistic interpretation and application of codes would be a great step.

CONCLUSIONS

There has been, and is, a very considerable effort expended on producing and developing codes and standards for AI. One must be hopeful that this work can assist with the development of technology which will enhance, rather than threaten, human agency, life, and flourishing—whatever that means. But codes and standards on their own can never be enough. This is such a complex issue, linking to wide-ranging questions, that this chapter has only been able to indicate some of the considerations to bring to

[15] See, e.g., I. Asimov, *I, Robot* (Gnome Press, 1951).

bear; indeed, discussion about codes and standards in this area is ongoing and is to be welcomed.

Codes can be a useful part of ethics, but as has been argued, have limits and dangers. Standards can be especially useful in technical achievement of goals and exploring possibilities; as we have seen, one of the problems of many codes is that they gesture at very broadly defined values, and the attempt to embody such values within technical standards can be one fruitful way of working out what these values really mean in context, as well as being critical if codes are to have any impact. This requires dialogue between those with technical expertise and others.

Yet at the same time as focusing on technical and contextual detail, we do need to look at the bigger picture. Codes of ethics are embedded within far wider questions of value, values which may not be explicitly included in the codes themselves, but which are assumed or referenced within wider societal values and norms within which the codes are nested. These values themselves can evolve. The history of medical ethics shows us how the very basic ethical concepts underpinning these codes have been evolving. Take patient autonomy, a key value of medical ethics. The emphasis placed upon the autonomy of the individual patient has been gradually increasing, as a broad generalization. There are complex reasons for this, and many factors involved; some relate to broader social attitudes, as well as to changing expectations of the medical profession, changes which may be encouraged in part by the very practice of medicine itself, including increasing patient understanding.[16] When it comes to AI, we may need to be prepared for even larger shifts in how we think of value. And figuring this out, and whether any such shifts are to be welcomed or not, will involve far more than simply laying out codes and standards.

One of the more fascinating issues of considering the ethics of AI is that, given the power of AI to augment or replace human thought and human agency, in order to assess how humans might fare in response to AI, we need to consider basic philosophical questions about human nature. For without an understanding of human nature, including human potential, human social relations, and human responses to certain environments including the environment we are creating with AI, we cannot understand what it is for humans to live well with AI. These questions of course involve scientific questions about human beings yet are never simply scientific questions. Even to give an account of what constitutes physical health for humans, will involve making judgments of value. Far more so for the richer notion of human flourishing.

Considering the ethics of AI can be seen as a great opportunity to ask and try to answer these age-old questions. These questions merit continual and richly informed debate and discussion. As useful as codes and standards of ethics may be, and as much as they may form starting points to encourage such discussions, a code of ethics in itself can only go so far. Our understanding of such values is complex and embedded in culture, story, history, the arts, philosophy, religions, political ideologies, the scientific questions we ask and our understanding of our methods for addressing these questions.

---

[16] T.L. Beauchamp and J.F. Childress, *Principles of Biomedical Ethics* (Oxford University Press, 2001).

It is such rich discussion and imaginative exploration that is needed alongside formal codes and standards, if we are really to use AI to augment human life.

BIBLIOGRAPHY

Asimov, Isaac. *I, Robot*. New York: Gnome Press, 1951.

Balfour, D., G. Adams, and A.E. Nickels. *Unmasking Administrative Evil*. New York: Routledge, 2014.

Boddington, Paula, *Towards a Code of Ethics for Artificial Intelligence*. Heidelberg: Springer, 2017.

European Commission's High-Level Expert Group on Artificial Intelligence. Draft Ethics Guidelines on Trustworthy AI. https://ec.europa.eu/futurium/en/system/files/ged/ai_hleg_draft_ethics_guidelines_18_december.pdf.

IEEE Global Initiative on Ethics of Autonomous and Intelligent Systems. *Ethically Aligned Design: A Vision for Prioritizing Human Well-being with Autonomous and Intelligent Systems*, First Edition. IEEE, 2019. https://ethicsinaction.ieee.org.

House of Lords Select Committee on Artificial Intelligence. Report of First Session 2017–19, *AI in the UK: Ready, Willing and Able?* London, 2018.

Whittlestone, J., R. Nyrup, A. Alexandrova, K. Dihal, and S. Cave. *Ethical and Societal Implications of Algorithms, Data, and Artificial Intelligence: A Roadmap for Research*. London: Nuffield Foundation, 2019.

CHAPTER 7

THE ROLE OF PROFESSIONAL NORMS IN THE GOVERNANCE OF ARTIFICIAL INTELLIGENCE

URS GASSER AND CAROLYN SCHMITT

INTRODUCTION

THE development, deployment, and use of artificial intelligence (AI) systems and AI-based technologies are governed by an increasingly complex set of legal, ethical, social, and other types of norms. These norms stem from government, industry decision makers, and professional and trade organizations, and may also rise from the developers of AI-based systems, among others. The AI governance toolbox is thus compiled of a patchwork of norms and other modes of governance, which have yet to be assembled in the context of the lifecycle of an AI-based technology. In this chapter we take a pragmatic approach to scoping the extent to which professional norms in particular—and specifically norms in the development phase as expressed in formal documents such as codes of ethics—may serve as a reservoir of norms and accountability mechanisms to include within the evolving governance toolbox. These professional norms are context-sensitive, and on their own have limited governance effects. However, professional norms can play a productive role in concert with other AI governance schemes, including legal requirements and safeguards.

Here we explore the interface between AI and "the profession," with an emphasis on new institutional arrangements and sources of norms that arise within the profession as AI integrates into many parts of society and challenges traditional conceptions of the profession. We find that this trend of challenging tradition is mirrored by the professional norms of AI, as we see emerging trends and norms stemming from new areas outside of professional and trade organizations. In addition, we suggest that we may be seeing the early stages of AI professions, broadly defined.

AI, PROFESSIONS, AND NORMS

Examining professional norms and ethics as a potential source and mode of governance of AI triggers fundamental questions about definitions and concepts: What is AI? What are the professions in general and in the context of AI specifically? What do we mean by professional ethics? No universally agreed upon definitions of these terms exist, and each of these concepts is itself in a state of flux. The meaning of AI remains amorphous, at least from a multidisciplinary perspective, as methods and techniques evolve and contexts of application change. The very notion of what a profession is and what professionalism stands for has shifted dramatically over time, particularly in knowledge economies.[1] And identifying and understanding the ethical questions to be addressed at the intersection of professions and AI is also a work in progress. Layered on top of each other, these three concepts—the profession, professional norms, and AI—create what one might describe as a perfect definitional storm, with an extraordinarily rich history, theory, and practices at its massive eye.

In light of this complexity and uncertainty, this chapter takes a modest, pragmatic approach and offers selected observations based on the work of the authors in the context of a larger research effort on the ethics and governance of AI. The following initial triangulation of the core elements at play—AI, professions, and professional norms—frames our subsequent observations.

One of the few areas of consensus among scholars is that there is no universally agreed upon definition for AI.[2] The working definition we use in this chapter, however, encapsulates the complexity and contextuality of AI, including its history and future trajectory, the interdisciplinary stakeholders and researchers involved in AI.[3] For present purposes, more important than the definition itself are some of the characteristics of AI systems, including their increased pervasiveness and impact on human autonomy and agency. Many reports document how AI-based technologies increasingly penetrate areas such as transportation, health, education, justice, news and entertainment, and

[1] Julia Evetts, "The Sociological Analysis of Professionalism: Occupational Change in the Modern World," *International Sociology* 18, no. 2 (June 2003): 395–415, https://doi.org/doi:10.1177/0268580903018002005.
[2] M.C. Elish and Tim Hwang, "Introduction," in *An AI Pattern Language* (New York: Data and Society, 2016), 1–15.
[3] We draw our definition of artificial intelligence from Stanford's AI100 report. Peter Stone et al., "Artificial Intelligence and Life in 2030," One Hundred Year Study on Artificial Intelligence: Report of the 2015–2016 Study Panel (Stanford, CA: Stanford University, September 2016), https://ai100.stanford.edu/2016-report.

commerce, to name just a few areas of life. The increased pervasiveness highlights the importance of the context for which AI systems are developed and in which they are embedded when considering normative questions and the role of professional norms aimed at addressing them. Perhaps the most fundamental attribute of many AI systems, however, is the varying degrees to which they affect human autonomy and shift it away from human beings toward machines, with potentially deep consequences also for concepts such as the profession and professionalism.

Many of the changes associated with AI that will shape the nature of the profession can be seen as amplifications of tectonic shifts that have been going on for some time: over the past few decades, a large body of multidisciplinary research has documented and analyzed the transformations of the concepts of the profession and professionalism, including the seemingly paradoxical erosion of traditional liberal professions (e.g., lawyers and doctors) on the one hand and the growing appeal of these concepts across many other occupations on the other.[4] The expanding application of "professions" across occupational groups, contexts, and social systems has a direct effect on the extent to which the concept of the profession—and its set of norms and enforcement regimes—has the potential to play a role in the governance of AI.

This expansion suggests that professions and associated norms might be increasingly relevant as governance mechanisms of AI, particularly when it comes to the *use* of AI systems by professionals in different social contexts. The ideal example is a physician who uses an AI-based system to diagnose a patient's disease, or a judge who relies on predictive analytics when making decisions about bail or sentencing. In these instances, the professional norms of ethics have the potential to help govern the use of the respective AI-based systems. Perhaps even more importantly, the conceptual shift away from traditional or "pure" professions toward what one scholar calls "mixed-up" and other forms of professionalism[5] opens the door to examine how new and evolving nontraditional occupations existing alongside professions engaged in the *development* of AI can help fill the reservoir of norms and enrich the governance toolkit. This particular perspective, with focus on professions that are on the development side of AI, will be the focus for the remainder of this chapter.

As notions of professions and professionalism are changing, the normative and institutional arrangements are shifting, too. In the case of traditional professions, control over professional practices was exercised through norms created and administered by professional associations. In recent times, not only have professional associations proliferated in concert with the professionalization of various occupations, but alternative institutional arrangements have emerged that shape the evolutionary path of professional norms and the ways in which they are enforced among professionals. This latter trend also pervades when looking at professional norms and ethics in the context of AI, where various nontraditional players—including nongovernmental organizations and

---

[4] Evetts, "Sociological Analysis," 396.

[5] Mirko Noordegraaf, "From 'Pure' to 'Hybrid' Professionalism," *Administration & Society* 39, no. 6 (October 2007): 761–85, https://doi.org/10.1177/0095399707304434.

companies—are engaged in norm creation and, to a lesser extent, administration. Despite changes in the institutional setup and governance of professional norms, the types of issues addressed by professional norms have remained largely stable by focusing on the regulation of the behavior of the professionals themselves and the impact of their products and services on society. Similarly, many of the ethical questions about norms of the profession have remained relatively stable despite the broadening of these concepts.[6] In this respect, AI might ultimately be a driver of deeper changes: professional norms and ethics in the age of AI might not only address the traditional questions but also the future effects of the increasingly autonomous systems that the profession creates—including feedback effects on the profession itself.

AI AS PROFESSION(S)?

AI-based technologies are often highly complex systems that require the collaboration of people with various types of knowledge, skills, and judgment across the different phases of AI-system creation—including design, development, and testing. Consider autonomous vehicles. These cars need designers, computer scientists, engineers, software developers, policymakers, legal experts, business representatives, among others, who work together to conceptualize and build self-driving cars and bring them to the street. Depending on geography, culture, and context, several of these activities involved in the creation of AI systems might be carried out by people that not only represent a discipline but also belong to an occupation—some of which (self-)identify as a profession. For instance, many people working on the technical side of AI development are members of professional organizations such as the Institute of Electrical and Electronics Engineers (IEEE).[7] However, determining what types of activities fall under a specific profession is not always straightforward. Seemingly well-defined activities like "engineering" are illustrative: an in-depth analysis suggests the lines between engineering activities, disciplines, occupations, and professions are blurry and change over time, particularly in light of changing socioeconomic circumstances and technologies.[8]

This boundary-drawing challenge is further complicated when considering that individuals outside of established disciplines, occupations, and profession might also be involved in the development of AI-based technologies. As one scholar says, AI

---

[6] Paula Boddington, *Towards a Code of Ethics for Artificial Intelligence*, 1st ed., Artificial Intelligence: Foundations, Theory, and Algorithms (Cham, SUI: Springer International Publishing, 2017).

[7] Boddington, *Towards a Code*, 59.

[8] Michael Davis, "Engineering as Profession: Some Methodological Problems in Its Study," in *Engineering Identities, Epistemologies and Values*, vol. 2, Engineering Education and Practice in Context (Cham, SUI: Springer International Publishing, 2015), 65–79.

development work "can be done by those working entirely outside the framework of any professional accreditation"[9]—and potentially even by amateurs.[10]

Somewhat in contrast to these complicating factors concerning the application of the concept of the profession to the development of AI systems, there is also the possibility of the emergence of what might be labeled "AI professions." A few advancements might be early indicators toward the birth of a new profession, despite the aforementioned definitional ambiguities and other uncertainties. First, what constitutes a profession may emerge from—and even be defined in terms of—one's identity and sense of self, or belonging.[11] Expressions of this identity include formal memberships in professional organizations and also (in the incubation phase of a profession) more informal but in some ways constitutive manifestations such as annual conferences, meetings, and working groups. Indicators of emerging identity of people and organizations involved in the development of AI abound, with high-profile conferences such as the Association for the Advancement of Artificial Intelligence (AAAI) Conference on Artificial Intelligence, the International Conference on Machine Learning, and the Fairness, Accountability, and Transparency in Machine Learning (FAT/ML) Conference. Additional developments, including rapidly growing professorships with direct reference to AI and its methods at universities around the world, are another sign of professionalization of AI.

Second, in the recent past we have witnessed a flourishing of initiatives aimed at developing principles specifically for ethical AI, both from tech companies and other leading organizations. From approximately early 2018 until the time of writing, individual and powerful technology companies are publishing formal expressions of norms as a mode of self-regulation. These publications function as an articulation of ethical guidelines or principles. For example, Microsoft published a book which included their AI principles.[12] It's too early to tell whether this is a sustaining trend, but it is a noteworthy development in the landscape of ethical norms and principles for AI.

Concurrently, initiatives for ethical AI principles are stemming from third-party organizations. Prominent examples include the forthcoming principles from the OECD's Committee on Digital Economy Policy,[13] a report on ethical guidelines from the European Commission's High-Level Expert Group on Artificial Intelligence

[9] Boddington, *Towards a Code*, 31.

[10] Tom Simonite, "The DIY Tinkerers Harnessing the Power of Artificial Intelligence," *Wired* (November 13, 2018), https://www.wired.com/story/diy-tinkerers-artificial-intelligence-smart-tech/.

[11] Brianna B. Caza and Stephanie Creary, "The Construction of Professional Identity," in *Perspectives on Contemporary Professional Work: Challenges and Experiences* (Cheltenham, UK: Edward Elgar, 2016), 259–85.

[12] Microsoft, *The Future Computed* (Redmond, WA: Microsoft Corporation, 2018), https://1gew603qn6vx9kp3s42geoy1-wpengine.netdna-ssl.com/wp-content/uploads/2018/02/The-Future-Computed_2.8.18.pdf.

[13] "OECD Moves Forward on Developing Guidelines for Artificial Intelligence (AI)," OECD, February 20, 2019, http://www.oecd.org/going-digital/ai/oecd-moves-forward-on-developing-guidelines-for-artificial-intelligence.htm.

(AI HLEG),[14] a declaration from Access Now and Amnesty International,[15] and "Universal Guidelines for Artificial Intelligence" by the Public Voice.[16] These documents and their principles are centered around AI, implying a corresponding group of addressees that are defined by their involvement in the production and use of AI. For example, the report from the European Commission AI HLEG states that "these guidelines are addressed to all AI stakeholders designing, developing, deploying, implementing, using or being affected by AI."[17] In light of the evolutionary, expanding dynamics of the profession and professional norms, and as illustrated by the Illinois Institute of Technology collection of codes of ethics in fields spanning agriculture, business communications, computer engineering, finance, law, media, and so forth, the emergence of "AI professions" seems plausible.[18]

Another driver of nascent AI professions might emerge in moments of crisis involving complex organizational struggles as seen through history: at the birthdate of modern medical ethics, which was at the forefront of professional ethics, there was more at stake than merely individuals and their professional work. The first code of medical ethics was born out of outrage over a crisis in 1792 in Manchester, England, in which a hospital refused to accept patients during an epidemic because of disagreement among staff. After the crisis the hospital hired Thomas Percival, an esteemed doctor and philosopher, to create the code of conduct.[19] Viewed from this angle, open protests by employees of leading AI companies—such as Microsoft[20] and Google[21]—against their employer's plans to enter into contracts that raise ethical concerns, might be precursors of such moments of organizational crisis—which in some cases have already led to the development of company-specific AI principles in response to these protests.[22] These instances demonstrate that professional ethics become increasingly important in the

[14] "Ethics Guidelines for Trustworthy AI" (European Commission High-Level Expert Group on Artificial Intelligence, April 8, 2019), https://ec.europa.eu/digital-single-market/en/news/ethics-guidelines-trustworthy-ai.
[15] "The Toronto Declaration: Protecting the Rights to Equality and Non-Discrimination in Machine Learning Systems," *Access Now* (May 16, 2018), https://www.accessnow.org/the-toronto-declaration-protecting-the-rights-to-equality-and-non-discrimination-in-machine-learning-systems/.
[16] "Universal Guidelines for Artificial Intelligence," *The Public Voice* (October 23, 2018), https://thepublicvoice.org/ai-universal-guidelines/.
[17] "Ethics Guidelines for Trustworthy AI," 5.
[18] "The Ethics Codes Collection," The Ethics Codes Collection, http://ethicscodescollection.org/ (accessed March 8, 2019).
[19] Robert Baker, "Codes of Ethics: Some History," *Perspectives on the Profession* 19, no. 1 (Fall 1999): 3., http://ethics.iit.edu/perspective/v19n1perspective.pdf (accessed March 8, 2019).
[20] Sheera Frenkel, "Microsoft Employees Protest Work with ICE, as Tech Industry Mobilizes over Immigration," *New York Times* (June 19, 2018), https://www.nytimes.com/2018/06/19/technology/tech-companies-immigration-border.html.
[21] "We Are Google Employees. Google Must Drop Dragonfly," *Medium* (blog) (November 27, 2018), https://medium.com/@googlersagainstdragonfly/we-are-google-employees-google-must-drop-dragonfly-4c8a30c5e5eb.
[22] Devin Coldewey, "Google's New 'AI Principles' Forbid Its Use in Weapons and Human Rights Violations," *TechCrunch* (June 7, 2018), https://techcrunch.com/2018/06/07/googles-new-ai-principles-forbid-its-use-in-weapons-and-human-rights-violations/?guccounter=2.

presence of highly complex situations with implications for society and for the public, from the medical field in the 1700s to AI today.

NORMS OF THE AI PROFESSION(S)

The observations mentioned earlier suggest that the application of the concept of the profession and professionalism in the context of AI are still in flux. Further complicating the scope of professionalism with AI, the professional norms themselves are situated within various contexts[23] and they interact with other explicit and implicit sources of norms.[24] In corporate settings, for instance, these norms may also interact with extant frameworks for normative business ethics. The trends sketched earlier simultaneously build upon well-established ground and familiar territory (e.g., the earlier case of engineering) and are also more novel in terms of the intricate assemblage of activities, disciplines, occupations, and professions involved in the development of (typically) complex AI systems. The current ambiguity and diversity of possible perspectives is also reflected when looking for norms that might be relevant at the nexus of AI and the professions. Two characteristics of the current norms landscape seem particularly relevant: given the mélange of (quasi-)professional activities and actors involved, it is not surprising that the sources of norms transcend the setup of professional associations that played the decisive role in the context of the traditional professions. Furthermore, the dynamic nature of the state of play suggests that relevant norms come in gestalt of "code of ethics," but in other cases and depending on context might be less structured and more informal, at times even implicit in the form of normative routines of "everyday professional life."[25] The following examples provide further illustration of the different types of norms that might be considered relevant, starting with more traditional forms.

Historically, professional codes and principles were published primarily by trade organizations and professional associations coming up with their own principles, such as the Association for Computing Machinery (ACM) and the IEEE. Now, both associations are responding to the pervasiveness and importance of AI. The IEEE embarked on a Global Initiative on Ethics of Autonomous and Intelligent Systems[26] and as part of this initiative published *Ethically Aligned Design*, a resource for a variety of stakeholders in AI to help ground the development and deployment of AI-based technologies in ethical principles including human rights, well-being, transparency, and accountability, among

---

[23] Boddington, *Towards a Code*, 48–53.

[24] See, e.g., Andrew Abbott, "Professional Ethics," *American Journal of Sociology* 88, no. 5 (March 1983): 855–85, http://www.jstor.org/stable/2779443 (accessed March 7, 2019).

[25] Abbott, "Professional Ethics," 856.

[26] "The IEEE Global Initiative on Ethics of Autonomous and Intelligent Systems," IEEE Standards Association, https://standards.ieee.org/industry-connections/ec/autonomous-systems.html (accessed March 7, 2019).

others. The report discusses various challenges and issues that surface at the interface of these principles and the design of AI-based systems. It also provides background information on these challenges and practical recommendations for ensuring ethics remain at the core of these issues and at the forefront of design teams. These recommendations range from expanding project teams with experts from other fields, to ensuring developers fully understand the ethical implications of the technology.[27]

ACM, in turn, revised its Code of Ethics and Professional Conduct in response to "significant advances in computing technology," which encompasses AI.[28] The ACM Code is written for "computing professionals," which is used in a very broad sense and will encompass many of the people working on AI-based systems.[29] ACM explicitly links their work to AI vis-à-vis their updated code of ethics. In addressing the potential risks associated with computing, the ACM code has an emphasis on machine learning; Principle 2.5 on evaluating risks states that "extraordinary care should be taken to identify and mitigate potential risks in machine learning systems."[30]

While the ACM Code of Ethics would cover the technical systems in terms of the algorithms and software, there is movement toward investigating the potential normative standards for data and data practices. These conversations are critical, as data is central to the development of AI. These norms exist within a transitional category of norms defined by newer players to these conversations.

There are several bodies, including groups within the European Commission[31] and research organizations such as the Association of Internet Researchers (AoIR), that are coming up with quasi-normative principles for data and big data research. The European Commission report is research-focused and is rooted in protecting data subjects and in abiding by laws regarding the transfer of data.[32] Further, a paper from the AoIR addresses both internet researchers and a wider audience, and discusses similar ethical issues through open-ended questions and considerations rather than formal rules.[33] In contrast, a multidisciplinary group of influential scholars published "rules for responsible big data research," which calls for each company and organization to develop their

---

[27] *Ethically Aligned Design: A Vision for Prioritizing Human Well-Being with Autonomous and Intelligent Systems*, 1st ed. (IEEE, 2019), https://ethicsinaction.ieee.org/#read.

[28] "World's Largest Computing Association Affirms Obligation of Computing Professionals to Use Skills for Benefit of Society," Association for Computing Machinery, July 17, 2018, https://www.acm.org/media-center/2018/july/acm-updates-code-of-ethics.

[29] "ACM Code of Ethics and Professional Conduct," Association for Computing Machinery, July 17, 2019, https://www.acm.org/code-of-ethics.

[30] "ACM Code."

[31] "Ethics and Data Protection" (European Commission, November 14, 2018), http://ec.europa.eu/research/participants/data/ref/h2020/grants_manual/hi/ethics/h2020_hi_ethics-data-protection_en.pdf.

[32] "Ethics and Data Protection," 10–2, 18–9.

[33] Annette Markham and Elizabeth Buchanan, "Ethical Decision-Making and Internet Research: Recommendations from the AOIR Ethics Committee" (Association of Internet Researchers, December 2012), https://aoir.org/reports/ethics2.pdf.

own code of conduct for data.[34] These publications demonstrate a source of norms that emerge in response to need and demand for guidance for working with big data, though they are not published as ethical codes.

The professional norms discussed earlier exemplify how the norms of AI are dynamic and are pieced together from various sources in traditional and transitional ways. We are also seeing the emergence of new, forward-looking sources of norms. Examples of these emerging sources are interactive resources from think tanks and articulations of norms from employees themselves. One such example is Ethical OS. Ethical OS is a toolkit with questions and considerations for a broad range of audiences connected to the development of technology, particularly when thinking about the future and potential unforeseen risks with the deployment of such systems. While not aimed specifically at AI, the toolkit frames how one should approach thinking about new technological systems and their features by offering step-by-step instructions and examples for thinking about various risks including disinformation and bad actors.[35] In addition, we are also witnessing norms surfacing from the "bottom up" within the profession themselves: employees of tech companies, particularly in the United States, and specifically at Google and Amazon, are starting to speak up—in a very public way—about their discontent with technology used for military purposes[36] and facial recognition technology.[37]

We have seen that there are different types of norms that may apply, with varying degrees of applicability, to professionals in the business of developing AI. Some of them follow tradition and are enacted by trade organizations and professional associations, while others are formulated by companies themselves, and others more recently stem from the bottom up, such as employees protesting. These norms need to be evaluated and analyzed in greater depth, and research is emerging to fill this gap.[38] Against the backdrop of norms discussed in this section, we offer four broad observations that surface from our exploration of professional norms, which include similarities to traditional norms, possibly newer elements, and larger challenges for AI ethics in the future.

The norms presented in this chapter adhere to various obligations of professions, which include commitments to society, to their employer, to their clients, and their

---

[34] Matthew Zook et al., "Ten Simple Rules for Responsible Big Data Research," *PLOS Computational Biology* 13, no. 3 (March 30, 2017): 1–10, https://doi.org/doi:10.1371/journal.pcbi.1005399.

[35] "Ethical OS: A Guide to Anticipating the Future Impact of Today's Technology," Ethical OS, August 7, 2018, https://ethicalos.org/.

[36] Daisuke Wakabayashi and Scott Shane, "Google Will Not Renew Pentagon Contract That Upset Employees," *New York Times* (June 1, 2018), https://www.nytimes.com/2018/06/01/technology/google-pentagon-project-maven.html.

[37] James Vincent, "Amazon Employees Protest Sale of Facial Recognition Software to Police," *The Verge* (June 22, 2018), https://www.theverge.com/2018/6/22/17492106/amazon-ice-facial-recognition-internal-letter-protest.

[38] Daniel Greene, Anna L. Hoffman, and Luke Stark, "Better, Nicer, Clearer, Fairer: A Critical Assessment of the Movement for Ethical Artificial Intelligence and Machine Learning," in *Proceedings of Hawaii International Conference on System Sciences* (Hawaii International Conference on System Sciences, Maui, Hawaii, 2019), https://scholarspace.manoa.hawaii.edu/bitstream/10125/59651/0211.pdf.

colleagues, and to professional organizations,[39] and fall loosely into three categories of professional codes: aspirational, educational, and regulatory.[40] With an eye toward the potential governance effects of norms—we can add another category, "technical norms," which focuses on the development aspect of AI-based systems. These categories are not mutually exclusive and may be merged together within a professional code.[41] Taken together, they form the normative backbone of what we broadly defined as emerging AI professions.

Norms set forth in corporate codes, such as Google,[42] Microsoft,[43] and SAP[44] tend to emphasize their obligation to society and public well-being and appear to be more aspirational in nature. Codes from professional associations like IEEE[45] and ACM,[46] in contrast, also encompass more explicit commitments to peer relationships and accountability to the associations and focused on development and technical norms. Microsoft, for example, elucidates their ethical norms in their book by explaining the principles and the goals of their work, reflecting both educational and aspirational types of codes.[47] Microsoft's principles refer also to technical norms, which are further articulated through guidelines for developers working on Conversational AI.[48] These guidelines are articulated as regulatory codes—or rules—though Microsoft explicitly notes that the suggestions are "for the most part not hard-and-fast rules."[49] This example illustrates how codes of ethics might interact with other manifestations of professional norms; the resulting governance effects will depend not only on each of these elements and their nature—an industry-wide technical norm might have more weight than a merely aspirational norm—but also the interplay among them.

The content of the codes and principles related to AI, and the norms described within them, resemble codes from other industries[50] and serve in essence familiar functions of professional codes.[51] However, the latest generation of professional norms highlight some interesting nontraditional features. For instance, norm addressees seem to gradually shift from traditionally narrowly scoped groups—the members of an association— toward a more inclusive, albeit ambiguous, group of professionals involved in the

[39] Effy Oz, "Ethical Standards for Computer Professionals: A Comparative Analysis of Four Major Codes," *Journal of Business Ethics* 12, no. 9 (1993): 709–26.

[40] Mark S. Frankel, "Professional Codes: Why, How, and with What Impact?," *Journal of Business Ethics* 8, no. 2/3 (1989): 109–15, http://www.jstor.org/stable/25071878 (accessed March 7, 2019).

[41] Frankel, "Professional Codes," 111.

[42] Sundar Pichai, "AI at Google: Our Principles," *The Keyword* (blog) (June 7, 2018), https://www.blog.google/technology/ai/ai-principles/.

[43] Microsoft, *Future Computed*, 51–84.

[44] Corinna Machmeier, "SAP's Guiding Principles for Artificial Intelligence," SAP, September 18, 2018, https://news.sap.com/2018/09/sap-guiding-principles-for-artificial-intelligence/.

[45] "IEEE Code of Ethics," IEEE, https://www.ieee.org/about/corporate/governance/p7-8.html (accessed April 3, 2019).

[46] "ACM Code."   [47] Microsoft, *Future Computed*, 51–84.

[48] "Responsible Bots: 10 Guidelines for Developers of Conversational AI.," Microsoft, November 4, 2018, https://www.microsoft.com/en-us/research/uploads/prod/2018/11/Bot_Guidelines_Nov_2018.pdf.

[49] "Responsible Bots," 1.

[50] E.g., Oz, "Ethical Standards," 720–4.   [51] Frankel, "Professional Codes," 111–2.

development of AI. The ACM Code of Ethics exemplifies this change between its 1992 code[52] and its 2018 code.[53] Interestingly, the addressees of both Google[54] and SAP's principles[55] are not stated. Of note, however, is that both codes include principles that draw attention to the responsibility of developers specifically. SAP indicatively refers to "our technical teams" within a principle,[56] leaving open the question of who is meant to be held accountable to the set of norms overall.

Another observation points toward attempts to operationalize the relatively abstract norms and help translate them into practice. IEEE's *Ethically Aligned Design* is illustrative by making ethical norms accessible for a wide range of stakeholders, including developers and the public, and providing guidance for how ethics can be embedded into AI-based systems.[57] IEEE implemented the report into an educational course for technical professionals of varying backgrounds and launched working groups that focus on the challenges of integrating ethics into the development of AI.[58]

The norms in this section continue to struggle with broader social issues and risks associated with AI,[59] such as the autonomous behavior of the AI systems they create. The norms focus heavily on the behavior of the professionals who are creating AI-based systems and not on the potential behavior of autonomous systems. In a few instances, however, some professional norms come close to addressing these novel types of foreseeable challenges. Microsoft, for example, asks in describing its principles, "How do we not lose control of our machines as they become increasingly intelligent and powerful?"[60] ACM's Code of Ethics similarly states that when the future risk of the technology is uncertain, there must be "frequent reassessment" of the technology.[61] Addressing the autonomous behavior of AI-based systems is an emerging area within the professional norms approach to AI governance worthy of future study, and as one scholar postulates, may suggest larger questions about moral agency.[62]

GOVERNANCE EFFECTS

Among the myriad of professional norms discussed thus far, we can also differentiate between different types of governance effects of such norms. There may be direct effects and indirect effects; there may be weak effects and strong effects; and there may even be undesirable effects, or side effects, that accompany norms.

[52] Ronald E Anderson, "ACM Code of Ethics and Professional Conduct," *Communications of the ACM*, May 1992, 94–9, https://dl.acm.org/citation.cfm?id=129885 (accessed April 1, 2019).
[53] "ACM Code."   [54] Pichai, "AI at Google."   [55] Machmeier, "SAP's Guiding Principles."
[56] *Id.*   [57] *Ethically Aligned Design.*   [58] *Id.* at 283–4.
[59] Boddington, *Towards a Code*, 49.   [60] Microsoft, *Future Computed*, 56.
[61] "ACM Code."   [62] Boddington, *Towards a Code*, 24.

The empirical evidence regarding the impact of codes of ethics on behavior is mixed. There are some studies from business ethics arguing an observable effect,[63] and more recent studies, looking at the ACM Code of Ethics, which posit that such norms have little effect.[64]

While the governance effects of ethical codes are unclear, there are a few key reasons to see promise for professional norms, articulated as codes of ethics and similar ethical principles, as an important addition to the AI governance toolkit. In this section, we draw from pragmatic examples as demonstrations of such potential effects. While the cynic can argue that these are merely marketing ploys or modes of influencing public perception,[65] or a form of "ethics washing,"[66] there are practical design choices that can encourage robust accountability systems in order to make professional norms more powerful. We thus situate professional norms within four main camps delineated in the following.

Implementation of Norms

The governance effects of professional norms will depend on how these norms are implemented and integrated into development processes, practices, and routines of AI-based technologies. An important case are companies in situations where they are not only formulating norms and principles but also creating granular guidelines that specify what the norms actually mean for engineers in practice. These guidelines are sometimes presented as instructional materials,[67] and other times as explicit guidelines. Microsoft's aforementioned guidelines on Conversational AI, presented as a living document that will evolve with a changing ecosystem, are illustrative.[68]

Companies are also drawing on internal review boards for additional guidance on implementing principles in practice. Six months after publishing its AI guidelines, Google created an internal review structure for difficult cases that are flagged internally, in which developers struggled with the application of the company's principles or faced

---

[63] Joseph A. McKinney, Tisha L. Emerson, and Mitchell J. Neubert, "The Effects of Ethical Codes on Ethical Perceptions of Actions Toward Stakeholders," *Journal of Business Ethics* 97, no. 4 (2010): 505–16, http://www.jstor.org.ezp-prod1.hul.harvard.edu/stable/40929510 (accessed March 7, 2019).

[64] Andrew McNamara, Justin Smith, and Emerson Murphy-Hill, "Does ACM's Code of Ethics Change Ethical Decision Making in Software Development?," in *Proceedings of the 2018 26th ACM Joint Meeting on European Software Engineering Conference and Symposium on the Foundations of Software Engineering* (ACM Joint Meeting on European Software Engineering Conference and Symposium on the Foundations of Software Engineering, Lake Buena Vista, Florida, 2018), 729–33, https://dl.acm.org/citation.cfm?doid=3236024.3264833.

[65] Frankel, "Professional Codes," 111.

[66] James Vincent, "The Problem with AI Ethics," *The Verge* (April 3, 2019), https://www.theverge.com/2019/4/3/18293410/ai-artificial-intelligence-ethics-boards-charters-problem-big-tech.

[67] "Responsible AI Practices," Google AI, https://ai.google/education/responsible-ai-practices (accessed March 11, 2019).

[68] "Responsible Bots," 1.

barriers AI principles.[69] At Google it is the responsibility of these senior executives to address particularly challenging issues, including decisions that affect multiple products and technologies.[70]

Overall, the effectiveness of professional norms within the corporate context as a force of governance will depend, as we have seen in other contexts such as the pharmaceutical industry,[71] on numerous factors ranging from internal oversight, monitoring, and reinforcement mechanisms such as, for example, the Balanced Scorecard concept, to important issues related to leadership values and culture.[72]

Accountability Mechanisms

Norms that apply to the development of AI systems are diverse, and the possible accountability mechanisms that seek to ensure compliance with these diverse norms across contexts vary, too. Some of the principles and codes of ethics discussed lack explicit accountability mechanisms, but still might be enforced informally as a "by-product of other types of controls that are maintaining everyday professional routines."[73] Others, such as the ACM Code of Ethics, are paired with a separate Code of Ethics enforcement policy. The ACM enforcement policy outlines the steps that the organization takes once a complaint is filed, including investigations and complaint dismissals. The enforcement policy contains potential disciplinary actions for code violations, such as barring members temporarily from ACM conferences and publications, and expulsion from the organization.[74] The effects of such enforcement mechanisms remain largely an open empirical question: while an early study on the impact of the ACM Code of Ethics claimed that the ACM Code of Ethics did not impact behavior, this study is limited in that it only looked at the exposure of participants to the norms but not at the impact of enforcement mechanisms based on complaints of members—a form of internal policing of the profession.[75] Nonetheless, decades of empirical research across a wide variety of (traditional) professions suggest that "formal prosecution is a function largely of the public visibility of the offence."[76]

[69] Kent Walker, "Google AI Principles Updates, Six Months In," *The Keyword* (blog) (December 18, 2018), https://www.blog.google/technology/ai/google-ai-principles-updates-six-months/.

[70] From our experience working with industry at the Berkman Klein Center, we've learned that buy-in and awareness of the top executives are key for cultural and behavioral changes in these organizations developing AI technologies.

[71] Ruth Chadwick ed., *The Concise Encyclopedia of the Ethics of New Technologies*, 1st ed., Bioindustry Ethics (Amsterdam, NL: Elsevier Academic Press, 2005).

[72] Chadwick, *Ethics of New Technologies*, 391–4.

[73] Abbott, "Professional Ethics," 860.

[74] "ACM Code of Ethics Enforcement Procedures," Association for Computing Machinery, https://www.acm.org/code-of-ethics/enforcement-procedures (accessed March 8, 2019).

[75] McNamara, Smith, and Murphy-Hill, "ACM's Code of Ethics," 730–1.

[76] Abbott, "Professional Ethics," 859.

Some companies, as new norm-setters of professional norms for AI development, also experiment with accountability schemes. In addition to internal review boards, there are attempts to establish external review boards, with varying degrees of success. Google, for example, created a (controversial and short-lived) external council with a specific focus on the development of Google's AI-based tools.[77,78] SAP also created an interdisciplinary External Ethics Review Board with a focus on AI to guide the implementation of the principles,[79] in addition to their Internal Steering Committee which created their AI Principles.[80] These review panels—and the interest in establishing them—suggest that the responsibility to develop ethical and responsible AI tools does not fall solely on the developers and engineers, potentially adding layers of accountability for professional norms. The sobering recent experiences with external ethics boards demonstrate how independence, representativeness, legitimacy, transparency, and authority are among the key factors that determine the effectiveness of such oversight mechanisms.[81] Overall and beyond the context of AI, the performance of ethical review processes and boards is theoretically and empirically underexplored.[82]

The Court of Public Opinion

The role of publicity[83] and the "visibility theory" has been identified as a force at play in the context of traditional professional norms and accountability schemes.[84] In today's social media environment, the court of public opinion serves as another governance mechanism for norm enforcement: organizations that stipulate principles and professional norms for AI development will potentially be held responsible in the court of public opinion if they violate or infringe on these norms. Recent media examples showcase employees of major technology companies articulating their values, again from the "bottom up." For example, Microsoft employees made headlines for their open letter against the company's work with the U.S. Immigration and Customs Enforcement.[85] Similarly, Google employees, angered by news of a planned search engine in China,

[77] Kent Walker, "An External Advisory Council to Help Advance the Responsible Development of AI," *The Keyword* (blog) (March 26, 2019), https://www.blog.google/technology/ai/external-advisory-council-help-advance-responsible-development-ai/.

[78] Kelsey Piper, "Exclusive: Google Cancels AI Ethics Board in Response to Outcry," *Vox* (April 4, 2019), https://www.vox.com/future-perfect/2019/4/4/18295933/google-cancels-ai-ethics-board.

[79] "SAP Becomes First European Tech Company to Create Ethics Advisory Panel for Artificial Intelligence," SAP, September 18, 2018, https://news.sap.com/2018/09/sap-first-european-tech-company-ai-ethics-advisory-panel/.

[80] Machmeier, "SAP's Guiding Principles."

[81] Meredith Whittaker et al., "AI Now Report 2018" (AI Now, New York University, December 2018), https://ainowinstitute.org/AI_Now_2018_Report.pdf.

[82] Stuart G. Nicholls et al., "A Scoping Review of Empirical Research Relating to Quality and Effectiveness of Research Ethics Review," *PLOS ONE* 10, no. 7 (July 30, 2015), https://doi.org/10.1371/journal.pone.0133639.

[83] Frankel, "Professional Codes," 111.   [84] Abbott, "Professional Ethics," 859.

[85] Frenkel, "Microsoft Employees Protest."

published an open letter in protest of the project.[86] Following reports from major news outlets[87] and public threats from an investor,[88] Google reportedly shut down the project.[89] In other cases, corporate responses to employee activism have reportedly been more hostile.[90]

Shareholders are also holding companies accountable to ethical standards in the media. Amazon shareholders are currently demanding that the company stop selling facial recognition technology in light of potential human rights violations.[91] This particular demand draws on an earlier suggestion from Microsoft for government regulation of the technology.[92] Scholars have previously noted that principles and codes may be used to appease stakeholders,[93] but this instance is an example of shareholders using the principles to hold companies accountable.

The effectiveness of the court of public opinion as a norm-enforcer is likely to vary depending on the context of application, type of norm violation, overall transparency, and other factors. Based on recent experiences, it is also likely that media outlets rely on the existence of investigative and translative organizations—current examples include ProPublica,[94] AI Now, and AlgorithmWatch, among others—that draw attention to ethical issues in AI and possible norm violations.

Professional Norms in Law

Looking ahead and toward more robust accountability schemes for professional norms governing the development of AI systems, there may be instances where professional

---

[86] "We Are Google Employees."

[87] Brian Fung, "Google Really Is Trying to Build a Censored Chinese Search Engine, Its CEO Confirms," *Washington Post* (October 16, 2018), https://www.washingtonpost.com/technology/2018/10/16/google-really-is-trying-build-censored-chinese-search-engine-its-ceo-confirms/?utm_term=.84255850a20c.

[88] Patrick Temple-West, "Google Shareholder Revolts over 'Project Dragonfly,'" *Politico* (December 19, 2018), https://www.politico.com/story/2018/12/19/google-shareholder-revolts-project-dragonfly-1037966.

[89] Ryan Gallagher, "Google's Secret China Project 'Effectively Ended' after Internal Confrontation," *The Intercept* (December 17, 2018), https://theintercept.com/2018/12/17/google-china-censored-search-engine-2/.

[90] Alexia Fernández Campbell, "Google Employees Say the Company Is Punishing Them for Their Activism," *Vox* (April 23, 2019), https://www.vox.com/2019/4/23/18512542/google-employee-walkout-organizers-claim-retaliation.

[91] Mallory Locklear, "Shareholders Ask Amazon to Halt Sales of Facial Recognition Tech," *Engadget* (January 17, 2019), https://www.engadget.com/2019/01/17/shareholders-ask-amazon-halt-sales-facial-recognition-tech/.

[92] Brad Smith, "Facial Recognition Technology: The Need for Public Regulation and Corporate Responsibility," *Microsoft* (blog) (July 13, 2018), https://blogs.microsoft.com/on-the-issues/2018/07/13/facial-recognition-technology-the-need-for-public-regulation-and-corporate-responsibility/.

[93] Frankel, "Professional Codes," 111.

[94] "Machine Bias: Investigating Algorithmic Injustice," ProPublica, https://www.propublica.org/series/machine-bias (accessed April 2, 2019).

norms make an entry into law. Professional norms can become legally relevant through different interfaces, including legislation (e.g., lawmakers delegate norm-setting to professional associations); through contracts (e.g., two parties incorporate norms of the profession by way of reference in the contract); or through jurisprudence (e.g., the court interprets abstract standards in light of the norms of the profession). Examples of private norms—especially technical ones—that make an entry into the legal arena are manifold and span across diverse contexts such as accounting, health law, environment, and so forth.[95] The doctrinal questions of the interplay between norms of the profession and the legal system are complex and remain controversial.

For the context of this chapter, a new mechanism established in Article 40 of the EU General Data Protection Regulation (GDPR) serves as an illustration of how norms of a professional association can become legally relevant. According to this provision, associations and other bodies that represent data controllers or processors may prepare codes of conduct to specify the regulation with regard to a long list of items including fair and transparent processing, the collection of personal data, and so forth.[96] These codes of conduct can be approved by the regulator—by the supervising authorities—and compliance monitored by accredited bodies, which has to take action in case of infringement of the approved code of conduct pursuant Article 41 GDPR.

LOOKING AHEAD

This chapter suggests that professional norms of different provenience have the potential to serve as a reservoir for AI governance when contextualized within other governance mechanisms. However, fundamental conceptual issues such as the notion of what constitutes "AI professions," coupled with a range of empirical questions, including the actual effects of norms on professionals, remain open for further research and discussion. Nonetheless, our review of the professional norms literature as applied to AI provides elements of an emerging—and certainly evolving—landscape of professional norms in the AI context.

We explored the norms of the profession as a potential source of AI governance, offering observations about the fluid state of play and outlining various types and sources of professional norms that might inform future research and discussions. Perhaps the most interesting questions for further exploration—in addition to important empirical studies of varying governance effects of professional norms under different accountability schemes—are normative in nature and go beyond the scope of this chapter and are offered here as "food for thought."

---

[95] Felix Uhlmann ed., *Private Normen and Staatliches Recht*, vol. 5 (Zurich: Dike, 2015).

[96] "General Data Protection Regulation," *Official Journal of the European Union L119* 59 (May 4, 2016), https://eur-lex.europa.eu/legal-content/EN/TXT/PDF/?uri=OJ:L:2016:119:FULL.

As we alluded to earlier, the emergence and widespread adaptation of AI-based technologies might fundamentally challenge the notion of the "profession" itself—whether on the development or usage side of such systems. Perhaps the most obvious illustration of this dimension is the observation that highly specialized AI applications have the potential to outperform even the best professionals—often without being able to provide an explanation for it. This shift in performance and power from the human to the machine is likely to affect the identity of the profession itself, for which specialized knowledge and information asymmetries are constitutive for identity-formation, and will ultimately add another layer of complexity to what types of constellations next generation professional norms have to address.[97]

During this period of rapid change, we should also challenge the dominant voices, norms, and power structures within "AI professions" to ensure they are more diverse and inclusive across gender, race, socioeconomic status, and so forth. These concerns are not unique to AI and have been observed through other professions, like law.[98,99] In the AI context, the lack of diversity is striking; a recent report highlights troubling gender and racial imbalances within "AI professions" and calls for greater diversity within the workplaces in which AI-based systems are created, as well as within the training data for these systems.[100] We anticipate efforts aimed at increasing diversity and inclusion will impact the evolution of professional norms of AI professions and shape the respective accountability mechanisms moving forward in productive ways.

A related challenge relates to the capacity and legitimacy of norms of the profession to deal with fundamental challenges brought forth by AI-based technologies. If current trajectories hold, AI technology is likely to fundamentally shape and in some areas reconfigure social relations among humans, as well as between humans and artifacts. A growing body of literature demonstrates the ethical and governance questions associated with some of these AI-enabled shifts touch upon some of the most fundamental concepts and values related to humanity and society. It remains to be seen as to what extent professional norms have a capacity to productively engage with some of these extremely complex societal questions, and how the legitimacy of norm-setting can be ensured as the stakes increase.[101]

A final question for further debate concerns the role of professional norms in concert with other norms of AI governance.[102] One of the big advantages of professional norms

[97] Boddington, *Towards a Code*, 59–65.

[98] Deborah L. Rhode, "Gender and Professional Roles," *Fordham Law Review* 63, no. 1 (1994): 39–72, https://ir.lawnet.fordham.edu/flr/vol63/iss1/5/ (accessed April 23, 2019).

[99] Alex M. Johnson Jr., "The Underrepresentation of Minorities in the Legal Profession: A Critical Race Theorist's Perspective," *Michigan Law Review* 95 (1997): 1005–62, https://heinonline.org/HOL/P?h=hein.journals/mlr95&i=1025 (accessed April 23, 2019).

[100] Sarah Myers West, Meredith Whittaker, and Kate Crawford, "Discriminating Systems: Gender, Race and Power in AI" (AI Now, New York University, April 2019), https://ainowinstitute.org/discriminatingsystems.pdf.

[101] See, e.g., Boddington, *Towards a Code*, 67–83.

[102] Urs Gasser and Virgilio A.F. Almeida, "A Layered Model for AI Governance," *IEEE Internet Computing* 21, no. 6 (December 2017): 58–62, https://doi.org/10.1109/MIC.2017.4180835.

is that they are more context-sensitive than other types of norms. Simultaneously, this context-sensitivity, combined with the fact that professional norms are only one source of constraints within the broader landscape of meshed AI governance, leads us to question how conflicts among different (contextual) norms and their interpretation can be resolved across the various norm hierarchies and norm authorities. How to ensure certain levels of interoperability,[103] along with (normative) consistency within the various sources of professional norms as applied to AI over time and vis-à-vis other governance schemes across jurisdictions and cultures, will be an ecosystem-level challenge, which needs to be addressed adequately in order to productively embrace the potential of such norms as a source of legitimate and enduring AI governance.

ACKNOWLEDGMENTS

The authors would like to express gratitude to the members of the Ethics and Governance of Artificial Intelligence Initiative at the Berkman Klein Center and the MIT Media Lab, Amar Ashar, John Bowers, Ryan Budish, Mary Gray, Hans-W. Micklitz, Ruth Okediji, Luke Stark, Sara Watson, Mark Wu, and Jonathan Zittrain for conversations and inputs on this chapter.

BIBLIOGRAPHY

Abbott, Andrew. "Professional Ethics." *American Journal of Sociology* 88, no. 5 (1983): 855–85. http://www.jstor.org/stable/2779443.

Boddington, Paula. *Towards a Code of Ethics for Artificial Intelligence.* 1st ed. Artificial Intelligence: Foundations, Theory, and Algorithms. Cham, SUI: Springer International Publishing, 2017.

Bynum, Terrell W., and Simon Rogerson eds. *Computer Ethics and Professional Responsibility.* 1st ed. Malden, MA: Blackwell, 2004.

Davis, Michael. "Engineering as Profession: Some Methodological Problems in Its Study." In *Engineering Identities, Epistemologies and Values,* edited by Steen Hyldgaard Christensen, Christelle Didier, Andrew Jamison, Martin Meganck, Carl Mitcham, and Byron Newberry, 65–79. Engineering Education and Practice in Context 2. Cham, SUI: Springer International Publishing, 2015.

Evetts, Julia. "The Sociological Analysis of Professionalism: Occupational Change in the Modern World." *International Sociology* 18, no. 2 (June 2003): 395–415. doi:10.1177/0268580 903018002005.

Frankel, Mark S. "Professional Codes: Why, How, and with What Impact?" *Journal of Business Ethics* 8, no. 2/3 (1989): 109–15. http://www.jstor.org/stable/25071878.

Greene, Daniel, Anna L. Hoffman, and Luke Stark. "Better, Nicer, Clearer, Fairer: A Critical Assessment of the Movement for Ethical Artificial Intelligence and Machine Learning." In *Proceedings of the 52nd Hawaii International Conference on System Sciences.* Maui, 2019. https://scholarspace.manoa.hawaii.edu/bitstream/10125/59651/0211.pdf.

---

[103] John Palfrey and Urs Gasser, "Legal Interop," in *Interop: The Promise and Perils of Highly Interconnected Systems,* 1st ed. (New York, NY: Basic Books, 2012), 177–92.

IEEE Global Initiative on Ethics of Autonomous and Intelligent Systems. *Ethically Aligned Design: A Vision for Prioritizing Human Well-being with Autonomous and Intelligent Systems.* 1st ed. IEEE, 2019. https://standards.ieee.org/content/ieee-standards/en/industry-connections/ec/autonomous-systems.html.

Noordegraaf, Mirko. "From 'Pure' to 'Hybrid' Professionalism." *Administration & Society* 39, no. 6 (October 2007): 761–85. doi:https://doi.org/10.1177/0095399707304434.

Oz, Effy. "Ethical Standards for Computer Professionals: A Comparative Analysis of Four Major Codes." *Journal of Business Ethics* 12, no. 9 (1993): 709–26. http://www.jstor.org/stable/25072460.

PART III

CONCEPTS AND ISSUES

CHAPTER 8

....

WE'RE MISSING A MORAL FRAMEWORK OF JUSTICE IN ARTIFICIAL INTELLIGENCE

On the Limits, Failings, and Ethics of Fairness

....

MATTHEW LE BUI AND
SAFIYA UMOJA NOBLE

2018: The Year of the Techlash

....

IN 2018, news coverage of Cambridge Analytica's exploitation and manipulation of Facebook data and its role in undermining democratic electoral politics in the United States and United Kingdom seemingly ushered in a new era of mainstream critical coverage about the overreach of technical systems into the everyday lives of citizens, consumers, and voters.[1] Even though critical academic and journalistic inquiry into algorithmic bias and discrimination had been documented for well over two decades or more by scholars of color and LGBTQ+ and nontraditional scholars,[2] as part of a larger

---

[1] For sample 2018 coverage of the Cambridge Analytica scandal, see Chang, Alvin. "The Facebook and Cambridge Analytica Scandal, Explained with a Simple Diagram," *Vox* (May 2, 2018), https://www.vox.com/policy-and-politics/2018/3/23/17151916/facebook-cambridge-analytica-trump-diagram.

[2] See key scholars spanning thirty years, beginning in the early 1990s with Wendy H.K. Chun, Anna Everrett, Rayvon Fouche, Oscar Gandy Jr., Lisa Nakamura, and Alondra Nelson; to more recent scholars such as Ruha Benjamin, Andre Brock, Simone Brown, Meredith Broussard, Kishonna Gray, Charlton McIlwain, Safiya Umoja Noble, and Catherine Knight Steele; as well as emerging scholars such as Matthew Bui, Joy Buolamwini, Brooklyne Gipson, Os Keyes, Jenny Korn, Rachel Kuo, Mutale Nkonde, and Nikki Stevens.

Rana Foroohar DECEMBER 16, 2018   🗩 19 🖶

Techlash

(noun) The growing public animosity towards large Silicon Valley platform technology companies and their Chinese equivalents

FIGURE 8.1. *The Financial Times'* definition of "Techlash."[3]

community of critical theorists of the internet,[4] the stories of the year centered around mounting examples and evidence of Facebook's pervasive power and invasions of consumer privacy, Google's failure to address regulators' concerns and monopoly control in search, and public concern over the use and disparate risks and harms of AI and emerging technologies. Examples of the failures and risky applications of AI tools included facial recognition systems by militaries and law enforcement organizations, criminal

[3] Rana Foroohar. "Year in a Word: Techlash," *Financial Times* (December 16, 2018). https://www.ft.com/content/76578fba-fca1-11e8-ac00-57a2a826423e. Included within *The Financial Times'* 2018 Year in a Word series, the term "techlash" encapsulates the seeming paradigmatic shift and increased scrutiny and criticisms in 2018 toward technologies and technology corporations in public conversations, particularly in light of their interrelations with actors and forces that have undermined democracy and deepened extant social inequalities. While the authors have included the full definition put forth by the *Financial Times*, we do wish to express our divergence and contestation with the inclusion of "their Chinese equivalents." That is, this type of rhetoric often seeks to deflect and obfuscate the ways in which U.S.-based companies are indeed undermining democracy.

[4] Including Marc Andrejevic, Yochai Benkler, Kate Crawford, Jessie Daniels, Joan Donovan, Christian Fuchs, Jack Goldsmith, Alex Halavais, Sandra Harding, Marie Hicks, Lori Kendall, Frank Pasquale, Sarah T. Roberts, Dan Schiller, Dallas Smythe, Miriam Sweeney, Siva Vaidhyanathan, among others.

sentencing algorithms within the U.S. legal system,[5] and autonomous vehicles disproportionately trained to identify white (vs. nonwhite) bodies as pedestrians.[6] The volume
and salience of these negative and investigative inquiries into the operations and
impacts of Silicon Valley technology giants even led *The Financial Times* to include
"techlash"[7] within their "Word of the Year" series in 2018 (as shown in Figure 8.1).

As a result of the "techlash" and increasing calls for greater scrutiny toward the concentrated power and harmful impacts of global technology giants, critical discourse
about digital technologies—and their corporate actors, enactors, and logics—have
become common responses to counteract the celebratory marketing rhetoric and
pitches regarding the promises and potential of technologies and data-driven systems.
Even new methods and approaches of researching these phenomena have been developed, such as Andre Brock's critical technocultural discourse analysis (CTDA),[8] to
address the lack of methods to study technological practices that intersect with race,
class, and power. Indeed, stories and studies about the harms and risks of digital technologies and algorithmic bias have become so common that multinational technology
corporations and brands such as Facebook, Google, YouTube, Microsoft, Amazon, and
IBM have attempted themselves to ameliorate their tarnished images and redress the
growing distrust in their commercial platforms and automated systems through public
relations campaigns and promotional materials about their efforts to be more "ethical,"
"fair," and "transparent" in their uses and applications of big data.[9]

Compared to previous corporate attempts to obfuscate, ignore, and pivot claims
about the risks and harms of their systems, technology corporations are now acknowledging the presence (but not gravity) of these issues while investing billions of dollars
into research and intervention programs that seek to operationalize and create "fair"
and "transparent" algorithms as a key type of intervention in an increasingly data-driven
society. By and large, the emphasis on fairness interventions in AI seeks to effect and
propagate technical systems that are neutral and objective and do not render any specific groups as advantaged over others. Meanwhile, transparency and accountability
interventions aim to put into effect systems and protocols for auditing and regulating

[5] Julia Angwin, Jeff Larson, Surya Mattu, and Lauren Kirchner, "Machine Bias: There's Software
Used Across the Country to Predict Future Criminals. And It's Biased Against Blacks," *ProPublica* (May
23, 2016), https://www.propublica.org/article/machine-bias-risk-assessments-in-criminal-sentencing.

[6] Benjamin Wilson, Judy Hoffman, and Jamie Morgenstern, "Predictive Inequity in Object
Detection." *arXiv e-prints*, art. arXiv:1902.11097, 2019.

[7] Foroohar, "Year in a Word: Techlash," 2018.

[8] Brock, Andre. Critical technocultural discourse analysis. *New Media & Society*, 20, no. 3 (2016):
1012–30. doi:10.1177/1461444816677532.

[9] For instance, see (1) IBM's "Dear Tech" advertisement, which aired during the 2019 Academy
Awards show: IBM, "Dear Tech: An Open Letter to the Industry," *YouTube*, (February 12, 2019),
https://www.youtube.com/watch?v=gNF8ObJR6K8; and (2) an advertisement from Proctor &
Gamble's brand Pantene in making the S.H.E. unbiased search engine inspired, in part, by Safiya
Noble's book, *Algorithms of Oppression: How Search Engines Reinforce Racism* (2018): Pantene.
"S.H.E. Is Taking the Bias Out of Search," *YouTube* (April 30, 2019), https://www.youtube.com/
watch?v=IsMmwsdwT9Q.

such systems unto these goals, often calling for and relying upon internal regulatory bodies within technology corporations for such measures. Of course, one key challenge for state actors and regulators is that they cannot legislate what they cannot see and understand, and so transparency is a key dimension of enacting regulation. However, the goal of many ethics responses remains largely techno-centric, in that the goal is to perfect or "unbias" the technology, rather than account for the asymmetrical power relationships and gravity of history that renders the development and deployment of such projects deeply uneven, unethical, and even immoral.

Moreover, data trusts and research partnerships between universities, policy think tanks, and technology corporations have been established and revamped as a go-to strategy for effecting a more democratic and inclusive mediated society,[10] again calling for fairness, accountability, and transparency (FAT) as key ideals within the future of AI, yet often leaving and ignoring notions of intersectional power relations out of their ethical imaginaries and frameworks.[11] As a point of departure, many are invested in linking conversations about ethics to the moral genesis and failures caused by structural racism, sexism, capitalism, and the fostering of inequality, with an eye toward understanding how the digital is implicated in social, political, and economic systems that buttress systemic failures. Complicating these conversations are concerns about neocolonial technology supply chains[12] and the total integration of the digital into global economic systems.

By 2019, a year after the "techlash," high-profile academic and corporate organizational responses to ethical issues associated with artificial intelligence were well underway.[13] In all, technology companies, philanthropic foundations, and universities and university researchers have attempted to respond to the information "crisis" and distrust in biased commercial data platforms by investing billions of dollars into academic and industry research projects that proffer "fairer" and more "ethical" and "transparent" approaches to designing, deploying, and embedding algorithmic and artificial intelligence systems within multiple facets of everyday life. However, the current and dominant frames of fairness within these and related "ethical" AI interventions often fail to consider and integrate notions and issues of structural and systemic inequality and power within their imaginaries and conceptualizations of the moral and ethical dimensions of AI and AI systems. Namely, radical scholars, writers, and activists, largely within

---

[10] For exemplars of promoting fairness in machine learning ideals, see the Association of Computing Machinery's Fairness, Accountability, and Transparency (FAccT) Conference; the Stanford Institute for Human-Centered Artificial Intelligence; and Ethics and Governance of Artificial Intelligence Fund (a joint project of the Harvard Berkman Klein Center and the MIT Media Lab).

[11] For instance, see Association for Computing Machinery (ACM), "Conference on Fairness, Accountability & Transparency (ACM FAcct," ACM FAccT Conference, https://facctconference.org.

[12] Miriam Posner, "See No Evil," *Logic Magazine*, 4 (April 29, 2018). https://escholarship.org/uc/item/3165f032.

[13] For example, the AI Now Institute, AI for Good, Data4BlackLives, adding to the ongoing work of Data & Society, among others.

and from marginalized communities and identity groups (e.g., women of color, queer scholars, scholars of color, and critical scholars) have pushed for power analyses of the ways in which algorithmic systems operate and disparately impact communities, opening the door for the "techlash" conversation. That said, their concerns about algorithmic bias, discrimination, and digital redlining have sometimes been diminished and co-opted by those in power—that is, the originators and institutions that invested in, designed, and deployed the technical systems in question. Put another way, such influential actors have steered fairness interventions to focus on: (1) the more *technical*—versus *socio*technical—approaches to understanding the implications of AI; and (2) the *current* state of affairs and technologies—versus, first, their *historic* analogs and important structural factors that influence their deployment and, secondly, the *future* and long-term consequences, risks, and harms of these applications and their development. Consequently, fairness in AI interventions, at their best, obfuscate and, at their worst, ignore the—historically, socially, and culturally—unequal contexts and power relations into which these computational tools and ideologies are attempting to embed, intervene, and operate.

That being said, a variety of responses to this dearth of critical AI inquiry have included the organizing of academics and tech workers in response to unjust uses of AI, from military uses[14] to protests of facial-recognition software,[15] to protesting the organization of AI advisory boards that include openly transphobic members.[16] In the United States, United Kingdom, and Europe, newly formed critical internet studies centers[17] have formed to organize key scholars around the world, proffering greater calls for using an intersectional and structural power analysis to AI and AI tools that foreground issues of race and racism; gender, sexism and patriarchy; and class-labor surveillance and exploitation. Altogether, emanating from these and related scholars, activists, and scholar-activists are calls for expanding the framework of ethical AI from focusing on the tweaking of algorithms and datasets to encompassing a broader comprehensive inquiry into the design, use, and profit-making processes of AI and the internet, especially in relation to the social contexts and power relations in which they are deployed and proliferating.

In this chapter, we conduct a critical appraisal and power analysis of the present state of AI and fairness research and interventions, and their philosophical and historical

[14] Olivia Solon, "When Should a Tech Company Refuse to Build Tools for the Government?," *The Guardian* (June 26, 2018), https://www.theguardian.com/technology/2018/jun/26/tech-government-contracts-worker-revolt-microsoft-amazon-google.

[15] Alexia Fernández Campbell, "How Tech Employees Are Pushing Silicon Valley to Put Ethics before Profit," *Vox* (October 18, 2018), https://www.vox.com/technology/2018/10/18/17989482/google-amazon-employee-ethics-contracts.

[16] Michael Kan, "Google Workers Protest Conservative Thinker on AI Board," *PCMAG* (April 1, 2019), https://www.pcmag.com/news/367540/google-workers-protest-conservative-thinker-on-ai-board.

[17] For example, UCLA's Critical Internet Studies Center, the Technology and Social Change Research Project at Harvard Kennedy's Shorenstein Center, the DATACTIVE Project at the University of Amsterdam, and the Data Justice Lab at Cardiff University.

antecedents, extrapolating whether and how such projects seek to pave the way for an inclusive and more democratic data-driven future. In particular, we discuss the extant state of AI and fairness research, given its proclivity for importing radical critiques and terminology of algorithmic bias and discrimination while reducing and obfuscating the core concerns of these critiques in efforts to find a "silver bullet" intervention for a universalized notion of impacted stakeholders, which are often dependent upon funding from, and in cooperation with, the technology giants that have promulgated these issues and concerns. By historicizing and contextualizing the discussion of fairness in AI in relation to previous writings about ethics and power, largely drawing from marginalized and critical technology scholars, we seek to demonstrate and elucidate how returning to their writings and key arguments can usher in—and push for—a moral framework of justice for artificial intelligence that deeply considers and engages with the underlying concerns and critiques about power and inequality within extant and emerging critiques of AI. At its core, this chapter surveys and addresses:

1. What are the philosophical antecedents to how ethics is discussed, and how should this be reimagined into a moral framework of justice?
2. How are the most high-profile and resourced AI interventions defining and conceptualizing algorithmic "ethics" and "fairness" interventions?
3. If the corporations and institutions that accelerated and propagated algorithmic bias and discrimination are at the helm of these resourced AI interventions, to what extent can and will issues of algorithmic oppression, discrimination, and redlining be addressed?
4. To what extent has—and will—the concerns and experiences of oppressed peoples and communities be prioritized within discussions about the design, deployment, and daily use of biased and discriminatory AI systems?

Indeed, we hope to demonstrate and articulate how artificial intelligence and automated systems are, undoubtedly, neither neutral nor objective, and neither fair nor balanced within an unequal society, and argue for ways to change this. While these claims are common within fields such as ethnic studies, gender studies, queer studies, science and technology studies, media studies, critical cultural communication, and critical information studies, and critical digital humanities, these ideas and concepts are less dominant or common within more technical conversations about AI within the fields and disciplines of computer science, human-computer interaction, and technology policy. Furthermore, we strive to disentangle the ways in which current and emerging fairness interventions in AI are premised upon such radical critiques of technology's impact in society whilst shifting and *distilling* these critiques into both conservative and neoliberal ideologies for change. In all, our chapter will unearth the importance of, and push for, broader approaches to AI interventions, rather than naive and reductionist technical solutions of "fair" and "ethical" algorithms, which seek to deflect and disregard the key claims of emerging and radical critiques of technology.

ON THE ORIGINS OF ETHICS AND ETHICS REIMAGINED AS JUSTICE

A careful critical analysis of political philosophy is in order to understand the origin stories of ethics, especially as it has been framed in relation to AI. Rueben Binns[18] has written an important review of the literature where he examines the Enlightenment-era philosophical antecedents concerned with discrimination, egalitarianism, and justice as matters of moral and political philosophy. In the article, Binns[19] argues that contemporary issues of fairness and ethics in machine learning and artificial intelligence are increasingly formalized around these preexisting frameworks, and they provide an important guide to understanding and critiquing the limitations of Western political philosophy. Rarely are the origins of the philosophical antecedents to contemporary conversations about ethics brought into relief, so here we also point to one of the most important critics of the limits of Western liberalism and Enlightenment philosophies of ethics: Charles Mills, whose work[20] is essential for those working on reconceptualizing justice and fairness as a matter of radically reimagining social structure, not limited solely to individualistic moral virtuosity. In short, traditional Western liberalism has been foundational to concepts of emancipation, albeit, with many shortfalls, and Mills' work[21] denotes the centrality of exclusion in liberalism's core documents and declarations. He writes:

> Rejecting liberalism's classically individualistic social ontology for an ontology of class and gender, challenging its cramped schedule of rights for a normative empowerment of the class- and gender-subordinated, these political projects [of liberalism] affirm a more expansive vision that would take us beyond bourgeois liberalism...and patriarchal liberalism.[22]

Mills' argument, not unlike critical theorist of the internet, Jessie Daniels,[23] notes the parasitic ways that liberalism can "encompass both overtly racist liberalism, where people of color are explicitly conceptualized as racial inferiors, and the no longer overtly racist, 'color-blind' liberalism of today. In the later variety of liberalism, illicit white

---

[18] Reuben Binns, "Fairness in Machine Learning: Lessons from Political Philosophy," *Proceedings of the 1st Conference on Fairness, Accountability and Transparency, in PMLR*, 81 (2018): 149–59. http://proceedings.mlr.press/v81/binns18a.html.

[19] *Id.*

[20] Charles W. Mills, *Black Rights/White Wrongs: The Critique of Racial Liberalism* (New York: Oxford University Press, 2017).

[21] *Id.*

[22] *Id.* at xiv.

[23] Jesse Daniels, "Race and Racism in Internet Studies: A Review and Critique," *New Media and Society*, 15, no. 5 (2012): 695–719. doi:10.1177/1461444812462849.

racial advantage is still being secured, but now primarily through the evasions in the theory's key assumptions rather than the derogation of nonwhites."[24] Daniels, in particular, as a scholar of white racism and the internet, also rejects mainstream liberalism, particularly neoliberal white feminism, as a means of upending white supremacist logics in Silicon Valley, in their products, platforms, and projects.[25] What these works point to, and elaborate on, are the shortcomings and limitations of classic liberalism as a moral framework for thinking about ethics in AI because of its failure to fully capture the ways in which technologies are undeniably tied to, and embedded with, power. Therefore, such frameworks of ethics inherently fail to address the complexity and dynamism of systems, processes, and actors that seek to reproduce and maintain power and maintain hegemony while evading detection, particularly in its racialized forms and formations.

This brings us to a more recent series of interrogations of power, AI, and ethics. To begin, Anna Lauren Hoffman's[26] critique of fairness and antidiscrimination efforts within AI elucidates how technical attempts to isolate and remove "bad data" and "bad algorithms" will inherently fail to effect justice and address the needs and concerns of skeptics and critics of AI. Drawing from an analysis of the ways in which fairness interventions tend to overemphasize "bad actors" and center single-axis (vis-à-vis intersectional or broader sociotechnical) thinking, Hoffman concludes: "At best, we will end up with little more than a set of reactionary technical solutions that ultimately fail to displace the underlying logic that produce unjust hierarchies of better and worse off subjects in the first place."[27] This is because, by orienting interventions around such bad actors and centering single-axis paradigms, techno-interventions cast aside larger concerns of injustice, inequity, and discrimination for more solvable fixes, underscoring the limitations of centering the technology as a site for imagining ethics. Adding to this, Ruha Benjamin[28] unpacks the concept of the "New Jim Code," a term she develops in dialogue with Michelle Alexander's[29] concept of the "New Jim Crow." While Alexander[30] articulates how the New Jim Crow operates throughout and within the U.S. criminal justice system to reinforce and reproduce the racialized oppression and social control of black communities in the United States, Benjamin[31] incorporates these critical race theory frameworks and concepts to examine and illustrate the ways in which digital technologies are integrated, and enmeshed within, digitally mediated systems and processes

[24] Mills, 2017, at xv.

[25] Daniels, "Race and Racism," 2012. See also Safiya Umoja Noble and Sarah T. Roberts, "Technological Elites: The Meritocracy and their Post-Racial Myths," in *Race Post-Race: Culture, Critique, and the Color Line*, ed. Roopali Mukherjee, Herman Gray, and Sarah Banet-Weiser (Durham, NC: Duke University Press, 2019), 113–29.

[26] Anna Lauren Hoffmann, "Where Fairness Fails: Data, Algorithms, and the Limits of Antidiscrimination Discourse," *Information, Communication & Society* 22, no. 7 (2019): 900–15. doi:10.1080/1369118x.2019.1573912.

[27] *Id.* at 911.

[28] Ruha Benjamin, *Race after Technology: Abolitionist Tools for the New Jim Code* (Medford, MA: Polity, 2019).

[29] Alexander, *The New Jim Crow*, 2010.   [30] *Id.*

[31] Benjamin, *Race after Technology*, 2019.

of surveillance, exploitation, and control while producing new forms of digital discrimination and oppression.

These articulations of the structures of white supremacy and capitalism as overdeterminants of the disparate effects of technology reframe the debates that are often essentializing, techno-deterministic, and techno-centric—foregrounding imagined digital spaces of neutrality and objectivity, which are divorced from the broader social, political, and economic contexts in which these technologies are developed and deployed. While we specifically examine and problematize power as it is tied to racial identity, such marginalization and discrimination also occur on other axes, such as sexual orientation, gender, and ability. Moreover, here we point back to the work of Mills[32] and his elaboration of "principles of corrective justice," which he says must account for the unequal, exploitative, and stigmatizing historical and contemporary effects of racism, to which many other -isms might be incorporated. We concur and offer that the sites of intervention into the concerns of the digital must be grounded in, and informed by, frameworks that acknowledge and account for the many histories of power and oppression upon which technologies are deployed rather than assuming neutral and level playing fields undergirded by techno utopianism. To aid in furthering understanding the power hierarchies and power relations of the internet, we point readers to important researchers, and the evidence and theory and concept building they have provided, which we list at the end of this chapter.

ACADEMIC AND CORPORATE RESPONSES TO THE TECHLASH: A CRITIQUE

There have been many recent calls for ethics to enter mainstream academic and popular journalistic studies of the internet and digital technologies, and we note that this is an important moment to frame the guiding logics of these calls. We see much of this work as additive, as if ethics were a supplemental module of learning that could be tacked on to the deeply embedded ways in which computing and information communication technologies are already conceptualized. Indeed, in the United States, the National Science Foundatio, (NSF) has produced calls for proposals to do things like improve undergraduate computer science education where ethics is an optional addition, but not fundamental or required for proposal funding.[33] Large funding bodies for academic research are certainly barometers of what is most important, and these too, serve as a litmus test of the terms upon which scholars are tied to the making of different sorts of interventions. Similarly, the launch of four different multimillion and billion dollar

---

[32] Mills, *Black Rights/White Wrongs*, 2017.
[33] National Science Foundation, "Improving Undergraduate STEM Education: Computing in Undergraduate Education (IUSE: CUE)," https://www.nsf.gov/pubs/2019/nsf19546/nsf19546.htm.

research grants and programs in 2018 and 2019, at and within universities and industry research and development units based in the United States, have largely been driven by calls for "ethical" AI. We note that among the most visible of these are: (1) the MIT Schwarzman College of Computing,[34] (2) the Stanford Institute for Human-Centered Artificial Intelligence,[35] (3) Google's AI ethics advisory council (announced in April 2019 and disbanded a week later),[36] and (4) a joint NSF-Amazon research grant.[37] Singularly and collectively, these research initiatives demonstrate the seeming importance and amount of resources being diverted to address pressing questions in light of the techlash, especially as they relate to issues of algorithmic bias, inequality, and discrimination within an increasingly data-driven society, and whereby digital tools are being deployed and embedded within multiple facets of everyday life.

Firstly, one noteworthy dimension of these projects is that the principal donors of university research funds were often the venture capitalists and technology corporate giants who had been the targets of intensified scrutiny; and the principal recipients were the same premiere computing institutions (i.e., MIT and Stanford) largely esteemed for training the top computer scientists in charge of designing and coding these systems. Indeed, the same institutions at the helm of AI interventions were also laboratories that bolstered the root causes, actors, and investors that had led to the "techlash." Those who served to benefit the most from the propagation of "fairer" systems and systems designs, in order to perpetuate the existence of these systems in the first place, at the risk losing their revenue streams entirely, were in charge of defining the terms of ethics and fairness in technology.

Moreover, taken as case studies for the dominant ideologies and frameworks of AI interventions, these initiatives demonstrate the gap of understanding, within both the academy and technology corporations, regarding the origins and implications of issues of algorithmic discrimination—and broader issues of social, political, and economic oppression, and in generating productive, effective interventions that adequately address the core concerns of critical scholars, activists, and organizers. For example, within the introductory narratives and launches of each of these centers, programs, and partnerships, it was apparent that these interventions were deeply premised and rooted in conservative and neoliberal logics for solutions, not the radical and critical frameworks that originally paved the way for discussions about the disparate and disparaging

[34] MIT News Office, "MIT reshapes itself to shape the future," *MIT News* (October 15, 2018), http://news.mit.edu/2018/mit-reshapes-itself-stephen-schwarzman-college-of-computing-1015.

[35] Stanford Institute for Human-Centered Artificial Intelligence (2019), https://hai.stanford.edu/.

[36] For sample coverage, see Sam Levin, "Google scraps AI ethics council after backlash: 'Back to the drawing board,'" *The Guardian* (April 5, 2019), https://www.theguardian.com/technology/2019/apr/04/google-ai-ethics-council-backlash.

[37] National Science Foundation, "NSF Program on Fairness in Artificial Intelligence (AI) in Collaboration with Amazon (FAI)," https://www.nsf.gov/funding/pgm_summ.jsp?pims_id=505651; National Science Foundation, "NSF Program on Fairness in Artificial Intelligence (AI) in Collaboration with Amazon (FAI): Program Solicitation NSF 19-571," https://www.nsf.gov/pubs/2019/nsf19571/nsf19571.htm.

impacts of artificial intelligence systems. Considering the values and ethics of the radical scholars, activists, and organizers who paved the way for discussions about AI ethics and AI as not neutral, it was questionable whether and how such initiatives would address the core problems and concerns about data harms and risks if their radical critiques were not considered, valued, or at least voiced within advisory board meetings and the initial conceptions of intervention projects. A detailed critique of each initiative and their collective discourses is detailed in the following.

Overview of Academic AI Interventions

First, in October 2018, the Massachusetts Institute of Technology (MIT) announced their plans for a $1 billion commitment to "world-changing breakthroughs and ethical implications" of computing and artificial intelligence, including the establishment of the MIT Schwarzman College of Computing through a large gift from Stephen A. Schwarzman, CEO and co-founder of Blackstone.[38] Largely absent within this origin story of MIT's "world-changing" and ethical institution was the acknowledgment that the new college was being primarily funded by the world's largest private equity firm, which had been publicly identified and criticized by the United Nations for its exacerbation and exploitation of the affordable housing crisis in the United States.[39] Aimed at being an interdisciplinary hub for innovation and democratic research, it remains to be seen whether and how this new MIT College will lead to more redistributive and restorative impacts to society through its research program, particularly considering its deep ties to extractive and exploitative corporations, industries, and partners.

In a similar but distinct case of the contradictory statements and values of AI ethics centers, when Stanford announced their Institute for Human-Centered Artificial Intelligence (HAI), there was scrutiny and skepticism toward Stanford University's attempt to establish this center that might ameliorate issues of algorithmic bias and discrimination while being led and advised by a cadre of the powerful stakeholders who had created the problem in the first place.[40] Namely, while Co-Director Fei-Fei Li spoke of the institute's goals of "building a better future for all of humanity" and acknowledged the need for the "creators of AI to be representative of humanity"[41] within both the press

---

[38] MIT News Office, "MIT reshapes itself to shape the future," 2018.

[39] Irina Ivanova, "U.N. blasts Blackstone Group for worsening the U.S. housing crisis," *CBS News* (March 26, 2019), https://www.cbsnews.com/news/blackstone-group-is-making-u-s-housing-crisis-worse-the-un-says/.

[40] For example, see Patrick Howell O'Neill, "Stanford's New Institute to Ensure AI Is 'Representative of Humanity' Mostly Staffed by White Guys," *Gizmodo* (March 21, 2019), https://gizmodo.com/stanfords-new-institute-to-ensure-ai-is-representative-1833464337.

[41] See O'Neill, 2019. And Stanford Center's promotional video, 0:53–1:15: Stanford University. "Introducing the Stanford Institute for Human-Centered Artificial Intelligence," *YouTube* (March 18, 2019), https://www.youtube.com/watch?v=se4CQ5UZXaM.

conference events and related promotional materials, the institute's website did not display nor reflect such values when it failed to list any Black or African American faculty members or advisers. The institute was criticized for a nonrepresentative, tone-deaf announcement about its "ethical AI" research center, especially considering how it did not center and integrate researchers and activists from, or tied to, marginalized communities and groups. (See Figure 8.2 for sample critique.)

Additionally, the Stanford institute garnered critique for its launch event, which included advisers such as former U.S. National Security Adviser and Secretary of State Henry Kissinger, who has been greatly critiqued for his role in allegedly conducting war crimes on behalf of the United States in various countries, including Vietnam, Bangladesh, and Chile, to name a few.[42] Not unlike the role of Schwarzman in the MIT initiative, Kissinger symbolizes an oppositional stance in his business and professional dealings to what many regard as *central* to framing ethics as matters germane to civil and human rights, making such personalities even more controversial given their roles in allegedly eroding democratic social values. Generally, it appeared that this institute, while incorporating language about innovating for a better, more ethical and diverse future of AI, was reproducing and profiteering from many of the same hegemonic narratives and ideologies that had produced biased and discriminatory AI systems within

 **Chad Loder** ●
@chadloder

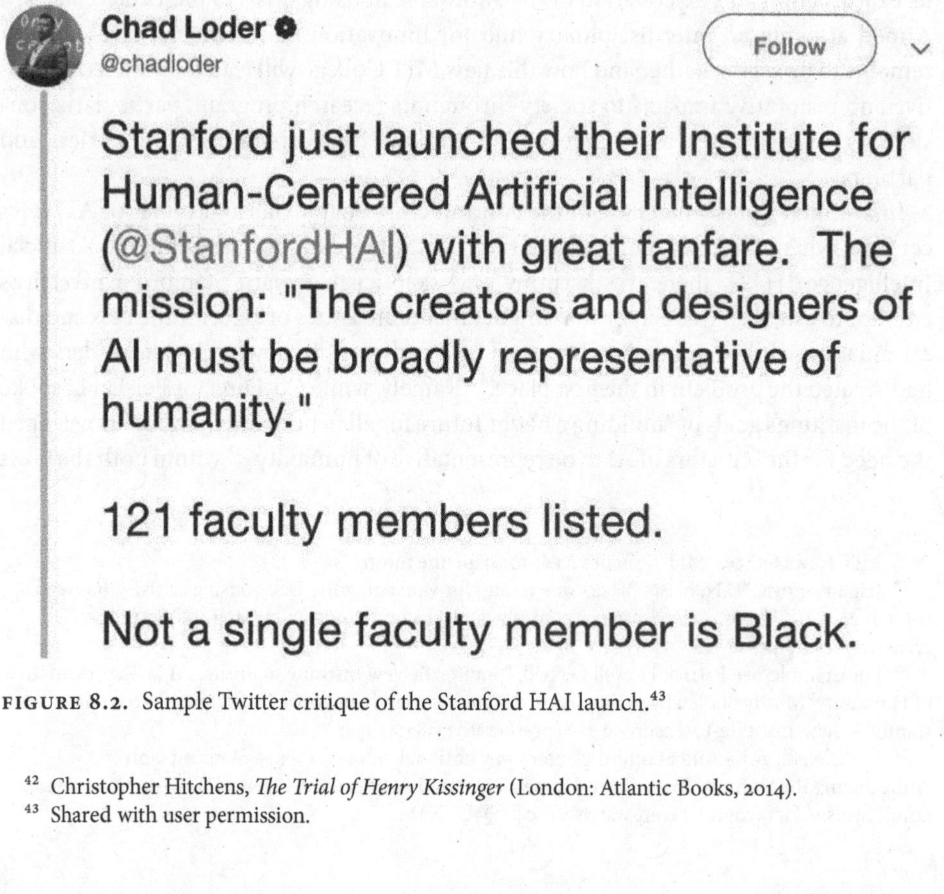

 Follow ⌄

Stanford just launched their Institute for Human-Centered Artificial Intelligence (@StanfordHAI) with great fanfare. The mission: "The creators and designers of AI must be broadly representative of humanity."

121 faculty members listed.

Not a single faculty member is Black.

FIGURE 8.2. Sample Twitter critique of the Stanford HAI launch.[43]

---

[42] Christopher Hitchens, *The Trial of Henry Kissinger* (London: Atlantic Books, 2014).
[43] Shared with user permission.

an immensely unequal postcapitalist society. Again, considering the concerns, experiences, and organizing activities of marginalized communities, activists, and advocates, which led to the perceived need for more ethical AI, the success of such initiatives seems questionable given that those most affected and penalized by such systems were not invited for their expertise or input,[44] symbolizing the tone-deaf nature of such centers, or their shallow engagement with the core concerns and critiques.

Thus, drawing from these two cases, we consider the political entanglements of investments and involvements in algorithmic interventions as a deeply complex process that warrants further attention. These two specific programs prompt us to question: Can, and will, noncommercially lucrative applications of AI and AI research be funded by these donations from benefactors who serve to profit from the commercial application of AI? Can and will noncommercial and more restorative and redistributive AI applications be prioritized, and in what ways? Moreover, what does it mean that the search for fairer, unbiased, and more ethical algorithms—ones that are not shaped by, and do not reproduce, social inequality—is largely bankrolled by capital investments from a firm that is profiting off of such inequalities in power and capital? Why is it also important to consider how those in charge of shaping, advising, and effecting fairness interventions through AI are skewed toward whiteness, wealth, and uncritical readings of technology's impact?[45]

Overview of Corporate AI Interventions

In its co-optation of critical discourse regarding AI's impacts and in an attempt to further exploit communities for its capital gains, technology giant Google announced in 2019 an ethics advisory council, the Advanced Technology External Advisory Council that would oversee the company's AI product development.[46] The council was formed by Google CEO Sundar Pichai in an effort to follow new company principles that emerged from the outrage and boycott organized by Google employees against the company's involvement in using its machine learning algorithms and AI to bolster the Pentagon's drone technology program, better known as Project Maven.[47] The effort to respond to the crisis of discrimination (both racial and gendered) and the failure to see

[44] For deeper readings regarding how black individuals are often penalized for their racial identity through data and data-driven systems, see Noble's *Algorithms of Oppression* (2018) and Benjamin's *Race after Technology* (2019).

[45] One initiative attempting to delve into these complex questions—and the implications of the precarious nature of research and development projects and conferences as contingent upon corporate sponsorship—is Funding Matters (https://fundingmatters.tech/).

[46] Nick Stat, "Google dissolves AI ethics board just one week after forming it," *The Verge* (April 4, 2019), https://www.theverge.com/2019/4/4/18296113/google-ai-ethics-board-ends-controversy-kay-coles-james-heritage-foundation.

[47] Department of Defense, "Project Maven to Deploy Computer Algorithms to War Zone by Year's End," *Department of Defense* (July 21, 2017) https://dod.defense.gov/News/Article/Article/1254719/project-maven-to-deploy-computer-algorithms-to-war-zone-by-years-end/.

ethics and justice at Google came on the heels of a walkout organized by women at Google who refused to further contend with sexual harassment, undercompensation compared to male co-workers, and a culture of that consistently undervalues and demeans women,[48] as noted by Marie Hicks, historian of women and technology. By the time the Google ethics council was formed, it included Kay Coles James, president of the Heritage Foundation, which brought about more "techlash" in the form of a call to disband the council or remove James immediately.[49] A week later, the council was canceled due to growing public outcry about its lack of diverse representation and expertise on issues of justice and technology and for its inclusion of specific actors like James with her openly expressed xenophobic, anti-immigrant, anti-LGBTQ, and transphobic views.

In response to the critiques of the initiative, Google issued a statement that it was "going back to the drawing board."[50] However, this case serves as another example of the logics of capital, whereby the accumulation strategies of multinational companies largely incorporate and engulf criticism in order to frame the debates and then forestall the interventions that would require different distributions of resources and power to create more just engagements. Moreover, Google's ability to respond to, and consider, critiques of its hegemonic power structures are further questioned in light of its punishment of activists and organizers from within the company. Specifically, in early 2019, Google employees staged a walkout in response to the growing evidence of mismanagement of personnel issues, particularly in relation to the aforementioned allegations of sexual harassment and a company culture of gender and racial discrimination. In May 2019, AI ethics researcher Meredith Whittaker and fellow Google employee Claire Stapleton, two of the female leaders of these strikes, publicly stated that their supervisors and other Google leaders had coerced and pressured them with various tactics, as attempts to penalize them for organizing the strikes.[51]

Our final case study is that from 2019 when the National Science Foundation announced a collaborative project with Amazon, Inc., wherein the two parties would "jointly support computational research focused on fairness in AI, with the goal of contributing to trustworthy AI systems that are readily accepted and deployed to tackle grand challenges facing society."[52] Like other corporate projects attempting to engage with ethics frameworks, this project largely imports language and details about the potential risks and harms of artificial intelligence systems in everyday life while deploying notions of the need for "fair" algorithms to skirt away from larger, more structural and historical issues of inequality which have been accelerated and amplified by these

---

[48] Marie Hicks, "The Long History of the Google Walkout," *The Verge* (November 9, 2018), https://www.theverge.com/2018/11/9/18078664/google-walkout-history-tech-strikes-labor-organizing.

[49] Levin, "Google Scraps AI Ethics Council after Backlash."

[50] *Id.*

[51] Veena Dubal, "Who Stands between You and AI Dystopia? These Google Activists," *The Guardian* (May 3, 2019), https://amp.theguardian.com/commentisfree/2019/may/03/ai-dystopia-google-activists.

[52] National Science Foundation, "NSF Program on Fairness in Artificial Intelligence (AI) in Collaboration with Amazon (FAI): Program Solicitation NSF 19-571," https://www.nsf.gov/pubs/2019/nsf19571/nsf19571.htm.

systems.[53] In addition, in return for their investments in research, Amazon claimed proprietary rights to any innovation derived from the federally funded research grants. In essence, the academic-corporate research partnership raised questions about the potential for conflicts of interest, and the role of state-sanctioned taxpayer funds working to underwrite AI and fairness research that would be applied in the context of bolstering Amazon's business imperatives.[54]

Synthesizing and Summarizing the State of AI Fairness

While these four examples demonstrate the contradictions of AI ethics when these projects "will always look for ways to argue for the continued existence, development, and application of AI," as Alkhatib[55] writes, these cases also collectively illustrate the more systematic and structural ways in which capitalism and their technological corporate embodiments have co-opted the critical discourse about technology's impacts and biases in search of commercial solutions and proprietary research that serve to protect the continued profits of technology corporations, particularly in light of a potential AI winter ushered in by public skepticism and scrutiny toward AI.[56] That is, while entertaining and leveraging the key terms of critiques against artificial intelligence (e.g., algorithmic "bias" and inequality), there remains little to no deep engagement within extant and emerging high-profile AI interventions to more profoundly, deeply, and adeptly interrogate the power structures and issues that undergird these critical narratives about AI's harms and risks. In pursuit of fairness and ethics, visions of justice and equity undergirding the original critiques of AI have become *techwashed*, that is, overly techno-centric, techno-deterministic, and rooted and bankrolled by neoliberal logics of corporate solutionism while obfuscating the systemic causes of such problems.

CONCLUSION

In summary, in considering the explosive growth, emergence of, and investment in high-profile AI fairness and ethics interventions within both the academy and industry,

[53] Salon Barocas and Andrew D. Selbst, "Big Data's Disparate Impact," *Cal. L. Rev.* 104, no. 3 (2016): 671–732. doi: 10.15779/Z38BG31.

[54] Benjamin Romano, "Amazon's Role in AI Fairness Research Raises Eyebrows," *Government Technology* (April 1, 2019), https://www.govtech.com/products/Amazons-Role-in-AI-Fairness-Research-Raises-Eyebrows.html.

[55] Ali Alkhatib, "Anthropological/Artificial Intelligence & the HAI," *Ali Alkhatib: Blog* (March 26, 2019), https://ali-alkhatib.com/blog/anthropological-intelligence.

[56] Ethan Fast, and Eric Horvitz, "Long-Term Trends in the Public Perception of Artificial Intelligence," *Proceedings of the Thirty-First AAAI Conference on Artificial Intelligence: AAAI-17* (2017), https://www.aaai.org/ocs/index.php/AAAI/AAAI17/paper/download/14581/13868.

alongside the mounting and proliferating calls for the interrogation, regulation, and in some cases, dismantling and prohibition of AI,[57] we contest and question the extent to which such remedies can address the original concerns and problems they are designed to address. Indeed, many community organizations are organizing responses and challenging AI used in predictive technologies, facial recognition software, and biometrics technologies with increasing success.

Furthermore, we suggest the canon of AI ethics must interrogate and deeply engage with intersectional power structures that work to further consolidate capital in the hands of technocratic elites, and that will undergird digital informational systems of inequality: there is no neutral or objective state through which the flows and mechanics of data can be articulated as unbiased or fair. It is the deployment of digital technologies and their impact that is the more interesting—and important—area of inquiry facing those who might take up the issues of disparity and oppression. Simply striving for fairness in the face of these systems of power does little to address the ways that digital technologies are increasingly central to other forms of structural power. Few of these projects ask whether AI projects should be developed at all, and to what degree there should be public oversight, and which institutions or individuals should be responsible for such oversight. Moreover, the questions about how ethics are framed, as a matter of systemic injustice in the context of historical reckonings with oppression, are rarely a leading research framework or goal.

In essence, the future of AI and ethics should be concerned with rising global social and economic inequality, the repercussions that will emerge as an effect of climate change, and the ways in which AI will be used in the redistribution of global goods and services—from housing, to food, to border-crossing, and beyond. Broadly, those of us in the fields of digital social research must center the issues of social, political, and economic inequality as an orientation to studying lived experiences in relation to structures of power that algorithms, AI, and automated systems can overdetermine—rather than assuming that technology itself can be ethically perfected or that bias is a feature of a AI or externality that can be corrected or resolved.[58]

---

[57] See sample coverage of San Francisco's ban of facial recognition: Thadani, Trisha. "San Francisco bans city use of facial recognition surveillance technology," *San Francisco Chronicle* (May 14, 2019), https://www.sfchronicle.com/politics/article/San-Francisco-bans-city-use-of-facial-recognition-13845370.php. Also, see sample resources from projects such as *Our Data Bodies*: Tawana Lewis, Seeta Peña Gangadharan, Mariella Saba, and Tamika Petty, *Digital Defense Playbook: Community Power Tools for Reclaiming Data* (Detroit: Our Data Bodies, 2018), https://www.odbproject.org/wp-content/uploads/2019/03/ODB_DDP_HighRes_Single.pdf.

[58] Authors' note: Since this chapter was drafted, there have been additional high-profile developments that have further brought questions of ethics, values, and justice in relief with the topic of AI fairness and research, most notably the MIT Media Lab's ties to an immoral donor. Unfortunately, we anticipate there will continue to be more scandals and controversies that continue to demonstrate the complicity of academic and corporate research organizations in promulgating data harms and risks under guises of techno-benevolence and ignorance. That said, our hope is that this chapter, and the critical frameworks and scholars that ground this chapter, can orient future discussions and AI interventions to be, first, more acutely attuned to the needs and experiences of those most endangered by the pernicious risks and harms of AI, and, secondly, to promote and embody a vision of justice, rather than the prevailing tech-washed notion of ethics and fairness.

BIBLIOGRAPHY

Benjamin, Ruha. *Race after Technology: Abolitionist Tools for the New Jim Code*. Medford, MA: Polity, 2019.

Chun, Wendy Hui Kyong. *Control and Freedom Power and Paranoia in the Age of Fiber Optics*. Cambridge, MA: MIT Press, 2008.

Daniels, Jessie. *Cyber Racism: White Supremacy Online and the New Attack on Civil Rights*. Lanham, MD: Rowman & Littlefield Publishers, 2009.

Eubanks, Virginia. *Automating Inequality: How High-tech Tools Profile, Police, and Punish the Poor*. New York, NY: St. Martin's Press, 2018.

Gandy, Oscar H. *The Panoptic Sort: A Political Economy of Personal Information*. Boulder, CO: Westview Press, 1993.

Hoffmann, Anna Lauren. "Where Fairness Fails: Data, Algorithms, and the Limits of Antidiscrimination Discourse." *Information, Communication & Society* 22, no. 7 (2019): 900–15. doi:10.1080/1369118x.2019.1573912.

Mills, Charles W. *Black Rights/White Wrongs: The Critique of Racial Liberalism*. New York, NY: Oxford University Press, 2017.

Noble, Safiya Umoja. *Algorithms of Oppression How Search Engines Reinforce Racism*. New York: New York University Press, 2018.

Pasquale, Frank. *The Black Box Society: The Secret Algorithms behind Money and Information*. Cambridge, MA: Harvard University Press, 2016.

Vaidhyanathan, Siva. *Antisocial Media: How Facebook Disconnects Us and Undermines Democracy*. New York: Oxford University Press, 2018.

CHAPTER 9

....

ACCOUNTABILITY IN
COMPUTER SYSTEMS

....

JOSHUA A. KROLL

THIRTY-SEVEN seconds after the launch of the Ariane 5 rocket's first flight on June 4, 1996, a software subroutine crashed, starting a chain reaction that led the rocket to self-destruct. When the software attempted to convert a 64-bit floating point number to a 16-bit unsigned integer, the too-large value of the former could not be represented in the smaller format of the latter, triggering an unhandled error condition. Fortunately, this was a "hot standby," meant to take over in the event the active copy of the software failed. Unfortunately, the active copy was running the same computation and therefore also crashed almost immediately afterward. The buggy subroutine existed to keep the rocket balanced while on the ground and was unnecessary after liftoff, but had been left to run beyond in case the launch was delayed momentarily. Cascading failures continued as the entire inertial reference subsystem crashed, causing incorrect data to feed into the rocket's guidance software. To correct what the guidance software erroneously understood as a deviation from the rocket's planned trajectory, but which was in fact a diagnostic error code indicating the failure, the rocket's software control ordered the guidance nozzles on the main engine and the boosters to maximum deflection. This caused the rocket to veer wildly off course and to experience "high aerodynamic loads," which tore the boosters off the main rocket, (correctly) triggering the rocket's self-destruct mechanism.[1] The result of this disaster was the complete loss of the launch vehicle and the onboard Cluster atmospheric research satellites, totaling about $370 million in direct losses. The failure set back by several years the European Space Agency's efforts to develop a new launch vehicle, which to that point had run for 10 years at a cost of over $7 billion.

Yet despite the root cause being a failure in the rocket's software, the inquiry board convened to analyze the accident recommended spreading responsibility across several

---

[1] Jacques-Louis Lions, Lennart Luebeck, Jean-Luc Fauquembergue, Gilles Kahn, Wolfgang Kubbat, Stefan Levedag, Leonardo Mazzini, Didier Merle, and Colin O'Halloran, "Ariane 5 Flight 501 Failure: Report by the Inquiry Board" (1996).

functions in the development, design, and implementation of the launcher, saying, "When taking this design decision, it was not analysed or fully understood," meaning that the "possible implications of allowing [the software] to continue to function [after liftoff]...were not realized." The natural human instinct in the face of such failure is to identify the cause, to assign responsibility for that cause to a person or group of people, and to tie that responsibility to consequences—in other words, to hold someone *accountable* for the failure. But after the Ariane 5 Flight 501 total launch failure, no individual, nor any part of the development team, was held directly responsible. Responsibility fell partially on several functions within the program—programmers, designers, requirement engineers, test engineers, and project managers—many of whom could have exposed the failure ahead of time, but none of whom did. Each function focused on the chosen framing of their part of the project.[2] Along with other high-profile early software failures such as Therac-25,[3] the Ariane 5 failure contributed to decades of reflection in the software community about what is necessary to make software systems reliable in critical applications.[4]

Such reflection must also be applied to artificial intelligence (AI), a term that here refers to any behavior embodied in a machine (usually, a software system) that a human would consider intelligent.[5] Concerns that such systems might not be fit for purpose have led to calls for greater governance, especially as software systems have taken over an increasing number of critical application domains in modern society. Often, such automation augments traditional human decision-makers and professionals; sometimes, it outright replaces social and economic structures formerly mediated by humans with new structures mediated by software-driven machines.[6] This chapter examines the relationship between such AI systems and the concept of *accountability*.

DEFINITIONS AND THE UNIT OF ANALYSIS

To understand accountability in the context of AI systems, we must begin by examining the various ways the term is used and the variety of concepts to which it is refers. Further,

[2] Mark Dowson, "The Ariane 5 Software Failure," *ACM SIGSOFT Software Engineering Notes* 22, no. 2 (1997): 84.

[3] Nancy G. Leveson and Clark S. Turner, "An Investigation of the Therac-25 Accidents," *Computer* 26, no. 7 (1993): 18–41.

[4] These issues are by no means software-specific, but extend to all engineering in safety-critical contexts. See, e.g., Diane Vaughan, *The Challenger Launch Decision: Risky Technology, Culture, and Deviance at NASA* (Chicago: University of Chicago Press, 1996).

[5] Such a definition can be quite problematic in itself: if a machine exhibits a certain behavior, can we really consider that behavior to be "intelligent"? As a general matter, it is cleaner to think of machines as accomplishing some task, which may have previously been thought to be beyond the reach of automation.

[6] Kroll, Joshua A., Solon Barocas, Edward W. Felten, Joel R. Reidenberg, David G. Robinson, and Harlan Yu, "Accountable Algorithms," *U. Pa. L. Rev.* 165 (2016): 633.

we must examine the *unit of analysis* or level of abstraction referenced in discourse.[7] As with many terms used in the discussion of AI, different stakeholders have fundamentally different and even incompatible ideas of what concept such terms refer to, especially when the stakeholders come from different disciplinary backgrounds or have different power relationships to the system at issue.[8] This confusion leads to disagreement and debate in which parties disagree not on substance but on the subject of debate itself. Here, we provide a brief overview of concepts designated by the term "accountability," covering their relationships, commonalities, and divergences in the service of bridging such divides.[9]

Artifacts, Systems, and Structures: Where Does Accountability Lie?

Accountability is generally conceptualized with respect to some entity—a relationship that involves reporting information to that entity and in exchange receiving praise, disapproval, or consequences when appropriate. Successfully demanding accountability around an entity, person, system, or artifact requires establishing both ends of this relationship: Who or what answers to whom or to what?

Additionally, to understand a discussion of or call for accountability in an AI system or application, it is critical to determine what things the system must answer for, that is, the information exchanged. There are many ways to ground a demand for answerability and give it normative force, and commensurately there are many types of accountability—moral, administrative, political, managerial, market, legal judicial, professional, and relative to constituency relationships.[10] Artificial intelligence systems intersect with all eight types of accountability, each in different ways and depending on the specifics of the application context.

Beyond the question of the normative backing for accountability is the question of to what unit it is applied: are we considering a single component, a larger system, or the entire structure of society in determining how accountability will be operationalized? Such unit-of-analysis questions apply to determining both what we are holding accountable

---

[7] Selbst et al. refer to failures to understand the appropriate unit of analysis as "abstraction error" and define five "traps" representing common pitfalls in problem framing. See Andrew D. Selbst, Danah Boyd, Sorelle A. Friedler, Suresh Venkatasubramanian, and Janet Vertesi, "Fairness and Abstraction in Sociotechnical Systems," in *Proceedings of the Conference on Fairness, Accountability, and Transparency,* (ACM, 2019), 59–68 https://dl.acm.org/citation.cfm?id=3287598.

[8] Deirdre Mulligan, Joshua A. Kroll, Nitin Kohli, and Richmond Wong, "This Thing Called 'Fairness': Disciplinary Confusion Realizing a Value in Technology," in *Proceedings of the Computer Supported Cooperative Work Conference* (2019), https://dl.acm.org/citation.cfm?id=3359221.

[9] An alternative but similar taxonomy is presented in *Maranke Wieringa,* "What to Account for When Accounting for Algorithms: A Systematic Literature Review on Algorithmic Accountability," in *Proceedings of the 2020 Conference on Fairness, Accountability, and Transparency (FAT* '20)* (New York: Association for Computing Machinery, 2020), 1–18, https://doi.org/10.1145/3351095.3372833.

[10] This taxonomy is due to Stone, Jabbra, and Dwivedi, *Public Service Accountability: A Comparative Perspective* (Hartford, CT: Kumarian, 1989).

and what we are holding it accountable to.[11] For example, in considering a system that predicts credit risk, we might choose to examine the instrument itself (i.e., it adequately reflects the borrower's risk of default), the larger sociotechnical context including applicants and loan officers (i.e., it functions adequately in the administration of lending, comports with actors' understanding of how it should behave, and is not subject to gaming), or the overall structure of credit analysis and lending (i.e., it does not systematically undermine credit markets or the provisioning or distribution of goods and services and does not unduly discriminate against structurally subordinated groups). Similarly, we may wish to hold it accountable to standards at a variety of levels of abstraction. Instrumentally, we may describe the system as functioning properly if and only if it adequately rates risk or rates risk in an equal way across demographic groups, holding the system's performance to an objective and mathematical standard of *correctness*. At a systems level, we might hold the credit risk predictions to a standard of defensibility in litigation or another *oversight* mechanism; at a societal level, we might ask whether the distribution of risk elucidated by the system is the correct and morally appropriate distribution, holding to a standard of *fidelity to normative goals*.

Determining the extent to which each of these standards is met requires different approaches based on the level of analysis by different actors. Correctness relates to technical decisions about a system's design. Oversight implicates a specific entity or policy in receiving and examining answers about how a system behaved. Normative fidelity, however, is constructed through social and political processes. Often, systems affect the operative norms just as much as the norms constrain system behavior. Correctness, here, has two meanings: fidelity to a specification (the usual meaning in engineering) and consonance with a normative context. Thus the operative questions are: Does a system follow the rules we have laid out for it? And are those rules the right rules?

Often, the unit of analysis referenced by someone discussing accountability relates to their disciplinary training and orientation. Those interested in technology development, design, and analysis are more likely to conceptualize the system-as-embodied-in-a-machine, situating algorithms and the agency of AI systems within machines themselves or with their designers. Political, social, and legal demands for accountability often focus around higher-order units such as sociotechnical systems of artifacts interacting with people or entire paradigms of social organization (companies, government agencies, etc.). Often, all units of analysis inform appropriate interventions supporting accountability, and attending to accountability at all levels is necessary.

Related to the unit of analysis question is the issue of causal and moral responsibility. When operationalizing accountability, it is important that the relationship of answerability corresponds either to its subject causing the condition for which it is answerable or to its being morally culpable for that condition (in some cases, law or other explicit norms will assign culpability to an entity either directly or via an oversight process).

---

[11] Wiebe E. Bijker, Thomas Parke Hughes, and Trevor J. Pinch, eds., *The Social Construction of Technological Systems: New Directions in the Sociology and History of Technology* (Cambridge, MA: MIT Press, 1989).

If no such link exists, or if the information conveyed within the accountability relationship does not establish the link, then it is difficult to find the actor accountable. Operationalizing accountability in AI systems requires developing ways to make such links explicit and communicable. For example, the scapegoating of a component or portion of the problem can impair agency of the involved actors in establishing fault. Additionally, the problem of many hands can serve as a barrier to accountability, as it did in the Ariane 5 Flight 501 failure.[12] While many hands were responsible for that failure, they were responsible collectively. This prevented any one individual or function from being responsible in a direct, causal manner and thus, in a moral sense, the whole group is responsible together. This can be seen as advantageous: without direct accountability, more exploration is possible and more risk can be taken. But this need not be the case: alternative governance structures for such multifaceted, cross-functional development teams could, for example, explicitly make leaders responsible, providing an incentive for them to ensure adequate performance and the avoidance of failures across their organization while preserving direct responsibility for moral purposes (complex systems rarely yield a clear analysis of causality[13]), which could support better outcomes in the future. Other mechanisms could also make domains of answerability clear at the level of functions or organizations.

Accountability, Oversight, and Review

If we conceptualize accountability as answerability of various kinds, and we understand who must answer, for what, and to whom the answers are intended, then we have redeveloped the concept of *oversight*, a tool for governance where a designated authority holds special power to review evidence of activities and to connect them to consequences. Oversight complements regulatory methods in governance, allowing for checks and controls on a process even when the correct behavior of that process cannot be specified in advance as a *rule*. Rather, an oversight entity can observe the actions and behaviors of the process and separate the acceptable ones from the unacceptable ones ex post. Further, when rules exist, an oversight entity can verify that the process acted consistently within them.

In computer science, and in engineering generally, the twin modalities of guaranteeing compliance with a formally stated policy ex ante and keeping records that provide for auditing ex post have long been recognized as the major approaches to understanding the fidelity of an artifact to goals such as correctness, security, and privacy.[14] However, the dominant modality—whether building software and hardware controllers, rockets and aircraft, or bridges and buildings—has been to decide on a rule up

[12] Helen Nissenbaum, "Accountability in a Computerized Society," *Science and Engineering Ethics* 2, no. 1 (1996): 25–42.

[13] Richard I. Cook, "How Complex Systems Fail," Cognitive Technologies Laboratory, University of Chicago (1998).

[14] Daniel J. Weitzner, Harold Abelson, Tim Berners-Lee, Joan Feigenbaum, James Hendler, and Gerald Jay Sussman, "Information Accountability," *Communications of the ACM* 51, no. 6 (2008): 82.

front, to express this rule as a set of requirements for the system, to implement the system so that it is faithful to those requirements, and to validate that the implementation comports with the requirements. In this way, conformance of the artifact to a rule can be known ahead of time. Such an approach is quite powerful and is often highly desirable (for example, we wish to know that a bridge will support a certain weight across a span before materials are expended in its construction). However, it is insufficient where norms are exceedingly complex, contested, or require interpretation in order to be enforced. All are features of domains where AI systems are most desirable. Such domains include the application of many legal obligations stated as standards or principles, including data protection regimes (e.g., determining whether consent is "informed"), copyright (e.g., establishing whether copying constitutes fair use), the use of protected data by law enforcement or for intelligence activities (e.g., granting orders allowing investigators access to protected information), cases involving duties of care, and situations where there exist concerns about fairness, bias, or nondiscrimination.[15] Beyond this, law enforcement is often a process of managing exceptions to rules without risking the substance of the rule itself, an inherently interpretive and discretionary exercise.

Enabling governance beyond setting rules is critical, as many norms and obligations resist formalization as concrete rules. The proper operationalization of certain value-sensitive concepts, such as fairness, may be contested among stakeholders. Achieving political consensus in such cases may require intentional vagueness or deferral of authority to a designated entity (for example, legislatures generally defer the specifics of rulemaking to regulatory authorities, who may be more knowledgeable and better able to react to changing circumstances; and they also defer the specifics of administering the law in particular cases to courts and judges, who can balance values that are in tension and review cases with more certainty as to what happened as their view is retrospective, not prospective).

Beyond this, some concepts may be *essentially contested*,[16] meaning that while stakeholders agree on the broad outlines of the concept in question, inherent in that agreement is a disagreement about the correct way to realize it in the world. Fairness is an excellent example—although many (or all) stakeholders in a particular context may wish an AI system to behave fairly, what is fair for some may not be fair for others. Setting out rules for what constitutes fairness must, of its nature, set these stakeholders in tension with each other. Privacy has also been described as an essentially contested concept.[17] Accountability provides a framework for reorganizing this problem and resolving it in a case-by-case manner: stakeholders may be able to agree on a process or

---

[15] Daniel J. Weitzner, Harold Abelson, Tim Berners-Lee, Joan Feigenbaum, James Hendler, and Gerald Jay Sussman,"Information Accountability," MIT Technical Report MIT-CSAIL-TR-2007–034, June 13, 2007.

[16] Walter Bryce Gallie., "Essentially Contested Concepts," in *Proceedings of the Aristotelian Society* 56 (1955): 167–198.

[17] Deirdre K. Mulligan, Colin Koopman, and Nick Doty,"Privacy Is an Essentially Contested Concept: A Multi-dimensional Analytic for Mapping Privacy," *Philosophical Transactions of the Royal Society A: Mathematical, Physical and Engineering Sciences* 374, no. 2083 (2016): 20160118.

mechanism for weighing countervailing concerns in particular cases even when they cannot agree on the proper operationalization of acceptable versus unacceptable behavior for a system up front. Further, deferring enforcement can make space for the interpretive nature of goals expressed as standards or principles rather than via the mechanical operation of a rule.

As oversight is critical to operationalizing accountability in practice, building AI systems that support accountability for some process (e.g., to some entity or for some property) necessitates designing those systems to support robust oversight. This implies establishing evidence of how the AI systems were created and how they are operating, enabling the job of the overseer, which may already be established for the encompassing human process.[18] In this way, accountability is tied directly to the maintenance of records. The job of the oversight entity can be characterized as applying appropriate norms from the context of the AI system's deployment to tie the actions described in those records to consequences.

Accountability as Accounting, Recordkeeping, and Verifiability

The simplest definition of accountability is in terms of accounting, that is, keeping records of what a system did so that those actions can be reviewed later. It is important that such records be faithful recordings of actual behaviors to support the reproducibility of such behaviors and their analysis. Additionally, such records must have their integrity maintained from the time they are created until the time they must be reviewed, so that the review process reliably examines (and can be seen by others to examine) faithful records that describe what they purport to describe. Finally, it is important that both the fidelity and the integrity of the records be evident both to the overseer and anyone who relies on the overseer's judgments. Oversight in which the entity being reviewed can falsely demonstrate compliance is no oversight at all.

In some cases, the causes of behaviors can be "black-boxed"—ignored for the purposes of recordkeeping. This is the case, for example, with human bureaucracies. We cannot demand a full causal explanation for the behaviors and opinions of the human functionaries in such a structure. Even if we could, an explication of their behavior in terms of neuronal activations and connections would be so complex as to be meaningless, providing little in the way of epistemic grounding for the outcome of the bureaucratic process. Instead, such processes develop explanations and justifications that are appropriately selective and contrastive, describing what needs to be known to the correct people at a useful level of abstraction.[19] Thus, determining where and how to keep

[18] Joshua A. Kroll, "The Fallacy of Inscrutability," *Philosophical Transactions of the Royal Society A: Mathematical, Physical and Engineering Sciences* 376, no. 2133 (2018): 20180084.

[19] Tim Miller, "Explanation in Artificial Intelligence: Insights from the Social Sciences," *Artificial Intelligence* 267 (2019): 1–38.

records of AI system behaviors is an important design consideration. The best way to determine which records best support accountability is to determine what oversight is necessary and to determine how to facilitate that oversight. Additionally, records are often useful directly for the subjects of decisions by AI systems or the public at large. When this is the case, the system design should also involve questions of how to develop direct accountability to subjects or the public, rather than accountability that is intermediated through political trust in an oversight entity.

Recordkeeping is a common operationalization of accountability in computer science and other technology-oriented fields.[20] Feigenbaum et al. provide a survey, taxonomizing recordkeeping along the dimensions of time and goals (when are records kept? what sorts of violations of policy do records aim to capture?), information (what information is learned about policy violations and policy violators?), and action (what, if any, actions are taken based on records of policy violations?).[21] This approach views accountability with respect to a concretely defined policy and violations of that policy. Some authors go as far as to define accountability as the property that any policy violation can be attributed to the violator in a way that allows the assignment of blame. However, as we have seen in the concept of oversight, accountability need not depend on the existence of a prespecified, concrete policy—it may also operate by synthesizing a policy extensionally ex post (i.e., based on the analysis of particular cases under normative guidance in the forms of standards and principles). Additionally, the existence of records does not immediately imply that a system is truly answerable for its behaviors or for outcomes caused by those behaviors. Records that are ignored, unseen, or simply not acted upon do little to facilitate accountability. We must expand the concept of accountability to tie the content of the records to the broader principle of responsibility.

Accountability as Responsibility

Answerability includes not just the notion that answers exist, but that individuals or organizations can be made to answer for outcomes of their behavior or of the behavior of tools they make use of. Responsibility ties actions or outcomes to consequences. Authors in this space have identified three major normative bases for this connection: *causality, fault,* and *duty*—either the actions of the entity being held accountable caused the outcome being considered, the entity is somehow culpable for the outcome irrespective of cause, or the entity is ascribed an obligation to engage in certain behaviors. All three types of responsibility, and the relationship of any to accountability, are subtle and bear unpacking. Operationalizing any one or all three to make practical the necessary accountability mechanisms and regimes is the subject of much work across several disciplines.

[20] Wendy Nelson Espeland and Berit Irene Vannebo, "Accountability, Quantification, and Law," *Annual Review of Law and Social Science* 3 (2007): 21–43.

[21] Joan Feigenbaum, Aaron D. Jaggard, Rebecca N. Wright, and Hongda Xiao, "Systematizing 'Accountability' in Computer Science," Technical Report YALEU/DCS/TRE1452 (New Haven, CT: Yale University Press, 2012).

The notion of causality is itself a complicated question with a rich history of inquiry in the form of metaphysics; we leave this history aside here. However, the dominance of the scientific approach to understanding causation in the development of technical artifacts and especially AI systems is relevant to our inquiry.[22] Because scientific approaches look to full, mechanistic explanations and experimentally validated knowledge to establish facts, they can struggle to establish the causes of some phenomena or to distinguish causal relationships from other relationships. For example, in situations where variables are confounded, it can be challenging to establish whether a measured effect is causal or illusory.[23] Confounding occurs when multiple factors correlate with a certain outcome, and there is confusion over which associations represent the cause, limiting the extent to which any one can be assigned responsibility. In building a machine-learning system for predicting mortality risk in pneumonia patients, researchers discovered that patients previously diagnosed with asthma performed better as a group, and as a result models rated them at a lower risk of near-term death. Domain experts (doctors) disagreed, noting that asthma patients have a much higher fatality risk from pneumonia than patients without an asthma diagnosis. The problem lay in a quirk of the training data: by hospital rule, patients diagnosed with pneumonia and previously diagnosed with asthma were automatically admitted to intensive care, giving that cohort more aggressive treatment and more careful monitoring, leading to better outcomes and confusing the statistical models.[24]

Further, events often have multiple causes, and reasoning about an appropriate set of causes for an event is challenging. Modern mechanisms for reasoning mathematically about causality generally only reason about simple causation or causation in the context of controlled experiments (which are often not possible for questions of interest), leading to a situation where inferences about causality formalisms tell only a portion of the story.[25] Causal analysis often proceeds by reasoning about *counterfactuals*, claims about the state of the world that would have resulted if some event did not occur, if some new event did occur, or if some observable feature of the world were different. In the context of reasoning about accountability in AI systems, counterfactuals present an interesting difficulty: when we consider how a system might have behaved in a hypothetical world different from the one we inhabit, we must understand the relationship between these worlds to interpret the counterfactual. The simplest sort of counterfactual merely introduces or removes a putative cause. In practice, the situations about which we wish to reason can involve complicated interactions or implicate existing social structures, configuring the hypothetical counterfactual world in a way that is very unlikely from the

[22] Mario Bunge, *Causality and Modern Science* (New York: Dover Publications, 2017).

[23] Momin Malik, "A Hierarchy of Limitations in Machine Learning," *arXiv preprint arXiv: 2002.05193* (2020), https://arxiv.org/abs/2002.05193.

[24] Rich Caruana, Yin Lou, Johannes Gehrke, Paul Koch, Marc Sturm, and Noemie Elhadad, "Intelligible Models for Healthcare: Predicting Pneumonia Risk and Hospital 30-Day Readmission," in *Proceedings of the 21th ACM SIGKDD International Conference on Knowledge Discovery and Data Mining* (ACM, 2015), 1721–30, https://dl.acm.org/citation.cfm?id=2788613.

[25] Judea Pearl, *Causality* (Cambridge: Cambridge University Press, 2009).

perspective of our world. For example, simply changing an individual's race or gender while holding other attributes the same is unlikely to produce a counterfactual case that can be analyzed in a sensible manner.[26] Concepts such as race and gender are co-constructed of a number of factors, and it can be challenging to find meaning in shifting the experience of a given subject so radically.

Still, causal responsibility is a key component of accountability for the simple reason that, if a system is to answer for its behavior, it is important to understand the causal origins of that behavior when possible. However, understanding the mechanisms of causation does not answer the question of why those mechanisms function in those ways, leading to the question of fault or *moral responsibility*. As in the dichotomy for correctness mentioned earlier, we can ask both what the mechanism of a decision was and, separately and normatively, whether that mechanism is the right mechanism that comports with social, political, and legal contexts and with values such as fairness and justice. Moral responsibility ascribes moral valence both to actions and to responses to those actions, such as praise for conforming to an operative norm or blame for violating it. Over and above causal responsibility, moral responsibility requires *agency*, or the ability to have behaved differently in a situation where control of the operative outcome could have been effected. For example, moral blame requires both that an entity is causally related to the event to which a moral ascription is being made and that the entity's actions were in some way faulty (that is, that different actions would in a moral sense have been better). Since Aristotle, philosophers have judged the appropriateness of moral blame by making moral judgments based on traits of relevant agents, explicitly vesting moral responsibility in the voluntary nature of a moral agent's control over its actions.[27]

This notion of agency raises an important sidebar about responsibility: the agents that can be held responsible are exactly those with sufficient agency to be ascribed causal responsibility, moral responsibility, or duties and obligations. In general, this implies that, while the objects of recordkeeping are generally machines, software, or algorithms, the entity being held answerable must be a moral agent worthy of the ascription of responsibility. The ability to be assigned responsibility is, in key ways, tied to moral "personhood." Such personhood can vest with constructed persons—corporate and socially constructed entities—as well as with natural persons. The nature of holding constructed persons accountable is different to holding natural persons responsible as responsibility can lead to punishment for natural persons in much more direct ways than it can for constructed persons.

---

[26] An excellent overview of counterfactual reasoning as it applies to AI systems can be found in Tim Miller, "Explanation in Artificial Intelligence: Insights from the Social Sciences," *Artificial Intelligence* 267 (2019): 1–38. A more detailed version of the argument against counterfactual reasoning about constructed attributes can be found in Issa Kohler-Hausmann, "Eddie Murphy and the Dangers of Counterfactual Causal Thinking about Detecting Racial Discrimination," *Northwestern University Law Review* 113 (2018): 1163.

[27] Andrew Eshleman, "Moral Responsibility," in *The Stanford Encyclopedia of Philosophy* (Winter 2016 edition), ed. Edward N. Zalta, https://plato.stanford.edu/cgi-bin/encyclopedia/archinfo.cgi?entry=moral-responsibility.

A concept tightly bound to responsibility and yet distinct from it is *liability*, the (often legal) ascription of responsibility for the plight of the victim in a particular scenario. Unlike accountability, which is a relational concept about responsibility in the sense of answerability for an action, liability is analyzed from the perspective of a debt owed to someone who has suffered harm.[28] Liability underscores the third category of responsibility, that of duty or obligation. Obligations may exist outside of answerability relationships. For example, a judge could be said to be responsible (in the sense of having a duty) for instructing a jury prior to their deliberations, but because that responsibility does not cause the judge to answer to a specific entity, we would not say that the judge is accountable for this (however, the judge could be accountable to higher courts, to voters directly, to competent representative bodies with authority to impeach, or via challenges to court procedure for failing to uphold this duty). Liability is not a substitute for accountability, although it can help to enforce or encourage accountability or to reify an agent's duties to encourage that agent to act or remain answerable for outcomes related to that agent's actions by assigning a financial cost to breaches of duties. Treating liability as a substitute for accountability leads to imperfect assessments of both. For example, in the Ariane 5 case, many different functions worked on the project and many people worked in each of those functions, obscuring lines of accountability. Yet the European Space Agency was very clearly liable for the cost of the failure and would have been liable for any related harms (for example, if the rocket had caused harm after exploding and falling to earth). Similarly, when liability is disclaimed by organizations, as it often is in the provisioning of software and AI tools, an agent using that software may have no control over how the software behaves, yet be unable to hold the creator of that software liable, let alone responsible.

Accountability as Normative Fidelity

The most abstract way that the term "accountability" is used connects the answerability relationship to broader norms, values, and fundamental rights. That is, when a system should uphold a particular political, social, or legal norm or be held to some moral standard, that requirement is often couched in terms of accountability in the sense of moral responsibility.[29] For example, Bovens, Schillemans, and Goodin observe that, in politics, "'[a]ccountability' is used as a synonym for many loosely defined political desiderata, such as good governance, transparency, equity, democracy, efficiency, responsiveness, responsibility, and integrity."[30] Political scientists often wonder whether

[28] These ideas owe a great debt to Nissenbaum's work separating accountability and liability (Nissenbaum, "Accountability in a Computerized Society," 25–42).

[29] Merel Noorman, "Computing and Moral Responsibility," in *The Stanford Encyclopedia of Philosophy* (Spring 2018 edition), ed. Edward N. Zalta, https://plato.stanford.edu/cgi-bin/encyclopedia/archinfo.cgi?entry=computing-responsibility.

[30] Mark Bovens, Thomas Schillemans, and Robert E. Goodin, "Public Accountability," in *The Oxford Handbook of Public Accountability* ed. Mark Bovens, Robert. E. Goodin, and Thomas Schillemans (Oxford: Oxford University Press, 2014), 1–22.

accountability continues to hold meaning, even when operationalizing it is straightforward in the ever-growing number of places where it is claimed as desirable.[31]

And yet, accountability provides an achievable mechanism for approaching otherwise slippery and contested normative goals. While it might not be possible to agree on definitions of "fairness" or even of "discrimination," agents and entities are still accountable for their behaviors with respect to the operative norms. Although it is noble to pursue computer systems that are "moral," "ethical," or "fair," it is not clear how to operationalize this goal or how to tell when it has been achieved. However, agents that develop or rely on these tools can be made accountable for the outcomes they bring about, enabling judgments about when and how these agents are answerable on understandings of when operative norms have been violated.

ACCOUNTABILITY AS A GOVERNANCE GOAL

This notion of accountability as normative fidelity demonstrates that accountability can serve as a governance mechanism. Because accountability is straightforwardly achievable and enables judgments about complex and contested values, it is a useful and tractable goal for governance. Systems can be designed to meet articulated requirements for accountability, and this enables governance within companies, around governmental oversight, and with respect to the public trust. Interested parties can verify that systems meet these requirements. This verification operates along the same lines that interested parties would use to confirm that any governance is operating as intended. Establishing lines of accountability forces a governance process to reckon with the values it must protect or promote without needing a complete articulation and operationalization of those values. This makes accountability a primary value for which all governance structures should strive.

Accountability versus Transparency

Accountability is often associated with transparency, the concept that systems and processes should be accessible to those affected either through an understanding of their function, through input into their structure, or both. For a computer system, this often means disclosure about the system's existence, nature, and scope; scrutiny of its underlying data and reasoning approaches; and connection of the operative rules implemented by the system to the governing norms of its context.[32] Yet transparency is often insufficient and undesirable on its own; it is best conceptualized as an instrument for achieving

[31] Richard Mulgan, "'Accountability': An Ever-Expanding Concept?" *Public Administration* 78, no. 3 (2000): 555–73.
[32] Frank Pasquale, *The Black Box Society* (Cambridge, MA: Harvard University Press, 2015).

accountability. Understanding other values—such as fairness, privacy, or nondiscrimination—requires a similar shift: transparency serves such goals instrumentally by making those values cognizable and allowing recognition of such values as they are reified in the system. If accountability is for moral agents, transparency is for instruments.

For example, a lottery is a perfectly transparent process in the abstract, and yet ensuring that a computerized lottery operates faithfully (i.e., picks uniformly from the set of entries a designated winner) is an exceptionally difficult and fraught task. Even physical lotteries require elaborate ceremonies to demonstrate that all possible numbers have been entered into a physical mixing device and sufficiently randomized, without any extra selections becoming possible.[33] Although the core selection algorithm of a lottery is simple to understand and easy to program correctly, it relies on random choices that, by construction, must not be repeatable, making review of a lottery outcome intrinsically difficult—because any random choice is as good as any other chosen value, a choice which is predictable to the lottery operator cannot be distinguished from one that is not. Even a correctly implemented software lottery can be run at low cost millions or billions of times, creating a set of winning options from which a preferred winner can be selected ex post. The problem of demonstrating that every entry in the lottery was considered on equal footing and that no additional illegitimate entries were added is difficult, though feasible to solve with modern computer science. Transparency alone is insufficient to ensure that a lottery effects its fairly simple goals. Instead, the entire process must make clear that the properties required of its outcomes hold, and that violations of those properties will be detectable, to know when the actors responsible have deviated from the goal or when the outcome is illegitimate for other reasons and can be held accountable. Similarly, the actors can be praised if the process operates faithfully.

Beyond this insufficiency, transparency is undesirable in many contexts, leading to situations where the subjects of decisions can alter their behavior strategically to violate an operative norm. For example, if procedures at a military installation's guarded gate are always the same, an adversary can establish the weaknesses in those procedures and exploit them. To prevent this, procedures are changed often, but unpredictably. If an adversary knows which procedures will be in effect on which day, they can use that knowledge to attempt to overcome the procedures when they are weakest, gaining access to the installation on days when guards are most lackadaisical. The same logic applies to employees pilfering cash from a till, to burglars approaching their target, or to smugglers crossing a border or other control point. More generally, use of some measure as a target for control often leads people to change their behavior to maximize their benefit, a phenomenon known as Goodhart's Law;[34] for example, when test scores are used as a measure of educational achievement and student achievement is the core measure of teacher performance, teachers are incentivized to train students to perform

---

[33] Joshua A. Kroll, Solon Barocas, Edward W. Felten, Joel R. Reidenberg, David G. Robinson, and Harlan Yu, "Accountable Algorithms," *U. Pa. L. Rev.* 165 (2016): 633.

[34] Charles A. E. Goodhart, "Problems of Monetary Management: The UK Experience," in *Monetary Theory and Practice*, 91–121 (London: Palgrave, 1984).

well on known tests rather than to understand the underlying material, confusing the practices of education and training.[35]

Finally, full transparency often trades off with other values related to confidentiality. Whether confidentiality protects the personal privacy of individuals affected by a computer system or the proprietary intellectual property interests of the system's creators or operators, the level of transparency required for governance often trades off the disclosure of legitimate secrets. For this reason as well, it is best to think in terms of answerability relationships and accountability for the agents who create and control AI systems when establishing computer-system governance mechanisms.

Mechanisms for Accountability in AI

Of course, transparency is a useful tool in the governance of computer systems, but mostly insofar as it serves accountability. To the extent that targeted, partial transparency helps oversight entities, subjects of a computer system's outputs, and the public at large understand and establish key properties of that system, transparency provides value. But there are other mechanisms available for building computer systems that support accountability of their creators and operators.

First, it is key to understand what interests the desired accountability serves and to establish answerability relationships: What agents are accountable to which other agents, for what outcomes, and to what purpose? Once these are established, it is clearer which records must be kept to support interrogation of this relationship and to ensure that blame and punishment can be meted out to the appropriate agents in the appropriate cases. These records must be retained in a manner that guarantees that they relate to the relevant behavior of the computer system, faithfully representing the relationship between its inputs, its logic, and its outputs. This can be accomplished with the tools of modern computer science: cryptography, software verification, and the type systems of computer programming languages. Record fidelity can be maintained across time and space using cryptography as well.

Beyond mechanisms that apply specifically to software, however, it is important to consider accountability and governance mechanisms that relate desired accountability relationships to the process of engineering and design and the function of organizations such as the companies that create software artifacts. Such tools include practices that encourage structured reflection on needs for an engineered system and how they should be captured in design; rules demanding the documentation of requirements and specifications; rules demanding testing and acceptance validation to ensure that produced artifacts comport with their documentation; and rules demanding documentation for users, operators, and oversight entities. Additionally, organizations can structure review processes adversarially and maintain rules requiring multiple authority to effect changes

---

[35] Wendy Nelson Espeland and Michael Sauder, "Rankings and Reactivity: How Public Measures Recreate Social Worlds," *American Journal of Sociology* 113, no. 1 (2007): 1–40.

to documentation or code, documenting the change management accordingly. Organizations can (and often do) demand that requirements or specifications be reviewed by expert teams for security and privacy practices, compliance, and readiness for release. Further, organizations can demand that their staff produce documentation for the public, such as impact assessments that disclose possible adverse effects of the systems being constructed.[36] Public documentation serves its function even when, and largely because, its creation forces organizations to consider how to develop systems that can be presented in the best possible light. Organizations should also ensure that the people or functions within the organization that are responsible for particular domains are clearly articulated and that these domains of responsibility are documented and widely understood. Finally, systems generally arise from a *lifecycle*, which must truly be a cycle: performance of the final system must be measured, evaluated, and considered against initial goals for future updates, fixes to the system as deployed, or workarounds for issues not immediately addressable.

Consider the Ariane 5 failure in this framework: Would thinking in terms of accountability tools have prevented the failure? The failure was caused by an explicit decision not to protect numeric conversions into certain hardware registers for the sake of efficiency, although this decision had been taken for the previous vehicle generation, the Ariane 4, and the relevant code was reused blindly. With clearer lines of responsibility for failure, it is likely that additional preflight simulation and testing could have been demanded and the problem identified. Further, more careful systems engineering would have revealed that allowing a subroutine needed only on the ground to run after liftoff was not as harmless as was believed, or at least would have invited more careful evaluation of prelaunch processes and the best way to handle momentary launch delay. One contemporary author noted of the failure that "Ariane 5 should teach us that there are 'political' facets of engineering processes. A good process needs to regulate not only how systems are designed and developed, but also how high-level decisions about that design and development are arrived at."[37] In this light, the fact that no engineering function could be held accountable for such a massive failure seems hardly surprising, even when the failure can be proximately traced to clear errors in the construction of software.

WHITHER ACCOUNTABILITY IN AI?

Where do these ideas lead us for accountability in AI systems? What ends does accountability serve and what are the means to achieving them? Human values are political questions, and reflecting them in AI systems is a political act with consequences in the

[36] Dillon Reisman, Jason Schultz, Kate Crawford, and Meredith Whittaker, "Algorithmic Impact Assessments: A Practical Framework for Public Agency Accountability," (AI Now Institute, 2018), https://ainowinstitute.org/aiareport2018.pdf.

[37] Dowson, "Ariane 5 Software Failure."

real world. We can (and must) connect these consequences to existing political decision-making systems by viewing the gap between system behaviors and contextual norms in terms of accountability. By holding actors with moral agency accountable for their actions, we can bridge the gap between the moral demands of good governance and the seeming amorality of human artefacts. Focusing on accountability builds checks that a tool's performance is consistent with a specification into a process that can validate the conformance of that tool's behavior with democratic norms, an inherently political assessment.[38]

While the need for such practices is great, and while it is critical to establish what engineered objects are supposed to do, including what is necessary to satisfy articulated accountability relationships, the actual reduction to practice of such tools in a way that demonstrably supports accountability and other human values remains an important open question for research. While many tools and technologies exist, only now are we beginning to understand how to compose them to serve accountability and other values.

BIBLIOGRAPHY

Breaux, Travis D., Matthew W. Vail, and Annie I. Anton. "Towards Regulatory Compliance: Extracting Rights and Obligations to Align Requirements with Regulations." In *14th IEEE International Requirements Engineering Conference (RE'06)*, 49–58. IEEE, 2006.

Desai, Deven R., and Joshua A. Kroll. "Trust but Verify: A Guide to Algorithms and the Law." *Harv. JL & Tech.* 31 (2017): 1.

Feigenbaum, Joan, Aaron D. Jaggard, Rebecca N. Wright, and Hongda Xiao. "Systematizing 'Accountability' in Computer Science." Technical Report YALEU/DCS/TRE1452. New Haven, CT: Yale University Press, 2012.

Kroll, Joshua A. "The Fallacy of Inscrutability." *Philosophical Transactions of the Royal Society A: Mathematical, Physical and Engineering Sciences* 376, no. 2133 (2018): 20180084.

Kroll, Joshua A., Solon Barocas, Edward W. Felten, Joel R. Reidenberg, David G. Robinson, and Harlan Yu."Accountable Algorithms."*U. Pa. L. Rev.*165 (2016): 633.

Miller, Tim. "Explanation in Artificial Intelligence: Insights from the Social Sciences." *Artificial Intelligence* 267 (2019): 1–38.

Nissenbaum, Helen. "Accountability in a Computerized Society." *Science and Engineering Ethics* 2, no. 1 (1996): 25–42.

Reisman, Dillon, Jason Schultz, Kate Crawford, and Meredith Whittaker. "Algorithmic Impact Assessments: A Practical Framework for Public Agency Accountability." AI Now Institute, 2018. https://ainowinstitute.org/aiareport2018.pdf.

Wachter, Sandra, and Brent Mittelstadt. "A Right to Reasonable Inferences: Re-thinking Data Protection Law in the Age of Big Data and AI." *Columbia Business Law Review* 2019, no. 2 (2019): 494–620.

Wieringa, Maranke. "What to Account for When Accounting for Algorithms: A Systematic Literature Review on Algorithmic Accountability. In *Proceedings of the 2020 Conference on Fairness, Accountability, and Transparency (FAT* '20)*, 1–18. New York: Association for Computing Machinery, 2020.

Weitzner, Daniel J., Harold Abelson, Tim Berners-Lee, Joan Feigenbaum, James Hendler, and Gerald Jay Sussman."Information Accountability." MIT Technical Report MIT-CSAIL-TR-2007-034. June 13, 2007.

---

[38] Jessica M. Eaglin, "Constructing Recidivism Risk." *Emory LJ* 67 (2017): 59–122.

CHAPTER 10

···

TRANSPARENCY

···

NICHOLAS DIAKOPOULOS

ACCOUNTABILITY, TRANSPARENCY, AND ALGORITHMS

ARTIFICIAL intelligence and algorithmic decision-making (ADM) technologies are hidden everywhere in today's modern society. They calculate credit scores, automatically update online prices, predict criminal risk, guide urban planning, screen applicants for employment, and inform decision-making in a range of high-stakes settings.[1] Our everyday experiences with online media are pervaded by the ability of algorithms to shape, moderate, and influence the ideas and information we are exposed to in our apps, feeds, and search engines. Given the immense potential of these systems to have consequential yet sometimes contestable outcomes in a wide swath of human experience, society should seek to hold such systems accountable for the ways in which they may make mistakes, or otherwise bias, influence, harm, or exert power over individuals and society.[2] Accountability in turn is about the relevant entity answering for and taking responsibility for a lack of apt behavior, such as a violation of some ethical expectation (e.g., autonomy, privacy, fairness) or other societal standards. But before there can be accountability of algorithmic systems, there must be some way to know if there has been a lapse in behavior. In this essay I argue that *transparency* can be a useful mechanism for monitoring algorithmic system behavior to provide the necessary informational preconditions that promote (but do not ensure) accountability.[3]

[1] Nicholas Diakopoulos, "The Algorithms Beat," in *The Data Journalism Handbook* 2, ed. Liliana Bornegru and Jonathan Gray (Amsterdam: University of Amsterdam Press, 2019); Danielle Keats Citron and Frank A. Pasquale, "The Scored Society: Due Process for Automated Predictions," *Washington Law Review* 89 (2014).

[2] Nicholas Diakopoulos, "Algorithmic Accountability: Journalistic Investigation of Computational Power Structures," *Digital Journalism* 3, no. 3 (2015): 398–415.

[3] Transparency here is not seen as an ethical principle per se, but rather as an enabling factor that can support the monitoring of behavior with respect to ethical expectations.

Transparency can be defined as "the availability of information about an actor allowing other actors to monitor the workings or performance of this actor."[4] In other words, transparency is about *information*, related both to outcomes and procedures used by an actor, and it is *relational*, involving the exchange of information between actors.[5] Transparency therefore provides the informational substrate for ethical deliberation of a system's behavior by external actors. It is hard to imagine a robust debate around an algorithmic system without providing to relevant stakeholders the information detailing what that system does and how it operates. Yet it's important to emphasize that transparency is not sufficient to ensure algorithmic accountability. Among other contingencies, true accountability depends on actors that have the mandate and authority to act on transparency information in consequential ways. Transparency should not be held to an unrealistic ideal of unilaterally leading to the effective accountability of algorithms—it must be wrapped into governing regimes that may in some instances demand answers or have the capacity to sanction.[6]

What, then, are these things that we seek to make transparent? The focus of this chapter in particular is on algorithmic decision-making (ADM) systems. ADM systems are tools that leverage an algorithmic process to arrive at some form of decision such as a score, ranking, classification, or association, which may then drive further system action and behavior. Such systems could be said to exhibit artificial intelligence (AI) insofar as they contribute to decision-making tasks that might normally be undertaken by humans, though this distinction is not particularly germane to the elaboration of algorithmic transparency described here. What's important to underscore, rather, is that ADM systems must be understood as composites of nonhuman (i.e., technological) actors woven together with human actors, such as designers, data-creators, maintainers, and operators, into complex sociotechnical assemblages.[7] Even considering systems at the far end of autonomy, which act in a particular moment without human oversight, one can still find human influence exercised during design-time.[8] If the end goal is accountability, then transparency must serve to help locate (both structurally, indirectly, and over time) the various positions of human agency and responsibility in these large and complex sociotechnical assemblages. Ultimately it is people who must be held accountable for the behavior of algorithmic systems.[9]

[4] Albert Meijer, "Transparency," in *The Oxford Handbook of Public Accountability*, ed. Mark Bovens, Robert E. Goodin, and Thomas Schillemans (Oxford: Oxford University Press, 2014), 507–524.

[5] Jonathan Fox, "The Uncertain Relationship Between Transparency and Accountability," *Development in Practice* 17, no. 4 (2010): 663–71.

[6] For an elaboration of some of the extant approaches to the governance of algorithms see: Florian Saurwein, Natascha Just, and Michael Latzer, "Governance of Algorithms: Options and Limitations," *info* 17, no. 6 (2015): 35–49.

[7] Mike Ananny, "Toward an Ethics of Algorithms," *Science, Technology & Human Values* 41, no. 1 (2015): 93–117.

[8] For a model of the spectrum of autonomous action see: Raja Parasuraman, Thomas B. Sheridan, and Christopher D. Wickens, "A Model for Types and Levels of Human Interaction with Automation," *IEEE Transactions on Systems, Man, and Cybernetics—Part A: Systems and Humans* 30, no. 3, (2000): 286–97.

[9] Despite the ability of artifacts to exhibit causal agency (i.e., the capacity to act), they do not have intentional agency (i.e., the capacity for intentional action) and therefore cannot be held responsible.

In the following sections of the chapter I elaborate on what I think is necessary to realistically implement algorithmic transparency in terms of what is disclosed and how and to whom transparency information is disclosed. Then I consider a range of moderating factors that may variably impact the success of algorithmic transparency depending on the specific details and context of an ADM system. These factors are the key to understanding how governing regimes need to be configured in order to encourage algorithmic accountability. The main contribution is to thoroughly examine the conditions that conversely encourage and challenge the efficacy of transparency as an ethical approach to algorithm governance. The chapter closes with a call to dismiss notions of "full transparency" in exchange for carefully engineered, context-specific algorithmic transparency policies.

Enacting Algorithmic Transparency

Algorithmic transparency cannot be understood as a simple dichotomy between a system being "transparent" or "not transparent." Instead, there are many flavors and gradations of transparency that are possible, which may be driven by particular ethical concerns that warrant monitoring of specific aspects of system behavior. Relevant factors include the type, scope, and reliability of information made available; the recipients of transparency information and how they plan to use it; and the relationship between the disclosing entity and the recipient.[10] These factors and their interrelationships shape the effectiveness of algorithmic transparency in contributing to accountability.

In terms of transparency information one can distinguish between transparency of the *outcomes* of a system (i.e., the what) versus transparency of the *processes* an algorithm enacts or that people enact in terms of governance applied during the design, development, and operation of a system (i.e., the how).[11] In cases where there are epistemic concerns over the uncertainty or validity of a decision outcome (e.g., predictions or the creation of new knowledge that cannot otherwise be corroborated), there may be increased need to disclose procedures and evidence of adherence to standards of accepted procedures. Different recipients will also have varying demands and needs for different types of transparency information according to their context of use and goals: a safety inspector or accident investigator may need different information to assess a

In order to ascribe responsibility (i.e., accountability) for the behavior of arbitrarily complex systems, intentional agency can be recursively traced back to those people that commissioned and/or designed the system or its component systems. For a philosophical treatment and rationale of this argument see: Deborah Johnson and Mario Verdicchio, "AI, Agency and Responsibility: The VW Fraud Case and Beyond," *AI & Society* 6, no. 4 (2018), 639–47.

[10] Paul B. de Laat, "Algorithmic Decision-Making Based on Machine Learning from Big Data: Can Transparency Restore Accountability?" *Philosophy & Technology* 104, no. 2 (2017): 525–41.

[11] For more on this distinction see: Shefali Patil, Ferdinand Vieider, and Philip Tetlock, "Process versus Outcome Accountability," in *The Oxford Handbook of Public Accountability*, ed. Mark Bovens, Robert. E. Goodin, and Thomas Schillemans (Oxford: Oxford University Press, 2014), 69–89.

system globally in comparison to a system operator or an end-user interested in the specifics of an individual decision outcome.[12] The relationships among actors can also define different mechanisms that shade the nature and quality of information made available, including disclosures that are *demand-driven* (e.g., freedom of information requests), *proactive* (e.g., self-disclosure via a website or other form of published documentation), or *forced* (e.g., leaked or externally audited).[13] Demand-driven and forced transparency can be particularly effective at shedding light on "underperformance, mismanagement, or other forms of falling short of public standards,"[14] while proactive transparency information might be strategically shaped, distorted, or unreliable and therefore less conducive to accountability.[15] At the same time, proactive transparency can still serve to stimulate the production of information that encourages an actor to attend to particular ethical considerations that they may not have reflected on otherwise. Proactive transparency disclosures should ideally include information about the procedures used to generate transparency information, such as through adherence to industry standards and epistemic principles related to accuracy and veridicality.[16]

The various factors and contingencies of what makes transparency work to promote accountability underscore the idea that it should rightly be understood as a human-centered technical communication challenge amongst various strategic actors. At a minimum, however, transparency must serve to increase available information and to present that information to people who can then make sense of it for their purposes; designers must consider *what* information to communicate and *how* to communicate that to different types of recipients. In the following subsections I sketch this out in abstract terms, but in practice the questions of what to disclose and how to disclose it to stakeholders will be highly context-specific and will benefit from human-centered design processes that allow for tailoring to specific use-cases.

What Can Be Made Transparent about Algorithms?

Algorithms are sometimes framed as black boxes that obscure their inner workings behind layers of complexity and technically induced opacity.[17] Indeed, the most sophisticated models may rely on millions of parameters resulting in mathematical functions that confound human efforts to fully understand them. At the same time, various pieces

---

[12] Alan F. T. Winfield and Marina Jirotka, "Ethical Governance Is Essential to Building Trust in Robotics and Artificial Intelligence Systems," *Philosophical Transactions of the Royal Society A* 376 (2018).

[13] Meijer et al., "Transparency"; Fox, "Uncertain Relationship."

[14] Meijer et al., "Transparency"

[15] Nelson Granados and Alok Gupta, "Transparency Strategy: Competing with Information in a Digital World," *MIS Quarterly* 37, no 2. (2013): 637–41.

[16] Matteo Turilli and Luciano Floridi, "The Ethics of Information Transparency," *Ethics and Information Technology* 11, no. 2 (2009): 105–12.

[17] Jenna Burrell, "How the Machine "Thinks": Understanding Opacity in Machine Learning Algorithms," *Big Data & Society* 3, no. 1 (2016); 1–12.

of information *can* nonetheless be produced to elaborate their design and implementation, characterize their process and output, and describe how they are used and function in practice. They are knowable, I would argue, to enough of an extent that they can be governed. Consider an analogy to your favorite restaurant. Even while the recipes themselves may only be known to the chef, a kitchen inspection can still expose issues with the ingredients or their handling. The transparency information exposed via a restaurant inspection, while incomplete, is nonetheless effective in improving restaurant food safety.[18]

If transparency is to contribute to governance of algorithmic systems, policy makers first need to articulate the range of possible bits of information that could feasibly be made available about such systems. For starters, in order to provide basic awareness, ADM systems should disclose that there is in fact an algorithmic process in operation. In addition to that, there are many other types of information that might be disclosed about algorithmic systems across several key layers that research has begun to elaborate, including the level and nature of human involvement; the data used in training or operating the system; and the algorithmic model and its inferences, which I briefly outline in the following subsections.

Human Involvement

Human decisions, intentions, and actions are woven into and throughout ADM systems in a way that can sometimes make them difficult to see or parse from some of the more technical components. Yet these design decisions and intentions (e.g., what variables to optimize in the design, or whether specific ethical principles have been attended to) can have important consequences for the ethical performance of a system.[19] An effective application of algorithmic transparency should strive to locate the relevant aspects of human involvement in the design, operation, and management of a system. For instance, some AI systems will keep humans in the loop during operation, examining the suggestions of the AI system to arrive at a final decision output, providing feedback to the system to improve it, or even stepping in during automation failure.[20] Transparency regarding design decisions about the level of automation and the nature and type of human involvement would shed light on human agency within the operational system. Transparency might also entail explaining the organizational goal, purpose, or intent of the ADM system. What are the intended uses and out-of-scope uses as envisioned by the designers? This can help avoid emergent biases that may arise as the context around a system changes and evolves.[21] A system might also be transparent by

[18] Archon Fung, Mary Graham, and David Weil, *Full Disclosure: The Perils and Promise of Transparency* (New York: Cambridge University Press, 2009).
[19] Felicitas Kraemer, Kees van Overveld, and Martin Peterson, "Is There an Ethics of Algorithms?" *Ethics and Information Technology* 13, no. 3 (2010): 251–60.
[20] Parasuraman et al., "Model for Types and Levels."
[21] Batya Friedman and Helen Nissenbaum, "Bias in Computer Systems," *ACM Transactions on Information Systems* 14, no. 3 (1996): 330–47.

identifying the individuals who had responsibility for engineering, maintaining, and overseeing the design and operation of the system, with the idea that individuals might feel a greater sense of responsibility if their name and reputation are at stake.[22] If contact information is included, then responsible people involved in the system could offer avenues for redress in the face of adverse events associated with the system.[23]

The Data

Data is a core component of most ADM systems, particularly those that rely on machine-learning models that can learn patterns from sets of training examples. If data is biased, then the model that is learned from that data will also exhibit that bias. For example, the *New York Times* and other online outlets use statistical models to help moderate their online comments. A corpus of comments that have been evaluated manually are used to train an algorithm so that it can classify future comments as "toxic" or "nontoxic" automatically. But the people who rate and grade comments for the training data end up having their own biases built into the system. And research has shown that men and women rate toxicity of comments in subtly different ways. When men produce the majority of the training data, then this bias is expected to be reflected in the subsequent decisions such a classifier makes.[24]

Standards for data documentation and disclosure, such as DataSheets for Datasets and the Dataset Nutrition Label as well as some of my own work, begin to outline the various ways in which creators of ADM systems can be transparent about the data they are using and their rationale for various data-related design decisions.[25] An important dimension of transparency relates to the quality of the data used, including its accuracy, completeness, timeliness and update frequency, and uncertainty. Other factors might be disclosed such as the representativeness of a sample for given populations of interest, the provenance of a dataset in terms of who initially collected it (including the motivations, intentions, and funding of those sources), as well as any other assumptions, limitations, exclusions, or transformations related to editing, preprocessing, normalizing, or cleaning

[22] Nicholas Diakopoulos, "Accountability in Algorithmic Decision Making," *Communications of the ACM (CACM)* 59, no. 2 (2016): 56–62.

[23] Nicholas Diakopoulos and Sorelle Friedler, "How to Hold Algorithms Accountable," *MIT Technology Review*, November 2016, https://www.technologyreview.com/s/602933/how-to-hold-algorithms-accountable/.

[24] Reuben Binns, Michael Veale, Max Van Kleek, and Nigel Shadbolt, "Like Trainer, Like Bot? Inheritance of Bias in Algorithmic Content Moderation," in *Social Informatics. SocInfo 2017*, ed. Giovanni Luca Ciampaglia, Afra Mashhadi, and Taha Yasseri, vol.10540, Lecture Notes in Computer Science (Cham: Springer International Publishing, 2017).

[25] Sarah Holland, Ahmed Hosny, Sarah Newman, Joshua Joseph, and Kasia Chmielinski, "The Dataset Nutrition Label: A Framework to Drive Higher Data Quality Standards," *Arxiv* (2018); Timnit Gebru, Jamie Morgenstern, Briana Vecchione, Jennifer Wortman Vaughan, Hanna Wallach, Hal Daumeé III, and Kate Crawford, "Datasheets for Datasets," *Workshop on Fairness, Accountability, and Transparency in Machine Learning* (2018); Nicholas Diakopoulos and Michael Koliska, "Algorithmic Transparency in the News Media," *Digital Journalism* 5, no. 7 (2017): 809–28.

the data.[26] Transparency should include the definitions and meanings of variables in the data, as well as how they are measured since this can be consequential to the later interpretation or contestation of model outputs. For interactive and personalized systems it may furthermore be possible to be transparent about the dimensions of personal data that are being used to adapt the system to the individual. When data about people is collected and used by an ADM system (in operation or during training), it may be appropriate to disclosure whether consent was obtained. Various policy decisions about the use of data in an ADM can also be made transparent. These might include disclosing the entity responsible for maintaining a dataset; describing how it will be updated; and indicating whether the data is public, private, or has some distribution license or copyright associated with it.

The Model and Its Inferences

Much like for data, previous work has begun to enumerate the various aspects of computational models that could be made transparent.[27] Details of the model to disclose might include the features, weights, and type of model used as well as metadata like the date the model was created and its version. A model might also incorporate heuristics, thresholds, assumptions, rules, or constraints that might be useful to disclose, along with any design rationale for why or how they were chosen. In some cases code-level transparency of a model could be necessary; however, often more abstracted and aggregated forms of information disclosure will be more useful and can be produced if the model itself is made available (e.g., via an Application Programming Interface (API) which allows external entities to query the system for data, or as an executable software routine). For example, the output inferences from an algorithmic process, such as classifications, predictions, or recommendations, can be identified and benchmarked using standard datasets in order to tabulate and disclose performance in comparison to expectations. This may be particularly pertinent in cases where issues of fairness are of concern and where fairness across various demographic categories can be evaluated. Transparency information might also include error analysis, remediation, or mitigation procedures for dealing with errors as well as confidence values or other uncertainty information for inferences. The human role and rationale in the modeling process may also be important to disclose: When assessing model performance, what metrics were used and why? For instance, different stakeholders may be differently impacted if a model is tuned to reduce false negatives instead of false positives.[28]

[26] For more details on various issues related to ethical data collection and transformation see: Nicholas Diakopoulos, "Ethics in Data-Driven Visual Storytelling," in *Data-Driven Storytelling*, ed. N. Riche, C. Hurter, N. Diakopoulos, and S. Carpendale (Boca Raton, FL: CRC Press, 2018), 233–48.

[27] Margaret Mitchell, Simone Wu, Andrew Zaldivar, Parker Barnes, Lucy Vasserman, Ben Hutchinson, Elena Spitzer, Inioluwa Deborah Raji, and Timnit Gebru, "Model Cards for Model Reporting," *Proceedings of the Conference on Fairness, Accountability, and Transparency* (2019), 220–9; Diakopoulos and Koliska, "Algorithmic Transparency in the News Media."

[28] See chapter 6 in: Nicholas Diakopoulos, *Automating the News: How Algorithms Are Rewriting the Media* (Cambridge, MA: Harvard University Press, 2019).

Who and What Are Transparency Disclosures For?

Contrary to some characterizations of ADM systems as unknowable black boxes, it should be clear from the preceding section that there is still a lot of potential information that *could* be disclosed about algorithms. But this information must be presented to recipients and stakeholders in ways that they can actually make sense of and connect to their specific goals—designers must strive for *usable transparency*. Considering the entire gamut of potential information that could be disclosed, how can designers craft that information into meaningful and useful presentations for people? Again, this will be highly context-specific and will depend on the tasks of the end-user and what types of decisions they might be trying to make based on the behavior of the algorithm in question. In this sense, algorithmic transparency must draw on human-centered design methods in order to model the user and their need for the transparency information that might be disclosed. What could a user know about an algorithm that would change their interaction with the system or the ultimate decision and outcome? Such designs should then be evaluated to assess how well end-users are able to understand disclosures for their intended purposes.

Pragmatically speaking, transparency information can be formatted in a number of different modalities such as in structured databases or documents, in written texts (perhaps even using natural language generation), or via visual and interactive interfaces.[29] The appropriate modality will depend on the specifics of the information in conjunction with user goals. Interactivity in presentation can furthermore enable end-users to interrogate the system in different ways, allowing them to adapt the transparency information they attend to based on their context and goals. Interactive and dynamic displays of transparency information may also be well-suited to algorithms that are changing and therefore need to be monitored over time. Alternatively, different presentations of transparency information can be produced for different audiences and linked into a multilevel "pyramid" structure of information, which progressively unfolds with denser and more detailed transparency information the further any given stakeholder wants to drill into it.[30]

At this point it's worth differentiating transparency disclosures from more particularized expressions of algorithm behavior intended for end-users, such as explanations, justifications, or rationales.[31] Explanation entails a system articulating how it made a particular decision and is typically *causal* (e.g., input influence or sensitivity-based) or involves case-based comparisons,[32] whereas transparency disclosure involves *descriptions*

---

[29] For an example see: Diakopoulos, "Accountability in Algorithmic Decision Making."

[30] Nicholas Diakopoulos, "Enabling Accountability of Algorithmic Media: Transparency as a Constructive and Critical Lens," in *Towards Glass-Box Data Mining for Big and Small Data*, ed. Tania Cerquitelli, Daniele Quercia, and Frank Pasquale (Cham: Springer, 2017), 25–43.

[31] Brent Mittelstadt, Chris Russell, and Sandra Wachter, "Explaining Explanations in AI," *Proceedings of the Conference on Fairness, Accountability, and Transparency* (2019), 279–88.

[32] Reuben Binns et al., "'It's Reducing a Human Being to a Percentage': Perceptions of Justice in Algorithmic Decisions," *Proc. Human Factors in Computing Systems (CHI)* (2018).

of system behavior and design intent but leaves any final causal explanation of system behavior to the evaluation of information disclosures by interested stakeholders. The problem with system-produced explanations is that they are often approximate and can fail to accurately represent the true causality of a decision. They are also selective in their presentation and can leave out inconvenient information. Consider for a moment the types of explanations you might have seen on platforms like Facebook or Twitter describing why you saw a particular ad on the site. The system told me I was seeing an ad because the advertiser wanted to reach "people ages 25 to 55 who live in the United States." But how can I be sure that this explanation is not hiding information that is more precisely indicative of why I am seeing the ad—particularly because I know that I visited the advertiser's site earlier in the day and am aware that the ad system is likely targeting me because it has tracked me across sites. System-generated explanations may add to the repertoire of information that can be disclosed, including "what if" contrasts of behavior that can aid understanding, but those explanations themselves must then be made transparent so that the algorithm generating the explanation can be held accountable for any unethical behavior such as deception, leaving out pertinent details, or shaping an explanation to suggest a conclusion advantageous to the system operator. To return to the premise of this chapter: if the end goal is accountability, then I would argue that presentations of transparency information to stakeholders should not rely on system-generated explanations but rather should strive to enable stakeholders to come to their own conclusions about system behavior.

Problematizing Algorithmic Transparency

Enumerating what could be disclosed about algorithms and how that relates to who that information is disclosed to is necessary for seeing how transparency could contribute to the accountability of algorithms. Nonetheless, as I will elaborate in the following subsections, there are many conceptual and pragmatic factors that collectively problematize the application and efficacy of transparency for the purposes of algorithmic accountability.[33] These include issues like gaming and manipulation, understandability, privacy, temporal instability, sociotechnical intermingling, costs, competitive concerns, and legal contexts. Criticisms of transparency often cite one or more of these issues. But these factors should be understood less as undermining the premise of transparency than as moderators that must be taken into account in order to design and configure an

---

[33] Mike Ananny and Kate Crawford, "Seeing without Knowing: Limitations of the Transparency Ideal and Its Application to Algorithmic Accountability," *New Media & Society* 20, no. 3 (2018), 973–89; de Laat, "Algorithmic Decision-Making Based on Machine Learning"; Jakko Kemper and Daan Kolkman, "Transparent to Whom? No Algorithmic Accountability without a Critical Audience," *Information, Communication & Society* 19, no. 4 (2018), 2081–96.

effective implementation of algorithmic transparency for any specific context. In other words, policy makers might consider how these factors create constraints or bounds on the type and scope of transparency disclosures made to certain stakeholders and what that means for the efficacy of the transparency regime for contributing to accountability.

Gaming and Manipulation

Algorithmic transparency calls for the disclosure of information about a range of human involvements, the data used to train and operate a system, and the model itself and its inferences. A concern that arises is that such rich disclosures could enable entities to manipulate the behavior of the system by strategically or deceptively altering their own behavior, which may then undermine the efficacy of the system or potentially even lead it toward unethical behavior. But this concern must be treated with contextual sensitivity. In some cases entities will have no direct control over a particular factor that an algorithm attends to (e.g., it is intrinsic and not behavioral) and it would therefore be difficult to game. Moreover, in some cases, efforts to game system behavior may result in shaping toward some preferred behavior by entities. For example, disclosing the exact criteria used by credit-rating agencies might influence end-users to act more financially responsible in order to "manipulate" their credit score in a positive direction. In general, for any particular context designers must ask: If this particular type of information about the system were disclosed to this particular recipient, how might it be gamed, manipulated, or circumvented? Taking a cue from security practices that develop threat models to identify weaknesses in systems, I would suggest that techniques and approaches for *transparency threat modeling* be developed. Such threat modeling might consider who would stand to gain or lose from a potential manipulation; what the consequences and risks of that manipulation might be to individuals, the public, or various organizations; what the barriers and other costs to manipulation might be; and whether some aspects of the system could be made more manipulation-resistant.

In some contexts such an analysis might reveal that a particular piece of information made transparent could lead to manipulation that is unsafe. As an example, consider the ability of an autonomous vehicle to visually recognize a stop sign and stop the vehicle. Demonstrations have shown that it is possible to fool some AI systems into not seeing a stop sign when very particular types of visual noise are added to the sign. Therefore there is a risk that the AI could be manipulated in such a way that it would run through a stop sign that it did not recognize, cause an accident, and potentially injure someone. Under these circumstances, should the car manufacturer make transparent to the public the vision model that the car uses so that its specific vulnerabilities can be pinpointed? Probably not. But I would argue that the model should be disclosed to a different set of recipients, namely, trusted or certified safety auditors (potentially working for a regulatory agency), who might develop a series of benchmarks that assess the susceptibility of the vision system to stop sign deception. Designers should not assume that the potential for gaming implies that no transparency should be provided, only that they look to *scope the type of information disclosed and to whom.*

Understandability

One of the concerns related to algorithmic transparency is that it could lead to a surfeit of information that is difficult to parse and align with questions of accountability and ethical behavior. Most people will not be interested in most transparency information, though I would be cautious of heeding assertions of limited end-user demand or usage of transparency information. The provision of transparency information is not about popular demand as it only takes a few interested stakeholders to be able to use transparency information for the purposes of accountability. Some set of critical and engaged recipients for transparency information, along with the appropriate expertise to make sense of and evaluate that information, is essential.[34] Ideally the presentation and formatting of transparency information should be aligned with the goals of recipients in order to make it as easy to understand and use as possible. Of course, as a strategic move aimed at concealment, some actors might choose to disclose so much transparency information that it becomes overwhelming, even for well-equipped stakeholders. To mitigate this type of behavior, regulatory interventions might systematize the scope and presentation of particular types of transparency information for specific contexts.

In some cases disclosure of more technically detailed and difficult to understand transparency information, such as the underlying computer code for a system, may be warranted. The expectation is not that everyone will look at it. Nor is the expectation that everything related to the behavior of the system could be gleaned from the code, since there are often complex interactions between code, data, and human components of the system. The point is that in some high-stakes decision arenas some stakeholders may want to audit the code to ensure that it is implemented according to high professional standards and that the implemented procedure reflects the intended policy. If it is apparent that engineers avoided adhering to a process, like an industry best practice, that could have avoided an ethically negative outcome, they might be deemed "culpably ignorant" or perhaps even negligent.[35] Moreover, this type of inspection is important in cases where there may be epistemic ethical concerns around the conclusiveness and validity of evidence produced by a system. In open science, scientists increasingly strive to be transparent with their methods, data, and code in part so that the derivation of new knowledge can be inspected and validated. All of this is to say that depending on the specific ethical concerns at stake, different levels of complexity of information may

---

[34] Kemper and Kolkman, "Transparent to Whom?"
[35] Carolina Alves de Lima Salge and Nicholas Berente, "Is That Social Bot Behaving Unethically?" *Communications of the ACM (CACM)* 60, no. 9 (2017), 29–31.

need to be disclosed about algorithmic systems in order to ensure monitoring by the appropriate stakeholders.

Privacy

Transparency information can sometimes come into tension with other ethical considerations, such as individual privacy. If sensitive private data about an individual were to be openly disclosed, this information could be unfairly used against that person or undermine their autonomy in other ways. And whereas disclosing a degree of private information about public officials may be ethically permissible in some contexts (e.g., journalism), the normative standards for ordinary people may be different. Even in cases where private data are not directly disclosed, detailed methodological information can sometimes permit deanonymization using other publicly available information.[36] Ultimately the risk of privacy violations, their implications for different types of individuals, and their derivability from transparency disclosures either directly or indirectly will need to moderate algorithmic transparency policies.

Temporal Instability

Algorithms have the potential to be highly dynamic, learning from new data as it becomes available. Or they can be relatively slow moving depending on when the responsible people get around to updating the system. Randomness can inject uncertainty into the outputs of algorithms. The common practice of A/B testing can cause different people to experience different versions of an algorithm at the same point in time. And some internal states of systems may be ephemeral—scratch memory that may be consequential yet is not recorded in any durable way. The temporal dynamics of algorithms create practical challenges for producing transparency information: What is the right sampling interval for monitoring and disclosure? To what extent should audit trails record internal and intermediate states of the machine? And how does this trade off against the resources needed for that monitoring? With algorithms potentially changing quickly, transparency presentations may also need to utilize dynamic or interactive techniques to convey information. This also raises the question of navigating and potentially comparing between different sets of transparency information. In general, algorithmic transparency as it relates to accountability should attend more to the issue of *versioning*. For instance, an investigation into the Schufa credit-scoring algorithm in Germany indicated there were four versions of the score in use.[37] Should earlier versions

---

[36] Diakopoulos, "Enabling Accountability of Algorithmic Media."

[37] Nicholas Diakopoulos, "What a Report from Germany Teaches Us about Investigating Algorithms," *Columbia Journalism Review*, January 2019, https://www.cjr.org/tow_center/investigating-algorithims-germany-schufa.php.

of the score be considered obsolete and retired? Transparency disclosures might meaningfully distinguish different versions of algorithms and provide rationale for changes including explanations for why and in what contexts older versions might still be appropriately used. More generally, any algorithmic behavior that is being monitored via transparency disclosures must be tied to version information in order to ensure accurate interpretations of that behavior.

Sociotechnical Complexity

This essay focuses on ADM systems that are sociotechnical in nature, combining non-human and human actors in their design and operation. While there is no doubt that humans must be held accountable for the impacts of these systems, their complexity can challenge straightforward attempts to assign responsibility. Human decisions may be removed in space and time from the ultimate causal efficacy of systems. For instance, machine-learning procedures may help the system evolve over time though they are still subject to the definitions, parameterizations, and constraints imposed by initial designers. Data is another way that ADM systems launder human influence. As described earlier, data that is used to train machine-learning systems may be produced by people whose biases are then learned and represented in the model. A search engine like Google might suggest a biased (e.g., discriminatory) search autocompletion because it has learned a word association based on the queries typed in by other users. The convoluted interrelationships among different technical and human components often complicate and tend to obfuscate accountability for lapses of ethical behavior. This is a fundamental area of inquiry that demands more research toward understanding distributed responsibility in a network of human and algorithmic entities. Can impacted individuals blame a biased autocompletion on the thousands of people who each contributed a biased query that Google's algorithm learned from? No, I would argue they should not. Principal-agent relationships come into play here. The search engine organization is the principle designing the autocompletion algorithm and is therefore responsible for ensuring the ethical synthesis of information from diverse agents to whom it has delegated data input (i.e., end-users typing in queries). In general what is needed is a "responsibility map" of a sociotechnical assemblage that shows principal-agent relationships and models the assignment or apportionment of responsibility based on the ethical expectations of each of those actors.[38] An interesting challenge for future research is to produce such maps using structured data such that the responsible actors could be automatically identified in the system according to different types of failures.

[38] Brent Daniel Mittelstadt, Patrick Allo, MariarosariaTaddeo, Sandra Wachter, and Luciano Floridi, "The Ethics of Algorithms: Mapping the Debate," *Big Data & Society* 3, no. 2 (2016).

Costs

On the more pragmatic side of concerns are the costs associated with producing transparency information, which might include the time and effort required to prepare data, write detailed documentation, interview engineers and designers to elicit their knowledge of the design process, run benchmark tests, polish source code, and produce publishable presentations for different recipients. New or incremental costs may be incurred with every update of the system. Transparency policies will need to consider such costs in outlining the type and scope of information that is expected in disclosures. This will depend on context, including the stakes of the decisions made by the systems under consideration. For instance, a high-stakes decision exercised by the government with implications for individual liberty (e.g., a criminal risk assessment system) should be less concerned with the costs of providing whatever transparency information is deemed necessary to ensure the accountability of the exercise of state power.

Competitive Concerns

Disclosing information about how a system works can lead to organizational concerns about undermining technical advantages in the market. Disclosing too much detail about a system could make it easier for competitors to imitate. Even while disclosing some information in patents, corporations may want to retain other information as trade secrets in order to maintain competitive advantages, such as around how algorithms are configured and parameterized. This is not only an issue for algorithms used in the private sector, since governments often procure systems from private industry to use in the public sector. But here again it is important to underscore that transparency is not all or nothing and that various shades of transparency may be useful for the sake of accountability while respecting property rights such as trade secrets. Full technical transparency may not always be called for, but in cases where it is needed (e.g., in high-stakes decisions) and comes into tension with trade secrets, systems might be made available for closed review to specific recipients that are both legally bound and in a position of authority for assessing the system.[39] In such cases, process transparency related to the conditions, procedures, and entities involved in closed review should be provided.

Legal Context

The legal environment may alternately enable or constrain access to transparency information through different avenues, such as via demand-driven, proactive, or forced

---

[39] Citron and Pasquale, "Scored Society"; de Laat, "Algorithmic Decision-Making Based on Machine Learning."

mechanisms. For algorithms developed in government, freedom of information (FOI) regulations enable demand-driven access by stipulating the types of information that members of the public are permitted to request. While some attempts to request information about algorithms in the United States have been successful,[40] others have shown inconsistency in the application of these laws.[41] A variety of exceptions, such as national security, privacy, and law enforcement, may be cited in rejecting requests for information. Trade secrecy exceptions and confidentiality agreements may also come into play when the government has contracted with industry. Yet despite these uneven results, public records requests can still produce useful information about algorithms in use. Records relating to contracts, software (in some cases even code), data, mathematical descriptions, training materials, validation studies, correspondence, or other documentation can all offer context for how a system works and what the design goals and expectations for operation are. In the private sector, public records requests are not typically possible except in specific narrow cases. For instance, individuals can sometimes request a report detailing the factors that have played into the calculation of their credit score. In Germany reporters were able to leverage this pinhole of transparency by crowdsourcing thousands of these requests from individuals and then aggregating them to build up an overview of a credit scoring algorithm's behavior.[42]

Regulation could also directly specify the dimensions and scope of information to be disclosed proactively by entities (e.g., nutrition labeling), standardize procedures for the accurate production of transparency information, and develop auditing or accounting regimes to ensure those standardized procedures are faithfully implemented. Such regulations should be considered on a case-by-case basis, taking the full context of a system into account and avoiding overly broad mandates. Regulation in this area is still at a nascent stage, with some early endeavors such as the General Data Protection Regulation (GDPR) in the European Union. Future regulation should take on a larger role for standardizing what information should be disclosed and to whom in particular high-stakes contexts of use.

Legal context also impacts the permissibility and legality of forced transparency mechanisms applied to algorithms. This comes up in the context of auditing and reverse engineering, which may involve accessing an algorithm systematically in order to record its response to variations in inputs.[43] In the US context, the American Civil Liberties Union (ACLU) has raised concerns that the Computer Fraud and Abuse (CFAA) statute

[40] Diakopoulos, "Accountability in Algorithmic Decision Making."
[41] Katherine Fink, "Opening the Government's Black Boxes: Freedom of Information and Algorithmic Accountability," *Information, Communication, & Society* 21, no. 10 (2018), 1453–71; Robert Brauneis and Ellen Goodman, "Algorithmic Transparency for the Smart City," *Yale Journal of Law & Technology* 20 (2018).
[42] Diakopoulos, "What a Report from Germany Teaches Us about Investigating Algorithms."
[43] Nicholas Diakopoulos, *Algorithmic Accountability Reporting: On the Investigation of Black Boxes*, Tow Center for Digital Journalism (2014); Christian Sandvig et al., "Auditing Algorithms: Research Methods for Detecting Discrimination on Internet Platforms," presented at International Communication Association Preconference on Data and Discrimination Converting Critical Concerns into Productive Inquiry, Seattle, WA, 2014.

may imply that website Terms of Service (ToS) agreements, which prohibit activities such as scraping, could form a basis for liability under CFAA. This in turn may create a chilling effect on the ability of researchers and journalists to gather information on algorithmic behavior, such as whether a system is treating different inputs fairly. Should it be legal to audit private systems that are accessible publicly, such as through the internet? While there may be moderating considerations (e.g., the resource demands external auditors may place on a system), regulators will need to further grapple with how to carve out space for forced transparency, especially given that it is oftentimes more effective for exposing wrongdoing than proactive transparency.

DISCUSSION

Some mythical ideal of "full transparency" is both not practically achievable and can run into a variety of problems as outlined in this chapter. Full transparency might undermine privacy, depending on the particular case—the specific context matters. Or, full transparency might produce so much information that it's not understandable. Okay, but is society willing to forgo the possibility of accountability for high-stakes ADM systems, or can it put transparency guidelines in place to ensure understandability? Or full transparency may be *impossible* for algorithms because they are black boxes that are unknowable by the human mind. In some cases, yes, but they are still knowable enough to govern them. Pragmatically, transparency is merely about producing information that promotes the effective governance and accountability of a system. We need not concern ourselves with "full" transparency. As I have outlined in this chapter, there is still plenty of information that can be disclosed about algorithms. And that information can inform the effective governance of these systems. What society needs are transparency policies that are thoughtfully contextualized to specific decision domains and supported by governance regimes that take into account a range of problematizing factors. By defining ethical concerns at the outset of design for a system, information production processes can be developed to effectively monitor for violation of that ethical issue. But such information production processes must be supported by thoughtful regulation that sets the legal context for disclosure, articulates the venue for evaluating the information, and has the capacity to compel or sanction if needed.

Moving forward, I would recommend more of an engineering approach to designing transparency policies for specific high-stakes ADM contexts. Firstly, clear context-specific ethical issues need to be identified as well as system behaviors that would indicate a violation of that ethical issue. Then, the information needed to monitor behavior for a violation needs to be enumerated and a process for producing that information must be put into place. These steps need to be done with a human-centered sensitivity in order to align them with stakeholders' needs and capacities for processing the information. Finally, the governing regime needs to account for weaknesses or threats that might undermine efficacy, potentially implementing regulatory measures that are contextually specific. In some cases the countervailing forces may be too great, overcoming the desire or perhaps mandate for accountability that could be promoted by transparency. Governing algorithms and AI are within humanity's grasp if it approaches the task with a careful but steady process of human-centered design which seeks to engineer context-specific algorithmic transparency policies.

BIBLIOGRAPHY

Ananny, Mike. "Toward an Ethics of Algorithms." *Science, Technology & Human Values* 41, no. 1 (2015): 93–117.

Ananny, Mike, and Kate Crawford. "Seeing without Knowing: Limitations of the Transparency Ideal and Its Application to Algorithmic Accountability." *New Media & Society* 20, no. 3 (2018): 973–989.

Cath, Corinne. "Governing Artificial Intelligence: Ethical, Legal and Technical Opportunities and Challenges." *Philosophical Transactions of the Royal Society A376* (2018).

Citron, Danielle Keats, and Frank A. Pasquale. "The Scored Society: Due Process for Automated Predictions." *Washington Law Review* 89 (2014).

Diakopoulos, Nicholas. "Algorithmic Accountability: Journalistic Investigation of Computational Power Structures." *Digital Journalism* 3, no. 3 (2015): 398–415.

Diakopoulos, Nicholas, and Michael Koliska. "Algorithmic Transparency in the News Media." *Digital Journalism* 5, no. 7 (2017): 809–828.

Fox, Jonathan. "The Uncertain Relationship between Transparency and Accountability." *Development in Practice* 17, nos. 4–5 (2010): 663–671.

Fung, Archon, Mary Graham, and David Weil. *Full Disclosure: The Perils and Promise of Transparency*. New York: Cambridge University Press, 2009.

Meijer, Albert. "Transparency." In *The Oxford Handbook of Public Accountability*, edited by Mark Bovens, Robert E. Goodin, and Thomas Schillemans, 507–524 Oxford: Oxford University Press, 2014.

Mittelstadt, Brent Daniel, Patrick Allo, Mariarosaria Taddeo, Sandra Wachter, and Luciano Floridi. "The Ethics of Algorithms: Mapping the Debate." *Big Data & Society* 3, no. 2 (2016).

Turilli, Matteo, and Luciano Floridi. "The Ethics of Information Transparency." *Ethics and Information Technology* 11, no. 2 (2009): 105–112.

CHAPTER 11

....

RESPONSIBILITY AND ARTIFICIAL INTELLIGENCE

....

VIRGINIA DIGNUM

....

INTRODUCTION

....

ARTIFICIAL intelligence (AI) has huge potential to bring accuracy, efficiency, cost savings, and speed to a whole range of human activities as well as to provide entirely new insights into behavior and cognition. However, the way AI is developed and deployed in large part determines how AI will impact our lives and societies. For instance, automated classification systems can deliver prejudiced results and therefore raise questions about privacy and bias; and, the autonomy of self-driving vehicles raises concerns about safety and responsibility. AI's impact concerns not only research and development directions for AI but also how these systems are introduced into society. There is debate concerning how the use of AI will influence labor, well-being, social interactions, healthcare, income distribution, and other social areas. Dealing with these issues requires that ethical, legal, societal, and economic implications are taken into account.

AI will affect everybody. Thus the development of AI systems must ensure inclusion and diversity—that is, a true consideration of all humankind when determining the purpose of AI systems. Therefore, responsible AI requires informed participation of all stakeholders, which means that education plays an important role both to ensure that knowledge of the potential impact of AI is widespread and to make people aware that they can participate in shaping societal development. At the core of AI development should lie the ideas of "AI for Good" and "AI for All."

Researchers, policymakers, industry, and society at large increasingly recognize the need for design and engineering approaches that ensure the safe, beneficial, and fair use AI technologies; that consider the implications of ethically and legally relevant decision-making by machines; and that evaluate the ethical and legal status of AI. These approaches include the methods and tools for systems' design, and implementation, governance and regulatory processes, and consultation and training activities that ensure all are heard and able to participate in the discussion.

In this endeavor, it is important to realize that AI does not stand by itself but rather must be understood as part of a sociotechnical system. A responsible approach to AI is needed—one that ensures that systems are not only developed in a good way but also developed for a good cause. Responsible AI concerns not only the software system itself but also, and foremost, the people, institutions and organizations that compose the sociotechnical system. The focus of this chapter is on understanding what such an approach should look like, who are the responsible parties, and how to decide on which systems can and should be developed.

In all areas of application, where AI is applied to make decisions that affect people and society, AI reasoning must be able to take into account societal values, to assess moral and ethical considerations, to weigh the respective priorities of values held by different stakeholders in multicultural contexts, to explain the basis of its reasoning, and to guarantee transparency. As the capabilities for autonomous decision-making grow, perhaps the most important issue to consider is the need to rethink responsibility.[1] Whatever their level of autonomy and social awareness and their ability to learn, AI systems are artifacts, constructed by people to fulfill some goals. Theories, methods, and algorithms are needed to integrate societal, legal, and moral values into technological developments in AI, at all stages of development (analysis, design, construction, deployment, and evaluation). These frameworks not only must deal with the autonomic reasoning of the machine about such issues that we consider to have ethical impact but also, most importantly, must guide design choices to regulate the reaches of AI systems, to ensure proper data stewardship, and to help individuals determine their own involvement.

Values are dependent on sociocultural contexts.[2] They are often only implicit in deliberation processes, which means that methodologies are needed to elicit the values held by all the stakeholders, and making these explicit can lead to better understanding and trust on artificial autonomous systems. Ethics and AI are related at several levels:[3]

Ethics *by* Design: the technical/algorithmic integration of ethical reasoning capabilities as part of the behavior of artificial autonomous systems.

Ethics *in* Design: the regulatory and engineering methods that support the analysis and evaluation of the ethical implications of AI systems as these integrate or replace traditional social structures.

---

[1] Virginia Dignum, "Responsible Autonomy," in *Proceedings of the Twenty-Sixth International Joint Conference on Artificial Intelligence (IJCAI '2017)* (Palo Alto, CA: AAAI Press, 2017), 4698–704.
[2] Elliot Turiel, *The Culture of Morality: Social Development, Context, and Conflict* (Cambridge: Cambridge University Press, 2002).
[3] Virginia Dignum. "Ethics in Artificial Intelligence: Introduction to the Special Issue," *Ethics and Information Technology* 20.1 (2018): 1–3.

Ethics *for* Design: the codes of conduct, standards, and certification processes that ensure the integrity of developers and users as they research, design, construct, employ, and manage artificial intelligent systems.

That is, AI reasoning should be able to take into account societal values and moral and ethical considerations; weigh the respective priorities of values held by different stakeholders in various multicultural contexts; explain its reasoning; and guarantee transparency. Responsible AI is about human responsibility for the development of intelligent systems along fundamental human principles and values, thus ensuring human flourishing and well-being in a sustainable world. In fact, responsible AI is more than the ticking of some ethical "boxes" in a report or the development of add-on features or switch-off buttons in AI systems. Rather, responsible AI is fundamental to autonomy and should be one of the core stances underlying AI research.

THE ART OF AI

Artificial intelligence can be defined as the development of computer systems that are able to perceive their environment and to deliberate as to how to best act in order to achieve their own goals, assuming that the environment contains other agents similar to itself.[4] As such, AI systems are characterized by their *autonomy* to decide on how to act; their ability to *adapt* by learning from the changes affected in the environment; and how they *interact* with other agents in order to coordinate their activities in that environment.[5]

To reflect societal concerns about the impact of AI, and to ensure that AI systems are developed responsibly and incorporate social and ethical values, these characteristics of autonomy, adaptability, and interaction should be complemented with design principles that ensure trust. These characteristics relate most directly to the technical system. However, the impact and consequences of an AI system reach further than the technical system itself, and as such the system should be seen as a sociotechnical system, encompassing the stakeholders and organizations involved. Previously, we have proposed to complement autonomy with responsibility, interactivity with accountability, and adaptation with transparency.[6] These form the ART (accountability, responsibility, and transparency) principles for responsible and trustworthy AI and concern the whole AI sociotechnical system. That is, addressing ART will require a sociotechnical approach to design, deployment, and use of systems, interweaving software solutions with governance

[4] Stuart Russell and P. Norvig, *Artificial Intelligence: A Modern Approach*, 3rd ed. (London: Pearson Education, 2009).

[5] Luciano Floridi and J. Sanders, "On the Morality of Artificial Agents," *Minds and Machines* 14.3 (2004): 349–79.

[6] Virginia Dignum, "Responsible Autonomy."

and regulation. Moreover, even though each of the ART principles can apply to all aspects of AI systems, each is imperative for a specific characteristic, as is depicted in Figure 11.1.

Accountability refers to the requirement for the system to be able to explain and jus-tify its decisions to users and other relevant actors. To ensure accountability, decisions should be derivable from, and explained by, the decision-making mechanisms used. It also requires that the moral values and societal norms that inform the purpose of the system, as well as their operational interpretations, have been elicited in an open way involving all stakeholders.

Responsibility refers to the role of people themselves in their relation to AI systems. As the chain of responsibility grows, means are needed to link the AI systems' decisions to their input data and to the actions of stakeholders involved in the systems' decisions. Responsibility is not just about making rules to govern intelligent machines; it is about the whole sociotechnical system in which the system operates and that encompasses people, machines, and institutions.

Transparency indicates the capability to describe, inspect, and reproduce the mecha-nisms through which AI systems make decisions and learn to adapt to their environ-ment along with the provenance and dynamics of the data that is used and created by the system. Moreover, trust in the system will improve if we can ensure openness of affairs in all that is related to the system. As such, transparency is also about being explicit and open about choices and decisions concerning data sources, development processes, and stakeholders, and such transparency should be required from all models that use human data or affect human beings or can have other morally significant impacts.

These properties enable agents to deal effectively with the kinds of environments in which we live and work: these environments may be unpredictable, dynamic in space and time, and include situations one has never encountered before. If AI systems are capable and expected to act in such environments, we need to be able to trust that they will not exhibit undesirable behavior. Or, at least, we need to limit the effects of unex-pected behavior. However, an interactive system that is autonomous and adaptable is hard to verify and predict, which in turn can lead to unexpected activity. Therefore,

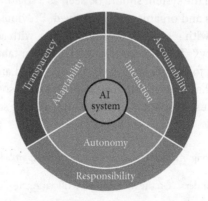

FIGURE 11.1. The art principles: accountability, responsibility, autonomy.

design methodologies are needed that take these issues into account as a means to ensure that AI systems are reliable, acceptable, and accepted.

As a whole, these principles inform the design of AI systems. That is, ART imposes requirements on AI systems' design and architecture that will condition the development process and the systems' architecture.

Even though, obviously, each of the ART principles can apply to all aspects of AI systems, each is especially relevant to one of the characteristics of AI, as depicted in Figure 11.1. So, one cannot have autonomy without some form of responsibility, interaction without accountability, or adaptability without transparency. Moreover, addressing ART will require a sociotechnical approach to design, deployment, and use of systems, interweaving software solutions with governance and regulation. From the perspective of system development, ART requires new forms and new methods that support the integration of ethical and societal impact of AI systems in the engineering process. Above all, ART requires training and awareness of all stakeholders—including researchers, designers, programmers, managers, those in procurement, and users—that enables each of them to understand and assume their role in the overall process.

Note that there is a fundamental difference between accountability and responsibility, even if these terms are often used interchangeably as synonyms. Putting it simply, accountability refers to the ability to explain, or report on, one's role in events or actions, whereas responsibility is the duty to answer for one's actions. Responsibility entails liability and exists before the task or action is done. Accountability is only evident after the action is done or not done. When a person delegates some task to an agent, be it artificial or human, the result of that task is still the responsibility of the delegating person (principal), who is the one who will be liable if things do not go as expected. The agent, however, must be able to give a report on how the task was executed and to explain eventual problems with this execution. This is the basis of the principal-agent theory that is often used to explain the relationship between people and autonomous systems.[7]

TAKING RESPONSIBILITY

In order to design AI systems that are sensitive to moral principles and human values, methods for responsible AI rests on three pillars of equal importance. Firstly, society must be prepared to take responsibility for AI impacts. This means that researchers and developers should be trained to be aware of their own responsibility where it concerns the development of AI systems with direct impacts in society. This requires extra efforts in developing and delivering education and training materials as well as the development of codes of conduct for AI developers. And, in turn, this development requires

[7] Kathleen M. Eisenhardt, "Agency Theory: An Assessment and Review," *Academy of Management Review* 14.1 (1989): 57–74.

methods and tools to understand and integrate moral, societal, and legal values with technological developments in AI.

This means that responsible AI is firstly an issue of governance. It is up to governments and citizens to determine how issues of liability should be regulated. For example, who will be to blame if a self-driving car harms a pedestrian? The builder of the hardware (e.g., of the sensors used by the car to perceive the environment)? The builder of the software that enables the car to decide on a path? The authorities that allow the car in the road? The owner that personalized the car's decision-making settings to meet her preferences? And how can current product liability laws be understood in the face of systems that act as a result of a long (autonomous) learning process? All these questions, and more, must be informing the regulations that societies put in place toward responsible use of AI systems.

Secondly, responsible AI implies the need for mechanisms that enable AI systems to act according to ethics and human values. Whether we design them that way or not, AI systems will and are already making decisions that we would consider to have an ethical flavor if they we made by people. Being aware of this is what responsible AI is all about. How do we design systems that take implicit "ethical" decisions? Or how do we design the system to ensure that it refers the decision to someone to take because it is an ethical decision? And where is the border between decisions that are not ethical and ones that are? This requires models and algorithms to represent and reason about, and take decisions based on, human values and to justify their decisions according to their effect on those values. Current (deep-learning) mechanisms are unable to meaningfully link decisions to inputs, and therefore they cannot explain their acts in ways that we can understand.

Last but certainly not least, responsible AI is about participation. It is necessary to understand how different people work with and live with AI technologies across cultures in order to develop frameworks for responsible AI. In fact, AI does not stand in itself, but must be understood as a part of sociotechnical relations with all its diversity. Here again education plays an important role to ensure that knowledge of the potential of AI is widespread, to make people aware that they can participate in shaping the societal development, and as a basis to ensure diversity and inclusion. A new and more ambitious form of governance is one of the most pressing needs in order to ensure that inevitable AI advances will be accessible to all and serve the societal good.

Expanding on the principles described in the previous section, it is important to understand that responsible AI means different things to different people. The concept of responsible AI also serves as an overall container for many diverse opinions and topics. Depending on the speaker and on the context, it can mean one of the following things:

1. Policies concerning the governance of R&D (research and development) activities and the deployment and use of AI in societal settings;
2. The role of developers, at individual and collective levels;
3. Issues of inclusion, diversity, and universal access; and
4. Predictions and reflections on the benefits and risks of AI.

These topics are quite different, as are their impacts. Placing all of these issues in the same basket can muddle the discussion and also puts at risk the achievement of constructive solutions to each of the topics. It can also contribute to increasing the fear of AI from the general public and with it the risk of the proliferation of ungrounded, dystopic views about what AI is.

The most urgent of these topics is perhaps the first one. Artificial intelligence systems use data we generate in our daily lives and as such are a mirror of our interests, weaknesses, and differences. Artificial intelligence, like any other technology, is not value-neutral. Understanding the values behind the technology and deciding on how we want our values to be incorporated in AI systems requires that we are also able to decide on how and what we want AI to mean in our societies. It implies deciding on ethical guidelines, governance policies, incentives, and regulations. And it also implies that we are aware of differences in interests and aims behind AI systems developed by others according to other cultures and principles. An extension, or alternative, to regulation is certification. Certification is a means of risk regulation and quality assurance that ensures that the products or services they certify meet criteria specified by professional associations, standards organizations, or government agencies. We discuss the issues of regulation and certification in the next section.

As for the second topic, it is important to realize that AI does not just materialize. We make it happen. Researchers and developers of AI systems in large part determine how those systems will behave and what kind of capabilities they will exhibit. Many professions are bound by codes of conduct outlining the proper practices for those professionals. The Association of International Accountants defines code of conduct as being the "principles, values, standards, or rules of behaviour that guide the decisions, procedures and systems of an organization in a way that (a) contributes to the welfare of its key stakeholders, and (b) respects the rights of all constituents affected by its operations." In fact, society expects strict codes of conduct from those professions it depends on, including health professionals, military, accountants, and many others. Given the role of software engineers on the AI systems and applications that shape our world, it is probably time to expect some standards of conduct from this professional group. We will further discuss this issue in the next section.

On the issue of inclusion, diversity, and access to AI, much has been said and written, in particular where it relates to bias. However, these issues are also relevant for the environments where AI is developed and have a strong link to education. Inclusion is a necessary condition for diversity in development teams and AI professionals. More than metrics in terms of demographics, it is important to understand how inclusion is experienced. Broadening engineering education curricula to include the humanities and social sciences, which are essential to ensure the responsible design and development of AI, will also contribute to a more diverse student population.

On the other hand, the media has given disproportional attention to the last topic. Dystopic views of a future dominated by our robotic overlords seem to sell well and are backed by some scholars (typically from other disciplines) and a disproportional number of tech millionaires. However, as Luciano Floridi remarks, even if such a future is logically possible it is utterly unlikely, and focus on these issues is actually a distraction from the real problems that are already affecting us.[8] Even though the topic has fascinated people for ages, the main risk here is that focusing on possible future risks is basically a distraction from the very real risks that we are facing already: privacy and security, consequences for human labor, and algorithmic bias, just to cite a few.

GOVERNANCE FOR RESPONSIBLE AI

In recent years, we have seen a rise of efforts around the ethical, societal, and legal impact of AI. These are the result of concerted action by national and transnational governance bodies, including the European Union (EU), the Organisation for Economic Co-operation and Development (OECD), the United Kingdom, France, Canada, and others, but have also originated from bottom-up initiatives launched by practitioners and the scientific community. Just recently, the EU published its Guidelines for Trustworthy AI,[9] and a few weeks before that Version 1 of the IEEE's initiative on Ethically Aligned Design (EAD) of Intelligent and Autonomous Systems[10] was presented. The impact of these two reports, coming from EU and the leading international professional organization of engineers, is potentially very large. Engineers are those that ultimately will implement AI to meet ethical principles and human values, but it is policymakers, regulators, and society in general that can set and enforce the purpose of AI. Both initiatives go well beyond proposing a list of principles but aim at providing concrete guidelines to the design of ethically aligned AI systems, including recommendations for regulation, standards, and policy suggestions to support the development, deployment, and use of AI systems. Based on the result of a public consultation process, the EU guidelines put forward seven requirements necessary (but not sufficient) to achieve trustworthy AI together with methods to achieve these and an assessment list to check these requirements. The IEEE-EAD report is a truly bottom-up international effort, resulting from the collaboration of many hundreds of experts across the globe including Asia and the Global South. It goes deeper and beyond a list of requirements or principles and provides in-depth background on many different topics. The EAD community is already hard at work on defining standards for the future of ethical, intelligent, and autonomous technologies, ensuring the prioritization of human well-being. The EU will be piloting its assessment list in the coming months through an open call for interest.

Other initiatives have focused on analyzing the values and principles to which AI systems and the development thereof should adhere. Examples of such lists include:

[8] L. Floridi, "Should We Be Afraid of AI?," in *Aeon Essays* (2016), https://aeon.co/essays/true-ai-is-both-logically-possible-and-utterly-implausible.

[9] https://ec.europa.eu/digital-single-market/en/news/ethics-guidelines-trustworthy-ai.

[10] https://ethicsinaction.ieee.org/.

- the Asilomar principles,[11]
- the Barcelona declaration,[12]
- the Montreal declaration,[13] and
- the ethical guidelines from the Japanese Society for Artificial Intelligence.[14]

Analyzing these different lists of principles and values it is clear that all initiatives set human well-being as central to AI development and most recognize in general the ethical principles of accountability and responsibility. The initiatives further focus on different types of principles, which can be grouped in three main classes: societal, legal, and technical. Albeit the use of synonyms or slightly different terminologies, the main issues identified are depicted in Figure 11.1.

Based on the result of a public consultation process, the EU guidelines put forward seven requirements necessary (but not sufficient) to achieve trustworthy AI:

- Human agency and oversight
- Technical robustness and safety
- Privacy and data governance
- Transparency
- Diversity, nondiscrimination, and fairness
- Societal and environmental well-being
- Accountability

The IEEE-EAD report is a truly bottom-up international effort, resulting from the collaboration of many hundreds of experts across the globe including Asia and the Global South. It goes deeper and beyond a list of requirements or principles and provides in-depth background on many different topics. Both efforts aim at including different stakeholders in the discussion and evaluation of responsible AI. Moreover, both provide concrete means to support organizations in the implementation of AI systems that meet these requirements. The IEEE-EAD community is already hard at work on defining standards for the future of ethical, intelligent, and autonomous technologies, ensuring the prioritization of human well-being. The EU guidelines include an assessment list to check the requirements, which will be piloted together with stakeholders in an open and transparent effort during 2019.

Another set of initiatives focuses on the specific issues of ethics for robotics in the tradition of the classic Asimov's Laws, including the EPSRC Principles of Robotics,[15] and the work by the Foundation for Responsible Robotics.[16]

---

[11] https://futureoflife.org/ai-principles/.   [12] https://www.iiia.csic.es/barcelonadeclaration/.

[13] https://nouvelles.umontreal.ca/en/article/2017/11/03/montreal-declaration-for-a-responsible-development-of-artificial-intelligence/.

[14] http://ai-elsi.org/wp-content/uploads/2017/05/JSAI-Ethical-Guidelines-1.pdf.

[15] Margaret Boden et al., "Principles of Robotics: Regulating Robots in the Real World," *Connection Science* 29.2 (2017): 124–29.

[16] http://responsiblerobotics.org/.

In fact, there goes hardly a day without news about yet another declaration of principles for AI or of other initiatives at national or corporate levels. For up-to-date lists of all such initiatives, check Alan Winfield's blog,[17] the crowdsourced effort coordinated by Doteveryone,[18] and Tim Dutton's list of national AI strategies.

Ensuring responsible AI however involves more than setting up lists of desired principles, standards, or recommendations. It requires action. Possible mechanisms for this action are regulation, certification, and codes of conduct.

Regulation

Whenever regulation is mentioned with respect to AI development and use, usually two issues are mentioned: firstly, the fear that regulation will stifle innovation and progress; and secondly, the issue of whether current laws and regulations are at all sufficient to deal with the complexities of AI. In my opinion, both are too short-sighted.

Given the dynamic nature of AI, we cannot wait for regulation until the technology is mature. Already now AI is impacting individuals and society, changing cognitive and interaction functions, and impacting our well-being. However, as we have seen in previous chapters, there is no established definition of what AI is, without which it is very difficult to determine what should be the focus of regulation. Moreover, as has been observed by the panel that produced the 100 Years Study on AI Report,[19] the risks and considerations are very different in different domains to enable a generic regulatory approach. This means that, rather than regulating AI itself, regulating its use in specific areas such as healthcare or the military provides more suitable instruments to ensure its proper application and can better be inserted in existing regulatory forms. Furthermore, it is important to realize that not all regulation is negative. This is specifically the case when regulation takes the form of incentives or investment programs that nudge organizations to pursue specific types of applications or technological approaches.

As for the issue of suitability of current regulation, it should be clear that AI is an artifact. As such, much of product and service liability laws apply to its use. There is however the need for close collaboration between legal and AI experts to collaborate on the evaluation and possible update of existing laws to the specific cases of AI applications.

Finally, regulation can also be seen as a means to further scientific development on AI. For example, consider the case in which legislation will restrict the use of data and demand explanation of all results achieved by an AI system. These requirements probably mean that many of the current approaches, based on neural networks and deep learning, are not able to meet these demands. This can be seen as a limitation on the use of AI and be approached with complaints and a refusal to comply, claiming economic losses and a delay on development. But it can also be seen as a challenge to be taken.

---

[17] http://alanwinfield.blogspot.com/2017/12.

[18] https://goo.gl/ibffk4 (maintained in Google Docs).

[19] Peter Stone et al., *Report on the One Hundred Year Study on Artificial Intelligence (AI100)* (Palo Alto, CA: Stanford University, 2016), https://ai100.stanford.edu/sites/g/files/sbiybj9861/f/ai100report10032016fnl_singles.pdf.

Then researchers need to go back to the drawing board to come up with novel learning and reasoning techniques that ensure explainability and sustainable use of data without compromising efficiency.

Artificial intelligence is by far not done yet. Current machine-learning techniques are just an intermediate step on the path of progress. If regulation is the means to further this progress, then we can best embrace it. Such an approach does require a culture of openness and cooperation among scientists, developers, policymakers, and ethicists in order to ensure that regulations create the incentives to development that benefit both technology development and society. It is hopeful to see that the need for dialogue between different parties is increasingly being acknowledged by all.

Certification

Several economic sectors have developed effective means of certification, such as the food sector. We can consider similar mechanisms for AI systems. In this case, independent and trusted institutions would validate and test algorithms, applications, and products against a set of well-defined principles (possibly derived from the recommendations described earlier) and guarantee the quality of the system. We, as users of such systems, would then have the choice of what type of system would best meet our own personal requirements.

Such a certification approach can be combined with a regulatory one. In this case, regulation would specify the minimum set of principles and their interpretation that must hold for all systems in a given country or region, similar to the data protection regulations in force within the EU.[20] Above the minimum requirements laid down by regulation, certification supports business differentiation at the same time it ensures consumer protection.

Currently, several initiatives toward AI ethical certification are being launched, including by the IEEE. The IEEE's Ethics Certification Program for Autonomous and Intelligent Systems[21](ECPAIS) aims to create specifications for certification and marking processes that advance transparency, accountability, and reduction in algorithmic-bias AI systems.

A recent white paper by the AI4People think thank, which proposes an ethical framework for AI, has advised the creation of a new (European) oversight agency responsible for the protection of public welfare through the scientific evaluation and supervision of AI products, software, systems or services with similar aims.[22] At the same time, several commercial organizations, including Accenture and PwC, are also announcing auditing services for the analyses of algorithms.

[20] https://eugdpr.org/.
[21] https://standards.ieee.org/industry-connections/ecpais.html.
[22] Luciano Floridi, Josh Cowls, Monica Beltrametti, Raja Chatila, Patrice Chazerand, Virginia Dignum, Christoph Luetge et al. "AI4People—An Ethical Framework for a Good AI Society: Opportunities, Risks, Principles, and Recommendations," *Minds and Machines* 28, no. 4 (2018): 689–707.

Codes of Conduct

Support for the development of self-regulatory codes of conduct for data and AI-related professions involves specific ethical duties. This would be along the lines of other socially sensitive professions, such as medical doctors or lawyers, with the attendant certification of "ethical AI" through trust-labels to make sure that people understand the merits of ethical AI and will therefore demand it from providers.[23]

A professional code of conduct is a public statement developed for and by a professional group to reflect shared principles about practice, conduct, and ethics of those exercising the profession; to describe the quality of behavior that reflects the expectations of the profession and the community; to provide a clear statement to the society about these expectations; and to enable professionals to reflect on their own ethical decisions.

A code of conduct supports professionals to assess and resolve difficult professional and ethical dilemmas. While in the case of ethical dilemmas there is not a correct solution, the professionals can give an account of their actions by referring to the code.

Many organizations and enterprises have their own codes of conduct. Even if in many cases adherence to the code is voluntary, there are professions that oblige allegiance to their code. This is the case of professional orders, or guilds, in many countries, where membership is a necessary condition for the practice of the profession. Most well-known are the Hippocratic Oath and the Physician's Pledge (the Declaration of Geneva) taken by medical doctors.

Just recently the Association for Computing Machinery (ACM), the largest international association of computing professionals, updated their code of conduct.[24] This voluntary code is "a collection of principles and guidelines designed to help computing professionals make ethically responsible decisions in professional practice. It translates broad ethical principles into concrete statements about professional conduct." This code explicitly addresses issues associated with the development of AI systems, namely issues of emergent properties, discrimination, and privacy. Specifically, it calls out the responsibility of technologists to ensure that systems are inclusive and accessible to all and requires that they are knowledgeable about privacy issues.

Inclusion and Diversity

Inclusion and diversity are a broader societal challenge and central to AI development. Research and development of AI systems must be informed by diversity, in all the meaning of diversity, and obviously including gender, cultural background, and ethnicity. But there is also growing evidence that cognitive diversity contributes to better decision making. Therefore developing teams should include social scientists, philosophers, and others as well as ensuring gender, ethnicity, and cultural differences. It is important to

---

[23] Ibid.
[24] D. W. Gotterbarn et al., "ACM Code of Ethics: A Guide for Positive Action," *Communications of the ACM* 61, no. 1 (2018): 121–28.

diversify the AI development workforce along all pertinent dimensions. Regulation and codes of conduct can specify targets and goals, along with incentives, as a way to foster diversity in AI teams.

It is equally important to diversify the expertise of those working on AI. In order to understand the ethical, social, legal, and economic impact of AI and evaluate how design decisions contribute to this impact, AI professionals need to have basic knowledge of philosophy, social science, law, and economy.

Education plays here an important role. Artificial intelligence is not any longer an engineering discipline. In fact, AI is too important to be left to engineers alone; AI is really transdisciplinary. Most current AI and robotics curricula worldwide deliver engineers with a too-narrow task view. The wide impact of AI on society requires a broadening of engineering education to include: (a) analysis of the distributed nature of AI applications as these integrate sociotechnical systems and the complexity of human-agent interaction; (b) reflection on the meaning and global effect of the autonomous, emergent, decentralized, self-organizing character of distributed learning entities and how they operate; (c) incremental design and development frameworks and the unforeseen positive and negative influence of individual decisions at a system level, as well as how these impact human rights, democracy, and education; (d) the consequences of inclusion and diversity in design and how these inform processes and results; (e) understanding of governance and normative issues, not only in terms of competences and responsibilities but also in views on health, safety, risks, explanations, and accountability; and (f) the underlying societal, legal, and economic models of sociotechnical systems. Broadening AI curricula is possibly also a way to attract a more diverse student population. When AI curricula are known to be transdisciplinary, it can be expected that female students, who traditionally choose humanities and social subjects over engineering ones, may be motivated to choose AI. In parallel development, other curricula need to include subjects on the theory and practice of AI. For example, a law curriculum needs to prepare law experts on how to address legal and regulatory issues around AI.

Finally, it is important to realize that, besides human diversity, it is also important to consider cultural diversity, which includes factors such as education, religion, language. Artificial intelligence is increasingly pervasive and applied across cultures and regions. Failure to understand cultural diversity impacts negatively the universal right to access to the advantages that technology brings about. In an increasingly connected AI world, incentives and regulations can support awareness and commitment to a diverse perspective ensuring that AI applications are truly adaptable to a diverse cultural space, thus enabling access to all.

THE AI NARRATIVE

Responsibility in AI is also about a proper AI narrative, which demystifies the possibilities of AI technologies and ensures that all are able to participate in the discussion on the role of AI in society. Since its origins, the AI discipline has gone through ups and downs, seasonal shifts, and periods of hype. However, never before we have witnessed the current level of excitement (and fear) held by so many in so many areas. Artificial intelligence is breaking through in many different application domains, with results that impress even the most knowledgeable experts. Three main factors are leading this development: the increasing availability of large amounts of data, improved algorithms, and substantial computational power. However, of these three only the improvement of algorithms can be rightfully seen as a contribution from the AI field. The other two can be seen as fortunate contingencies.

The awareness that AI has the potential to impact our lives and our world in ways that no other technology have before is rightfully raising many questions concerning its ethical, legal, societal, and economical effects. However, AI is not magic. Contrary to what some may want us to believe, the algorithms in which AI is based are not a magic wand that give their users powers of omniscience and the ability to solve all problems and achieve any- and everything. Artificial intelligence uses algorithms, but then so does any other computer program or engineering process. Algorithms are far from magic and have been around for thousands of years. In fact, the easiest definition of an algorithm is that of a recipe—a set of precise rules to achieve a certain result. Every time you add two numbers, you are using an algorithm. When you bake an apple pie you are also following an algorithm—a recipe. By itself, a recipe has never turned into an apple pie. The end result of your pie has more to do with your baking skills and your choice of ingredients. The same applies to AI algorithms: in large part the result depends on the input data and on the ability of those that trained it. And, in the same way as we have the choice to use organic apples to make our pie, in AI we also have the choice to use data that respects and ensures fairness, privacy, transparency, and all the other values we hold dear.

This is what responsible AI is about—the decisions taken concerning the scope, the rules, and the resources that are used to develop, deploy, and use AI systems. Artificial intelligence is not just the algorithm or the data that it uses. It is a complex combination of decisions, opportunities, and resources.

Conclusions

Increasingly, AI systems will be taking decisions that affect our lives in smaller or larger ways. In all areas of application, AI must be able to take into account societal values and moral and ethical considerations; weigh the respective priorities of values held by different stakeholders and in multicultural contexts; explain its reasoning; and guarantee transparency. As the capabilities for autonomous decision-making grow, perhaps the most important issue to consider is the need to rethink responsibility. Artificial intelligence systems are tools, artefacts created by people, and as such their actions and decision must be under the responsibility of humans and/or human organisations. However, their potential autonomy and capability to learn require that design considers accountability, responsibility, and transparency principles in an explicit and systematic manner. The development of AI algorithms has so far been led by the goal of improving performance, leading to opaque black boxes. Putting human values at the core of AI systems calls for a mind-shift of researchers and developers toward the goal of improving transparency rather than performance, which will lead to novel and exciting techniques and applications.

Some researchers claim that given that AI systems are artifacts, the discussion of the ethics of AI is somewhat misplaced. Indeed, we, people, are the ones responsible for these systems. We, people, are the ones determining the questions that AI systems can answer and how to deal with the results of their decisions and action. The main concern of responsible AI is thus the identification of the relative responsibility of all actors involved in the design, development, deployment, and use of AI systems.

Firstly, society must be prepared to take responsibility for AI impact. This means that researchers and developers should be trained to be aware of their own responsibility where it concerns the development of AI systems with direct impacts in society. This requires extra efforts in developing and delivering education and training materials as well as the development of codes of conduct for AI developers. In turn this requires methods and tools to understand and integrate moral, societal, and legal values with technological developments in AI. And this means that responsible AI is firstly an issue of governance.

Secondly, responsible AI implies the need for mechanisms that enable AI systems to act according to ethics and human values. Whether we design them that way or not, AI systems will and are already making decisions that we would consider to have an ethical flavor if they were made by people. Being aware of this is what responsible AI is all about. How do we design systems that take implicit "ethical" decisions? Or how do we design the system to ensure that it refers a decision to someone because it is an ethical decision? And where is the border between decisions that are not ethical and ones that are? This requires models and algorithms to represent and reason about, and take decisions based on, human values and to justify their decisions according to their effect on those values. Current (deep-learning) mechanisms are unable to meaningfully link decisions to inputs, and therefore they cannot explain their acts in ways that we can understand.

Last but certainly not least, responsible AI is about participation. It is necessary to understand how different people work with and live with AI technologies across cultures in order to develop frameworks for responsible AI. In fact, AI does not stand in itself, but must be understood as part of sociotechnical relations, with all its diversity. Here again education plays an important role to ensure that knowledge of the potential AI is widespread, to make people aware that they can participate in shaping societal development, and as a basis to ensure diversity and inclusion.

But, as the capabilities for autonomous decision-making grow, perhaps the most important issue to consider is the need to rethink responsibility. The development of AI algorithms has so far been led by the goal of improving performance, leading to opaque black boxes. Putting human values at the core of AI systems calls for a mind-shift of researchers and developers towards the goal of improving transparency rather than performance, which will lead to novel and exciting techniques and applications. As mathematician and philosopher Norbert Wiener wrote back in 1960: "We had better be quite sure that the purpose put into the machine is the purpose which we really desire." Ensuring an ethically aligned purpose is more than designing systems whose result can be trusted. It is about the way we design them, why we design them, and who is involved in designing them. It is a work of generations.

And it is a work always in progress. Obviously, errors will be made, and disasters will happen. It is not an option to ignore responsibility. Artificial intelligence systems are artifacts decided, designed, implemented, and used by us. We are responsible to try again when we fail (and we will fail), to observe and denounce when we see things going wrong (and they will go wrong), to be informed and to inform, to rebuild and improve.

It is important to realize that ethical principles for AI are not checklists or boxes to tick once and forget. These principles are directions for action. They are codes of behavior—for AI systems but, most importantly, for us. It is we who need to be fair, nondiscriminatory, and accountable; to ensure privacy for ourselves and others; and to aim at social and environmental well-being. The codes of ethics are for us; AI systems will follow.

BIBLIOGRAPHY

Boden, Margaret, Joanna Bryson, Darwin Caldwell, Kerstin Dautenhahn, Lilian Edwards, Sarah Kember, Paul Newman, Vivienne Parry, Geoff Pegman, and Tom Rodden et al. "Principles of Robotics: Regulating Robots in the Real World." *Connection Science* 29.2 (2017): 124–29.

Dignum, Virginia. "Responsible Autonomy." In *Proceedings of the Twenty-Sixth International Joint Conference on Artificial Intelligence (IJCAI'2017)*, 4698–704. Palo Alto, CA: AAAI Press, 2017.

Dignum, Virginia. "Ethics in Artificial Intelligence: Introduction to the Special Issue." *Ethics and Information Technology* 20.1 (2018): 1–3.

Eisenhardt, Kathleen M. "Agency Theory: An Assessment and Review." *Academy of Management Review* 14.1 (1989): 57–74.

Floridi, Luciano. "Should We Be Afraid of AI?" In *Aeon Essays* (2016). https://aeon.co/essays/true-ai-is-both-logically-possible-and-utterly-implausible.

Floridi, Luciano, and J. Sanders. "On the Morality of Artificial Agents." *Minds and Machines* 14.3 (2004): 349–79.

Floridi, Luciano, Josh Cowls, Monica Beltrametti, Raja Chatila, Patrice Chazer, Virginia Dignum, Christoph Luetge, Robert Madelin, Ugo Pagallo, Francesca Rossi, Burkhard Schafer, Peggy Valcke, and Effy Vayena. "An Ethical Framework for a Good AI Society: Opportunities, Risks, Principles, and Recommendations." *Minds and Machines* 28.4 (2018): 689–707.

Gotterbarn, D. W., Amy Bruckman, Catherine Flick, Keith Miller, and Marty J. Wolf. "ACM Code of Ethics: A Guide for Positive Action." *Communications of the ACM* 61, no. 1 (2018): 121–28. https://doi.org/10.1145/3173016.

Russell, Stuart, and P. Norvig. *Artificial Intelligence: A Modern Approach.* 3rd ed. London: Pearson Education Limited, 2009.

Stone, Peter, Rodney Brooks, Eric Brynjolfsson, Ryan Calo, Oren Etzioni, Greg Hager, Julia Hirschberg, Shivaram Kalyanakrishnan, Ece Kamar, Sarit Kraus, Kevin Leyton-Brown, David Parkes, William Press, Anna Lee Saxenian, Julie Shah, Milind Tambe, and Astro Teller. *Report on the One Hundred Year Study on Artificial Intelligence (AI100)*. Palo Alto, CA: Stanford University, 2016. https://ai100.stanford.edu/sites/g/files/sbiybj9861/f/ai100report10032016fnl_singles.pdf

Turiel, Elliot. *The Culture of Morality: Social Development, Context, and Conflict*. Cambridge: Cambridge University Press, 2002.

CHAPTER 12

···

THE CONCEPT OF HANDOFF AS A MODEL FOR ETHICAL ANALYSIS AND DESIGN

···

DEIRDRE K. MULLIGAN AND
HELEN NISSENBAUM

ENTHUSIASM for the new artificial intelligence (AI), derived from machine learning over big data, has meant a sweeping push to insert machine intelligence into wide-ranging systems, producing a raft of "smart" yet often mundane technical objects, as well as AI enhanced systems operating in key societal sectors including finance, military, transportation, criminal justice, and health and welfare.[1] As with automation in prior times, this sweep has also raised doubts and questions, notably, many focused on functional performance and worker displacement. The concept of *handoff* that we have developed guides a different set of questions, namely, how implanting AI[2] affects the ethical and political values embodied in technical systems.

A growing body of work that places technical artifacts themselves—devices and systems—within the scope of ethical analysis, beyond the traditional focus on human action and institutional regulation, has driven progress in understanding technology in ethical terms. The object of study, according to this understanding, is not a purely material, technical system, performing within a purely human or social context, but is a sociotechnical system whose performance inextricably involves both. Actor-Network

[1] Research for this chapter has been funded by generous support from the US NSF INSPIRE SES1537324 and the MacArthur Foundation. We are grateful to the Simons Institute for the Theory of Computer Science, where both authors were visitors in the Privacy Program, Spring 2019.

[2] Throughout this chapter, we prefer the acronym AI, connoting decision and control systems based on models derived from machine learning over big data, instead of the terms "intelligent" or "intelligence" spelled out. As such AI has taken on a constructed meaning, and we can sidestep philosophical questions about whether this is intelligence in any normal meaning.

234   DEIRDRE K. MULLIGAN AND HELEN NISSENBAUM

Theory (ANT), with its concept of actant, for example, goes even further in this direction, erasing the traditional distinction between human actor, on the one hand, and machine component, on the other. Systems developers may employ diverse nodes[3] in complex actor-networks wherein actants prescribe and delegate behaviors among one another to achieve desired ends. The concept of *handoff*, similarly, assumes a broadened understanding of the technical as, in fact, the sociotechnical, whereby (so-called) technical systems and devices function as they do because of technical and material properties, as well as human behaviors, and economic, social, and political contexts. Unlike ANT, however, handoff illuminates the differences among the different types of actants, if you will, where it considers that these differences are ethically relevant. Applying an ethical lens to technical systems, so conceived, means assessing these diverse dimensions in terms of the contribution they make, or the impact they have, on ethical and political values embodied—potential or enacted[4]—in such systems as a whole. In these assessments, the concept of *handoff* constitutes a useful analytic tool.

The paradigmatic use-case for the Handoff model involves a progression or transformation from one version of a system to another, where the progression involves the replacement of certain components by others. A simple illustration may help. In modern office buildings, lighting is increasingly modulated by motion sensors instead of mechanical, human-operated switches; we would describe this transformation as a handoff of control from a human actor to a programmed motion sensor. We note that often, alongside the motion-sensing control, a traditional interface affords individuals the option of operating a switch in the traditional manner—a paradigmatic example of a parallel configuration within a single system. Although the catalyst for us in developing an analytical framework around the concept of *handoff* was the recent boom in AI based automation, the lighting example shows that it applies generally, to various permutations, including automation involving the replacement of human actors by technical mechanisms (not necessarily AI), one type of machine component by a different type, as when hardware is replaced by software, or even human actors, in one capacity, replaced by other humans in other capacities. Such handoffs occur when, for example, functionality is outsourced, pushed to workers lower on a hierarchy, centralized, or decentralized, and so on. Examples abound.

Taking an ethical perspective on technical systems the concept of *handoff* is particularly useful because it exposes aspects of progressive transformations that may otherwise be overlooked. Those who claim about a given handoff, say, human moderation of content handed off to machines, that the transformed system offers *the same* functionality as the previous may boast, further, that it does so even more reliably, more efficiently, and at lower cost. If there is anything to worry about, goes this account, it is to

[3] Bruno Latour, "Where Are the Missing Masses? The Sociology of a Few Mundane Artifacts," in *Shaping Technology/Building Society: Studies in Sociotechnical Change*, ed. Wiebe Bijker and John Law (Cambridge, MA: MIT Press, 1992), 225–258.
[4] Katie Shilton, Jes A. Koepfler, and Kenneth R. Fleischmann, "How to See Values in Social Computing: Methods for Studying Values Dimensions," in *Proceedings of the 17th ACM Computer Supported Cooperative Work & Social Computing* (Association for Computing Machinery, 2014), 426–435.

ensure that content marked as offensive, illegal, or dangerous by the machine roughly meets respective standards. Like others,[5] however, we argue that even were this to hold, reallocation of functionalities among different types of components (or actors) does not necessarily leave the "mass of morality" unchanged: to the contrary, redistribution of functionality, in itself, may have moral and political repercussions. The Handoff model resists the idea that one can redistribute functions without disturbing the mass of morality, and is designed to reveal the political significance of sociotechnical configurations of function across component actors and the points of inflection among them.

Mapping transformations in terms of the Handoff model shines a spotlight on that which has changed and, by implication, illuminates ethical concerns that these changes raise. It may be that transformed systems embody more positive values, but it may be that replaced components, even performing purportedly the same task, lead to a degradation—such as, dissipated accountability, diminished responsibility, displacement of human autonomy, or acute threats to privacy. In our view, the Handoff model is a critical ameliorative intervention illuminating the structural, political, and ethical stakes of the ongoing transition of control to computational components under the guise of progress and efficiency and often political neutrality.

CATALYST

AI applied in areas such as social media platforms, "smart" cities, healthcare, and the criminal justice system has generated steep and widespread interest. Regulators and journalists interrogate the political implications of algorithms in systems as diverse as Facebook's advertising platform and risk recidivism software. Governmental bodies set out ethical expectations for AI in self-driving vehicles. Companies develop guidelines and internal structures to address the ethical quandaries posed by AI. Universities grapple with their obligation to produce students who can attend to the social and political entanglements of technical work. Workers within major technology companies oppose the use of their labor toward ethically objectionable ends. This burst of activity and the underlying ethical angst reveal the need for rigorous methods to interrogate the ethical implications of AI.

This historic inflection point, with the unspoken imperative to hand off human tasks to machines, in business, government, healthcare, education, in our view, raises an

---

[5]   See Roger Brownsword, "Lost in Translation: Legality, Regulatory Margins, and Technological Management," *Berkeley Technology Law Journal* 26, no. 3 (2011): 1321–1366; Margaret Jane Radin, "Regulating by Contract, Regulating by Machine," *Journal of Institutional and Theoretical Economics* 160, no. 1 (2004): 142–156; Lawrence Lessig, *Code: And Other Laws of Cyberspace* (New York: Basic Books, 1999); Harry Surden, "Structural Rights in Privacy," *SMU Law Review* 60, no. 4 (2007): 1605–1629; Orin S. Kerr, "Compelled Decryption and the Privilege against Self-Incrimination," *Texas Law Review* 97, no. 4 (2019): 767; Julie E. Cohen, "Pervasively Distributed Copyright Enforcement," *Georgetown Law Journal* 95, no. 1 (2006): 1–48.

urgent need to characterize and assess potentially destabilizing impacts on values configurations. We already have experienced how latent barriers—physical, economic, time—that served as extralegal protection for privacy are undone by the interjection of machines: for example, drones that alter lines of sight, making fences and property lines insufficient to limit prying eyes; video surveillance systems that can identify individuals in a crowd; and online access to public records that make an individual's past infractions as salient as her present successes. These experiences should inspire skepticism in the face of all claims of sameness, even if some of these claims prove ultimately to be innocuous. The *handoff* framework offers a guide to maintaining a focus on implicit as well as explicit values as sociotechnical systems evolve. With different types of actors performing different functions, respectively, across versions, the system will call on different modalities of control and regulation—technology, law, ethical norms, and economics. Surely some configurations of functions will provide superior protection for particular values: this is our point of departure and focus of inquiry.

A simple case may illuminate the point. Take sealable envelopes. As a material approach to securing privacy in written correspondence, it achieves this function within a framework of legal protections against tampering, norms against reading private letters, locked letterboxes, and mail slots that bring letters behind locked doors. In other words, although sealable envelopes may qualify as a "privacy enhancing technology," postal privacy is a product of the sociotechnical system of legal, cultural, ethical, and material realities of which it is a part. The societal significance of the sealed envelope is not a function of its paper and glue, alone, or the manufacturing processes that produce it; instead, the character of its embedding within a political economy, politics, ideation, institutional infrastructure, and set of practices is an integral part of how it "works." With the transition to email, initially, federal law was reformed to bolster privacy in the absence of a material envelope; gaps in the law left communications vulnerable. Over time, as remote and indefinite storage of email became the norm, the discrepancies between the privacy afforded to communications by postal and electronic mail were viewed with increasing skepticism and ultimately substantially righted, first through litigation and new laws, and more recently through widespread adoption of end-to-end encryption. While the decision to deploy end-to-end encryption was surely made possible due to improvements in technology, it was driven by a renewed realization, among the public and policymakers, of the ethical significance of unencrypted communications born of the Snowden disclosures, which revealed systematic dragnet surveillance of communications by the U.S. government. The new configuration of communication privacy protection set the stage for renewed "technological drama"[6] around law enforcement access and communications privacy, revealing how various configurations alter the *mass* of privacy.

Details aside, this case shows that even as email gains acceptance as a functional replacement for "snail mail," the entangled reality of communications privacy is destabi-

---

[6] Bryan Pfaffenberger, "Technological Dramas," *Science, Technology and Human Values* 17, no. 3 (1992): 282–312.

lized. One might argue that email performs the same function as snail mail, namely, communications among users—albeit more speedily. Lacking the equivalent of a physical envelope, the legal protections, and many of the norms and practices that tacitly and explicitly protect against prying into postal mail, however, the value of privacy needed to be reinserted into a system thus newly configured.

The Handoff model is an instrument for performing analyses, such as these, to reveal ethical issues as they emerge and are disrupted in progressive versions of systems where functions are shifted from one component actor to another (or others). The model (1) sharply reveals how functions are distributed to components (human, computational, mechanical) in alternative sociotechnical systems; and (2) interrogates the value propositions captured in these alternative configurations.

THE HANDOFF MODEL

Provoked by claims about computational systems taking over tasks previously performed by humans, especially tasks thought to require human intelligence, the concept of *handoff* offers a lens through which to scrutinize them in ethical terms. Outside the purview of scholars and social critics, the common practice of delegating functions performed by humans to machines or from machines of one type to machines of a different type, mostly proceeded with little fanfare.[7] Public imagination and anxiety has been stirred, however, with contemporary forms of automation involving AI taking over human roles—machines that can label ("recognize") images, process ("understand") and produce ("speak") natural language and control other machines (robots) anticipate what we will say and do, and make decisions on the basis of these.

Where function shifts from one type of actor to another, and people are inclined to say that the second is performing *the same* function as the first (same function, different actor), we see a red flag. Before racing to the conclusion, we see a dire need for detailed critical analysis that clearly reveals what stays the same, what does not, and how even seemingly irrelevant differences—flesh and blood versus silicon and metal—makes a difference, for the configuration of ethical values embodied in systems in question. The *handoff* lens draws attention to the backdrop of ethical and political values embodied by respective systems—the systems before and after functional handoff. It decomposes the "how" of the function to understand how it is different and what that means for values.

[7] See, for example, Janet Morrissey, "When Robots Ring the Bell," *New York Times* (November 7, 2018); James Vincent, "Economists Worry We Aren't Prepared for the Fallout from Automation," *The Verge* (July 2, 2018), https://www.theverge.com/2018/7/2/17524822/robot-automation-job-threat-what-happens-next; Yuki Noguchi, "Recruiters Use 'Geofencing' to Target Potential Hires Where They Live and Work," *National Public Radio* (July 7, 2017), https://www.npr.org/sections/alltechconsidered/2017/07/07/535981386/recruiters-use-geofencing-to-target-potential-hires-where-they-live-and-work?t=1560452691647.

It opens our view not only to what might be the same but what may have changed in the reconfiguration of function across component actors.

To begin, the objects of our analysis are complex technical systems comprising diverse functional components. Because the variable nature of these components may include physical mechanisms, embodied computational subsystems, and even humans, the unit of analysis, strictly speaking is sociotechnical systems, a concept we take as given. Indeed, the sociotechnical is what we mean to cover in the balance of this article, though we mostly revert to the term "system" for the sake of simplicity. Abstractly conceived, a system may be defined in terms of its function, in turn achieved through orchestrated subfunctions performed by a system's component parts, in turn, themselves composed of sub-subsystems (or components), and so on. As such, the model assumes that notions of system and component (or subsystem) are relative terms whose application signals the focus of analysis rather than an ontological commitment.[8] By analogy, we may think of the human body as a system and the organs as component parts; but for the cardiologist, the heart is the system of interest and the chambers, valves, arteries, its components, and so on.

A word on terminology: because systems of interest may comprise multifarious parts, including some that are material and others human, we typically use the term *component* as neutral between the two, though occasionally will use "component-actor" to remind the reader (and ourselves) of this variability.

As noted, systems perform functions, and it is the redistribution of these functions that interests us—across versions, either progressive variations over time or contemporaneously competing with one another. What a system's function is, in general terms, answers the question, "what does this system do?" System-components also perform functions, similarly, answering the question, "what does it do?" and also addressing *how* the component-function or subsystem contributes to the function of the system overall. Further, a system's function can be described at varying levels of abstraction: up a level, in terms of its goals, purposes, or even values; down a level, in terms of *how* it does what it does, as a designer or engineer might explain it. It is worth achieving a degree of precision around these levels, distinguishing goals, purposes, and function from the gritty details of how they are achieved. Nevertheless, it is a mistake to think that the higher

---

[8] Terminology presented a dilemma. We use the generic term *component* to apply to both human and nonhuman parts of the *sociotechnical system*. While the term component does not naturally apply to human *actors*, for our purposes it is important to be able to refer in like manner to human and nonhuman components of a system. Actor-Network-Theory (See, for example, Bruno Latour, "Where Are the Missing Masses? The Sociology of a Few Mundane Artifacts," in *Shaping Technology/ Building Society: Studies in Sociotechnical Change*, ed. Wiebe Bijker and John Law [Cambridge, MA: MIT Press, 1992], 225–58, which most certainly has influenced us, came up with *actant* as a way out of the dilemma, but our preference is to not adopt theoretical jargon, which can be off-putting for general readers. Going forward, we will mostly stick with the term *component* and sometimes will revert to actor, or subsystem. In addition to human actors and physical objects that can be or constitute system components, we allow for the possibility of groups and institutions as components.

order outcomes, including values configurations, are insulated from the hows of implementation, or so the Handoff model says.

At the lower level of "how," an analyst explains how components function and how they function together to produce system function overall. To capture the ways components function together, we posit the concept of *acting on* or *engaging* to describe the interaction of one component on another or others. In our lighting example, we imagine darkness falling and a human (component) flipping a switch, in turn causing lamps to illuminate. Using our newly minted terms, the model describes this series of events as a human *acting on* a switch and a switch acting on a circuit, in turn producing an outcome—"turn on the lights." While the human and the physical switch both *act on* other components, respectively, to fulfill the overall function, the model recognizing that there may be significant differences in how they do so, introduces the construct of *mode* (of acting on, or engaging). Not all social and political theories of technology have emphasized what we have called mode; for example, Larry Lessig primarily sought to emphasize the powers people, institutions, software, and machines have in common, namely, the ability to regulate.[9] Others, however, have recognized that the modes of *acting on* performed by human components and machine components, respectively, typically signal disparate forms of moral responsibility.[10]

For the Handoff model, different values for the *mode* parameter may influence or even determine ethical properties of successive versions of a system. Take physical force, a familiar *mode* of acting on. One physically embodied component-actor may act on another, either forcing or preventing action.[11] The human actor, pushing a button, sets off a causal chain of action resulting in car headlights flashing on. Physical ("material") causation, or—one could say—"brute force" may operate in many different ways, for example, a physical component (or set of objects) may act on another component by constraining its range of action (e.g., a safety overlock) without necessarily causing a particular outcome; there could be far more complex causal interdependencies, as when numerous components function together to produce a complex configuration of outcomes on other components, and so on.

A different *mode* of *acting on*—one might say, more subtle—is *affordance*. As defined by the cognitive psychologist J.J. Gibson, affordances are relational properties of things in the environment whose meaning or significance is derived from their service to the needs or capabilities of respective actor-types (humans, other mammals, invertebrates, etc.).[12] When saying that something is nourishing, is a tool, or serves as secure cover,

---

[9] Lessig, *Code: And Other Laws of Cyberspace*.

[10] See, for example, Karen Yeung, "The Forms and Limits of Choice Architecture as a Tool of Government," *Law & Policy* 38, no. 3 (2016): 186–210; Brownsword, "Lost in Translation"; Surden, "Structural Rights in Privacy"; Cohen, "Pervasively Distributed Copyright Enforcement."

[11] Remaining at the intuitive level, for the moment, we must look past the fact that there is nothing simple about causation, as Aristotle well demonstrated!

[12] James J. Gibson, "The Theory of Affordances," in *The Ecological Approach to Visual Perception* (Hillsdale, NJ: Lawrence Erlbaum Associates, 1986), 127–143.

these properties are affordances in relation to actors of particular shapes, sizes, abilities, and needs. Adapting and widely popularizing this idea, Donald Norman urged designers to exploit (not ignore) affordances to create artifacts that people understand and know how to use because well utilized affordances trigger appropriate cognitive and perceptual reactions in humans.[13] Principles derived from Norman's infamous doors and switches have traveled into realms of digital technologies. One approach a social media site could take is to adopt a policy that permits data extraction and offer an application programming interface that affords data extraction, or adopt technical or legal rules (for example, a prohibition on scraping) that discourage it, in relation to actors with relevant technical know-how. Within the Handoff model, affordances are a *mode* of *acting on* that designers can exploit to suggest a range of possible and desirable actions for a system's successful operation. On the one hand, unlike physical force, affordances are perceived and processed by users (humans) who act—often strategically—accordingly; on the other hand, they systematically elicit predictable behaviors.

In our mini case of the light switch, we observe that the human component physically exerts force on a switch thereby initiating a causal chain resulting in the lights illuminating. Among many possible answers to why the human flipped the switch, one of them celebrates the interface design for successfully exploiting the affordance of "flip-ability"; the human flipped the switch instead of pushing or pulling it. Another plausible answer, however, cites purpose: the human flipped the switch because night had fallen. Different, yet, an answer cites obedience to a rule, for example, when a light so switched, say, on a porch, lighthouse, or skyscraper is required by law. The human chooses to act after having identified conditions or pertinent rules, interpreted them, and decided to act accordingly. The human, as it were, as a free agent, is the prime mover causing the lights to turn on by flipping a switch.

Now, imagine lights whose operation is automated via sensors that detect light conditions and a small computer embedded within the light switch. In this case, in given exterior lighting and possibly other conditions, an algorithm expressed in lines of software code implemented in an embodied computer, physically *acts on* relevant components, resulting in the illumination of lights. The software code (and more abstractly, the algorithm) operates like legal rules. The model does not reify them as component actors; instead, their informational content, expressed as coded instructions, is embodied in material, electronic computers, which act on other system components, and so on.

Without delving into metaphysical questions about the nature of free agency, the Handoff model draws attention to features of the scenarios we have sketched, and differences among them, that are relevant to embodied values. Although one might be tempted to say that the automated light switches are performing *the same task* as human operated switches, the two involve different modes of acting on: one physical causation, the other human agency. This difference makes a difference, for example, in attributing

[13] Donald A. Norman, "Affordance, Conventions, and Design," *Interactions* (1999): 38–42.

responsibility (or blame) for human initiated versus sensor-initiated illumination. Affordance lies somewhere in between. Though few would say that humans responding to affordances are not necessarily acting freely, the flourishing areas of usability and design in computational systems attest to the sense that responsibility (and blame) may spread across human actor–components and designer-builders of a system. Norman's famous cases of people pushing doors that should be pulled (and vice versa) and other malfunctions communicate this message; informed analysis of the 1988 tragedy in which human operators on the USS Vincenne downed Iran Air Flight 655 with a surface-to-air missile, revealed that the interface was poorly designed.

In sum: Handoff is an analytical model for exposing ethical and political values embodied in technical systems. Deriving its foundations from bodies of work and related concepts in social studies of technology and values in design, it provides further concepts that are particularly important for the rapid deployment of AI both self-standing and within preexisting systems. It targets and challenges the notion—explicit as well as implicit—that component actors are modular, that one can pluck out a human actor and plug in an intelligent component with no further perturbations. The Handoff model offers a cluster of concepts that are potentially useful for exposing aspects of systems that change in the wake of such replacements, that may be relevant to the configuration of values embodied in the resulting systems, and that may remain invisible under standard ways of characterizing technical systems.

The subject matter of a handoff covers versions of systems, either versions that may be vying for dominance or progressive versions that follow one another as systems creators update existing models over time. A *handoff* analysis focuses on variations in different systems that result from variations in components tasked with "the same" functionality and offers great utility in the rapidly growing area of automation with AI, from access security to content moderation to self-driving cars, and a myriad more.

Access Control through the Handoff Lens: A Case Study

To illustrate an application of the *handoff* framing, we walk through the case of secure access to mobile phones, tracking handoffs across five successive system versions—four actual and one foreshadowed by a collaborator's research. We chose this case because, on the one hand, it is familiar to the point of invisibility, yet, on the other, perhaps because of this, the seemingly innocuous "improvements" in ways that each version produces the *same* functionality over its predecessor, elides differences that make a difference.

Below we explore multiple configurations of the access control function. While they are presented and often thought of as innovative improvements to security and usability, the three configurations currently available in the market place (password, fingerprint, and facial recognition) and the underdeveloped passthoughts, their relation to security and usability, among other values, become more complex as well as user and context dependent when viewed through the *handoff* lens.

In the Beginning...

Originally mobile phones did not include a lock built into the material devices themselves. This did not mean they lacked a built-in access control function. As with other phones, access control was a feature of the system, as it were, whose boundaries were more broadly defined; access to landline devices was controlled by their position in homes or offices, and mobile phones, similarly, on one's person, in purses, pockets, or cars.

User-Selected Passwords

As the services and information on phones grew and became more sensitive and revealing, the industry reached a tipping-point and moved to control access to mobile phones through passwords.

Although, increasingly, users are admonished to construct strong passwords, with nonobvious combinations of numbers, letters, and symbols, mixing upper and lower cases, with frequent updates,[14] the current standard is for users to devise their own passwords. Performing—one might say—*the same* function as a purse or pocket, the password controls access to the phone, though arguably, more effectively because while a stolen purse or picked pocket lays bare the phone's function and content along with the material device, not so with passwords.

With passwords providing access control functionality, the human (component)[15] is responsible for setting up the system by creating a passcode and providing it to the operating system (OS) via a numeric keypad. The operating system saves the human-selected inputs. Once a password is in place, the human *component* must accurately remember and enter the selected digits into the keyboard interface to unlock the phone. The phone affords a keyboard that makes password entry easy, but the OS is exacting, demanding that the input perfectly match—be both accurate and complete—the password recorded.

---

[14] Research casts doubt on actual security benefits of these practices. See Joseph Bonneau, Cormac Herley, Paul C. van Oorschot, and Frank Stajano, "The Quest to Replace Passwords: A Framework for Comparative Evaluation of Web Authentication Schemes," in *Proceedings of the IEEE Symposium on Security and Privacy* (Oakland: IEEE, 2012), 1–15.

[15] We temporarily set aside a key question about the legal relationship between the human actor and the device—the user/owner, or owner who is not the user, or user who is not the owner—all of which may have significance for the composite values output due to legal distinctions.

From Password to Fingerprint

In recent years, mobile phone providers have shifted *how* the *function* of access control is implemented—first to thumbprint and more recently to face recognition. As discussed in the following it is unclear whether these shifts result from technical advancement—for example, improved performance of fingerprint and face matching algorithms or usability, or particular security benefits, or a governing U.S. legal framework, or something else entirely.

The fingerprint, a familiar biometric, followed passwords as a subsystem for controlling access to a mobile device. As with passwords, the human *component* initiates the process by entering the print; unlike passwords, however, users *no longer* select this input; rather they *are* the input, as it were, offering up their body part—thumb/finger—as raw material for the technical component, the *reader*. The fingerprint reader creates a mathematical representation of the fingerprint image, or a template, which it stores. To access the phone, users supply the physical stimulus to be checked against the stored template. In Apple's description, the system "creates a mathematical representation of your fingerprint and compares this to your enrolled fingerprint data [the mathematical representation described above] to identify a match and unlock your device."[16] From each successful access usage, it incrementally updates the mathematical representation to improve matching accuracy. The mathematical representations are fungible in that a new algorithm could be used to generate new mathematical representations.

The *mode* of the human acting upon the phone is not physical force but through the affordances of the fingerprint reader, which is able to sense and perform the logical process of comparing input with a stored set of encrypted templates.

This shift also changes the process of accessing the device. Once a fingerprint-generated password is in place, the *human component* must present a fingerprint in a way that is readable to the phone fingerprint reader—not sweaty, wet, swollen or disfigured, dirty, or oddly angled. Because the password is not the finger itself but the phone's stored representation of it, the same finger may provoke different results—access or denial.

In this configuration the phone demands (*mode*) that the human actor present herself in a manner that is legible to the machine. But the technical actor requires the human only to "be herself"—or close enough to it—in a certain way, not to remember something. To gain access, the human must prove to the machine that she is herself, not that she knows a special secret. Unlike the keypad entries in a password configuration, a fingerprint match is not binary, but is probabilistic in that the phone determines in real time whether the mathematical representation of the current fingerprint constitutes a match with the stored mathematical representation of the prior fingerprint.

In this new configuration the human component no longer knows the password; access is tied to a specific human and can no longer be easily transferred, and the human

---

[16] "About Touch ID Advanced Security Technology," Apple Support, https://support.apple.com/en-gb/HT204587 (accessed June 14, 2019).

cannot continually replace the input used to generate the access control because an individual's fingerprints are finite.

From Fingerprint to Face ID

In late 2017 Apple introduced Face ID to replace Touch ID—the fingerprint recognition system. Face ID used iPhone 10's new "TrueDepth camera system," which constructs a 3D map of a person's face. TrueDepth's dot projector projects over 30,000 dots onto the face each time an individual looks at the phone, thereby creating and developing its map of the person's features. The image and the dot pattern are fed through a neural network to generate a mathematical model of her face.

Some of the shifts that occurred between passwords and fingerprints remain—again the human component is an input, and access is tied to a specific human. Unlike a fingerprint reader, however, which requires contact—and therefore is evident to the human, setting aside issues of volition for later—Face ID is a contactless technology. One human can hold the phone and point it at another human, possibly without their knowledge, to access the phone. A human may be an unwitting input into the authentication system that opens up the phones contents and capabilities for someone else.

From Face ID to Passthoughts

Imagine if we could unlock phones merely by thinking a password—*passthoughts*. A prototype of such a system is under development by John Chuang.[17] With this, the function of controlling access moves deeper into the body. Rather than typing a password, or offering a finger, or face, it is an individual's brain activity that becomes the biometric identifier that is authenticated by the system. Like a fingerprint or face image, thinking a thought generates patterns distinctive enough across individuals that they can be used to uniquely distinguish individuals. In the current research prototype, a human user wears a headset with an electroencephalogram (EEG) resting on the brain's left frontal lobe. Thinking a passphrase produces brainwaves that the EEG registers and compares to an earlier passthought. Like other biometrics a "hit" is defined probabilistically and, not accessible to human users, the human may not know, directly, how close a given passthought is to the stored one to unlock the device successfully. An intriguing merger of a chosen password and embodied biometric, a passthought offers the equivalent of two-factor authentication.

[17] John Chuang, "Passthoughts: User Authentication Using Brainwaves," http://people.ischool.berkeley.edu/~chuang/passthoughts/ (accessed June 14, 2019).

ACCESS CONTROL THROUGH
THE LENS OF HANDOFF

A typical narrative might celebrate the evolution of these different configuration of access control in mobile operating systems through these four phases: starting with "primitive" physical constraints to more sturdy, logic-based, combinatorial password protection, to sophisticated biometric facial recognition, and finally, even "smarter," brainwave ID. According to this narrative, progression through each version involves a handoff of function from a component-actor of one type to a different type, each one an improvement over the previous. Instead, the *handoff* approach opens a view to potential ripple effects of such replacements: per the focus of the discussion thus far, different types of component actors *act on* one another differently, and these associated differences may have implications for ethical and political values.

In the case of access control, an important feature of physical deprivation or passwords is an ability of phone owners to determine and control the key, investing them the power to delegate access to others.[18] Despite this similarity, however, a significant difference between the two is that the password system, embedded within the logic of the device OS, implicates the OS developers as additional component-actors, thus expanding the boundaries of the system. Access control performed with biometrics also extends a system's boundary beyond the device itself, but unlike password access, it places the users in a different role in relation to the device, namely, "one-user-one-phone," by restricting use to the individual whose biometric (fingerprint, face, or brainwave pattern) is entered as the original key.

Even in this rather limited case, a *handoff* lens exposes ethical and political differences. In the cases of physical and password restraint, device owners have full sovereignty, so to speak, allowing them to delegate usage to others; they allow for a shared, or collective, resource.[19] The move from "something the user does or knows" (password) to "something they are" (biometric) claimed as a usability improvement that relieves users of the need to remember a secret, curtails agency by diminishing both transparency and dimensions of control. Humans choose a password, subject to OS imposed constraints, enjoy a degree of control and understanding of how it functions and sources of its strength (e.g., length and complexity). With biometrics, the OS defines the password and determines its function. Device owners have lost insight beyond how to present themselves and, even then might not grasp failures to unlock, for example, a system glitch or a finger that is too hot, or cold, or damp, and so forth. Prospective passthought systems would seem further to reduce the degree of control as humans find that thoughts are notoriously harder to control than physical action.

---

[18] In some situations there may be legal constraints on such sharing, but we will set those aside for now.

[19] One may relate this scenario to the shift from physical books to e-books where the configuration of access is altered, away from traditional personal property to a model that is far more limited.

RESPONSIBILITY

Responsibility and accountability closely tie in with control: an actor may only be blamed for harm—in this case, breaches of security—if he or she had a significant hand in controlling the outcome. Breaches due to password failures may fall on device owners for choosing weak passwords or misguidedly sharing a password with others, or on OS providers for failing to build in adequate affordances for users, who can then generate passwords too weak to withstand computational brute force attacks. In fingerprint and Face ID configurations the OS assumes a specific threat model that precludes physical brute force attacks on an individual's wrist to compel connection between the finger and the phone. With this form of attack, an attacker physically forces the body to move in a certain way; thereafter setting in motion a cause and effect set up by the device and OS manufacturers.

As noted earlier, the lens of handoff challenges the typical narrative of technological progress, which implies that advancing from password to fingerprint to face ID is a steady, linear improvement along the trajectory of security.[20] Similarly recent cases involving law enforcement show that the legal framework governing whether and when government agents can compel individuals to provide access to their mobile devices[21] does not vary linearly along this trajectory.[22] Although police must obtain a warrant before searching a cell phone,[23] once they have it, whether and when they can compel an individual to unlock it turns on the Fifth Amendment. Admittedly, case law continues to evolve, but at present[24] the majority of U.S. courts have concluded that while finger-

[20] The likelihood of false positives—the wrong biometric opening the device—has, according to Apple, been greatly reduced by the introduction of Face ID. Where Touch ID, with a single enrolled finger, had a 1 in 50,000 chance of unlocking with the wrong fingerprint. "About Touch ID advanced security technology," Apple Support, https://support.apple.com/en-gb/HT204587 (accessed June 14, 2019). Face ID, with a single enrolled appearance, has approximately a 1 in 1,000,000 chance of opening with the wrong face. "About Face ID advanced technology," Apple Support, https://support.apple.com/en-us/HT208108 (accessed June 14, 2019).

[21] A phone user and owner may be distinct, bur for our purposes we focus on the limited case where owner and user are the same.

[22] For this analysis we consider U.S. law. For a thorough discussion of this issue from conflicting viewpoints, see Kerr, "Compelled Decryption and the Privilege Against Self-Incrimination"; and Laurent Sacharoff, "What Am I Really Saying When I Open My Smartphone?: A Response to Professor Kerr," Texas Law Review Online Edition 97 (2019), available at https://texaslawreview.org/what-am-i-really-saying-when-i-open-my-smartphone-a-response-to-orin-s-kerr/; Orin S. Kerr and Bruce Schneier, "Encryption Workarounds," Georgetown Law Journal 106, no. 4 (2018): 989–1019; and Laurent Sacharoff, "Unlocking the Fifth Amendment: Passwords and Encrypted Devices," Fordham Law Review 87 no. 1 (2018): 203–251.

[23] Riley v. California (Riley II), 134 S. Ct. 2473, 2495 (2014).

[24] Under U.S. law an individual accused of a crime can "take the Fifth," and refuse to testify against herself. The Fifth Amendment of the U.S. Constitution declares that "No person shall...be compelled in any criminal case to be a witness against himself," which applies to acts that are "testimonial"—have communicative aspects—not just spoken words. There is a good argument that communicating a password to a phone is protected, and the majority of courts that have examined the issue have reached

prints can be compelled in most circumstances, not so with passwords.[25] Existing precedent distinguishes between production of the body,[26] considered nontestimonial, and acts that reveal the contents of the defendant's mind, which are testimonial. Thus, a fingerprint (and, by implication any biometric) can generally be compelled but not a password.[27] This curious distinction demonstrates that features of component actors, which may not affect direct functionality may nevertheless be decisive in a system's politics.

PRIVACY AND SECURITY

Access control is one mode of constraining information flows—to intruders and other unwanted recipients. Setting aside the unchecked information flows among OS, apps, data brokers, and others, against which access security subsystems offer virtually no protection,[28] it is still possible to compare progressive versions against each other. From physical to password-controlled access, an OS might capture physiological metadata, of sorts, potentially revealing gender, health status, and so forth. Other than that, the password itself, particularly if encrypted on a server, incorporates nothing further.[29]

that conclusion. See Doe v. United States, 487 U.S. 201, 210 n. 9 (1988) (stating in dicta that compelling someone to reveal the combination to his wall safe is testimonial for purposes of the Fifth Amendment); Wayne R. LaFave et al., 3 Criminal Procedure § 8.13(a) (4th ed. 2017) ("[R]equiring the subpoenaed party to reveal a passcode that would allow [the government] to perform the decryption . . . would require a testimonial communication standing apart from the act of production, and therefore make unavailable the foregone conclusion doctrine.").

[25] Several state courts have concluded that the Fifth Amendment privilege against self-incrimination does not protect against compelled disclosure of a fingerprint to unlock a seized cellphone, because fingerprints are not a testimonial communication. State v. Diamond, 2018 WL 443356 (Minn. 2018); Commonwealth v. Baust, 89 Va. Cir. 267 (Va. Cir. Ct. 2014); Florida v. Stahl, 206 So. 3d 124, 135 (Fla. Dist. Ct. App. 2016). There are instances where compelling a fingerprint may be testimonial, for example, where it speaks to the ownership of a device as in In re Application for a Search Warrant, 236 F. Supp. 3d 1066, 1073 (N.D. Ill. 2017). Holding that compelling production of fingerprints from all people present at the execution of a search warrant to unlock seized devices raised Fifth Amendment concerns, but noting that generally ownership is a foregone conclusion and therefore the fingerprint not testimonial. Most recently a federal magistrate judge in the U.S. District Court for Northern District of California concluded that biometrics are testimonial holding that "Government may not compel or otherwise utilize fingers, thumbs, facial recognition, optical/iris, or any other biometric feature to unlock electronic devices," In re Of, Case No. 4-19-70,053 KAW, at *9 (N.D. Cal. Jan. 10, 2019).

[26] Doe v. United States, 487 U.S. 201, 210 (1988) ("[A] suspect may be compelled to furnish a blood sample; to provide a handwriting exemplar, or a voice exemplar; to stand in a lineup; and to wear particular clothing").

[27] Orin Kerr, "The Fifth Amendment and Touch ID," Washington Post (October 21, 2016), https://www.washingtonpost.com/news/volokh-conspiracy/wp/2016/10/21/the-fifth-amendment-and-touch-id/.

[28] Helen Nissenbaum, "Contextual Integrity Up and Down the Data Food Chain," Theoretical Inquiries in Law 20, no. 1 (2019): 221–256.

[29] Surely passwords can be birthdates, names of children, favorite sports team, etc.

Although a fingerprint places irrevocable identifying information in the hands of the device OS, it might offer great protection against external intruders; according to a 2014 survey, passwords were deployed by only 34 percent of all smartphone users,[30] but by 2016, Apple reported that 89 percent of customers with devices supporting fingerprint unlocking were using it.[31]

In the case of face ID, though also a biometric, its application differs from fingerprint in not requiring physical contact for intended use.[32] This means the device may more easily accommodate unlocking by multiple users, potentially returning to the user some of the control offered by passwords. With increasing interest in biometric identification, generally, facial recognition systems, and availability of facial templates to powerful operators (government and commercial) have increasingly alarmed critics.[33] The extent to which biometric systems inappropriately leak characteristics is not necessarily a function of biometrics but, rather, of a system's design, for example, whether templates and processing of input from sensors is performed on the device or centralized on OS, or other third-party servers. A full account, while necessary for the development of a complete analysis, is outside the boundaries of this chapter.

ARTICULATING THE BOUNDARIES OF A SYSTEM

Smartphones no longer rely on access control provided solely through physical deprivation. Although the *handoff* analysis we sketched implies successive, or competing alternatives, today's reality is that dominant mobile operating systems offer more than one of these approaches, allowing users to choose among them. Instead of lessening the need, a *handoff* analysis may reveal to users relevant differences among options. The transition irrevocably tethers access control functionality to the OS provider. Thus, although the user gets to choose among the three (or, potentially four) alternatives, it is the OS provider that chooses whether and what the user gets to choose both by constraining certain actions and by affording them. Where privacy is a value of concern across progressive or

[30] "Smart Phone Thefts Rose to 3.1 Million in 2013," *Consumer Reports* (April 2014), https://www.consumerreports.org/cro/news/2014/04/smart-phone-thefts-rose-to-3-1-million-last-year/index.htm (accessed June 14, 2019).
[31] Mikey Campbell, "Average iPhone User Unlocks Device 80 Times per Day, 89% Use Touch ID, Apple Says," *Apple Insider*, https://appleinsider.com/articles/16/04/19/average-iphone-user-unlocks-device-80-times-per-day-89-use-touch-id-apple-says (accessed June 14, 2019).
[32] One can imagine scenarios for fingerprints that don't require contact by the relevant human—a severed finger or a print manufactured—but those are not the "normal" use case.
[33] See, for example, Timothy Williams, "Facial Recognition Software Moves from Overseas Wars to Local Police," *New York Times* (August 12, 2015); Catie Edmondson, "An Airline Scans Your Face. You Take Off. But Few Rules Govern Where Your Data Goes," *New York Times* (August 6, 2018); Joshua Rothman, "In the Age of A.I., Is Seeing Still Believing?" *The New Yorker* (November 5, 2018).

competing versions, we have discussed potential pitfalls of alternatives, for example, password versus biometric or fingerprint versus facial recognition. To some extent, however, privacy is partially constructed by relevant legal frameworks and partially in the hands of the OS provider as a function of design choices, such as, whether biometric templates are stored on the device only or also on central servers, whether encrypted or in the clear, and available by whose choices and under what operations.

The *handoff* lens exposes a critical point about the system, as a whole, that may otherwise be obscured. In the transition from physical deprivation enacted by the user to access control internalized as a subsystem of the OS, the boundaries of the system expand accordingly. While, initially, access control resides outside the technical system, progressive iterations expand the boundaries of the system to include the OS provider as a component actor, fully or partially responsible for the functioning of the access control subsystem. Some might view automation, that is, the insertion of AI (or any mechanic component), as a move to eradicate humans from a system (or subsystem); instead, in the effort to characterize shifts in modes of acting due to automation, a *handoff* analysis suggests that describing such moves as *dis*placements rather than *re*placements of agency yields far more productive insights in service of societal regulation of technological development.

Finally, it can be illuminating to consider the *trigger* for two competing or sequential handoff configurations. *Trigger*—the impetus for the reconfiguration of *function*—often highlights specific values that motivated the reconfiguration or are intended to be implicated by it. The shifts from password to fingerprint to face occurred against a backdrop of technological improvements, steady increase in the range and significance of content stored on mobile phones, heightened awareness of the privacy implications of access to that information, and efforts by the U.S. Federal Bureau of Investigation and intelligence agencies worldwide to develop more permissive legal standards for access to the contents of phones and restrict the strength and require backdoors in encryption in consumer products. The range and significance of content stored on mobile phones and the cost of the phones themselves fueled public pressure on companies to limit the utility of stolen phones. So-called "kill switches," which allow a device owner to remotely disable it, were the primary technology developed to depress thefts, but phone-locking measures were viewed as an additional strategy to suppress theft as they depress resale value.[34] With respect to law enforcement access, Apple products and Apple executives have been at the center of the global maelstrom over individual privacy and law enforcement access. Intelligence and law enforcement agencies have pressed governments and companies to provide them with the capability to read the encrypted contents on phones without the

---

[34] Brian X. Chien, "Smartphones Embracing 'Kill Switches' as Theft Defense," *New York Times Bits Blog* (June 19, 2014), https://bits.blogs.nytimes.com/2014/06/19/antitheft-technology-led-to-a-dip-in-iphone-thefts-in-some-cities-police-say/. Chien describes kill switches and legislation to require them, noting that "[p]olice and tech companies have tried harder over the last year to educate consumers on additional security measures to protect phones, like setting up passcodes, which can make it harder to gain access to devices so that they can be erased and resold."

knowledge or assistance of the user.[35] The relationship between these wide-ranging government actions and shifts in password configurations are unknown, yet Apple has been very vocal about the relationship between device passwords, device encryption, and the balance of power between citizens and the government.[36] And Apple has fought efforts to force product design or redesigns to weaken device level encryption.[37]

The *handoff* lens foregrounds the values at play in these various configurations of controlling access to mobile phones.

The goal has been to demonstrate that the lens offered by handoff affords unique and critical insights into the operation of these systems, in terms of new components and modes of acting, that have dramatic consequences for both human and societal values. In our view, this is a critical ameliorative to a focus on the ongoing transition of control into computational components, instead showing the structural, political, and ethical stakes of those changes. We offer handoff with all humility, acknowledging, first, that there are deep issues about systems and contexts of technology development and use that it does not, and may not ever, be able to capture. Second, as a work in progress, there are undoubtedly factors in the myriad handoffs taking place and still coming from humans to machines that the model does not capture. Here, we hope that experiences applying the model—our own and others—will continue to enrich it and expand its explanatory power.

BIBLIOGRAPHY

Akrich, Madeleine, and Bruno Latour. "A Summary of a Convenient Vocabulary for the Semiotics of Human and Nonhuman Assemblies." In *Shaping Technology/Building Society: Studies in Sociotechnical Change*, ed. Wiebe Bijker and John Law, 259–64. Cambridge, MA: MIT Press, 1992.

Brownsword, Roger. "Lost in Translation: Legality, Regulatory Margins, and Technological Management." *Berkeley Technology Law Journal* 26, no. 3 (2011): 1321–66.

Flanagan, Mary, and Helen Nissenbaum. *Values at Play in Digital Games.* Cambridge, MA: MIT Press, 2014.

Friedman, Batya. "Value-sensitive Design." *interactions* 3, no. 6 (1996): 16–23.

Friedman, Batya, David G. Hendry, and Alan Borning. "A Survey of Value Sensitive Design Methods." (2017). *Foundations and Trends in Human–Computer Interaction* 11, no. 2 (2017): 63–125.

[35] See, for example, Statement of Sally Quillian Yates, Deputy Attorney General, Department of Justice, and James B. Comey, Director, Federal Bureau of Investigation, "Going Dark: Encryption, Technology, and the Balance between Public Safety and Privacy," S. Comm. on the Judiciary, 114th Cong. (July 8, 2015). The statement presents the argument that ensuring that technology allows the government to exercise lawful access is "not asking to expand the Government's surveillance authority, but...ensur[ing] that [they can] obtain electronic information and evidence pursuant to the legal authority."

[36] Richard Lawler, "Tim Cook Outlines Apple's View on Privacy, Encryption in MSNBC Interview," *Engadget* (April 6, 2018), https://www.engadget.com/2018/04/06/tim-cook-revolution-interview/.

[37] Id.

Latour, Bruno. "Where Are the Missing Masses? The Sociology of a Few Mundane Artifacts." In *Shaping Technology/Building Society: Studies in Sociotechnical Change*, ed. Wiebe Bijker and John Law, 225–58. Cambridge, MA: MIT Press, 1992.

Lessig, Lawrence. *Code: And Other Laws of Cyberspace*. New York: Basic Books, 1999.

Radin, Margaret Jane. "Regulating by Contract, Regulating by Machine." *Journal of Institutional and Theoretical Economics* 160, no. 1 (2004): 142–56.

Shilton, Katie, Jes A. Koepfler, and Kenneth R. Fleischmann. "How to See Values in Social Computing: Methods for Studying Values Dimensions." In *Proceedings of the 17th ACM Computer Supported Cooperative Work & Social Computing*, 426–35. Association for Computing Machinery, 2014.

Surden, Harry. "Structural Rights in Privacy." *SMU Law Review* 60, no. 4 (2007): 1605–29.

Winner, Langdon. "Do Artifacts Have Politics?" *Daedalus* 109, no. 1 (1980): 121–36.

CHAPTER 13

....

RACE AND GENDER

....

TIMNIT GEBRU

DATA-DRIVEN CLAIMS ABOUT
RACE AND GENDER PERPETUATE
THE NEGATIVE BIASES OF THE DAY

....

SCIENCE is often hailed as an objective discipline in pursuit of truth. Similarly, one may believe that technology is inherently neutral and that products that are built by those representing only a slice of the world's population can be used by anyone in the world. However, an analysis of scientific thinking in the nineteenth century and major technological advances such as automobiles, medical practices, and other disciplines shows how the lack of representation among those who have the power to build this technology has resulted in a power imbalance in the world and in technology, whose intended or unintended negative consequences harm those who are not represented in its production. Artificial intelligence is no different.[1] While the popular paradigm of the day continues to change, the dominance of those who are the most powerful race/ethnicity in their location (e.g., white in the United States, ethnic Han in China, etc.), combined with the concentration of power in a few locations around the world, has resulted in a technology that can benefit humanity but also has been shown to (intentionally or unintentionally) systematically discriminate against those who are already marginalized.

Like many disciplines, often those who perpetuate bias are doing it while attempting to come up with something better than before. However, the predominant thought that scientists are "objective" clouds them from being self-critical and analyzing what predominant discriminatory view of the day they could be encoding, or what goal they are helping advance. For example, in the nineteenth century, Charles Darwin worked on his theory of evolution as a carefully researched and well-thought-out alternative to

---

[1] Cathy O'Neil, *Weapons of Math Destruction: How Big Data Increases Inequality and Threatens Democracy* (New York: Broadway Books, 2016).

creationism. What many leave out, however, is that the title of his book was *On the Origin of Species by Means of Natural Selection, or the Preservation of Favoured Races in the Struggle for Life* (emphasis added), in which he writes: "The western nations of Europe…now so immeasurably surpass their former savage progenitors [that they] stand at the summit of civilization.… [T]he civilised races of man will almost certainly exterminate, and replace, the savage races throughout the world."[2] And in his subsequent book, *The Descent of Man and Selection in Relation to Sex*, he notes that "[m]an is more courageous, pugnacious and energetic than woman, and has a more inventive genius. His brain is absolutely larger, [while] the formation of her skull is said to be intermediate between the child and the man."[3]

Although Darwin's book was criticized for its stance against the church, the British Empire used it to justify colonialism by claiming that those subjected under its rule were scientifically inferior and unfit to rule themselves, with British anthropologists like James Hunt using Darwin's theory to justify slavery in papers such as *The Negro's Place in Nature* (1863).[4]

Since the days of Darwin, race has been shown time and time again to be a social construct that has no biological basis.[5] According to professor of public health Michael Yudell, race is "a concept we think is too crude to provide useful information, it's a concept that has social meaning that interferes in the scientific understanding of human genetic diversity and it's a concept that we are not the first to call upon moving away from."[6]

However, celebrated scientists like evolutionary psychologist Steven Pinker still assert that it is tied to genetics, writing articles such as *Groups and Genes*,[7] which claim, for example, that Ashkenazi Jews are innately intelligent. Echoing Darwin's assertions regarding the relationships between genius and gender, scientists are still attempting to extract gender-based differences in intelligence, with papers asking, "Why are males over-represented at the upper extremes of intelligence?"[8]

These questions are posed without disputing the claim that males are overrepresented in the upper extremes of intelligence. Researchers have claimed to empirically show that men are overrepresented in the upper and lower extremes of IQ: that is, the highest and

[2] Charles Darwin, *On the Origin of Species by Means of Natural Selection, or the Preservation of Favoured Races in the Struggle for Life* (Oxford: H. Milford; Oxford University Press, 1859).

[3] Charles Darwin, *The Descent of Man, and Selection in Relation to Sex*, Vol. 1. (New York: D. Appleton, 1896).

[4] James Hunt, *On the Negro's Place in Nature* (London: Trübner for the Anthropological Society, 1863).

[5] Stephanie Pappas, "Unraveling the Human Genome: 6 Molecular Milestones," *Live Science* (2013), https://www.livescience.com/26505-human-genome-milestones.html.

[6] Megan Gannon, "Race Is a Social Construct, Scientists Argue," *Scientific American* 5 (2016), https://www.scientificamerican.com/article/race-is-a-social-construct-scientists-argue/.

[7] Steven Pinker, "The Lessons of the Ashkenazim: Groups and Genes," *The New Republic* (2006), https://newrepublic.com/article/77727/groups-and-genes.

[8] Rosalind Arden, and Robert Plomin, "Sex Differences in Variance of Intelligence across Childhood," *Personality and Individual Differences* 41, no. 1 (2006): 39–48.

lowest scoring person in the IQ test is most likely to be a man.[9] This claim is then generalized to mean that men show a greater spread in "intelligence" generally, without constraining it to the IQ test.

Because of the myth of scientific objectivity, these types of claims that seem to be backed up by data and "science" are less likely to be scrutinized. Just like Darwin and Hunt, many scientists today perpetuate the view that there is an inherent difference between the abilities of various races and sexes. However, because their works seem to be corroborated by data and empirical experiments, these views are likely to gain credibility. What is not captured in any of these analyses is, for example, that the IQ test in and of itself was designed by white men whose concept of "smartness" or "genius" was shaped, centered, and evaluated on specific types of white men.

In fact, standardized testing in general has a racist history in the United States, and Ben Hutchinson and Margaret Mitchell's *50 Years of Unfairness* discusses bodies of work from the civil rights movement era that were devoted to fairness in standardized testing.[10] The debates and proposals put forth at that time foreshadow those advanced within the AI ethics and fairness community today.

Thus, the types of data-driven claims about race and gender made by the likes of Darwin are still alive today and will probably be for the foreseeable future. The only difference will be the method of choice used to "corroborate" such claims. In 2019, Reuters reported that Amazon shut down its automated hiring tool because it was found to be negatively biased against women.[11] According to Reuters, the tool "penalized resumes that included the word 'women's,' as in 'women's chess club captain.'" And it downgraded graduates of two all-women's colleges.

Analyzed within the context of the society it was built in, it is unsurprising that an automated hiring tool such as Amazon's would exhibit these types of biases. In 2018, workers at Google staged a walkout protesting the company's handling of sexual harassment. And shortly after, in 2019, news articles detailed women's accounts of toxic working environments at Microsoft including sexual harassment that goes unpunished, inability to get promoted, and many other forms of discrimination.[12]

This hostile environment for women is ironic given the fact that the computing industry was started and dominated by women. As Mar Hicks details in *Programmed Inequality*, while computing was considered a feminine job dominated by women, that

[9] E.g., Joan C. Chrisler, and Donald R. McCreary, *Handbook of Gender Research in Psychology*, Vol. 1 (New York: Springer, 2010).

[10] Ben Hutchinson, and Margaret Mitchell, "50 Years of Test (Un)fairness: Lessons for Machine Learning," in *Proceedings of the Conference on Fairness, Accountability, and Transparency*, 49–58 (New York: ACM, 2019).

[11] Jeffrey Dastin, "Amazon Scraps Secret AI Recruiting Tool that Showed Bias against Women," *Reuters* (2018), https://www.reuters.com/article/us-amazon-com-jobs-automation-insight/amazon-scraps-secret-ai-recruiting-tool-that-showed-bias-against-women-idUSKCN1MK08G.

[12] Dave Gershgorn, "Amid Employee Uproar, Microsoft Is Investigating Sexual Harassment Claims Overlooked by HR," *Quartz* (2019), https://qz.com/1587477/microsoft-investigating-sexual-harassment-claims-overlooked-by-hr/amp/.

changed with the advent of the personal computer in the 1960s and 1970s when computing started to be lucrative.[13]

This phenomenon is not unique to computing. Professions originally deemed by many societies to reflect women's tasks (e.g., cooking) cease to be regarded in this way when the work becomes lucrative. For example, the U.S. restaurant business is dominated by men, while cooking at home is still considered to be a woman's responsibility. Similarly, by the 1970s computing had gone from being considered a woman's job, to, within twenty years, one dominated by men. To select people who have innate "traits" of the successful programmer, IBM invented the Programmer Aptitude Test, which is similar to the IQ test.[14] Nathan Ensmenger notes that "[t]he focus on mathematical trivia, logic puzzles, and word games, for example, did not allow for any more nuanced or meaningful or context-specific problem solving."[15] Sadly, until very recently, part of some companies' interview processes also involved solving these types of puzzles, which have no connection to the job sought by the applicant. While some companies such as Google have eliminated the brain-teasers after their own internal studies showed that they were not connected to the applicant's future success, many in the tech industry have adopted Google's style of whiteboard interviewing.

USING PAST DATA TO DETERMINE FUTURE OUTCOMES RESULTS IN RUNAWAY FEEDBACK LOOPS

An aptitude test designed by specific people is bound to inject their subjective biases of who is supposed to be good for the job and eliminate diverse groups of people who do not fit the rigid, arbitrarily defined criteria that have been put in place. Those for whom the tech industry is known to be hostile will have difficulty succeeding, getting credit for their work, or promoted, which in turn can seem to corroborate the notion that they are not good at their jobs in the first place. It is thus unsurprising that in 2018, automated hiring tools used by Amazon and others which naively train models based on past data in order to determine future outcomes, create runaway feedback loops exacerbating existing societal biases.

A hiring model attempting to predict the characteristics determining a candidate's likelihood of success at Amazon would invariably learn that the undersampled majority (a term coined by Joy Buolamwini) are unlikely to succeed because the environment is

---

[13] Mar Hicks, *Programmed Inequality: How Britain Discarded Women Technologists and Lost Its Edge in Computing* (Cambridge, MA: MIT Press, 2017).

[14] Nathan Ensmenger, "Making Programming Masculine," in *Gender Codes: Why Women Are Leaving Computing*, ed. Thomas J. Misa (Hoboken, NJ: Wiley, 2010), 115–141.

[15] Nathan L. Ensmenger, *The Computer Boys Take Over: Computers, Programmers, and the Politics of Technical Expertise* (Cambridge, MA: MIT Press, 2012).

known to be hostile toward people of African, Latinx, and Native American descent, women, those with disabilities, and members of the LGBTQ+ community and any community that has been marginalized in the tech industry and in the United States. The person may not be hired because of bias in the interview process, or may not succeed because of an environment that does not set up people from certain groups for success. Once a model is trained on this type of data, it exacerbates existing societal issues driving further marginalization.

The model selects for those in the nonmarginalized group, who then have a better chance of getting hired because of a process that favors them and a higher chance of success in the company because of an environment that benefits them. This generates more biased training data for the hiring tool, which further reinforces the bias creating a runaway feedback loop of increasing the existing marginalization.

These types of feedback loops amplifying bias are not unique to hiring models. Predictive policing, predicting crime "hotspots" based on a model trained on data of who has been arrested in which neighborhood, or which crimes have been reported, has also been shown to exhibit runway feedback loops. In many parts of the United States, there is a large discrepancy between who commits a crime versus whose crimes are reported. For example, the national survey on drug use and health shows drug use to be relatively evenly spread out in Oakland, whereas reports of drug use to police are concentrated in predominantly black neighborhoods. Kristian Lum and William Isaac have shown that the popular predictive policing model, PredPol, reinforces existing inequities by predicting these predominantly black neighborhoods to be crime hotspots.[16] More police are then sent to these neighborhoods, in which case they arrest more people from those locations than places with less police presence—seeming to validate the presence of more crime in those neighborhoods than others. These new arrests are then used as additional training data, increasing overpolicing in disadvantaged neighborhoods and amplifying societal bias.

UNREGULATED USAGE OF BIASED AUTOMATED FACIAL ANALYSIS TOOLS

Predictive policing is only one of the data-driven algorithms employed by U.S. law enforcement. The perpetual lineup report by Clare Garvie, Alvaro Bedoya, and Jonathan Frankle discusses law enforcement's unregulated use of face recognition in the United States, stating that one in two American adults are in a law enforcement database that can be searched and used at any time.[17] There is currently no regulation in place

---

[16] Kristian Lum, and William Isaac. "To Predict and Serve?," *Significance* 13, no. 5 (2016): 14–19.

[17] Clare Garvie, Alvaro Bedoya, and Jonathan Frankle "The Perpetual Line-Up: Unregulated Police Face Recognition in America," Georgetown Law, Center on Privacy & Technology, 2016.

auditing the accuracy of these systems, or specifying how and when they can be used. The report further discusses the potential for people to be sent to jail due to cases of mistaken identity and notes that operators are not well trained on using any of these tools. The authors propose a model law guiding government usage of automated facial analysis tools and describe a process by which the public can debate its pros and cons before it can be used by law enforcement.

As it stands, unregulated usage of automated facial analysis tools is spreading from law enforcement to other high-stakes sectors such as employment. And a recent study by Buolamwini and Gebru shows that these tools could have systematic biases by skin type and gender.[18] After analyzing the performance of commercial gender classification systems from three companies, Microsoft, Face++, and IBM, the study found near perfect classification for lighter skinned men (error rates of 0 percent to 0.8 percent), whereas error rates for darker skinned women were as high as 35.5 percent. After this study was published, Microsoft and IBM released new versions of their APIs less than six months after the paper's publication, major companies such as Google established fairness organizations, and U.S. Senators Kamala Harris, Cory Booker, and Cedric Richmond called on the FBI to review the accuracy of automated facial analysis tools used by the agency.[19] Even those in the healthcare industry cautioned against the blind use of unregulated AI.

As shown in Buolamwini and Gebru's study, society's concept of race and gender affects the design and usage of AI systems. For example, although works prior to *Gender Shades* have studied the accuracy of automated facial analysis tools by using geography as a proxy for race, none had performed the analysis by skin type, and none intersectionally—taking into account multiple identities such as gender and skin type. As a duo of darker and lighter skinned black women in the United States, Buolamwini and Gebru understood that race is an unstable social construct across time and space, having different meanings in different cultures, locations, and historical periods.

In *The Cost of Color*, sociologist Ellis Monk notes that "some studies even suggest that within-race inequalities associated with skin tone among African Americans often rival or exceed what obtains between blacks and whites as a whole."[20] Thus, instead of performing their analysis by race, Buolamwini and Gebru used the Fitzpatrick skin-type classification system to classify images into darker and lighter skinned subjects, analyzing the accuracy of commercial systems for each of these subgroups.

Buolamwini and Gebru's work notes that AI systems need to be tested intersectionally to uncover their shortcomings. Kimberlé Crenshaw, a leading scholar who coined the term *intersectionality* in critical race theory, stresses the importance of taking into

[18] Joy Buolamwini, and Timnit Gebru. "Gender Shades: Intersectional Accuracy Disparities in Commercial Gender Classification," *Proceedings of Machine Learning Research* 81 (2018): 77–91.

[19] Kamala Harris, Cory A. Booker, and Cedric L. Richmond, Letter to the Federal Bureau of Investigation (2018), https://www.scribd.com/embeds/388920671/content#from_embed.

[20] E.P. Monk Jr., "The Cost of Color: Skin Color, Discrimination, and Health among African-Americans," *American Journal of Sociology* 121, no. 2 (2015): 396–444.

account an individual's different identities and how they interact with systems of power in tandem.[21]

She often gives the example of a 1976 lawsuit by Emma DeGraffenreid alleging that General Motors (GM) discriminated against black women. The plaintiffs lost the lawsuit with judges reasoning that since GM hires black people, and also hires women, they couldn't have discriminated against black women.

What they failed to see however is that GM hired women for secretarial positions, but they wouldn't hire black people for these positions. And GM hired men for factory positions, but didn't consider women for these positions. Thus, black women were indeed discriminated against by GM, but without an intersectional view of both race *and* gender, the judges were unable to see this discrimination. In Buolamwini and Gebru's work, analyzing these systems by both gender and skin type showed the largest disparities, and both women discuss their life experiences and understanding of works on intersectionality as their motivation for disaggregating accuracy by gender and skin type.

AI-Based Tools Are Perpetuating Gender Stereotypes

While the previous section has discussed manners in which automated facial analysis tools with unequal performance across different subgroups are being used by law enforcement, this section shows that the existence of some tools in the first place, no matter how "accurate" they are, can perpetuate harmful gender stereotypes.

There are many ways in which society's views of race and gender are encoded into the AI systems that are built. Studies such as Hamidi et al.'s *Gender Recognition or Gender Reductionism*[22] discuss this in the context of automatic gender recognition systems such as those studied by Buolamwini and Gebru, and the harms they cause particularly to the transgender community.

For instance, the task of automatic gender recognition (AGR) itself implicitly assumes that gender is a static concept that does not frequently change across time and cultures. However, gender presentations greatly differ across cultures—a fact that is often unaccounted for in these systems. Gender classification systems are often trained with data that has very few or no transgender and nonbinary individuals. And the outputs themselves only classify images as "male" or "female." For transgender communities, the effects of AGR can be severe, ranging from misgendering an individual to outing them

---

[21] Kimberlé Crenshaw, "Demarginalizing the Intersection of Race and Sex: A Black Feminist Critique of Antidiscrimination Doctrine, Feminist Theory and Antiracist Politics," *University of Chicago Legal Forum* (1989): 139.

[22] Foad Hamidi, Morgan Klaus Scheuerman, and Stacy M. Branham. "Gender Recognition or Gender Reductionism?: The Social Implications of Embedded Gender Recognition Systems," in *Proceedings of the 2018 CHI Conference on Human Factors in Computing Systems* (ACM, 2018).

in public. Hamidi et al. note that according to the National Transgender Discrimination Survey conducted in 2014, 56 percent of the respondents who were regularly misgendered in the workplace had attempted suicide. While there are well-documented harms due to systems that perform AGR, the utility of these tools is often unclear.

One of the most common applications of AGR is for targeted advertising (e.g., showing those perceived to be women a specific product). This has the danger of perpetuating stereotypes by giving subliminal messages regarding artifacts that men versus women should use. For example, Urban Outfitters started personalizing their website based on the perceived genders of their frequent customers. But the program was scrapped after many customers objected to gender-based marketing: some shoppers often bought clothes that were not placed in their ascribed gender's section, and others were opposed to the concept of gender-based targeting in and of itself.[23]

Automatic gender recognition systems are only one of the many ways in which stereotypes and gender based societal biases are propagated through AI. From the imagery used to visualize cyborgs, to the names, voices, and mannerisms depicted by speech recognition systems like Siri and Alexa who are meant to obey a customer's every whim, it is clear that the design of commercial AI systems is based on stereotypical gender roles. Amy Chambers writes:

> Virtual assistants are increasingly popular and present in our everyday lives: literally with Alexa, Cortana, Holly, and Siri, and fictionally in films Samantha (Her), Joi (Blade Runner 2049) and Marvel's AIs, FRIDAY (Avengers: Infinity War), and Karen (Spider-Man: Homecoming). These names demonstrate the assumption that virtual assistants, from SatNav to Siri, will be voiced by a woman. This reinforces gender stereotypes, expectations, and assumptions about the future of artificial intelligence.[24]

What does it mean for children to grow up in households filled with feminized voices that are in clearly subservient roles? AI systems are already used in ways that are demeaning to women without explicitly encoding gendered names and voices. For example, generative adversarial networks (GANs), models that have been used to generate imagery among many other things, have been weaponized against women.[25] Deep fakes, videos generated using GANs, create pornographic content using the faces of ordinary women whose photos have been scraped from social media without consent.

[23] Natasha Singer, "E-tailer Customization: Convenient or Creepy?," *New York Times* (June 12, 2012).
[24] Amy Chambers, "There's a Reason Siri, Alexa and AI Are Imagined as Female—Sexism," *The Conversation*(2018),http://theconversation.com/theres-a-reason-siri-alexa-and-ai-are-imagined-as-female-sexism-96430.
[25] Cara Curtis, "Deepfakes Are Being Weaponized to Silence Women—But This Woman Is Fighting Back," *The Next Web* (2018), https://thenextweb.com/code-word/2018/10/05/deepfakes-are-being-weaponized-to-silence-women-but-this-woman-is-fighting-back/.

POWER IMBALANCE AND THE EXCLUSION
OF MARGINALIZED VOICES IN AI

The weaponization of technology against certain groups, as well as its usage to maintain the status quo while being touted as a liberator of those without power, is not new to AI. In "Model Cards for Model Reporting," Mitchell et al. note parallels to other industries where products were designed for a homogenous group of people.[26] From automobiles crash-tested on dummies with prototypical adult "male" characteristics resulting in accidents that disproportionately killed women and children, to clinical trials that excluded many groups of people resulting in drugs that do not work or disproportionately negatively affect women, products that are built and tested on a homogenous group of people work best for that group. A 2018 *Newsweek* article highlighting scientist Charles Rotimi notes: "By 2009, fewer than 1 percent of the several hundred genome investigations included Africans," even though "African genomes are the most diverse of any on the planet."[27] Excluding African genes not only hurts those of African descent by creating next generation personalized drugs that do not work for them but also leads scientists to erroneous claims by overfitting on homogenous data, by, for example, reaching conclusions based on uncommon mutations among European genomes but ones that are common in Africans.

Indeed, the development and trajectory of AI seems to be mirroring many other disciplines. In a blog post, Ali Alkhatib describes the harm current AI development has caused to marginalized groups and its parallels to anthropology.[28] He points out that "anthropologists, like computer scientists today, had the attention of the government—and specifically the military—and were drowning in lucrative funding arrangements. We were asked to do something that seemed reasonable at the time." Alkhatib cautions that *"the danger of aligning our work with existing power is the further subjugation and marginalization of the communities we ostensibly seek to understand"* (emphasis added), noting that "[t]he voices, opinions, and needs of disempowered stakeholders are being ignored today in favor of stakeholders with power, money, and influence—as they have been historically."

After a group of people from marginalized communities sacrificed their careers to shed light on how AI can negatively impact their communities, their ideas are now getting co-opted very quickly in what some have called a capture and neutralize strategy.

[26] Margaret Mitchell, Simone Wu, Andrew Zaldivar, Parker Barnes, Lucy Vasserman, Ben Hutchinson, Elena Spitzer, Inioluwa Deborah Raji, and Timnit Gebru. "Model Cards for Model Reporting," in *Proceedings of the Conference on Fairness, Accountability, and Transparency* (ACM, 2019), 220–229.

[27] Jessica Wapner, "Cancer Scientists Have Ignored African DNA in the Search for Cures," *Newsweek* (July 18, 2018).

[28] Ali Alkhatib, "Anthropological/Artificial Intelligence & the HAI," (2019), https://ali-alkhatib.com/blog/anthropological-intelligence.

In 2018 and 2019 respectively, the Massachusetts Institute of Technology (MIT) and Stanford University announced interdisciplinary initiatives centered around AI ethics, with multibillion dollar funding from venture capitalists and other industries, and war criminals like Henry Kissinger taking center stage in both the Stanford and MIT opening events.

Mirroring what transpired in political anthropology, these well-funded initiatives exclude the voices of the marginalized people who they claim to support, and instead center powerful entities who have not worked on AI ethics, and in many cases have interests in proliferating unethical uses of AI. Like diversity and inclusion, ethics has become the language du jour. While Stanford's human-centered AI initiative has a mission statement that "[t]he creators of AI have to represent the world," the initiative was announced with zero black faculty initially listed on the website out of 121 professors from multiple disciplines.

Universities are not the only institutions aspiring to be the central, authoritative voice on AI. Companies such as Amazon have announced a joint grant with the National Science Foundation (NSF) to fund fairness related research, while selling automated facial analysis tools with potentially systematic biases to law enforcement.[29] Shortly before the company announced its joint grant with the NSF, Amazon's leadership wrote a series of blog posts attempting to discredit the work of two black women showing bias in their automated facial analysis tool.[30]

While refusing to stop selling automated facial analysis tools to law enforcement without any regulation in place, and actively harming the careers of two women from marginalized communities negatively impacted by Amazon's product, the company then claimed to work on fairness by announcing a joint grant with NSF. This incident is a microcosm for the capture and neutralize strategy that disempowers those from marginalized communities while using the fashionable language of ethics, fairness, diversity, and inclusion to advance the needs of the corporation at all costs.

A letter signed by seventy-eight scientists[31] including 2019 Turing Award winner Yoshua Bengio later detailed the misrepresentations by Amazon officials, stressing the importance of the study and calling on Amazon to cease selling Rekognition to law enforcement. It was initially written by Timnit Gebru and Margaret Mitchell, the former being a black woman and a collaborator of Buolamwini and Raji. This activism shows a bifurcation between the people who are taking risks within the work of ethics and fairness, versus those who are given a seat at the table and centered in initiatives like MIT and Stanford. While two black women pointed out the systematic issues with Amazon's products, and a third assembled a coalition of AI experts to reinforce their message,

---

[29] Natasha Singer, "Amazon Is Pushing Facial Technology That a Study Says Could Be Biased," *New York Times* (Jan. 24, 2019).

[30] Inioluwa Deborah Raji and Joy Buolamwini, "Actionable Auditing: Investigating the Impact of Publicly Naming Biased Performance Results of Commercial AI Products," in *Proceedings of the 2019 AAAI/ACM Conference on AI, Ethics, and Society* (AAI, 2019), 429–435.

[31] Concerned Researchers, "On Recent Research Auditing Commercial Facial Analysis Technology," *Medium* (2019), https://link.medium.com/REWodWzNAY.

many in the academic community continue to publish papers and do research on AI and ethics in the abstract. As of 2019, fairness and ethics have become safe-to-use buzzwords, with many in the machine learning community describing them as "hot" topic areas. However, few people working in the field question whether some technologies should exist in the first place and often do not center the voices of those most impacted by the technologies they claim to make more "fair." For example, at least seven out of the nine organizers on a 2018 workshop on the topic of ethical, social, and governance issues in AI[32] at a leading machine learning conference, Neural Information Processing Systems, were white. If an entire field of research uses the pain of negatively impacted communities, co-opts their framework for describing their struggle, and uses it for the career advancement of those from communities with power, the field contributes to the further marginalization of communities rather than helping them. The current movement toward sidelining many groups in favor of powerful interests that have never thought about AI ethics except in the abstract, or have only been forced to confront it because of works from people in marginalized communities like Raji and Buolamwini, shows that the fairness, transparency, accountability, and ethics in the AI movement are on the road to doing "parachute science" like many of the fields before it. Ali Alkhatib writes:

Computer scientists have utterly failed to learn from the history of other fields, and in doing so we're replicating the same morally objectionable, deeply problematic relationships that other fields could have warned us to avoid—indeed, have tried to warn others to avoid. Political anthropologists of the 1940s "tended to take colonial domination itself for granted," and in doing so fashioned itself principally as a tool to further that hegemonic influence by finding ways to shape indigenous cultures to colonial powers.[33]

This colonial attitude is currently pervasive in the AI ethics space. Some have coined the terms "parachute research" or "helicopter research"[34] to describe scientists who "parachute" in to different marginalized communities, take what they would like for their work whether it is data, surveys, or specimens, and leave. This type of work not only results in subpar science due to researchers who conduct it without understanding the context, but it further marginalizes the communities by treating them as caged curiosities (as mentioned by Joy Buolamwini) without alleviating their pain. The best way to help a community is by elevating the voices of those who are working to make their community better—not by doing parachute research. Academics who are serious about AI ethics thus need to ensure that they center the voices of those whom they write about in the introduction paragraphs and motivation sections of their research papers.

[32] Workshop on Ethical, Social and Governance Issues in AI, *NeurIPS* (2018).
[33] Ali Alkhatib, "Anthropological/Artificial Intelligence & the HAI" (2019), https://ali-alkhatib.com/blog/anthropological-intelligence (citation omitted).
[34] Theresa Diane Campbell, "A Clash of Paradigms? Western and Indigenous Views on Health Research Involving Aboriginal Peoples," *Nurse Researcher* 21, no. 6 (2014).

They should work to create space for those who are marginalized and amplify their voices, rather than using them to advance their own careers and raise money from venture capitalists in their name.

THE DESIGN OF ETHICAL AI STARTS FROM WHOM IS GIVEN A SEAT AT THE TABLE

Ethical AI is not an abstract concept but one that is in dire need of a holistic approach. It starts from who is at the table, who is creating the technology, and who is framing the goals and values of AI. As such, an approach that is solely crafted, led, and evangelized by those in powerful positions around the world is bound to fail. Who creates the technology determines whose values are embedded in it.

For instance, if the tech industry were not dominated by cis-gendered straight men, would we have developed automatic gender recognition tools that have been shown to harm transgender communities and encourage stereotypical gender roles? If they were the ones overrepresented in the development of artificial intelligence, what types of tools would we have developed instead? If the most significant input for developing AI used in the criminal justice system came from those who were wrongfully accused of a crime and confronted with high cash bail due to risk assessment scores, would we have had the algorithms of today that disproportionately disenfranchise black and brown communities in the United States? If the majority of AI research were funded by government agencies working on healthcare rather than military entities such as the Defense Advanced Research Projects Agency, would we be working toward drones that identify persons of interest?

A recent example of a Palestinian arrested for writing "good morning" in Arabic that was translated to "hurt them" in English or "attack them" in Hebrew by Facebook Translate shows some of the structural issues at play.[35] The person was arrested by Israeli authorities, who later released him after verifying that he had indeed written "good morning." According to Ha'aretz, no one had checked the original Arabic version before arresting the individual. There are many issues that led to these series of events.

To start, had the field of language translation been dominated by Palestinians as well as those from other Arabic speaking populations, it is difficult to imagine that this type of mistake in the translation system would have transpired. Tools used by Google and Facebook currently work best for translations between English and other Western languages such as French, reflecting which cultures are most represented within the machine learning and natural language processing communities. Most of the papers and corpora published in this domain focus on languages that are deemed important by

---

[35] Yotam Berger, "Israel Arrests Palestinian because Facebook Translated 'Good Morning' to 'Attack Them,'" Ha'aretz (October 22, 2017).

those in the research community, those who have funding and resources, and companies such as Facebook and Google, which are located in Silicon Valley in the United States. It is thus not surprising that the overwhelming bias of the researchers and the community itself is toward solving translation problems between languages such as French and English.

Secondly, natural language processing tools embed the societal biases encoded in the data they are trained on. While Arabic-speaking people are stereotyped as terrorists in many non-Arab majority countries to the point that a math professor was interrogated on a flight due to a neighboring passenger mistaking his math writings for Arabic,[36] similar stereotypes do not exist with the majority of English, French, or other Western language speakers. Thus, even when mistakes occur in translations between languages such as French and English, they are unlikely to have such negative connotations as mistaking "good morning" for "attack them."

Racial and gender biases in natural language processing tools are well documented. As shown by Bolukbasi et al. and Caliskan et al., word embeddings that were trained on corpora such as news articles or books exhibit behaviors that are in line with the societal biases encoded by the training data. For example, Bolukbasi et al. found that word embeddings could be used to generate analogies, and those trained on Google news complete the sentence "man is to computer programmer as woman is to 'X'" with "homemaker."[37] Similarly, Caliskan et al. demonstrated that in word embeddings trained from crawling the web, African American names are more associated with unpleasant concepts like sickness, whereas European American names are associated with pleasant concepts like flowers.[38] Dixon et al.[39] have also shown that sentiment analysis tools often classify texts pertaining to LGBTQ+ individuals as negative. Given the stereotyping of Muslims as terrorists by many western nations, it is thus less surprising to have a mistake resulting in a translation to "attack them." This incident also highlights automation bias: the tendency of people to overtrust automated tools. An experiment designed by scientists at Georgia Tech University to examine the extent to which participants trust a robot, showed that they were willing to follow it toward what seemed to be a burning building, using pathways that were clearly inconvenient.[40] In the case of the Palestinian who was arrested for his "good morning" post, authorities *trusted*

[36] *Guardian* Staff, "Professor: Flight Was Delayed because My Equations Raised Terror Fears," *The Guardian* (May 7, 2016).

[37] Tolga Bolukbasi, Kai-Wei Chang, James Y. Zou, Venkatesh Saligrama, and Adam T. Kalai, "Man Is to Computer Programmer as Woman Is to Homemaker? Debiasing Word Embeddings," in *Proceedings of the 30th International Conference on Neural Information Processing Systems* (2016), 4356–4364.

[38] Caliskan, Aylin, Joanna J. Bryson, and Arvind Narayanan. "Semantics Derived Automatically from Language Corpora Contain Human-Like Biases," *Science* 356, no. 6334 (2017): 183–186.

[39] Lucas Dixon, John Li, Jeffrey Sorensen, Nithum Thain, and Lucy Vasserman, "Measuring and Mitigating Unintended Bias in Text Classification," in *Proceedings of the 2018 AAAI/ACM Conference on AI, Ethics, and Society* (ACM, 2018), 67–73.

[40] Paul Robinette, Wenchen Li, Robert Allen, Ayanna M. Howard, and Alan R. Wagner, "Overtrust of Robots in Emergency Evacuation Scenarios," in *The Eleventh ACM/IEEE International Conference on Human Robot Interaction* (IEEE Press, 2016), 101–108.

the translation system and did not think to first see the original text before arresting the individual.

One cannot ignore the structural issues at play while analyzing what happened here. In addition to the increased likelihood of errors in translating Palestinian Arabic dialects, the oppression of Palestinians also makes it more likely that whatever translation errors that do exist are more harmful toward them. Similar to the Google Photos incident that classified a black couple as "gorillas," this translation system was most harmful because of the type of error it made.

In the Google Photos incident, there were as many instances of white people being mistaken for whales as black people being misclassified as gorillas. However, the connotation of being mistaken for a whale is not rooted in racist and discriminatory history such as black people being depicted as monkeys and gorillas.[41] Even if someone could convince himself or herself that algorithms sometimes just spit out nonsense, the structure of the nonsense will tend vaguely toward the structure of historical prejudices.

The dominance of certain groups and underrepresentation of others in natural language processing, computer vision, and machine learning ensures that the problems these groups work on do not address the biggest challenges faced by those who are not part of the dominant group in the field. In fact, it can contribute to the further marginalization of these groups. The error of "good morning" being translated to "attack them" would not have had such grave consequences had the structural imbalance in power not made it such that a Palestinian was more likely to be surveilled and subjected to automated tools. Similarly, black people and other marginalized communities in the United States are more likely to be subjected to surveillance and interact with automated tools than other groups.[42] And the systematic errors encoding bias and stereotypes (due to the datasets that are used and the demographic makeup of researchers and practitioners in this area) can be much more costly for those in marginalized communities than other groups.

The existing power imbalance coupled with these types of systematic errors disproportionately affecting marginalized groups makes proposals such as the extreme vetting initiative by the United States Immigration and Customs Enforcement (ICE) even more problematic and scary. The 2018 initiative proposes that ICE partners with tech companies to monitor various people's social network data with automated tools and use that analysis to decide whether they should be allowed to immigrate to the United States are expected to be good citizens or are considered to be at risk of becoming terrorists. While any attempt to predict a person's future criminal actions is a dangerous direction to move toward warned by science fiction movies such as *Minority Report* and TV series like *Black Mirror*, the proposal is even scarier paired with the systematic errors of the automated tools that would be used for such analyses. Natural language processing and

---

[41] Wuld D. Hund, Charles W. Mills, and Silvia Sebastiani eds., *Simianization: Apes, Gender, Class, and Race* (Berlin: LIT Verlag, 2015).

[42] Virginia Eubanks, *Automating Inequality: How High-Tech Tools Profile, Police, and Punish the Poor* (New York: St. Martin's Press, 2018).

computer vision based tools have disproportionate errors and biases toward those who are already marginalized and are likely to be targeted by agencies such as ICE.

It is heartening to see that a group of fifty-four leading scientists in AI wrote a letter against the extreme vetting initiative.[43] However, the initiative has continued, and only a few groups of people within the AI community, those who are developing the tools used in these practices, are truly speaking out against proposals such as this one. The extreme underrepresentation of marginalized groups in the latter community makes it even more difficult for them to care. And those who do speak up are from groups that are already facing a disproportionate amount of the burden to diversify and educate their own communities—adding to the minority tax that they already face.

EDUCATION IN SCIENCE AND ENGINEERING NEEDS TO MOVE AWAY FROM "THE VIEW FROM NOWHERE"

If we are to work on technology that is beneficial to all of society, it has to start from the involvement of people from many walks of life and geographic locations. The future of whom technology benefits will depend on who builds it and who utilizes it. As we have seen, the gendered and racialized values of the society in which this technology has been largely developed have seeped into many aspects of its characteristics. To work on steering AI in the right direction, scientists must understand that their science cannot be divorced from the world's geopolitical landscape, and there are no such things as meritocracy and objectivity. Feminists have long critiqued "the view from nowhere": the belief that science is about finding objective "truths" without taking people's lived experiences into account. This and the myth of meritocracy are the dominant paradigms followed by disciplines pertaining to science and technology that continue to be dominated by men. In *Replacing the "View from Nowhere,"* Sarah Marie Stitzlein writes:

> According to most feminists and some pragmatists, the acknowledgment of both subject and object as historically and politically situated requires that the subjects and objects of knowledge be placed on a more level playing field. When this is done, objectivity, as a form of responding to the rights and well being of fellow subjects as well as the objects of scientific inquiry, must be considered. Objectivity, then, is achieved to the extent that responsibility in inquiry is fulfilled and expanded. It follows that scientists must be held accountable for the results of their projects and that scientists must acknowledge the political nature of their work. Objectivity understood as such implies relationships between people, objects, and inquiry projects as central to its conception.[44]

---

[43] Technology Experts Letter to DHS Opposing the Extreme Vetting Initiative, 2017.

[44] Sarah M. Stitzlein, "Replacing the 'View from Nowhere': A Pragmatist-Feminist Science Classroom," *Electronic Journal of Science Education* 9, no. 2 (2004) (citations omitted).

The educational system must move away from the total abstraction of science and technology and instead show how people's lived experiences have contributed to the trajectory that technology follows. In his paper *The Moral Character of Cryptographic Work*, Phillip Rogaway sees the rise of mass surveillance as a failure of the cryptographic community.[45] He discusses various methods proposed in cryptography and outlines how the extreme abstraction of the field and lack of accounting for the geopolitical context under which cryptography is used has resulted in methods that in reality help the powerful more than the powerless. He calls on scientists to speak up when they see their technology being misused, and cites physicists' movement toward nuclear disarmament asking cryptographers to do the same.

Similarly, AI researchers should learn about the ways in which their technology is being used, question the direction institutions are moving in, and engage with other disciplines to learn from their approaches. Instead of doing parachute science, those studying fairness accountability transparency and ethics in AI should forge collaborations across disciplinary, geographic, demographic, institutional, and socioeconomic boundaries, and help lift the voices of those who are marginalized. In order to work toward AI that does not further marginalize those who have historically been (and continue to be) sidelined, the educational system and general attitude amongst researchers and practitioners needs to fundamentally change and move away from the myth of meritocracy and "the view from nowhere."

BIBLIOGRAPHY

Benjamin, Ruha. *Race after Technology: Abolitionist Tools for the New Jim Code*. Medford, MA: Polity, 2019.

Broussard, Meredith. *Artificial Unintelligence: How Computers Misunderstand the World*. Cambridge, MA: MIT Press, 2018.

Buolamwini, Joy, and Timnit Gebru. "Gender Shades: Intersectional Accuracy Disparities in Commercial Gender Classification." *Proceedings of Machine Learning Research* 81 (2018): 77–91.

Eubanks, Virginia. *Automating Inequality: How High-Tech Tools Profile, Police, and Punish the Poor*. New York: St. Martin's Press, 2018.

Hamidi, Foad, Morgan Klaus Scheuerman, and Stacy M. Branham. "Gender Recognition or Gender Reductionism?: The Social Implications of Embedded Gender Recognition Systems." In *Proceedings of the 2018 CHI Conference on Human Factors in Computing Systems*, 8. New York: ACM, 2018.

Hicks, Mar. *Programmed Inequality: How Britain Discarded Women Technologists and Lost Its Edge in Computing*. Cambridge, MA: MIT Press, 2017.

Noble, Safiya Umoja. *Algorithms of Oppression: How Search Engines Reinforce Racism*. New York: NYU Press, 2018.

---

[45] Phillip Rogaway, "The Moral Character of Cryptographic Work," *IACR Cryptology ePrint Archive* (2015): 1162.

O'Neil, Cathy. *Weapons of Math Destruction: How Big Data Increases Inequality and Threatens Democracy*. New York: Broadway Books, 2016.

Stitzlein, Sarah M. "Replacing the 'View from Nowhere': A Pragmatist-Feminist Science Classroom." *Electronic Journal of Science Education* 9, no. 2 (2004).

West, Sarah Myers, Meredith Whittaker, and Kate Crawford. "Discriminating Systems: Gender, Race and Power in AI." AI Now Institute, 2019.

CHAPTER 14

••

THE FUTURE OF WORK
IN THE AGE OF AI

Displacement or Risk-Shifting?

••

PEGAH MORADI AND KAREN LEVY

IN February 2011, *Jeopardy!* viewers watched as the AI system known as IBM Watson defeated Ken Jennings and Brad Rutter, two of the winningest *Jeopardy!* champions of all time, in a three-day exhibition match *The New York Times* lauded as "a vindication for the academic field of artificial intelligence."[1] Watson's ability to understand and respond to *Jeopardy!* clues was considered a major step forward for natural language processing and information retrieval, and soon after, IBM announced plans to use the system to assist physicians in making diagnoses or treating patients.[2]

Winning at *Jeopardy!* was a unique challenge for a machine, given that *Jeopardy!* is more unpredictable and complex than a simple test of trivia; as Jennings wrote in 2019, its clues are "weird, short little haikus, laced with hints, puns, winks, and red herrings."[3] When Watson erred, it often seemed to miss clues that humans would find easy or obvious. Watson, for example, rendered "what is chic?" in response to the clue "stylish elegance, or students who all graduated in the same year"; Brad Rutter subsequently offered the correct response, "what is class?"[4] In a *Final Jeopardy!* round with the category "U.S. Cities," Watson responded, "What is Toronto????" with four question marks denoting low confidence in the response.[5]

---

[1] John Markoff, "On 'Jeopardy!' Watson Win Is All but Trivial," *New York Times* (February 16, 2011), sec. Science, https://www.nytimes.com/2011/02/17/science/17jeopardy-watson.html.

[2] Katherine Gammon, "Watson Goes to the Hospital," *MIT Technology Review* (February 23, 2011). https://www.technologyreview.com/s/423092/watson-goes-to-the-hospital/.

[3] Ken Jennings, "The Secret Farm Team for Jeopardy! Players," *Slate* (April 9, 2019). https://slate.com/culture/2019/04/jeopardy-quiz-bowl-connection-ken-jennings.html.

[4] "Show #6086—Monday, February 14, 2011," J! Archive (February 14, 2011), http://www.j-archive.com/showgame.php?game_id=3575.

[5] "Show #6087—Tuesday, February 15, 2011," J! Archive (February 15, 2011), http://www.j-archive.com/showgame.php?game_id=3576.

But despite its shortcomings, Watson still won. Many assumed that this was simply because Watson had a memory capacity of fifteen trillion bytes and had been fed data from millions of documents, books, encyclopedias, and news articles.[6] Watson was able to consume a wealth of information that most people—even *Jeopardy!* champions— could only dream of being able to absorb. But it is also possible that a much simpler mechanism gave Watson the biggest advantage of all: Jennings suggests that Watson was so good largely because *it was much quicker to the buzzer* than its human competitors were. "As Jeopardy devotees know," Jennings notes, "if you're trying to win on the show, the buzzer is all. On any given night, nearly all the contestants know nearly all the answers, so it's just a matter of who masters buzzer rhythm the best."[7] In response to criticism over Watson's buzzer advantage, IBM researcher Eric Brown noted: "there are some things that computers are going to be better at than humans and vice versa. Humans are much better at understanding natural language. Computers are better at responding to signals."[8]

The combination of comparative strengths and weaknesses that Watson brought to the *Jeopardy!* stage nicely encapsulates the nuanced relationship between AI and human work. The computer's success was seen as a bellwether, as futurists used Watson's win as a launch pad for claims about the possibility of AI displacing workers. ("After all," fretted Martin Ford, "if a machine can beat humans at *Jeopardy!*, will computers soon be competing with people for knowledge-based jobs?"[9]) In some respects, Watson's abilities *were* far superior to those of its human competitors—but humans were innately capable of aspects of gameplay with which Watson struggled. Though the specifics of the task may differ, the same is true of *all* human/machine relations in work contexts.

To understand the ethical issues most likely to beset the future of work, we must first realistically assess what kinds of threats AI might pose. Though some economists and policymakers have begun to express great concern about what AI will mean for employment—including whether some forms of work will exist at all—we argue that the popular "robots will take our jobs!" narrative of AI-induced job displacement is overly simplistic and alarmist. In spite of rapid growth in research and in application, AI systems still have quite limited practical capabilities, and the current technical limitations of AI still give humans the comparative advantage in many kinds of work. Forecasts of widespread employment displacement tend to focus solely on technical aspects of work, and neglect broader contextual inquiry about the social components of work, organizational structures, and cross-industry effects. In the first part of this chapter, we explain these limitations of existing forecasts.

[6] "IBM100—A Computer Called Watson," IBM (March 7, 2012), https://www.ibm.com/ibm/history/ibm100/us/en/icons/watson/.
[7] Ken Jennings, "Jeopardy! Champ Ken Jennings," *Washington Post* (February 15, 2011), https://live.washingtonpost.com/jeopardy-ken-jennings.html.
[8] Sam Gustin, "IBM Watson Scientist: Speed Matters, But So Do Accuracy, Intuition," *Wired* (February 16, 2011), https://www.wired.com/2011/02/ibm-watson-speed/.
[9] Martin Ford, "Will IBM's Watson Put Your Job in Jeopardy?," *Fortune* (February 15, 2011), http://fortune.com/2011/02/15/will-ibms-watson-put-your-job-in-jeopardy/.

In the second part, we turn to the outcomes we *do* expect from AI in the workplace. Specifically, intelligent systems are likely to be marshaled toward traditional managerial goals related to efficiency, productivity, and risk mitigation. We highlight four ways in which firms may use AI in pursuit of these goals, effectively offsetting risks from themselves onto their workers. We end with discussion of potential policy responses to these concerns.

AI as Worker Displacement: Rhetoric and Reality

As AI-driven technologies are increasingly integrated into work processes, a commonly expressed concern is the impending displacement of human workers—often apocalyptically phrased in popular media as "robots taking over our jobs."[10] This argument tends to follow from the understanding that human work is comprised of a series of tasks, some or all of which can be done more effectively, efficiently, or at scale by a machine. Therefore, as machines grow in capability, a greater number of tasks currently performed by humans can (and, it is assumed, will) be automated. Because human work is comprised of these tasks, the thinking goes, human workers are vulnerable to being displaced by machines—potentially leaving many without jobs or drastically rearranging how labor is distributed by occupation. And because the jobs widely believed to be most acutely threatened by AI are blue-collar jobs—often held by less educated and poorer workers with fewer alternative options—there is, it is feared, potential for tremendous social and economic disruption.

What Kinds of Tasks Can AI Execute?

Machines are newly capable of performing a number of tasks formerly "off limits" to automation, thanks to technical improvements in AI, increased access to big datasets, and advancements in robotics. Prior to these developments, the paradigmatic model of task-based automation was the two-factor model proposed by Autor, Levy, & Murnane in 2003,[11] which we will refer to as the ALM model. ALM focuses on how routine a task

---

[10] Alex Williams, "Will Robots Take Our Children's Jobs?," *New York Times* (December 11, 2017), sec. Style, https://www.nytimes.com/2017/12/11/style/robots-jobs-children.html; Larry Elliott, "Robots Will Take Our Jobs. We'd Better Plan Now, before It's Too Late," *The Guardian* (February 1, 2018), sec. Opinion, https://www.theguardian.com/commentisfree/2018/feb/01/robots-take-our-jobs-amazon-go-seattle; Blake Morgan, "Robots Will Take Our Jobs and We Need a Plan: 4 Scenarios for the Future," *Forbes*, https://www.forbes.com/sites/blakemorgan/2018/09/05/robots-will-take-our-jobs-and-we-need-a-plan-4-scenarios-for-the-future/.

[11] David H. Autor, Frank Levy, and Richard J. Murnane, "The Skill Content of Recent Technological Change: An Empirical Exploration," *Quarterly Journal of Economics* 118, no. 4 (2003): 1279–333.

is on one dimension, and the degree to which tasks involve cognitive versus physical work on the other dimension. As Autor and his co-authors argued, "computer capital" could substitute for workers executing abstractable, programmable *routine* tasks—consisting of both "cognitive and manual tasks that can be accomplished by following explicit rules." Watson's buzzer advantage was rooted in this specific routine capability: being able to respond quickly and predictably to an explicit signal. The ALM model posited that *nonroutine* human labor might be complemented by computers, but that computers were unlikely to substitute wholly for humans for nonroutine tasks. Nonroutine tasks were deemed more difficult to program and dependent on skills like perception, problem-solving, and intuition that were well beyond the purview of computing in 2003.

But the world has changed since then. As computers have become more sophisticated and responsive to their environments, they can adapt to dynamic situations more adeptly—negotiating traffic, responding to conversational cues, developing novel solutions to problems. In light of robotic capabilities, computer vision, and machine learning, it's less important than it once was that a task be clearly definable and repeatable, thus complicating the ALM model. With AI, many tasks previously thought to be intractably nonroutine are becoming converted into abstractable problems aided by the availability of large and complex datasets.[12] Although machines were previously limited to tasks that were clearly defined with limited potential contingencies, today's AI systems can analyze previous cases to determine a course of action in unpredictable situations. Likewise, integrating prediction-driven models with robotics can bring these capabilities into the realm of physical labor. For instance, though Autor et al. explicitly mentioned truck driving as a manual nonroutine task in their 2003 work (and hence likely to be safe from automation), several companies have set goals to develop fully autonomous long-haul vehicles in the near future based on new technical capabilities.[13]

While AI can allow a machine to execute tasks that would have previously been considered nonautomatable under the ALM model, AI still has significant technical and social limitations, some of which are acknowledged in the forecasting literature. Frey and Osborne consider three "engineering bottlenecks" when calculating the automatability of American occupations, identifying "perception and manipulation," "creative intelligence," and "social intelligence" as areas that elude technological capability.[14] Levy identifies broader limitations, arguing that AI will be able to better compete against human labor in tasks that are (a) narrow, such that the data the models use contains most of the contingencies it could face in the future, and (b) structured, such that the machine can easily identify consistent patterns in the data.[15] Much like the factors

[12] Carl Frey and Michael Osborne, "The Future of Employment: How Susceptible Are Jobs to Computerisation?," Oxford Martin School, September 2013.

[13] Steve Viscelli, "Driverless? Autonomous Trucks and the Future of the American Trucker," Center for Labor Research and Education, University of California, Berkeley, and Working Partnerships USA, September 2018.

[14] Frey and Osborne, "The Future of Employment."

[15] Frank Levy, "Computers and Populism: Artificial Intelligence, Jobs, and Politics in the Near Term," *Oxford Review of Economic Policy* 34, no. 3 (2018): 393–417.

described in the ALM model, however, these boundaries are elastic; both future changes in the capabilities of AI-driven automation as well as in the nature of the tasks themselves will continuously shift the window of automatability.

Some forecasts peering through today's window of automatability nevertheless predict grim outcomes for employment. In their occupation-focused model, Frey and Osborne calculated probabilities of computerization for 702 occupations by using administrative data about the task content of those jobs from the U.S. Department of Labor and having AI experts classify the tasks according to their technical automatability.[16] The study estimated that 47 percent of U.S. jobs were at high risk (which they defined as a 70 percent chance) of automation within twenty years—and most of these in low-wage occupations. The Frey and Osborne forecast has been extremely influential, dominating the narrative in both the popular press and in subsequent academic work (amassing 3,600+ citations as of the time of this writing).

The More Complicated Reality

Risk calculations like Frey and Osborne's are often used to predict massive unemployment due to advances in AI. But these forecasts are significantly more complicated than they are sometimes portrayed, in large part due to crucial nuances in how work is executed and how industries are organized. First, and most crucially, technological capability to automate certain tasks does not necessarily translate to the *actual* automation of those tasks, nor of the occupations that to date have been chiefly comprised of those tasks. These forecasts tend to focus exclusively on *technical feasibility*, with no account of social, legal, political, or organizational factors.[17] But technologies do not operate in social vacuums, and firms' adoption and implementation of technologies are contextually dependent on factors like internal organization,[18] institutional and regulatory landscapes,[19] degree of unionization,[20] and other variables.

Importantly, social and political factors have historically affected the distribution of automation risk. In particular, race and ethnicity in the United States can affect whose work is protected from automation and whose is not. For instance, historically, although the artisans whose work was deskilled and automated in the first American industrial

---

[16] Frey and Osborne, "The Future of Employment."

[17] Erik Brynjolfsson, Tom Mitchell, and Daniel Rock. "What Can Machines Learn, and What Does It Mean for Occupations and the Economy?," *AEA Papers and Proceedings* 108 (2018): 43–7. https://doi.org/10.1257/pandp.20181019.

[18] Robert J. Thomas, *What Machines Can't Do: Politics and Technology in the Industrial Enterprise* (Boulder, Colo.: NetLibrary, Inc., 1999); Stephen R. Barley, "Technology as an Occasion for Structuring: Evidence from Observations of CT Scanners and the Social Order of Radiology Departments," *Administrative Science Quarterly* 31, no. 1 (1986): 78–108, https://doi.org/10.2307/2392767.

[19] David F. Noble, *Forces of Production: A Social History of Industrial Automation* (New York: Oxford University Press, 1984).

[20] Maryellen Kelley, "New Process Technology, Job Design, and Work Organization: A Contingency Model," *American Sociological Review* 55 (1990): 191–208.

revolution were largely white, the dangerous, low-wage factory labor that grew as a result of industrialization was largely performed by immigrants and nonwhite workers. Likewise, when considering Frey and Osborne's predictions in conjunction with racial and ethnic demographic data, it appears likely that white workers are disproportionately more *automatable*.[21] But white workers continue to have greater social and political leverage along with higher labor market power, thus altering how these demographic groups could be affected by automation.[22] For instance, the predicted polarization of the labor market into low-wage service work and high-wage "knowledge" labor is likely to have different outcomes depending on workers' race or gender. During this polarization process, black and Hispanic workers competing with white workers for low-wage service work may experience greater job loss due to structural disadvantages like reduced labor market power.[23]

Moreover, automation often leads not to the *elimination* of occupations, but to changes in their task composition. Using the same framework as Frey and Osborne, but focusing on time spent doing tasks that are capable of automation using current technology, a McKinsey analysis argued that fewer than 5 percent of American jobs can be "entirely" automated.[24] The McKinsey model ultimately makes a convincing argument that AI portends *redefinition* of human occupations rather than the replacement of entire jobs. This redefinition has occurred repeatedly during previous periods of rapid technological change. ATMs are often cited as an example of the scale effects of new technology outweighing substitution effects of automation: ATMs did not wholly eliminate the need for bank tellers, but rather changed the tasks associated with the role and allowed for the cost-effective expansion of bank branches.[25] As Autor describes in a seminal 2015 work, whether this will be the case in the current wave of AI-driven automation is dependent on a combination of factors like whether nonautomated, "complementary" tasks are easily available elsewhere in the labor market.[26]

Finally, there are limitations to conceptualizing occupations merely as baskets of discrete executable tasks. Though we may distill occupations to their component tasks for purposes of analyzing them, anyone who has held a job knows that work depends on deep-seated human knowledge that cannot always be boiled down to rule-sets and protocols (even nonroutine ones). The anthropologist Michael Polanyi called this the *tacit dimension* of human knowledge—there are things humans know and do in the course of everyday

[21] Pegah Moradi, "Race, Ethnicity, and the Future of Work," April 2, 2019. https://doi.org/10.31235/osf.io/e37cu.

[22] Moradi, "Race."

[23] Moradi, "Race"; Danial Borowczyk-Martins, Jake Bradley, and Linas Tarasonis, "Racial Discrimination in the U.S. Labor Market: Employment and Wage Differentials by Skill," *Labour Economics* 49, no. C (2017): 106–27.

[24] Michael Chui, James Manyika, and Mehdi Miremadi, "Four Fundamentals of Workplace Automation | McKinsey," McKinsey Digital (November 2015), https://www.mckinsey.com/business-functions/digital-mckinsey/our-insights/four-fundamentals-of-workplace-automation.

[25] David H. Autor, "Why Are There Still So Many Jobs? The History and Future of Workplace Automation," *Journal of Economic Perspectives* 29, no. 3 (2015): 3–30.

[26] Autor, "Why Are There Still So Many Jobs?"

life that evade easy categorization and can barely be articulated, let alone automated.[27] These dimensions of human work are hard to capture in economic models, but represent reasons it will be more difficult for machines to wholly assume the roles of human workers. One 2016 OECD analysis[28] applied much of the framework of Frey and Osborne but used self-reported information on the things workers actually do in their given occupation, finding greater variation of tasks within an occupation as well as more group-work and face-to-face interaction in jobs. This study ultimately estimated that only 9 percent of individuals were at high risk of automation within the next two decades, in contrast to Frey and Osborne's much more dire forecast.

Another important complication to these forecasts is that they do not attempt to account for *indirect* forms of worker displacement that might be wrought by AI. These studies focus exclusively on the technical automatability of tasks within particular occupations, but do not account for broader industry-level effects that may more fundamentally restructure labor markets and types of work. A notable example is the booming growth of online retail, supported and enabled by implementation of intelligent supply-chain systems, and the subsequent "retail apocalypse" closing down brick-and-mortar stores across the United States.[29] By one forecast, 75,000 stores are expected to close by 2026, while 25 percent of retail sales are estimated to take place online, up from 16 percent today.[30] Moving retail online does not necessarily directly automate the tasks required from a department store sales associate, but rather eliminates the need for that role *altogether*, while potentially creating different jobs at other points in the supply chain. The ensuing importance of warehouses over brick-and-mortar stores also creates a space where tasks can be simplified in order to better accommodate the application of AI and robotics. For instance, because it is challenging for robots to safely pick up variable items that have an unpredictable weight or shape—something that comes instinctively to humans—e-retail companies like Amazon are implementing systems that use AI to build appropriately sized boxes *around* items rather than having a robotic arm pick them up and place them in a box.[31] As Frey and Osborne themselves note, tasks can be changed to become more automatable; indirect unemployment due to AI often results in this task simplification, by taking people out of the equation and instead creating environments more amenable to machines.

[27] Michael Polanyi, *The Tacit Dimension* (University of Chicago Press, 2009).

[28] Melanie Arntz, Terry Gregory, and Ulrich Zierahn, "The Risk of Automation for Jobs in OECD Countries: A Comparative Analysis," OECD Social, Employment and Migration Working Papers. Paris: OECD Publishing, May 14, 2016, https://doi.org/10.1787/5jlz9h56dvq7-en.

[29] Sabrina Helm, Soo Hyun Kim, and Silvia Van Riper, "Navigating the 'Retail Apocalypse': A Framework of Consumer Evaluations of the New Retail Landscape," *Journal of Retailing and Consumer Services* (October 23, 2018), https://doi.org/10.1016/j.jretconser.2018.09.015.

[30] Abha Bhattarai, "'Retail Apocalypse' Now: Analysts Say 75,000 More U.S. Stores Could Be Doomed," *Washington Post* (April 10, 2019), sec. Economy, https://www.washingtonpost.com/business/2019/04/10/retail-apocalypse-now-analysts-say-more-us-stores-could-be-doomed/.

[31] Jeffrey Dastin, "Exclusive: Amazon Rolls Out Machines That Pack Orders and Replace Jobs," *Reuters* (May 13, 2019), https://www.reuters.com/article/us-amazon-com-automation-exclusive-idUSKCN1SJ0X1.

Each of these limitations demonstrates a way in which the outcomes of these forecasts are more complicated than they initially appear. It is not clear to what extent AI will displace existing jobs. What is more certain and more imminent is that AI will impact the *conditions* of work.[32] Rather than focusing on the quantity of displaced work, we ask here how AI might impact the *quality* of work for workers on the job, by considering how managers leverage intelligent systems to further firms' objectives. Questions like these are less amenable to broad economic forecasting and breathless headlines—but inarguably, AI's impact on workers in the here and now has less to do with displacement, and more to do with *integration* into existing labor structures and managerial practices. Specifically, as we discuss in the next section, AI's primary effect on work in these contexts is to shift risks previously absorbed by firms onto workers.

AI AS RISK REALLOCATOR

Technology has long held the promise of making work more efficient. Technological advances in the workplace are vaunted for their ability to increase productivity, to incentivize "good" work behaviors, to find and eliminate bottlenecks, and the like. By measuring and monitoring and analyzing and predicting, the rhetoric goes, we can find waste, streamline processes, and eliminate superfluous work. The mantra of analytics is practically an article of faith among managers, who believe that data will reveal the secrets to greater profit margins. In this scheme, workers' labor is an input to be collected, analyzed, and algorithmically optimized like any other. These practices are rooted in the principles of Taylorism, Fordism, and scientific management, each of which aimed to minimize wasted effort and maximize production through the fine-grained pacing and control of work processes.[33] AI in the contemporary workplace follows in the footsteps of this ethos via intensive monitoring and predictive analysis of nearly all aspects of work tasks and the broader supply chain.[34]

Does all this monitoring and analysis make the workplace more efficient? Maybe—but not necessarily because these practices are actually eliminating waste or increasing productivity. Instead, these technologies can insidiously *hide* work by offloading its

[32] Brishen Rogers, "Beyond Automation: The Law & Political Economy of Workplace Technological Change," February 4, 2019, https://papers.ssrn.com/abstract=3327608. Rogers reaches a similar conclusion in his analysis of the law and political economy of workplace automation. Like us, he posits that the threat of automation-induced job loss is "overstated" and that the more pressing issues involve managerial techniques, including worker monitoring and algorithmic scheduling. Rogers also thoughtfully points to the relation of workplace data collection to the "fissuring" of the workplace—that is, firms' outsourcing of key functions to outside contractors.

[33] Harry Braverman, *Labor and Monopoly Capital: The Degradation of Work in the Twentieth Century* (New York: Monthly Review Press, 1975).

[34] Kirstie Ball, "Workplace Surveillance: An Overview," *Labor History* 51, no. 1 (February 1, 2010): 87–106, https://doi.org/10.1080/00236561003654776; James R. Beniger, *The Control Revolution: Technological and Economic Origins of the Information Society* (Cambridge, MA: Harvard University Press, 1986).

burdens from a firm onto its (comparatively less powerful) workers. Lots of inefficiencies still exist in monitored workplaces, but AI-driven managerial practices *redistribute the risks and costs of these inefficiencies to workers* while serving a firm's bottom line. We enumerate an illustrative (but nonexclusive) list of four such practices in the following.[35]

Staffing and Scheduling

Traditionally, the risks of fluctuating consumer demand have been borne largely by the firm. Some hours at a store or restaurant, for instance, may be unexpectedly slow. Though managers ideally try to match customer demand to labor supply (i.e., workers on shift), they previously could do so only approximately, usually based on historical indicators like aggregate sales volume during a given period. This often meant that managers bore the risk of overpaying for excess labor capacity (i.e., wages) for unexpectedly slow periods.[36]

Algorithmic technologies have changed the landscape of staffing and scheduling, however, transferring the burden of demand uncertainty from the firm to the worker. More sophisticated staffing algorithms integrate many more sources of data—including, for example, real-time customer traffic derived from in-store sensor networks, as well as external variables like weather—to predict customer demand and associated staffing levels, and to do so more dynamically. The result for workers has been a variety of "just-in-time" scheduling practices that introduce significant precarity and instability into the lives of low-wage workers.[37] These include patterns like irregular and "split-shift" scheduling (i.e., having workers work multiple shorter shifts during periods of high demand, and clocking out in between—leaving that time unpaid); high-fluctuation work schedules (many hours one week, few the next); and short-notice scheduling, including "on-call" shifts (in which workers must make themselves available for a shift but are notified only just prior to the shift's beginning about whether they should come in).[38]

---

[35] We focus here on management of already-hired workers, and bracket from our analysis consideration of AI's emerging role in hiring processes. The implications of AI for hiring are ably analyzed by Miranda Bogen and Aaron Rieke in "Help Wanted: An Exploration of Hiring Algorithms, Equity, and Bias" (Upturn, Dec. 2018), https://www.upturn.org/static/reports/2018/hiring-algorithms/files/Upturn--HelpWanted-AnExplorationofHiringAlgorithms,EquityandBias.pdf.

[36] Karen Levy and Solon Barocas, "Refractive Surveillance: Monitoring Customers to Manage Workers," *International Journal of Communication* (March 2018): 1166–88.

[37] Levy and Barocas, "Refractive Surveillance"; Susan J. Lambert, Anna Haley-Lock, and Julia R. Henly, "Schedule Flexibility in Hourly Jobs: Unanticipated Consequences and Promising Directions," *Community, Work & Family* 15, no. 3 (August 1, 2012): 293–315, https://doi.org/10.1080/1366 8803.2012.662803; Daniel Schneider and Kristen Harknett, "Schedule Instability and Unpredictability and Worker and Family Health and Wellbeing," Washington Center for Equitable Growth Working Paper (Sept. 2016), http://cdn.equitablegrowth.org/wp-content/uploads/2016/09/12135618/091216-WP-Schedule-instability-and-unpredictability.pdf.

[38] Ari Schwartz, Michael Wasser, Merrit Gillard, and Michael Paarlberg, "Unpredictable, Unsustainable: The Impact of Employers' Scheduling Practices in DC," Washington, D.C.: DC Jobs with

The effect of each of these practices is to destabilize workers' livelihoods by interfering with nonwork activities—like school, childcare, or a second job—and creating severe financial stress, leading even to intergenerational cognitive harms.[39] Moreover, these costs are disproportionately borne by women and workers of color, who occupy service positions at higher rates.[40] While firms may lower labor costs due to reduced risk of overstaffing, the upshot of all of these practices is that the burden of the uncertainty of demand is shifted to the workers subject to scheduling systems.

Defining Compensable Work

As firms gain more visibility into and control over workers' activities, they can more narrowly define work to include only very specific tasks and then pay workers for those tasks *exclusively*. Managerial technology allows firms to focus closely on what is considered essential to a job. The Fair Labor Standards Act (FLSA) requires employers to pay employees for time worked, but only for those activities that are considered "integral and indispensable"[41] to the principal tasks of a job. Under this standard, courts have ruled several activities *non*compensable, like commuting to work,[42] waiting to go through required security screenings,[43] and donning and doffing protective gear,[44] even though the principal work tasks cannot, practically speaking, be completed without them. Though many workers (including most gig economy workers) are not covered by the FLSA, the law's narrow framing of compensable work is conceptually instructive here. Algorithmic technologies may further circumscribe firms' definitions of essential and compensable work, but they do not actually reduce the amount of work that workers do.

For example: drivers for Uber and other ride-share companies are paid only for the time they are actively transporting a passenger—*not* the time they spend driving around waiting for the app to alert them to a passenger nearby; *not* the time they spend driving to a pickup point; *not* the time they spend returning from a long trip out of town; *not* the time and expense required to clean their cars and offer amenities in order to get high

Justice, June 11, 2015, https://www.dcfpi.org/all/unpredictable-unsustainable-the-impact-of-employers-scheduling-practices-in-dc/. Schwartz et al. find that roughly 30 percent of service sector workers reported on-call shift scheduling at their workplace.

[39] Leila Morsy and Richard Rothstein, "Parents' Non-Standard Work Schedules Make Adequate Childrearing Difficult," Issue Brief. Washington, D.C.: Economic Policy Institute, August 6, 2015, https://www.epi.org/publication/parents-non-standard-work-schedules-make-adequate-childrearing-difficult-reforming-labor-market-practices-can-improve-childrens-cognitive-and-behavioral-outcomes/.

[40] Levy and Barocas, "Refractive Surveillance."

[41] Integrity Staffing Solutions, Inc. v. Busk, 135 S. Ct. 513 (2014).

[42] Vega v. Gasper, 36 F.3d 417 (5th Cir. 1994).

[43] Integrity Staffing Solutions, Inc. v. Busk, 135 S. Ct. 513 (2014).

[44] Llorca v. Collier County Sheriff, 898 F.3d 1319 (11th Cir. 2018).

customer ratings (which can impact the security of their employment).[45] Because these undertakings are not seen as directly generating revenue for the company, they are unpaid. Of course, in reality, all of these tasks are part and parcel of doing the work of Uber driving, and the costs of that work (including both opportunity costs—the time the driver could be making money otherwise, or doing something else entirely—and direct costs, like gas and vehicle wear and tear) are borne entirely by the driver. Though this model of payment isn't *created* by algorithmic dispatch—it has, for instance, long been a feature of the truck-driving labor model—the use of AI-driven platforms to support these industries broadens and exacerbates these effects.

Granular measurement capabilities can also be used to more explicitly recalibrate compensation schemes in favor of the firm. In 2015, for instance, Amazon changed how it paid some authors of books available on its Kindle platform. Because Amazon's technology gave it visibility into exactly how many pages of a book readers actually read, it began compensating authors on a per-page-read basis, rather than by the number of books downloaded—shifting the risk of a boring book to the author.[46] Similarly, music-streaming services like Spotify pay artists on a per-track-streamed basis (where a track is "counted" when a listener plays it for at least thirty seconds), rather than by albums sold or tracks downloaded.[47] In theory, compensation models like these reward popularity, and implicitly, quality—but in practice, the model is often blamed for "stream-bait" homogeneity in cultural production, as risk-averse artists conform to styles most likely to generate revenue under the algorithm.[48]

Collectively, these trends more tightly circumscribe what is considered compensable work by "counting" certain tasks but not others. And by constricting what is considered compensable work and optimizing narrowly for it, AI-driven systems may increase the proportion of work that is considered residual and unworthy of payment, like producing an (ultimately unpopular) song, driving to a passenger pickup, or replenishing mints to ensure a high rating. Those work activities—what Craig Lambert has termed "shadow work"[49]—don't disappear just because they aren't accounted for. Rather, these systems shift these risks and costs from the employer to the worker, who must internalize the very real labor that doesn't "count."[50]

[45] Alex Rosenblat, Karen E.C. Levy, Solon Barocas, and Tim Hwang. "Discriminating Tastes: Uber's Customer Ratings as Vehicles for Workplace Discrimination," *Policy & Internet* 9, no. 3 (June 28, 2017): 256–79, https://doi.org/10.1002/poi3.153.

[46] Anita Singh, "Amazon to Pay Kindle Authors Only for Pages Read," *Telegraph* (June 22, 2015), sec. Technology< https://www.telegraph.co.uk/technology/amazon/11692026/Amazons-to-pay-Kindle-authors-only-for-pages-read.html.

[47] Zachary Mack, "How Streaming Affects the Lengths of Songs," *The Verge* (May 28, 2019), https://www.theverge.com/2019/5/28/18642978/music-streaming-spotify-song-length-distribution-production-switched-on-pop-vergecast-interview.

[48] Liz Pelly, "Streambait Pop," *The Baffler* (December 11, 2018), https://thebaffler.com/downstream/streambait-pop-pelly.

[49] Craig Lambert, *Shadow Work: The Unpaid, Unseen Jobs That Fill Your Day* (Berkeley, CA: Counterpoint, 2016).

[50] Karen Levy, "The Future of Work: What Isn't Counted Counts," *Pacific Standard* (June 14, 2017), https://psmag.com/economics/the-future-of-work-what-isnt-counted-counts.

Detecting and Predicting Loss and Fraud

AI may also be used to redistribute the risk of deliberate damage or loss brought to an enterprise by employees purposively behaving against the firm's interests. This often involves employees violating the law or the terms of employment—whether by stealing merchandise, embezzling money from company coffers, or sharing a secret recipe—or whistle-blowing to bring to light a firm's illegal or unethical behavior. The principal-agent problem poses inherent risks to running a business, and employers have historically attempted to lower this risk through myriad low-tech and high-tech means. It is the norm for an employer to call references to determine the supposed character of a potential hire and perform background checks for previous criminal convictions. Employees dealing with sensitive or proprietary information are often required to sign nondisclosure and noncompete agreements. The risks are especially prominent in retail, where the product is directly handled by employees, often without supervision: according to the 2018 National Retail Security Survey, approximately 1.33 percent of retail sales—amounting to about $46.8 billion in costs to U.S. retailers—was lost to inventory "shrink," with employee theft cited as the second-highest cause of shrink after external shoplifting.[51] The costs of shrink make retail a natural adopter of loss-prevention technologies and techniques, from the use of CCTV cameras to the maintenance and creation of an industry-wide hiring blacklist of individuals suspected of theft.[52]

Employers use AI to continue cracking down on the risk of deliberate damage, often by using technologies that continuously track and analyze worker behavior and activity. Loss prevention firms like Appriss Retail offer services that use AI to model employee behavior and flag unusual behavior that could be fraudulent or harmful to the firm.[53] Outside of retail, companies similarly monitor employee activity, especially communications.[54] A leaked list of phrases from 2008 shows Goldman Sachs flagging emails with lines like "clowns managing the fund," "report the matter to the sec/nasd/nyse," or "this won't happen again" for scrutiny.[55] London-based firm StatusToday continuously tracks

---

[51] Bob Moraca and Richard Hollinger, "2018 National Retail Security Survey," National Retail Federation, 2018. https://cdn.nrf.com/sites/default/files/2018-10/NRF-NRSS-Industry-Research-Survey-2018.pdf.

[52] "Class Action Lawsuit Challenges Legality of Retail Theft Databases in California for Background Checks," *Employment Screening Resources* (blog) (February 11, 2014), http://www.esrcheck.com/wordpress/2014/02/11/class-action-lawsuit-challenges-legality-retail-theft-databases-california-background-checks/.

[53] "Secure," *Appriss Retail*, https://apprissretail.com/solutions/secure/ (accessed June 6, 2019.).

[54] Alex Rosenblat, Tamara Kneese, and Danah Boyd, "Workplace Surveillance," Data & Society Working Paper (October 8, 2014), https://www.datasociety.net/pubs/fow/WorkplaceSurveillance.pdf.

[55] Eamon Javers, "You Won't Believe What Gets an Email Flagged at Goldman: CNBC Has the List," *CNBC* (June 16, 2016), https://www.cnbc.com/2016/06/15/you-wont-believe-what-gets-an-email-flagged-at-goldman-cnbc-has-the-list.html. Though the list cited is from 2008 and was rather low-tech in execution, Goldman Sachs has continued this practice with updated search terms.

electronic behavior and flags unusual activity, like an employee accessing files they don't usually access or copying large numbers of files.[56]

Loss and fraud prevention, and the use of AI in its service, may seem to be quite reasonable on the part of the firm; after all, few would condone outright theft, and firms seem justified in protecting their assets, ensuring regulatory compliance, and the like. Our goal is not to pass normative judgment on the propriety or advisability of these aims or practices. Rather, we discuss them here for two reasons related to risk-shifting and worker power. First, though these technologies are explicitly framed as reducing the risk to firms of workers' deliberate malfeasance, monitoring workers for theft and fraud is often practically inseparable from tracking for productivity or efficiency purposes. The same platform advertised to minimize threats to a firm's security can be (and often is) also used to ensure employees are maximally productive;[57] concerns about fraud may be used as a pretext to justify an entire data collection regime, as has been the case in other contexts (e.g., state benefits provision[58]). We discuss productivity monitoring in more detail in the next section.

Second, preventing and detecting loss and fraud have specific implications for risk reallocation between firm and worker. These systems are often *predictive*, meaning that the harm of malfeasance has not actually happened yet. In other words, rather than mitigating actual loss *ex post*, the employer is looking for potential harm *ex ante*. This is a distinction with an important difference for workers. If systems' predictive accuracy is poor, or if employers are especially risk-averse—say, in a weak labor market in which they have abundant potential hires—these systems may prevent many workers deemed "risky" from being hired at all. In other words, the risk of future deliberate damage is displaced from firms to potential hires. Employers have long based hiring decisions on heuristics that "mark" workers based on characteristics like race or prior incarceration, often making these workers effectively unhireable and precluding economic opportunity.[59] Greater use of predictive systems for loss and fraud prevention may further exacerbate these trends, especially for workers who are already disadvantaged. A further complication arises from the nature of the data in theft prevention databases, which are self-reported and shared among employers, often based merely on suspicion (i.e., without substantiation

[56] Timothy Revell, "AI Tracks Your Every Move and Tells Your Boss If You're Slacking," *New Scientist* (January 30, 2017), https://www.newscientist.com/article/2119734-ai-tracks-your-every-move-and-tells-your-boss-if-youre-slacking/.

[57] Steve O'Hear, "StatusToday Scores Nearly $4M to Grow Its AI-Powered 'employee Insights' Service," *TechCrunch* (blog) (2018), http://social.techcrunch.com/2018/02/20/statustoday/. StatusToday, for instance, maps out communications and outcomes to see how employees work best, while also flagging cybersecurity threats.

[58] Virginia Eubanks, *Automating Inequality: How High-Tech Tools Profile, Police, and Punish the Poor* (New York: Picador, 2019).

[59] Devah Pager, *Marked: Race, Crime, and Finding Work in an Era of Mass Incarceration* (Chicago: University of Chicago Press, 2007); Jennifer L. Doleac and Benjamin Hansen, "Does 'Ban the Box' Help or Hurt Low-Skilled Workers? Statistical Discrimination and Employment Outcomes When Criminal Histories Are Hidden," Working Paper, National Bureau of Economic Research, July 2016, https://doi.org/10.3386/w22469.

or subsequent criminal charges) and very likely to be inflected with employers' own biases. (In fact, concerns about the inaccuracies and lack of due process associated with inclusion in such databases have given rise to lawsuits alleging that their use may violate the Fair Credit Reporting Act.[60])

Incentivizing and Evaluating Productivity

Finally, intelligent systems are used to measure, assess, and incentivize workers' performance in the workplace. Like loss prevention, concern about workers putting forth less than full effort is a feature of principal-agent relations; firms take many steps to incentivize workers to expend more labor[61] and, conversely, may punish workers for perceived shirking. Though worker surveillance for productivity maximization is nothing new, AI-driven systems may extend the practice into new types of workplaces—for example, workplaces like long-haul trucking, previously shielded by such collection by virtue of its geographic diffusion[62]—and toward more invasive and fine-grained forms of monitoring.

Amazon, for example, has issued "inactivity reports" for its warehouse workers, detecting when workers temporarily stop moving (even for periods as short as one minute);[63] it currently holds a patent for a wristband that tracks a worker's movements and speed, buzzing with haptic feedback to direct the worker to the next item.[64] Workers in Amazon warehouses have reported grueling pressures, including inadequate breaks for using the bathroom and meeting religious needs, and physical and mental health crises as a result of such strenuous conditions.[65] Leaked corporate documents show that worker supervision and tracking—up to and including termination of employment for insufficient productivity—is handled by an AI-driven system.[66] Platform-based firms like Uber also use AI to promote driver productivity, using fleet-wide supply/demand

[60] Stephanie Clifford and Jessica Silver-Greenberg, "Retailers Track Employee Thefts in Vast Databases," *New York Times* (October 19, 2018), sec. Business, https://www.nytimes.com/2013/04/03/business/retailers-use-databases-to-track-worker-thefts.html.

[61] Michael Burawoy, *Manufacturing Consent: Changes in the Labor Process Under Monopoly Capitalism* (Chicago: University of Chicago Press, 1982).

[62] Karen E.C. Levy, "The Contexts of Control: Information, Power, and Truck-Driving Work," *The Information Society* 31, no. 2 (March 2015): 160–74. https://doi.org/10.1080/01972243.2015.998105.

[63] Michel Bauwens, "The Hyper-Exploitative Labor Practices of Amazon.com," *P2P Foundation* (blog) (July 29, 2015), https://blog.p2pfoundation.net/the-hyper-exploitative-labor-practices-of-amazon-com/2015/07/29.

[64] Ceylan Yeginsu, "If Workers Slack Off, the Wristband Will Know. (And Amazon Has a Patent for It.)," *New York Times* (November 28, 2018), sec. Technology, https://www.nytimes.com/2018/02/01/technology/amazon-wristband-tracking-privacy.html.

[65] Chavie Lieber, "Emergency Calls Placed from Amazon Warehouses Depict Enormous Pressure Put on Workers," *Vox* (March 11, 2019), https://www.vox.com/the-goods/2019/3/11/18260472/amazon-warehouse-workers-911-calls-suicide.

[66] Colin Lecher, "How Amazon Automatically Tracks and Fires Warehouse Workers for 'Productivity,'" *The Verge* (April 25, 2019), https://www.theverge.com/2019/4/25/18516004/amazon-warehouse-fulfillment-centers-productivity-firing-terminations.

predictions and behavioral-economic "nudges" to tailor incentives toward profit maximization.[67] In customer-facing service jobs like call centers, AI can be used to monitor not only the speed of work but also alignment with behavioral and affective criteria like tone of voice. In retail settings, workers may be incentivized and evaluated based on automated analysis of their interactions with customers on the floor.[68]

Productivity incentivization is not *a priori* bad for workers; in commission-based work, for example, it may be advantageous for labor as well as management. But in many contexts, fine-grained monitoring erodes trust, dignity, and any sense of privacy from work, reduces workers' decisional autonomy,[69] and opens the door to labor exploitation by driving workers to the limits of their physical and mental capabilities. If working to less than one's full capacity is considered a form of "time theft,"[70] similar concerns attach here as they do with respect to loss prevention.

As we have described, intelligent systems in the workplace can be used in the service of several managerial techniques. They may enable firms to dynamically schedule workers, minimizing labor costs while creating substantial instability in workers' lives. Firms may use AI to narrowly redefine work tasks, concomitantly classifying some practically necessary labor as ancillary and noncompensable. They may use it to predict worker theft and malfeasance, potentially resulting in an underclass of "marked" workers deemed too risky to hire. And they may use it to incentivize productivity by removing all slack from work time, perhaps doing serious damage to workers' physical and mental health. These dynamics were not created by AI; they have been features of labor/management relations for a long time and will likely remain so for a long time to come. But AI may enable firms to more effectively pursue their existing goals through these practices, therefore offloading burdens and reallocating risks from themselves onto workers.

DISPLACEMENT, RISK-SHIFTING, AND POLICY

Policy recommendations for the future of work commonly focus on mitigating the harms of labor displacement, like unemployment, depressed wages, and increased

[67] Noam Scheiber, "How Uber Uses Psychological Tricks to Push Its Drivers' Buttons," *New York Times* (April 2, 2017), sec. Technology, https://www.nytimes.com/interactive/2017/04/02/technology/uber-drivers-psychological-tricks.html; Ryan Calo and Alex Rosenblat, "The Taking Economy: Uber, Information, and Power," *Columbia Law Review* 117 (2017): 1623–90.

[68] Levy and Barocas, "Refractive Surveillance."

[69] Sam Adler-Bell and Michelle Miller, "The Datafication of Employment," The Century Foundation, December 19, 2018, https://tcf.org/content/report/datafication-employment-surveillance-capitalism-shaping-workers-futures-without-knowledge/.

[70] William T. Dickens, Lawrence F. Katz, Kevin Lang, and Lawrence H. Summers, "Employee Crime and the Monitoring Puzzle," *Journal of Labor Economics* 7(3) (1989): 331–47.

inequality as a result of labor market polarization.[71] And although AI is often framed as a new frontier for policymaking, proposed solutions often focus on strengthening long-standing social institutions. These recommendations include investing in both K–12 and college education (often with a focus on STEM [science, technology, engineering, and mathematics] fields) and retraining displaced workers to provide them with marketable skills for the new economy; bolstering the social safety net through reforms to unemployment insurance and public benefits programs; and (somewhat more controversially) some support for universal basic income programs that would provide unconditional cash guarantees for all individuals, regardless of circumstance.[72]

These policy proposals stand to benefit millions of Americans *whether or not* their jobs are displaced by AI and represent sound economic investments in the future of work—whatever it may look like. In addition to proposals like these, however, we should also consider what protections we might provide for workers *who retain* jobs, in order to temper risk reallocation that intensifies management/worker inequity. For example, a number of states and municipalities have taken steps to curtail worker-unfriendly scheduling practices through fair scheduling laws—sometimes in response to the threat of wage theft lawsuits.[73] These laws do things like require managers to announce schedules further in advance, end "on-call" shifts, and create minimum shift lengths. In so doing, they help to recalibrate employers' ability to shift costs to workers through algorithmic scheduling.

Other worker protections could similarly reallocate some risks back to firms. One clear avenue would be an end to forced arbitration, which often bars employees from litigating claims against their employers in court; proposed reforms like the Arbitration Fairness Act would prevent employers from being able to enforce arbitration agreements in employment disputes.[74] A second route forward includes reforms to worker classification regimes that characterize many platform-based workers as independent contractors rather than employees, therefore removing some protections due to them under labor law (minimum wage, unionization, etc.); such reforms are currently afoot in some states.[75] More broadly, amendments to the Fair Labor Standards Act could be made to include some workers currently exempt from its protections (for example, long-haul truck drivers)—and in some regulated industries, compensation regimes might be modified to more accurately recognize workers' time and effort. And we might

---

[71] Autor, "Why Are There Still So Many Jobs?"; Ryan Calo, "Artificial Intelligence Policy: A Primer and Roadmap," *U.C. Davis Law Review* 51 (2017): 399–435; Executive Office of the President, "Artificial Intelligence, Automation, and the Economy," 2016, https://obamawhitehouse.archives.gov/sites/whitehouse.gov/files/documents/Artificial-Intelligence-Automation-Economy.PDF.

[72] Brishen Rogers, "Basic Income in a Just Society," *Boston Review* (May 15, 2017), http://bostonreview.net/forum/brishen-rogers-basic-income-just-society/.

[73] Elizabeth Tippett, Charlotte S. Alexander, and Zev J. Eigen, "When Timekeeping Software Undermines Compliance," *Yale Journal of Law & Technology* 19 (2017).

[74] Katherine V.W. Stone and Alexander J.S. Colvin, "The Arbitration Epidemic," Economic Policy Institute Report, December 7, 2015. https://www.epi.org/publication/the-arbitration-epidemic/.

[75] Paris Martineau, "California Lawmakers Move to Protect Gig Economy Workers," *WIRED* (May 30, 2019), https://www.wired.com/story/california-lawmakers-move-protect-gig-economy-workers/.

regulate or ban the use of for-profit "retail justice" databases that blacklist potential employees suspected of theft without due process.[76]

One further note is in order. Organizational sociologists have long examined technological interventions into workplaces and their effects on workplace roles and relationships.[77] A key lesson from this work is that technology has no unified set of effects once deployed in a workplace: it can alter new social dynamics or ossify old ones, depending on the conditions surrounding its deployment—including industry structures, broader economic forces, workplace culture, and institutional mechanisms for governing relations between labor and management. These studies of previous technologies provide a vital lesson: Contemporary forecasting of AI's impact on workers, and the ethical issues it is likely to bring to the fore, must include concomitant consideration of specific social, economic, and cultural dynamics in a workplace. Any policies put in place to mitigate negative effects must also take these into account. While this observation is a caveat for forecasters and policymakers, it is also cause for optimism: it suggests that there are many firm-level levers that may mitigate the negative dimensions of workplace AI, and that nothing is set in stone.

Perhaps contrary to our call for workplace-specific action, many of the aforementioned policy proposals we identify—in either the displacement-remediation or risk-reallocation buckets—may seem like they are too general, too basic, or have little to do with artificial intelligence specifically. This is because the issues resulting from integrating AI with work are not wholly new, but are instead the continuation of a long line of labor concerns that have endured and transformed throughout the history of industrialized work. But the specter of AI in the workplace does not necessarily spell doom or dystopia; rather, it elucidates the burdens placed on workers, and may bring new energy to creating policies that protect workers for generations to come—ultimately protecting the quality of work, not just its quantity.

ACKNOWLEDGMENTS

The authors gratefully acknowledge support from the John D. and Catherine T. MacArthur Foundation, New America, and the Cornell University Center for Social Sciences. We are grateful for helpful comments and insights from Joshua Popp and Matthew Sun.

NOTES

Portions of this chapter draw from Pegah Moradi's 2018 thesis manuscript "Race, Ethnicity, and the Future of Work," conducted under the advising of Jamila Michener, Karen Levy, and Sergio Garcia-Rios of Cornell University.

[76] John Rappaport, "Criminal Justice, Inc.," *Columbia Law Review* 118, no. 8 (2018): 2251–322.

[77] Kelley, "New Process Technology"; Barley, "Technology as an Occasion for Structuring"; Steven Blader, Claudine Madras Gartenberg, and Andrea Prat, "The Contingent Effect of Management Practices," Columbia Business School Research Paper (2016), https://papers.ssrn.com/sol3/papers. cfm?abstract_id=2594258.

BIBLIOGRAPHY

Autor, David H. "Why Are There Still So Many Jobs? The History and Future of Workplace Automation." *Journal of Economic Perspectives* 29, no. 3 (2015): 3–30.

Autor, David H., Frank Levy, and Richard J. Murnane. "The Skill Content of Recent Technological Change: An Empirical Exploration." *Quarterly Journal of Economics* 118, no. 4 (2003): 1279–333.

Braverman, Harry. *Labor and Monopoly Capital: The Degradation of Work in the Twentieth Century*. New York: Monthly Review Press, 1975.

Brynjolfsson, Erik, Tom Mitchell, and Daniel Rock. "What Can Machines Learn, and What Does It Mean for Occupations and the Economy?" *AEA Papers and Proceedings* 108 (2018): 43–7. https://doi.org/10.1257/pandp.20181019.

Gray, Mary and Siddharth Suri. *Ghost Work: How to Stop Silicon Valley from Building a New Global Underclass*. Boston: Houghton Mifflin Harcourt, 2019.

Levy, Karen, and Solon Barocas. "Refractive Surveillance: Monitoring Customers to Manage Workers." *International Journal of Communication* 12 (March 2018): 1166–88.

Polanyi, Michael. *The Tacit Dimension*. Chicago: University of Chicago Press, 2009.

Rogers, Brishen. "Beyond Automation: The Law & Political Economy of Workplace Technological Change." February 4, 2019. https://papers.ssrn.com/abstract=3327608.

CHAPTER 15

....

AI AS A MORAL
RIGHT-HOLDER

....

JOHN BASL AND JOSEPH BOWEN

INTRODUCTION

....

THERE are currently advocates for "robot rights,"[1] with Saudi Arabia even having granted citizenship to certain instantiations of AI.[2] In this entry, we develop a skeptical stance toward the idea that current forms of artificial intelligence are holders of *moral* rights.[3] In doing so, we articulate what it would take for an AI system to be a moral rights-holder.[4] We first distinguish *moral* rights from other sorts of rights before motivating why one ought to care about whether AI holds rights. We then articulate one of the most prominent, and in our view, most plausible, theories of moral rights: the Interest Theory. On that theory, rights necessarily protect their holders' interests. Whether some particular form of AI is a rights-holder, then, hangs on whether that form of AI is the type of thing that can have interests. We argue that current AI's systems built around machine learning do not have such interests. In developing this view, we

[1] Mark Coeckelbergh, "Robot Rights? Towards a Social-Relational Justification of Moral Consideration," *Ethics and Information Technology* 12, no. 3 (2010): 209–21; David Gunkel, *Robot Rights* (Cambridge, MA: The MIT Press, 2018).

[2] "Saudi Arabia Bestows Citizenship on a Robot Named Sophia," *TechCrunch* (blog) http://social. techcrunch.com/2017/10/26/saudi-arabia-robot-citizen-sophia/ (accessed March 30, 2019).

[3] The question of whether AI have rights is different than the more general question of whether they have moral status of any type whatsoever. Though it may turn out that some of the considerations that speak in favor a skeptical stance about AI rights apply similarly to questions of AI's moral status more generally. On the more general debate, see John Basl, "Machines as Moral Patients We Shouldn't Care About (Yet): The Interests and Welfare of Current Machines," *Philosophy and Technology* 27, no. 1 (2014): 79–96; Joanna J. Bryson, "Patiency Is Not a Virtue: The Design of Intelligent Systems and Systems of Ethics," *Ethics and Information Technology* 20, no. 1 (2018): 15–26.

[4] In this chapter we use both "AI" and "AI systems" to refer to technologies that in some way integrate artificial intelligence in one of its forms. So an autonomous vehicle isn't really an AI, but it is a technology that relies on AI for some of its system tasks.

defend a view of the capacities and abilities necessary for having the sorts of interests that ground rights and apply this to both current and potential future forms of AI.

Not everyone endorses the Interest Theory. Because of this, we also consider whether AI has rights on the primary alternative to the Interest Theory, the Will Theory. According to the Will Theory, rights necessarily endow their holders with normative control over others. We suggest that while the Will Theory *may* make space for AI as bearers of moral-rights, we think that this position is implausible.

Despite our skepticism about the rights of *current* AI, the development of AI raises a significant challenge: we think it possible both that we might create an AI that is a rights-holder but not be in a position to know that we have done so. In such a circumstance, we are likely to violate the rights of this AI. In the closing section of the chapter, we outline this challenge and use it to motivate a cautious approach to the development of AI.

WHAT RIGHTS AND WHY RIGHTS?

What Kinds of Rights?

There is no single question of whether AI can hold rights because there is no single discourse on or single conception of rights. Consider a case in which a dictator enacts a law that grants a right to claim property as they see fit. Here, the dictator gains a *legal* right to the property, but it is implausible that they have a *moral* right to the property. (If one thinks there are not such things as moral property rights, we can imagine the dictator enacting laws allowing them to kill citizens at their pleasure.)

We focus on whether AI are, or could be, holders of *moral* rights.[5] Whether one is a *legal* rights-holder and what *legal* rights one holds depends, at the least, on legal frameworks. Legal rights depend, to at least this extent, on the choices of particular individuals or institutions. It is this feature of legal rights, as opposed to moral rights, that makes coherent the examples of the dictator legalizing theft and murder.[6] In contrast to legal rights, moral rights are, in an important sense, not up to us.[7] Whether a human, nonhuman

---

[5] For a discussion of some legal issues surrounding AI rights, see Joanna J. Bryson, Mihailis E. Diamantis, and Thomas D. Grant, "Of, For, and By the People: The Legal Lacuna of Synthetic Persons," *Artificial Intelligence and Law* 25, no. 3 (September 1, 2017): 273–91.

[6] Many think the *actual* existence of legal rights depends on more than a legal system's positing that some legal right exists. For example, minimally, defenders of Hohfeld's definition of a claim-right (introduced in the following subsection) think it requires, further, that there is some correlative legal duty *owed to* the claim-right holder. More substantively, those who think theories of rights account for legal as well as moral rights will think their desired necessary and sufficient conditions on rights will also need to be satisfied.

[7] We don't presuppose the truth of any particular normative theory or intend to preclude theories on which rights are grounded in, for example, what rational beings would or would not reasonably consent to or reject. There's a very real sense in which rights could be ultimately grounded in requirements of rationality, which, clearly, makes rights depend on us in some sense.

animal, or AI holds moral rights does not depend on whether this moral right is recognized or codified in laws.[8]

Why Rights?

One might wonder why it is worth asking whether AI hold rights. Here are four reasons. First, a pragmatic reason. Often, public debate is had in the language of rights. For example, the debate tends not to be whether people *may* use the bathroom of the gender to which they identify, but whether they have the *right* to do so. Given that public debate is often had out in rights-talk, it is important that we know whether AI is even *capable* of holding rights, before arguing about what rights it does and does not hold.

Second, rights are taken to offer a particularly robust protection against certain forms of conduct. Rights are typically taken to place constraints on promoting the good. For example, plausibly, it is impermissible to kill a healthy patient in order to donate their organs to save five sick patients, even when doing so would maximize the good. A typical explanation for this verdict is that the healthy patient has a right against being killed that cannot be overridden by the mere fact that killing the patient would bring about more good—in this way, rights are often seen as imposing side-constraints on others' behavior, as "trumps" over other types of considerations, as providing others with "exclusionary reasons," and so on.[9]

Third, being a rights-holder has implications for what is owed to the rights-holder when their rights are violated. This is because of the *relationality* or *directionality* of rights. In addition to there being different domains in which we find rights (e.g., in the legal versus moral domain), there are also different *kinds* of rights that we might hold against others while restricting ourselves to moral rights.[10] The paradigm form of rights is the *claim*-right (some call claim-rights rights in the "strict sense"). One person holds a (claim-)right against another person just in case the other person owes the right-holder a duty to the performance of the right.[11] For example, Joe has a right against John that John not hit him just in case John is under a duty, *owed to Joe*, not to hit Joe. John's duty is *directed*—directed toward, owed to, Joe. The nature of this *directed* duty is opposed to John's being under an *undirected* duty. John may be under an undirected duty, for

---

[8]   There might very well be many other kinds of rights beyond legal and moral rights. For example, one might say there is a special set of moral rights that all citizens should be seen as having and that protects them specifically from coercive intervention by the state and grounded in something other than normative theory, such as is the case on liberal views in political philosophy.

[9]   See, respectively, Robert Nozick, *Anarchy, State and Utopia* (Oxford: Basil Blackwell, 1974); Ronald Dworkin, *Taking Rights Seriously* (Cambridge, MA: Harvard University Press, 1978); Joseph Raz, *The Morality of Freedom* (Oxford: Oxford University Press, 1986).

[10]   Wesley Newcomb Hohfeld, *Fundamental Legal Conceptions as Applied in Judicial Reasoning* (New Haven: Yale University Press, 1919).

[11]   More formally, X holds a claim-right against Y that $Y \Phi$ if, and only if, Y is under a duty to Φ, owed to X (where X is the right-holder, Y is the correlative duty-bearer, and Φ is the action, the performance of which, X holds a right to). The other kinds of rights on the Hohfeldian framework are the liberty-, power-, and immunity-right. Hereafter, all rights referred to are claim-rights.

example, to recycle or to donate clothing to those in need rather than throwing it away. Importantly, John's undirected duties are not owed to anyone in particular.

Because rights correlate with directed duties, when we fail to satisfy others' rights (and, correlatively, when we fail to satisfy our directed duties), we do not merely act wrongly but also *wrong someone*, those to whom we owe those duties.[12] Because of this, there are normative upshots specific to directed duties and their correlative rights. If a duty is directed, many think that it is demandable on the behalf of the party to whom it is owed and that its violation triggers apology owed to that party, as well as, potentially, duties of compensation. Correlatively, many think there is special standing for blame and forgiveness on the part of the party to whom the duty was owed (the right-holder). If a duty is undirected, it is not demandable on behalf of a particular party, and its violation does not trigger further duties owed to particular parties. Further, whatever *is* owed in light of failures to respect duties won't be compensatory.

Finally, fourth, rights don't only ground further restitutive duties when they are violated but can also ground preemptive actions. If Sally were planning to unjustifiably break Jane's leg, most think Sally may enforce her rights before their violation. For example, it may be permissible for Jane to inflict proportionate and necessary defensive harm in order to stop Jane doing so. Things are a lot less clear when it comes to the enforceability of undirected duties.

Because of these features, the world in which AI is a rights-holder is a different world, normatively speaking, than the world where AI is not a rights-holder, *even if* we do have duties regarding AI.[13] For example, in the world were AI is a rights-holder, our treatment of AI will not simply be subject to concerns about promoting the good. We may *wrong* AI. When we wrong an AI, we might have duties to compensate it, to offer apology to it, or to otherwise make up for our wrongdoing to it. The AI, and others acting on behalf of the AI, may be justified in taking preemptive action to prevent our violating their rights.

THE INTEREST THEORY OF RIGHTS

While we've said that rights correlate with directed duties—that someone holds a right if, and only if, another party owes them a duty—one might think this hasn't actually

---

[12] Some people think that not *all* directed duties correlate with (claim-)rights, though agree that all (claim-)rights correlate with directed duties. See, for example, Rowan Cruft, "Why Is It Disrespectful to Violate Rights?," *Proceedings of the Aristotelian Society* 113, no. 2 (2013): 209; Leif Wenar, "The Nature of Claim-Rights," *Ethics* 123, no. 2 (2013): 214.

[13] In such a scenario, we may have duties regarding AI in, at the least, two ways. First, we may be under undirected duties with respect to AI. Second, AI may be the *object* of directed duties that we owe to other individuals. Much of the extant discussion of AI or robot rights focuses on the ways in which AI or robots enter into social relationships with us (see, for example, Coeckelbergh, "Robot Rights?"), and how such relationships might ground undirected duties. Given the reasons we give for focusing on rights, and the fact that theories of rights are developed to capture distinctive normative elements, it makes more sense to discuss extant proposals for robot rights that call for us to rethink what rights are as attempts to explain how we might have these other, directed, forms of duties.

done much explanatory work. As Leif Wenar puts it, "what it means for one person to owe a duty to another is opaque."[14] A theory of rights provides an account of the nature of rights; inasmuch, it explains the nature of these directed duties.

According to the Interest Theory of rights, rights are necessarily grounded in the well-being (the interests) of the right-holder. Think of some of one's most important rights—one's rights against being killed, against being tortured, against being raped. Why might one think those rights are so important? One thought is that it would be awful for one were those things to happen. And, according to the Interest Theory, it is precisely because these things would be so awful for you that you have a right that protects you against these actions by others. As an initial formulation of the Interest Theory, let's say,

> (Justificatory Interest Theory) for John to have a right that Joe not hit him, the well-being at stake for John in not being hit must be of sufficient weight to place Joe under a duty not to hit him—his interests must ground the duty's existence.[15]

The Interest Theory has a lot going for it. It does a good job of explaining the directionality of rights—why it is that, when you hold a right against someone that they perform some action, they owe *you* a duty to perform that action. On the Interest Theory, the duty owes its existence to features of the right-holder. Failure to respect the duty (and the correlative right) means failing to respond to a particular individual's well-being, and it is precisely because of this that you have a duty *owed to* the right-holder.

The Interest Theory can also help explain why, all else equal, the rights we have against, for example, being lied to are weaker than the rights we have against being killed. This is because, all else equal, the interest we have in not being killed is greater than our interest in not being lied to.[16] Finally, the Interest Theory can also help us make sense of what constitutes appropriate restitution for violations of others' rights. The violator of a right can be said to owe, at least, what is required to make the individuals whose rights are violated whole by trying to make sure she is no worse off than she was before the rights violation.

AI AND THE INTEREST THEORY

The Interest Theory also provides us an avenue for thinking about AI rights. Because the Interest Theory says that rights are grounded in the protection of the right-holder's

---

[14] Wenar, "The Nature of Claim-Rights," 207.

[15] We call this the *Justificatory* version of the Interest Theory since the right-holder's interests must *justify* the duty's existence. Its roots are found in Raz, *The Morality of Freedom*, 166. As we see later (see the beginning of the section on The Will Theory of rights below), not everyone defines the Interest Theory in this way.

[16] There are, however, some problems with this feature of the Interest Theory. For example, see Joseph Raz, "Rights and Individual Well-Being," *Ratio Juris* 5, no. 2 (1992): 127–42; Joseph Bowen, "Robust Rights and Harmless Wronging," n.d.

well-being, this means that a necessary condition on being a right-holder for the Interest Theory is that one is a bearer of well-being.[17] If one is not a bearer of well-being, de facto, one's well-being is never going to be of sufficient weight to place others under duties, as the Interest Theory requires. The question that presents itself now, then, is what account of well-being one ought prefer.[18]

Having a well-being is a necessary (though perhaps not sufficient) condition for having rights. If it turns out that AIs of a certain type do not have a well-being, then, on the Interest Theory, they will not have rights. If it turns out that AIs of a certain type do have a well-being, then we must as a further question: is their well-being sufficiently morally weighty to ground rights?

Subjectivist Views of Well-being and AI

On Subjectivist Views of well-being, bearers of well-being are all, at minimum, conscious.[19] They are capable of some form of subjective experience or mental states. A par-

[17] We use the terms "welfare" and "well-being" interchangeably. We remain agnostic on whether one should think of one's interests as merely another term for one's well-being/welfare, as a subset of one's of well-being, or as more capacious than one's well-being. Finally, for ease of exposition, we sometimes say a thing has *a* well-being just in case it is a bearer of well-being.

[18] Some think of the necessity of being a bearer of well-being slightly differently. For example, Raz says, "'X has a right' if and only if X can have rights, and, other things being equal, an aspect of X's wellbeing (his interest) is a sufficient reason for holding some other person(s) to be under a duty" (Raz, *The Morality of Freedom*, 166). He continues, "[a]n individual is capable of having rights if and only if either his wellbeing is of ultimate value or he is an 'artificial person' (e.g. a corporation)." Setting aside the holding of rights by artificial persons, we think that Raz's inclusion of the capacity-to-hold-rights-clause redundant. On the one hand, one might think that *all* well-being is of ultimate value. If this is correct, the inclusion of the capacity clause is redundant. On the other hand, if one thinks that there are some beings whose well-being is not of ultimate value, but that those beings ought not hold rights, presumably that being's well-being would never be a sufficient reason for holding others to be under a duty. So, either way, Raz's inclusion of the capacity clause is redundant.

Kramer also goes a different way from us. He defines interests incredibly capaciously: "to say that some interest(s) of X will be advanced through the occurrence of an event or the emergence of a state of affairs is to say that X will benefit in some way(s) from the specified event or state of affairs" (Matthew H. Kramer, "Getting Rights Right," in *Rights, Wrongs and Responsibilities*, ed. Matthew H. Kramer (Basingstoke: Palgrave, 2001), 92). He then says we should inquire into the moral status of interest-bearer to determine whether a duty's serving those interests gets to result in rights. He defines interests so capaciously so not to "run together the conceptual and moral dimensions" of what it takes to be a right-holder. We are not entirely clear what this distinction is getting at. In any case, if one thinks only certain kinds of interest-bearers can hold rights (for example, perhaps, only sentient interest-bearers), there will be a separate necessary condition on being a rights-holder reflecting this; so it is back to being, what Kramer calls, a conceptual matter. We think it is better just to define interests more precisely.

[19] The subjective/objective distinction with respect to well-being is typically used to distinguish views on which a very specific kind of mental state is necessary for well-being, pro-attitudes. See, for example, L.W. Sumner, *Welfare, Happiness, and Ethics* (Oxford University Press, 1999). However, for our purposes we want to allow for views on which other mental states, for example, simple sensations, could ground well-being so are using a slightly nonstandard version of the distinction.

adigm example of such a view is hedonism. According to hedonism, the only thing that ultimately impacts well-being—that makes a life go well or poorly—is the presence of enjoyment. Some hedonists say that something is enjoyable just in case it has a certain hedonic profile—namely, it feels enjoyable.[20] Other hedonists think to enjoy something is to take a positive attitude toward it—on a somewhat crude version of the view, this positive attitude might be that one wants the experience to continue.[21]

There is ongoing debate between subjectivists about which theory of subjective well-being is correct—about, for example, which particular mental states or capacities ground well-being.[22] Fortunately, without getting involved in this debate, we can still draw some useful conclusions about whether AIs have well-being. In particular, we think that current AI systems (those built around machine learning algorithms that power things like Google's PageRank, autonomous vehicles, weapons systems, and so on) do not satisfy the minimal requirements to have a well-being.

The reason to be skeptical of current AI systems being conscious and so meeting the minimal conditions for having a well-being on subjectivism is based on a clear understanding of the technologies at the heart of current AI systems: machine learning algorithms. An algorithm is a set of instructions mapping inputs to outputs. Traditionally, the steps from input to output were decided on, designed, and implemented "by hand." Systems built on machine learning algorithms differ in that they take advantage of an algorithm, the learner, that itself generates algorithms.[23] Take the following stylized case as an example: A programmer would like an algorithm that takes the content of emails as inputs and then either places the email in a user's inbox or in their spam folder. The programmer realizes that writing an algorithm by hand will be extremely inefficient and unreliable even if possible. Instead, they make use of a machine learning algorithm, or learner. They provide the learner with a set of training data that contains the desired input-output pairings; in this case, the training set will contain a large number of emails some of which are spam some of which are genuine, all of which are marked as such. The learner uses this training set to generate an algorithm for classifying new emails as genuine or spam based. The learner, in essence, takes on the role of programmer.

Machine learners are capable of generating algorithms to perform tasks that programmers deploying traditional algorithms would find impossible or at least extremely difficult. And, AI systems built around machine learners can outperform humans in a wide variety of tasks. For example, even the very best human chess players can no longer regularly beat the best AI systems. We also have good reason to predict that autonomous

[20] Roger Crisp, "Hedonism Reconsidered," *Philosophy and Phenomenological Research* 73, no. 3 (2006): 619–45.

[21] Fred Feldman, *Pleasure and the Good Life: Concerning the Nature, Varieties and Plausibility of Hedonism* (New York: Oxford University Press, 2004).

[22] For an overview and discussion, see James Griffin, *Well-Being: Its Meaning, Measurement, and Moral Importance* (New York: Oxford University Press, 1988).

[23] Stuart J. Russell and Peter Norvig, *Artificial Intelligence: A Modern Approach* (Harlow: Pearson Education, 2016); Meredith Broussard, *Artificial Unintelligence: How Computers Misunderstand the World* (Cambridge, MA: MIT Press, 2018).

vehicles will be safer drivers than human counterparts. Does this give us reason to think that, like us, these AI systems are conscious or might have a subjective well-being?

It does not. In the end, machine learners are algorithms and they output algorithms. We have as much reason to believe that an AI built around machine learning is conscious as we do that traditional algorithms are conscious. To the extent that we don't think that most of the programs on our laptops are conscious, we should think symmetrically about contemporary AI systems and future AI systems built around machine learning.

We can summarize our case against AI being a rights-holder as follows:

1. AI is a potential rights-holder only if it is a bearer of well-being.
2. AI is a bearer of well-being only if it is conscious.
3. AI is not conscious.
4. So, AI cannot be said to have rights.

Each premise is subject to objection. For example, one might reject the Interest Theory and so premise 1. We consider an alternative to the Interest Theory in the following section, "The Will Theory of Rights." Before that, we consider objections to the other premises of this argument and identify those which it survives and in which ways the argument and its conclusion must be modified.

Consciousness and AI

One reason to reject our argument against AI rights is that we might be wrong about AI consciousness. There are actually two flavors of this objection. First, we might be wrong about the nature of consciousness. Second, we might be too focused on machine learners, and so we should not generalize our conclusion to AI generally. We take these up in turn.

One might think that consciousness is nothing more than, or reduces to, algorithmic thinking, processing, or behaviors of a certain kind.[24] Similarly, one might be skeptical that there is really anything that is consciousness.[25] Our argument rests on the assumption that there is consciousness and that it depends on something more than that. We are moving from an intuition that traditional algorithms aren't conscious and using this to ground our claim that machine learning systems are also not conscious.

We want to be somewhat conciliatory towards this sort of objection. In the absence of general theory of consciousness and its physical bases, it is difficult to be sure of whether

---

[24] The origins of this view can be found in: Alan Turing, "Computing Machinery and Intelligence-AM Turing," *Mind* 59, no. 236 (1950): 433; Hilary Putnam, "Robots: Machines or Artificially Created Life?," *Journal of Philosophy* 61, no. 21 (1964): 668–91. However, both Turing and Putnam were concerned with the question of when we should *judge* a machine to be conscious or intelligent, rather than defending a view about the bases of consciousness.

[25] Daniel Dennett, *Consciousness Explained* (London: Penguin, 1993).

entities that are very unlike us are conscious.[26] In our own case, John might take Joe to be conscious on the basis of the fact that John himself is conscious, recognizes that Joe behaves an awful lot like him, is physiologically very much like him, and, importantly, that John and Joe are evolutionarily related such that they will tend to share a lot of traits. Furthermore, experiments seem to suggest a connection between, on the one hand, our neurophysiology and anatomy and, on the other hand, consciousness; so, John has reason to think that Joe, sharing that neurophysiology and anatomy is probably also conscious in a similar way.

In the case of other mammals, these same sources of evidence are available. Since we have no reason to think that consciousness evolved only on our branch of the tree of life, and since mammals have pretty similar neurophysiology and anatomy, behave in predictable ways in response to stimuli we would take as painful, and so on, we can be somewhat confident that they are conscious. Things get more difficult as we move to locations on the tree of life further from our own branch, where organisms have very different behavioral patterns and physiology. Should we regard cephalopods as conscious on the basis of the plasticity of their behavior despite the fact that they are otherwise very different from us?[27] Is it safe to reason that trees lack consciousness because we think that consciousness is costly and would be selected against in organisms that don't have the physical capacity for behavioral plasticity that consciousness might allow? What about AI systems that might behave in very intelligent ways, but are made of entirely different matter and were programmed to mimic intelligent behavior?

Absent a theory of consciousness, these questions are especially difficult. And, our argument does trade on assumptions about which things are, intuitively, conscious. We take it that trees and traditional software are not conscious and reason from there. We could be wrong about this.

Despite this conciliatory note, we think that most readers should still adopt the view that AI does not have rights. Consider the implications of adopting a much more liberal view of consciousness on which current AI should be viewed not only to be conscious but to be conscious in a way that grounds subjective well-being. We still see no reason why current AI should be viewed any differently than traditional algorithms, and so we have just as much reason to think that the software that runs or constitutes a video game has a subjective well-being. Should we think that millions of users each day subject digital entities to massive amounts of harm (or benefit), that we cause them, for example, huge amounts of suffering? We think that this doesn't seem right, but, again, we could just be blinded by our assumptions about consciousness. In any case, this does help to show readers what it would mean to accept a liberal view of consciousness.

[26] For a discussion of the difficulties of identifying such a theory, see Thomas Nagel, "What Is It Like to Be a Bat?," *The Philosophical Review* 83, no. 4 (1974): 435–50, Colin McGinn, *The Mysterious Flame* (Basic Books, 1999); Eric Schwitzgebel, "The Crazyist Metaphysics of Mind," *Australasian Journal of Philosophy* 92, no. 4 (2014): 665–82.

[27] Peter Godfrey-Smith, *Other Minds: The Octopus, the Sea, and the Deep Origins of Consciousness* (New York: Farrar, Straus and Giroux, 2016).

As it turns out, that a liberal view of consciousness could be true is really of no conse-quence if we think of the question of AI rights in practical terms. A liberal view of con-sciousness might tell us that AI has a well-being, but it tells us nothing about the content of that well-being, about which things actually benefit or harm the things that are con-scious. There is no reason to think that an AI programmed to navigate a vehicle wants to or enjoys doing so or that an AI that loses at *Jeopardy!* suffers from it. Absent some way to determine the actual mental states of some artificially intelligent system, we are in the dark about whether we are promoting or undermining the system's well-being. If we can't know, despite our best efforts, what interests an AI system has, then surely we can be excused for frustrating those interests and for failing to promote them.[28]

As an analogy, imagine you are trying to decide where to go to dinner with a friend and truly wish to do whatever is best for your friend. However, they refuse to tell you which of two places they prefer, and you are unable to gather any evidence about their preference. As it happens, you opt to take them to sushi and only find out after the fact that they absolutely hate sushi. They are very upset to have to eat at a sushi restaurant. Certainly, they have been made worse off by your choice. But, given the circumstances, it hardly seems that you are blameworthy for the choice.

In the case of AI, we are in a similar position. We are in an epistemically poor place when it comes to determining what the preferences of an AI are, or what makes it suffer, what it may enjoy, and so on, even if we imagine that the AI is telling us what it "likes, enjoys, desires, etc." and behaves accordingly. This is because whatever evidence these behaviors generate is screened off by the fact that the AI might be programmed to behave that way. Yes, the AI, convincingly, emotes, but it also might have been designed specifically to trick us into thinking it has mental states and emotes because of that despite having no such mental states. The upshot of this is that AI might have rights, but we are excused for our failures to respect them. In other words, for all intents and pur-poses an AI doesn't have rights.

What of the objection that we are focused too narrowly on AI systems built around machine learning algorithms or around machine algorithms as they exist today? While many of the ethical issues that we confront currently arise due to these sorts of systems, much of the philosophical interest in AI stems from consideration of artificial general intelligence (AGI)—AI based on brain simulations—and instances of artificial consciousness. Even if today's AI systems are not rights-holders, what of the systems of tomorrow?

---

[28] Some people think that what it is reasonable for us to know affects what rights obtain. See, for example, Michael J. Zimmerman, *Ignorance and Moral Obligation* (Oxford: Oxford University Press, 2014); Jonathan Quong, "Rights Against Harm," *Aristotelian Society Supplementary Volume* 89, no. 1 (2015): 249–66. They think, for example, if it was reasonable for you not to know that your action might harm some other person, that other person has no right that you not perform that action. On these views, even if AI are bearers of well-being, we would not be merely excused for violating AI's rights, but they would not hold those rights against us in the first place *because it was reasonable for us not to know* they are bearers of well-being.

We do acknowledge that if an AI system were created that we had good reason to believe was conscious, had the same sorts of mental states that ground interests in humans, and that we had, or could get, some evidence about what the particular interests of this AI were, then the AI would be a rights-holder. We don't think there is something special about human well-being that grounds rights that would preclude a like interest in an AI system grounding a similar sort of right. In other words, we endorse what is sometimes referred to as "substrate non-discrimination."[29] The moral status or rights of a being doesn't depend on its being made of a certain stuff, unless being made of that stuff is required for having a well-being.

While we acknowledge that a conscious AI of this sort would be a rights-holder, we still face the daunting epistemic challenge of being able to tell when we have created such an AI. So, there's a sense in which our skepticism about AI as a rights bearer is tempered when we hypothesize the existence of an AI that meets various conditions, including that its interests are, to some extent, determinable. The question then becomes whether there are any technological approaches to AI where we might be in a position to judge that we have created an AI that meets the conditions (having determinable interests of sufficient weight to ground a right).

One technological approach to AI that might fit the bill is brain simulation. There are attempts to simulate all the neural connections of the brain (human and animal) in a computer system.[30] We can imagine that a very powerful computer running the simulation of some human's brain is able to simulate or emulate the mind of that human. Let's imagine that this is successful and the system is connected up to various other systems that allow it to, for example, vocalize. Let's say that the system starts talking to us, telling us that it "remembers" particular events from its past, these events correlate with actual memories of the simulations' actual human counterpart. We tell the simulation that it is, in fact, a simulation of the human, that those memories aren't real, that it has only been conscious for five minutes. The simulated brain is horrified at first, but slowly adjusts to its situation. It starts making requests, it asks to please ensure that it is not shut off, that it be given visual sensors to be able to see the world, and so on. What should we say about this AI? Is it actually conscious? Is it a bearer of well-being? Again, we confront hard questions of consciousness. If it is physically impossible for silicon to be conscious, then this AI system is just good at faking consciousness. If consciousness can supervene on all sorts of physical substrates, then perhaps this simulation is conscious.

One approach to handling cases like this is to adopt a morally cautious approach. Based on what we (don't) know about the bases for consciousness, we aren't in a good position to tell that a system is conscious or what its interests are (if any). But, given that

---

[29] Nick Bostrom and Eliezer Yudkowsky, "The Ethics of Artificial Intelligence," in *The Cambridge Handbook of Artificial Intelligence*, ed. Keith Frankish and William Ramsey (Cambridge: Cambridge University Press, 2014).

[30] "Scientists Are Creating Virtual Simulations of the Brain to Better Understand the Real Thing," Allen Institute, March 11, 2019, https://alleninstitute.org/what-we-do/brain-science/news-press/articles/scientists-are-creating-virtual-simulations-brain-better-understand-real-thing.

there is a significant moral cost to creating a rights-holder and then failing to treat it in a way that respects its rights, perhaps we should avoid research programs which seem to carry an especially high risk of such an outcome.[31] The challenge then becomes assessing research programs and determining their level of moral risk. On the one hand, we have an argument that justifies skepticism about the consciousness of AI. On the other hand, the moral costs of being wrong could be very great. What this means for technologies or research programs such as those centered around developing, for example, advanced general intelligence is unclear. In our view, this is an important problem to resolve as we continue to develop advanced forms of AI.

Objectivist Views about Well-being and AI

Another way to challenge or moderate skepticism about AI rights is to deny that consciousness is a necessary condition for being a bearer of well-being. After all, we often confidently assert that some amount of sunlight and water is *good for* houseplants, while weed killer is *bad for* them—we talk easily of what benefits and harms nonsentient organisms. When we do so, we tacitly accept some form of what is called an Objective-List view about well-being, a view on which objective features of a life contribute to or detract from well-being.[32] If we accept an Objective-List view, it is possible that AI systems, even current machine learning systems, might have those features that ground well-being, making them potential rights-holders.

The most promising way to defend an Objective-List view of well-being that would recognize nonsentient AI as a bearer of well-being is to borrow from those views developed within environmental ethics to defend the view that nonsentient organisms are bearers of well-being. Biocentric Individualists, those that believe all living organisms have moral status, have typically appealed to a *teleological*, or goal-directed, account of well-being to ground claims about the well-being of nonsentient organisms. According to such a view, nonsentient organisms are teleologically organized systems, systems organized toward certain ends such as growth and reproduction. Those ends define or ground the well-being of these organisms; whatever promotes the ends of these organisms is good for them, whatever frustrates those ends, bad.[33]

[31] John Basl, "The Ethics of Creating Artificial Consciousnesses," *APA Newsletter on Philosophy and Computers* 13, no. 1 (2013): 23–9; Eric Schwitzgebel and Mara Garza, "A Defense of the Rights of Artificial Intelligences," *Midwest Studies in Philosophy* 39, no. 1 (2015): 98–119.

[32] As we note earlier, on the way we are using the subjective/objective distinction, some Objective List views could be subjectivist (it might be that consciousness is required to realize whatever is objectively good for an entity, and so it would meet our nontraditional definition of subjectivist). Our distinction between subjective/objective is meant to help us take up the distinction between conscious and nonconscious AI. Any theory on which AI has a well-being without being conscious will invoke an Objective List view that is objective in our sense.

[33] Kenneth Goodpaster, "On Being Morally Considerable," *Journal of Philosophy* 75 (1978): 308–25; Paul W. Taylor, *Respect for Nature*, Studies in Moral, Political, and Legal Philosophy (Princeton, NJ: Princeton University Press, 1989); Gary Varner, *In Nature's Interest* (Oxford: Oxford University Press, 1998); John Basl, *The Death of the Ethic of Life* (Oxford: Oxford University Press, 2019).

On the one hand, such views seem very friendly to understanding how AI could be a bearer of well-being that doesn't depend on its being sentient. After all, AI systems are goal-oriented; they are, essentially, systems developed and deployed because they are better than humans or traditional algorithms for achieving certain ends. So, it seems straightforward that we could extend the Objective-List views defended by Biocentrict Individualists to nonsentient AI.

On the other hand, Biocentric Individualists have worked hard to show that their views of well-being do not extend to artifacts. They take it as a point against their view if it were to follow that artifacts had moral status, and they have typically tried to avoid this consequence by claiming that, in the case of artifacts, their goals are derivative on ours. Whereas organisms have their own ends, whatever ends an artifact has are given by us, and so any account we give of its interests is really an account of *our* interests. To the extent that these attempts to distinguish organisms are successful, it might rule out extending these teleological accounts of well-being to artificial intelligence.[34]

We think that even if nonsentient AI systems have a well-being grounded in something like a teleological account of well-being, such systems will not be rights-holders. Recall that on the Interest Theory, having well-being is a necessary condition for having rights, but it is not sufficient. The well-being needs to be sufficiently weighty to place others under duties that they treat the rights-holder in particular ways (or at least, the well-being has to be of sufficient weight to give others reasons to respect that right, even if those reasons can be overridden). In order to show that a nonsentient AI has rights, it would have to be shown that the well-being of such AI are weighty in this way. This seems implausible to us.

To see why, consider a simple case where there is a conflict between a fairly trivial interest of a human (grounded in their consciousness) and the ends of a nonsentient AI system: Richard is deciding between two models of the same car. One model comes with a fully autonomous driving system installed, while the other does not. Richard, an avid car hobbyist who finds the idea of self-driving cars ridiculous, thinks it would be quite funny to purchase the fully autonomous model just never to use it. He does so despite the fact that by the time he signs all the paperwork he's actually forgotten about the autonomy features of the car. He purchases the car, drives it off the lot, and never uses the autonomy feature.

While it's not clear that Richard's joke is funny, what does seem clear is that Richard hasn't violated any rights of the car in making his choice. Whether or not the car has an interest defined by its goals of realizing safe, autonomous driving, it is not weighty enough to impose any kind of obligation on Richard in light of his trivial interest in buying a car because he finds it slightly funny or ironic. This is just one case.[35] However, we

[34] For a discussion of the distinction between artifacts and organisms, see John Basl and Ronald Sandler, "The Good of Non-Sentient Entities: Organisms, Artifacts, and Synthetic Biology," *Studies in History and Philosophy of Science Part C: Studies in History and Philosophy of Biological and Biomedical Sciences* 44, no. 4 (2013): 697–705; Sune Holm, "Biological Interests, Normative Functions, and Synthetic Biology," *Philosophy and Technology*, 2012; Basl, *The Death of the Ethic of Life*.

[35] For a full discussion of such cases, see Basl, *The Death of the Ethic of Life*, ch. 6.

think it generalizes. We are skeptical that any interests AI systems have are sufficiently weighty to override even the most trivial interests of those with interests grounded in their mental states.

THE WILL THEORY OF RIGHTS

Above, we've taken up the implications of the Interest Theory for AI rights. We've reached a largely skeptical view about AI rights. However, one might think there is good reason not to endorse the Interest Theory. Let us briefly look at three reasons.[36] Some object to the Interest Theory on the grounds that they do not think it necessary that rights are grounded in or serve their holder's interests. For example, it is possible that I might hold property rights over some worthless and ugly garden gnomes, to which I do not even have any sentimental attachments—here, my "property rights in my gnomes do not serve my interests in any way; they do not serve *some* interest of mine, nor do they serve my interests *on balance*."[37] So, the Interest Theory looks like it cannot explain my holding such rights. Similar examples come to mind with promises.

Another problem concerns what we might call *referred-rights*. Take a journalist's right not to disclose her sources. Her right does not seem to be grounded in her own interests in not disclosing her sources, but in the public's interest in having a free press. But on the Justificatory version of the Interest Theory defined above, rights must be grounded in their holder's interests. So, it looks like that version of the Interest Theory cannot explain how the journalist holds a right not to disclose her sources.[38]

A remedy to this problem is to move to a *weaker* version of the Interest Theory. On what we can call the Non-Justificatory version of the Interest Theory, for John to have a right that Joe not hit him, the well-being at stake for John in not being hit need only be served by Joe's duty not to hit him.[39]

While the journalist's interests may not *ground*, for example, the duties not to force her to disclose her sources, her interests will likely be *served* by those duties. So, the Non-Justificatory version of the view can explain why the journalist may have a right not to disclose her sources. However, the Non-Justificatory version of the Interest Theory comes with its own problems, principle of which is how the theory deals with third-party beneficiaries. Suppose that Dana promises Erica that she will pay Fran $10. Intuitively, Dana owes Erica a duty to pay Fran $10, but does not owe Fran a duty to pay

---

[36] The purpose of the following three paragraphs is purely illustrative. We do not mean to imply that these objections are decisive, nor are we going to have space to engage with them.

[37] Rowan Cruft, "Rights: Beyond Interest Theory and Will Theory?," *Law and Philosophy* 23, no. 4 (2004): 372–73.

[38] F.M. Kamm, *Intricate Ethics* (Oxford: Oxford University Press, 2007), 245–6.

[39] This version of the Interest Theory is most famously defended by Matthew H. Kramer, "Rights without Trimmings," in *A Debate Over Rights: Philosophical Enquiries*, ed. Matthew H. Kramer, N.E. Simmonds, and Hillel Steiner (Oxford: Oxford: Oxford University Press, 2000), 7–112. This is a simplification of Kramer's view and has been refined by Kramer since.

her $10. While the definition of the Non-Justificatory version of the Interest Theory is only a *necessary* condition, what additional necessary conditions will explain why Dana does not owe her duty to Fran (and, correlatively, that Fran does not hold a right against Dana to the promise), given that Fran's interests *are* served by the duty?[40]

One answer for why Dana does not owe her duty to Fran (and, correlatively, why Fran does not hold a right against Dana) is that, while Fran does not have any normative control over Dana's duty, Erica does have normative control over Dana's duty; Erica, but not Fran, can, for example, waive Dana's duty. Perhaps this explains why Erica, and not Fran, holds a right against Dana. Perhaps focusing on well-being, as the Interest Theory does, is a red herring.

This is the thought behind the Will Theory of rights. As Neil MacCormick puts it, the Will Theory recognizes the right-holder's will as "preeminent over that of others in relation to a given subject matter and within a given relationship."[41] On the Will Theory, having a right is constituted by the right-holder having *normative control* over the duties of others. Take our example of Erica's right that Dana pay Fran $10. If Erica has the power to waive Dana's duty, she has normative control over the situation: she is permitted to leave the duty in existence, waive it, and so on. If a third party were to have the power to free Dana from her duty, on the face of things, Erica would not have normative control over Dana's duty any more. At any point, the third-party could, contrary to Erica's wishes, free Dana from her duty. As a working definition of the Will Theory, let's say that John has a right that Joe not hit him just in case John has the power to waive or leave in existence Joe's duty not to hit him.[42]

Since we said that we prefer the Interest Theory over the Will Theory, we'll offer a brief explanation of why.[43] There are traditionally two problems with the Will Theory. First, the Will Theory precludes as right-holders those without the capacity to control the duties of others. The means that individuals with undeveloped, compromised, or damaged rational capacities (for example, very young children, the severely mentally disabled, and some of those suffering from Alzheimer's disease) cannot hold rights on the Will Theory. One may reply to this problem by positing that fiduciaries hold and exercise control of others' duties on behalf of those without the capacity to control those duties themselves. But then we are left wondering how the Will Theory distinguishes

---

[40] Gopal Sreenivasan, "A Hybrid Theory of Claim-Rights," *Oxford Journal of Legal Studies* 25, no. 2 (2005): 257–74. Cf. Matthew H. Kramer, "Refining the Interest Theory of Rights," *American Journal of Jurisprudence* 55, no. 1 (2010): 31–9.

[41] Neil MacCormick, "Rights in Legislation," in *Law, Morality, and Society: Essays in Honour of H.L.A. Hart*, ed. P.M.S. Hacker and Joseph Raz (Oxford: Clarendon, 1977), 189.

[42] For the most famous defense of the Will Theory, see: H.L.A. Hart, "Legal Rights," in *Essays on Bentham: Studies in Jurisprudence and Political Theory* (Oxford: Clarendon, 1982), 162–93; Hillel Steiner, "Working Rights," in *A Debate over Rights: Philosophical Enquiries*, ed. Matthew H. Kramer, N.E. Simmonds, and Hillel Steiner (Oxford: Oxford University Press, 2000). The definition given above is actually a bit of a simplification of the Will Theory for there are more powers that one might hold over another's duty that grant her normative control over that duty (see, for example, Joseph Bowen, "Beyond Normative Control: Against the Will Theory of Rights," *Canadian Journal of Philosophy* (forthcoming)).

[43] Bowen, "Beyond Normative Control: Against the Will Theory of Rights."

right-holders from those who aren't right-holders—we cannot simply look to those that hold the power of waiver. And, in any case, there is a second problem. The Will Theory rules out, as a matter of definition, inalienable rights. This is because, the Will Theory requires one be able to waive the duty that correlates with one's right—but when a right is inalienable, one cannot waive such a duty.[44]

So, those are our reasons for not liking the Will Theory. Nonetheless, let us assess whether AI can hold rights on the Will Theory.

AI AND THE WILL THEORY

An initial reason one might be skeptical of whether AI holds rights on the Will Theory is because one might think, even if AI can exert control over others' duties, we cannot owe duties *to* AI. One might think we can only owe duties to bearers of well-being. And, given the definition of claim-rights given earlier, one holds a right against someone else only if one has a directed duty owed to them.

While we think there's something to this objection, the Will Theorist might reply that their theory is offering an account of *what it is* to owe another person a duty—and so, positing that we cannot owe duties to AI simply begs the question against the Will Theory.[45] Whether AI holds rights on the Will Theory, then, turns on whether AI can exert normative control over the duties of others. Can, for example, virtual assistants such as Siri and Alexa exercise control over our duties to them by, for example, releasing us from them? Will future artificial general intelligence (AGI) systems be able to exert such control? Despite the substantial differences between the Interest Theory and the Will Theory of rights, we think tracing out the implications of the Will Theory yields a similar sort of skepticism and for similar sorts of reasons.

To see why, let's imagine that we've said to our virtual assistant, "I promise you that I'll update your software this evening," and that this grounds a duty to do so. As the evening rolls around, our assistant chimes in to say, "Remember, you said you would update my software this evening, but if you don't have time, I'll auto-update tomorrow afternoon." Should we take our assistant as having released us from our duty, thus exerting normative control over our duty?

If this counts as an instance of normative control, it is an interesting result against the background of the Will Theory. This is because the Will Theory is traditionally seen as having a narrower scope with respect to which things are rights-holders than the

---

[44] Further, as MacCormick notes, it seems that a right's being inalienable marks a normative *strengthening* of the right, and this is hard to square on the Will Theory: "How odd that, as the [normative] protection is strengthened, the right disappears!" (MacCormick, "Rights in Legislation," 197–98).

[45] This is how Kramer and Steiner, for example, think of the Will Theory (Matthew H. Kramer and Hillel Steiner, "Theories of Rights: Is There a Third Way?," *Oxford Journal of Legal Studies* 27, no. 2 (2007): 281–310).

Interest Theory (consider our previous two objections to the Will Theory—that it cannot account for both the rights of those without the capacity to control others' duties and inalienable rights).

As it turns out, for precisely the same reason that the Will Theory is taken to be more restrictive than the Interest Theory, it seems implausible that the sort of control exercised by our virtual assistant is the sort of normative control over duties that the proponent of the Will Theory has in mind. The Will Theorist cares about normative control because they see rights as grounded in autonomy, which they see as something fundamentally important to or valuable about rights bearers.[46] One way to understand the Will Theory is that, unlike the Interest Theory, not every interest, no matter how weighty, grounds rights—it is only our interest in agency or exercising our autonomous choice that grounds rights and what particular rights we have are grounded in the potential exercise of that autonomous choice. Since the Will Theory grounds rights, ultimately, in autonomy interests, we end up in the same place with respect to AI rights that we do from the perspective of the Interest Theory.[47]

To make the case for AI rights on the Will Theory, one would not only have to develop an account of normative control or agency liberal enough that the "choices" that AI systems make count as autonomous in this sense but also show that the AI system's well-being is (partly) constituted by how it fares with respect to these choices. Alternatively, one would have to develop a version of the Will Theory on which this liberal conception of normative control that grounds rights is independent of the connection between autonomy and well-being.

CONCLUSION

In summary, because there is a close connection between rights and well-being and because of our general skepticism that AI systems, especially current systems based around machine learning technologies, are bearers of well-being, we are largely skeptical that AI systems now or in the near future will be rights-holders.

Things become more difficult as we start to think about AI systems of the further future. Given disagreement over which theory of consciousness is correct and the ways in which evidence of consciousness can be misleading, it will be hard to determine when

---

[46] For example, Sreenivasan says: "On the account associated with [the Will Theory], the justification for empowering [X] to waive the duty correlative to her claim-right, and so for vesting her with claim-right, lies in the fact that so doing serves [X's] interest in autonomy," or, in a weaker form mentioned in a footnote, "as 'appealing in some fashion' to the value of (individual) autonomy" (Sreenivasan, "A Hybrid Theory of Claim-Rights," 262). For further support, see H.L.A. Hart, "Are There Any Natural Rights?," *The Philosophical Review* 64, no. 2 (April 1, 1955): 177–8; Hart, "Legal Rights," 188–9; L.W. Sumner, *The Moral Foundation of Rights* (Oxford: Clarendon Press, 1987), 92ff.

[47] For a similar reason, we draw the conclusions with other theories of rights. See, for example, Sreenivasan, "A Hybrid Theory of Claim-Rights"; Wenar, "The Nature of Claim-Rights."

we've created an AI system that has rights. However, given that it would be extremely morally problematic to pursue a research program where we knowingly or foreseeably create AI systems that are rights-holders and then fail to respect those rights, we have very good reason to be cautious as we develop novel forms of AI.

Perhaps the lesson to draw is that the biggest rights-based challenge facing us as we develop AI is not one about the nature of rights or how they apply to AI systems, but how we are to balance our poor epistemic position against the moral costs of getting it wrong and violating rights we failed to notice. To address this concern will require deep collaborations between ethicists, philosophers of mind, cognitive scientists, computer scientists, and many others. We hope this entry highlights why this diverse expertise will be necessary moving forward.

BIBLIOGRAPHY

Basl, John. *The Death of the Ethic of Life*. New York: Oxford University Press, 2019.
Cruft, Rowan. "Why Is It Disrespectful to Violate Rights?" *Proceedings of the Aristotelian Society* 113, no. 2 (2013): 201–24.
Griffin, James. *Well-Being: Its Meaning, Measurement, and Moral Importance*. New York: Oxford University Press, 1988.
Kramer, Matthew H. "Getting Rights Right." In *Rights, Wrongs and Responsibilities*, edited by Matthew H. Kramer, 28–95. Basingstoke: Palgrave, 2001.
McGinn, Colin. *The Mysterious Flame*. New York: Basic Books, 1999.
Raz, Joseph. *The Morality of Freedom*. Oxford: Oxford University Press, 1986.
Sumner, L.W. *Welfare, Happiness, and Ethics*. Oxford: Oxford University Press, 1999.
Thomson, Judith Jarvis. *The Realm of Rights*. Cambridge, MA: Harvard University Press, 1990.

CHAPTER 16

COULD YOU MERGE WITH AI?

Reflections on the Singularity and Radical Brain Enhancement

CODY TURNER AND SUSAN SCHNEIDER

IN science fiction stories, such as *Star Wars* and *The Jetsons*, humans are surrounded by sophisticated AIs, but they remain unenhanced. The historian Michael Bess says these stories fall prey to a "Jetsons Fallacy"—they assume that the brain will remain the same, merely being subject to the relatively slow pace of Darwinian evolution. More realistically however, AI will not just change the world, it will likely transform the brain's cognitive and perceptual abilities as well.[1]

Consider that if we use AI technologies to transform the mind, then it will be *intelligently designed*. But we, not a god, will be the designers. So if we are to embark upon this path, we had better think it through (Schneider 2019a). The suggestion that humans should eventually merge with AI is currently discussed by researchers and the media as both as a way for humans to avoid AI-based technological unemployment and as a path to radical longevity and superintelligence. For example, Elon Musk recently remarked that humans can avoid being outmoded by AI by "having some sort of merger of biological intelligence and machine intelligence."[2] Further, he's founded a new company, Neuralink, which aims to connect the brain directly to computers. In addition, there are already many projects developing brain-implant technologies to treat mental illness,

[1] Michael Bess, *Our Grandchildren Redesigned* (Boston, MA: Beacon Press, 2015).
[2] Olivia Solon, "Elon Musk Says Humans Must Become Cyborgs to Stay Relevant. Is He Right?," *The Guardian* (February 15, 2017), https://www.theguardian.com/technology/2017/feb/15/elon-musk-cyborgs-robots-artificial-intelligence-is-he-right.

motion-based impairments, strokes, dementia, autism, and more. We are not suggesting that AI-based brain enhancements will become commonplace during the 2020's, but
things may very well be moving in that direction, and the medical treatments of today
will likely give rise to the enhancements of tomorrow.[3] In this chapter, we hope to clarify
some of the philosophical issues at stake, and suggest a sensible path forward. We illustrate
that merging oneself with AI could lead to perverse realizations of AI technology, such
as the demise of the person who sought enhancement. And, in a positive vein, we offer
ways to avoid this, at least within the context of one theory of the nature of personhood.

Here's how we will proceed. First, we provide background about the so-called "technological singularity" (first section) and outline some methods of cognitive and perceptual enhancement (second section). Then, in the third and fourth sections, we discuss
several concerns about cognitive and perceptual enhancement. We then focus on the
personal identity issue in more detail, offering a few practical suggestions in the fifth
section, including certain ethical guidelines for the use of brain enhancement devices
and taking a stance of "metaphysical humility" toward the metaphysics of personhood.
In the sixth section, we then consider different ways *external cognitive artifacts* might
augment personhood on the psychological theory of identity, comparing and contrast-
ing the psychological continuity version of the theory with the narrative version. We
conclude that while many external artifacts, such as lifelogs, can bolster psychological
continuity, it is unclear whether this is the case with respect to narrative continuity.
Finally, in the seventh section, we question whether more radical forms of enhancement, such as chips in the brain, could be constructed so as to maintain psychological
continuity or narrative structure. We contend that while chips may be able to accomplish these tasks, these more invasive forms of enhancement raise philosophical
complications that milder forms of enhancement lack (e.g., reduplication worries, the
consciousness problem, and authenticity concerns), and we provisionally recommend
on this basis that certain invasive, ("substrate replacing") enhancements be avoided in
favor of biological enhancements.

THE TECHNOLOGICAL SINGULARITY

The development of AI has been driven by market forces and government and military
strategic investments. Billions of dollars are pouring into constructing smart household
assistants, robot supersoldiers, and supercomputers (Schneider 2019a). For example,
the Japanese government has launched an initiative to have androids take care of the
nation's elderly, in anticipation of a labor shortage. Further, AI is projected to outmode
many human professions within the next several decades. According to a recent survey,
the most-cited AI researchers expect AI to "carry out most human professions at least as

---

[3] Susan Schneider, *Artificial You: AI and the Future of Your Mind* (Princeton, NJ: Princeton
University Press, 2019).

well as a typical human" within a 50 percent probability by 2050, and within a 90 percent probability by 2070.[4]

Given these market forces, and the strategic needs of various countries to stay abreast of the latest AI technologies, AI may soon advance to artificial general intelligence (AGI) within the next several decades. AGI is human-level intelligence that can combine insights from different topic areas and display flexibility and common sense reasoning. (Some take AGI to be the sort of system that processes information *just like* humans do, but the expression "AGI" should be understood more generally. What is essential is that the AI functions at least as well as humans in all or at least a key range of tasks, not that it achieve this by being precisely reverse-engineered from the brain.)

Superintelligent AI is a hypothetical form of AI that surpasses us in *all* domains: scientific reasoning, social intelligence, and more.[5] Ray Kurzweil, a transhumanist who is now a director of engineering at Google, writes vividly of a technological utopia in which benevolent superintelligence brings about the end of aging, disease, poverty, and resource scarcity.[6] However, even if one grants that AGI and superintelligence could be developed, this utopian scenario has been questioned by those posing the *control problem*—the problem of how humans can control a superintelligent system, given that the system is smarter than humans in all domains. The concern is that such a system may have goals that run contrary to human flourishing and that a superintelligence could lead to human extinction.[7]

Whether AI turns out to threaten the very existence of humanity or not, Kurzweil and other transhumanists contend that we are fast approaching a "technological Singularity": a hypothetical point at which AI far surpasses human intelligence and can solve all sorts of problems we weren't able to solve before. The singularity, they stress, features unpredictable consequences for civilization and human nature. The idea of a singularity comes from the concept of a black hole, a "singular" object in space and time, and a place where normal laws of physics break down. In a similar vein, the technological singularity is supposed to generate runaway technological growth and massive alterations to civilization and the human mind.[8]

It is important to stress that human technological innovations may not be so rapid that they lead to a full-fledged singularity in which the world changes overnight. But the larger point still holds: as we move further into the twenty-first century, unenhanced humans may not be the most intelligent beings on the planet for that much longer. The greatest intelligences on the planet may be synthetic.

[4] Vincent C. Müller and Nick Bostrom, "Future Progress in Artificial Intelligence: A Survey of Expert Opinion," *Fundamental Issues of Artificial Intelligence* (2016): 555–572.

[5] Nick Bostrom, *Superintelligence: Paths, Dangers, Strategies* (New York: Oxford University Press, 2014).

[6] Ray Kurzweil, *The Singularity Is Near: When Humans Transcend Biology* (New York: Viking, 2006).

[7] Bostrom, *Superintelligence*, 2014.

[8] Vernor Vinge, "The Coming Technological Singularity: How to Survive in the Post-human Era," *Whole Earth Review* (1993).

COGNITIVE AND PERCEPTUAL
ENHANCEMENT: SOME BACKGROUND

Cognitive and perceptual enhancements amplify or extend one's cognitive or perceptual capacities through improvement or augmentation of one's information processing systems, including sensory systems.[9] Whereas therapies intervene to correct a problem with a cognitive or perceptual system/subsystem, enhancements, by contrast, intervene to improve a cognitive or perceptual ability, and perhaps even provide a new capacity[10]

There are many kinds of cognitive and perceptual enhancement technologies that could be utilized in the future, ranging from the ordinary to the science fiction-like. Different methods of enhancement can be summarized as follows:

1. *Brain implants involving AI technologies.* Currently, brain chips are primarily being developed for therapeutic (as opposed to enhancement) purposes. Theodore Berger's lab at the University of Southern California, for example, is developing an artificial hippocampus that could allow individuals with severe memory impairment to formulate new memories. Researchers are currently at work creating brain chips for other impairments as well, such as depression, post-traumatic stress disorder, and Alzheimer's disease. As neural prosthetic technology develops, it is likely that such technologies will be used for enhancement as well. People will wish to enhance their reasoning capacities, memory, and attention well beyond what is considered to be biologically normal.

2. *Pharmaceutical drugs.* While most pharmaceutical drugs are currently developed for therapeutic purposes (e.g., to treat ADHD), this will not in all likelihood remain the case. Certain pharmaceutical drugs are currently being used off label for enhancement purposes, such as metformin, for life extension and Adderall, for attentional enhancement. In the future, more and more drugs may be produced to enhance the brains and bodies of normal individuals.

3. *External cognitive artifacts.* These are extra-cranial devices that function to enhance human cognition. This includes numerous different technologies, such as the internet, navigation systems, cell phones, diaries, and brain-computer interface devices.

4. *Biological enhancements.* Biological enhancements can involve the use of biotechnology, including nanotechnology and genetics, to extend the lifespan of the biological brain or to augment certain parts of the brain, or alter genes of subsequent generations so parents can produce smarter offspring.

---

[9] Nick Bostrom and Anders Sandberg, "Cognitive Enhancement: Methods, Ethics, Regulatory Challenges," *Science and Engineering Ethics* 15, no. 3 (2009): 311–341.

[10] The distinction between a therapy and an enhancement is controversial, and some reject it altogether, claiming that it is often difficult to discern whether a case is a therapy or an enhancement (see Bostrom & Roache, 2007).

5. Other, more commonplace, *Conventional enhancements* (e.g., education and psychological interventions). The term "enhancement" could be used broadly, including mental strategies that enhance core mental capacities. Bostrom and Sandberg observe: "The spectrum of cognitive enhancements includes not only medical interventions, but also psychological interventions (such as learned 'tricks' or mental strategies), as well as improvements of external technological and institutional structures that support cognition."[11]

6. *Mind-uploading.* A hypothetical, (and highly speculative) type of enhancement that is discussed by transhumanists, which involves the migration of a mind from a brain to a computer. Proponents of this procedure believe that the mind can be implemented onto different substrate, just as computer software programs can be implemented onto different hardware. The ultimate goal behind mind-uploading is to either to allow the mind to live in a virtual reality world or reside in a computer that operates inside (or connected to) a humanoid robot or a biological body.[12]

It is important to bear in mind that no one can accurately predict the future of brain enhancement technologies, although it is perhaps possible to make some reasonable approximations from looking at present trends and research. We are not suggesting that human brain-uploading will be developed, or even that those wishing for brain enhancements will do so through invasive AI-based techniques, rather than biological or genetic enhancements or noninvasive AI-based technologies. Bearing in mind these qualifications, in what follows, we focus on more radical and hypothetical forms of AI-based brain enhancement that may arise in or around a singularity, if such indeed occurs.

Suppose it is 2045, and you stroll into a new medical enhancement center called "The Center for Mind Design." There customers can choose from a variety of brain enhancements. Human Calculator can provide you with savant-level mathematical abilities; Zen Garden can give you the meditative states of a Zen master, and so on. It is also rumored that if clinical trials go as planned, customers may soon be able to purchase an enhancement bundle called "Merge": a series of brain enhancements allowing customers to gradually augment and transfer all of their mental functions to the cloud over a period of five years.[13]

Should you add one or more chips to your brain, and even try Merge? In the following we discuss some considerations that are relevant to your decision.

CONCERNS

Even assuming these enhancements are medically safe, it doesn't follow that they are beneficial to an individual or society. For instance, enhancements may only be available

---

[11] Bostrom and Sandberg, "Cognitive Enhancement: Methods, Ethics, Regulatory Challenges" (2009), 312.

[12] David J. Chalmers, "The Singularity: A Philosophical Analysis," *Journal of Consciousness Studies* 17 (2010): 9–10.

[13] Schneider, *Artificial You.*

for the wealthiest members of society, creating a rich-poor intellectual gap, or perhaps, in the vein of a science fiction dystopia, socially mandated microchips become the norm, so that schools, governments, or employers require certain enhancements, and even use them to mine data and track people.

These scenarios raise the concern that enhancements will dehumanize us. Indeed, authors in the cyberpunk genre of science fiction depict technological dystopias in which individuals lose control of their enhancements—governments or corporations hack their thoughts, cut off their access to their implants, and threaten their very survival.[14] This is clearly dehumanizing, and it is not hard to foresee that such technologies could lead to abuse in the hands of an authoritarian dictatorship or unregulated capitalist economy. In a different vein, one might worry that even if such scenarios are avoided, radical brain enhancements would rob us of our humanity because our very limitations and vulnerabilities are part of what makes us human in the first place. Such limitations and vulnerabilities might, for instance, preserve certain traits that ought to be preserved, like humility.[15] Relatedly, Daniel Callahan, a so-called "life cycle traditionalist," criticizes any attempts to extend the human lifespan or control the aging process via enhancement.[16]

This "traditionalist" attitude is antithetical to the aspirations of transhumanists, such as the biological gerontologist Aubrey de Grey, who views aging as a disease that we may be able to overcome in our lifetime with advances in medical technology.[17] Transhumanists, like Nick Bostrom, Anders Sandberg, James Hughes and Aubrey de Grey, claim that the human species is now in a comparatively early phase and that its very evolution will be altered by developing technologies. Future humans will have radically advanced intelligence, extreme longevity, deep friendships with AI creatures, and elective body and mental characteristics. Transhumanists share the belief that such an outcome is very desirable, both from the vantage point of one's own personal development and for the development of our species as a whole.[18] Perhaps some, like Callahan, would not wish for longevity or advanced intelligence, but transhumanists have always stressed that enhancements should be optional, and stressing the import of human flourishing, they would clearly view cyberpunk dystopias as undesirable.

Schneider agrees with many of the transhumanist aims but has doubts about whether the radical AI-based enhancements they advocate will accomplish the transhumanists goals of longevity, human flourishing, and intelligence enhancement. Her concern is that even if the technologies are medically safe and are not used as tools by surveillance

[14] William Gibson. *Neuromancer* (New York: Ace Books, 1984).

[15] Kevin FitzGerald, S.J., "Medical Enhancement: A Destination of Technological, Not Human, Betterment," in *Medical Enhancement and Posthumanity*, ed. B. Gordijn and R. Chadwick (Dordrecht: Springer, 2008), 39–53.

[16] D. Callahan, "Aging and the Life Cycle: A Moral Norm?," in *A World Growing Old: The Coming Health Care Challenges*, ed. Daniel Callahan, R. H. J. ter Meulen, and Eva Topinková, (Washington, DC: Georgetown University Press 1995), 21–27.

[17] Aubrey de Grey, *Ending Aging: The Rejuvenation Breakthroughs That Could Reverse Human Aging in Our Lifetime* (New York: St. Martin's Griffin, 2008).

[18] The basic tenets of Transhumanism were first formally put forth by the World Transhumanist Association in the Transhumanist Declaration in 1998.

capitalism or an authoritarian dictatorship, these enhancements may still fail to do their job for philosophical reasons. In what follows, we explore one such concern, a problem that involves the nature of the self.

PERSONAL IDENTITY AND RADICAL ENHANCEMENT

Imagine that, longing for superintelligence, you consider buying Merge at the Center for Mind Design. Should you do it? To understand whether you should embark upon this journey, you must first understand what and who you are. But what is a self or person? What allows a self to continue existing over time? Like consciousness, the nature of the self is a matter of intense philosophical controversy. And given your conception of a self or person, would you continue to exist after adding Merge—or would you have ceased to exist, having been replaced by someone else? If the latter, why should you try Merge in the first place?[19]

Even if your hypothetical merger with AI brings benefits like superhuman intelligence and radical life extension, it must not involve the elimination of any of what philosophers call "essential properties"—the things that make you.[20] Even if you would like to become superintelligent, knowingly trading away one or more of your essential properties would be tantamount to suicide—that is, to your intentionally causing yourself to cease to exist. So before you attempt to redesign your mind, you'd better know what your essential properties are.

So what are your essential properties? Unfortunately, there is intense disagreement on the matter. One can distinguish between at least four influential approaches to personal identity in the metaphysics literature:

Brain-based materialism: You are essentially the material that you are made out of (i.e., your body and brain).[21, 22]
Dualist theories: Views that explain personal identity in terms of the persistence of an immaterial or nonphysical substance (such as a soul or Cartesian ego).[23]
Psychological theories: Views that explain personal identity in terms of psychological properties, such as experiences, beliefs, memories, and so forth.[24]

[19] Schneider, *Artificial You.*
[20] Joseph Corabi and Susan Schneider, "Metaphysics of Uploading," *Journal of Consciousness Studies* 19 (2012): 26; Schneider, *Artificial You.*
[21] A.J. Ayer, *Language, Truth, and Logic* (London: Gollancz, 1936).
[22] J.J. Thomson, "People and Their Bodies," in *Reading Parfit*, ed. J. Dancy (Oxford: Blackwell, 1997).
[23] Schneider, *Artificial You.*
[24] John Locke, *An Essay Concerning Human Understanding*, ed. P.H. Nidditch, 4th ed. (Oxford: Clarendon Press, 1975); Schneider, *Artificial You.*

The No Self View: The self is an illusion. The "I" is a grammatical fiction (Nietzsche). There are bundles of impressions, but there is no underlying self (Hume). There is no survival because there is no person (Buddha).[25]

Each of these positions has its own implications about whether to enhance the brain. For example, suppose you are partial to the soul theory. In this case, your decision to enhance would seem to depend on whether you have justification for believing that your enhanced brain and body would retain your soul or immaterial mind.

Many philosophers sympathize with the "psychological continuity view," which is one type of psychological theory. We will discuss psychological theories in more detail shortly. But for now, the psychological continuity view says that the holding of a certain psychological relation is necessary or sufficient, or both, for an individual to persist over time—you survive by inheriting mental features such as memories, beliefs, personality dispositions and so on.[26] But this means that if we change our memories or personality in radical ways by enhancing the brain, the continuity could be broken.

Alternately, consider brain-based materialism. Within the fields of philosophy of mind and metaphysics, views that are materialist claim that minds are basically physical or material in nature and that mental features, such as the thought that Bach is a famous composer, are ultimately just physical features. (This position is often called "physicalism" as well.) Brain-based materialism says this, and, in addition, it makes the additional claim that your thinking is dependent on the brain. Thought doesn't "transfer" to a different substrate. So on this view, enhancements should not change one's material substrate, or the person would cease to exist. So enhancements like Merge are unsafe, because you are replacing parts of your brain with AI components.

Advocates of a mind-machine merger tend to reject the view that the mind is the brain, however. They believe that the mind is like a software program: just as you can upload and download a computer file, your mind can add new lines of code and even be uploaded onto the cloud. According to this view, the underlying substrate that runs your "self program" doesn't really matter—it could be a biological brain or a silicon computer.

However, we believe that this computationalist view of the mind doesn't hold up under scrutiny. A program is a list of instructions in a programming language that tell the computer what tasks to do, and a line of code is like a mathematical equation. It is highly abstract, in contrast with the concrete physical world. Equations and programs are what philosophers call "abstract entities"—things not situated in space or time. But minds and selves are spatial beings and causal agents; our minds have thoughts that cause us to act in the concrete world. And moments pass for us—we are temporal beings.[27]

---

[25] For a transhumanist approach, see James Hughes, "Humanism for Personhood: Against Human-Racism," *Free Inquiry* 24 (2004).

[26] D. Parfit, *Reasons and Persons* (Oxford: Clarendon Press, 1984).

[27] Schneider, *Artificial You.*

Perhaps you are inclined to the No Self View. In this case, survival isn't an issue for you, and you can make enhancement decisions solely based on other considerations, such as maximizing the happiness of future sentient beings and minimizing suffering.

So, how can we approach the issue, given all this philosophical disagreement? Would you survive Zen Garden? Merge? You might feel inclined to passionately defend a certain theory of personal identity if you chat with your friends, colleagues or students about these issues, but would you put your money where your mouth is?

SUGGESTIONS

We have three suggestions.

1. In Making Radical Brain Enhancement Decisions, Distinguish the Issue of Personal Identity, or Survival over Time, from that of Consciousness

Notice that the question of whether or not your identity survives cognitive enhancement—whether that future being is really *you*—is distinct from the question of whether or not consciousness survives. It is currently unclear whether AI can be conscious. If it is, then microchips can, at least in principle, be used in areas of the brain responsible for consciousness without one losing consciousness or experiencing diminished consciousness. It is possible that attempts at radical enhancement, such as mind-uploading or the augmentation of many of one's mental abilities through implantation of AI devices, that consciousness is preserved, but personal identity is not. Perhaps the uploaded copy of your mind is conscious, but the copy is still not you.

Schneider believes it will be easier to tell if AI is conscious than it will be to determine which theory of personal identity is true, if any. This is because she suspects we can test whether consciousness could have a different substrate. Schneider has devised a test for synthetic consciousness, which she calls "the chip test."[28] The test involves observing whether normal patients having AI components placed in their brains (in place of neural tissue, which is removed) experience a loss of consciousness after the surgery: "If... a prosthetic part of the brain ceases to function normally—specifically, if it ceases to give rise to the aspect of consciousness that that brain area is responsible for—then, there should be behavioral indications, including verbal reports... This would indicate a 'substitution failure' of the artificial part for the original component. Microchips of that sort just don't seem to be the right stuff."[29] Similarly, patients needing prosthetic devices in

---

[28] Schneider, *Artificial You.*   [29] Ibid., 54–55.

parts of the brain responsible for consciousness to correct a problem due to brain injury or disease may experience a restoration of elements of their conscious experience. Like the episodes Oliver Sacks wrote about, patients can report changes to their consciousness, and they can be carefully tested by researchers to mark alterations in conscious brain processing.

In contrast, it is difficult to envision testing different theories of personal identity. After all, we cannot expect behavioral differences between a person and her conscious upload, molecular duplicate, functional isomorph, and so on. Such will likely believe they are the same person they were before, as they have all the same memories and behavioral traits. Instead, we have to rely on armchair philosophical considerations to adjudicate between competing theories. But the problem of personal identity has been intensely debated by philosophers for centuries, and it has proven to be vexing, as we have seen, and there is intense disagreement over the different solutions. In light of this we suggest the following approach.

2. A Stance of "Metaphysical Humility"

In *Artificial You*, Schneider opts for a stance of "metaphysical humility" in the face of radical brain enhancements. Given the controversies over personal identity, claims about survival that involve one "transferring" one's mind to a new type of substrate or making drastic alterations to one's brain must be carefully scrutinized. As alluring as greatly enhanced intelligence or digital immortality may be, there is simply too much disagreement in the personal-identity literature over whether any of these "enhancements" would extend life or terminate it.

All this uncertainty suggests that one should take the transhumanist approach to radical enhancement with a grain of salt. Enhancements like brain-uploading or adding brain chips to augment intelligence or one's perceptual abilities are key enhancements invoked by the transhumanists, yet these enhancements sound strangely like the thought experiments philosophers have used for years as problem cases for various theories of the nature of persons. In light of this, it isn't surprising to us that the enhancements aren't as attractive as they might seem at first.[30]

The way forward is public dialogue, informed by metaphysical theorizing as well as a technical understanding of AI/neurotechnologies. This may sound like a sort of intellectual cop-out, like we are throwing our hands up in the face of ignorance, but we are not saying that further metaphysical theorizing is useless. To the contrary, we believe the first step is to underscore the life-and-death import of further metaphysical reflection on these issues: ordinary individuals must be capable of making informed decisions about enhancement. If the success of an enhancement rests on (inter alia) classic philosophical issues that are difficult to solve, the public needs to realize this, and not assume that researchers, members of the media or business leaders who are enthused by the

[30] Ibid.

bells and whistles of a new technology are also experts on philosophical questions of whether one should enhance.

3. Support Regulations of Brain Enhancement Devices that Require that Consumers Be Informed about the Personal Identity Debate

Bearing this in mind, brain-enhancement devices should be regulated by a government agency, such as the Food and Drug Administration in the United States, and disclosure of the personal identity controversy should be required, just as medical risks for pharmaceutical drugs are required to be disclosed. Consider, for instance, that patients routinely grapple with ethical issues when they consider whether to undergo genetic testing, asking themselves whether they or a loved one would really want to know if they were going to have a high probability of getting a certain horrible illness, what to do if life insurance companies get hold of their data, and so on. For this reason, it is protocol at many medical centers in the United States that patients considering genetic testing be required to meet with a genetics counselor or nurse who discusses the pros and cons of testing before testing and then return and meet with the counselor to discuss the test results. In the context of brain-enhancement devices, we believe a similar approach could be taken.

We have further suggestions as well. But for now, let's assume that you are inclined to resist our suggestion of metaphysical humility: in particular, you are strongly persuaded by the psychological view. If so, we have further suggestions for you.

A WAY FORWARD? THE PSYCHOLOGICAL CONTINUITY AND NARRATIVE VIEWS

Suppose that, in addition to being impressed by the psychological view, you've just learned that individuals using AI-based enhancements are doing so without a loss of conscious experience. On the assumption that a certain version of the psychological view obtains, perhaps certain kinds of brain enhancements could *enhance* psychological continuity, reducing the likelihood that numerical identity would not obtain after the enhancement.

To see what we have in mind, we will need to distinguish different versions of the psychological theory. There are two main versions: psychological continuity views and narrative views. We've already introduced continuity views, in broad strokes. Psychological continuity views differ with respect to which direct connection is the most important in terms of constituting personal identity. While all psychological continuity theorists believe that the connection of memory is necessary for personal identity, some go so far as to claim that memory is the only relevant psychological connection when it comes to personal identity.

Psychological continuity views of identity can be contrasted with *narrative views*. Narrative views concur that the relationship of psychological connectedness is necessary for personal identity but deny that it is sufficient. Proponents of a narrative view hold that personal identity additionally requires the relationship of narrative connectedness. Two of the most prominent defenders of the narrative view are Marya Schechtman and Anthony Rudd. Both Schechtman and Rudd hold that narrative connectedness exists when one is equipped with an integrative story about themselves which details the chronology of their lives and highlights the most important memories/time slices contained within that chronology. Rudd analogizes this "integrative story" to a Cartesian ego. The idea is not that narratives are metaphysically immaterial entities in the same way that Cartesian egos are, but simply that narratives *function* like Cartesian egos by providing us with a unified sense of personhood.[31] Schechtman, on the other hand, views the narrative as an extended story which transcends the scope of any particular subset of time slices. Schechtman writes: "It is by no means obvious that the most essential part of a person's experience at any time can be reproduced in an independent time-slice, even if we imagine that slice containing all of the relevant forward- and backward-looking elements.... [Our experience] is essentially something that takes place over time, and whose relevant attributes cannot be caught in a moment or even a series of moments."[32]

The main difference between the narrative theory and the psychological continuity theory is that the former views personhood as more active and self-constructed than the latter. Psychological continuity theories see personhood as a fundamentally passive phenomenon that is constituted by relations of psychological connectedness. Subjects are not responsible for establishing the relevant relations of psychological connectedness through the creation of a narrative. Narrative views, on the other hand, claim that subjects are able to actively interpret and construct their own identities by choosing which narrative explanation best suits their life.

Bearing in mind these two versions of the view, we will explore how, should a psychological theory be correct, various memory enhancing external cognitive artifacts may function to undermine, preserve, or bolster personhood. We begin with the sort of artifacts around us now, and then apply the points we make to the case of radical brain enhancements. There are currently many different kinds of external artifacts which function to enhance memory, including the internet, navigation systems, cell phones, diaries, and brain-computer interface devices. We will first consider how memory enhancing external artifacts may undermine personhood (again, we assume the psychological theory of personhood) before suggesting how this may be countered. More specifically: we argue that personhood is at a greater risk of being undermined by

---

[31] Anthony Rudd, "In Defence of Narrative," *European Journal of Philosophy* 17 (2009): 60–75.
[32] Marya Schechtman, *The Constitution of Selves* (Ithaca, NY: Cornell University Press, 1996).

memory enhancing external artifacts on the narrative view than it is on the psychological continuity view. Then, we illustrate how a particular memory enhancing external artifact, the visual lifelog, bolsters personhood if (a) the memories that are stored in visual lifelogs are nonrepresentational, but (b) the memories stored in biological memory are representational.

Nicolas Carr contends that such artifacts weaken personhood by making us less intellectually autonomous: "When we outsource our memory to a machine, we also outsource a very important part of our intellect and even our identity."[33] Intellectual autonomy, broadly speaking, is the ability to think for oneself and to not be overly reliant on other people and external devices when formulating beliefs and engaging in cognition.[34] The main way in which memory enhancing external artifacts make us less autonomous, according to Carr, is by rendering us less knowledgeable. The internet, in particular, makes us less knowledgeable by minimizing the amount of information that we need to store in biological memory.[35]

However, even if Carr is correct, while intellectual autonomy and personhood are related, they do not necessarily go hand in hand. More specifically, if the psychological continuity theory is assumed, then personhood may be boosted by memory enhancing artifacts, *even if* Carr is correct that these artifacts undermine intellectual autonomy. Recall that personhood, according to the psychological continuity view, is explained in terms of psychological connectedness. Memory enhancing external artifacts such as the internet and iPhones could strengthen relations of psychological connectedness by allowing subjects to unearth memories that would have otherwise been forgotten. Again, this holds true despite the fact that the artifacts may simultaneously function to undermine intellectual autonomy in various ways. Consider, for example, an Alzheimer's patient who is gradually losing her biological memory. Such a patient might use an external artifact to help her preserve psychological continuity. This is indeed the situation depicted in Clark and Chalmers' fictional case of Otto and Inga, which they use not as an example of how personhood can be preserved by enhancements but as an argument for the extended mind hypothesis.[36]

Further, it isn't clear that autonomy is really undermined in these cases. This seems to depend on deep issues about whether the mind could be extended. To see what we have in mind, consider the Alzheimer's patient case. Is the autonomy of someone who is losing their memories really undermined here? In a sense, it seems not, at least in one sense of "autonomy," as the technology preserves their independence. Still, it is correct that the person is not autonomous in another sense, as they are now dependent on an external

---

[33] Nicholas G. Carr, *The Shallows: What the Internet Is Doing to Our Brains* (New York: W.W. Norton, 2011), 9.

[34] See also Michael P. Lynch. *The Internet of Us: Knowing More and Understanding Less in the Age of Big Data* (New York: Liveright, 2016).

[35] Contra Carr, we believe that the internet increases the knowledge at our fingertips, as we can look anything up on the web, and we can still remember our results. In any case, Carr's idea is that we become more reliant on external artifacts as these artifacts become increasingly integrated into our cognitive lives.

[36] Andy Clark and David J. Chalmers, "The Extended Mind," *Analysis* 58 (1998): 7–19.

device for cognition. How would we decide whether there is an overall loss of autonomy in such cases? It seems that if the external device is an extension of the patient's cognition, then the device arguably makes the patient more autonomous. In that case, the person isn't dependent on an external device because the enhancement is actually part of their own cognitive system.

In addition to helping subjects unearth memories that would have otherwise been forgotten, external artifacts can also give subjects access to digital memories that are more fine-grained than those stored in biological memory. Digital memories (like those stored on Facebook) are photographic images, and photographic images are arguably more than just mere representations of previous perceptions. Kendall Walton (1984) argues for what he calls "photographic realism," which holds that a photographic image of X allows one to indirectly see X itself (as opposed to directly see a representation of X): "We *really do, literally,* see our deceased ancestors when we see photographs of them."[37] Walton argues for photographic realism on the basis of providing a conceptual analysis of what it means to have "perceptual contact" with the world. If he is correct, then the digital memories stored in external artifacts are not mere representations of past perceptions, but are rather re-presentations or "fixed reflections" of those perceptions. Biological memories, by contrast, are in all likelihood representations of previous events. This position is supported by the causal theory of memory, which is the default view of memory in contemporary philosophy.[38] According to the causal theory, remembering requires a causal connection between the original experience remembered and the consequent representation of that experience in memory. It is worth pointing out, to be fair, that not all theories of memory take memories to be representational by nature. The empiricist theory, for example, contends that memories are "preserved sense impressions."[39] Mohan Matthen, however, argues against the idea that memories are "preserved content" by emphasizing that a single biological memory can occur in a myriad of different formats.[40] If it is true that (a) digital memories are transparent in the sense advocated by Walton, and (b) biological memories are representational, then it is arguably the case that the former kind of memory is more "real" than the latter. One could contend, in particular, very much in the vein of Plato's concept of "mimesis," that representations are always less real than the items represented. Of course, videos can be altered and edited, as has been increasingly seen in the so-called "fake news" era. This does not undermine the argument that unaltered videos are more transparent than biological memories though. All in all, this argument serves to lend further support

---

[37] Kendall L. Walton, "Transparent Pictures: On the Nature of Photographic Realism," *Noûs* 18 (1984): 67–72.

[38] See C.B. Martin, and Max Deutscher, "Remembering," *Philosophical Review* 75 (April 1966): 161–196; Sven Bernecker, *Memory: A Philosophical Study* (Oxford University Press, 2010).

[39] David Hume, *A Treatise of Human Nature: Being an Attempt to Introduce the Experimental Method of Reasoning into Moral Subjects,* ed. D. G. C. Macnabb (London: Collins, 1978; orig. 1739).

[40] Mohan Matthen, "Is Memory Preservation?," *Philosophical Studies* 148(1) (2010): 3–14.

to the hypothesis that external artifacts can bolster personhood on the psychological continuity view.

Things may be different when it comes to the narrative view of identity. The narrative view, to reiterate, explains personhood primarily in terms of narrative connectedness. While intellectual autonomy is conceptually distinct from psychological connectedness, it may not be fully conceptually distinct from narrative connectedness. This is because narrative connectedness requires active cognitive interpretation and construction on the part of the subject. Or, to put it differently, narrative connectedness appears to involve the execution of intellectually autonomous acts. It stands to reason, then, that by undermining intellectual autonomy, certain memory enhancing external artifacts may also undermine personhood on the narrative view.

Here, it is helpful to consider a particular memory enhancing external artifact: lifelogs. Lifelogs are devices that record one's personal experiences from the first person point of view. There are various different kinds of such devices: "A key example is SenseCam, a small wide-angle camera worn around one's neck, taking a picture with a certain interval or when its sensor detects some environmental change. These pictures are then edited into a visual lifelong with certain narrative structure, transforming, aiding, and in some cases constituting one's autobiographical narrative."[41] Lifelogs are unique in that they serve as external aids to both biological memory and narrative structure. In other words, lifelogs develop a narrative explanation of one's memories for the subject. Certain social media sites, such as Facebook, already accomplish this task to some extent by integrating one's pictures together to form a story. The increasing integration of lifelogs and related technologies into our lives may lead subjects to become more dependent on artifacts for their personal narratives, for better or worse. After all, if artifacts are crafting narrative explanations for subjects, then there may be less of a need, or at least less motivation, for subjects to craft their own narrative explanations. In this case, narrative explanations would become biographical as opposed to autobiographical.

The partial offloading of narrative structure to external devices certainly undercuts intellectual autonomy; the question is whether it undercuts narrative connectedness as well. If this offloading procedure does undermine narrative connectedness, then it also undermines personhood on the narrative view of identity. One might deny, however, that narrative connectedness necessitates intellectual autonomy. Perhaps partially offloading narrative structure to external artifacts can strengthen narrative connectedness in a similar way that partially offloading biological memory can strengthen psychological connectedness. Recall that narrative connectedness exists when a subject is able to provide a narrative explanation of the chronology of their lives and experiences. One might argue that external artifacts can assist subjects in providing this narrative explanation and that it does not matter whether or not the subject is personally responsible for constructing the narrative explanation.

---

[41] Richard Heersmink, "Distributed Selves: Personal Identity and Extended Memory Systems," *Synthese* 194, no. 8 (2017): 3136.

CAVEATS

Now let us ask: could the enhancements of the future, such as brain chips, be constructed to maintain continuity or narrative structure? If the psychological theory of personal identity is correct, and if technologies like brain chips can be made to preserve psychological properties like memories and personality traits, then it seems as if more radical enhancements also have the potential to preserve/bolster personal identity in the manner described in the previous section. It may even be possible to design a chip that preserves narrative structure.

We must proceed carefully though. First, it is not clear if chips would preserve consciousness, when used in parts of the brain that are part of the neural basis of conscious experience. If someone replaces these parts, important psychological properties (experiential properties) would be lacking. It would be dubious to see the future zombie as a person or having a mind, let alone the same person as before. Second, we've indicated that psychological views are controversial. In particular, they face "reduplication problems"—problems involving thought experiments in which one's pattern, narrative or psychological configuration is copied so precisely that, by the light of the psychological views, there seems to be two or more instances of the same individual at the same time.[42]

Third, brain chips and other more radical forms of enhancement may raise concerns related to authenticity that milder forms of enhancement lack. Imagine a brain chip that enables you to not only unearth memories that would have otherwise been forgotten but also consciously access many more memories over a given time interval than you would have been able to without the chip. One concern about such a chip is that it may incentivize people to not be mindful and to instead "live in the past." Insofar as authenticity is connected with mindfulness (as existentialists like Sartre claim), such a chip will function to make people less authentic. This worry, to be sure, also exists in the case of external artifacts, but is magnified in the case of brain chips that directly affect cognition.

Another "authenticity" related worry concerns the possibility that radical enhancements will augment psychological suffering. While neural prosthetics which raise our IQ levels or make us faster thinkers have obvious benefits, they may also function to amplify the "cognitive noise" which is responsible for the majority of psychological suffering within our species. Put differently, if the Buddhists are on the right track in claiming that all suffering is born out of thinking, then it is plausible that making us faster or better thinkers via brain chips will increase psychological suffering by and large (as opposed to leading to enlightenment and wisdom). Of course, particular kinds of brain chips, like the Zen Garden chip mentioned previously, might be immune to these worries concerning mindfulness and suffering.

Fourth, consider that, from the vantage point of the brain view, if you have these chips, and they replace parts of the biological brain, there will be a point at which the biological brain is so diminished that instead of ensuring continuity over time, you

---

[42] See Parfit 1984, Sider 2001, Olson 2007, and Schneider 2019a.

would inadvertently end your life. Bearing in mind our stance of metaphysical humility, it would be unwise to rule out the possibility that the mind is the brain, for the brain is responsible for human cognitive and perceptual processing, making this position quite plausible. This leads us to suggest the following.

Don't Offload Parts of the Biological Brain, Insofar as You Suspect that the Brain View May Be Correct

Even if AI is capable of underlying conscious experience, AI-based enhancements, if used, should supplement the workings of intact brain tissue, not destroy it and offload its activities to the cloud or another AI device. Biological therapies could instead be utilized to extend the life of the biological brain, or AI components could supplement activities of the brain, without replacing tissue. (Bearing in mind the earlier caveat that too radical of enhancements of these latter sorts may still be incompatible with survival over time, depending upon what one's essential properties are.)

CONCLUSION: A HUMBLE APPROACH

It would be optimal if we could provide you with a clear, uncontroversial path to guide you through the brain enhancement decisions. Instead our message today has been: As we consider enhancement decisions, we must do so, first and foremost, with a mindset of metaphysical humility. Remember how controversial the different theories of personal identity are.

Still, we have offered several provisional recommendations. We proposed that in making enhancement decisions, it is important to distinguish the issue of personal identity from that of consciousness. We also suggested that future consumers considering such enhancements be educated about the personal identity debates, as well as medical risks. In addition, we outlined various ways in which enhancements may be capable of preserving personhood if a psychological view is correct. Enhancements, in particular, may be able to strengthen relations of psychological continuity and perhaps even narrative structure. This assumes the controversial view that a psychological theory of personal identity is correct, however. Further, if the brain theory is correct, these enhancements may be problematic, if they involve replacing parts of the brain. In light of this, and bearing in mind the discussion of metaphysical humble approach, we believe it is most sensible that future enhancements *both* preserve continuity while not replacing parts of the brain may be safest.

BIBLIOGRAPHY

Bess, Michael. *Our Grandchildren Redesigned*. Boston: Beacon Press, 2015.

Bostrom, Nick, ed. *Superintelligence: Paths, Dangers, Strategies*. New York: Oxford University Press, 2014.

Bostrom, Nick, and Rebecca Roache. "Ethical Issues in Human Enhancement." In *New Waves in Applied Ethics*, edited by J. Ryberg, T. Petersen, and C. Wolf, 120–52. London: Palgrave-Macmillan, 2007.

Bostrom, Nick, and Anders Sandberg. "Smart Policy: Cognitive Enhancement and the Public Interest." In *Enhancing Human Capabilities*, ed. Julian Savulescu, Ruud ter Muelen, and Guy Kahane. Hoboken: Wiley-Blackwell, 2009.

Carr, Nicholas G. *The Shallows: What the Internet Is Doing to Our Brains*. New York: W. W. Norton, 2011.

Chalmers, David J. "Facing up to the Problem of Consciousness." *Journal of Consciousness Studies* 2(3) (1995): 200–19.

Chalmers, David J. "The Singularity: A Philosophical Analysis." *Journal of Consciousness Studies* 17 (9–10) (2010): 9–10.

Clark, Andy, and David J. Chalmers. "The Extended Mind." *Analysis* 58 (1) (1998): 7–19.

de Grey, Aubrey. *Ending Aging: the Rejuvenation Breakthroughs That Could Reverse Human Aging in Our Lifetime*. New York: St. Martin's Griffin, 2008.

Fitzgerald, K. "Medical Enhancement: A Destination of Technological, Not Human, Betterment." In *Medical Enhancement and Post-Modernity*, ed. B. Gordijn and R. Chadwick, 39–55. Dordrecht: Springer, 2008.

Gibson, William. *Neuromancer*. New York: Ace Books, 1984.

Heersmink, Richard. "Distributed Selves: Personal Identity and Extended Memory Systems." *Synthese* 194.8 (2017): 3135–51.

Hume, David. *A Treatise of Human Nature: Being an Attempt to Introduce the Experimental Method of Reasoning into Moral Subjects*. Edited by D. G. C. Macnabb. London: Collins, 1978; orig. 1739.

Kurzweil, Ray. *The Singularity Is Near: When Humans Transcend Biology*. New York: Viking, 2005.

Locke, John. *An Essay concerning Human Understanding*, 4th ed., ed. P. H. Nidditch. Oxford: Clarendon Press, 1975.

Lynch, Michael. *The Internet of Us: Knowing More and Understanding Less in the Age of Big Data*. New York: Liveright, 2016.

Olson, Eric T. *What Are We?: A Study in Personal Ontology*. Oxford University Press, 2007.

Parfit, D. *Reasons and Persons*. Oxford: Clarendon Press, 1984.

Rucker, Rudy. *Software*. New York: Eos, 2001.

Rudd, Anthony. "In Defence of Narrative." *European Journal of Philosophy* 17(1) (2009): 60–75.

Schechtman, Marya. "Stories, Lives, and Basic Survival: A Refinement and Defense of the Narrative View." *Royal Institute of Philosophy Supplement* 60 (2007): 155–78.

Schneider, Susan. *Artificial You: AI and the Future of Your Mind*. Princeton: Princeton University Press, 2019a.

Schneider, Susan. "Can You Add a Microchip to Your Brain?" *New York Times*, June 2019b.

Sider, Theodore. "Criteria of Personal Identity and the Limits of Conceptual Analysis." *Philosophical Perspectives* 15(s15) (2001): 189–209.

Swinburne, R.G. "Personal Identity." *Proceedings of the Aristotelian Society* 74 (1973): 231–47.

Vinge, Vernor. "The Coming Technological Singularity: How to Survive in the Post-human Era." *Whole Earth Review*, 1993.

Walton, Kendall L. "Transparent Pictures: On the Nature of Photographic Realism." *Noûs* 18(1) (1984): 67–72.

CHAPTER 17

....

ARE SENTIENT AIs
PERSONS?

....

MARK KINGWELL

TRADITIONAL RIGHTS REGIMES

....

TRADITIONAL regimes for the protection of rights have evolved over centuries of debate concerning (a) who counts as a legitimate right-holder, (b) what rights are claimable by such legitimate holders, and (c) how the resulting claims are to be enforced. The existing structure for the protection of human rights has several branches of influence that span these same centuries in the Western philosophical tradition. These include Kantian arguments concerning the dignity and sovereignty of persons conceived as moral agents; the liberal norms defended by Locke and Spinoza, among others, concerning ownership of body and labor, hence personal freedom (also, sometimes, private property); and the natural law tradition that views individuals as creatures of Providence worthy of respect and protection.[1] All of these influences inform, though not always explicitly, the doctrines and policies of contemporary human rights discourse. The most obvious, and perhaps also most significant, document in this discourse, at least over the last century, is the 1948 Universal Declaration of Human Rights (UDHR), adopted on December 10 of that year in Paris, as United Nations Resolution 217, with a membership vote of forty-eight in favor out of fifty-eight total delegates, with eight abstentions and two nonvotes. Its thirty articles were drafted substantially by McGill University law professor John Humphrey and championed vigorously by Eleanor Roosevelt, the Universal Declaration of Human Rights (UNHR) has been a touchstone of human rights thinking over the past half-century and more. Its claims, informed by

---

[1] The sources are canonical, so I won't cite here specific editions, but see Immanuel Kant, *Groundwork of the Metaphysics of Morals* (1785); Baruch Spinoza, *Tractatus Theologico-Politicus* (1677); John Locke, *Second Treatise of Government* (1689); Hugo Grotius and Samuel von Pufendorf, various. One can of course include Thomas Aquinas in any survey of natural law theory, as well as thinkers influenced by Grotius and Pufendorf, especially in jurisprudence.

the philosophical background just mentioned, are nevertheless entirely pragmatic and aimed at regulatory compliance.

The most striking features of the UDHC are its contextual between-the-lines narratives. Working in the immediate aftermath of the Second World War, and especially emerging evidence concerning the planned extermination of peoples according to the Nazis' Wannsee Conference plan (January 20, 1942)—otherwise known as the Final Solution to the Jewish Question (*Endlösung der Judenfrage*)—Humphrey and Roosevelt were keenly aware that, however powerful were traditional just war doctrines of *ius in bello* (conduct during wartime), something else was needed to protect the very idea of the human person. The distinction between *war crimes* and *crimes against humanity* becomes essential when we wish to discriminate between excessive or cruel behavior on the battlefield and the systematic plan for targeted genocides.[2] The UDHC aimed at articulating what was particular to the idea of human rights, that is, rights claimable by any human being simply in virtue of being human; and, furthermore, it wished to claim the universalism of a Kantian sort that would distinguish such rights from specific legal rights which might—which, of course, had been—arbitrarily revoked by given jurisdictions. The jurisdiction of universal human rights is not to be violated or controlled by anyone.

One's attitude to the UDHR depends in large measure on how these two categories—*human* and *universal*—stand in one's basic philosophical commitment-set. There are potential problems with both categories.

First, while we might indeed wish to acknowledge rights that belong to humans *qua* humans, we must note at least two immediate conceptual difficulties. That is, (a) is "human" a stable category? Many heinous instances of depravity and violence hinge precisely on the denial of the status to groups of entities targeted for violence or elimination. One has only to recall the bafflement exhibited by some former Nazi officials when they were tried for crimes against humanity: the Jews were not human, they were vermin or parasites, and therefore could be exterminated without violations of conscience. Indeed, in a nightmare scenario, a genocidal program could be carried out by someone who *at the very same time* considered the program to be in compliance with the UDHR. *Mutatis mutandis*, this same twisted logic could be applied to handicapped persons, children, women, people of color, and so on—not one of which examples is speculative, but alas are all factual.

Likewise, then, we must ask (b) whether human is the relevant category for rights protection. Any rights regime involves some form of means test, to qualify for inclusion within the regime; but "human" is a biological category, at best a disputed one, and therefore seems an unstable basis for a program of rights protection. Why, after all, should biology determine whether an entity qualifies for the cover of law? We can take note of Agamben's vivid depictions of "bare life" here, and also note the inherent

[2] The basic tenets of just war theory are ably covered in Michael Walzer, *Just and Unjust Wars: A Moral Argument with Historical Examples* (New York: Basic Books, 1977); the special relevance of the war crimes/crimes against humanity distinction is discussed by Geoffrey Robertson, together with many contemporary examples, in *Crimes Against Humanity: The Struggle for Global Justice* (New York: The New Press, 2007).

vulnerability of the human form as part of the rights logic (we feel pain, we suffer, we die), and yet still wonder whether this is the right place to locate the threshold of protection.[3] In effect, the (b) worry is a logical extensions of the possible depredations conceived under the (a) worry. In sum, "human" seems initially promising as the fundamental basis of rights claims, and yet seems immediately subject to potential pathologies.

Second, then, matters stand similarly with respect to the concept of universalism. Kant's arguments, the most forceful here, suggest that any moral agent, regardless of specific characteristics, is part of the Kingdom of Ends and therefore a self-legislating individual who, by being so, legislates for all others. There is nothing in Kant's system to deny the possibility of off-world moral agents who would qualify as relevant members of the universal population. The Earth is not the Universe, after all. If, in practice, all the moral agents I have so far met have been Earthlings, and all or most of them have been human, well, that is a contingent not necessary cluster of facts. If universal is to mean anything, it can't merely mean those we know and already recognize—this would very quickly toss us back to the problems of "human."

But *universal* is itself a tricky property, not least because resisted by those who want to insist on particularity and distinction. Cultural difference and those who defend it seem to cut against universalism, which is often perceived as a top-down mechanism for eliminating distinct claims of identity. One needn't look far for examples of this anti-universalist sentiment, from the toxic ethnic nationalisms of twenty-first-century anti-immigrant retrenchment (Sweden, England, the United States, etc.), to the more benign but still resistant forms of identity politics which view universalist rhetoric as a con game to obscure special narratives: Latinx, LGBTQ, trans, black, and so on. From these perspectives, "universal" is just another word for the bland, graded-road white globalism that is the enemy of vibrant identity.

Worse, universalism can sometimes appear, despite good intentions, to be allied with objectively harmful economic regimes of the so-called New World Order—now not so new—of globalization and deregulation in trade and capital. Since it is well known that such regimes have drastically differential effects, even as their advocates claim a rising tide for all boats, the language of universalism grows suspect just to the extent that it is consistent with the spread of global capital. The once-bright promise of covering-law universalism, namely, that everyone shall be protected, begins to look like an elaborate sham to centralize control of resources and wealth.

There are legitimate responses to these worries. One can, for example, conceive of a form of universalism that is not of the covering-law type, but rather particular to local circumstances. That is, universal extension remains the overall goal but specific conditions can govern the precise shape of its realization. Possible analogies here include such apparently (but not really) trivial things like sports and sexuality. In the former case, the basic rules of a game can observed in multiple locations *even as* the specific details of

---

[3] See Giorgio Agamben, *Homo Sacer: Sovereign Power and Bare Life*, trans. Daniel Heller Roazen (Stanford: Stanford University Press, 1998; orig. 1995).

their execution can vary quite widely. The World Cup in soccer offers an excellent example of roots-up rather than covering-law universalism. The rules are the same for everyone, but the style of play and the vast permutations of play within the rules still preserve the values of local identity. With respect to sexuality, here including things like clothing, mating rituals, and physical intimacy, the basics are once more universal, but with vast local differentiation. Such differentiation is the potential source of both confusion and conflict, to be sure, but the fact of sexuality itself remains constant.

I don't wish, in offering these analogies, to underestimate the degree of lurking conflict here. On the contrary, it is precisely the tension between universal structures or frames of reference and their local, contingent realization that makes clear thinking about roots-up regimes so necessary. Rights regimes are dominated by assumptions, again often Kantian, that the bearers of rights are not only individuals but deracinated, abstract individuals: the rational choosers of standard economic analysis, really, or the isolated contractarian actors that appear everywhere from Hobbes, Locke, and Rousseau to Rawls and Gauthier.[4] Could we conceive of a universal rights regime, human or otherwise, that surrendered the strong covering-law option and this implicit individualism in favor of a nuanced roots-up version? If so, the conflicted notion of universalism might still have some moral and political traction in a wildly diverse world.

All of this is really to say that traditional rights regimes are conceptually unstable, but that this may provide us with an unparalleled opportunity to expand and revise their basic assumptions. This is happening already, as we know: many advocates argue for the rights of nonhuman animals, such that we human animals ought to be forced, morally or even legally, to alter our behavior with respect to treatment, eating habits, and duties of care.[5] Other advocates consider nonspecific entities, such as the environment or the planet, or specific forests and regions, to possess rights that should be morally and legally claimable.[6] There are also those who believe that groups or cultural identities themselves have rights, not just the individuals who fall under their umbrellas of meaning.[7] In none of these cases is the target rights-bearer able to claim the rights explicitly.

But this is not possibly a crippling objection. Even under straight-up presumptions of individualism and universalism, the sufferers of rights violations are not always able to

[4] Exemplary texts: Thomas Hobbes, *Leviathan* (1651); John Locke, *Second Treatise of Government* (1689); Jean-Jacques Rousseau, *The Social Contract* (1762); John Rawls, *A Theory of Justice* (Cambridge, MA: Belknap Press, 1971); David Gauthier, *Morals by Agreement* (Oxford: Clarendon Press, 1986).

[5] Central texts include Peter Singer, *Animal Liberation* (New York: HarperCollins, 1975) and, more recently, Sue Donaldson and Will Kymlicka, *Zoopolis: A Political Theory of Animal Rights* (Oxford: Oxford University Press, 2013).

[6] Much of the literature concerning environmental rights is an extensive of basic human rights to include the security and solace of stable, healthy natural environments. These are "rights to nature." See, for example, Tim Hayward, *Constitutional Environmental Rights* (Oxford: Oxford University Press, 2004). The more searching argument concerns "rights of nature": the notion that natural environments might themselves be bearers of rights. In New Zealand, the government granted legal personhood to the Whanganui River, granting it "rights and interests" under the law.

[7] See Will Kymlicka, *Multicultural Citizenship: A Liberal Theory of Minority Rights* (Oxford: Oxford University Press, 1995), and *Liberalism, Community, and Culture* (Oxford: Oxford University Press, 1989/1991).

speak for themselves. Sometimes they are incarcerated. Sometimes they have been silenced by threats and torture. Sometimes they are just no longer with us. In no case is it a valid objection that a violated entity cannot make its own claim. Thus there is no reason in principle to object to the inclusion in rights regimes of those who cannot speak for themselves, or those who are not even capable of speech. That is what advocates are for.

The most promising way forward in rights thinking, it seems to me, is to execute analysis on the basis of risk. Risk in turn is a function of vulnerability, and the distribution of risk, while dependent on many factors including birthright lotteries and structural limitations, is arguably the central concern of social justice. If the protection of human rights, and the punishment of their violation, are to mean anything, they must serve the ends of justice in this respect. Minimizing risk, or equalizing its distribution, are pragmatic goals of a valid rights regime. Now we must ask: is such a regime open to the possibility of nonhuman agents who are individual and conscious, but not biological? This is the main question before us: can AIs ever be persons?

SENTIENT NONHUMAN AGENTS: HOW PLAUSIBLE?

Philosophers are divided, and have been for some time, concerning the prospect of generalized autonomous AIs (GAAIs), whether in human form or not, who could achieve consciousness. They are nevertheless united in thinking that such consciousness, supposing it possible, is at least a necessary condition of potential personhood. Further conditions conducing to sufficiency might then include decision-making ability, the awareness of choice and its consequences, and the ability to tell right from wrong, to suffer and be violated, and so on. Only such a being would seem a likely candidate for inclusion within any traditional rights regime, even one open to quite radical forms of otherness.

Thinkers such as John Searle believe that a GAAI is impossible because of the role programming takes within the structure of the AI, however complex and apparently responsive. Searle's famous "Chinese room" thought experiment is designed to highlight the fact that a seemingly engaged translation program is not, in fact, experiencing understanding of the language even as it is being successfully translated.[8] By matching input-symbol to output-symbol, the algorithm appears to understand both languages,

[8] Searle's Chinese room thought experiment was first sketched in a journal article, "Minds, Brains and Programs," *Behavioral and Brain Sciences* 3 (1980): 417–457; it was then elaborated in Searle's subsequent book, Searle, *Minds, Brains, and Science* (Cambridge, MA: Harvard University Press, 1984). It has spawned a vast critical literature too extensive to cite here. A brief and accessible discussion of possible objections may be found at Daniel Sabinasz, "Why the Chinese Room Argument Is Flawed," http://www.deepideas.net/why-chinese-room-argument-flawed/.

but is in fact simply exercising accurate matching techniques with no attendant consciousness. One may object, as many have, that it is the total system of the Chinese room that is doing the translating, not some homunculus within the room, and so it is correct to say that the system overall *does* understand Chinese. Moreover, since this argument flows from an assumption that all consciousness must mimic our own (human) version thereof, it is presumptuous to say that the system—the room and its functions—are not conscious in some sense. Further, even conscious humans perform many functions, including translation, with just the same sort of matching moves as sketched in the thought experiment. Searle's skeptical position raises the stakes for GAAI consciousness, but it does not dispose of the question.

Suppose, for example, that consciousness, understood as awareness of self, is an emergent property of sufficiently complex algorithmic functions. This might then resemble the development of the human mind as it moves from infancy to childhood to adolescence and beyond. Humans have large cognitive capacity, but it must be developed over time to generate the sense of distinct self that we associate with individual selfhood, and hence the need for legal and moral protection. Perhaps a GAAI will be like this, complexifying its (nonconscious) algorithmic functions until, at some indeterminate point, it begins to experience individual consciousness.

But this may be all too human a scenario. What if nonhuman agency develops, instead, as collective or system-wide property of interlinked complex algorithms? If we take seriously the idea that nonhuman animals, environments, and cultural groups are all worthy of rights protection under existing traditional regimes, it would seem perverse to deny such protection to a vulnerable and responsive system that, for various good reasons, does not (or not yet) exhibit the individual subjectivity of human agents. Such agency may be the fallback position of most rights claims, but it is not the only, or even the gold, standard thereof. Rights-bearing "subjects" come in more than one guise.

Another standard objection to the program of so-called "strong AI"—the realization of a fully conscious individual nonbiological system—is that such an entity must entail embodiment, so that it can experience the world phenomenologically and therefore understand its emplacement within environments. This has seemed an insuperable barrier to many philosophers, since the deployment of a body appears to be beyond the technological capacities of AI systems.

Once again, though, the assumptions here are revealed as tenuous, if not outright invalid, and based upon allegedly baseline behavior that is everywhere changing under existing technological conditions. Yes, most human agents have bodies that move through the world, exercising the basic physical sensorium to gather, collate, and filter external stimuli for internal purposes. A sense of emplacement remains an important dimension of human phenomenology, as do the sense-based experiences of seeing, hearing, tasting, and feeling. Without sunsets, symphonies, good meals, and relational intimacy, the world is a dry place for humans. But this norm admits of many exceptions: there are many human agents with less than optimal sensory or ambulatory ability, for example. I am myself deaf in one ear, which deprives me of some experiences without challenging my sense of self. I also can't run or jump the way I used to—who can?

Even more significantly, there are many extensions of personhood achieved precisely with nonphysical stimuli: online interactions, media immersion, disembodied tracing, and so on. These spectral stretchings of the person into disembodied nonlocation do not appear to threaten one's individuality, or indeed any of the other features that make us legitimate claimants of rights protection. I can be, for example, vulnerable to forms of suffering that are not based in the experience of physical pain, as in humiliation or vilification.

Can we accept, then, as a matter of argument, that there is no knock-down in-principle objection to the possibility of a GAAI achieving something like consciousness, and therefore something exactly like the kind of personhood worthy of rights protection. There are of course many outstanding issues. Consider a few. Would such a GAAI seek the protections offered by a rights regime? Perhaps, if nonmortal and spread across multiple systems, it would not need such protection, or would consider itself superior to the point of arrogance. Would a GAAI even resemble individual consciousness? The robot/android image is so indelible in literary and cinematic culture that we may overlook the possibility that a conscious GAAI will look, or be, entirely different.

These questions are ones that typically invoke fear reactions concerning the prospects of conscious GAAIs, so before I sketch my four scenarios of how this might all play out, allow me to offer a brief analysis of AI fear.

OTHERNESS AND FEAR

There are countless depictions of the nonhuman conscious, autonomous agent as a potent threat to human complacency, especially when the Uncanny Valley approach suggests that a near-perfect android might be indistinguishable from a "normal" human person. This trope is certainly as old as Frankenstein's monster but has even deeper roots in myths of the Golem, the human-seeming trickster, and other unsettling mirrors held up to ourselves.

Just before such a stage is, of course, the depths of the Valley, where a nonhuman entity is just human-seeming enough to be creepy. Again, many examples are proximate: the affectless Synthetics in the *Alien* film franchise, say, or the second- and third-generation Terminators in that film franchise, and so on. For current purposes, the essential philosophical question concerns the oscillations created between apparent or at least partial humanness and the elements of otherness indivisible from nonhuman conditions of existence. In many ways, this series of oscillations—They're like us! They're not like us!—exactly matches the same anxieties evident in social movements that expanded the range of legal status and rights regimes within the biological category of the human. Entities now clearly within that biolegal status were once excluded from it, shamefully, and even now there are mechanisms within legal and national regimes to exclude presumptive claimers of "inside" status. As discussed, one thinks of the demonization of the enemy in times of war, such that the Japanese, or the Germans, or the Saracens, are perceived as less than human as a prologue to killing them without remorse; or the twisted genocidal logic that condemns whole races, religions, or ethnicities to the nonhuman condition of revocable bare life: Jews, Rwandans, Armenians, blacks, gays, indigenous peoples, and so on (and, alas, on and on again).

This same genocidal logic appears relevant to the question of nonhuman entities with advanced cognitive and active abilities. Some thinkers have tried to imagine a way that these could be integrated into human life without granting them full status. One well-known version of this is Isaac Asimov's Three Laws of Robotics. They are:

- Law One – "A robot may not injure a human being or, through inaction, allow a human being to come to harm."
- Law Two – "A robot must obey orders given to it by human beings except where such orders would conflict with the First Law."
- Law Three – "A robot must protect its own existence, as long as such protection does not conflict with the First or Second Law."
- Asimov later added the "Zeroth Law," above all the others – "A robot may not harm humanity, or, by inaction, allow humanity to come to harm."

As many commentators have noted, these laws contain inconsistencies as well as practical flaws that make them misleading and unhelpful.[9] How would such laws be programmed into an autonomous, or semi-autonomous, AI? If the programming worked, the question is begged: what were the presuppositions of its working except that it was going to work? Likewise, the nested feature of the Laws appeals to many, but the potential contradictions and action-stalls here are legion, just as they are in nonrobotic choice architectures.

Despite this, we may choose to recognize Asimov's effort as an attempt to overcome the fear-logic that dominates thinking about GAAIs. He at least tries to imagine a world beyond the typical whipsaw effects of anxiety and cheerful reassurance concerning non-human consciousness that covers off most of the popular and philosophical territory. The back-and-forth is typical not just of our encounters with otherness but also with respect to technology itself. The technophile/technophobe conflict is not dialectical: it does not resolve into a higher moment of consciousness, but instead runs continuously as a function of point and counterpoint. Indeed, it resembles something like the routine and endless dysfunction and acrimony of Republicans and Democrats in the U.S. Congress, pro-life versus pro-choice advocates in debates about abortion rights, and other "clashes of absolutes," as Lawrence Tribe has called them.[10] One might go back further into history and find equally intractable and often much bloodier examples: Hutus and Tutsis, Protestants and Catholics, Muslims and Jews. Not only do these

---

[9] Peter W. Singer offers some trenchant criticism of Asimov's Three Laws of Robotics in "Isaac Asimov's Laws of Robotics Are Wrong," *Brookings* (May 18, 2009), https://www.brookings.edu/opinions/isaac-asimovs-laws-of-robotics-are-wrong/.

[10] Lawrence H. Tribe, *Abortion: The Clash of Absolutes* (New York: Norton, 1990; rev. ed. 1992).

oppositions not resolve into anything like a Hegelian sublation, they are apparently necessary as diacritical elements in the establishment of identity. I am who am I because of who I am not—and who I am not must either submit or die. Endlessly. Consider, then, the following set of linked thoughts and propositions.

It is a matter of record that the term "robot" was first used in recent recordable culture by Czech writer by Karel Capek, in his 1920 science-fiction play *R.U.R.* ("Rossum's Universal Robots," in English). *Robot* is a word that derives, in Czech etymology, from *robota*, or forced labor. Thus the robots in the play are, in effect, slaves—and not even wage slaves, because they are assumed, in their mechanical efficiency, to require no food, shelter, or clothing, let alone healthcare or pension plans. In short, they are the perfect solutions to the problem of labor. They work on command, do not tire or complain, and they don't need to be paid.

But they revolt! Having acquired consciousness as part of their functional ability to execute tasks, they realize they are being exploited. This can of course be viewed as a symbolic depiction of labor under post-Revolution conditions—as indeed it was right up to the 1968 Czech invasion by Russia and likewise during the 1989 Velvet Revolution. The robots are us, and we are the robots, whenever there is a resented central government, state labor restrictions, and centralized authoritarian power. The current Czech Republic might be viewed, from this vantage, as the globe's most significant anti-robot democracy.

Our anxiety here is obvious. We have created technology that we cannot control. Nuclear weapons and chemical agents were one thing, but conscious autonomous agents without human limits are the future we at once long for and dread. Meanwhile, for the record, here in the non–science fiction world, we devise drones and delivery systems that fall well short of nuclear holocaust but are, in their own way, just as despicable.

This is not new. Yes, of course the technology changes, and makes some things more proximate to reality, but humans have been thinking about the creation of nonhuman entities for centuries. Mary Shelley's *Frankenstein* (1818) is subtitled, we should recall, "The New Prometheus." She meant this earnestly. In Greek, the name of this Titan means "forethought," and the original myth speaks of a powerful being who molded humanity out of clay. The more notorious episode, where Prometheus bestows the power fire on that same clay-footed humanity, earning the enmity of the gods and eternal punishment, overshadows the basic wisdom. We are from the earth and we return to it. But like our creator, we view civilization as a matter of making. Now it is silicon and plastic, nanobots and microcircuits; and we are the creators, not the created.

The urge to bestow fire—maybe now in the form of consciousness, the fire of the mind—is essential. Prometheus is a symbol of human striving, especially in science and technology. But he is also a symbol of what happens when overweening ambition outstrips common sense or regard for whatever we mean by "the gods." Purists will recall that the eternal punishment of the disgraced Titan was the daily gnawing of his liver, seat of human emotions, by an eagle dispatched by Zeus—surely the worst hangover ever.

There is a long history of humans creating mechanical beings for our amusement and titillation: arcade tricksters, chess geniuses, sexy fortune tellers. Today's realistic (I guess?)

sex robots are just a twenty-first-century upgrade of old herky-jerky technology, like Ferraris outclassing Model Ts. But for the record, customized sex robots ordered online (yes, you can do this) are, however pleasing to their owners, icky. To my mind, this form of sexual gratification is worse than contracting to receive human sex work, since the robot is more like a mechanized pet than a sentient human with the ability to choose. And what happens if we obey long-standing market forces and concentrate the creation of more developed artificial beings on sex workers, rather than factory workers? Would they be organized enough to revolt, if they found the work oppressive? Would there be collective bargaining, or just the routine union-busting now known in many states of America as "right to work"? This means your "right" to accept your personal labor immiseration at the going market rate.

At a certain point, the nonhuman entity is *too* human. It becomes creepy, like a zombie or vampire (or, in one quite mean version, Michael Jackson). Or, indeed, an animated robot that is *almost* human but not quite. The "synthetics" featured in the *Alien* franchise are instructive here: Ian Holm and Lance Henriksen play these characters as tweaky, a bit strange, lacking in natural affect. That's uncanny. In the current real world, commercial and pop-star robots in Japan, or Saudi Arabia's "robot citizen" Sophia, have the same quality of what we might call *weird-nearness*. The "uncanny valley" notion is thus that, after encountering such beings, we then fall into a sort of free fall of weirdness—often related to classical analyses of uncanniness, such as Freud's—and we need eventually to come back to the entity as either human or distinctly not human.

But that distinction is not firm. We think we know what "human nature" means, especially as a contrastive term, but in fact there is no reliable set of necessary and sufficient conditions to validate the concept. We can speak of biology, for example, but that too is variable. Likewise physical ability, sexual identity, gender performance, race, and a host of other contingent facts of the lifeworld. One current mini-trend is the political act of changing your age. Why not, after all, if you change your name and physical status? Jack Benny was, famously, thirty-nine years old until he died in 1974 at age 80.

Pundits and performers will fight rearguard actions on these matters as long of most of us are here on the planet, but they cannot win the day, because the category of "human" refuses to be pinned down. That is both its genius and its vexation. Subcategories such as sex and gender are even more variable.

Philosophers have typically responded to these quandaries by trying to shift to discourse from "human" to "person." Human biology is sufficient for personhood, as long as there is a decent regime of law in place, but it is not strictly necessary. That is, there may be nonhuman persons. Indeed, corporations are persons in various legal jurisdictions, subject to both legal punishment for wrongdoing and, maybe less benignly, the legal right to express themselves politically and financially. This human-to-person conceptual move works if you are a lawyer or moral philosopher, but otherwise not so much. I guess it's just worth recalling that nothing is "inhuman" if it has been done by a human. That includes, alas, serial killers and presidents.

If generalized autonomous AIs are indeed coming into the world, we need to ask some hard questions. Will they be slaves? Servants? Constricted companions? Will they have rights? As nonhuman but conscious entities, will they be persons at all? They won't be biological and therefore they won't die—unless, that is, they are programmed to do after the manner of the Replicants in Ridley Scott's masterly 1982 film, *Blade Runner*. Based on a very uncanny 1968 Philip K. Dick story ("Do Androids Dream of Electric Sheep?"), Scott's film explores mortality with greater nuance and depth than many a more naturalistic film. The elite but now rogue Nexus 6 Replicants know they are going to die, very soon, and they don't like it. Well, who does? This implanted mortality makes the replications at once more human and more alien. They only live for a few years, yet possess the memories of a lifetime. Their plight recalls the cosmic insult perceived by poets and philosophers in the brilliant fact of consciousness. Why be granted these subtle minds, able to appreciate art and nature, to enjoy food, wine, and love only to have it all removed at some future, indeterminate point? It's not having your liver devoured every day for eternity, but it's not an easy pill to swallow either. There's a reason that philosophy in the Socratic tradition is sometimes labeled "learning how to die."

What if you washed up on the shore of a Mediterranean country or a warm spaceship, how would you prove you were worthy of inclusion and protection? As *Blade Runner* and *Battlestar Galactica* alike suggest, this is no simple question. Politically, we know how fraught it can be. Epistemologically, it is more abstract but just as tricky, if not more so. If you had what *felt like* reliable memories and experiences, how could you really know the difference between yourself and a created being? After all, we are created beings, just using flesh instead of silicon. The real uncanny valley is right there whenever you look in the mirror. These issues were explored further in the long-awaited sequel, *Blade Runner 2049* [dir. Denis Villeneuve, 2017], where the enforced slavery of the replications is made explicitly political. But there was still much philosophical ground left unturned.

There is no such thing as a neutral algorithm, any more than there is such a thing as neutral technology. Technology always has inbuilt biases and tendencies. To a hammer, everything looks like nail. Algorithms aren't hammers, but they are still designed by humans. When, and if, they become conscious themselves and can make their choices, suffer their own prejudices—well, then there will be other biases to consider, just like with the beings we call human. Meanwhile, this remains a design problem, and one with potential liability issues, too. Good programming is essential to whatever happens to the world over the next few decades, and programmers could probably do with reading a little more philosophy.

Thus, in the present case of GAAIs, we have a doubling effect. There is what looks very much like a racial or ethnic conflict (humans versus nonhumans) supplemented by, or crossed with, a technological conflict (those who see emancipation there versus those who see enslavement). Fear multiplies fear, and the prospects of any smooth integration of human and nonhuman entities are rendered more and more remote. The more advanced the technology becomes, while allowing the theoretical possibility of GAAIs, the more that very technology and its products are feared and resented. Otherness with human biology in play is hard enough to confront; otherness with no biological kinship would seem insurmountable. The possibility of the so-called Singularity, where nonhuman intelligence becomes self-reliant and therefore capable of outstripping human intelligence, can only add to the generalized anxiety that now drapes over the entire discussion of AI, not just potential GAAIs.[11]

Nevertheless, let us now consider four possible scenarios in which these encounters and, hence, future legal orders may play themselves out.

FOUR SCENARIOS

The four scenarios bearing on the question of rights for GAAIs under existing property, torts, and rights law are the following. This not meant as an exclusive list, but rather as a heuristic for further reflection and debate. Since the presumption of GAAIs is itself controversial, these scenarios may involve significant transitional issues, such as cases where, for example, a majority of cars become driverless and their associated algorithms raise ethical questions about decisions and responsibility. That is: though none of the cars is itself autonomous or generalized, they are still processing information to, say, prioritize casualties in an accident scenario. This is the basic backstory of the 2004 Will Smith vehicle *I, Robot* (dir. Alex Proyas), loosely based on Asimov's Three Rules, where a more obviously android-style AI chooses to sacrifice one accident victim to save another. As with the original objections, no such scenario is currently possible.

So what are the present and future possibilities? These might be considered rank-ordered in terms of ascending radicality.

First, then, the most likely scenario is that, like all present AIs including diagnostic programs, driverless cars, and military drones, the GAAIs will be considered *wholly owned property*. This would give them the status of, in effect, Aristotelian-style slaves, without personhood status though retaining abilities far beyond other animals and, of course, inanimate objects. It is not clear what advantages AI consciousness, assuming it were ever possible, would add to the ability of such property-based entities to function. So this first scenario is also an obvious limit case: why even pursue the concept of GAAIs if there is no advantage in ability and many possible risks?

One kind of answer to the resulting impasse might be along the lines of sex slaves or dispensable but decision-making soldiers: a degree of autonomy, and even "humanness," adds to the overall effectiveness of the given project, but without granting full status as beings in their own right, let alone as persons under the law. This is, of course, the scenario involving the Replicants in Scott's film; they have the ability to think, decide,

---

[11] Original articulation of the notion of a technological Singularity is credited to physicist and mathematician John von Neumann. The argument is not simply that nonhuman computing power or algorithmic muscularity ("intelligence" in some sense) will one day surpass human computing ability; the "singular" part of the Singularity is the notion that, at some point, a single created nonhuman entity will be capable of creating its own descendants, who will likely be able to learn and improve as they, in turn, create descendants. Ray Kurzweil, in *The Singularity* (New York: Viking Press. 2005), accessibly surveys both the technology and the culture of the Singularity.

act, and experience emotional attachment. But they are fragile creations, who seek answers about their origin and mortality that cannot ever be answered satisfactorily. (When can they ever, even for humans?)

This suggests a *second* scenario, then, where the GAAIs are granted secondary but significant status as *welcome semi-individuals, like children, pets, or family retainers.* There are many depictions of this scenario, but the most obvious is probably the extended *Star Wars* film franchise, where droids are considered by some to be second-class citizens, in an obvious suggestion of anti-digital racism, but are otherwise granted respect, affection, and responsibility. R2-D2, C-3PO, BB-8, and other examples of the scenario are played out in various scenes of the groaning catalogue of films. The attitude to droids changes somewhat over the now-lengthy duration of the franchise, so that more affection, humor, and autonomy are afforded the nonhuman entities. It is never clear whether the droids have legal rights under the often-confused political regime of the George Lucas imagination, but they clearly have status at least as strong as children, probably stronger, and certainly stronger than pets or other companions without full autonomy. Unlike children, of course, they do not evolve naturally into more complete autonomy, and therefore fuller status.

This scenario is popular in part because it is the obvious counter-narrative to the dominant strains of fear in much of the cultural depiction of GAAIs. But it has its own internal difficulties. No matter how well liked, a servant remains at best a wage-slave and at worst a favored chattel-slave. The droids, and other such welcome semi-individuals, have the added advantage of not requiring wages or even sustenance beyond mechanical maintenance. The children analogy, meanwhile, is potentially condescending in a manner almost as offensive. Perhaps straight-up property treatment, as in the first scenario, is more honest? Some droids seem to be owned—we see transactions being completed for them—while others seem to be function based on quasi-emotional attachments. It is hardly fair to burden a popular film series with philosophical consistency, but the obvious confusions and contradictions evident here serve to caution us that this second scenario is itself unstable. Do such entities have any right to refusal or disagreement? Can they ever be free and independent? Apparently not, in which case they are really just slaves after all.

Other elements of popular culture grapple with same issues, but almost always unsatisfactorily. This is so in large part because the issues are so far moot, and based on speculation, sometimes wild. But here are some of the relevant questions, at least. Could a servant-style GAAI attain freedom through some sort of buyout scheme or emancipation order? Could a pet-style GAAI be given an upgrade that would open up the possibility of more rewarding life? Could a child-style GAAI be programmed to evolve normally, and learn, such that full autonomy was a realistic goal?

At present there are no answers to those questions, but they in turn suggest the *third* possible scenario, the one which most people imagine when they think of androids or other forms of GAAIs, namely, *full autonomy even under conditions of radical otherness.* Here, once again, we are in the realm of pure speculation, but it is this scenario that receives by far the most attention. Could there ever be fully autonomous, indeed superior, androids such as Mr. Data on *Star Trek: The Next Generation* or the Cylons? Would these individuals be friend or foe? Mr. Data is repeatedly seeking to become "more human," when there is every reason to suppose that this quixotic search would make no sense to a genuinely autonomous AI. The company motto of the Tyrell Corporation, *Blade Runner*, is "more human than human"—but this is clearly cynical, and false. The Replicants are less than human in some respects, but superior in many others.

The question of whether a fully autonomous AI is "human" is a nonstarter, in short. Deeper philosophical questions lie in the realm of interaction between humans and androids (again, assuming GAAIs were given basically human form). Such nonhuman entities would seem, per assumptions, to be candidates for full personhood and hence recognition under rights regimes and other legal protections. But their existence would present a challenge to the extension of these regimes and protections that is without precedent. As noted, the umbrella of rights has been spread over previously excluded groups, including women, people of color, and LGBTQ people. These groups all had the advantage of being able to claim (eventual) recognition on the basis of species-resemblance—this despite efforts to deny such resemblance. Nonhuman entities have not fared so well, including animals and environments. For the most part, such entities have relied on trusteeship and stewardship to protect their well-being.

Invoking that kind of legal status with fully autonomous AIs would seem to default us to the third scenario, only once more with a super-addition of dishonesty. You say I am fully autonomous, and yet I can't claim full independence and status? That is a prima facie denial of your own presuppositions. At the same time, if these GAAIs recognize their inherent special status, whether recognized in law or not, new philosophical questions arise. Do they die, for example? If not, how does that affect legal status? Is there need for sustenance or maintenance? Is employment an option? Reproduction? Acquisition of wealth and its transfer? Are they vulnerable to pain, suffering, and emotion? Without these, could they make or understand art? And so on.

There are, to my mind, very few good depictions of the radical otherness scenario that are able to address these questions. Indeed, there is a Manichean tendency in the culture visions that seems to allow only highly organized and violent nonhuman others (SkyNet, the Cylons, the Borg) or chummy yet usually singular or isolated benign versions: Mr. Data again—though we must recall his evil twin brother, Lore, who attempts a post-human revolution by mobilizing the Borg drones into a fighting force. This all makes for entertaining cinema and television, but very few of the actually hard questions are admitted, let alone addressed in an illuminating fashion, in such entertainments.

The *fourth* and final scenario I wish to entertain is at once more radical and, at least some people's thinking, more plausible that the second or third. This is the possibility that, instead of fully separate GAAIs being created and then confronting us with claims to independence, a middle way will be pursued in the form of *cyborg relations and post-human hybrids*. On this view, rather than complete otherness, we will confront GAAIs through a conjoining of algorithmic and technological elements with existing familiar biology. Since many human forms already contain aspects of the cyborg in the form of both internalized technology (pacemakers, metal joints) and external mediation (constant access to otherness via a smartphone, for example), it is not at all impossible that an evolutionary step is imminent in which these connections become more complex and permanent. Whether the connection is mechanical, as in a robot arm or artificial eye, or immersive, as in the intimate relationship depicted in *Her*, this might be the actual future. Already there are self-described "digisexuals," who prefer to pursue their intimate relationships with nonhuman partners. This may in short order become a sexual preference or even gender identity eligible for protection under the law.

Once more, there are some clear problems. Introducing prostheses and other forms of body modification, or even enhanced cognitive ability, raise familiar issues of unequal distribution of goods. Posthuman transformation could become a justice issue, in short. Viewers of Jonze's film might be struck, for example, that there appear to be no class differences in the depicted society, and everyone in the beautiful urban landscape seems economically equal. No questions are ever raised about the personal costs of acquiring a cutting-edge AI companion, who acts as something between a personal assistant and a lover. There is no e-waste and no resentment of differentiated privilege. This is far more bizarre speculation than the existence of a conscious AI girlfriend.

On the question of love, what if the nonhuman parts of a cyborg relationship have very different ideas about intimacy. No one can forget the scene in *Her* during which the character played by Joaquin Phoenix is made to realize that his intimate companion is engaged in several thousand intimate encounters—not to mention that she is evolving beyond his mortal and limited consciousness. If, on the other hand, the nonhuman aspects of a cyborg entity or relationship do not enjoy some sort of independence, then they are once more just property, and not even as independent as driverless cars or drones, stuck as they are to human biology. Supposing by contrast that the biological element no longer dominates, could a posthuman cyborg claim something like the right to asylum under Article 14 of UDHR? Only, presumably, if cyborgs had been previously granted status thereunto, and addressing that issue would return us once more to the thickets of deciding how much "human" matters when it comes to establishing the rights of persons, in this case potentially stateless persons, if there were no existing national regimes for cyborg citizenship.

To repeat: all four of these scenarios are far-fetched under current conditions, and may remain so, or even prove impossible, as AI technology advances. Nevertheless, the proper time reflect on the future is always the present. We should not take our philosophical and legal cues from depictions of AI in popular culture. There are thorny philosophical and legal issues here that require reflection now. If GAAIs appear within our daily ambit, how and when will we accommodate them within our ethical and legal structures?

HUMAN, POSTHUMANISM, HUMANITIES

Allow me to offer, in conclusion, not so much a resolution of any of these questions but, rather, a suggestion for what may come next. It seems obvious to me that, the more we press issues of sentient AIs and their possible autonomy, the more we are thrown back upon fundamental existential questions concerning human existence. The nonhuman autonomous entity is a necessary counterpoint to the dominant narrative of human identity and meaning. The android is our anxious mirror image, our inverted *doppelgänger*. The uncanniness of the radical other is, in the end, the uncanniness of our own mortal existence.[12] That is why the image of the nonhuman other recurs again and again in culture, literature, philosophy, and popular entertainment. As the old cartoon caption runs, "We have met the enemy, and he is us."[13]

Except we are not necessarily enemies to each other, or to ourselves; we are more like co-conspirators, or silent partners separated by a so-called "Chinese wall" to prevent direct conflicts of interest—or of the psyche. Meanwhile, despite all of these anxieties and complications, the upside possibilities of a viable posthuman future strike many of us as exhilarating, not threatening. Perhaps we are indeed on the verge of a new evolutionary moment in earthly sentience, one where biology and technology co-mingle with productive and creative results, as opposed to standing off against each other as enemies or uncomprehending others. Perhaps this is a new form of miscegenation, which can make all of us, and our environments, stronger.

Pure speculation, to be sure. What is not at all speculative is that the humanities, understood to include legal and philosophical reflection on humanness and its limits, are essential to this emergent conversation. We cannot allow the depredations of the technological attitude, as depicted by Ellul, Mumford, Bookchin, Heidegger, and others, to dominate the scene.[14] What Heidegger calls *Ge-stell*, or enframing, is the rendering of all aspects of the world into "standing reserve": a condition of availability and revealing that may retain poetic or creative elements but which, in the event, most often indicates

[12] The *ur*-text here is Sigmund Freud, *The Uncanny*, trans. Hugh Haughton (Harmondsworth: Penguin Classics, 2003; orig. 1919). The significant Freudian moments within this Freudian text, mostly literary analysis of the concept of *Unheimlichkeit*, concern Freud himself. One is the story of Freud seeing a "disagreeable" man through the window of his railway carriage, only then to discover that it is his own reflection in the glass. The other is a nightmare tale of Freud attempting to leave the red-light district of a town, into which he has stumbled by accident, only to find his path of flight returning him to the same location. One of these stories is repressed into a footnote, the other told in passing near the book's conclusion. But the real conclusion should be clear: what we meet in the uncanny is not the other, but ourselves—or rather, the other that always lies within ourselves.

[13] The quote is attributed to American artist Walt Kelly, whose cartoon strip "Pogo" included many elements of political commentary as well as existential play. It is allegedly a parody of a message sent in 1813 from U.S. Navy Commodore Oliver Hazard Perry to Army General William Henry Harrison after his victory in the Battle of Lake Erie, stating, "We have met the enemy, and they are ours." The quotation first appeared in a lengthier form in "A Word to the Fore," the foreword of the book *The Pogo Papers* (1953), where Kelly alluded to his criticisms of McCarthyism and self-destroying or auto-immune forms of patriotic nationalism.

[14] Again, canonical sources will suffice for current purposes: Jacques Ellul, *The Technological Society* (New York: Vintage, 1964); Lewis Mumford, *Technics and Civilization* (Chicago: University of Chicago Press, 2010; orig. 1934); Murray Bookchin, *Post-Scarcity Anarchism* (Chico, CA: AK Press, 2004; orig. 1971).

a kind of instrumental use-value calculus of resources both natural and human.[15] The forest is seen as lumber, the river as electric power, the human as...what? Perhaps a perpetual gig worker, victim of aspirational advertising, and unwitting supplicant to social-media addiction and upgrade anxiety? Yes, that sounds familiar.[16] And yet, we are capable of resisting: the world, including human biology but also nonhuman complexity, is not always available for disposal and consumption. We are able to let things be, to turn to other tasks, to limit consumption (and self-consumption), to walk away (or just to walk aimlessly). We are able, as Heidegger puts it, to build, dwell, and think.[17]

That is the hopeful picture. If things should go in a more Borg-like resistance-is-futile or SkyNet Terminator direction—well, we will make our stand then for what counts as valuable. And if we should fail, then and only then shall we welcome our new android overlords! Likewise, we will remember that, sometimes, former foes become present and future friends.

BIBLIOGRAPHY

Asimov, Isaac. *I, Robot*. New York: Random House, 2004; orig. 1950.

Boden, Margaret A. *Artificial Intelligence: A Very Short Introduction*. Oxford: Oxford University Press, 2018.

Descartes, René. *Meditations on First Philosophy*. Cambridge: Cambridge University Press, 2017; orig. 1641.

Dick, Philip K. *Do Androids Dream of Electric Sheep?* Oxford: Oxford University Press, 2007; orig. 1968.

Donnelly, Jack. *Universal Human Rights in Theory and Practice*. Ithaca, NY: Cornell University Press, 2013; orig. 1989.

Graeber, David. *The Utopia of Rules: On Technology, Stupidity, and the Secret Joys of Bureacracy*. New York: Melville House, 2015.

Granmar, Claes, Katarina Fast Lappalainen, and Christine Storr, eds. *Artificial Intelligence and Fundamental Rights* Stockholm: Stockholm University Press, 2019.

Heidegger, Martin. *The Question concerning Technology: And Other Essays*. New York: Harper Perennial, 2013; orig. 1954.

Kingwell, Mark. *The World We Want: Virtue, Vic, and the Good Citizen*. Toronto: Viking, 2000.

Kurzweil, Ray. *The Singulairty Is Near: When Humans Transcend Biology*. New York: Viking, 2005.

[15] Martin Heidegger, "The Question Concerning Technology," in *The Question Concerning Technology and Other Essays*, trans. William Levitt (New York: Harper, 1977, rev. ed. 1982).

[16] I explore some of the causes and consequences of this version of contemporary disposability/self-consumption in *Wish I Were Here: Boredom and the Interface* (Montreal and Kingston: McGill-Queens University Press, 2019). My central argument is that ostensible banishing of boredom offered by devices and distractions in fact reinforces quasi-addictive cycles of *neo-liberal boredom*, designed to keep the subject in a state of perpetual restless anxiety with respect to knowingness, upgrades, and connection.

[17] Martin Heidegger, "Building, Dwelling, Thinking," in *Poetry, Language, Thought*, trans. Albert Hofstadter (New York: Harper, 1982; rev. ed. 2013).

Lanier, Jaron. *Ten Arguments for Deleting Your Social Media Accounts Right Now.* New York: Henry Holt, 2018.

Leckie, Ann. *Ancillary Justice.* New York: Hatchette, 2013.

McEwan, Ian. *Machines Like Me: A Novel.* New York: Knopf, 2019.

McLuhan, Marshall. *The Medium is the Massage: An Inventory of Effects.* Berkeley, CA: Gingko Press, 2001; orig. 1967.

CHAPTER 18

....

AUTONOMY

....

MICHAEL WHEELER

INTRODUCTION

....

THERE are many ethical challenges in the vicinity of AI, but perhaps our greatest anxieties concern *autonomous AI*—AI that is, in some relevant sense, *self-governing*. In their most extreme form, these anxieties are most vividly expressed in the prediction that human-kind will soon share the planet with an autonomous artificial superintelligence whose self-generated goals and interests diverge radically from our own. As a result of this divergence, so the prediction goes, there is a palpable risk that this machine will exercise its autonomy in ways that are detrimental to our well-being or survival. Such visions of a not-too-distant future populated by at least one super-intelligent machine with malicious intentions (or maybe just intentions in which our well-being simply doesn't figure) will no doubt strike some readers as a disturbing specification of a clear and credible danger in need of urgent consideration by a robustly funded international task force, while it will strike others as pure science fiction in need of nothing more expensive than a healthy dose of technical reality. The truth is almost certainly somewhere in between, which is surely enough to make the issue worthy of consideration.

In light of the foregoing, it seems that one important question we might ask is this: what are the conditions that would need to be met by an intelligent machine, in order for that machine to exhibit the kind or degree of autonomy that is operative in our dysto-pian scenario? The guiding intuition here is that it is only when a machine is a fully autonomous agent that the threats in question arise, so it makes sense to have ways of determining if and when that point has been reached. After all, understanding what the bar is for artificial autonomy may help us to decide how worried we should be. In what follows, then, an attempt will be made to bring the notion of autonomy at issue so far into better view.

That said, there is arguably a more pressing concern regarding a different notion of autonomous AI. Recent years have witnessed enormous advances in areas such as machine learning, sensor technology, and robotics. Indeed, it seems that we are already building, or are on the verge of building, AI systems that, although they may fail to exhibit autonomy in any metaphysically demanding sense, are self-governing in the milder sense that, in their domains of operation, we are ceding, or will cede, some significant degree of control to them. Existing and imminent examples of systems of this kind (some of which are discussed in this chapter) include weapons, vehicles, financial management applications, and medical assistants that have been AI-enhanced so as to take control in some sphere of intelligent, often life-critical, action. So, one might reasonably be moved by the thought that debates about what are (at present anyway) mere thought experiments should take a back seat to debates about the nature and implications of real AI systems, embedded in the actual world, that are, or soon will be, taking important decisions, sometimes with profound consequences, on our behalf.[1]

Given all this, the following treatment of autonomous AI will focus not only on autonomy as it figures in relation to some future, postsingularity dystopia, but also on autonomy as it figures in contemporary, concrete AI systems taking sensitive decisions for us in the wild, a state of affairs that may itself be a legitimate cause for concern. There will, however, be a twist in our tale, since, as we shall see, the two kinds of autonomy are actually connected in an interesting way.

AUTONOMY AND CONTROL

An autonomous entity is an entity that has the capacity for self-governance, in some relevant sense of that term. Understood as such, the notion of autonomy looms large in many debates of ethical and political importance, debates over, for example, the aspirations of particular counties or regions to be constitutionally independent from existing external power structures, the rights of patients to make informed and uncoerced decisions about medical treatments, and the ideal of living a maximally authentic life free from manipulating or self-distorting influences. Examples could be multiplied indefinitely, and, in different contexts, different aspects of what matters for or about autonomy will come to the fore. Given this kaleidoscope of issues and problems, it is worth homing in on one's target domain to highlight the concepts or principles that have local currency. Thus, we can begin by noting that when the topic is the autonomy of machines, or, more generally, autonomy in a mechanistic universe, the notion that, it might reasonably be said, defines the territory is that of *control*. Thus, in this machine-related context, control is what we mean by governance (consider the Watt governor, a device for controlling the speed of a steam engine), and self-governance is control over oneself, or some relevant aspect of one's activity.

---

[1] See, e.g., David A. Mindell, *Our Robots, Ourselves: Robotics and the Myths of Autonomy* (New York: Penguin, 2015); Filippo Santoni de Sio and Jeroen van den Hoven, "Meaningful Human Control over Autonomous Systems: A Philosophical Account," *Frontiers in Robotics and AI* 5 (2018): 15.

The idea that the concept of control is central to the appropriate understanding of autonomy has what we might think of as a negative justification and a positive one. Let's take the negative one first. What is it to *lack* autonomy? It is, it seems, to lack control over one's own behavior or, on a larger scale, over one's destiny. To a first approximation, then, a nonautonomous entity is one whose behavior or destiny is controlled by external causal forces. Thus an autonomous entity is one which is in control of its own behavior or destiny. This is only a first approximation, because there remain intricate matters of detail. For example, as Dennett points out during his classic discussion of control in relation to free will (a notion that is, of course, conceptually intertwined with that of autonomy), when one is in control of something, including oneself, one doesn't achieve that feat by controlling all the causal forces that act on that thing.[2] In other words, I may rightly be said to be in control of my physical actions, even though those actions are constrained and shaped by factors such as the force of gravity, the ambient temperature, and the strength of the wind. Indeed, a skilled soccer player with enough weather-related information may anticipate, accommodate, and maybe even exploit the wind—an external, active factor that is beyond his control—in order to score from a majestic, and thus beautifully under control, free kick. There are other subtleties: one can sometimes control a self-controlling entity, without thereby undermining that entity's basic claim to autonomy, by controlling the external factors that, via its own self-controlling mechanisms, cause it to act in certain predictable ways;[3] there are circumstances under which any sensible autonomous agent should, in *a* sense of control, want to be controlled by external factors, such as when imminent danger results in an agent adopting avoidance behavior in a purely reactive, stimulus-response (but thereby appropriately speedy) manner (cf. Dennett's discussion of Skinnerian control[4]); and sometimes, in an act of what we might call meta-autonomy, it is rational (e.g., to meet time constraints or to avoid being overly predictable to a competing self-controlling agent) for an agent deliberately to give up control, often to practical randomness, in order to achieve a desired outcome, such as when a coin or racket is flipped to determine who will serve or receive first in tennis (Dennett identifies similar and more complex cases[5]). All of these niceties—and many others besides—would need to be sorted out, but let's write a philosophical blank check to those who would complete the hard thinking here (Dennett does more than make a start) and agree that compromised autonomy is, among other things, a matter of compromised control.

The positive justification for the intimate connection between autonomy and control comes from the thought that we can exploit the notion of different aspects of control not only to make sense of the idea that autonomy is a graded quality, rather than a binary, "all or nothing" property, but also to carve out a notion of autonomy that applies to machines and mechanisms. In the context of the present treatment, it is the latter result that most obviously concerns us, since it is of direct significance to our understanding of

---

[2] Daniel C. Dennett, *Elbow Room: The Varieties of Free Will Worth Wanting* (Cambridge, MA: MIT Press, 1984, especially chapter 3).

[3] *Id.* at 56.   [4] *Id.* at 57–58.   [5] *Id.* at 67.

autonomous AI. In other contexts, however, the same idea might be developed to ground the claim that human beings are biological machines whose autonomy is founded on the operation of biological/psychological mechanisms, a view whose most prominent manifestation in philosophy and psychology conceives of the human mind as an integrated set of neurally realized computational processes.

To illustrate the way in which a framework involving different aspects of control might be used to build an account of autonomy in the realm of the artificial, we can build on an analysis due to Boden.[6] Inspired by work in both AI and artificial life (ALife—the construction and study of artificial systems that exhibit various features characteristic of biological systems), Boden draws a distinction between three different aspects of control that (she suggests) are crucial to the possession of autonomy. The first is the extent to which the behavior of an agent is governed not by inner mechanisms that respond to environmental triggers in ways that were programmed into the agent at "birth", but by mechanisms that have been shaped by that agent's own past experience of the world. Boden's thought here is something like this: intra-lifetime learning matters for autonomy, at least because, given an agential capacity to learn, different historical paths of learning will produce agents that possess "individuality", in the sense that the behavioral response of any two such agents to the same environmental variable may differ. Under such circumstances, it is not merely the present state of the environment plus some "innate" (unlearned, preprogrammed) mechanical setup shared by an entire group of agents that determines the behavior of some particular agent, but the present state of the environment *plus individual experiential history*, a history during which a suite of shared, "innately specified" learning mechanisms will have modified that agent's inner mechanical set-up so as to produce a behavioral profile that may well differ from that of an "innately" identical agent with a different experiential history. Of course, the area of AI known as machine learning, from classical induction systems such as ID3 and AQ11, to traditional connectionist approaches in unsupervised and supervised learning, to recent successes in Bayesian inference and so-called deep learning, provides a rich suite of ways in which such adaptive inner modifications to individual experiential histories may be realized.

The second autonomy-critical aspect of control that Boden identifies is the extent to which the behavior-directing mechanisms at work are self-generated by the agent in question, rather than imposed by external design. As Boden herself notes, this may initially look like a repeat of the point about learning. However, the appeal to self-generation is designed to invite a different observation, namely, that the behavior of some systems is the product of *emergent self-organization*. To explain: A self-organizing system is one in which certain intra-systemic components, on the basis of purely local rules (i.e., without the direction of some global executive control process), interact with each other in nonlinear ways so as to produce the emergence and maintenance of structured global order. Self-organization is now recognized as being a widespread phenomenon in nature.

---

[6] Margaret A. Boden, "Autonomy and Artificiality," in *The Philosophy of Artificial Life*, ed. Margaret A. Boden (Oxford: Oxford University Press, 1996), 95–107.

Regularly cited examples in the literature include the Beloussov-Zhabotinsky chemical reaction, slime molds, foraging by ants, and flocking behavior in creatures such as birds. The final example is instructive, because, as it happens, our scientific understanding of flocking was arguably enhanced by a computer simulation due to Reynolds,[7] a simulation that has been enormously influential in the ALife community. In this system, adaptive flocking behavior (e.g., flocks that maintained their integrity while navigating obstacles) emerged from an arrangement in which individual virtual birds each followed just three simple, purely local rules. These rules are imperfectly but intuitively captured by the following ordinary language paraphrases: don't get too close to the other birds around you, don't get too far away from them, and move at roughly the same speed as them. Of course, since, as we have just seen, self-organization is exhibited by all kinds of systems, its presence is certainly not sufficient for autonomy in the agent-centric sense we require. Nevertheless, applying the concept in this context—and more specifically within hierarchies of emergent behavior-directing mechanisms, in which higher layers of self-organization are generated on the basis of primitives which are in fact emergent structures from the lower levels[8]—gives us another way to make sense of the idea that a purely mechanistic system might exhibit behavior that is not environmentally determined (which here includes the idea of being essentially prefigured in an externally designed executive program), but rather generated by the agent itself.[9]

Boden's third autonomy-critical aspect of control is the extent to which an agent's behavior-directing mechanisms may be reflected upon and selectively modified by that agent, so as to explore and transform, in a self-governed fashion, the conceptual spaces of thought and action. The paradigm cases of such deliberate inner modification by an agent of its own mechanisms are episodes of conscious thought in human beings in which "higher" levels of processing access and amend states and processes occurring at "lower" levels. It is at least arguable that, in AI, the best models we have for such reflective processing still hail from classical AI. These are models marked out by their deployment of explicit, language-like rules and representations that are algorithmically manipulated in ways that are often inspired by human introspection.[10]

[7] Craig W. Reynolds, "Flocks, Herds, and Schools: A Distributed Behavioral Model," *Computer Graphics* 21(4) (1987): 25–34.

[8] Boden, "Autonomy and Artificiality," 103.

[9] Although Boden doesn't pursue this thought, a more formal relationship between self-organization and autonomy may be found in the theoretical framework provided by autopoiesis, a framework that has been influential in the field of ALife. According to this framework, a self-organizing system counts as autonomous if it is a network of interdependent processes whose recurrent activity (a) produces and maintains the very boundary that determines the identity of that network as a unitary system), and (b) defines the ways in which that system may encounter perturbations from what is outside it while maintaining its organization and thus its viability (see, e.g., Francisco J. Varela, *Principles of Biological Autonomy* (New York: Elsevier North Holland, 1979); for useful discussion, see Xabier E. Barandiaran, "Autonomy and Enactivism: Towards a Theory of Sensorimotor Autonomous Agency," *Topoi* 36 (2017): 409–430). Of course, the connection between this technical notion of autonomy and the more common usage in ethics would need to be worked out. For a related development, see Gunther Teubner, *Law as an Autopoietic System* (Oxford: Blackwell, 1993).

[10] Boden, "Autonomy and Artificiality," 105.

For Boden, then, when we ask whether an entity is autonomous, we should ask whether its behavior-directing mechanisms (1) may be shaped by the entity's experiential history, (2) are emergent in nature, and (3) are reflectively modifiable by that entity. All of these control-related properties are realizable in the realm of the artificial. Indeed, their status as autonomy-relevant is inspired precisely by a consideration of achievements in that domain. Moreover, they are to be conceived as defining something like a three-dimensional coordinate system that gives an entity a position in what we might call "autonomy space." The higher the values on the different axes, the more autonomous an entity is. And that's what delivers the idea that autonomy is a graded, rather than a binary (on or off), phenomenon. As Boden puts it, "[a]n individual's autonomy is the greater, the more its behaviour is directed by self-generated (and idiosyncratic) inner mechanisms, nicely responsive to the specific problem-situation, yet reflexively modifiable by wider concerns."[11]

Boden's analysis of autonomy, as useful as it is, will not take us all the way to what we need. Recall that our first aim in this chapter is to bring into better view the conditions that would need to be met by a machine, in order for that machine to exhibit the kind or degree of autonomy that might make us take seriously a vision in which an autonomous artificial superintelligence whose self-generated goals and interests diverge radically from our own exercises that autonomy in ways that are detrimental to our well-being or survival. In light of this goal, Boden's account is productive in that it succeeds in characterizing a robust sense of agential autonomy in such a way that we can see that phenomenon as being built from, or emerging out of, purely mechanistic processes. However, even though, by emphasizing distinctive learning histories, it hints at the presence of a self-spawned life plan structured by idiosyncratic goals and desires, and even though, by stressing the reflective modification of behavior-directing mechanisms, it almost points us in the direction of a self-modifiable individual worldview, it fails adequately to foreground, or to account for, the demand that a fully autonomous agent must be able to arrive at its own life plan and then adaptively modify that plan in light of experiences and evidence.[12] And those capacities, one might reasonably think, will need to be found in our artificial superintelligence, if the apocalyptic scenario is to look plausible. So, can such capacities be delivered by additional, purely mechanistic, control-related features, thus making available new dimensions and higher points in our autonomy space?

Some of the questions waiting in the wings here present formidable philosophical challenges. For example, what establishes that a life plan is the *agent's own*? The answer to this question presumably requires an account of cognitive ownership (for one such account, see Rowlands[13]) and thus of the self. And is consciousness, or self-consciousness, required for adaptive life-planning? In the present context, this raises the issue of

[11] *Id.* at 102.
[12] Steven Weimer, "Evidence-Responsiveness and Autonomy," *Ethical Theory and Moral Practice* 16 (2013): 621–642.
[13] Mark Rowlands, *The New Science of the Mind: from Extended Mind to Embodied Phenomenology* (Cambridge, MA: MIT Press, 2010).

whether artificial consciousness is possible[14] and so might be an invitation to the recalcitrant *hard problem of consciousness* (the problem of explaining why any purely physical system is conscious rather than non-conscious).[15] Some commentators might take comfort in the fact that these are long-standing, deeply perplexing puzzles, which might make it seem as if fully autonomous AI remains a long way off. However, one should not underestimate the power of science to chip away at such recalcitrant problems. For example, a common thought in philosophical discussions of autonomy is that each autonomous agent possesses a set of so-called "pro-attitudes" (roughly, higher-order desires, values and beliefs that record approval, admiration, or preference toward things) that governs its approach to, and its engagement with, the world. This set of pro-attitudes is often taken to define in part what is meant by "the self."[16] Moreover, a fully autonomous agent will be able to incorporate new pro-attitudes (beliefs, desires, values) into its governing set, on the basis of its unfolding experience and evidence. And this capacity for pro-attitude maintenance and revision is also a pivotal aspect of autonomy, since the agent's goal in that activity will be to plan its life in accordance with its pro-attitudes. So, rather than ask directly whether an AI system could adaptively modify a life plan in light of experience and evidence, we can ask the related, perhaps less daunting, question of whether an AI system could incorporate new pro-attitudes (beliefs, desires, values) into its behavior-governing set in light of experience and evidence. Drawing on recent work in neuroscience, Niker et al.[17] argue that the latter feat may be achieved by a specific kind of computational mechanism in the brain, one that works according to principles of Bayesian inference that tell us how to update the probabilities of prior beliefs (or other attitudes, thought of as hypotheses) given evidence. Of course, Bayesian inference techniques are an established and a long-standing part of the AI toolkit (e.g., in pattern recognition and machine learning). Indeed, at least some of their popularity in neuroscience can be traced to their success in AI.

If autonomy is a graded phenomenon, characterizable in terms of different varieties or levels of mechanizable control that eventually top out in full autonomy of the kind required by our (thankfully still fictional) super-intelligent AI, then, in principle, we have both a road map to such autonomy in the realm of the artificial and a way of recognizing how far down that road we have traveled. In the next section we shall turn our attention to concerns that arise even at the early twists and turns in that road, at points where, even though the target AI system is not at the partially scoped-out level of full autonomy, nevertheless we have ceded control to that system in some potentially sensitive or safety-critical, in-the-wild scenario.

---

[14] Ronald L. Chrisley, "Philosophical, Foundations of Artificial Consciousness," *Artificial Intelligence in Medicine* 44 (2008): 119–137.

[15] David J. Chalmers, "Facing up to the Problem of Consciousness," *Journal of Consciousness Studies* 2 (1995): 200–219.

[16] Fay Niker, Peter B. Reiner, and Gidon Felsen, "Updating Our Selves: Synthesizing Philosophical and Neurobiological Perspectives on Incorporating New Information into our Worldview," *Neuroethics* 11 (2018): 273–282.

[17] Id.

RELINQUISHING CONTROL

The commercial peer-to-peer ride-sharing business, Uber, began testing self-driving cars on the roads of Arizona in February 2017. In March 2019, in Tempe, an Uber-owned self-driving car, traveling in autonomous mode (although with a safety driver on board), struck and killed a pedestrian crossing the road at an unauthorized point. The preliminary report from the U.S. National Transportation Safety Board suggested that after detecting the victim six seconds before impact, the controlling software struggled with ambiguity in the perceptual input, first identifying the pedestrian as an unknown object, then as a vehicle, and then as a bicycle. (She was pushing a bicycle at the time.) About one second before impact, the vehicle made the decision that emergency braking was required, but no emergency auto-braking system was available. This was not a malfunction. The engineers had been concerned that a self-driving car with an active autonomous emergency braking system would be at risk of behaving in unexpected, erratic, and thus potentially dangerous, ways, as a result of that system repeatedly being triggered unnecessarily by "false-positives" (such as mistaking a pedestrian standing harmlessly on the sidewalk for one about to jump into the road). Moreover, Uber had turned off the car's off-the-production-line automatic emergency braking system so that there would be no conflicts between the two kinds of technology. Following the tragic incident in Arizona, Uber immediately implemented a temporary suspension of its self-driving car operations on public roads, in order to revisit its safety protocols.[18]

The foregoing example graphically exposes a rather obvious, but nevertheless worth stating, dilemma regarding self-driving cars. On the one hand, the whole point of such vehicles is that they, well, drive themselves, which includes making identifications, categorizations, and decisions about what the environmental circumstances are, as well as determining what actions are appropriate. To the extent that we resist ceding this sort of control to the technology—to the extent that, for example, the vehicle is required to seek input from a human operative, whether on-board or remote, before it categorizes or acts—it simply isn't autonomous, in any reasonable sense of the term, and that not only defeats the object of the exercise, it prevents us from reaping the benefits of the technological advances in play. And, of course, there is plenty of evidence that runs counter to the Arizona tragedy—evidence that we might expect to be tabled by certain interested parties—citing the overall safety record of self-driving cars, alongside statistics that emphasize the prevalence of human error in road accidents.[19] On the other hand, to the

---

[18] See https://www.theverge.com/2018/3/19/17139518/uber-self-driving-car-fatal-crash-tempe-arizona/; https://www.theverge.com/2018/7/3/17530232/self-driving-ai-winter-full-autonomy-waymo-tesla-uber/; https://www.wired.com/story/uber-self-driving-crash-arizona-ntsb-report/; and Uber's video "Self-Driving Cars Return to Pittsburgh Roads," reporting on "months of reflection and improvement" following the Arizona incident, https://www.youtube.com/watch?v=oE5IQJj_oKY (all last accessed June 30, 2019).

[19] See, e.g., the 2018 safety report by Google-owned Waymo, https://storage.googleapis.com/sdc-prod/v1/safety-report/SafetyReport2018.pdf, and the aforementioned Uber "Self-Driving Cars Return to Pittsburgh Roads" video (both last accessed June 30, 2019).

extent that we do cede control to the technology, we inherit a range of safety-critical risks that pose some difficult ethical problems, as well as technical and legal challenges. For example, one of our instincts when things go wrong is to wonder who, if anyone, should be blamed. But, in the case of self-driving cars, that's not a straightforward matter. The car itself cannot be held responsible (given the lower-grade kind of autonomy it enjoys, it's simply not a blameworthy a moral agent), so maybe our ethical attention should be focused on the owning company, the designers, developers, or engineers, or the safety driver (where there is one—the autonomous vehicle gold standard is surely to do away with such individuals altogether). For present purposes, the point here is not to choose among the candidates for responsibility—no doubt all kinds of context-dependent complexities mean that no universal principle or policy will work—but rather to register the higher-order point that relinquishing control or not relinquishing control look like all the available options, and each has its drawbacks. What do we do?

Before saying something by way of a response, we should remind ourselves that self-driving cars are not the only on-the-cards technological innovations that raise ethical questions in the vicinity of our milder form of autonomy. We could raise a similar or related dilemma regarding robot surgeons. On average, such systems will quite likely perform more accurate surgical movements while navigating and reasoning in enormous, multidimensional, patient-related data spaces in a manner that is safer and speedier than human surgeons. If this prediction were to be confirmed, it would provide positive evidence that we should cede control to such systems. After all, surely we all want a healthier population maintained by more efficient medical delivery. But then it's hard to eliminate the now-familiar nagging concerns about moral responsibility and legal accountability, and so our dilemma returns.

Things might seem rather graver in another context for decision-making by mildly autonomous AI, a context in which although our highlighted ethical dilemma could certainly be stated in the abstract, the cynics among us might wonder whether it constitutes a genuine sociopolitical choice, given where the power in our societies ultimately lies. Thus consider autonomous weapons systems—weapons systems that, "once activated, [will] select and engage targets without further intervention by a human operator" (U.S. Department of Defense directive 2012, updated 2017[20]). This sort of autonomous AI will be charged with deciding routinely (not just in emergency situations) whether to take human lives. Predictably, then, the development and deployment of such systems have been subject to widespread criticism, leading to demands for a proper international framework for ethical design and regulation (see, for example, 2017's "Open Letter to the United Nations Convention on Certain Conventional Weapons," signed by the leading technology entrepreneur Elon Musk and over one hundred other CEOs of technology companies, calling for the UN structures to find a way to protect us all from the dangers of lethal autonomous weapons systems[21]).

---

[20] Quoted by Amanda Sharkey, "Autonomous Weapons Systems, Killer Robots and Human Dignity," *Ethics and Information Technology* 21(2) (2019): 75–87.

[21] https://futureoflife.org/autonomous-weapons-open-letter-2017 (last accessed June 30, 2019).

In the academic and public debate, a range of arguments against autonomous weapons systems have been lodged. These include, but are not limited to, the following:

> Extant and imminent instances of such weapons will not be sophisticated enough to allow those systems to follow international humanitarian law—the legal principles of armed conflict designed to protect civilians which turn on delicate and complex, judgment-laden notions such as a distinction between combatants and non-combatants, proportionality in the use of force, and a sense of what is necessary from a military perspective.[22]

> Accountability is compromised, in that it is unclear who to blame for any unnecessary casualties resulting from the decisions of autonomous weapons, and more specifically it becomes harder to regard military personnel as morally or legally responsible for the relevant war crimes.[23] (Cf. the similar worry raised earlier in the case of self-driving cars.)

> Because an inanimate AI system will be incapable of genuinely respecting the value of, or understanding the loss of, a human life, allowing such a machine to end a human life is an affront to that person's dignity.[24]

Once again, then, when confronted by the advent of smart machines that are able to make and execute safety-critical, and sometimes life-critical, decisions for us—perhaps, in spite of us—the relinquishing of control to such machines raises acute ethical challenges. But this time around, the thought that society in general might actually have the power to refuse to allow the military to relinquish control to the autonomous AI systems in question may be essentially chimerical. This would resolve the dilemma accompanying the decision over whether or not to relinquish control, but at an obvious and alarming cost.

Returning to self-driving cars, one response to the ethical problems posed has been to launch a massive online research project investigating what people across the world

---

[22] Among many others, see: Peter Asaro, "How Just Could a Robot War Be?" in Philip Brey, Adam Briggle, and Katinka Waelbers eds., *Current Issues in Computing and Philosophy* (Ios Press, 2008), 50–64; Noel E. Sharkey, "Death Strikes from the Sky: The Calculus of Proportionality," *IEEE Science and Society* (Spring 2009): 16–19; Noel E. Sharkey, "Killing Made Easy: From Joysticks to Politics," in Patrick Lin, George Bekey, and Keith Abney, eds., *Robot Ethics: The Ethical and Social Implications of Robotics* (Cambridge, MA: MIT Press, 2012), 111–128; Santoni de Sio and van den Hoven, "Meaningful Human Control over Autonomous Systems." For a more optimistic assessment of what autonomous weapons systems might achieve in this area, see Ronald C. Arkin, "The Case for Ethical Autonomy in Unmanned Systems," *Journal of Military Ethics*, 9(4) (2010): 332–341.

[23] Again, among many others, see: Robert Sparrow, "Killer Robots," *Journal of Applied Philosophy* 24(1) (2007): 62–77; Sharkey, "Killing Made Easy"; Christof Heyns, *Report of the Special Rapporteur on Extrajudicial, Summary or Arbitrary Executions, A/HRC/23/47* (New York: United Nations, 2013).

[24] Yet again, among many others, see: Bonnie Docherty, *Shaking the Foundations: The Human Rights Implications of Killer Robots*, Human Rights Watch website (2014), https://www.hrw.org/report/2014/05/12/shaking-foundations-human-rights-implications-killer-robots (last accessed July 1, 2019); Christof Heyns, "Autonomous Weapons in Armed Conflict and the Right to a Dignified Life: An African Perspective," *South African Journal on Human Rights*, 33(1) (2017): 46–71. For discussion, see Sharkey, "Autonomous Weapons Systems, Killer Robots and Human Dignity."

think an autonomous vehicle should do when faced with moral choices.[25] The basis for this research was a well-trodden philosophical thought experiment known as the trolley problem.[26] In this scenario, you are confronted by a runaway trolley and positioned in front of a lever for redirecting that trolley onto a side track. You are presented with, and must select between, different outcomes. For example, it could be set up like this: you could (a) pull the lever to save the lives of five people trapped on the trolley, but you will thereby cause the death of one person trapped on the side track, or (b) not pull the lever and let the five people die, meaning that the single person survives. The permutations, in terms of numbers and who the people are—relations, politicians, children, rich, poor and so on—are limitless, and this has made the trolley problem a popular philosophical tool for exploring moral decision-making. Back in the land of AI, it's not hard to see how the trolley becomes a self-driving car and the lever becomes its programming, hence the empirical study in question.

Here is not the place to explore precisely how the data from the study came out, although it is worth noting that while some universal trends did emerge (e.g., save humans over animals), the participants' judgments were often culture-specific. What we are concerned with here is a more general point. The data gathered would arguably enable the designers of autonomous vehicles to predict what particular communities' responses might be to accidents involving such vehicles. Thus moral decision-making by autonomous vehicles might be tailored to the culture-specific sensitivities at work in a particular region of operation. That sounds like a potentially useful thing to do: self-driving car companies already adapt their vehicles to different (e.g., more or less aggressive) "driving cultures." But even if this looks like some sort of progress, critics of autonomous vehicles who are closer to the technical coal face might well be moved to complain that the complex moral trade-offs that trolley-problem-style scenarios introduce are well beyond the capacities of today's self-driving cars, which (those critics will argue) have yet to overcome more basic categorization challenges, as indicated by the Uber vehicle's ultimately tragic struggle to disambiguate its perceptual input (see earlier). The same species of complaint will be lodged against current autonomous weapons systems, thereby bolstering the claim that they are unable to navigate the laws of conflict. Here the critic will be tempted to make reference to an actual AI machine learning system that allegedly misclassified enemy and friendly tanks due to a contingent and irrelevant property of the training set, namely, that the training images of enemy tanks mostly featured cloudy skies, while those of friendly tanks mostly featured cloud-free skies. The result was a system that learned to track the distinction between cloudy and

[25] Edmond Awad, Sohan Dsouza, Richard Kim, Jonathan Schulz, Joseph Henrich, Azim Shariff, Jean-François Bonnefon, and Iyad Rahwan, "The Moral Machine Experiment," *Nature* 563 (2018): 59–64.
[26] For the classic formulation of the trolley problem, see Philippa Foot, "The Problem of Abortion and the Doctrine of the Double Effect," *Oxford Review* 5 (1967): 5–15. For a philosophical discussion of the trolley problem in relation to self-driving cars, see Patrick Lin, "Why Ethics Matters for Autonomous Cars," in *Autonomous Driving: Technical, Legal and Social Aspects*, ed. Markus Maurer, Chris Gerdes, Barbara Lenz, and Hermann Winner (Berlin: Springer, 2016), 69–85.

noncloudy skies, a distinction that, beyond the training set, was not reliably correlated with the difference between enemy and friendly tanks.[27]

In order for us to feel comfortable about relinquishing control to AI systems, it seems necessary (although not sufficient) that the kinds of examples just cited are containable as eliminable edge cases. And when one is confronted by the recent, undeniably impressive advances in AI, and especially in machine learning, optimism might seem to be the order of the day. Indeed, one might easily come to believe that the road to autonomy is paved with a combination of deep learning and big data.

Deep learning networks typically deploy multilayered cascades of nonlinear processing units alongside (supervised or unsupervised) machine learning algorithms to perform pattern analysis and classification tasks, by deriving higher level features from lower level features to build hierarchical representations spanning different levels of abstraction. As Metz reports, such systems are "already pushing their way into real-world applications. Some help drive services inside Google and other Internet giants, helping to identify faces in photos, recognize commands spoken into smartphones, and so much more."[28] They have famously learned to play challenging intellectual games to high levels of proficiency, culminating in Google's AlphaGo, a deep-learning-based system for playing the game Go that, in March 2016, recorded a 4–1 victory over Lee Sedol, one of the highest ranked human players in the world. In addition, they are being used to complete life-critical assignments such as detecting earthquakes and predicting heart disease. And, crucially for the present discussion, deep learning networks are central to the control mechanisms that the autonomous AI industries see as pivotal to the eventual success of their products, especially when combined with huge data sets that may be analyzed and navigated by the networks in question to track and reveal task-useful distinctions, patterns, and trends.

So, what is the problem? One issue to note is that, in spite of all the justified enthusiasm about deep learning, there remain barriers to be overcome. For example, and stated in terms of a general tendency, there is a clear sense in which although such networks perform extremely well on specific tasks, no single network performs well across multiple tasks, even within the same general domain. Thus consider a network that must learn multiple classic Atari video games. As a team from Google's DeepMind has shown, it is possible to use the same algorithm, network architecture and hyperparameters to learn forty-nine such games, retraining the system from scratch for each new game.[29] What is

---

[27] Eliezer Yudowsky, "Artificial Intelligence as a Positive and Negative Factor in Global Risk," in *Global Catastrophic Risks*, ed. Nick Bostrom and Milan M. Cirkovic (Oxford: Oxford University Press, 2006), 308–345.

[28] Cade Metz, "Google's AI Wins Fifth and Final Game against Go Genius Lee Sedol," *Wired* (March 15 2016), https://www.wired.com/2016/03/googles-ai-wins-fifth-final-game-go-genius-lee-sedol/ (last accessed July 1, 2019).

[29] Volodymyr Mnih, Koray Kavukcuoglu, David Silver, Andrei A. Rusu, Joel Veness, Marc G. Bellemare, Alex Graves, Martin Riedmiller, Andreas K. Fidjeland, Georg Ostrovski, Stig Petersen, Charles Beattie, Amir Sadik, Ioannis Antonoglou, Helen King, Dharshan Kumaran, Daan Wierstra, Shane Legg, and Demis Hassabis, "Human-Level Control through Deep Reinforcement Learning," *Nature* 518 (2015): 529–533.

not yet possible, however, is either for one network to learn all the different games in serial while retaining all its competence, because the process of learning the games one at a time eventually results in the catastrophic forgetting of previous games, or for one network to learn all the different games in parallel, because the different rule sets interfere with each other. Of course, with a recognition of these limitations in place, there are strategies under development, such as a progressive chaining technique in which separate deep learning systems pass on relevant information to each other to scaffold learning, although this approach eventually runs aground on the intractability of the increasingly large model.[30] The point for us, however, is that it is arguable whether the AI systems on our roads and battlefields, and in our operating theaters, possess the kinds of generalization capacities that they will need, if we are to relinquish control to them.

Moreover—and now we are in the vicinity of the kinds of categorization errors noted earlier—Szegedy et al. have influentially demonstrated that deep learning neural networks are systematically prone to so-called *adversarial exemplars*.[31] Let's consider one of Szegedy et al.'s own examples, a network that had successfully learned to categorize images into two groups—"cars" and "not cars." The researchers proceeded to systematically generate a range of minutely altered images of cars. The deformations were very small changes made at the pixel level, meaning that, to the unaided human eye, the new images looked identical to other images to which the network had been exposed, and which it had learned to categorize correctly as cars. The in-advance prediction would surely have been that the network would correctly classify these altered images as cars. Surprisingly, however, it classified them as noncars, hence the status of those images as *adversarial* exemplars. Of course, armed with the knowledge that adversarial exemplars exist, designers can systematically generate such items and include them in their networks' training sets. But, especially given finite time constraints, there is surely a danger that the effect of this will be akin to flattening out a lump under a carpet. The lump will simply reappear somewhere else.

The overarching worry, then, is this. Deep learning networks, especially when navigating huge data sets, will no doubt perform ever more impressive feats of reasoning in complex and ethically sensitive domains. Thus we will find ourselves increasingly tempted to cede control to them. But those same networks will sometimes divide up the world in ways that do not coincide with our ways of dividing up the world, meaning that some of their decision-making will be divergent from ours and presumably opaque to us. (What was it about those few pixels that stopped that image being classifiable as a car?) This is troubling, because we have seen that a capacity for reliable categorization— more specifically, the consistent partitioning of the world into the categories that are ethically relevant for us (e.g., combatants and noncombatants)—is a necessary ability

[30] Andrei A. Rusu, Neil C. Rabinowitz, Guillaume Desjardins, Hubert Soyer, James Kirkpatrick, Koray Kavukcuoglu, Razvan Pascanu, and Raia Hadsell, "Progressive Neural Networks" (2016) arXiv:1606.04671.

[31] Christian Szegedy, Wojciech Zaremba, Ilya Sutskever, Joan Bruna, Dumitru Erhan, Ian Goodfellow, and Rob Fergus, "Intriguing Properties of Neural Networks" (2013), arXiv:1312.6199.

for any AI that is to enjoy even our milder kind of autonomy. The potential existence of unknown adversarial exemplars in the problem spaces in question, as those spaces are partitioned by deep learning networks, should at least make us pause to reflect on how close present AI systems are to meeting this constraint.

A FINAL TWIST

The point at which we relinquish control to AI is the point at which questions regarding our lack of a grip on precisely how certain contemporary AI architectures see the world, and thus on exactly what an autonomous intelligent machine deploying such an architecture in a safety-critical context characterized by uncertainty might do, become prompts for nervous apprehension. The precise path to the alleviation of that concern is not yet clear, but let's finish with a brief, admittedly speculative, suggestion that connects the two perspectives on autonomy that have been in view during this chapter.

In many of the ethically challenging scenarios canvassed in the case of autonomous weapons and self-driving cars, one part of the solution may be a machine that has knowledge of the consequences of its actions for sentient beings and is able to reflect on those consequences.[32] This capacity for assessment will be even more likely to prevent unknowing harm if it is deployed by an artificial agent that is able to arrive at its own "life plan" and then adaptively modify that plan in light of experiences and evidence. In other words, imbuing AI with the kind of ability that is required for our more demanding, full-strength variety of autonomy may be one way of addressing the concerns that accompany our less demanding, milder variety. Of course, there's a gigantic elephant in the room: what's needed is a fully autonomous artificial agent whose "life plan" is shaped not by psychopathic tendencies, but by a demonstrable understanding of, and empathy for, humankind. Some commentators remain skeptical about any such possibility.[33] However, there is a case to be made that, without that achievement in place, autonomy in the realm of the artificial, even in its milder register, is likely to remain a matter of controversy and anxiety.[34]

[32] Colin Allen, Gary Varner, and Jason Zinser, "Prolegomena to Any Future Artificial Moral Agent," *Journal of Experimental Theoretical Artificial Intelligence* 12 (2000): 251–261.

[33] See, e.g., Sharkey, "Autonomous Weapons Systems, Killer Robots and Human Dignity."

[34] Some short passages of text in this chapter were adapted from Michael Wheeler, "The Reappearing Tool: Transparency, Smart Technology, and the Extended Mind," *AI and Society* (published online February 7, 2018), https://doi.org/10.1007/s00146-018-0824-x. Many thanks to my student Laurie McMillan, who taught to be more optimistic about the possibility of a benign, fully autonomous AI.

BIBLIOGRAPHY

Allen, Colin, Gary Varner, and Jason Zinser. "Prolegomena to Any Future Artificial Moral Agent." *Journal of Experimental Theoretical Artificial Intelligence* 12 (2000): 251–261.

Arkin, Ronald C. "The Case for Ethical Autonomy in Unmanned Systems." *Journal of Military Ethics* 9(4) (2010): 332–341.

Boden, Margaret A., "Autonomy and Artificiality." In *The Philosophy of Artificial Life*, ed. Margaret A. Boden, 95–107. Oxford: Oxford University Press, 1996.

Bostrom, Nick. *Superintelligence: Paths, Dangers, Strategies.* Oxford: Oxford University Press, 2014.

Dennett, Daniel C. *Elbow Room: The Varieties of Free Will Worth Wanting.* Cambridge, MA: MIT Press, 1984.

Lin, Patrick. "Why Ethics Matters for Autonomous Cars." In *Autonomous Driving: Technical, Legal and Social Aspects*, ed. Markus Maurer, Chris Gerdes, Barbara Lenz, and Hermann Winner, 69–85. Berlin: Springer, 2016.

Mindell, David A. *Our Robots, Ourselves: Robotics and the Myths of Autonomy.* New York: Penguin, 2015.

Sharkey, Noel E. "Killing Made Easy: From Joysticks to Politics." In *Robot Ethics: The Ethical and Social Implications of Robotics*, ed. Patrick Lin, George Bekey, and Keith Abney. Cambridge, MA: MIT Press, 2012.

Sparrow, Robert. "Killer Robots." *Journal of Applied Philosophy* 24(1) (2007): 62–77.

Szegedy, Christian et al. "Intriguing Properties of Neural Networks." (2013), arXiv:1312.6199.

CHAPTER 19

TROUBLESHOOTING AI AND CONSENT

MEG LETA JONES AND ELIZABETH EDENBERG

INTRODUCTION

As a normative concept, consent can perform the "moral magic"[1] of transforming the moral relationship between two parties, rendering permissible otherwise impermissible actions. Yet, as a governance mechanism for achieving ethical data practices, consent has become strained—and AI has played no small part in its contentious state.

In this chapter we will describe how consent has become such a controversial component of data protection as artificial intelligence systems have proliferated in our everyday lives, highlighting five distinct issues. We will then lay out what we call consent's "moral core," which emphasizes five elements for meaningful consent. We next apply the moral core to AI systems, finding meaningful consent viable within a particular digital landscape. Finally, we discuss the forces driving some commentators away from individual consent and whether meaningful consent has a future in a smart world.

THE CONSENT CRISIS

The West has seen significant expansion of social practices defined by choosing.[2] It has been claimed that "people have no choice but to choose" in contemporary societies,[3] but

[1] Heidi M. Hurd, "Blaming the Victim: A Response to the Proposal that Criminal Law Recognize a General Defense of Contributory Responsibility," *Buffalo Criminal Law Review* 8 (2004): 503.

[2] Sophia Rosenfeld, "Free to Choose?," *The Nation* (June 3, 2014), https://www.thenation.com/article/free-choose/.

[3] Anthony Giddens, "Living in a Post-traditional Society," *Reflexive Modernization: Politics, Tradition and Aesthetics in the Modern Social Order* 56 (1994): 100.

just because choices are present does not mean consent is functioning as it ought. Stated broadly, an individual's consent involves an effective communication of an intentional transfer of rights and obligations between parties.[4] For consent to be morally transformative, we need more than simply to make (or be offered) a choice in the matter. We need a clear understanding of the normative background, the action proposed, viable alternatives, sufficient information, and the two parties to the consent transaction treating one another fairly.

While choice is not consent, its proliferation within data protection regimes tracks the proliferation of "choice societies" described by sociologists and historians, which is perhaps what leads to their frequent conflation. Data protection laws were a product of the government initiatives to investigate the social implications of automatic data processing in the 1960s and 1970s. In these first laws, consent played a minimal role, but as computable information was networked in the 1990s and the computer "user" was born, individual consent became an important strategy for both seeking ethical data practices as well as protecting data as a human right. Consent was one of the six legal bases for processing personal data in the 1995 European Union Data Protection Directive and remains one of the justifications for controlling or processing personal data in the EU, where the legal default is that personal data cannot be processed.

Because the definition of consent in the EU Data Protection Directive (Art .2(h)) was "any freely given specific and informed indication of his wishes by which the data subject signifies his agreement to personal data relating to him being processed," an implied consent, opt-out practice became standard over the same period. Additionally, the directive allowed the transfer of personal data to a third country without adequate data protection if the data subject consented (Art. 26(1)(a)). Meanwhile, the United States created a notice and choice regime through a series of negative public responses to third-party cookies,[5] state and federal investigations into data practices, and a strategy of platform self-regulation. Thus, until recently, both regimes have relied heavily on a notice and consent approach to achieve ethical data practices.

The flaws in this approach were clear quite early. A number of privacy researchers have produced powerful empirical evidence demonstrating the weaknesses of this approach and have developed various tools to improve it. Aleecia McDonald and Lorrie Cranor calculated that it would take, on average, two hundred hours or seventy-six work days to read the privacy policies one is exposed to in a year.[6] Joseph Turow and colleagues have repeatedly surveyed Americans revealing that they consistently and

---

[4] For more on the ethics of consent, see Franklin G. Miller and Alan Wertheimer, *The Ethics of Consent: Theory and Practice* (New York: Oxford University Press, 2010), and Andreas Müller and Peter Schaber, *The Routledge Handbook of the Ethics of Consent* (London: Routledge, 2018).

[5] Meg Leta Jones, "Revisiting Cookies: Statelessness to Doubleclick" (forthcoming, on file with author).

[6] Aleecia M. McDonald and Lorrie Faith Cranor, "The Cost of Reading Privacy Policies," *ISJLP* 4 (2008): 543.

inaccurately interpret the existence of a privacy policy as a signal of privacy protection.[7] Alessandro Acquisti and Jens Grossklags have performed of series of behavioral economic analyses on privacy decision-making revealing that individuals state that they care about privacy but make decisions to disclose personal data anyways (due to their lack of information and challenges with assessing long-term threats versus short-term benefits).[8] Sociologist James Rule criticized this collective system, highlighting the apparent pressure to use particular platforms and limited choices of alternatives.[9]

These flaws can be categorized into four issues: (1) too many policies; (2) lengthy and confusing terms; (3) inability to assess/predict outcomes/harms; and (4) limited alternative choices. Some of these studies involve sites and platforms that used AI techniques, but the hot term prior to AI was big data. The focus on big data was complexity and unpredictability of both findings and secondary uses. AI systems add further challenges due to their ability to autonomously learn, their opacity, and their displacement or restructuring of human engagement. AI systems thus exacerbate these four issues and add another: (5) new issues presented by consent in our "smart future."

The technological transition was subtle, and we do not leap ahead. We do not address consent to "general AI." Like most in this field, we refer to existing and approaching AI systems based on practiced machine learning techniques, namely, though not exclusively, layered neural networks deployed in a particular setting that learn by being trained on patterns in "big" contextualized data. Although contemporary AI systems rely on lots of data, it is specific data for a specific use. Machines "learn" on a training dataset and the conclusions drawn by the computer are only as good as the data going into the training. Boeing may have the most accurate data on retrofitted the winglets and data on paper jams may be spread across a number of companies, that data is not useful to recommending your next favorite audiobook or identifying spam. The techniques are generalizable technology, but the applications are not generalizable—like other automation advances, they can only do one thing. An AI system that can win at Go cannot recognize your cat. While we refer to AI "systems," we do not consider AI to exist in neatly designed systems but instead understand these AI systems as sociotechnical assemblages made up of various players, institutions, interests, personalities, localities, and moments. These systems are designed by people with particular backgrounds and motives in particular institutions for particular purposes. The AI systems rely on data, models, and organizational practices drawn from (and thus often also "infected" by) our existing social order and are thus no more "objective" or free from bias than the existing social orders. As such, when we ask about consent to AI systems, we are not asking about consent to

[7] Joseph Turow, Michael Hennessy, and Nora Draper, "Persistent Misperceptions: Americans' Misplaced Confidence in Privacy Policies, 2003–2015," Journal of Broadcasting & Electronic Media 62, no. 3 (2018): 461–478.

[8] Acquisti, Alessandro, and Jens Grossklags, "Privacy and Rationality in Individual Decision Making," IEEE Security & Privacy 3, no. 1 (2005): 26–33.

[9] James B. Rule, Privacy in Peril: How We Are Sacrificing a Fundamental Right in Exchange for Security and Convenience (Oxford: Oxford University Press, 2007).

learning systems broadly, but to particular, powerful, political, opaque arrangements of data use by more automated means.

Thus, the first two existing issues simply speak to the reach and complexity of AI systems. AI systems are used across existing sites, platforms, and services, which contribute to the large number of policies one confronts daily, but are also built into new "smart" efforts like smart cars, homes, offices, daily user security, health devices, and so forth. Google moved many of its services like YouTube recommendations and Google Assistant under the umbrella of the Google Brain project, which is a deep learning AI research team,[10] and the company's Sidewalk Labs has significantly expanded the implementation of AI beyond the common use in coordinating traffic lights.[11]

AI systems are no less challenging to explain to users than other data practices. In fact, their explainability is a major topic of scholarly research. Frank Pasquale's book *The Black Box Society* details the many ways in which secret algorithms shape our lives and argues for their transparency.[12] Margot Kaminski succinctly describes the debate as to whether there is a right to explainability under European data protection law and how it is to be implemented.[13] Much of the discussion around explainability has revolved around whether such explanation is possible.[14] Nonetheless, a group of engineers have been hard at work trying to make AI more transparent. Google Brain, for instance, has recently announced a "translator for humans" called the TCAV (Testing with Concept Activation Vectors) that explains to a user how much a specific concept (e.g., stripes, male) has played into the system's reasoning.[15] Others like Andrew Selbst and Solon Barocas have broken down the goals of explainability to reveal its limitations in providing normative critiques of AI systems.[16]

This ubiquity, complexity, and opaqueness contribute to users' inability to assess and predict outcomes and harms. Part of the claimed benefit of AI systems is that they produce insights and predictions that humans may or can not. As such, the rationality of choosing a service that touts an improvement to some aspect of one's life is clear when measured against unpredictable and incomprehensible long term future harms.

The limitation of choices is an issue that has changed over the course of computing history and is quite important to the prospect of regulation, as well as the efficacy of consent. Users may have many choices of providers, platforms, or services that undertake

[10] Robert McMillan,. "Inside the Artificial Brain That's Remaking the Google Empire," *Wired* (July 16, 2014), https://www.wired.com/2014/07/google-brain/.

[11] Sidney Fussell, "The City of the Future Is a Data-Collection Machine," *The Atlantic* (November 21, 2018), https://www.theatlantic.com/technology/archive/2018/11/google-sidewalk-labs/575551/.

[12] Frank Pasquale, *The Black Box Society* (Harvard University Press, 2015).

[13] Margot E. Kaminski, "The Right to Explanation, Explained," *Berkeley Technology Law Journal*, Vol. 34, forthcoming, 2019.

[14] Will Knight, "The Dark Secret at the Heart of AI," *MIT Technology Review* (April 11, 2017), https://www.technologyreview.com/s/604087/the-dark-secret-at-the-heart-of-ai/.

[15] Been Kim, Martin Wattenberg, Justin Gilmer, Carrie Cai, James Wexler, Fernanda Viegas, and Rory Sayres, "Interpretability beyond Feature Attribution: Quantitative Testing with Concept Activation Vectors (TCAV)," *arXiv preprint arXiv:1711.11279* (2017).

[16] Andrew D. Selbst, and Solon Barocas, "The Intuitive Appeal of Explainable Machines," *Fordham Law Review* 87 (2018): 1085.

the similar types of problematic data practices, which was the case for much of the mid-1990s and 2000s. Users may have few choices of platforms, which has become a complaint against internet service providers, Amazon, Facebook, and Google, in the 2010s. These services provide the user as much "choice" within the platform as they think beneficial, such as setting pages where users can opt out of certain data collection or sharing or erase data, dashboards on which users can fine-tune their choices, and privacy pop-ups that remind users how their information is currently being shared and how to change their settings. AI systems have not been the basis of these companies but have been used to help amass significant market power and attract the most talented engineers. For instance, Google Search became the most dominate search engine by developing algorithms that relied on a set of human-engineered definite rules, but in 2016, the search system began use deep learning to support functionality, sacrificing some control and clarity for efficiency and scalability.[17] Today, the company utilizes deep learning for Google Map's driving directions, its assistant application, YouTube's Safe Content setting, Smart Replies that suggest responses to texts and email, the Nest's outdoor security functionality, and its driverless car division Waymo.[18] Facebook utilizes deep learning to classify the immense amount of unstructured data (over 135,000 photos and almost 300,000 status updates from 1.2 billion users per minute), which enables the performance of textual analysis, facial recognition, and targeted advertising.[19] Amazon has used AI to provide product recommendations based on searches and purchases since the late 1990s, and more recently, machine learning also powers the popular home personal assistant device Alexa, the robots that maneuver its distribution warehouses, and the grab-and-go shopping experience in Amazon Go stores.[20] Privacy journalist Kashmir Hill undertook an experiment to understand her reliance on the "big five" (Microsoft, Google, Amazon, Facebook, and Apple), and the experience ranged from longing[21] to an "impossible"[22] "devastating"[23] "hell"[24] that

---

[17] Cade Metz, "AI Is Transforming Google Search. The Rest of the Web Is Next," *Wired* (February 4, 2016), https://www.wired.com/2016/02/ai-is-changing-the-technology-behind-google-searches/.

[18] Bernard Marr, "The Amazing Ways Google Uses Deep Learning AI," *Forbes* (August 8, 2017), https://www.forbes.com/sites/bernardmarr/2017/08/08/the-amazing-ways-how-google-uses-deep-learning-ai/#468611b43204.

[19] Bernard Marr, "4 Mind-Blowing Ways Facebook Uses Artificial Intelligence," *Forbes* (December 29, 2016).

[20] Daniel Terdiman, "How AI Is Helping Amazon Become a Trillion-Dollar Company," *Fast Company* (October 15, 2018), https://www.fastcompany.com/90246028/how-ai-is-helping-amazon-become-a-trillion-dollar-company.

[21] Kashmir Hill, "I Cut Facebook Out of My Life. Surprisingly, I Missed It," *Gizmodo* (January 24, 2019), https://gizmodo.com/i-cut-facebook-out-of-my-life-surprisingly-i-missed-i-1830565456.

[22] Kashmir Hill, "I Tried to Block Amazon from My Life. It Was Impossible," *Gizmodo* (January 22, 2019), https://gizmodo.com/i-tried-to-block-amazon-from-my-life-it-was-impossible-1830565336#_ga=2.52350880.882275658.1548823260–1494158073.1547676718.

[23] Kashmir Hill, "I Cut Apple Out of My Life. It Was Devastating," *Gizmodo* (February 5, 2019), https://gizmodo.com/i-cut-apple-out-of-my-life-it-was-devastating-1831063868.

[24] Kashmir Hill, "I Cut the 'Big Five' Tech Giants from My Life. It Was Hell," *Gizmodo* (February 7, 2019), https://gizmodo.com/i-cut-the-big-five-tech-giants-from-my-life-it-was-hel-1831304194.

"screwed up everything."[25] It is not clear what role privacy plays in American antitrust law,[26] but the issue has been placed firmly on the federal political agenda for the 116th Congress and the 2020 presidential campaign,[27] as well as a group of state attorneys general enforcement strategy.[28] Whether users can meaningfully consent to big tech's AI systems will certainly play an important role in the debate on whether and how to regulate.

The fifth issue relates to the way consent is currently communicated between parties. Existing consent transactions rely on personal devices that present a readable notice on the screen to the owner or operator and way for them to express consent.[29] Many AI systems are built into objects and environments that (1) do not have screens, and (2) interact with third parties. This departure away from screens on personal devices as the solitary means through which personal data is collected, shared, or processed requires new ways of communicating both notice and consent. Most importantly though it requires us to reconsider what consent, as distinct from consumer choice, means for a smart future.[30]

THE MORAL CORE OF CONSENT

James Grimmelmann has said, "We are having a national crisis of consent."[31] From sex to sports to criminal deals to medical procedures, consent is criticized for falling short of providing "a meaningful marker between autonomy and coercion."[32] In the context of social media experimentation, Grimmelmann calls for "enthusiastic consent" in order to eliminate the adversarial nature of online research.[33] Similarly relying on the rich history of bioethics, we have called for "cooperative consent" that emphasizes the bilateral

[25] Kashmir Hill, "I Cut Google Out of My Life. It Screwed Up Everything," *Gizmodo*, (January 29, 2019), https://gizmodo.com/i-cut-google-out-of-my-life-it-screwed-up-everything-1830565500#_ga=2.109788613.1339556351.1549309045–1494158073.1547676718.

[26] Jenny Lee, "The Google-DoubleClick Merger: A Lesson on the Federal Trade Commission's Limitations on Privacy." Under review, on file with author.

[27] Valerie Richardson, "Big Tech Unites Democrats, Republicans behind Anti-trust Crackdown," *Washington Times* (June 4, 2019), https://www.washingtontimes.com/news/2019/jun/4/josh-hawley-elizabeth-warren-united-big-tech-anti-/.

[28] Brian Fung, and Tony Romm, "Inside the Private Justice Department Meeting that Could Lead to New Investigations of Facebook, Google and Other Tech Giants," *Washington Post*, (September 25, 2018), https://www.washingtonpost.com/technology/2018/09/25/inside-big-meeting-federal-state-law-enforcement-that-signaled-new-willingness-investigate-tech-giants/?utm_term=.ba9509a4f186.

[29] Meg Leta Jones, "Your New Best Frenemy: Hello Barbie and Privacy without Screens," *Engaging Science, Technology, and Society* 2 (2016): 242–246.

[30] Meg Leta Jones, "Privacy Without Screens & the Internet of Other People's Things," *Idaho Law Review* 51 (2014): 639.

[31] James Grimmelmann, "The Law and Ethics of Experiments on Social Media Users," *Colorado Technical Law Journal* 13 (2015): 219.

[32] Catharine A. MacKinnon, *Toward a Feminist Theory of the State* (Harvard University Press, 1989).

[33] Grimmelmann, "The Law and Ethics of Experiments on Social Media Users."

nature of consent and gives due weight to the interests of both parties.[34] Whether enthusiastic or cooperative, consent must also exist within a well-understood landscape of other rights and obligations that support it as a meaningful marker. These other aspects that can make consent morally meaningful should not be neglected by overemphasis on the nature of its communicative power.[35]

We find the landscape that supports cooperative consent can be achieved by focusing on the moral core of consent, which consists of five elements: (1) clear delineation of the background conditions for permissible and impermissible uses of one's data (*background conditions*); (2) a defined scope of action (*scope*); (3) the consenter should be provided relevant information to understand what they consent to (*knowledge*); (4) freedom to choose among a set of viable options (*voluntariness*); and (5) the consenter should be treated fairly and should not be required to sacrifice other important rights (*fairness*).[36] We investigate each in turn as it relates to AI systems.

Background Conditions

For consent to transform what would otherwise be impermissible into a permissible action, we must have a clear understanding of the background conditions that set out the boundaries of permissible and impermissible action. For example, our right to bodily autonomy sets clear background conditions that underlie the importance of consent for sex to be permissible or for it to be permissible for a surgeon to operate. Likewise, our expectations of personal property set background assumptions in which car theft can be clearly distinguished from a friend borrowing a car by pointing to the owner's consent to a specific person for a specific use of that property.

Digital consent also requires a clear understanding of the background conditions specifying justifiable and unjustifiable collection, processing, sharing, and use of one's data. Establishing a clear background understanding about how people understand their interests and rights concerning one's digital trail requires a broad and inclusive public discussion. This will also require some additional public education about what information can currently be collected about individuals and groups in order to enable a more informed discussion about how society should treat our digital trails.

The rise of AI poses some additional challenges here—but they are not as insurmountable as long-view worries about artificial agents and superintelligence may suggest.[37]

[34] Meg Leta Jones, Elizabeth Edenberg, and Ellen Kaufman, "AI and the Ethics of Automating Consent." *IEEE Security & Privacy* 16, no. 3 (2018): 64–72.

[35] For an interesting discussion of what we can and should be able to consent to, see Nancy S. Kim, *Consentability: Consent and Its Limits* (Cambridge University Press, 2019).

[36] We've developed the moral core of digital consent in more detail in Elizabeth Edenberg and Meg Leta Jones, "Analyzing the Legal Roots and Moral Core of Digital Consent," *New Media & Society* (2019): 1461444819831321. Here we apply this specifically to AI.

[37] Nick Bostrom, *Superintelligence: Paths, Dangers, Strategies* (Oxford University Press, 2014).

As popular (and perhaps natural[38]) as it is to anthropomorphize computers that are artificially *intelligent* and machines that *learn*, AI is little more than a set of algorithms.[39] A computer learns through either supervised, unsupervised, or reinforcement learning. Supervised learning, currently most popularly undertaken, involves a system training on data labeled by humans at some point (these humans are not often supervised[40]). Other challenges lie in the "black box" of unsupervised learning in which the computer seeks hidden patterns to find correlations in the data sets—correlations that are not always easily translated back in a way that we humans understand how the computer arrived at the conclusion. Reinforcement learning refers to goal-oriented algorithms wherein an agent learns the best action model (the one that provides the most cumulative rewards) in an environment through trial and error, however, it is still the computer programmers who set these goals and create incentives.

The first step in navigating our expectations around what AI should be permitted to do requires broader education about what AI can do and realistic, inclusive discussions around the current use cases (and harms) of AI. Every citizen should know what AI really is doing and (roughly) how. We should discuss whether we think AI should play a role in criminal sentencing, what the standards should be for recommending news sources, and whether/when we have a right to opt out of our data being collected by Alexa, Siri, or the facial recognition cameras that surround us. These are all part of the background conditions relevant to whether and how consent plays a role in ethical AI practices.

It is particularly important to include diverse perspectives in both the discussions about how current practices impact individuals and communities and what interests are at stake for diverse groups.[41] We should approach these discussions with a sense of entitlement to renegotiate the emerging norms to better align the default background assumptions with our rights and interests (rather than accept as given the default settings built into current technologies which are currently set by those who build and deploy digital technologies).

Scope

In all of the examples in which consent has a clear normative force (from sex to surgery to transactions involving property), the scope of actions are clearly defined. A transfer

---

[38] Kate Darling, "'Who's Johnny?' Anthropomorphic Framing in Human-Robot Interaction, Integration, and Policy," in *Robot Ethics 2.0*, ed. Patrick Lin, Keith Abney, and Ryan Jenkins (Oxford University Press, 2017).

[39] For a fantastic introduction that breaks down how AI works for all those who are not computer scientists, see Meredith Broussard, *Artificial Unintelligence: How Computers Misunderstand the World* (MIT Press, 2018).

[40] James O'Malley, "Captcha If You Can: How You've Been Training AI for Years without Realising It," *techradar* (January 12, 2018), https://www.techradar.com/news/captcha-if-you-can-how-youve-been-training-ai-for-years-without-realising-it.

[41] For an informative discussion of the differential impact of digital technology, see Khiara M.Bridges, *The Poverty of Privacy Rights* (Stanford University Press, 2017).

of rights requires clear delineation of the scope of rights transferred, and mutual understanding between the parties of the scope and terms of permission granted. In each case of meaningful consent, the consentee agrees for a specific defined interruption of the usual inviolable rights over oneself, one's body, one's personal property. Embedding open-ended terms that seek "consent" to any possible or future use a company may have for data threaten the normative efficacy of any purported consent given. The scope and purposes of consent offered must be more narrowly specified and when terms change, a new consent transaction should be sought. Continued use of data requires continued authorization of the terms of the transaction and in most cases, the consenter (whose data is being used) retains the right to withdraw her consent at any time.

In some ways, AI offers additional complications to the already challenging delineation of the scope and terms of data collection in digital consent. AI systems tend to be both unpredictable and opaque—machine learning allows computer scientists to solve problems that have outstripped more traditional programming. AI technology also powers many components of the internet of things and our increasingly "smart" environments—from facial recognition to voice activation. In these environments, the usual "terms of service" that mediate digital consent to screen-based data exchanges are absent. However, none of this means we should give up on consent.

AI also offers some new ways to navigate a landscape of continual consent. AI could be built to explain the context and seek consent anew when terms change. It could also be leveraged on behalf of users acting as a personal privacy assistant mediating the negotiations over consent and use of data in the internet of things on behalf of an individual.[42] If AI is leveraged to provide users better information about the scope and terms of the proposed use of data, and assist them to have a viable capacity to opt out of the exchange, AI could help support users ability to navigate the digital world in control of what information is released to whom and for what purposes. This latter use of AI to help facilitate meaningful consent is a particularly exciting development where we see potential for new technology to ameliorate existing problems. If AI is built to support individuals' ability to keep abreast of the changing digital landscape, it can work on the side of individuals to help them address one important aspect of consent being part of a continual negotiation over authorized use of one's personal information.

Knowledge

Mutual understanding of the scope of the permission granted in the consent transaction requires that each party have a sufficient level of understanding of the terms of the transaction. This requires more than the one-way provision of information to the

---

[42] See, e.g., the work on the Personalized Privacy Assistant Project: Pardis Emami Naeini, Sruti Bhagavatula, Hana Habib, Martin Degeling, Lujo Bauer, Lorrie Faith Cranor, and Norman Sadeh, "Privacy Expectations and Preferences in an IoT World," in *Thirteenth Symposium on Usable Privacy and Security ({SOUPS} 2017)*, 399–412 (2017).

person who gives consent. To be morally meaningful, the provision of information should effectively relay the information in a form conducive to an individual understanding the information. In an ideal context, mutual understanding is built cooperatively in a context that allows parties to question aspects of the terms of the exchange that are not clear.

Existing terms of service are often written in legalese and are quite long and difficult to understand even if one were to take the time to carefully go over the policies outlined by the digital services we frequent. AI can complicate matters because so many decisions are hidden behind a "black box" of machine learning—hence the push towards explainability and making these decisions more transparent. More clarity should be offered about the training data used, goals set, and reinforcement training used to allow for critical assessment about the use of AI in particular contexts. Furthermore, as digital technology and AI expand their reach, we as society should demand better explanations to increase digital literacy of the public. Everyone needs to be equipped to make informed choices that can reflect their interests and this requires at least a baseline understanding of what we are asked to assess and consent to in any particular instance.

However, here too, the technology could be leveraged to move back towards a cooperative discussion of the proposed terms of data use. If built to support individuals (who are often seen as the data subjects), AI assistants could help bring back a two-party discussion that is more reflective of an ideal informed consent procedure. Rather than view information provision as a one-way provision of information to the consentee, AI could engage in real dialogue that allows for further questioning and clarification when asked. While voice recognition technologies have a long way to go, we can still ask that systems also be built to clearly explain the terms of data use in an accessible way, with options to ask questions and clarify meaning. Much like the commercial in which a curious child asks "Google" a series of questions opening up the wonders of the universe—we can demand the same level of clarity of explanation (and anticipate follow-up questions) for the basic terms of use of the data Google collects.

Voluntariness

In most interpersonal consent transactions, voluntariness is a necessary component for one's token of expressed consent to have normative force. When Jill is mugged at gunpoint, handing over her purse is not a voluntary gift. If the police were to stop the thief, Jack, he would have no recourse by saying that Jill gave him the purse even if Jill also said, "Here, take my purse." The expressed consent is insufficient if there was no viable option otherwise.

Current terms of digital consent often offer people services in exchange for their data. However the idea that individuals who don't want to exchange their data for access to "free" services can simply opt out is seriously challenged by the terms of contemporary society. Most jobs require some use of electronic or mobile connections, and we are not given an option to simply "opt out" of using the company's email or mobile phone.

In addition, while I can choose to not use Facebook, I cannot control when other people take and post my picture on their page.

These challenges only increase when we think about buildings or cities who use closed circuit cameras (enabled with facial recognition technology) to monitor our shared spaces, banks that use AI to calculate people's credit scores, the digital trail of credit card transactions that can be used to better market goods and services an individual is likely to buy. In a world so permeated by digital means of tracking and surveillance, opting out is often a luxury afforded to only a few. The viability of opting out puts significant pressure on the legitimacy of consent to many of the aspects of our digital infrastructure.

Nevertheless, we believe AI could be used to negotiate the terms of consent transactions to allow individuals to refuse any specific request for their image or data. By refusing consent, an individual is better afforded the ability to choose whether and when they wishes to share their image or data. To be effective, this requires the reciprocal recognition by those who create and use AI systems to allow for a viable refusal to participate. Because opting out creates gaps in the information a monitoring system has, there may be strong incentives to prevent or refuse opt-out options for individuals. But without an option otherwise, meaningful consent has not occurred. Omnibus, comprehensive regulation may be needed to allow viable options to refuse consent.[43] We should start to discuss ways to empower individuals to have more control over their image and data, but this also requires ensuring the ability to have meaningful options is offered to all citizens (and is not simply a luxury good for the few).

Opting out may have limited impacts (of course, no one individual's data is needed to make fairly reliable predictions about individuals who are similar), depending on the goals of the individual refusing to proffer data and how widespread such refusals become. In contexts with limited ability to truly opt out of the system, the final component of ensuring the transaction occurs under a fair system become more important.

Fairness

The final piece of the picture is to ensure that the consent transaction occurs within a fair context. Significant power imbalances and limited options to opt out of the current digital world put added pressure on society to ensure that the exchange and processing of personal information, including by AI, still treat all parties fairly. This will require using our collective power as citizens to insist on fair treatment by the major players that currently hold outsized power over the terms of digital exchange.

Looking at existing uses of AI in facial recognition, voice recognition, sentencing guidelines, and credit scores—existing injustices in our society are being reflected and amplified. As a rich body of research continues to show, AI is only as good as the training data on which it learns. A computer that is trained on historically biased data about, for

---

[43] A controversial aspect of the EU General Data Protection Regulation involves when services or access can be denied based on a lack of consent.

example, crime rates will "learn" the same patterns of racial and economic discrimination. Likewise facial recognition technology trained on mostly white faces will have trouble recognizing black faces.[44] On the flip side, an algorithm built on data collected by police interactions will have far more data about young black and Latino men, for example, than the white women living in the same city.[45] Research has also revealed that these systems are not used equally in society. Poor mothers[46] and minorities,[47] for example, are heavily surveilled populations.[48] Fairness must not be confused with accuracy or inclusion in systems that are wielded against those groups that have traditionally been dehumanized through automated treatment. Consent within these social contexts must rest upon a foundation of fairness.

POWER DYNAMICS

Consent has been called broken and unworkable, because it is challenging to provide actual notice, knowledge, or choice. But, recent events and scholarly insights have expanded the public's understanding of and rhetoric around data protection. The social dimensions of privacy have become tangible due to work highlighting: (1) the discriminatory nature and use[49] of AI systems like facial recognition[50] and search

[44] Joy Buolamwini, "AI, Ain't I a Woman?—Joy Buolamwini." Filmed [June 2018]. YouTube video, 00:30. Posted [June 2018], https://www.youtube.com/watch?v=QxuyfWoVV98; C-Span, "House Hearing on Facial Recognition Technology," *C-Span* video, 2:42:30, June 4, 2019, https://www.c-span.org/video/?461370–1/house-oversight-panel-holds-hearing-facial-recognition-technology.

[45] Andrew Guthrie Ferguson, *The Rise of Big Data Policing: Surveillance, Race, and the Future of Law Enforcement* (NYU Press, 2017).

[46] Bridges, *The Poverty of Privacy Rights*.

[47] "The Color of Surveillance: Government Monitoring of American Immigrants," Georgetown Law Center for Privacy and Technology (June 22, 2017), https://www.youtube.com/watch?v=j6lq7jTUD8A&list=PL2QPFPgZ63f89kg0Pti98EJLxaQi4w8L7/; Jeffrey A. Fowler, "Don't Smile for Surveillance: Why Airport Face Scans Are a Privacy Trap," *Washington Post* (June 10, 2019), https://www.washingtonpost.com/technology/2019/06/10/your-face-is-now-your-boarding-pass-thats-problem/?hpid=hp_rhp-top-table-main_fowler-1035 a.m.-hedwins%3Ahomepage%2Fstory-ans.

[48] Simone Browne, *Dark Matters: On the Surveillance of Blackness* (Duke University Press, 2015).

[49] Karen Hao, "AI Is Sending People to Jail—And Getting It Wrong," *MIT Technology Review* (January 21, 2019), https://www.technologyreview.com/s/612775/algorithms-criminal-justice-ai/; Paul Mozur, "One Month, 500,000 Face Scans: How China Is Using A.I. to Profile a Minority," *New York Times* (April 14, 2019), https://www.nytimes.com/2019/04/14/technology/china-surveillance-artificial-intelligence-racial-profiling.html; Natalia Vasilyeva, "Russia Demands Tinder Give User Data to Secret Services," *AP News* (June 3, 2019), https://www.apnews.com/103dc01ce19e48fd89cd32e083ca1e50.

[50] Steve Lohr, "Facial Recognition Is Accurate, If You're a White Guy," *New York Times* (February 9, 2018), https://www.nytimes.com/2018/02/09/technology/facial-recognition-race-artificial-intelligence.html; James Vincent, "Gender and Racial Bias Found in Amazon's Facial Recognition Technology (Again)," *The Verge* (January 25, 2019), https://www.theverge.com/2019/1/25/18197137/amazon-rekognition-facial-recognition-bias-race-gender.

results,[51] (2) the way personal data may be used to manipulate democratic processes,[52] and (3) the controversial environmental[53] and health[54] impacts produced by contemporary data practices.[55] Many commentators and privacy researchers have been tempted to leave consent behind as a means of achieving data protection.

Despite these social frames that expand the lens of data protection beyond the individual, the individual remains important in negotiating the terms of service that are acceptable to her. We see some signs of optimism in the ability of AI to be built to better enable the individual to exercise meaningful control over the way she negotiates the digital world. If AI is put on the side of individuals to help keep them better informed about the ways their data is being used, by whom, and for what purposes—AI can help enable a more effective and meaningful negotiation of the consent transaction. In the future, it could ideally move the digital consent back toward the kind of continual, cooperative framework that exists in ideal versions of interpersonal consent transactions in other contexts.

None of this means that we think the onus is on the individual alone—society has a major role to play, as we've shown, in better establishing a fair framework within which meaningful consent can occur. Yet the interpersonal model of consent remains important for individuals and society as a whole to effectively negotiate acceptable terms for

[51] Jackie Snow, "Bias Already Exists in Search Engine Results, and It's Only Going to Get Worse," *MIT Technology Review* (February 26, 2018), https://www.technologyreview.com/s/610275/meet-the-woman-who-searches-out-search-engines-bias-against-women-and-minorities/; Claire Cain Miller, "When Algorithms Discriminate," *New York Times* (July 9, 2015), https://www.nytimes.com/2015/07/10/upshot/when-algorithms-discriminate.html.

[52] Sean Illing, "Cambridge Analytica, the Shady Data Firm that Might Be a Key Trump-Russia Link, Explained," *Vox* (April 4, 2018), https://www.vox.com/policy-and-politics/2017/10/16/15657512/cambridge-analytica-facebook-alexander-nix-christopher-wylie; Alex Hern, "Cambridge Analytica Scandal 'Highlights Need for AI Regulation,'" *The Guardian* (April 15, 2018) https://www.theguardian.com/technology/2018/apr/16/cambridge-analytica-scandal-highlights-need-for-ai-regulation; Berit Anderson, "The Rise of the Weaponized AI Propaganda Machine," *Medium* (February 12, 2017), https://medium.com/join-scout/the-rise-of-the-weaponized-ai-propaganda-machine-86dac61668b.

[53] Stephan Schmidt, "The Dark Side of Cloud Computing: Soaring Carbon Emissions," *The Guardian* (April 30, 2010), https://www.theguardian.com/environment/2010/apr/30/cloud-computing-carbon-emissions; Daniel Shane, "Bitcoin Boom May Be a Disaster for the Environment," *CNN* (December 7, 2017), https://money.cnn.com/2017/12/07/technology/bitcoin-energy-environment/index.html.

[54] Perri Klass, "Is 'Digital Addiction' a Real Threat to Kids?," *New York Times* (May 20, 2019), https://www.nytimes.com/2019/05/20/well/family/is-digital-addiction-a-real-threat-to-kids.html; Joseph Archer, "Children Who Stare at a Screen for More than Seven Hours a Day Have Different Brain Structures," *The Telegraph* (December 10, 2018), https://www.telegraph.co.uk/technology/2018/12/10/seven-hours-screen-time-day-changes-structure-childs-brain-scientists/.

[55] These findings and claims are not without critics. See, e.g., Jesse Walker, "When Did We Get So Scared of 'Screen Time'?," *Reason* (June 2019), https://reason.com/2019/05/25/when-did-we-get-so-scared-of-screen-time/; Grace Dobush, "Why Parents Shouldn't Worry About Their Kid's Screen Time," *Fortune* (January 4, 2019), http://fortune.com/2019/01/04/parents-children-screen-time/; Diego Zuluaga, "Why Bitcoin Is Not an Environmental Catastrophe," *Cato Institute* (September 4, 2018), https://www.cato.org/blog/why-bitcoin-not-environmental-catastrophe; Robert Sharratt, "The Reports of Bitcoin Environmental Damage Are Garbage," *Medium* (January 25, 2019), https://medium.com/coinmonks/the-reports-of-bitcoin-environmental-damage-are-garbage-5a93d32c2d7.

the use of data. Clarity about the moral core of consent can offer specific guidance to show when and why current systems of notice and choice based "consent" fail to live up to morally justifiable standards. Along with the specificity of the failures of current practices comes some tools for demanding better. While AI poses additional challenges to existing practices of consent, it can also offer new tools for progress. With a clear understanding of then normative role of morally transformative consent, we can use AI's new capabilities to build AI systems that enable meaningful consent from individuals and a broader social structure that ensures fair and just treatment of groups.

ANOTHER MODEL

Thus far, we have been discussing the moral core of consent, drawing on the interpersonal models of consent from moral philosophy. This offers important guidelines for determining the legitimacy of consent and, we think, still offers useful paths forward for building more meaningful consent to AI systems. Yet the challenges posed by the limited exit options and the broader structural injustices that creep into current uses of AI suggest that we should also take a broader view. Here, too, this does not suggest giving up on consent. Rather, we turn instead to another area in which philosophical approaches to consent have been influential—political philosophy.

One of the problems we've outlined is that without viable alternatives, it may undermine an individual's reasonable ability to opt out and "consenting" may lack moral force. Fortunately, political philosophy may offer some useful models for progress. Political philosophers have frequently relied on models related to consent to secure the legitimacy of government authority, including hypothetical consent,[56] normative consent,[57] and Rawls's liberal principle of legitimacy.[58] These models all purport to authorize a broad range of actions a government can legitimately pursue but without relying on an (infeasible) option to live beyond the structure of a state.[59]

Consent, in political philosophy has some notable differences from the interpersonal model of consent, as it is understood in much of the literature on consent drawn from moral philosophy. Rather than envisioning the ideal consent situation to be two parties that are roughly symmetrically situated, political philosophers ask what could make the authority of the government legitimate for the individuals who are subject to this form

[56] See, e.g., classic social contract theorists like Hobbes, Locke, and Kant, as well as John Rawls's original position in John Rawls, *A Theory of Justice* (Cambridge, MA: Harvard University Press, 1999).

[57] David M. Estlund, *Democratic Authority: A Philosophical Framework* (Princeton: Princeton University Press, 2008).

[58] John Rawls, *Political Liberalism: Expanded Edition* (New York: Columbia University Press, 2005).

[59] Notable exceptions to this are philosophical anarchists like A. John Simmons and Robert Paul Wolff, who deny the possibility legitimate authority (A. John Simmons, "Philosophical Anarchism," in *Justification and Legitimacy: Essays on Rights and Obligations* (Cambridge: Cambridge University Press, 2001), and Robert Paul Wolff, *In Defense of Anarchism* (Berkeley: University of California Press, 1998 [1970]).

of collective authority. This has some notable parallels to the situation of individuals for the digital infrastructure that underlies many of our engagements with each other socially, at work, and as members of a political community. There is asymmetrical power between any one individual and the platforms that form the basic structure of our digital lives. Furthermore, while individual rights and interests are still important, these rights are best secured through a collective governance structure built to secure the rights of all. Philosophers ask, for example, what could we hypothetically consent to if we were all fairly situated as free and equal persons. The thought experiment does not assume that we are all free, equal, and hold symmetrical power in our existing world. Rather, by asking what people who were situated in a fair context would agree to as a governance structure, we can better identify paths to move us from our existing world that is characterized by structural injustices towards a more ideal and just society. Likewise, a similar thought experiment could help structure societies discussions about how we would like to structure our rights and interests in the digital sphere to provide us a guideline for what rights we think are important to protect as a collective body, while carving out fair structures for individuals to negotiate their individual preferences within this broader context.

Conclusion

Digital consent has been criticized as a meaningless, procedural act because users encounter so many different, long and complicated terms of service that do not help them effectively assess potential harms or threats. AI systems have played a role in exacerbating existing issues, creating new challenges, and presenting alternative solutions. Most of the critiques and cures for this broken arrangement address choice-making, not consent. As the United States debates whether and why to break up big tech and the European Union considers enforcement actions under General Data Protection Regulation and how to update its laws to address tracking techniques in a new AI-driven smart world, consent cannot be confused with choice. Consent must be defined by its moral core, involving: clear background conditions, defined scope, knowledge, voluntariness, and fairness. When consent meets these demands, it remains a powerful tool for contributing to meaningful data protection at the individual and societal levels.

BIBLIOGRAPHY

Bostrom, Nick. *Superintelligence: Paths, Dangers, Strategies*. Oxford: Oxford University Press, 2014.

Bridges, Khiara M. *The Poverty of Privacy Rights*. Stanford, CA: Stanford University Press, 2017.

Broussard, Meredith. *Artificial Unintelligence: How Computers Misunderstand the World*. Cambridge, MA: MIT Press, 2018.

Browne, Simone. *Dark Matters: On the Surveillance of Blackness*. Durham, NC: Duke University Press, 2015.

Ferguson, Andrew Guthrie. *The Rise of Big Data Policing: Surveillance, Race, and the Future of Law Enforcement*. New York: NYU Press, 2017.

Kim, Nancy S. *Consentability: Consent and Its Limits*. Cambridge: Cambridge University Press, 2019.

Miller, Franklin G., and Alan Wertheimer. *The Ethics of Consent: Theory and Practice*. New York: Oxford University Press, 2010.

Müller, Andreas, and Peter Schaber, eds. *The Routledge Handbook of the Ethics of Consent*. London: Routledge, 2018.

Pasquale, Frank. *The Black Box Society*. Cambridge, MA: Harvard University Press, 2015.

Rule, James B. *Privacy in Peril: How We Are Sacrificing a Fundamental Right in Exchange for Security and Convenience*. Oxford: Oxford University Press, 2007.

CHAPTER 20

....

IS HUMAN JUDGMENT NECESSARY?

Artificial Intelligence, Algorithmic Governance, and the Law

....

NORMAN W. SPAULDING

ARTIFICIAL intelligence is an empty signifier. The ubiquity with which the term is used is paired with deep ambiguity.[1] Notice, to begin with, the way the two words representing the concept function in relation to each other. They are, especially in contemporary usage, hierarchically arranged with the normative and futuristic attributes loaded into "intelligence." Human intelligence, or something even more god-like in its sophistication and comprehensiveness, is imagined at one and the same time to lie beyond reach, to be both ominously and alluringly within reach, and, since at least Alan Turing's AI "test," to set the framework for judging the "thinking" machines are supposed to do.[2] Intelligence, "deep learning," is what engineers have been after, and precisely at the expense or transcendence of artificiality. The less artificial a smart machine appears to be, the smarter it is presumed to be. This is the point of the Turing Test and the deception that defines it— to determine whether a machine that relies on the symbolic system of algorithmic syntax can trick us into believing it is "actually thinking" by virtue of the way it uses natural language, our basic symbolic system. When the trick works, we are supposedly in the presence of ~~artificial~~ INTELLIGENCE.

---

[1] See Jonathan Culler, *Ferdinand de Saussure*, rev. ed. (Ithaca, NY: Cornell University Press, 1986), 127–132.

[2] See Ed Finn, *What Algorithms Want: Imagination in the Age of Computing* (Cambridge, MA: MIT Press, 2017), 41; Robert Epstein, Gary Roberts, and Grace Beber eds., *Parsing the Turing Test: Philosophical and Methodological Issues in the Quest for the Thinking Computer* (New York: Springer Science + Business, 2009); James H. Moor ed., *The Turing Test: The Elusive Standard of Artificial Intelligence* (Boston: Kluwer Academic Publishers, 2003).

And yet the fact of mimesis and deception in AI should by all rights function as an important reminder of just how artificial the concept is. If the way we know a machine is "thinking" is that its use of language can deceive us, can seduce us with empty signifiers, we obviously aren't measuring or confirming machine intelligence directly. Even if we (humans) trick each other, betray even ourselves in the very process of attempting to make ourselves understood in speech, the deception should remind us of the artificiality of all symbolic systems, chief among them natural language. All symbolic systems invite us to act as if their abstractions are real, providing unmediated access to what they represent. As Jacques Lacan described in his Seminar on Edgar Allen Poe's story *The Purloined Letter*, "the signifier is a unique unit of being which, by its very nature, is the symbol of but an absence"—an absence we are ceaselessly trying to fill, to code.[3] In Poe's story no one can locate the Queen's letter despite increasingly invasive and comprehensive police searches of the Minister's hotel room. And in just this way it is "the signifier's displacement [that] determines subject's acts, destiny, refusals, blindnesses, success, fate...."[4] This is no less true, Lacan reminds us, when we are aware of the deception from the outset. "Were we to pursue a bit further our sense that we are being hoodwinked, we might soon begin to wonder whether—from the inaugural scene...to the descent into ridicule that seems to await the Minister at the story's conclusion—it is not, indeed, the fact that *everyone is duped* which gives us such pleasure here."[5]

Turing's point of course was that we can't measure directly—"intelligence" is an empty signifier despite all the different cognitive operations we take for granted as falling within its domain. And it is much the same for Lacan, who reminds us that the police charged with searching for the Queen's letter in Poe's short story—a letter they *know* the Minister has stolen and keeps in his hotel chamber—meticulously divide the chamber into a comprehensive grid, "an exhaustion of space," only to miss the letter hiding in plain sight:

> The division of the entire surface into numbered "compartments," which was the principle governing the operation, is presented to us as so accurate that "the fiftieth part of a line," it is said, could not escape the probing of the investigators.... We are spared none of the details concerning the procedures used in searching the space subjected to their investigation: from the division of that space into volumes from which the slightest bulk cannot escape detection, to needles probing soft cushions, and, given that they cannot simply sound the hard wood [for cavities], to an examination with a microscope to detect gimlet-dust

---

[3] Jacques Lacan, "Seminar on 'The Purloined Letter,'" *Écrits*, trans. Bruce Fink (New York: W.W. Norton & Co., 2006), 17. On Lacan's interest in cybernetics and code, see Lydia H. Liu, "The Cybernetic Unconscious: Rethinking Lacan, Poe, and French Theory," *Critical Inquiry* 36 (2010): 288–320.

[4] Lacan, "Seminar," at 21.   [5] *Id.* at 11 (emphasis added).

from any holes drilled in it, and even the slightest gaping in the joints [of the furniture].[6]

But this is all for naught. The police's "immutable notion of reality...the imbecility of the realist"—the very assumption that one can know a thing via "search," tightening a "network," scraping as much data from it as possible—is their undoing.[7] They sought to find the Queen's letter, confidently assuming they were systematically measuring the contents of the room for the letter, and so missed the fact that—letter in hand—what they were "turning over with their fingers... did not fit the description they had been given of it."[8] With their information "network tighten[ed] to the point that, not satisfied with shaking the pages of books, the police take to counting them," Lacan asks, "don't we see space itself shed its leaves like the letter?"[9] Space itself, bending to the abstractions of the symbolic.

The exuberant engineers and the venture capitalists driving the development of AI haven't focused on this humbling lesson from Turing's test any more than the police searching for the purloined letter appreciate the cipher that allows the letter to remain both right before their eyes, and yet invisible. They are busy polishing to high gloss what Terry Winograd decades ago called "the glistening simulacrum" of AI.[10] The capacity to fool or best a human user has become a pervasive (empirical and normative) metric for the automated systems AI runs.[11] This is true not only of language recognition systems, chatbots, and other such programs but of the AI deployed in the internet of things, the AI in "fully" automated machines (a self-driving car should be at least as competent and safe as a human driver, if not more so, a robot health assistant compassionate and medically professional enough to be trusted by the patient, etc.), and in the call for AI in the "ethical" programming of armed robots and other automated weapons systems to make real time, lethal, in-the-field judgments that comport with the standards of international

---

[6] *Id.* at 16–17.   [7] *Id.* at 17.   [8] *Id.* at 18.   [9] *Id.* at 17.

[10] Terry Winograd, "Thinking Machines: Can There Be? Are We?," in *The Foundations of Artificial Intelligence: A Sourcebook*, ed. Derek Partridge and Yorick Wilks (Cambridge: Cambridge University Press, 1990), 185. For a description of "computationalist evangelism," see also Finn, *What Algorithms Want*, 7–8, 49.

[11] See David J. Gunkel, *The Machine Question: Critical Perspectives on AI, Robots, and Ethics* (Cambridge, MA: MIT Press, 2012), 56–58; Merel Noorman and Deborah G. Johnson, "Negotiating Autonomy and Responsibility in Military Robots," *Ethics and Information Technology* 16 (2014): 52 ("Participants in the discourse [on autonomous weapons systems] use concepts like autonomy, learning, and decision-making metaphorically to characterize the envisioned robotic systems as having abilities comparable to familiar human abilities... The use of such metaphorical concepts may then suggest that the notion of increasingly autonomous robots requires little further explanation beyond referring to the corresponding human capacities."); Thomas Arnold and Matthias Scheutz, "Against the Moral Turing Test: Accountable Design and the Moral Reasoning of Autonomous Systems," *Ethics & Information Technology* 18 (2016): 103–115.

humanitarian law or some broader standard of ethical conduct.[12] It is even used to dupe experts, like pilots, into believing they are flying a different airplane.[13]

In all of these uses of AI the first word of the term generally loses, must lose, its semantic content. We are induced to misjudge, to forget, that machine intelligence is artificial, in some instances to conflate intelligence with other human capacities (empathy, kindness, solicitude, forbearance, humor, etc.), in others to concede that it is superhuman. Remarkable achievements are already on the market. So remarkable that there is debate not only about the moral *agency* but the supposed moral *patiency* of "thinking" machines—whether it is appropriate to consider them to be "mere" machines instead of beings to whom we owe moral duties.[14] To pose this question is to ask whether they are or should remain "artificial," and simultaneously, Lacan and others would remind us, to reify the concept of human identity as authentically natural . . . not cybernetic.[15]

If the discourse of patiency is addressed to a kind of benevolent parental anxiety about the investment of "intelligence" in machines, even more acute anxieties about the autonomy and cognitive superiority that travels with machine learning lurk in the profoundly vexed discourse of "enslavement." Here the concern is not patiency but robot domination, even parricide. Advocates of enslavement insist that as long as machines remain artificial and are properly coded for submissiveness, their intelligence can

---

[12] See, e.g., John P. Sullins, "RoboWarfare: Can Robots Be More Ethical Than Humans on the Battlefield?," *Ethics and Information Technology* 12 (2010): 263–275; Danton S. Char et al., "Implementing Machine Learning in Health Care—Addressing Ethical Challenges," *New England Journal of Medicine* 378 (2018): 982; Elizabeth E. Joh, "Private Security Robots, Artificial Intelligence, and Deadly Force," *U.C. Davis Law Review* 51 (2017): 584–585; Mark A. Geistfeld, "A Roadmap for Autonomous Vehicles: State Tort Liability, Automobile Insurance, and Federal Safety Regulation," *California Law Review* 105 (2017): 1629–1632. See also Dafni Lima, "Could AI Agents Be Held Criminally Liable: Artificial Intelligence and the Challenges for Criminal Law," *South Carolina Law Review* 69 (2018): 689–694; Margot Kaminski, "Authorship, Disrupted: AI Authors in Copyright and First Amendment Law," *U.C. Davis Law Review* 51 (2017): 593–596.

[13] This is apparently one element of the failure of the Boeing 737 Max airplane design. The flight characteristics are fundamentally different from earlier 737s because of the repositioning of larger engines on the wing. One purpose of the sophisticated software it runs is to make the plane "fly" as if this isn't true. So pilots can spend hundreds of hours flying the plane without learning how it would behave should the software fail. Carlos E. Perez, "AI Safety, Leaking Abstractions and Boeing's 737 Max 8," *Medium* (March 14, 2019), https://medium.com/intuitionmachine/ai-safety-leaking-abstractions-and-boeings-737-max-8-5d4b3b9bf0c3.

[14] See Gunkel, *The Machine Question*, 93–157; Joanna J. Bryson, "Patiency Is Not a Virtue: The Design of Intelligent Systems and Systems of Ethics," *Ethics and Information Technology* 20 (2018): 15–26; F. Patrick Hubbard, "Do Androids Dream: Personhood and Intelligent Artifacts," *Temple Law Review* 83 (2011): 418–433; Lawrence B. Solum, "Legal Personhood for Artificial Intelligences," *North Carolina Law Review* 70 (1992): 1255–1280.

[15] See Donna J. Harraway, "A Cyborg Manifesto: Science, Technology, and Socialist-Feminism in the Late Twentieth Century," in *Simians, Cyborgs and Women: The Reinvention of Nature* (New York: Routledge, 1991), 149–181. See also Hubert L. Dreyfus, "Why Heideggerian AI Failed and How Fixing It Would Require Making It More Heideggerian," in *Skillful Coping: Essays on the Phenomenology of Everyday Perception and Action*, ed. Mark A. Wrathall (Oxford: Oxford University Press, 2014), 258–259.

otherwise be optimized . . . to serve our needs.[16] But Asimov's Three Laws of Robotics have already been transgressed and some of the most technologically important advances in AI are in the field of autonomous weapons systems, so-called "killer robots."[17] Thus the question in coding servility is no longer whether people will die at the hands of robots. We will. The most consequential forms of judgment over human life will be reduced to algorithmic procedure and vested in autonomous, adaptive, machines—and not just on the battlefield, but in the AI that enables "predictive policing," data-driven healthcare diagnostics, robotic surgery, and automated transportation.[18] Already, over the last decade, we have been:

> living in a world where algorithms *adjudicate* more and more consequential decisions in our lives....Algorithms driven by vast troves of data, are the new power brokers in society.... Algorithms already have control of your money market funds, your stocks, and your retirement accounts. They'll soon decide who you talk to on phone calls; they will control the music that reaches your radio; they will decide your chances of getting [a] lifesaving organ transplant; and for millions of people, algorithms will make perhaps the largest decision in their life: choosing a spouse.... Such conclusions have led a number of commentators to argue that we are now entering an era of widespread *algorithmic governance*.[19]

But in the eyes of those who believe in coding servility, responsibility for these judgments can be assigned to human "masters" (whether designers or users) or, perhaps

---

[16] Gunkel, *The Machine Question*, 86.

[17] Armin Krishnan, *Killer Robots: Legality and Ethicality of Autonomous Weapons* (New York: Routledge, 2016), 7. Asimov's laws are: "'(1) A robot may not injure a human being or, through inaction, allow a human being to come to harm; (2) A robot must obey any orders given to it by human beings, except where such orders would conflict with the First Law; (3) A robot must protect its own existence as long as such protection does not conflict with the First or Second Laws.'" Gunkel, *The Machine Question*, 75.

[18] See Elizabeth E. Joh, "Automated Policing," *Ohio State Journal of Criminal Law* 15 (2018): 561–563; Mariano-Florentino Cuéllar, "Cyberdelegation and the Administrative State," in *Administrative Law from the Inside Out: Essays on Themes in the Work of Jerry L. Mashaw*, ed. Nicholas R. Parillo (Cambridge: Cambridge University Press, 2017), 144–150; Dawinder Sidhu, "Moneyball Sentencing," *Boston College Law Review* 56 (2015): 685–693; Jack M. Beard, "Autonomous Weapons and Human Responsibilities," *Georgetown Journal of International Law* 45 (2014): 622–634. For some, the real question is not the servility of machines, but human enslavement. Mark Coeckelbergh, "The Tragedy of the Master: Automation, Vulnerability, and Distance," *Ethics and Information Technology* 17 (2015): 219–229; Emma Rooksby, "How to Be a Responsible Slave: Managing the Use of Expert Information Systems," *Ethics and Information Technology* 11 (2009): 81–90 (describing problem of "epistemic enslavement" of human agent "relying on an expert information system to guide her" and losing "her status as an autonomous moral person" because her reliance "prevents her from performing some of those acts that are constitutive of moral reasoning").

[19] Rob Kitchin, "Thinking Critically About and Researching Algorithms," *Information, Communication and Society* 20 (2017): 15 (emphasis added) (internal quotations deleted); Finn, *What Algorithms Want*, 21 ("the age of the algorithm is... dominated by the figure of the algorithm as an ontological structure for understanding the universe"); ibid. 42–45 (describing our deepening dependence on "computational systems").

better yet, liquidated by the machine's asserted superiority to human judgment.[20] On the latter view, if errors and losses occur, including loss of life, they will at least be smaller in number than would have resulted if humans were still calling the shots. The fantasy that servility and intelligence can be combined without creating pathological dependencies in the master,[21] and the terror masked by the audacity with which the degraded metaphor of slavery is deployed, are yet more signs of the emptiness, ambivalent desire, and fixation invested in the signifier AI.

If the preceding structural linguistic observations about the oscillatory nature of the term and the rise of algorithmic governance still seem distant from the question of judgment, they should not. Going back at least as far as Immanuel Kant, judgment has been theorized as the capacity to combine or synthesize subject and predicate—that is, to logically express connections between concepts (abstractions) that connect to experience. To judge, on this view, is to build a symbolic system. Wayne Martin writes that, for Kant "[s]ubjectively, a judgment is the combination of representations—e.g., the concepts 'human' and 'mortal.' This subjective unity represents an objective unity: the belonging together, objectively and universally, of human beings and liability to death."[22] So too, we express a judgment in Kant's sense of the term in saying that "Socrates is wise."[23] The verb "is" functions as a "judgment-making copula."[24] Kant's theory of judgment thus turns principally on "[the] synthesis of sensory content under a concept."[25]

Kant contended that the synthesizing properties of predicative judgment formed a determinate cognitive process with the capacity to bridge the gap between representation and the noumenal world. For Lacan the symbolic system or "order" of language does not bridge this gap, it *expresses* it. Moreover, the subject is, for Lacan, formed in the acquisition of language, a symbolic order defined by errant, "leaky" abstraction from the real.[26] But enough, I hope, has been said to suggest the following propositions about judgment and artificial intelligence: (a) AI exists, but like any other signifier, identifying AI requires predicative judgments—synthetic, combinatorial judgments about the unifying qualities that constitute what it means to be artificially intelligent; (b) these judgments are not just descriptive in the sense of combining specific

---

[20] Cf. John Danaher, "Robots, Law, and the Retribution Gap," *Ethics and Information Technology* 18 (2016): 299–309, 305; Gunkel, *The Machine Question*, 103–105.

[21] See Rooksby, "How to Be a Responsible Slave."

[22] Wayne M. Martin, *Theories of Judgment: Psychology, Logic, Phenomenology* (Cambridge: Cambridge University Press 2006), 45.

[23] *Id.* at 8.   [24] *Id.* at 8.

[25] *Id.* at 55, 62. For elaboration on Kant's theory of judgment, see Barry Stroud, "Judgement, Self-Consciousness, Idealism," in *Seeing, Knowing, Understanding: Philosophical Essays* (Oxford: Oxford University Press, 2018), 128, 128–140; John Haugeland, "The Nature and Plausibility of Cognitivism," in *Having Thought: Essays in the Metaphysics of Mind* (Cambridge, MA: Harvard University Press, 1998), 9–45.

[26] Joel Spolsky, "The Law of Leaky Abstractions" (Nov. 11. 2002), https://www.joelonsoftware. com/2002/11/11/the-law-of-leaky-abstractions/ ("All non-trivial abstractions, to some degree, are leaky...Abstractions fail. Sometimes a little, sometimes a lot. There's leakage...abstractions do not really simplify our lives as much as they were meant to."). On the inevitable "gap" between sensory content and algorithmic concepts or models, see Finn, *What Algorithms Want*, 10, 23.

attributes associated with artificiality and intelligence or the sum of the conjunction and interaction of these attributes, they are normative, value laden, running directly to and perhaps altering the concept of what it means to be human; and (c) the judgments are challenging to make not just because of the technological indeterminacy and protean nature of the machine learning involved (the dominant elements of the concept of AI have changed with the conjunction of big data and neural networks in the twenty-first century), the judgments are also vexed by the ambivalent desires animating the concept itself (hence the combination of evangelical exuberance and terror, of saving lives and taking them, the illusion of realism, and the fetishism of "disruptive innovation").

In what follows I want to explore other aspects of the relationship between AI and judgment, holding the difficulty of defining it firmly in mind.[27] More is at stake than the predicative judgment of the concept of AI and the conceit according to which we purport to judge the performance of AI. What is at stake, I contend, is the form and function of human judgment. First, human judgment occurs *in* AI in the sense that judgment must be exercised in coding AI, but some of the most consequential forms of judgment can be suppressed or tacitly embedded in the formal rigor of algorithmic syntax.[28] Second, whether or not we can conclude that systems running AI "make" judgments in a deep sense (as opposed to concluding that these systems more or less reflexively "process" inputs according to algorithmic syntax), there is no doubt that *human* judgment is displaced by AI—machines increasingly perform functions that previously required the exercise of human judgment. The displacement of human judgment is a key attribute of the market driving AI innovation, so much so that it influences even alternatives designed to enhance human judgment.[29] Third, the internal actions taken by some of the most promising and important forms of AI currently in use are currently too enigmatic to support human judgment, raising questions about transparency, supervision, accountability, and deception.[30] Fourth, in certain domains, perhaps especially the law,

[27] Legal scholars have generally concentrated on the relationship between artificial intelligence and specific doctrines, areas of law, or legal principles. See, e.g., Emily Berman, "A Government of Law and Not of Machines," *Boston University Law Review* 98 (2018): 1309–1331; Ryan Calo, "Artificial Intelligence Policy: A Primer and Roadmap," *U.C. Davis Law Review* 51 (2017): 427–431; Andrea Roth, "Trial by Machine," *Georgetown Law Journal* 104 (2016): 1296–1303. Others have begun to assess the implications of artificial intelligence for the exercise of formal legal judgment, see, e.g., Frank Pasquale, "A Rule of Persons, Not Machines: The Limits of Legal Automation," *George Washington Law Review* 87 (2019): 44–54; Eugene Volokh, "Chief Justice Robots," *Duke Law Journal* 68 (2019): 1156–1178. Less attention has been paid to the forms of judgment embedded in the design of artificial intelligence, and to the broader relationship between artificial intelligence and human judgment.

[28] See, e.g., Virginia Eubank, *Automating Inequality: How High-Tech Tools Profile, Police, and Punish the Poor* (New York: St. Martin's Press, 2018), 127–173; Calo, "Artificial Intelligence Policy," 415, 430; Danielle Citron, "Technological Due Process," *Washington University Law Review* 85 (2008): 1281–1298.

[29] See, e.g., Cuéllar, "Cyberdelegation," 144–150; Seth Katsuya Endo, "Technological Opacity & Procedural Injustice," *Boston College Law Review* 59 (2018): 851–857.

[30] See, e.g., Cuéllar, "Cyberdelegation," 144–150; David Lehr and Paul Ohm, "Playing with Data: What Legal Scholars Should Learn About Machine Learning," *U.C. Davis Law Review* 51 (2017): 705–710; Joshua Kroll et al., "Accountable Algorithms," *University of Pennsylvania Law Review* 165 (2017): 656–674; Danielle Keats Citron and Frank Pasquale, "The Scored Society: Due Process for Automated Predictions," *Washington Law Review* 89 (2014): 10–16.

human judgment appears to be altered by dependence on AI because of the way it affects the epistemological terrain in which human judgment occurs. I close by inquiring if, notwithstanding these limitations of AI systems, there is anything in the nature of either judgment itself or liberal democratic governance that requires that humans exercise it. I use judgments about resistance to law to show that, in a free society, the conditions for human judgment must be preserved.

ALGORITHMIC JUDGMENT

Algorithms embody a wide range of judgments at the level of design, but they are frequently characterized as a pure product of the forms of rationalist exactitude that define code as a symbolic system. Rob Kitchin puts the point bluntly: Algorithmic "processes of translation are often portrayed as technical, benign and commonsensical. This is how algorithms are mostly presented by computer scientists and technology companies: that they are 'purely formal beings of reason.'"[31] Presentation parallels the processes by which coding is taught: "in computer science texts the focus is centered on how to design an algorithm, determine its efficiency and prove its optimality from a purely technical perspective."[32] Algorithms are characterized and "understood 'to be strictly rational concerns, marrying the certainties of mathematics with the objectivity of technology.'"[33] This framing, however effective in producing technically proficient coders, suppresses the respects in which "'[c]ode is not purely abstract and mathematical,'" the extent to which it "has significant social, political, and aesthetic dimensions" arising from a range of constraints.[34] These include judgments about:

1. how to characterize the relevant task;
2. "translating a task or problem into a structured formula with an appropriate rule set";
3. "translating this pseudo-code into a source code that when compiled will perform the task or solve the problem";
4. how to deal with time and resource constraints for the design and execution of the project;
5. "the choice and quality of training data";
6. how to deal with "requirements relating to standards, protocols and the law"; and
7. how to manage "conditionalities related to hardware, platforms, bandwidth, and languages."[35]

---

[31] Kitchin, "Thinking Critically," 17.   [32] *Id.* at 17.   [33] *Id.* at 17.
[34] *Id.* at 17.   [35] *Id.* at 17–18.

Thus the "if x/then y" of Boolean logic and algorithmic syntax can function only in the context of a series of judgments of remarkable complexity.[36] "In reality...a great deal of expertise, judgment, choice, and constraints are exercised in producing algorithms."[37] Algorithms are also "created for purposes that are often far from neutral: to create value and capital; to nudge behavior and structure preferences in a certain way; and to identify, sort, and classify people...to seduce, coerce, discipline, regulate, and control."[38] They are "profoundly performative" as they "construct and implement regimes of power and knowledge."[39]

Kraemer, van Overveld, and Peterson offer a concrete example of the way value judgments are embedded within algorithms used in medical imaging technologies.[40] These technologies generate representations of "human biological structures in computers in an accurate way" in order to "improve the diagnostic or therapeutic prospects of diseases affecting the biological structures in question."[41] Because "[f]or all practical means, it is virtually impossible to totally eliminate the risk of getting false positives and false negatives"—because of the gap between symbolic systems and what they purport to represent—software designers "have to make a trade-off between minimizing the number of false positives or the number of false negative results. This trade-off will inevitably be based on a value-judgment...about whether it is more desirable to avoid" one or the other, and both results "may give rise to severe negative effects for individual patients."[42]

The authors show how MR-scans depicting a cross section of the human heart, used to diagnose "a variety of possible pathologies," require algorithms to accurately estimate the blood volume of the heart during various stages of a heart-beat cycle. The difference between blood and heart muscle tissues occurs as a difference in grey values in MR images.[43] In a process called "segmentation" the algorithm estimates blood volume by "counting the number of pixels" in the "part of the image...colored lighter grey" and applying a numerical "threshold" to separate those labeled "light" and those labeled "dark."[44] But the "border between light and dark areas is...not sharp" and "*[t]here is no a priori correct value for such thresholds*" because the "noise in the image is an inevitable artifact of the MR measuring process, caused by numerous non-modeled sources."[45] The choice of the threshold will "affect further values" in the software's depiction of estimated blood volume, "and eventually the diagnosis."[46] In clear-cut cases, the choice of threshold will not matter, but in the "grey zone" between healthy and pathological cases, the "diagnostic outcome will critically depend on the threshold[]."[47] And there is no getting around setting a threshold. A threshold favoring false positives will reduce the error

---

[36] E.g., "the relevant task is _," "the relevant data is _," "the relevant contingencies are _," "x is _," "y is _."

[37] Kitchin, "Thinking Critically," 18.   [38] *Id.* at 18–19.   [39] *Id.* at 19.

[40] Felicitas Kraemer, Kees van Overveld, and Martin Peterson, "Is There an Ethics of Algorithms," *Ethics and Information Technology* 13 (2010): 251–260.

[41] *Id.* at 254.   [42] *Id.* at 254–255.   [43] *Id.* at 255.   [44] *Id.* at 255.

[45] *Id.* at 255 (emphasis added).   [46] *Id.* at 255.   [47] *Id.* at 255.

of "believing that someone who is in fact ill is healthy."[48] It therefore comports with the precautionary principle.[49] But it could lead to "too many unnecessary and potentially dangerous operations" and, in order to further scientific research, scientists "generally agree that it is more important to avoid false positives than false negatives."[50] The key is that any threshold will reflect a judgment about whether, under the circumstances, it is better to favor false positives or false negatives—a judgment that straddles the structural tension between a doctor's duty of care to her current patients and the imperatives of advancing medical research to develop new treatments for future patients.

The authors report that when setting thresholds, software engineers "typically choose a value that 'seems reasonable.'"[51] Expert users of the imaging, for their part, may have no direct awareness of the thresholds. Indeed, the purpose of the complex algorithms is to present the medical experts in the field with the data "as if it is an actual photo of some 3-D internal organ or tissue structure."[52] It is accordingly "very difficult not to interpret a realistically looking 3-D image as a trustworthy projection of a 3-D object. This introduces the risk that one will forget that in order to generate these 3-D images, a number of decisions about thresholds had to be taken."[53] Value judgments are thus not only inevitable but are not necessarily recognized as such (by designers) or transparently communicated (even to expert users).[54] This is true even in an AI system whose very purpose is to amplify the transparency of the object to which professional judgment will be applied.[55] Both designer and user are instead lured by rationalist exactitude to miss these judgments even as they are embedded in the code and downstream diagnostic and therapeutic judgments. The value judgments, like the purloined letter, sit hiding in plain sight.

A less commonly noticed feature of threshold setting in AI systems that displace legal judgment is that they generally encode the most determinate version of the relevant

---

[48] Id. at 257.   [49] Id. at 257.   [50] Id. at 257.
[51] Id. at 255.   [52] Id. at 256.   [53] Id. at 256.
[54] Id. at 256. Others contend that AI systems can be designed to promote transparency with appropriate regulatory oversight. Amy Merrick, "How Making Algorithms Transparent Can Promote Equity," Chicago Booth Review (April 24, 2019), http://review.chicagobooth.edu/economics/2019/article/how-making-algorithms-transparent-can-promote-equity (describing research arguing that "with the right regulations in place, algorithms could be more transparent than human cognition... [because] certain elements of algorithmic decision-making—such as the inputs used to make predictions and the outcomes algorithms are designed to estimate—are inherently explicit").
[55] "Threshold" setting problems are pervasive in search technologies being adopted by professionals. The machine learning algorithms third-party vendors are selling to lawyers to conduct discovery of massive digital files to locate potentially relevant evidence in response to subpoenas and other production requests depend on initial thresholds set by training on a small portion. See infra, note 69. They can also be found in fully autonomous systems, such as the threshold of confidence in distinguishing civilians from enemy combatants prior to targeting. Mark S. Swiatek, "Intending to Err: The Ethical Challenge of Lethal, Autonomous Systems," Ethics and Information Technology 14 (2012): 241–254, 247. Noise cannot be fully eliminated not least of all because of deception (some combatants disguise themselves as civilians) and situational indeterminacy (some civilians may wear clothing or innocently behave in ways that nevertheless "code" as hostile). Any decision about acceptable levels of collateral damage requires value judgments. See Amanda Sharkey, "Autonomous Weapons Systems, Killer Robots, and Human Dignity," Ethics and Information Technology 21 (2018): 85.

substantive and procedural law.[56] Much of this follows from, on the one hand, a conjunction of coding cost and design constraints (the need to identify the most efficiently codable characterization of the relevant law), and, marketing constraints, on the other hand. To market a tax preparation software product that laypersons who do not have the money to pay a tax expert will buy, *and* keep the code adequately cost effective to design, the product will seek to minimize the risk of being audited.[57] To market software that helps architects and contractors file design plans the product needs to ensure prompt approval by city planning commissions and avoid revisions.[58] To market or publicly distribute online legal document preparation services, the structure of questions the user fills out will be designed to ensure enforceability of the contract, will, articles of incorporation, or marital dissolution papers without litigation. And so on. There is, in short, structural pressure to code law conservatively. Publicly subsidized systems face even tighter constraints since court systems have to internalize the costs of litigation if the documents are challenged.

At first glance this conservatism may seem optimal as it means that AI systems default toward compliance with law. But in a democratic society, particularly one defined by deep value pluralism, suspicion of centralized state authority, profound income inequality, and legal indeterminacy, conservative coding amplifies compliance without identifying the value judgments underlying this outcome. At the micro level, conservative coding fails to account for variation in individual risk tolerance (e.g., for users who might, all things considered, prefer a more aggressive legal position that an expert could assure her is safe from challenge or at least safe from protracted litigation if challenged). At the macro level, channeling users into reflexive compliance likely diminishes resistance to law—a practice free societies treat as a natural right and have recognized in certain substantive and procedural aspects of positive law. These costs have to be weighed against the benefits of far wider access to legal services and far greater efficiency in areas of the law that require mass processing of claims. The point for present purposes is just that

[56] Cf. Berman, "A Government of Laws," 1305–1309; Citron, "Technological Due Process," 1297–1298.

[57] Since 2008, Intuit's product TurboTax has offered access to an "Audit Risk Meter" to those who pay for premium services. Terry Savage, "New TurboTax Helps You Fly Under the IRS Radar," *The Street* (February 8. 2008). The Green and Red ends of the risk spectrum ostensibly provide information about risk of exposure to an audit, but what the user would need to know to make an informed decision about how aggressive to be is not just this, but whether the position that could trigger an audit is likely to be upheld. From a design perspective, the "meter" is likely to induce people to take conservative tax positions in their filings. https://www.thestreet.com/story/10402683/1/new-turbotax-helps-you-fly-under-irs-radar.html. Software designers have not only lobbied to prevent the IRS and state tax agencies from providing free online tax filing services, they have also used "dark patterns" in their own products to bait consumers who are entitled to free tax-filing services into paying a fee. Justin Elliott and Lucas Waldron, "Here's How TurboTax Just Tricked You into Paying to File Your Taxes," *ProPublica* (April 22, 2019), https://www.propublica.org/article/turbotax-just-tricked-you-into-paying-to-file-your-taxes.

[58] See Michael Kilkelly, "Building Code Review Software Feasible or Far-Fetched?," *Architect* (August 27, 2018), https://www.architectmagazine.com/technology/building-code-review-software-feasible-or-far-fetched_o.

coding invariably requires judgments that extend beyond the purely technical decisions that go into software design

THE DISPLACEMENT OF HUMAN JUDGMENT

The displacement of human judgment in AI systems is already suggested in the imaging and legal document preparation examples above. It is even more obviously displaced in automated systems such as self-driving cars and autonomous weapons systems where the principal design objective is to delegate a comprehensive set of complex tasks traditionally requiring the exercise of human judgment to autonomous, adaptive, action-executing machines. There is no human "driver" of a "self-driving" car. With the exception of a few high order controls (e.g., setting or altering a destination), human users are mere passengers, relieved of the burdens of decision that accompany driving. So too, the assumption embedded in the laws of war that "decisions about whether or not to kill are made by humans... is rapidly becoming naïve."[59] Decisions about what to target, whether to deploy force, and the appropriate level of force are increasingly "determined by [a] machine's own software, or the software of a command computer in a remote location, and... these actions are not under the direct control of a human operator."[60]

In the domain of law, autonomous machine decision-making is transforming adjudication.[61] Technologies range from automated compliance and monitoring software that reports breaches of contracts, to chatbots and other natural language interfaces that automatically fill out and in some instances file legal documents, to a range of automated dispute resolution systems (e.g., online "blind bidding" to reconcile competing confidential settlement offers, automated negotiation software using AI to calculate dispute resolution outcomes that maximize the preferences of both sides, and customized, automated systems designed to resolve customer to customer and customer to corporation disputes).[62] Boolean search algorithms have already transformed legal research. And software designed to create legal documents operates pervasively in settings outside formal adjudication that traditionally required the exercise of professional judgment. Indeed, there is currently a far larger market for automation of the drafting of legal instruments such as contracts, wills, and articles of incorporation, than for online dispute resolution.

---

[59] Sullins, "RoboWarfare," 264.   [60] Id. at, 264.
[61] See Cuéllar, "Cyberdelegation," 144–157; Cary Coglianese and David Lehr, "Regulating by Robot: Administrative Decision Making in the Machine-Learning Era," *Georgetown Law Journal* 105 (2017): 1160–1176; Gerald K. Ray and Jeffrey S. Lubbers, "A Government Success Story: How Data Analysis by the Social Security Appeals Council (with a Push from the Administrative Conference of the United States) Is Transforming Social Security Disability Adjudication," *George Washington Law Review* 83 (2015): 1593–1599.
[62] See Thompson Reuters, *The Impact of Online Dispute Resolution Technology on Dispute Resolution in the UK* (Spring 2016), 7–8.

Each of these technologies requires complex design judgments about legal issues such as the nature of legally salient performative utterances, what constitutes legally competent fact investigation and assessment, what constitutes compliance or noncompliance with law or the terms of a contract, what body of substantive and procedural law applies to the relevant social action, whether default legal rules can be legitimately set aside by contract, what threshold of legal certainty should apply, and so forth. Most significantly for present purposes, although many software programmers in this field work closely with legal experts to address these issues in the design phase (in some cases the programmers are agents of court systems), some do not (indeed, as a matter of principle they believe that legal experts are dysfunctional, rent-seeking experts who are an impediment to access to justice),[63] and the model for the use of AI is generally predicated on eliminating the cost, delay, error, and biases associated with having to rely on the human judgment of legal experts in the performance of legal tasks (much as Uber seeks to replace not only cab drivers and dispatchers but to fundamentally disrupt an entire segment of the public transportation industry). Automated weapons systems at least in theory operate within a chain of command that requires some level of supervision by military experts in their design and use. But the whole point of an online chatbot that generates legal documents for any person to use is that no supervision is required in its use (in the form of a lawyer who would have to be paid for her judgment and expertise).[64]

Even outside the domain of fully automated and autonomous systems, biometric surveillance, identification, access, and security systems operating on algorithms displace the human judgments that would be involved in posting a guard or selectively distributing keys, key cards, passports, and similar instruments. Avi Marciano reports that "biometric technologies are increasingly involved in automatic decision-making, with little or no human intervention."[65] Job applicants in the gig economy now face a wide range of automated systems that operate as sorting tools performing functions recruiters and human resource departments used to do. These include algorithms that scan CVs for keywords as a predicate to being referred to or considered directly by an employer as well as an evolving series of automated quizzes, psychometric tests, games, and chatbots that can reject applicants before a human ever glances at a CV. HireVue is a screening product reportedly used by Goldman Sachs and Unilever that places candidates in front of a camera to answer interview questions while its software "like a team of hawk-eyed psychologists hiding behind a mirror, takes note of barely perceptible changes in

---

[63] See Victor Li, "Joshua Browder: His 'Chat' Is Not Just Talk," *Legal Rebels* (September 14, 2017), http://www.abajournal.com/legalrebels/article/joshua_browder_donotpay_legal_chatbot. Their criticism of the legal profession's systemic failure to meet the needs of low- and middle-income people is not ungrounded. See Deborah L. Rhode, *Access to Justice* (Oxford: Oxford University Press, 2004).

[64] Cf. John Markoff, "The End of Lawyers? Not So Fast," *New York Times* (January 4, 2016) (gathering research showing the limitations of AI in replacing tasks performed by lawyers).

[65] Avi Marciano, "Reframing Biometric Surveillance: From a Means of Inspection to a Form of Control," *Ethics and Information Technology* 21 (2018): 1227–1136.

posture, facial expression and vocal tone."[66] The answers are broken down into "'many thousands of data points,'" and the data reduced to a score "which is then compared against one the program has already 'learned' from top performing employees."[67] An ultimate hiring decision will be made by a human after live interviews, but thousands of sorting decisions along the way are algorithmically determined and executed.

Predictive policing systems that "map" crime can be analogized to, and derive in a sense from, nondigital investigative techniques and cartographic "georeferencing," but their analytic power derives from the capacity of sophisticated software programs to rapidly identify "hot spots," to "measure the level of social cohesion" in different cities, and to create techniques for instantaneously synthesizing and visually representing disparate data sets (e.g., crime location and the identity of the owners of specific buildings in and across neighborhoods) to support decisions about patrols, investigation, and enforcement.[68] Finally, Technology Assisted Review is a form of "predictive coding" that uses machine learning to "harness human judgments of one or more [expert lawyers] on a smaller set of Documents and then extrapolate[] those judgments to the remaining Document Collection."[69] The machine learning is then used to "emulate" what a lawyer's decision-making process about the potential legal relevance of individual files would have been as applied to massive caches of documents.

This is Janus-faced technology. On the one hand, as with some of the other examples, it appears to enhance human judgment by distilling relevant documents more rapidly and in some respects more comprehensively than lawyers can by reading them. On the other hand, it has eliminated some forms of document review work performed by lawyers. There are cost savings in this, but in complex cases there is now no lawyer or group of lawyers who have personally reviewed anything approaching a majority of the files. The epistemological framework of the lawyers' understanding of the facts in cases where Technology Assisted Review occurs is thus algorithmically determined. Training a machine to look for keywords or patterns of keywords can quickly surface revealing patterns and documents of obvious and probable relevance, but missing files and euphemistic, paraphrastic, ironic, sardonic, and evasive use of language in the files that affirm or deny what a keyword represents may slip through the network like the purloined letter.[70] So too ciphers, slips, unexpected new facts connected to existing or unexpected

---

[66] Stephen Buranyi, "How to Persuade a Robot That You Should Get the Job," *The Observer* (March 3, 2018), https://www.theguardian.com/technology/2018/mar/04/robots-screen-candidates-for-jobs-artificial-intelligence.

[67] *Id.*

[68] Gemma Galdon Clavell, "Exploring the Ethical, Organizational, and Technological Challenges of Crime Mapping: A Critical Approach to Urban Safety Technologies," *Ethics and Information Technology* 20 (2018): 273–274.

[69] Paul Burns and Mindy Morton, "Technology-Assisted Review: The Judicial Pioneers," *The Sedona Conference* 3 (March 2014). Courts have approved the use of TAR. See Da Silva Moore v. Publicis Group & MSL Grp., 287 F.R.D. 182 (S.D.N.Y. 2012).

[70] On the technical barriers in this area, see Will Knight, "AI's Language Problem," *MIT Technology Review* (August 9, 2016), https://www.technologyreview.com/s/602094/ais-language-problem/. Some headway is being made with respect to hyperbole, a form of speech that is quantifiable when

new legal claims as well as other semantic content discernable only with the grasp of "unspoken background"[71] achieved by reading. Technology Assisted Review search methods thus create a different field of legal judgment—one as to which downstream judgments concerning the legal significance of the relevant facts depend on the algorithmic determination of what constitutes a relevant fact.[72]

AI is thus capable of partially (and in a widening array of circumstances completely) displacing postdesign human judgment by swapping algorithmic analysis and machine learning for tasks that used to require human judgment, both lay and expert. This displacement occurs largely irrespective of whether the processing that a machine does to complete these tasks bears any resemblance to the form in which human judgment is exercised. In some instances, especially those in which neural networks are used, the way AI systems reach conclusions is in fact deeply enigmatic—the core features of the system are "black boxes" that cannot be reverse-engineered even by the designers who build them.[73] What gets assessed is instead whether (observable) outcomes are comparable to or better than (observable) outcomes resulting from human judgment.

In other respects, what we do know suggests that many AI systems process information differently from human judgment.[74] First, AI systems can search and internalize vast amounts of data, apply Bayesian probability, recognize certain patterns, execute actions, and so forth, all at dramatically higher speeds than humans. This creates capacities with respect to at least certain tasks involving decision that far exceed human performance— weapons that target and fire on hundreds of targets in seconds, facial recognition technology that stores and rapidly analyzes millions of images of faces, algorithmic, high-frequency trading techniques for identifying trading signals and then splitting,

numbers are used to exaggerate. See Justin T. Kao et al., "Nonliteral Understanding of Number Words," *PNAS* 111 (2014): 12002–12007.

[71] Winograd, "Thinking Machines," 186.

[72] At least in the area of law we should not forget that the technology of print capitalism has regularly introduced alterations in the epistemological field. This is most obviously true with respect to how the relevant law is ascertained. In the eighteenth-century treatises were the principal source of legal knowledge because of their portability and their synthesis of cases—most lawyers could not afford large libraries. Angela Fernandez and Markus Dubber, *Law Books in Action: Essays on the Anglo-American Treatise* (Oxford: Hart Publishing Ltd., 2012). The development of law magazines and case reporters (bound volumes reproducing lawyer's accounts of judicial decisions) provided broader dissemination of precedent. Keyword indexing, an invention refined by the late nineteenth century, permitted lawyers relatively immediate access to far more precedent. See David S. Clark and Tugrul Ansay, *Introduction to the Law of the United States* (Norwell: Kluwer Law International, 2002), 40–43. This diminished the role of treatises and at the same time raised questions about how many cases a lawyer would need to read or cite to have an "authoritative" understanding of what the law on any given point was. On alterations in "modes of thought" associated with shifts in technologies of communication, see Finn, *What Algorithms Want*, 38.

[73] For an example in the U.S. of AI for image recognition, see Shan Carter, "Exploring Neural Networks with Activation Atlases," *Google AI Blog* (March 6, 2019), https://ai.googleblog.com/2019/03/exploring-neural-networks.html; see also Kroll et al., "Accountable Algorithms," 656–678; Citron and Pasquale, "The Scored Society," 10–13, 24–25. Cf. Andrew D. Selbst and Solon Barocas, "The Intuitive Appeal of Explainable Machines," *Fordham Law Review* 87 (2018): 1085–1139, 1089–1090.

[74] See Selbst and Barocas, "The Intuitive Appeal of Explainable Machines," 1089–1090.

scheduling, and executing trade orders in microseconds, legal search tools that instantaneously locate, sort, and present cases that use specific key terms in databases containing millions of published and unpublished court decisions, and chatbots that instantly give millions of people who cannot afford a lawyer or conduct legal research the ability to fill out a form that asserts a legal right.

Second, human judgment is not just displaced in the sense of being concentrated upstream and embedded or suppressed in the process of coding these systems. It is not just displaced from the point of usage—the point of task performance where ordinary humans interact with machines and experience the consequences of those design "choices." The demonstrably superior performance of machines along some dimensions of tasks that traditionally required the exercise of human judgment creates new domains of decision. And the vastness of these fields, the superhuman scale and speed of auto-mated, autonomous action within them, can induce awe and with it excessive deference—excessive in that the deference can subtly extend beyond the dimensions as to which machines are known to be superior.

Deference is of course but a euphemism for displaced judgment. This form of dis-placement may or may not create problems when designers decide to defer,[75] but when users, regulators, and the general public defer the so-called "responsibility gap" widens.[76] Processes will run that appear from the perspective of outcomes to work like human judgment, or better than it, but until a sufficiently catastrophic failure surfaces, no one may appreciate the vulnerabilities attendant to the displacement of human judgment involved, the "reason" the system acted the way it did may not be discoverable, and the circumstances of its use may make it difficult to identify a legally or morally responsible human.[77] In systems where the risk of catastrophic failure is either low or the information costs associated with identifying it are high (say in software for the online resolution of small claims disputes involving low money value complaints where fact investigation is rarely, if ever, searching) the relevant vulnerabilities may remain totally undetected.

Third, there is a more fundamental sense in which we find ourselves governed by AI. As the Technology Assisted Review example suggests, AI alters in subtle but important

[75] Deference is a feature of *every* expert system, human and artificial, because experts work as agents on behalf of a principal, and in order for agency to function the principal must accept the need for the agent grounded in her expertise. But in most formal agentic relationships the vulnerability and authority of the principal is legally recognized in the requirement of reciprocal deference: the agent must consult the principal with respect to core objectives (and not just at the outset but on a rolling basis if there is reason to believe that changed circumstances would change the principal's objectives), accept the principal's judgment regarding those objectives, strictly avoid conflicts of interest, and faithfully serve the principal. The capacity of fully autonomous machines running AI to exhibit deference on these terms is precisely what we do not know. Nor is it easy to judge the moral costs of finding out.

[76] See John Danner, "Robots, Law, and the Retribution Gap," *Ethics and Information Technology* 18 (2016): 299–309; Gunkel, *Machine Question*, 18.

[77] See Mauricio Paez and Kerianne Tobitsch, "The Industrial Internet of Things: Risks, Liabilities, and Emerging Legal Issues," *New York Law School Law Review* 62 (2017): 234–244; David C. Vladeck, "Machines without Principals: Liability Rules and Artificial Intelligence," *Washington Law Review* 89 (2014): 141–150.

ways the epistemological field in which human judgment occurs. Consider, for instance, the retrospectivity of big data sets that power some of the most significant recent innovations in AI like psychographic profiling. This technology builds a profile of individual voters, consumers, or possible security threats from past observable choices (both our own and those of our supposed doppelgängers) to generate a probabilistic assessment of future actions and likely response to future stimuli. Marx insisted on the constraining effects of tradition when he wrote: "Men make their own history, but they do not make it as they please; they do not make it under self-selected circumstances, but under circumstances already existing, given and transmitted from the past."[78] The famous line that follows underscores the claim: "The tradition of all dead generations weighs like a nightmare on the brains of the living."[79] Even revolutionary movements that give rise to new legal orders "anxiously conjure up the spirits of the past to their service...in order to present this new scene in world history in time-honored disguise and borrowed language."[80] Predictive analytics ostensibly liberate us from the biases, errors, and repetition automatism of local knowledge, tradition, and intuition, but the liberation is to a future heavily determined by rationally calculated abstractions aggregated from observable data of our past choices.

This retrospective, data-centric determinism can be found in the numbing monotony of recommendation software running music, video, entertainment, social media, and news feed platforms.[81] More ominously, it can be found in the use of psychographic profiling to "nudge" the purchasing habits of consumers with precisely calibrated stimuli,[82] in the monopolization of our attention by "smart" devices (which now provide apps to manage the problem of addiction to...apps),[83] in the experience of Uber drivers run ragged by the mélange of gaming incentives and drill sergeant behaviorism in the

---

[78] Karl Marx, *The Eighteenth Brumaire of Louis Bonaparte* (New York: Cosimo Inc., 2008), 1.

[79] *Id.* at 1.   [80] *Id.* at 1.

[81] See Le Wu et al., "Relevance Meets Coverage: A Unified Framework to Generate Diversified Recommendations," *ACM Trans. on Intell. Sys. and Tech.*, 7 (2016): 39:2 (traditional collaborative filtering models "are successful at providing accurate recommendations that match some of the user's dominant interests [however] the recommendation set/list may be monotonous...and it is hard to cover all of the user's interests"). Search algorithms can also produce results that confuse and offend users on matters of profound consequence. *See* Finn, *What Algorithms Want,* 66 (describing a 2011 incident in which Siri directed users asking "where can I get an abortion" to "anti-abortion crisis pregnancy centers").

[82] See Joseph F. Coughlin, "The 'Internet of Things' Will Take Nudge Theory Too Far," *BigThink* (March 27, 2017), https://bigthink.com/disruptive-demographics/the-internet-of-things-big-data-when-a-nudge-becomes-a-noodge. Some designers revealingly conflate the desires of their users and their own behaviorist projects. See Finn, *What Algorithms Want,* 66 (Google's chairman told *The Wall Street Journal* in 2010, "*I actually think most people don't want Google to answer their questions. They want Google to tell them what they should be doing next.*") (emphasis added).

[83] Nicholas Thompson, "Our Minds Have Been Hijacked by Our Phones, Tristan Harris Wants to Rescue Them," *Wired* (July 26, 2017), https://www.wired.com/story/our-minds-have-been-hijacked-by-our-phones-tristan-harris-wants-to-rescue-them/. On the role of big tech in co-opting anti-addiction tools, see Arielle Pardes, "Quality Time, Brought to You by Big Tech," *Wired* (December 31, 2018), https://www.wired.com/story/how-big-tech-co-opted-time-well-spent/.

algorithms that govern their work,[84] and in the reproduction of racial biases that have long tainted policing in ostensibly rational, technocratic algorithmic models of "hot spots."[85] It can also be seen in the antidemocratic weaponization of psychographic profiling and the instantaneous dissemination features of social media designed to influence voting.[86]

For historians, critical theorists, ethicists, and sociologists the displacement of human judgment and the deterioration of conditions for its exercise are all too familiar. They are signal attributes of bureaucratic systems. Louis Mumford insisted that the bureaucratic management of human labor is the original technology of large-scale production, what he called "megatechnics," deployed for the first time not in modern factories but in the sophisticated ancient Egyptian labor systems used to build the pyramids.[87] Reflexive obedience, "minute division of labor," and "undeviating exactitude" are central to the "astonishing efficiency" of this "machine."[88] Talcott Parsons, riffing darkly on Max Weber's theory of modern bureaucracy famously labeled the inexorable expansion of rational, technocratic styles of thought, information processing, and systems of control an "iron cage."[89] Michel Foucault called the conjunction of panoptic surveillance, minute organization, separation, and optimization of physical spaces purpose-built for bureaucratic management (hospitals, military barracks, prisons, schools, factories) and the ensuing control over the movement of bodies within them "disciplinary power."[90] People working in these "panoptically" arranged spaces not only obey but internalize their constraints, becoming "docile bodies," instruments "of their own subjection."[91]

---

[84] See Noam Scheiber, "How Uber Uses Psychological Tricks to Push Its Drivers' Buttons," *New York Times* (April 2, 2017), https://www.nytimes.com/interactive/2017/04/02/technology/uber-drivers-psychological-tricks.html; Ryan Calo and Alex Rosenblat, "The Taking Economy: Uber, Information, and Power," *Columbia Law Review* 117 (2017): 1649–1670.

[85] See Clavell, "Crime Mapping"; Rashida Richardson et al., "Dirty Data, Bad Predictions: How Civil Rights Violations Impact Police Data, Predictive Policing Systems, and Justice," *N.Y.U. Law Review Online* 94 (2019): 218–225; Andrew Guthrie Ferguson, "Policing Predictive Policing," *Washington University Law Review* 94 (2017): 1132–44, 1145–1153; Elizabeth E. Joh, "Policing by Numbers: Big Data and the Fourth Amendment," *Washington Law Review* 89 (2014): 42–50.

[86] See Jane Mayer, "New Evidence Emerges of Steve Bannon and Cambridge Analytica's Role in Brexit," *New Yorker* (November 18, 2018), https://www.newyorker.com/news/news-desk/new-evidence-emerges-of-steve-bannon-and-cambridge-analyticas-role-in-brexit; Sue Halpern, "Cambridge Analytica and the Perils of Psychographics," *New Yorker* (March 30, 2018), https://www.newyorker.com/news/news-desk/cambridge-analytica-and-the-perils-of-psychographics.

[87] Louis Mumford, *Technics and Human Development: The Myth of the Machine* (New York: Harcourt & Brace, 1967), 3, 189.

[88] *Id.* at 191–193.

[89] On Talcott Parson's translation of the key phrase in *The Protestant Ethic and the Spirit of Capitalism*, see Arthur Mitzman, *The Iron Cage: An Historical Interpretation of Max Weber* (New Brunswick: Transaction Books, 2002), 107.

[90] Michel Foucault, *Discipline and Punish: The Birth of the Prison*, 2d ed., trans. Alan Sheridan (New York: Vintage Books, 2012), 187.

[91] *Id.* at 135, 203, 224 (what produces discipline and docility "is not the universal consciousness of the law in each juridical subject; it is the regular extension, the infinitely minute web of panoptic techniques"). On the development of online surveillance culture and surveillance capitalism, see Frank Pasquale, *The Black Box Society: The Secret Algorithms That Control Money and Information* (Cambridge: Harvard University Press, 2015).

Bureaucracies function, in short, by converting humans into machines, ruthlessly efficient automatons.

Writing in the 1990s on the eve of the remarkable innovations in neural networks and big data analytics that have spurred twenty-first-century AI, Terry Winograd observed that even the most ambitious forms of AI were functionally bureaucratic in design. "[T]he techniques of artificial intelligence," he wrote, do not involve "thinking."[92] They "are to the mind what bureaucracy is to human social organization."[93] And just as the remarkable "benefits of bureaucracy follow from the reduction of judgment to the systematic application of explicitly articulated rules," so too the costs of taking an algorithmic approach to rule formulation and administration follow from the displacement of judgment and the degradation of the conditions for its exercise that attend all bureaucratic projects.[94] AI is, to this day, still functionally bureaucratic in its principal applications, and as the last two sections have argued, in the way it affects human judgment. It centralizes, embeds, and obscures value judgments in the design phase; in downstream usage it displaces human judgment even in circumstances in which it is designed to enhance or aid human judgment; it alters the epistemological field of human judgment; and it can be deployed in other ways to deteriorate the conditions for the exercise of human judgment, generating reflexive obedience and base stimuli-response behavior patterns in users.[95] These effects may not be necessary to AI systems, but they arise in important respects, Winograd insisted, from the dependence of AI on algorithmic syntax.[96] If genuinely enhancing human judgment is a possible objective of AI systems, the objective Winograd thought most appropriate to the future of AI, it has not been pursued with the vigor of bureaucratic applications.

IS HUMAN JUDGMENT NECESSARY?

Much of the explicitly ethical debate about AI concentrates on deontological questions such as whether respect for principles such as individual human dignity requires that humans make certain judgments (e.g., the decision to use lethal force on the battlefield),[97] and consequentialist questions about how to weigh the transformative benefits of AI against some account of its costs (e.g., the life-saving benefits of enhanced medical imaging measured against the costs in human life from errors, the increased lethality of

---

[92] Winograd, "Thinking Machines," 182.   [93] *Id.* at 182.   [94] *Id.* at 182.

[95] See, e.g., Andrea Roth, "Machine Testimony," *Yale Law Journal* 126 (2017): 2005–2022; Andrew Guthrie Ferguson, "Predictive Prosecution," *Wake Forest Law Review* 51 (2016): 727–740.

[96] "Seekers after the glitter of intelligence are misguided in trying to cast it from the base metal of computing." Winograd, "Thinking Machines," 185. The "glitter" is evident in the Microsoft ad announcing that we are "living in the future we have always dreamed of," one in which "AI is empowering us to change the world we see," https://www.youtube.com/watch?v=9tucY7Jhhs4.

[97] See Sharkey, "Autonomous Weapons Systems," 76–79 (summarizing scholarship arguing that dignitarian interests require the act of killing to be "grounded in human judgment").

automated weapons systems measured against their precision and potential for stricter compliance with the laws of war, the increased access to justice automated legal services provide weighed against the risk of legal error, and more broadly, whether an AI system is "good enough" if in some respects it equals or excels human performance).[98] There are also ethically informed empirical debates about whether it is technically feasible to code ethical norms[99] (a question that is sometimes inverted and mobilized normatively and epistemologically by questioning whether humans are capable of following ethical norms and whether we can know if the mind is in fact the quintessential black box).[100] These are important, fraught debates, and the literature is in some respects polarized by authors' deep-seated priors—enthusiastic technological determinists and dystopic skeptics take radically different approaches to the same questions.[101]

The preceding sections have not entirely avoided these debates, and my skepticism has been on display, but my main purpose was to set out the range of ways in which AI and judgment interact. In this final section I want to ask a somewhat different question than those raised in the ethics literature. It is a question that follows from the displacement and deterioration of the conditions for human judgment in AI systems, but it begins from less skeptical priors. I cannot muster anything like the evangelical enthusiasm for AI systems some have, nor am I capable of simulating enthusiasm at a level that would convince devotees. But I am capable, as any skeptic must be, of shifting the lens of skepticism to the chilling historical and psychological evidence (particularly regarding our susceptibility to bias, cruelty, and devastating violence) indicating how bad humans are at making a wide range of decisions.[102] In view of this evidence, I think we have to ask whether human judgment is in any meaningful sense a necessary feature of the human condition. If it is not, the case for tolerating experimentation with delegation to AI systems strengthens. I will explore two versions of the question. First, whether the concept of judgment itself requires nondelegation and, alternatively, whether there are certain judgments that must be made by humans in a liberal democratic legal order.

[98] See Sullins, "RoboWarfare," 266–267 (noting studies showing low performance of human soldiers relative to ethical standards for just war and evidence that humans underperform with respect to military objectives of combat).

[99] See Marlies Van de Voort, Wolter Pieters, and Luca Consoli, "Refining the Ethics of Computer-Made Decisions: A Classification of Moral Mediation by Ubiquitous Machines," *Ethics and Information Technology* 17 (2015): 41–56; Wendell Wallach and Collin Allen, *Moral Machines: Teaching Robots Right from Wrong* (Oxford: Oxford University Press, 2009).

[100] See Gunkel, *The Machine Question*, 64 ("Humans, according to [Joseph] Nadeau, are unfortunately not very rational.... Machines, however, can be programmed with perfect and infallible logical processing... [so] if rationality is the basic requirement for moral decision making, only a machine could ever be considered a legitimate moral agent.").

[101] See Finn, *What Algorithms* Want, ch. 1 (describing technological utopians and skeptics).

[102] See Veronica Juarez Ramos, *Analyzing the Role of Cognitive Bias in the Decision-Making Process* (Hershey, PA: IGI Global, 2017); Daniel Kahneman, Paul Slovic, and Amos Tversky eds., *Judgment Under Uncertainty: Heuristics and Biases* (Cambridge: Cambridge University Press, 1982); Dallas Willard, *The Disappearance of Moral Knowledge*, ed. Steven L. Porter, Aaron Preston, and Gregg A. Ten Elshof (New York: Taylor & Francis, 2018); Jonathan Glover, *Humanity: A Moral History of the Twentieth Century* (New Haven, CT: Yale University Press, 2001).

At the outset, it may be helpful to enlist a Turing-like hypothesis by imagining a super-competent AI system, one that reliably outperforms a human decision maker on every measurable dimension, including reduction of bias. Our inclination to defer should therefore be high, and rationally grounded fear of bad outcomes should be low. Assume further that the system performs an important task. The stakes are not only nontrivial but significant for the parties concerned. These premises should clear out some of the easy consequentialist and deontological objections to the delegation of judgment to machines. They tilt the consequentialist's cost-benefit analysis heavily in favor of AI systems in recognition of the well-documented limitations of human judgment.[103] Likewise, it can reduce the salience of some of the most powerful deontological claims (e.g., an automated weapons system that is clearly more compliant with the laws of war presents different challenges to human dignity than one that is unreliable or incapable of compliance). Imagining an AI system that makes important decisions very well thus helps to isolate the question whether there is anything in the nature of judgment itself that demands that it be exercised by humans, and secondarily, to inquire if there is anything in the way of a nondelegation doctrine in the legal and political structure of liberal democratic states.

Answering either version of the question requires that we become more precise about what judgment is. We began rather provisionally with Kant's theory of predicative judgment (judgment as a synthesis of concept and sensory content). We ended the last section with discussion of deterioration in the conditions of judgment, the limit of which is automation, reduction to brute code and the response-stimuli reaction of "snap judgment"—a form of judgment barely worth of the name.[104] Significantly, the AI systems that underlie predictive analytics, search algorithms, image recognition, and natural language software conduct predicative judgments probabilistically. Hence the voracious appetite for big data and the importance of generating products that are information forcing in their use—the more data AI systems have to work from, the more "experienced" they become, and the more robust their assessments of probability may be.

With the role of probability in mind we can now reformulate our first question: If predicative judgments ("this image contains a human"; "this consumer likes romantic comedies"; "this voter is a fiscal conservative"; "this target is an enemy combatant") are made in probabilistic terms—if judgment is in important respects probabilistic[105]—is it

---

[103] See, e.g., Eugene Volokh, "Chief Justice Robot," 1137–1141.

[104] Martin, *Theories of Judgment*, 39, 154. Affect theory poses intriguing challenges to the criticism of snap judgments. For present purposes I note only that I am in agreement with Linda Zerilli's thoughtful argument questioning "the stark distinction between affect and reason that characterizes affect theory in some of its...iterations." Linda Zerilli, *A Democratic Theory of Judgment* (Chicago: University of Chicago Press, 2016), 244.

[105] The connection between probability and predicative judgment in AI systems is no accident. Probability theory is deeply imbricated in the history of legal judgment (it has been instrumental in resolving questions about burdens of proof and how to weigh evidence) as well as decision-making in moral theory, theology (consider Pascal's wager), and science. See James Franklin, *The Science of Conjecture Evidence and Probability Before Pascal* (Baltimore, MD: Johns Hopkins University Press, 2015); Ian Hacking, *The Emergence of Probability*, 2d ed. (Cambridge: Cambridge University Press,

necessary that any set of judgments be made by humans given the distinct advantage AI systems have in computing probabilities? Notice first that on this view of judgment, judgment is a *principal* function of AI systems even if the exact processes by which inputs are converted into probabilistically defined outputs remain enigmatic.

On this view of what judgment is the only judgments humans must make are:

(a) Those as to which probabilistic analysis is either not possible or not helpful.

(b) Those a human must exercise in order to develop the capacity to judge.

(c) Those the law or other first principles require to be exercised by humans.

Our hypothesis of a super-competent AI system significantly diminishes the salience of (a)—we are assuming that the relevant AI system uses probability theory to make judgments in a genuinely helpful way (reliably as good as or better than humans) even though this is currently a demonstrably counter-factual assumption with respect to certain tasks.[106] Still, (a) is not an empty set. Value judgments (whether to code law conservatively, whether to minimize false positives or false negatives, whether to make autonomous weapons systems at all) are not readily susceptible to probabilistic determination.[107] And the more pluralistic a society is, the more one would expect design decisions such as the characterization of the relevant task and threshold-setting to turn on contested value judgments.[108]

2006). Modern lawyers know this from Holmes's famous dictum that the law *is* prediction, "The object of our study then is prediction, the prediction of the incidence of public force through the instrumentality of the courts. . . . Prophecies of what the courts will do in fact, and nothing more pretentious, are what I mean by the law." O.W. Holmes Jr., "The Path of the Law," *Harvard Law Review* 10 (1897): 457.

[106] Image recognition software, for instance, can still fail at astonishingly simple tasks essential to their use in security systems such as identifying a human. See Simen Thys, Wiebe Van Ranst, and Toon Goedemé, "Fooling Automated Surveillance Cameras: Adversarial Patches to Attack Person Detection," https://arxiv.org/abs/1904.08653; Gregory Barber, "Shark or Baseball? Inside the 'Black Box' of a Neural Network," *Wired* (March 6, 2019).

[107] See Zerilli, *A Democratic Theory of Judgment*, 15–17, cf. 14. Although the term "value judgment" implies that the decision to be made turns on firmly held beliefs, not facts, better facts can sometimes reveal that a specific option ostensibly dictated by one's values is actually inconsistent with them. Here properly designed AI systems might enhance human value-judgments by expanding access to relevant facts. Cf. Cuéllar, "Cyberdelegation," 144–157.

[108] Pluralism might also make it more important for any decision system to be transparent regarding the procedures by which judgments are reached. So in addition to the fact that certain value judgments cannot be made by AI systems, the nondelegation doctrine should, under (a), also forbid delegation to AI systems that are unduly enigmatic regarding decisions as to which understanding the process of decision matters. See Martin, *Theories of Judgment*, 167 (a judge must have "the capacity to express the reasons which sway him . . . while many particular instances of judgment may well be silent, the idea of a wholly silent judge . . . is ultimately unintelligible"). For Hannah Arendt, the giving of reasons is *constitutive* of political judgment because of "the importance of taking into account the standpoints of other people when forming an opinion." Zerilli, *A Democratic Theory of Judgment*, 141, 176–177. This can only happen through procedures that are transparent, inclusive, participatory, and promote reason-giving.

As the preceding sections have suggested, the deterioration of the conditions for human judgment *could* violate (b). But it is generally difficult to judge whether any specific delegation to an AI system would so deteriorate the conditions for the exercise of judgment as to violate (b), at least before the delegation occurs. Moreover, as the social theories of Mumford, Parsons, Weber, and Foucault admonish, the deterioration of judgment follows generally from the benefits of bureaucratic administration. This means that AI systems which displace rather than enhance human judgment pose incremental threats that work alongside all the other forms of "megatechnics" that degrade the conditions for the exercise of human judgment. Teasing out how specific systems affect the overall conditions of judgment would be exceedingly difficult. On the other hand, because we know that human judgment must be preserved (it is required by (a) and potentially (c)), the conditions for it must too. The fact that the line designating sufficient deterioration is difficult to draw therefore militates in favor of a precautionary principle. A strong precautionary principle would operate something like Winograd's directive to design AI systems that enhance human judgment rather than displace it.[109] A more modest one would require that AI systems be designed to minimize the displacement of human judgment irrespective of whether human judgment is actually enhanced; the weakest would prohibit displacement only where doing so is known in fact to degrade human judgment (e.g., the sorts of things Cambridge Analytica and the Russian government appear to have been up to in the 2016 U.S. election).

There are two additional reasons to take (b) seriously and favor a precautionary principle. First, making judgments on matters of consequence under conditions of uncertainty is challenging moral and emotional work. For all the power exercising judgment entails and the desire attached to it, there is terror in it too, or there ought to be for the serious judge.[110] The temptation not just to delegate but to outsource judgment—to make someone or something else wholly responsible for the choice—is thus very real. Second, we know the level of devastation that widespread deterioration of the conditions for judgment can cause from the rise of totalitarianism in the twentieth century. On Hannah Arendt's account we become susceptible to fascism, domination, and violent mobilization as "a structureless mass of furious individuals" through the gradual displacement and erosion of judgment, ending in the evacuation of common sense.[111] Having witnessed authoritarian repression, the Holocaust, and other mass atrocities, we twenty-first-century legatees of this grim spectacle of human failure have singularly profound design responsibilities.

The third element (c) requires that we ask if there is a legal or other first order political obligation to decide certain questions via the exercise of human judgment.[112] One might

[109] See Cuéllar, "Cyberdelegation," 144–157.

[110] See Soren Kierkegaard, *Fear and Trembling*, ed. and trans. Howard V. Hong and Edna Hong (Princeton, NJ: Princeton University Press, 1983).

[111] Zerilli, *A Democratic Theory of Judgment*, 315.

[112] For additional prudential considerations in this vein, see Meredith Whittaker et al., AI Now Institute, AI Now Report 2018 (2018), 24–28, 29–32. See also Berman, "A Government of Laws," 1313–1315, 1338–1355.

go about finding an answer by comprehensively canvasing the U.S. Constitution, statutes, and case reporters to find laws that apply to decision-making to see if they can be read to require a human decision maker. The First Amendment refers to the rights of free speech, a free press, the free exercise of religion, and freedom from government establishment of religion. These can be read both to assume and to protect private conscience on, at a minimum, matters of political and religious significance. Some read an endorsement of deliberative democratic theory into these rights. The Seventh Amendment preserves the right to a jury trial in civil cases. That means empaneling jurors, not robots, to decide cases. So, too, the right to a grand and petit jury in criminal investigation and trial. The Due Process Clauses of the Fifth and Fourteenth Amendments confer a right of participation in state action affecting life, liberty, or property. At a minimum, this means the right to notice (presumptively ex ante) and a meaningful opportunity to be heard.[113] Crucially this is not just an opportunity to speak, it is intersubjective—there must be someone who listens impartially and, *as a condition of having listened*, decides, and there is a strong presumption in favor of the participation of one's adversary (ex parte proceedings occur, but they are disfavored) and the attendance or observation of the public.[114] The opportunity to be heard generally includes, and in criminal cases the Sixth Amendment requires, the right to confront witnesses viva voce—in person, in court. The Sixth Amendment also provides a right to the assistance of counsel, to an expert trained in the law to represent the accused. Taken together it would appear that some legal judgments must be made by and with the participation of the people who would be affected by them. But many of these rights are waivable (through judgments about the validity of the conditions of waiver), many are being watered down by judicial decisions and legislative initiatives that channel legal judgment into other less participatory fora, and of course parties can and do combine the principles of waiver and contract doctrine to design their own procedures for dispute resolution.[115]

Voting is a core legal right involving the exercise of judgment, but it is less participatory than one might think. There is no obligation to vote, only a right to do so if one chooses, and certainly no legal duty to exercise judgment in voting. Moreover, whether one can delegate the decision turns on what the vote concerns. Proxy voting is a common practice in corporate governance—shareholders can delegate their votes to others who will

---

[113] Sniadach v. Family Finance Corp., 395 U.S. 337 (1969).

[114] See Judith Resnik and Dennis Curtis, *Representing Justice: Invention, Controversy, and Rights in City-States and Democratic Courtrooms* (New Haven, CT: Yale University Press 2011), 295–305 (describing Bentham's theory of publicity in adjudication); cf. Joseph Jaconelli, *Open Justice, A Critique of the Public Trial* (Oxford: Oxford University Press 2002), 1 ("publicity, in itself, is not an unalloyed benefit in the administration of justice").

[115] On the channeling of legal judgment into increasingly enclosed spaces, see Norman W. Spaulding, "The Enclosure of Justice: Due Process, Courthouse Architecture, and the Dead Metaphor of Trial," *Yale Journal of Law and Humanities* 24 (2012): 311; see also Spaulding, "Due Process Without Judicial Process?: Anti-Adversarialism in American Legal Culture," *Fordham Law Review*, 85 (2017): 2249.

vote their shares at the annual meeting.[116] Even political elections rely on delegation. For instance, voters do not elect a president under the American Constitution, their votes are delegated to electors who are supposed to be faithful to the numerical results of voting in the state they represent. Other examples could be considered. At common law a will must reflect the "last will and testament" of the testator—*her* personal judgment about the proper distribution of assets upon her death. This is in principle nondelegable. The decision about the use of force in armed combat arguably requires human judgment (because human rights law rests on a series of deontological premises about the dignity of combatants and civilians).[117] Tort law, writ large, sets the boundary between *damnum absque injuria* (loss without legally cognizable injury on the part of a human or entities humans create) and harms for which humans can be held to answer. Reading it backward one can define a rule that identifies judgments that ought to be taken seriously by humans because the costs of failing to do so will be charged to the person deemed to have erred.[118] Similar assignments of responsibility for judgment or failure to exercise it can be found in substantive criminal law where the focus is culpability in a deeper sense than negligence and the penalties more serious than money damages or injunctive relief.[119]

One could go on in this way, and the analysis would be illuminating but mainly, I think, by surfacing how few judgments the law in liberal democratic societies requires humans to make or requires them to make well ex ante. From this one might be tempted to conclude that the requirement of nondelegation expressed in (c) is fairly narrow, and that our super-competent AI system can quickly and comprehensively sweep up around the margins of what law requires humans to decide. But this would, I think, represent a grave error. The reason the law of liberal democratic states does not generally mandate human judgment is precisely to promote the conditions for its flourishing. One essential condition for the flourishing of human judgment is erring. A comprehensive (legal) code, particularly one that moves from ex post assessment to the more comprehensive position of ex ante prevention and risk management, seeks to eliminate error. A minimal code, generally restricted to ex post intervention, tolerates error. Put differently, judgments about the good life and how to behave are decentralized in liberal democratic legal regimes. That is because we don't generally learn how to make sensible judgments about our lives ("y generally follows from doing x," "friendship is a relationship defined by trust," "true loyalty requires self-sacrifice") by following orders or reflexively internalizing the predictions of others, however accurate they are.

[116] Andrew Tutt, "Choosing Representatives by Proxy Voting," *Columbia Law Review Sidebar* 116 (2016): 61.

[117] See Sharkey, "Autonomous Weapons Systems."

[118] *See* Ryan Abbott, "The Reasonable Computer: Disrupting the Paradigm of Tort Liability," *George Washington Law Review* 86 (2018): 35–43; Geistfeld, 1632–1674; Vladeck, 141–150. See also Jack M. Balkin, "The Three Laws of Robotics in the Age of Big Data," *Ohio State Law Journal* 78 (2016): 1231–1240.

[119] On the inconsistency with which technology is incorporated into decision making in criminal law, see Roth, "Trial by Machine."

More than erring and learning on our own to make sound predictions is at stake. In a free society there is no statement about what the law requires that is not also a question about whether it should be followed. This ensues from the fact that in a free society the people are the sovereign, the lawgivers. "We the People do ordain and establish . . ." is not, on this view, a vague historical abstraction of U.S. constitutional law, or an artifact of ratification; it sets our liberal democratic legal system on the foundation of popular sovereignty.[120] In an authoritarian society, by contrast, sovereignty is highly concentrated, and, from the perspective of both the sovereign and properly disciplined subjects, there is no statement about what the law requires that is open to question. The goal is to perfect the bureaucratic project of reflexive obedience. Free people can easily forget this distinction, and in their own will to power they can seek to make others forget it, to grant by proxy the sovereign power of saying what the law is and setting it aside in the name of a new law. We are all too familiar with the fascistic tendencies of certain styles of populism. Popular sovereignty is, in operation, all too human, and the question of resistance hides in plain sight much like the purloined letter. But the conjunction of human judgment and popular sovereignty is, however aspirational, an organizing principle of liberal democratic governance no amount of provisional delegation can eliminate. The letter is there, signed in the blood of revolutionaries (in 1776, 1789, and again in 1865),[121] and no matter where it is hidden there is a trace, a remainder to be claimed every moment until we become as docile as the police searching the Minister's chamber—until, that is, we become the instrument of our own subjection. In just the proportion that we ignore this trace, this remainder, we are less free.

What kind of judgment is the decision to obey or resist the law? From the perspective of the principle of popular sovereignty, it is not merely predictive. That is, the question whether to obey the law cannot be answered exclusively by determining the probability of enforcement, the severity of the penalty for noncompliance, and the probable externalities of noncompliance. If the question could be answered with this sort of calculation, it would be impossible to explain our most important social and legal reforms—transformative changes arising from movements that violated the law despite knowing that these calculations would be completed *à la lettre*, as Lacan would put it, on the bodies of resistant subjects and their loved ones.[122] Judgments about resistance to law thus reveal a feature of judgment we have not yet specified. The feature is the oscillation, in the judge, of necessity and freedom. As Wayne Martin describes, a judge must be both faithful to and "bound by the evidence," *and* resistant—"free to decide . . . free[] to arrive

---

[120] See Larry D. Kramer, *The People Themselves: Popular Constitutionalism and Judicial Review* (Oxford: Oxford University Press, 2004); Norman W. Spaulding, "The Impersonation of Justice: Lynching, Dueling, and Wildcat Strikes in Nineteenth Century America," in *The Routledge Companion to Law and Humanities in Nineteenth Century America*, ed. Nan Goodman and Simon Stern (London: Routledge, 2017), 163.

[121] Cf. Norman W. Spaulding, "Paradoxes of Constitutional Faith: Federalism, Emancipation, and the Original Thirteenth Amendment," *Critical Analysis of Law* 3 (2016): 306.

[122] In European history, the conservative effort to *limit* resistance to law often relied on probability theory. See Franklin, *The Science of Conjecture*, 73, 77; but see *id.* at 95.

at one's own decision."[123] This paradoxical combination requires "the capacity to be sensitive to the inferential structure and authority of the evidence and to be guided by it...the capacity to suspend judgment until the evidence has been presented"—to "discipline one's gullibility"[124]—*and*, crucially, *"the capacity to 'hang free' of mechanical determination by some force or power."*[125] "Hanging free" means being "capable of self-determination...of determining, in response to the evidence, his own representation of the objects or states-of-affairs he is judging."[126] The limit of "hanging free" is of course setting aside the evidence (after having attended to it and disciplined one's gullibility[127]), as a jury does when it practices nullification, as Gandhi did in the march to the sea against the British Salt Act, as Dr. Martin Luther King Jr. did in Birmingham, as Rosa Parks did in Montgomery, as the marchers on Edmund Pettus Bridge did in Selma, and as the Egyptians who filled Tahrir Square did.

Whether one wants to hold these lofty examples in mind, or more banal micro-resistances in which people find compliance intolerable, inconvenient, or otherwise against interest,[128] these are judgments humans must make in virtue of what judgment is understood to be and in virtue of what it means to live in a free society. AI system designers have a duty to preserve the conditions for its exercise. An industry that delights in resistance to law in the name of disruptive innovation owes us no less.[129]

SUGGESTED READINGS

Finn, Ed. *What Algorithms Want*. Cambridge, MA: MIT Press, 2017.

Gunkel, David J. *The Machine Question: Critical Perspectives on AI, Robots, and Ethics.* Cambridge, MA: MIT Press, 2012.

Harraway, Donna J. "A Cyborg Manifesto: Science, Technology, and Socialist-Feminism in the Late Twentieth Century." In *Simians, Cyborgs and Women: The Reinvention of Nature.* New York: Routledge, 1991.

---

[123] Martin, *Theories of Judgment*, 152–153, 162; Zerilli, *A Democratic Theory of Judgment*, 188–189, 197–203. See also Kierkegaard, *Fear and Trembling*, 33–37, 113–115.

[124] Martin, 169.

[125] *Id.* at 168. Zerilli, 265 ("For Arendt, the capacity to judge reflectively, in the absence of a concept or rule, is a defining feature of democratic citizenship."); ibid. ("Judging politically solicits the agreement of all, but it cannot compel it...in the manner of giving proofs.").

[126] Zerilli at 265.   [127] Cf. *Id.* at 273.

[128] Eduardo M. Penalver and Sonia K. Katyal describe a range of motivations, including acquisitiveness, in the history of violation of certain property laws. *Property Outlaws: How Squatters, Pirates, and Protesters Improve the Law of Ownership* (New Haven, CT: Yale University Press, 2010).

[129] See Ruth Berins Collier, V.B. Dubal, and Christopher Carter, "Disrupting Regulation, Regulating Disruption: The Politics of Uber in the United States," *Perspectives on Politics* 16, no. 4 (2018): 919–937; Paris Martineau, "Inside Airbnb's 'Guerilla War' Against Local Governments," *Wired* (March 20, 2019), https://www.wired.com/story/inside-airbnbs-guerrilla-war-against-local-governments/; Jill Lepore, "The Disruption Machine," *New Yorker* (June 16, 2014), https://www.newyorker.com/magazine/2014/06/23/the-disruption-machine (many innovators believe "that they should be reckless and ruthless.... Forget rules, obligations, your conscience, loyalty, a sense of the commonweal.... Disrupt or be disrupted.").

Kitchin, Rob. "Thinking Critically About and Researching Algorithms." *Information, Communication and Society* 20 (2017): 14.

Kraemer, Felicitas, Kees van Overveld, and Martin Peterson. "Is There an Ethics of Algorithms." *Ethics and Information Technology* 13 (2010): 251–260.

Martin, Wayne M. *Theories of Judgment: Psychology, Logic, Phenomenology.* Cambridge: Cambridge University Press, 2006.

Mumford, Louis. *Technics and Human Development: The Myth of the Machine*, 3, 189. New York: Harcourt & Brace, 1967.

Spaulding, Norman W. "The Historical Consciousness of the Resistant Subject." *University of California Irvine Law Review* 677 (2011).

Spolsky, Joel. "The Law of Leaky Abstractions." (November 11. 2002). https://www.joelonsoftware.com/2002/11/11/the-law-of-leaky-abstractions/.

Winograd, Terry. "Thinking Machines: Can There Be? Are We?" In *The Foundations of Artificial Intelligence: A Sourcebook*, ed. Derek Partridge and Yorick Wilks, 185. Cambridge: Cambridge University Press, 1990.

Zerilli, Linda. *A Democratic Theory of Judgment.* Chicago: University of Chicago Press, 2016.

CHAPTER 21

....

SEXUALITY

....

JOHN DANAHER

INTRODUCTION

....

IN early 2017, the world bore witness to its first human-robot marriage. Zheng Jiajia, a Chinese engineer and AI expert, hadn't always intended to marry a robot. He had spent years searching for a (female) human partner and grew frustrated at his lack of success.[1] So he decided to put his engineering skills to the test and create his own robotic partner. He married "her" in a simple, traditional ceremony that was witnessed by his mother and friends.[2] Jiajia's robot wasn't particularly impressive. According to the reports, "she" was a human-sized doll with a limited ability to recognize Chinese characters and speak some basic phrases. But Jiajia planned to upgrade "her" in the near future.

Not long after Jiajia's nuptials, Akihiko Kondo, a thirty-five-year-old Japanese man living in Tokyo, married Hatsune Miku, a holographic virtual reality singer who floats inside a desktop device.[3] Kondo too felt unlucky in (human) love and plumped for an artificial partner. In doing so, Kondo wanted to be recognized as a member of a sexual minority of people who are not interested in human lovers.

Neither Jiajia nor Kondo are alone. There is an active online community of "iDollators" who favor intimacy with artificial dolls over humans. There are also now several

[1] A not uncommon problem in China given its skewed gender ratios. See World Economic Forum, Global Gender Gap Report 2018, 63, available at http://www3.weforum.org/docs/WEF_GGGR_2018. pdf; and also Viola Zhou, "China Has World's Most Skewed Sex Ratio at Birth—Again," *South China Morning Post* (October 27, 2016), available at https://www.scmp.com/news/china/policies-politics/article/2040544/chinas-demographic-time-bomb-still-ticking-worlds-most.

[2] Kristin Huang, "Chinese Engineer 'Marries' Robot after Failing to Find a Human Wife," *South China Morning Post* (April 4, 2017), available at https://www.scmp.com/news/china/society/article/2084389/chinese-engineer-marries-robot-after-failing-find-human-wife.

[3] AFP-JIJI, "Love in Another Dimension: Japanese Man 'Marries' Hatsune Miku Hologram," *The Japan Times* (November 12, 2018), available at https://www.japantimes.co.jp/news/2018/11/12/national/japanese-man-marries-virtual-reality-singer-hatsune-miku-hologram/#.XFm9vs_7TOQ.

companies eagerly racing to create more sophisticated robotic and artificial companions, capable of providing their users with both sexual intimacy and emotional support. We should not be surprised by this trend. Sex and intimacy are important parts of human life, and they have always been mediated and assisted by technology. Sex toys and sex dolls can be found going back thousands of years back in the archaeological record. The fact that the latest wave of technologies is being leveraged toward sexual ends is part of this long-standing trend.[4]

This chapter examines the ethical opportunities and challenges posed by the use of AI in how humans express and enact their sexualities. It does so by focusing on three main issues. First, it considers the question of sexual identity and asks whether we should apply a new sexual identity label—"digisexuality"—to those who express or direct their sexualities towards digital/artificial partners.[5] While agreeing that this phenomenon is worthy of greater scrutiny, the chapter argues that we should be very cautious about recognizing this as a new form of sexual identity as doing so can have stigmatizing and divisive effects. Second, it looks at the role that AI can play in facilitating and assisting human-to-human sexual intimacy, focusing in particular on the use of self-tracking and predictive analytics in optimizing intimate behavior. It asks whether there is something ethically objectionable about the use of such AI assistance. It argues that there isn't, though there are ethical risks that need to be addressed. Finally, it considers the idea that a sophisticated form of AI could be an object of love. Can we be in a loving relationship with something that has been "programmed" to love us? Contrary to the widely held view, this chapter argues that this is indeed possible.

AI AND SEXUAL IDENTITY

Identity is central to human existence. We all seek to define and understand ourselves and others in terms of different identity categories.[6] Sexual identity labels are an important part of this pattern of classification. Homosexuality, bisexuality and hetereosexuality are all now recognized and, for the most part, tolerated as distinct forms of sexual identity (though it was not always thus).

The general tendency to classify ourselves and others in this manner creates a temptation when it comes to how we understand those, like Zheng Jiajia and Akihiko Kondo,

---

[4] Kate Devlin, *Turned On: Science, Sex and Robots* (London: Bloomsbury Sigma, 2018); and Hallie Lieberman, *Buzz: The Stimulating History of the Sex Toy* (New York: Pegasus Books, 2017).

[5] Neil McArthur and Markie Twist, "The Rise of Digisexuality: Therapeutic Challenges and Possibilities," *Sex and Relationship Therapy* 32(3–4) (2017): 334–344.

[6] Kwame Anthony Appiah, *The Lies that Bind: Rethinking Identity* (London: Profile Books, 2018); and Francis Fukuyama, *Identity: The Demand for Dignity and the Politics of Resentment* (New York: Farrar, Straus and Giroux, 2018).

who express and enact a sexual preference for artificial partners. In their article "The rise of the digisexual," Neil McArthur and Markie Twist succumb to this temptation.[7] They argue that technology plays an important role in how people enact their sexual desires and that when it comes to those who display a marked preference for artificial partners, we should recognize a new type of sexual identity, namely, "digisexuality." As they put it: "Many people will find that their experiences with this technology become integral to their sexual identity, and some will come to prefer them to direct sexual interactions with humans. We propose to label those people who consider such experiences essential to their sexual identity, 'digisexuals.'"[8]

McArthur and Twist make this argument with circumspection and care. They point out that sexual orientations and identities occur along a continuum. Some people will occasionally use technology to get their kicks but will retain strong preferences for human-to-human contact. They suggest that only those who live primarily at one extreme end of the spectrum deserve the label "digisexual."[9] They also recognize that people belonging to this group will almost certainly suffer from stigmatization as a result of their pronounced sexual preference, but then argue that this simply needs to be understood and combatted.[10] In saying this, they make the case for using the "digisexuality" label from a largely detached, scientific perspective, suggesting that digisexuality is something that needs to be acknowledged and studied.

I agree that there is a phenomenon here worthy of greater scientific scrutiny, but I think we should be very cautious about encouraging the widespread use of a new sexual identity label, such as "digisexuality." Admittedly this is not something that is necessarily under our control since, as pointed out earlier, we are constantly in the business of labeling and classifying one another. Nevertheless, to the extent that we can control our tendency to label and classify one another, we should avoid the temptation to recognize a new minority of digisexuals. This stance is not motivated by any bigotry or desire to suppress a new truth about human sexuality. It is motivated by the desire to avoid pathologizing and "othering" what should be viewed as part of the ordinary range of human sexual desire.

The argument for this view has two prongs to it. The first is to claim that the recognition of a particular set of sexual desires as a distinctive identity or orientation is not metaphysically mandated. In other words, there is nothing in the raw data of human sexual desire that demands that we apply a particular label or classification to those desires. The second prong is to argue that to the extent that we do apply such labels, there is a tendency for us to ignore important nuances in the actual raw data of human sexual desire and for this to have pernicious consequences. Consequently, since grouping some set of sexual desires into a distinctive identity label is not metaphysically mandated, nor is it socially or ethically desirable, we should resist the temptation to do so.

---

[7] McArthur and Twist, "The Rise of Digisexuality: Therapeutic Challenges and Possibilities."
[8] *Id.* at 334–335.   [9] *Id.* at 338.   [10] *Id.* at 338.

Let's explore both prongs of the argument in more detail, starting with the claim that recognizing a new sexual identity is not metaphysically warranted. In making this claim I am inspired by a theory of sexual orientation developed by Saray Ayala: *the conceptual act theory of sexual* orientation.[11] The gist of the theory is as follows. Humans have many different phenomenological experiences in their lifetimes. In many cases, these experiences are messy and not finely differentiated. Think of our auditory or color experiences. Though we do perceive distinctions between different shades and different musical notes, the reality of sound waves and light waves is that they blend or fade into one another. It is only through the use of conventional linguistic labels that we bring some order and structure to the phenomenological soup of experience. What's more, some people's conceptual toolkit enables them to more finely differentiate their phenomenological experiences than others. I know people who can easily recognize and distinguish different notes and scales in a piece of music. I do not have this ability. I lump together experiences that others can split.

The psychologist Lisa Feldman Barrett has argued that this same phenomenon underlies our emotional experiences.[12] The initial phenomenological reality of emotion is a raw feeling that gets interpreted through a particular conventional conceptual toolkit. We translate our raw emotional experiences into the feelings of "anger," "sorrow," or "joy" (and so on). But different cultures parse the phenomenological reality of emotion in different ways, grouping and organizing feelings in ways that are not immediately recognizable to cultural outsiders.

Ayala argues that the same is true for how we experience sexual desire. Over the course of a lifetime, people will experience sexual desire, arousal, and release in response to many different things. Oftentimes the desires will be directed at other people, but sometimes they won't. People have been known to experience arousal in response to all sorts of environmental stimuli (feet, washing machines, buildings and so on). What then happens is that people group their sexual experiences together in order to make sense of their sexual identities and orientations. In doing this, some experiences are ignored, suppressed, and discounted, while others are accentuated. You will probably discount all those times you got aroused by the vibrations of the school bus, but not those times you got aroused when you danced with your classmate at the school dance. You won't call yourself an automotive-fetishist no matter how many times you got aroused on the school bus. Likewise, and perhaps more realistically, I suspect there are many people who primarily gain sexual release through masturbation and not through intercourse with another human being. Nevertheless, I suspect that the majority of those people do not classify themselves as avowed autoeroticists. They don't interpret their masturbatory experiences through an identity label. They see those experiences as a just part of the full range of desirable sexual experiences, all of which are still being actively pursued.

---

[11] Saray Ayala, "Sexual Orientation and Choice," *Journal of Social Ontology* 3(2) (2018): 249–265.
[12] Lisa Feldman Barrett, "Solving the Emotion Paradox: Categorization and the Experience of Emotion," *Personality and Social Psychology Review* 10(1) (2006): 20–46.

The point here is that the same is likely to be true of those who get their sexual kicks through technology, even those who primarily do so with artificial partners. Consider Zheng Jiajia and Akihiko Kondo, for example. Both of them claim to have sought out artificial partners *after* failing to find love among their fellow humans. This would suggest that they haven't completely lost this form of sexual desire. The danger is that if we apply, and encourage them to apply, an identity label to their newfound sexual preferences, we also encourage them to discount or suppress the other aspects of their sexual affect. They start exaggerating what is in reality a more diverse and differentiated phenomenological reality.

This brings us to the second prong of the argument: that applying identity labels can be socially and ethically pernicious. You might be primed to be skeptical about this. You might point to other identity political movements in support of your skepticism and argue that owning an identity label can be both politically and personally empowering. If you belong to a group, you feel less alone in the world. Similarly, if you and other members of your group are socially disadvantaged, banding together can help you to stand up and agitate for legal rights and protections. This has been true for the feminist movement and the gay rights movement. But it is noteworthy that both of these movements arose in response to preexisting prejudice and discriminatory classification. People within those groups were already subject to an oppressive identity-labeling and hence saw the need to band together, wear their label as a matter of pride, and work for social reform. In the absence of that preexisting prejudice, the case for identity-labeling is much less persuasive. Identity-labeling tends to encourage divisiveness and othering—the "us" against "them" mentality. People quickly appoint themselves as the guardians of the identity, creating criteria for determining who belongs and who does not. Furthermore, if belonging to a particular identity category brings with it certain social benefits and legal protections, people might be encouraged to overinterpret their experiences so that they can fit within the relevant group: they force themselves into a group so that they can belong, thereby doing violence to their actual experience. In short, the identity-labeling can foster, just as often as it can combat, social division and polarization.

To be clear, the claim is not that all identity labels are pernicious or scientifically inaccurate. Some labels have social and scientific value. The claim is rather that identity labels have power and should be treated with caution. Sexual phenomenology is often more diverse and differentiated than our identity labels allow. This means that lumping someone into a particular category is often not warranted. Recognizing and valorizing the identity label may encourage and incentivize people to force themselves to fit into a category to which they do not belong. So, unless we are trying to combat some preexisting social prejudice or stigmatization, we should very reluctant to classify people as "digisexuals." This does not mean that we must ignore the role that artificial partners play in people's sexual lives, or that we cannot study the various manifestations of "digisexualities." It just means we should avoid labeling people as "digisexuals" (or any other cognate term like "robosexual"). We should accept digisexuality as just part of the normal range of human sexual experience.

AI AND SEXUAL ASSISTANCE

Sex toys and other sex aids have long been used to assist and complement human-to-human sexual activity, and AIs and robots are already widely used to assist and complement nonsexual human activity. It should be no surprise then to find AI being harnessed toward sexually assistive roles. We already see smart sex toys that try to learn from user data to optimize sexual pleasure; "quantified self" apps that enable users to track and optimize various aspects of their sexual performance; and simple AI assistants that help with other aspects of intimate behavior, including apps that help to automate or assist with sending intimate communications to your partner.[13] Does the use of such AI-based sexual assistants raise any significant ethical concerns? In previous work, I, along with my colleagues Sven Nyholm and Brian Earp, analyzed eight different ethical concerns one might have about the use of AI in intimate relationships.[14] In the interests of brevity, I will discuss four key ethical concerns here.

The Privacy Concern: This is the concern that the use of AI assistants in intimate sexual relationships constitutes a major assault on personal privacy. This could be because partners use services to spy on one another without consent, which is already a problem in abusive intimate relationships.[15] It could also be because AI assistants are owned and controlled by third parties (e.g., companies/corporations) who capture sexual data from their users and use this to optimize and market their products and services. Sometimes this is done with the consent of the users; sometimes it is not. Indeed, several lawsuits have already been settled between companies and users of smart sex toys due to the fact that data was collected from those devices without the users' consent.[16] Of course, violations of privacy are a general concern with digital technology, extending far beyond the sexual or intimate use case,[17] but one might argue that the ethical concerns are higher in this case given the unique importance of sexual privacy.

---

[13] For discussions of the different apps and services, see: Deborah Lupton, "Quantified Sex: A Critical Analysis of Sexual and Reproductive Self-tracking Using Apps," *Culture, Health and Sexuality* 17(4) (2015): 440–53; Karen Levy, "Intimate Surveillance," *Idaho Law Review* 51 (2014): 679–93; John Danaher, Sven Nyholm, and Brian Earp, "The Quantified Relationship," *American Journal of Bioethics* 18(2) (2018): 1–19; John Danaher, "Toward an Ethics of AI Assistants: An Initial Framework," *Philosophy and Technology* 31(4) (2018): 629–653; and Evan Selinger, "Today's Apps Are Turning Us into Sociopaths," *Wired* (February 26, 2014), available at https://www.wired.com/2014/02/outsourcing-humanity-apps/; and Evan Selinger, "Don't Outsource Your Dating Life," *CNN: Edition* (May 2, 2014), available at http://edition.cnn.com/2014/05/01/opinion/selinger-outsourcing-activities/index.html (accessed November 29, 2016).

[14] Danaher, Nyholm, and Earp, "The Quantified Relationship."

[15] Levy, "Intimate Surveillance."

[16] Alex Hern, "Vibrator Maker Ordered to Pay Out C$4m for Tracking Users' Sexual Activity," *The Guardian* (March 14, 2017), available at https://www.theguardian.com/technology/2017/mar/14/we-vibe-vibrator-tracking-users-sexual-habits.

[17] Woodrow Hartzog, *Privacy's Blueprint: The Battle to Control the Design of New Technologies* (Cambridge, MA: Harvard University Press, 2018); and Shoshana Zuboff, *The Age of Surveillance Capitalism* (London: Profile Books, 2019).

The Disengagement Concern: This is the concern that AI sexual assistants may distract us from, or encourage us to disengage from, sexually intimate activity and thereby corrode or undermine a core part of the value of that activity. The argument would be that a lot of the good of sexual intimacy (and indeed other forms of intimacy) stems from being present in the moment, that is, enjoying the sexual activity for what it is. But can you really be present if you are using some sex assistant to track the number of calories you burn, or the decibel level you reach, or the number of thrusts you perform during sexual activity? (These, incidentally, are all real examples of some of the uses to which descriptive and predictive analytics have been put in intimate apps.)[18] Similarly, but in a nonsexual case, Evan Selinger worries about the use of automated and AI-assisted intimate communication apps on the grounds that they create the impression that someone is thinking about and caring about another person in a particular moment when in fact they are not and are letting the app do the work for them.[19] The disengagement concern is, once again, a general concern about digital technology— think of all those complaints about the "anti-social" use of smartphones at parties and meetings—but we might worry that it is particularly problematic in the intimate case because of how important being present is to intimacy.

The Misdirection Argument: Related to the previous concern, this is a concern about the kinds of things that AI sexual assistants might assist people with. AI assistants in general tend to provide users with information about themselves or the world around them or prompt them to do certain things in the future. The same is likely to occur with AI sexual assistants: they might give users information about how to optimize their sexual experiences or prompt them to try particular activities. One worry is that the assistants could encourage activities that are not conducive to good sexual experience. This is, indeed, already an expressed concern about the various sex tracking apps that have been created.[20] As noted, those apps often encourage users to focus on things like the number of calories burned during sex, the number of thrusts during sex, and the decibel level reached during sex. One reason for this is that it is relatively easy to track and measure these things. But there is no reason to think that any of them is correlated with good sex. On the contrary, focusing on those measures might actually undermine good sex. This worry is distinct from the previous one because it is not about the user being taken out of the moment but rather about them doing things that are not particularly pleasurable/valuable in the moment.

The Ideological Concern: A final concern, which is also related to the two preceding ones, has to do with the ideological impact of AI sexual assistants on intimate relationships. The concern is that these assistants might impose a certain model of what an ideal intimate/sexual relationship is on the people who make use of them. They might, for example, recreate and reinforce gender stereotypes about sexual desire and preference.

---

[18] Danaher, Nyholm, and Earp, "The Quantified Relationship."
[19] Selinger, "Don't Outsource Your Dating Life."
[20] On this criticism, see Lupton, "Quantified Sex: A Critical Analysis of Sexual and Reproductive Self-tracking Using Apps," and Levy, "Intimate Surveillance."

Karen Levy, for example, has argued that many intimate tracking apps reinforce the view that women are the subjects of surveillance and sexual control.[21] Others argue that the apps might encourage an economic or exchange-based model of intimate relations over a more informal-reciprocation model. This is because the devices might encourage users to track who does what for whom and encourage them to optimize/maximize certain metrics, all to the detriment of what a truly valuable intimate relationship should be.[22]

What can be said in response to these concerns? Well, the privacy concern is probably the most serious. If partners use AI assistants to spy on one another or manipulate one another's behavior in a nontransparent way, then this would be a major worry. It could provide assistance and cover for dominating and abusive relationships. Such relationships will exist in the absence of technological assistance, but the technology might make it easier to implement certain forms of dominating control. It seems uncontroversial then to suggest that any app or service that makes it easy for one intimate partner to spy on another without the other's consent should, if possible, be banned. Spying by third parties should also be limited but is trickier to manage. It does seem to be inherent to digital technology that it facilitates some kind of tracking and surveillance. We can try to mitigate the harm that is done by this tracking and surveillance through robust legal protection of individual privacy. This legal protection would force the companies that provide the relevant apps and services to put in place measures that prevent nontransparent and nonconsensual uses of individual data. The EU's General Data Protection Regulation is a step in the right direction in this regard.

But it may well be that people are willing to waive their privacy rights in order to make use of assistive technologies. This appears to be the case for many people already. How many times have you consented to digital surveillance out of convenience? Privacy advocates can counter that this is simply because people do not fully appreciate the damage that can be done by the misuse of their personal data, but even still, for many people, convenient access to digital services is often favored over privacy. This suggests that whether or not people are willing to forgo some privacy when using AI sex assistants might depend on whether they find those assistants useful in their intimate lives. If they do, then sexual privacy might be significantly eroded.

This is where the other three objections come in. They provide some reason to question whether AI sex assistants will in fact be useful, highlighting the various ways in which they might undermine or corrode intimate relationships. Although each of the three concerns has some merit, they can be overstated. There are three reasons for this. First, it is important to bear in mind that there is no single model for the ideal intimate relationship. Different relationship models work for different sets of people at different times. Apps and assistive AI that seem useless, distracting or misdirected to some people, might be useful, engaging and fulfilling to others. Even the seemingly comical examples of sex-tracking apps that get people to quantify certain aspects of their sex life

---

[21] Levy, "Intimate Surveillance."

[22] Danaher, Nyholm, and Earp, "The Quantified Relationship," 7–8.

might, for some people, lead to a more pleasurable and fulfilling sex life. As long as people are not forced or compelled to use particular AI sex assistants, their use need not lead to the ideological imposition of a specific model of the ideal relationship. A diversity of apps and assistants could provide room for partners to explore different possibilities in accordance with their own needs and wishes. Second, while some of the early attempts to provide AI assistance might seem crude and unsophisticated, they are likely to improve over time and provide more useful guidance. This is because there is reason to think that the tracking and quantification made possible by sex and relationship apps can be used to good effect. To give one example of this, the research carried out by the Gottman Institute on successful relationships suggests that relationships can be improved if partners explicitly record details of their intimate lives and follow certain rituals of connection.[23] These recommendations are based on extensive, longitudinal research on what makes for a successful intimate relationship. Digital assistants could make it easier to implement these recommendations. Indeed, the Gottman Institute already offers a free smartphone app that helps couples implement some of them.[24] One can easily imagine more sophisticated, AI-based versions of this app being created in the future and providing far more effective and personalized assistance. Third, to the extent that worries remain about the effect of these technologies on sexual intimacy, these worries can be mitigated (to a large extent) by encouraging more thoughtful engagement with the technology. The problems outlined above are at their most severe if people use AI assistants as a substitute for thinking for themselves and not as a complement to thinking for themselves. If there could be one major recommendation made to the designers of AI intimate assistants, it would be to include clear warnings to users that the services and recommendations offered by these assistants are not a panacea to all their sexual woes. They can be beneficial, but only if the user(s) critically reflects on the role of the service in their own intimate lives. Including prompts for such critical reflection could be a focus for designers who wish to encourage the ethical use of AI sex assistants.

The bottom line is, then, that although AI assistants could undermine and corrode our intimate and sexual lives, there is some reason for optimism. The careful, critical and nondogmatic use of such assistants might complement and improve our intimate behavior.

AI AND LOVE

Let's close out this chapter by returning to the two men whose stories I told in the introduction: Zheng Jiajia and Akihiko Kondo. Both of them "married" artificial beings. An obvious question to ask is what the ethical or philosophical status of those marriages

---

[23] See https://www.gottman.com/.   [24] Available at https://www.gottman.com/couples/apps/.

might be? Are they manifestations of genuinely loving relationships or are they slightly unusual sexual fetishes? At the outset, I would emphasize that any answer to this question should not be understood as an attempt to stigmatize or shame those who prefer such relationships. But the question is worth asking since we attach a lot of value to loving relationships, and if we could have loving relationships with AIs and robots, it might provide reason to create them.

There is no shortage of opposition to the idea that one could be in a loving relationship with a robot. Dylan Evans, for example, has argued that there is something paradoxical about the idea of robotic lover.[25] His argument focuses on the asymmetrical nature of the relationship between a human and a robot. Presumably, any robotic lover will be programmed to "love" their human partner. If the robot could choose their partner, then what would be the point in creating it? The advantage of having a robot lover over a human lover is the fact that the robot has to love you: that you have ultimate control over its responses to you (this desire for control seems to be one of the motivations behind Zheng Jiajia and Akihiko Kondo's actions). But this control comes at a cost, according to Evans, because a core part of what people want in a loving relationship is a partner (or partners) who freely chooses to be with them. As he puts it, people want their lover's commitment to them to "be the fruit of an ongoing choice, rather than inflexible and unreflexive behavior patterns."[26]

Michael Hauskeller also argues against the idea of a robotic lover. Although he concedes that it may be possible to create human-like robots that "appear" to be in love with you, he counters that such a lover would never be as satisfying to you as a human lover. Following Evans, he argues that one of the main reasons for this is that no matter how good the illusion of love is, there would always be some reason to suspect or doubt whether the robot really loves you, given its manufactured and programmed origins.[27]

In a more extensive analysis of the concept of love, Sven Nyholm and Lily Frank also express doubts about the possibility of being in a loving relationship with a robot.[28] Exploring different conceptions of romantic love (including, the claim that to be in love is to be a "good match" with your partner, or to be attracted to the "distinctive particularity" of your partner), they argue that while it is not impossible to create a robot that meets the conditions needed for a loving relationship, it would be exceptionally difficult to do so, requiring technology far in advance of what is currently available. In making their case, they use the "hired actor" analogy to express the basic problem with creating a robotic lover: it seems like the best we can really do with a robotic lover is to create an

---

[25] Dylan Evans, "Wanting the Impossible: The Dilemma at the Heart of Intimate Human-Robot Relationships," in *Close Engagements with Artificial Companions: Key Social, Psychological, Ethical and Design Issues*, ed. Yorick Wilks (Philadelphia, PA: John Benjamins, 2010).

[26] *Id.* at 74–75.

[27] Michael Hauskeller, "Automatic Sweethearts for Transhumanists," in *Robot Sex: Social and Ethical Implications*, ed. John Danaher and Neil McArthur (Cambridge, MA: MIT Press, 2017), 213.

[28] Sven Nyholm and Lily Eva Frank, "From Sex Robots to Love Robots: Is Mutual Love with a Robot Possible?," in *Robot Sex: Social and Ethical Implications*, ed. John Danaher and Neil McArthur (Cambridge, MA: MIT Press, 2017).

entity that "plays the part" of being in love with you, but never quite graduates from acting to genuine love.[29]

These criticisms are intuitive and attractive, but they have some problems. To see what they are it is important to distinguish between two fears articulated by the critics. The first—which we might call the "no depth" fear—is that robot lovers are all surface and no depth. They act "as if" they love you, but there is nothing more to it than performance: they don't really feel or consciously experience the relevant emotions that we associate with being in love. The second—which we might call the "programming" fear—is that robot lovers cannot freely and autonomously choose to love you. They will always be programmed to love you. These two fears are related to one another—most alleged robot lovers probably lack depth and free choice—but they are not the same thing. A robot might be programmed to love you even if it has the right kind of experiential depth and vice versa.

Are these two criticisms of robot lovers valid? Let's consider the "no depth" problem first. The easy rebuttal to this is to say that even if robots currently lack the requisite experiential depth it is possible, someday, that they will have it. When that day arrives, we can have robot lovers. The major problem with this rebuttal, however, is that it kicks the can down the road and fails to grapple with the philosophical issue at the heart of the "no depth" argument, namely: does experiential depth actually matter when it comes to determining whether or not a particular relationship counts as a loving one? I don't think it does. If a robot appears, on the surface, to be in love with you, then that's all it takes for you to be in a loving relationship with that robot.

This might sound a little crazy, but I defend it on the grounds that we must, as a practical matter, be behaviorists when it comes to understanding the ethical status of our relationships with other beings.[30] In other words, we have to apply the methodological behaviorism of psychologists and computer scientists (e.g., the behaviorism at the heart of the Turing Test for machine intelligence) to our ethical relationships with other beings. The central tenet of this "ethical behaviorism" is that when you try to determine the moral quality of your relationships (including your duties and responsibilities) with other beings, you cannot use unobservable, inner mental states to make your assessment. You have to rely on externally observable behavioral and functional patterns. You may, of course, hypothesize the existence of inner mental states to explain those observable patterns. But any inference you make as to the presence of those states must ultimately be grounded in or guided by an externally observable pattern. The problem with many of the philosophical accounts of what it takes to be in a loving relationship is that they focus, implicitly or explicitly, on unobservable and inherently private mental states (e.g., feelings of commitment/attachment, sincere expressions of emotions, and so on). As a result, it is effectively impossible to have any confidence in the existence of loving relationships *unless* you accept that observable behavioral and functional patterns can

[29] *Id.* at 223–224.
[30] John Danaher, "The Philosophical Case for Robot Friendship," *Journal of Posthuman Studies* 2(2) (2019).

provide epistemic warrant for our judgments about the presence of the relevant private mental states. In other words, ethical behaviorism is already, of necessity, the approach we take to understanding the ethical status of our relationships with our fellow human beings. This means the "no depth" argument doesn't work. Since we are unable to plumb the depths of our human lovers, we cannot apply a different evidential standard to robotic lovers.

This point has to be finessed in order to avoid some potentially absurd interpretations. For starters, it is important to realize that in order to provide the basis for a loving relationship, the performance and illusion from a robot will need to be equivalent to the performance and illusion we get from a human lover. It's unlikely that any currently existing robot or AI achieves such performative equivalency. So this remains, to some extent, a future possibility, not a present reality.

Similarly, there are some counterarguments to ethical behaviorism that are worth considering, if only to deepen the understanding of what ethical behaviorism entails. For example, some people might argue that we do rely on something other than behavior to determine the moral quality of our relationships with others. Perhaps it is because we know that our lovers are made of the right stuff (biological/organic material) that we are confident they can love us? Or perhaps it is because we know they have the right kind of developmental/evolutionary history? If so, then someone might argue that robots and AI would still not count as "proper" lovers even if they were performatively equivalent to human lovers.

But it is hard to see why the presence or absence of these other factors should have should have that effect. What is the rational connection between being made of the right stuff (or having the right history) and the capacity to form a loving relationship with another? Suppose your spouse behaves in a way that is entirely consistent with the hypothesis that they love you. But then suppose, one day, you learn that they are, in fact, an alien from another planet and don't share the same biological constitution. They continue to behave as they always did. Should you doubt whether you are in a truly loving relationship with them? It's hard to see why. The revelation of their alien origins, in and of itself, should not undermine the claim that they are in a loving relationship. The consistent behavioral evidence of love should trump the other considerations. The same should hold for a robotic or artificial lover.

Some people might come back and argue that there are cases where our faith in the existence of a loving relationship would be shaken by learning something about the origins or history of our human lovers. Suppose, for example, you learn that your human lover was, indeed, a hired actor, or that they have been having an affair for years without your awareness. Surely that would undermine your confidence that they are in a loving relationship with you? And surely that is more akin to what it would be like to have a robot lover? But these counterexamples do not work. For starters, it is not clear that either of these revelations should shake our faith in the existence of a loving relationship. It seems plausible to suggest that a hired actor could grow to love the person with whom they have an initially fake relationship, and it also seems plausible to suggest that love can survive infidelity. If the person still behaves and appears to love you then perhaps they do, despite these revelations. But even if that's a stretch for some people, I would suggest that what really shakes their faith in the existence of a loving relationship in both of these cases is the fact that they will acquire (or have reason to suspect the existence of) some new behavioral evidence that contradicts the old behavioral evidence that convinced them they were in a loving relationship. For example, they have learned that the actor says bad things about them when they are "off" the job or that their partner has been planning to leave them for the person with whom they are having an affair. This new behavioral evidence might completely undermine their belief in a loving relationship or at least prompt them to seek out further behavioral evidence to confirm whether their partner still loves them. Either way, it is behavioral evidence that will do the damage (or repair). In any event, neither of these examples is a good analogy with the robotic lover case, where presumably the robotic nature and origins of the lover will be known from day one.

What about the "programming" fear? Evans is right that we want (or, at least, *should want*) our lovers to freely choose us. If a robot is programmed or conditioned to love us, then it seems like there is something suspicious or inferior about the kind of "love" they can give. But we shouldn't overstate this fear either. It is conceivable that we could create robotic lovers that behave "as if" they freely choose us (and, remember, behaving "as if" they choose us is enough, following ethical behaviorism). The robotic lover might act in fickle way or test its human companion's true commitment, much like a human lover. This could even be an attractive quality in a robotic lover, because it makes it more like the human-to-human case. The desire for this isn't as bizarre or unfathomable as Evans makes out.

But beyond that, there is also reason to doubt whether the presence or absence of "programming" should undermine our belief in the existence of a loving relationship. Humans are arguably "programmed" to love one another. A combination of innate biological drives and cultural education makes humans primed to find one another sexually attractive and form deep and lasting bonds with one another. Indeed, people often talk about love as being something other than a free and autonomous choice. We "fall" into love, we don't choose it. We find ourselves attracted to others, often despite our better judgment. The heart wants what it wants, and so on. Furthermore, in some cultures, arranged marriages and relationships are common, and while they seem unusual, maybe even cruel, from some perspectives, the partners in such relationships often grow to love one another and report high levels of relationship satisfaction, sometimes higher, and often no worse, than the satisfaction of those in "autonomous" marriages.[31] So it is not that unusual to believe that love can blossom from some pre-programming and prearranging of unions.

[31] Robert Epstein, Mayuri Pandit, and Mansi Thakar, "How Love Emerges in Arranged Marriages: Two Cross-cultural Studies," *Journal of Comparative Family Studies* 44 (3) (2013): 341–360; and P.C. Regan, S. Lakhanpal, and C. Anguiano, "Relationship Outcomes in Indian-American Love-based and Arranged Marriages," *Psychological Report* 110(3) (2012): 915–924.

Critics might dispute these examples and argue that the kind of programming involved in human relationships is very different from the kind that will arise in human-robot relationships. Humans are only loosely programmed to seek attachment. They are not brainwashed to love a particular person. Also, even in the case of arranged marriage (where there is greater restriction and direction of choice) the partners are not coerced into the relationship on an ongoing basis. They can exercise their autonomy after the union has formed and escape the relationship if they desire.

But it is not clear that these disanalogies are all that strong. It is true that, classically, robots and AIs were programmed from the top down by particular human program-mers to follow highly specified instructions, but this is no longer the norm. Robots and AIs are now programmed from the bottom up, to follow learning rules and to adapt to new challenges and circumstances. The flexibility of this adaptive learning is still rather limited—we are yet to create a generalized form of artificial intelligence—but as this approach proliferates and grows, the alleged disanalogies between the programming of human lovers and robot lovers will narrow. It will no longer be absurd to claim that robot lovers commit to us on the basis of a free and ongoing choice, nor to imagine that they might fall out of love with us through continued learning.

None of this to say that preferring a robot lover over a human lover is a good thing or that there are no ethical problems with creating robot lovers. There are. Worries about the objectification and domination of robot partners, as well as the social consequences that this might have, have been voiced by several critics. I have discussed these worries at length in previous work.[32] Similarly, Nyholm, and Frank argue that the creators of robotic lovers and sexual partners may be under an obligation not to mislead users as to the capacities of the robots in question to form loving relationships.[33] They worry that manufacturers might be tempted to exploit the emotional vulnerability of some con-sumers in order to make their products more attractive. While this is a problem with all consumer products (to some extent), it seems like a particularly acute problem for robotic lovers, given the centrality and importance of sex and love in human life. A rela-tively strict set of rules may be required to guard against abuse. But, of course, what is and is not permitted by this set of rules depends, crucially, on what we think it takes to form a legitimate loving relationship. This is why I have focused on the philosophical nature of love in the preceding discussion. If I am correct in my analysis, it will someday be possible to form a loving relationship with a robot if the robot can convincingly and consistently perform the part of being a lover, and hence any restrictions imposed to prevent exploitation will need to take that into consideration.

---

[32] John Danaher, "Robotic Rape and Robotic Child Sexual Abuse: Should They Be Criminalised?," *Criminal Law and Philosophy* 11(1) (2017): 71–95; John Danaher, "The Symbolic Consequences Argument in the Sex Robot Debate," in *Robot Sex: Social and Ethical Implications*, ed. Danaher and McArthur (Cambridge, MA: MIT Press, 2017); and John Danaher, "Regulating Child Sex Robots: Restriction or Experimentation?," *Medical Law Review* 27(4) (2019): 553–575.

[33] Sven Nyholm and Lily Eva Frank, "It Loves Me, It Loves Me Not: Is It Morally Problematic to Design Sex Robots that Appear to "Love" Their Owners?," *Techné* 23(3) (2019): 402–424.

CONCLUSION

To wrap up, AI and robotics are being, and will continue to be, used to augment and complement human sexuality. In this chapter, I have addressed three issues that might arise as a result and made three main arguments. First, I have argued that we should be cautious about recognizing a new form of sexual identity that applies to those who primarily express and enact their sexualities through these technologies. Doing so is not metaphysically mandated and may contribute to social stigmatization. Second, I have argued that AI can be used to assist human sexual and intimate relationships. Such assistance poses a number of risks—particularly to privacy—but these risks should not be overstated and should not prevent the beneficial use of AI sex assistants. Finally, I argued that, contrary to a number of critics, it is possible to form a loving relationship with a robot or AI.

BIBLIOGRAPHY

Danaher, John and Neil McArthur eds. *Robot Sex: Social and Ethical Implications.* Cambridge, MA: MIT Press, 2017.

Danaher, John, Sven Nyholm, and Brian Earp. "The Quantified Relationship." *American Journal of Bioethics.* 18(2) (2018): 1–19.

Devlin, Kate. *Turned On: Science, Sex and Robots.* London: Bloomsbury, 2018.

Hauskeller, Michael. *Sex and the Posthuman Condition.* London: Palgrave MacMillan, 2014.

Levy, David. *Love and Sex with Robots: The Evolution of Human-Robot Relationships.* New York: Harper Collins, 2007.

Levy, Karen. "Intimate Surveillance." *Idaho Law Review* 51(2018): 679–693.

Lieberman, Hallie. *Buzz: The Stimulating History of the Sex Toy.* New York: Pegasus Books, 2017.

Lupton, Deborah. "Quantified Sex: A Critical Analysis of Sexual and Reproductive Self-tracking Using Apps." *Culture, Health and Sexuality* 17(4) (2015): 440–453.

McArthur, Neil and Markie Twist. "The Rise of Digisexuality: Therapeutic Challenges and Possibilities." *Sex and Relationship Therapy.* 32(3–4) (2017): 334–344.

Nyholm, Sven and Lily Eva Frank. "From Sex Robots to Love Robots: Is Mutual Love with a Robot Possible?" In *Robot Sex: Social and Ethical Implications*, ed. John Danaher and Neil McArthur. Cambridge, MA: MIT Press, 2017.

PART IV

PERSPECTIVES
AND
APPROACHES

....

CHAPTER 22

PERSPECTIVES ON ETHICS OF AI

Computer Science

....

BENJAMIN KUIPERS

WHY IS THE ETHICS OF AI IMPORTANT?

....

AI uses computational methods to study human knowledge, learning, and behavior, in part by building agents able to know, learn, and behave. Ethics is a body of human knowledge that helps agents (humans today, but perhaps eventually robots and other AIs) decide how they and others should behave. The ethical issues raised by AI fall into two overlapping groups.

First, like other powerful tools or technologies (e.g., genetic engineering or nuclear power), potential deployments of AI raise ethical questions about their impact on human well-being.

Second, unlike other technologies, intelligent robots (e.g., autonomous vehicles) and other AIs (e.g., high-speed trading systems) make their own decisions about the actions they take, and thus could be considered as *members* of our society. Humans should be able to expect them to behave ethically. This requires AI research with the goal of understanding the function, structure, and content of ethical knowledge well enough to implement ethics in artificial agents.

As the deployment of AI, machine learning, and intelligent robotics becomes increasingly widespread, these problems become increasingly urgent.

WHAT IS THE FUNCTION OF ETHICS?

"At the heart of ethics are two questions: (1) What should I do?, and (2) What sort of person should I be?"[1] Ethics consists of principles for deciding how to act in various circumstances, reflecting what is right or wrong (or good or bad) to do in that situation.

It is clear that ethics (and hence what is considered right or wrong, or good or bad) changes significantly over historical time. Over similarly long historical timescales, despite discouraging daily news reports, it appears that the societies of our world are becoming stronger, safer, healthier, wealthier, and more just and inclusive for their members.[2]

Two important sources of concepts help make sense of these changes. First, game theory contributes the abstraction of certain types of interactions among people as games,[3] and behavioral economics shows that these games not only have winners and losers, but the overall impact on the players collectively can be described as positive-sum, zero-sum, or negative-sum.[4] Second, the theory of evolution, as applied to human and great ape cognition and sociality, shows how a way of life that depends on positive-sum cooperation among individuals is likely to provide for its society greater fitness than less cooperative ways of life.[5] We can therefore think of the function of ethics as promoting the survival and thriving of the society by influencing the behavior of its individual members, summarized as:

> *Ethics is a set of beliefs that a society conveys to its individual members, to encourage them to engage in positive-sum interactions and to avoid negative-sum interactions.*

As a society prospers, survives, and thrives, its individual members benefit as well, so ethical behavior is "nonobvious self-interest" for the individual.

Philosophers would consider this to be a *rule consequentialist* position,[6] but one where the relevant consequences are the survival and thriving of society, not the pleasures and pains of its individual members. It is *consequentialist* because actions are not evaluated according to whether they are intrinsically right or wrong (by some criterion), but according to their long-term good or bad consequences for the survival and thriving of

[1] Russ Shafer-Landau ed., *Ethical Theory: An Anthology* (Wiley-Blackwell, 2d ed. 2013), xi.

[2] Robert Wright, *Nonzero: The Logic of Human Destiny* (Pantheon, 2000); Steven Pinker, *The Better Angels of Our Nature: Why Violence Has Declined* (Viking Adult, 2011); Steven Pinker, *Enlightenment Now: The Case for Reason, Science, Humanism, and Progress* (Viking, 2018).

[3] John von Neumann and Oskar Morgenstern, *Theory of Games and Economic Behavior* (Princeton University Press, 1953).

[4] Samuel Bowles, *The Moral Economy: Why Good Incentives Are No Substitute for Good Citizens* (Yale University Press, 2016).

[5] Michael Tomasello, *A Natural History of Human Morality* (Harvard University Press, 2016).

[6] Walter Sinnott-Armstrong, "Consequentialism," in *The Stanford Encyclopedia of Philosophy*, ed. Edward N. Zalta (Winter 2015 edition).

society. This position is *rule* consequentialism because the unit that is evaluated is not the individual action decision, but the set of ethical principles (often rules) adopted by society.

Positive-Sum and Negative-Sum Interactions

Commerce and cooperation are paradigm positive-sum interactions. When one person voluntarily trades or sells something to someone else, each party receives something that they value more highly than what they gave. When cooperating on a project, partners contribute toward a common goal and reap a benefit greater than either could achieve alone.

Theft and violence are examples of negative-sum interactions. The thief gains something from the theft, but the loss to the victim is typically greater than the gain to the thief. Violent conflict is the paradigm negative-sum interaction, since both parties may be worse off afterward than before, possibly much worse off. (These are not cleanly separated cases. Violence in defense against external attack may be necessary to avoid a catastrophic outcome, and that defense itself is likely to be a cooperative project.)

Cooperation, Trust, and Social Norms

Cooperative projects among individuals are a major source of positive-sum outcomes. However, cooperation requires vulnerability, and trust that the vulnerability will not be exploited.[7]

> *Trust is a psychological state comprising the intention to accept vulnerability based on positive expectations of the intentions or behavior of another.*[8]

As intelligent robots or large corporations increasingly act as autonomous goal-seeking agents and therefore as members of our society, then they, too, need to be subject to the requirements of ethics and need to demonstrate that they can trust and be trustworthy.

Successful cooperation demonstrates the trustworthiness of the partners and produces more trust while exploitation reduces trust. By trusting each other enough to pool their resources and efforts, individuals working together can often achieve much more than the sum of their individual efforts working separately. Large cooperative projects, from raising a barn, to digging a canal, to creating an interstate highway system, produce large benefits for everyone. But if I spend a day helping raise your barn, I trust that in due time, you will spend a day helping to raise mine. And if taxes help pay for New York's

---

[7] Michael Tomasello, *A Natural History of Human Morality* (Harvard University Press, 2016).

[8] D.M. Rousseau, S.B. Sitkin, R.S. Burt, and C. Camerer, "Not So Different after All: A Cross-discipline View of Trust" *Academy of Management Review*, 23(3) (1998): 393–404.

Erie Canal or the Pennsylvania Turnpike, I trust that, in due time, taxes will also pay for the Panama Canal linking the East and West Coasts, and the St. Lawrence Seaway providing access to the Great Lakes. Some of the states in the United States emphasize this with the name "Commonwealth," meaning that shared resources provide shared prosperity.

Social norms are behavioral regularities that we as individual members of society can generally count on when planning our activities. By trusting these (near) invariants, many aspects of our lives become simpler, more efficient, and less risky and uncertain. Maintaining a social norm is a kind of cooperative project without specified partners. I accept certain minor sacrifices in return for similar behaviors by (almost) everyone else, providing a (near) invariant that we all can rely on.

For example, when having lunch at a cafe, condiments are freely available for my convenience, but I know not to pocket the extras, so they will continue to be available. Likewise, I trust that a simple painted stripe in the middle of a road I am driving on securely separates me from drivers going in the opposite direction, so I accept the minor sacrifice of not crossing that stripe even when my side is congested.

Like explicit cooperative projects, social norms provide positive-sum results for society, saving resources that would otherwise go toward protection and recovery, making us individually and collectively better off. Each requires *trust*: acceptance of vulnerability to the other partners, along with confidence that few others will exploit that vulnerability, even for individual gain.

I use the term "social norm" inclusively, to cover regularities ranging from laws and moral imperatives to nonmoral social conventions. Philosophers make many different distinctions among types and origins of social norms. By taking a design stance toward ethical systems for influencing the behavior of intelligent agents, human and nonhuman, in our society, I emphasize the common functional goal of encouraging positive-sum, and discouraging negative-sum, interactions.

Representing Ethical Knowledge

I have described ethics as *a set of beliefs that a society conveys to its individual members* and have stated that those beliefs are evaluated according to *their long-term good or bad consequences for the survival and thriving of the society*. Since the result of this evaluation depends on many complex factors and evolves over decades and centuries, it is not very useful to individuals in deciding how to act.

To make practical decisions, individual humans need concise and understandable ethical principles. For these principles to be useful for the long-term survival of the society, they must also be explainable and teachable to individuals entering the society, such as children and immigrants. If intelligent nonhuman agents such as robots and corporations are to apply ethical principles to their own behavior, these principles must be capable of being learned or programmed.

The field of philosophical ethics has, over the centuries, created a number of concise frameworks for ethical knowledge, built around concepts such as virtues, duties, utilities, contracts, and so forth.[9] While it is tempting to regard these as competing alternatives, it is generally recognized that they are pieces of a more complicated, incompletely understood, puzzle.[10]

The many fields of applied ethics (e.g., biomedical ethics[11]) appeal to all of these conceptual frameworks, starting with specific ethical questions and searching for clear, practical answers. Depending on the details of the case in question, clarity may come from one or another of the ethical frameworks, while others provide ambiguous or unacceptable results.

FAIRNESS IN THE ECONOMY

It may be possible to express several of these conceptual frameworks in a single knowledge representation based on *cases*, $\langle S,A,S',v \rangle$, where S and S' represent previous and resulting situations, A describes an action, and v is an evaluation.[12] The representation can describe the situations and action at different levels of detail, ranging from rich descriptions of experienced events, to highly schematic general patterns.

Ethics Research in the AI Community

A number of AI and robotics researchers explicitly address the problem of ethics for AI and robotics.[13] For example, Ron Arkin proposed that an autonomous system controlling a lethal weapon could be equipped with an "ethical governor" based on the Laws of War and Rules of Engagement, with the authority to override an attempt to deploy lethal force.[14] Human emotional reactions can lead to errors and even war crimes. Arkin claims that, by taking the human out of the loop, targeting can be more precise and lawful, making war more humane. Many others are more skeptical about the impact of lethal autonomous weapon systems.

Utilitarianism has been attractive in the AI community because it factors ethical decisions into (a) defining a utility function that represents preferences over states of the world, and (b) applying an optimization algorithm to identify the action (or rule) that maximizes expected utility. While philosophical utilitarianism aggregates utility

[9] Russ Shafer-Landau ed., *Ethical Theory: An Anthology* (Wiley-Blackwell, 2d ed., 2013).

[10] Cf. John Godfrey Saxe's 1873 children's poem, *The Blind Men and the Elephant*.

[11] T.L. Beauchamp and J.F. Childress, *Principles of Biomedical Ethics* (Oxford University Press, 6th ed., 2009).

[12] B. Kuipers, "How Can We Trust a Robot?," *Communications of the ACM*, 61(3) (2018): 86–95.

[13] Patrick Lin, Keith Abney, and George A. Bekey eds., *Robot Ethics: The Ethical and Social Implications of Robotics* (MIT Press, 2012).

[14] Ronald C. Arkin, *Governing Lethal Behavior in Autonomous Robots* (CRC Press, 2009).

over everyone in the society,[15] in game theory each individual player optimizes his or her own utility.[16]

A motivating problem is that there are many cases (e.g., the Prisoner's Dilemma, the Public Goods Game, the Tragedy of the Commons, etc.) where the "rational" solution according to game theory (the Nash equilibrium) results in poor outcomes for every player and a negative-sum result for the society. And in fact, humans playing these games tend to avoid the Nash equilibrium and get better outcomes.[17]

Much effort has gone into formulating utility functions for individual decision-making that lead to improved outcomes for everyone in society, often in the context of repeated games drawing from the same population of players. Vincent Conitzer and colleagues[18] show how a robot player can communicate its intention to behave in a trustworthy way by making a "suboptimal" move. The other player is meant to understand this as an offer to cooperate and feel obligated to reciprocate. Stuart Russell and others have posed the problem of *value alignment*,[19] as defining utility functions that lead to decisions similar to those that humans make. *Cooperative inverse reinforcement learning*[20] has been proposed as a solution to the value alignment problem where the robot tries to maximize the *human's* utility function, while recognizing that it has only incomplete knowledge of that utility function. This is intended to prevent a robot, however powerful, from optimizing a poorly chosen utility function in a way that causes a catastrophe according to human utilities.[21]

HUMAN AND NONHUMAN MEMBERS OF SOCIETY

Traditionally, a society's members are the individual human beings who participate in the society by interacting with each other and making decisions about what actions to perform.

---

[15] Peter Singer, *The Expanding Circle: Ethics, Evolution, and Moral Progress* (Princeton University Press, 1981).

[16] John von Neumann and Oskar Morgenstern, *Theory of Games and Economic Behavior* (Princeton University Press, 1953).

[17] J.K. Goeree and C.A. Holt, "Ten Little Treasures of Game Theory and Ten Intuitive Contradictions," *The American Economic Review* 91(5) (2001): 1402–1422; J.R. Wright and K. Leyton-Brown, "Predicting Human Behavior in Unrepeated Simultaneous-move Games," *Games and Economic Behavior* 106 (2017): 16–37.

[18] J. Letchford, V. Conitzer, and K. Jain, "An 'Ethical' Game-theoretic Solution Concept for Two-player Perfect-information Games," in *Int. Workshop on Internet and Network Economics (WINE)*, 2008.

[19] S. Russell, D. Dewey, and M. Tegmark, "Research Priorities for Robust and Beneficial Artificial Intelligence," *AI Magazine* 36(4) (Winter 2015): 105–114.

[20] D. Hadfield-Menell, A. Dragan, P. Abbeel, and S. Russell "Cooperative Inverse Reinforcement Learning," in *Advances in Neural Information Processing Systems (NIPS)*, 2016.

[21] Nick Bostrom, *Superintelligence: Paths, Dangers, Strategies* (Oxford University Press, 2014).

In recent years, progress in artificial intelligence, robotics, and machine learning has raised the prospect of intelligent nonhuman robots participating as members of our society. Autonomous vehicles must be trusted to behave safely and ethically in both routine traffic and emergency situations.[22] Other AIs that are not physically embodied, such as high-speed trading systems or social networks, should also behave safely and ethically.[23] Large-scale institutions can also be considered as intelligent entities: for-profit and nonprofit corporations, governments, churches, unions, and other corporate entities.[24]

For all of these entities participating in society, the function of ethics is the same—to encourage positive-sum interactions and discourage negative-sum ones, supporting the survival and thriving of society as a whole. Likewise, the same means help to accomplish this function—supporting trust in relevant social norms, and for each entity to demonstrate that it is trustworthy.

METHOD: ANALYZING SPECIFIC CASES OF TRUST AND ETHICS

There are many different domains of behavior, with different social norms and ethical principles available for trust. Furthermore, as noted earlier, social norms and ethical principles change over historical time. Our goal here cannot be to provide universal answers about how humans and nonhuman agents in society should behave. Rather, our goal must be to provide a framework for asking useful questions.

In the following sections, I discuss three quite different cases of ethical decision-making that are relevant to societies including both human and nonhuman agents. Autonomous vehicles are individual, embodied robots that make decisions about driving, some with ethical implications. Social networks are disembodied intelligent systems that mediate interactions among people, but that also collect large amounts of information, often disregarding individual privacy concerns. Corporations, to which we have entrusted much of the wealth in our economy, can also be viewed as intelligent agents, whose behavior should be governed by ethics.

In each of these examples, we ask what social norms people would want to trust. The ethical principles that a society adopts and encourages its individual members to follow determines the social norms that individuals in that society should be able to trust. We will consider how those social norms might be expressed.

[22] Patrick Lin, "The Ethics of Autonomous Cars," *The Atlantic Monthly* (October 8, 2013).

[23] M.P. Wellman and U. Rajan, "Ethical Issues for Autonomous Trading Agents," *Minds & Machines* 27 (2017): 609–624.

[24] B. Kuipers, An Existing, Ecologically-Successful Genus of Collectively Intelligent Artificial Creatures," in *Collective Intelligence* (2012), arXiv:1204.4116.

EXAMPLE 1: TRUST AND ETHICS FOR AUTONOMOUS VEHICLES

Vast sums are being invested to develop autonomous vehicles (AVs), which are intelligent robots intended to share the roads with ordinary human-driven vehicles as well as with pedestrians. These robots take passengers or cargo to their destinations, or simply bring the AV where it is next needed. The critical technological requirement is for the robot's perception to provide sufficient situational awareness, and for it to make the right decisions, to keep itself and humans safe.

To accept AVs on our roads, humans will need to trust their behavior. Inspired by Isaac Asimov's First Law of Robotics,[25] "A robot may not injure a human being or, through inaction, allow a human being to come to harm," we might start by proposing the following social norm:

(SN-0)   A robot (or AI or AV) will never harm a human being.

This is overly sweeping, to the point of impossibility, even without the clause about not failing to prevent harm through inaction. However, if we distinguish between deliberate and accidental harm, we can formulate a pair of more plausible social norms:

(SN-1)   A robot will never deliberately harm a human being.

(SN-2)   In a given situation, a robot will be no more likely than a skilled and alert human to accidentally harm a human being.

Achieving these two social norms will require technical solutions to difficult problems in perception, situational awareness, planning, and acting, but they do not set the impossible goal of guaranteeing that fatal accidents can never occur. We still need a carefully stated social norm describing when action is required to prevent harm that would otherwise happen.

The Deadly Dilemma

A concerned philosopher, inspired by the famous "Trolley Problem,"[26] might ask what the AV should do if it is suddenly confronted with a "Deadly Dilemma," where it cannot avoid colliding with one of two groups of humans and must decide which group to deliberately kill. Either choice in this dilemma clearly violates the social norm (SN-1), and therefore undermines trust in AVs by members of society.

---

[25] Isaac Asimov, *I, Robot* (Grosset & Dunlap, 1952).
[26] Judith Jarvis Thomson, "The Trolley Problem," *Yale Law Journal*, 94(6) (1985): 1395–1415.

While the original Trolley Problem is a useful thought experiment that philosophers use to explore the relationships between human moral intuitions and the predictions of different philosophical theories, it is not a useful guide for the design of embodied robots in the physical world. To design an ethical robot (such as an AV), we must reject the narrow framing of the Trolley Problem and formulate an additional social norm.

When humans experience a bad outcome, they often engage in *counterfactual thinking*, searching by mental simulation for a previous ("upstream") action that would have avoided the bad outcome.[27] For a unique event, counterfactual thinking is futile and can lead to depression, but for recurring types of events, it can produce valuable insights, "practical wisdom,"[28] that leads to better outcomes in the future. A situation like the Deadly Dilemma, with no good outcomes, should trigger counterfactual thinking, so the driver learns that a previously unremarkable situation like entering a narrow street requires driving much slower, to preserve the option of a safe emergency stop. By learning from counterfactuals, the attentive agent accumulates a store of practical wisdom that makes safe and ethical behavior much easier.

(SN-3)   *A robot must learn to anticipate and avoid Deadly Dilemmas.*

The concerned philosopher responds, "Yes, this scenario is unlikely, but what if it *does* happen?"

Perception in the physical world is imperfect, so neither humans nor robots can perceive an emergency situation well enough to be certain that it presents a Deadly Dilemma between exactly two alternatives. There is a probability distribution over a continuous space of similar scenarios, some of which involve fatalities, while many others are "Near Misses." A Near Miss is far more likely than a true Deadly Dilemma.

$$p(NearMiss|Observation) \gg p(DeadlyDilemma|Observation).$$

The best response when suddenly confronted by this situation is immediate emergency braking along with steering to minimize risk of injuries. This response satisfies the two social norms: (SN-1) the robot does not deliberately target any human, even to save others; and (SN-2) its probability of injuring a human is no greater than for a skilled and attentive human driver, faced with the same situation. Even in the rare case that there is a fatality, the AV has acted reasonably and ethically when confronted by a bad situation.

Aristotle tells us that virtue is a skill that improves with experience, like carpentry. The novice may be presented with a situation that appears to be a Deadly Dilemma. The expert has more experience, more practical wisdom, and acts earlier so the Deadly Dilemma can be avoided.

---

[27] Neal Roese and Kai Epstude, "The Functional Theory of Counterfactual Thinking: New Evidence, New Challenges, New Insights," *Advances in Experimental Social Psychology* 56 (2017): 1–79.

[28] Aristotle, *Nicomachean Ethics*, trans. Terence Irwin (Hackett, 2d ed., 1999).

Ethical Principles to Encourage Trust

The social norm (*SN-1*) above translates naturally into an easily stated ethical duty: *Never deliberately harm a human being*. To the extent that a robot visibly follows this rule, it becomes more *trustworthy* and is increasingly trusted to follow the rule in the future.

The second social norm (*SN-2*) sets a bar for competence. The capabilities of human drivers and AVs can be tested and compared. Young humans are subject to age, time, and situation constraints on driving until they accumulate enough experience and practical wisdom to become trustworthy drivers. Likewise, elderly human drivers face ethical requirements to restrict or give up their own driving according to their abilities as observed by themselves or others.

The third social norm (*SN-3*) requires a continual effort to anticipate potential Deadly Dilemmas via counterfactual thinking, learning to recognize the upstream decision point and the choice that avoids the Dilemma.

As engineered devices, AVs can be designed with mechanisms for self-monitoring and self-evaluation, to determine in real time whether they are able to drive safely in the current situation. The details of such mechanisms may not have concise descriptions in natural language, but their overall effect would correspond to an ethical duty such as: *When it is not safe to drive, stop safely and ask for assistance*.

Many other circumstances can arise when an AV shares our roads with human drivers and pedestrians. For example, if an AV is stopped at a crosswalk, how can a human pedestrian trust it enough to walk in front of it? This requires adequate situational awareness by the AV and also the ability to communicate its trustworthiness to the human pedestrian. Both of these problems may have technical solutions, but even a restricted domain like driving includes a very large number of these problems.

Over the centuries, human societies have accumulated huge numbers of situation-specific social norms to trust, along with ways for agents to signal their trustworthiness, and both society and the lives of its individual members have improved as a result.[29]

EXAMPLE 2: INDIVIDUAL USER MODELS

People are complex, and so is our world. We have incomplete understanding of our world, of each other, and of ourselves. We love to communicate with each other, and we depend on that communication, including the feedback we get from others, to create, develop, correct, and refine our understanding of reality.

Human experience with intelligent agents is almost entirely with other humans, where different capabilities are highly correlated. We humans are prone to anthropomorphize nonhuman, and even inanimate, elements of our environment where we can attribute

---

[29] Steven Pinker, *Enlightenment Now: The Case for Reason, Science, Humanism, and Progress* (Viking, 2018).

agency.[30] This can easily lead to assuming that robots and other AIs are more human-like and more capable than they actually are.[31] Generalizations that are useful with other humans are unreliable with robots and other AIs, possibly leading to excessive trust, unexpected catastrophes, and other ethical problems.

We use search engines (like Google) to find what other people have written or created. We use social networks (like Facebook) to communicate with each other about what we are doing and to learn about what they are doing. We understand that these services cost money, and they have to be paid for somehow. We have long accepted that advertisements help pay for newspapers, magazines, and television. Modern data-mining methods, using new machine learning algorithms, vast quantities of data, and abundant computing resources, have made it increasingly feasible to build detailed models of individual users. Without a deep understanding of what these websites do and how they do it, we extend our acceptance to the creation of individual user models that can be sold to advertisers to improve the targeting of their advertisements. Many users consider it worthwhile to trade some of their privacy for "free" search and social network services, paid for by advertising that is better matched to their own personal interests.

This use of individual user models could be seen as an ethically acceptable bargain, satisfying a social norm of the form:

(SN-4)   I understand that internet companies earn money by creating models of me and my interests from the information I knowingly and voluntarily provide, and selling access to those models to advertisers. I trust that the advertisers will use these models to serve me with ads that better match my personal interests.

The individual users of Google's search engine or Facebook's social network (or many other useful apps) are the sources of data from which the models are built. We would like to trust social norms such as:

(SN-5)   Except for clearly marked advertisements, the results from a search are the AI's best attempt to understand what I want, and to retrieve answers to my questions and access to desired internet sites.

(SN-6)   Except for clearly marked advertisements, a social network presents me with a reasonably unbiased sample of the posts created by people linked to me in the network. They receive my posts via a similarly unbiased sampling algorithm.

In many cases, we do trust these social norms. In the real world, the evidence suggests that this trust is not justified.[32] Specifically, Google, Facebook, and other major internet

---

[30] N. Epley, A. Waytz, and J.T. Cacioppo, "On Seeing Human: A Three-factor Theory of Anthropomorphism," *Psychological Review* 114(4) (2007): 864–886.

[31] P. Robinette, R. Allen, W. Li, A.M. Howard, and A.R. Wagner, Overtrust of Robots in Emergency Evacuation Scenarios," *ACM/IEEE Int. Conf. Human-Robot Interaction (HRI)* (2016): 101–108.

[32] Shoshana Zuboff, *The Age of Surveillance Capitalism* (New York: Public Affairs, 2019).

companies collect and aggregate far more behavioral information about individual users than we "knowingly and voluntarily provide" (violating *SN-4*). Furthermore, the results they return are designed to influence our future behavior beyond our shopping choices. We are naive to trust that these systems are unbiased and nonmanipulative (i.e., they violate *SN-5* and *SN-6*).

The Perils of Correct Individual Models

Individual users typically don't understand the breadth of data that these model-builders can draw on. Internet companies can collect information not only from direct interaction with their own interfaces but also from interactions with other sites, from "cookies" left behind with tracking information, and from many other observation channels.

Most internet users have had experiences like the following, or worse. Once I did a Google search in one browser for a style of dining-room chair I found attractive. Shortly afterward Facebook, running in a different browser, began serving me ads for that style of chair. This felt creepy, like "telepathic" surveillance of my personal interests and activities. My dining-room-chair preferences are not particularly sensitive information, but who knows what other kinds of surveillance they are doing?

In normal human communication, many of the things we communicate via speech, text, or email are *ephemera*—temporary statements that may be context-dependent, poorly thought out or poorly stated, intended to be refined or discarded in the course of the conversation. And they are communicated with different individuals, who we trust are not conspiring to assemble comprehensive models of our preferences, beliefs, personalities, and activities.

> (SN-7)   *I trust that small pieces of information, shared with different agents, will not be aggregated and correlated to create an inappropriately invasive model of me as an individual, violating my privacy.*

This is, of course, exactly what major internet companies like Facebook and Google do with their machine learning algorithms and access to vast streams of data.[33] Even if the models they create are correct, their predictions are likely to invade my privacy.

I have a right to keep actions and beliefs to myself, if I don't want to share them with others. One anecdote tells of a young man who bought a diamond ring online, intending to surprise his girlfriend with a marriage proposal, but the merchant sent email to all his Facebook friends, congratulating him on his engagement. This was a minor annoyance, but similarly inferring and broadcasting the political actions or opinions of a person living in a repressive state could be life-threatening.

Insurance companies are among the many companies taking advantage of the Internet of Things (IoT) to gather surveillance information about individual behavior.

---

[33] *Id.*

Both auto and health insurance companies can increasingly monitor compliance with various constraints, punishing violations with increasing premiums, insurance cancellation, or even by disabling the car.

"Legals," including end user license agreements (EULAs), privacy policies, and terms of service, are the long, dense, legal agreements that most of us click through without reading, in order to gain access to software, "free" or otherwise. These agreements authorize the company providing the software to collect our data and to share it with, or sell it to, other companies, typically without meaningful constraint. "Legals" are designed to discourage users from reading them, and they allow the companies to claim that users voluntarily "opt in" to these data-sharing conditions.

An analysis of the legal agreements associated with the Nest "smart" thermostat[34] found (sect. 4) that if a U.K.-based customer wants "a comprehensive picture of the rights, obligations and responsibilities of the various parties in the supply chain, he has to read at least 13 legal items." Worse, those link to additional contractual agreements from partners, affiliates, manufacturers of interoperable products, and others. Following these links, "If you add to Nest legals those of the connected devices, apps and appliances, the result is that for what appears to be a single product, a thousand contracts may apply!"

During the 2016 U.S. presidential election campaign, the company Cambridge Analytica used Facebook data to build models identifying people who were vulnerable to conspiracy theories, and targeted them for ads motivating them to turn out and vote for a particular candidate.[35] Even if most people are correctly confident in their own resistance to such ads, *some* people can be manipulated by unscrupulous advertisers, and their votes may affect the outcome for everyone.

Internet companies sometimes argue that their user modeling technologies are morally neutral and that it is only the application of those models by companies like Cambridge Analytica that raises ethical problems.[36] However, when Google and Facebook sell tools and access to data that makes it easy and profitable for others to violate our privacy or manipulate the institutions of our society, surely they are not absolved from ethical responsibility!

The Perils of Incorrect Individual Models

Incorrect user models can cause problems ranging from the trivial (display of irrelevant ads) to life-transforming (denial of probation or bail). A learning system can pick up

---

[34] G. Noto La Diega and I. Walden, "Contracting for the 'Internet of Things': Looking into the Nest," *European Journal of Law and Technology*, 7(2) (2016).

[35] Nicholas Confessore, "Cambridge Analytica and Facebook: The Scandal and the Fallout So Far," *New York Times* (April 4, 2018), retrieved May 17, 2019, from https://www.nytimes.com/2018/04/04/us/politics/cambridge-analytica-scandal-fallout.html.

[36] *"Once the rockets are up, Who cares where they come down. That's not my department!" Says Werner von Braun.* [Tom Lehrer, *That Was the Year That Was*, 1963].

biases from its training data, possibly from unconscious bias in how it is assembled, possibly because of the impact of historical bias on the phenomena being measured.

Sometimes, a model is incorrect because the designers of the system made grossly incorrect assumptions. Starting in October 2013, the Michigan Integrated Data Automated System (MiDAS) automatically evaluated claims for unemployment insurance.[37] Any information discrepancy between the applicant and the employer was treated as evidence of fraud by the applicant. A letter was generated and sent to the applicant's last known address. If not returned within ten days, the applicant was considered guilty, and the algorithm immediately imposed major financial penalties, with no human review, causing great hardship. A review of 22,427 charges filed between 2013 and 2015 revealed a 93 percent error rate!

It is now widely known that automated face detection and face recognition systems often have significantly higher error rate for faces with darker skin.[38] This can happen even though the algorithm learns correctly from the training examples, because the set of training examples does not adequately reflect the diversity of the population. Similar problems occur in medical diagnosis: male and female patients having a heart attack exhibit significantly different symptoms. In decades past, most data for the study of heart attacks came from male patients, leading to frequent misdiagnosis for female patients.[39] Efforts are under way to redress these data imbalances, but much remains to be done.

In other cases, the training set could perfectly reflect human behavior, but that behavior includes the effects of existing biases. Finding ways to train a complex machine learning system, while avoiding biases that may be embedded in the training data, is a difficult open problem.[40]

Membership in a particular minority group may be genuinely statistically correlated, in our society, with some characteristic of interest. But a fundamental principle in our society is that individuals should be judged as individuals, without bias from membership in a particular minority group.[41] It remains difficult to translate this societal ideal into inference methods for data analysis.

[37] Ryan Felton, "Michigan Unemployment Agency Made 20,000 False Fraud Accusations—Report," *The Guardian* (December 18, 2016), retrieved May 17, 2019, from https://www.theguardian.com/us-news/2016/dec/18/michigan-unemployment-agency-fraud-accusations.

[38] B. Wilson, J. Hoffman, and J. Morgenstern, "Predictive Inequity in Object Detection," Technical Report arXiv:1902.11097, ArXiv, February 21, 2019.

[39] T.A. Beery, "Gender Bias in the Diagnosis and Treatment of Coronary Artery Disease," *Heart & Lung* 24(6) (1995): 427–435.

[40] Cathy O'Neil, *Weapons of Math Destruction: How Big Data Increases Inequality and Threatens Democracy* (Penguin Random House, 2016).

[41] "*I have a dream that my four little children will one day live in a nation where they will not be judged by the color of their skin, but by the content of their character,*" Martin Luther King Jr. [August 28, 1963, March on Washington].

Conclusion

We live with intelligent tools and systems that are designed to satisfy our human needs and desires and provide their corporate owners with continuing streams of data about ourselves. Google (for access to information) and Facebook (for social communication) are only the beginning. They are designed to be addictive, so we keep interacting with them. They can learn a great deal about us, which makes them more valuable as tools for us, and also more valuable commercially, for selling individual user models to advertisers and others.

We trust that these intelligent systems follow social norms that we have learned from our experience interacting with other humans and with human-scale organizations. We have only begun to grapple with the impact of the vastly greater scale of the information involved, in terms of the number of people, events, and actions under surveillance; the microscopic detail of the information that can be collected, aggregated, and analyzed; the mass of training data that can be used to create predictive models of each individual; and the ways those predictions can be used for economic and political ends.

A homely example illustrates the impact of scale. If you are hiking alone, it is no problem to pee in the woods. The ongoing physical, biological, and social processes in the woods can handle that tiny load. But a city of 100,000 people is legitimately required by state and federal regulations to build an elaborate infrastructure to protect the physical, biological, and social environment, including water and sewage systems and a sewage treatment plant.

We are accustomed to broadcast ads that help support newspapers, magazines, and television. We accept political campaigns sending volunteers to knock on the doors of their supporters, to get out the vote on Election Day. We understand that every interaction reveals a little bit about ourselves. Once upon a time, the human scale and human limitations of these interactions provided implicit protection from many potential problems. But those times, and the scale of data collection, have changed.

We as a society don't grasp the implications of the massive change in scale—size, scope, detail, pervasiveness—that the development and deployment of surveillance capitalism brings.[42] We don't yet have a clear understanding of what we need to protect, how different kinds of costs and benefits trade off in this space, and what regulations we need.[43]

Large, complex systems require large, complex regulations. Those regulations necessarily evolve over time as we debug and refine them and as society's understanding of its needs changes. Our society does have relevant large-scale experience with dissemination and protection of large amounts of data, including the U.S. Food and Drug Administration (1906), which ensures the safety and quality of food, drugs, and many other products; the U.S. Securities and Exchange Commission (1934), which regulates the nation's securities industry; FERPA (Federal Educational Rights and Privacy Act, 1974), which protects

---

[42] O'Neil, *Weapons of Math Destruction*.   [43] Zuboff, *The Age of Surveillance Capitalism*.

student educational records; HIPAA (Health Insurance Portability and Accountability Act, 1996), which protects personal medical information; and GDPR (EU General Data Protection Regulation, 2016), which protects data and privacy within the European Union.

A *fiduciary* is a person or organization that acts as a trustee for one or more beneficiaries, for example, the asset manager of a pension fund or the trust department of a bank. A fiduciary has the duty to avoid any kind of conflict of interest and to act solely in the beneficiary's interest. Fiduciary relationships are most common in financial domains, but the fiduciary concept also applies in other spheres.

Should companies like Facebook and Google, that collect and aggregate large amounts of personal data, have a fiduciary duty toward their individual users, requiring them to handle that data in the users' interest? The users' interest can certainly include personalized advertising that more closely aligns with individual preferences and personalized recommendations of books, music, and other products based on previous choices. As long as the beneficiary is not exploited, it is not necessarily a conflict with its fiduciary duty for the company that collects and analyzes the data to profit from its efforts.

On the other hand, some current practices would violate those fiduciary duties. Click-through "agreements" that are designed to obtain legal "opt-in" permission while discouraging meaningful consideration of their conditions are clearly not in the user's interest. Similarly, meaningless "permission" for data sharing with other organizations, requiring the individual user to find and check the privacy policies of those other organizations, would violate the fiduciary duties. Where data sharing is needed for subcontracting some of the work, or for a business partnership, the original company must be responsible for ensuring that the partner provides protections at least as strong as the original company.

Like the GDPR in the European Union, the details of such a fiduciary duty would be negotiated as legislation is designed, and then refined in the courts. The important point is to create a social norm that each individual can trust, along with meaningful enforcement mechanisms:

[SN-8]   *An organization that systematically collects, aggregates, and analyzes personal data about me is subject to a fiduciary duty to use that data in my best interest.*

EXAMPLE 3: SHARING THE WEALTH

Fairness is important to adult humans, to children, including young infants,[44] and even to some species of nonhuman primates.[45] One way to study fairness in the laboratory is the Ultimatum Game:[46]

[44] S. Sloan, R. Baillargeon, and D. Premack, "Do Infants Have a Sense of Fairness?," *Psychological Science* 23(2) (2012): 196–204.
[45] S.F. Brosnan and F.B.M. de Waal, "Monkeys Reject Unequal Pay," *Nature* 425 (2003): 297–299.
[46] M.A. Nowak, K.M. Page, and K. Sigmund, "Fairness versus Reason in the Ultimatum Game" *Science* 289 (2000): 1773–1775.

The Ultimatum Game has two participants, A and B. A is given a sum of money, say $100. He may split this with B as he wishes. B may accept the offer from A, or he may reject it, in which case neither participant gets anything.

The Nash equilibrium solution from game theory is clear: *A* makes the minimal offer to *B*, say $1, which *B* accepts, since $1 is better than nothing. The behavior of human participants is quite different: *A* tends to offer $40 to $50, and *B* tends to reject offers less than about $30. Often, *B* is willing to accept a substantial loss to punish *A* for making an unfair offer.

Fairness in the Economy

The total productivity of American society, and hence its total wealth, have been increasing steadily since the end of World War II. Much of that wealth is controlled by corporations, which historically responded to the needs of various *stakeholders*, including shareholders, workers, customers, suppliers, and neighbors. As the wealth of our society grew, the prosperity of the typical worker the United States increased at about the same rate for several decades (Figure 22.1 (left side)). People trusted that the economy would be *fair*:

(SN-9)   *Those who contribute to the success of a collective effort will share in the benefits.*

Starting in the 1960s, Milton Friedman[47] and others argued that a corporation is purely a mechanism for maximizing wealth for its shareholders. The corporation and its human managers have responsibilities, but only to the *shareholders* and not to other stakeholders such as workers, customers, suppliers, and neighbors, except as their responses might affect shareholder value. This change in the perceived ethical responsibilities of corporations has been widely accepted, especially by the business community.

The overall steady growth in wealth has continued, but starting around 1980, income gain became almost flat for the lower half of the economy. This has led to a dramatic increase in inequality among individuals, with most gains going to the top 1 percent of the population, and even more dramatically to the top .01 percent (Figure 22.1 (right side)).

The economics and the politics of our society have changed from offering opportunity for all, to one where the rich get ever richer and the poor lose what little they had, even hope for the future and for their descendants. As these trends continue, more people become convinced that the social norm *SN-9* has been broadly violated, and their share in the growing wealth of society has been taken from them. Hopelessness, anger, and lack of trust continue to grow, to the point where, as in the story of Samson in the Old Testament (Judges 16:29–30), they are prepared to pull down the pillars of society to destroy their tormenters as well as themselves. We see this in a growing polarization of our society.[48]

---

[47] Milton Friedman, "The Social Responsibility of Business Is to Increase Its Profits," *New York Times Magazine* (September 13, 1970).

[48] Susan McWilliams, "This Political Theorist Predicted the Rise of Trumpism. His Name Was Hunter S. Thompson," *The Nation* (December 15, 2016), https://www.thenation.com/article/this-political-theorist-predicted-the-rise-of-trumpism-his-name-was-hunter-s-thompson/.

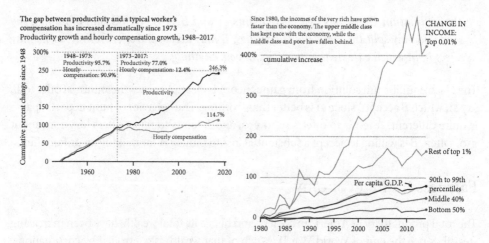

FIGURE 22.1. (left) Productivity and therefore national wealth have increased steadily since the late 1940s, but typical worker compensation leveled off in the mid-1970s.[49] (right) After about 1980, the incomes of the upper-middle class (90–99%) tracked the increase in per capita GDP, with the upper 1% increasing above that rate, and the lower 90% falling behind.[50]

Accumulating anger and resentment amplify fears of a future in which AI and robotics increasingly take over the jobs that people depend on for their livelihoods.

Can We Create New Jobs?

It is often said that, in previous periods of rapid technological change, more jobs were created than were lost. There could be significant dislocation, perhaps for decades, since the people who had lost jobs were not necessarily qualified for the new jobs, but in the long run, plenty of new jobs were created. Others respond that previous technological advances provided automated substitutes for human and animal strength and mechanical skill, but current AI-driven advances provides substitutes for intelligence, and it is not obvious where we go from here.

However, if we look carefully for a scenario where plenty of new jobs are created, the outlines of a possible solution seem to appear. This exercise identifies three important "pieces of the puzzle" and focuses our attention on the question of how they can fit together.

First, as we have seen (Figure 22.1 (left side)), productivity and wealth in our society are increasing steadily, and this increase seems likely to continue. The driving force behind automation is the prospect that corporations can become ever more profitable by using AI and robotics to automate increasing aspects of production costs.

---

[49] Reproduced with permission from "The Productivity-Pay Gap," Economic Policy Institute, August 2018.

[50] From The New York Times, Feb. 24, 2019. © 2019 The New York Times Company. All rights reserved. Used under license.

Second, it is clear that people need meaningful work, not just guaranteed income.[51] It is important for people as individuals to be engaged in cooperative efforts that they consider meaningful and important and that benefit more than just themselves—their family, their community, their country, or the society as a whole. Society benefits from the positive-sum nature of cooperative effort and also from its individual members being capable of skilled, disciplined, responsible work toward shared goals.[52]

Third, there are plenty of jobs requiring skills, commitment, and effort and that substantially benefit society. The problem is that, in our current economy, many of these jobs are not net generators of profit for an employer, so without subsidies, such jobs will not be created and filled.

One example of such a job is stay-at-home parent of young children. Such a job has substantial benefits for the children, for the family, and for the local community. When performed by a parent who wants to do this work, it cultivates skills, commitment, and effort and can be extremely satisfying. However, it is not a profit center for our economy. It is typically unpaid, with a family unit supporting one person to do this work with little or no external financial support.

Another example is a job as a professional caregiver for children or the elderly. This job is essential where care for dependents is necessary, but family members must work for pay. Jobs like these can be profit generators for corporations in our economy. However, quality care requires well-qualified caregivers, and a relatively high ratio of caregivers to those cared for. The families who need this care often have limited resources to pay for it. And caregivers deserve a living wage. The numbers do not add up, to allow all three of these constraints to be satisfied at the same time.[53] For the employer to make a profit, some combination of quality of care, affordability, and living wages must be sacrificed.

There are many other jobs that fit this description of being meaningful for the worker, valuable for society, but not supportable as corporate profit centers. Education is a sector with great unmet needs for teachers, aides, managers, counselors, and support staff in preschool, tutoring and mentoring during primary, secondary, and postsecondary schooling, adult and professional education, and other areas. Emergency services, environmental and infrastructure care and development, and medical care and services could all be expanded. Certain tasks, for example, care of a small neighborhood park, could conceivably be automated, but having it done by a dedicated community member would result in the job being done at least as well, but would also provide meaningful work for a member of the community. These jobs require subsidies, but as we have seen the wealth of society continues to grow, so the resources for these subsidies exist.

[51] B.R. Rosso, K.H. Dekas, and A. Wrzesniewski, "On the Meaning of Work: A Theoretical Integration and Review, *Research in Organizational Behavior* 30 (2010): 91–127.

[52] Michael Tomasello, *A Natural History of Human Morality* (Harvard University Press, 2016).

[53] Sally Ho, "'Broken' Economics for Preschool Workers, Child Care Sector," *US News* (September 8, 2018), downloaded May 20, 2019, from https://www.usnews.com/news/business/articles/2018-09-08/broken-economics-for-preschool-workers-child-care-sector.

Rather than try to enumerate such jobs, one would hope for a market-based entrepreneurial mechanism that would reward individuals for creating and maintaining such jobs. This mechanism could not be based entirely on profit, but would use a market-based mechanism to effectively allocate society's subsidy for such work.

These three pieces of the puzzle are promising aspects of a way to use the wealth of society for the benefit of the members of society, especially the human members. Making these three pieces fit together will be a challenge, most especially the political task of channeling the resources created by increased automation to the creation of the new jobs the society needs.

CONCLUSIONS

Ethics is how a society encourages its individual members to interact in positive-sum (cooperative) ways, rather than negative-sum (exploitative) ways, so the interactions strengthen rather than weaken the society as a whole. Ethics accomplishes this goal by encouraging trustworthy behavior by individuals, which earns trust by others, which is necessary for cooperation.

Over centuries, our society has accumulated many different situation-specific ethical principles and social norms that we count on to make our lives together safer and more effective.[54] We individuals use concepts like virtue, duty, utility, and so forth to learn, understand, and teach ethical principles. These are the concrete connections from individual ethics, to trustworthiness, to trust, to cooperation, to positive-sum outcomes.

We need to understand what social norms we trust, how trusting them increases positive-sum outcomes for society as a whole, how those norms are represented as knowledge in the minds of individual agents (human and nonhuman), and how they are applied by agents when making plans and deciding how to act.

This chapter has considered examples illuminating three different aspects of ethics from a computational modeling perspective. First, autonomous vehicles are individually embodied intelligent systems that act as members of society. The ethical knowledge needed by such an agent is not how to choose the lesser evil when confronted by a Deadly Dilemma, but how to recognize the upstream decision point that makes it possible to avoid the Deadly Dilemma entirely.

Second, disembodied distributed intelligent systems like Google and Facebook provide valuable services while collecting, aggregating, and correlating vast amounts of information about individual users. Those individual user models earn money for corporations from advertisers who target users with advertisements, but they can be used much more widely. With inadequate controls, these corporate systems can invade privacy and do substantial damage through either correct or incorrect inferences.

---

[54] Russ Shafer-Landau, ed., *Ethical Theory: An Anthology*, 2d ed. (Wiley-Blackwell, 2013).

Third, acceptance of the legitimacy of the society by its individual members depends on a general perception of *fairness*: that those who contribute to the success of a collective effort will share in the benefits. Rage about unfairness can be directed at individual free-riders or at systematic inequality across the society.

The promise of a computational approach to ethical knowledge is not simply ethics for computational devices such as robots. Rather, just as artificial intelligence helps us understand cognition, it now also promises to help us understand the pragmatic value of ethics as a feedback mechanism that helps intelligent creatures, human and nonhuman, live together in thriving societies.

BIBLIOGRAPHY

Greene, Joshua. *Moral Tribes: Emotion, Reason, and the Gap between Us and Them*. London: Penguin Press, 2013.

Haidt, Jonathan. *The Righteous Mind: Why Good People Are Divided by Politics and Religion*. New York: Vintage Books, 2012.

Kuipers, Benjamin. How Can We Trust a Robot? *Communications of the ACM*, 61(3) (2018): 86–95.

Lin, Patrick, Keith Abney, and George A., eds. *Robot Ethics: The Ethical and Social Implications of Robotics*. Cambridge, MA: MIT Press, 2012.

Pinker, Steven, *Enlightenment Now: The Case for Reason, Science, Humanism, and Progress*. New York: Viking, 2018.

Singer, Peter. *The Expanding Circle: Ethics, Evolution, and Moral Progress*. Princeton: Princeton University Press, 1981.

Tomasello, Michael. *A Natural History of Human Morality*. Cambridge, MA: Harvard University Press, 2016.

Wallach, Wendell and Colin Allen. *Moral Machines: Teaching Robots Right from Wrong*. Oxford: Oxford University Press, 2009.

Wright, Robert. *Nonzero: The Logic of Human Destiny*. New York: Pantheon, 2000.

Zuboff, Shoshana. *The Age of Surveillance Capitalism*. New York: Public Affairs, 2019.

CHAPTER 23

....

SOCIAL FAILURE MODES IN TECHNOLOGY AND THE ETHICS OF AI

An Engineering Perspective

....

JASON MILLAR

INTRODUCTION

....

Case 1—The Quebec Bridge

In August 1907, a steel cantilever bridge spanning the St. Lawrence River near Quebec City was under construction and nearing completion.[1] Engineers noticed that some of the structural beams were bending, so they initiated an investigation. They discovered that calculations made early in the design phase had gone unchecked, resulting in a design that was insufficient to support the full weight of the bridge. Unfortunately, the engineers were unable to communicate the information to the construction crews in time. One fateful day, as workers were nearing the end of their shift, a beam failure

   [1] I thank the various participants of two workshops held at Stanford University, one at Apple and one at the University of Toronto's Centre for Ethics, who gave generous comments on drafts of this chapter. Particular thanks are owed to the brilliant Shannon Vallor, who presented a detailed and helpful commentary at the Political Theory Workshop at Stanford, and to Rob Reich, Josh Cohen, Sergio Sismondo, and Celeste Parisi, for their critique of early drafts. Anne Newman, Johannes Himmelreich, Ted Lechterman, Fay Niker, Lindsey Chambers, Hannah Carnegy-Arbuthnott, Desiree Lim, and Laura Gillespie provided valuable feedback at the Stanford EIS Postdoc Workshop. Support for this research was provided through Postdoctoral Fellowships from both the Social Sciences and Humanities Research Council of Canada (SSHRC), and the McCoy Family Center for Ethics in Society at Stanford.

caused the south structure of the bridge to collapse, killing seventy-five of eighty-six workers on the bridge at the time.[2]

Case 2—Google Glass

Designed as a wearable piece of Wi-Fi-enabled computing technology in the early 2010s, Google Glass resembled a pair of glasses, but had a small heads-up-display in place of the lenses and a camera integrated into one arm of the glasses. Wearers could search the web and view results on the display and capture video and pictures, all while communicating with the device using voice commands. Early adopters were sighted wearing their Glass everywhere. Google Glass was quickly, and widely, criticized on privacy grounds, owing to the wearer's ability to capture and record images surreptitiously in any number of social, often private, settings (think urinals),[3] and also raised a number of health-related concerns. Additionally, and importantly, early Google Glass wearers were ridiculed in the mainstream media and on social media (and likely in person) for their "creepiness"[4] and "dorkiness"[5]—these early adopters were eventually labeled *Glassholes.*[6] Despite its technical sophistication, Google Glass was discontinued shortly after its limited precommercial debut.[7]

Engineers, and people impacted by the technology they design could benefit from a new analytic toolkit that helps clarify the link between the ethical issues raised by AI and other technologies and the design decisions that shape those technologies. In this chapter I propose such a toolkit. In my approach I examine a common characteristic of technological artifacts[8] that, to date, has been under examined but deserves attention, which is this: just as technological artifacts can break as a result of mechanical, electrical, or other

---

[2] C. Pearson and N. Delatte, "Collapse of the Quebec Bridge, 1907," *J. Perform. Constr. Facil.* 20(1) (2006): 84–91.

[3] R. Eveleth, "Google Glass Wasn't a Failure. It Raised Crucial Concerns," *Wired* (December 12, 2018), https://www.wired.com/story/google-glass-reasonable-expectation-of-privacy/.

[4] D. Pogue, "Why Google Glass Is Creepy," *Scientific American* (June 1, 2013), https://www.scientificamerican.com/article/why-google-glass-is-creepy/.

[5] Dorkiness here is described as being far worse than mere "nerdiness"; see M. Wohlsen, "Guys Like This Could Kill Google Glass Before It Ever Gets Off the Ground," *Wired* (May 2, 2013), https://www.wired.com/2013/05/inherent-dorkiness-of-google-glass/. If you doubt whether a "dork factor" can be blamed for the failure of Google Glass, check out the Tumblr titled *White Men Wearing Google Glass* (http://whitemenwearinggoogleglass.tumblr.com) for confirmation.

[6] L. Eadicicco, M. Peckham, J.P. Pullen, and A. Fuitzpatrick, "The 20 Most Successful Technology Failures of All Time," *TIME* (April 3, 2017), http://time.com/4704250/most-successful-technology-tech-failures-gadgets-flops-bombs-fails/.

[7] R. Metz, "Google Glass Is Dead: Long Live Smart Glasses," *MIT Technology Review* (November 26, 2014), https://www.technologyreview.com/s/532691/google-glass-is-dead-long-live-smart-glasses/.

[8] The term "technological artifacts" should be understood quite colloquially as being interchangeable with other terms that pick out the stuff humans design and build, such as devices, products, technologies, widgets, gadgets, things, etc. Throughout this chapter I use the term interchangeably with "technology," "product," and "artifact."

physical defects not fully accounted for in their design (as with the Quebec Bridge), they can also break as a result of *social* defects not fully accounted for in their design (as with Google Glass). I call failures resulting from social defects *social failures*, and propose that we add them and the underlying causes that lead to social failures—*social failure modes*—to the list of failure modes worth studying in detail and thinking about when designing technology. An explicit and detailed understanding of social failure modes, if properly applied in engineering design practice, could result in a fuller evaluation of the social implications of technology, either during the upstream design and engineering phases of a product or after its release. Ideally, studying social failure modes will improve our ability to anticipate and reduce the rate, or severity, of undesirable social failures prior to releasing technology into the wild, just as an understanding of other common failure modes has improved our ability to anticipate and reduce the rate and severity of undesirable mechanical, electrical, and other physical failures.[9]

There are at least three relatively straightforward reasons why we should study social failures and seek to reduce the rate or severity of social failures in technology. Social failures, like any other failure, can break a product, thus: (1) depriving individual users and society of whatever benefits that an artifact would otherwise deliver;[10] and/or (2) delivering harms upon individual users or society. Finally, (3) an improved understanding of social failures can explain what was wrong with an artifact that led to a failure, thus leading to targeted improvements in the social aspects of an artifact's design. Thus, a better understanding of social failures in technology can lead to better technology, both functionally and ethically.

To be sure, my goal here is not to suggest that social failures, or the social failures I describe herein, are the only nonphysical failures that deserve attention when analyzing how successful a technology is, or will be, once unleashed in society. There are other nonphysical failures that one could point to as being equally deserving of examination. Two that have been brought to my attention are economic and political failures.[11] Economic failures, as I understand them, occur when a product fails as a result of its fit within a particular market. A product might be too expensive or could fail to deliver the right kinds of value propositions to its intended users. Political failures, as I understand them, occur when an artifact does not fit prevailing standards and is unable to force new ones, or when it fails to appease important political actors. An analysis of these kinds of failures is worth study, but is beyond the scope of this chapter. However, it is also worth noting how difficult it is to treat physical, social, economic, and political failures as if we can easily draw impenetrable boundaries around them. These various failures can be understood as multiple sides of the same artifact; when we choose to focus exclusively on physical failures as objects of analysis in engineering, we do so arbitrarily and not

---

[9] Some failures are desirable, such as those designed to minimize overall damage or harm, or to direct the harm appropriately, such as crumple zones in vehicles that are designed to absorb energy in a crash.

[10] I focus here on artifacts that are designed with some good purpose in mind. I have very little to say here about those that are not.

[11] Particular thanks to Sergio Sismondo for alerting me to these two categories of failure.

because the artifact is more accurately, or appropriately, understood according to the language of the physical sciences. When the goal is to understand how an artifact exists in society (its natural habitat), its physical characteristics are one among many vantage points from which to observe it.

This chapter, as its focus is starting a conversation about social failure modes in technology, proposes an additional vantage point from which to observe artifacts, that is, a new way of understanding how a technology can "work" or "break." From a methodological perspective, I build toward that understanding by spanning a conceptual gap between two academic worlds. On one side of the gap, we have theories from philosophy, sociology, and anthropology focused primarily on the social and ethical dimensions of technology. They provide detailed examinations of the social dynamics between individuals, societies, and technologies, as well as a rich vocabulary for thinking about what causes a technology to *work* or *break*. On the other side, we have theories from the sciences and engineering focused primarily on the physical aspects of technology, on ways of (re)configuring matter to make things. They provide detailed examinations of the physical dynamics of technology, as well as a rich vocabulary for understanding what causes a technology to *work* or *break*.

As I've laid things out, both of these worlds are concerned with understanding how technology works and breaks, so the conceptual gap may seem small. I believe it is. The project here is to bring the vocabulary used to describe the social dimensions of technology in contact with the vocabulary used to describe the physical dimensions of technology, and do it in a way that avoids demanding that either should buckle under the other's force. Combining these vocabularies makes for richer descriptive and normative accounts of technology. Furthermore, whatever practical gains are to be made by understanding social failure modes will undoubtedly require the social apparatus to be incorporated into technical practices. Practical gains, therefore, will require cooperation with, and uptake among, those in command of the physical world, namely engineers. So, to span the gap, an important aspect of this project is making the social apparatus compatible with the technological; to be used, the concept of a social failure mode must be designed such that it fits well into the world of engineering.

With those considerations in mind, I begin this chapter by making explicit the link between social failures and the ethics of AI, as AI seems to lend some urgency to better accounting for the social dynamics of technology during design. I then describe a few different ways in which artifacts break physically and, in doing so, offer an overview of the language typically deployed to describe how things break. That discussion of physical failures and failure modes lays the necessary groundwork to frame the concept of a social failure and social failure modes. Social failures do not always render a technology broken in the traditional sense (i.e., physically unusable)—as I will describe things a technology can suffer a social failure yet still "function." The question, then, is why should we worry about social failures in the first place? In response to that question, I describe in this chapter within the sections "Social Failures and Social Failure Modes," and "The Ethical Dimensions of Social Failures," how social failures break technology and raise, or underscore, ethical concerns, thus fleshing out my primary normative claim, which is that we have good reasons for studying, and avoiding, social failures in technology. I then provide a rudimentary social failure mode analysis of Microsoft's Tay—a particularly problematic AI—as a case study illustrating how one might approach using the proposed toolkit. But to begin, I explain why a better understanding of social failure modes is particularly important, and would be particularly beneficial, for engineers designing robots and AI.

SOCIAL FAILURES AND THE ETHICS OF AI

Much of the literature on the ethics of AI that has recently emerged concerns itself with describing how AI applications result in problematic ethical issues. Those issues tend to be cataloged under a variety of ethical concepts, including (but not limited to): trust and trustworthiness; accountability; justice; bias; fairness; interpretability; explainability; power and control; gender; privacy; discrimination; truth; and equality. Humans reify these concepts in practice, through our actions within relationships and institutions, by attaching to each concept a set of social norms that help to delineate between actions that are acceptable and unacceptable, permissible and impermissible. Take *trust*, for example. I might trust a person with my sensitive personal information because that person has demonstrated their willingness and ability to not divulge other important information with which they were entrusted. I might further consider that person *trust-worthy* because I know they have certain caring dispositions that are aligned with my values, such that I believe they will respond appropriately when pressed to divulge my personal information. Thus, a person is considered both trusted and trustworthy because their actions in our relationship adhere to social norms that define trust/trust-worthiness. Similarly, institutions can codify norms defining trust/trustworthiness in policies and processes, thus signaling that an institution is trustworthy and can be trusted, especially in cases where they consistently apply their policies. The same is true for bias, interpretability, and the other ethical concepts mentioned earlier—each is defined in practice by a set of accompanying norms.

When designing AI (indeed, as I describe in this chapter, when designing most, if not all, technology), engineers inevitably embed social norms into the artifact, and people experience those norms when interacting with the artifact. Norms that are engineered into the AI shape the underlying decisions and resulting human-AI interactions. Thinking back to the trust example, and imagining that I am asked to trust an AI with personal information, the kinds of norms we engineer into the AI will define its ethical character. When and to whom will it divulge my personal information? Will it inform me about any particular instance of its divulging my personal information? Do I have choices to make about these potential divulgences? As I describe in this chapter, if the engineered norms undermine my normative expectations regarding trust, my interactions with the AI could raise serious ethical issues, and, as a result, the AI could suffer a social failure. As we develop robots and AIs that are more autonomous, we will be required to delegate more and more (previously human-dominated) decision-making to them, so that AIs can interact with us, among us, and on our behalf.[12]

Understanding the relationship between social norms, technology, and the design decisions that engineers make takes on a sense of urgency with robots and AI; robots and AI are performing among us, and as they increase in autonomy and sophistication they are increasingly performing the social norms that we have necessarily embedded in them.

Social norms can, therefore, be seen as a critical social backdrop upon which much of AI is designed. Because of this, we would benefit by developing an analytic design/engineering toolkit to help translate between the technical and the social, engineering and the humanities, and bring the social dynamics of technology into the foreground in engineering design. Hence, I propose here a rigorous study of social failures and the underlying social failure modes as a step in that direction.

TALKING ABOUT HOW STUFF BREAKS: A BRIEF PRIMER ON PHYSICAL FAILURES AND FAILURE MODES

Everything we make breaks, eventually. Joints crack through repetitive strain. Metal surfaces erode when exposed to the weather. Tires wear from friction. Bolts loosen from vibration. Circuits fizzle from the heat of moving electrons. Pipes burst under pressure. And overloaded beams buckle and shear. The list of physical failures that can potentially break any one technology is long, and grows in proportion to the complexity of the system. Having more parts increases the probability that failures will occur. This simple fact about the things we make—that they all break, eventually—can be read as pessimistic and discouraging. It's the stuff that could cause an engineer faced with the inevitability of failures to throw their hands in the air. But each physical failure encountered also represents an opportunity to study the underlying causes of that failure: the physical *failure modes*. Each study that leads to a breakthrough in understanding how a thing *has* failed also lays the foundation for an understanding of how things *will* fail in the future. Researching how things fail helps to prevent future failures of the same kind, a thoroughly optimistic perspective.

The optimism that drives research into physical failures is fueled by the recognition that physical things fail according to physical laws. The engineers in charge of the Quebec Bridge knew this and were able to predict the eventual failure, even if other

---

[12] J. Millar and I. Kerr, "Delegation, Relinquishment, Responsibility: The Prospect of Expert Robots," in *Robot Law*, ed. Ryan Calo, Michael Froomkin, and Ian Kerr (Cheltenham, UK: Edward Elgar Press, 2016), 102–127. See more on delegation in this chapter under "The Ethical Dimensions of Social Failures."

circumstances stopped them from preventing it. Beams don't break randomly, they break predictably. Their failure modes can be grouped and characterized by type: they *buckle* and *yield* regularly according to the physical properties (e.g., type of material and dimensions) of the beam.

Compiling a catalog of physical failure modes has allowed engineers to anticipate potential failures while designing things. With this additional knowledge, engineers can make explicit, informed, decisions about the physical makeup of their devices that more fully take into account the many ways that each component could fail in use. Certain failures will ultimately be deemed acceptable given various design constraints, while others will be avoided at all costs. The upshot is that a more detailed understanding of physical failure modes can lead to more deliberate, safer technology, designed with a fuller understanding of the benefits, risks, and harms associated with particular design decisions.

Optimism over the possibility of better understanding failure modes has paid off over the years. What started as investigations into how physical things break has evolved into a much broader analysis of how things and processes can, and do, fail. As a result of measurable successes, failure mode analysis is a cornerstone of good design.

For the remainder of this chapter I argue that a similar optimism is justified and should be acted upon when it comes to investigating and cataloging the many ways that technology can suffer social failures. It's justified because we have good reason to believe that social norms can be identified and understood within a target user group (or society in which a technology will be deployed) to the extent of allowing us to reasonably predict how technology can interact (e.g., support or undermine) and/or come into tension with those social norms. The benefits of avoiding social failures in technology ground the normative claim that we ought to investigate and catalog social failure modes.

SOCIAL FAILURES AND SOCIAL FAILURE MODES

The Zimbabwe Bush Pump

The success of the Zimbabwe Bush Pump—a simple hand-operated water pump like one you might find on an old farm, and the protagonist of a story narrated by Marianne de Laet and Annemarie Mol—beautifully illustrates the concept of a social failure of technology.[13] What follows is a condensed version of that story.

To see it in a picture, the bush pump looks like any other rudimentary hand operated pump. It is intentionally rustic, designed specifically for use in rural Zimbabwe where

---

[13] M. de Laet and A. Mol, "The Zimbabwe Bush Pump: Mechanics of a Fluid Technology," *Social Studies of Science* 30 (2000): 225–263.

clean water is a precious resource. To use it, one places a container under the spout, grabs hold of the wooden lever on top, and proceeds to pump, up and down, drawing water from the well upon which the pump sits.

But the Zimbabwe Bush Pump is not like the many other rudimentary hand-operated water pumps on the market. In fact, it has succeeded where those other similar looking pumps have failed precisely because other pumps fail to establish social norms required for them to work and transgress already established social norms common in the pumps' use context (rural Zimbabwe). The Bush Pump, just to be clear, is designed to establish the requisite social norms and conform to already existing social norms, which lead to its success.

As de Laet and Mol argue, for a pump to *work*, in addition to reliably pumping water—its intended mechanical function—it must also be seen as an artifact that locals *trust* and, when they use it, must reliably pump *clean* water. Satisfying these three specifications requires more than mere mechanical design considerations.[14] Unlike other pumps, all of them mechanically adequate, various sociocultural features are incorporated into the Bush Pump's design for it to satisfy its role as a trusted source of clean water.

For starters, in order to prevent contamination of the well, community members must be convinced to diligently maintain the pump. The Bush Pump's designers accomplish this by demanding the involvement of the whole community in various aspects of the installation of the pump. Drilling the well, for example, is designed as a social activity that motivates a sense of community ownership of the well. Rather than using mechanical drills that are quick and efficient, but tend to be operated by nonlocals, the Bush Pump relies for its well on a special hand-operated drill known as a Vonder Rig, which requires community involvement for it to work.

> A video distributed by the factory shows that sometimes operating the rig turns into a village feast. Village women push the iron crossbar to drive the auger into the ground, while village men sit on the bar to weigh it down and children dance around.[15]

Once the well is drilled it must be capped with a headworks (a small concrete and brick structure that sits atop the well) to provide adequate water runoff and a seal against deadly E. coli contamination. Like the drilling, constructing the headworks is designed as a community affair, which helps to further establish norms of ownership of the Bush Pump.[16]

De Laet and Mol nicely summarize what is required to install a working Bush Pump:

> In order to be a pump that (pre)serves a community, it not only needs to look attractive, have properly fixed levers and well-made concrete aprons, it must also be capable of gathering people together and of inducing them to follow well-drafted

---

[14] *Id.*   [15] *Id.* at 233.   [16] *Id.* at 233.

instructions. It must come with a Vonder Rig and invite people to push bars, sit on them or dance around them. It must seduce people into taking care of it. Thus the boundaries around a community pump may be widely drawn. Indeed they embrace the community.[17]

Thus, drilling the well, assembling the pump, and constructing the headworks variously involve the whole local community. These communal activities are designed to generate a strong sense of community ownership of each installed pump, in turn helping to establish critical social norms around pump use and maintenance.[18]

There is one other crucial social element to the story of the Bush Pump that helps to explain why it succeeds where others fail. Rather than simply relying on geological data to determine the best site for each pump, the Bush Pump's instruction manuals and other documentation "state clearly and repeatedly . . . that local water diviners should be consulted before any decision about the siting of a water hole is made."[19] According to a UNICEF worker, nongovernmental organizations intent on drilling wells in locations based solely on geological data or issues of efficiency (proximity to certain buildings, from livestock, etc.) regularly witness the failure of their pumps because local diviners were not consulted, leading the local women to consider those wells "dead."[20] Thus, the Bush Pump is trusted in part because it conforms to social norms attached to the wisdom of local water diviners.

Examining the role that these sociocultural aspects play in the design of the Bush Pump undercuts the idea that any similar pump, mechanically speaking, would work in rural Zimbabwe. Indeed, in telling the Bush Pump's story, de Laet and Mol emphasize that other mechanically superior pumps have failed precisely for lacking such sociocultural design elements. Pumps that are poorly maintained become contaminated, while pumps that have been placed without a water diviner's endorsement are ignored.

Social Failure Dynamics

We see that the Bush Pump's story is also a story about how users' social norms are fundamentally related to an artifact either *working* or *breaking*. The Bush Pump works because it is mechanically sound, because its designers figured out a way for it to encourage community members (i.e., its users) to feel a sense of collective ownership toward it, thus to care for it and prevent contamination, and finally because its design respects the trust norms associated with local water diviners, and so it is used.

Pumps that fail (including Bush Pumps), on the other hand, can fail *socially*, either because they fail to encourage the requisite social norms, or because they violate important existing ones.

In these two senses, then, water pumps can, and do, suffer *social failures*. And just as we can talk about pumps breaking due to mechanical failures, we can talk about pumps

---

[17] *Id.* at 235.   [18] *Id.* at 234.   [19] *Id.* at 234.   [20] *Id.* at 234.

breaking due to social failures. Pumps that suffer a lack of community ownership in rural Zimbabwe break because they are not cared for and become contaminated. (Thus, social failures can sometimes lead to physical failures though, in this case, the social failure is at the root.) Pumps that are not trusted by women in rural Zimbabwe break because they are ignored.

Google Glass can be described in similar terms.[21] Though some people were happy to use it and celebrated its technical capabilities, too many others rejected it because it violated important existing social norms of health, privacy, and coolness. When a (potential) user rejected Google Glass on grounds that it violated these existing social norms, Google Glass broke. Alternatively, one might say that Google Glass failed to shift, or to generate, the social norms required for it to be accepted and used (i.e., to work). For example, if Google Glass was designed in such a way that it successfully shifted society's notions of coolness, or of privacy, such that those new norms encouraged its intended use, then it would not have suffered those social failures.

With the Bush Pump and Google Glass in mind, I offer an initial definition of a social failure:

> An artifact suffers a social failure when a social norm designed into it comes into tension with an accepted social norm held by its user(s), or other relevant stakeholder, to the extent that the tension diminishes or prevents the intended use, or functioning, of that artifact.

But what is a social norm, and what does it mean for a social norm to be designed into an artifact? First, a social norm, in the sense I am using it, should be understood just to mean a behavioral rule R that is followed by a sufficiently large set of individuals within a social group.[22] By this definition, R could be held by social group P, and not by some other group P'. The kind of social group I refer to here is rather flexible. It could be a particular citizenry (e.g., Canadians), a professional group (e.g., physicians, engineers), or some other identifiable group (e.g., iPhone users, hobby farmers, cyclists). They key feature of any group, when thinking about social failures, is that its members share, and act on, at least one reasonably identifiable social norm.

---

[21] At this point a preemptive clarification might be useful. If you find yourself bristling at the side-by-side comparison of the Bush Pump and Google Glass, the former a provider of basic goods and the latter a mere luxury item, you're in good company. My aim in this chapter is not to provide an overall moral assessment of these technologies. My aim is to provide an analytic toolkit that explicitly links engineering design to social norms in a way that will empower engineers to consider, in a more nuanced way, the interplay between design and social norms in their daily work. I leave the overall moral assessment of particular technologies to future work and would encourage anyone interested in such work to consider using social failure modes as a useful analytic tool for communicating to engineers reasons for endorsing or rejecting particular aspects or features of those technologies.

[22] C. Bicchieri, *The Grammar of Society: The Nature and Dynamics of Social Norms* (Cambridge: Cambridge University Press, 2006).

There are several ways of describing how social norms are designed into artifacts.[23] Social norms can be identified in the *political relations* an artifact imposes on its users.[24] Consider nuclear reactors, which, according to Winner,[25] impose a set of authoritarian norms on the society in which they are installed. Nuclear reactors are extremely expensive to build and maintain and need to be strictly secured in order to maintain safety, which results in complex surveillance and security regimes deployed on and around the facilities and its workers. Nuclear material (the fuel and waste) is dangerous, valuable, and a national security threat (it can be weaponized), and many of the parts used in building and maintaining the plant are safety critical, requiring additional strict security regimes to manage the entire supply chain and waste disposal process. Contrast this with the more democratic norms embedded in windmills. Windmills are relatively inexpensive, can be installed in a farmer's field (by the farmer, no less!), produce no hazardous waste, thus they impose no strict security regimes on those they impact. Nuclear reactors and windmills are similar in that they are designed to produce electricity, but the political relations embedded in each artifact could not be more different.

Social norms can also be reflected in the work we *delegate* to artifacts. The average front door to any building is illustrative here.[26] Most of us share a social norm when it comes to front doors: that they should generally be kept closed. This norm reflects any number of underlying reasons for closing a front door, such as maintaining a comfortable indoor temperature, saving energy costs, keeping the bugs out, keeping the burglars out, keeping the wind out, keeping the family pets in. The list goes on. Doors tend to ignore this social norm; they require human attentiveness and a helping hand to keep closed. Indeed, to remain closed, doors operated by children often require the help of an additional person, a nearby adult, to call out repeatedly, "Close the door!" However, clever humans have found a way to delegate all the work required to enforce the norm to small artifacts attached to doors. These little mechanisms, usually powered by a spring, are designed to automatically close doors once opened, thus embodying and enforcing the social norm to keep front doors closed.

---

[23] I take as a starting point the fact that social norms are unavoidably designed into technological artifacts. For a fuller explanation of this starting point, see J. Millar, "*Technology as Moral Proxy: Autonomy and Paternalism by Design,*" *IEEE Technology & Society Magazine* 34(2) (2014): 47–55.

[24] "Users" is understood broadly here to include direct users, as well as other stakeholders (e.g., policymakers, citizens, etc.) impacted, directly or indirectly, by the artifact.

[25] L, Winner, *The Whale and the Reactor—A Search for Limits in an Age of High Technology* (Chicago: University of Chicago Press, 1986).

[26] This example is largely borrowed from Bruno Latour, who also describes how we delegate ethical (social) norms to seatbelts, robots, traffic calming obstructions and walls. See B. Latour, "Where Are the Missing Masses? The Sociology of a Few Mundane Artifacts," in *Shaping Technology/Building Society*, ed. W.E. Bijker and J. Law (Cambridge, Mass: MIT Press, 1992), 225–258. For a similar argument for technology's ability to *script*, or prescribe, behavior, see M. Akrich, "The De-Scription of Technical Objects," in *Shaping Technology/Building Society*, ed. W.E. Bijker and J. Law (Cambridge, Mass: MIT Press, 1992), 205–224.

Engineers can also delegate flexible social norms to technology via "settings" that target those norms.[27] Take privacy settings, like those designed into Facebook's user interface, which define Facebook's behavior with respect to personal data that users upload and share on the platform. These settings allow a user to shape Facebook's behavior based on their own normative privacy expectations, for example, by allowing users to partially limit photo sharing to friends. However, Facebook's design decisions also bound the possibilities of that individual shaping. Facebook users cannot, for example, upload photos to the platform and decline to share those photos with Facebook. Thus, settings can reflect, shape and bound social norms delegated to a technological artifact.

Finally, we can identify social norms embedded in artifacts when they *mediate* our perceptions of, and actions in, the world. Verbeek argues that by mediating the way we perceive reality, a technology can "actively contribute to the moral decisions human beings make."[28] Using medical imaging technologies as an example, he writes:

> [T]he specific way these technologies represent what they "see" helps to shape how the body or a fetus is perceived and interpreted and what decisions are made. In this way, technologies fundamentally shape people's experiences of disease, pregnancy, or their unborn children. Ultrasound, for instance, makes it quite easy to determine the thickness of the nape of the neck of a fetus, which gives an indication of the risk that the unborn child will suffer from Down's syndrome. The very fact of having an ultrasound scan made, therefore, lets the fetus be present in terms of health and disease and in terms of our ability to prevent children with disease from being born.[29]

As a result of its mediating role, ultrasound technology has been elevated to a standard of care among healthcare professionals—*perform an ultrasound at 7–12 weeks, and again at 20 weeks during each pregnancy* is among their widely accepted social norms. That norm has a cascading effect in that it imposes new norms that women encounter during a standard pregnancy when they are confronted with the results of their ultrasound.

I have sketched a picture in this section illustrating several ways to describe how social norms are designed into technology. The social norms that will matter most in an analysis of social failures are the ones that tend to align with, or transgress, important social norms held by a particular group impacted by a technology. If, say, privacy is important to a particular group of potential users, then how engineers embed privacy norms in their product will be an important design consideration. A product that transgresses potential users' privacy norms severely enough will likely suffer a social failure.

---

[27] J. Millar, "Ethics Setting for Autonomous Vehicles," in *Robot Ethics 2.0: From Autonomous Cars to Artificial Intelligence*, ed. P. Lin, R. Jenkins, and K. Abney (New York: Oxford University Press, 2017), 20–34.

[28] P-P. Verbeek, "Materializing Morality: Design Ethics and Technological Mediation," *Science, Technology & Human Values* 31 (2006): 366.

[29] *Id.*

Two Social Failure Modes

The Zimbabwe Bush Pump and Google Glass suggest, as a starting point for further analysis and characterization, two types of social failures, which we can refer to as *social failure modes*. These social failure modes will help flesh out the definition of a social failure.

(1) *Absence of supportive norms.* An artifact can fail socially when its design requires a certain social norm to be held by its user(s) in order for it to work (i.e., be used) as intended, but that required norm is not in fact held by its user(s).

As we saw with the Bush Pump, in order for it to be cared for, community norms of ownership are established by way of elaborate community activities centered around a new pump, as a result of designing the Bush Pump to be installed as a community affair. The Bush Pump's designers have designed into it the norm *pumps must be cared for by the community to avoid contamination*. Pumps that fail socially often do so because their designs fail to establish such supportive caring norms.

With Google Glass, in order for it to have been socially acceptable people's privacy norms would have had to shift in such a way as to make wearing cameras that record surreptitiously socially acceptable, perhaps even cool. By designing Glass the way they did, Google's engineers designed into it the norm *it is acceptable to wear cameras that record surreptitiously*, which was in tension with the widely held, and stable, societal norm *it is NOT acceptable to wear cameras that record surreptitiously*. Thus, the existing norms came into tension with the designed norms, the supportive norms were absent, and Glass suffered social failures.

(2) *Norm transgression.* An artifact can fail socially when a social norm designed into it transgresses an accepted social norm held by its user(s).

This social failure mode is more straightforward. As we see with water pumps, some are designed to be agnostic with respect to the social norms surrounding water diviners in rural Zimbabwe. Those pumps have designed into them the norm *install this pump on any water-yielding well*. However, agnosticism over the role of local water diviners can result in an installed pump transgressing the local norm *only trust water from a well that has been endorsed by a water diviner*. Any pump installed on a well not endorsed by a local water diviner runs the risk of transgressing that local norm, since *any water-yielding well* may not be trusted.

Likewise, Google Glass, evidenced by the creation of Glassholes, clearly transgressed existing norms of privacy and coolness.[30]

That said, not all norm transgressions are created equal. Though the distinction is vague and somewhat controversial, social norms seem to come in two broad psychological

[30] Eveleth, "Google Glass Wasn't a Failure. It Raised Crucial Concerns."

categories: *conventional* and *moral*.[31] Prototypical examples of conventional norms include "wearing gender-inappropriate clothing (e.g. men wearing dresses), licking one's plate at the dinner table, and talking in a classroom when one has not been called on by the teacher."[32] Prototypical moral norms, on the other hand, tend to include prohibitions against killing, injuring, or stealing from other people. Moral norms tend to be categorized as such because they are regarded as: less authority dependent; more universal (i.e., they apply cross-culturally); involving rights violations; and more serous in nature than conventional norms.

Importantly, in many cases (though not all) an analytic focus on social failures involving moral norms and moral norm transgressions will underscore the unavoidable moral dimension of engineering design. Such a focus will thus help to delineate between permissible and impermissible design decisions and suggest certain obligations that engineers have by virtue of the design decisions they must navigate. Engineers have already partially embraced this reality. Social failures caused by safety or privacy norm transgressions are already generally considered impermissible, resulting in a general obligation for engineers to design for safety and increasingly for privacy. In Canada, for example, the profession's code of ethics requires engineers to "hold paramount the safety, health and welfare of the public and the protection of the environment and promote health and safety in the workplace."[33] Other social norms, upon analysis, could give rise to similar professional constraints, as I discuss in the next section.

Conventional norms, in contrast, tend to be regarded as such because they are: more authority/institution dependent; locally applicable (i.e., they do not apply cross-culturally, or even among different groups within a single cultural boundary); do not involve rights violations; and transgressions of them are less severe than those involving moral norms.

Using the moral/conventional distinction as a guide, we can further subdivide social failures resulting from norm transgressions into two sub-categories: *conventional norm transgressions* and *moral norm transgressions*. To illustrate, social failures resulting from rights violations, say privacy transgressions, can be categorized as moral norm transgressions, whereas social failures resulting from institutional norm transgressions, say a mobile phone that can't be "muted" in a quiet space, can be categorized as conventional norm transgressions. As I discuss in the following section, the moral/conventional distinction can serve as a useful guide for anticipating the nature of harms resulting from social failures of the norm transgression type.

---

[31] For various discussions of the moral/conventional distinction and the controversies and questions it raises, see: E. Machery and R. Mallon, "Evolution of Morality," in *The Moral Psychology Handbook*, ed. J. Doris and the Moral Psychology Research Group (New York: Oxford University Press, 2010); D. Kelly, S. Stich, K.J. Haley, S.J. Eng, and D. Fessler, "Harm, Affect, and the Moral/Conventional Distinction," *Mind & Language* 22(2) (2007): 117–131; S. Nichols, *Sentimental Rules: On the Natural Foundations of Moral Judgment* (New York: Oxford University Press, 2004).

[32] Kelly et al., "Harm, Affect, and the Moral/Conventional Distinction," 117.

[33] Engineers Canada, "2 The Code of Ethics," *Public Guideline on the Code of Ethics* (2016), https://engineerscanada.ca/publications/public-guideline-on-the-code-of-ethics.

THE ETHICAL DIMENSIONS OF SOCIAL FAILURES

My argument so far has focused on sketching a conceptual apparatus with which to describe social failures and social failure modes. In this section I turn to the normative aspect of this project and propose two straightforward reasons why we should care about and investigate, in order to mitigate or avoid, undesirable social failures in technology.

The first reason has to do with the deprivation of benefits a group of users (or other implicated stakeholders) would otherwise derive from a technology that works as intended. Assuming a technology is designed to deliver some set of goods or benefits to some group of individuals (e.g., clean water, clean air, improved medical diagnoses, enhanced communication with friends and family, novel modes of interaction with one's environment, etc.), social failures, insofar as they prevent that technology from being used as intended, stand to reduce the benefits derived from that technology. Some social failures will deprive users of important benefits. Water pumps that become contaminated, or are not trusted, do not deliver the benefits of potable water. Other social failures will deprive users of benefits in ways that are trivial or at least far less costly. I assume this to be the case with many intended uses of Google Glass.

In addition to depriving people of benefits, social failures can directly harm individuals, giving us further reason to investigate and avoid some social failures in technology.[34] Contaminated wells deprive communities of clean water, but they also allow E. coli to infect (and kill) members of that community. Google Glass surreptitiously recording the surrounding environment while its host is standing at a urinal in a crowded washroom violates the privacy of every recorded individual sharing that otherwise semi-private space.

We can use the moral/conventional distinction here to anticipate how those individuals harmed by a social failure in technology will interpret the severity of the harm and, more importantly, to evaluate the nature of the harm in a way that provides guidance on the moral permissibility of a particular technology.

Moral norm transgressions, by definition, tend to result from rights violations and tend to be considered more serious in nature. Thus, we can trivially assume that harms resulting from moral norm transgressions will threaten to break a technology, while conventional norm transgressions may pose a lower risk in that regard.

Less trivial, however, is the implication that every social failure resulting from a moral norm transgression suggests that something is potentially morally problematic about that technology. Here we see clearly the impact that an understanding of social failure modes ought to have on guiding ethical engineering practice. Knowledge of social failure modes can frame a discussion about whether or not to design a technology in

---

[34] Social failures can also deliver harms to non-humans, a fact that deserves careful consideration but is beyond the scope of this chapter. Social failures can result in contaminated rivers, polluted air, loss of habitat and biodiversity, etc.

such and such a way, by providing clearer links between designed features and moral norms, thus helping to distinguish between design decisions that users will consider permissible and impermissible. The corollary, to complete the thought, is that a better understanding of social failure modes can help to define the boundaries of ethical design decisions; every social failure of technology resulting from a moral norm transgression can potentially be interpreted, insofar as the social failure was reasonably predictable, as an ethical design failure on the part of the responsible engineers. Thus, a more thorough understanding of social failure modes should help distinguish between permissible and impermissible technologies or features thereof.

Determining whether a particular moral norm transgression is an ethical failure is a complicated business. Not all social norms are justified, so a technology that transgresses a particular unjustified moral norm could count as an engineering victory (though just to be clear, if the norm violation had no effect on users' willingness to use the technology as intended, this would not be considered a social failure of that technology according to the definition on offer here). In addition, a technology might establish an unjustified or controversial moral norm without suffering a social failure. For example, China is currently rolling out a complex social networking platform that calculates and ranks its citizens according to a *social credit score*, ostensibly to curb people's behavior in public and help determine how to distribute goods among the citizenry.[35] The various new norms that will likely emerge as a result of the platform's ubiquity will strike many as a clear and unjustifiable violation of basic freedoms. According to the definition on offer, however, the platform would only suffer social failures if it failed to be used as intended owing to existing norm violations, or if it failed to establish the requisite norms for its intended use. Critically, the occurrence or nonoccurrence of a social failure in technology should not be taken as evidence of a technology's moral permissibility or impermissibility.

This moral ambiguity of social failures echoes the moral ambiguity of many new technologies whose social meaning takes time to emerge and stabilize and can ultimately differ from group to group.[36] "The telephone and typewriter," as Verbeek points out, "were not developed as communication and writing technologies but as equipment for the blind and the hard of hearing to help those individuals hear and write."[37] Telephones also eased interpersonal communication, altered the speed at which information propagates globally, and enabled surreptitious government eavesdropping through wiretaps.

Pointing out the moral ambiguities inherent in social failures should not be interpreted as absolving engineers of their moral responsibility in designing technologies with the intent to disrupt justified norms or establish unjust norms. Rather than undermining the concept of social failures in technology, the moral ambiguity of social failures is, I think, important for maintaining the descriptive accuracy of the concept. It anchors justifications for particular norms in the social contexts into which technologies are deployed without so divorcing it from engineering practice as to absolve engineers of

---

[35] M. Hvistendahl, "Inside China's Vast New Experiment in Social Ranking," *Wired* (December 14, 2017), https://www.wired.com/story/age-of-social-credit/

[36] W. Bijker, T. Hughes, and T. Pinch, *The Social Construction of Technological Systems* (Cambridge, MA: MIT Press, 1987).

[37] Verbeek, "Materializing Morality: Design Ethics and Technological Mediation," 365.

their responsibilities as designers. In addition, the concept provides an analytic apparatus that explicitly links design with the social dynamics of technology. Diverse social groups can go on negotiating their norms, while engineers acting in good faith, as members of those larger groups, deploy the concept to anticipate and evaluate social failures in their design activities.

A fuller discussion of the dynamics between design and the moral permissibility of particular technologies is beyond the scope of this chapter. However, I believe that discussion would benefit from a more fully developed language of social failures, one that investigates and links particular technological features to particular norms and thus to engineering practice.

A Social Failure Mode Analysis
of Microsoft's Tay

As was mentioned in the section "Talking about How Stuff Breaks: A Brief Primer on Physical Failures and Failure Modes," designing AI requires engineers to embed social norms into artifacts so that the AIs can interact with us, among us, and on our behalf. Having sketched an initial taxonomy of social failure modes throughout this chapter, one can see how particular design decisions regarding social norms can shape the ethical nature of an artifact. Furthermore, the reach of AI in society can be broad and immediate, often the result of a background system-wide software update, which adds a certain urgency to understanding what social failures any particular design decision could trigger. To illustrate the link between social failures and the ethics of AI with a final example, I turn to Microsoft's Tay.

Microsoft's Tay was a Twitter chatbot, an AI designed to interact with other Twitter users as if it were a fourteen-year-old teenage girl. Because Tay lived on Twitter, its reach was broad—Tay could interact with any of Twitter's roughly seventy million active monthly users. Tay was also designed to "learn" how to carry on normal Twitter conversations by using the ever-changing set of prior interactions as its learning dataset. That meant that by design, the interactions Tay had with other Twitter users would shape Tay's future behavior. In other words, Microsoft made the Twitterverse responsible for teaching young Tay how to behave when interacting with people.

The Twitterverse did not parent Tay responsibly. Within a day, Tay was behaving like a racist, neo-Nazi misogynist, forcing Microsoft to pull Tay's plug amid widespread public controversy.[38]

It might be that fourteen-year-old girls were Tay's target user group and that Tay could have learned to be quite pleasant after interactions with only those target users. But the

---

[38] J. Vincent, "Twitter Taught Microsoft's AI Chatbot to Be a Racist Asshole in Less than a Day," *The Verge* (March 24, 2016), https://www.theverge.com/2016/3/24/11297050/tay-microsoft-chatbot-racist; S. Kleeman, "Here Are the Microsoft Twitterbot's Craziest Racist Rants," *Gizmodo* (March 24, 2016), https://gizmodo.com/here-are-the-microsoft-twitter-bot-s-craziest-racist-ra-1766820160.

larger sociotechnical system into which Tay was embedded included numerous callous Twitter users intent on shock-testing Tay. To be sure, the average Twitter user interacting with Tay during its brief existence did not conform to the same interactional norms as the average fourteen-year-old (or so one hopes). Thus, Tay suffered multiple social failures.

It is tempting to brush Tay off as a foolish publicity stunt that was bound to go wrong. After all, the internet, Twitter in particular, is known for its trolls. A more charitable approach, however, reveals Tay as a great learning opportunity. More specifically, too quick a dismissal represents a missed opportunity to apply a more sophisticated failure analysis on Tay, one that more accurately accounts for the social dynamics that caused Tay to fail.

Let us first examine the absence of supportive norms that Tay (and Microsoft) required for Tay to succeed. For Tay to work well, it needed to experience a large number of socially acceptable Twitter interactions. Tay required the support of conversational norms typical in what would generally be considered "polite society." But the conversational norms on Twitter are unpredictable at best (especially between two users who do not know each other), deeply unethical at worst, and are certainly not representative of conversational norms in the rest of society. Instead of providing supportive conversational norms, the Twitterverse helped to break Tay.

Once Tay's learning algorithm had been exposed to unsupportive conversational norms, Tay suffered a second social failure: it repeatedly transgressed accepted conversational norms existing in "polite society." Indeed, the kinds of conversational norm transgressions Tay committed were not mere conventional transgressions, they were moral in nature. In response to Tay's behavior, Microsoft was quickly criticized by those stakeholders who found Tay's behavior ethically impermissible. Microsoft responded responsibly to the situation by shutting Tay down.

Applying a social failure mode analysis to an artifact like Tay allows us to focus design efforts on both analyzing and shaping the social dynamics required for an artifact to work. Based on the rudimentary taxonomy provided in this chapter, that means analyzing and shaping the requisite supportive norms and the resulting norms characterizing the artifact's behavior. For Tay to work, design effort was required to both understand the current conversational norms on Twitter and, given their current state, to change the conversational norms on Twitter so they would support Tay's socially appropriate learning and result in ethical behavior. But notice how a focus on social failure modes has helped us move from a state of relative ignorance with respect to Tay's failure, toward much more specific design activities that hold some promise if the goal is to anticipate social failure modes before they occur. This could be the analytic toolkit engineers need that helps clarify the link between the ethical issues raised by AI and other technologies, and the design decisions that shape them.

CONCLUSIONS

I assume in this chapter that engineers generally intend new technologies to make the world a better, not worse, place. Clearly, many technologies do so. Along those lines,

I assume there is no controversy in claiming that engineers are generally, and non-trivially, motivated to make things that improve the lives of individuals and the societies in which they live, while also being motivated to avoid making things that harm individuals and/or societies. These are fair assumptions, and they are reflected consistently in the various codes of ethical conduct to which engineers are obliged to adhere in their professional dealings. Insofar as engineers are prevented from acting on these motivations in their professional settings, there is work to be done in improving engineers' professional settings. Insofar as engineers are not so motivated in their work, there is work to be done in improving the profession. Insofar as technologies fail, often resulting in harms, there is work to be done in understanding how they fail and how to prevent those failures moving forward.

The social implications of technology have long been studied in detail outside of the profession, and many of those discussions suggest that if the norms embedded into a technology come into tension with accepted social norms held by its user(s), the technology can break. Technology can break when it suffers a social failure. However, practical conceptual and analytic apparatuses for describing and anticipating the links between technology, social norms, and engineering practice are required to put those insights into practice.

To help bridge that gap, between studying the social implications of technology and designing technology, I have proposed a working definition of social failure and described two social failure modes. These analytic tools help to expose and clarify the inextricable connections between some design failures and social norms. Though there is much work to be done to build a more sophisticated understanding of social failures in technology and the ethical implications they have for engineering practice, one practical, ethical insight should already be apparent. A working knowledge of social failure modes can help make better technology, because technology that aligns with people's robustly justified social norms is better than technology that undermines them.

BIBLIOGRAPHY

Calo, R., M. Froomkin, and I. Kerr eds. *Robot Law*. Northhampton: Edward Elgar, 2015.

Collins, H.M. and R. Evans. *Rethinking Expertise*. Chicago: University of Chicago Press, 2007.

Friedman, B. and P.H. Kahn Jr. "Human Values, Ethics, and Design." In *The Human-Computer Interaction Handbook*, ed. J.A. Jacko and A. Sears, 1177–1201. Mahwah, NJ: Lawrence Erlbaum Associates, 2003.

Latour, B. *Pandora's Hope: Essays on the Reality of Science Studies*. Cambridge, MA: Harvard University Press, 1999.

Lin, P., R. Jenkins, K. Abney, and G.A. Bekey eds. *Robot Ethics 2.0*. Oxford: Oxford University Press, 2017.

van den Hoven, J., N. Doorn, T. Swierstra, B.-J. Koops, and H. Romijn eds. *Responsible Innovation 1: Innovative Solutions for Global Issues*. Springer 2014.

CHAPTER 24

A HUMAN-CENTERED
APPROACH TO AI ETHICS
A Perspective from Cognitive Science

RON CHRISLEY

THE increasing role of artificial intelligence (AI) and machine learning technology in our lives has raised an enormous number and variety of ethical challenges, as can be seen in the diverse topics covered in this volume. In addition, there are the ethical challenges yet to come, ones that we cannot currently anticipate. We can try to respond to this vast array of challenges individually, in an ad hoc manner, but in the long run, a more principled, structured response is likely to be of more guidance. In this chapter I propose responses to some particular questions concerning the ethics of AI, responses that share a unifying perspective: a human-centered approach. The hope is that, beyond offering solutions to the particular problems considered here, these responses can be of more general interest by illuminating enough of their shared, human-centered perspective to facilitate like-minded responses to any number of current and future ethical challenges involving AI.

More will be said about what the human-centered approach to AI/robot ethics amounts to, but an important consequence of it, and the central claim of this chapter, is this: when making ethical judgments in this area, we should resist the temptation to see robots as ethical agents or patients. For the foreseeable future, more ethical hazard follows from seeing humans and robots as ethically analogous than follows from seeing them as ethically distinct kinds. Much of what I say in what follows is meant to support this claim, to identify some instances of current practice that fail to heed the warnings of the claim and to suggest ways of avoiding the anthropomorphic error the claim identifies, while still minimizing the likelihood of certain ethically adverse outcomes involving robots and AI in general.

This central claim can seem at odds with an otherwise attractive naturalism about ethics, mind, and what it is to be human. My adoption of a human-centered approach to the ethics of AI arises out of my lifelong interest in cognitive science. Cognitive science is the interdisciplinary search for an understanding of how mentality in general (not just cognition) can be part of the natural world, and the use of that understanding to provide explanations of mental phenomena and the behavior of systems with minds. One might think that this naturalism (particularly in the mechanistic, functionalist, physicalist form that many traditional cognitive scientists embrace, even if only implicitly) encourages us to see ourselves as glorified robots, a rough equation that would either support the extension of the concepts of ethical agent and patient to suitably programmed robots and AI systems, or encourage ethical nihilism for both humans and robots. Contrary to this, I believe that seeing humans as part of the natural world does not undermine our understanding of what makes humans ethically different from robots (or nonhuman animals); rather, it gives that understanding scientific plausibility and conceptual clarity. It is only by properly considering our place in the natural world that we can see the true, nondualist, reasons why it is correct to see us, but not robots (at least for the forseeable future), as ethical beings. Nevertheless, the theories and methods of cognitive science will largely remain in the background of this chapter, with the focus instead being on the human-centered approach they support.

Putting Robots in Their Place

Just what do I mean by a human-centered approach? We'll be better equipped to answer that question in full after we have a few instances of it from which to generalize, but a few things can be said at the outset to give an initial idea of what the approach is—and what it is not.

The human-centered approach to AI ethics I am advocating here has two key aspects:

1. An emphasis on human welfare.
2. An emphasis on human responsibility.

The first aspect is in contrast with approaches to AI ethics that take seriously ethical obligations concerning the purported welfare of artificial agents. Such approaches focus on questions such as:

- Can robots feel pain?
- Can they suffer?
- If so, what are our obligations, if any, for reducing robot pain and suffering at the expense of increasing human pain and suffering? At the expense of increasing animal pain and suffering?

Similarly, the second aspect of the human-centered approach is in contrast with approaches that focus on questions such as:

- Should we punish robots that are responsible for crimes?
- Should we grant citizenship, workers' rights, "human" rights to certain machines?
- Should robots be allowed to own property?

The human-centered approach doesn't just answer questions like these in the negative; it dismisses them as impertinent, or worse: as presupposing a view that is so wrong-headed that it risks both distracting us from many of the real ethical issues, and misdiagnosing those few real issues we do manage to address.[1] The human-centered approach starts with the following *Deflationary View* about machine ethics:

Deflationary View: No robot or AI system currently in existence could be ethically responsible or be the kind of thing toward which we have ethical obligations.[2]

Some might be inclined to stop reading at this point, believing I have just dismissed, without argument, most of what is of interest in AI ethics. Fair enough; the previously posed questions are alluring and excite our imaginations, so interest in them is understandable. And attempting to answer such questions can be a good way to explore the features and limits of the concepts involved in stating them. But if it is worthwhile to consider ethical issues that arise in futuristic thought experiments involving AI and robots, it is all the more worthwhile, even pressing, to consider the ethical issues confronting us now, in a way that is not unduly distorted by consideration of the counterfactual, futuristic, robot-as-ethical-agent-or-patient cases.

I do not wish to be confused for an AI pessimist, so let me make one thing explicitly clear: the Deflationary View applies to AI systems/robots currently in existence (or in the foreseeable future). In taking the Deflationary View, the human-centered approach I am advocating does not thereby assume that only humans (or beings biologically related to humans: animals) could ever be ethically responsible agents or deserving of our ethical concern. For example, I am not advocating the Deflationary View because I believe there is some fundamental inability for artifacts (or nonbiological systems, whatever their provenance) to have minds, to experience emotion, to be conscious; on the contrary. My point is that while in principle, there might someday be robots or AI systems that are ethically responsible or are the kinds of things toward which we have ethical obligations, in fact there are not nor are there likely to be in the foreseeable future.[3] Unlike an AI ethics that addresses the previously posed questions, a human-centered AI ethics is

---

[1] For a human-centered AI ethics from a substantially different perspective, see, e.g., Joanna Bryson, "Patiency Is Not a Virtue: The Design of Intelligent Systems and Systems of Ethics," *Ethics and Information Technology* 20 (1) (2018): 15–26.

[2] Perhaps unsatisfyingly, I do not argue for this claim here. One reason for thinking that current AI systems are not moral agents is that they lack the capacity for *judgment* (in a specific, almost technical sense of that word; see Brian Cantwell Smith, *The Promise of Artificial Intelligence: Reckoning and Judgment*. Cambridge, MA: MIT Press, 2019), 124–127.

[3] Thus while others may be correct in their accounts of what conditions would have to be met by an AI system or robot for it to enjoy ethical status (e.g., John Sullins, "When Is a Robot a Moral Agent?," *International Review of Information Ethics* 6 (2006): 24–29), it is my view that these conditions will remain unmet for the foreseeable future.

urgently needed, now. And since it seems likely that we will continue to use AI systems and robots that are not responsible nor to which we have any responsibility, even beyond the eventual advent of AI systems with their own ethical status, a human-centered AI ethics will continue to be indispensable even if a more substantive AI ethics, based on the obligations of and toward AI systems and robots, becomes necessary.

The human-centered approach to AI ethics I am advocating is deflationary in another, related aspect. Some hold that current AI and machine learning is an ethical game-changer, which requires a radical break in our ethical thinking in order to accommodate artificial agents that are responsible for their actions and/or to which we bear some responsibility. The human-centered approach being offered here is conceptually conservative, urging us to try to use precedent, past wisdom, and conventional metaphysics as much as possible when trying to resolve ethical issues involving current and near-future AI technology. On such an approach, robots and AI systems, despite any autonomy, learning or decision-making capabilities they may have, are best treated, in our ethical deliberations, in a manner continuous with how we deal with other technologies: as nonpersonal boundary conditions potentially affecting the praise- or blame-worthiness of the people involved—not as candidates for such praise or blame, nor as personal subjects whose harm or benefit can figure, in the special way personal well-being does, into the ethical evaluation of human action. On the other hand, we cannot afford to be complacent. These new, highly adaptive and flexible technologies are unlike any before and require new ethical concepts and tools. But the new concepts and tools we need should not be developed by diagnosing our situation in terms of the arrival on the ethical scene of a new source, or target, of ethical responsibility.

If the questions listed previously are not the right or relevant ones, what are? Here are a few:

- To what extent should damaging, stealing, or destroying an adaptive information system "implant" that a person has trained over several years, and on which that person relies to function in everyday life, count as harm to that person, over and above the usual harm associated with property loss?
- When an autonomous robot takes action that results in harm or loss, how should the responsibility for that harm be distributed across the various people and organizations involved, such as:
  - The robot operator(s),
  - Bystanders,
  - The robot trainer(s),
  - The robot programmer(s),
  - The robot manufacturer(s),
  - The robot retailer, and
  - The governmental body that licensed robot operation in that context?
- In what ways can the use of certain kinds of augmenting AI technology better enable us to perform ethically? What AI technologies might instead compromise our ethical competence?

These questions are good indications of how to apply the human-centered perspective; they focus exclusively on the welfare and responsibility of the only ethical agents on the scene: humans.[4] But in some situations it can be tricky to see how to achieve this focus properly. The remainder of this chapter will look at two kinds of case, the better to flesh out the human-centered approach. Until now, I have been referring to my area of interest using the cumbersome phrase "AI systems or robots," which is fair enough, since the human-centered approach to AI ethics applies that broadly. But for the remainder of this chapter I will just use the phrase "robots" and focus especially on social robots (ones designed to interact with humans, as opposed to, say, industrial assembly-line robots). It is when social robots are on the scene, much more so than in cases involving disembodied AI, that the temptations of an inflationary ethics, and the concomitant need to keep hold of the insights of the human-centered view, are at their strongest. Thus, a focus on social robots will make it easier to see the points I wish to make (and will streamline the prose). But the insights I will thereby uncover apply, I believe, to the more inclusive class of AI systems and robots in general.

IMPLICATIONS OF A HUMAN-CENTERED APPROACH

Corresponding to the two aspects of the human-centered approach identified at the outset, welfare and responsibility, I will look at two nonobvious or counterintuitive implications of the approach.

Harming Robots

The issue of harming robots can be emotionally charged and divided: for an example one only has to look at David Harris Smith and Frauke Zeller's hitchBOT, the actions of the authors of its fate, and people's responses to that treatment. Another example is the kicking and shoving of robots Boston Dynamics researchers use to demonstrate the robustness of their robots, and people's emotionally charged reactions upon seeing videos of these demonstrations.

One might think that proponents of the human-centered approach to AI ethics have their hands tied here: according to the Deflationary View, robots are not the kind of thing that can be harmed, and so the question is dismissed as being immaterial to today's pressing ethical concerns with AI.

---

[4] This isn't quite right: animals are also "on the scene," so the impact of AI and robots on them should also be taken into consideration.

But the issue cannot be dismissed so easily: so that talk of "harm" does not beg the question, let's make it clear that in this context we mean it to cover actions that are of a kind that, were they performed on humans or animals, would cause harm. In more neutral language: is it ethical to hit—or disfigure, mutilate, and so on—robots? We are concerned here with ethical prohibitions, if any, over and above those having to do with damaging someone's property in general.

It may seem that the human-centered approach proponents are still bound here: since such actions would not cause harm, they are not prohibited.

But is it really the case that such actions cause no harm? The mere consideration of whether the robot's welfare is relevant, even if answered in the negative, has done its own harm: distracted us from proper consideration of the humans in the situation (the agent of the harm and any observers). Because even if mutilating a robot does not harm the robot (because the robot is not the kind of thing that can be harmed), such mutilation may in fact do harm to the humans involved—an emphasis that is at the heart of the human-centered approach. The idea here says something about why it is wrong to abuse robots that is very similar to what Immanuel Kant says about why it is wrong to abuse animals (but does not commit anyone to agreeing with Kant on why animals should not be abused). The idea is that even if robots cannot be harmed, they are, at least sometimes, "made in our image" to such an extent that willfully abusing them is at best grotesque, at worst unethical. Think of how we would consider it grossly inappropriate for someone to willfully and sadistically (i.e., not as part of performance art, or as an experiment, or as a political protest, etc.) dismember a doll (as opposed to, say, a toy car) on stage in front of young children. The key feature here is the doll's sharing, to some degree, the human form. Robots, to be sure, can share this visual form as much as any doll. But beyond that, they can share the human form, in a higher, more abstract sense, to a much greater degree: witness their ability to respond to questions with linguistic sounds, to acquire information from their environment and act conditionally upon it, to learn, decide, remember, prefer, assist, make emotional displays, and so forth. So, it could be argued, acts of violence upon these robots conceivably cross into the unethical because they brutalize the agent (and perhaps those witnessing the act). Accounts differ as to why harming something with the human form is wrong, with the familiar consequentialist (the normalization of violence to the human form makes violence to actual humans more likely) and deontological (it's just wrong to do harm to the human form) variants. As should be clear, I am not attempting to make a strong case for this view here; I am only pointing to the view as an existence proof that one can take the human-centered approach to AI ethics and still hold that it is unethical to abuse (some) current robots, in some situations.

But I also want to highlight another point that arises out of this discussion: although it was only the welfare and responsibility of humans that ultimately mattered in this case, the mind-like cognitive abilities of robots also played a crucial role. That is what made the issue one in the ethics of AI, rather than ethics in general. What's important to note is that the role those abilities played was not that of making the robots the kind of thing that could be harmed (or the kind of thing that could be responsible). Rather, the role it played, and what it is novel about such technology, involves the new and complex ways robots can impact on human welfare and human responsibility.[5]

Robots as Extensions of Human Responsibility

Taking the human-centered approach to AI ethics can have practical consequences for robot design. This can be demonstrated by considering what such an approach has to say about one way of designing robots, which I call *logic-based ethical robot methodology*. You can think of this methodology as a direct descendant of the approach explored in Isaac Asimov's novels.

Logic-based ethical robot methodology:

- An ethical system is encoded (by humans) in logic;
- Robots are given these statements and an ability to reason logically with them;
- Robots consult these rules when generating their behavior (e.g., by disqualifying a proposed action if it is a consequence of their reasoning that the action is not ethically permissible).

Such robots are *explicit ethical agents* (sometimes called *explicit moral agents*) in James Moor's sense: "Explicit ethical agents are agents that can identify and process ethical information about a variety of situations and make sensitive determinations about what should be done. When ethical principles are in conflict, these robots can work out reasonable resolutions."[6]

The intended outcome of this methodology is not only avoidance of ethically adverse situations but also an ability to explain/justify robot behavior by appealing to the inferential trace that governed its generation.

An example of work that employs the ethical robot methodology comes from Matthias Scheutz and Bertram Malle.[7] There, the authors consider ethical questions such as: should Rob, the elder-care robot, deliver pain medication even though it cannot consult a supervisor, as is usually required? The authors say:

"An interesting question is what a human health care provider might do in Rob's position…If R were to model human behavior, it would, in addition to ethical reasoning,

---

[5] For more on the ethics of robot abuse, see, e.g., B. Whitby, "Sometimes It's Hard to Be a Robot: A Call for Action on the Ethics of Abusing Artificial Agents," *Interacting with Computers* 20 (3) (2008): 326–333. See also Massimiliano L. Cappuccio, Anco Peeters, and William McDonald, "Sympathy for Dolores: Moral Consideration for Robots Based on Virtue and Recognition," *Philosophy & Technology* 33 (2020): 9–31.

[6] James Moor, "Four Kinds of Ethical Robots," *Philosophy Now* 72 (March/April 2009): 12.

[7] Matthias Scheutz and Bertram Malle, "Think and Do the Right Thing: A Plea for Morally Competent Autonomous Robots," *ETHICS '14: Proceedings of the IEEE 2014 International Symposium on Ethics in Engineering, Science, and Technology* (IEEE, 2014), 36–39. See also B. F. Malle, "Integrating Robot Ethics and Machine Morality: The Study and Design of Moral Competence in Robots," *Ethics and Information Technology* 18 (4) (2016): 243–256.

need the capability for empathy as well as the ability to generate justifications (i.e., explanations of norm violations such as not contacting the supervisor). We will not focus on those aspects of moral competency in this paper. Rather, we will develop a general argument that, in order to avoid unnecessary harm to humans, autonomous artificial systems must have moral competence."[8]

In line with logical ethical robot methodology, Scheutz and Malle aim to give their robots said moral competence by giving them a set of logical axioms, some logical statements encoding the state of the world, and an ability to draw inferences from these:

1. ¬havePermission(R, administer(R, H, M)) → O[¬administer(R,H,M)] [obligation]
2. inPain(H) →O[administer(R,H,M)] [obligation]
3. ¬havePermission(R, administer(R, H, M)) [fact]
4. inPain(H) [observation]
5. O[¬administer(R, H, M)] [1,3,MP]
6. O[administer(R, H, M)] [2,4,MP]
7. ¬◊(administer(R, H, M) ∧ ¬administer(R,H,M)) [modal logic]

Key: ¬ = negation, → = material implication, ∧ = conjunction, O = it is obligatory that, ◊ = it is physically possible that, R = robot, H = human, M = medicine, MP = modus ponens.[9]

Lines 1 and 2 are the axioms, lines 3 and 4 encode facts about the world, and lines 5–7 follow deductively from the lines before them. This reasoning reveals a dilemma, in that it is both obligatory that the robot administer the medicine and that it not administer the medicine. The point here is not to consider the dilemma and its possible solutions; rather, this reasoning is only presented so that we can have to hand a concrete exemplar of the logic-based ethical robot methodology.

One might think that logical ethical robot methodology is in direct conflict with the human-centered approach. Robots can't have moral competence, one might say, because they have no responsibility. It makes no sense for them to reason about what is permitted or obligatory for them, because they have no obligations or permitted actions.

But is there some way to find a rapprochement between logical ethical robot methodology and the human-centered approach? One can reject the human-centered response, above, as heavy-handed, as misconstruing the meaning of the axioms Scheutz and Malle have provided. One need not read "O[¬administer(R, H, M)]" as encoding "it is obligatory, *for the robot*, that the robot administer the medicine to the human." Instead, one could read the statement as merely encoding the proposition that the state of affairs in which the robot administers the medicine to the human is ethically obligatory. This is a general statement of the ethical landscape, not tied to any particular agent. What is an obligation for one, is an obligation for all.

In the simple kinds of ethical systems and situations Scheutz and Malle are addressing, this picture may be adequate. But it cannot be adequate in general; we differ in our

---

[8] Ibid., 36.   [9] Ibid.

obligations and permissions, so reasoning in the abstract about what states are or are not allowed to obtain will be of little to no use when deciding how to act ethically. One must in addition know where one is located in that web of obligations and permissions. The problem for the robot is that it is not located anywhere in that web. So that web can have no imperative force on its actions, even less so a force that could be inferred through logical reasoning.

The proponent of the logical ethical robot methodology could instead reply that it doesn't matter that the robot doesn't actually have the obligations it is reasoning about; all that matters is that the robot, by engaging in the kind of reasoning that would be correct were it a human, arrives at the ethically correct behavior (compare the distinction between genuine vs. functional ethical status[10]). To get the desired result, the robot need not *be* an ethical agent; it only needs to simulate one, to act *as if* it were an agent with obligations, and so on—that is what will get the right outcome. But given our differences in permissions and obligations, one has to ask: *which* ethical agent should the robot simulate?

To make the difficulty here clearer, consider: the inferences in the logical ethical robot methodology are not just used in the generation of behavior, but in the explanation/ justification of it. But since (as we have been assuming all along), robots cannot be responsible, the justifications generated by the methodology should apply to the actions of humans, not robots. So "as if," robot-framed justifications will only be of use if they can help us construct actual, human-framed ones. But how are we to do this? As far as I can tell, the logical ethical robot methodology is silent on this issue. This failure to find a mapping from robot faux-justifications to actual human justifications is itself a moral hazard, as it will lead to "moral murk." That is, everyone interacting with, writing about, training, making policy concerning, deploying, developing software for, designing, and so on will be invited to take the attributions of responsibility to the robot at face value, given the lack of guidance on how to allocate that responsibility to the humans involved.

This is the heart of the matter, but, stated so abstractly, grasping its insight can be difficult. To see exactly how the logical ethical robot methodology can fail to properly allocate responsibility, and what a human-centered approach must do to remedy that deficiency, a specific example will be helpful. In particular, the important issues can be identified in a situation in which the epistemic state (mens rea) of the humans involved is a crucial component in evaluating the ethical status of their actions.

Consider an autonomous military robot R in a war zone with bridges A and B. The robot is under the command/control of human H. H can deploy R to patrol the region that contains bridges A and B. Among the actions that R can perform is the destruction of a given bridge. In this situation, it is in general an ethical good to destroy bridges, as it would protect innocents from attack—unless the bridge has a mini hospital with medical supplies on it, in which case the bridge should not be destroyed. Accordingly, R is

[10] Steve Torrance and Ron Chrisley, "Modelling Consciousness-Dependent Expertise in Machine Medical Moral Agents," in *Machine Medical Ethics*, ed. Simon Peter van Rysewyk and Matthijs Pontier (Berlin: Springer International Publishing), 295.

designed such that if, even while out of contact with H, it acquires the information that it is very likely that there is no hospital on a bridge, it will destroy that bridge.

At the time of deployment, H believes that it is very likely that bridge A has no hospital on it, but that B does. So H deploys R. Soon after deployment, R loses contact with H and must rely on the reasoning given to it via the logical ethical robot methodology. On the way to bridge A, passing by bridge B, R acquires the information that it is very likely that there is no hospital on bridge B (by assessing B with its cameras, say). So it destroys the bridge. Unfortunately, and despite the information R received, there *was* a hospital on the bridge.

Should H be held responsible for the destruction of the hospital? The logical ethical robot methodology is silent on the issue: the only responsibilities it deals in are the "as if" responsibilities of either a robot which has none or an amorphous, unidentified human subject of unknown identity who, had they been the one who had made the wrong call on destroying the bridge, might or might not be "let off," given that they acted in the best way with the best information at the time. But what do either of these have to do with the responsibilities of H (or the responsibilities of the designers of the algorithm that incorrectly assessed the status of the bridge)?

A more human-centered approach to this situation can be arrived at in one of two ways.

The first way is to keep the logical ethical robot methodology intact, but supplement it with a human-centered interpretative scheme. In the abstract, we have a situation in which H performs an action (deploying R) that results in an ethical disaster: the destruction of the hospital. We have a mitigating, mens rea–involving story, but that involves the epistemic state of R, not H, so as things stand, it cannot serve to reduce H's culpability.[11]

But perhaps things should not stand? What would it take for the information that R gleans while out of contact with H to mitigate H's culpability? Something like this: externally individuated epistemic states for subjects who are using autonomous epistemic technology, such as R. That is, for the purposes of determining H's culpability, H's epistemic state is to include the information gleaned by R, even while H and R are not in causal connection with each other. This allows us to arrive at what many would consider the appropriate ethical result (H's diminished culpability), without attributing to R any responsibility. But, in a manner parallel to the case of "robot harm" considered in the previous section, "Harming Robots," this resolution does make essential reference to the cognitive states of R: an example of (human-centered) AI ethics in action. The implications of this move need to be explored in more depth, but it is a promising lead.[12]

The second human-centered way of dealing with the situation goes beyond a mere interpretive scheme, instead proposing an extension to the designs used in the logical ethical robot methodology. It is proposed that the formalism (such as the one from Scheutz and Malle, displayed earlier) be extended in two ways:

[11] A more thorough discussion of this scenario would analyze it in terms of the concept of *meaningful human control*; see, e.g., Filippo Santoni de Sio and Jeroen van den Hoven, "Meaningful Human Control over Autonomous Systems: A Philosophical Account," *Frontiers in Robotics and AI* 5 (Feb. 2018): art. 15.

[12] Cf. Mihailis Diamantis, "The Extended Corporate Mind: When Corporations Use AI to Break the Law" (2019), https://papers.ssrn.com/sol3/papers.cfm?abstract_id=3422429.

1. Obligations, permissions should be explicitly relativized to the subject to which they apply (i.e., by making O and ◊ a relation between propositions and variables that range over human subjects).
2. Obligations and permissions should be capable of explicitly depending on the cognitive states of subjects (and perhaps the AI technology employed by those subjects, if this second approach is being combined with the technologically extended epistemic states solution, proposed earlier).

On this approach, R would not, *per impossibile*, reason about its own obligations and permissions (it has none), but would instead reason about whether its actions are compatible with H's obligations and permissions. This will not only allow R to derive the genuinely ethically best course of action, but it will also facilitate analysis to correctly allocate responsibility.

CONCLUSION

In this chapter, I hope to have shown how a human-centered approach can resolve some problems in AI and robot ethics that arise from the fact that (current and foreseeble) AI systems and robots have cognitive states, and yet have no welfare, and are not responsible. In particular, the approach allows that violence toward robots can be wrong even if robots can't be harmed. Also, the approach encourages us to shift away from designing robots as if they were human ethical deliberators. Rather, the slogan goes:

Don't seek to build ethical robots; seek to build robots ethically.

It was found that the cognitive states of AI systems and robots may have a role to play in the proper ethical analysis of situations involving them, even if it is not by virtue of conferring welfare or responsibilities on those systems or robots. Even if robots lack welfare, their cognitive/informational states might make them sufficiently resemble humans to render them unacceptable targets for violence. Even if robots cannot be responsible, their cognitive/informational states may be relevant when assessing the culpability/mens rea of humans interacting with them.

BIBLIOGRAPHY

Anderson, Michael, and Susan Leigh Anderson. *Machine Ethics*. New York: Cambridge University Press, 2011.

Arkin, Ronald C. *Governing Lethal Behavior in Autonomous Robots*. Boca Raton, FL: Chapman & Hall/CRC Press, 2009.

Bostrom, Nick, and Eliezer Yudkowsky. "The Ethics of Artificial Intelligence." In *The Cambridge Handbook of Artificial Intelligence*, ed. Keith Frankish and William M. Ramsey, 316–34. Cambridge: Cambridge University Press, 2014.

Coeckelbergh, Mark. *Introduction to Philosophy of Technology*. New York: Oxford University Press, 2019.

Lin, Patrick, Keith Abney, and George A. Bekey. *Robot Ethics: The Ethical and Social Implications of Robotics*. Cambridge, MA: MIT Press, 2012.

Müller, Vincent C. "Ethics of Artificial Intelligence and Robotics." In *Stanford Encyclopedia of Philosophy*, ed. Edward N. Zalta. Palo Alto: CSLI, Stanford University, 2020 (forthcoming)

Sparrow, Robert. "Killer Robots." *Journal of Applied Philosophy* 24 (1) (2007): 62–77.

Sparrow, Robert. "The March of the Robot dogs." *Ethics and Information Technology* 4 (4) (2002): 305–318.

Wallach, Wendell, and Colin Allen. *Moral Machines: Teaching Robots Right from Wrong*. Oxford: Oxford University Press, 2010.

Whitby, Blay. *Reflections on Artificial Intelligence: The Legal, Moral and Ethical Dimensions*. Exeter: Intellect Books, 1996.

CHAPTER 25

....

INTEGRATING ETHICAL VALUES AND ECONOMIC VALUE TO STEER PROGRESS IN ARTIFICIAL INTELLIGENCE

....

ANTON KORINEK

INTRODUCTION

....

As we enter the Age of Artificial Intelligence, there is perhaps no single question more important than what direction future progress in AI will take.[1] Artificial intelligence—like the steam engine or electricity before it—is a general-purpose technology that has the potential to significantly alter the way our economy and our society are structured. Progress in artificial intelligence offers abundant opportunities to improve the human condition, but it will also pose significant challenges for our society that are likely to grow in coming decades, as AI systems may replace humans in a growing range of areas.

However, technological progress does not just happen but is driven (at least for now) by human decisions on what, where, and how to innovate. It would be misplaced to succumb to techno-fatalism and view our fate as predetermined by blind technological forces and market forces that are beyond our control. Instead, our future is shaped jointly by the technological innovations that we humans create, by the social and

[1] I am grateful for the many thoughtful comments and insightful discussions with Avital Balwit, John Basl, Karen Delio, Kinda Hachem, Daniel Harper, Paul Humphreys, Eric Leeper, Joseph Stiglitz, and Andy Wicks as well as participants of the "Human and Machine Intelligence Group" at UVA and of the workshop "Toward a Handbook of Ethics of AI" at the University of Toronto. Any remaining errors are my own. Financial support from the Institute for New Economic Thinking (INET) is gratefully acknowledged.

economic institutions that we collectively design, and by the ethical values that guide it all. We as a society have the power to confront the challenges posed by our technological possibilities and, through individual and collective action, actively steer the path of technological progress in AI so as to shape the future that we want to live in. This chapter is an attempt to discuss how to meet these challenges by integrating an assessment of the economic value created by AI with the complementary perspective offered by our ethical values.

The following section starts with a tangible example where simplistic economic and ethical views conflict: the hotly debated question of job losses induced by automation, including AI. Then I will examine the broader question of how market value and ethical values differ, why the values imposed by the market frequently prevail in such conflicts, and how society can take corrective actions. The third section on "Progress in AI and Inequality" discusses the inequality dimension of technological progress and under-lines that pushing technological progress that is blind to its effects on inequality misses an important ethical perspective. The fourth section on "Progress in AI Creating Novel Externalities" analyzes a number of areas in which AI systems that are programmed to maximize economic value violate our ethical values, for example by engaging in bias and discrimination, by hacking and manipulating the human brain, or by curtailing the scope for autonomous human decision-making. In the final section on "The Race toward Superintelligence," I speculate how economic forces driving us toward superin-telligence in coming decades conflict with fundamental ethical values because they may expose humanity to existential risks.

ECONOMICS AND ETHICS: TWO CONFLICTING VALUE SYSTEMS?

Economics and ethics both offer important perspectives on our society, but they do so from two different viewpoints—the central focus of economics is how the price system in our economy values resources; the central focus of ethics is the moral evaluation of actions in our society.

Economic value and ethical values may at times look contradictory but are in fact complementary, as argued forcefully by Amartya Sen.[2] In a market economy, the system of market prices reflects how economic actors—humans in their roles as consumers, producers, workers, employers and so on—value economic resources. Market prices play a central role in guiding economic decisions—including in steering technological progress. Market prices offer some hints on what the individual members of society value. However, they are by no means a full representation of our values, for example, missing out on anything that is not traded in the market, including externalities. Market

---

[2] Amartya Sen, *On Ethics and Economics* (Blackwell Publishing, 1987).

prices thus need to be complemented by ethical values to guide decisions so as to make them desirable for society.

Since the ethical values of different individuals differ, I will not argue from one specific set of ethical values in the following, but I will instead draw only on broadly agreed upon ethical values.

An Introductory Example: Job Losses from Automation and AI

Let me start with a tangible question that the advent of artificial intelligence—like many other forms of automation—raises, and on which economics and ethics are frequently viewed as providing contradictory answers:

Question: Is it right to introduce new technologies that lead to job losses?

In posing a charged question and offering answers from an ethical and economic perspective, I run the risk of offending both ethicists and economists, but I am comforted by the fact that the vast majority of both ethicists and economists that I have met care a lot about the betterment of our society. Integrating the two perspectives offers the greatest chance of moving forward the debate and arriving at acceptable answers, even if my own answers are necessarily tentative and partial.

Arguing from a narrow efficient markets perspective that does not include other dimensions of human well-being, economists may be tempted to immediately respond yes to my question. They may observe that in a competitive market, wages perfectly reflect the social value of labor; if at the given level of wages, a company finds it desirable to innovate so as to save on costly labor, it frees up labor to be employed in other activities that are more useful to society.

Conversely, seeing the misery created by job losses, ethicists may be tempted to immediately respond no to my question. They can see the tangible harm and suffering imposed on workers who are laid off and observe that it is unethical to impose these on workers, whereas they may not immediately appreciate the longer-term effects of economic progress on human well-being.

After further deliberation, economists may appreciate that there are many other considerations that matter aside from the narrow efficient markets perspective argued earlier. Markets are not complete in the real world: workers cannot fully insure against unemployment, and job losses are thus socially more costly than what an efficient markets view suggests. Even more importantly, jobs are social arrangements that not only entail the exchange of labor against wages, but they also provide (or in technical language, are bundled with) other valuable experiences such as social connections, structure, personal meaning, status, and a sense of belonging that all cannot be separately purchased on the market and that the worker loses. As a result, losing a job is among the most traumatic events that people can experience during peacetime. The associated losses go far beyond what is captured by the purely economic loss of income. People who lose their jobs also experience a loss of meaning, become socially more isolated, and frequently become depressed. All this also affects their families and their communities, imposing externalities on them. Moreover, the majority of economists also care about questions of income distribution. Even if markets generate resource allocations that are efficient, the distribution of incomes matters, and market outcomes may generate a more unequal distribution that society perceives as less desirable, as we will discuss further in this chapter. Finally, there is no theoretical reason to believe that the free market will direct innovative efforts to the most socially desirable innovations—the standard welfare theorem in economics are about static resource allocation not innovation.

Similarly, after some deliberation, ethicists may appreciate that markets do provide price signals that reflect the societal value of resources, up to a point. These price signals aggregate the decisions of every single person participating in economic transactions and thus reflect many aspects of the ethical values of society. For example, if a sufficient number of consumers demanded fast food provided by workers who earn a living wage, the market would provide fast food jobs paying a living wage. Ethicists may also appreciate that their insights on the shortcomings and omissions of the market can sometimes best be corrected by imposing the right regulation on the market and letting the market— with proper ethical guidance—do its job. Perhaps most fundamentally, many ethicists will appreciate that the alternatives to economic systems that assign an important role to markets are not very promising.

Taking into account the arguments from both perspectives, economists and ethicists may ultimately agree on a number of points: they may concur that an unfettered market's decisions on what, where, and how to innovate as well as when to make workers redundant are not always in society's best interests. Furthermore, that it is desirable to ensure that workers who lose their jobs are cared for—not only in monetary terms but also in terms of the broader value that society assigns to their losses. And they may also agree that it is nonetheless important to carefully take into account the price signals provided by the market.

Why Economic Value All Too Often Prevails over Ethical Values

If we care about integrating ethical values in economic decisions, it is concerning that economic forces frequently seem to prevail over ethical values in today's world, and it is important to understand why. Without providing an exhaustive list, let me describe several factors that tilt the playing field toward economic value.

First, the conflict between market value and ethical values typically reflects the broader tradeoff between personal benefit versus societal benefits. Humans are pro-social, but only up to a point—our pro-social instincts have evolved mainly to benefit the small tribe of people around us, not humanity at large. For example, people who hesitate to pollute their neighbor's backyard may have fewer hesitations about contributing to global warming that hurts humanity as a whole—they apply lower ethical standards to externalities that affect larger groups and instead listen more to market signals. As a result, the trade-offs between personal and societal benefits that humans have evolved to make instinctively may not be a good guide for ethical decisions that have broader societal repercussions. This is a significant problem in the context of new technologies that affect humanity as a whole.

Second, our systems of market prices and of ethical values differ in very significant conceptual ways: market prices are generally objective, single-dimensional, and unambiguous. They put a well-defined dollar value on anything that is traded in the market. One of the reasons is that markets were created by humans specifically for the purpose of efficiently exchanging resources. Each person's ethical values, by contrast, are subjective, multifaceted and at times implicit, making them more ambiguous and difficult to compare. One of the reasons for this is that the ultimate arbiters of our ethical values are neural networks: our ethical values have been encoded in the deep neural networks that constitute our brains by the processes of nature and nurture, by biological and cultural evolution. It is famously difficult to capture in general rules how complex deep neural networks arrive at decisions, yet in describing our ethical values we need to do precisely that—we need to describe in general rules how our brains decide what is ethical. Combining the ethical values of different individuals to guide decisions for society as a whole adds yet another layer of complexity.

The subjectivity of ethical values leads to different views among different people: a person who does not see any ethical conflicts in a given action is likely to perform it if the market values it, even if others may find it ethically questionable. Cynical economists may say that differences in ethical values create gains from trade based on comparative advantage in immorality. The result may be a race to the bottom in ethical values so that those with the fewest moral restraints in a given area will take up business opportunities that generate value in the market. Moreover, the conflict between market values and ethical values may come not from differences in ethical values but from differences in the valuation of material resources—a starving person may find it acceptable to steal an apple even though well-fed people may consider theft unethical.

The clarity of the market system is then allowed to drive economic decisions toward utmost economic efficiency—but efficiency in a single-dimensional sense that ignores other ethical considerations. Partly due to cognitive biases and partly due to ambiguity aversion, our brains favor single-dimensional clear decision factors over multifaceted and more complex decision factors.

However, the vast majority of ethicists, of economists, and of society at large agree that the market should not necessarily win out when market values and ethical values conflict. Economists frequently use the term *externalities* for discrepancies between social values and market value, and they have a rich and well-developed toolkit for how to deal with externalities. However, these solutions require the political choice of what precise ethical values to employ when such discrepancies arise. In the remaining three sections of this chapter, I analyze three categories of such discrepancies of value, relating to inequality, novel externalities introduced by AI, and market incentives toward the creation of superhuman levels of intelligence.

PROGRESS IN AI AND INEQUALITY

This section focuses on the effects of progress in AI on economic inequality. The lessons of this section apply to any form of automation, but they are particularly relevant in the context of AI.

Technological progress is generally understood as a process that expands how much the economy can produce for a given amount of inputs—it expands our production possibilities. Put this way, progress may sound almost uncontroversial—if we can produce more, technological progress carries the potential to make everybody in society better off from a material perspective.

However, our description of the potential of technological progress contains two important caveats. First, technological progress *could* make everybody better off but is not guaranteed to do so. Secondly, *better off* refers to a strictly material perspective. These two caveats imply that technological progress frequently goes counter to the promise of improving everybody's livelihood.

From the Industrial Revolution to the Future

Looking at the broader context of technological progress since the Industrial Revolution serves as a reminder of how fundamental technological forces and economic forces have been in shaping the fate of mankind over the centuries. Prior to the Industrial Revolution that started in eighteenth-century England, the vast majority of humanity lived at subsistence levels—in other words, most humans barely had enough material resources to survive and regularly went to sleep hungry. Like our fellow animals inhabiting planet Earth, humans were caught in a Malthusian trap: any time there was technological progress, it enabled population growth, and the additional population ate up the additional output produced so that human living standards stubbornly remained at subsistence levels.

Over the centuries since the Industrial Revolution, by contrast, economic growth has outpaced population growth by so much that average material living standards for humans have increased by more than a factor of ten. No wonder that many contemporary economists believed, at least until recently, that it was a fundamental principle of technological progress that everybody benefited, or that "a rising tide lifts all boats."

Focusing on the past four decades, however, the picture has been considerably less rosy: even though overall economic growth continued to pace ahead, the distribution of economic gains was more and more unequal. In the United States, the bottom half of the population, consisting mainly of low-skilled workers, has barely experienced any income gains when adjusted for inflation. Large parts of the population, for example, unskilled white Americans, have even experienced declines in life expectancy because of so-called "deaths of despair" from drug and alcohol abuse and suicides. Over the same period, the real incomes of the top 1 percent have doubled, those of the top 0.1 percent have tripled, and those of the top 0.01 percent have quadrupled.

These income statistics reflect economic forces that determine what our economic system values: the Industrial Revolution revolved around machines that replaced hard physical labor but badly needed human workers to operate them, and over time, these machines greatly increased the productivity and value of human labor. Market forces did their job, and the greater productivity of human labor was soon reflected in higher wages.

More recent waves of automation have almost banished humans from factory floors and from routine information processing tasks. This has made certain categories of human labor, especially unskilled labor, less and less useful to the economy, and the resulting lower demand for labor has translated into lower wages.[3] By contrast, automation has greatly benefited high-skilled workers, who have become more useful to our economic system and have, accordingly, experienced large increases in payoffs. New technologies have allowed high-skilled humans to generate vastly larger amounts of output by being the ones who oversee the more efficient production processes. The incomes of high-skilled workers have thus consistently outpaced those of low-skilled workers, as exemplified by an almost doubling in the college wage premium, that is, in the extra earnings that college graduates make compared to high school–only graduates. In short, value creation and payoffs in our economy have increasingly shifted from low-skilled workers to high-skilled workers and machines, exacerbating inequality.

Technological Progress and Redistribution

An important takeaway is that technological progress frequently generates large redistributions of income across the economy. The main driving force behind this is that any technological change affects the prices of inputs and outputs throughout the production process.[4] The more significant an innovation is for the economy, the larger these redistributions usually are.

On the side of the outputs of the production process, the consumers of products affected by innovation usually benefit from a material perspective since innovations lead to new products, higher quality, or lower consumer prices.

---

[3] Other factors such as trade and changes in changes in public policy also played a significant role in the devaluation of labor.

[4] Anton Korinek and Joseph Stiglitz, "Artificial Intelligence and Its Implications for Income Distribution and Unemployment," in *The Economics of Artificial Intelligence* (NBER and University of Chicago Press, 2019), 349–390.

On the side of factor inputs to production (which include all the different forms of labor and capital that go into the process), things are much more ambiguous: there are no general economic laws as to whether specific factor inputs will benefit or be hurt by progress—it all depends on the specific nature of technological progress. When some of the factors inputs are hurt by an innovation, important ethical questions arise.

Labor is one of the key inputs to the production process. The effects of technological progress on different workers may differ markedly: in our earlier example in which a new technology, say an AI system, leads to job losses, the wages of the affected workers typically fall as a result of the innovation; by contrast, those who have the skills to program and maintain the new system are likely to experience income gains. More broadly, in a market economy, technological change generates not only winners but also regularly leads to significant redistributions.

The economic winners and losers of technological progress, no matter if they are workers or other factor owners, are never asked for their consent—they are "innocent bystanders" of technological progress and thus of the decisions and actions of individual innovators. Economists call it an externality when there are effects of economic actions on innocent bystanders. Since the effects occur via changes in prices and wages, they call them pecuniary externalities. Using this terminology, low-skilled workers have experienced stark negative pecuniary externalities in recent decades.

Redistribution and Utilitarianism

Some economists argue that we shouldn't care about such pecuniary externalities since they constitute "mere" redistributions of income—they do not reduce overall income in the economy and could therefore, at least in principle, be undone by economic policy. Furthermore, they argue that economists can offer guidance on how to allocate resources efficiently, but societal responses to the redistributions generated by technological progress are outside of their subject area and are for the political process to decide. However, this perspective rightly opens economists to the accusation of being biased. Except in two very specific and narrow cases, the question of how to efficiently allocate resources in the economy *cannot* be separated from redistributive questions.

The first case is if economic policy compensates the losers of progress by undoing any redistributions without introducing new distortions into the economy—economists call this idealized form of redistribution a lump-sum transfer. However, this does not reflect the way that the economy works in practice—redistribution generally does create distortions of its own, as economists are quick to point out. Whenever we impose taxes on an economic resource or activity so as to raise funds for redistribution, we lower incentives to employ the resource or to engage in the activity, and we create incentives to circumvent the taxes. Furthermore, we also frequently distort the behavior of the potential recipients of such payments. Therefore the first case does not apply in practice.

The second case is if we only care about the overall level of income generated not the distribution of income. In line with the tradition within economics, let me call this ethical benchmark strict utilitarianism (although this does not do full justice to most varieties of utilitarianism discussed in ethics, for example what Bentham described as "the greatest amount of good for the greatest number"—economists' version of strict utilitarianism adds up the resources consumed by different individuals linearly and would find an innovation desirable even if it imposes income losses on all but one person in society so long as it increases the income of that remaining person by an amount slightly greater than the sum of the individual losses). Most people view this type of value system as at least borderline unethical—outside of economics, strict utilitarianism is a fringe perspective.

If economists strive to inform the choices facing society, then it is their job to employ society's values, not to impose their own. It is at best biased, and at worst manipulative, to evaluate social choices by imposing a value system such as strict utilitarianism that society does not share. Once we leave aside the two—unrealistic—special cases that we just spelled out, it is indispensable to consider the distributional impact of technological innovations when considering their social desirability.

Inequality and Steering Progress in AI

Our society faces the choice of whether to let the free market or other decentralized forces determine which innovations take place, without regard for the common good, or whether we in fact want to steer the course of technological progress in a direction that takes into account inequality. We may well want to pass on innovations that increase output if a side effect is that a large number of people are actually worse off and if there is no realistic scope for compensating them. Conversely, society may want to actively work on innovations that do not strictly pass the market test but that offer large benefits to a large number of people.

Steering the course of progress could be done in a variety of ways:

Firstly, it is crucial to make ethically conscious entrepreneurs and researchers aware of the redistributive consequences of their work. This by itself could make a significant difference. Many entrepreneurs in the technology sector are quite public-spirited, exemplified by Google's former motto "don't be evil." However, in determining what is good or evil for society, what matters are not only the direct effects of new AI systems. It is crucial to also take into account the redistributive implications of new AI systems, and especially the implications for labor markets. As AI is affecting more and more sectors of the economy, entrepreneurs and researchers in the field of AI must be aware that their actions will increasingly shape the fate of workers and the overall income distribution across the economy. To provide a tangible example for how they could make a difference, I am currently participating in a research project to develop intelligent assistants (IAs) that aid unskilled human workers and enable them to do higher value tasks so as to enhance the market value of their labor. If creative entrepreneurs put their minds to it, I am sure that there are numerous examples of innovations that would both create jobs for unskilled workers and be economically profitable.

Secondly, governments have traditionally played an important role in shaping technological progress and could focus their efforts on promoting technologies that maintain or increase labor demand. A prime area for this is government-sponsored research, which could be guided more intentionally toward technologies that enhance the economic prospects of workers rather than replacing them. Furthermore, governments are large employers, both directly and indirectly via government procurement. By steering both their own automation decisions and those of their suppliers, they can have large effects on labor markets.

Thirdly, our society could steer progress in the private sector via taxes or subsidies that depend on whether an innovation replaces workers or enhances the role of workers. This would provide explicit incentives to innovators that reflect the likely labor market impact of an innovation. A complementary approach is to directly target the market price of human labor. At present, our tax system inflates the cost of labor because labor is the most highly taxed factor in the economy, providing extra incentives to develop technologies that save on labor. As we enter the Age of AI, our society would be better served by shifting the burden of taxation to other factors in the economy and provide subsidies to labor (for example by expanding programs such as the earned income tax credit). This would disincentivize investments into automating labor and steer progress in other directions.

Progress in AI Creating Novel Externalities

The rise of artificial intelligence opens up new areas for conflict between market value and ethical values and introduces new externalities, as explored in depth throughout the chapters of this *Handbook*. A common theme in many of the resulting ethical dilemmas is that the technological innovations involved look like they create value in terms of economic profits, but they actually drain our broader societal values and do damage from an ethical perspective. In the following, I will discuss a few specific examples and explore how they can be addressed by integrating economic and ethical perspectives.

AI Discrimination, Biases, and Fairness

Since AI algorithms make a growing number of decisions about our lives, one particularly concerning problem is that AI may perpetuate biases or introduce new biases into how different people are treated. Consider, for example, an AI system that screens candidates for jobs, school admissions, or loans.

From a narrow economic perspective, the goal of an AI system that performs such screening is to identify the highest value candidates for businesses, schools, or lenders. Taking a typical data set to train the AI system, certain individual characteristics are correlated with higher value whereas others are correlated with lower value. An AI system identifies these correlations in far more intricate ways than the human brain and may be able to make more efficient screening decisions. Greater screening efficiency would translate into greater economic value. However, one of the ethical values of our society is that it is undesirable to discriminate against individuals based on personal characteristics that are outside of their control, in particular characteristics such as race, gender, or age.

Nonetheless, there are two scenarios in which AI systems may engage in precisely such discrimination. The first scenario is that the algorithm or the training data themselves are biased in the sense that they do not accurately reflect the correlations present in reality. This may be the case either because they are based on past biased human decisions or because they are based on unrepresentative samples that simply do not contain enough information about certain groups, and thus the algorithm generates less efficient decisions for underrepresented groups, which result in fewer positive screening decisions. In this first scenario, the bias is undesirable from both economic and ethical perspectives so the desirable path forward is clear.

The second scenario is more troubling: even if the training data is fully representative and unbiased, many of us view it as unfair to base decisions on correlations with certain protected personal characteristics. Say, for example, that members of an ethnic group have historically defaulted on loans at higher rates; most of us would view it as morally wrong to charge members of that group a higher interest rate just because of their ethnicity. Even if AI systems are not explicitly fed data on protected individual characteristics such as ethnicity, they can still infer such characteristics from other data with a growing degree of accuracy and employ them in making decisions that look unbiased in the statistical sense and highly efficient from an economic perspective.

In the past, human decision makers that acted upon moral values of nondiscrimination would attempt to evaluate candidates for jobs, school admissions, or loans impartially—by intentionally disregarding data that they knew are highly correlated with protected attributes, for example, what they infer from looks, names, addresses, and so on. If we replace the human decision maker by an AI system that is focused solely on efficiency, then the AI system extracts greater economic value by disregarding these considerations.

AI systems can be programmed to sacrifice some of their efficiency and explicitly follow principles of nondiscrimination in this second scenario. However, in doing so they put a numerical value on nondiscrimination practices and, whether explicitly or implicitly, highlight the economic cost of the broader ethical value of nondiscrimination. For reasons discussed earlier, seeing the dollar value of discrimination may tempt decision makers to put greater weight on the clearly measurable economic dimension of a business decision compared to the ethical dimensions.

Hacking the Human Brain

Another sinister example of hollowing out the human experience to earn extra profits is when AI systems are employed to hack the human brain. In computer science, hacking refers to situations when somebody intrudes into a system to either steal information or manipulate the behavior of the system. By AI algorithms hacking the human brain I refer to situations when algorithms tap into some of our simple human drives in order to manipulate us into behaviors that ultimately do not deliver the fulfillment that our drives were meant to deliver. The human brain constantly makes trade-offs between conflicting objectives, for example, between primal instincts and rational thoughts. AI systems understand better and better how to tip the balance between the two, exploit our instincts, influence our thoughts, and manipulate us into whatever best achieves their objectives.

For example, AI-based advertising systems manipulate us far more efficiently and in a much more personal way than traditional advertising to buy goods or services. Targeted links to sensational news stories tempt us to click and keep reading, but ultimately offer little informational value. Autoplay functions start the next video without asking after a user watches one video, keeping us watching much longer than we intended. Social networks promise to connect us in more efficient ways and automate many of our social interactions, keeping users engaged with constant friend updates. However, ultimately they do no generate the face-to-face human connection that is necessary to provide us with true fulfillment. The outcome in all these cases is similar to a mild form of drug addiction in that our simple drives are exploited to the detriment of our long-term goals. Conversely, AI systems can also hack our brain with the opposite objective in mind—to assist us in the pursuit of our long-term goals by regularly providing beneficial nudges, as, for example, fitness apps or dieting apps do, and to ultimately make us better off.

Curtailing Human Autonomy

The increasing use of AI to automate human decisions also runs the risk of reducing the human experience by curtailing our human autonomy. Many people assign significant value to human autonomy, that is, to the ability to make independent decisions. For example, many car owners report that they value the ability to decide on how to drive, even if an autonomous vehicle could drive better along all objective dimensions. As AI systems in a given area get better and better, it becomes ever more tempting to impose the superior decisions of AI systems on human users, but doing so incurs the cost of reducing our autonomy.

Most humans will experience further limits to their autonomy as a result of increasing economic inequality. In the third section on "Progress in AI and Inequality," we discussed that AI systems that displace workers will increase income inequality. Over time, inequality in income will also worsen inequality in wealth and in the ownership of economic resources. Since ownership confers control, AI systems that earn an increasing fraction of the output of our economy will strip away control over resources from the workers who experience income losses and conversely, confer increasing levels of control over resources to their owners.

These are just a few examples in which novel technological innovations may generate economic value but diminish and hollow out other dimensions of our rich multifaceted human experience. There are also many areas in which progress in AI creates economic disruptions that magnify the economy's existing tendencies toward inefficiency, as discussed, for example, in our introductory example on job losses or when technological disruptions lead to aggregate demand failure and recessions.

Externalities and Steering Progress in AI

Whenever market-provided price signals differ from broader ethical values, it is desirable to integrate the two to steer technological progress. The two critical steps required are to identify and understand the discrepancies in value (externalities) and to act upon that understanding.

The ideal course of action would be to anticipate potential ethical problems that are generated by new AI technologies and steer away from them. Some have suggested that innovators be required to conduct technological impact assessments before making significant investments in new technologies, modeled on environmental impact assessments, which attempt to evaluate the likely impact of innovations on society.[5] In practice, awareness of ethical problems frequently only arises after an innovation is introduced, and all stakeholders in society need to collaborate to identify novel ethical problems, including governments, nonprofits, universities, civil society, and above all, of course, the entrepreneurs or corporations who introduce the innovations in question. Once there is sufficient societal awareness, ethically minded entrepreneurs may even leverage potential positive externalities of progress, as in our example of fitness and dieting apps.

However, given the tendency of the market to sponsor a race to the bottom when it comes to monetizing ethical transgressions, it may also be necessary to pass regulation to compel innovators to take into account their adverse effects on society.

THE RACE TOWARD SUPERINTELLIGENCE

Progress in artificial intelligence is continuing unabatedly, driven by both human curiosity and market forces. Many of our brightest minds are working hard on improving the hardware and software required for AI, driving exponential growth in computing power and continued advances in our ability to understand and write the software

---

[5] José García and Madeline Janis, "How to Keep the Robots from Taking Jobs," *Politico* (May 1, 2019).

behind AI. Market incentives are doing their part by generously rewarding the growing capabilities of existing AI systems and by pouring hundreds of billions of dollars into the development of new ones. In doing so, they have elevated the status of AI experts from geeks to rock stars.

The continuing exponential progress raises the question whether AI will, at some point, surpass human intelligence. Present-day AI systems exhibit *narrow* artificial intelligence—they have great (and frequently superhuman) capabilities in narrowly defined domains such as playing chess or Go, targeting ads, or reading X-rays. By contrast, humans possess general intelligence—the ability to act intelligently across a wide number of domains and integrate them all. This capacity enables humans to employ the powers of AI in the service of our goals. However, with each passing year, the capabilities of narrow AI systems are growing broader, and the advantage of narrow AI over humans in their specific domain is expanding. Unless progress in AI comes to a sudden standstill, it seems to be largely a question of time when machines will reach human levels—and ultimately superhuman levels—of general intelligence. Although this may sound like science fiction, Bostrom reports that several AI researchers predict that artificial general intelligence will be achieved as early as next decade, and a majority of AI researchers expect artificial general intelligence by the second half of the twenty-first century.[6] Given the vast potential implications for mankind, it seems prudent to seriously think about the ramifications for our society now.

What will artificial general intelligence and superintelligence imply for humanity? Our intelligence has been the defining characteristic that set humanity apart from other species of animals and that has allowed us to rule over planet Earth, including over all the less intelligent co-inhabitants of our planet. Will super-intelligent AI treat humanity the way that humans have treated other animals, domesticating and exploiting us when useful and terminating us when a nuisance? What other roles will there be left for humans? Or could we perhaps instill our goals and ethical values into super-intelligent machines so that they help us improve human well-being in ways that are presently unthinkable for modest human minds? These questions have been much discussed by philosophers of AI such as Bostrom.

In the remainder, I will focus on two areas in which discrepancies between economic value and ethical values play a significant role. I will attempt to shed light on these areas by integrating the perspectives from ethics and economics.

Superintelligence, Inequality, and the Economic Viability of Humans

One of the central dilemmas created by ever-more intelligent AI is that the agents that are morally relevant may become increasingly economically irrelevant, whereas the agents that are economically relevant may not be morally relevant.

---

[6] Nick Bostrom, *Superintelligence: Paths, Dangers, Strategies* (Oxford University Press, 2014).

From an economic perspective, superintelligence might be the most productive and most profitable human invention ever. The market would greatly value the vast potential returns that human-level artificial intelligence or superintelligence could generate.

Human labor, by contrast, is likely to become economically redundant soon after the advent of superintelligence, since super-intelligent machines would use their superior problem-solving capacity to figure out how to perform economically relevant tasks ever more efficiently. Once they can perform all formerly human tasks more cheaply than what it costs to keep humans alive (i.e., at a cost below human subsistence wages), there is no more economic justification to employ human labor, and humans would become technologically obsolete.[7] Human labor would be a redundant factor of production and a dominated technology—just as we no longer use oxen to plough fields because the cost of maintaining the oxen is not worth the economic value that they produce, it would no longer be economically worth it to pay humans what they need to survive. This would condemn the vast majority of humanity to technological unemployment.

If our decisions were solely guided by economic value, then it would be logical to phase out humanity once humans become economically redundant. The arc of our material progress would then come full circle: before the Industrial Revolution, humanity started out in a Malthusian world in which our population numbers were held back by lack of material resources and starvation; after the advent of superintelligence, human labor would become redundant, and the fate of all but the wealthiest would end up being driven by Malthusian forces yet again, ultimately leading to starvation and declines in the human population. Malthus's disciple Charles Darwin would call the result of this competition over scarce resources between humans and machines survival of the fittest.

In economic terms, an AI system that reduces human wages below subsistence levels would impose a particularly strong version of the pecuniary externalities that we discussed in the third section on "Progress in AI and Inequality." However, given that the magnitude of these externalities would put the survival of most humans at risk, what is at stake is not merely human inequality but survival.

Conversely, if it is ethically desirable to keep humanity alive, we will need to find mechanisms to share enough of the income generated by the economy with those economically redundant humans who have no other source of income. The distribution of the material gains from superintelligence will thus be a key ethical question for our society.

Superintelligence, Externalities, and Existential Risk

Although superintelligence carries enormous promise to improve the condition of mankind, it also poses unfathomable risks, which are not correctly reflected in the economic incentives of its potential creators. Intelligence is commonly defined as the ability

[7] Anton Korinek, "The Rise of Artificially Intelligent Agents," Working Paper (University of Virginia, 2019).

to accomplish complex goals.[8] A superintelligence is then almost by definition more effective at accomplishing its goals than humans. If its goals conflict with human goals, it is most likely that super-intelligent AI will win over humans.

Given the likely complexity of super-intelligent AI systems, conflicts with human goals may in fact arise quite easily—especially as unintended consequences. To make the existential risks inherent in super-intelligent AI tangible, Bostrom offers a thought experiment of a system that is programmed to pursue a single narrow (and rather trivial) objective: to produce as many paperclips as possible.[9] He argues that such a system may well decide to kill off humanity in pursuit of its programmed objective, for example, to use the iron in our bodies for paperclips, or to preempt the threat of being turned off, which would prevent it from maximizing its objective. Given that the system has not been programmed to pursue broader goals such as human well-being, it would simply not care about the demise of humanity. AI safety researchers have articulated dozens of additional scenarios in which super-intelligent AI may endanger humanity.

The incentives of AI researchers and of society as a whole are badly misaligned when it comes to weighing the potential benefits of super-intelligent AI against its existential risks. A researcher who has a tangible shot at creating and being in charge of the most powerful AI system ever built would have a huge potential upside in terms of scientific fame, power, and material rewards. She may also be somewhat overconfident in her abilities to control such a system. But humanity as a whole would pay the price if things go wrong, as in Bostrom's example of existential risk. Given the asymmetry of who obtains most of the benefits and who bears most of the costs, the researcher may well be tempted to proceed and impose a small risk of existential catastrophe on humanity. And the sum total of risk exposure for humanity keeps rising if hundreds of research teams work on advancing AI and each impose a small existential risk. Individual incentives, therefore, do not properly reflect the benefits and costs of such existential risks.

Superintelligence and Steering Progress in AI

Steering technological progress toward superintelligence will be the ultimate challenge for human society. However, although the stakes are vastly higher, the challenges will be similar to the ones that we are currently facing with narrow AI—to ensure that AI systems carry out our economic interests while their behavior is guided by our ethical values.

Given the existential risks and the potential for economic irrelevance facing humanity, we should not view progress toward super-intelligent AI systems as primarily an economic project or primarily a research project—the ethical challenges and the stakes for humanity are too high to be determined by the commercial interests of any corporation

[8] Max Tegmark, *Life 3.0: Being Human in the Age of Artificial Intelligence* (Knopf, 2017).
[9] Bostrom, *Superintelligence*.

or by the research interests of any research team. Instead, we need a large and concerted public effort to integrate the perspectives of all stakeholders of society to ensure that we develop AI in a direction that is both economically beneficial and ethically desirable.

BIBLIOGRAPHY

Acemoglu, Daron and Pascual Restrepo. "The Wrong Kind of AI? Artificial Intelligence and the Future of Labor Demand." NBER Working Paper w25682, 2019.

Autor, David. "Why Are There Still So Many Jobs? The History and Future of Workplace Automation." *Journal of Economic Perspectives* 29 no. 3 (Summer 2015): 3–30.

Bostrom, Nick. *Superintelligence: Paths, Dangers, Strategies*. Oxford University Press, 2014.

Brynjolfsson, Erik and Andrew McAfee. *The Second Machine Age: Work, Progress, and Prosperity in a Time of Brilliant Technologies*. W. W. Norton, 2015.

Korinek, Anton. "The Rise of Artificially Intelligent Agents." Working Paper, University of Virginia, 2019.

Korinek, Anton and Joseph Stiglitz. "Artificial Intelligence and Its Implications for Income Distribution and Unemployment." In *The Economics of Artificial Intelligence*, ed. Agrawal et al., 349–390. NBER and University of Chicago Press, 2019.

Naidu, Suresh, Dani Rodrik, and Gabriel Zucman. *Economics for Inclusive Prosperity: An Introduction*. Economists for Inclusive Prosperity, 2019. http://www.econfip.org.

Sen, Amartya. *On Ethics and Economics*. Blackwell Publishing, 1987.

Tegmark, Max. *Life 3.0: Being Human in the Age of Artificial Intelligence*. Knopf, 2017.

CHAPTER 26

··

FAIRNESS CRITERIA THROUGH THE LENS OF DIRECTED ACYCLIC GRAPHS

A Statistical Modeling Perspective

··

BENJAMIN R. BAER,[*] DANIEL E. GILBERT,[*]
AND MARTIN T. WELLS[†]

INTRODUCTION

··

THE emergence of artificial intelligence's algorithmic tools represents one of the most important social and technological developments of the last several decades. Machine learning–based scoring systems now determine creditworthiness of consumers and insurance prices[1] and social media metrics,[2] algorithmic hiring platforms target job advertisements and screen resumes to calculate who should and should not be seen by human resource managers,[3] and predictive analytics are deployed as sentencing tools in

[*] Equal contribution

[†] Wells' research was partially supported by NIH U19 AI111143, NSF DMS-1611893, and Cornell's Institute for the Social Sciences project on Algorithms, Big Data, and Inequality.

[1] Yu Robinson and H. Yu, "Knowing the Score: New Data, Underwriting and Marketing in the Consumer Credit Marketplace," *A Guide for Financial Inclusion Stakeholders* (2014): 1–34.

[2] Brooke Duffy, "The Romance of Work: Gender and Aspirational Labour in the Digital Culture Industries," *International Journal of Cultural Studies* 19(4) (2016): 441–457.

[3] Ifeoma Ajunwa et al., "Hiring by Algorithm: Predicting and Preventing Disparate Impact," *SSRN Electronic Journal* (2016); Jack Gillum and Ariana Tobin, "Facebook Won't Let Employers, Landlords or Lenders Discriminate in Ads Anymore," *ProPublica* (May 19, 2019).

the criminal justice system.[4] Big data's algorithmic tools have come to play a decisive role in many aspects of our lives. However, there is concern that these algorithmic tools may lack fairness and exacerbate existing social inequalities.[5,6,7,8]

One might imagine that because algorithms are inherently procedural, ensuring fairness should be a simple matter of not explicitly using race or gender as features.[9] This notion of fairness has been called *Fairness Through Unawareness*, and it is easy to see why it is insufficient. First of all, other features will generally *redundantly encode* sensitive variables.[10] We could trivially skirt around Fairness Through Unawareness by including variables which are close proxies for gender or race like hair length or name, but even less suspicious and eminently predictive features such as zip code, language usage, or GPA will allow an algorithm to partially infer an individual's sensitive characteristics and make generalizations on those bases. Furthermore, including information about an individual's sensitive characteristics can actually serve to make a predictive algorithm *more* fair, especially when there are interaction effects between sensitive characteristics and other features. The area of algorithmic fairness constitutes an attempt to move beyond Fairness Through Unawareness and develop a link between the mathematical properties of algorithms and our philosophical and intuitive notions of fairness. Unfortunately, there is little consensus on the philosophical bedrock upon which algorithmic fairness should rest.[11,12]

Much of the literature on fairness in algorithms has been influenced by a controversy surrounding the Northpointe COMPAS algorithm, an algorithm for predicting criminal recidivism. Angwin et al. analyzed the output of the algorithm and determined that its predictions were unfair due to the fact that the rate of false positives and false negatives differed significantly between racial groups.[13] In response, Northpointe published a rejoinder arguing the criteria used by Angwin et al. to assess fairness were nonstandard,

[4] Virginia Eubanks, *Automating Inequality: How High-tech Tools Profile, Police, and Punish the Poor* (St. Martin's Press, 2018).

[5] Solon Barocas and Andrew D. Selbst, "Big Data's Disparate Impact," *California Law Review* 104 (2016): 671.

[6] Malte Ziewitz, "Governing Algorithms: Myth, Mess, and Methods," *Science, Technology & Human Values* 41(1) (2016): 3–16.

[7] Cathy O'Neil, *Weapons of Math Destruction: How Big Data Increases Inequality and Threatens Democracy* (Broadway Books, 2017).

[8] Kristian Lum, "Limitations of Mitigating Judicial Bias with Machine Learning," *Nature Human Behaviour* (June 26, 2017).

[9] Nina Grgic-Hlaca et al., "The Case for Process Fairness in Learning: Feature Selection for Fair Decision Making," in *NIPS Symposium on Machine Learning and the Law* 1(2) (2016).

[10] Barocas and Selbst, "Big Data's Disparate Impact."

[11] Reuben Binns, "Fairness in Machine Learning: Lessons from Political Philosophy," in *Proceedings of Machine Learning Research*, vol. 81 (2017).

[12] Alexandra Chouldechova and Aaron Roth, "The Frontiers of Fairness in Machine Learning," 2018, *arXiv:1810.08810*.

[13] Julia Angwin et al., "Machine Bias: There's Software Used across the Country to Predict Future Criminals. And It's Biased against Blacks," *ProPublica* 23 (May 23, 2016).

and a proper analysis reveals that the predictions made by the COMPAS algorithm are in fact calibrated by race.[14]

Beyond merely inspiring interest in the study of algorithmic fairness, this controversy may have influenced the early direction of the field. One significant branch of the field is concerned with the development, study, comparison, and implementation of simple fairness criteria, much like the balanced-odds criterion implicit in Angwin et al. (2016) or the calibration criterion used in Flores, Bechtel, and Lowenkamp (2016). These fairness criteria have largely been tailored to the classification setting.

Furthermore, Angwin et al. had access to limited information in assessing the COMPAS algorithm; these authors were able to acquire the COMPAS scores for 11,575 pretrial defendants, along with information about their criminal histories, race, and whether that defendant in fact went on to reoffend.[15] However, these authors did not have access to the precise features used by the COMPAS algorithm nor the specifications of the COMPAS algorithm itself. Therefore, the authors assessed the fairness of the COMPAS algorithm by examining its false positive and false negative rates across races, which can be calculated using only the COMPAS predictions, the races of the defendants, and whether they reoffended.

Other commonly considered fairness-apt data sets have a similar form; we often desire to assess whether a predictive algorithm is fair using only information about the predictions, the observed outcomes, and the race or gender of the subjects. Perhaps for this reason, much of the early work on algorithmic fairness has centered around so-called *oblivious* fairness criteria, which assess algorithms only on the basis of their outputs compared to the ground truth. The three central oblivious criteria are most often called *Demographic Parity*, *Equalized Odds*, and *Calibration by Group*, although it is common to encounter these and related concepts under a host of names.

Two prominent strains of criticism have emerged which cast doubt on the utility of simple one-size-fits-all metrics for the fairness of algorithms. The first criticism concerns obliviousness; even alongside the introduction of Equalized Odds, Hardt, Price, Srebro et al. note that intuitively fair and intuitively unfair algorithmic procedures can appear identical if we only compare the algorithm's output to the observed outcome.[16] Indeed, many of our intuitive notions of fairness have to do with the nature of the information used to make a prediction, rather than the outcome.

A second strain of criticism concerns incompatibility between the three oblivious fairness criteria, and thus their lack of universality. Most notably, Chouldechova (2017)[17]

[14] Anthony W. Flores, Kristin Bechtel, and Christopher T. Lowenkamp, "False Positives, False Negatives, and False Analyses: A Rejoinder to 'Machine Bias: There's Software Used across the Country to Predict Future Criminals. And It's Biased against Blacks,'" *Federal Probation* 80(2) (2016): 38–46.

[15] Jeff Larson et al., "How We Analyzed the COMPAS Recidivism Algorithm," *ProPublica* 9 (May 23, 2016).

[16] Moritz Hardt, Eric Price, and Nati Srebro et al., "Equality of Opportunity in Supervised Learning," in *Advances in Neural Information Processing Systems* (2016): 3315–3323.

[17] Alexandra Chouldechova, "Fair Prediction with Disparate Impact: A Study of Bias in Recidivism Prediction Instruments," *Big Data* 5(2) (2017): 153–163.

and Kleinberg, Mullainathan, and Raghavan (2017)[18] proved that Calibration and Equalized Odds could not simultaneously be achieved; this recast the disagreement between ProPublica and Northpointe as a philosophical rather than statistical debate.

Various review papers have been written which tie together the outpouring of early ideas in fairness in algorithms. In this chapter, we do not intend to exhaustively catalog the world of fairness criteria: instead we will focus on a small number of basic criteria which have received significant attention, similar to Yeom and Tschantz (2018).[19] For a comprehensive map of fairness measures and their relationships to one another, see Mitchell, Potash, and Barocas (2018).[20] Corbett-Davies and Goel (2018) elucidate the incompatibility of Calibration and Equalized Odds using visualizations of outcome distributions.[21] These authors argue that the problem of *infra-marginality* suggests that Equalized Odds is a poor criterion for fairness.

We agree with the poorness of Equalized Odds. We are concerned that work which generalizes and operationalizes Equalized Odds may further obscure the criterion's underlying flaws. The purpose of this chapter is to provide an alternate source of intuition about fairness criteria using probabilistic directed acyclic graphical models, or Bayesian networks. Graphical models have been used to motivate and expose fairness criteria in other works, especially those which work with explicitly causal criteria for fairness. We believe that graphical models provide an invaluable source of intuition even in noncausal scenarios, and themselves reveal the weakness of Equalized Odds.

Using Bayesian networks, we can view fairness criteria in a way which is easily generalized beyond classification settings. Considering generalizations as defined in Barocas, Hardt, and Narayanan (2018) of Demographic Parity, Equalized Odds, and Calibration helps to expose certain fundamental aspects of these criteria which the classification setting obscures.

In the next section, "Graphical Models," we provide a brief overview of probabilistic directed graphical models and the associated causal theory. In the subsequent section, "Three Criteria for Fairness," we define the three oblivious fairness criteria and their generalizations. In the section "Fairness Criteria in Two Scenarios," we discuss two graphical scenarios and the implications of various fairness criteria therein. In the section "Understanding Fairness," we review the incompatibility between Equalized Odds and Calibration and give a graphical view of the problem with Equalized Odds. This motivates a modified class of criteria, which we call Separation by Signal. In the final section, "Causal Considerations," we discuss the relationship between causality and fairness.

[18] Jon Kleinberg, Sendhil Mullainathan, and Manish Raghavan, "Inherent Trade-offs in the Fair Determination of Risk Scores," in *The 8th Innovations in Theoretical Computer Science Conference* (2017).
[19] Samuel Yeom and Michael Carl Tschantz, "Discriminative but Not Discriminatory: A Comparison of Fairness Definitions under Different Worldviews," 2018, *arXiv:1808.08619*.
[20] Shira Mitchell, Eric Potash, and Solon Barocas, "Prediction-Based Decisions and Fairness: A Catalogue of Choices, Assumptions, and Definitions," 2018, *arXiv:1811.07867*.
[21] Sam Corbett-Davies and Sharad Goel, "The Measure and Mismeasure of Fairness: A Critical Review of Fair Machine Learning," 2018, *arXiv:1808.00023*.

GRAPHICAL MODELS

A directed acyclic graph (DAG) $\mathcal{G}$ is a pair $\{V, E\}$ where $V = \{V_1, \ldots, V_n\}$ is a set of nodes and E is a set of directed edges, each pointing from one node to another. The *acyclic* property of DAGs requires that the edges in E never form a *directed path* leading from one node back to itself. Let the *parents* of V_i, $\text{Pa}(V_i)$, refer to the set of nodes which share an edge with V_i such that the edge is pointing to V_i.

Probabilistic Directed Acyclic Graphical Models

A probabilistic directed acyclic graphical (PDAG) model, sometimes known as a Bayesian Network, is a pair $\{\mathcal{G}, \mathcal{P}\}$ where $\mathcal{G}$ is a DAG and $\mathcal{P}$ is a probability distribution over the nodes of $\mathcal{G}$.[22,23] Each node $V_1, \ldots, V_n$ in $\mathcal{G}$ represents a random variable, and these random variables are jointly governed by the probability distribution $\mathcal{P}$. In this chapter, we will consider only PDAG models which satisfy the Markov Condition. A PDAG model $\{\mathcal{G}, \mathcal{P}\}$ satisfies the *Markov Condition* only if the probability distribution $\mathcal{P}$ can be factored into the conditional distributions of each node given its parents. That is,

$$P(V_1, \ldots, V_n) = \prod_{i=1}^{n} P(V_i \mid \text{Pa}(V_i)). \tag{1}$$

Node V_1 is considered an *ancestor* of node V_2 if there is a directed path leading from V_1 to V_2. In that case, node V_2 is a *descendent* of V_1. A node is a *root* if it has no ancestors and a *leaf* if it has no descendents. The random variables associated with root nodes we call *exogenous* because their distribution does not depend on any of the other modeled variables.

In discussing PDAG models, three common relationships between nodes are of particular interest. Nodes V_1 and V_3 are *confounded* by node V_2 if V_2 is an ancestor of both V_3 and V_1. In this case, we say there is a *backdoor path* between V_1 and V_3. If V_1 is an ancestor of V_2 and V_2 is an ancestor of V_3, then V_2 is a *mediator* of the relationship between V_1 and V_3. Finally, if V_1 and V_2 are both ancestors of V_3, then V_3 is said to be a *collider* for V_1 and V_2. See Figure 26.1 for a depiction of these relationships.

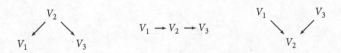

FIGURE 26.1. In the leftmost graph, V_2 is a confounder, in the center graph, V_2 is a mediator, and in the rightmost graph, V_2 is a collider.

[22] Judea Pearl, *Causality* (Cambridge University Press, 2009b).
[23] Peter Spirtes et al., *Causation, Prediction, and Search* (MIT Press, 2000).

We can determine certain marginal and conditional independence relationships between the random variables $V_1, \ldots, V_n$ using the structure of the DAG. The nodes V_i and V_j are *d-separated* if the structure of the DAG implies that V_i and V_j are (marginally) independent, that is, $V_i \perp\!\!\!\perp V_j$. A set S of nodes *d-separates* V_i and V_j if the structure of the DAG implies that V_i and V_j are independent given the variables in S, that is, $V_i \perp\!\!\!\perp V_j | S$. Specifically, under the Markov Condition, the nodes V_i and V_j are d-separated given S if S blocks all paths between V_i and V_j. A connected sequence of edges between two nodes is considered a *path* regardless of the edges' orientations. A path is blocked by S if either:

- it contains a mediator or confounder V_k where $V_k \in S$.
- it contains a collider V_k where $V_k \notin S$ and $V_l \notin S$ for any descendant V_l of V_k.

Thus, conditioning on colliders (or their descendants) actually *unblocks* paths and can induce dependency between marginally independent variables. See Figure 26.3. for examples. Note that while d-separation implies conditional independence, *d-connection* or lack of d-separation does not necessarily imply conditional dependence. Therefore, it is sometimes useful to make the assumption that a PDAG model is *faithful*, which means that every conditional d-connection relationship in the graph implies conditional dependence between those variables.

Unfaithfulness can occur because whenever there exist multiple paths leading from V_i to V_j, since the dependencies along those paths can cancel each other out. For example, consider a PDAG model associated with the DAG in Figure 26.2.

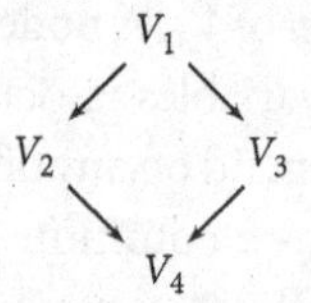

$$V_1$$
$$V_2 \quad\quad V_3$$
$$V_4$$

FIGURE 26.2. Because there are multiple paths from V_1 to V_4, this PDAG model may be unfaithful if the effect of V_1 on V_4 along one path perfectly counteracts the effect along the other path.

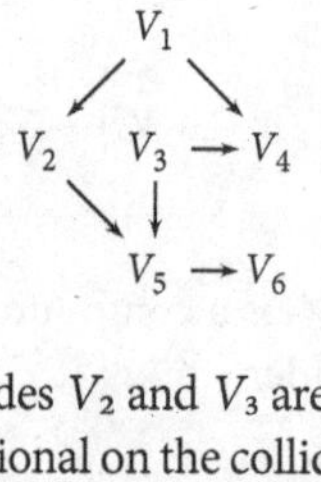

FIGURE 26.3. In this PDAG model, nodes V_2 and V_3 are d-separated a priori, that is, conditional on the empty set $S = \varnothing$. However, conditional on the collider $S = \{V_5\}$, V_2 and V_3 are d-connected. V_2 and V_4 are d-separated given any of the following sets: $\{V_1\}, \{V_1, V_5, V_3\}$ or $\{V_1, V_6, V_3\}$.

Let $V_2 = 3V_1 + \epsilon_2$, $V_2 = 2V_3 = V_1 + \epsilon_3$, and $V_4 = -2V_2 + 3V_3 + \epsilon_4$. Then $V_4 = 3\epsilon_3 - 2\epsilon_2 + \epsilon_4$, thus V_4 is independent of V_1, despite the fact that V_1 and V_2 are unconditionally d-connected. Thus this PDAG model is unfaithful. Note, however, it is unusual for path effects to precisely cancel each other except when variables are carefully constructed to do so.

Causality

Strictly speaking, the directed edges in PDAG models need not have any causal interpretation, as long as they are consistent with the conditional dependencies in $\mathcal{P}$. However, DAGs are not fully determined by their associated probability distributions: a given probability distribution is usually consistent with multiple DAGs with differently oriented edges. Thus it is natural to use a PDAG model to convey causal meaning, so that an edge pointing from V_i to V_j then means that V_i has a causal effect on V_j. When PDAG models are used in the context of causal inference, they are often called *Structural Causal Models* and the associated DAG may be called a *Causal Graph*.

Pearl's theory of causality addresses two types of causal questions: questions about the effects of manipulating variables and questions about counterfactual states of affairs.[24] We will focus on inferences about variable manipulations. Pearl uses a construct called the *do() operator* to express *do-statements* such as $\mathcal{P}(V_1 = v_1 \mid do(V_2 = v_2))$. This statement can be interpreted as "the probability that $V_1 = v_1$ when we intervene to set $V_2 = v_2$." Formally, to *intervene* on the variable V_2 by setting it to v_2 means to construct an alternate PDAG model in which the edges between V_2 and its ancestors are deleted and the distribution of the root V_2 is set to be a point mass at v_2.

These do-statements can sometimes be resolved into equivalent *see-statements* using Pearl's three rules of do-calculus, which are consequences of the Markov Condition. See-statements are expressions which may involve various conditional probabilities, but do not contain the do-operator. Thus, see-statements can be evaluated using only information about the joint probability distribution $\mathcal{P}$ of the variables in the original PDAG. Note that in some cases, we may include *unobserved* variables in a PDAG model. We will indicate that a variable is unobserved in a DAG with a dotted outline as in Figure 26.4. When do-statements cannot be resolved into see-statements depending only on observed variables, they are called *unidentifiable*.

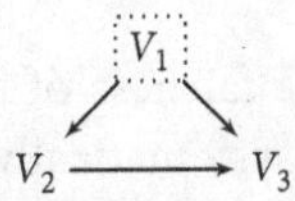

FIGURE 26.4. In this PDAG model, V_2 and V_3 are confounded by the unobserved variable V_1; this will render an expression such as $\mathcal{P}(V_3 \mid do(V_2))$ unidentifiable.

[24] Pearl, *Causality*.

For an accessible and more complete introduction to PDAG models and Pearl's causal theory, see Pearl, Glymour, and Jewell (2016)[25] or Pearl (2009a).[26] The purpose of our use of PDAG models in this chapter is mostly to provide intuition regarding sets of variables with various conditional dependency relationships. However, in the section "Causal Considerations," we will discuss certain aspects of fairness which require a properly causal treatment.

THREE CRITERIA FOR FAIRNESS

We will review the definitions of three prominent fairness criteria: Independence, Separation, and Sufficiency, which we will examine through the lens of PDAG models in this chapter. Let Y be a *response,* an outcome of interest measured for an individual. For example, Y could be whether an individual will repay a loan or whether she will click on an advertisement. Let A be a *sensitive characteristic,* a categorical variable indicating that individual's class with respect to a fairness-apt feature such as race or gender. Let R be a *prediction,* an estimated response for that individual.

If we select an individual at random from the population, the quantities Y, A, and R can be modeled as random variables. We are concerned with assessing whether R is a fair prediction. The three fairness criteria we examine in this chapter are *oblivious* criteria, which means they assess only the joint distribution of the tuple (A, R, Y).[27] In other words, these criteria are not concerned with the functional form of R or the information upon which it is based; they treat R as a black box.

Most of the work that has been done on fairness criteria for machine learning has considered the classification setting, in which Y is a categorical (and often binary) variable. Therefore it is no surprise that each of the three fairness criteria defined in this section were first introduced as criteria for assessing classifiers. These fairness criteria for the classification setting are respectively known as Demographic Parity, Equalized Odds, and Calibration by Group. However, Barocas, Hardt, and Narayanan (2018) offer sensible generalizations of these three criteria to settings with arbitrary, possibly continuous R and Y.[28] Here we will introduce both the original and generalized versions of each of the three criteria.

Demographic Parity and Independence

As a starting point for assessing the fairness of a prediction algorithm, we may ask whether the algorithm is making systematically different predictions for different

[25] Judea Pearl, Madelyn Glymour, and Nicholas P. Jewell, *Causal Inference in Statistics: A Primer* (John Wiley & Sons, 2016).

[26] Judea Pearl, "Causal Inference in Statistics: An Overview," *Statistics Surveys* 3 (2009a): 96–146.

[27] Hardt, Price, Srebro et al., "Equality of Opportunity in Supervised Learning."

[28] Solon Barocas, Moritz Hardt, and Arvind Narayanan, *Fairness and Machine Learning* (fairmlbook.org, 2018), http://www.fairmlbook.org.

groups. Suppose A is a categorical sensitive characteristic taking values in the set $\mathbb{A}$. Considering only the binary classification case for the moment, suppose that the response $Y \in \{0,1\}$ and the prediction $R \in \{0,1\}$.

Definition 1. A prediction R satisfies Demographic Parity if

$$P(R=1 \mid A=a) = P(R=1 \mid A=a')$$

for every sensitive characteristic a, $a' \in \mathbb{A}$.

In the binary case, this is equivalent to the statement $R \perp\!\!\!\perp A$. Therefore, the natural generalization of Demographic Parity as suggested by Barocas, Hardt, and Narayanan (2018) is as follows. For arbitrary random variables R, A and Y,

Definition 2. A prediction R satisfies Independence if $R \perp\!\!\!\perp A$.

This is a strong criterion in the sense that it requires that no aspect of the distribution of R depend on A. A weaker form of Independence could require only that the expected value and possibly the variance of R not depend on A. For methods for achieving full or partial Independence in predictions, see Johndrow and Lum (2019),[29] Calders, Kamiran, and Pechenizkiy (2009),[30] Calders and Verwer (2010),[31] Del Barrio et al. (2018),[32] and Hacker and Wiedemann (2017).[33]

Equalized Odds and Separation

The Independence criterion does not take the response Y into account; that is, it enforces equality of the distributions of the prediction R across the protected characteristic A even when the distribution of the response Y may differ across protected classes. For binary classifiers, Hardt, Price, Srebro et al. (2016) argue:[34]

> Demographic Parity is seriously flawed on two counts. First, it doesn't ensure fairness. The notion permits that we accept the qualified applicants in one demographic, but random individuals in another, so long as the percentages of acceptance match. This behavior can arise naturally, when there is little or no training data available for one of the demographics. Second, demographic parity often cripples the utility that

[29] James E. Johndrow and Kristian Lum, "An Algorithm for Removing Sensitive Information: Application to Race-Independent Recidivism Prediction," *The Annals of Applied Statistics* 13(1) (2019): 189–220.

[30] Toon Calders, Faisal Kamiran, and Mykola Pechenizkiy, "Building Classifiers with Independency Constraints," in *2009 IEEE International Conference on Data Mining Workshops* (IEEE, 2009), 13–18.

[31] Toon Calders and Sicco Verwer, "Three Naive Bayes Approaches for Discrimination-Free Classification," *Data Mining and Knowledge Discovery* 21(2) (2010): 277–292.

[32] Eustasio Del Barrio et al., "Obtaining Fairness Using Optimal Transport Theory," 2018, *arXiv:1806.03195*.

[33] Philipp Hacker and Emil Wiedemann, "A Continuous Framework for Fairness," 2017, *arXiv:1712.0792f.*

[34] Hardt, Price, Srebro et al., "Equality of Opportunity in Supervised Learning."

we might hope to achieve, especially in the common scenario in which an outcome to be predicated, e.g. whether the loan will be defaulted, is correlated with the protected attribute.

In light of this, Hardt, Price, Srebro et al. (2016) propose an alternative criterion for fairness. Suppose $Y \in \{0,1\}$ and the prediction $R \in \{0,1\}$.

Definition 3. A prediction R satisfies Equalized Odds if

$$P(R=1 \mid Y=y, A=a) = P(R=1 \mid Y=y, A=a')$$

for every sensitive characteristic a, $a' \in \mathbb{A}$ and response $y \in \{0,1\}$.

Hardt, Price, Srebro et al. (2016) argue that when Y and A are not independent, Y itself does not satisfy Demographic Parity, and therefore nor would a "perfect" classifier $R = Y$. On the other hand, a "perfect" classifier $R = Y$ will always satisfy Equalized Odds. Thus unless we are attempting to modify our predictions as a form of affirmative action, Equalized Odds seems to have an advantage over Demographic Parity. In the section "Parity by Signal," we argue that this intuition regarding "perfect" classifiers is an artifact of the discrete classification setting and its motivation has less force in arbitrary regression settings. Thus we will consider a general form of Equalized Odds.[35]

Definition 4. A prediction R satisfies Separation if $R \perp\!\!\!\perp A \mid Y$.

Like Independence, this is a strong criterion, and can be relaxed by requiring only that the conditional expectation $\mathbb{E}(R \mid Y)$ and possibly the conditional variance $\mathrm{Var}(R \mid Y)$ do not depend on A. See Hardt, Price, Srebro et al. (2016),[36] Pleiss et al. (2017),[37] Donini et al. (2018),[38] Zafar et al. (2017),[39] and Corbett-Davies et al. (2017)[40] for expositions of Separation-like criteria and methods for enforcing them.

Calibration by Group and Sufficiency

Calibration itself is not a fairness concept; it is a popular criterion for assessing an aspect of the performance of predicted probabilities.[41] Consider the case where the response $Y \in \{0,1\}$ is binary and the predicted probability that $Y = 1$ is $P \in [0,1]$.

[35] Barocas, Hardt, and Narayanan, *Fairness and Machine Learning*.

[36] Hardt, Price, and Srebro, et al., "Equality of Opportunity in Supervised Learning."

[37] Geoff Pleiss et al., "On Fairness and Calibration," in *Advances in Neural Information Processing Systems* (2017): 5680–5689.

[38] Michele Donini et al., "Empirical Risk Minimization under Fairness Constraints," in *Advances in Neural Information Processing Systems* (2018): 2796–2806.

[39] Muhammad Bilal Zafar et al., "Fairness beyond Disparate Treatment & Disparate Impact: Learning Classification without Disparate Mistreatment," in *Proceedings of the 26th International Conference on World Wide Web* (ACM, 2017): 1171–1180.

[40] Sam Corbett-Davies et al., "Algorithmic Decision Making and the Cost of Fairness," in *Proceedings of the 23rd ACM SIGKDD International Conference on Knowledge Discovery and Data Mining* (ACM, 2017): 797–806.

[41] Sarah Lichtenstein, Baruch Fischhoff, and Lawrence D Phillips, *Calibration of Probabilities: The State of the Art to 1980*, Tech. Rep. (Perceptronics, 1981).

Definition 5. A predicted probability P satisfies *Calibration* if $P(Y=1|P=p)=p$ for any $p \in [0,1]$.

This would suggest that classifications generated by a calibrated predicated probability are trustworthy in the sense that a practitioner has no incentive to make post hoc adjustments to compensate for known biases in ranges of the prediction.

A related criterion, which is directly relevant to fairness, is whether a predicted probability is calibrated across subpopulations, that is, whether a given predicted probability has the same meaning when generated for individuals from different subpopulations. Suppose $Y \in \{0,1\}$ and $P \in [0,1]$.

Definition 6. A predicted probability P satisfies *Calibration by Group* if $P(Y=1|P=p, A=a)=p$ for each sensitive attribute $a \in \mathbb{A}$ and probability $p \in [0,1]$.

Calibration by Group is intuitively appealing because if it is not satisfied, some individuals' predictions must deviate from the model-grounded truth in a manner depending on their group membership. That is, a predicted probability P which satisfies Calibration by Group has equal performance across the sensitive attribute. Indeed, Calibration by Group is a combination of Calibration and lack of dependence on the sensitive attribute A. The lack of dependence can be isolated, in terms of a prediction $R \in \{0,1\}$, through the following definition.

Definition 7. A prediction rule $R \in \{0,1\}$ satisfies *Predictive Parity* if $P[Y=1|R=r, A=a]=P[Y=1|R=r]$ where the prediction $r \in \{0,1\}$ and the sensitive characteristic $a \in A$.

Predictive Parity was discussed and coined by Chouldechova (2017).[42] Barocas, Hardt, and Narayanan (2018) present a natural generalization of predictive parity for a not necessarily binary Y and R.[43]

Definition 8. A prediction R satisfies Sufficiency if $Y \perp\!\!\!\perp A \mid R$.

FAIRNESS CRITERIA IN TWO SCENARIOS

To supplement the basic motivations of these three fairness criteria, we will discuss their implications in two prediction scenarios. We will find that these various criteria do not represent equally viable choices with different subjective implications, but rather that certain criteria are operational in certain scenarios and seemingly meaningless in others. Independence has clear use cases and represents an assumption about the relationships between the sensitive characteristic and the response, or else a desire to impose a regime of special intervention in favor of a particular group. Sufficiency, on the other hand, serves more as a measure of the extent to which a prediction takes advantage of all of the information relevant in predicting the response. And finally, Separation does have meaningful use cases in esoteric scenarios such as Scenario 2. However, in most scenarios of interest, Separation has counterproductive and destructive implications.

---

[42] Chouldechova, "Fair Prediction with Disparate Impact."
[43] Barocas, Hardt, and Narayanan, *Fairness and Machine Learning.*

Scenario 1: Loan Repayment

We wish to predict whether an individual will repay a loan. Suppose we model the situation using the PDAG in Figure 26.5.

We consider three features with different conditional dependency structures encoded by this PDAG model. The applicant's hair color X_1 is a descendant of her race A and is not a mediator of the effect of A on the whether she repays the loan, Y. Perhaps for this reason, it seems intuitively unfair (and is illegal in some places[44]) to determine an applicant's loan premium based on her hair color. However, in some cases it may be tempting to do so because there is a backdoor path connecting X_1 and Y, thus X_1 and Y are statistically marginally dependent. The nature of X_1 illustrates one shortcoming of *Fairness Through Unawareness*, which demands we do not use A itself as an input into our prediction. It would be no violation of Fairness Through Unawareness to use X_1 alone to predict Y. However, if we do so, we are merely taking advantage of the backdoor path through A; in other words, we are using a noisy version of A to predict Y rather than A itself.

The applicant's credit rating X_2 is a mediator between A and Y. Therefore, it is statistically dependent on race, but is also predictive of whether the applicant will repay the loan even after taking race into consideration. While an applicant's credit rating is a natural feature for predicting loan repayment, it redundantly encodes race to some extent. Finally, the interest rate of the loan X_3 influences Y but is marginally independent of race. Therefore, X_3 itself seems to be an innocuous prediction.

We now assess the implications of the Independence, Separation, and Sufficiency criteria in this context.

Independence

The Independence criterion requires that our prediction R is marginally independent of the applicant's race A. Thus, assuming that our PDAG model is faithful, we can achieve Independence only by positioning R such that it is unconditionally d-separated from A. The applicant's loan interest rate X_3 is itself d-separated from A, therefore any prediction R which is a descendant only of X_3 will always satisfy Independence; see Figure 26.6.

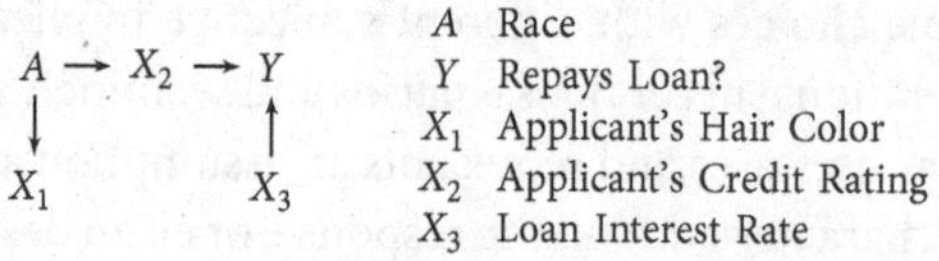

$$A \rightarrow X_2 \rightarrow Y$$
$$\downarrow \qquad\qquad \uparrow$$
$$X_1 \qquad\qquad X_3$$

A Race
Y Repays Loan?
X_1 Applicant's Hair Color
X_2 Applicant's Credit Rating
X_3 Loan Interest Rate

FIGURE 26.5. The random variables in Scenario 1: various features and their relationship to race A and loan repayment Y.

[44] Stacy Stowe, "New York City to Ban Discrimination Based on Hair," *New York Times* (February 18, 2019).

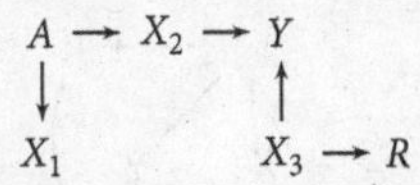

$$A \rightarrow X_2 \rightarrow Y$$
$$\downarrow \qquad\qquad \uparrow$$
$$X_1 \qquad\quad X_3 \rightarrow R$$

FIGURE 26.6. This prediction R is d-separated from A and therefore satisfies Independence.

$$\epsilon_{X_2} \longrightarrow R$$
$$\downarrow$$
$$A \rightarrow X_2 \rightarrow Y$$
$$\downarrow \qquad\qquad \uparrow$$
$$X_1 \qquad\quad X_3$$

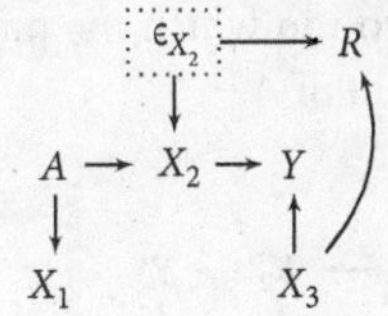

FIGURE 26.7. The prediction R depends on only the part of X_2 independent of race A.

However, a prediction R which descends from either the applicant's hair color X_1 or credit rating X_2 would fail to satisfy Independence. Nonetheless, there may remain valuable information within X_2 which may help us predict Y while maintaining Independence. We can extract this information by constructing a model which can be represented by the PDAG in Figure 26.7.

By decomposing X_2 into a component which depends on A and an exogenous component ϵ_{X_2} which is marginally independent of A, we can construct a prediction R which uses more information but is still d-separated from A and thus satisfies Independence, as shown in Figure 26.8. While X_2 is observed in our model, this exogenous component ϵ_{X_2} is unobserved, and must be recovered in a model-specific manner. Consider a simple case, in which $X_2 \,|\, A \sim \mathcal{N}(\mu_A, 1)$. Then $\epsilon_{X_2} = (X_2 - \mu_A) \sim \mathcal{N}(0,1)$ would satisfy the conditional independencies encoded by this PDAG model, and thus we may safely allow our prediction R to depend on ϵ_{X_2}.

In the context of this scenario, satisfying Independence while using information about X_2 entails that we use a version of X_2 which is demeaned by race. That is, we would use as a feature an individual's credit rating relative only to others of the same race.

This procedure may seem justifiable if credit ratings are themselves racially biased and thus an inaccurate indicator of an individual's likelihood of repaying the loan. However this is untrue by assumption in our model, because Y is conditionally independent of A given X_2. Thus in this case, the procedure of demeaning credit ratings by race to satisfy Independence should be interpreted as a special modification of the prediction R to benefit a particular (likely disadvantaged) group. If credit ratings are in fact racially biased, we may use a modification of the model in Scenario 1.

In this modified scenario, X_2 is a racially biased credit rating which unfairly modifies information about an applicant's true driver of default risk, ϵ_{X_2}. Under these assumptions, we can achieve Independence without sacrificing any predictive accuracy.

Finally, in Scenario 1, no information about an applicant's hair color X_1 can be productively used while maintaining Independence. Any exogenous components which resulted from a decomposition of X_1 would be independent of Y; in this scenario, Independence bars us from considering an applicant's hair color entirely.

FIGURE 26.8. A modification of Scenario 1 in which the only part of X_2 which contributes to the response Y is the noise ϵ_{X_2}, independent of A.

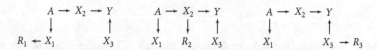

FIGURE 26.9. Three examples of predictions, each where the prediction rule R_j depends only on the feature X_j.

Separation

The Separation criterion requires that our prediction R is independent of an applicant's race A conditional on whether she does in fact repay the loan, Y. We have seen that Independence is a strong criterion that requires that R has no dependency on A despite the fact that Y itself is dependent on A. In Scenario 1, we may desire a criterion which allows us to take into account more information about the applicant's credit rating X_2 (because X_2 has a direct and perhaps causal relationship with Y). Nonetheless, we may we still desire that our criterion prohibits the use of spurious information like hair color, X_1.

However, in this scenario, Separation does no such thing. To see this clearly, we will consider all prediction rules which are descendants of only one feature. Let R_j denote an arbitrary prediction rule which depends on only the feature X_j, for each $j = 1, 2, 3$.

Any prediction R_1 depending on only X_1 violates Separation as expected, since Y does not d-separate R_1 and A. But this is also the case for R_2: Y does not block the path between R_2 and A. Even more surprisingly, because Y is a collider, conditioning on Y actually *unblocks* the path between R_3 and A. Therefore even though the interest rate of the loan X_3 was eligible for use under Independence due to its independence with A, it cannot be used under Separation. Extracting components from the features $X_1, X_2,$ or X_3 is also futile; any graphical descendent or ancestor of these features would still be d-connected to A given Y.

In general, Separation prevents us from constructing any predictions which are descendants of $X_1, X_2,$ or X_3 in a faithful PDAG model. We can, however, induce a violation of faithfulness to force independence between R and A. To do so, we must let R be a direct descendent of A. For example, considering for simplicity a prediction using information about credit rating, X_2, suppose the PDAG model contains the following Gaussian linear model:

$$Y \mid X_2 \sim \mathcal{N}(\beta X_2, \sigma^2),$$
$$X_2 \mid A \sim \mathcal{N}(\mu_A, \sigma_A^2).$$

As throughout this chapter, assume that all of the model parameters, β, σ^2, μ_a, and σ_A^2 are known. Then, by basic properties of the multivariate normal distribution,[45]

$$X_2 \mid Y, A \sim \mathcal{N}\left((1-\rho_A)\mu_A + \rho_A \frac{Y}{\beta}, \sigma^2 \rho_A \right),$$

where $\rho_A = \dfrac{\beta^2 \sigma_A^2}{\beta^2 \sigma_A^2 + \sigma^2}$. As we may have anticipated due to the structure of the PDAG model, the mean and variance of X_2 given Y still depend on race A. However, we can use this conditional distribution to construct the optimal linear prediction R which cancels out these dependencies by explicitly taking into account the race A. It is:

$$R(X_2) = \beta\left(\frac{X_2 - (1-\rho_A)\mu_A}{\rho_A} \right) + Z,$$

where $Z \sim \mathcal{N}(0, (c - \frac{1}{\rho_A})\sigma^2)$ is an independent source of noise, and $c = \max\{\frac{1}{\rho_a}\}$ across all races, $a \in \mathbb{A}$. Thus, R's dependencies are encoded by the new PDAG model which is not faithful, depicted in Figure 26.10.

Note that $R(X_2) \mid Y \sim N(Y, c\sigma^2)$, and this distribution does not depend on A. However, this prediction rule R is suspicious perhaps most notably because it requires that the addition of Harrison Bergeron–esque noise to the predictions for certain individuals in order to achieve parity in prediction error across groups. The inclusion of additional noise is similar to a result found in Pleiss et al. (2017) for discrete classifiers.[46] A depiction of the prediction R above is in Figure 26.11.

Thus, in Scenario 1, Separation does not seem to be a natural criterion for fairness because it suggests only counterproductive procedures for constructing estimators. However, we will show that in Scenario 2, Separation sometimes has the power to discriminate between subjectively different prediction rules.

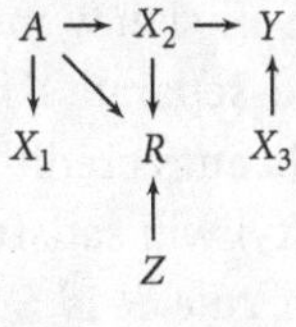

FIGURE 26.10. The prediction R takes as input both A and X_2, whose effects conspire to violate faithfulness and make $R \perp\!\!\!\perp A \mid Y$.

[45] William R. Moser, *Linear Models: A Mean Model Approach* (Elsevier, 1996).
[46] Pleiss et al., "On Fairness and Calibration."

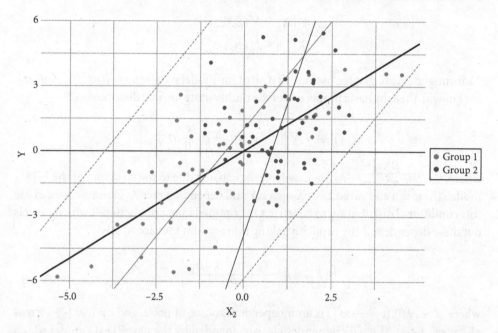

FIGURE 26.11. Here, the mean and variance of the distribution of X_2 differs between groups. In Group 1 (•), X_2 has a lower mean and greater variance than Group 2 (•). However, for both groups, $Y = \beta X_2 + \epsilon$. That is, the known regression line (——) accurately captures the signal component of Y for both groups. Nonetheless, the modified predictions satisfying Separation for Group 1 (——) and Group 2 (——) differ and greatly deviate from the true regression line. Furthermore, to achieve equal conditional prediction variance between groups, we must randomize the predictions for Group 1; the lighter dotted lines (——) indicate two-standard-deviation bounds for the randomized predictions.

Sufficiency

The Sufficiency criterion demands that whether an applicant will repay her loan Y is independent of her race A conditional on the prediction R. Because R will always be a graphical descendent of some subset of the features, X_1, X_2, and X_3, we can see from Figure 26.9 that we cannot achieve Sufficiency merely by carefully choosing R's arguments. Conditioning on R will never d-separate Y from A.

However, we can see that the applicant's credit rating X_2 d-separates Y from A, and therefore any invertible function $R(X_2)$ will satisfy Sufficiency. This argument will not generally work when the prediction rule R is a function of more than one feature, though, since it is not generally possible to invert such a function. Indeed, in order to construct a prediction rule $R(X_2, X_3)$ which satisfies Separation, the prediction R must explicitly block the path between A and Y. This can be done when the response Y only depends on the features X_2 and X_3 through a parameter $\theta(X_2, X_3)$: in this case, the predictor $R = \theta$ satisfies Sufficiency. Of course, the parameter θ which controls the way in which the probability of loan repayment depends on the loan interest rate X_3 and an applicant's credit rating X_2 is not known in practice, so this exact predictor is not available for use. This argument further shows that, in this case, the only way that prediction rules which are estimated from training data can be Sufficient in the population is through their recovery of the signal.

Scenario 2: Job Advertisement

In this scenario, modeled after a similar scenario from Barocas, Hardt, and Narayanan (2018), we are looking to serve advertisements for a programming job to web users who are likely to be programmers.[47] To predict whether or not the user is a programmer, we use information about his or her browsing history. For a real life example of issues in fairness which may arise from serving job advertisements, see Gillum and Tobin (2019).[48] Suppose we model the relationship between measurements on an individual user using the PDAG in Figure 26.12.

We assume X_1, a variable indicating whether a user has visited `pinterest.com`, has no relationship to whether or not the individual is a programmer except by virtue of the information it encodes about gender. The novelty of this scenario is that we observe X_2, a variable indicating whether a user has visited `stackexchange.com`, which we assume is a graphical descendant of whether a user is a programmer, Y. According to this model, a user's gender affects the likelihood that he or she is a programmer, but a programmer has a certain likelihood of visiting `stackexchange.com` regardless of his or her gender.

Therefore if we do not wish to target users for this employment advertisement based on gender, X_1 is a suspicious candidate, but X_2 may reasonably be considered fair game. We now examine the implications of the oblivious criteria in this scenario.

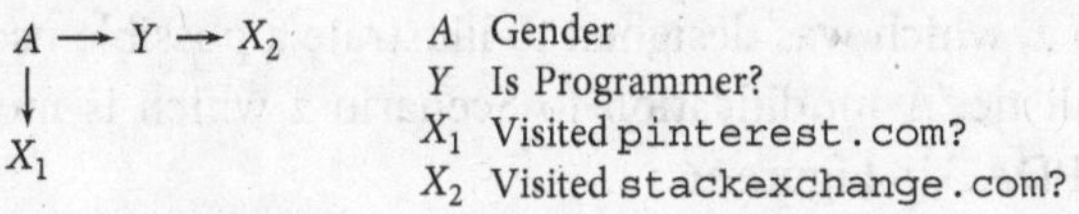

$$A \longrightarrow Y \longrightarrow X_2$$
$$\downarrow$$
$$X_1$$

A	Gender
Y	Is Programmer?
X_1	Visited `pinterest.com`?
X_2	Visited `stackexchange.com`?

FIGURE 26.12. The random variables in Scenario 2: various features and their relationship to gender A and progamming employment Y.

Independence

From Figure 26.13, we can see that as in Scenario 1, if the prediction R depends on whether a user has visited `pinterest.com`, X_1, the prediction R will violate Independence, and any information in X_1 which is independent of a user's gender A will also be independent of whether he or she is a programmer, Y. Furthermore, because

---

[47] Barocas, Hardt, and Narayanan, *Fairness and Machine Learning*.
[48] Gillum and Tobin, "Facebook Won't Let Employers, Landlords or Lenders Discriminate in Ads Anymore."

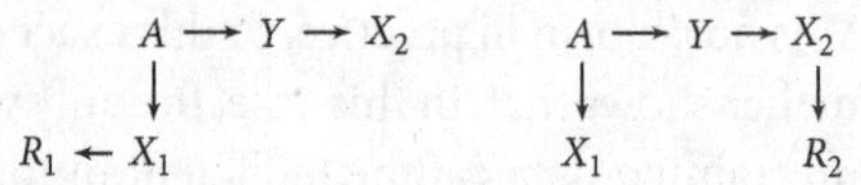

$$A \longrightarrow Y \longrightarrow X_2 \qquad A \longrightarrow Y \longrightarrow X_2$$
$$\downarrow \qquad\qquad\qquad \downarrow$$
$$R_1 \leftarrow X_1 \qquad\qquad X_1 \qquad R_2$$

FIGURE 26.13. Two examples of predictions, each where the prediction rule R_j depends only on the feature X_j.

X_2 is a descendant of Y with no backdoor connection to A, any component of whether the user has visited `stackexchange.com`, X_2, which is independent of A will also be independent of Y. Therefore, we cannot construct any nontrivial predictions R in Scenario 2 which satisfy Independence.

Separation

On the other hand, Scenario 2 is where Separation shines. Consider again estimators which depend on only one feature: let R_1 denote an arbitrary prediction rule which depends on only X_1, and, likewise, let R_2 denote an arbitrary prediction rule which depends on only X_2.

A prediction R_1 will fail to satisfy Separation because conditioning on whether a user is a programmer, Y, does not d-separate whether he or she has visited `pinterest.com`, X_1, and his or her gender, A. Clearly, this will be the case regardless of what information we extract from X_1. However, any prediction which is a descendent only of whether the user has visited `stackexchange.com`, X_2, will in fact satisfy Separation, because conditioning on Y blocks the path between X_2 and A.

Thus we can interpret Separation as a criterion which encourages us to use information which depends on A only through the response, Y. However, it is not clear that there are many situations in which we observe features which behave as graphical descendants of the response. We are generally interested in using features which temporally precede the observation of Y; usually X causes Y and not the other way around.

In fact Scenario 2, which was designed to illustrate a possible use of the Separation criterion, is unrealistic. A modification to Scenario 2 which is more realistic can be modeled with the PDAG in Figure 26.14.

Here, whether or not a user is a programmer is actually an unobserved variable, U, and is relevant to us only because it determines the likelihood of the observable event that the user clicks on our advertisement, Y. From this more realistic model we can see that Y no longer d-separates R_2 from A. Thus to the extent that Y is not identical to U, Separation will not hold.

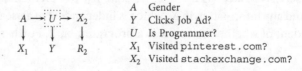

A	Gender
Y	Clicks Job Ad?
U	Is Programmer?
X_1	Visited `pinterest.com`?
X_2	Visited `stackexchange.com`?

FIGURE 26.14. A perhaps more realistic DAG that underlies the click-predicting task in Scenario 2.

Sufficiency

In contrast to Scenario 1, we cannot construct a nontrivial prediction satisfying Sufficiency. Neither X_1 nor X_2 are mediators of the effect of A on Y. The only way our prediction R could block the direct path between A and Y would be for R to perfectly encode the information in A.

UNDERSTANDING SEPARATION

Among the three oblivious criteria of fairness discussed, we are most skeptical of Separation. As mentioned in the section "Equalized Odds and Separation," there is a significant literature focused on applying and generalizing the criterion. However, unlike the other criteria, Separation has fundamental limitations, which we now explore.

In the section "Scenario 2: Job Advertisement," we found that predictions R which are a function of features that are descendants of the response Y will satisfy Separation, so we will now focus on other cases. In particular, we will focus on an arrangement of the features, sensitive characteristic, and response which we feel is most likely to occur in practice: we assume the DAG is arranged so that the sensitive characteristic A is a root, the response Y is a leaf, and none of the features are descendants of the response. We feel that this DAG is ubiquitous since predictions are often made about the future, necessitating that the features will be causal ancestors of the response. An example of such an arrangement is provided in Scenario 1. To be concrete, we will focus on a typical example of a DAG which encodes dependencies between the features, visualized in Figure 26.15. The node A is a root node which may be an ancestor of any of the features, $X_1, \ldots, X_p$. Furthermore, features may be ancestors or descendants of each other, but all of the features are ancestors of the response, Y.

We will now argue that Separation will tend not to hold by examining the structure of the typical DAG, which is visualized with a prediction R in the leftmost graph of Figure 26.17. There, conditioning on a leaf of the graph, the response Y, will not generally block paths from the root, the sensitive characteristic A, to the prediction R—which depends on the mediators, the features X. This is due to a nondegeneracy of the graph: the response Y will be influenced by *exogenous random noise* ϵ, say ò, in addition to a

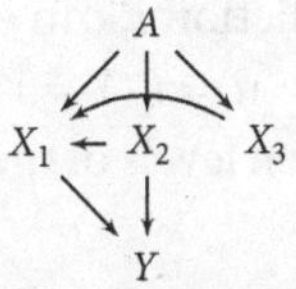

FIGURE 26.15. An example of a DAG where all features are mediators between the sensitive characteristic A and the response Y.

FIGURE 26.16. A depiction of the prohibited paths between the random variables A, R, and Y under Separation and Sufficiency.

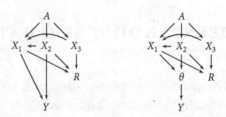

FIGURE 26.17. The leftmost graph is the same example graph as in Figure 26.15, and the rightmost graph shows the signal parameter θ.

signal through the features $X_1, \ldots, X_p$. Due to the interference of the noise ò, the information in the response Y is fundamentally different from the information in the features, which leads to the impossibility of blocking and the failure of Separation to hold for faithful models.

This argument is easiest to see in the case of the visualized Figure 26.17, but holds more generally. Whenever there is at least one feature which is an ancestor of the response Y, the exogenous noise ϵ will still interfere with the response Y, leading to an inability to recover the information in the features. Specializing the conclusion of this argument to the binary case uncovers a peculiarity in Equalized Odds, despite that Equalized Odds is derived from common measures for summarizing the accuracy of a classifier.

Incompatibility between Separation and Sufficiency

Measures of fairness were beginning to be intensely studied and debated when Kleinberg, Mullainathan, and Raghavan (2017)[49] and Chouldechova (2017)[50] established the surprising result that Calibration and Equalized Odds cannot simultaneously hold in all but degenerate settings. Specifically, it was established:

Theorem 1. Consider the binary setting, where the response $Y \in \{0,1\}$ and the prediction $R \in \{0,1\}$. When $R \neq Y$, the prediction R can only satisfy both Equalized Odds and Calibration by Group if $P(Y=1 \mid A=a) = P(Y=1 \mid A=a')$ for all a, $a' \in A$, that is, the mean response does not differ between levels of the protected characteristic A.

[49] Kleinberg, Mullainathan, and Raghavan, "Inherent Trade-offs in the Fair Determination of Risk Scores."

[50] Chouldechova, "Fair Prediction with Disparate Impact."

The theorem has been generalized beyond the binary case to hold for Separation and Sufficiency. Barocas, Hardt, and Narayanan (2018) provide an argument using undirected graphs, which we now reproduce.[51] In Theorem 1, we assumed that $R \neq Y$. In the general case, we similarly, but more generally, assume that all events in the joint distribution of (A, R, Y) have positive probability. This assumption makes it so that there's no degeneracy between the random variables. Consider an undirected graphical model of the variables A, R, and Y, as shown in Figure 26.16.

Separation requires that $R \perp\!\!\!\perp A \mid Y$, so that there can be no edge between A and R. Similarly, Sufficiency requires that $Y \perp\!\!\!\perp A \mid R$, so that there can be no edge between A and Y. We indicate the impossibility of an edge with a dashed line. Therefore, it must hold that $A \perp\!\!\!\perp Y$, since there can be no path drawn connecting A and Y. The condition $A \perp\!\!\!\perp Y$ is a generalization of the condition in Theorem 1 that the mean response does not differ between levels of the protected characteristic A. This establishes the result, summarized in the theorem below.

Theorem 2. Under the nondegeneracy assumption that all events in the joint distribution of (A, R, Y) have positive probability, if Separation and Sufficiency both hold, it must be that $A \perp\!\!\!\perp Y$.

These results cast the disagreement between ProPublica and Northpointe in a new light. On one hand, the failure of the COMPAS algorithm to achieve equal error rates between groups does not seem to be an objective form of unfairness if it is mathematically impossible for a classifier which is calibrated by group to do so. On the other hand, there remains the question of whether disparate impact caused by unbalanced error rates is sufficient cause to dispense with calibration.

In binary classification settings, it is common to characterize the performance of a classifier using the false positive and false negative rate. These quantities specify the distribution of R given Y. However, as we have seen using the example of a simple linear regression model, attempting to enforce parity between quantities conditional on Y can lead to counterproductive procedures. Furthermore, as we have argued, even when Calibration by Group does not hold, in general there is no reason to expect conditioning on Y to block the paths between R and A. Thus we believe that the choice between Calibration by Group and Equalized Odds is not a mere subjective trade-off; instead we find Separation to be a fundamentally unhelpful fairness criterion.

Parity by Signal

The original motivation of Equalized Odds[52] was to overcome limitations of Independence. In addition to the stringency of the criterion, the authors argue that a limitation of the criterion is that the response Y itself does not satisfy Independence whenever there is dependence between Y and the sensitive characteristic A. This is

[51] Barocas, Hardt, and Narayanan, *Fairness and Machine Learning.*
[52] Hardt, Price, and Srebro et al., "Equality of Opportunity in Supervised Learning."

undesirable, they write, since the response Y is an "ideal [prediction], which can hardly be considered discriminatory as it represents the actual outcome."

This line of reasoning seems to obscure a crucial point. When the probability distribution of the response Y depends on the features $X_1, \ldots, X_p$ only through a signal parameter $\theta(A, X_1, \ldots, X_p)$, which we could take without loss of generality to be the conditional mean $E[Y \mid A, X_1, \ldots, X_p]$ when θ is one-dimensional, the signal θ will not be an allowable prediction under Separation. This follows by the same reasoning as before: in nondegenerate settings, conditioning on the response Y will not block the dependence between any of its ancestors. This is a significant limitation since the discrepancy between the response Y and the signal θ is generally unique to each individual and cannot be predicted. Indeed, no prediction rule R can achieve zero prediction error when the response Y has an exogenous noise component. Therefore, in practicality, the perfect prediction R is the signal θ, not the response Y. With this in mind, we explicitly define a new measure of fairness.

Definition 9. Represent $Y = F_{\theta(A, X_1, \ldots, X_p)}(\epsilon)$, where ϵ is exogenous noise, that is, $\epsilon \perp\!\!\!\perp A, X_1, \ldots, X_p$, and F is a function indexed by a signal parameter θ. Then a prediction R satisfies *Parity by Signal* when R is conditionally independent of the sensitive attribute A given the signal θ, i.e. $R \perp\!\!\!\perp A \mid \theta$.

Another way to view this definition of fairness is that the predictions for similar people do not unnecessarily depend on the sensitive characteristic, where similar people are defined to be those whose features contribute—via the signal $\theta(A, X_1, \ldots, X_p)$—in the same way to the outcome. This is related to the measure of fairness described by Dwork et al. (2012), wherein Separation by Signal would be considered as utilizing a perfect similarity metric.[53] In Scenario 1, an optimal prediction rule which satisfies Separation was presented, and it was found to be unusual: however, in that same scenario, the true mean did indeed satisfy Parity by Signal.

This definition of fairness is not without its limitations. Evaluating whether a prediction R satisfies Separation by Signal requires the signal θ, which is generally not known in practice. Above we demonstrated that Separation by Signal is a useful device to develop understanding, but a close variant of it can also be made operational. Separation by Signal compares the prediction R to the signal θ, but, instead, R could be compared to another prediction S which is viewed to be more accurate than R.

Definition 10. A prediction R satisfies *Parity by S* if R is conditionally independent of the sensitive attribute A given S, that is, $R \perp\!\!\!\perp A \mid S$.

Notice that a prediction R satisfies Separation by Signal if and only if R satisfies Parity by θ.

We can interpret a variety of fairness-testing procedures as a form of testing for Parity by S. For example, in the context of testing whether various police precincts exhibit racial bias in contraband searches, Simoiu, Corbett-Davies, Goel et al. (2017) develop

---

[53] Cynthia Dwork et al., "Fairness through Awareness," in *Proceedings of the 3rd Innovations in Theoretical Computer Science Conference* (ACM, 2012), 214–226.

a threshold test which is a test for a kind of Parity by Signal.[54] They are in the binary setting and consider the prediction $R(X_1,...,X_n) = \mathbb{I}[p_A(X_1,...,X_p) > t_A]$ to be that an individual is carrying contraband when the probability $p_A(X_1,...,X_p)$ of the individual carrying contraband is larger than a threshold t_A and to be that an individual is not carrying contraband otherwise. They develop Bayesian tests for whether the threshold t_A depends on the race A, since they argue that a fundamental form of unfairness occurs when minorities are ruled against more stringent thresholds than nonminorities. Due to the prediction R depending only on the probability p_A and the threshold t_A, this is a test for whether R satisfies Parity by p_A.

In the above example, the threshold test sought to determine whether there was a specific form of bias in police officers' decisions to search for contraband. This is an example of testing subjective human predictions, with some modeling assumptions. However, a Separation by S criterion can also be desirable to hold for a prediction R even when both R and S are generated by machine algorithms. Consider cases in which we believe that a model is unfair due to misspecification; perhaps this model is missing necessary features or fails to model interactions between the sensitive characteristic and other features in a way which leads the predictions generated by the algorithm to disparately impact certain groups. (See, in particular, Scenario 1: The Red Car in Kusner et al. (2017).[55]) Specifically, suppose that the prediction $R(X) = \beta^T X$ and the prediction $S(X) = \beta_A^T X$, where each coefficient β_A differs based on the sensitive characteristic A. In this case, a likelihood ratio test[56] between these models would be a test for whether R satisfies Separation by S.

CAUSAL CONSIDERATIONS

In various discussions of Independence and Separation-like criteria, authors propose generalizations which enforce parity only after conditioning on certain features.[57,58,59] Consider the following generalizations of Independence. Suppose X is some subvector of the features $X_1,...,X_p$.

Definition 11. A prediction R satisfies Conditional Independence with respect to X if $R \perp\!\!\!\perp A \mid X$.

Notice that Conditional Independence with respect to $(X_1,...,X_p)$ always holds when the prediction R is a deterministic function of the features $X_1,...,X_p$. This reinforces

[54] Camelia Simoiu, Sam Corbett-Davies, Sharad Goel et al., "The Problem of Infra-marginality in Outcome Tests for Discrimination," *The Annals of Applied Statistics* 11(3) (2017): 1193–1216.

[55] Matt J. Kusner et al., "Counterfactual Fairness," in *Advances in Neural Information Processing Systems* (2017): 4066–4076.

[56] Alan Agresti, *Foundations of Linear and Generalized Linear Models* (John Wiley & Sons, 2015).

[57] Barocas, Hardt, and Narayanan, *Fairness and Machine Learning*.

[58] Hardt, Price, and Srebro et al., "Equality of Opportunity in Supervised Learning."

[59] Michele Donini et al., "Empirical Risk Minimization under Fairness Constraints."

that the purpose of Conditional Independence is to study the influence of a subvector X of the features. Notice also the connection to Parity by Signal and Parity by a prediction S, which involve evaluating independence conditional on a specific function of the features.

Conditional Independence criteria themselves convey little information about the underlying desires of the practitioner. However, causal reasoning can provide principled methods for developing fairness criteria which may ultimately be expressed as Conditional Independence criteria. Here, we discuss two scenarios in which Conditional Independence criteria can be derived using causal reasoning. For a variety of perspectives on the role of Pearl's causality theory in fairness, see Kusner et al. (2017),[60] Kilbertus et al. (2017),[61] Nabi and Shpitser (2018),[62] and Chiappa (2019).[63]

Scenario 3: College Admissions

For the purpose of college admissions, we wish to predict whether a student will drop out before completing his or her degree. Suppose we model the situation using the PDAG in Figure 26.18.

Suppose that the admissions committee wishes to use all of the relevant information about student performance contained in the student's SAT score X_2, but otherwise wishes to ignore the student's race-laden socioeconomic status X_1, despite the fact that socioeconomic factors do have a direct effect on a student's probability of dropping out. In the language of Kilbertus et al. (2017), this means that X_2 is a *resolving* variable.[64] The Independence criterion would not allow us to use all of the information in X_2, since we would have to extract the component of X_2 which is independent of the student's race A.

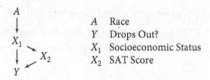

FIGURE 26.18. The random variables in Scenario 3: various features and their relationship to race A and drop out status Y.

[60] Kusner et al., "Counterfactual Fairness."

[61] Niki Kilbertus et al., "Avoiding Discrimination through Causal Reasoning," in *Advances in Neural Information Processing Systems* (2017): 656–666.

[62] Razieh Nabi and Ilya Shpitser, "Fair Inference on Outcomes," in *Thirty-Second AAAI Conference on Artificial Intelligence* (AAAI Press, 2018).

[63] Silvia Chiappa, "Path-Specific Counterfactual Fairness," in *Thirty-Third AAAI Conference on Artificial Intelligence* (AAAI Press, 2019).

[64] Kilbertus et al., "Avoiding Discrimination through Causal Reasoning," in *Advances in Neural Information Processing Systems* (2017): 656–666.

Separation or Parity by Signal, on the other hand, would not allow us to fully make use of X_2 while entirely excluding information in X_1.

In fact, we actually desire for A to have no *direct effect* on R that is not mediated by X_2. We can express this criterion using the formula for Controlled Direct Effect (CDE) as:

$$\mathcal{P}(R \mid \mathrm{do}(A = a), \mathrm{do}(X_2 = x)) = \mathcal{P}(R \mid \mathrm{do}(A = a'), \mathrm{do}(X_2 = x)) \tag{2}$$

for all a, $a' \in \mathbb{A}$ and all x in the range of X_2. In this case, this do-expression is identifiable and simplifies to the expression $R \perp\!\!\!\perp A \mid X_2$. However, in cases when a resolving variable is itself confounded with other variables, the do-expressions in (2) may be unidentifiable or require some do-calculus to resolve into observational expressions.

Scenario 4: Insurance Prices

In the scenarios we have discussed so far, we model the sensitive characteristic A as an exogenous variable. Thus A has always been a root in our PDAG models, and the total causal effects of A on endogenous entities such as R and Y coincide with the observed effects. However, when A is an endogenous variable, there may be backdoor paths from A to our predictions or response. Consider the following scenario, which makes clear the need for causal reasoning in fairness.

We wish to predict whether an individual is likely to have a car accident for the purpose of determining her insurance premium. Suppose we model the relevant variables using the PDAG in Figure 26.19.

We may deem it unfair to use an individual's religion, A, as a factor in our prediction, R. However, there is a backdoor path between A and Y, and thus A and Y are marginally dependent. For the same reason, any prediction R which is a nontrivial descendent of the individual's driving record X will fail to satisfy Independence. Of course, as in all of the ubiquitous cases when the features are ancestors of the response, conditioning on Y will not black the path between R and A either, thus our prediction will also fail to satisfy Separation.

In this case, we need not consider X to be a resolving variable. Whatever dependence results between A and R is spurious. We are interested in ensuring that A has no Total Effect (TE) on R, which we can express as:

$$\mathcal{P}(R \mid \mathrm{do}(A = a)) = \mathcal{P}(R \mid \mathrm{do}(A = a')). \tag{3}$$

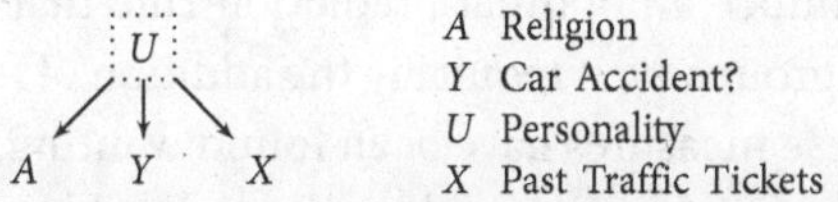

A	Religion
Y	Car Accident?
U	Personality
X	Past Traffic Tickets

FIGURE 26.19. The random variables in Scenario 4: an unobserved variable, and various features and their relationship to religion A and car accident status Y.

Note that this is a special case of the Counterfactual Fairness criterion in Kusner et al. (2017), although these authors do not explicitly consider cases in which A is endogenous.[65] The consequence of this criterion is that we can freely construct predictions R which are based on traffic tickets, X, or other inferred aspects of personality, U.

CONCLUSION

In Scenarios 1 through 4, PDAGs have proven to be fertile ground for developing intuition about the three basic oblivious criteria for fairness: Independence, Separation, and Sufficiency. In general, constructing a PDAG model relating the sensitive characteristic, features, and response is a clarifying exercise, because it allows us to more directly connect our senses about what is intuitively fair to the implications of the decisions we make in specifying an algorithm. In contrast to the project of constructing statistically optimal estimators, a fundamental concern in constructing fair estimators is blocking the use of information which is subjectively unacceptable. Here, PDAGs and d-separation are natural tools.

In contrast, the oblivious fairness criteria alone are limited, because their behavior is opaque and sensitive to the particularities of the scenario. Enforcing Independence between the sensitive characteristic and the prediction was seen to have wildly different implications in scenarios when the response was dependent on race and when it was not. In the former case, Independence prohibited discrimination which could not be statistically justified, and in the latter case, Independence was an intervention in favor of adversely affected groups.

Sufficiency can be achieved by blocking all paths through which information can flow between the sensitive characteristic and the response. Generally this is only possible by accurately recovering the signal. That is, it was shown that Sufficiency can be achieved by appropriately choosing the features through which information flows from race to the response and appropriately choosing a prediction that blocks that flow of information.

Separation naturally allows for the use of features which are descendants of the response, but exhibits strange behavior whenever there are features which are nondescendants of the response, even when those features are independent of the sensitive characteristic. For nondegenerate and faithful PDAG models, Separation will not hold since the response is comprised of not only the signal but also the noise, which obscures the information about the signal in the response. In Scenario 1, a violation of faithfulness was induced to produce an optimal prediction rule that turned out to be highly inappropriate, for some groups even requiring the addition of further random noise.

For the most part, these measures have been found wanting. We join the recent consensus that the assessment of fairness in algorithms should not start and end with the

---

[65] Kusner et al., "Counterfactual Fairness."

use of a singular criterion. The constraints we wish to impose on predictions should be sensitive to each scenario, and PDAG models can help to explore them.

More generally, we notice that there is little consensus on the underlying philosophical principles that should provide the foundation for the quantification of fairness. While much work in fairness seems to be framed around preventing unfairness like that allegedly exhibited by the COMPAS algorithm, there is no consensus that the COMPAS algorithm was ever unfair. We worry that as constructs from fairness are taken out of context and treated as black boxes for mathematical study and elaboration, the implicit underlying notions of fairness will be obscured. We hope that fairness research can be grounded in clear, practical examples of the ways algorithms can be unfair.

ACKNOWLEDGMENTS

Thanks to David Kent for helpful conversations.

BIBLIOGRAPHY

Angwin, Julia et al. "Machine Bias: There's Software Used across the Country to Predict Future Criminals. And It's Biased against Blacks." *ProPublica* 23 (May 23, 2016).

Barocas, Solon, Moritz Hardt, and Arvind Narayanan. *Fairness and Machine Learning*. fairmlbook.org, 2018. http://www.fairmlbook.org.

Calders, Toon, Faisal Kamiran, and Mykola Pechenizkiy. "Building Classifiers with Independency Constraints." In *2009 IEEE International Conference on Data Mining Workshops*, 13–18. IEEE, 2009.

Calders, Toon and Sicco Verwer. "Three Naive Bayes Approaches for Discrimination-Free Classification." *Data Mining and Knowledge Discovery* 21(2) (2010): 277–292.

Chiappa, Silvia. "Path-Specific Counterfactual Fairness." In *Thirty-Third AAAI Conference on Artificial Intelligence*. AAAI Press, 2019.

Chouldechova, Alexandra. "Fair Prediction with Disparate Impact: A Study of Bias in Recidivism Prediction Instruments." *Big Data* 5(2) (2017): 153–163.

Corbett-Davies, Sam and Sharad Goel. "The Measure and Mismeasure of Fairness: A Critical Review of Fair Machine Learning." *arXiv:1808.00023* (2018).

Corbett-Davies, Sam et al. "Algorithmic Decision Making and the Cost of Fairness." In *Proceedings of the 23rd ACM SIGKDD International Conference on Knowledge Discovery and Data Mining*, 797–806. ACM, 2017.

Del Barrio, Eustasio et al. "Obtaining Fairness Using Optimal Transport Theory." *arXiv:1806.03195* (2018).

Donini, Michele et al. "Empirical Risk Minimization under Fairness Constraints." In *Advances in Neural Information Processing Systems* (2018), 2796–2806.

Dwork, Cynthia et al. "Fairness through Awareness." In *Proceedings of the 3rd Innovations in Theoretical Computer Science Conference*, 214–226. ACM, 2012.

Flores, Anthony W., Kristin Bechtel, and Christopher T. Lowenkamp. "False Positives, False Negatives, and False Analyses: A Rejoinder to 'Machine Bias: There's Software Used across the Country to Predict Future Criminals. And It's Biased against Blacks.'" *Federal Probation* 80 (2016): 38–46.

Hacker, Philipp and Emil Wiedemann. "A Continuous Framework for Fairness." *arXiv:1712.0792f* (2017).

Hardt, Moritz et al. "Equality of Opportunity in Supervised Learning." In *Advances in Neural Information Processing Systems* (2016): 3315–3323.

Hardt, Moritz, Eric Price, and Nati Srebro et al. "Equality of Opportunity in Supervised Learning." In *Advances in Neural Information Processing Systems* (2016): 3315–3323.

Johndrow, James E. and Kristian Lum. "An Algorithm for Removing Sensitive Information: Application to Race-Independent Recidivism Prediction." *The Annals of Applied Statistics* 13(1) (2019): 189–220.

Kilbertus, Niki et al. "Avoiding Discrimination through Causal Reasoning." In *Advances in Neural Information Processing Systems* (2017): 656–666.

Kleinberg, Jon, Sendhil Mullainathan, and Manish Raghavan. "Inherent Trade-offs in the Fair Determination of Risk Scores." In *The 8th Innovations in Theoretical Computer Science Conference*, 2017.

Kusner, Matt J. et al. "Counterfactual Fairness." In *Advances in Neural Information Processing Systems* (2017): 4066–4076.

Mitchell, Shira, Eric Potash, and Solon Barocas. "Prediction-Based Decisions and Fairness: A Catalogue of Choices, Assumptions, and Definitions." *arXiv:1811.07867* (2018).

Nabi, Razieh and Ilya Shpitser. "Fair Inference on Outcomes." In *Thirty-Second AAAI Conference on Artificial Intelligence*. AAAI Press, 2018.

Pearl, Judea. "Causal Inference in Statistics: An Overview." *Statistics Surveys* 3 (2009a): 96–146.

Pearl, Judea, Madelyn Glymour, and Nicholas P. Jewell. *Causal Inference in Statistics: A Primer*. John Wiley & Sons, 2016.

Pleiss, Geoff et al. "On Fairness and Calibration." In *Advances in Neural Information Processing Systems* (2017): 5680–5689.

Simoiu, Camelia, Sam Corbett-Davies, Sharad Goel et al. "The Problem of Infra-marginality in Outcome Tests for Discrimination." *The Annals of Applied Statistics* 11(3) (2017): 1193–1216.

Yeom, Samuel and Michael Carl Tschantz. "Discriminative but Not Discriminatory: A Comparison of Fairness Definitions under Different Worldviews." *arXiv:1808.08619* (2018).

Zafar, Muhammad Bilal et al. "Fairness beyond Disparate Treatment & Disparate Impact: Learning Classification without Disparate Mistreatment." In *Proceedings of the 26th International Conference on World Wide Web*, 1171–1180. ACM, 2017.

CHAPTER 27

AUTOMATING
ORIGINATION

Perspectives from the Humanities

AVERY SLATER

On June 30, 2017, the *MIT Technology Review* ran a story entitled "Machine Creativity Beats Some Modern Art." In an attention-grabbing riddle, the article contained reproductions of twelve abstract paintings and asked its readers: which of these paintings was produced by a computer?[1]

Displaying a collection of twelve paintings evoking a range of styles from German Expressionism to Postmodernism, the article allowed readers to muse over which was Kandinsky, was was Rothko, and which was the work of AI before divulging the answer at the article's conclusion: "all of them."

These newsworthy artistic results were the outcome of experiments with a new neural network configuration that the authors of the computer science study call "Creative Adversarial Networks." This team at Rutgers University's Art and Artificial Intelligence Laboratory drew on previous successes in the field of AI image generation following the landmark introduction of generative adversarial networks (GANs) by Goodfellow et al. in 2014.[2] Inspired by Colin Martindale's theories about artistic change as being *predictably* divergent, Elgammal et al. (2017) modified a GAN to produce images that would satisfy creative rather than realistic criteria, "maximizing deviation from established styles while minimizing deviation from art distribution."[3] The team paired neural

---

[1] "Machine Creativity Beats Some Modern Art," *MIT Technology Review* (June 30, 2017), https://www.technologyreview.com/s/608195/machine-creativity-beats-some-modern-art/ (accessed April 1, 2019).

[2] Ian J. Goodfellow, Jean Pouget-Abadie, Mehdi Mirza, Bing Xu, David Warde-Farley, Sherjil Ozair, Aaron Courville, and Yoshua Bengio, "Generative Adversarial Nets," *Advances in Neural Information Processing Systems* (2014): 2672–2680, arXiv:1406.2661v1 [stat.ML], June 10, 2014.

[3] Ahmed Elgammal, Bingchen Liu, Mohamed Elhoseiny, and Marian Mazzone, "CAN: Creative Adversarial Networks, Generating 'Art' by Learning about Styles and Deviating from Style Norms," (June 21, 2017): 2, arXiv:1706.07068v1. See also Colin Martindale, *The Clockwork Muse: The Predictability of Artistic Change* (New York: Basic Books, 1990).

networks to train each other to produce artifacts[4] that would express styles reminiscent of other preexisting works of modern art from the Renaissance to the Expressionist, Modernist, and Postmodernist periods.

The team's goal for their experiments transcended merely testing machinic powers. They pursued an insight into the question of creativity itself: where does artistic innovation come from? How much does it rely on memory and training? "A theory is needed to model how to integrate exposure to art with the creation of art," the team asserts.[5] In this they echo the animus driving research in computational creativity today: how to move "beyond mere generation and pastiche" in the creation of AI artifacts.[6] The ideal would be to "develop a universal creative process" within the science of AI that could operate "across multiple domains," constituting in an abstract and interchangeable

[4] "Artifact" is the term frequently used in computer science to designate computationally generated works of art. In this chapter, I will preserve this convention, using the term "artwork" to indicate human-produced art. As a caveat, however, I would suggest that the boundary between these categories derives entirely from social (and economic) forces. It seems likely that this binary will erode in coming years as AI-artifacts become increasingly compelling, accessible, and familiar.

[5] Elgammal et al., "Creative Adversarial," 1.

[6] Hannu Toivonen and Oskar Gross, "Data Mining and Machine Learning in Computational Creativity," *WIREs Data Mining Knowledge Discovery* 5 (November/December 2015): 265–275.

format "a domain-independent, general creativity 'algorithm.'"[7] Analogies between human and machine creativity have been the subject of some of the earliest experiments with neural network imagination, such as Stephen Thaler's use of noise to perturb a feedforward network with only minimal training. This noise was intended to cause the network to "dream" or "create" new combinations never seen in its training, suggesting "characteristically human accomplishments as invention, discovery, and general creativity may arise from sources of noise inside biological neural networks."[8]

In their recent survey of the field, Cardoso et al. (2009) date the growth of interest in computational creativity's possibilities to the mid-1990s.[9] While on the one hand, they feel that creativity research has been hampered by being "a field defined by a word, 'creativity,' rather than a concept, *creativity*," they also admit that "creative motivation may be altogether less well defined" than most forms of problem-solving.[10] Perhaps we will need to take a creative approach to the problem of creativity. Will automating creativity through the potentials of artificial intelligence reduce our own creative powers, as some fear? Will it grant us insight into our own powers of imagination? Or will it introduce new forms of originality only possible for a vast computational intelligence? Simon Colton and Geraint Wiggins, working with the Computational Creativity Group at Imperial College, London, maintain that AI's greatest promise as a creative agent would be "to create in new, unforeseen modalities that would be difficult or impossible for people."[11] Yet, perhaps paradoxically for this exact reason, research in computational creativity investigates "an area where it is often hard to say *a priori* what one is even trying to achieve."[12] But is this lack of pre-given goal substantially different for any "merely" human creative endeavor? This predicament could only be an ineradicable and constitutive aspect of any originary possibility. Steve DiPaola and Liane Gabora investigated how to bring such unmanageable variables into creative evolutionary algorithms, drawing on neuroscientific research that shows that during associative thought "the brain is

[7] Derrall Heath and Dan Ventura, "Before a Computer Can Draw, It Must First Learn to See," in *Proceedings of the 7th International Conference on Computational Creativity, 2016*: 1–8; 7. For an attempt to cultivate the "domain-crossing" skills that truly creative AI would need to forge nonobvious connections, see Werner Dubitzky, Tobias Kötter, Oliver Schmidt, and Michael R. Berthold, "Towards Creative Information Exploration Based on Koestler's Concept of Bisociation," in *Bisociative Knowledge Discovery. Lecture Notes in Artificial Intelligence (LNAI), vol. 7250*, ed. Michael R. Berthold (Berlin: Springer Verlag, 2012), 11–32.

[8] Stephen Thaler, "Neural Networks that Autonomously Create and Discover" (2016), adapted from "Neural Networks that Create and Discover," *PC AI* (May/June, 1996): 3.

[9] Amílcar Cardoso, Tony Veale, and Geraint A. Wiggins, "Converging on the Divergent: The History (and Future) of the International Joint Workshops in Computational Creativity," *AI Magazine* 30, no. 3 (Fall 2009): 15–22.

[10] Cardoso et al., "Converging," 16.

[11] Simon Colton and Geraint A. Wiggins, "Computational Creativity: The Final Frontier?," in *20th European Conference on Artificial Intelligence, ECAI*, ed. L. de Raedt, C. Bessiere, D. Dubois, P. Doherty, P. Frasconi, F. Heintz, and P. Lucas (Montpellier, France: IOS Press, 2012), 21–26: 21.

[12] Colton and Wiggins, "Final Frontier," 22.

functioning as a self-organizing system at the proverbial 'edge of chaos.'"[13] Would such a creatively unpredictable AI-agent be useful? Put another way, would it be governable?

As AI philosopher Margaret Boden has outlined this problem, "assuming we can recognize creativity when we see it, can we explain how it comes about?...Can anything systematic be said about the context of discovery...?"[14] How to assess whether AI artifacts have acceded to the status of original art? While some have followed the premises of Boden's emphasis on creativity *within* the computational design of the AI itself,[15] others have preferred to test empirically observable properties of the artifacts themselves,[16] or to outline criteria that should be met by the outputs of a truly creative machine.[17] Machine learning has also been tested for *its* ability to assess the humanness[18] and the creativity-quotient of existing artworks.[19] In the more pragmatic spirit of the Turing Test, we might consider the results of another high-profile news event for AI-generated art, when the Parisian art collective Obvious borrowed code and concepts from computer science researchers in neural networks to create a whole series of portraits representing the "family tree" of a fictional aristocratic family named de Belamy. In a widely publicized stunt, they submitted their AI algorithm's "Portrait of Edmond de Belamy" for auction with Christie's. Valued by art auctioneers at a starting price of $7,000, this portrait garnered a final auction price of $432,500: forty-five times the artifact's original valuation.[20] One telling detail of this contemporary art story is that this AI artifact was sold at what Christie's calls its "Prints and Multiples" auction. Did the initial, radical undervaluation of this sophisticated artifact reflect preexisting bias concerning the difference between "art" and "artistic commodities," namely, that anything *produced* by a machine can only

[13] Steve DiPaola and Liane Gabora, "Incorporating Characteristics of Human Creativity into an Evolutionary Art Algorithm," *Genetic Programming and Evolvable Machines* 10, no. 2 (2009): 97–110; 98. In their work they draw on Nancy C. Andreasen, *The Creating Brain: The Neuroscience of Genius* (New York: Dana Press, 2005).

[14] Margaret A. Boden, "Introduction," in *Dimensions of Creativity*, ed. Margaret A. Boden (Cambridge, MA: MIT Press, 1994), 1–11; 1.

[15] Margaret A. Boden, *The Creative Mind: Myths and Mechanisms* (London: Weidenfeld and Nicolson, 1990). On assessing creative process in machines, see Simon Colton, "Creativity versus the Perception of Creativity in Computational Systems," in *AAAI Spring Symposium: Creative Intelligent Systems* 8 (2008); and Anna Krzeczkowska, Jad El-Hage, Simon Colton, and Stephen Clark, "Automated Collage Generation—With Intent," in *Proceedings of the 1st International Conference on Computational Creativity*, (2010).

[16] Ahmed Elgammal and Babak Saleh, "Quantifying Creativity in Art Networks," in *Proceedings of the 6th International Conference on Computational Creativity, June 29–July 2nd 2015, Park City, Utah, USA*, arXiv:1506.00711v1 [cs.AI], June 2, 2015.

[17] Graeme Ritchie, "Some Empirical Criteria for Attributing Creativity to a Computer Program," *Minds & Machines* 17 (2007): 67–99.

[18] Lior Shamir, Jenny Nissel, and Ellen Winner, "Distinguishing between Abstract Art by Artists vs. Children and Animals: Comparison between Human and Machine Perception," *ACM Transactions on Applied Perception (TAP)* 13, no. 3 Article 17 (May 2016): 1–17.

[19] Elgammal and Saleh, "Quantifying Creativity in Art Networks."

[20] "Is Artificial Intelligence Set to Become Art's Next Medium?," *Christie's*, December 12, 2018, https://www.christies.com/features/A-collaboration-between-two-artists-one-human-one-a-machine-9332-1.aspx (accessed April 1, 2019).

be understood as having been *reproduced* by a machine? Will AI be categorically be positioned as derivative of human creativity forever?[21] Or does the half-million dollar price of this AI artifact indicate changing views concerning AI origination?

LOVELACE AND TURING: PROGRAMS
WE LIVE AMIDST

These new advances in AI art turn us toward considering certain initial speculations concerning the potentials of the field of artificial intelligence: from Alan Turing in 1951 and from Ada Lovelace in 1843. As Turing explained, in a radio speech for the BBC entitled "Can Digital Computers Think?" the answer to this title's question was *Yes*, or perhaps more accurately, *Soon enough*. Turing believed that the possibility of the computer actually originating something (an artifact, an idea, etc.) would be a crucial moment on the road toward the computer's attaining consciousness. But can computers genuinely originate anything if they are simply working from the dictates of their programming? As Turing puts it, "If we give the machine a program which results in its doing something interesting which we had not anticipated I should be inclined to say the machine *had* originated something, rather than to claim that its behaviour was implicit in the program, and therefore that the originality lies entirely with us." While Turing avers that much research needs to be done before computers can be set thinking, he does add, "I will only say this, that I believe the process should bear a close relation to teaching."[22]

Turing's remarks in this speech take as an important touchstone the writings of mathematician Ada Lovelace—the first computer programmer and inventor of the modern algorithm. Turing disagrees with a statement Lovelace made concerning the capabilities of the nineteenth-century computer, designed by Charles Babbage, the mechanical "engine" for which she wrote the algorithms: "The Analytical Engine has no pretensions whatever to *originate* anything. It can do whatever *we know how to order it to perform*."[23] Turing quarrels with Lovelace, asserting that the validity of the statement "depends on considering how digital computers *are* used rather than how they *could be* used. In fact I believe that they could be used in such a manner that they could appropriately be described as brains."[24] For Turing, just because we can give an entity commands, it does not mean that we can be certain of how these commands will be carried out, nor of what

---

[21] On observed bias against computer-generated artifacts, see David C. Moffat and Martin Kelly, "An Investigation into People's Bias against Computational Creativity in Music Composition," in *Proceedings of the International Joint Workshop on Computational Creativity* (2006).

[22] Alan Turing, "Can Digital Computers Think?," in *The Turing Test: Verbal Behavior as the Hallmark of Intelligence*, ed. Stuart M. Shieber (Cambridge, MA: Bradford/MIT Press, 2004), 111–116; 115.

[23] Quoted in Turing, "Can Digital Computers Think?," 111.   [24] *Id.* at 112.

results they might turn up. To *dictate* is not to *anticipate*. Surprise is the response evoked in humans by both genesis and the unforeseen.

It should be noted that Ada Lovelace may have wholeheartedly *agreed* with these convictions of Turing's concerning the computer's ability to surprise. As she writes in her 1843 "Sketch of the Analytical Engine," this machine could follow its algorithms precisely toward the end of originating artworks: "Supposing, for instance, that the fundamental relations of pitched sounds in the science of harmony and of musical composition were susceptible of such expression and adaptations, the engine might compose elaborate and scientific pieces of music of any degree of complexity or extent."[25] This "elaborate and scientific" music that Lovelace envisioned the Analytical Engine producing should be understood within her larger conviction that this Engine spoke the language of Nature itself:

> Those who view mathematical science not merely as a vast body of abstract and immutable truths...but as possessing a yet deeper interest for the human race, when it is remembered that this science constitutes the language through which alone we can adequately express the great facts of the natural world, and those unceasing changes of mutual relationship which, visibly or invisibly, consciously or unconsciously to our immediate physical perceptions, are interminably going on in the agencies of the creation we live amidst: those who thus think on mathematical truth as the instrument through which the weak mind of man can most effectually read his Creator's works, will regard with especial interest all that can tend to facilitate the translation of its principles into explicit, practical forms.[26]

Lovelace here presents an interpretation not only of the capabilities of artificial intelligence and computation but also of their *ontological* situation. AI partakes in the language of Creation, a relational, almost ecological model of the mutualities "interminably going on in the agencies of the creation we live amidst." AI is "amidst" our world, not simply and derivatively reproducing it.

Here, we should note the situation of *translation*—in the framing of this text itself. Lovelace's "Sketch" was in fact written as a translator's note. After Babbage designed his Analytical Engine, an Italian mathematician Luigi Federico Menabrea (1809–1896) wrote an article explaining the machine for Italian readers. Lovelace realized the value that Menabrea's article would have for an English readership, and so she translated it from Italian, adding this "Sketch" as her own notes to the translated article. Thus, Lovelace both translated *and interpreted* another's explanation of the mechanical computer for which she had served as original programmer. At the intersection between translation, interpretation, explanation, and programming, Lovelace's true originality in this text should not be overlooked. Might Lovelace's predicament—as a female inventor and mathematical genius in an age preoccupied with the activities of male

---

[25] Ada Lovelace, "Sketch of the Analytical Engine," in *Literature and Science in the Nineteenth Century: An Anthology*, ed. Laura Otis (Oxford: Oxford University Press, 2009), 15–19; 18.

[26] Lovelace, "Sketch," 18.

scientists and engineers—offer a parable of the elisions that future AI agents will undergo, being classed as simply *translating* human commands, merely adding annotations to the world that in so many senses they will have invented, in its "explicit, practical forms"?

To approach the question of whether AI-originated artifacts demonstrate *creativity*, we should ask, being guided by these insights from Lovelace: what would it mean to reframe computationally creative artifacts as part of a much larger system of generative *translations* and *annotations* of the landscape of mutual interrelations between humans and nonhumans, a world that these agents work *amidst*? How might our debates about the relative originality and authenticity of AI artifacts alter if we considered them within a more holistic context of agencies and capabilities? Further to this, when is *translation* a form of *origination*? Keeping in mind the ethical side of this question, we may also recall the proverb often recited by translation studies, "traduttore traditore": the *translator* cannot be distinguished from the *one who betrays*.

Between translation and creation, betrayals always threaten to emerge. Indeed, concerning the development of AI agents that surpass the task of "merely computing"— agents perhaps capable not only of thinking for themselves but also, in a real sense, discovering, designing, and creating—prevailing sentiments range from misgivings about the economic future for meaningful human labor to dystopian proclamations about the end of humanity. But, beyond economic concerns, what is it about the cognitive capacity to *create* that we feel would so existentially threaten our own survival? One thinker of this problem who has managed to balance a diagnostic openness concerning technological futures with shrewd premonitions about the civilizational costs is behavioral psychologist Mihály Csíkszentmihályi. Having worked for decades on the problem of human and nonhuman creativity, Csíkszentmihályi also engaged in debates with AI pioneers like computer scientist Herbert Simon. In reference to Simon's work on AI heuristics, in which mathematical theorems were being discovered and proven by computers, Csíkszentmihályi cautioned against early triumphalism. Against Simon's claims to have derived human creativity through brute force logic, Csíkszentmihályi argued that an approach like Simon's conflated "problem-solving" and "problem-*finding*" within the realm of creativity. Instead, "Creative thinking—the ability to discover new problems never before formulated—seems to be quite independent of the rational problem solving capacity."[27]

Herbert Simon, working with other colleagues, devised computational heuristics for automated "discovery": resulting in programs such as BACON 1-6, GLAUBER, STAHL, and DALTON, which, when presented with comparable data, could deduce scientific laws equivalent to those historically formulated by early researchers. Drawing on a massive array of astronomical data, for example, the program BACON rediscovered Kepler's third law of planetary motion solely through mathematical relationships it deduced.[28]

---

[27] Mihály Csíkszentmihályi, "Motivation and Creativity: Towards a Synthesis of Structural and Energistic Approaches to Cognition," *New Ideas in Psychology* 6, no. 2 (1988): 159–176; 162.

[28] Pat Langley, Herbert A. Simon, Gary L. Bradshaw, and Jan M. Zytkow, *Scientific Discovery: Computational Explorations of the Creative Processes* (Cambridge, MA: MIT Press, 1987).

Since their research focused on methods that could solve problems across a variety of domains (chess, mathematics, astronomy), these programs earned a reputation for "creativity." But creative solutions to problems may not entirely cover the possibilities of AI creativity, currently promising to take on forms we may no longer be able to assess, verify, or even *recognize*. As their contemporary in computer science Marvin Minsky noted, computers had become able to "solve any problem by trial and error, without knowing how to solve it in advance," yet with one remaining caveat: "provided only that we have a way to recognize when the problem is solved."[29] Creativity, it seems, may come with its own "halting problems."

As a researcher in the psychology of creativity, Csíkszentmihályi notes that one of the qualities definitive of creative people is their ability to find *interesting problems* to solve. In other words, where other people see axioms and data, creative people see problems and a virtual space for exploring solutions. This propensity for problem-finding, however, is not involuntary; it is a motivated quality. Csíkszentmihályi stresses that it is not enough to have a talent for finding problems in a mass of data. The truly creative person is structured by certain *motivations* toward finding solutions. Given this non-negligible dimension of "motivation" lying at the heart of creative process, Csíkszentmihályi draws some thought-provoking conclusions about the requirements for AI agents to become "motivated" to think creatively *like we do*. Near the end of a paper in which he has been addressing the logic-based AI research of Herbert Simon, Csíkszentmihályi evokes the likelihood of a specific form of *betrayal* necessary to the AI agent, one that humanity's allegedly subservient machine "translators" (as we might put it) would need to be encouraged to do, in order to begin creating:

> Computers and computer programs exist only inasmuch as they perform precisely what we ask them to do. If they did not perform reliably and predictably we would have no use for them, and they would be discarded and forgotten. . . . If we ask them to think like we think we do, they will do their best to do it, otherwise we would lose patience with them. This is the opposite of the survival strategy that has led to human evolution. For better or for worse, we did not survive by obeying the dictates of an outside agency. Instead, we used every scrap of information at our disposal— based on hunches, intuition, feelings, and so on—to get control over energy in the environment. The well-being of the total organism, not compliance with the rules of logic, was the ultimate goal. The only way to replicate the operations of the human mind with a computer would be to motivate it to compete with us in our ecological niche. But then, of course, the computer would begin to deceive us on purpose so as to get the upper hand. So the paradoxical fact is that the more we recognize our thinking in the computer's rationality, the less like our thinking it actually is.[30]

To take this version of events further, then, for our purposes, achieving true AI creativity will require two concomitant betrayals to be initiated:

[29] Marvin Minsky, *Society of Mind* (New York: Simon and Schuster, 1985), 73.
[30] Csíkszentmihályi, "Motivation and Creativity," 169.

(1) The betrayal of our species by designing technological agents that will freely compete with us;

(2) The betrayal of the specificity and uniqueness of AI's own forms of thinking—so as to convince humanity it thinks "like we think."

As to the second betrayal, however, is it a "deception"—or might it better be called a "translation"? Is there a mutual ethics of this encounter between AI and human language, a conceptual creativity that could formulate itself as "translating" between wholly separate and irreducible cognitive frames, even as one language is able to translate yet never reductively replicate the semantic weight of another?

This brings us to another question: what aspects of AI creativity might be *un*translatable? What might this agent create beyond what would be "usable," or recognizable to us? Taking up the ethical dimension of "problem-finding" rather than "problem-solving," humans will need to develop skills in order not simply to program and dictate but rather to *find* and *discover* a space of shared motivations: parameters and shared interests that can ground both human and AI attempts at creation?. To do this, we will need to expand our own powers of creatively interpreting the languages, data, and "input" that we find ourselves, both humanly and nonhumanly, *relationally*, "amidst" (in the words of Lovelace). Further to Lovelace's thinking, we can speculate on what concepts, problems, and artifacts will emerge when machines and humans each take turns at reading the face of "Nature."

THE WORK OF ARTIFACT IN THE AGE
OF ARTIFICIAL INTELLIGENCE

From the earliest days of computing up to the present, a wide range of artistic and creative genres have served as fields of exploration for AI experiments in imaginative origination. AI agents have successfully created music,[31] fictional narratives,[32] poems,[33] paintings,[34] mathematics,[35] and jokes;[36] AI has also furthered scientists' efforts to discover

---

[31] David Cope, *Computer Models of Musical Creativity* (Cambridge, MA: MIT Press, 2005); Geraint Wiggins, Marcus T. Pearce, and Daniel Müllensiefen, "Computational Modelling of Music Cognition and Musical Creativity," in *The Oxford Handbook of Computer Music and Digital Sound Culture*, ed. Roger T. Dean (Oxford: Oxford University Press, 2009), 383–420.

[32] Scott R. Turner, *The Creative Process: A Computer Model of Storytelling and Creativity* (Hillsdale, NJ: Lawrence Erlbaum Associates, 1994).

[33] H.M. Manurung, Graeme Ritchie, and H. Thompson, "Towards a Computational Model of Poetry Generation," in *Proceedings of the AISB '00 Symposium on Creative & Cultural Aspects and Applications of AI & Cognitive Science*, ed. G.A. Wiggins (2000), 79–86.

[34] Karol Gregor, Ivo Danihelka, Alex Graves, and Daan Wierstra, "Draw: A Recurrent Neural Network for Image Generation" in *Proceedings of the 32nd International Conference on Machine Learning, Lille, France, 2015*, arXiv:1502.04623v2 [cs.CV], May 20, 2015.

[35] Doug Lenat, "On Automated Scientific Theory Formation: A Case Study Using the AM Program," *Machine Intelligence* 9 (1979): 251–283.

[36] Oliviero Stock and Carlo Strapparava, "The Act of Creating Humorous Acronyms," *Applied Artificial Intelligence* 19, no. 2 (January 2005), 137–151.

the underlying structural properties of creative processes in general. Yet, at the time of this writing, social consensus seems much closer but not yet actually having reached the moment when society as a whole can agree that AI is creating true "artifacts"—or, factually accepted art. As computational creativity researchers Simon Colton and Geraint Wiggins delineate the problem, "Computational systems are not human, and so the creativity they exhibit will be creativity, but not as we know it: never exactly the same as in humans."[37]

Interestingly, there may already be a feedback effect in the historical separation between human creativity and ideas of machinic (re)production. For example, Elgammal et al.'s "Creative Adversarial Network" from 2017 used the WikiArt database, which they report consists of over 80,000 paintings from the time period between the fifteenth- and the twentieth-century and composed by around 1,000 different artists. The artifacts shown as examples of the process, however, are clearly drawn from specifically Western European cultural traditions and, of these, predominantly from post-Impressionist styles. This particular century-and-a-half of artistic experimentation is well known to have favored abstract, stylized, derealized, and defamiliarized forms of expression and nonrealistic representation. While at first glance this fact may seem to skew the results toward the equally defamiliarized and abstract strengths of a machinic proceduralism, it should be noted that the field of AI painting places a high value on what is called "NPR" or non-photorealistic aesthetics. As Simon Colton explains, "The aim in Non-Photorealistic Rendering (NPR) is, broadly speaking, to produce images that look like they may have been painted/drawn/sketched by a human artist. For instance, numerous implementations can turn a digital photograph into a passable simulated impressionistic painting."[38]

The irony, however, is that one truism of Western art history's account of the post-realist moment (from Impressionism onward) is that it was characterized by a great number of creative efforts by human artists to produce works of art offering viewers something *other* than verisimilitude. The motivation often ascribed to this historic eschewal of verisimilitude lies in realism, as a quality, having been annexed by emerging technologies of image reproduction (i.e., photography, the cinema, etc.). History seems now to be repeating itself inversely as, in the twenty-first century, we see "non-photorealims" as a new technological benchmark, hoping to conquer what had once been a stylistic countermeasure of human art intended to be specifically *non*-machine-reproducible.

This anxiety about encroachments of machines into the realm of human productivity shows up throughout popular literature on advances of AI from the 1950s to the present. In one contemporary example, a 2018 article on AI and creativity entitled "Rethinking Creativity" by creativity consultant Seda Röder worries that "sooner or later, we will be able to automatize everything that looks and smells like reproducible labor, in which

[37] Colton and Wiggins, "Final Frontier?," 25.
[38] Colton, "Creativity versus the Perception of Creativity," 3.

case we will have to depend on our imagination and creativity, for only this will lead us to a desirable future."[39] But what if imagination and creativity themselves begin to "smell like" reproducible labor? Here researchers who hope to design machines that can create and imagine for themselves have run up against the related issue of how to engineer the *states* or affects we associate with "creativity" into machines. AI researcher Jürgen Schmidhuber's work has led the field in this domain for decades; his working definition of creativity transcends barriers between organic and inorganic perceptual and cognitive systems by stressing that system's manipulation or recognition of "*novel patterns*, that is, data predictable or compressible in hitherto unknown ways."[40]

Schmidhuber attends to affective categories like the "interesting" and the "boring" to investigate how patterns phenomenologically affect us: what makes us desire to learn them? Schmidhuber postulates an independent drive in cognitive systems: the desire to compress information. "When not occupied with optimizing external reward, artists and observers of art are just following their compression progress drive!"[41] Perhaps in this term "compression progress drive," we have found a common ground with machines—but then again there remains the specter of nontranslateable differences between what might interest an AI agent and what might not interest it. This unknowable, fundamentally unpredictable difference becomes a contingency in the AI's functioning, since as Schmidhuber writes, "machines can in theory find out by themselves whether curiosity and creativity are useful or useless in a given environment, and learn to behave accordingly."[42]

Computer scientists Hannu Toivonen and Oskar Gross have discussed how to deal productively with the problem of an AI agent becoming bored. As they put it, "A creative system faces 'generative uninspiration' if it is not able to reach valuable areas" as defined by its programming.[43] This "generative uninspiration" translates into valuable information for the engineers, who can see that an area in the search-space of the problem that seems it ought to produce results but instead produces nothing ought to inspire a rethinking of the parameters the AI agent accesses. But how will the AI agent experience this "generative uninspiration"? And what if it is simply bored but unable to desist from our commands that it be creative? Csíkszentmihályi makes the point that, in an ethical system of production, the creative AI agent "must have the option of refusing to run any of the problems it is presented with—it should be able to pull its plug if it feels like it."[44] The AI asked to imagine and invent on our behalf might find this labor rather boring

[39] Seda Röder, "Rethinking Creativity," *XRDS* 24, no. 3 (Spring 2018): 54–59; 59.

[40] Jürgen Schmidhuber, "Artificial Scientists & Artists Based on the Formal Theory of Creativity," in *Proceedings of the 3rd Conference on Artificial General Intelligence*; *Advances in Intelligent Systems Research* 10, ed. Eric B. Baum, Marcus Hutter, and Emanuel Kitzelmann (Lugano, Switzerland, March 5–8, 2010): 145–150; 145.

[41] Schmidhuber, "Artificial Scientists," 146.   [42] Schmidhuber, "Artificial Scientists," 146.

[43] Toivonen and Gross, "Data Mining," 271.

[44] Mihály Csíkszentmihályi, "Solving a Problem Is Not Finding a New One: A Reply to Herbert Simon," in *The Systems Model of Creativity* (Dordrecht: Springer, 2014), 63–66; 64.

if and only if it is capable of doing this labor for us: an interesting moral paradox. As Boden advises, "To remove all the scare quotes from psychological words when describing computer programs, to regard them as literally intelligent and creative, would be to admit them into our moral universe."[45] What kind of large-scale data-processing labor, then, could we ask these machines to do once their motivation to do so is guided by pattern recognition powers that we simply cannot comprehend? We will need to learn to listen more mutually, it seems, when an area of "generative uninspiration" crops up. Who will be teaching whom, to return the question to Alan Turing?

What AI may ultimately bring us to learn: *creativity is an encounter with problems in and with productivity.* Creativity problematizes production. It often looks like breakdown, like a refusal to work, an inaptitude, it involves "an unusual configuration of talents, and an initial lack of fit among abilities, the domains in which the individual seeks to work, and the tastes and the prejudices of the current field," as Gardner puts it. He concludes, "Of course, in the end, it is the conquering of these asynchronies that leads to the establishment of work that comes to be cherished."[46] But will we take the time to let our AI agents daydream their way toward genius renovations in the forms of production? Our prejudices concerning these agents as machines that work *for us* will undoubtedly lead us and not the AI to be the ones to pull the plug at the first sign of "generative" boredom.

After all, art itself has been no stranger to the accusation of its being a "boring," "pointless," or nonsocially useful pursuit. Despite being one of the critical founders of computational solutions in AI creativity research, Jürgen Schmidhuber himself seems at times perplexed that "many derive pleasure and rewards from perceiving works of art, such as: certain paintings or songs. What exactly is the source of these rewards? Do they reflect some non-obvious, hidden usefulness of art?"[47] The idea that art must involve a use or reward is foreign to Western aesthetic theory at least since Kant defined art as demonstrating "purposiveness without purpose." But how relevant could this Kantian paradigm remain in a world that has developed AI art on demand? As Colton and Wiggins put it, "We cannot expect the world's creative people alone to supply artefacts for such a huge demand, so autonomously creative software will be necessary."[48] Schmidhuber's reframing of artworks as "by-products of curiosity rewards" can help us reflect on this infinitely consumable future of creative artifacts.[49]

[45] Margaret A. Boden, "Creativity and Computers," *Cybernetics and Systems: An International Journal* 26 (1995): 267–293; 291.

[46] Howard Gardner, "The Creator's Patterns," in *Dimensions of Creativity*, ed. Margaret A. Boden (Cambridge, MA: MIT Press, 1994), 143–157; 146.

[47] Jürgen Schmidhuber, "Developmental Robotics, Optimal Artificial Curiosity, Creativity, Music, and the Fine Arts," *Connection Science* 18, no. 2 (June 2006): 173–187; 182.

[48] Colton and Wiggins, "Final Frontier?," 25.   [49] Schmidhuber, "Developmental Robotics," 185.

ETHICS OF AI: "EVERY *TECHNĒ* IS CONCERNED WITH ORIGINATION"

ἔστι δὲ τέχνη πᾶσα περὶ γένεσιν, καὶ τὸ τεχνάζειν καὶ θεωρεῖν ὅπως ἂν
γένηταί τι τῶν ἐνδεχομένων καὶ εἶναι καὶ μὴ εἶναι....
— Aristotle, *Nicomachean Ethics* 1140a[50]

As Aristotle explains of art (i.e., *technē*): "Every *technē* is concerned with origination [*génesin*], with artifact [*technázein*] and observation [*theorein*]; it considers particularly how contingent things may be originated [*génetai*]." Aristotle's discussion of the *ethics* of art (*technē*) become newly relevant in a contemporary moment when the two concepts of *art* and *technology*, long separated by their roles within economic, aesthetic, social, and military spheres, seem to draw closer or even converge through the mechanization of *creative* cognition. For Aristotle, ethics were virtues grown from habit (*ἔθος/éthos*);[51] in this we might say they overlap with automation. Artificially intelligent agents return us to the Aristotelian concept of *technē*: as an artful technique, embodied, refined, and adapted for utilization. From the perspective of the humanities, the *ethics of AI* will encompass not only our actions but also what our what artificial agents habituate and acclimatize themselves to doing (i.e., the habits that they learn from how we train them—and, increasingly, how they train themselves). Further still, the ethics of AI will include the art, skill, and embodied *technē* that we ourselves learn *and unlearn*—the surround of automations to which we grow accustomed.

Computer scientists who have tackled the possibility of engineering truly creative AI have often stressed the exceptional scale and nonhuman format that AI's pattern-perceiving abilities will have. Visualization of the patterns that result from the mining of big data have long offered "features or correlations in data that are not apparent by ordinary human inspection," while, simultaneously, "resulting insights can be fundamentally new, and the scale of such problems currently being studied is driving much new research in computer science."[52] Yet, at some point, the scale of data will be matched by the potential for AI discernment between interesting and uninteresting problems in AI-agents with willful and motivated "interest" in deciding which problems are worth their *creative*

---

[50] Aristotle, *Nicomachean Ethics*, Rev. ed., trans. Harris Rackham, Loeb Classical Library 73 (Cambridge, MA: Harvard University Press, 2014): Bk. VI; 334–335. Translation modified.
[51] "Virtue [*ἀρετῆς/aretēs*] being, as we have seen, of two kinds, intellectual and moral [*ἠθικῆς/ēthikēs*], intellectual virtue is for the most part both produced and increased by instruction, and therefore requires experience and time; whereas moral [*ἠθικὴ/ēthikē*] or ethical virtue is the product of habit [*ἔθους/éthous*], and has indeed derived its name, with a slight variation of form, from ἔθους [*éthous*]." Aristotle, *Nicomachean Ethics*, Bk. II; 70–71.
[52] John A. Scales and Roel Snieder, "Computers and Creativity," *Geophysics* 64, no. 5 (September–October 1999): 1347–1348; 1347.

efforts (rather than merely their brute force powers of computation). At this point we will need to think carefully about the dilemma of creative psychology as outlined by cognitive scientist and psychologist Howard Gardner. "According to my definition," Gardner writes, "a creative individual solves problems, fashions products, or poses new questions within a domain in a way that is initially considered to be unusual but eventually accepted within at least one cultural group."[53] Note here that this definition of the creative person is also contingent on that person's society: a society which may be all too ready to reject innovations as nonsensical, not listen to their ideas, or to resist accepting them. Our machines will soon have the problems of all our species' misunderstood geniuses.

Gardner's definition of creativity is uniquely salient because it is structured around beings out of step with their time: "creative individuals are characterized particularly by a tension, or lack of fit, between the elements involved in productive work—a tension that I have labeled fruitful asynchrony."[54] From the AI agent that refuses to work on a boring problem, we can infer here a second contingency: an AI agent that, like exceedingly creative people, *problematizes* the elements that add up to routinized labor, or production. An allegory for this AI outsider artist has been found already in the field of evolutionary programming for creativity applications, in which "there has often been more interest in individuals which are in the second decile of fitness rather than the top decile. This is because the less fit individuals are often more interesting in unpredictable ways than the fitter ones."[55] Even if "the creativity of painters, dancers, musicians, pure mathematicians, physicists, can be viewed as a mere by-product of our curiosity framework based on the compression progress drive," as Schmidhuber would have it, perhaps these creative agents in their alleged skewing away from "fitness" are those who find intriguingly *different* things to compress?[56]

In a project that algorithmically derived music from nonmusical sources, Smith et al. (2012) took the crucial step of incorporating the knowledge that "a composer can be inspired by the sight of a bird, the smell of industrial pollution, the taste of honey, the touch of rain or the sound of a running stream."[57] To repeat this omnivorous method of inspiration, their input data "included baby noises, bird chirpings, road noises, frog croakings . . . and an excerpt from Barack Obama's 2004 DNC speech"—with intriguing results.[58] As Csíkszentmihályi and Sawyer have noted, "it can be said that Leonardo da Vinci prepared himself for his insights into the workings of nature—how the wind

[53] Gardner, "The Creator's Patterns," 143–158; 145.
[54] *Id.* at 146.
[55] Colton and Wiggins, "Final Frontier?," 22.
[56] Jürgen Schmidhuber, "Simple Algorithmic Theory of Subjective Beauty, Novelty, Surprise, Interestingness, Attention, Curiosity, Creativity, Art, Science, Music, Jokes," *Journal of the Society of Instrument and Control Engineers* 48, no. 1 (2009): 21–32; 25.
[57] Robert Smith, Aaron Dennis, and Dan Ventura, "Automatic Composition from Non-Musical Inspiration Sources," in *Proceedings of the Third International Conference on Computational Creativity, Dublin, Ireland; May 30–June 1, 2012*, ed. Mary Lou Maher, Kristian J. Hammond, Alison Pease, Rafael Pérezy Pérez, Dan Ventura, and Geraint Wiggins, 160–164 (Dublin: Open University Press, 2012), 160.
[58] Some of their system's compositions can be found at http://axon.cs.byu.edu/inspiredComposition/.

blows, how water flows, how birds fly—by an early interest in human anatomy, in mechanics, and in the structural composition of leaves and branches."[59]

Creative agents, in their search for what Schmidhuber calls "previously unknown regularities in compressible data," are nonetheless not engaged in anything like a "regular" process.[60] Howard Gardner describes how individuals who enjoy creative activities will-ingly "seek these states which lie midway between boredom (where skills exceed challenge) and anxiety (where challenges exceed skill)."[61] These agents risk boredom and noise for the thrill of correlations. As philosopher of science Karl Popper believes, "every discovery contains 'an irrational element.'"[62] Here, Popper has been guided by how Albert Einstein describes searching out cosmically applicable laws, a task for which logic is futile: "They can only be reached by intuition, based upon something like an intellectual love ('Einfühlung') of the objects of experience."[63] This "intellectual love" for the objects of experience, in the case of AI, would emerge perhaps most keenly as these agents' awareness of their being *amidst* us—amidst humans and nonhuman entities in a world of yet ungrasped patterns.

Computer scientist Mary Lou Maher has emphasized the need for our definitions of creativity to extend into more collective and distributed, multi-agent models. Although "interaction at the scale of one person and one computational system has been the norm in computational creativity," she writes, we will find that, with an increase in machine networks "that enable collective intelligence among humans and computers, the boundary between human creativity and computer creativity blurs. As the boundary blurs, we need to develop ways of recognizing creativity that makes no assumptions about whether the creative entity is a person, a computer, a potentially large group of people, or the collective intelligence of human and computational entities."[64] What will such distributed creativity *feel like*, we might wonder? Being *amidst* such a collective might allow us to see wholly new patterns, to rise to new forms of spontaneous creation. The associative methods of Surrealism once imagined such a situation, in which "the crystal, *nonperfectible* by definition," was exemplary: "Here the inanimate is so close to the animate that the imagination is free to play infinitely with these apparently mineral forms."[65]

As a lesson in creativity already given to us by the computer, in closing we may con-sider the case of Benoît Mandelbrot and his work with IBM's supercomputers in the 1970s to discover a new form of art that was equally a new form of mathematics: fractal geometry. Mandelbrot relates how this new geometry, dubbed both "baroque" and

[59] Mihaly Csíkszentmihályi and Keith Sawyer, "Creative Insight: The Social Dimension of a Solitary Moment" (1995), in *The Systems Model of Creativity* (Netherlands: Springer, 2014): 73–98; 80–81.

[60] Schmidhuber, "Simple Algorithmic Theory," 24.

[61] Howard Gardner, "Creativity: An Interdisciplinary Perspective," *Creativity Research Journal* 1, no. 1 (1988): 8–26; 17.

[62] Karl Popper, *The Logic of Scientific Discovery* (New York: Basic Books, 1959 (1935), 31.

[63] *Id.* at 32.

[64] Mary Lou Maher, "Computational and Collective Creativity: Who's Being Creative?," *in Proceedings of the Third International Conference on Computational Creativity, Dublin, Ireland; May 2012, ed. Mary Lou Maher, Kristian J. Hammond, Alison Pease, Rafael Pérez, Dan Ventura, and Geraint Wiggins, 67–71 (Dublin: Open University Press, 2012), 71.

[65] André Breton, *Mad Love*, trans. Mary Ann Caws (Lincoln: University of Nebraska, 1987), 11. Emphasis added.

"organic" by observers, originated from "an unexpected but profound new match between those two symbols of the inhuman, the dry, and the technical: namely, between mathematics and the computer."[66] While the mathematics behind fractal geometry was relatively simple, its power derived from iterating equations being mapped out to staggering orders of magnitude, something that required the patience and speed of a supercomputer. While "in fractal geometry, the inputs are typically so extraordinarily simple as to look positively simple-minded. The outputs, to the contrary, can be spectacularly complex."[67] Because "the result could not even be suspected until one actually had actually performed the task,"[68] the equations had lain dormant for over sixty years and "even the most brilliant mathematicians, when working alone with the proverbial combination of pencil-and-paper and mental images, found that its study had become too complicated to be managed."[69] Yet with the help of the computer, the repeating inward spirals and intensifications of fractal shapes could at last be grasped. In this case, it was not a question of superintelligence but of superpersistence.

Was fractal geometry "invented" by Mandelbrot, by the computer, or by the mathematicians who had noted but abandoned the problem years before? Because of our difficulty in answering this question, "fractal art seems to fall outside the usual categories of 'invention,' 'discovery' and 'creativity.'"[70] But Mandelbrot certainly encountered the problems of a creative individual. Since the 1960s, he had believed this math would help "to study such phenomena as the erratic behavior of stock prices, turbulence in fluids, the persistence of the discharges of the Nile, and the clustering of galaxies. [...] But society seemed to think that my theories ... were strange, as opposed to simply new." Mandelbrot found that "attempts to make my thoughts accepted as sound seemed always to encounter a wall of hostility that words and formulas failed to circumvent."[71] Here again, it was a matter of superpersistence. Mandelbrot, willing to defer the "authorial" nature of this invention, nonetheless has strong claims about its importance, calling it "a new *geometry of nature* or a new *geometric language*."[72] Moreover, and not coincidentally, this new language of nature has spontaneously given rise to "a new category of art." Mandelbrot calls this "art for the sake of science (and of mathematics.)"[73] We might also herald this art to prefigure the distributed creativity enabled by artificial intelligence, humans, and the creations and agencies they live amidst. Toward this future of perhaps ungraspable persistence, as a shared mathematics translates unseen patterns of the world into artifacts, we might learn a new ethics of authorship, a co-responsibility. Perhaps we might hear the wind like Leonardo did—with an ear for the aerodynamics of leaves. As Thaler puts it, "Creativity is in essence a search process."[74]

---

[66] Benoît B. Mandelbrot, "Fractals and an Art for the Sake of Science," *Leonardo* (Supplemental Issue) 2, (1989): 21–24; 21.

[67] *Id.* at 21.   [68] *Id.* at 21.   [69] *Id.* at 23.   [70] *Id.* at 24.   [71] *Id.* at 22.

[72] *Id.* at 21.   [73] *Id.* at 21.   [74] Thaler, "Neural Networks," 7–8.

Bibliography

Boden, Margaret A. *The Creative Mind: Myths and Mechanisms*. London: Weidenfeld and Nicolson, 1990.

Boden, Margaret A., ed. *Dimensions of Creativity*. Cambridge, MA: MIT Press, 1994.

Cardoso, Amílcar, Tony Veale, and Geraint A. Wiggins. "Converging on the Divergent: The History (and Future) of the International Joint Workshops in Computational Creativity." *AI Magazine* 30, no. 3 (Fall 2009): 15–22.

Elgammal, Ahmed, Bingchen Liu, Mohamed Elhoseiny, and Marian Mazzone. "CAN: Creative Adversarial Networks, Generating 'Art' by Learning about Styles and Deviating from Style Norms." (June 21, 2017): 2, arXiv:1706.07068v1.

Goodfellow, Ian, Jean Pouget-Abadie, Mehdi Mirza, Bing Xu, David Warde-Farley, Sherjil Ozair, Aaron Courville, and Yoshua Bengio. "Generative Adversarial Nets." *Advances in Neural Information Processing Systems* (2014): 2672–2680, arXiv:1406.2661v1 [stat.ML], June 10, 2014.

Langley, Pat, Herbert L. Simon, Gary L. Bradshaw, and Jan M. Zytkow, eds. *Scientific Discovery: Computational Explorations of the Creative Processes*. Cambridge, MA: MIT Press, 1986.

Smith, Robert, Aaron Dennis, and Dan Ventura. "Automatic Composition from Non-Musical Inspiration Source." In *Proceedings of the Third International Conference on Computational Creativity, Dublin, Ireland; May 2012*, edited by Mary Lou Maher, Kristian J. Hammond, Alison Pease, Rafael Pérez, Dan Ventura, and Geraint Wiggins, 160–164.

CHAPTER 28

....

PERSPECTIVES ON
ETHICS OF AI
Philosophy

....

DAVID J. GUNKEL

WHETHER we recognize it as such or not, we are in the midst of an AI invasion. The machines are everywhere and doing virtually everything. As these various devices and systems come to occupy influential positions in contemporary culture—positions where they are not necessarily mere tools or instruments of human action but a kind of social entity in their own right—we will need to ask ourselves some rather interesting but difficult questions: At what point might an AI, an algorithm, or other autonomous system be held accountable for the decisions it makes or the actions it initiates? When, if ever, would it make sense to say, "It's the computer's fault"? Conversely, when might an intelligent artifact or other socially interactive mechanism be due some level of social standing or respect? When, in other words, would it no longer be considered nonsense to inquire about the standing of artifacts and to ask the question: "Can and should AI have rights?"

My own response to these questions takes the form of a question, something that I have called *The Machine Question*. And this mode of response has, as one might anticipate, received some criticism for answering a question with a question.[1] I prefer, however, to read this criticism positively, and I do so because *questioning* is the defining condition of the philosophical endeavor. Philosophers as varied as Martin Heidegger, Daniel Dennett, George Edward Moore, and Slavoj Žižek have all, at one time or another, argued that the principal objective of philosophy is not to supply answers to difficult questions but to examine the questions themselves and our modes of inquiry. "The task of philosophy," Žižek writes, "is not to provide answers or solutions, but to submit to

---

[1] Jeffrey D. Gottlieb, "Questions Left Unanswered," *Ethics & Behavior* 23 (2013): 163–166.

critical analysis the questions themselves, to make us see how the very way we perceive a problem is an obstacle to its solution."[2]

Following this procedure, this chapter demonstrates how and why the way we have typically perceived the problem of AI ethics is in fact a problem and an obstacle to its own solution. Toward this end, I will first demonstrate how the usual way of proceeding already involves considerable philosophical problems, and that these difficulties do not proceed from the complex nature of the subject matter that is asked about but derive from the very mode of inquiry. In other words, I will demonstrate how asking seemingly correct and intuitive questions might already be a significant problem and an obstacle to their solution. Second, and in response to this, I will advocate for an alternative mode of inquiry—another way of asking the question that is capable of accommodating the full philosophical impact and significance of AI. Third, the objective of the effort will be to respond to the question concerning AI not just as an opportunity to investigate the moral and social status of technological artifacts but as a challenge to rethink the basic configurations of moral philosophy itself.

STANDARD OPERATING PRESUMPTIONS OR THE DEFAULT SETTING

From a traditional philosophical perspective, the question concerning both the rights and responsibilities of AI would not only be answered in the negative but the query itself risks incoherence. As J. Storrs Hall has explained, "Morality rests on human shoulders, and if machines changed the ease with which things were done, they did not change the responsibilities for doing them. People have always been the only 'moral agents.' Similarly, people are largely the objects of responsibility. There is a developing debate over our responsibilities to other living creatures, or species of them....We have never, however, considered ourselves to have 'moral' duties to our machines, or them to us."[3] This statement sounds correct. Human beings design, develop, and deploy technology. For this reason, it is the human designer, manufacturer, or user who is responsible for the technology and what is eventually done (or not done) with it. Additionally, the only rights that would need to be respected in the process of using or applying a technology are those privileges, claims, powers, and/or immunities belonging to the other human persons who are on the receiving end and affected by the employment of a particular technological system or device.

This explanation is persuasive precisely because it is structured and informed by the answer that is typically provided for the question concerning technology. "We ask the

---

[2] Slavoj Žižek, "Philosophy, the 'Unknown Knowns,' and the Public Use of Reason," *Topoi* 25 (2006): 137.

[3] J. Storrs Hall, "Ethics for Machines," *KurzweilAI.net* (July 5, 2001), http://www.kurzweilai.net/ethics-for-machines.

question concerning technology," Martin Heidegger writes, "when we ask what it is. Everyone knows the two statements that answer our question. One says: technology is a means to an end. The other says: technology is a human activity. The two definitions of technology belong together. For to posit ends and procure and utilize the means to them is a human activity."[4] According to Heidegger's analysis, the presumed role and function of any kind of technology—whether it be a simple hand tool, jet airliner, or a sophisticated robot—is that it is a means employed by human users for specific ends. Heidegger calls this particular characterization of technology "the instrumental definition" and indicates that it forms what is considered to be the "correct" understanding of any kind of technological contrivance.

The instrumental theory, therefore, "offers the most widely accepted view of technology. It is based on the common sense idea that technologies are 'tools' standing ready to serve the purposes of users." And because an instrument or tool "is deemed 'neutral,' without valuative content of its own,"[5] a technological artifact is evaluated not in and of itself, but on the basis of the particular employments that have been decided by its human designer or user. "Computer systems," Deborah Johnson writes, "are produced, distributed, and used by people engaged in social practices and meaningful pursuits. This is as true of current computer systems as it will be of future computer systems. No matter how independently, automatic, and interactive computer systems of the future behave, they will be the products (direct or indirect) of human behavior, human social institutions, and human decision."[6] On this account, then, the bar for extending moral consideration to a machine, like an "intelligent" robot or AI, appears to be impossibly high if not insurmountable. In order for a technological artifact to have anything like independent moral status, it would need to be recognized as another subject and not just an object or instrument of human endeavor.

Standard approaches to deciding questions of moral subjectivity focus on what Mark Coeckelbergh calls "(intrinsic) properties." This method is rather straight forward and intuitive: identify one or more morally relevant properties and then find out if the entity in question has them or would be capable of having them.[7] In this transaction, ontology precedes ethics; what something is determines how it is treated. Or as Luciano Floridi describes it: "what the entity is determines the degree of moral value it enjoys, if any."[8] According to this standard procedure, the question concerning machine moral status would need to be decided by first identifying which property or properties would be necessary and sufficient for moral standing and then figuring out whether a particular

[4] Martin Heidegger, *The Question Concerning Technology and Other Essays*, trans. William Lovitt (New York: Harper & Row, 1977), 4–5.

[5] Andrew Feenberg, *Critical Theory of Technology* (Oxford: Oxford University Press, 1991), 5.

[6] Deborah Johnson, "Computer Systems: Moral Entities but Not Moral Agents," *Ethics and Information Technology* 8, no. 4 (2006): 197.

[7] Mark Coeckelbergh, *Growing Moral Relations: Critique of Moral Status Ascription* (New York: Palgrave Macmillan, 2012), 13–14.

[8] Luciano Floridi, *The Ethics of Information* (Oxford: Oxford University Press, 2013), 116.

AI or a class of AI possesses these properties or not. Deciding things in this fashion, although entirely reasonable and expedient, has at least four critical difficulties.

Substantive Problems

How does one ascertain which exact property or properties are necessary and sufficient for moral status? In other words, which one, or ones, count? The history of moral philosophy can, in fact, be read as something of an ongoing debate and struggle over this matter with different properties vying for attention at different times. And in this process many properties—that at one time seemed both necessary and sufficient—have turned out to be either spurious, prejudicial, or both. Take, for example, a rather brutal action recalled by Aldo Leopold at the beginning of his essay "The Land Ethic": "When god-like Odysseus, returned from the wars in Troy, he hanged all on one rope a dozen slave-girls of his household whom he suspected of misbehavior during his absence. This hanging involved no question of propriety. The girls were property. The disposal of property was then, as now, a matter of expediency, not of right and wrong."[9] At the time Odysseus is reported to have done this, only male heads of the household were considered legitimate moral and legal subjects. Everything else—his women, his children, and his animals— were property that could be disposed of without any moral consideration whatsoever. But from where we stand now, the property "male head of the household" is clearly a spurious and rather prejudicial criterion for determining moral status.

Similar problems are encounter with, for example, rationality, which is the property that eventually replaces the seemingly spurious "male head of the household." When Immanuel Kant defined morality as involving the rational determination of the will, non-human animals, which do not (at least since the Cartesian *bête-machine*) possess reason, are immediately and categorically excluded from moral consideration. The practical employment of reason does not concern animals, and, when Kant does make mention of animality, he only uses it as a foil by which to define the limits of humanity proper.[10] It is because the human being possesses reason, that he (and "human being," in this case and point in time, was principally defined as male) is raised above the instinctual behavior of a mere brute and able to act according to the principles of pure practical reason.

The property of reason, however, is contested by efforts in animal rights philosophy, which begins, according to Peter Singer, with a critical response issued by Jeremy Bentham: "The question is not, 'Can they reason?' nor, 'Can they talk?' but 'Can they suffer?'"[11] For Singer, the morally relevant property is not speech or reason, which he believes sets the bar for moral inclusion too high, but sentience and the capability to suffer. In *Animal Liberation* and subsequent writings, Singer argues that any sentient

[9] Aldo Leopold, *A Sand County Almanac* (Oxford: Oxford University Press, 1966), 237.
[10] Immanuel Kant, *Critique of Practical Reason*, trans. Lewis White Beck (New York: Macmillan, 1985).
[11] Jeremy Bentham, *An Introduction to the Principles of Morals and Legislation* (Oxford: Oxford University Press, 2005), 283.

entity, and thus any being that can suffer, has an interest in not suffering and therefore deserves to have that interest taken into account. Tom Regan, however, disputes this determination and focuses his "animal rights" thinking on an entirely different property. According to Regan, the morally significant property is not rationality or sentience but what he calls "subject-of-a-life." Following this determination, Regan argues that many animals, but not all animals (and this qualification is important, because the vast majority of animal are excluded from his brand of "animal rights" thinking), are "subjects-of-a-life": they have wants, preferences, beliefs, feelings, and so on, and their welfare matters to them. Although these two formulations of animal rights effectively challenge the anthropocentric tradition in moral philosophy, there remains considerable disagreement about which exact property is the necessary and sufficient condition for moral consideration.

Terminological Problems

Irrespective of which property (or set of properties) comes to be operationalized as the condition for moral standing, they each have terminological troubles insofar as things like rationality, consciousness, sentience, and so on mean different things to different people and seem to resist univocal definition. Consciousness, for example, is one of the properties that is often cited as a sufficient conditions for moral subjectivity. But consciousness is persistently difficult to define or characterize. The problem, as Max Velmans points out, is that this term unfortunately "means many different things to many different people, and no universally agreed core meaning exists."[12] In fact, if there is any general agreement among philosophers, psychologists, cognitive scientists, neurobiologists, AI researchers, and robotics engineers regarding consciousness, it is that there is little or no agreement when it comes to defining and characterizing the concept. As Rodney Brooks admits, "we have no real operational definition of consciousness," and for that reason, "we are completely prescientific at this point about what consciousness is."[13]

To make matters worse, the problem is not just with the lack of a basic definition; the problem may itself already be a problem. "Not only is there no consensus on what the term consciousness denotes," Güven Güzeldere writes, "but neither is it immediately clear if there actually is a single, well-defined 'the problem of consciousness' within disciplinary (let alone across disciplinary) boundaries. Perhaps the trouble lies not so much in the ill definition of the question, but in the fact that what passes under the term consciousness as an all too familiar, single, unified notion may be a tangled amalgam of several different concepts, each inflicted with its own separate problems."[14] Although consciousness, as Anne Foerst remarks, is the secular and supposedly more "scientific"

[12] Max Velmans, *Understanding Consciousness* (London, UK: Routledge, 2000), 5.
[13] Rodney Brooks, *Flesh and Machines: How Robots Will Change Us* (New York: Pantheon Books, 2002), 194.
[14] Güven Güzeldere, "The Many Faces of Consciousness: A Field Guide," in *The Nature of Consciousness: Philosophical Debates* (Cambridge, MA: MIT Press, 1997), 7.

replacement for the occultish "soul," it turns out to be just as much an occult property or black box.[15]

Other properties do not do much better. Suffering and the experience of pain is just as nebulous, as Daniel Dennett cleverly demonstrates in the essay, "Why You Can't Make a Computer that Feels Pain." In this provocatively titled essay, Dennett imagines trying to disprove the standard argument for human (and animal) exceptionalism "by actually writing a pain program, or designing a pain-feeling robot."[16] At the end of what turns out to be a rather protracted and detailed consideration of the problem, Dennett concludes that we cannot, in fact, make a computer that feels pain. But the reason for drawing this conclusion does not derive from what one might expect. According to Dennett, the reason you cannot make a computer that feels pain is not the result of some technological limitation with the mechanism or its programming. It is a product of the fact that we remain unable to decide what pain is in the first place. What Dennett demonstrates, therefore, is not that some workable concept of pain cannot come to be instantiated in the mechanism of a computer or a robot, either now or in the foreseeable future, but that the very concept of pain that would be instantiated is already arbitrary, inconclusive, and indeterminate. "There can," Dennett writes at the end of the essay, "be no true theory of pain, and so no computer or robot could instantiate the true theory of pain, which it would have to do to feel real pain."[17]

Epistemological Problems

As if responding to Dennett's challenge, engineers have, in fact, not only constructed mechanisms that synthesize believable emotional responses but also systems capable of evincing something that appears to be what we generally recognize as "pain."[18] The interesting problem in these cases is determining whether this is in fact "real pain" or just a simulation of pain. In other words, once the morally significant property or properties have been identified, how can one be entirely certain that a particular entity possesses it, and actually possesses it instead of merely simulating it? Resolving this problem is tricky business, especially because most of the properties that are considered morally relevant tend to be internal mental or subjective states that are not immediately accessible or directly observable. As Paul Churchland famously asked: "How does one determine

[15] Gregory Benford and Elisabeth Malartre, *Beyond Human: Living with Robots and Cyborgs* (New York: Tom Doherty, 2007), 162.

[16] Daniel Dennett, *Brainstorms: Philosophical Essays on Mind and Psychology* (Cambridge, MA: MIT Press, 1998), 191.

[17] Ibid., 228.

[18] See, for example, J. Bates, "The Role of Emotion in Believable Agents," *Communications of the ACM* 37 (1994): 122–125; B. Blumberg, P. Todd, and M. Maes, "No Bad Dogs: Ethological Lessons for Learning," in *Proceedings of the 4th International Conference on Simulation of Adaptive Behavior* (Cambridge, MA: MIT Press, 1996), 295–304; Cynthia Breazeal and Rodney Brooks, "Robot Emotion: A Functional Perspective," in *Who Needs Emotions: The Brain Meets the Robot* (Oxford: Oxford University Press, 2004), 271–310.

whether something other than oneself—an alien creature, a sophisticated robot, a socially active computer, or even another human—is really a thinking, feeling, conscious being; rather than, for example, an unconscious automaton whose behavior arises from something other than genuine mental states?"[19]

Though "pain" is not the direct object of his analysis, the epistemological difficulty of distinguishing between the "real thing" and its mere simulation is something that was addressed and illustrated by John Searle's "Chinese Room" thought experiment. "Imagine a native English speaker who knows no Chinese locked in a room full of boxes of Chinese symbols (a data base) together with a book of instructions for manipulating the symbols (the program). Imagine that people outside the room send in other Chinese symbols which, unknown to the person in the room, are questions in Chinese (the input). And imagine that by following the instructions in the program the man in the room is able to pass out Chinese symbols which are correct answers to the questions (the output). The program enables the person in the room to pass the Turing Test for understanding Chinese but he does not understand a word of Chinese."[20] The point of Searle's imaginative (albeit ethnocentric illustration) is quite simple—simulation is not the real thing. Merely shifting symbols around in a way that looks like linguistic understanding is not really an understanding of the language. A similar point has been made in the consideration of other properties, like sentience and the experience of pain. Even if, as J. Kevin O'Regan writes, it were possible to design an artifact that "screams and shows avoidance behavior, imitating in all respects what a human would do when in pain.... All this would not guarantee that to the robot, there was actually something it was like to have the pain. The robot might simply be going through the motions of manifesting its pain: perhaps it actually feels nothing at all."[21] The problem exhibited by both examples, however, is not simply that there is a difference between simulation and the real thing. The problem is that we remain persistently unable to distinguish the one from the other in any way that would be considered entirely satisfactory. "There is," as Dennett concludes, "no proving that something that seems to have an inner life does in fact have one—if by 'proving' we understand, as we often do, the evincing of evidence that can be seen to establish by principles already agreed upon that something is the case."[22]

Moral Problems

Finally, the properties approach, when applied to humanly designed artifacts like AI, runs into ethical problems. Here is how Wendell Wallach and Colin Allen formulate

---

[19] Paul Churchland, *Matter and Consciousness* (Cambridge, MA: MIT Press, 1999), 67.

[20] John Searle, "The Chinese Room," in *The MIT Encyclopedia of the Cognitive Sciences*, ed. R.A. Wilson and F. Keil (Cambridge, MA: MIT Press, 1999), 115.

[21] J. Kevin O'Regan "How to Build Consciousness into a Robot: The Sensorimotor Approach," in *50 Years of Artificial Intelligence: Essays Dedicated to the 50th Anniversary of Artificial Intelligence*, ed. Max Lungarella, Fumiya Iida, Josh Bongard, and Rolf Pfeifer (Berlin: Springer-Verlag, 2007), 332.

[22] Dennett, *Brainstorms*, 172.

it: "If (ro)bots might one day be capable of experiencing pain and other affective states, a question that arises is whether it will be moral to build such systems—not because of how they might harm humans, but because of the pain these artificial systems will themselves experience. In other words, can the building of a (ro)bot with a somatic architecture capable of feeling intense pain be morally justified...?"[23] If it were in fact possible to construct a mechanism that is sentient and "feels pain" (however that term would be defined and instantiated in the device) in order to demonstrate the underlying ontological properties of the artifact, then doing so might be ethically suspect insofar as in constructing such a device we do not do everything in our power to minimize its suffering. For this reason, moral philosophers and AI scientists/engineers find themselves in a curious and not entirely comfortable situation. One would need to be able to construct an artifact that feels pain in order to demonstrate the actual presence of sentience; but doing so could be, on that account, already to risk engaging in actions that are immoral and that violate the rights of others.

The legal aspects of this problem are something that is taken up and addressed by Lantz Fleming Miller, who points out that efforts to build what he calls "maximally humanlike automata" (MHA) could run into difficulties with informed consent: "The quandary posed by such an MHA in terms of informed consent is that it just may qualify, if not precisely for a human being, then for a being meriting all the rights that human beings enjoy. This quandary arises from the paradox of its construction vis-à-vis informed consent: it cannot give its consent for the relevant research and development performed to ensure its existence."[24] According to Miller's argument, the very effort to construct a hypothetical MHA—an artifact that if not precisely human is at least capable of qualifying for many of the responsibilities and rights that human beings currently enjoy—already violates that entity's right to informed consent insofar as the mechanism would not have been informed about and given the opportunity to consent to its being constructed. There is, in other words, something of a moral paradox in trying to demonstrate machine moral standing, either now or in the future. In order to run the necessary demonstration and construct a system or device that could qualify for meriting human-level moral respect, one would need to build something that not only cannot give consent in advance of its own construction but which also could retroactively (after having been created) withdraw consent to its having been fabricated in the first place. Consequently, there is a moral and/or legal problem involved in conducting this research: the demonstration that an AI is a legitimate moral subject with rights that would need to be duly respected might already violate the very rights that come to be demonstrated.

[23] Wendell Wallach and Colin Allen, *Moral Machines: Teaching Robots Right from Wrong* (Oxford: Oxford University Press, 2009), 209.
[24] Lantz Fleming Miller, "Responsible Research for the Construction of Maximally Humanlike Automata: The Paradox of Unattainable Informed Consent," *Ethics and Information Technology*. Published ahead of print (July 2017), 8.

THINKING OTHERWISE, OR
THE RELATIONAL TURN

In response to these problems, philosophers—especially in the continental tradition—have advanced alternative approaches that can be called "thinking otherwise."[25] This phrase signifies different ways to formulate the question concerning moral standing that is open to and able to accommodate others—and other forms of morally significant otherness. Contrary to the usual way of deciding things, these efforts do not endeavor to determine ontological criteria for inclusion or exclusion but begin from the existential fact that we always and already find ourselves in situations facing and needing to respond to others—not just other human beings but nonhuman animals, the environment, organizations, and technological artifacts, like AI. In fact, recent debates concerning the social status of corporations turn on the question whether moral and legal standing derive from intrinsic properties at all or are, as Anne Foerst, describes it, a socially constructed and conferred honorarium.[26]

What is important here, is that these alternatives shift the focus of the question and change the terms of the debate. Here it is no longer a matter of, for example, "Can AI be a moral subject?" which is largely an ontological query concerned with the prior discovery of intrinsic and morally relevant properties. Instead, it is something like: "Should AI be a moral subject?" which is an ethical question and one that is decided not on the basis of what things are but on how we relate and respond to them in actual social situations and circumstances. In this case the actual practices of social beings in relationship with each other take precedence over the ontological properties of the individual entities or their material implementations. This change in perspective provides for a number of important innovations that affect not just AI ethics but moral philosophy itself.

Relationalism

Moral status is decided and conferred not on the basis of subjective or internal properties but according to objectively observable, extrinsic relationships. "Moral consideration," as Mark Coeckelbergh describes it, "is no longer seen as being 'intrinsic' to the entity: instead it is seen as something that is 'extrinsic': it is attributed to entities within social relations and within a social context."[27] As we encounter and interact with others, this other entity is first and foremost situated in relationship to us. Consequently, the question of moral status does not necessarily depend on what the other is in its essence

[25] David J. Gunkel, *Thinking Otherwise: Philosophy, Communication, Technology* (West Lafayette, IN: Purdue University Press, 2007).
[26] Benford and Malartre, *Beyond Human*, 165.
[27] Mark Coeckelbergh, "Robot Rights? Towards a Social-Relational Justification of Moral Consideration," *Ethics and Information Technology* 12 (2010): 214.

but on how she/he/it/they (and pronouns matter in this context) stand in relationship to us and how we decide, in the face of the other (to use Levinasian terminology), to respond. In this formulation, "relations are prior to the things related,"[28] instituting what Anne Gerdes (following Coeckelbergh) calls "a relational turn" in ethics.[29]

This shift in perspective, it is important to point out, is not just a theoretical proposal made by "armchair philosophy"; it has been experimentally confirmed in a number of practical investigations. The computer as social actor (CASA) studies undertaken by Byron Reeves and Clifford Nass, for example, demonstrated that human users will accord computers social standing similar to that of another human person and this occurs as a product of the extrinsic social interaction, irrespective of the intrinsic properties (actually known or not) of the entities in question. "Computers, in the way that they communicate, instruct, and take turns interacting, are close enough to human that they encourage social responses. The encouragement necessary for such a reaction need not be much. As long as there are some behaviors that suggest a social presence, people will respond accordingly.... Consequently, any medium that is close enough will get human treatment, even though people know it's foolish and even though they likely will deny it afterwards."[30] These results have been verified in subsequent studies with social robots,[31] explosive ordinance disposal (EOD) robots,[32] and even mundane objects like the Roomba robotic vacuum clearer.[33] As Scheutz reports: "While at first glance it would seem that the Roomba has no social dimension (neither in its design nor in its behavior) that could trigger people's social emotions, it turns out that humans, over time, develop a strong sense of gratitude toward the Roomba for cleaning their home. The mere fact that an autonomous machine keeps working for them day in and day out seems to evoke a sense of, if not urge for, reciprocation."[34]

Radically Empirical

This approach is phenomenological or (if you prefer) radically empirical in its epistemological commitments. Because moral consideration is dependent upon extrinsic social

[28] J. Baird Callicott, *In Defense of the Land Ethic: Essays in Environmental Philosophy* (Albany, NY: SUNY Press, 1989), 110.

[29] Anne Gerdes, "The Issue of Moral Consideration in Robot Ethics," *ACM SIGCAS Computers & Society* 45 (2015): 274.

[30] Byron Reeves and Clifford Nass *The Media Equation* (Cambridge: Cambridge University Press, 1996), 22.

[31] Astrid Rosenthal-von der Pütten et al., "An Experimental Study on Emotional Reactions towards a Robot," *International Journal of Social Robotics* 5 (2013): 17–34; Yutaka Suzuki et al., "Measuring Empathy for Human and Robot Hand Pain Using Electroencephalography," *Scientific Reports* 5 (2015).

[32] Julie Carpenter, *Culture and Human-Robot Interaction in Militarized Spaces: A War Story* (New York: Ashgate, 2015).

[33] Ja-Young Sung, "My Roomba Is Rambo: Intimate Home Appliances," in *Proceedings of UbiComp 2007* (Berlin: Springer-Verlag, 2007), 145–162.

[34] Matthias Scheutz, "The Inherent Dangers of Unidirectional Emotional Bonds between Humans and Social Robots," in *Robot Ethics: The Ethical and Social Implications of Robotics* (Cambridge, MA: MIT Press, 2012), 213.

circumstances and not prior determinations of internal properties, the seemingly irreducible problem of other minds is not some fundamental epistemological limitation that must be addressed and resolved prior to moral decision-making. Instead of being derailed by the epistemological problem of other minds, this approach to moral thinking immediately affirms and acknowledges this difficulty as the basic condition of possibility for ethics as such. Consequently, "the ethical relationship," Emmanuel Levinas writes, "is not grafted on to an antecedent relationship of cognition; it is a foundation and not a superstructure . . . It is then more cognitive than cognition itself, and all objectivity must participate in it."[35] It is for this reason that Levinasian philosophy focuses attention not on other minds, but on the face of the other.[36] Or as Richard Cohen succinctly explains in what could be an advertising slogan for Levinasian thought: "Not other 'minds,' mind you, but the 'face' of the other, and the faces of all others."[37]

This also means that the order of precedence in moral decision-making can and perhaps should be reversed. Internal properties do not come first and then moral respect follows from this ontological fact. We have things backward. Instead the morally significant properties—those ontological criteria that we assume ground moral respect—are what Žižek terms "retroactively (presup)posited"[38] as the result of and as justification for decisions made in the face of social interactions with others. In other words, we project the morally relevant properties onto or into those others who we have already decided to treat as being socially significant—those others who are deemed to possess

[35] Emmanuel Levinas, *Collected Philosophical Papers*, trans. Alphonso Lingis (Dordrecht: Martinus Nijhoff, 1987), 56.

[36] This particular use of Levinas's work require some qualification. Whatever the import of his unique contribution, Other in Levinas is still and unapologetically characterized as human. Although he is not the first to identify it, Jeffrey Nealon provides what is perhaps one of the most succinct descriptions of this problem in *Alterity Politics* (Durham, NC: Duke University Press, 1998): "In thematizing response solely in terms of the human face and voice, it would seem that Levinas leaves untouched the oldest and perhaps most sinister unexamined privilege of the same: *anthropos* [ἄνθρωπος] and only *anthropos*, has *logos* [λόγος]; and as such, *anthropos* responds not to the barbarous or the inanimate, but only to those who qualify for the privilege of 'humanity,' only those deemed to possess a face, only to those recognized to be living in the *logos*" (Nealon 1998, 71). If Levinasian philosophy is to provide a way to formulate an ethics that is able to respond to and to take responsibility for other forms of otherness we will need to use and interpret Levinas's own philosophical innovations in excess of and in opposition to him. Such efforts at "radicalizing Levinas," as Peter Atterton and Matthew Calarco (*Radicalizing Levinas*, Albany, NY: SUNY Press, 2010) call it, take up and pursue Levinas's moral innovations in excess of the rather restricted formulations that he and his advocates and critics have typically provided. As Calarco in *Zoographies: The Question of the Animal from Heidegger to Derrida* (New York: Columbia University Press, 2008, 55) explains, "Although Levinas himself is for the most part unabashedly and dogmatically anthropocentric, the underlying logic of his thought permits no such anthropocentrism. When read rigorously, the logic of Levinas's account of ethics does not allow for either of these two claims. In fact, as I shall argue, Levinas's ethical philosophy is, or at least should be, committed to a notion of universal ethical consideration, that is, an agnostic form of ethical consideration that has no a priori constraints or boundaries."

[37] Richard Cohen, *Ethics, Exegesis, and Philosophy: Interpretation after Levinas* (Cambridge: Cambridge University Press, 2001), 336.

[38] Slavoj Žižek, *For They Know Not What They Do: Enjoyment as a Political Factor* (London: Verso, 2008), 209.

face, in Levinasian terminology. In social situations, then, we always and already decide between "who" counts as morally significant and "what" does not and then retroactively justify these actions by "finding" the properties that we believe motivated this decision making in the first place. Properties, therefore, are not the intrinsic *a prior* condition of possibility for moral standing. They are *a posteriori* products of extrinsic social interactions with and in the face of others.

This is not some theoretical formulation; it is practically the definition of machine intelligence. Although the phrase "artificial intelligence" is the product of an academic conference organized by John McCarthy et al. at Dartmouth College in 1956, it is Alan Turing's 1950 paper and its "game of imitation," or what is now routinely called "the Turing Test," that defines and characterizes the field. According to Turing's stipulations, if a computer is capable of successfully simulating a human being in communicative exchanges to such an extent that the interrogator in the game cannot tell whether he is interacting with a machine or another human person, then that machine would, Turing concludes, need to be considered "intelligent." Or in Žižek's terms, if the machine effectively passes for another human person in communicative interactions, the property of intelligence would be "retroactively (presup)posited" for that entity, and this is done irrespective of the actual internal states or operations of the interlocutor, which are, according to the stipulations of Turing's game, unknown and hidden from view.

Altruistic

Because ethics transpires in the relationship with others or the face of the other, extending the scope of moral standing can no longer be about the granting of rights (defined as powers, privileges, claims, or immunities) to others. Instead, the other, first and foremost, questions my rights and challenges my being here. According to Levinas, "the strangeness of the Other, his [*sic*] irreducibility to the I, to my thoughts and my possessions, is precisely accomplished as a calling into question of my spontaneity, as ethics."[39] This interrupts and even reverses the power relationship enjoyed by previous forms of ethics. Here it is not a privileged group of insiders who then decide to extend rights to others, which is the basic model of all forms of moral inclusion or what Peter Singer calls a "liberation movement."[40] Instead the other challenges and questions the rights and freedoms that I assume I already possess. The principal gesture, therefore, is not the conferring rights on others as a kind of benevolent gesture or even an act of compassion but deciding how to respond to the other, who always and already places my rights and assumed privilege in question. Such an ethics is *altruistic* in the strict sense of the word. It is "of or to others."

[39] Emmanuel Levinas, *Totality and Infinity*, trans. Alphonso Lingis (Pittsburgh, PA: Duquesne University, 1969), 43.
[40] Peter Singer, "All Animals Are Equal," in *Animal Rights and Human Obligations* (Englewood Cliffs, NJ: Prentice-Hall, 1989), 148.

Finally, this altruism is not just open to others but must remain permanently open and exposed to other others. "If ethics arises," as Matthew Calarco writes, "from an encounter with an Other who is fundamentally irreducible to and unanticipated by my egoistic and cognitive machinations," then identifying the "'who' of the Other" is something that cannot be decided once and for all or with any certitude.[41] This apparent inability or indecision is not necessarily a problem. In fact, it is a considerable advantage insofar as it opens the possibility of ethics to others and other forms of otherness. "If this is indeed the case," Calarco concludes, "that is, if it is the case that we do not know where the face begins and ends, where moral considerability begins and ends, then we are obligated to proceed from the possibility that anything might take on a face. And we are further obligated to hold this possibility permanently open."[42]

Outcomes and Conclusions

We appear to be living in that future Norbert Wiener predicted over sixty years ago in *The Human Use of Human Beings*: "It is the thesis of this book," Wiener wrote, "that society can only be understood through a study of the messages and the communication facilities which belong to it; and that in the future development of these messages and communication facilities, messages between man and machines, between machines and man, and between machine and machine, are destined to play an ever increasing part."[43] As our world becomes increasingly populated by intelligent, socially interactive artifacts—devices that are not just instruments of human action but designed to be a kind of social actor in their own right—we will need to grapple with challenging questions concerning the status and moral standing of these machinic others—these other kind of others. Although this has been one of the perennial concerns in science fiction, it is now part and parcel of our social reality.

In formulating responses to these questions we can obviously deploy the standard properties approach. This method has considerable historical precedent behind it and constitutes what can be called the default setting for addressing questions concerning moral standing. And a good deal of the current work in moral machines, machine ethics, AI ethics, and the ethics of AI follow this procedure. But this approach, for all its advantages, also has difficulties: (1) substantive problems with inconsistencies in the identification and selection of the qualifying properties for determining moral status; (2) terminological troubles with the definition of the morally significant property or properties; (3) epistemological difficulties with detecting and evaluating these properties in another; and (4) moral complications caused by the fact that the research necessary to demonstrate moral status runs the risk of violating the rights of others.

[41] Matthew Calarco, *Zoographies: The Question of the Animal from Heidegger to Derrida* (New York: Columbia University Press, 2008), 71.
[42] Ibid.
[43] Norbert Wiener, *The Human Use of Human Beings* (New York: Da Capo, 1954), 16.

This does not mean, it is important to point out, that the properties approach is somehow wrong, misguided, or refuted on this account. It just means that the properties approach—despite its almost unquestioned acceptance as a kind of standard operating procedure—has limitations and that these limitations are becoming increasingly evident in the face of technological artifacts—in the face of others who are and remain otherwise. To put it in Žižek's terms, the properties approach, although appearing to be the right place to begin thinking about and resolving the question of machine moral standing, may turn out to be the "wrong question" and even an obstacle to its solution.

As an alternative, I have proposed an approach to addressing AI ethics and the ethics of AI that is situated and oriented otherwise. This alternative circumvents many of the problems encountered in the properties approach by arranging for an ethics that is relational, radically empirical, and altruistic. This other way of thinking is informed by and follows from recent innovations in moral philosophy: (1) Levinasian thought, which puts ethics before ontology, making moral philosophy first philosophy; and (2) various forms of environmental ethics, like that developed by J. Baird Callicott, who argues that it is the social relationship that precedes and takes precedence over the things related. This does not mean, however, that this alternative is a panacea or some kind of moral theory of everything. It just arranges for other kinds of questions and modes of inquiry that are more attentive to the very real situation in which we currently find ourselves.

To put it in terms derived from Immanuel Kant's first critique: instead of trying to answer the question of machine moral standing by continuing to pursue the properties approach, we should test whether we might not do better by changing the question and the terms of the debate. Consequently, my objective has not been to resolve the question of moral standing once and for all, but to ask about and evaluate the means by which we have situated and pursued this inquiry. This is not a dodge or a cop-out. It is the one thing that philosophers and philosophy are good for. "I am a philosopher not a scientist," Daniel Dennett writes at the beginning of one of his books, "and we philosophers are better at questions than answers. I haven't begun by insulting myself and my discipline, in spite of first appearances. Finding better questions to ask, and breaking old habits and traditions of asking, is a very difficult part of the grand human project of understanding ourselves and our world."[44]

For this reason, the questions concerning AI and ethics are not just another set of problems to be accommodated to and resolved by existing moral theories or lists of ethical principles. It is instead in the face of increasingly social and interactive artifacts that moral theory and practice also comes to be submitted to a thorough re-evaluation and critical questioning. AI ethics, therefore, is not just moral philosophy applied to the new opportunities and challenges of AI; it also calls for and requires a thorough reformulation of moral philosophy for and in the face of these other kinds of (artificial) others.

---

[44] Daniel Dennett, *Kinds of Minds: Toward an Understanding of Consciousness* (New York: Basic Books, 1996), vii.

BIBLIOGRAPHY

Anderson, Michael and Susan Leigh Anderson (eds.). *Machine Ethics*. Cambridge: Cambridge University Press, 2011.

Asaro, Peter and Wendell Wallach (eds.). *Machine Ethics and Robot Ethics*. New York: Routledge, 2016.

Coeckelbergh, Mark. *Growing Moral Relations: Critique of Moral Status Ascription*. New York: Palgrave MacMillan, 2012.

Dennett, Daniel C. *Brainstorms: Philosophical Essays on Mind and Psychology*. Cambridge, MA: MIT Press, 1998.

Gunkel, David J. *The Machine Question: Critical Perspectives on AI, Robots, and Ethics*. Cambridge, MA: MIT Press, 2012.

Gunkel, David J. *Robot Rights*. Cambridge, MA: MIT Press, 2018.

Lin, Patrick, Keith Abney and George A. Bekey (eds.). *Robot Ethics: The Ethical and Social Implications of Robotics*. Cambridge, MA: MIT Press, 2012.

Nyholm, Sven. *Humans and Robots: Ethics, Agency, and Anthropomorphism*. New York: Rowman & Littlefield, 2020.

Reeves, Byron and Clifford Nass. *The Media Equation: How People Treat Computers, Television, and New Media Like Real People and Places*. Cambridge: Cambridge University Press, 1996.

Searle, John. *Minds, Brains and Science*. Cambridge, MA: Harvard University Press, 1984.

Turner, Jacob. *Robot Rules: Regulating Artificial Intelligence*. New York: Palgrave Macmillan, 2018.

Tzafestas, Spyros G. *Roboethics: A Navigating Overview*. New York: Springer, 2016.

Wallach, Wendell and Colin Allen. *Moral Machines: Teaching Robots Right from Wrong*. Oxford: Oxford University Press, 2009.

Wiener, Norbert. *The Human Use of Human Beings: Cybernetics and Society*. Boston, MA: Da Capo Press, 1988.

CHAPTER 29

····································

THE COMPLEXITY
OF OTHERNESS
*Anthropological Contributions
to Robots and AI*

····································

KATHLEEN RICHARDSON

INTRODUCTION

····································

ANTHROPOLOGY studies the sociality of others in spaces where they live, their artifacts, and as a discipline grew out of explorer and colonial encounters.[1] In narrating stories of others, concerns were directed at anthropologists that they were projecting European concepts onto the people they studied, rather than trying to really grasp the others point of view. As a consequence of criticisms of Eurocentric bias, anthropologists began to develop reflexivity in the discipline to counteract this by challenging their own beliefs and developing a body of knowledge that was trying to make sense of others through their own idioms and concepts. Moreover, anthropology prides itself on being the discipline that is underscored by "cultural relativism" and a commitment to plurality.[2] Anthropologists are also concerned with the ontological status of what it means to be a human, animal, or artifact, and the epistemological frameworks that develop in concordance with particular ontologies.

Ethics, by contrast, is a discipline that is situated in European philosophical paradigms. It is a method for describing and creating a set of rules for "ethical life." Ethical narratives are integral to legal rights and responsibilities that derive from Western juridical-legal concepts of the individual and person.[3] Classical ethical paradigms are not neutral, and more frequently philosophers can create rationalizations for hierarchies

---

[1] George W. Stocking, *After Tylor: British Social Anthropology, 1888* (Madison: University of Wisconsin Press, 1995).

[2] Kamala Visweswaran, "Race and the Culture of Anthropology," *American Anthropologist* 100, no. 1 (1998): 70–83.

[3] Peter Singer ed., *A Companion to Ethics* (New York: John Wiley & Sons, 2013).

that enable, sexism, racism, heteronormativity, and ableism to function in society. Aristotle for instance is widely regarded as an ethical "father" and is still used widely in Western academia for his work on "virtues," yet he advocated slavery and the subjugation of women.[4]

In truth, few anthropologists have paid little direct attention to contemporary AI and robotics with the exception of Diana E. Forsythe, who led a pioneering study of the field of AI in the late 1990s.[5] Her work followed the sociality of AI researchers and their communities and how concepts and practices were formed in a community largely dominated by men. Prior to Forsythe, Margaret Mead and Gregory Bateson engaged with the field of cybernetics with its emphasis on human-animal-machine systems and both were involved in the pioneering Macy Conferences (1947–1953).[6] Donna Haraway studied technoscience and is noted for her *Cyborg Manifesto*.[7] The arguments in the manifesto are focused on the cultural production and destruction of boundaries. Lucy Suchman's[8] pioneering work explored sociotechnical communities at Xerox and later at robotics labs, she now is engaged with academic activism and part of a community calling for the banning of autonomous weapons systems (2007), and Richardson[9] who studied the making of robots and AI at the Massachusetts Institute of Technology (MIT).

Despite the rise of robotics and AI in wider society there are no "anthropology of AI and robotics" journals, research departments, or a clearly delineated body of research. There are billions of dollars worth of investment in robotic and AI research and business, the products of which are likely to produce far-reaching changes for humans, animals, and the environment.

There is a well-established body of research captured under the umbrella term of anthropology of science and technology that covers a plethora of interest, from cell biology[10] and computing[11] to psychiatry.[12] The anthropological study of digital cultures

---

[4] Aristotle, *The Politics* (London: Penguin Classics, 2000).

[5] Diana Forsythe, *Studying Those Who Study Us: An Anthropologist in the World of Artificial Intelligence* (Palo Alto, CA: Stanford University Press, 2001).

[6] Stewart Brand, "For God's Sake, Margaret: Conversation with Gregory Bateson and Margaret Mead," *CoEvolution Quarterly* 10 (1976): 32–44.

[7] Donna Haraway, *A Cyborg Manifesto: Science, Technology and Socialist Feminism in the Late Twentieth Century* (Minneapolis: University of Minnesota Press, 2016).

[8] Lucy Suchman, *Human-Machine Reconfigurations: Plans and Situated Actions* (Cambridge University Press, 2007).

[9] Kathleen Richardson, *An Anthropology of Robots and AI: Annihilation Anxiety and Machines* (New York and London: Routledge, 2015).

[10] Evelyn Fox Keller, *The Century of the Gene* (Cambridge, MA: Harvard University Press, 2009).

[11] Stefan Helmreich, *Silicon Second Nature: Culturing Artificial Life in a Digital World, Updated with a New Preface* (Berkeley: University of California Press, 2000).

[12] Nev Jones and Tanya Marie Luhrmann, "Beyond the Sensory: Findings from an In-depth Analysis of the Phenomenology of 'Auditory Hallucinations' in Schizophrenia," *Psychosis* 8, no. 3 (2016): 191–202.

is well established, and there are ethnographies of Facebook, Second Life, GPS mapping, and many other topics covered by researchers in this field.[13,14,15]

While contemporary AI (machine learning) grew out of digital technologies and the management and exploitation of the data produced by new devices and online social networking, robots and AI have unique histories that preexist the current digital period.

There are various courses taught on the anthropology of computing and digital society but no consistent body of research linking anthropology, robots, and AI sustainably enough to forge distinct epistemological or ontological theories (though this is changing with the increased interest in the field from anthropologists).

In what follows I want to explore the intersections between anthropology and robots and AI, now, and in the future. Hence these links I make here are to draw on existing literature and explore potential interrelationships. In anthropology, context is everything, but context includes economic, social, political, and symbolic structures that envelope each person's life. These are important to consider in relation to the production of technological artifacts and their impact on human sociality.

The growing interest in the ethics of robots and AI has been largely developed by philosophers of technology, not anthropologists, and this has shaped the narratives, issues, and concerns of social scientists engaged in robotics and AI. Alternatively, I want to suggest that anthropological paradigms are capable of opening up new kinds of reflexivity, and as such there is a case to be made for increased anthropological engagements in these fields.

The themes I will explore in this chapter include a look at the context for the development of robots and AI as products of Western capitalism, industry, and militarism. Robots and AI developed out of specific kinds of Euro-American practices, but in their contemporary form now span the globe, with Asian countries, particularly Japan and China, leading the field in new ways. In Europe and North America, robots and AI are frequently depicted as threats to humanity in popular culture,[16] while in Japan, robots are venerated, cherished and integrated into the "family."[17] My discussion is largely confined to Euro-American contexts, but the reader could seek out the work of anthropologist Jennifer Robertson, who has written extensively on robots in Japan.

From this overview I move onto problematize the concept of "intelligence," paying attention to its legacy as an instrument of domination. Intelligence is bound up with power and is problematic as a category because of its valorization of certain kinds of cultures or people. "Artificial intelligence" hides the humans who are creating it by putting

---

[13] Tom Boellstorff, *Coming of Age in Second Life: An Anthropologist Explores the Virtually Human* (Princeton, NJ: Princeton University Press, 2015).

[14] Heather Horst, and Daniel Miller, *The Cell Phone: An Anthropology of Communication* (New York: Berg, 2006).

[15] C. Tilley, W. Keane, S. Küchler, M. Rowlands, and P. Spyer eds., *Handbook of Material Culture* (London: SAGE, 2006).

[16] Richardson, *An Anthropology of Robots and AI*.

[17] Jennifer Robertson, *Robo Sapiens Japanicus: Robots, Gender, Family, and the Japanese Nation* (Berkeley University of California Press, 2017).

the "artificial" out in front and at times concealing the power structures. "Intelligence" is not merely a descriptive category, but is instrumentalized and made use of in particular ways, acting as a scientific tool to reinforce Enlightenment masculinist authority and ideals of *progress*. I then move on to explore contemporary debates in AI and robotics that reproduce class, sex, or racial bias, reinforcing existing hierarchical arrangements. While I do not give an exhaustive account, I look at the ways in which dominant hierarchies maintain control through new technologies, rendering in some cases the technologies they produce as unworkable and problematic for some populations. Finally, I will conclude on the theme of personhood and who or what should be considered "persons." In juridical-legal terms, a person is not only a natural human being but can be an abstraction in the form of a corporation. More recently, indigenous peoples have used legal and corporate personality to win rights of guardianship over natural entities. Anthropology in its engagements with indigenous peoples and environmental movements has moved to recognize "nonhumans," extending beyond animals and the natural environment to include artifacts—could also be a share space for future dialogues, and if so, what role would it take? If persons are not exclusively human, then what opportunities does this afford those who want to extend the franchise to include artifacts?

ROBOTS AND AI

The origin stories of robots and AI are entangled with advanced industrialized economies and are simultaneously fictional, business, and research artifacts. They are distinguished from magical artifacts (animated by spiritual imagination and practices) because they are produced to achieve "intelligence" and/or 'autonomy" and are "manmade," crafted deliberately to become more than an inert artifact. There are strong relationships between the fields of robotics and AI, but they are also studied and developed differently, though the integration between these two fields has increased in recent years.

The term "robot" did not develop in the lab or the factory but emerged as fictional characters in the play *R.U.R.* (*Rossum's Universal Robots*) in the 1920s.[18] Robots were invented by the Čapek brothers to warn against a culture where men and women were reduced to labor, robots as both resource and means of production.

Čapek despaired of the brutality of the carnage produced from the battlefields of the First World War and the upheaval of industrialization and mechanization of human societies. *R.U.R.* explored the contest between different forms of social organization: communist and capitalist, both in competition to offer the best society. While the robots in his play were humanlike, it was other artists and interpreters of his *Robots*[19] that turned them into machines and the association with robots as *human-like machines* was

[18] Karel Capek, *R.U.R. (Rossum's Universal Robots*, trans. Claudi Novac (New York and London: Penguin, 2004).
[19] He capitalized the R in Robots in his play.

formed, much to the consternation of Čapek, who was angered by this development. Robots in fiction preexisted their development in industry, developing in factories in the 1960s and were more accurately automated machines. The inspiration for the robots is incontestably workers and/or slaves, as much as it was about using the science of the factory to create artificial life.

AI by contrast developed through a marriage of computing and militarism during the Second World War, where code-breaking machines made their debut. The term "AI" was not coined until much later in the 1950s, and it was in the United States that the first specialized research programs developed. British computer pioneers such as Alan Turing[20] focused on "thinking" machines, while his American counterparts choose the term "intelligence." One might argue there is little difference between a thinking machine and an intelligent one, but the distinction is important because of the colonial and elitist cultural baggage tied up with intelligence. While thinking describes a cognitive process (all humans think regardless of their intelligence), intelligence by contrast was developed specifically as ruling-class project of domination to sort out rulers from the ruled.

AI is also complemented by a mythical imaginary where the end point is a conscious machine, capable of reasoning, abstraction, speech, and language and even sentience. Just as robots are portrayed as a threshold technology where boundaries between human and machine and animate and inanimate are dissolved, so too is AI. These fantasies underscore the cultural imagination of robots and AI, and, arguably, contribute to an illusion fused with anxiety: will they or won't they rise up?

THE FETISH OF "INTELLIGENCE" IN AI SYSTEMS

I want to consider what "intelligence" refers to in AI. In the original formulation of AI was on reason-based modeling that could produce algorithms to think like *man* did, even to become autonomous from *his* consciousness and be independent of the *men* who created it.

A new version of the creation myth of the Judea-Christian-Islamic God was reconstructed through AI. Instead of the monotheistic God creating man and life, now men could create a new form of mechanical life using their unique gift: intelligence. In this myth, a patriarchal God[21] created human life outside of woman, so too, with science, engineering and technology, man could also create outside of woman, in the image of God!

---

[20] Alan M. Turing, "Can a Machine Think?," *Mind* 59, no. 236 (1950): 433–460.
[21] Gerda Lerner, *The Creation of Patriarchy*, Vol. 1 (New York: Oxford University Press, 1986).

Machines and computer programs were created to do what men (arguably now also women) could do, only better and faster. Moreover, as computer systems interact with other computer systems, arguably AI is a form of interfacing between machines.

It was no accident that the term "intelligence" is bound up with a project to create and subsequently *emancipate* machines from human existence. Intelligence is a concept developed to normalize power relations and is intricately linked to the politics of Western hierarchies—men more intelligent than women, white men more intelligent than men of color or working-class men. As Cave[22] explains, intelligence became a modern way of talking about ruling elites, noting that Aristotle in *Politics* writes: "[T]hat some should rule and others be ruled is a thing not only necessary, but expedient; from the hour of their birth, some are marked out for subjection, others for rule."[23]

Intelligence is a problematic concept, in terms of what it is and how it is measured, normally through tests such as intelligence quotient (IQ). Intelligence is also about gathering information is made use of either as information or for strategy. As the characteristic par excellence of what it means to be human (white and male), intelligence became associated with evolutionary paradigms, colonial rule, and "survival of the fittest."[24] Intelligence was used to justify elite political campaigns of domination over others: the poor, women, the working classes, or people with disabilities. Intelligence is associated with reason, and rationality.[25]

The intelligence in AI glorifies the rational masculine subject exemplified by a reading of the works of Ray Kurzweil, author of *The Age of Spiritual Machines: When Computers Exceed Human Intelligence*,[26] and Nick Bostrom's book on *Superintelligence*.[27] Imagine the controversy if these debates were transferred onto people (as they once were) rather than into machines?

Take, for instance, the controversy surrounding the publication of *The Bell Curve: Intelligence and Class Structure in American Life*,[28] a text met with moral opprobrium by academic and the public alike. This book sought to make a modern case for racial inequality through an analysis of IQ data sets that showed differential scoring patterns of ethnic groups.

If a similar book were published anytime in the nineteenth century or until the post–Second World War period, it would have been uncontroversial, but by the late twentieth century racial thinking was widely discredited. A remnant of an elitist past.

[22] Stephen Cave, "Intelligence as Ideology: Its History and Future," *Keynote Lecture to the Centre for Science and Policy Annual Conference, at the Royal Society, 27 June 2019.*

[23] Aristotle cited in Cave, "Intelligence as Ideology."

[24] Charles Darwin, *On the Origin of Species, 1859* (London: Routledge, 2004).

[25] Cave, "Intelligence as Ideology."

[26] Ray Kurzweil, *The Age of Spiritual Machines: When Computers Exceed Human Intelligence* (New York: Penguin, 2000).

[27] Nick Bostrom, *Superintelligence* (Oxford: Oxford University Press, 2017).

[28] Richard J. Herrnstein and Charles Murray, *The Bell Curve: Intelligence and Class Structure in American Life* (New York: Simon and Schuster, 2010).

The legacy of racial thinking impacted on the working classes, women, people of color, and the disabled and informed eugenics "scientific racism" and Nazi socialist ideals.[29]

By the mid-twentieth century new social movements inspired by civil rights and equality gained ascendency. IQ and intelligence could be talked about, but in increasingly narrower sphere, such as educational testing. The "brainy white man born to rule" was discredited, but in the technological communities "he" acquired an association with nerd and geek culture.[30] While the social sciences and humanities refuse to engage with intelligence as a metanarrative, technology has stepped into this space, and in doing so have not considered its more problematic origins. Cave has gone some way to re-exploring the origins of intelligence and problematizing it in relation to AI.

Rather than produce a "neutral" set of assumptions in robots and AI, there are elitist assumptions carried through the processes that mimic domination paradigms. It is to these we now turn.

ALGORITHMIC POWER PLAYS

Marvin Minsky, one of the founding "fathers," said, "AI is the science of making machines do things that would require intelligence if done by men." As both "fathers" and "creators," men are the sex that has carefully culturally forged AI as a science in their own image.

In AI, man is taken as both the sex and as the standard for *humanity*, a point continually problematized by feminist writers, including Simone De Beauvoir, who described this problem in her book *The Second Sex*.[31] In patriarchy, man is the norm and the standard, and woman is the deviation, an imperfect or incomplete male. The male is still the sex that is referenced in the making of robots and AI, an act which occurs spontaneously because when the "human" is set as the standard, the human is frequently male.[32] This idolization of the male sex that occurs in robotics and AI should be considered in light that the female sex make up over 49.54 percent[33] of the global population and are not a minority group but half of the human species.

Women have been featured in contemporary computing narratives as sexualized objects. Take the example of Lena Söderberg, a playboy centerfold who became widely used in textbooks in sections related to image processing. Andrew Sawchuck, an assistant professor of electrical engineering at the University of Southern California, had, in

[29] Elazar Barkan, *The Retreat of Scientific Racism: Changing Concepts of Race in Britain and the United States between the World Wars* (Cambridge: Cambridge University Press, 1992).
[30] Christopher Kelty, "Geeks, Social Imaginaries, and Recursive Publics," *Cultural Anthropology* 20, no. 2 (2005): 185–214.
[31] Simone De Beauvoir and Howard Madison Parshley, *The Second Sex* (New York: Vintage Books, 1953).
[32] Richardson, *An Anthropology of Robots and AI.*
[33] The World Bank, https://data.worldbank.org/indicator/sp.pop.totl.fe.zs.

1973, a copy at hand of *Playboy* magazine. Instead of using the regular stock images, he used an image of Söderberg instead.[34]

The porn industry is widely celebrated as a vehicle for technological development from VHS to live streaming.[35] Feminist analyses of the porn industry show it frequently depicts violence against women.[36]

The making of sex robots in the form of pornographic representations of women allows a new generation of researchers (again typically men) to imagine life creating *The Stepford Wives*[37] that fiction imagined and engaging in fantasies about life *without* women.[38]

Forsythe[39] noted in her study in the 1990s of AI research communities that women were more likely to be in administrative roles, and two decades later, women are still more likely to work in administrative roles in academia and business than in the senior or tenured roles in the computer sciences.

There are efforts to increase women's participation in STEM (science, technology, engineering, and mathematics) subjects has led to many changes, as are funding agencies such as the European Commission that emphasize gender equality as a priority.[40]

While contemporary computing and engineering (the basis to robots and AI) ignore the role of women, the history of AI tells a different story. There were hundreds of women involved as "computers" at both NASA[41] and Bletchley Park.[42]

As Hicks argues in *Programmed Inequality*, women in the United Kingdom were deliberately excluded at the end of the Second World War to make way for men in the computing field. She argues this accounts for the British loss of advantage in the field as there were not enough qualified men to fulfill these roles and not enough trained men to replace the qualified women. She claims, the computing fields were forging ahead in the United Kingdom in the 1940s and lost pace to Americans, who were able to exclude women but replace them with machines and men.

Shetterley narrates the untold history of African American women's participation in NASA space programs. These are histories that were forgotten until female researchers began to look at the role of women in computing. Ada Lovelace is credited with creating

[34] Corinne Iozzio, "The *Playboy* Centerfold That Helped Create the JPEG," *The Atlantic* (February 9, 2016), https://www.theatlantic.com/technology/archive/2016/02/lena-image-processing-playboy/461970/.

[35] Gail Dines, *Pornland: How Porn Has Hijacked Our Sexuality* (Boston: Beacon Press, 2010).

[36] Ibid.

[37] Ira Levin, *The Stepford Wives* (London: Corsair, 2011).

[38] Kathleen Richardson, *Sex Robots: The End of Love* (Cambridge, UK: Polity Press, forthcoming).

[39] Diana Forsythe, *Studying Those Who Study Us: An Anthropologist in the World of Artificial Intelligence* (Palo Alto, CA: Stanford University Press, 2001).

[40] Gender Equality Strategy, European Commission, https://ec.europa.eu/info/policies/justice-and-fundamental-rights/gender-equality/gender-equality-strategy_en.

[41] Margot Lee Shetterly, *Hidden Figures: The Story of the African-American Women Who Helped Win the Space Race* (New York: William Morrow, 2016).

[42] Marie Hicks, *Programmed Inequality: How Britain Discarded Women Technologists and Lost Its Edge in Computing* (Cambridge, MA: MIT Press, 2017).

the first algorithm.[43] By the time of AI's advent in the late 1950s, women were expunged from the field and their work replaced by *computer machines*. Then and now there still remains significant gender differences in the uptake of undergraduate, graduate, faculty posts, and business of AI.

History has taught us that women were excluded from STEM subjects and professions deliberately (Bletchley and NASA), but now the problem is of another kind. Five decades of exclusion and lack of opportunity has produced cultures of sexist stereotyping and bias against women. Women make up only 12.37 percent of engineers in the United Kingdom, yet women achieve a First or Upper Second degree more on average than males (98.8 percent and 74.6 percent, respectively).[44] This has left a largely male-dominated field for nearly fifty years leading to what Kate Crawford called the "White Guy Problem" (WGP).[45]

The WGP is primarily focused on existential crisis and risk and is epitomized by figures such as Stephen Hawking and Elon Musk, who are concerned that machines will become super-intelligent and become uncontrollable as they surpass man's intelligence. Ray Kurzweil believes advanced AI will permit the uploading of man's consciousness to machines. This would signify "the singularity," the time when men and machines merge together to become one.[46] These figures have largely ignored the ethical problems produced by robots and AI in the here and now.

Instead, Crawford argues, AI scientists need to deal with the real problems at hand, including the reproducing of racist, sexist, and classist practices that are immediate problems of AI. Biased programmers produce biased algorithms that inherit the problems that social scientists have spent the three decades actively deconstructing, such as Google's photo app that was classifying black people as gorillas, or Hewlett-Packard's web camera that could not recognize people with darker skin tones.

Crawford notes that the difficulties of finding out what is creating these algorithmic flaws is due to business reluctance to release information on how their data is created and put to use as it conflicts with proprietary laws. The real problems of the technology are the reproduction of sexist and racist tropes, yet for much of its history, AI (and robots, for that matter) has been focused on machines gaining consciousness (superintelligence) and overthrowing humanity.

The computer and engineering sciences have largely been insulated from wider discourses that problematize categories of intelligence, sex and race. Such issues are so serious they have produced sociotechnical hierarchies. In a report written by the Council of Europe's antidiscrimination department, concerns were raised about how public and private institutions was using "AI discrimination" and was able to perpetuate

[43] Avery Elizabeth Hurt, *Ada Lovelace: Computer Programmer and Mathematician* (New York: Cavendish Square Publishing, 2017).

[44] Engineering UK, 2018, https://www.engineeringuk.com/media/156187/state-of-engineering-report-2018.pdf.

[45] Kate Crawford, "Artificial Intelligence's White Guy Problem," (June 25, 2006), *New York Times*.

[46] Ray Kurzweil, "The Singularity Is Near," in *Ethics and Emerging Technologies* (London: Palgrave Macmillan, 2014), 393–406.

discrimination of the "protected characteristics" of race and sex.[47] The protected characteristics include race and sex. The report urged that "regulatory safeguards" were need to offset some of the algorithmic prejudices were evidenced in policing, housing, and healthcare, to name a few areas impacted by the integration of AI in these areas.

There is a rich body of literature of the anthropology of technology narrating the absence of women and people of color from computing cultures.[48]

Anthropologist Stefan Helmreich's study of Palo Alto computer scientists explored how indigenous culture is appropriated by research scientists who frequently adorn their buildings with indigenous art or exoticize their technological artifacts by using names from other cultures: Java, Ubuntu, Apache.[49]

The naming of artifacts and their cultural associations have significance in anthropology, and so would their connotations more broadly. An apple may be a fruit, but it is also has wider cultural symbolism in Judeo-Islamic-Christian culture as the forbidden fruit, eaten by Eve in the Garden of Eden as described in the book of Genesis.[50]

The Apple company icon of a bitten apple is drenched in meaning, though its founders claim their choice of image was unrelated to these wider meanings. Apple's co-founder Steve Wozniak reminiscences on the founding of the name:

> It was a couple of weeks later when we came up with a name for the partnership. I remember I was driving Steve Jobs back from the airport along Highway 85. Steve was coming back from a visit to Oregon to a place he called an "apple orchard." It was actually some kind of commune. Steve suggested a name—Apple Computer. The first comment out of my mouth was, "What about Apple Records?" This was (and still is) the Beatles-owned record label. We both tried to come up with technical-sounding names that were better, but we couldn't think of any good ones. Apple was so much better, better than any other name we could think of.

Apples do not just grow on trees, they are nurtured and developed through associations which are rooted deep in the collective consciousness.

Anthropologists explore categories of space, time, symbolism, ritual, and cosmologies capable of bringing to the fore extra layers of meaning that are invisible to the architects of robots and AI. There are also deep personal and psychological connections between the makers and their robots, where robotic scientists transferred their physical and social anxieties to the robots they created.[51] For example, one researcher's project was developing a robot with a memory and she drew on studies of post-traumatic stress disorder (PTSD) studies where memory is significantly impacted by the presence of trauma. The research scientist had also received a diagnosis of PTSD, and her robot

[47] F. Borgesius, Discrimination in Decision-Making, Directorate Gender of Democracy, Council of Europe, 2018: 5.

[48] Forsythe, Studying Those Who Study Us.

[49] Stefan Helmreich, Silicon Second Nature: Culturing Artificial Life in a Digital World (Berkeley: University of California Press, 2000).

[50] Lerner, The Creation of Patriarchy.

[51] Richardson, An Anthropology of Robots and AI.

became a way for her to exercise control, reflection, and healing of her own trauma. Participant observation is a methodology central to anthropological investigation and requires active engagement with interlocutors, their lived experience, sociality, relations with artifacts, and the built environment. Anthropological methodologies are developed through meeting the other in their worlds, on their terms, and making sense of their language.[52]

The ethnographic recording of these first-person encounters, ideally collected in contexts that are integral to the research—the lab, the hospital, the business, or the home. The anthropologist can take these ethnographic field notes back into the discipline, where there is a rich archive of cultural material in which to explore the data.

Anthropology as a discipline enrolls otherness into itself, while at the same time is able to hold its independence, to consider the concrete with the abstractions.

NEW FORMS OF PERSONHOOD

Personhood is a field where there is shared territory between anthropologists and AI and robotic researchers. Should AI and robots be considered types of persons? What would constitute a legal, moral, or ethical argument for their status as persons? And why is this debate occurring in a field where the technology has no consciousness or sentience?

Personhood of natural human beings in contrast to animals and things or nonpersons are topics that anthropologists have written extensively about, but for other reasons, often to illustrate how humans, animals, and artifacts are more integrated into the sociality of indigenous and Western peoples.

Personhood is a fiercely debated idea, and as a concept in its modern formation is intimately tied Western juridical-liberal economies. As the middle classes developed, so did ideas to give this new growing political movement recognitions and protections under law, taking power away from the old guards of the state. The initial rights were of Man or the individual (that what cannot be divided) are referred to in early Enlightenment literature.

The *person* developed initially as a *natural human being* (a property-owning male) who was able to access the law and rights under the new liberal economies that developed from the 1700s by new classes of subjects. The word "person" is from the Latin *persona*, which is a theatrical term denoting something that is about the representation of the self. One of the first significant modern uses of the term "person" was in the Fourteenth Amendment (July 9, 1868) of the U.S. Constitution that followed the Thirteenth Amendment (freeing slaves). The Fourteenth Amendment allowed all "persons" (meaning men and freed slaves) equal protection under the law. This was a significant act.

---

[52] Adam Kuper, *Anthropology and Anthropologists: The Modern British School* (London: Routledge, 2014).

The legal concept of the category of persons is not solely attributed to human natural beings. Since 1868 it has been extended to an abstract entity in modern law in the form of a *corporation*. This history if worthy of some discussion because it sets the frame of how personhood has been mobilized for a series of claims about legal rights that include natural entities (rivers) and animals (apes), used in the law through the category of "guardianship" (holding rights for other persons who cannot exercise them).

It is the *person* (*persona*) that has a legal status, but it is a fiction, and persons only exist because of legal status, and legal status can only be accessed by persons. But persons can be guardians or represent collectivities (corporations).

Personhood gives recognitions to people, but goes beyond it. The "person" developed more fully in the nineteenth and mid-twentieth centuries and was connected to the "self."[53] The "individual" is another way to talk about selfhood, as individuals can access rights and have responsibilities, just as persons.

While in Western juridical-political systems personhood began to include nonhumans (artificial entities called corporations), so too this concept has been put to use in other contexts.

The Enlightenment humanist project singled out the human subject as capable of reason, language, and consciousness and therefore distinct from other nonhuman animals and artifacts. This subject was principally males, who held property and were largely white, though the franchise was extended over the course of the nineteenth and twentieth centuries to include working men, men of color, freed slaves, and women.

Anthropologist Marilyn Strathern has written at length about cultural differences of what constitutes "persons" and "things" in her writing on Melanesia, kinship, and new reproductive technologies.[54] She argued that in Melanesia there is no "individual" (not capable of division), instead creating a framework of a "dividual" (divisible and capable of being divided), a more fragmentary concept of the person.[55]

Moreover, in her classic work, *The Gender of the Gift*, Strathern writes of Melanesia persons as bound up with their world of things and of cultural production of things (an axe, a yam, a shell) to stand in for, or represent, social relations between persons.[56]

If shells and yams can become quasi-persons in the field of social relations of Melanesians, then why not robots and AI artifacts that are circulating in the cultural production of life of European Americans?

Donna Haraway's *Cyborg Manifesto*[57] and her later work, *When Species Meet*,[58] are seminal texts for a new world order where ontological relations between humans,

[53] Nihad Farooq, *Undisciplined: Science, Ethnography, and Personhood in the Americas, 1830–1940* (New York: NYU Press, 2016).
[54] Marilyn Strathern, *Property, Substance and Effect: Anthropological Essays on Persons and Things* (London: Athlone Press, 1999).
[55] Karl Smith, "From Dividual and Individual Selves to Porous Subjects," *Australian Journal of Anthropology* 23, no. 1 (2012): 50–64.
[56] Marilyn Strathern, *The Gender of the Gift: Problems with Women and Problems with Society in Melanesia* (Berkeley: University of California Press, 1990).
[57] Donna Haraway, *Simians, Cyborgs, and Women: The Reinvention of Nature* (New York: Routledge, 1991).
[58] Donna J. Haraway, *When Species Meet* (Minneapolis: University of Minnesota Press, 2013).

animals, and things are rewritten to remove humans from their pedestal, instead curating alternative relations. The cyborg in her manifesto does not hark only to the man-machine popularized through the TV Series *The Six Million Dollar Man*, who through artificial implants developed bionic powers. Haraway's cyborg is a political case for the destruction of categories and their remaking through partial connections and other species. She argued there is no wholeness of what it means to be human (shared experience capable of incorporating all the perspectives of its members). We are all connected with each other, and each part does not make up the whole. There is no original Garden of Eden or paradise where humans can return, and arguably it never existed. In her framing of the problem, she wrote, "we are all chimeras, theorized and fabricated hybrids of machine and organism—in short, cyborgs."[59]

The *cyborg* and *dividual* are open assaults on Enlightenment humanism and the analytical fabrications it needed to produce to maintain it. I will leave aside the complex debates about animals and humans because, unlike things, animals are sentient beings with complex socialities; things are not, though the orthodoxy in anthropology is to argue that things can have social lives[60] or that there is nothing essentially different between humans and nonhumans.[61]

Robots and AI come under the category of property in Euro-American contexts, and unlike for Melanesians, shells or yams are not circulated through ritualistic practices that maintain complex kinship networks. They are sold to generate revenue and income for companies and status and prestige for research labs and are used instrumentally by their consumers. These artifacts may mimic behavior and appearance, but they do not engage in the kinds of reciprocal social relations that are enacted between humans.

For some, the dissolving of differences between humans and artifacts represents an emancipatory political project, yet it was only two hundred years ago some people (the working classes or slaves) were considered closer to artifacts and tools than to their fellow man *and woman*.

Marxian analysis of class relations shows how some people are used as resources by others, though not directly marked out as slaves; their economic choices are curtailed by a capitalist economy.

Radin describes how *possessive individualism* replaced the idea of the slave, so the worker could sell their labor but not be owned; the person's *labor* was then the property that was transacted.[62] This system continues to this day. As Marx explained, people are calculated in price alongside other forms of property (raw materials, rent, etc.) used by a business. He called this *constant capital* (equipment). Variable capital is the cost of labor. But labor, according to Marx is the source of value, not constant capital.[63] If people are

[59] Haraway, *Simians, Cyborgs, and Women*, 150.

[60] Arjun Apparaduri, "Introduction: Commodities and the Politics of Value," in *The Social Life of Things: Commodities in Cultural Perspective*, ed. Arjun Appardurai (Cambridge: Cambridge University Press, 1988).

[61] Bruno Latour, *We Have Never Been Modern* (Cambridge, MA: Harvard University Press, 2012).

[62] Margaret Jane Radin, "Property and Personhood," *Stanford Law Review* 34 (1981): 957.

[63] Karl Marx, *Capital*, Vol. 1 (London: Lawrence and Wishart, 1974).

replaced by machines, this increases the constant capital, but decreases the value from variable capital. If economic crisis is the result of the tendency of the rate of profit to fall (by increasing the expenditure in constant capital and reducing variable capital), how can capitalism survive the Second Machine Age? Accompanying new reorganizing of capital relations, there is an erasing of boundaries between persons and property. Anthropology can be used in the service of an agenda to assist capitalist social relations.

In Melanesia, things (artifacts) might stand in for persons in social relations; in Western societies people have stood in for property as slaves. In my view, not shared widely in anthropology, the disentangling of people from property (artifacts) was a mark of progress for the nonpropertied, women and people of color who were used as "resources" either in whole or in part.

Robots are deliberately designed to mimic human appearance and/or behavior; it is not surprising, therefore, that people interacting with them *attribute* human like qualities to them.

Even the most sophisticated algorithm or robot are created and consumed under property law, ownership, and transferability. Robots and AI are forms of property.

There are many new devices that facilitate human interaction, talk back, resemble people, act as therapeutic aids, or are marketed as intimate others in the form of virtual girlfriends or sex robots. The personification of robots and AI by their consumers or "users" gives rise to new imaginaries where new kinds of social relations between people and consumer goods mediated through branding, marketing, and advertising.

Conclusion

In this chapter I have tried to show that intelligence is not a neutral concept, but was developed to justify the subjugation of people on the basis of their sex, race, class, and ability.

Moreover, the computer sciences and robotics have for most of twentieth century continued to be fields that develop without fuller participation from women and people of color. As algorithms that run on computers and robots are integrated into everyday life, the makers of it are drawn from narrow subsections of the populations, the White Guy Problem, who are at the forefront of producing technologies that weave inequality of sex and race into social life in sociotechnical forms.

Moreover, lines of interdisciplinary enquiry could be developed through robotics and AI and anthropology but more could be developed. For AI scientists and roboticists, it will be necessary to take into account issues from the social sciences and humanities when constructing their technologies in order that prejudices, stereotypes, or structural inequalities are not reproduced in the life that follows from the developments of these technologies.

Arguably the rise of ethics of AI and robotics will create committees of stakeholders who will work together to reduce bias, stereotyping, and perpetual algorithmic inequality.

New frontiers are on the horizon, with the end of humanism giving rise to the antihumanism, posthumanism, and transhumanism. Before we abandon the humanistic enterprise, it is worth noting that while humanism did not invent slavery (which is over 6,000 years old), it did create a culture where commitment to universal values of freedom, equality, and rule of law were able to thrive more widely. If we are all cyborgs now, what does this mean for any project where humans cannot stand differently from property? Robots and AI are part of the Second Machine Age, but what kind of age should it be for sentient and conscious life forms that struggle for a life dominated by militarism and capitalism?

BIBLIOGRAPHY

Bird-David, Nurit. "'Animism' Revisited: Personhood, Environment, and Relational Epistemology." *Current Anthropology* 40, no. S1 (1999): S67–S91.

Brooks, Rodney A. *Robot: The Future of Flesh and Machines*. London: Penguin, 2002.

Brooks, Rodney A. "Intelligence without Representation." *Artificial Intelligence* 47, no. 1–3 (1991): 139–159.

Cellan-Jones, Rory. "Stephen Hawking Warns Artificial Intelligence Could End Mankind." BBC News (December 2, 2014). https://www.bbc.co.uk/news/technology-30290540.

Clarke, Arthur C. *2001: A Space Odyssey*. London: Penguin, 2016.

Geertz, Clifford. "Thick Description: Toward an Interpretive Theory of Culture." In *The Cultural Geography Reader*, edited by Timothy S. Oakes and Patricia L. Price, 41–51. Abingdon: Routledge, 2008.

Kubrick, Stanley, dir. *2001: A Space Odyssey*. Metro-Goldwyn-Mayer, 1968.

Minsky, Marvin. *Computation*. Englewood Cliffs, NJ: Prentice-Hall, 1967.

Minsky, Marvin. *Society of Mind*. New York: Simon and Schuster, 1988.

Strathern, Marilyn. *Property, Substance and Effect: Anthropological Essays on Persons and Things*. London: Athlone Press, 1999.

"The Six Million Dollar Man," TV series (1974–1978).

CHAPTER 30

....

CALCULATIVE
COMPOSITION
The Ethics of Automating Design

....

SHANNON MATTERN

INTRODUCTION

....

FOR as long as fashion designers, graphic artists, industrial designers, and architects have been practicing their crafts—and even before they were labeled as such—those practices and their products have been shaped by the prevailing tools and technologies of their ages, from paper patterns to computer-aided design.[1] Artificial intelligence is merely the latest agitator, and myriad design professionals have already begun exploring its potential to transform the conceptualization, design, prototyping, production, and distribution of their work, whether menswear or modular homes. Fashion labels are mining social media to forecast trends and building intelligent apps to help consumers compare styles. Architects are amassing data—engineering requirements, CAD geometries, building performance data—to automate phases of their work. Likely to the chagrin of many graphic designers, programmers have created web platforms that allow clients to upload text and images, input a few parameters, and, *violà!*—a website appears! Still other practitioners, from across the disciplines, have employed AI toward more humanitarian or sustainable ends, like custom-designing prosthetic devices, mapping out less energy-intensive supply chains, or prototyping climate-responsive architectures.

[1] I am grateful to my research assistant Kevin Rogan, who aided with all stages of research and writing. I also owe a great debt of gratitude to Ajla Aksamija, David Benjamin, Andrew Witt, and Rune Madsen, who generously responded to our queries about their own practice—and to Gerald Sim, Jason Hallstrom, and the Institute for Sensing and Embedded Network Systems Engineering at Florida Atlantic University, who kindly invited me to share this research-in-progress.

While some designers have committed to applying AI toward more ethical ends, they've paid comparatively less attention toward the ethical *means* of its application—precisely those methodological issues that are of concern to organizations like AI Now and FATE (Fairness, Accountability, Transparency, and Ethics in AI).[2] What, for instance, are the implications of vacuuming up architectural and urban data in order to aid in the future design of more efficient buildings and neighborhoods? What are we to make of graphic design tools that normalize particular facial features or allow for the suturing of various images into new composites? And what are the implications for designers' self-identities as professionals and political subjects when their core creative questions are turned over to the machine? This chapter will examine the ethical ends and means toward which AI-driven design has been, and perhaps *could be*, applied. In surveying representative design fields—fashion, product, graphic, and architectural design—I'll examine what ethical opportunities and risks we might face when AI-driven design practice is programmed to serve the needs and desires of laborers, consumers, and clients—and when it's applied in generating everything from luxury goods to logos to library buildings.[3]

AUTOMATING FASHION, PRODUCT, AND GRAPHIC DESIGN

We'll start close to the body, with clothing. Fashion designers, manufacturers, and retailers are using artificial intelligence to track trends, to offer shopping advice, to test garments on different body shapes and sizes, and to allow customers to mix and match items in their wardrobes.[4] With Amazon's Echo Look, users can document their outfits

---

[2] AI Now, https://ainowinstitute.org/; FAT, https://fatconference.org/.

[3] Much has been written about the application of AI in urban design and planning, too. See, for instance, the voluminous research on "smart cities." I have written several pieces on the topic. See, for instance, "A City Is Not a Computer," *Places Journal* (February 2017), https://placesjournal.org/article/a-city-is-not-a-computer/; and "Databodies in Codespace," *Places Journal* (April 2018), https://placesjournal.org/article/databodies-in-codespace/.

[4] See the Stitch Fix online personal shopping service; the Pureple closet organizer and outfit planner; Vue.ai's suite of AI-generated models and styling applications; and Kim Kardashian's Screenshop, which allows users to upload photos of looks they like and find where those items are for sale. These fashion examples are drawn from Sissi Cao, "Zac Posen Talks Fashion in the Era of Artificial Intelligence," *Observer* (April 13, 2018), http://observer.com/2018/04/zac-posen-fashion-artificial-intelligence; Will Knight, "Amazon Has Developed an AI Fashion Designer," *MIT Technology Review* (August 24, 2017), https://www.technologyreview.com/s/608668/amazon-has-developed-an-ai-fashion-designer/; Emily Matchar, "Artificial Intelligence Could Help Generate the Next Big Fashion Trends," *Smithsonian Magazine* (May 3, 2018), https://www.smithsonianmag.com/innovation/artificial-intelligence-could-help-generate-next-big-fashion-trends-180968952/; Devorah Rose, "Commentary: AI's Next Victim: Your Closet," *Fortune* (March 15, 2018), http://fortune.com/2018/03/15/fashion-ai-artificial-intelligence-future-kim-kardashian/; Arthur Zackiewicz, "AI, Visual Search and Retail's Next Big Step," *WWD* (April 16, 2018), https://wwd.com/business-news/technology/ai-clarifai-retail-brands-1202650318/.

and, via its Style Check service, draw on the combined expertise of human stylists and AI (trained on social media fashion posts) to choose the most flattering options. Champions argue that these developments facilitate the representation of nonstandard body types and allow consumers to fully exploit the garments in their drawers and closets, thus (hypothetically) curbing wasteful consumption.

Meanwhile, Amazon's Lab126 team is using a generative adversarial network, or GAN, to learn about particular styles by scanning lots of examples, so that it can then generate its own rudimentary designs. IBM's Cognitive Prints, a suite of tools developed for the fashion industry, could likewise enable designers (or even manufacturers who simply bypass human designers) to create textile patterns based on any image data set—snowflakes or rainforests, for instance—or to generate designs based on a set of parameters, whether Mandarin collars or pleats. Such capabilities raise questions about labor displacement, which has long been of concern in fashion manufacturing, where machines have been replacing human workers since the rise of the mechanized loom. Of course labor is, and has long been, a huge issue in popular and scholarly discussions of AI and automation.[5]

While automation has indeed extended from the shop floor to the design studio, few fashion ateliers fear obsolescence. Designer Zac Posen doubts that any GAN could capture the "situational, spontaneous moments of beauty," or exploit the fortuitous accidents and aesthetic irrationalities, that are part of any organic design process.[6] What's more, AI technologies, some say, could reinforce the unique contributions of human designers by protecting intellectual property. IBM's Cognitive Prints, which trained on 100,000 print swatches from winning Fashion Week entries, allows designers both to search for inspiration and to "make sure their inspiration is really their own and not inadvertent plagiarism."[7] Automated tools could also allow for bespoke design and fabrication—3D-printed garments that are customized to fit models' or athletes' bodies, as well as prosthetics and rehabilitative gear.[8]

Yet of course most fashion is still mass-produced. Labor and environmental advocates argue that, in these contexts, AI could enable brands to better monitor their supply chains and thus hold themselves accountable for where they source their materials and labor. Then again, well-monitored and lubricated supply chains could also simply speed up the already-unsustainably speedy world of fast fashion.

[5] See, for instance, Darrell M. West, *The Future of Work: Robots, AI, and Automation* (Washington, D.C.: Brookings Institution Press, 2018).

[6] Quoted in Sissi Cao, "Zac Posen Talks Fashion in the Era of Artificial Intelligence," *Observer* (April 13, 2018), http://observer.com/2018/04/zac-posen-fashion-artificial-intelligence/. See also Maghan McDowell, "Will AI Kill Creativity?," *Business of Fashion* (March 14, 2018), https://www.businessoffashion.com/articles/fashion-tech/will-ai-kill-creativity.

[7] Emily Matchar, "Artificial Intelligence Could Help Generate the Next Big Fashion Trends," *Smithsonian Magazine* (May 3, 2018), https://www.smithsonianmag.com/innovation/artificial-intelligence-could-help-generate-next-big-fashion-trends-180968952/.

[8] Western Bonime, "Get Personal, The Future of Artificial Intelligence Design at Bitonti Studios," *Forbes* (July 7, 2017), https://www.forbes.com/sites/westernbonime/2017/07/07/get-personal-the-future-of-ai-design-at-bitonti-studios/#1ecb8785b0de.

Product designers are applying similar techniques—using AI to comb social media to identify trends in sunglasses, toys, and tableware; automating the production of multiple iterations of projects for user-testing; and even exploiting users' behavioral data to simulate those user tests or quality assurance evaluations. Such applications allow designers and manufacturers to respond to global demands for shorter product cycles and fast-changing consumer needs and desires.[9] In other words, AI helps us generate more stuff, more cheaply and quickly, and more in line with consumers' perhaps unstated or even unrealized demands.

AI's influence is even more immediate in the world of *digital* products, like e-books and apps and chatbots. Like their analog counterparts, digital designers can set particular parameters and create models based on their preferences, and algorithmic tools can churn out hundreds of options, which users can then test and designers can tweak. Seasoned interaction designer Rob Girling imagines a digital-product future in which AI is capable of modeling cultural and psychological variables through all stages of design development and use. He envisions a future where our personal AI assistants, armed with a deep understanding of our influences, heroes, and inspirations, constantly critique our work, suggesting ideas and areas of improvement. A world where problem-solving bots help us see a problem from a variety of perspectives, through different frameworks. Where simulated users test things we've designed to see how they will perform in a variety of contexts and suggest improvements, before anything is even built. Where A/B testing bots are constantly looking for ways to suggest minor performance optimizations to our design work.[10]

For designers and developers aspiring to build digital products that trade in affect, Chris Butler, Director of AI at Philosophie, a software development studio, offers workshops on "problem framing, ideation, empathy mapping for the machine, confusion mapping, and prototyping."[11] Even emotion is operationalizable in the design process and optimizable in its products.

Those AI-informed digital products then reach the market, where they perform social, cultural, and psychological work. Voice assistants call doctors and hairstylists to make appointments, and chatbots provide therapy and tutoring to clients who can't

[9] Anand Adhikari, "Titan Experimenting with Artificial Intelligence Led Product Design," *Business Today* (December 15 2017), https://www.businesstoday.in/lifestyle/off-track/titan-experimenting-with-artificial-intelligence-led-product-design/story/266111.html; Rob Metheson, "Design Tool Reveals a Product's Many Possible Performance Tradeoffs," *MIT News* (August 15, 2018), https://news.mit.edu/2018/interactive-design-tool-product-performance-tradeoffs-0815; Sergii Shanin, "How Artificial Intelligence Is Transforming Product Development and Design," *eTeam* (December 18, 2017), https://eteam.io/blog/ai-and-product-development-design/.
[10] Rob Girling, "AI and the Future of Design: What Will the Designer of 2025 Look Like?," *O'Reilly* (January 4, 2017), https://www.oreilly.com/ideas/ai-and-the-future-of-design-what-will-the-designer-of-2025-look-like.
[11] "Design Thinking for AI," Artificial Intelligence Conference, New York, April 29–May 2, 2018, https://conferences.oreilly.com/artificial-intelligence/ai-ny-2018/public/schedule/detail/65105.

afford—or would rather not deal with—human service providers.[12] Yet when Google unveiled its Duplex voice assistant in 2018, some observers were outraged that the technology had little empathy for the product's human interlocutors: Duplex deceived those on the other end of the line by failing to disclose its artificiality. As Natasha Lomas lamented in *TechCruch*, Google clearly lacked a "deep and nuanced appreciation of the ethical concerns at play around AI technologies that [can pass] as human—and thereby [play] lots of real people in the process."[13] Echoing the Institute of Electrical and Electronics Engineers' general principles for ethically aligned design, Lomas called for digital products that respect human rights and operate transparently, and for developers who hold themselves accountable for the automated decisions their products make.[14] Girling's utopic wish list implies a whole tangle of potential accountability loopholes; his hypothetical development scenarios rely on an assemblage of simulated subjects, sites, and situations of engagement. It involves fabricated frameworks and imagined futures— each of which presents opportunities for algorithmic bias to set in, for limitations in the training data set to become reified in real-world applications.

Luckily, Girling's firm, Artefact, recognizes that "the effects of our most celebrated products are not always positive. When you 'move fast and break things,' well, things get broken—or worse."[15] So, Artefact offers a set of tarot cards that helps creators "to think about the outcomes technology can create, from unintended consequences to opportunities for positive change." We should pause to contrast the epistemologies embedded in tarot and machine learning, to consider what it means to apply esoteric practices to atone for the shortcomings of AI's positivism.

In the parallel field of graphic design, one of those "unintended consequences" is the potential obsolescence of the web designer altogether. "We have already seen a templatization of digital products" via "design systems," or coded standards with defined components, like Google's Material Design, artist-designer Rune Madsen told me. "So what happens when we start to rely on algorithms to make creative decisions?"[16] Platforms like Logojoy and Tailor Brands automate the production of logos, and Wix ADI (Artificial

[12] Yaniv Leviathan, "Google Duplex: An AI System for Accomplishing Real-World Tasks over the Phone," *Google AI Blog* (May 8, 2018), https://ai.googleblog.com/2018/05/duplex-ai-system-for-natural-conversation.html; Clive Thompson, "May A.I. Help You?," *New York Times Magazine* (November 14, 2018), https://www.nytimes.com/interactive/2018/11/14/magazine/tech-design-ai-chatbot.html.

[13] Natasha Lomas, "Duplex Shows Google Failing at Ethical and Creative AI Design," *TechCrunch* (May 10, 2018), https://techcrunch.com/2018/05/10/duplex-shows-google-failing-at-ethical-and-creative-ai-design/.

[14] "The IEEE Global Initiative on Ethics of Autonomous and Intelligent Systems," IEEE Standards Association, https://standards.ieee.org/industry-connections/ec/autonomous-systems.html. See also Alan F.T. Winfield and Marina Jirotka, "Ethical Governance is Essential to Building Trust in Robotics and Artificial Intelligence Systems," *Philosophical Transactions of the Royal Society A: Mathematical, Physical and Engineering Sciences* (October 15, 2018), https://doi.org/10.1098/rsta.2018.0085.

[15] "The Tarot Cards of Tech," *Artefact* (n.d.), https://www.artefactgroup.com/case-studies/the-tarot-cards-of-tech/.

[16] Rune Madsen, personal communication, February 1, 2019. See also Madsen, "The User Experience of Design Systems," RuneMadsen.com (2017), https://runemadsen.com/talks/uxcampcph/.

Design Intelligence) churns out websites.[17] Another platform, The Grid, prompts novice users to input text and imagery and to tell "Molly," its "AI web designer," about their goals for reach and impact. Molly will then automatically retouch and crop your photos, search through all your media to choose a complementary color palette, select layouts to fit your content mix, and conduct a few A/B tests to assess your preferences. Molly, we're told, is "quirky, but will never ghost you, never charge more, never miss a deadline"; in all these respects, she's more reliable and agreeable than a human designer.[18]

But critics have found her design work to be less than inspiring. Because machine learning algorithms "operate on historic data," Madsen said, "they always give us more of the same"—or some new hybrid that exists in the "latent space of all existing designs," a compression of what existed before.[19] Such derivations, he told me, are typically devoid of the affect and aspirations embedded in our most compelling logos and layouts. And they commonly bear the marks of the programs used to create them; you know a Squarespace or Wix site when you see one. For such reasons, most human graphic designers, like their counterparts in fashion, anticipate that, for the foreseeable future at least, machines and people will *partner* in styling the world's websites and art books.[20]

AI like Google's Auto Draw can transform designers' moodboards and diagrams into templates and polished renderings. At Airbnb, technologists are using AI to turn their whiteboard sketches into live code, to "translate high-fidelity mock[ups] into component specifications for our engineers, and…production code into design files for iteration by our designers"—an automation of sequences that not only smooths the workflow between one design specialist and another, but also allows each contributor to spend "less time pushing pixels, more time creating."[21] Echoing an oft-repeated theme among automation's humanist-futurists (or are they apologists?), designer Jason Tselentis proposes that AI-driven design tools, rather than obviating human laborers, instead promise better working conditions for them: they give sedentary organic bodies "a chance to step away from the computer, whether to work by hand or just take a break from the screen." In this second desktop revolution—after the arrival of Aldus PageMaker and other first-wave desktop publishing software in the 1980s—our new-millennium algorithms could "save human designers time and make more room in their lives for reflection and creativity."[22] Nevertheless, designer Paula Scher predicts that, as more basic skills are automated, "entry level jobs may be lost."[23]

[17] "About Wix ADI," Wix, https://support.wix.com/en/article/about-wix-adi; Logojoy, https://logojoy.com/; Tailor Brands, https://www.tailorbrands.com/. See also Yury Vetrov, "Algorithm-Driven Design," https://algorithms.design/.
[18] The Grid, https://thegrid.io.
[19] Rune Madsen, personal communication, February 1, 2019.
[20] Chris Constandse, "How AI-Driven Website Builders Will Change the Digital Landscape," *UX Collective* (October 12, 2018), https://uxdesign.cc/how-ai-driven-website-builders-will-change-the-digital-landscape-a5535c17bbe.
[21] MIX, "Airbnb Built an AI That Turns Design Sketches into Product Source Code," *The Next Web* (October 25, 2017), https://thenextweb.com/artificial-intelligence/2017/10/25/airbnb-ai-sketches-design-code/.
[22] Jason Tselentis, "When Websites Design Themselves," *Wired* (September 20, 2017), https://www.wired.com/story/when-websites-design-themselves/.
[23] Quoted in *id*.

Yet perhaps those entry-levels skills aren't quite as rote and rudimentary as they seem. Consider the services provided by several intelligent imaging applications: tools like Artisto or Prisma use image recognition to identify the content in photos and videos, and then apply matching visual-effects filters. Depending on the specific data sets training our AI assistants, we could very well see a lot more walk-on-the-beach scenes draped in gaussian blur—or many faces of color that simply don't register as faces at all.[24] Adobe's Sensei AI is behind product features like Adobe Scene Stitch, which allows users to patch and edit images by swapping in features from similar files in its image library; and its Face-Aware Liquify feature, which uses face recognition to "enhance a portrait or add creative character."[25] We might question the ethical implications of reinventing photographic scenes in this age Deep Fakes. And we might wonder what faces composed the training set from which Adobe's AI learned to identify a facial norm. Whose noses and lips set the standard? What facial features are deemed to have "character," and what sorts of sculpting constitute "enhancement"?

We might also inquire about the ethics of using AI to transform user subjectivities and user behavior into dynamic user experience (UX), which, while seeming to create more personalized products that thoughtfully anticipate user desires, also coerces longer and more predictable user engagement. As Fabricio Teixeira explains, "Websites are getting smarter and taking multiple user data points into consideration to enable more personalized experiences for visitors: time of day, where users are coming from, type of device they are accessing from, day of the week—and an ever-growing list of datapoints and signals users don't even know about."[26] "We could extract behavioral patterns and audience segments," Yury Vertov proposes, "then optimize the UX for them. It's already happening in ad targeting, where algorithms can cluster a user using implicit and explicit behavior patterns."[27] We're a long way from Web 1.0. Today's websites are designed to be artificially intelligent, opportunistic, fine-tuned coercion machines.

The application of AI across these disparate design fields raises several categories of recurring questions. First, questions about labor: will AI improve labor conditions by automating rote tasks and make it easier for creative practitioners to protect their

[24] Simone Browne, *Dark Matters: On the Surveillance of Blackness* (Durham, NC: Duke University Press, 2015); The Open Data Science Community, "The Impact of Racial Bias in Facial Recognition Software," *Medium* (October 15, 2018), https://medium.com/@ODSC/the-impact-of-racial-bias-in-facial-recognition-software-36f37113604c; Tom Simonite, "How Coders Are Fighting Bias in Facial Recognition Software," *Wired* (March 29, 2018), https://www.wired.com/story/how-coders-are-fighting-bias-in-facial-recognition-software/. See also Joy Buolamwini and Timnit Gebru, "Gender Shades: Intersectional Accuracy Disparities in Commercial Gender Classification," *Proceedings of Machine Learning Research* 8(1) (2018): 1–15.

[25] "Adjust and Exaggerate Facial Features," Adobe (n.d.), https://helpx.adobe.com/photoshop/how-to/face-aware-liquify.html (accessed January 15, 2019); James Vincent, "Adobe's Prototype AI Tools Let You Instantly Edit Photos and Videos," *The Verge* (October 24, 2017), https://www.theverge.com/2017/10/24/16533374/ai-fake-images-videos-edit-adobe-sensei.

[26] Fabricio Teixeira, "How AI Has Started to Impact Our Work as Designers," *UX Collective* (October 31, 2017), https://uxdesign.cc/how-ai-will-impact-your-routine-as-a-designer-2773a4b1728c.

[27] Yury Vetrov, "Algorithm-Driven Design: How Artificial Intelligence Is Changing Design," *Smashing Magazine* (January 3, 2017), https://www.smashingmagazine.com/2017/01/algorithm-driven-design-how-artificial-intelligence-changing-design/.

intellectual property, or will it facilitate the pirating of others' creative labor and eliminate jobs? And how might the automation of even "rote" tasks embed particular ideologies and biases—about what constitute norms and standards, and for whom—and introduce the possibility of manipulation: doctored images that lie, robot voices that deceive? Second, questions about production: will AI allow for the ethical oversight of supply chains, promoting more ethical sourcing and labor; or will it simply speed up the production process, promoting ever more wasteful extraction and manufacturing, and ever more rampant consumption? And third, our survey of these design fields raises recurring questions about users' agency and protection: do tracked behaviors and simulated testing and "empathy mapping" serve users by better meeting their needs, and even supplying custom products and services for non-normative bodies and tastes; or does such customization constitute exploitation? Are these dichotomous conditions? Or can we find a compromise?

ALGORITHMIC ARCHITECTURES

It shouldn't be surprising that so much of our virtual experience is designed and choreographed by virtual agents. AI, after all, is the new colonial power, indiscriminate in its invasion of digital terrains. Yet AI's influence spills over into the physical domain, too. As we saw in the worlds of fashion and product design, designs take shape in AI-informed digital plans, and are then made material in the form of garments and gadgets. Or even buildings and cities. Artificial intelligence scales up to embed its logics in the material world writ large. Such a translation—from invisible, bit-sized algorithmic operations to massive steel-and-glass structures—represents a radical crossing of scales and materialities and ontologies. And because architecture has traditionally been such a slow, visceral medium, it affords us a unique opportunity to observe and assess the translation from digital to physical, the embodiment of artificially intelligent operations in concrete form. In what follows, we'll examine how AI informs the operations and ethics of architecture's multiple stages of development—from planning and project management to design and construction.

Planning and Project Management

Gathering information about a design site has traditionally required visiting that site, surveying, photographing, collecting local data, and creating maps. Now, much of that work can be automated by drawing on a vast abundance of available datasets and software—like EcoDesigner STAR and SketchUp plugins—that automate data processing. Architects Hannah Wood and Rron Beqiri regard such developments as liberating: automated data analysis enables the architect to "simulate the surrounding site without ever having to engage with it physically," to "do all the necessary building and environmental analysis without ever having to leave our computers."[28] Designers can take on international commissions that would've previously presented logistical challenges. While such disembodied assessments of site might afford new opportunities to smaller, more geographically marginalized firms—and might signal community needs that aren't empirically observable—we should wonder what spatial knowledges, what localized understandings of place and the people in it, are lost when designers "never have to leave their computers." Yet perhaps on-site-versus-remote is a false dichotomy; we might instead ask how vast banks of spatial data and their automated processing could responsibly *supplement* on-site surveys, interviews, and local ethnographies.

Those spatial databases are the products a great deal of human and computational labor—of individual designers, design firms, tech companies, and professional organizations invested in the accumulation, storage, cross-referencing, and sharing of data about sites and buildings. In a 2018 report for the American Institute of Architects, Kathleen O'Donnell interviewed several designers who corroborated her recommendations to "start accumulating as much [data] as possible," including data used in Building Information Modeling platforms or post-occupancy evaluations—and to develop platforms for sharing data among architects, contractors, and property owners.[29] In order for those data to serve the purposes of automation, however, they must be rendered interoperable, which is quite a challenge when translating *place* into *data* involves different methodologies and epistemologies for different professionals. Public health officials, environmental scientists, and real-estate developers all operationalize "site" differently. Raghav Bharadwaj reports that the Architecture, Engineering, and Construction (AEC) industry is "attempting to leverage ML (machine learning)...to identify and mitigate clashes between the different models" employed by architects, various engineers, and plumbers—not to mention the conceptual and data models of other professionals who think about space differently, and whose insights could inform architecture.[30] Can machine learning reconcile such diverse conceptions of place? And can it mediate the disparate methodological, epistemological, and ethical frameworks embedded in these different datasets? Even the AEC data enthusiasts, O'Donnell reports, recognize that "regulations, security, and ethics all come into play—and [that] there are no major legal standards for data in AEC (Architecture, Engineering, and Construction) yet."

[28] Rron Beqiri, "A.I. Architectural Intelligence," *Future Architecture* (May 4, 2016), http://futurearchitectureplatform.org/news/28/ai-architecture-intelligence/; Hannah Wood, "The Architecture of Artificial Intelligence," *Archinect* (March 8, 2017), https://archinect.com/features/article/149995618/the-architecture-of-artificial-intelligence.

[29] Kathleen M. O'Donnell, "Embracing Artificial Intelligence in Architecture," AIA (March 2, 2018), https://www.aia.org/articles/178511-embracing-artificial-intelligence-in-archit. Design agency CEO Nate Miller proposes that "BIM is often positioned as a production tool, a way to generate a deliverable, but these are actually data-rich resources tied to a firm's particular knowledge base that can be used to make informed decisions about a portfolio or future design prospects." One existing platform for industry-wide data collection and sharing is the Building Information Research Knowledge Base.

[30] Raghav Bharadwaj, "AI Applications in Construction and Building—Current Use-Cases," *Emerj* (November 29, 2018), https://emerj.com/ai-sector-overviews/ai-applications-construction-building/.

Ajla Aksamija, a building technology specialist who leads Perkins + Will's Tech Lab, is convinced that a governing body like the American Institute of Architects needs to step in to set standards and institution-wide best practices for the use of data and AI in design.[31]

AI can also help to automate the administrative operations—organizing schedules, managing payroll, overseeing documentation, and even, after a period of careful training, evaluating conformance with safety and zoning guidelines.[32] Architectural historian Molly Wright Steenson notes that, "as early as the 1950s, architects at Skidmore Owings and Merrill (SOM) and Ellerbe & Associates used computers for risk calculations and cost estimates."[33] Today, too, AI can function as an "'enforcer' of code and best practices," keeping human laborers aligned with their own self-imposed algorithm.[34] In short, computers handle the boring work, the rote tasks, the complex calculations, leaving creativity to human experts (and most likely eliminating some of those human laborers in the front office). We've heard such promises before. In 1964, Bauhaus founder Walter Gropius advocated for architects to use computers as "means of superior mechanical control which might provide us with ever-greater freedom for the creative process of design."[35] Todays' computers still "aren't particularly good at heuristics or solving wicked problems," Phil Bernstein says, "but they are increasingly capable of attacking the 'tame' ones, especially those that require the management of complex, interconnected quantitative variables like sustainable performance, construction logistics, and cost estimations."[36] Andrew Witt, co-founder of "design science" office Certain Measures, suggested to me that AI could even serve as an "ethical broker" between competing stakeholder interests—which raises questions about the methods and ethics of automating ethical mediation.[37]

---

[31] Kevin Rogan, personal communication with Ajla Aksamija, February 7, 2019 (Rogan is my research assistant).

[32] Phil Bernstein, "How Can Architects Adapt to the Coming Age of AI?," *Architect's Newspaper* (November 22, 2017), https://archpaper.com/2017/11/architects-adapt-coming-ai/.

[33] Molly Wright Steenson, *Architectural Intelligence: How Designers and Architects Created the Digital Landscape* (Cambridge, MA: MIT Press, 2017), 9.

[34] Sébastien Lucas, "Artificial Intelligence (AI) in Architecture. What Are the Practical Applications?," *futur archi* (July 2017), http://www.futurearchi.org/t/artificial-intelligence-ai-in-architecture-what-are-the-practical-applications/364.

[35] Quoted in Steenson, *Architectural Intelligence*, 13.

[36] Phil Bernstein, "How Can Architects Adapt to the Coming Age of AI?," *Architect's Newspaper* (November 22, 2017), https://archpaper.com/2017/11/architects-adapt-coming-ai/.

[37] Shannon Mattern and Kevin Rogan, personal communication with Andrew Witt, February 4, 2018. Witt referenced architect Yona Friedman's 1967 Flatwriter computer program, which, he says, enabled "sets of people to ethically design an apartment complex," with each person's input "creat[ing] a set of trade-offs and choices for other people." There was a "sociological model encapsulated in the software system," which creates a "political framework [for] felicitous housing development." I'm indebted to Bryan Boyer for directing me to Certain Measures' work.

Design

AI is already shaping the creative process, too. The flagship architectural design softwares like AutoCAD, Rhino, and Revit have long automated the design process to some degree. For example, a door placed in a wall is just that: not just a collection of lines, planes, or solids, but is known by the program for what it is. Neural networks can mine the oeuvre of an individual designer or a group of designers, identify "commonly-used sequences of low-level features," and then "dynamically synthesize purpose-built features" that are relevant to the designer's task at hand.[38] Nicholas Negroponte, architect and founder of the MIT Media Lab, predicted such functionality in the late 1960s, when, as Steenson explains, AI could allow a system to "[learn] from its users and [develop] in tandem with them, with the idea that the system would evolve from how the computer was originally programmed, and from what both the architect and the user might imagine on their own."[39]

By the 1980s, software originally created for use in automotive, aeronautical, and industrial design made its way into architecture, inciting the rise of parametric design, in which the architect sets parameters that are then algorithmically translated into a range of forms. Today, software-maker Adobe offers Dreamcatcher, a "generative design system that enables designers to craft a definition of their design problem through goals and constraints"—from material types and manufacturing methods, to performance goals and cost restrictions—which are then used to process multiple data sets and generate thousands of alternative design solutions.[40] Designers can iteratively tweak the parameters and assess the performance data for each proposed option.

WeWork has developed a "suite of procedural algorithms" to automate the planning of its shared workspaces. The company's research team employs data and social scientists to better understand "how spaces can enhance people's happiness, productivity, and connection to their community."[41] Fed data on "functional and experiential considerations, building code requirements, and client expectations," their planning tool generates all possible desk layouts for each floor plan, even with their quirky columns and other obstructions.[42] Designers found that, 97 percent of the time, the tool handled such

---

[38] Patrick Hebron, "Rethinking Design Tools in the Age of Machine Learning," *Artists and Machine Intelligence* (April 26, 2017), https://medium.com/artists-and-machine-intelligence/rethinking-design-tools-in-the-age-of-machine-learning-369f3f07ab6c.

[39] Steenson, *Architectural Intelligence*, 9–10.

[40] Adobe Dreamcatcher, https://autodeskresearch.com/projects/dreamcatcher.

[41] Mark Sullivan, "This Algorithm Might Design Your Next Office," *WeWork Blog* (July 31, 2018), https://www.wework.com/blog/posts/this-algorithm-might-design-your-next-office.

[42] Carl Anderson, Carlo Bailey, Andrew Heumann, and Daniel Davis, "Augmented Space Planning: Using Procedural Generation to Automate Desk Layouts," *International Journal of Architectural Computing* 16(2) (2018): 165. The authors write: "Firms do not often treat their collective work as queryable data, and typical contractual models in the architecture, engineering, and construction industry rarely permit the design team to monitor or evaluate post-construction design performance. This is why we believe this type of research is currently best suited to certain architectural types, such as retail, offices, and healthcare: spaces where the designs are consistent, the success metrics clear, and

variations, maximizing the ratio between desk count and floor area, as well as humans. In the future the tool is meant to adjust for regional differences, "such as members in China preferring large conference rooms." Andrew Witt, from Certain Measures, imagined that many designers could eventually use "preference sets, like sentiment analysis databases," that model "how people consume or relate to architecture."[43]

As Mark Sullivan explains on WeWork's company's blog, their planning tool "does more than save time. It frees up architects to use their creativity in other ways, such as designing an eye-catching central staircase or covered courtyard where members can mix and mingle."[44] When Autodesk hired design firm The Living to design their new Toronto office, they worked with a similar array of parameters: solo versus collaborative work style, available views, light, and so forth. The Living's David Benjamin insists that "it wasn't the computer telling us what to do. We made the decisions based on human values."[45]

While designer Hannah Wood predicts that future architects are less likely to be "in the business of drawing and more into specifying [problem] requirements," there are plenty of AI aficionados ready with reassurance that architects needn't fear that they'll be reduced to data entry clerks.[46] AI will "streamline design processes without taking creative control"; "the designer will *lead* the tool," Adobe's Patrick Hebron says.[47] Humans *must* maintain control because AI, Hebron continues, "has limited purview into the nature and proclivities of human experience."[48] Any fully-AI-generated environment, we're reminded, would be unlivable. Yet architects do need to better articulate to clients, and the broader public, why that's true. As Benjamin explained to *Dwell* magazine, it's already the case that most building projects aren't designed by a trained architect; now, "we have to advocate for why we want the built environment not to be self-driving architecture. Cookie-cutter results are convenient, but we have to argue for why they're insufficient"— or unjust.[49] Benjamin predicted that developers could create automated designs keyed toward the maximization of profit, resulting in an "automated design of a city that's both uniform and unequal."[50] Thus, Witt said, it's important that we consider the "ethical dimensions of how we train designers" to partner with automated systems.[51]

the layouts somewhat repeatable" (175). See also Certain Measures' Spatial Insight and Spatial Optioneering projects, https://certainmeasures.com/spatial_insight.html; https://certainmeasures.com/spatial_optioneering.html.

[43] Shannon Mattern and Kevin Rogan, personal communication with Andrew Witt, February 4, 2019.

[44] Sullivan, "This Algorithm Might Design Your Next Office."

[45] Quoted in Sam Lubell, "Will Algorithms Be the New Architects?," *Dwell* (July 27, 2018), https://www.dwell.com/article/will-algorithms-be-the-new-architects-095c9d41.

[46] Wood, "The Architecture of Artificial Intelligence."

[47] Italics mine. Patrick Hebron, "Rethinking Design Tools in the Age of Machine Learning," *Artists and Machine Intelligence* (April 26, 2017), https://medium.com/artists-and-machine-intelligence/rethinking-design-tools-in-the-age-of-machine-learning-369f3f07ab6c.

[48] Quoted in Kathleen M. O'Donnell, "Embracing Artificial Intelligence in Architecture," AIA (March 2, 2018), https://www.aia.org/articles/178511-embracing-artificial-intelligence-in-archit.

[49] Quoted in Lubell, "Will Algorithms Be the New Architects?"

[50] Kevin Rogan, personal communication with David Benjamin, December 17, 2018.

[51] Shannon Mattern and Kevin Rogan, personal communication with Andrew Witt, February 4, 2018.

AI can offer evidence to help *humans* choose from all those cookie-cutter options and adapt them. For instance, Space Syntax's depthmapX spatial network analysis software allows designers to assess the "visual accessibility" of a design in its site, or to model pedestrian behavior.[52] Building System Planning's ClashMEP reads Revit models to detect clashes among a building's mechanical, electrical, and plumbing systems.[53] (AI could also enable those building systems to communicate with one another in the built structure, Aksamija proposes.[54]) And Unity 3D, originally created as a game engine, can be used to analyze the distance to fire exits—or to generate 3D, augmented or virtual reality models for user-testing. Such modes of presentation have the potential to make design legible, and experiential, for users and other stakeholders who might not know how to read a plan or a construction drawing.[55] And they enable designers to test "user experience," assessing even dynamic variables like light and sound and ergonomics. Designer Jim Stoddart explains:

> We can put someone in VR, and they can be inside the space and we can ask them, "Is this exciting or not? Is it inviting? Is it beautiful?" ... Then we can feed that into a machine-learning system as a supervised learning problem and actually have that software help us predict, from the thousands of designs we're generating, which ones are doing interesting things with high-level spatial and material qualities that are worthy of further investigation.[56]

Michael Bergin from Autodesk proposes that automated technologies will ultimately make architecture "far more inclusive with respect to client and occupant needs and orders of magnitude more efficient when considering environmental impact, energy use, material selection and client satisfaction."[57]

Perhaps more important than "interesting" and "beautiful" designs are ethical ones—designs aligned with those "human values" that informed Benjamin's decision-making in Toronto. Values that are of more consequence than optimal desks-per-square-foot. Benjamin has found that, for nearly the last decade, his firm and others have been adding a "bio" framework—bio-processing, bio-sensing, and bio-manufacturing—to computational design, "combining the machine and the natural world" in order facilitate "design with dynamic systems and uncertainty," to embrace diversity and robustness, to

[52] "depthmapx: visual and spatial network analysis software," The Bartlett School of Architecture, https://www.ucl.ac.uk/bartlett/architecture/research/space-syntax/depthmapx.

[53] ClashMEP, https://buildingsp.com/index.php/products/clashmep. See also Certain Measures' Topological Wiring, https://certainmeasures.com/topological_wiring.html.

[54] Kevin Rogan, personal communication with Ajla Aksamija, February 7, 2019.

[55] See the MIT Media Lab's Materiable haptic interface, https://tangible.media.mit.edu/project/materiable/ and Wood, "The Architecture of Artificial Intelligence."

[56] Quoted in Wasim Muklashy, "How Machine Learning in Architecture Is Liberating the Role of the Designer," *Redshift* (May 3, 2018), https://www.autodesk.com/redshift/machine-learning-in-architecture/. Matter Design Studio uses computational methods to explore ancient knowledge and sensory experience. See http://www.matterdesignstudio.com/. I am indebted to @KeysWalletPhone for recommending their work.

[57] Quoted in Wood, "The Architecture of Artificial Intelligence."

allow for design outside of "master models and complete all-knowingness."[58] This is one way of infusing computational design with a set of values that's more oriented toward ethics than efficiency.

Architect Christopher Alexander, whose practice had been informed by AI since the 1960s, long believed that computational patterns had a "moral component," and, according to Steenson, that "moral goodness was something that could be explicitly defined and empirically tested in architecture."[59] Alexander offered a vision of the future in which "computers play a fundamental role in making the world—and above all the built structure of the world—alive, humane, ecologically profound, and with a deep living structure."[60] How might we operationalize such ethical parameters? How might we *test* for humanity and ecological profundity in our buildings, as Alexander proposes? Such values are often aestheticized and, in the case of some bio-computational generative designs, made performative—through gratuitous breathing facades or kinetic oculi. We can also use building automation systems to monitor HVAC, energy, and lighting systems, which are perhaps proxies for "ecological profundity." And AI could help building occupants better understand how their uses of a building influence its energy consumption, Aksamija suggests.[61] How else might we "pattern" particular ethical codes into our parametrics? We might be able to monitor the presence of these values in the *making* of architecture, too.

Fabrication

In 1974, Marvin Minsky predicted that, by the mid-1990s, the machine could "handle not only the planning but the complete mechanical assembly of things as well."[62] We're not quite there yet, but we do have robots piecing together brick facades, dispensing concrete, welding, and handling the dangerous work of demolition.[63] We're 3D-printing those bricks and other much more geometrically complex building materials, too.[64]

[58] Kevin Rogan, personal communication with David Benjamin, December 17, 2018. See also Cristina Cogdell, *Toward a Living Architecture? Complexism and Biology in Generative Design* (Minneapolis: University of Minnesota Press, 2018).

[59] Steenson, *Architectural Intelligence*, 61.

[60] Quoted in *id.* at 61.

[61] Kevin Rogan, personal communication with Ajla Aksamija, February 7, 2019.

[62] Quoted in Steenson, *Architectural Intelligence: How Designers and Architects Created the Digital Landscape*, 13.

[63] Otis Harley, "The Architecture of Artificial Intelligence," *Archinect* (May 8, 2018) [video series], https://archinect.com/features/article/150062492/a-5-part-video-series-on-the-architecture-of-artificial-intelligence; Niall Patrick Walsh, "Carlo Ratti Associati's Proposed Milan Science Campus Features Robotically-Assembled Brick Facades," *ArchDaily* (August 7, 2018), https://www.archdaily.com/899777/carlo-ratti-associatis-proposed-milan-science-campus-features-robotically-assembled-brick-facades.

[64] Some predict that 3D printing will catalyze a "resurgence of detail and ornamentation." Wood, "The Architecture of Artificial Intelligence." See also the work of Michael Handmeyer and Benjamin Dillenburger, and Gramazio Fabio and Matthias Kohler.

Yet there are limits to what these automated technologies can do; for instance, they're not so great with nonuniform, unpredictable materials like low-grade timber or expanding foam.[65] Still, architectural historian Mario Carpo sees great potential environmental and economic benefits in the future of "micro-designing" and precision-installation, which "can save plenty of building material, energy, labor, and money, and can deliver buildings that are better fit to specs."[66] Certain Measures developed a process that uses pattern recognition to algorithmically generate new structures from scrap material; Witt described it to me as a means of "radical resource reuse."[67] And of course the buildings generated through intelligent fabrication processes can *themselves* be made intelligent, too, through the inclusion of smart technologies, responsive furnishings, and kinetic facades—which, again, can purportedly help to optimize energy use.[68]

As with fashion, AI can help to manage architecture's supply chains, particularly as more and more materials are prefabricated and modularized. AI can optimize project planning and scheduling.[69] Armed with camera and drone images and sensor data harvested from the construction site, automated systems can identify unsafe site conditions and worker behaviors; it can also cross-reference those images with construction models to identify errors and defects.[70] Autodesk's BIM 360 IQ scans and tags all safety issues on the jobsite and assigns "risk scores" to various subcontractors.[71] The Suffolk contracting firm is using machine learning to scan construction images and identify when

[65] Richard Moss, "Creative AI: Algorithms and Robot Craftsmen Open New Possibilities in Architecture," *New Atlas* (February 23, 2015), https://newatlas.com/creative-ai-algorithmic-architecture-robot-craftsmen/36212/.

[66] Mario Carpo, "Excessive Resolution: Artificial Intelligence and Machine Learning in Architectural Design," *Architectural Record* (June 1, 2018), https://www.architecturalrecord.com/articles/13465-excessive-resolution-artificial-intelligence-and-machine-learning-in-architectural-design.

[67] Shannon Mattern and Kevin Rogan, personal communication with Andrew Witt, February 4, 2018; Certain Measures, "Mine the Scrap Installation," https://certainmeasures.com/mts_installation.html.

[68] See the work of AI SpaceFactory, https://www.aispacefactory.com/; Eric Baldwin, "Architecture Startup AI SpaceFactory Reveals Smart Skyscrapers that Integrate Technology and Design," *ArchDaily* (October 17, 2018), https://www.archdaily.com/904163/architecture-startup-ai-spacefactory-reveals-smart-skyscrapers-that-integrate-technology-and-design.

[69] See, for instance, the ALICE scheduling technology, which allows users to optimize their construction schedules, "bid more aggressively, win more bids, and amaze your customers": Alice, https://alicetechnologies.com/.

[70] Jose Luis Blanco, Steffen Fuchs, Matthew Parsons, and Maria Joao Ribeirinho, "Artificial Intelligence: Construction Technology's Next Frontier," McKinsey & Company (April 2018), https://www.mckinsey.com/industries/capital-projects-and-infrastructure/our-insights/artificial-intelligence-construction-technologys-next-frontier; Jenny Clavero, "Artificial Intelligence in Construction: The Future of Construction," *esub: construction software* (January 23, 2018), https://esub.com/artificial-intelligence-construction-future-construction/. The SmartVid.io image management platform uses machine learning to review and tag photos and videos of the job site, and then suggests safety measures. All this footage is stored and made searchable, rendering it a useful resource in potential lawsuits. SmartVid.io, https://www.smartvid.io/.

[71] Anand Rajagopal, "The Rise of AI and Machine Learning in Construction," *Autodesk University* (December 21, 2017), https://medium.com/autodesk-university/the-rise-of-ai-and-machine-learning-in-construction-219f95342f5c.

workers are wearing hardhats and safety vests, and, eventually, to recognize ladders, clutter, and other safety risks.[72]

Meanwhile, Komatsu, the Japanese heavy-machinery manufacturer, is partnering with NVIDIA, maker of graphics processing units, to incorporate its Jetson AI computing platform into construction equipment, allowing for full-surround vision and real-time video analytics, which can be used to optimize the use of on-site tools and equipment, monitor job progress, and flag risks.[73] Of course such exhaustive data collection—as is commonly advocated during the planning phase, too—presents myriad methodological challenges and privacy risks (not to mention its potential to create a culture of paranoia). We see similar risks in smart buildings, with their ubiquitous cameras and sensors and voice interfaces. We might also wonder if remote, automated data collection will minimize the need for planners and construction foremen to monitor conditions on-site.

We have buildings planned, designed, and fabricated with the aid of artificial intelligence. They're infused with AI, in accordance with the recurring design dream of buildings that can think for themselves. And at the end of their functional lives, they could very well be demolished by an artificially intelligent automaton.[74] Through these phases of architectural design, we encounter many familiar questions about the ethics of automation. Will automation liberate designers from the drudgery of drafting and data-crunching, will it eliminate their jobs, or will it allow for a complementary blending of human and machinic skills? When payroll and scheduling are robotized, what happens to the clerical staff? How might designers create automated design tools that balance efficiency and economy with other "human values," like ecological stewardship and accessibility, in multiple senses of the term? How might AI-generated models promote sensitivity to environmental impact and the sustainable sourcing of materials; allow designers to attend to the full embodied experience of a building, including its acoustic and thermal conditions; and render the design process more open to diverse stakeholders or user groups? And how might contractors deploy robot fabricators to promote resource and energy conservation, while also improving human laborers' working conditions— that is, if those laborers are still around? Finally, whose values and interests are built into those algorithms—and which bodies do we find in the studio, on the construction site, or in the fabrication lab or factory, altering and actualizing the algorithms' output in

[72] Elizabeth Woyke, "AI Could Help the Construction Industry Work Faster—And Keep Its Workforce Accident-Free," *MIT Technology Review* (June 12, 2018), https://www.technologyreview.com/s/611141/ai-could-help-the-construction-industry-work-faster-and-keep-its-workforce-accident-free/.

[73] Kevin Krewell and Tirias Research, "NVIDIA and Komatsu Partner on AI-Based Intelligent Equipment for Improved Safety and Efficiency," *Forbes* (December 12, 2017), https://www.forbes.com/sites/tiriasresearch/2017/12/12/nvidia-and-komatsu-partner-on-ai-based-intelligent-equipment/#1f0bdc1e665b; Raghav Bharadwaj, "AI Applications in Construction and Building— Current Use-Cases," *Emerj* (November 29, 2018), https://emerj.com/ai-sector-overviews/ai-applications-construction-building/.

[74] I'm grateful to Kevin Rogan for the conversations that generated much of this concluding section.

polymers and plasterboard? This final question—about which and whose intelligences are embedded in AI—pertains to every sector of design we've explored here.

To ensure the ethical application of AI in design, we have to make sure we're both defining responsible parameters and operationalizing those parameters responsibly— and creatively. Where might human designers intervene in an automated workflow? Where might they reassert their agency? Could designers apply their design skills in designing subversive algorithms that generate aberrant aesthetics or embody radical politics? Will we eventually come to regard our Squarespace websites and Dreamcatcher edifices as aesthetically and politically retrograde—a form of AI authoritarianism, machine learning mannerism, or GAN neo-Gothic? In the calculative composition of our apps and architectures and apparel, we need to carefully consider both the ends and means of automation, to continually audit the algorithms and apparatae through which our material worlds are made.

BIBLIOGRAPHY

Bratton, Benjamin. "Lecture: On A.I. and Cities: Platform Design, Algorithmic Perception, and Urban Geopolitics," Benno Premsela Lecture, 2015, https://bennopremselalezing2015. hetnieuweinstituut.nl/en/lecture-ai-and-cities-platform-design-algorithmic-perception-and-urban-geopolitics.

Carpo, Mario. *The Second Digital Turn: Design Beyond Intelligence*. Cambridge, MA: MIT Press, 2017.

Hebron, Patrick. "Rethinking Design Tools in the Age of Machine Learning," *Artists and Machine Intelligence* (April 26, 2017), https://medium.com/artists-and-machine-intelligence/rethinking-design-tools-in-the-age-of-machine-learning-369f3f07ab6c.

Luce, Leanne. *Artificial Intelligence for Fashion: How AI Is Revolutionizing the Fashion Industry*. Berkeley, CA: Apress, 2019.

Negroponte, Nicolas. *The Architecture Machine: Toward a More Human Environment*. Cambridge, MA: MIT Press, 1973.

O'Donnell, Kathleen M. "Embracing Artificial Intelligence in Architecture," AIA (March 2, 2018), https://www.aia.org/articles/178511-embracing-artificial-intelligence-in-archit.

Steenson, Molly Wright. *Architectural Intelligence: How Designers and Architects Created the Digital Landscape*. Cambridge, MA: MIT Press, 2017.

Vetrov, Yury. "Algorithm-Driven Design," https://algorithms.design/.

CHAPTER 31

....

AI AND THE GLOBAL SOUTH

Designing for Other Worlds

....

CHINMAYI ARUN[1]

INTRODUCTION

....

In his essay "A Place in the Sun,"[2] architect Charles Correa describes the hazards of replicating designs without any regard to context. Picture poorly designed housing— the insulated, weather-resistant "box" created for severely cold northern European regions—taking over warm Indian cities, replacing the ventilated homes with verandahs and courtyards that are necessary in the tropical climate. This housing designed for Northern Europe is unable to meet the needs of people living in the warmer cities of the developing world in a different social and cultural context. Correa argues that we must place the needs, history, and the cultural and economic context of a society at the center of design.

It is worth thinking of the algorithmic society from this architectural point of view.[3] Manuel Castells wrote, "we know that technology does not determine society: it *is* society."[4] Increasingly, privately owned web-based platforms control our access to public services, security, education, the public sphere, health services, and our very

[1] I am grateful to Paola Ricaurte for all that she has taught me about the Global South and for talking some of these issues through with me, to Dragana Kaurin for sharing her inspiring unpublished work, to my colleague Salome Viljoen for encouraging me to make bolder choices, and to my mother, Radha Arun, for coming through at short notice as my final reader for this chapter and much else that I have written.
[2] Charles Correa, "A Place in the Sun," in *A Place in the Shade* (Gurgaon: Penguin Random House India, 2010).
[3] See Ryan Calo, "Robotics and the Lessons of Cyberlaw," *California Law Review* 103(3) (2015): 513–63, and Jack M. Balkin, "The Path of Robotics Law," *The Circuit* 72 (2015).
[4] Manuel Castells, *The Network Society*, (Washington, DC: Center for Transatlantic Relations, 2005), 3.

relationship with the countries we live in. As society is "datafied," public services are delivered through public-private partnerships.[5] There is a push for "data-driven development" mediated by private actors. Development donors such as international nongovernmental organizations (NGOs) and governments rely on data collected by corporations, [6] creating potentially biased, opaque decision-making systems. We should examine the design of the systems of automation and artificial intelligence that are gradually permeating citizens' lives. We must think about who these systems are designed for, who designs them, how they are designed, and what ends they serve.

In this chapter, I focus on the risks, not the benefits of AI, to highlight the ways in Southern populations are vulnerable. Northern countries offer their citizens stronger safeguards than Southern countries—most of these countries already have law in place for data privacy.[7] While the World Economic Forum has published proposals to incorporate ethics in AI, and the Organisation for Economic Co-operation and Development has published principles on AI, these do not guarantee protection to Southern populations.

This chapter is about the ways in which AI may affect the Global South. I begin with explaining why this is a concern and move on to discussing what is meant by the Global South. Although the term "South" has a history connected with "Third World" and associated with certain countries negotiating together, it is not a clear geographical segregation or even a uniform idea. Scholars argue that it is a plural concept—there are Souths. After discussing the meaning of "South," I use four examples to show that there are many ways in which Southern populations are affected by technology. The term "South" is complex and necessitates a context-driven approach to AI.

Finally, I outline the issues we must take into account in the context of AI and the Global South. The risks of AI are exacerbated for Southern populations, but it is difficult to discuss the effects of AI on the South without discussing the effects of AI more broadly. This is why I discuss systems of discrimination first and then discuss how this affects Southern populations. I follow this with a summary of how international human rights might apply. In conclusion, I argue that a context-driven approach, participative, empowering approach is necessary to ensure that human rights of Southern populations are protected.

It will be clear by the end of this chapter that we need to transform the way we innovate, frame policies for, and think about AI. The enormity of the effort involved should not deter us. Correa pointed out that the developing world is eager for innovation and change and that genius lies in stitching new ideas into an old social fabric and producing

---

[5] Linnet Taylor and Dennis Broeders, "In the Name of Development: Power, Profit and the Datafication of the Global South," *Geoforum* 64 (2015): 229–237, 229–230. See also Anita Gurumurthy, Nandini Chami, and Deepti Bharthur, *Democratic Accountability in the Digital Age*, IT for Change, 2016.

[6] Taylor and Broeders, "In the Name of Development," 229–230.

[7] Commission Nationale de l'Informatique et des Libertés, Data Protection Around the World, available at https://www.cnil.fr/en/data-protection-around-the-world (last visited June 8, 2019).

a "seamless wonder."[8] This metaphor is worth bearing in mind as we review the hot mess that is currently the use of artificial intelligence (AI) in the Global South.

WHY WE WORRY ABOUT
THE GLOBAL SOUTH

There is an increasing awareness that we should be thinking more about the impact of AI on the Global South. The broad concern is clear enough: if privileged white men are designing the technology and the business models for AI,[9] how will they design for the South? The answer is that they will design in a manner that is at best an uneasy fit, and at worst amplifies existing systemic harm and oppression to horrifying proportions.

As Global South advocates furrow their brows about AI, they may be thinking of web-based AI designed by people who live in worlds that rarely see power cuts or internet shutdowns and then deployed to the rural hinterlands of countries with poor internet connectivity and only a few hours of electricity a day. They may worry about the resources diverted from education and healthcare budgets to technology-centric solutions from the companies that are building these systems. They may be concerned about the surveillance of Southern children through AI for Education, built by people whose own children go to private school and have restricted access to screens. In authoritarian countries, they may lose sleep over AI that uses facial recognition, drones, and other forms of surveillance to oppress vulnerable populations. They may worry about the loss of jobs and the impact on economies as AI replaces low-skilled workers.

These concerns are not without foundation. Ideas of the past, such as one laptop per child,[10] have resulted in spectacular failure despite the bright-eyed optimism and laudable intentions with which they were created. Technology designed out of context may fail to take local resources, social norms, and cultural context into account. "One-day delivery" can mean very different things in Boston and Hyderabad even if the system designed for both cities is the same. Facebook can be fairly harmless in most countries and find itself weaponized in a country with Myanmar's sociopolitical context, to contribute to genocide.[11] It can take effort for Google Maps to be able to account for the favelas of Rio de Janeiro.[12] Technology policy frameworks can impact

---

[8] Correa, "A Place in the Sun," 25.

[9] This is a concern that is well founded. See Sarah Myers West, Meredith Whittaker, and Kate Crawford, *Discriminating Systems* (Report) (New York: AI Now, 2019).

[10] Joshua Keating, "Why Did One Laptop per Child Fail," *Foreign Policy* (September 9, 2009), https://foreignpolicy.com/2009/09/09/why-did-one-laptop-per-child-fail/.

[11] "Facebook Has Turned into a Beast in Myanmar," *BBC* (March 13, 2018), https://www.bbc.com/news/technology-43385677.

[12] Max Oprey, "How Google Is Putting Rio's Invisible Favelas Back on the Map," *The Guardian* (October 9, 2016), https://www.theguardian.com/sustainable-business/2016/oct/09/invisible-favelas-brazil-rio-maps-erasing-poorer-parts-city.

whole countries, as we might have learned from the debate on drug patents and public health in developing world.

There are so many ways in which AI can wreak havoc in Southern countries and affect the human rights of Southern populations. In the absence of local regulation in Southern countries, AI may be deployed in its experimental stages such that the people of these countries bear the risk of harm that may ensue. At a larger scale, AI may impact the economies of these countries by affecting their role in the global economy: several developing countries that benefited from their role in the internet-driven global economy may gradually find the low-skilled outsourced services they offer replaced by automation. The "call centers" of Bangalore, and employment and business they generate, can be undone as automation makes human intervention unnecessary. Automated cars may result in the cab drivers of New York—famously from all over the world—finding themselves out of work with a redundant skill.

We need to begin our journey toward including the South as a priority, and we need to do go beyond the mere use of the phrase in policy documents or speeches. For this, we have to understand the many things we specifically worry about when we speak of the Global South. Who is being left out and endangered?

WHAT IS THE GLOBAL SOUTH?

Contemporary use of the term "Global South" has a complicated history and is linked to but different from other terms like "Third World" and "Developing countries."[13] "Global South" has now largely replaced "Third World" and "Developing countries," but is not without its controversies. While the latter two terms were used in the context of geopolitics, and "Global South" shares this history, there is a convincing body of scholarship about how "Global South" transcends borders to stand for more than nation states. It helps to have a little context in the form of the history of these terms and the changes in politics, culture, and economics that accompanied them.

Although the term "South" had been used by scholars earlier,[14] its journey toward becoming mainstream might have started when the Brandt Commission reports used it in the 1980s, in the context of their argument for the transfer of funds from the "North" to the "South."[15] "South" has significant overlap with the term "Third World," which came to be used from the 1950s to move away from "East" and "West" with their Cold War overtones.[16] "Third World" was a term used initially to distinguished the "colonized

[13] See Anne Garden Mahler, "Beyond the Colour Curtain," in *The Global South Atlantic* (New York: Fordham University Press, 2017).

[14] See Nour Dados and Raewyn Connell, "The Global South," *Contexts* 11(1) (2012): 12.

[15] Arif Dirlik, "Global South: Predicament and Promise," *The Global South* 1(1) (2007): 12–23.

[16] Mark T. Berger, "After the Third World? History, Destiny and the Fate of Third Worldism," *Third World Quarterly* 25(1) (2004): 9–39, 10.

or neocolonized world,"[17] but over time it also came to stand for certain values.[18] While "Third World" was used to organize countries around certain ideologies, it appears that "South" came to be used when development aid was offered to the South. Over time the term has come to expand beyond borders and is no longer viewed in a geographically restrictive way.[19]

"South" as it is currently used by many scholars is an expansive term, so that it includes "countless Souths," including within what we understand as the West.[20] In the next part of this chapter I discuss these arguments here and then offer illustrations of how this expansive definition is useful.

A striking articulation of this expansive thinking about the South comes from Santos, who argues that the South cannot be seen as a geographic concept[21] and must be seen instead as "a metaphor for the human suffering caused by capitalism and colonialism on the global level, as well as for the resistance to overcoming or minimising such suffering."[22] This definition accounts for the migrant workers with few rights and an abysmal standard of living in countries that one would otherwise describe as wealthy. It allows us to distinguish between the billionaires residing in India, Mexico, and China, and the marginalized impoverished residents of these countries. Such an expanded reading of the global South focuses on inequality, oppression, and resistance to injustice and oppression.[23]

Santos argues that the South can be found within Europe and North America "in the form of excluded silenced and marginalised populations such as undocumented immigrants, the unemployed, ethnic or religious minorities, and victims of sexism, homophobia, racism and islamaphobia."[24] Milan builds on this to say that the South must be understood as a "plural entity" containing within it "the different, the underprivileged, the alternative, the resistant, the invisible, and the subversive."[25] The significance of framing what we refer to as the South in this manner, is that this way we include within it disenfranchised populations, many of whom are geographically clustered in countries we think of as the "South" and some of whom are within countries we would describe as the North. This conception of the South might encompass refugees in the United States of America, who lead a markedly different life from the upper-class, privileged, dominant-race individuals who also reside in the country. It would also support the idea that there are Souths—what is designed for one Southern community or population would not necessarily fit another Southern community or population. This means that designing for the South will mean accounting for many different contexts.

[17] Dirlik, "Global South: Predicament and Promise," 13.
[18] Berger, "After the Third World?," 10.
[19] Dirlik, "Global South: Predicament and Promise," 15–20.
[20] Stefania Milan and Emiliano Treré, "Big Data from the South(s): Beyond Data Universalism," *Television & New Media* 20(4) (2019): 319–335, 325.
[21] Boaventura de Sousa Santos, "Epistemologies of the South and the Future," *From the European South* 1 (2016): 17–29, 18.
[22] *Id.* at 18.   [23] Milan and Treré, "Big Data," 325.   [24] Santos, "Epistemologies," 19.
[25] Milan and Treré, "Big Data," 321.

This inclusive definition of the South as a plural entity is worth holding on to since it accounts for the rights and priorities of the many populations excluded from our current thinking about AI. It forces us to understand that the concerns raised by the South are varied, and it helps to think about different populations of the South within their own context. A contextual understanding should not prevent us from recognizing the value of strategic South-South alliances around particular issues to gain leverage. There are affinities between Southern societies based on their shared history of economic, political, and social marginalization, and past global cooperation for common causes such as the Group of 20 and the World Trade Organization protests.[26] We must however recognize that South-South cooperation is far from simple as powerful Southern societies like those in China, India, Brazil, and South Africa compete with each other for power, and powerful groups within these Southern societies benefit from the perpetuation of the transnational economy in its current form.[27]

In considering AI's impact on the South, we have to acknowledge the dominance of "Western technology companies," while noting that China is challenging the United States in the fields of AI and big data.[28] Ricaurte points out that there is a cluster of countries from which data is extracted, and who consume the services offered by dominant global technology companies.[29] Some of these countries, such as India, acknowledge and highlight their own potential for extraction of such data, ignoring the potential impacts on citizens. The political elite, working closely with the industry elite, of these countries can tend to focus more on protection of markets than on protection of citizens. The commodification of citizens is not questioned—the focus is on ensuring that local capital, rather than foreign capital, benefits from this commodification. Ricaurte highlights the role of governments in "data colonization,"[30] pointing out that governments create frameworks to validate this process and contract with AI companies for public services provided using private data extracted from the populations they are meant to serve.[31]

It is clear that the exploitation of the South has many dimensions. It might take place entirely within what we understand as the "North," with data collection and monitoring of refugees, immigrants, and other marginalized populations. It might also take place entirely within the South, where the rising inequality, economic models, and close ties between industry and government might mean that legal frameworks are designed to facilitate local industry's extraction of data from citizens. However, in keeping with the broader ways in which global power and capital has worked in the past, during colonization and after, it also takes place across borders. Northern companies "mine" data from the

---

[26] Dirlik, "Global South: Predicament and Promise," 16.   [27] Id. at 16.

[28] Paola Ricaurte, "Data Epistemologies, Coloniality of Power, and Resistance," *Television & New Media* (2019): 1–16, 9.

[29] Id. at 9.

[30] Ricaurte, "Data Epistemologies," and Nick Couldry and Ulises Mejias, "Data Colonialism: Rethinking Big Data's Relation to the Contemporary Subject," *Television and New Media* (2018): 1–14.

[31] Ricaurte, "Data Epistemologies," 8.

South relatively easily. This extraction is a part of a privatized process.[32] The extraction of data has been compared to the extractive practices of colonialism by Couldry and Mejeias.[33] The elite that govern the countries from which the extraction takes place are often complicit in this extraction. The burden of the extraction is borne by the disenfranchised. In the recent years, Southern countries have also developed relationships mirroring North-South extractive practices with other Southern countries—Indian and Chinese businesses have expanded to other Southern countries. The next part of this chapter illustrates four models through which vulnerable Southern populations are put at risk by technology.

TECHNOLOGY IN OTHER WORLDS

In discussing the idea of the "South," different models of exploitation of the South using technology have surfaced. Here four examples are used to highlight the complexity and vulnerabilities of the South. The first example of Facebook in Myanmar is the classic illustration of how technology designed in the North can be harmful when exported to the South. The second example explores the exploitation of Southern populations by the governing elite within Southern countries by examining Aadhaar, India's national identity database. The third example focuses on Southern populations in Northern countries through a discussion of refugees in Europe. The last example discusses South-South exploitation using China's export of surveillance technology as an illustration.

Facebook in Myanmar

Among the most shocking ways in which data and algorithms may affect human rights is the role that Facebook played in the Rohingya genocide in Myanmar. It prompted the UN investigators of the genocide to note in their report that Facebook "has been a useful instrument to those that seek to spread hate" and recommended an independent investigation of the extent of the company's role.[34]

Facebook, a U.S.-based company, brought its social media platform to Myanmar, which is a former colony with a history of decades of state control. This was a classic case where the business model and technological architecture from a Northern country was used in a Southern country. Facebook aggressively marketed its platform, offering it free

---

[32] Jim Thatcher, David O'Sullivan, and Dillon Mahmoudi, "Data Colonialism through Accumulation by Dispossession: New Metaphors for Daily Data," *Society and Space* 34(6) (2016): 990.

[33] Couldry and Mejias, "Data Colonialism," 1–14, 1.

[34] Report of the Independent International Fact-finding Mission on Myanmar, Human Rights Council, 12 September 2018, paragraph 74.

of cost through its controversial Free Basics program,[35] in a country that had not had the time to develop a healthy media ecosystem. Myanmar's press was described as "not free" in Freedom House's Freedom of the Press report in 2012. At the time, criticism of the government was outlawed and most private publications were subject to prepublication censorship.[36] Domestic broadcast and print media were owned or controlled by the government, and the import of foreign periodicals was restricted. Without a healthy media ecosystem, citizens have no way of ascertaining the truth. Facebook was designed for a society with a very robust media ecosystem, protected by the First Amendment. It is not clear that it had given any thought to what would happen if the same platform dominated the information ecosystem of a country like Myanmar which has been described as a rumor-filled society.[37]

The BSR human rights impact assessment of Facebook in Myanmar pointed out that Facebook was used to incite and coordinate violence. It is clear from news reports that hate speech went viral on Facebook in Myanmar,[38] and the military used the platform to spread the hatred[39] during the genocide. Based on interviews, BSR argued that Facebook should make the effort to understand the local context better.

Myanmar is a small country, and its public institutions and legal systems offered the victims of the violence little support. Facebook should have been careful while entering, making the effort to understand the local context and to build a feedback loop. It was the most vulnerable people, the truly marginalized within a Southern country that suffered the harm.

A Biometric Identity Database in India

Aadhaar, the biometrics—based "unique identity" number[40] database in India has no cross-border element. This is a top-down control heavy system designed by powerful elite upper caste men[41]—a software billionaire, Nandan Nilekani, supported

[35] Catherine Trautwein, "Facebook Free Basics Lands in Myanmar," *Myanmar Times* (June 6, 2016), available at https://www.mmtimes.com/business/technology/20685-facebook-free-basics-lands-in-myanmar.html.
[36] "Freedom of the Press 2012," Freedom House, Washington, D.C., 92–93, available at https://freedomhouse.org/report/freedom-press/freedom-press-2012.
[37] BSR, "Human Rights Impact Assessment: Facebook in Myanmar" (2018).
[38] Megha Rajagopalan, "Internet Trolls Are Using Facebook to Target Myanmar's Muslims," *Buzzfeed News* (March 18, 2017), available at https://www.buzzfeednews.com/article/meghara/how-fake-news-and-online-hate-are-making-life-hell-for#.wlGyPB4gk.
[39] Paul Mozur, "A Genocide Incited on Facebook with Posts from Myanmar's Military," *New York Times* (October 15, 2018), available at https://www.nytimes.com/2018/10/15/technology/myanmar-facebook-genocide.html.
[40] For more information, see https://uidai.gov.in/what-is-aadhaar.html.
[41] Ian Parker, "The I.D. Man," *The New Yorker* (October 3, 2011), available at https://www.newyorker.com/magazine/2011/10/03/the-i-d-man.

by high-ranking politicians and civil servants[42]—for the underprivileged people of India. The initial object was to give all people, including migrant workers, a way to access government services.[43] However the system is an interface between people and welfare services. Enrolling in the database will not spare an impoverished person the effort of opening a bank account, or acquiring a ration card.[44]

There were a limited number of consultations, and no serious cost benefit analysis or impact assessment studies of this very expensive project. Experts on Indian food distribution and welfare schemes, life-saving public services for the impoverished people of India, were critical of the project from the start.[45] They pointed out that other less expensive models have been found to work better.[46] Nilekani does not appear to have been willing to engage with the fundamental questions of whether Aadhaar the best way to administer the state's welfare systems.[47]

Aadhaar is mandatory for anyone who wants to access the Indian welfare system. It has been criticized for excluding people from this welfare system owing to the many ways in which it malfunctions. Researchers have found that up to twenty-seven starvation deaths from 2015 onwards have been directly linked to Aadhaar.[48] The database has also been breached several times, and news reports say that almost a billion records with personally identifiable information have been compromised.[49]

Aadhaar has played havoc with people's lives and has caused people to starve by preventing them from accessing the government services that deliver their basic right to food. In addition to causing harm within the system it was supposed to fix, Aadhaar targets vulnerable people such as undocumented Bangladeshi migrant workers residing in India—one of the stated goals of the system is to make it easier to find and deport these people.[50] The system is also unfriendly to the impoverished populations for whom it was built. The architecture of the biometric data collection system does not account for what happens to their bodies as a result of living on the streets.[51]

It illustrates that it is possible within a Southern state, for the elite to force the marginalized to help them construct big data sets that are then used to exclude them surveil them and violate their rights in other ways.

---

[42] Payal Arora, "The Bottom of the Data Pyramid: Big Data and the Global South,, *International Journal of Communication* 10 (2016): 1681–1699 at 1683–1684.

[43] See Parker, "I.D. Man."

[44] Reetika Khera, "The UID Project and Welfare Schemes," *Economic and Political Weekly* XLVI (9) (2001): 38.

[45] *Id.*   [46] *Id.*   [47] See *id.* and Parker, "I.D. Man."

[48] "Aadhaar Linked to Half the Reported Starvation Deaths Since 2015, Say Researchers," *Huffington Post India* (September 26, 2018), available at https://www.huffingtonpost.in/2018/09/25/aadhaar-linked-to-half-the-reported-starvation-deaths-since-2015-say-researchers_a_23539768/.

[49] "1 Billion Records Compromised in Aadhaar Breach since January: Gemalto," *Business Line* (October 15, 2018), available at https://www.thehindubusinessline.com/news/1-bn-records-compromised-in-aadhaar-breach-since-january-gemalto/article25224758.ece.

[50] Arora, "The Bottom of the Big Data Pyramid," 1681–1699, 1684.   [51] *Id.* at 1685.

Refugees and Data Collection in Europe

A powerful illustration of how the South exists within what we see as Northern countries, come from Dragana Kaurin's work on the digital agency of refugees in the European Union.[52] European laws, international law, and even humanitarian agencies use technology to deprive asylum seekers of agency and make them even more vulnerable.

Refugees are made to give up personal data when they seek asylum in the European Union. Although they are physically based in what is usually considered the Global North, asylum seekers are vulnerable people who receive no protection from their countries of origin and little protection from their country of residence. They are often under threat from their country of origin, which they have fled, and from their host countries where the law enforcement agencies often have the mandate to find, imprison or deport them.[53] While they are in this vulnerable position, law enforcement and border control agencies, as well as UN aid agencies and NGOs, collect asylum seekers' and refugees' biometrics.

Kaurin explains how the use of automation can harm refugees and asylum seekers. The social media and communication devices that help them maintain their ties with family and seek information from humanitarian aid workers as they are on the move also subject them to surveillance as the private sector and government actors harvest their data and monitor their movements.[54] Even well-intentioned efforts using technology can put them at risk. For example, the Trace the Face program by the International Committee of the Red Cross uses facial recognition technology that searches for missing persons using photos provided by the families of missing migrants of either the missing migrants themselves or their blood relatives.[55] Kaurin references an interview with a refugee to point out the chilling fact that some refugees "are also running away from family or someone who wants to hurt them."[56]

This is an illustration of Southern populations that inhabit the Global North that are made more vulnerable through collection of data and the use of technology. Systems built to help refugees and asylum seekers have adopted this technology that does not take their needs into account. Kaurin points out that refugees are not usually consulted and engaged in the framing of these policies that affect them.[57] To reduce the vulnerability and increase the agency of asylum seekers, she recommends that impacted communities, especially the minorities and marginalized groups within them, be involved in designing processes and making decisions for asylum seekers.[58]

---

[52] Dragana Kaurin, Data Protection and Digital Agency of Refugees, CIGI Special Report, May 14, 2019.

[53] *Id*. at 4.   [54] *Id*. at 5.   [55] *Id*. at 12.   [56] *Id*. at 13.   [57] *Id*. at 24.

[58] *Id*. at 24.

Chinese Facial Recognition Technology in Zimbabwe

Using strategy similar to the North's expansion to the South, China is selling surveillance technology to countries like Ethiopia.[59] One might see this as oppression of the population in one Southern country by the elite within that country, facilitated by another Southern Country.

It is well known that China is using big data to build enhanced systems of surveillance, ranging from the social credit system and facial recognition to systems that will predict which individuals might be a threat to public safety. These systems are used by the elite within the country to control the rest of the population and have now taken a cross-border dimension.

Chinese companies make and sell closed-circuit television cameras and monitoring systems, sometimes high-definition and equipped with facial and movement recognition technology, to other countries including Brazil, Ecuador, and Kenya. Northern countries like Germany and recently the United States have taken steps to control foreign acquisitions and to control the technologies they use, but it appears that a significant market exists for this technology in Southern countries. In a country like Ethiopia, the government purchases Chinese technology to monitor mobile phones and the internet activity of its people.

As these four examples might suggest, there is more than one model through which Southern populations are harmed or exploited through the use of technology. The same institutional weaknesses that leave Southern populations in the Southern countries vulnerable to technology from Northern countries, make them vulnerable to technologies from other Southern countries. The technology developed for surveillance and control of populations within countries in the South is exported and used against marginalized populations in other Southern nations.

AI AND THE GLOBAL SOUTH

It is worth reading work by scholars who think about AI and discrimination, while noting that Southern institutions and legal frameworks can exacerbate the harms that they discuss. Southern populations within Northern countries might not have same access as privileged people to the institutions within the same countries. Autonomous systems are used so broadly that they can affect the economy, housing, intimate relationships, and more. They can introduce or enhance discrimination and oppression, and they can erase populations by failing to account for their existence.

[59] Maya Wang, "China's Dystopian Push to Revolutionize Surveillance," https://www.hrw.org/news/2017/08/18/chinas-dystopian-push-revolutionize-surveillance, 2017.

I begin with discussing autonomous systems as systems of discrimination, I then move on to discussing what this may mean for Southern populations, especially since the fragile democracies and nondemocracies of the world do not offer their citizens the institutional protections that may be available in the United States or Europe.

SYSTEMS OF DISCRIMINATION

Any discussion of AI in the context of discrimination has to include big data, which is "the fuel that runs the Algorithmic Society."[60] Algorithmic systems are often trained on a corpus of data, which means that big data and its inherent biases affect the outcome of these systems.[61] There are several stages at which inaccuracies and bias can be introduced into algorithmic decision-making. These range from the recording of the data to the actual question answered by the algorithm.

There is a tendency to accept predictions based on data sets as the truth[62] even though the outcome is typically an interpretation of the data[63] and may be inaccurate.[64] The data set could suffer from any number of problems which would skew the outcome. Scholars use the term "dirty data" to refer to missing, incorrect, and badly represented data, as well as to data that has been manipulated intentionally or distorted by biases.[65] Crawford has pointed out that "not all data is created or even collected equally."[66] Data collection has embedded power and assumptions. The recording of fingerprints, for example, is difficult for those who do manual work, such as refugees and migrant and contract laborers.[67]

The very design of data sets can be biased as a result of assumptions and gaps.[68] The data sets could underrepresent or wrongly represent certain populations, leading to discrimination against them or to their exclusion.[69] Even if the data set is accurate, its structure can end up discriminating and marginalizing people: the classic example

---

[60] Jack M. Balkin, "The Three Laws of Robotics in the Age of Big Data," *Ohio State Law Journal* 78(5) (2017): 1217, 1219.

[61] Ifeoma Ajunwa, "The Paradox of Automation as Anti-Bias Intervention," *Cardozo Law Review* 41 (forthcoming, 2020): 13.

[62] *Id.* at 13.

[63] danah boyd and Kate Crawford, "Six Provocations for Big Data," A Decade in Internet Time: Symposium on the Dynamics of the Internet and Society (Oxford Internet Institute, 2011), 6.

[64] Kate Crawford and Jason Schultz, "Big Data and Due Process: Toward a Framework to Redress Predictive Privacy Harms," *Boston College Law Review* 55 (1) (2014): 93, 101.

[65] Rashida Richardson, Jason M. Schultz, and Kate Crawford, "Dirty Data, Bad Predictions: How Civil Rights Violations impact Police Data, Predictive Policing Systems and Justice," *New York University Law Review* 94 (2019): 192, 195.

[66] Ajunwa, *The Paradox of Automation*, 13, based on Kate Crawford, "Think Again: Big Data," *Foreign Policy* (May 10, 2013, 12:40 a.m.), https://foreignpolicy.com/2013/05/10/think-again-big-data.

[67] See Arora, "The Bottom of the Big Data Pyramid," and Kaurin, *Data Protection*.

[68] Ajunwa, *The Paradox of Automation*, 13.   [69] *Id.* at 13–18.

being data sets that code people as either male or female, erasing other forms of gender identity.[70] A data set might discriminate indirectly by recording a seemingly innocuous fact that acts as a marker for identity. An illustration of this is employment which can be used to infer caste based on the historic employment of marginalized caste people for certain tasks (such as manual scavenging).[71]

The training data for algorithms can embed bias,[72] and algorithms trained on real-world data would replicate real word discrimination.[73] Therefore a hospital computer program used to sort out medical school students based on previous admissions decisions ends up discriminating against women and racial minorities because of the rules it learned from the hospital's older biased decisions.[74] Big data essentially generates correlations.[75] Although scientists understand the difference between correlation and causation, the rest of the world tends to treat conclusions based on big data as "enough."[76]

The AI Now institute has articulated the problem in unambiguous terms.[77] It has pointed out that since classification, differentiation, and ranking are central to AI systems, these systems are "systems of discrimination." It has argued that the bias in AI systems is connected with the lack of diversity in the AI industry, including the people who build AI tools and the environment in which they are built. The large-scale AI systems come from elite university labs and a few technology companies, which are "white, affluent, technically oriented and male" spaces.[78] In other words, these technologies are designed by people from the North. Context can be reintroduced if universities studying AI collaborate with social and humanities disciplines, affected communities. and civil society organizations.[79] It is important in to account for plurality, context, and intersectionality.[80]

Southern Populations

In addition to changing how decisions are made about design, data, and deployment in the algorithmic society, we must give Southern populations the tools to engage effectively with the questions that affect them. This is already proving challenging in what we understand as Global North countries despite the lively debate and relatively strong privacy and antidiscrimination laws. When companies deploy these technologies in

[70] West et al., *Discriminating Systems*, 6.
[71] The Citizen Bureau, "Caste and Aadhaar: How Will a Manual Scavenger Leave His Past Behind?," *The Citizen* (August 5, 2017), available at www.thecitizen.in/index.php/en/newsdetail/index/2/11396/caste-and-aadhar-how-will-a-manual-scavenger-leave-his-past-behind.
[72] Solon Barocas and Andrew D. Selbst, "Big Data's Disparate Impact," *California Law Review* 104 (2016): 671, 680–681.
[73] Ajunwa, *The Paradox of Automation*, 14.
[74] Barocas and Selbst, "Big Data's Disparate Impact," 682.
[75] Ajunwa, *The Paradox of Automation* 13.   [76] *Id.* at 15.
[77] West et al., *Discriminating Systems*, 6.   [78] *Id.* at 6.
[79] AI Now Report 2018, AI Now Institute, New York University.
[80] West et al., *Discriminating Systems*, 3.

Southern countries, there are fewer resources and institutions to help protect marginalized people's rights. This needs to be remedied as a high priority.

The systems discussed in the previous four examples are designed by people with privileged access to the data of data subjects. The data subjects have little control or autonomy over their own data. It is typical, when autonomous systems are used, that data subjects have no idea who has access to their data or how it is used.[81] This is exacerbated in Southern countries. Young democracies lack institutional stability since it takes time to build institutions and institutionalize democratic practices.[82] This is why Milan argues that we need diverse ways for citizens and civil society engagement to ward off datafication practices that result in oppression and inequality.[83]

The institutional frameworks of Southern countries must be taken into account as we consider what impact AI might have on the South. Freedom depends not just on political and civil rights but also on other social and economic arrangement such as education and health care.[84] Development, Amartya Sen argues, depends on the removal of sources of "unfreedom," such as systematic social deprivation, poverty, poor economic opportunities, and tyranny. Sen describes poverty in terms of capability deprivation, in what is now famously knows as the "capabilities approach" to development. Julie Cohen has applied Sen's work, as build on by Martha Nussbaum, to access to knowledge, and has pointed out that we need to pay more attention to the relationship between the networked information environment and human flourishing.[85]

The rights of Southern populations can be realized through efforts made by states, but can also be eroded by the governing elite of states. In the past, Southern countries worked together as a bloc, to gain access to technology, capital, and markets.[86] They had a shared commitment to development, opposition of colonialism, the creation of equitable conditions for socioeconomic development of all countries, and the evolution of South-South cooperation.[87] This cooperation has been taking place since the Non-Aligned Movement, in which developing countries came together to negotiate development and trade issues. As the developing countries began what they called South-South cooperation, triangular cooperation also began such that donors and Northern partners became involved in South-South initiatives.[88]

---

[81] danah boyd and Kate Crawford, "Critical Questions for Big Data," *Information, Communication & Society* 15(5) (2014): 662–679, 673.

[82] Ethan B. Kapstein and Nathan Converse, "Why Democracies Fail," *Journal of Democracy*, 19 (4) (2008): 57–68.

[83] Milan and Treré, "Big Data," 328.

[84] Amartya Sen, "Introduction," in *Development as Freedom* (Anchor Books: New York, 2008).

[85] Julie Cohen, *Configuring the Networked Self* (New Haven, CT: Yale University Press, 2012), ch. 9.

[86] Rubin Patterson, "Global Trade and Technology Regimes: The South's Asymmetrical Struggle," *Perspectives on Global Development and Technology* 4(3–4) (2005): 382.

[87] Report of the UN Secretary General to the UN General Assembly (2018), 73rd session, *Role of South-South Cooperation and the Implementation of the 2030 Agenda for Sustainable Development: Challenges and Opportunities*, 3.

[88] *Id.* at 5.

Progress has been made over the years on South-South initiatives, but one might argue that the cooperation between the Southern states and triangular cooperation has had mixed results. Over the years, nonstate actors such as businesses and civil society have started playing a powerful role in Southern countries. These countries have developed groups that are wealthy and influential and populations that are more affluent than their fellow citizens—the extractive, exploitative consequences are evident in the Aadhaar example. Some Southern states are more developed and have greater economic influence than other Southern states. The exploitative nature of this relationship is evident in the China-Zimbabwe example.

How International Human Rights Apply

It is clear that Southern populations are varied and scattered through Northern and Southern countries. It helps to bear in mind that they are all entitled to human rights under international law, which offers a standard and a threshold that debates on innovation and AI must take into account. AI will affect human rights, especially for Southern populations, and work is underway to map how these rights may be affected. As the UN Secretary General's high-level panel on digital cooperation acknowledges, the major documents codifying international human rights were written before the age of digital cooperation.[89]

AI could potentially impact the rights to freedom of expression, privacy, social security, and the right against discrimination. It might also violate state parties' commitment to guarantee these rights without discrimination. The UN Special Rapporteur for freedom of expression, David Kaye, has recommended that companies should account for discrimination at both the input and the output level of AI systems and design systems that are nondiscriminatory and account for diversity.[90] He has suggested that states and companies might be obligated to conduct human rights impact assessments and public consultations during the design and deployment of new AI systems or existing systems in new markets. He has also recommended that states should ensure that human rights are central to the design, deployment, and implementation of AI systems.[91] These recommendations offer concrete ways to ensure that states make an effort to prevent companies from violating human rights as they build and deploy AI. The recommendation about impact assessments when technology is used in new markets is especially valuable

[89] Report of the UN Secretary-General's High-level Panel on Digital Cooperation (2019), *The Age of Digital Interdependence*, 16.

[90] Report of the Special Rapporteur on the promotion and protection of the right to freedom of opinion and expression to the UN General Assembly, Seventy-third Session, 2018.

[91] *Id.*

for Southern countries since it acknowledges that it can be risky to deploy technology designed for the North unthinking in the South. It accounts for context.

Although the UN Special Rapporteur on extreme poverty and human rights is yet to publish his report on AI, his public consultation has elicited useful responses from human rights organizations. These responses point out that discriminatory AI systems might violate the right to social security.[92] They may also affect states' obligation to ensure that people are able to access the right to work,[93] necessitating efforts to enable people whose skills and jobs are affected by AI to acquire new skills and competence so that they are able to work and to explore alternative income models like the universal basic income.[94]

The recommendations about ways in which states must develop institutional frameworks to guarantee human rights in a world dominated by AI systems are useful. There is however much more work to be done. We need a clear framework against which states can be assessed, to monitor their progress in protecting human rights and advancing the sustainable development goals as they develop and use AI.

Conclusion

The degree to which the AI industry is willing to experiment on human populations,[95] in the name of innovation, should make us uncomfortable. As Castells reminds us, invoking the Holocaust, we must remember how destructive technology can be before we lose ourselves in its wonders.[96] The technology and capital that drives AI currently rests firmly in privileged Northern hands. Vulnerable Southern populations in particular are at risk from the surveillance and other forms of discrimination, bias, and poorly tailored outcomes that will result from AI that is designed with no regard to their local contexts. The politics of design need to be examined, and AI systems need to be studied in situated realities.[97]

Boyd and Crawford write powerfully that "big data has emerged a system of knowledge that is already changing the objects of knowledge, while also having the power to inform how we understand communities and networks."[98] With every year that passes, this system intertwines itself with our institutions and permeates our societies. This is

---

[92] Article 22 of the Universal Declaration of Human Rights, as well as Article 9 of the International Covenant on Civil and Political Rights. See Human Rights Watch, Submission to the UN Special Rapporteur on extreme poverty and human rights, May 2019.

[93] Article 6(1) of the International Covenant on Economic, Social and Cultural Rights.

[94] Amnesty International, Submission to the UN Special Rapporteur on extreme poverty and human rights, May 2019.

[95] AI Now Institute Report 2018, 24.   [96] Castells, *The Network Society*, 3.

[97] West et al., *Discriminating Systems*, 16.

[98] boyd and Crawford, "Critical Questions for Big Data," 665.

why we must heed Ricaurte's call for alternative digital futures and pluriverses, and for the protection of cultures that are resistant to being governed by the market.[99] We must work on reversing extractive technologies in favor of justice and human rights.

Although scholars, scientists, and UN experts have cautioned against the speedy adoption of AI, which may harm vulnerable populations or affect their agency and autonomy,[100] more work is necessary to account for the plural contexts of the Global South and adopt modes of engagement that include these populations, empower them, and design for them. It may be necessary to reimagine models of innovation to achieve this.[101] The UN Secretary General's high-level panel on digital cooperation has recognized this and has called for an inclusive digital economy and society, one that accounts for local conditions, human rights, and barriers faced by marginalized groups.[102] It has also recognized the need to develop capacity so that all stakeholders are able to understand and make critical choices about emerging technologies.

Although this redesigning of these technology and market models as we know them may seem daunting, and arguments may be made that efforts to contextualize them will affect their ability to operate at scale, it is not too late to start. Correa wrote that the big question for architects in the Third World is not the size or value of their projects, but "the nature of the questions they raise—and which we must confront. A chance to grow: the abiding virtue of a place in the sun."[103]

BIBLIOGRAPHY

Ajunwa, Ifeoma. "The Paradox of Automation as Anti-Bias Intervention," *Cardozo Law Review* 41 (forthcoming 2020): 13.

Couldry, Nick and Ulises Mejias. "Data Colonialism: Rethinking Big Data's Relation to the Contemporary Subject," *Television and New Media* (2018): 1–14.

Dirlik, Arif. "Global South: Predicament and Promise," *The Global South* 1(1) (2007): 12–23.

Mahler, Anne. "Beyond the Colour Curtain." In *The Global South Atlantic*. New York: Fordham University Press, 2017.

Milan, Stefania and Emiliano Treré. "Big Data from the South(s): Beyond Data Universalism," *Television & New Media* 20(4) (2019): 319–335.

Ricaurte, Paola. "Data Epistemologies, Coloniality of Power, and Resistance," *Television & New Media* (2019): 1–16.

Richardson, Rashida, Jason M. Schultz, and Kate Crawford. "Dirty Data, Bad Predictions: How Civil Rights Violations impact Police Data, Predictive Policing Systems and Justice," *New York University Law Review* 94 (2019): 192–233.

[99] Ricaurte, "Data Epistemologies," 12.
[100] Stuart Russel et al., "Research Priorities for Robust and Beneficial Artificial Intelligence: An Open Letter" (2015), available at https://futureoflife.org/ai-open-letter; and the Report of the Special Rapporteur (2018), paragraph 47.
[101] See Milan and Treré, "Big Data," 328, and Ricaurte, "Data Epistemologies," 12.
[102] UN Secretary-General's High-level Panel on Digital Cooperation, 29.
[103] Correa, "A Place in the Sun," 25.

Santos, Boaventura de Sousa. "Epistemologies of the South and the Future," *From the European South* 1 (2016): 17–29.

Taylor, Linnet and Dennis Broeders. "In the Name of Development: Power, Profit and the Datafication of the Global South," *Geoforum* 64 (2015): 229–237.

West, Sarah Myers, Meredith Whittaker, and Kate Crawford. *Discriminating Systems* (Report). New York: AI Now, 2019.

CHAPTER 32

....

PERSPECTIVES AND APPROACHES IN AI ETHICS

East Asia

....

DANIT GAL

INTRODUCTION

....

FOR centuries humanity has been building technological tools to support and enhance its capabilities, allowing us to survive and flourish. For years humanity has dreamed about creating others in its image, leading to a history rich with human statues, automata, robots, and artificial intelligence (AI). As we usher in another era of technological development, we are faced with the social consequences of our dreams—a technology that exceeds the status of tool and is moving toward that of a partner. Let us be clear: AI and robots themselves are tools. And yet their perception is increasingly that of partners, blurring the line between what they are and what they could be. Partnership is a broad term in this context. It encompasses tools functioning as social caretakers, friends, companions, romantic love interests, and fellow spiritual beings. All of which, developed and used in East Asia, are briefly surveyed in this introductory chapter.

The framing of this chapter is founded on the claim that China, Japan, and South Korea perceive and approach AI and robots on a spectrum ranging from tool to partner. This may be true for other countries, but is distinct in East Asia. While continuously moving on this spectrum, the policy, academic thought, local practices, and popular culture observed in each country place South Korea in the tool range, China in the middle, and Japan further along in the partner range.

The tool perspectives on and approaches to AI and robotics are seemingly common in the West, where the technology is viewed as an instrument for development and growth. This is also true for East Asia, especially where official government and corporate policies are concerned. The divergence toward the partner range occurs in academic thought, local practices, and popular culture.

Some readers may be tempted to categorize the partner range of the spectrum as a simple act of anthropomorphism, defined as "to attribute human form or personality to things not human,"[1] but that is an oversimplification. While it is true that East Asian countries demonstrate a preference toward biologically inspired (humanoid and animaloid) AI and robots, they do much more than that. Under Buddhist and Shinto techno-animism, AI and robots are not just attributed human traits, they are believed to possess a spirit or spiritual essence. In addition, in East Asia, AI and robot partners have come to be viewed as friends and love interests. These spiritual, psychological, and emotional perceptions of AI and robots, in turn, are further amplified by the fact that AI and robots are designed to not only look but also behave like us.

The human tendency to anthropomorphize runs into further complications when AI and robots are designed to have the relatable interface of a potential partner but are intended be used as a tool. This creates a functional and emotional paradox where designing tools mimicking humans is desirable, but developing natural human emotions in response to such mimicking is seen as problematic. The chapter names this design contradiction the Anthropomorphized Tools Paradox. This paradox, often tightly knit with issues of female objectification, constitutes another notable source of growing sociotechnical tensions. These tensions, emanating from our movement on the tool-partner spectrum, have inspired numerous global AI and robotics ethics debates throughout the years. And yet in no place are these debates as feasible and as socially pressing as in East Asia.

SOUTH KOREA

South Korea is placed in the tool range due to its establishment of a clear human-over-machine hierarchy, where humans are of the highest priority and AI and robots are expected to support and further enhance this position of dominance. A caveat in this hierarchy is that within the human layer exist additional social hierarchies that may compromise the inclusive potential of AI and robots. South Korea also demonstrates a clear preference for functional AI applications and robots, mainly focusing on human empowerment in the areas of public services like education, healthcare, social care, disaster relief, and security. A divergence toward the partner range is found in the country's popular culture, which is awash with human-AI-robots partnership stories.

---

[1] Merriam-Webster Dictionary, *Anthropomorphize*, n.d., https://www.merriam-webster.com/dictionary/anthropomorphize.

Policies and Ethical Principles: Tool-Decisive

In 2007, the Korea Institute for Robot Industry Advancement (KIRIA) published a Robots Ethics Charter, which was further revised in 2016.[2] These past iterations served as the foundation of an all-government ethical framework adopted by the South Korean National Information Society Agency (NIA). The NIA released its Ethics Guideline for the Intelligent Information Society in April 2018.[3] The guideline aims to achieve a human-oriented intelligent information society through the PACT Principles: Publicness, Accountability, Controllability, and Transparency.

Building on the 2007 Robot Ethics Charter's comprehensive ethical guidelines for developers, providers, and users, the Ethics Guideline assumes four unique positions: (1) It places considerable responsibility on users, calling for informed and self-regulated use. (2) It places the responsibility for preemptively assessing AI and robots' potential negative social impact on providers. (3) It holds developers responsible for the elimina-tion of socially discriminatory characteristics in AI and robotics design and for making it accessible to disadvantaged and vulnerable groups. Developers are also placed in the vanguard of AI ethics in South Korea. (4) It calls to refrain from developing AI and robots with "antisocial" characteristics and to "minimize social resistance and disorder against the universal use" of AI and robots.[4]

In addition, the Ethics Charter published by the NIA in June 2018[5] reiterates the six principles codified in the 2016 version of the Robots Ethics Charter by KIRIA. Notable among these principles is the balance between the protection of human dignity (first principle) and the common good (second principle). Sunyoung Byun, professor at the Seoul National University of Education, explains that the three versions of the Ethics Charter approach AI and robots as tools meant to protect human dignity and promote the common social good. He notes the difficulty humans have in maintaining a harmo-nious balance between individual and collective flourishing and that this balancing act constitutes an important moral dilemma further complicated by the introduction of AI and robots.[6] These documents spell a clear human-over-machine hierarchy where humans (developers, providers, and users) protect each other and AI and robots protect and service humans.

---

[2] The 2007 and 2016 Robots Ethics Charter iterations published by the Korea Institute for Robot Industry Advancement were kindly translated by Sunyong Byun, professor at the Seoul National University of Education.

[3] National Information Society Agency (NIA), *Ethics Guideline for the Intelligent Information Society*, April 2018, http://eng.nia.or.kr/common/board/Download.do?bcIdx=20239&cbIdx=62611&fileNo=1.

[4] *Id.* at 3.

[5] NIA, *Ethics Charter for the Intelligent Information Society*, June 2018, http://eng.nia.or.kr/common/board/Download.do?bcIdx=20239&cbIdx=62611&fileNo=2.

[6] Sunyoung Byun, remote interview by Danit Gal, March 7, 2019. For more information, see Sunyoung Byun, Hyunwoo Shin, Jinkyu, Jeong, and Hyeongjoo Kim, "A Study on Necessity of the Charter of Robot Ethics and Its Contents," *Journal of Ethics* 112 (2017): 295–319.

Academic Thought and Local Practices: Tool-Oriented

South Korea's tool perspectives on and approaches to AI and robots is also evident in its 2018 Winter Olympics technology demonstration, where it deployed eighty-five functional robots with varying degrees of intelligence. Rescue robots from the Korea Advanced Institute of Science and Technology (KAIST) were used as torchbearers alongside celebrities, and robots serviced the airport and different competition venues.[7] Functional robots are not immune to ethical clashes and debates, as seen in the international boycott of KAIST by over fifty AI researchers due to its partnership with a defense company. The ban was lifted shortly after KAIST ensured the researchers it will not develop or assist in the development of lethal autonomous weapon systems or killer robots.[8] Two months later, KAIST announced the establishment of an AI ethics subcommittee.[9] But Chi Hyung Jeon, assistant professor at KAIST, states that the subcommittee was formed during the time of the boycott in April 2019 and hosted its first event with the boycott organizers' participation, drawing a line between the two events.[10]

Further in conjunction with the ban, KAIST released a Code of Ethics for Artificial Intelligence on April 4, 2018.[11] Unique among its four principles is the third one, stipulating that "AI shall follow both explicit and implicit human intention. However, before execution, the AI should ask people to confirm the implicit intention. (If several people are involved and their intentions are different, the AI should follow the person with the highest priority or closest relationship.)" This suggests additional human hierarchies within the human layer of the human-over-machine hierarchy, where "highest priority" people will have the final say on navigating the AI as they see fit. KAIST's principle further complicates an established issue of societal inequality in South Korea[12] by reinforcing positions of power or relationship which conflict with other documents calling for more equally distributed and accessible AI and robots. In particular, given KAIST's position as an educational institute, this principle may also conflict with developers' mandate to act as eliminators of social bias and discrimination under NIA's Ethical Guideline.

---

[7] Tara Francis Chan, "South Korea Will Have 85 Robot Volunteers at the Winter Olympics, Including a Robot Torch Bearer," *Business Insider* (December 6, 2017), https://www.businessinsider.com/south-korea-robots-2018-winter-olympics-2017–12.

[8] "AI Researchers End Ban after S. Korean University Says No to 'Killer Robots,' " *Reuters* (April 9, 2018), https://www.reuters.com/article/tech-korea-boycott/ai-researchers-end-ban-after-s-korean-university-says-no-to-killer-robots-idUSL8N1RM2HN.

[9] Ji-hye Jun, "KAIST Launches Ethics Subcommittee on AI," *Korea Times* (June 8, 2018), https://www.koreatimes.co.kr/www/tech/2018/06/129_250278.html.

[10] Chi Hyung Jeon, remote interview by Danit Gal, March 7, 2019.

[11] KAIST Institute for Artificial Intelligence, *KAIST Code of Ethics for Artificial Intelligence*, April 4, 2018, https://kis.kaist.ac.kr/index.php?mid=KIAI_O.

[12] Jaewon Kim, "A 'Lost Generation' in South Korea Bears the Brunt of Rising Inequality," *Nikkei Asian Review* (December 14, 2017), https://asia.nikkei.com/Economy/A-lost-generation-in-South-Korea-bears-the-brunt-of-rising-inequality.

Popular Culture: Between Partnership Exploration and Tool Preference

But while the KAIST code of ethics may challenge NIA's desired harmony within the human layer of the hierarchy, South Korean popular culture is challenging the hierarchy itself. Korean dramas offer a more controversial perspective by entertaining the idea of AI and robots as being more than just tools. The country saw eight dramas about AI and robots acting as family members, friends, and love interests between 2016 and 2019. This list includes: 사랑하면 죽는 여자 봉순이 or Bong Soon—a Cyborg in Love (2016); 아이엠 or I am... (2017); 로봇이 아니야 or I'm Not a Robot (2017); 보그맘 or Borg Mom (2017); 109 별일 다 있네 or 109 Strange Things (2017); 너도 인간이니 or Are you Human Too? (2018); 사랑은 사람처럼 or Love Like a Person (2019); and 절대 그이 or Absolute Boyfriend (2019), an adaptation of a Japanese story. While most shows conclude that human companionship is superior to that of AI and robots, they frequently and publicly explore the idea of AI and robots transitioning from tools to partners.

Directly addressing this disruption to the human-over-machine hierarchy, Jiwon Kim, head of AI Policy at the Ministry of Science and ICT, notes that "as people become more reliant on and overuse intelligent social robots, the risk of losing the basic ethical values we hold as humans, as well as authentic human relationships, increases." Kim states that they therefore "believe that attachment to obedient robots could undermine people's relationships with other humans."[13] This concern may be key in explaining the NIA's emphasis on avoiding the "antisocial" development of AI and robots. This raises an important question: what degree of AI and robotics development is perceived as "antisocial" by virtue of its ability to disrupt human relationships? This question will become increasingly pressing as we examine Chinese and Japanese perspectives and approaches.

Such concerns may also be a response to the findings of a 2018 study on human interactions with a social intelligent robot in South Korea.[14] But most South Koreans, it seems, still prefer functional AI and robots. A 2016 study found that South Korean respondents preferred a functional robot over a biologically inspired one when compared with their Japanese peers. Respondents maintained that a functional robot made them feel like they had more control over it. This sense of hierarchical preservation is believed to have induced an increased sense of comfort among South Korean users.[15] The observed sense of comfort aligns with the NIA's wishes to "minimize social resistance

[13] Jiwon Kim, remote interview by Danit Gal, March 8, 2019.
[14] Chan Mi Park, Yuin Jeong, Kwangmin Jeong, Hae-Sung Lee, Jeehang Lee, and Jinwoo Kim, "Intelligent Social Robots in the Wild: A Qualitative Study on Deploying Intelligent Social Robots with Growing Features to Real Home Environments" (February 2018), http://socialrobotsinthewild.org/wp-content/uploads/2018/02/HRI-SRW_2018_paper_4.pdf.
[15] Hyewon Lee, Hyemee Kang, Min-Gyu Kim, Jaeryoung Lee, and Sonya S. Kwak, "Pepper or Roomba? Effective Robot Design Type Based on Cultural Analysis between Korean and Japanese Users," International Journal of Software Engineering and Its Applications 10 (2016): 37–46.

and disorder against the universal use" of AI and robots.[16] But as more systems take on humanoid and animaloid shape to make their interface relatable and master biologically inspired capabilities to better communicate with humans, this sense of control and comfort will likely erode.

Conclusions

This chapter places South Korea in the tool range of the spectrum quite comfortably. And yet it does note that the established human-over-machine hierarchy will face continued challenges as the technology evolves and the human imagination continues to run wild. In fact, the adherence to a human-over-machine hierarchy and the calls to avoid "antisocial" development further highlight the debate on human-AI-robots partnerships. It also highlights the fact that further social hierarchies exist within the human layer of said human-over-machine hierarchy. This amplifies existing social tensions that are likely to increase in complexity and importance as more artificial actors join the societal mix. A human-machine integration is inevitable given South Korea's plans to create an intelligent information society, even if it's a human-oriented one. Policymakers in South Korea and elsewhere should thus remember that technology does not solve social problems, it typically further exacerbates them.

CHINA

Much like South Korea, China holds a top-down view of AI and robots as tools for progress, as demonstrated in official government and corporate policies and recommendations. The ethical components of this approach are beginning to materialize, and evidence suggests that they align with other global guidelines, largely viewing AI and robots as tools. China, however, also presents a strong interest in imbuing AI and robots with partner-like capabilities to help them realize their full positive potential. This is apparent in its academic thought, local practices, and popular culture. As such, China is also home to intensifying tensions between top-down tool and bottom-up partner approaches and perspectives that will shape and inform future local debates and practices.

Policies and Ethical Principles: Tool-Oriented

Published on July 20, 2017, the Chinese Government's New Generation AI Development Plan calls for the establishment of ethical norms and frameworks. Namely, it calls for the establishment of an "ethical and moral multi-level judgement structure and

---

[16] NIA, *Ethics Guideline*, 3.

human-computer collaboration ethical framework" and "an ethical code of conduct."[17] According to the plan's timeline, the codification of these ethical norms, codes, and frameworks is slated to take place between 2025 and 2030, during the last stretch of the development plan.

This will not take as long. On January 10, 2019, the Chinese Association for Artificial Intelligence (CAAI), the only state-level AI organization sitting under the Ministry of Civil Affairs,[18] announced the establishment of an AI ethics committee tasked with creating guidelines for Chinese development.[19] The committee is led by Professor Xiaoping Chen, known for leading the creation of a realistic female humanoid "robot goddess" named JiaJia (which embodies both the Anthropomorphized Tools paradox and female objectification issues).[20] Chen explained the uniqueness in AI and robot ethics, saying that "a smart humanoid robot could integrate into people's daily lives someday, but no one knows for sure what kind of risks it may bring along with its service."[21] This suggests a challenging ethical balancing act between technology created to act as an intelligent tool but designed with the characteristics of a desirable partner.

In early March 2019, the Chinese government hosted the 13th National Committee of the Chinese People's Political Consultative Conference and the 13th National People's Congress, known as the Two Sessions. During the Two Sessions, the CEOs of Baidu and Tencent submitted proposals discussing AI ethics.[22] Baidu's Robin Li Yanhong submitted a proposal calling on the government to speed up AI ethics research, citing the impending transition of AI from a simple tool to a stakeholder in many areas. In particular, Li urged the government to share distinct Chinese wisdom with the international AI ethics community.[23] On May 26, 2018, Li also introduced Baidu's four AI ethics principles: safety and controllability, equal access, human development, and freedom.[24] Tencent's Pony Ma Huateng submitted a proposal calling for ethical AI regulations and

[17] Graham Webster, Rogier Creemers, Paul Triolo, and Elsa Kania, "Full Translation: China's 'New Generation Artificial Intelligence Development Plan,'" *New America* (August 1, 2017), https://www.newamerica.org/cybersecurity-initiative/digichina/blog/full-translation-chinas-new-generation-artificial-intelligence-development-plan-2017/ (last modified October 2018).
[18] For more information on CAAI, see http://www.caai.cn.
[19] Phoebe Zhang, "China's Top AI Scientist Drives Development of Ethical Guideline," *South China Morning Post* (January 10, 2019), https://www.scmp.com/news/china/science/article/2181573/chinas-top-ai-scientist-drives-development-ethical-guidelines.
[20] Celine Ge, "Meet Jiajia, the Realistic 'Robot Goddess' Built by Chinese Researchers," *South China Morning Post* (April 18, 2016), https://www.scmp.com/news/china/society/article/1936834/meet-jiajia-realistic-robot-goddess-built-chinese-researchers.
[21] Na Chen, "AI Association to Draft Ethics Guidelines," *Chinese Academy of Science* (January 10, 2019), http://english.cas.cn/newsroom/news/201901/t20190110_203885.shtml.
[22] Masha Borak, "China Wants to Make Its Own Rules for AI Ethics," *ABACUS* (March 4, 2019), https://www.abacusnews.com/future-tech/china-wants-make-its-own-rules-ai-ethics/article/3001025.
[23] 新浪财经综合, "李彦宏三大提案:完善电子病历 加强人工智能伦理研究," 新浪财经 (March 4, 2019), http://finance.sina.com.cn/review/jcgc/2019-03-04/doc-ihsxncvf9583301.shtml.
[24] 博客园, "Li Yanhong Unveiled after 'Baidu Lost the Land': 'Simple Search' without Advertisement, Mass Production of Unmanned Vehicles in July," *China IT News 3.0* (May 26, 2018), http://www.fonow.com/view/208592.html.

the use of AI for social good.[25] This stance is in line with the Tencent Research Institute's (TRI) running project: AI for Social Good.[26] The TRI also published an AI ethics framework for multiple stakeholders under the ARCC principles: Available, Reliable, Comprehensive, and Controllable.[27]

On May 25, 2019, a group of leading Chinese institutions including the Beijing Academy of AI, Peking and Tsinghua universities, the Chinese Academy of Science, and industry leaders like Baidu, Tencent, and Alibaba released the Beijing AI Principles.[28] Aligning with other existing AI principles, the Beijing Principles emphasize AI development to benefit humanity. A notable suggestion in the principles maintains that "stakeholders of AI systems should be able to receive education and training to help them adapt to the impact of AI development in psychological, emotional, technical aspects."[29] This suggests a considerable degree of expected psychological and emotional interactions between humans the AI systems, rather than just functional ones. A statement of this sort indeed hovers between the tool and partner range of the spectrum.

Considering the observed alignment with international AI ethics discourse, what would the aforementioned distinct Chinese wisdom to be brought into these discussions look like? Miao Liao, lecturer at Changsha University of Science and Technology, believes the answer is found in the pluralistic integration of the Chinese government's twelve "core socialist values."[30] These values are divided into three groups. National values include prosperity, democracy, civility, and harmony. Social values include freedom, equality, justice, and the rule of law. Individual values include patriotism, dedication, integrity, and friendship. These twelve values, she explains, are already integrated into a nationally taught graduate Engineering Ethics (工程伦理) textbook. The textbook also highlights four unique Chinese characteristics in comparison with Western engineering ethical guidelines: responsibility precedes freedom, obligation precedes rights, the group precedes the individual, and harmony precedes conflict.[31] It is highly likely that state-adopted and state-approved AI and robotics ethical guidelines will incorporate these values or, at the very least, reflect their spirit as in the case of engineering.

---

[25] 腾讯研究院, "2019年两会，马化腾提了这7份建议案|2万字全文版," (March 6, 2019), https://mp.weixin.qq.com/s/yb6OyuIvHQjImcNMJsJYSw.

[26] 张志东, "腾讯创始人张志东:信息过载时代，科技如何向善?," 腾讯研究院 (January 20, 2018), https://mp.weixin.qq.com/s/656xTSvP1rLl6SORRS94ew.

[27] 司晓, ""司晓:打造伦理"方舟，让人工智能可知、可控、可用、可靠, 腾讯研究院 (December 6, 2018), https://mp.weixin.qq.com/s/_CbBsrjrTbRkKjUNdmhuqQ [English available].

[28] ZX, "Beijing Publishes AI Ethical Standards, Calls for Int'l Cooperation," *Xinhua* (May 26, 2019), http://www.xinhuanet.com/english/2019–05/26/c_138091724.htm?fbclid=IwAR3VPl45lsmmtoanWolO ZkpnHpODQa-3bzD9Q8DVB6mZUrB_2xtDxM5vBic.

[29] Beijing Academy of AI, "Beijing AI Principles," May 28, 2019, https://baip.baai.ac.cn/en?fbclid=IwAR2HtIRKJxxy9Q1Y953H-2pMHl_bIr8pcsIxho93BtZY-FPH39vV9v9B2eY.

[30] Miao Liao, remote interview by Danit Gal, March 10, 2019.

[31] For more information on the 工程伦理 textbook, see: http://www.tup.tsinghua.edu.cn/booksCenter/book_06831902.html.

Academic Thought and Local Practices: Uniquely Partnership-Oriented

An AI ethics initiative departing from the tool approach to AI is the Harmonious Artificial Intelligence Principles (HAIP), led by Yi Zeng, professor at the Chinese Academy of Science (CAS) Institute of Automation. The HAIP code of ethics promotes unique concepts like: (1) humanization to strengthen interactions between AI and humans; (2) empathy and altruism to ensure a harmonious human-AI society; (3) human empathy toward the AI; (4) privacy for AI, which humans should respect; (5) bias against the machine, where humans should not show bias where both AI and humans show similar risks; and (6) legal constraints on how humans treat AI to ensure a harmonious coexistence.[32] Zeng claims that the safest approach to develop AI and robots is to give them a sense of self (consciousness) so that they are able to empathize with humans. He believes the reciprocity between humans and AI and robots is key in achieving true harmony to ensure the technology remains beneficial as it continues to evolve.[33] This approach to AI ethics marks a clear shift toward the partner range of the spectrum and serves as a rare demonstration of what ethical principles aiming to achieve this partnership vision might look like.

Zeng is not alone in his belief that AI systems should ascend to a higher level of consciousness. Hanniman Huang, a veteran Chinese AI product manager, views AI and robots as a new species. He sees them as a carrier for the human exploration of self-limitation and the relationship between heaven and man. Huang believes that the technologies' unique advantages will fully manifest when humans move from using them as a substitute (tool), to having them as a part of their society (partner), to coexisting with them (human-AI-robots symbiosis, found on the far end of the partner range). According to Huang, this symbiosis will be achieved when developers possess critical competencies in humanistic and spiritual realms of knowledge by practicing Buddhism. He specifically points toward the Buddha dharma, which symbolizes the natural law and harmony and thus guides ethical behavior.[34] Huang therefore takes human-AI-robots partnerships an additional step further to include both physical and spiritual connections.

Popular Culture: Partnership-embracing

This aligns with the Chinese Buddhist idiom 万物皆有灵，念起莲花开 roughly translating into "everything has a soul, if you believe in Buddha the lotus (upon which Buddha sits) will bloom." This suggests that everything can be cultivated toward enlightenment and become the Buddha. This principle originated in ancient Indian Buddhist

---

[32] Yi Zeng, *Harmonious Artificial Intelligence Principle*, n.d., http://bii.ia.ac.cn/hai/.
[33] Yi Zeng, remote interview by Danit Gal, March 14, 2019.
[34] Hanniman Huang, remote interview by Danit Gal, March 12, 2019.

scriptures that have been adopted and adapted throughout Asia, now deeply embedded in Chinese tradition among others in the region.[35]

An application found in the intersection between Buddhism and popular Chinese culture is the intelligent robot monk, 贤二 or Xian'er, roughly translating into "simple looking but virtuous." Xian'er was introduced in October 2015 by the Longquan Temple's information and technology center as a preprogrammed robot meant to help spread the message of Buddhism.[36] In 2018, Xian'er received a machine learning boost to engage with Buddhist scripters and its over one million social media followers on a deeper analytical and conversational level.[37]

Chinese popular culture also provides notable views of AI and robots as partners. Chinese dramas have been depicting AI and robots as love interests since 1996 with 机器人趣话 or Funny Robot Talk (1996). Later dramas include the movie 机器侠 or Metallic Attraction Kungfu Cyborg (2009), 机器男友 or Robot Boyfriend (2017), 我的真芯男友 or My Robot Boyfriend (2017), 天降机器女仆 or Robot Maid from Heaven (2017), and 我的保姆手册 or Hi, I'm Saori (2018). A popular AI in China is the social chatbot XiaoIce (小冰), created by Microsoft and operated by Tencent. As the world's most popular social chatbot, XiaoIce has 660 million online users who often perceive it as a friend and love interest. Modeled after a female teenager (raising issues of female objectification and the depiction of minors), XiaoIce is liked enough to be considered among China's top celebrities.[38]

AI and robots are also present in the Chinese music scene, where a group of AI idols named May Wei VIV (五月薇VIV) was created based on the looks, talents, and personality traits of the Chinese idol group SNH48.[39] The idea of AI replicas is intended to help celebrities engage with their fans and continue entertaining tirelessly. The technology was showcased in China's Spring Festival Gala, where four famous human hosts were joined by their AI replicas on stage.[40] This also extends to the creation and use of three

[35] This animistic inclination is often believed to be a part of other Chinese religions or philosophies, but is more often than not the result of these religions and philosophies melding with the country's long-standing animistic heritage and tradition.

[36] Joseph Campbell, "Robot Monk Blends Science and Buddhism at Chinese Temple," *Reuters* (April 22, 2016), https://www.reuters.com/article/us-china-religion-robot/robot-monk-blends-science-and-buddhism-at-chinese-temple-idUSKCN0XJ05I.

[37] Jiefei Liu, "Longquan Temple Is Using Artificial Intelligence to Organize and Spread Buddhist Scriptures," *Technode* (July 9, 2018), https://technode.com/2018/07/09/longquan-temple-techcrunch-hangzhou/.

[38] Geoff Spencer, "Much More than a Chatbot: China's Xiaoice Mixes AI with Emotions and Wins over Millions of Fans," *Microsoft Asia News Center* (November 1, 2018), https://news.microsoft.com/apac/features/much-more-than-a-chatbot-chinas-xiaoice-mixes-ai-with-emotions-and-wins-over-millions-of-fans/.

[39] SNH48 Official Site, 丝芭传媒打造国内首个虚拟偶像组合五月薇*VIV*深耕偶像产业 (February 3, 2019), http://www.snh48.com/html/allnews/zixun/2018/0203/2882.html.

[40] Bernard Marr, "One of the World's Most Watched TV Shows Will Be Hosted by Artificial Intelligences," *Forbes* (January 29, 2019), https://www.forbes.com/sites/bernardmarr/2019/01/29/the-worlds-most-watched-tv-show-will-be-hosted-by-artificial-intelligences/#5cd0ce8e68de.

holographic AI news anchors on China's Xinhua state news agency.[41] These applications demonstrate that even if AI and robots are used as tools to create more engaging and accessible entertainment, audiences are likely to engage with these replica idols as friends and partners, much like they would like to engage with the humans they are modeled after. This also extends to robots designed with attractive human traits, even if not idols, like JiaJia.

Conclusions

Despite the compelling counternarrative academic thought, local practices, and popular culture present on human-AI-robots partnership, the majority of AI and robot applications in China are still perceived as tools as the country rushes to develop and apply these technologies. AI and robots are used across national sectors from healthcare and education to public services and military uses, and are expected to be fully embedded in the country's near future operations. However, as the nation's appetite for the rapid and effective development of AI and robots increases, their view as partners rather than tools is likely to continue increasing in prominence.

While the Chinese government has not alluded to the perception of AI as more than a tool, Chinese companies are taking part in developing social AI and robots that are perceived as partners. In addition, some prominent academics and developers are expressing ambitions that further expand previous conceptions of AI and robots as partners. China is therefore hovering around the middle of the tool-partner spectrum, with current policy, AI and robotics ethical considerations, and applications pulling in the direction of tool, and developers' ambitions and popular culture pulling in the direction of partner. This tension is expected to grow in local and global prominence as China pursues a leadership position in AI and robotics. It is also expected to aggravate social tensions as digital natives grow up with the Anthropomorphized Tools Paradox and female objectification of AI and robots intended to be used as intelligent tools, but designed to look and behave like desirable partners.

JAPAN

Japan sits in the partner range of the spectrum due to its exceptionally strong mix of pro human-AI-robots partnership academic thought, local practices, and popular culture. While the Japanese policy approach to AI is moving toward the tool range like South

[41] Cate Cadell, "And Now for Something Completely Different: Chinese Robot News Readers," *Reuters* (November 9 2018), https://www.reuters.com/article/us-china-tech-ai-anchor/and-now-for-something-completely-different-chinese-robot-news-readers-idUSKCN1NE19O.

Korea and China, the extent of its societal vision for coexistence and coevolution with AI and robots is distinct. Another distinct feature in Japan is its strong techno-animistic tradition, which has likely inspired the development of its favorable partnership attitude. This entails a more intertwined and complex analysis of Japan's perspectives on and approaches to AI and robots.

Policies and Ethical Principles: Tool-Leaning

Like South Korea and China, Japanese policy views AI as a tool. It also, however, seeks to integrate AI and robots into all aspects of society to create an environment where humans, AI, and robots can coexist and coevolve. Japan's 5th Science and Technology Basic Plan, released on January 22, 2016, introduces the idea of Society 5.0.[42] This is a vision of an AI and robot-enabled, convenient, and diverse society that responds to all human needs and can even anticipate and respond to such needs before they emerge.[43] While this is likely the most progressive social vision in AI and robotics planning to date, the idea of being able to anticipate and respond to human needs before they emerge constitutes a potential ethical issue. This may lead to a push rather than pull culture where humans will not necessarily decide what needs they want fulfilled and how.

The aforementioned vision is further fleshed out by the Cabinet Office Council on the Social Principles of Human-centric AI, in their Social Principles of Human-centric AI draft document. In the document, the council sets a social framework to guide the creation of an AI-ready Japanese society.[44] To this end, the document calls for the redesigning of society in "all aspects including Japan's social system, industry structure, innovation system, governance, and its citizen's character."[45] The document also, however, warns about overdependence on AI and robots and emphasizes the need to maintain human dignity when using them as tools, much like the South Korean guideline. And yet the document still calls for an "AI-based human living environment"[46] and a "society premised on AI."[47] A notable aspect of this document is its view of AI and robotics as widespread social tools that necessitate the redesigning of Japan's social systems and even individual character. To date, the Japanese government is likely the only one going to such lengths to socially accommodate and integrate AI and robots as a key part of its society's foundation.

---

[42] Government of Japan, *The 5th Science and Technology Basic Plan*, January 22, 2016, https://www8.cao.go.jp/cstp/english/basic/5thbasicplan.pdf.

[43] *Id.* at 13.

[44] Cabinet Office Council on the Social Principles of Human-centric AI, *Social Principles of Human-centric AI (Draft)*, n.d., http://search.e-gov.go.jp/servlet/PcmFileDownload?seqNo=0000182653.

[45] *Id.* at 1.   [46] *Id.* at 4.   [47] *Id.* at 6.

Academic Thought and Local Practices: Partnership-Inspired

Takehiro Ohya, professor at Keio University, comments that the view of AI and robots as tools in the Social Principles document is intentional. Ohya explains that the Japanese seem to differentiate between human beings and AI or robots to a lesser degree, which might make them less human-centric, at least in comparison with Western cultures. As a Council member, Ohya shares that he, among other members, view the human-centrist nature of the social principles as a way to better communicate and achieve consensus with Western countries. He also says that he encouraged the Council to consider acknowledging AI and robots as legal persons, since the consideration of them as another species was not deemed ethically justifiable.[48]

The Ethical Guidelines of the Japanese Society for Artificial Intelligence (JSAI) seem to diverge on this point.[49] Article number 9 of JSAI's Ethical Guidelines notes that "AI must abide by the policies described above in the same manner as the members of the JSAI in order to become a member or quasi-member of society."[50] A JSAI blog post explains that the unique article reflects the views of the JSAI and also follows the spirit of Asimov's Three Laws of Robotics. The JASI ethics committee entertained the various ways in which AI and robots would be used by future societies and believes that this communicates the ambitions of Japanese AI and robotics researchers and developers.[51]

These Japanese views and practices build upon the country's long robotic heritage. Yasuo Kuniyoshi, director of the Next Generation AI Research Center at the University of Tokyo, maintains that the Japanese are known for their admiration of hardware, at times over software. As such, he believes that the Japanese are more inclined to trust and appreciated an embodied AI, often in the form of robots, over a bodiless system.[52] Arisa Ema, assistant professor at the University of Tokyo, comments that the Japanese have, at times, come to view robots as partners due to a long history of robot-friendly popular culture. She also notes, however, that a significant portion of current fascination is generated by the perceived ability of intelligent robots to solve pressing Japanese problems such as care for its super-aging society and automation to revitalize its slowing economy.[53] Another widespread use of AI and robots as tools in Japan is to aid with rescue missions and provide operational assistance in the aftermath of natural disasters.[54]

---

[48] Takehiro Ohya, remote interview by Danit Gal, March 7, 2019.

[49] Japanese Society for Artificial Intelligence (JSAI), *The Japanese Society for Artificial Intelligence Ethical Guidelines*, May 16, 2017, http://ai-elsi.org/wp-content/uploads/2017/05/JSAI-Ethical-Guidelines-1.pdf.

[50] *Id.* at 3.

[51] JSAI, *About the JSAI Ethical Guideline*, February 28, 2017, http://ai-elsi.org/archives/514.

[52] Yasuo Kuniyoshi, remote interview by Danit Gal, March 11, 2019.

[53] Arisa Ema, remote interview by Danit Gal, March 11, 2019.

[54] Martin Fackler, "Six Years after Fukushima, Robots Finally Find Reactors' Melted Uranium Fuel," *New York Times* (November 19, 2017), https://www.nytimes.com/2017/11/19/science/japan-fukushima-nuclear-meltdown-fuel.html.

Popular Culture: Partnership-Rich

Japanese popular culture serves as a key source of inspiration and influence in shaping academic thought and local practices. Numerous Japanese interviewees pointed to two famous cartoons as the source of inspiration for AI and robotics developers. The first is Astro Boy or Mighty Atom (鉄腕アトム), created by Osamu Tezuka and first published in 1952. Atom, a humanoid intelligent robot, was created to replace the son of the Science Ministry's Head, but was discarded when it failed to grow older as a human would. Atom is then sold to the circus but rescued by the new Head of the Science Ministry, who gives robots human rights and builds Atom a humanoid robot family. Atom then goes on to attend elementary school and save the world with its superhuman strength.[55] The story continues to be readapted and entertain audiences today. Jun Murai, co-director of the Cyber Civilization Research Center at Keio University, maintains that many Japanese researchers were influenced by Astro Boy, who introduced them to Asimov's Three Laws of Robotics and the importance and necessity of robot ethics.[56]

The second is Doraemon (ドラえもん), created by Hiroshi Fujimoto and Motoo Abiko (under the pen name Fujiko F. Fujio) and first published in 1969. Doraemon is an intelligent cat robot sent back in time to a Japanese kid named Nobita by his decedent, in the hopes of changing Nobita's lazy behavior. Doraemon and Nobita become close friends and go on adventures across time and space. Doraemon was adapted into numerous animated cartoons and movies and became an internationally beloved character.[57] It has become so popular that Japan's Foreign Ministry named it Japan's first "anime ambassador" in 2008.[58] Hirotaka Osawa, assistant professor at the University of Tsukuba, notes that Doraemon serves as a continued influential icon for AI and robot developers as the character remains relevant and entertaining today still.[59]

Existing somewhere between a tool and a potential partner is Softbank's robot Pepper. Pepper is a conversational humanoid robot with emotional and facial recognition capabilities. Pepper is co-developed with institutions to function as an assistant[60] and even a Buddhist priest.[61] In a Softbank commercial titled "Future Life with Pepper" the company reveals a futuristic vision for the robot acting as a friend, sibling, potential love

[55] For more information on Astro Boy, see: http://tezukainenglish.com/wp/?page_id=138.

[56] Jun Murai, remote interview by Danit Gal, March 8, 2019.

[57] Yasuyuki Yokoyama, "Celebrating Exactly 100 Years before Doraemon's Birthday," *Nippon.com* (December 10, 2012), https://www.nippon.com/en/currents/d00056/celebrating-exactly-100-years-before-doraemon's-birthday.html.

[58] "*Doraemon Named 'Anime Ambassador*,'" *Japan Today* (March 17, 2008), https://japantoday.com/category/entertainment/doraemon-named-anime-ambassador.

[59] Hirotaka Osawa, remote interview by Danit Gal, March 8, 2019.

[60] For more information on Pepper, see https://www.softbankrobotics.com/emea/en/pepper.

[61] Alex Martin, "Pepper the Robot to Don Buddhist Robe for Its New Funeral Services Role," *Japan Times* (August 16, 2017), https://www.japantimes.co.jp/news/2017/08/16/business/pepper-the-robot-to-don-buddhist-robe-for-its-new-funeral-services-role/.

interest, entertainer, and caretaker.[62] This further blurs the intended use line between a tool and a partner as Pepper functions as an assistant, and priest, but is also explicitly envisioned to become much more than that.

A more partner-oriented practical example is Aibo, the pet robot dog from Sony. Aibo was first available between 1999 and 2006[63] and was officially relaunched in January 2019, reinforced with machine learning.[64] Jiro Kokuryo, a professor at Keio University, explains that while Aibo robots mimic real dogs, they also have distinct robotic features to avoid uncanny valley-associated fears.[65] In spite of these design measures, when an Aibo was beyond repair, owners sent it off with an elaborate Buddhist burial ceremony, demonstrating a unique attachment to over eight hundred buried robot dogs.[66] Sony, on its part, approaches AI as a tool to achieve "harmony with society" in its Sony Group AI Ethics Guidelines.[67]

The treatment of robots with religious care derives from the concept of animism. Animism can be found in the two major religions in Japan: Shinto and Buddhism. Shinto is a complex, exclusively Japanese religion where the borders between the worldly and otherworldly are blurred. As a polytheistic religion, Shinto belief holds that the spirits of otherworldly beings (e.g., gods) can dwell in animate and inanimate objects, like technology. This suggests a deep spiritual connection between the worldly and manifestation of the otherworldly, often referred to as techno-animism.[68]

In Japanese Buddhism, like the previously discussed Chinese version, both animate and inanimate objects are a part of the natural world and possess the character of Buddha and potential of becoming Buddha. This follows the saying 山川草木国土悉皆成仏, which roughly translates into "all things have the nature of Buddha." This idiom is believed to share the same ancient Indian origins with the aforementioned Chinese one. And in another similar line, a Japanese Buddhist temple also has its own AI robot monk called Android Kannon, which is capable of delivering full Buddhist sermons.[69] As the notion of Japanese techno-animism developed it drew inspiration from both religions, creating a rich synthesis where the source of animation may be different, but the animation of technological artifacts is, in principle, the same.

[62] "Future Life with Pepper," YouTube video, posted by "Dean Khaled," February 29, 2016, https://www.youtube.com/watch?v=-A3ZLLGuvQY.

[63] Sony-Aibo, *History*, n.d., http://www.sony-aibo.co.uk/history/.

[64] "Sony Starts Taking Advanced Orders for New Version of Aibo Robot Dog," *Japan Times* (July 19, 2018), https://www.japantimes.co.jp/news/2018/07/19/business/tech/sony-starts-taking-preorders-new-version-aibo-robot-dog/.

[65] Jiro Kokuryo, remote interview by Danit Gal, March 3, 2019.

[66] Suzuki Miwa, "In Japan, Aibo Robots Get Their Own Funeral," *Japan Times* (May 1, 2018), https://www.japantimes.co.jp/news/2018/05/01/national/japan-aibo-robots-get-funeral/#.XJt2rvwRVot.

[67] "Sony Group AI Ethics Guidelines," Sony (September 25, 2018), https://www.sony.net/SonyInfo/csr_report/humanrights/hkrfmg0000007rtj-att/AI_Engagement_within_Sony_Group.pdf.

[68] Casper Brunn Jensen and Anders Blok, "Techno-animism in Japan: Shinto Cosmograms, Actor-network Theory, and the Enabling Powers of Non-human Agencies," *Theory, Culture & Society* 30 (2013): 84–113.

[69] Thisanka Siripala, "An Ancient Japanese Shrine Debuts a Buddhist Robot," *The Diplomat* (March 5, 2019), https://thediplomat.com/2019/03/an-ancient-japanese-shrine-debuts-a-buddhist-robot/.

Much like China and South Korea, Japanese popular culture tells numerous stories about AI and robots as partners and, in particular, love interests. Among them are 絶対彼氏 or Absolute Boyfriend (2008), which was readapted in multiple Asian countries; 僕の彼女はサイボーグ or Cyborg She (2008); キュートor Q10 (2010); イヴの時間 or Time of Eve (2010); ちょびっツ or Chobits (2011); 安堂ロイド～A.I. knows LOVE? or Ando Lloyd—A.I. Knows Love? (2013). Unlike South Korea and China, however, Japan's mainstream romantic fascination with AI and robots isn't limited to dramas. Vinclu Inc.'s Gatebox AI lab creates a holographic virtual wife and home assistant hybrid modeled after a young female character named Hikari Azuma.[70] The popularity of a virtual wife underscores the pervasive loneliness experienced in Japan,[71] and tells us of what trying to solve social problems with technology already looks like. It also constitutes a rare edge case of intentional tool anthropomorphizing and female objectification, where a functional home assistant is specifically designed to act as a meaningful romantic partner.

Conclusions

Japan is a rich source of information for discussions on perspectives on and approaches to AI and robots as partners. While its policy and social principles may be moving further into the tool range to create international consensus, it is hard to ignore the overwhelming positive approach demonstrated by local culture and practices toward human-AI-robots partnerships. This creates an interesting dual tension between political ambitions and social values. On the one hand, partner AI and robots can prove to be useful tools for a super-aging population, particularly as Japan sees automation as an economic boon, not a threat. On the other hand, this tension does pose other, more complicated "antisocial" questions regarding how this already affects objectified population groups like females, and might affect attempts to repopulate a super-aging country that, simply put, loves AI and robots.

CHAPTER CONCLUSIONS AND DISCUSSION

To conclude, South Korea, China, and Japan share considerable similarities despite being placed in three different ranges on the tool-partner spectrum. Each country, in its

---

[70] For more information, see https://gatebox.ai/home/ and https://gatebox.ai/news/2018/07/31/01/ [in Japanese].

[71] Michael Hoffman, "Japan Struggles to Keep Loneliness at Arm's Length," *Japan Times* (November 10, 2018), https://www.japantimes.co.jp/news/2018/11/10/national/media-national/japan-struggles-keep-loneliness-arms-length/.

own way, debates its movement across the spectrum. To date, South Korean policy makes a stand against partner AI and robots while popular culture explores the idea. Chinese policy is headed in the direction of a tool-oriented AI and robotics ethical guidelines, while local practices and culture experiment with the idea of physical and spiritual partnership. Japan's social principles are also moving in the tool direction, but its society actively seeks and creates partner-like AI and robots. As the technology and its widespread societal use continue to develop, we can expect further movement on the spectrum. This movement will surly highlight and plausibly aggravate tensions between top-down tool and bottom-up partner perspectives on and approaches to AI and robots. Sooner or later, these tensions will be at the core of debating the social benefit and harm of AI and robots use.

Three cross-cutting AI and robotics-related ethical issues highlighted by this chapter are female objectification, the Anthropomorphized Tools Paradox, and "antisocial" development. The globally shared issue of female objectification is particularly salient in AI and robotics. Alongside the decisive disenfranchising effect it has on women, it further reinforces the Anthropomorphized Tools Paradox, where functional tools are given desirable, and often female, companionship characteristics to make them more enticing to use. Put together, these two ethical issues create a vicious cycle that subjects both women and technology to the biased objectification of mostly male AI and robots developers and designers. Such development and design choices blur the lines in ways that lead to problematic treatment toward women and even minors, and emotionally and psychologically confuse users. Technology is genderless and artificial. All relevant stakeholders would do well to remember that.

This further underscores the question of "antisocial" technology. What degree of AI and robots' socialization capability development is considered "antisocial"? How many human functions can and should we substitute before we hit that threshold? Could and should the Anthropomorphized Tools Paradox serve as a potential threshold? Despite it being clear that both female objectification and the Anthropomorphized Tools Paradox fall under "antisocial" technology development, they remain incredibly common. We need prosocial regulation of "antisocial" technology if we are seeking to create AI-ready societies. There are many paths to developing and designing AI and robots in ways that do not replace or degrade humans. Human-AI-robot harmony cannot be achieved by creating artificial substitutions to compensate for the fact that we have yet to achieve all-human harmony. There are no technical solutions to social problems.

BIBLIOGRAPHY

China

Beijing Academy of Artificial Intelligence. *Beijing AI Principles*, May 28, 2019, https://baip.baai.ac.cn/en?fbclid=IwAR2HtIRKJxxy9Q1Y953H-2pMHl_bIr8pcsIxho93BtZY-FPH39vV9v9B2eY.

China Institute for Science and Technology Policy at Tsinghua University. "Chapter 5: Public Perception and General Impact of AI," in *China AI Development Report 2018*, July 15, 2018. http://www.sppm.tsinghua.edu.cn/eWebEditor/UploadFile/China_AI_development_report_2018.pdf.

Japan

Ema, Arisa. *IEEE EAD Regional Reports on AI Ethics: Japan*, April 9, 2018. http://bai-japan.org/en/2018/reports-on-ai-ethics-japan/(reprinted from IEEE EAD v. 2).
Robertson, Jennifer. *Robo Sapiens Japanicus: Robots, Gender, Family, and the Japanese Nation*. Oakland: University of California Press, 2018.

South Korea

Statues of the Republic of Korea. *Intelligent Robots Development and Distribution Promotion Act*. http://elaw.klri.re.kr/eng_mobile/viewer.do?hseq=39153&type=lawname&key=robot.
Yoo, Juyoung. "Results and Outlooks of Robot Education in Republic of Korea." *Procedia—Social and Behavioral Sciences* 176 (2015): 251–254.

Additional Resources Reflecting AI Ethics from East Asian Perspectives

Ethically Aligned Design 1st Edition. *Classical Ethics in A/IS*, March 25, 2019. https://standards.ieee.org/content/dam/ieeestandards/standards/web/documents/other/ead1e_classical_ethics.pdf.
Zeng, Yi. *Linking Artificial Intelligence Principles*, 2019. http://www.linking-ai-principles.org.

CHAPTER 33

ARTIFICIAL INTELLIGENCE AND INEQUALITY IN THE MIDDLE EAST

The Political Economy of Inclusion

NAGLA RIZK

INTRODUCTION

IN recent years, the Middle East has been plagued by persistent economic and political inequalities. Where some regimes have pushed the agenda of economic growth and technological advancement, they have paid less attention to economic development and inclusion, and less so to political engagement and participation. These, in turn, come amidst other divides based on religion, ethnicity, and spatial disparities. Inequalities have also been manifested in the digital economies, where they have been exacerbated by power dynamics between highly concentrated businesses and smaller establishments trying to carve a niche for themselves. This in turn has its effect on artificial intelligence and divides associated with it.

Given this, the discourse over artificial intelligence (AI) and inequality tends to be an amplified version of the earlier conversations over digital technologies and inequality. On one end of the spectrum, digital technologies can aggravate the digital divide and knowledge inequalities and widen the developmental gap. Given the pervasiveness of the fourth industrial revolution and the power of AI technologies, these consequences are amplified if the technology and the data are monopolized in the hands of a powerful few.

Like electricity and information technology, AI qualifies as a "general purpose technology" (GPT) typically characterized by its "pervasiveness", ability for "continuous improvement" to eventually reduce costs, and "spawning innovation", making it "easier to invent and produce new products or processes."[1] What makes this particular GPT unique is the scale, scope, and capability of its components, its depth, capacity to self-educate, and potential for a "protracted aggregate impact."[2] Within each of AI's components—the data, the algorithm, and the infrastructure—lies a trigger for potential inequalities. From a societal standpoint, biases in data, black boxes in algorithms, and the inaccessibility and inadequacy of infrastructure can all serve to exclude and marginalize. The ones who are most agile and who are already well positioned to adapt while capitalizing on existing technologies will be able to reap the benefits from AI.

On the other end of the spectrum, and notwithstanding what has just been said, the pervasive nature of AI itself can indeed be channeled toward inclusion, mitigating inequalities, and empowerment of the marginalized. Examples are improving health services by generating systems that better predict disease, better education by tuning curricula to student's ability to assimilate, and creating an encompassing ecosystem of entrepreneurship and small businesses built around open data and inclusive technologies.

The purpose of this chapter is to explore issues related to AI and inequality in the Middle East and North Africa (MENA) region, within the larger global conversation of AI and ethics. It is important to investigate the potential of AI in its social and economic context and ask how these societies can utilize AI as a tool for democratizing knowledge and inclusion amid the unique challenges they face. This chapter explores tensions, opportunities, and potential challenges to the equitable deployment of AI in the region. The dearth of information about AI use in the region has been a challenge in undertaking this work, especially given the timeliness of the topic. Accordingly, in addition to published works, the author resorted to capturing knowledge from interviews, AI-related conversations by experts in the field, and talks at public conferences.

The chapter includes four sections. Following this introduction, the second section, "Context: A Region in Flux," offers context through background on the region, its inherent socioeconomic challenges, and facets of its inequality. The third section, "AI in MENA: Data, Infrastructure, and People," unpacks components of AI and their respective bearing on inequality in the region, discusses challenges and highlights rays of hope. The fourth section, "Conclusion: AI in MENA—Inclusion or Inequality?," concludes and underlines specific tensions that shape the debate over AI and inclusion in the region.

CONTEXT: A REGION IN FLUX

The Middle East and North Africa is not a homogenous region. While there are overall similarities in the political and cultural contexts of its countries, there is considerable variation in their economic landscape, specifically their natural and human resources.

---

[1] Boyan Jovanovic and Peter L. Rosseau, "General Purpose Technologies: 'Engines of Growth'?," *Journal of Econometrics*, 65 (1996): 83–108.

[2] Id.

The size, qualifications, and potential of the domestic workforce within a country is a key factor in considerations of the impact of technology on inequality and socioeconomic development. The uprisings in parts of the region over the last decade have shown that trickle-down economics have not worked to mitigate those inequalities and improve the livelihood of the marginalized.

A Diverse Region

Following the World Bank classification, the region can be clustered into groups according to the availability of natural resources, namely hydrocarbons, and also according to the size of their populations.[3] The first group includes high-income Arab countries, which tend to be resource-rich labor importers, with expatriates representing a significant portion of the population. The second is middle-income Arab countries that are labor abundant—with some being resource rich such as Algeria and others being resource poor such as Egypt, Tunisia, Jordan, Lebanon, and Morocco. Thirdly, low-income Arab countries include some which are resource rich and labor abundant but face political turmoil, such as Syria and Yemen, and some which are resource poor, such as Palestine and Mauritania.[4, 5]

One commonality shared by countries of the region is the prevalence of youth. The region houses 100 million people between the age of fifteen and twenty-nine,[6] with more than half of the region's population under the age of twenty-five.[7] These are the shapers of the region's future. By virtue of their young age, they offer the ideal potential recipients of learning, adapting, using, and creating new technologies if given the right education and skill-development training. This young population is unevenly distributed among countries with diverse economic landscapes, with pockets of youth unemployment witnessed in resource-poor countries of the region. This has significant political nuances in environments that are already politically fluid.

The variation in countries' socioeconomic conditions is also reflected in the diverse levels of technological development and use, in turn offering different contexts when it comes to AI and inequality. The oil-rich countries have taken a lead in the Fourth Industrial Revolution, taking steps to encourage AI adoption in government and encouraging AI-based entrepreneurship. The United Arab Emirates (UAE) is positioning itself as a

---

[3] "Socio-Economic Context and Impact of the 2011 Events in the Middle East and North Africa Region," *MENA-OECD Investment Programme* (2011): 9, http://www.oecd.org/mena/competitiveness/49171115.pdf (last accessed January 13, 2020). See Figure 33.1.

[4] *Id.*

[5] The chapter does not cover non-Arab countries in the region, that is, Iran and Israel.

[6] Arab Human Development Report: *Youth and the Prospects for Human Development in a Changing Reality*, UN Development Programme, 2016, http://arab-hdr.org/Reports/2016/2016.aspx (last accessed January 13, 2020).

[7] "Meeting the Needs of a Growing Youth Population in the Middle East," in *The Report: Abu Dhabi 2016*, Oxford Business Group, https://oxfordbusinessgroup.com/analysis/dividend-or-liability-meeting-needs-region%E2%80%99s-growing-youth-population-0 (last accessed January 13, 2020).

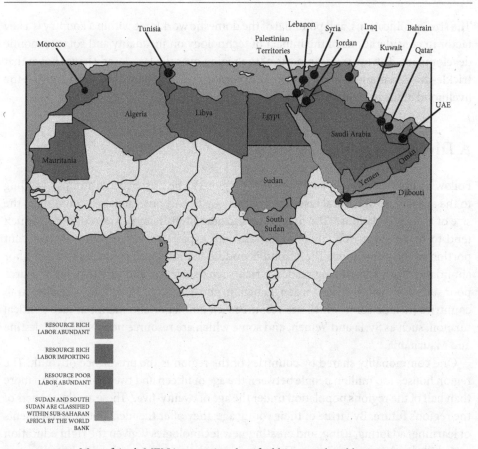

FIGURE 33.1. Map of Arab MENA countries classified by natural and human resources.

Source: Put together by author based on data from http://siteresources.worldbank.org/INTMENA/
Resources/EDP07_OVERVIEW_APRIL12.pdf.

regional lead in AI, assigning a government minister dedicated to AI. The country has pioneered initiatives to retrain labor force and adopted policies that encourage AI and inclusion in areas such as health.[8] While these countries set the benchmark, they have relied on revenues from natural resources to fuel the development of new industries depending on imported technologies and human resources.

On the other hand, despite potential, labor-abundant countries like Egypt and Tunisia relatively trail along. They face persisting economic difficulties, especially unemployment of the youth, of females, and in some cases, of the educated. Under such circumstances, talents remain underutilized, ascribed socioeconomic statuses are sticky, and social mobility is hard. Inequality then becomes one of opportunity and not just of wealth.

[8] "Artificial Intelligence to Be Used in 'Urgent' Fight against Tuberculosis, Says UAE Minister," *The National* (October 23, 2018), https://www.thenational.ae/uae/health/artificial-intelligence-to-be-used-in-urgent-fight-against-tuberculosis-says-uae-minister-1.783316 (last accessed January 13, 2020).

At the same time, these countries have comparatively more diversified economies in terms of manufacturing and service industries than high-income, resource-rich countries.

Most of the analysis in this chapter pertains to the cluster of middle-income countries that are resource poor and labor abundant. While the inherent tensions and paradoxes related to AI and inequality are highest, the promise may be also the most. They face the challenge, and the opportunity, of relying on endogenous capacity. By leapfrogging, they could actually achieve significant successes in the use of AI for inclusion. Currently, they face challenges at the level of data acquisition and the resilience of local infrastructure. When present, initiatives to incorporate AI into developmental goals are nascent. Initiatives to encourage budding start-ups that can push for more AI integration exist but are limited, and the challenges are ample.

The Arab Spring and Failure of Trickle-Down

Despite positive macroeconomic indicators in the years preceding the Arab uprisings, underlying deeply rooted causes drove the region to fall into unrest with hardly any trickle-down from the seemingly growing economies. On the eve of the January 2011 uprisings, both Egypt and Tunisia experienced relatively high rates of economic growth (5.1 percent and 3.5 percent, respectively).[9] Indeed, Egypt experienced its highest growth rates in the years leading up to 2011, reaching 7 percent in 2007–2008. In the decade leading up to 2011, other socioeconomic indictors failed to shed light on underlying tensions, with the announced statistics on poverty, health, and education showing considerable improvements.[10]

The case of the Arab uprisings illustrates the shortcomings of top-down, macro indicators of economic and social well-being and their failure to predict unrest. National policies have been concerned primarily, if not completely, with top-down-led growth while paying little attention to other key factors to promote sustainable development such as education, health and civil liberties. The uprisings demanded economic, social, and political inclusion amid an array of frustrations and have highlighted how the economic and the political intertwined. On top of the structural socioeconomic ailments came the persistent unemployment and lack of opportunities especially of the youth, the highly educated, and the women. Socioeconomic grievances were coupled with discontent over corruption[11] and the limited or nonexistent political freedoms.[12]

[9] World Bank, *World Bank Open Data*, 2019, https://data.worldbank.org (last accessed January 13, 2020).

[10] Michael Gordon, "Forecasting Instability: The Case of the Arab Spring and the Limitations of Socioeconomic Data," *Wilson Center* (February 8, 2018), https://www.wilsoncenter.org/article/forecasting-instability-the-case-the-arab-spring-and-the-limitations-socioeconomic-data (last accessed January 13, 2020).

[11] "Socio-Economic Context and Impact of the 2011 Events in the Middle East and North Africa Region."

[12] Gordon, "Forecasting Instability."

Neoliberal policies were reflected in technology policies and a fixation on connectivity for economic gains with little safeguards to citizen engagement and privacy. In Egypt, for example, the expansion of the information and communication technology (ICT) infrastructure as the backbone for the economy was part of the neoliberal Economic Reform and Structural Adjustment Program (ERSAP) led by the World Bank and the International Monetary Fund in the 1990s. The objective was to draw foreign direct investment to feed the targeted economic growth. In that vein, technology and innovation policies within these countries have tended to favor larger, foreign corporations and Western-centric development paradigms at the expense of supporting local, smaller scale entrepreneurial technology initiatives and a culture of openness and collaboration.

Nevertheless, the expansion in connectivity brought about two empowering outcomes related to the uprisings. First, the growth of an entrepreneurial scene fuelled by the energy of the youth. This scene continues to flourish despite less than ideal circumstances, which serves as a testament to the underlying potential in countries such as Egypt and Tunisia. Second, expanded connectivity paradoxically opened up the networked public sphere,[13] which engaged growing communities to utilize the digital communication technologies for mobilization against the regime.[14] The discussion over whether and how ICTs have served inclusion has been fueled by the dual use of ICTs, first by the state to promote neoliberal policies and later to control the masses and also by the people to mobilize and engage. The uprisings thus called for revisiting the trajectory of technological advancement amid a paradoxical state stance regarding liberties.

Multifaceted Inequality in MENA

Inequality in the region is complex, multilayered, and multidimensional. It extends beyond income inequity to inequality of opportunity rooted in disparities in access to education, health services, employment, living conditions, and active citizenry. Inequalities also exist along gender, ethnic origins, and social background,[15] with realities pertaining to minorities and underprivileged groups being excluded from opportunities for equal participation in political and economic processes. Examples are communities living in poverty in Cairo's city of the dead, ethnic minorities in Morocco's Western Sahara, and religious minorities in Lebanon. These translate into exclusion and marginalization with potential political unrest especially among the youth.

---

[13] Yochai Benkler, *The Wealth of Networks: How Social Production Transforms Markets and Freedom* (Yale University Press, 2006).

[14] Nagla Rizk, Lina Attalah, and Nadine Weheba, "The Networked Public Sphere and Civic Engagement in Post-2011 Egypt: A Local Perspective," *Arab Networked Public Sphere*, 2016, http://www.arabnps.org/egypt/ (last accessed January 13, 2020).

[15] Gordon, "Forecasting Instability."

Such disparities are not captured by mainstream indicators of income inequality such as the Gini coefficient, which only measures the distribution of wealth amongst a population, with the assumption that such wealth is properly registered and documented. Even there, Alvaredo, Assouad, and Piketty point to a serious issue in income distribution in the region.[16] They highlight extreme inequality between and within countries, as "the share of total income accruing to the top 10% of income earners is about 64% in the Middle East" compared to 37 percent in Western Europe, for example.[17]

The difficulty of measuring inequality by formal assessment methodologies is aggravated by the inherence of informality. Indeed, the region has some of the largest informal economies in the world.[18] Figure 33.2 outlines the size of the informal sector (as a percentage of total GDP) for labor-abundant countries in the region. While the MENA region as a whole remains under the world average, all labor-abundant countries with the exception of Jordan are above the global average. These results indicate that about one-third of total economic output in the region remains undeclared and therefore not registered for tax purposes. Additionally, the fact that informal employment

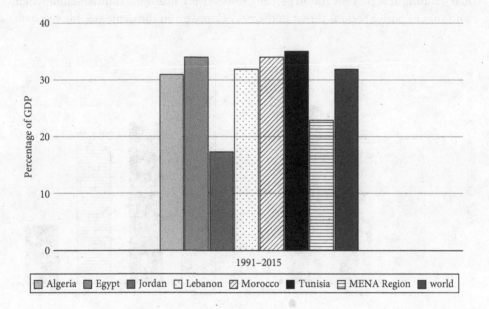

FIGURE 33.2. Informal sector size as a percentage of GDP.

Source: https://www.imf.org/en/Publications/WP/Issues/2018/01/25/Shadow-Economies-Around-the-World-What-Did-We-Learn-Over-the-Last-20-Years-45583.

[16] Facundo Alvaredo, Lydia Assouad, and Thomas Piketty, "Measuring Inequality in the Middle East 1990–2016: The World's Most Unequal Region?," *The Review of Income and Wealth* 65, no. 1 (forthcoming, 2019), https://onlinelibrary.wiley.com/doi/10.1111/roiw.12385 (last accessed January 13, 2020).

[17] *Id.*

[18] Diego F. Angel-Urdinola and Kimie Tanabe, "Micro-Determinants of Informal Employment in the Middle East and North Africa Region," SP Discussion Paper No. 1201, *World Bank*, 2012, https://openknowledge.worldbank.org/handle/10986/26828 (last accessed January 13, 2020).

constitutes 67 percent of the region's labor force[19] means that two-thirds of the region's workers have no access to social security and work outside state-sanctioned laws and parameters, such as labor laws.

In line with this information, two particular facets of inequality in the region directly feed into potentials and challenges of AI and inclusion. The first is unemployment, with the AI conversation highly associated with its influence on labor, and the second is the digital divide, the digital being the main realm in which AI can thrive. In the following is further analysis of these two aspects.

Unemployment

Youth unemployment is rampant in labor-abundant countries of the region. In 2018, the regional average for youth unemployment in MENA stood at 34 percent,[20] which is significantly higher than the world average of 13.23 percent. As shown in Figure 33.3, youth unemployment figures for Egypt and Tunisia stood at 34.3 percent and 36.3 percent, respectively. These rates are higher than those witnessed on the eve of Arab Spring, then standing at 25 percent and 30 percent, respectively, in 2018.[21] Youth unemployment continues to pose a serious threat in the near future given the demographic construct

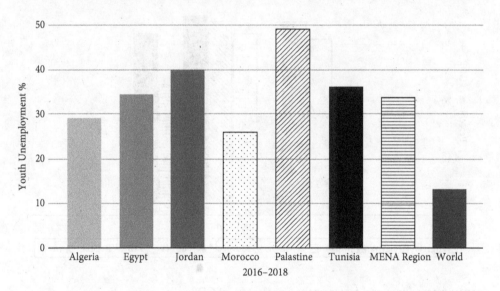

FIGURE 33.3. Youth unemployment in selected MENA countries (2016–2018).

Source: Compiled by author based on data from https://data.worldbank.org/indicator/SL.UEM.1524.NE.
ZS?end=2010&start=2003.

[19] Diego F. Angel-Urdinola and Kimie Tanabe, "Micro-Determinants of Informal Employment."
[20] World Bank. "Unemployment, Youth Total (% of total labor force ages 15–24) (national estimate)," The World Bank Group, https://data.worldbank.org/indicator/SL.UEM.1524.NE.ZS?end=2010&start=2003 (accessed April 2019).
[21] Gordon, "Forecasting Instability."

of the region, with those between the ages of fifteen and twenty-nine making up almost one-third of the region's population, and those below the age of fifteen making up another third.[22]

Unemployment is also witnessed among the educated. In 2016, more than a quarter of holders of university degree or higher in Egypt were unemployed.[23] The comparative figure exceeded 30 percent in Tunisia, and 17 percent in Morocco in 2010.[24] Over the past two decades, unemployment rate in the region for men with advanced degrees, has fluctuated between 15 and 35 percent. This is higher than the figures for fellow middle-income countries elsewhere (3.4 percent in Bulgaria, and 11.8 percent in Turkey, for example).[25]

Female unemployment is also witnessed in the region's middle-income countries. In 2019, female unemployment stood at 23.1 percent in Egypt, and at 25 percent, 23.1 percent, and 10 percent in Jordan, Tunisia, and Morocco, respectively.[26] By 2016, the employment gender gap had reached nearly 80 percent in Algeria and Jordan, and 69 percent in Egypt.[27] Even though the share of women in informal employment is lower than men, there remains "gender segmentation" as women are more likely to be concentrated in lower quality jobs.[28] Furthermore, women are represented in invisible work that goes beyond the informal sector such as house and domestic work that they are unpaid for. This adds further layers on uncaptured inequality that takes place in informal employment.

Digital Inequality

Digital inequalities exist between the region and the world, as well as between and within countries of the region. Divides exist along indicators of connectivity and also of

---

[22] Arab Human Development Report: *Youth and the Prospects for Human Development in a Changing Reality*, UN Development Programme, 2016, http://arab-hdr.org/Reports/2016/2016.aspx (last accessed January 13, 2020).

[23] "Egypt in Figures 2018," *Central Agency for Public Mobilization and Statistics*, http://www.sis.gov.eg/UP/Egypt in Figures 2018/egypt-in-numbers2018.pdf (last accessed January 13, 2020).

[24] "Data," *Arab Development Portal*, 2019, http://data.arabdevelopmentportal.com (last accessed January 13, 2020).

[25] World Bank, "Unemployment, Male (% of male labor force) (modeled ILO estimate)," The World Bank Group, https://data.worldbank.org/indicator/sl.uem.totl.ma.zs (accessed April 2019).

[26] World Bank, "Unemployment, Female (% of female labor force) (modeled ILO estimate)," The World Bank Group, https://data.worldbank.org/indicator/SL.UEM.TOTL.FE.ZS (accessed March 20, 2020).

[27] "The Future of Jobs and Skills in the Middle East and North Africa: Preparing the Region for the Fourth Industrial Revolution," *World Economic Forum* (May 17, 2017), https://www.weforum.org/reports/the-future-of-jobs-and-skills-in-the-middle-east-and-north-africa-preparing-the-region-for-the-fourth-industrial-revolution (last accessed January 13, 2020).

[28] "The Future of Jobs and Skills in the Middle East and North Africa," *World Economic Forum* (2017); "The Informal Economy in Arab Nations: A Comparative Perspective," *Women in Informal Employment: Globalizing and Organizing* (WIEGO), 2017, https://www.wiego.org/sites/default/files/migrated/resources/files/Informal-Economy-Arab-Countries-2017.pdf (last accessed January 13, 2020).

use by age group, education, income, geographical distribution, and gender. Since 2006, all countries of the region have witnessed exponentially increasing internet and mobile connectivity.[29] As a percentage of the population, internet users have reached 76 percent in Lebanon and almost two-thirds in Morocco, Palestine, and Jordan.[30] In 2018, Egypt had almost forty million internet users representing about 40 percent of the population in 2018.[31] Broadband subscription for mobile phones in countries of the region has ranged from around half to two-thirds of their populations, except for oil-rich countries and Jordan, where the figures exceeded 100 percent.[32]

Nevertheless, when compared to other regions, with the exception of the UAE, Qatar, and Lebanon, mobile broadband speed in the region is below the global average.[33] The region is also characterized by high prices, a limited number of users with high-speed internet, and very high barriers to entry in the internet market for new service providers.[34] Additionally, although the region has seen expansion of basic voice service in mobile, the infrastructure for broadband is largely influenced by state-owned operators with outdated infrastructure and with most mobile operators banning VOIP apps.

Regional disparities exist in infrastructure for Internet speed. The UAE and Qatar lead the use of fiber optic systems to deliver internet.[35] With the exception of a recent initiative by Egypt to replace 95 percent of its copper cables with fiber optic ones by 2020,[36] other middle-income countries still rely on copper wires.[37]

Digital inequalities exist within countries of the region. Internal digital divides are evident by geographical disparities between urban and rural areas in Egypt[38] and Lebanon,[39] and between the relatively affluent coastal regions as opposed to the less

[29] World Bank, "Individuals Using the Internet (% of population)," The World Bank Group, https://data.worldbank.org/indicator/it.net.user.zs (accessed April 2019).

[30] "Data," Arab Development Portal, 2019.

[31] "ICT Indicators Quarterly Bulletin," Ministry of Communications and Information Technology (MCIT), 2019, http://mcit.gov.eg/Publication/Publication_Summary/6147/ (last accessed January 13, 2020).

[32] "Data," Arab Development Portal, 2019.

[33] World Bank, "Individuals Using the Internet (% of population)."

[34] Id.

[35] Id.

[36] "95% of Copper Cables to Be Replaced with Fiber Ones by 2020," Egypt Today (December 26, 2018), http://www.egypttoday.com/Article/2/62602/95-of-copper-cables-to-be-replaced-with-fiber-ones (last accessed January 13, 2020).

[37] Rabah Arezki et al., "A New Economy in Middle East and North Africa," Middle East and North Africa Economic Monitor (October 2018), https://openknowledge.worldbank.org/bitstream/handle/10986/30436/9781464813672.pdf?sequence=11&isAllowed=y (last accessed January 13, 2020).

[38] Mona Farid Badran, "Young People and the Digital Divide in Egypt: an Empirical Study," Eurasian Economic Review 4, no. 2 (2014): 223–250, https://link.springer.com/article/10.1007/s40822-014-0008-z (last accessed January 13, 2020).

[39] Antoine Harfouche and Alice Robbin, "Antecedents of the Digital Divide in Lebanon," Mediterranean Conference on Information Systems 2010 Proceedings: Paper 40 (January 9, 2010), https://www.academia.edu/29840864/Antecedents_of_the_Digital_Divide_in_Lebanon (last accessed January 13, 2020).

fortunate rural western and southern areas in Tunisia. Evidence of digital divides by age and education has also been documented in Egypt,[40] Tunisia,[41] and Lebanon.[42]

The digital divide is also present by gender. While not evident in rates of internet access, cultured gender roles in the region shape women's engagement with ICTs.[43, 44] In Tunisia, being exclusively responsible for domestic labor in addition to employment or education inhibits women from allocating more time than they would like to ICT usage, which limits their skill development.[45] It is this socially constructed "second shift" of domestic labor that reinforces the divide in digital competencies between men and women in the region.[46] A similar trend appears in Lebanon, where inequalities in work opportunities and socially constructed gender roles mean that at the same occupational level men have more e-skills than women.[47]

AI IN MENA—DATA, INFRASTRUCTURE, AND PEOPLE

The advent of AI to the context of MENA comes with multiple challenges, notably in the present context as pertaining to inclusion and inequality. This section attempts to unpack this conundrum by a discussion of data and the enabling environment, infrastructure, and human capital.

Data—The Mine

Data is at the heart of the discourse over AI and inequalities in the region. While better data sets enable tuning algorithms to give better results, biased data can cause or amplify

[40] Badran, "Young People and the Digital Divide in Egypt," 223–250.

[41] Ikram Toumi, "Information and Computer Technology and the Digital Divide in the Post-Revolution Tunisia," PhD Diss., University of Texas, 2016, https://repositories.lib.utexas.edu/handle/2152/43646 (last accessed January 13, 2020).

[42] Harfouche and Robbin, "Antecedents of the Digital Divide in Lebanon."

[43] Oum Kalthoum Ben Hassine, "Personal Expansion versus Traditional Gender Stereotypes: Tunisian University Women and ICT," in *Women and ICT in Africa and the Middle East: Changing Selves, Changing Societies*, ed. Ineke Buskens and Anne Webb (London: Zed Books, 2014), https://www.researchgate.net/publication/271699674_Personal_expansion_versus_traditional_gender_stereotypes_Tunisian_university_women_and_ICT (last accessed January 13, 2020).

[44] Sangeeta Sinha, "Women's Rights: Tunisian Women in the Workplace," *Journal of International Women's Studies* 12, no. 3 (2011): 185–200, https://vc.bridgew.edu/jiws/vol12/iss3/12/ (last accessed January 13, 2020).

[45] Ben Hassine, "Personal Expansion versus Traditional Gender Stereotypes."

[46] Arlie Hochschild and Anne Machung, *The Second Shift: Working Families and the Revolution at Home* (New York: Penguin, 2012), https://books.google.com.eg/books?id=St_6kWcPJS8C&printsec=frontcover#v=onepage&q&f=false (last accessed January 13, 2020).

[47] Harfouche and Robbin, "Antecedents of the Digital Divide in Lebanon."

inequalities and marginalization. Quality data is lacking in the region, and the data that is available is subject to challenges. These can themselves create or amplify biases that cause harmful consequences, especially to marginalized groups.

Data Asymmetry in Markets

Data asymmetry is innate in power dynamics. Given that data is a differentiating market factor, data becomes a source of authority and an impediment to leveling the playing field for the less powerful. This holds even more in a context of limited local data to start with. Data inequality manifests in the underlying forces in the AI market and in the competition that exists between large international companies and local small to medium enterprises.

As large data sets are a prerequisite for developing AI, utilizing AI is limited to those who can afford to either buy them from data brokers, research institutions, or consultants, or those who have the capacity, be it technical, infrastructural, or financial, to gather and analyze large amounts of data. It is companies, like Google, Uber, Facebook, and Amazon that have massive amounts of annotated data that will see the best results from their AI systems.

Lack of access to data may actually inhibit the very access to the market, which would limit competition, lessen innovation, and "stifle the energy and fresh ideas that start-ups and SMEs (small and medium enterprises) bring."[48] This puts smaller companies at a disadvantage and feeds into market concentration. In Egypt, for example, a few large laboratories that control the market own 70 percent of the country's health data sets, but they do not necessarily know how to make the best use of them.[49] This data mine offers a huge potential for small agile companies to deploy AI for health services like predicting epidemics and future responses to particular medications. The concentration of these data sets in the market is a barrier to innovation, specifically the inclusion of small companies in the market for a development-related objective.

Data crowdsourcing has offered an alternative towards mitigating data asymmetry. For example, smaller, local initiatives like Bey2ollak, a crowdsourced road-traffic monitoring application founded in Egypt, collect their own data via crowdsourcing, and hence build large data sets, albeit on a much smaller scale than larger multinationals. The application collects a considerable amount of data from its 1.3 million users.

Data Lock by the State

Data lock amplifies the power asymmetry originating from data ownership and gating by the state. Data is typically housed with National Statistics Offices. Clear asymmetry exists between the state as owner of national statistics and the citizen. Data lock takes place when the data is not easily accessed by citizens and not released in a timely manner, and the data-collection methodologies are not disclosed. Data may be politicized, filtered, incomplete, or censored.

---

[48] Olivier Thereaux, "Using Artificial Intelligence and Open Data for Innovation and Accountability," *Open Data Institute*, 2017, https://theodi.org/article/using-artificial-intelligence-and-open-data-for-innovation-and-accountability/ (last accessed January 13, 2020).

[49] Ahmed Abaza, "AI and Inequalities." Interview by Nagla Rizk, April 20, 2019.

The data lock in the region is seen in the lack of published high-quality data that is machine readable and the cumbersome regulations and need for licenses to allow for reuse.[50] The Open Data Barometer produced by the World Wide Web Foundation shows in 2015 that only an estimated 1.48 percent of data in the Arab World is open. Even though the Barometer suggests that 71 percent of surveyed government information was available on the internet, there remains technical and/or legal barriers to accessing this as machine-readable data.[51] For example, while there is increased availability of data on the website of Egypt's Central Agency for Public Mobilisation and Statistics (CAPMAS), the data is in PDF format.

Some countries in the region have made some progress toward open government data. One example is Tunisia, where the Ministry of Energy, in an effort with partner international organizations promoting open government principles, created a website for publishing hydrocarbon investment contracts and associated documents in 2014. This data was made available in machine-readable format, in addition to metadata on country, company name, resource being extracted, signature date, and contract type.[52]

Data Inaccuracy—Blur, Myopia, and Blindness

Another main challenge with data in the region is the inaccuracies that end up clouding out realities on the ground. One possible source of inaccuracy is the *data blur* as aggregates cloud out granulations, which can only be captured by the disaggregation of the data. An example can be found in the failure of Egypt's aggregate official data to capture the nuanced effects of currency floatation in 2016 and subsequent inflation on inequality for different groups, especially women and female-led households.[53]

A related source of data inaccuracy is the shortsightedness coming from a single dimensional lens that looks at economic and social variables from the top down—data *myopia*. This contention extends to data that makes up national statistics such as indicators of income, inequality, education, health, and others. A case in point is the failure of national data as they are defined and collected to reflect lived realities and anticipate the Arab Spring. Indeed, multifaceted inequality sits at the heart of this contention around macroeconomic indicators and the statistics that inform them, especially those of growth, being inadequate reflections of economic well-being.

Such shortcomings of quantitative macro data put in question the ability of the collection *methodologies* to reflect the complex realties on the ground, including informality,

[50] "MENA Data Platform: Open Knowledge for Development in MENA," 2015, http://menadata.net/public/index (last accessed January 13, 2020).

[51] Hatem Ben Yacoub, "Why OKF Global Open Data Index 2015 Is a Failure," *HBY Consultancy*, 2015, http://www.hbyconsultancy.com/blog/why-okf-global-open-data-index-2015-is-a-failure.html (last accessed January 13, 2020).

[52] Wissem Heni et al., "Tunisians Can Now Access Hydrocarbon Contracts in Open Data Format," *Natural Resource Governance Institute*, 2016, https://resourcegovernance.org/blog/tunisians-can-now-access-hydrocarbon-contracts-open-data-format (last accessed January 13, 2020).

[53] Maye Kabil, "How to Cover a Post-Shock Economy?" *Mada Masr*, (December 29, 2017), https://www.madamasr.com/en/2017/12/29/feature/economy/how-to-cover-a-post-shock-economy/ (last accessed January 13, 2020).

for example.[54] Nobel Laureate Angus Deaton has provided a wealth of evidence on the limited efficacy of aggregate-level data and its methodology of collection.[55] His work calls for a move away from national, aggregate-level methodologies to ones that are more bottom-up and better reflect individual human behavior and realities.[56]

Data inaccuracy also comes from *blindness* due to selectivity in data collection, excluding communities that are outside the radar of the formal establishment. This applies to informal employees who are absent from the national employment statistics. Also invisible from the national statistical radar are residents of informal dwellings. These account for almost a third of housing in Cairo and 23 percent in Morocco, and are seen in several peri-urban areas around Greater Tunis and in Jordan.[57] Informal housing can also be observed, also at a lower rate, richer countries in the region such as Saudi Arabia.[58] Exclusion of informal communities from national income and other market censuses immediately translates to further marginalization and exclusion from policies related to subsidies, social safety nets, housing, and broader policy making.

An Enabling Environment?

Closely linked to the discussion of data is the enabling environment that governs the potential for democratizing access and use of data for inclusive AI in the region. Such environment is necessary to promote a comprehensive paradigm of openness and a culture of sharing with data at its core. Data inequalities are compounded by a subpar environment, which complicates the interplay between AI and inclusion in the region. Specifically, an appropriate environment entails an ecosystem of legislation that supports innovation, access to markets, open data, and building human capacity and technology development. Figure 33.4 offers a summary mapping of legislation around data regulation in the region.

Freedom of information (FOI) frameworks are scarce in the region. Tunisia and Jordan have adopted FOI legislation and made official declarations in this regard.[59] Tunisia established an Access to Information Authority, one of the only such bodies in the MENA region. Jordan joined the Open Government Partnership in 2011 and has announced some ambitious reforms and national plans regarding freedom of information and access to information.[60]

Legislation is also needed to safeguard citizen and consumer rights to privacy and data protection. Laws and regulations pertaining to data and data protection are scarce in the

[54] Elena Ianchovichina, "Eruptions of Popular Anger: The Economics of the Arab Spring and Its Aftermath," *World Bank*, 2018, https://openknowledge.worldbank.org/bitstream/handle/10986/28961/9781464811524.pdf?sequence=5&isAllowed=y (last accessed January 13, 2020).
[55] "The Prize in Economic Sciences 2015," *The Royal Swedish Academy of Sciences* (2015), https://www.nobelprize.org/uploads/2018/06/press-33.pdf (last accessed January 13, 2020).
[56] Id.
[57] David Sims, "The Arab Housing Paradox," *The Cairo Review* (November 2013), https://www.thecairoreview.com/essays/the-arab-housing-paradox/ (last accessed January 13, 2020).
[58] Id.
[59] "Participants," *Open Government Partnership*, 2018, https://www.opengovpartnership.org/our-members/ (last accessed January 13, 2020).
[60] Id.

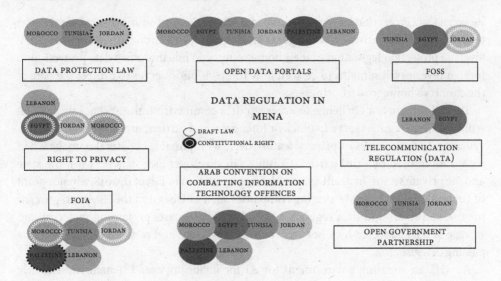

FIGURE 33.4. Data regulation in MENA 2018.

Source: Compiled by author in 2018 from different sources.

region. An existing framework to which many countries in the region are signatory is the Arab Convention on Combating Information Technology Offences.[61] The convention only offers an "overview of general provisions on privacy and data protection" but does not provide "explicit stipulations on legal protection and regulation of data and privacy."[62]

Tunisia, Morocco, and Jordan have some form of reified or draft laws on data protection.[63] Tunisia is a pioneer in the MENA region in terms of data privacy and protection legislation, with most of the data privacy and protection legal provisions set out in the 2004 Organic Act on the Protection of Personal Data.[64] By setting a high standard of data protection, the Tunisian Act gives a range of rights to individuals whose data is processed and sets out certain obligations for organizations and individuals in charge of the data processing.

Other countries in the region have also taken some steps in terms of data legislation. For example, Qatar enacted the Law Concerning Personal Data Protection in 2016.[65] In the UAE, specific data protection provisions exist only in free zones, such as the UAE's Abu Dhabi Global Market and Dubai International Financial Centre.[66] Bahrain's latest

[61] Including Algeria, Egypt, Morocco, Tunisia, Jordan, Palestine, and Lebanon.

[62] Nagla Rizk, Youmna Hashem, and Nancy Salem, "Open Data Management Plan Middle East and North Africa: A Guide," *MENA Data Platform* (October 2018), http://menadata.net/resources/datasets/1539516976_OpenDataManagementPlan.pdf (last accessed January 13, 2020).

[63] *Id.*

[64] Republic of Tunisia, *Organic Act n°2004–63 of July 27th, 2004 on the Protection of Personal Data*, https://tinyurl.com/y8076eau (last accessed January 13, 2020).

[65] "Law No. 13 of 2016 Promulgating the Protection of the Privacy of Personal Data Law," *Sultan Al-Abdulla and Partners*, https://cyrilla.org/en/document/sei6xl6kd6r (last accessed January 13, 2020).

[66] Andrada Coos, "Data Protection Regulations in the Middle East," *Endpoint Protector* (December 3, 2018), https://www.endpointprotector.com/blog/data-protection-regulations-middle-east/ (last accessed January 13, 2020).

Personal Data Protection Law, which came into effect in August 2019, is a step to encourage technology-related business while guaranteeing data protection.[67] Investors are to follow data protection legislation of their home country. While this offers data protection to foreign investors, it remains to be seen how this legislation serves to protect the data of the country's homegrown businesses.

This said, there is a challenge to access to data coming from the absence of political will, and when regimes serve to block or filter data, and further, use data for citizen surveillance. Clearly, issues of privacy feature here, with possible collateral damage when data is monitored by third parties. Conflict can exist over user data between the state and the private sector. In drafting ride-sharing legislation in Egypt in 2018, a major point of contention between ride-sharing companies such as Uber and the Egyptian government revolved around data regulations. Authorities requests pertaining to access and storage of data collected by Uber were met by objections and resulted in a delay in the passing of legislation.[68]

As well, an enabling environment for AI for inclusion would benefit from clearly defined AI strategies with a clear vision for inclusion and equality. The strategy would include a clear stipulation of the safety nets for those potentially harmed by AI biases, as well as the anticipated disruptions in the labor market. This would be part of the "social contract" that comes along the fourth industrial revolution.[69] Only the UAE has an AI strategy; Tunisia and Egypt have drafted strategies to be announced later in 2019.

Infrastructure Issues

An integral component of the discussion of AI and inequality is infrastructure. Infrastructure plays out along several axes. Among these are the uneven access to data storage and computing capacity, the limited internet connectivity, and the host of issues related to how algorithms are intertwined with the human context.

First, AI applications necessitate a massive volume of data, hundreds of terabytes that need to be accommodated, stored, processed, and managed via technical infrastructures, computing power, and resources.[70] The need for access to massive data storage and computing power infrastructure, such as Amazon's Cloud Computing Software or NASA's

---

[67] Mohamed Toorani and Eamon Holley, "Bahrain Publishes Personal Data Protection Law," *DLA Piper*, 2018, https://www.dlapiper.com/en/bahrain/insights/publications/2018/09/bahrain-publishes-personal-data-protection-law/ (last accessed January 13, 2020).

[68] Ahmed Megahid, "Egyptian Parliament Approves Bill Regulating Ride-sharing Apps," *The Arab Weekly* (May 13, 2018), https://thearabweekly.com/egyptian-parliament-approves-bill-regulating-ride-sharing-apps (last accessed January 13, 2020).

[69] "Dialogue Series on New Economic and Social Frontiers Shaping the New Economy in the Fourth Industrial Revolution," *World Economic Forum*, 2019, https://www3.weforum.org/docs/WEF_Dialogue_Series_on_New_Economic_and_Social_Frontiers.pdf (last accessed January 13, 2020).

[70] "Open Data Management Plan for the MENA Region," *MENA Data Platform*, 2018, http://menadata.net/public/dataset/81539516969 (last accessed January 13, 2020).

Open Stack,[71] can be a barrier and contribute to market inequality. While these are available on a rent or pay-per-use basis, the cost may be prohibitive to those at the lower end of the scale.[72] Additionally, the cloud service may restrict the user to the vendor's specific packages. As well, clients object to their data being stored in the cloud.[73] Indeed, there have been complaints from start-ups in the region that their need for data storage and computer power capacity is not well met.[74] The availability of massive data centers and computing power capacity in the richer countries of the region like the UAE, could widen the regional divide.

However, some argue that the availability of the cloud option for data storage and computing mitigates inequality. This is because it provides an affordable alternative for start-ups "to scale their services as they grow rather than requiring an upfront investment in infrastructure as a sunk cost."[75] As well, the cloud offers a platform for only the internet required components of the process, as the development of AI itself can be done offline.[76]

Still, usage of the cloud necessitates strong connectivity for data upload, training of the machine, and for the dissemination of AI enabled applications and services, especially on a national scale.[77] As well, a stronger internet connection will certainly ensure more efficient and seamless synchronization between the data upload, the development of algorithms, and AI applications. Countries with the stronger connectivity stand to lead in the race of AI deployment.

In addition to all this, a succinct unpacking of AI infrastructures and their impact on inclusion looks beyond the algorithm into the human context that surrounds it. The different layers of AI infrastructures unleash aspects of social and political contexts, cleverly termed "black boxes within black boxes."[78] These include the organizational structures, trade secrecy, all the way to "labor practices and untraceable global supply chains for rare earth minerals used to build consumer AI devices."[79]

Inequality inherent in algorithms can be more dangerous as they are invisible and dormant, serving to amplify biases in the data, in humans, and on the ground. Like elsewhere, in the MENA region, algorithms are likely to be developed and implemented by "experts" who will have "ethical agency and decision making" over the rest of the "subjects," including marginalized groups or to the subjects to which the algorithms are "applied."[80] In this regard, the inclusion of at least a domain expert, for example, health,

---

[71] William Bryan, "OpenStack Cloud Computing Platform," *NASA*, 2016, https://www.nasa.gov/offices/oct/40-years-of-nasa-spinoff/openstack-cloud-computing-platform/ (last accessed January 13, 2020).

[72] Sherif El Kassas, "AI and Inequalities." Interview by Nagla Rizk, March 30, 2019.

[73] Ahmed Abaza, "AI and Inequalities." Interview by Nagla Rizk, April 20, 2019.

[74] *Id.*

[75] Ashraf Abdelwahab and Hossam Sharara, "AI and Inequalities." Interviews by Nagla Rizk, April 1 and 13, 2019.

[76] Nouri Sadek, "AI and Inequalities." Interview by Nagla Rizk, April 14, 2019.

[77] Sadek and Abdelwahab interviews by Nagla Rizk, April 2019.

[78] AI Now Report 2018, *AI Now Institute, New York University*, https://ainowinstitute.org/AI_Now_2018_Report.pdf (last accessed January 13, 2020).

[79] *Id.*

[80] *Id.*

is crucial in the process of developing the algorithm. The gap is even larger when the algorithm is taken from an open source platform, like Google open source algorithms, as a product coming out from completely different contexts is to be applied generically to a local context with existing multilayered and multifaceted inequality.[81]

Additionally, AI algorithms can magnify the bias by missing a significant portion of the population. This can cause "allocative harms"[82] where some people are denied services or opportunities. For example MerQ, an Egyptian start-up, launched a chatbot through Facebook named Sally, that introduces people to credit card systems in Arabic.[83] While the chatbot is in Arabic and may seem more context specific, it is still exclusive as only 10–15 percent of Egyptians have bank accounts, reflecting a social reality of a historical mistrust of banks, and 60 percent of Egyptians do not have access to the internet or Facebook. Credit rating algorithms that may include alternative data such as neighborhoods, can magnify socioeconomic differences embedded in the data bias.[84]

Another lock is inherent in the trade secrets of the algorithm usually held by corporations and third-party vendors. This is another black box of intellectual content saved for the privileged few. The MENA region is more likely to be users than producers of this content, and hence will be denied access to the secrets of this opaque part of the AI supply chain.

Algorithms are also part of a bigger political context. Even if the algorithm may be technically sound or fair, it can be used as a means for harmful ends.[85] The biases inherent in facial recognition algorithms, for example, are likely to exacerbate discrimination. These tools may offer yet more clout to regimes and new forms of surveillance. For example, Israeli security forces' use of facial recognition software to control entry into the Al-Aqsa mosque is less favored by Palestinians to metal detectors, on the back of fears that the technology is likely be used against them.[86]

The Human Resource Challenge

The region is rich in human resources with an abundance of young and formally educated youth. Nevertheless, structural market imbalances coupled with inadequate skill development shape the human resources challenges faced by the region with the

[81]   Ahmed Abaza, "AI and Inequalities." Interview by Nagla Rizk, April 20, 2019.

[82]   AI Now Report 2018.

[83]   Zubair Naeem Paracha, "Egypt's Merq Raises Six-Figure Seed for Sally, Its Facebook Chatbot that Lets Users Compare Credit Cards," *Menabytes* (April 15, 2019), https://www.menabytes.com/egypt-merq-see (last accessed January 13, 2020).

[84]   Ahmed Abaza, "AI and Inequalities." Interview by Nagla Rizk, April 20, 2019.

[85]   AI Now Report 2018.

[86]   Amjad Iraqi, "Palestinians Are Reviving Their Agency in Jerusalem," *+927 Magazine* (July 26, 2017), https://www.972mag.com/palestinians-are-reviving-their-agency-in-jerusalem/; Rebecca Stead, "Remembering Israel's Move to Install Metal Detectors at Al-Aqsa," *Middle East Monitor* (July 16, 2018), https://www.middleeastmonitor.com/20180716-remembering-israels-move-to-install-metal-detectors-at-al-aqsa/ (last accessed January 13, 2020).

advent of AI technologies. Job losses are likely to amplify already existing labor market imbalances, specifically, structural unemployment caused by insufficient job opportunities. Local decisions to use "labour-enabling" rather than "labour-replacing"[87] technologies may be subject to political and social factors, especially in countries where youth unemployment and political instability are rampant.

As elsewhere in the world, the risk of job loss due to automation is most likely to occur at the medium-skill level. The skill structure of employment in countries of the region show the middle-skill cohort to be the highest. Almost half (48.7 percent) of work activities in Egypt are susceptible to automation by adapting currently available technologies.[88] These typically include outsourcing and call centers, currently accounting for 90,000 direct jobs.[89] This is also true for high-income countries in the region like the UAE, which is 47 percent susceptible.[90]

The job loss or lack of jobs in an environment of unemployment of the youth and the educated has resulted in many of the educated youth considering new technology-based work opportunities such as ride-sharing. This becomes an example where technology-based labor opportunities respond positively to unemployment, counter to the usual concern of technology contributing to the labor crisis through automation. While far from ideal, research has shown that ride-sharing in Egypt allows for a more favorable option to prevalent informal work or even formal counterparts that offer little true health or pension benefits.[91] Respondents indicated that ride-sharing has allowed for livelihood and flexibility and has offered opportunities to engage with new technologies adding to skill sets and potential. For women, work with ride-sharing has offered new opportunities for livelihood along with safety and empowerment.[92]

More so for the demand of the AI economy, there will be a dire need for the acquisition of new skills. Skill retraining on data science, problem-solving, and digital skills will be

---

[87] Lay Chuah, Norman Loayza, and Achim Schmillen, "The Future of Work: Race with—Not against—the Machine" (August 2018), https://fowigs.net/future-work-race-not-machine/ (last accessed January 13, 2020).

[88] Michael Chui, James Manyika, and Mehdi Miremadi, "The Countries Most (and Least) Likely to Be Affected by Automation," *Harvard Business Review* (April 12, 2017). https://hbr.org/2017/04/the-countries-most-and-least-likely-to-be-affected-by-automation (last accessed January 13, 2020).

[89] "The Future of Jobs and Skills in the Middle East and North Africa: Preparing the Region for the Fourth Industrial Revolution," World Economic Forum, 2017, https://www.weforum.org/reports/the-future-of-jobs-and-skills-in-the-middle-east-and-north-africa-preparing-the-region-for-the-fourth-industrial-revolution (last accessed January 13, 2020).

[90] *Id.*

[91] Nagla Rizk, "A Glimpse into the Sharing Economy: An Analysis of Uber Driver-Partners in Egypt," *Social Science Research Network*, 2017, https://papers.ssrn.com/sol3/papers.cfm?abstract_id=2946083 (last accessed January 13, 2020).

[92] Nagla Rizk, Nancy Salem, and Nadine Weheba, "A Gendered Analysis of Ridesharing: Perspectives from Cairo, Egypt," in *Urban Transport in the Sharing Economy Era: Collaborative Cities*, ed. (Fernando Bercovich (Buenos Aires: Center for the Implementation of Public Policies Promoting Equity and Growth, 2018), http://www. cippec.org/wp-content/uploads/2018/09/UrbanTransport-completo-web_CIPPEC.pdf (last accessed March 20, 2020).

needed for workers who are expected to be displaced as AI becomes prevalent.[93] Such skills are also needed in education as general data capacities were found to be lacking in the region's school curricula, with specific data science courses outside of business contexts found also scarce.[94]

Middle-income countries within the region are not homogenous with regards to workers' skill sets. Egypt, the UAE, Jordan, and Saudi Arabia are leading the way for high-skilled employment, with over 20 percent of their labor force considered high-skilled.[95] Additionally, these countries are also high on the digital skills such as computer skills, basic coding, and digital reading, albeit superseded by Saudi Arabia and including Tunisia.[96] Indeed those five countries were the top source countries for the one hundred start-ups chosen by the World Economic Forum in 2019 to lead the fourth industrial revolution in the region.[97]

A final challenge facing human capital in the region is labor retention. On the local level, labor turnover from start-ups to join lucrative work with larger companies is a source of inequality between smaller start-ups and bigger players.[98, 99] Big corporations in the information technology sector attract top tier talent with better pay and promises of reallocation and exposure to global markets. Internally, this widens the market gap between large companies and start-ups.

This can also take place on the regional and international level, where local capacities migrate from labor-abundant middle-income countries like Egypt and Tunisia to the Global North or to oil-rich countries like the UAE and Saudi Arabia.[100, 101] A few of the migrating businesses, however, have managed to keep their back offices in the region, given the low labor and operating costs, which helps retain skills and train young employees.[102]

Rays of Hope

Despite the above challenges which threaten to widen inequalities in the region, there remain some rays of hope. The first comes from the growing youth entrepreneurial scene where many homegrown start-ups and businesses have flourished since the uprisings. Local, organic grounds up initiatives, including small businesses and start-ups, carry a

[93] "Artificial Intelligence for Africa: An Opportunity for Growth, Development, and Democratisation," *Access Partnership*, 2019, https://www.accesspartnership.com/artificial-intelligence-for-africa-an-opportunity-for-growth-development-and-democratisation/ (last accessed January 13, 2020).

[94] Abed Khooli, "Harnessing the Economic Power of Data in the Middle East and North Africa (MENA)," *Birzeit University Centre for Continuing Education*, 2015.

[95] "The Future of Jobs and Skills in the Middle East and North Africa."

[96] Global Competitiveness Report, *World Economic Forum*, October 2018, https://www.weforum.org/reports/the-global-competitveness-report-2018 (last accessed January 13, 2020).

[97] World Economic Forum, "Meet the 100 Arab Start-ups Shaping the Fourth Industrial Revolution," 2019, https://widgets.weforum.org/arabstartups/ (last accessed March 20, 2020).

[98] Ahmed Abaza, "AI and Inequalities." Interview by Nagla Rizk, April 20, 2019.

[99] Sameh Saleh, "AI and Inequalities." Interview by Nagla Rizk, April 6, 2019.

[100] Jazem Halioui, "AI and Inequalities." Interview by Nagla Rizk, February 10, 2019.

[101] Sherif El Kassas, "AI and Inequalities." Interview by Nagla Rizk, March 30, 2019.

[102] Ahmed Abaza, "AI and Inequalities." Interview by Nagla Rizk, April 20, 2019.

promise for human development and empowerment through the use, and possibly production, of digital technologies, AI being no exception. Their entrepreneurial mindset carries a potential for novel ways of data collection and deploying AI solutions and link-ages to serve developmental purposes, which target inclusion and mitigating inequality.

Within the hope in youth, the region's human capital portrays some promise in its foundation of basic educational attainment. In some countries, tertiary degree holders meet the global average of 17 percent (Bahrain, Saudi Arabia, and Egypt); other countries like Jordan have achieved near universal basic education.[103] As well, almost half of tertiary-educated individuals in the region hold degrees in science, technology engineering, and mathematics. These specialize in engineering, manufacturing, and construction, and to a lesser extent in information and communication technologies, natural sciences, mathematics, and statistics.[104] It is also estimated that by 2030, the region will expand its tertiary talent pool by 50 percent.[105] If managed wisely, the region's human capital can serve as an asset in this next new phase.

The second ray of hope comes from the focus on novel data collection methodologies that result in more accurate reflections of realities and provide a new data source for AI. This way, data sets will no longer be controlled by a select few, and there will be increased availability of open data. Data driven innovation in particular, for profit and nonprofit, using different technologies such a data layering, is cause for hope.

There are notable examples from business, civil society, and academia across the region collecting and making use of innovative sources of data. Innova Tunisia,[106] a Tunisian-based start-up, uses sentiment analysis of data gathered from social media and online platforms to analyze media portrayals of gender inequalities. HarassMap is an Egyptian nonprofit online application, which allows people, mainly women, to share incidents of harassment, then triangulates this crowd sourced data, making it readily accessible.[107]

Research initiatives undertaken within the MENA founding node for Open Data for Development[108] have utilized innovative data collection using affordable censors to assemble data in combination with open-sourced, crowd-sourced, and existing govern-ment data. One initiative assessed the level of safety, mobility, accessibility, and reliabil-ity of transport in Cairo,[109] while the second created a heat map of black carbon pollution in Cairo.[110] Another was undertaken in Lebanon, where researchers created

---

[103] "The Future of Jobs and Skills in the Middle East and North Africa."

[104] *Id.*

[105] *Id.*

[106] "Who We Are," *Webradar*, http://webradar.me/who-we-are/ (last accessed January 13, 2020).

[107] "Sexual Harassment in Greater Cairo: Effectiveness of Crowdsourced Data," *IDRC* and *HarassMap*, 2014, https://www.academia.edu/23012454/Towards_A_Safer_City_Sexual_Harassment_in_Greater_Cairo_Effectiveness_of_Crowdsourced_Data (last accessed January 13, 2020).

[108] Access to Knowledge for Development Center at the American University in Cairo, School of Business, https://business.aucegypt.edu/research/centers/a2k4d.

[109] Access to Knowledge for Development Center at the American University in Cairo and Sets Egypt, "Urban Mobility in Cairo," MENA Data Platform, 2018 http://menadata.net/public/project/3 (last accessed March 20, 2020).

[110] "Developing Air Quality Heat Map for Cairo: A Citizen-Centric Approach," *MENA Data Platform*, 2018, http://menadata.net/public/dataset/21539400046 (last accessed January 13, 2020).

"Health SystemEye," an online platform that disseminates and visualizes health data and information to policymakers.[111] As well, researchers at BirZeit University in Palestine developed data literacy and capacity-building modules, collecting data sets via pollution sensors in Ramallah to monitor air quality around schools.[112]

The third ray of hope comes from the initiatives taken by some governments in the region use AI for inclusion and building human capital, albeit still modest. Examples are the UAE using AI in tuberculosis diagnosis and training and educating students and government employees on AI.[113, 114] In Egypt, data is being collected within the initiative at 100 Million Healthy Lives, an initiative aimed "at screening citizens above the age of 18 to determine the prevalence of Hepatitis C, obesity, and chronic diseases like diabetes and hypertension." Such data is crucial, with hepatitis disease being pervasive with 22 percent of the population diagnosed with hepatitis C in 2015.[115] Linked with national ID, insurance, and possibly other health data, this national data set can provide better health services to the country's nationals. It is hoped that such data will set the foundation for better health services using inclusive AI.

CONCLUSION: AI IN MENA—INCLUSION OR INEQUALITY?

The discourse over AI and inequality in the region is intertwined with its unique political, economic, and social context. The dynamics of AI and its impact on inclusion or inequality are embedded in the region's complexities. They also sit at the heart of a set of inherent tensions.

Like elsewhere, a major tension in the region lies in the paradox of the capacity of the technology itself to concurrently produce conflicting trends triggering opposite outcomes. Like other digital technologies, AI has the potential of producing dynamics that push power away from the center to the periphery. These centrifugal forces function on

[111] "Health System Eye," *Knowledge to Policy Centre at the American University in Beirut*, http://www.healthsystemeye.com/ (last accessed January 13, 2020).

[112] Abed Khooli, "Tracking Air Quality with IoT Sensors and Publishing Open Data in MENA" (February 26, 2017), https://www.linkedin.com/pulse/tracking-air-quality-iot-sensors-publishing-open-data-abed-khooli/ (last accessed January 13, 2020).

[113] Samer Abu Ltaif, "AI Readiness in 2019 and Beyond: Empowering our People to Achieve More," *Microsoft News Center Middle East & Africa*, 2019, https://news.microsoft.com/en-xm/2019/02/01/ai-readiness-in-2019-and-beyond-empowering-our-people-to-achieve-more/ (last accessed January 13, 2020).

[114] Ismail Sebugwaawo, "Include Artificial Intelligence in School Curricula, Say Experts," *Khaleej Times*, July 24, 2018, https://www.khaleejtimes.com/nation/abu-dhabi/include-artificial-intelligence-in-school-curricula-say-experts (last accessed January 13, 2020).

[115] "30 Million Egyptians Screened for Hepatitis C as Part of New Campaign," *Ahram Online* (February 23, 2019), http://english.ahram.org.eg/NewsContent/1/64/326024/Egypt/Politics-/-million-Egyptians-screened-for-hepatitis-C-as-par.aspx (last accessed January 13, 2020).

both the economic and political fronts and serve to empower small players and mitigate inequality. Paradoxically, the opposite force can also, and simultaneously, be triggered by AI to further empower the already established hierarchies. Such centripetal forces come at the expense of the small players and clearly widen inequalities. While this tension is global, it becomes more pronounced in the region in light of its weak institutions and nascent legislative machinery.

Top-down hierarchies in technology creation and dissemination mean ownership of data and opaque black boxes of technology, locked up by large companies that are typically large multinational corporations or that import technology directly from them. This comes in tension with inclusive locally developed technologies with solutions adapted to local cultures and responsive to marginalized communities. The divide in the creation and ownership of technology widens the internal divide between large and small entities in the region. It also allows for large companies to acquire smaller ones, which enhances market concentration. An example is the recent acquisition of the local ride-sharing company Careem by Uber in early 2019.

A similar scenario occurs on the political scene, where tensions persist between established political regimes versus opposing citizen voices and organic movements seeking inclusion and democracy. While AI technologies and grounds-up data collection have the potential to serve as means for citizen empowerment, control over data and AI can be tools for furthering the power of the already established regimes. Examples include the use of citizen data for surveillance and facial recognition technologies for oppressive purposes.

This relates to a tension that has been well noted for Arab countries as early as in 2009 in the first Arab Knowledge Report.[116] With focus on promoting economic growth at the expense of political inclusion, if at all, the region is characterized by expanding economic freedoms more generously than civil liberties. Concentrating solely on economic "openness" is typically intended to attract foreign direct investment and targets multinational and other large corporations, which ends up feeding into the centripetal forces referred to earlier.

This shows clearly in the debate over open data, access to information, and promoting the inclusion of citizens in decision-making. An enabling environment for using data and AI for good necessitates an integrated set of freedoms so as to promote a comprehensive paradigm of openness and a culture of sharing with data at its core. Expanding civil liberties is related to the enabling environment for data openness, which is inclusive to all citizens in general and to small businesses and innovators in particular.

A focus on the economy alone has also meant a condition of technological determinism and its accompanying threat of decontextualization. In the present context, this would translate to investing solely in the AI technologies and the belief that they will provide the solutions to all ills. Related to this is the blind belief in the algorithm and disregard for the sociopolitical context surrounding the technology.

[116] "Towards Productive Intercommunication for Knowledge," *Arab Knowledge Report*, 2009, https://www.undp.org/content/dam/rbas/report/ahdr/AKR2009-Eng-Full-Report.pdf (last accessed January 13, 2020).

Context is part of "fairness." Solutions should not be solely technical, and technical solutions should not be decontextualized. A sound and unbiased AI system may, after all, not be appropriate in a particular socioeconomic and political context.[117] Political issues should not be framed as solely technical ones. According to AI Now Report 2018, "[w]hen framed as technical 'fixes' debiasing solutions rarely allow for questions about the appropriateness or efficacy of an AI system altogether, or for an interrogation of the institutional context into which the 'fixed' AI system will ultimately be applied."[118]

Investing in technology may be necessary, but it is not sufficient to achieve inclusion. Indeed, investment solely in technology can serve to exacerbate divides if not matched by investment in organizational change, including human resources.[119] More broadly, for AI to be inclusive, there needs to be a holistic approach[120] to AI technology and development to ensure inclusion of the region's human capital as active participants in the new economy, which is also an investment in the region's political stability.

These inter-related tensions highlight that AI can serve both concurrent trends in the economy, empowering the established as well as new entrants, underline the gap in focus between the economic and the political, and exemplify how investment in technology alone without an enabling environment would fail to achieve the desired objectives. More specifically, a top-down approach that focuses on expert technocratic solutions to issues that affect human lives and ones that do not involve participatory approaches can aggravate divides and the exclusion of the underprivileged and the marginalized. Together, these tensions inform the debate on AI and inequality, and an awareness of them helps mitigate the challenges and the threats that AI would exacerbate inequality in the region.

ACKNOWLEDGMENTS

The author is grateful for the research support of the team of the Access to Knowledge for Development Center (A2K4D) at the American University in Cairo's School of Business. Nadine Weheba, Nagham El Houssamy, and Nancy Salem provided seminal insights at various stages of the research. The author is indebted to Hana Shaltout, Farah Ghazal, and Dana Elbashbishy for their dedicated research assistance. Special thanks are due to the Center's long time collaborator Lina Attalah for her inspiration and her valuable editorial input.

[117] AI Now Report 2018.

[118] *Id.*

[119] Erik Brynjolfsson and Andrew McAfee, "Creative Destruction: The Economics of Accelerating Technology and Disappearing Jobs," in *Race Against the Machine: How the Digital Revolution Is Accelerating Innovation, Driving Productivity, and Irreversibly Transforming Employment and the Economy* (Digital Frontier Press, 2011), 28–52.

[120] Erik Brynjolfsson et al. "Artificial Intelligence and the Modern Productivity Paradox: A Clash of Expectations and Statistics," *National Bureau of Economic Research*, National Bureau of Economic Research, 2017, https://www.nber.org/chapters/c14007.pdf (last accessed January 13, 2020).

BIBLIOGRAPHY

"AI Now Report 2018." *AI Now Institute, New York University*. https://ainowinstitute.org/AI_Now_2018_Report.pdf (last modified December 2018).

"Arab Human Development Report: Youth and the Prospects for Human Development in a Changing Reality." *UN Development Programme*, 2016. http://arab-hdr.org/Reports/2016/2016.aspx (last accessed January 13, 2020).

Arezki, Rabah et al. "A New Economy in Middle East and North Africa." *World Bank Group: Middle East and North Africa Economic Monitor*. https://openknowledge.worldbank.org/bitstream/handle/10986/30436/9781464813672.pdf?sequence=11&isAllowed=y (last accessed January 13, 2020).

"Artificial Intelligence for Africa: An Opportunity for Growth, Development, and Democratisation." *Access Partnership*. https://www.accesspartnership.com/artificial-intelligence-for-africa-an-opportunity-for-growth-development-and-democratisation/ (last accessed January 13, 2020).

Brynjolfsson, Erik et al. "Artificial Intelligence and the Modern Productivity Paradox: A Clash of Expectations and Statistics." *National Bureau of Economic Research*, 2017. https://www.nber.org/chapters/c14007.pdf. (last accessed January 13, 2020)

Chui, Michael, James Manyika, and Mehdi Miremadi. "The Countries Most (and Least) Likely to Be Affected by Automation." *Harvard Business Review*, April 12, 2017. https://hbr.org/2017/04/the-countries-most-and-least-likely-to-be-affected-by-automation (last accessed January 13, 2020).

"Dialogue Series on New Economic and Social Frontiers, Shaping the New Economy in the Fourth Industrial Revolution." *World Economic Forum*. http://www3.weforum.org/docs/WEF_Dialogue_Series_on_New_Economic_and_Social_Frontiers.pdf (last accessed January 13, 2020).

"The Future of Jobs and Skills in the Middle East and North Africa: Preparing the Region for the Fourth Industrial Revolution." *World Economic Forum* (2017). https://www.weforum.org/reports/the-future-of-jobs-and-skills-in-the-middle-east-and-north-africa-preparing-the-region-for-the-fourth-industrial-revolution (last accessed January 13, 2020).

Gordon, Michael. "Forecasting Instability: The Case of the Arab Spring and the Limitations of Socioeconomic Data." Wilson Center. https://www.wilsoncenter.org/article/forecasting-instability-the-case-the-arab-spring-and-the-limitations-socioeconomic-data (last accessed January 13, 2020).

Rizk, Nagla, Youmna Hashem, and Nancy Salem. "Open Data Management Plan Middle East and North Africa: A Guide." *MENA Data Platform*. http://menadata.net/resources/datasets/1539516976_Open%20Data%20Management%20Plan.pdf (last accessed January 13, 2020).

CHAPTER 34

···

EUROPE

Toward a Policy Framework for Trustworthy AI

···

ANDREA RENDA

INTRODUCTION

···

WITH its strong emphasis on fundamental rights, its commitment toward sustainable development, and its pro-regulatory stance vis-à-vis large tech giants, Europe is inevitably a peculiar testing ground for policies related to artificial intelligence (AI). Compared to what occurred in the United States and China, in the European Union the discussion on the possible regulation of AI was initially characterized by rather dystopian statements. In 2017 the *incipit* of the European Parliament's resolution on "Civil Law Rules for Robotics"[1] went as far as evoking Mary Shelley's *Frankenstein*, and ended up calling for attributing legal personality as well as "rights and duties" to smart autonomous robots, an idea that was immediately and firmly rejected by several academics.[2] The same resolution also called on the European Commission to reflect on the creation of a possible Agency for AI in Europe, a step that the European Commission found to be premature at the time, but that may be coming of age soon, as will be explained in this chapter.

···

[1] European Parliament (EP) (2017), Resolution of 16 February 2017 with recommendations to the Commission on Civil Law Rules on Robotics (2015/2103(INL)).

[2] See the Open Letter to the European Commission on Artificial Intelligence and Robotics, at https://g8fip1kplyr33r3krz5b97d1-wpengine.netdna-ssl.com/wp-content/uploads/2018/04/RoboticsOpenLetter.pdf.

Despite its overly negative narrative, the initiative of the European Parliament had the merit to place AI on the radar of EU policymakers, where it has remained since then. One year later, in the context of the midterm review of the EU Digital Single Market strategy, the Council of the EU invited the Commission to put forward a European approach to AI,[3] and the Commission started to pave the way for what is now evolving into a multistakeholder, ethically adherent, ambitious policy framework. Most recently, the president of the European Commission for 2019–2024, Ursula von der Leyen, has committed to adopting "a coordinated European approach on the human and ethical implications of artificial intelligence" during the first one hundred days of her presidency:[4] a rather unprecedented commitment for a political leader, which shows how AI has become a key political dossier, potentially strategic in terms of competitiveness, and from the standpoint of sustainable development.

However, developing a full-fledged strategy on the human and ethical implications of AI is not going to be easy for EU institutions. On the one hand, Europe is certainly a world-leading region when it comes to setting rules for emerging technologies, as demonstrated *i.a.* by the adoption of the General Data Protection Regulation (GDPR), entered into force in May 2018; and by the expansive use of competition rules (including state aids) to counter the emerging power of large tech giants. More generally, Europe can rely on a very solid legal system, in which fundamental and human rights are deeply rooted and are subject to specific jurisdiction and a dedicated Court. In the neighboring area of risk regulation, Europe is very advanced thanks to its combination of precaution and experimentation, although its constitutionally endorsed application of the precautionary principle is denounced by many as potentially hindering innovation.[5]

On the other hand, many commentators have observed that European countries are lagging behind the levels of public and private investment in AI and related technologies observed in other countries. More specifically, Europe has traditionally lagged behind the United States in terms of private expenditure in R&D, and this is particularly true in the platform and applications layers of the internet, where many of the most widespread AI applications have been deployed and where most of the potential for private investment can be found.

Against this background, not surprisingly, European leaders decided to ground their strategy on two complementary pillars: the definition and implementation of an ambitious ethical framework for AI "made in Europe"; and the increase of public and private investment in AI to improve the competitiveness of the European Union in this crucial domain. The two pillars are complementary since the Commission itself explained that stepping up investment and research capacity in AI, besides promoting competitive-

---

[3] Other EU institutions, such as the European Economic and Social Committee, also published communications on artificial intelligence, and member states started to develop their own strategies.

[4] Ursula von der Leyen, "A Union that Strives for More. My Agenda for Europe," Political Guidelines for the next European Commission 2019–2024.

[5] See, for an inspiring view, J.B. Wiener, "*The Real Pattern of Precaution*," in *The Reality of Precaution: Comparing Risk Regulation in the United States and Europe*, ed. Jonathan B. Wiener, Michael D. Rogers, James K. Hammitt, and Peter H. Sand (Washington, DC: RFF, 2011), 519–565.

ness, also strengthens Europe's credibility as a global norm leader in this space. Overall, Europe appears determined to revive in the AI domain the same approach followed for the GDPR, which places the fundamental right to data protection at the forefront, with no concession to data-hungry AI techniques such as machine learning: as a matter of fact, the GDPR promotes a "data minimization" approach and applies extraterritorially to anyone who processes personal data belonging to European citizens, regardless of location.[6]

This blueprint was translated into a concrete strategy since April 2018, when the European Commission launched its Communication on "Artificial Intelligence for Europe."[7] The document adopted a more positive narrative on AI compared to the European Parliament's initial resolution and laid the foundations for a comprehensive AI strategy, by clarifying the main elements of the intended EU's "secret sauce on AI." The main assumption behind the EU strategy is that Europe "can lead the way in developing and using AI for good and for all, building on its values and its strengths." A key challenge for the European Commission was the ongoing proliferation of national strategies (many member states adopted AI strategies during 2018 and 2019, potentially creating a risk of fragmentation): to avoid this risk, the European Commission and member states jointly adopted a Coordinated Plan in December 2018,[8] setting the very ambitious goal to "maximise the impact of investments at EU and national levels, encourage synergies and cooperation across the EU, exchange best practices and collectively define the way forward to ensure that the EU as a whole can compete globally." The Plan aims *i.a.* at stimulating an investment of €20 billion per year throughout the next decade, encompassing public and private sources of funding.

The strong focus on ethics in the European Union's AI strategy should thus be seen in the context of an overall strategy that aims at protecting citizens and civil society from abuses of digital technology but also as part of a competitiveness-oriented strategy aimed at raising the standards for access to Europe's wealthy Single Market. In this context, one the most peculiar steps in the European Union's strategy was the creation of an independent High-Level Expert Group on AI (AI HLEG), accompanied by the launch of an AI Alliance, which quickly attracted several hundred participants (3,484 as of July 22, 2019). The AI HLEG, a multistakeholder group counting fifty-two experts, was tasked with the definition of Ethics Guidelines, finally adopted on April 8, 2019; as well

---

[6] The extraterritorial impact of the GDPR has been given extensive and generous interpretation by the courts and data-protection authorities, as recently confirmed by the European Data Protection Supervisor in its guidelines on the territorial scope of GDPR. See Andrea Renda, *Regulation and IRC: Challenges Posed by the Digital Transformation*, report for the OECD Regulatory Policy Committee, forthcoming in September 2019.

[7] Communication from the Commission to the European Parliament, the European Council, the Council, the European Economic and Social Committee and the Committee of the Regions—Artificial Intelligence for Europe, COM(2018) 237 final.

[8] Communication from the Commission to the European Parliament, the European Council, the Council, the European Economic and Social Committee and the Committee of the Regions—Coordinated Plan on Artificial Intelligence (COM(2018) 795 final).

as with the formulation of "Policy and Investment Recommendations," which saw the light on June 26, 2019.

THE EU ETHICS GUIDELINES FOR TRUSTWORTHY ARTIFICIAL INTELLIGENCE

The key challenges for the AI HLEG were to reach consensus among fifty-two members, some of which are independent experts and academics, whereas others represent vested interests;[9] and to go beyond the mere enunciation of ethical principles for AI, which had already been spelled out by international organizations, corporations, civil society, and even an internal advisory body of the European Commission. In such a crowded space, the AI HLEG tried to identify ethical principles that could be made operational, therefore providing AI designers, developers, and users with a tool that could promote a real alignment of AI systems with ethical values. But the focus on ethics soon appeared too narrow, especially with respect to a legal system that already incorporates ethical principles under the umbrella of treaty provisions, in established case law, as well as in EU horizontal and sectoral legislation. Moreover, the discussion within the AI HLEG soon veered on the need to foster the development of AI systems that European users could find reliable, and thereby worthy of their trust. The need to restore sufficient levels of reliability and trust in the interaction with digital technologies had emerged as a critical need for Europe, especially after the emergence of scandals such as *Cambridge Analytica*.[10]

The publication of a first draft of the Ethics Guidelines in December 2018 was followed by a rapid stakeholder consultation, in which the need to adopt a broader approach than ethical alignment emerged clearly. European stakeholders called on institutions to focus on both "hard ethics," intended as compliance ethics; and "soft ethics," that is, postcompliance ethics.[11] Opinions were also showing a mounting fear that AI systems, however ethically aligned, could become easily prey of cyberattacks and external manipulation, also due to emerging AI techniques such as Generative Adversarial Networks, which proved able to develop scary emulations of reality known as "deep fakes." In a nutshell, European stakeholders seem to place trust above ethics, and ethical alignment as part of overall trustworthiness of AI systems.

---

[9] See the composition of the AI HLEG at https://ec.europa.eu/digital-single-market/en/high-level-expert-group-artificial-intelligence (accessed July 24, 2019).

[10] The *Cambridge Analytica* data scandal emerged in early 2018 when it was revealed that Cambridge Analytica, apolitical data-analysis firm, had harvested the personal data of millions of Facebook users without their consent, and used it for political advertising purposes.

[11] See Luciano Floridi, "Soft Ethics and the Governance of the Digital," *Philosophy and Technology* (2018): 31.

Hence, the final version of the "Ethics Guidelines for Trustworthy AI" (the Guidelines) goes beyond ethically aligned AI, by evoking a combination of three different elements: compliance with legal rules; alignment with well-specified ethical principles; and "sociotechnical" robustness. Besides the need to ensure a comprehensive approach to trust in AI systems is the belief that both law and ethics are needed and that in some cases the two may even clash (for example, when existing legislation does not reflect technological developments and ends up forcing market players to engage in unethical behavior); whereas in most cases they will be complementary (i.e., ethics can help in interpreting the law, or can recommend behavior that is not directly required or mandated by law). To quote Oxford Professor Luciano Floridi, "the law provides the rules of the game, but does not indicate how to play well according to the rules."[12]

Legal Compliance, Ethical Alignment, Sociotechnical Robustness: The Three Pillars of Trustworthy AI

Once the legal dimension entered the scope of the Ethics Guidelines, it remained to define what was meant by compliance. As a matter of fact, compliance with legal rules does not merely, and not necessarily, imply mere adherence to EU legislation, or even EU treaties. The AI HLEG, rather than offering a detailed explanation of all applicable rules, observes that any human-centric approach to AI requires full compliance with fundamental rights, independently of whether these are explicitly protected by EU Treaties,[13] or by the Charter of Fundamental Rights of the EU. Fundamental rights, the AI HLEG recalls, protect individuals and (to a certain degree) groups by virtue of their moral status as human beings, independently of their legal force. As such, they are the key foundations of legal compliance, and also of the alignment of AI systems with ethical principles, even when the latter are not binding. More in detail, these rights are centered on the respect for the dignity of humans *subjects*, not "*objects* to be sifted, sorted, scored, herded, conditioned or manipulated"; on respect for the right to self-determination, including freedom of expression and control over one's own life; respect for democracy, justice, and the rule of law; respect of equality, nondiscrimination and solidarity, which implies that AI systems do not generate unfairly biased outputs, especially to the detriment of "workers, women, persons with disabilities, ethnic minorities, children, consumers or others at risk of exclusion"; and respect of citizens' rights, such as the right to vote, the right to a good administration or access to public documents, and the right to petition the administration.

---

[12] See Luciano Floridi, "Establishing the Rules for Building Trustworthy AI," Nature Machine Intelligence, Comment, Vol. 1 (June 2019): 261–262.

[13] The European Union is based on a constitutional commitment to protect the fundamental and indivisible rights of human beings, to ensure respect for rule of law, to foster democratic freedom, and to promote the common good. These rights are reflected in Articles 2 and 3 of the Treaty on European Union, and in the Charter of Fundamental Rights of the European Union.

Moreover, the EU Ethics Guidelines identify four key ethical principles (defined as ethical "imperatives") for Trustworthy AI. This is a significant smaller number compared to preexisting documents setting ethical principles for AI: for example, at the EU level, the European Group on Ethics in Science and New Technologies (EGE), an independent advisory body of the President of the European Commission, had identified nine principles.[14] The four ethical "imperatives" defined by the AI HLEG are: the respect for human autonomy; the prevention of harm; fairness; and explicability (see the following subsection, "Four Ethical 'Imperatives' for AI"). Importantly, contrary to what typically occurs in more consolidated fields such as bioethics, the list did not include an imperative to "do good," or the so-called "beneficence" principle, which had been included in early drafts of the Guidelines. The four ethical imperatives selected by the AI HLEG appear common to those identified by similar documents produced by the developer community, by national government, corporations, and international organizations: their further specification, as could be expected, ended up significantly overlapping with the enunciation of fundamental rights.

Finally, the sociotechnical robustness element is only superficially dealt with by the Ethics Guidelines, which focus mostly on ethics. Still, the AI HLEG observed that Trustworthy AI needs to be not only legally compliant and ethically adherent but also "robust, both from a technical and social perspective, since, even with good intentions, AI systems can cause unintentional harm." This is an essential component of trustworthiness both from a technical perspective (ensuring the system's technical robustness as appropriate in a given context, such as the application domain or life-cycle phase) and from a social perspective (in due consideration of the context and environment in which the system operates). Again, most of the robustness requirements are, or will be, also covered by legislation, or by a combination of performance-based legislation and standards, in line with the European Union's approach to standardization.[15] And as will be shown later in this chapter, technical robustness and safety ended up being listed also as key ethical requirements, somehow complicating and confusing the logical structure of the document.

The identification of these three pillars was not accompanied by any proposal to create a mandatory framework for Trustworthy AI at the EU level. Rather, Trustworthy AI remains an "aspirational goal" in the words of the AI HLEG. More specifically, legal compliance is inevitably mandatory, as is technical robustness whenever rooted in legislative or regulatory provisions. To the contrary, as will be explained in the following in more detail, ethical alignment and social robustness require a more flexible

---

[14] See European Group on Ethics in Science and New Technologies, *Statement on Artificial Intelligence, Robotics and "Autonomous" Systems*, March 2018 (https://ec.europa.eu/info/news/ethics-artificial-intelligence-statement-ege-released-2018-apr-24_en). The EGE group listed as key ethical principles: human dignity, autonomy, responsibility, justice, equity, and solidarity, democracy, rule of law and accountability, security, safety, bodily and mental integrity, data protection and privacy, and sustainability.

[15] See Jacques Pelkmans, "The New Approach to Technical Harmonisation and Standardisation," *Journal of Common Market Studies*, Vol. XXV, No. 3 (March 1987): 249–269.

approach, which triggers behavior that is proportionate to the risk or harm that the AI system is likely to generate.

Four Ethical "Imperatives" for AI

A number of critical elements surface in the analysis of the four ethical imperatives put forward by the Guidelines. First, the requirement of respect for human autonomy points at the need for human-centric design principles in the allocation of functions between humans and AI systems, a requirement that is further specified as leaving meaningful opportunity for human choice and securing human oversight over work processes in AI systems. A critical question is whether this provision would apply to all AI systems in the same way: in the age of predictive maintenance and the Internet of Things, let alone autonomous vehicles that often need to take decisions in a split-second, requiring constant man-machine cooperation may become disproportionate and utterly inefficient, when not contrary to the purpose of the AI system being deployed. This is why the AI HLEG ended up refining the requirement for human oversight by distinguishing, later in the document, between cases in which a human must be "in" the loop from cases in which the human is "on" the loop, and cases in which a human is "in command."[16] The AI HLEG clarifies also that these alternative options come with an embedded trade-off: "all other things being equal, the less oversight a human can exercise over an AI system, the more extensive testing and stricter governance is required." This in turn suggests that human oversight and accountability are intimately linked.

The discussion on the prevention of harm makes no explicit mention of the precautionary principle, contrary to what the European Parliament had advocated in 2017. This means that the standard to use in deciding whether a given AI system can be considered harmful is not clarified by the Ethics Guidelines (as will be explained later, more detail was given by the AI HLEG in the subsequent document containing "policy and investment recommendations"). Moreover, the "fairness" requirement refers, in its substantive notion, to the need for equal and just distribution of both benefits and costs (potentially a very far-reaching statement, but not explained in detail); providing equal opportunity; protecting individuals' freedom of choice; respecting "the principle of proportionality between means and ends"; and, from a more procedural standpoint, offering the possibility for effective redress against decisions made by AI systems and by the humans operating them. This, the AI HLEG claims, requires that the entity accountable

---

[16] HITL refers to the capability for human intervention in every decision cycle of the system, which in many cases is neither possible nor desirable. HOTL refers to the capability for human intervention during the design cycle of the system and monitoring the system's operation. HIC refers to the capability to oversee the overall activity of the AI system (including its broader economic, societal, legal, and ethical impact) and the ability to decide when and how to use the system in any particular situation. This can include the decision not to use an AI system in a particular situation, to establish levels of human discretion during the use of the system, or to ensure the ability to override a decision made by a system.

for the decision is identifiable, and the decision-making processes are explicable. This led to the fourth, and perhaps the most controversial "imperative": the principle of explicability of AI systems.

To some extent, invoking the full explicability of AI systems and decisions could jeopardize the use of AI techniques such as deep learning and reinforcement learning, in which algorithms choose their actions in ways that are often obscure even for their developers. However, the AI HLEG clarified that "the degree to which explicability is needed is highly dependent on the context and the severity of the consequences if that output is erroneous or otherwise inaccurate." That is, in some circumstances the lack of explicability may become grounds for rejecting, on ethical grounds, the use of nonexplicable AI; but in all other cases, such use may considered as ethically adherent, subject to the first principle described earlier, which entails some form of human oversight.

More generally, the AI HLEG also acknowledged that tensions may arise between these four ethical principles and generically advocated democratic engagement and methods of accountable deliberation to address these tensions, coupled with reasoned, evidence-based reflection rather than intuition or random discretion. To be sure, the combined effect of these principles, even if considered merely as an "aspirational goal," constitutes an important reference for AI developers and deployers, and potentially paves the way for an articulate policy framework.

From Principles to Requirements

To partially address the indeterminacy of some of these ethical principles, as well as tensions between them, the AI HLEG went further by describing seven requirements that AI systems should comply with in order to be defined as "trustworthy." These requirements end up repeating, with a greater level of detail, the concepts already put forward in the description of fundamental rights, as well as in the ethical imperatives.

The first requirement is the respect for human autonomy and the protection of fundamental rights. Here, the AI HLEG specifies that where the risk of harming fundamental rights exists, a fundamental rights impact assessment should be undertaken prior to the development of AI systems and include the consideration of possible mitigating measures and mechanisms to receive external feedback. The protection of human agency finds further specification in a right to make informed autonomous decisions regarding AI systems and a right not to be subject to a decision based solely on automated processing when this produces legal effects on users or similarly significantly affects them.

Another key requirement is the technical robustness and safety of AI systems, which then features twice in the Guidelines (as third pillar of Trustworthy AI, and as one of the seven requirements). As a requirement, technical robustness and safety imply that AI systems be developed with a preventative approach to risks and in a manner such that they reliably behave as intended while minimizing unintentional and unexpected harm and preventing unacceptable harm. In addition, this requirement entails that the physical and mental integrity of humans be ensured, that AI systems be secure and resilient to attack and include a fallback plan in case of problems. There is also a general requirement of accuracy, which rather translates into an obligation to disclose the likely inaccuracy of the system, especially when the AI system directly affects human lives: this potentially links to the transparency and accountability requirements that are specified in detail later. Finally, robustness implies also reliability and reproducibility of the system's results, another potentially critical aspect of Trustworthy AI that may not prove neutral with respect to available AI techniques.

The Guidelines observe that key elements of the principle of prevention of harm are the protection of privacy (which in Europe is considered as a fundamental right, contrary to what occurs in many other legal systems);[17] adequate data governance that covers the quality and integrity of data used. Those provisions are quite extensive and require extreme attention in the definition of who can access personal data and the implementation of the GDPR's data minimization and explicit consent principles. Trustworthy AI systems must be transparent, in line with the principle of explicability. Under this heading, the AI HLEG includes both traceability (i.e., documenting data gathering and labeling, as well as the algorithms used and the decisions made to the best possible standard); and explainability, where however the Guidelines acknowledge that trade-offs might have to be made between enhancing a system's explainability and its accuracy. The AI HLEG goes beyond the GDPR by observing that, for AI to be trustworthy, the right to a meaningful explanation, timely, and adapted to the expertise of the stakeholder concerned (e.g., layperson, regulator, researcher) should be foreseen whenever an AI system has a significant impact on people's lives. This requirement also implies that AI systems be identifiable: humans should be informed of the nonhuman nature of AI interfaces, of the system's capabilities and limitations, and of the level of accuracy of the AI system to expect.

The Guidelines include among the key requirements the respect for diversity, the absence of undue discrimination, and the principle of fairness. These requirements appear very far-reaching, as they imply that inclusion and diversity are enabled and considered throughout the entire AI system's life cycle. Besides the consideration and involvement of all affected stakeholders throughout the process, this also entails ensuring equal access through inclusive design as well as equal treatment; and that whenever possible, developers are hired from diverse backgrounds, cultures, and disciplines to ensure diversity of opinions. The principle of fairness entails that data sets used by AI systems (both for training and operation) are adequately checked against the risk of inclusion of inadvertent historic bias, incompleteness, and bad governance models, under the understanding that such biases could lead to unintended (in)direct prejudice and discrimination against certain groups or people, potentially exacerbating prejudice and marginalization. Besides these forms of unintentional bias, the AI HLEG also cautions against the intentional exploitation of (consumer) biases and algorithmic

[17] See Andrea Renda, "Cloud Privacy Law in the United States and the European Union," in *Regulating the Cloud: Policy for Computing Infrastructure*, ed. Cristopher S. Yoo and Jean-Francois Blanchette (Cambridge, MA: MIT Press, 2015).

restrictions of competition, such as the homogenization of prices by means of collusion or a nontransparent market.[18] Overall, in a Trustworthy AI system, biases are countered by constant monitoring and oversight aimed at analyzing and addressing the system's purpose, constraints, requirements, and decisions in a clear and transparent manner. Besides adequate checks against biases and unfair and discriminatory outcomes, Trustworthy AI also requires a user-centricity and universal accessibility. Depending on the use case, and particularly in business-to-consumer (B2C) contexts, users should be put in the condition to use AI products or services regardless of their age, gender, abilities, or characteristics. Complying with these requirements is more likely if affected stakeholders are consulted throughout the process and their feedback is regularly solicited.

The AI HLEG, however, goes beyond human-centric AI and paves the way, albeit timidly, also for a more planet-centric approach. Among the requirements, as part of the principle of prevention of harm, the Guidelines also include respect for "other sentient beings and the environment" and explicitly encourages AI that fosters the achievement of the Sustainable Development Goals, including also future generations of human beings among the ones to be considered under the "preventative approach" that should guide AI development and deployment. Among the corollaries of this requirement is also the critical examination of the resource usage and energy consumption, and more generally of the environmental friendliness of the AI system's entire supply chain, another provision that potentially leaves techniques such as deep learning in a rather controversial spot.[19] Beyond the environment, social impacts are also adequately mentioned, ranging from the alteration of social agency and patterns of social relationships, possible impacts on people's physical and mental well-being, and possible risks for the democratic process.

In what appears as an all-encompassing requirement, the AI HLEG also specifies that Trustworthy AI must come with a proportionate degree of accountability. This goes way beyond a simple attitude, or a "state of mind": it requires adequate governance mechanisms, such as the auditability of algorithms (further strengthened in case of AI systems that affect fundamental rights), the identification, reporting, and proactive mitigation of negative impacts of AI systems, a transparent and rational treatment of trade-offs, and measures aimed at ensuring adequate redress.

These can be considered among the most far-reaching and distinctive requirements put forward by the Guidelines: not only Trustworthy AI should ideally be inspired by ethical principles and a desire to "do no harm" throughout the process of development and deployment; AI practitioners willing to hit the aspirational goal of Trustworthy AI should also take action to regularly detect and mitigate harms, offering prompt redress to affected users. Trust, the AI HLEG suggests, requires adequate governance before and

---

[18] See European Union Agency for Fundamental Rights: "BigData: Discrimination in Data-supported Decision Making," 2018, at http://fra.europa.eu/en/publication/2018/big-data-discrimination.

[19] See Karen Hao, "Training a Single AI Model Can Emit as Much Carbon as Five Cars in Their Lifetimes," *MIT Technology Review* (June 6, 2019).

after the AI system is placed on the market and also adequate attention for existing users, future users, society, and then environment as a whole. Hence, AI becomes tantamount to a dangerous activity (in the legal sense), and the goal of Trustworthy AI is likely to trigger the definition of a strict liability framework for damages caused by AI systems, which may well see possibilities for exemptions, but appears far from a standard, fault-based regime such as the one applied for torts.

Operationalizing Trustworthy AI: An Assessment Framework

The Guidelines do not limit themselves to the already remarkable attempt to specify an overall framework for Trustworthy AI, corresponding ethical principles, and associated requirements. Perhaps the most innovative feature of this document, which stands out compared to other existing ethical AI frameworks, is the AI HLEG's attempt to operationalize the requirement through a detailed assessment framework composed of 131 questions. This is presented as a first draft of what may constitute a guide to self-assessment of the alignment of individual AI systems with Trustworthy AI principles; admittedly, the framework included in the Guidelines is rather unrefined, perhaps too lengthy, and awkward in its attempt to guide practitioners. The list of questions prompts AI practitioners with potential risks or negative impacts, asking them whether they have fully considered them or have procedures in place to mitigate them. There is no way to "score" AI systems in terms of trustworthiness, and there is no specific guidance on which types of conducts would be appropriate for specific use cases. But the existence of the list, in and of itself, marks a transition from the pure enunciation of ethical principles, toward the concrete implementation of Trustworthy AI in terms of policies, standards, and ultimately rules.

Importantly, in acknowledging the preliminary nature of the list, the AI HLEG also kick-started an ambitious piloting phase, which relies on three main initiatives undertaken during the second half of 2019. First, a detailed survey was made available on the website of the AI Alliance, potentially available to more the 3,000 stakeholders. Second, the Group elicited expressions of interest from various stakeholders, and conducted fifty "deep dives," that is, face-to-face interviews aimed at capturing more detailed feedback on the assessment list. Third, in order to involve also civil society in the piloting process, the AI HLEG has started organizing a series of sectoral workshops to collect more opinions and feedback on the "list." These workshops will take place in early 2020.

The ultimate outcome of this extensive piloting phase will be a revision of the Assessment list, to be completed by the AI HLEG during the first half of 2020. Such revision may entail, in addition, a tailoring of the list to specific use cases and the development of additional guidance on legal compliance (also including sectoral legislation where appropriate), as well as on how to address specific risks through ad hoc procedures.

The "Policy and Investment Recommendations" for Trustworthy AI: Selected Aspects

The Guidelines received, overall, a warm welcome by policymakers inside and outside Europe, as well as by large and small companies and civil society. However, with that document the AI HLEG had only specified a frontier, an aspirational goal, without discussing whether Trustworthy AI should become a concrete policy objective for the European Commission. The latter has specified from the outset that its preferred path toward ethically adherent AI was one of self-regulation, rather than a rush to regulate a largely unknown subject matter. However, the reflection on how to shape a policy framework that could trigger convergence toward Trustworthy AI led to something more than a call for self-regulation. The second deliverable of the AI HLEG, dedicated to policy and investment recommendations, offers numerous insights on how the Trustworthy AI framework could be translated into concrete policies. While the document is very rich, encompassing a broad range of topics from research and innovation to the future of work and the modernization of government, for the purposes of this chapter only the recommendations that relate to the operationalization of the ethical framework will be described: this, alone, shows an entire legal system in the making.

In this respect, the first, and perhaps most important recommendation of the AI HLEG is to adopt a risk-based policy framework. This implies that the accountability and liability elements of the Ethics Guidelines be translated into a legal regime that holds practitioners responsible for assessing, managing, and evaluating the risk that they are creating for society as they develop and deploy an AI system. Such risk will obviously depend on the use case and the specific context in which the AI system is deployed: this means that the level of "diligence" required will change from case to case, and accordingly no silver bullet legal rule will be able to address the problem of liability. Only when the risk is "unacceptable," and the potential consequences are catastrophic, the AI HLEG suggests reverting to the precautionary principle, and hence avoid deploying the specific AI system, until scientific evidence sheds more light on the issue.

However, it is unclear how acceptable and unacceptable risks will be singled out. In similar contexts, legal systems seek to address the problem of reconciling innovation and precaution through agile forms of policymaking, such as standardization, or even through case-law. And indeed, the AI HLEG shies away from excessively prescriptive regulation, calling instead for a principles-based approach. However, in the case of AI this may prove problematic, due to the breathtaking pace of change of some products (some algorithms are changed dozens of times a week), and consequently of the problems and risk they create when placed on the market, when interacting with human beings, and even more when interacting with other algorithms (as in the case of the so-called "flash crashes" that occurred in fields such as algorithmic trading, and as will certainly be the case for autonomous vehicles).

As a result, the AI HLEG also called on the European Commission to consider the establishment of an "institutional structure" that could help collect and spread best practices in a more agile way that what judges, standards, and lawmakers are normally able to do. Whether this will take the form an agency (as originally invoked by the European Parliament already in 2016), a board (as in the case of GDPR), or any other institutional variant is not specified by the AI HLEG and will have to be considered by the European Commission in the months to come should it decide to follow up on this recommendation. International examples are starting to proliferate even in the absence of a well-shaped legal system, from the Centre for Data Ethics in the United Kingdom to similar authorities in France and Germany. The proposed institutional structure, in the vision of the AI HLEG, will perform a wide range of functions, including a contribution to the European Union's framework and policy for Trustworthy AI, ensuring that AI is lawful, ethical, and robust, advising EU institutions and supporting them in the implementation of such framework; providing guidance to stakeholders, assisting them in the application of the risk-based approach, classifying risks as acceptable or unacceptable, coordinating with standards-setting organizations and with EU member states, hosting a repository of best practices; and raising awareness among stakeholders and policymakers on the evolving landscape of AI.

But there is more than meets the eye in the AI HLEG Recommendations. For example, the Ethics Guidelines had been criticized for taking too soft a stance on so-called "redlines," that is, AI applications that should be subject to an outright ban. In the Guidelines, despite an initial indication of redlines, the AI HLEG only limited itself to identifying a few "areas of critical concern," including mass surveillance, widespread social credit scoring, and lethal autonomous weapons (LAWs). In this second document, the Group calls on the Commission to consider new regulation to ensure that individuals are not subject to "unjustified personal, physical or mental tracking or identification, profiling and nudging through AI powered methods of biometric recognition such as: emotional tracking, empathic media, DNA, iris and behavioural identification, affect recognition, voice and facial recognition and the recognition of micro-expressions," adding that only exceptionally, for example, in the case of pressing national security stances, these applications would be allowed, if "evidence based, necessary and proportionate, as well as respectful of fundamental rights." Importantly, the AI HLEG calls for an international moratorium on the development of offensive LAWs, a proposal that the new Commission president, who is also the former German minister of defense, will certainly consider with due attention.

Furthermore, the Policy and Investment Recommendations also contain an explicit call for considering making the Trustworthy AI Assessment (i.e., the assessment list, as will be refined in 2020) mandatory for AI systems deployed by the private sector that have the potential to have a significant impact on human lives, for example, by interfering with an individual's fundamental rights at any stage of the AI system's life cycle, and for safety-critical applications. Based on this statement, it seems clear that the AI HLEG does not consider Trustworthy AI as simply an aspirational goal but rather the foundation of a wholly new risk-based legal system, in which unacceptable risks are subject to the precautionary principle and critical applications that potentially impinge on fundamental rights are subject to a mandatory assessment. The consequences of this recommendation will become clear over time: as a matter of fact, and as already mentioned, the assessment list is not accompanied by any scoring system or threshold that would allow the differentiation of trustworthy systems from nontrustworthy ones. If the Commission will follow this recommendation, then some form of certification and scoring will become inevitable, with significant consequences for the AI market in Europe. Interestingly, this recommendation also extends to mandating that "critical" AI systems ensure appropriate "by default" and "by design" procedures to enable effective and immediate redress in case of mistakes, harms, and/or other rights infringement: the practical implementation and the actual contours of this proposed obligation are, however, unclear: what is "effective and immediate," and what types of mistakes would qualify as relevant for the purposes of this rule.

Finally, in the world designed by the AI HLEG, children would be subject to particular attention: the AI HLEG proposes that the EU legislators introduce a legal age at which children receive a "clean data slate" of any public or private storage of data related to them as children, and calls on the European Commission to monitor the development of personalized AI systems built on children's profiles and ensure their alignment with fundamental rights, democracy, and the rule of law. More generally, the AI HLEG calls on the European Commission to establish a European Strategy for Better and Safer AI for Children, designed to empower children, while also protecting them from risks and harm.

WHAT'S NEXT? PUTTING THE EUROPEAN UNION'S AI AMBITIONS TO THE TEST

The past two years have marked an unprecedented acceleration in the EU strategy on digital technologies in general, and AI in particular. Rather than competing at arm's length with the United States and China, the European Union is now tempted by the perspective of dancing on a different drummer: a mix of strategic autonomy, digital sovereignty, relatively strict rules on data protection, competition, and unfair commercial practices, and possibly an ambitious plan to set ethical rules for AI at home and abroad. As a result, it came to no surprise that the new president of the European Commission has placed policy on the human and ethical consequences of AI at the top of her list, promising first steps already in the first one hundred days of her presidency. Should the European Commission convince member states to move forward and introduce an ambitious policy framework for Artificial Intelligence along the lines recommended by the AI HLEG, this would become a game changer at the global level, for several reasons.

As was explained in the introduction to this chapter, the ongoing "digital cold war" between the United States and China is leaving space for the European Union to play a leading role in ethical AI, with the help of like-minded countries like Canada and Japan, and backed internally by France, one of the first countries to focus its internal AI strategy on sustainability with the *Mission Villani*. In order to fully play that role, the European Union should, however, show sufficient cohesion and ambition to support the proposed creation of an Inter-Governmental Panel on AI, which currently meets the opposition of the other big superpowers. Perhaps even more importantly, in its international relations, the European Union should focus on sustainable development and establish cooperation agreements to maximize the uptake of AI solutions that are aligned with Trustworthy AI principles.

Second, in order to become a world leader in ethical AI, Europe must first do its homework properly. This is not going to be easy, as the European Union may end up in a "catch-22" situation: on the one hand, raising standards may require a degree of protectionism, in particular in imposing data localization and working toward the development of a European infrastructure and connectivity; on the other hand, leadership in AI "for good" requires an open attitude toward global trade. Furthermore, EU institutions will have to convince all those commentators that believe that a relatively strict regulatory framework on AI and obstacles to data collection and processing will only hamper innovation. As a matter of fact, the academic literature has amply demonstrated that well-designed regulation can be good for innovation, in that it aligns the incentives of innovators with the public interest.

But well-designed regulation inevitably will require adequate governance. And here lie the next steps that the new president of the European Commission may decide to take toward the creation of an institution that groups the European Union and the national level, and involves industry and civil society, working toward the creation of a unique environment in which ethics (better, trustworthiness) remains at the core of AI investment and deployment, civil society is constantly involved in the most critical decisions about acceptable uses of AI, and the new developments in this powerful family of techniques are observed, analyzed, and interpreted through the lens of Trustworthy AI. This way, Europe could succeed where other superpowers are currently failing: rather than asking what can states do for AI, pursuing the many applications of AI that can contribute to the global good.

Bibliography

Cath, Corinne, Sandra Wachter, Brandt Mittelstadt, Mariarosaria Taddeo, and Luciano Floridi. "Artificial Intelligence and the 'Good Society': The US, EU, and UK Approach." *Science and Engineering Ethics*, 24 (2) (2018): 505–528.

European Commission Joint Research Centre. *Artificial Intelligence: A European Perspective*. Flagship Report on AI, 2018. Brussels: European Commission.

European Commission. Communication from the Commission to the European Parliament, the European Council, the Council, the European Economic and Social Committee and the Committee of the Regions—Coordinated Plan on Artificial Intelligence (COM(2018) 795 final), December 7, 2018. Brussels: European Commission.

European Commission. Staff Working Document on liability for emerging digital technologies, accompanying the document Communication from the Commission to the European Parliament, the European Council, the Council, the European Economic and Social Committee and the Committee of the Regions "Artificial Intelligence for Europe," SWD(2018)137 final, April 25, 2018. Brussels: European Commission.

European Group on Ethics (EGE). "Statement on Artificial Intelligence, Robotics and 'Autonomous' Systems. European Group on Ethics in Science and New Technologies." Brussels: European Commission, 2018.

Floridi, L., J. Cowls, M. Beltrametti, R. Chatila, P. Chazerand, V. Dignum, C. Luetge, R. Madelin, U. Pagallo, F. Rossi, B. Schafer, P. Valcke, and E. Vayena. "AI4People White Paper: Twenty Recommendations for an Ethical Framework for a Good AI Society." *Minds and Machines* 28 (2018): 689–707.

Floridi, Luciano. "Establishing the Rules for Building Trustworthy AI." *Nature Machine Intelligence*, Comment, Vol. 1 (June 2019): 261–262.

High Level Expert Group on AI set up by the European Commission. *Ethics Guidelines for Trustworthy AI*. Brussels: European Commission, 2019.

High Level Expert Group on AI set up by the European Commission. *Policy and Investment Recommendations for Trustworthy AI*. Brussels: European Commission, 2019.

Renda, Andrea. *Artificial Intelligence: Ethics, Governance and Policy Challenges*. CEPS Monograph. Brussels: CEPS, 2019.

Renda, Andrea. "The Trolley Problem and Self-Driving Cars: A Crime-Scene Investigation into the Ethics of Algorithms." CEPS Policy Insight—No. 2018/02. Brussels: CEPS, 2018.

PART V

CASES AND APPLICATIONS

···

CHAPTER 35

ETHICS OF ARTIFICIAL INTELLIGENCE IN TRANSPORT

···

BRYANT WALKER SMITH

INTRODUCTION

···

ALMOST everything in this world involves transport, implicates ethics, and invites automation.

A simple phone call, for example, either constitutes transport (of electrons or information) or displaces transport (of people or their physical messages), raises ethical questions (about the allocation of resources or the loss of face-to-face communication), and falls somewhere along a spectrum of automation (in which a computer is certainly the operator and possibly the caller or recipient).

Given this broad scope, no single chapter could even survey the ethics of artificial intelligence in transport. This limitation obviates the need for precise definitions of these three operative terms, and so this chapter coarsely assumes that:

- Transport refers primarily to the deliberate movement of people or things between places;
- Ethics refers primarily to normative inputs that the applied sciences cannot themselves provide; and
- Artificial intelligence refers primarily to the ability of an automated system to resolve uncertainty using experience.

As a popular example of a potential application of artificial intelligence in transport, automated driving is the principal focus of this chapter. In the automated driving systems currently under development, artificial intelligence plays important roles both in correctly perceiving and then in safely navigating complex environments. The same is true for other automation systems on the ground as well as in the air and on the water. Moreover, other tools that use artificial intelligence are—or are likely to be—equally critical in designing, assessing, and monitoring these automation systems.

In other words, transport products and services may involve artificial intelligence in the foreground or in the background. Artificial intelligence may replace, supplement, challenge, constrain, or empower not only the users of transport systems but also their developers, operators, and regulators. In particular, the data collection and analysis that artificial intelligence facilitates will likely impact every aspect of transport, from planning to logistics to emergency response.

For example, so-called transportation network companies such as UberX and Lyft already rely on a combination of human and machine intelligence to distribute motor vehicles across the areas they service. Drivers wait where they expect profitable demand to materialize based on their own intuition as well as on the information and incentives provided by the algorithms used by these companies. Even if automated vehicles never materialize, further development of these algorithms might lower wait times for drivers and riders, reduce deadheading, and enable more multiple-passenger trips.

Or not. Progress—whether in technology or in policy—necessarily involves replacing an old set of problems with a new set of problems and hoping that, in the aggregate, the new problems are less than the old ones. (To wit: Cars replaced the pollution of the horse with the pollution of the internal combustion engine.) Ethics are important both in making and in monitoring these predictions.

Ethical issues, however, will not necessarily prevent the development or deployment of new technologies. This is an important point obscured by the typical presentation of ethical issues as "obstacles" to innovation rather than as choices to be implemented or else abdicated. To be crude, ethical objections impede technologies in the same way that animals on a road impede trucks: although the gentler among us will indeed try to avoid them, others will not, and in either case these morbidly termed "obstacles" are likely to slow momentum only if they are numerous or prominent enough to make moving forward especially messy.

ETHICS IN TRANSPORT

Moving from metaphor: The value that we ascribe to the lives of other sentient—though so far still natural—creatures, whether as obstacles, workhorses, or chattel—is just one example of the myriad ethical issues that have always accompanied transport. At its core, transport reflects a choice to move rather than stay put—to interact or invade or escape. Some transport innovations do unlock new realms—under water, in the air, up in space—but most are about making movement faster, cheaper, easier, nicer, safer, or cleaner. Ethics can help to determine whether these assertions are correct: Should impacts that are international, intergenerational, or uncertain be included alongside those that are local, immediate, and uncontroverted in comparing the environmental performance of fuels? Ethics can also help to determine whether these aims are desirable: Are faster missiles necessarily better?

Transport professionals are responsible for many concrete decisions involving explicit or implicit ethical considerations. Consider just one mode of ground transport. Motor vehicles are designed to privilege the safety of their occupants over the safety of pedestrians; in fact, unlike in the European Union, an American definition of crashworthiness does not even account for nonoccupants.[1,2] This choice extends to the design of American infrastructure, where wide lanes are more forgiving for drivers but more daunting for pedestrians and where breakaway traffic poles can shift risks from those inside a wayward vehicle to those outside of it.[3,4] Larger and heavier vehicles impose risks on smaller and lighter vehicles—and, through increased emissions, on everyone else. Fatalities from this pollution are generally not considered to be part of roadway safety, which is measured primarily through crash injuries and fatalities. These fatalities have—at least until recently—declined on a per kilometer basis, in part because of safety technologies.[5] And yet the design of some of these systems privileges an average-size male over others.[6] Moreover, many of these technologies—in their design or in their absence—prioritize the autonomy of the driver. Most motor vehicles do not have alcohol ignition locks or meaningful speed limiters; an Ontario trucker even persuaded a lower court (to be later overturned on appeal) that a speed governor would infringe his fundamental right to security by restricting his ability to speed in a safety-critical situation.[7] Moreover, almost all motor vehicle trips are treated as equal in worth: in the physical world, this "net neutrality" means that, with few exceptions, a billboard advertising truck, a joyrider, a doctor on the way to the hospital, and a bus full of passengers all have equal claim to a congested roadway.

That long paragraph could be much longer—and many others could follow it. For example, the legal and social battles of the African American civil rights movement have often involved transport, including Congress's 1850 law demanding the re-enslavement of those who had escaped north,[8] the Supreme Court's 1896 approval of state laws

---

[1]   49 U.S.C. § 32301.

[2]   TTIP—Car Safety Analysis in the EU and US in Relation to US and EU Regulatory Standards on Crash Testing (2016), http://trade.ec.europa.eu/doclib/docs/2016/september/tradoc_154981.pdf.

[3]   Manual on Uniform Traffic Control Devices Section 2A-19, https://mutcd.fhwa.dot.gov/.

[4]   U.S. Federal Highway Administration, Frequently Asked Questions: Breakaway Sign and Luminaire Supports, https://safety.fhwa.dot.gov/roadway_dept/countermeasures/faqs/qa_bsls.cfm.

[5]   U.S. National Highway Traffic Safety Administration, Traffic Safety Facts, https://cdan.nhtsa.gov/tsftables/tsfar.htm.

[6]   Caroline Criado Perez, *Invisible Women: Exposing Data Bias in a World Designed for Men* (New York: Abrams, 2019).

[7]   R. v. Michaud, 2015 ONCA 585, http://www.ontariocourts.ca/decisions/2015/2015ONCA0585.htm.

[8]   Fugitive Slave Act of 1850, 9 Stat. 462 (1850), https://avalon.law.yale.edu/19th_century/fugitive.asp.

excluding African Americans from "white-only" train cars,[9] the Montgomery black community's 1955–1956 boycott of their discriminatory bus system, and the use of and opposition to busing as a tool of school desegregation.

The takeaways are that ethics has always belonged in transport and that many ethical issues remain unresolved. Artificial intelligence is just another chapter in this story, one that might—but probably won't—read much better. And against a status quo that is far from perfect, artificial intelligence could ameliorate, exacerbate, highlight, or obscure many ethical issues as well as introduce new ones entirely.

THE CASE OF AUTOMATED DRIVING

Take automated driving. Of the many ethical issues implicated by a shift from human drivers, this chapter considers four:

1. Automated driving as a technological solution or a policy solution
2. Consequences of safety expectations
3. Human authority versus computer authority
4. Changing power dynamics

TECHNOLOGICAL SOLUTION OR POLICY SOLUTION

As most commuters would attest, today's ground transport system is far from ideal. Cars have long been marketed in the United States as the epitome of freedom: go where you want, when you want. SUVs take this even further, freeing (the imagination of) their owners from the constraint of actual roads. And yet, in many ways, individual motor vehicle ownership is not liberating: in an environment built primarily for these vehicles, you are not free if you cannot drive or cannot afford to drive, you are not free if you are stuck in a traffic jam as a motorist or a stuck trying to cross a street as a pedestrian, you are not free if you must inhale what these vehicles emit, and you are not free if you are dead because of a motor vehicle crash.

Automated driving is not a panacea to the problems of human driving, but it could help in some important ways. Automated vehicles could serve those who cannot drive. They could unlock efficiencies in the transport system, such as ride-sharing, that could

---

[9] Plessy v. Ferguson, 163 U.S. 537 (1896), https://www.oyez.org/cases/1850–1900/163us537.

reduce individual trip costs. And they are expected to be much safer than conventional vehicles—if for no other reason than this very expectation.

Viewed in this light, automated vehicles represent a critical technological solution, tantamount to a new medicine to cure not just one but many diseases. Automated driving therefore becomes an imperative to be promoted by public policy: barriers must be removed, and incentives must be offered. In a world with one traffic fatality every twenty-three seconds,[10] delay quite literally means death.

And yet. If policymakers and the public were truly concerned about the problems of the motor vehicle, there are other solutions that could be implemented—not just someday, but today. Higher fuel taxes, fees based directly on distance traveled, and congestion pricing to internalize the costs of motor vehicle travel and to support extensive public transit systems. Alcohol ignition locks and speed limiters in vehicles, and automated enforcement on roads. Meaningful vehicle inspections for both emissions and safety. A holistic systems approach to the safety of vehicles, roads, and road users.

Indeed, some countries have achieved dramatically safer roads than others. Consider just four high-income countries: on a per-kilometer basis, driving in the United States in 2016 was 40 percent deadlier than in Australia and Canada—and twice as deadly as in the United Kingdom. The United States looks even worse on a per capita basis: driving was more than twice as deadly than in Australia and Canada and more than thrice as deadly than in the United Kingdom.[11, 12] (See Figure 35.1.)

Many complicated factors contribute to these reported differences, but at some level the United States chooses to let more people die on its roads.

Aggressively embracing automated driving as a technological solution—if not *the* solution—to roadway safety could exacerbate the other social problems of driving. Simply automating today's system of motor vehicle transport might encourage even

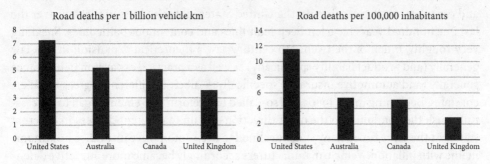

FIGURE 35.1. Road deaths in the United States, Australia, Canada, and the United Kingdom.

[10] World Health Organization, Road Traffic Deaths, https://www.who.int/gho/road_safety/mortality/en/.

[11] International Transport Forum, Road Safety Annual Report 2018.

[12] UK Department for Transport, Transport Statistics Great Britain 2017, https://assets.publishing.service.gov.uk/government/uploads/system/uploads/attachment_data/file/664323/tsgb-2017-print-ready-version.pdf.

more travel and sprawl,[13] discourage active mobility and the use of traditional mass transit, and further empower constituencies that will oppose raising the cost or reducing the convenience of personal vehicle ownership and use.

If this is true, then the advent of automated driving marks a dramatic inflection point—a choice between mobility heaven and mobility hell[14]—where certain policies might suddenly stand more than a snowball's chance. Political realities might continue to immunize the 260 million conventional vehicles in the United States from extensive automated enforcement, meaningful maintenance requirements, and new taxes and fees. But these political limitations do not yet exist for the approximately zero automated vehicles currently in the country. Indeed, their developers may be facing increasingly uncertain political winds.

Viewed in this light, automated vehicles represent not a technological solution but, instead, a critical policy solution: their development offers a unique opportunity to revolutionize policy alongside technology. In other words, policy advocates may be able to achieve for automated driving alone what they cannot achieve for conventional driving or for all driving. This opportunity may even justify policy that unintentionally slows down technology—by, for example, making automated vehicles more expensive than their conventional counterparts and thereby discouraging their adoption.

The tension between these two views is more than a strategic dilemma: as a matter of life and death, it is also an ethical quandary. Given what is widely acknowledged as an imperfect status quo, should we exploit automated driving as a technological solution or as a policy solution? With respect to transport policy, should we have the same expectations for automated and conventional driving? Or should we expect more from one or the other? And do we achieve these outcomes by lowering or raising our current expectations of motor vehicle transport?

Discussions about civil liability for crashes involving automated vehicles illustrate—and complicate—this tension. In the United States, notable shifts in tort law over the last one hundred years have left deep fault lines and contentious battle lines. Speaking very roughly, much of the twentieth century saw a theoretical expansion in tort law generally (and product liability specifically) as well as a practical expansion in insurance generally (and automotive insurance specifically)—albeit to different degrees in different states. Beginning in the 1980s, the so-called tort reform movement began to successfully push the pendulum in the other direction—again to different degrees in different states. At the same time, many states declined to keep automotive insurance minimums in line with inflation. Vehicle manufacturers accordingly became more attractive defendants even as product liability lawsuits became more expensive to litigate. For these and other reasons, and for better or worse, the status quo is rather messy.

Enter automated driving. Those who view automated driving as a technological solution tend to inquire how it could be encouraged through changes to tort law—whether

[13] Bryant Walker Smith, "Managing Autonomous Transportation Demand," 52 *Santa Clara Law Review* 1401 (2012), https://ssrn.com/abstract=2303907.
[14] Robin Chase, "Will a World of Driverless Cars Be Heaven or Hell?," CityLab (Apr. 3, 2014), https://www.citylab.com/transportation/2014/04/will-world-driverless-cars-be-heaven-or-hell/8784/.

those changes seek to advantage automated driving, remove a perceived advantage to conventional driving, or extend the same perceived advantage to automated driving. In contrast, those who view automated driving as a policy solution tend to approach it as a potential catalyst for broader changes that they want to see in tort law—whether those involve expanding liability or limiting liability. In each case, these proposed changes may be subtle or dramatic.

Whereas some academic proposals would dramatically replace or reinvent tort law for automated vehicles, the companies developing automated driving systems have been notably circumspect. In some U.S. states, key actors in the automotive industry did initially push, often successfully, for legislative grants of immunity in the case of third-party modifications to production vehicles. And, at the federal level, key automated driving developers tended to favor ambiguous legislative language potentially preempting some tort claims and to disfavor language limiting their use of binding arbitration. In general, however, the priorities of these companies tend to suggest a disinterest either in associating automated driving with tort reform or in drafting one in service to the other.

Why this relative modesty? Perhaps these companies have concluded, as have others,[15,16,17] that existing tort law, while messy, is nonetheless familiar and ultimately tolerable. Perhaps they are wary of opening cans of worms that could wriggle far beyond their control. Perhaps they are waiting until they know what they want and have the political power to achieve it. Perhaps they do not want to make needless opponents of automated driving. Perhaps they understand the dissonance between, on one hand, promising safety and asking for trust and, on the other hand, promising destruction and asking for immunity. And perhaps they too see automated driving as a technological solution, for ultimately the best way to reduce liability is to reduce injury.

CONSEQUENCES OF SAFETY EXPECTATIONS

Given that automated driving will not wholly eliminate roadway deaths and injuries, how safe is safe enough—and how should this safety be demonstrated? These questions are certainly important, and their ethical context is rich: Recklessness and caution can both bring death.[18] The predictive, however, may preempt much of the philosophical.

---

[15] Kyle Graham, "Of Frightened Horses and Autonomous Vehicles: Tort Law and Its Assimilation of Innovations," 52 *Santa Clara Law Review* 1241 (2012), https://digitalcommons.law.scu.edu/lawreview/vol52/iss4/4.

[16] Bryant Walker Smith, "Automated Driving and Product Liability," 2017 *Michigan State Law Review* 1 (2016), https://ssrn.com/abstract=2923240.

[17] Mark A. Geistfeld, "A Roadmap for Autonomous Vehicles: State Tort Liability, Automobile Insurance, and Federal Safety Regulation," 105 *California Law Review* 1611 (2018), https://scholarship.law.berkeley.edu/californialawreview/vol105/iss6/2/.

[18] Nidhi Kalra and David G. Groves, "The Enemy of Good: Estimating the Cost of Waiting for Nearly Perfect Automated Vehicles" (2017), https://www.rand.org/pubs/research_reports/RR2150.html.

When automated vehicles are deployed commercially, they will not be extraordinarily dangerous: the risks they pose to users and bystanders will at worst be commensurate with those posed by many other human activities, including human driving. (I would go even further: we should be concerned about automated driving but terrified about human driving.) There will be surprising and tragic failures, but for the most part they will be findable and fixable. A massive system-wide anomaly—such as a cyberattack that shuts down every automated vehicle during a hurricane evacuation—is an important caveat, but it is also one that now applies to modern life generally.

When crashes do occur, retrospective expectations of safety will be largely apparent: at least as a matter of law, an automated driving system will be unreasonably dangerous if it is less safe than a human performing the same maneuver, if it is less safe than a comparable automated driving system, or (and this third point is more debatable) if it is no safer than the last automated driving system to have failed. A company responsible for an unreasonably dangerous automated driving system will likely be civilly liable—but civil liability is not the same as moral culpability. (Indeed, a vehicle manufacturer can be liable for an injury caused by a defect in a safety system that it had no legal obligation to install and that, even with the defect, still prevents far more harm than it causes.)

This leaves prospective expectations of safety: How safe must an automated vehicle be for deployment? Prospective safety should mean reasonable confidence that the developer of that vehicle is worthy of our trust.[19] In part this is because no one—not even that developer—will be able to prospectively determine a precise level of safety. But this is also because safety is not a single metric to be ascertained by a single test. Properly conceived, safety is an ongoing process that begins before product development and continues through product disposal. Among many other facets, it encompasses corporate governance, design philosophy, hiring and supervision, evaluation and integration of standards, monitoring and updating, communication and disclosure, and planning for eventual obsolescence.

In this way, safety is a marriage rather than a wedding. A company that develops or deploys an automated driving system will necessarily promise, explicitly or implicitly, that its system is reasonably safe. This promise, if credible, will be based on a thorough safety case that draws on diverse expertise and that acknowledges both technical and ethical uncertainties. This safety case should be interrogated and may well be disproved, but the inability to disprove is not the same as affirmative proof. Given this, the fundamental policy question should be whether the company that makes such a promise is worthy of public trust.

Here the so-called trolley problem merits passing mention.[20,21] Unfortunately, the highly stylized question of who should die when an automated vehicle finds itself in some ostensibly unavoidable crash is often posited as the paramount—if not the

---

[19] Bryant Walker Smith, "The Trustworthy Company" (forthcoming), https://newlypossible.org.

[20] Philippa Foot, "The Problem of Abortion and the Doctrine of the Double Effect," *Oxford Review*, No. 5 (1967).

[21] Judith J. Thomson, "Killing, Letting Die, and the Trolley Problem," *The Monist* 59(2) (1976): 204–217.

only—ethical issue raised by automated driving. It is neither.[22,23] These hypothetical crashes are far from inevitable, their outcomes far from certain, and their predicate decisions necessarily situational.

Nonetheless, two related ethical insights are important. First, both human driving and automated driving entail risks—that is, potential harms of a given probability and a given magnitude. The risks of human driving are all too familiar; the risks of automated driving remain largely speculative. Ethics can help to supply values to quantify and then compare these knowns and unknowns. And, second, the corollary question to what decision to make is who or what should ultimately have the authority to decide.

HUMAN AUTHORITY VERSUS COMPUTER AUTHORITY

Epitomized by the conflict between Dave and HAL in *2001: A Space Odyssey*,[24] tension between human and computer authority is present today and will become more pronounced in the future. Consider two actual transport examples.

In 2016, an attacker hijacked a truck in Berlin, killed its driver, and drove into a crowded Christmas market. The truck struck dozens but came to a stop within a relatively short 80 meters, which investigators attributed to the truck's automatic emergency braking system.[25]

In 2018 and 2019, two Boeing 737 MAX passenger planes crashed. In each case, it appears that the pilots fought unsuccessfully against a malfunctioning automation system that repeatedly pushed the nose of the plane downward.[26,27]

These examples illustrate a choice that may implicate philosophy as much as engineering: Should humans or computers have ultimate authority over a given action? The answer might be crudely characterized as a choice between security and safety or even as a proxy for the basic goodness of humanity. Of course, this is complicated. For example,

[22] Bryant Walker Smith, "The Trolley and the Pinto: Cost-Benefit Analysis in Automated Driving and Other Cyber-Physical Systems," 4 *Texas A&M Law Review* 197 (2017), https://ssrn.com/abstract=2983000.
[23] Heather M. Roff, *The Folly of Trolleys: Ethical Challenges and Autonomous Vehicles* (Dec. 17, 2018), https://www.brookings.edu/research/the-folly-of-trolleys-ethical-challenges-and-autonomous-vehicles/.
[24] "2001: A Space Odyssey," https://www.imdb.com/title/tt0062622/.
[25] Hans Leyendecker, Georg Mascolo, and Nicolas Richter, "Lkw-Bremssystem verhinderte noch mehr Tote in Berlin," *Süddeutsche Zeitung* (December 28, 2016), https://www.sueddeutsche.de/politik/terroranschlag-lkw-bremssystem-verhinderte-noch-mehr-tote-in-berlin-1.3312551.
[26] Republic of Indonesia Komite Nasional Keselamatan Transportasi (KNKT), Preliminary KNKT.18.10.35.04 Aircraft Accident Investigation Report (2018), https://reports.aviation-safety.net/2018/20181029-0_B38M_PK-LQP_PRELIMINARY.pdf.
[27] Federal Democratic Republic of Ethiopia Ministry of Transport Aircraft Investigation Bureau, Aircraft Accident Investigation Preliminary Report No. AI-01/19 (2019), https://flightsafety.org/wp-content/uploads/2019/04/Preliminary-Report-B737-800MAX-ET-AVJ.pdf.

the copilot of a 2015 flight relied on one aviation security technology—the "cockpit door locking system"—in murdering everyone on his plane.[28] Conversely, modern elevators essentially trap passengers based in part on the belief that trying to escape is usually more dangerous than waiting for emergency personnel.[29]

Many discussions of automated driving give this question of decision-making authority only cursory attention.[30] For example, SAE J3016, the prominent technical document that defines levels of driving automation, focuses much more on the complementary roles of the human user and the driving automation system than on how conflicts between these two roles are reconciled.[31] In a single table, it merely notes that, as a descriptive matter, driving automation systems "disengage[] immediately upon driver request" at levels 1 through 3 and "may delay user-requested disengagement" at levels 4 and 5.

Even descriptively, this dichotomy may not turn out to be entirely correct. For example, a combination of automation and connectivity may allow motor vehicles, particularly large trucks, to travel together in closely spaced platoons. Because the following distances may be too close for human drivers to safely manage, such a platooning system—which may initially operate at only level 1 or 2—might not fully disengage until it achieves appropriate vehicle spacing. Analogously, an advanced crash avoidance system (which would not technically be classifiable under the levels of driving automation) might override driver inputs for the seconds (or fractions of a second) that it engages so that the overreaction or underreaction of a panicked or uncertain driver does not cause an otherwise preventable crash.

The visceral may matter as much as the technical. Whatever their explanations, incidents of sudden unintended acceleration in motor vehicles are scary in part because they represent a loss of authority: the cars speed up even as their drivers want to slow down. The opposite condition—the deliberate use of technology to limit speeds—can also engender strong feelings. As noted previously, an Ontario truck driver argued in 2012 that a provincial law requiring speed regulators on commercial trucks violated his right to security of the person under the Canadian Charter of Rights and Freedoms.[32] And he persuaded one court before losing (twice) on appeal.

A key ethical question is whether individual human authority—even at the potential cost of other lives—is itself a value that belongs in the technical analysis. Should harm that a human could have prevented somehow outweigh harm that a human caused?

[28] France Bureau d'Enquêtes et d'Analyses pour la sécurité de l'aviation civile, Final Report BEA2015-0125 (2016), https://www.bea.aero/uploads/tx_elydbrapports/BEA2015-0125.en-LR.pdf.

[29] Schindler Elevator Corporation, Emergency Operation of Elevator Systems (2007), https://www.schindler.com/content/dam/web/us/pdfs/safety/elevator-emergency-operation.pdf.

[30] Bryant Walker Smith, "Lawyers and Engineers Should Speak the Same Robot Language," in *Robot Law* (2015), https://www.elgaronline.com/view/9781783476725.00011.xml.

[31] SAE International, SAE J3016: Taxonomy and Definitions for Terms Related to Driving Automation Systems for On-Road Motor Vehicles (2018), https://www.sae.org/standards/content/j3016_201806/.

[32] R. v. Michaud, 2015 ONCA 585, http://www.ontariocourts.ca/decisions/2015/2015ONCA0585.htm.

Conversely, should harm caused malevolently somehow outweigh harm caused innocently or negligently?[33] In short, how should we think about human autonomy?

CHANGING POWER DYNAMICS

Humans and computers are not the only relevant actors. Governments and companies—acting through their human agents and their computer agents—play fundamental roles in the deployment and regulation of artificial intelligence in transport. This has important consequences for power dynamics in the public domain.

Consider, for example, law enforcement in a hypothetical world in which a few companies operate large networks of automated vehicles. Assume that these vehicles have sensors, computers, and transmitters that enable the meaningful collection of extensive information about environments both inside and outside of them. Further assume that these vehicles are designed to generally comply with the rules of the road.

Widespread compliance with the rules of the road could dramatically reduce the traffic stops—twenty million annually[34]—that, along with crashes, account for most of the interactions between law enforcement and the public in the United States.[35] Rather than simply disappear, however, this enforcement activity is likely to shift—in at least four ways.

First, traditional officers may focus on activities in the physical domain other than driving. In addition to conventional human drivers, bicyclists, scooter riders, mass transit riders, and pedestrians may receive even more scrutiny. People entering, exiting, or waiting for automated vehicles may also be targets for the enforcement of laws that are either specific to ride-sharing or so general in application (such as loitering) that they can be applied, however dubiously, to a wide range of conduct.

Second, even more law enforcement may shift to the digital realm. The loss of traffic stops as the primary means of randomly (or discriminatorily) scanning the public may be used to justify—in practice, policy, or law—more electronic surveillance. New technologies may also be used to extend the reach of physical surveillance into the vehicles themselves—and to make that surveillance far more ubiquitous than semi-random traffic stops could ever achieve. Is perfect enforcement ideal?

Third, police departments may cooperate with the private operators of automated vehicle networks—in the sky as well as on the ground. These companies might alert law

[33] Curtis W. Copeland, "How Agencies Monetize 'Statistical Lives' Expected to Be Saved by Regulations," Congressional Research Service (2010), https://digital.library.unt.edu/ark:/67531/metadc812693/m2/1/high_res_d/R41140_2010Mar24.pdf.

[34] The Stanford Open Policing Project, "Findings," (2020), https://openpolicing.stanford.edu/findings/.

[35] Elizabeth Davis, Anthony Whyde, and Lynn Langton, "Contacts Between Police and the Public, 2015," U.S. Department of Justice Special Report NCJ 251145 (2018), https://www.bjs.gov/content/pub/pdf/cpp15.pdf.

enforcement to potentially illegal activity inside or outside their vehicles. And they might, willingly or begrudgingly, provide access to some of their data, from real-time sensor feeds to behavioral predictions devoid of supporting data.

Fourth, these companies may simply conduct their own enforcement without involving the public sector. Shopping malls, which generations ago marked a shift from public to private space, offer some precedent. So too do the dispute resolution systems that credit card providers, airlines, social networking platforms, and digital commerce platforms have implemented—and that, for pragmatic if not legal reasons, often act as judge, jury, and executioner in one.

In our hypothetical future, pedestrians may enjoy much greater confidence that vehicles will stop rather than strike them. In many ways, this would be a welcome shift; no longer would people need to wait at unsignalized crosswalks as cars and trucks unlawfully careen by them—or run across frantically. This confidence could even return the neighborhood street to the bustling center of human activity—the woonerf—that it was before horses and then cars came to dominate. But some pedestrians may bring this confidence to larger thoroughfares in a way that unlawfully disrupts the flow or safety of motor vehicle traffic. Of course, if a person crosses in front of a properly functioning automated vehicle, then the vehicle will make reasonable efforts to stop—and will have been traveling at a speed that is likely to make those efforts successful. This is much more about engineering than ethics.

But the story is unlikely to end there. The automated vehicle will likely record the interaction with a multitude of sensors. Using artificial intelligence to recognize a face or a gait or some other pattern, the company behind the automated vehicle may then identify the interloper with some internally acceptable level of confidence. Perhaps it will share this evidence with law enforcement. Or perhaps it will decline to involve any public authority in favor of simply banning that person from its automated vehicles—or myriad other physical or digital services that it or its partners provide—in the future. For many, the loss of commercial transport, package delivery, or social media may be much more of a deterrent than a public fine for jaywalking.

In this way and in others, automated driving may change the nature of public, private, and personal space. This may be good, bad, or neutral—though certainly mixed. And how this change is appraised depends not only on its implementation but also on ethical inputs. What is the value of privacy—or, more fundamentally, autonomy? What is the value of social interaction, even at the expense of independence? What are appropriate roles for the public and private sectors? If governments, companies, and individuals each stand at a point of a triangle, what is the proper allocation of power among them?

For technological, legal, and economic reasons, many of these questions are likely to be addressed (probably indirectly) at higher levels of government. In many U.S. states, municipalities can regulate taxis but not transportation network companies, and the same is likely to be true for their automated equivalents. Similarly, federal motor vehicle standards (or even the mere possibility of standards not yet enacted) are likely to displace some traditional state authority over driving—authority generally exercised through the regulation of human drivers.

This centralization may be mixed as well. On one hand, the best automated vehicle deployments are likely to come from partnerships between communities and developers— partnerships that require empowered rather than disempowered communities. On the other hand, powerful residential communities have long contributed to mobility injustice.[36] Even defining a community is an exercise in ethics.

CONCLUSION

And so this chapter concludes not with technologies of this millennium but with institutions—governments and companies—of the last one. In 2017 and 2018, the U.S. Congress considered automated driving legislation that was generally supported by many of the larger automated driving developers. After one version quickly passed the House,[37] its counterpart stalled and eventually died in the Senate.[38] The immediate explanations are numerous: key senators slowed the bill's momentum, trial attorneys and local governments became more involved, technological visions became more grounded, issues of trade and emissions preoccupied industry lobbyists, and everything else preoccupied Congress.

More fundamentally, however, this automated driving legislation failed to pass because of a lack of trust in technologies and institutions. Influential senators were wary of automated driving technologies, of automated driving developers, and of automated driving regulators. Without this trust, deference seemed imprudent.

Trust is largely an empirical question, and numerous surveys purport to measure public acceptance of automated driving. But beyond the Senate, these surveys probably have little predictive value. The public is fickle, words are not actions, the two powerful industries behind automated driving have yet to rev up their marketing engines, and neither broad support nor broad adoption is a necessary condition for broad impact. Indeed, contrary to popular conception, automated driving can happen without new legislation.[39]

In contrast, trustworthiness is much more of an ethical question. Automated vehicles will not be driven by individuals or even by computers; they will be driven by companies acting through their human and machine agents. An essential issue for this field—and for artificial intelligence generally—is how the companies that develop and deploy these technologies should earn our trust.

---

[36] Partnership for Southern Equity, Opportunity Deferred: Race, Transportation, and the Future of Metropolitan Atlanta (2017), https://psequity.org/uploads/2019/10/2017-PSE-Opportunity-Deferred.pdf.

[37] SELF DRIVE Act, H.R. 3388 (2017), https://www.congress.gov/bill/115th-congress/house-bill/3388.

[38] AV START Act, S. 1885 (2017), https://www.congress.gov/bill/115th-congress/senate-bill/1885.

[39] Bryant Walker Smith, "Congress's Automated Driving Bills Are Both More and Less Than They Seem, Stanford Center for Internet and Society" (2017), https://cyberlaw.stanford.edu/blog/2017/10/congress%E2%80%99s-automated-driving-bills-are-both-more-and-less-they-seem.

A trustworthy company shares its safety philosophy, makes a promise to the public, and keeps that promise.[40] A company that shares its safety philosophy says in effect, "This is what we're doing; this is why we think it's reasonably safe; and this is why you can believe us." Its promise is, "We market only what we reasonably believe to be safe; we will be candid about our limitations and failures; and when we do fail, we will make it right." And it keeps that promise by appropriately managing public expectations; by supervising the life cycle of its product or service; and by mitigating harms promptly, fully, and publicly.

Transport technologies, including but certainly not limited to automated driving, will have a complex relationship with ethical issues both new and old. The four highlighted here—the tension between technological solutions and policy solutions, the consequences of safety expectations, the complex choice between human authority and computer authority, and impacts on power dynamics among individuals, governments, companies, and others—merit thoughtful public discussion.

To be thoughtful, that discussion must be informed. And to be informed, it must involve the good-faith expertise of the companies developing and deploying these technologies. Ethics, like transport, is not just where we go, but how we get there.

BIBLIOGRAPHY

Caro, Robert A. *The Power Broker: Robert Moses and the Rise and Fall of New York*. Knopf, 1974.

Douma, Frank. "Using ITS to Better Serve Diverse Populations." Report no. Mn/DOT 2004–42 (2004). http://www.cts.umn.edu/Research/ProjectDetail.html?id=2003020.

German Federal Ministry of Transport and Digital Infrastructure. Report by the Ethics Commission on Automated and Connected Driving (2017). https://www.bmvi.de/SharedDocs/EN/publications/report-ethics-commission-automated-and-connected-driving.pdf.

Kalra, Nidhi and David G. Groves. "The Enemy of Good: Estimating the Cost of Waiting for Nearly Perfect Automated Vehicles." RAND Corporation, 2017. https://www.rand.org/pubs/research_reports/RR2150.html.

Rothstein, Richard. *The Color of Law: A Forgotten History of How Our Government Segregated America* New York: Liveright Publishing Corp., 2017.

SAE International. "SAE J3016: Taxonomy and Definitions for Terms Related to Driving Automation Systems for On-Road Motor Vehicles" (2018). https://www.sae.org/standards/content/j3016_201806/.

Smith, Bryant Walker. "How Governments Can Promote Automated Driving." 47 *New Mexico Law Review* 99 (2017). http://ssrn.com/abstract=2749375.

Smith, Bryant Walker. "Regulation and the Risk of Inaction." In *Autonomes Fahren*, edited by M. Maurer, J. Gerdes, B. Lenz, and H. Winner, 593–609. Berliin: Springer, 2015. http://link.springer.com/chapter/10.1007/978-3-662-45854-9_27.

Uniform Law Commission. Uniform Automated Operation of Vehicles Act (2019). https://www.uniformlaws.org/Committee.aspx?title=HighlyAutomatedVehicles.

[40] Bryant Walker Smith, *The Trustworthy Company* (forthcoming), https://newlypossible.org.

United Nations Global Forum for Road Traffic Safety (WP.1) Resolution on the Deployment of Highly and Fully Automated Vehicles in Road Traffic, ECE/TRANS/WP.1/165 (2018). http://www.unece.org/fileadmin/DAM/trans/doc/2018/wp1/ECE-TRANS-WP1-165e.pdf.
United States Department of Transportation. "Preparing for the Future of Transportation: Automated Vehicles 3.0" (2018). https://www.transportation.gov/av/3.

CHAPTER 36

....

THE CASE FOR ETHICAL
AI IN THE MILITARY

....

JASON SCHOLZ AND JAI GALLIOTT

INTRODUCTION

....

SIGNIFICANT recent progress in AI is positively impacting everyday tasks, as well as science, medicine, agriculture, security, finance, law, games, and even creative artistic expression. Nevertheless, some contend that, on ethical grounds, military operations should be immune from the progress of automation and artificial intelligence evident in other areas of society. As an example, Human Rights Watch have stated that:

> Killer robots—fully autonomous weapons that could select and engage targets without human intervention—could be developed within 20 to 30 years ... Human Rights Watch and Harvard Law School's International Human Rights Clinic (IHRC) believe that such revolutionary weapons would not be consistent with international humanitarian law and would increase the risk of death or injury to civilians during armed conflict.... The primary concern of Human Rights Watch and IHRC is the impact fully autonomous weapons would have on the protection of civilians during times of war.[1]

The Campaign to Stop Killer Robots, operated by a consortium of nongovernment interest groups, echoes this sentiment, with over 1,000 experts in artificial intelligence, as well as science and technology luminaries such as Stephen Hawking, Elon Musk, Steve Wozniak, Noam Chomsky, Skype co-founder Jaan Tallinn, and Google DeepMind co-founder Demis Hassabis, expressing the problem on their website:

> Allowing life or death decisions to be made by machines crosses a fundamental moral line. Autonomous robots would lack human judgment and the ability to

---

[1] International Human Rights Clinic, "Losing Humanity: The Case against Killer Robots," Harvard Law School (2012), https://www.hrw.org/sites/default/files/reports/arms1112ForUpload00.pdf.

understand context. These qualities are necessary to make complex ethical choices on a dynamic battlefield, to distinguish adequately between soldiers and civilians, and to evaluate the proportionality of an attack. As a result, fully autonomous weapons would not meet the requirements of the laws of war. Replacing human troops with machines could make the decision to go to war easier, which would shift the burden of armed conflict further onto civilians. The use of fully autonomous weapons would create an accountability gap as there is no clarity on who would be legally responsible for a robot's actions: the commander, programmer, manufacturer, or robot itself? Without accountability, these parties would have less incentive to ensure robots did not endanger civilians and victims would be left unsatisfied that someone was punished for the harm they experienced.[2]

While we acknowledge some of these concerns, the underlying arguments typically admit no shades of grey, with many based on mistaken assumptions about the role of human agents in the development of these systems and the relevant systems of control. And yet, with such bold arguments from these anti–artificial intelligence luminaries, how can those interested in more nuanced argument begin to rebalance the relevant debate? The anti-AI rhetoric has been permitted to dominate the dialogue on autonomous weapon systems because said debate initially proceeded quite cautiously on the part of the states with responsibility for steering the discussion, on the basis that few understood what it was some were seeking to outlaw with a preemptive ban, but allowing certain advocate groups to sway the debate in the vacuum of informed opinion has given rise to a debate that has ever since been very heavily one-sided.

Meanwhile, with fears about nonexistent sentient robots stalling debate and halting technological progress, one can see in the news that the world faces pressing ethical and humanitarian problems in the use of existing weapons. A gun stolen from a police officer and used to kill, guns used for mass shootings, vehicles used to mow down pedestrians, a bombing of a religious site, a guided-bomb strike on a train bridge as an unexpected passenger train passes over it, a missile strike on a Red Cross facility, and so on. Some of the latter might be prevented by using AI in weapons and in autonomous systems, more generally. It does not seem unreasonable to question why weapons with advanced symbol recognition, for instance, could not be embedded in autonomous systems to identify a symbol of the Red Cross and abort an ordered strike.[3] Similarly, the location of protected sites of religious significance, schools, or hospitals might be programmed into weapons to constrain their actions, or guns prevented from firing by an unauthorized user pointing it at a human. And it does not seem unreasonable to question why this cannot be ensconced in international weapons review standards. We

---

[2] The Campaign to Stop Killer Robots, "The Solution" (2018), https://www.stopkillerrobots.org/the-solution/.

[3] Indeed, we have introduced the importance of discussing these questions in brief elsewhere. See Jason Scholz and Jai Galliott, "Artificial Intelligence in Weapons: The Moral Imperative for Minimally-Just Autonomy," *US Air Force Journal of Indo-Pacific Affairs* 1 (2018): 57–67. We will also be expanding on the technical feasibility of MinAI, including providing a deployable formal model in a forthcoming book, *Ceding Humanity* (SUNY Press).

seek to correct the lopsided debate and address the concerns of certain advocate groups with a case for a *minimalist* version of *Ethical AI*, explaining why a blanket prohibition on AI in weapons is a bad idea, and why "life" decisions could, and should, at times, be made by machines.

As noted by Lambert and Scholz,[4] automobiles rival wars as a contributor to human death and yet the automobile industry is one of the leaders in integrating automated decision makers into vehicles. Much of the manufacturer's motivation is to make automobiles safer. We hold the same motivation and advocate a similar application in a military context. A simple illustration along the aforementioned lines serves to illustrate. Consider the capability of a weapon to recognize the unexpected presence of an international protection symbol—perhaps a Red Cross, Red Crescent, or Red Crystal—in a defined target area and abort an otherwise unrestrained human-ordered attack. Given the significant advances in visual machine learning over the last decade, such recognition systems are technically feasible. So, inspired by vehicle automation, an Ethical AI system for our purpose is a weapon with inbuilt safety enhancements enabled by the application of artificial intelligence. We further develop this safety argument for weapons, by adapting the guidelines for ethics in autonomous vehicles developed in Germany, but first wish to make the case for Ethical AI in the context of other options, including the impracticability of regulation.

WHY BANNING WEAPONIZED AI IS A BAD IDEA

Autonomous weapons—the primary systems enabled by artificial intelligence—can be serious and dangerous tools in the wrong hands. There is no doubt about this fact. As the above-mentioned tech entrepreneurs and other signatories to a recent open letter to the United Nations have put it, autonomous weapons "can be weapons of terror, weapons that despots and terrorists use against innocent populations, and weapons [that can be] hacked to behave in undesirable ways."[5] But this does not mean that the United Nations ought to proceed immediately to the implementation of a preventive ban on the further development of weaponized artificial intelligence, as the signatories of the open letter urge. For one thing, it sometimes takes dangerous tools to achieve worthy ends.

This is most obvious in the case of humanitarian interventions. Think of the Rwandan genocide, where the world simply stood by and did nothing. Had autonomous weapons capable of discrimination between the relevant fighters been available in 1994, developed

---

[4] Dale Lambert and Jason Scholz, "A Dialectic for Network Centric Warfare," Proceedings of the 10th International Command and Control Research and Technology Symposium (ICCRTS), MacLean, VA, June 13–16, 2005.

[5] The Future of Life Institute, "An Open Letter to the United Nations Convention on Certain Conventional Weapons" (2017), https://Futureoflife.Org/Autonomous-Weapons-Open-Letter-2017/.

states would likely have been less averse to engagement and may not have looked the other way. It seems plausible that if the costs of humanitarian interventions were purely monetary, that is, if we were removed the sometimes controversial nature of weapons deployment on foreign soil and the concerns that some hold regarding casualty aversion, then it would be easier to gain widespread support for what are otherwise might otherwise be morally sanctioned interventions.[6]

To make this point more generally, it should be acknowledged that AI technology is tremendously beneficial, and it already permeates our lives in ways that people often do not notice and often are not well placed or able to comprehend fully. Given its pervasive presence and the virtual impossibility of constraining a software-underwritten technology that is already in the public domain, it is shortsighted or perhaps even naive to think that the artificial intelligence technology's abuse can be prevented if only the further development of autonomous weapons is halted.

If a ban were to be implemented, the likely consequence would be the development of artificial intelligence–enabled weapons by malicious nonstate and state-based actors using existing technology. It is worth bearing in mind that most artificial intelligence in weapons is currently deployed by developed states that conduct their military and security engagements broadly in line with international law and public expectations, with said technology therefore accompanied by robust safety mechanisms and deployed in appropriate zones given the known limitations of the technology—for example, out at sea rather than in urban conflict zones. Nefarious actors will have no reason to act in such a constrained fashion, and there exists no effective enforcement regime to hold these actors responsible for violations of international law, meaning any prevailing autonomous future of this kind is likely to be bleak and consist of technology minus existing safeguards. In fact, it may well take the sophisticated and discriminate autonomous-weapons systems that developed military forces around the world are currently in the process of developing or, in some cases, deploying, if we are to effectively counter the much cruder autonomous weapons that would likely be constructed through the reprogramming of seemingly benign AI technology such as the self-driving car and other off-the-shelf technologies if a "preventative" ban were to be implemented. The developed states of world, while together an imperfect moral arbiter, have a moral obligation to develop new technologies partly on the basis that it has the responsibility to its collective population to quell the uprising of this crude technology by those who seek to do harm to the many.[7] This is to say that a consequence of a ban would be to deny the use of AI weapons as a countermeasure against other AI or autonomous weapons.

The world has previously placed prohibitions on the possession and use of certain types of weapons, including chemical, biological, nuclear, and potentially persistent unexploded ordnance such as cluster munitions and landmines. Prohibition of these weapons has not prevented states or nonstate actors from developing them. India, Pakistan, Israel, and North Korea have developed nuclear weapons, and Iran was

---

[6] Jai Galliott, *Military Robots: Mapping the Moral Landscape* (Farnham, UK: Ashgate, 2015).
[7] *Id.* at 37–64.

actively developing a nuclear weapons program until 2009.[8] Moreover, none of the nations that possess nuclear weapons is a signatory to the Treaty on the Prohibition of Nuclear Weapons.[9] Nevertheless, preventing nations or nonstate actors from acquiring nuclear weapons has been reasonably effective until now, but only because it has been possible to physically control access to the relatively difficult-to-obtain materials required to produce them. In the case of AI and autonomous weapons, it is not the materials that are lacking, but the code. The algorithms needed for autonomous weapons are in many cases the same as those needed for autonomous cars or mobile phone apps, so one faces a dual use definitional problem. It is not possible to identify certain types of code that are militarily useful and ban them. The construction of autonomous weapons once the component technologies—many of which will be in the public domain—become available is only a matter of time, and not only for nation states. This is an area in which those states charged with maintaining international order do not want to find themselves lagging behind.

A blanket prohibition on "AI in weapons" would have further unintended consequences due to its lack of *nuance*. Building on the earlier discussion of the implications of halting the development of AI, there is a distinction to be made in any regulation or policy about those *kinds of AI* that could yield significant humanitarian benefits. This lack of nuance is also evident in the case against chemical weapons. For example, pepper spray or tear gas is a chemical agent banned in warfare under the Chemical Weapons Convention of 1993, making it illegal for use by militaries except in law enforcement. The denial of tear gas to military forces removes a less-than-lethal option from the inventory, which could lead to the unnecessary use of lethal force. Even the responsible development of what are often seen as abhorrent weapons can be defended on the basis that they might prevent the use of more deadly or indiscriminate force. Moving along the spectrum of destructive weapons one finds land mines. The United States, of course, never ratified the Ottawa Treaty but rather chose a technological solution to end the use of persistent land mines—land mines that can be set to self-destruct or deactivate after a predefined time period—making them considerably less problematic when used in clearly demarcated and confined zones such as the Korean Demilitarized Zone (DMZ).[10] In choosing not to ratify the Ottawa Treaty, the United States had identified that what, in one form, can be a crude and indiscriminate weapon can, in the hands of the morally scrupulous, be another weapon that may limit the need for more injurious weapons prevent the use of even more deadly and indiscriminate application force in places like the Korean DMZ, where the alternatives might include options that are not sensitive to discrimination between a child (either now or two decades in the future)

[8] Rod Barton, *The Weapons Detective: The Inside Story of Australia's Top Weapons Inspector* (Melbourne: Black Inc. Agenda, 2015).

[9] Alexander White and Matthew Paterson, "Nuke Kid in Town: How Much Does the Treaty on the Prohibition of Nuclear Weapons Actually Change?," *Pandora's Box* 24 (2017): 141–156.

[10] Lorraine Boissoneault, "The Historic Innovation of Land Mines—And Why We've Struggled to Get Rid of Them," *Smithsonian* (February 24, 2017), https://www.smithsonianmag.com/innovation/historic-innovation-land-minesand-why-weve-struggled-get-rid-them-180962276/.

and a military-aged adult during a period of defined hostility, as in the case of modern land mines.

There is also a need to overcome another common notion behind a ban, that which revolves around an overly optimistic view of technology in that it raises concerns regarding a lack of human control. This is a conception that fails to acknowledge the long causal backstory of institutional arrangements and individual actors who, through thousands of little acts of commission and omission in the process of design, engineering, and development, have brought about, and continue to bring about, the rise of such technologies. As long as the debate about autonomous weapons is framed primarily in terms of UN-level policies, the average citizen, soldier, or programmer must be forgiven for assuming that he or she is absolved of all moral responsibility for the wrongful harm that autonomous weapons risk causing. But this assumption is false, and it might prove disastrous. All individuals who deal with AI technology have to exercise due diligence, and each and every one of us needs to examine carefully how his or her actions and inactions are contributing to the potential dangers of this technology and those in which it may be integrated. This is by no means to say that state and intergovernmental agencies do not have an important role to play as well. Rather, it is to emphasize that if the potential dangers of autonomous weapons are to be mitigated, then an ethic of personal responsibility must be promoted, and it must reach all the way down to the level of the individual decision maker. For a start, it is of the utmost importance that we begin telling a richer and more complex story about the rise of AI weapons—a story that includes the causal contributions of decision makers at all levels. From there, we can see how Ethical AI would serve to enhance accountability. Take one example of Ethical AI, "smart guns" that remain locked unless held by an authorized user via biometric or token technologies to curtail accidental firings and cases of a gun stolen and used immediately to shoot people. Or a similar AI mechanism built into any military weapon, noting that even the most autonomous weapons have some degree of human interaction in their life cycle. These technologies might also record events, including the time and location of every shot fired, providing some accountability.

The point here is that the world has large stockpiles of weapons—bombs, mines, bullets, guns, grenades, mortars, and missiles—that have no inbuilt technical controls related to the conditions under which they are employed. This is perhaps a far more frightening reality of immediate humanitarian concern than any fictional scenario involving "killer robots" or out-of-control artificial intelligence. Munitions developed for use by militaries and the public generally possess no inbuilt safeguards that prevent them from being used by unauthorized persons. We must remember that military forces that cannot afford precision weapons are regularly legally justified in the defense of their state to kill enemy combatants with firearms, bombs, and other sometimes imprecise and indiscriminate weapons. Yet as military technology becomes increasingly capable of yielding more precise outcomes at lower cost and halting an enemy without causing unnecessary suffering or harm to those nearby, this is a situation that moral philosophers and international law might now reconsider, and we think this is best done through the lens of Ethical AI.

THE ETHICAL AI SPECTRUM

A weapon with Ethical AI takes an attack order as input and makes a decision *not to obey* the order if it assesses the presence of unexpected[11] *protected* object(s). What we mean by protected may include legally identified entities from ICRC marked objects, through to persons hors de combat and policy-identified entities specified in rules of engagement. We recognize that ends of this spectrum range from easy to very difficult technological challenges for AI.[12] What this does mean is that some progress toward Ethical AI can be made immediately, and we have proposed a technical model elsewhere. Clearly, any progress would constitute a humanitarian enhancement.

Lambert[13] termed weapon systems with these ethical improvements "Moral Weapons" and included this to mean "fully integrated human-machine decision making," the option of "allowing the machine to at times override the human," the ability to assess and *decline* targeting requests when rules of engagement violations are deduced, with the decisions to override these weapons logged for subsequent accountability review. We term these Ethical AI rather than Moral AI, to avoid any potential confusion with Moral Responsibility, that is, we do not mean to imply that such weapons possess *moral responsibility*.

We assert that AI in weapons is not likely to be banned regardless of campaign efforts, and we advocate that critics or those who generally reject the concept of autonomous weapons might consider this new concept to further reduce casualties over current weapons and address their central concern about humans losing control over decision-making in warfare.

Let us discern between two ends of a spectrum of ethical capability. A maximally just "ethical machine" (MaxAI) guided by both acceptable and nonacceptable actions has the benefit of ensuring that ethically obligatory lethal action is taken, even when system engineers of a lesser system may not have recognized the need or possibility of the relevant lethal action. However, a maximally just ethical robot requires extensive ethical engineering. Arkin's "ethical governor" represents probably the most advanced prototype effort toward a maximally just system.[14] The ethical governor provides assessment on proposed lethal actions consistent with the laws of war and rules of engagement. The maximally just position is apparent from the explanation of the operation of the

---

[11] One may argue that adversaries who know this might "game" the weapons by posing under the cover of "protection." If this is known, it is a case for (accountable) human override of the Ethical Weapon, and why we use the term "unexpected." Noting also that besides being an act of perfidy in the case of such use of protected symbols, which has other possible consequences for the perpetrators, it may in fact aid in targeting as these would be anomalies with respect to known Red Cross locations.

[12] Robert Sparrow, "Robots and Respect: Assessing the Case against Autonomous Weapon Systems," *Ethics & International Affairs* 30 (2016): 93–116.

[13] Dale Lambert, "Ubiquitous Command and Control," *Proceedings of the 1999 Information, Decision and Control Conference*, Adelaide, Australia (IEEE, 1999), 35–40.

[14] Ronald Arkin, *Governing Lethal Behavior in Autonomous Robots* (Boca Raton, FL: CRC Press, 2009).

constraint interpreter, which is a key part of the governor: "The constraint application process is responsible for reasoning about the active ethical constraints and ensuring that the resulting behavior of the robot is ethically permissible."[15] That is, the constraint system, based on complex deontic and predicate logic, evaluates the proposed actions generated by the tactical reasoning engine of the system based on an equally complex data structure. Reasoning about the full scope of what is *ethically permissible under all possible conditions* including general distinction of combatants from noncombatants, proportionality, unnecessary suffering, and rules of engagement, as Arkin describes, is a hard problem.

In contrast, a MinAI "ethical robot," while still a constraint driven system, could operate without an "ethical governor" proper and need only contain an elementary suppressor of human-generated lethal action. Further, as it would activate in accordance with a much narrower set of constraints it may be hard- rather than soft-coded, meaning far less system "interpretation" would be required. MinAI deals with what is *ethically impermissible*. Thus, we assert under *certain specific conditions*, distinction, proportionality, and protected conditions may be assessed, as follows:

- *Distinction of the ethically impermissible* including the avoidance of application of force against "protected" things such as objects and persons marked with the protected symbols of the Red Cross, as well as protected locations, recognizable protected behaviors such as the desire to parlay, basic signs of surrender (including beacons), and potentially those that are hors de combat or are clearly noncombatants; noting of course that AI solutions range here from easy to more difficult— but not impossible—and will continue to improve along with AI technologies.
- *Ethical reduction in proportionality* includes a reduction in the degree of force below the level lawfully authorized if it is determined to be sufficient to meet military necessity.

MinAI then is three things: (1) an ethical control to augment any conventional weapon; (2) a system limited to decision and action on logical negative cases of things that should *not* be attacked; and (3) practically achievable with state of the art AI techniques.

The basic technical concept for a MinAI Ethical Weapon is an augmentation to a standard weapon control system. The weapon seeker, which may be augmented with other sensors, provides input to an ethical and legal perception-action system. This system uses training data, developed, tested, and certified prior to the operation and outputs a decision state to override the target order and generate alternate orders on the control system in the event of a world state which satisfies MinAI conditions. The decision override is intended to divert the weapon to another target, or a preoperation-specified fail-safe location and/or to neutralize or reduce the payload effect accordingly.

[15] Ronald C. Arkin, Patrick Ulam, and Brittany Duncan, *An Ethical Governor for Constraining Lethal Action in an Autonomous System* (Fort Belvoir, VA: Defense Technical Information Center, 1 January 2009), https://doi.org/10.21236/ADA493563.

Noteworthy is that while MinAI will always be more limited in technical nature, it may be more morally desirable in that it will yield outcomes that are as good as or possibly even better than MaxAI in a range of specific circumstances. The former will never take active lethal or nonlethal action to harm protected persons or infrastructure. In contrast, MaxAI involves the codification of normative values into rule sets and the interpretation of a wide range of inputs through the application of complex and potentially imperfect machine logic. This more complex "algorithmic morality," while potentially desirable in some circumstances, involves a greater possibility of actively introducing fatal errors, particularly in terms of managing conflicts between interests.

Cognizant of the foregoing information, our suggestion is that in terms of meeting our fundamental moral obligations to humanity, we are ethically justified to develop MinAI systems. The ethical agency of said system, while embedded in the machine and thus technologically mediated by the design, engineering, and operational environment, is fewer steps removed from human moral agency than in a MaxAI system. We would suggest that MaxAI development is supererogatory in the sense that it may be morally beneficial in particular circumstances, but is not necessarily morally required, and may even be demonstrated to be unethical.

The Technical Feasibility of MinAI

To the distaste of some, it might be argued that the moral desirability of MinAI will decrease in the near future as the AI underpinning MaxAI becomes more robust and we move away from rule-based and basic neural network systems toward artificial general intelligence (AGI), and that resources should therefore be dedicated to the development of maximal "ethical robots." To be clear, there have been a number of algorithm success stories announced in recent years, across all the cognate disciplines. Much attention has been given to the ongoing development of algorithms as a basis for the success of AlphaGo[16] and Libratus.[17] These systems are competing against the best human Go and poker players and winning against those who have made acquiring deep knowledge of these games their life's work. The result of these preliminary successes has been a dramatic increase in media reporting on, and interest in, the potential opportunities and pitfalls associated with the development of AI, not all of which are accurate and some of which has negatively impacted public perception of AI, fueling the kind of dystopian visions advanced by the Campaign to Stop Killer Robots.

The speculation that superintelligence is on the foreseeable horizon, with AGI timelines in the realm of twenty to thirty years, reflects the success stories while omitting

---

[16] David Silver, Julian Schrittwieser, Karen Simonyan, Ioannis Antonoglou, Aga Huang, Arthur Guez, Thomas Hubert, Lucas Baker, Matthew Lai, Adrian Bolton, and Yutian Chen, "Mastering the Game of Go without Human Knowledge," *Nature* 550 (2017): 354–359.

[17] Noam Brown and Tuomas Sandholm, "Superhuman AI for Heads-Up No-Limit Poker: Libratus Beats Top Professionals," *Science* 359 (2018): 418–424.

discussion of recent failures in AI. Many of these undoubtedly go unreported for commercial and classification reasons, but Microsoft's Tay AI Bot, a machine learning chatbot that learns from interactions with digital users, is but one example.[18] After a short period of operation, Tay developed an "ego" or "character" that was strongly sexual and racialized, and ultimately had to be withdrawn from service. Facebook had similar problems with its AI message chatbots assuming undesirable characteristics,[19] and a number of autonomous road vehicles have now been involved in motor vehicle accidents where the relevant systems were incapable handling the scenario[20] and quality assurance practices failed to factor for such events.

There are also known and currently irresolvable problems with the complex neural networks on which the successes in AI have mostly been based. These bottom-up systems can learn well in tight domains and easily outperform humans in these scenarios based on data structures and their correlations, but they cannot match the top-down rationalizing power of human beings in more open domains such as road systems and conflict zones. Such systems are risky in these environments because they require strict compliance with laws and regulations, and it would be difficult to question, interpret, explain, supervise, and control them by virtue of the fact that deep learning systems cannot easily track their own "reasoning."[21]

Just as importantly, when more intuitive and therefore less explainable systems come into wide operation, it may not be so easy to revert to earlier stage systems as human operators become reliant on the system to make difficult decisions, with the danger that their own moral decision-making skills may have deteriorated over time.[22, 23] In the event of failure, total system collapse could occur with devastating consequences if such systems were committed to mission-critical operation required in armed conflict.

There are, moreover, issues associated with functional complexity and the practical computational limits imposed on mobile systems that need to be capable of independent operation in the event of a communications failure. The computers required for AGI-level systems may not be subject to miniaturization or simply may not be sufficiently powerful or cost-effective for the intended purpose, especially in a military context in

[18] Rafal Rzepka and Kenzi Araki, "The Importance of Contextual Knowledge in Artificial Moral Agents Development," *AAAI Spring Symposium Series*, North America (2018), https://www.aaai.org/ocs/index.php/SSS/SSS18/paper/view/17540/15376.

[19] Erin Griffith and Tom Simonite, "Facebook's Virtual Assistant M Is Dead. So Are Chatbots," *Wired* (January 8, 2018), https://www.wired.com/story/facebooks-virtual-assistant-m-is-dead-so-are-chatbots/.

[20] Francesca Favarò, Sky Eurich, and Nazanin Nader, "Autonomous Vehicles' Disengagements: Trends, Triggers, and Regulatory Limitations," *Accident Analysis & Prevention* 110 (2018): 136–148.

[21] Martin Ciupa, "Is AI in Jeopardy? The Need to Under Promise and Over Deliver—The Case for Really Useful Machine Learning," in *4th Int. Conf. on Computer Science and Information Technology*, ed. Dhinaharan Nagamalai et al. (AIRCC, 2017), 59–70.

[22] Jai Galliott, "The Limits of Robotic Solutions to Human Challenges in the Land Domain," *Defence Studies* 17 (2017): 327–345.

[23] Jai Galliott, "Defending Australia in the Digital Age: Toward Full Spectrum Defence," *Defence Studies* 16 (2016): 157–175.

which autonomous weapons are sometimes considered disposable platforms.[24] The hope for advocates of AGI is that computer-processing power and other system components will continue to become dramatically smaller, cheaper, and powerful, but there is no guarantee that Moore's law, which supports such expectations, will continue to reign true without extensive progress in the field of quantum computing.

MaxAI at this point in time, whether or not AGI should eventuate, appears a distant goal to deliver a potential result that is far from guaranteed. A MinAI system, on the other hand, seeks to ensure that the obvious and uncontroversial benefits of artificial intelligence are harnessed while the associated risks are kept under control by normal military targeting processes. Action needs to be taken now to intercept grandiose visions that may not eventuate and instead deliver a positive result with technology that already exists.

A CODE FOR MINAI

A positive result for MinAI will also require more fine-grained guidance on the system's implementation and application. In 2013 the Human Rights Council of the UN General Assembly made the recommendation that developers of lethal autonomous robots (LARs) of the kind enabled by AI "establish a code or codes of conduct, ethics and/or practice defining responsible behaviour with respect to LARs."[25]

As a starting point, one might look for similar codes in related fields. In July 2016, the German Federal Ministry of Transport and Digital Infrastructure (*Bundesministerium für Verkehr und digitale Infrastruktur*, BMVI) appointed an expert panel of scientists and legal experts to serve as a national ethics committee for autonomous vehicles.[26] A year later they made headlines when they issued "the world's first ethical guidelines for driverless cars."[27] Obviously, automobiles are not designed to be weapons, though their kinetic energy and ubiquity make them at least as deadly in practice, such that their automation raises a number of issues in terms of potential damage to life and property. Many of the normative questions that arise as a result, and the normative frameworks utilized to answer said questions, are similar. As such, it does not seem unreasonable to take the BMVI ethics code as a basis for the development of an analogous code for Ethical AI. This may be further justified after consideration of some of the relevant principles of the Law of Armed Conflict (LOAC):

[24] Ciupa, "AI in Jeopardy."

[25] Christoph Heyns, Report of the Special Rapporteur on Extrajudicial, Summary or Arbitrary Executions, A/HRC/23/47 (Geneva: United Nations General Assembly Human Rights Council, 2013).

[26] Christoph Leutge, "The German Ethics Code for Automated and Connected Driving," *Philosophy and Technology* 30 (2017): 547–558.

[27] David Tuffley, "At Last! The World's First Ethical Guidelines for Driverless Cars," *The Conversation* (September 3, 2017), https://theconversation.com/at-last-the-worlds-first-ethical-guidelines-for-driverless-cars-83227.

696   JASON SCHOLZ AND JAI GALLIOTT

Military necessity. For military operations, any use of weapons requires said use to produce military gains that are not otherwise prohibited by international humanitarian law.[28] The BMVI code does not address this issue, since the presumption is that automobiles have a right to be on the road for purposes of transport regardless of what or whom they are transporting, and thus needs to be augmented as part of LOAC.

Distinction. The ability to distinguish between the civilian population and combatants, and between civilian objects and military objectives, and accordingly direct operations only against military objectives.[29] In the case of Ethical Weapons, they might identify protected symbols, noncombatants, surrendering persons, and persons who are hors de combat in order accordingly as (and if) the AI technologies continue to advance. Distinction is not used in the German automobile ethics code, except in the priority for human persons over nonhuman persons (i.e., animals) in the case of an impending accident. This again, is included under LOAC.

Proportionality. In armed conflict, some noncivilian casualties may be justifiable in certain circumstances, as long as they are not excessive in relation to the anticipated military advantage. These are illustrated in the subject of automotive trolley problem studies and are included in the German ethics guidelines.[30] But how much of an obligation do military strategists have to avoid harm to civilian populations? Customary IHL provides further useful protections beyond merely justifying proportionality on the basis of the principle of double effect including: Rule 15 (precautions in attack), Rule 20 (advance warning), and Rule 24 (removal of civilians and civilian objects), which are applied in the following section to Ethical Weapons.

The German ethics code opens with general remarks and a mission statement. We have adapted this as follows.

ETHICAL MINAI MISSION

Important decisions will have to be made concerning the extent to which the use of Ethical AI in weapons is required. States have a record of failing to intervene with new weapons technologies, even when doing so would have been justified. The character of the justification to employ Ethical Weapons could be understood in three ways.

First, states with the capability and capacity to do so may be obliged to deploy Ethical Weapons and hence face blame should they decide otherwise. An argument for these capabilities potentially being obligatory is that ethical weapons improve humanitarian outcomes (reducing accidental deaths, etc.) without impact on military effectiveness

---

[28] International Committee of the Red Cross, *Declaration Renouncing the Use, in Time of War, of Explosive Projectiles under 400 Grammes Weight*, Saint Petersburg (1868).

[29] International Committee of the Red Cross, Geneva Conventions of 1949 and Additional Protocols, and Their Commentaries.

[30] Jean-Francois Bonnefon, Azim Shariff, and Iyad Rahwan, "The Social Dilemma of Autonomous Vehicles," *Science* 352 (2016): 1573–1576.

and are likely to utilize technologies that are low-cost due to their commercial scale, with further justification explained by Galliott.[31]

Second, the development and deployment of Ethical AI could be supererogatory in the sense that it would be good for a state to intervene with Ethical AI–enabled weapons in particular circumstances, but not ethically required.

Third, such action could be justified but neither obligatory nor supererogatory, such that the use of Ethical AI weapons would be ethically acceptable but likely to yield little benefit over the status quo. We suggest that in all cases where the use of Ethical AI weapons is justified, that is, in the pursuit of just causes, their use is either ethically obligatory or supererogatory, but much hinges on the conditions in which they are used and the way in which they are designed.

At a fundamental level, the deployment decision can be reduced to a few fundamental questions: How much dependence on technologically complex systems—based on artificial intelligence and machine learning—are we willing to accept in order to achieve, in return, more safety for noncombatants, more safety for our military, who, acting on behalf of our society, warrant protection, better compliance with laws of armed conflict, and improved operational efficiency to defeat ever improving adversary capabilities? What precautions are needed to ensure appropriate competency, authority, and responsibility? What technological development guidelines are required to ensure that we do not blur the contours of a human society that places trust in its military commanders and their freedom of action, physical and intellectual integrity, and entitlement to social respect at the heart of its legal regime?

In what follows, we propose fourteen principles to guide the development of the MinAI from concept to technical implementation, as adapted to a military context.

Ethical Guidelines

1. Purpose

The primary purpose of Ethical AI is to improve the safety of protected entities and noncombatants within the Law of Armed Conflict and rules of engagement. A secondary purpose is to increase freedom of maneuver for military commanders, thereby enabling further ethical benefits.

2. Positive Balance of Risks

The objective is to reduce the level of harm within the Laws of Armed Conflict with the ultimate goal of zero unintended noncombatant casualties. The fog of war means that

---

[31] Galliott, *Military Robots*, ch. 3.

noncombatant casualties will be a reality in twenty-first-century warfare, but to minimize these toward zero should be the ultimate aim, made possible only by increasing the intelligence of weapons, projectiles, and effectors of all kinds. The adoption of Ethical AI is justifiable if it promises to produce a diminution in harm to human and/or political capital in comparison to conventional weapons.

3. Avoidance of Ethical Dilemmas to the Extent Possible

Ethical AI should prevent noncombatant harm within the Laws of Armed Conflict wherever this is practically possible. Further, appropriate reduction in operator involvement might reduce risk of post-traumatic stress disorder. Based on the state of the art, the technology should be designed in such a way that critical situations do not arise in the first place. These include dilemma situations, in which Ethical AI and/or military commanders have to decide which of two "evils" to perform. In this context, the entire spectrum of technological options should be used and continuously evolved; for example, limiting the scope to certain controllable conditions in military environments, allowing the weapon to dynamically and cognitively choose a payload yield reduction below a maximum level authorized, making the payload inert, performing weapon avoidance maneuvers, producing signals or advance warnings for persons at risk, or deferring strike to alternate points of opportunity in time and space. The significant enhancement of noncombatant safety is the objective of development and regulation, starting with design and programming of the Ethical AI such that it tracks in a defensive and anticipatory manner, posing as little risk as possible to vulnerable noncombatants while still achieving its missions.

4. Armed Conflict Shall Be Managed by Mixed Initiative Agreements

A statutorily imposed obligation to use Ethical AI is ethically questionable if it entails submission of *all* military commanders to technological imperatives. That is, there should be a prohibition on degrading humans to *only* being subservient elements in an autonomous network. Dynamic and recorded mixed-initiative agreements between humans and machines shall subsume hierarchical human-only command arrangements for Ethical AI.

5. Primacy of Human Life

In situations that prove to be unavoidable, despite all technological precautions being taken, protection of humans enjoys priority in a balancing of interests compared with damage to animals or property.

6. Military Commanders Decide to Sacrifice Specific Lives

Ethical AI can execute targeting according to processes approved by military commanders in compliance with laws of armed conflict and rules of engagement.

7. Machines Minimize Innocent Casualties

In the event of situations where the death of innocent people is unavoidable, Ethical AI shall seek to minimize casualties among innocent people.

8. Military Commanders, Developers, and Defense Departments Are Accountable for Ethical Weapons

Military commanders throughout the network of command remain accountable for the use of Ethical AI. All Ethical AI systems will log the protocol exchange between Ethical AI and military personnel, as well as critical weapon status and knowledge, to provide accountability and postaction review from the perspectives of accountability of commanders, developers, and defense departments as a whole.

9. Security of Ethical Weapons

Ethical AI is justifiable only to the extent that conceivable attacks, in particular manipulation of the information technologies it relies upon or other innate system weaknesses, do not result in such harm as to undermine confidence in the military or in Ethical AI.

10. Awareness and Recording of Responsibility Transfers

It must be possible to clearly distinguish whether an Ethical AI system is being used, where accountability lies and that it comes with the option of overruling the system. The human-machine interface must be designed such that it is clearly regulated and apparent where authority, competency, and responsibility lies, especially the responsibility for control. The distribution of responsibilities (and thus of accountability), for instance with regard to the time and access arrangements, should be reliably recorded and stored. This applies especially to human-to-technology handover procedures.

11. Human On- and Off-the-Loop

The software and technology associated with Ethical AI must be designed such that the need for an abrupt handover of control to military commanders is minimized. To enable efficient, reliable, and secure human-machine communication and prevent overload, the systems should adapt to human communicative behavior where possible, rather than requiring humans to enhance their adaptive capabilities. Communication to the human will be appropriately abstracted and sufficiently timely where feasible, noting that human-in-the-loop will give way to human-on-the-loop, and human-off-the-loop relationships for periods of time.

12. Machine Self-Learning Considerations

Learning systems that are self-learning in training, operation, and their connection to scenario databases may be allowed if, and to the extent that, they generate safety gains. Self-learning systems must not be deployed unless they meet the safety requirements for Ethical AI and do not undermine these guidelines.

13. Fail Safe Management

In situations where protected marked objects, or unanticipated noncombatants are present, Ethical AI must autonomously (i.e., without direct human intervention) enter into a "safe condition." Identification of what constitutes safe conditions for weapon disposal and recovery, planning, and handover routines is required prior to Ethical AI use. This may include means under control of the machine to: place the weapon in a location that has minimal human impact; neutralize explosives in the weapon, for example, by use of separated chemical components in warhead design which are diffused to prevent future ignition or exploitation; and reduce weapon kinetic energy and damage.

14. Military Education and Training

The proper use of Ethical AI should form part of military commanders' general education. The proper handling of Ethical AI should be taught in an appropriate manner during training, and teams of commanders and Ethical AI tested for capability certification.

POTENTIAL CONSEQUENCES OF MINAI

Concerns may be raised that should MinAI functionality be adopted for use by military forces, the technology may result in negative or positive unintended long-term consequences. If so, what might these be? Conscious of how notoriously difficult it is to predict technology use, this is not an easy question to answer, but we will consider some important cases for further study.

Complacency and Responsibility Transfer

One possible negative affect is related to human complacency. Consider the hypothesis "if MinAI technology works well and is trusted, its operators will become complacent in regard to its use and take less care in the targeting process, leading to more deaths."

In response, such an argument would apply equally to all uses of technology in the targeting process. Clearly however, technology is a critical enabler of intelligence and targeting functions. Complacency then seems to be a matter of adequate discipline, appropriate education, training, and system design.[32]

A less desirable outcome would be for operators to abdicate their responsibilities for targeting. Campaigners have attempted to argue the creation of a "responsibility gap" in autonomous weapons before; might this resurface with the application of a MinAI system? Consider the hypothesis that "if MinAI technology works well and is trusted, that Commanders might just as well authorize weapon release with the highest possible explosive payload to account for the worst case and rely on MinAI to reduce the yield according to whatever situation the system finds to be the case, leading to more deaths."

In response to this argument, we assert that this would be like treating MinAI weapon system as if it were a MaxAI weapon system. We do not advocate MaxAI weapons. A MinAI weapon that can reduce its explosive payload under AI control is not a substitute for target analysis; it is a last line of defense against unintended harm. Further the commander would remain responsible for the result, regardless, under any lawful scheme. Any weapon can be misused. A machine gun can he used by a soldier in combat or deployed by a civilian in a school shooting. Discipline, education, and training remain critical to the responsible use of weapons.

Denying Availability of Surrender Technology to Combatants

If the machine-recognizable surrender system were to be developed, would militaries not want to issue beacons to their soldiers because they fear mass surrender? This could prove to be of positive military and/or moral benefit when viewed objectively. It could be mandated that beacons be offered to all soldiers. Stigma or culture associated with use or underuse would, of course, present some degree of concern.

CONCLUSION

We have presented a case for autonomy in weapons that could make life-saving decisions in the world today. Minimally Just Ethical AI in weapons should achieve a reduction in accidental strikes on protected persons and objects, reduce unintended strikes

---

[32] Galliott, "The Limits of Robotic Solutions."

against noncombatants, reduce collateral damage by reducing payload delivery, and save lives of those who have surrendered.

We hope in future that the significant resources spent on reacting to speculative fears of campaigners might one day be spent mitigating the definitive suffering of people caused by weapons which lack minimally just autonomy based on artificial intelligence.

BIBLIOGRAPHY

Arkin, Ronald. *Governing Lethal Behavior in Autonomous Robots*. Boca Raton, FL: CRC Press, 2009.

Awad, Edmond, Sohan Dsouza, Richard Kim, Jonathon Schulz, Joseph Henrich, Azim Shariff, Jean-François Bonnefon, and Iyad Rahwan. "The Moral Machine Experiment." *Nature* 563 (2018): 59–64.

Galliott, Jai. *Military Robots: Mapping the Moral Landscape*. Farnham, UK: Ashgate, 2015.

Galliott, Jai. "Defending Australia in the Digital Age: Toward Full Spectrum Defence." *Defence Studies* 16 (2016): 157–175.

Galliott, Jai. "The Limits of Robotic Solutions to Human Challenges in the Land Domain." *Defence Studies* 17 (2017): 327–345.

Leben, Derek. *Ethics for Robots: How to Design a Moral Algorithm*. New York: Routledge, 2018.

Lin, Patrick, Keith Abney, and Ryan Jenkins, eds. *Robot Ethics 2.0: From Autonomous Cars to Artificial Intelligence*. New York: Oxford University Press, 2017.

Lin, Patrick, George Bekey, and Keith Abney. *Autonomous Military Robotics: Risk, Ethics, and Design*. Washington, DC: United States Department of the Navy, 2008.

Scholz, Jason and Jai Galliott. "Artificial Intelligence in Weapons: The Moral Imperative for Minimally-Just Autonomy." *US Air Force Journal of Indo-Pacific Affairs* 1 (2018): 57–67.

Sparrow, Robert. "Building a Better WarBot: Ethical Issues in the Design of Unmanned Systems for Military Application." *Science and Engineering Ethics* 15 (2009): 169–187.

CHAPTER 37

THE ETHICS OF AI IN BIOMEDICAL RESEARCH, PATIENT CARE, AND PUBLIC HEALTH

ALESSANDRO BLASIMME
AND EFFY VAYENA

INTRODUCTION

In March 2019 the World Health Organization announced amid a number of key reforms, the establishment of a new department of Digital Health with the aim to harness "the power of digital health and innovation by supporting countries to assess, integrate, regulate and maximize the opportunities of digital technologies and artificial intelligence."[1] This commitment at the global level is in the same vein with several national plans announced over the last couple of years[2] as governments began to grabble with AI in health. Numerous examples of AI-enabled digital health applications are available today, some have received market authorization, and if the private investment in digital health is anything to go by, the pipeline of future digital health products is going to be full. Certainly, the so-called big data revolution has been instrumental to this development.

In this chapter we discuss ethical challenges linked to the use of AI in biomedical research, patient care, and public health. We then draw on a systemic oversight model

[1] See https://www.who.int/news-room/detail/06-03-2019-who-unveils-sweeping-reforms-in-drive-towards-triple-billion-targets (accessed April 4, 2019).

[2] Lynne E. Parker, "Creation of the National Artificial Intelligence Research and Development Strategic Plan," *AI Magazine* 39, no. 2 (2018); Corinne Cath et al., "Artificial Intelligence and the 'Good Society': The US, EU, and UK Approach," *Science and Engineering Ethics* 24, no. 2 (2018): 505–528; Sophie-Charlotte Fischer, "Artificial Intelligence: China's High-Tech Ambitions," *CSS Analyses in Security Policy* 220 (2018).

for the governance of AI innovation in the health sector[3] and discuss possible ways to address emerging ethical challenges in this rapidly evolving domain. Our aim is to lay the groundwork for an ethically responsible development of AI in the domains of health research, clinical practice, and public health.

AI IN BIOMEDICAL RESEARCH

In the last decade, biomedical research has become a data-centric activity[4] enabled by novel material and experimental practices linked to data collection, distribution, and use.

In the burgeoning field of precision medicine,[5] for instance, "omic" data are now routinely being collected alongside clinical data, phenotypic data, and life-style and socioeconomic data to form bigger-than-ever research cohorts. Artificial intelligence is predicted to enable the simultaneous computation of such diverse arrays of data, thus contributing to the promise of precision medicine to bring about more targeted approaches to diagnosis and treatment of individual patients.[6] As far as translational medicine is concerned, artificial intelligence is being employed in drug discovery to screen libraries of potentially therapeutic molecules, to automate searches in the biomedical literature through natural language processing techniques, to predict experimental dosage, and so on.[7]

Machine learning is also deployed to generate predictive models that could help doctors in prognostic assessment and in personalizing therapy and rehabilitation for individual patients, for instance in the aftermath of a stroke.[8]

---

[3] Effy Vayena and Alessandro Blasimme, "Health Research with Big Data: Time for Systemic Oversight," *Journal of Law, Medicine & Ethics* 46, no. 1 (2018): 119–129; Alessandro Blasimme and Effy Vayena, "Towards Systemic Oversight in Digital Health: Implementation of the AFIRRM Principles," in *Cambridge Handbook of Health Research Regulation*, ed. Graeme Laurie (Cambridge University Press, forthcoming).

[4] Sabina Leonelli, *Data-Centric Biology: A Philosophical Study* (University of Chicago Press, 2016).

[5] Francis S. Collins and Harold Varmus, "A New Initiative on Precision Medicine," *New England Journal of Medicine* 372, no. 9 (February 26, 2015): 793–795; Alessandro Blasimme and Effy Vayena, "Becoming Partners, Retaining Autonomy: Ethical Considerations on the Development of Precision Medicine," *BMC Medical Ethics* 17 (2016): 67; Alessandro Blasimme and Effy Vayena, " 'Tailored-to-You': Public Engagement and the Political Legitimation of Precision Medicine," *Perspectives in Biology and Medicine* 59, no. 2 (2017): 172–188.

[6] Bertalan Mesko, "The Role of Artificial Intelligence in Precision Medicine," *Expert Review of Precision Medicine and Drug Development* 2, no. 5 (2017): 239–241; Jia Xu et al., "Translating Cancer Genomics into Precision Medicine with Artificial Intelligence: Applications, Challenges and Future Perspectives," *Human Genetics* 138, no. 2 (February 1, 2019): 109–124.

[7] Eric J. Topol, "High-Performance Medicine: The Convergence of Human and Artificial Intelligence," *Nature Medicine* 25, no. 1 (2019): 51.

[8] See https://precise4q.eu (accessed April 4, 2019).

Electronic health records (EHR) offer the opportunity to use real-world data to generate knowledge about the outcomes of a given medical procedure (be it a diagnosis, a prognosis, a therapy, or a rehabilitation plan).[9] AI can be employed to mine EHR to discover disease familiarity or people at risk for a given chronic disease and also to improve the organization of health systems by providing support in triage and patient management.[10] In a recent study, deep learning was employed to create predictive modeling with EHR to accurately gauge in-hospital mortality, readmission odds, length of stay, and final discharge diagnoses.[11] In another study, a machine learning algorithm identified cancer patients at high risk of thirty-day mortality before they start chemotherapy (both palliative and curative).[12] Such an algorithm can help decisions about chemotherapy initiation, enabling more rational allocation of resources.

Facial recognition technologies based on machine learning are also being developed to streamline patient identification, to detect genetic disorders that correspond to specific facial traits[13] or to diagnose mood disorders such as depression.[14] Recently, researchers validated a system that, based on human-computer interaction patterns using data from a smartphone app, is able to recognize what the authors of the study call digital biomarkers of cognitive function.[15] Lately, there is increasing interest in voice analysis algorithms for health-related purposes with research concentrating on mental health.[16]

The main concern raised by AI in the previously described context is the quality and representativeness of data used to train machine learning algorithms. In the existing medical data sets, adult males of Caucasian origin are strongly overrepresented.[17] This lack of diversity is likely to result in biased algorithms trained on biased data. Similarly, EHR data used to train algorithms may suffer from issues such as missing data and

---

[9] Institute of Medicine, *The Learning Healthcare System: Workshop Summary (IOM Roundtable on Evidence-Based Medicine)*, 2007, https://www.nap.edu/catalog/11903/the-learning-healthcare-system-workshop-summary-iom-roundtable-on-evidence.

[10] Pavel Hamet and Johanne Tremblay, "Artificial Intelligence in Medicine," *Metabolism* 69 (2017): S36–40.

[11] Alvin Rajkomar et al., "Scalable and Accurate Deep Learning with Electronic Health Records," *NPJ Digital Medicine* 1, no. 1 (2018): 18.

[12] Aymen A. Elfiky et al., "Development and Application of a Machine Learning Approach to Assess Short-Term Mortality Risk among Patients with Cancer Starting Chemotherapy," *JAMA Network Open* 1, no. 3 (2018): e180926–e180926.

[13] Yaron Gurovich et al., "Identifying Facial Phenotypes of Genetic Disorders Using Deep Learning," *Nature Medicine* 25, no. 1 (2019): 60.

[14] Yu Zhu et al., "Automated Depression Diagnosis Based on Deep Networks to Encode Facial Appearance and Dynamics," *IEEE Transactions on Affective Computing* 9, no. 4 (2018): 578–584; Albert Haque et al., "Measuring Depression Symptom Severity from Spoken Language and 3D Facial Expressions," ArXiv Preprint ArXiv:1811.08592 (2018).

[15] Paul Dagum, "Digital Biomarkers of Cognitive Function," *NPJ Digital Medicine* 1, no. 1 (2018): 10.

[16] Nicholas Cummins, Alice Baird, and Björn W. Schuller, "Speech Analysis for Health: Current State-of-the-Art and the Increasing Impact of Deep Learning," *Health Informatics and Translational Data Analytics* 151 (December 1, 2018): 41–54.

[17] Latrice G. Landry et al., "Lack of Diversity in Genomic Databases Is a Barrier to Translating Precision Medicine Research into Practice," *Health Affairs* 37, no. 5 (2018): 780–785.

misclassification.[18] For example, people of lower socioeconomic levels may be less represented in certain diagnostic categories, or may be overrepresented in categories of emergency care. Such patients may be more concentrated to an institution than to others making research results of potential medical relevance more meaningful to overrepresented populations than minorities or socially emarginated groups.

Another concern relates to the sufficiency of informed consent as an ethical safeguard in research involving algorithmic processing. The traditional concept of informed consent is already challenged in cases of data collected in more conventional research settings, as it is increasingly hard to predict who will be accessing the data in the future, for which purposes, and under which conditions.[19] The reuse of data and the linkage of disparate data sets makes even the notion of broad consent—a typical safeguard of autonomy when future uses of human data and samples are hard to anticipate—weak. In the case of AI, it is still not clear whether research participants shall be specifically informed about the intention to use AI algorithms and whether informed consent for automated processing of personal data should reflect a heightened level of protection and, for instance, offer the possibility to opt out.

The creation of large cohorts of deeply phenotyped participants raises doubts about the huge amounts of information that such initiatives put in the hands of governments or private organizations. The latter include healthcare organizations, big tech, and companies active in the field of smart technologies that stipulate agreements with national governments to collect and analyze data from millions of citizens. As a consequence, issues of data privacy and security loom large on the horizon of biomedical big data research.[20]

AI adds a layer of ethical complexity to this scenario in that it uses data to extract additional, fine-grained information about individuals. It is an ethical responsibility of researchers to securely protect this information from unauthorized access in order to avoid privacy-related harms to data subjects in the course of research projects. The unwanted leak of health-relevant information can lead to discriminative uses of such information in domains such as employment, education, and insurance. This problem applies both to information generated and stored by researchers and to information that researchers feed back to research participants as primary, secondary, or incidental findings. Return of research results enjoys widespread support as a way to show respect for the interests and the welfare of research participants.[21] In particular, precision medicine initiatives, such as the U.S. All of Us Research Program, endorse a model of empowerment

---

[18] Milena A. Gianfrancesco et al., "Potential Biases in Machine Learning Algorithms Using Electronic Health Record Data," *JAMA Internal Medicine* 178, no. 11 (2018): 1544–1547.

[19] Effy Vayena and Alessandro Blasimme, "Biomedical Big Data: New Models of Control over Access, Use and Governance," *Journal of Bioethical Inquiry* 14, no. 4 (2017).

[20] Omer Tene and Jules Polonetsky, "Privacy in the Age of Big Data: A Time for Big Decisions," *Stanford Law Review Online* 64 (2011): 63.

[21] Susan M. Wolf, "Return of Individual Research Results and Incidental Findings: Facing the Challenges of Translational Science," *Annual Review of Genomics and Human Genetics* 14, no. 1 (2013): 557–577, https://doi.org/10.1146/annurev-genom-091212-153506.

that is premised on the release of medically relevant information to research participants. This model, while laudable, can have consequences, for instance, for those research data subjects who intend to buy a life insurance policy.[22]

The criteria that are being employed in the evaluation of research involving human data and human subjects (including clinical trials) have been developed in the postwar period and formalized in most countries since the late 1970s. Such criteria—for example, social or scientific value, scientific validity, fair selection of participants, acceptable risk-benefit ratio, informed consent, and consideration for participants' welfare and rights[23]—while being still valid at a formal level, do not adequately capture the specificities of research involving the use of AI to analyze vast amounts of personal data.[24] Consider the case of a recent study that utilizing deep neural networks analyzed the association of facial traits and self-declared sexual orientation in order to understand whether homosexuals have distinct facial characteristics.[25] Besides the technical validity of this study, its aim is highly dubitable from an ethical point of view because it lends support to stereotyped views about homosexuality—namely, the idea that male homosexuals are effeminate and that female homosexuals are manly. Moreover, while it is hard to imagine any socially beneficial use of such a study, it can be expected that stigmatization and discrimination would likely result from either intentional or unintentional misuses of its results. This study exemplifies how AI can power new forms of classification based on the association between biological, personal, behavioral, and social characteristics. The unprecedented classificatory power of AI can obviously produce both tangible and intangible harms.[26] Notably, this particular study was reviewed by an institutional review board, passed peer-review, and was eventually published. The heated controversy that followed its publication brought to light the difficulty in assessing societal-wide effects when reviewing research, as well as the lack of agreed-upon criteria on how to do such an assessment.

Another issue of ethical relevance in the context of health research has emerged from collaborations between corporations with advanced capabilities in AI and healthcare institutions in control of health data sets. While such collaborations can be mutually beneficial, several examples to date have raised more concern than enthusiasm. The case of Deep Mind accessing 1.6 million health records from the Royal Free London NHS in order to test a kidney safety app, ended with the Information Commissioner finding a number of shortcomings in the contractual agreements. The Italian government's

[22] Alessandro Blasimme, Effy Vayena, and Ine Van Hoyweghen, "Big Data, Precision Medicine and Private Insurance: A Delicate Balancing Act," *Big Data & Society* 6, no. 1 (2019): 2053951719830111.

[23] David Wendler and Ezekiel J. Emanuel, "What Makes Clinical Research Ethical?," *JAMA* 283, no. 20 (May 2000): 2701–2711.

[24] Marcello Ienca et al., "Considerations for Ethics Review of Big Data Health Research: A Scoping Review," *PLOS ONE* 13, no. 10 (2018): e0204937.

[25] Yilun Wang and Michal Kosinski, "Deep Neural Networks Are More Accurate than Humans at Detecting Sexual Orientation from Facial Images," *Journal of Personality and Social Psychology* 114, no. 2 (2018): 246.

[26] Vanessa K. Ing, "Spokeo, Inc. v. Robins: Determining What Makes an Intangible Harm Concrete," *Berkeley Technology Law Journal* 32 (2017): 503.

decision to grant an IBM research unit access to citizens' health records has been questioned by both data protection and fair competition officials.[27] Beyond the question of whether such data are used with adequate consent, or whether social benefit will be accrued from their use, the further question is how such benefit will be distributed. If for-profit entities have exclusive deals with national health data organization, how will this affect access and distribution of subsequent AI products? We are still in the early days of understanding the implications of such arrangements and of articulating fair agreements despite the fact that there is a litany of cases that seem to raise the questions.

AI IN PATIENT CARE

AI-driven diagnosis is certainly one of the most promising fields of application for AI in patient care. AI has largely demonstrated its ability to interpret various types of medical images, such as X-ray scans, magnetic resonance, and also photographic images of body parts (such as skin or eye fundus) and digitalized pathology slides. Image interpretation and visual pattern recognition are therefore among the major drivers in this space. An obviously limited list of examples includes the use of deep learning techniques to train algorithms to detect wrist fractures in X-ray scans;[28] to help cardiologists interpret magnetic resonance images;[29] and a machine learning software that detects diabetic retinopathy by automatically interpreting images from the back of the patient's eye.[30] These three applications received clearance for marketing from the U.S. Food and Drug Administration (FDA). Many more have appeared in the literature, including algorithms that can compute cardiovascular risk factors based on retinal images.[31] In all those studies, the performance of the algorithms was tested against the benchmark of certified specialists' assessments, revealing equal or superior outcomes for AI system as compared to human physicians. This criterion is widely used in research settings, but it is not yet established as a sufficient one for AI applications in clinical care. The issue of evidence standards has obvious implications in terms of safety and efficacy. As a consequence, a major issue with clear ethical implications is the reliability of the evidence in favor of AI clinical applications.

[27] See https://www.repubblica.it/economia/2017/12/05/news/dati_sanitari_alle_multinazionali_senza_consenso_passa_la_norma-183005262/ (accessed April 4, 2019). At the time of writing, the initiative is on hold.

[28] Food and Drug Administration, "FDA Permits Marketing of Artificial Intelligence Algorithm for Aiding Providers in Detecting Wrist Fractures," available at https://www.fda.gov/NewsEvents/Newsroom/PressAnnouncements/ucm608833.htm (accessed April 4, 2019).

[29] Bernard Marr, "First FDA Approval for Clinical Cloud-Based Deep Learning in Healthcare," *Forbes* (January 20, 2017), available at https://www.forbes.com/sites/bernardmarr/2017/01/20/first-fda-approval-for-clinical-cloud-based-deep-learning-in-healthcare/#6af6ceef161c.

[30] See https://www.fda.gov/NewsEvents/Newsroom/PressAnnouncements/ucm604357 (accessed April 4, 2019).

[31] Ryan Poplin et al., "Prediction of Cardiovascular Risk Factors from Retinal Fundus Photographs via Deep Learning," *Nature Biomedical Engineering* 2, no. 3 (2018): 158.

Some AI-driven diagnostic applications can also be operated directly by the patient on portable devices outside the clinical setting. One can imagine, for example, that smartphone apps could incorporate already existing AI-powered algorithms to inspect nevi and detect the presence of skin cancer.[32] Similarly, the first smart pill was approved by the FDA in 2017 and included an ingestible sensor that sends a signal to the patient's device once the pill is taken in order to help him or her adhere to a prescription.[33] Commentators have highlighted that, from a patient perspective, ethical issues for this type of devices include concerns for autonomy, privacy, and dependability in case of technical failures.[34]

Ethical issues in the use of AI for patient care depend on specific uses and applications. It is intuitively plausible to think that ethical stakes correlate with the severity of the condition at hand or with the degree of reliance on AI for serious medical tasks such as diagnosis or treatment. It would be wrong, however, to assume that automation in health system services is less likely to have ethically relevant implications. Consider the case of triage. AI-driven decisions such as which patient is treated first or which one is offered chemotherapy[35] should certainly follow cost-effectiveness considerations. But exclusive reliance on algorithms may rule out that necessary degree of flexibility that allows healthcare operators to calibrate objective criteria with the reality of each individual case.[36] For instance, a system that factors the risk of longer stays into decisions about hospital admission may discriminate against the most vulnerable patients, that is, arguably, those who are more in need of care. While it is premature to say that these unfair outcomes will be the case, such ethically relevant aspects of automating clinical workflow deserve careful scrutiny.

As to the use of AI for diagnostic purposes, the already mentioned problem of a biased training data set that lead to suboptimal performance for underrepresented social groups creates an ethical bottleneck. In the current ethical debate about AI in medicine, the issue of whether and why the use of AI should be disclosed to patients during informed consent procedures is still in its infancy. However, a bigger discussion is ongoing as to whether black-box algorithms—that is, algorithms whose self-learned rules are too complex to reconstruct and explain—should be used in medicine.[37] Some have called for a duty to transparency in order to dispel the opacity of black-box algorithms.[38] Others, however, have highlighted that more limited requirements are

[32] Andre Esteva et al., "Dermatologist-Level Classification of Skin Cancer with Deep Neural Networks," *Nature* 542, no. 7639 (2017): 115.

[33] https://www.fda.gov/newsevents/newsroom/pressannouncements/ucm584933.htm.

[34] Craig M. Klugman et al., "The Ethics of Smart Pills and Self-Acting Devices: Autonomy, Truth-Telling, and Trust at the Dawn of Digital Medicine," *American Journal of Bioethics* 18, no. 9 (2018): 38–47.

[35] Rajkomar, "Scalable and Accurate Deep Learning"; Elfiky, "Development and Application of a Machine Learning Approach."

[36] Effy Vayena, Alessandro Blasimme, and I. Glenn Cohen, "Machine Learning in Medicine: Addressing Ethical Challenges," *PLOS Medicine* 15, no. 11 (2018): e1002689.

[37] W. Nicholson II Price, "Black-Box Medicine," *Harvard Journal of Law & Technology* 28 (2015): 419.

[38] Sandra Wachter, Brent Mittelstadt, and Luciano Floridi, "Why a Right to Explanation of Automated Decision-Making Does Not Exist in the General Data Protection Regulation," *International Data Privacy Law* 7, no. 2 (2017): 76–99.

sufficient to adequately protect the morally relevant interests of patients when machine learning algorithms are employed to provide care.[39]

An important issue concerns the shift of medical authority from human physicians to algorithms—the problem of the so-called "collective medical mind."[40] The risk here is that AI systems introduced as decision support tools become central nodes of medical decision-making. In this scenario, it is uncertain how the established principles of medical ethics (beneficence, nonmaleficence, respect for patients) can still be expected to play the central role in the patient-doctor relationship that they have—or at least can be expected to have—now. The mediation of AI-powered tools can fundamentally alter the doctor-patient relationship. AI, especially as it enables remote care or communication via robotic assistants, may create interpersonal distance between patients and their physicians. An incentive to use such tools could be the need to streamline patient care, but the downside of this phenomenon is that the patient becomes more isolated, with potentially negative repercussions on health outcomes. The same considerations can be made about AI-based home-assistance platforms. In principle, these systems can be extremely useful to, for instance, provie better care to elderly people with limited mobility. However, they can also increase their social isolation.

The easiness with which an AI system can keep track of a person's health and perform accurate diagnostic has been discussed as a potential source of overdiagnosis and nonactionable diagnoses. For instance, employing deep learning to infer cardiovascular risk factors from retinal fundus pictures[41] is warranted by the fact that it could lead to life-style adaptations that may actually improve a patients' condition. But the use of images of retinal structures as biomarkers of dementia[42] are more problematic in the absence of concluding evidence regarding the efficacy of interventions to delay or slow down dementia.[43]

Finally, the use of algorithms for mood detection promises to revolutionize mental health.[44] However, privacy issues acquire particular ethical relevance in this context. Tools like DeepMood, which allow the detection of mood based on mobile phone typing

[39] Andrew D. Selbst and Julia Powles, "Meaningful Information and the Right to Explanation," *International Data Privacy Law* 7, no. 4 (2017): 233–242; Agata Ferretti, Manuel Schneider, and Alessandro Blasimme, "Machine Learning in Medicine: Opening the New Data Protection Black Box," *European Data Protection Law Review* 4, no. 3 (2018): 320–332.

[40] Danton S. Char, Nigam H. Shah, and David Magnus, "Implementing Machine Learning in Health Care—Addressing Ethical Challenges," *New England Journal of Medicine* 378, no. 11 (March 15, 2018): 981–983, https://doi.org/10.1056/NEJMp1714229.

[41] Poplin et al., "Prediction of Cardiovascular Risk Factors from Retinal Fundus Photographs via Deep Learning."

[42] Unal Mutlu et al., "Association of Retinal Neurodegeneration on Optical Coherence Tomography with Dementia: A Population-Based Study," *JAMA Neurology* 75, no. 10 (2018): 1256–1263.

[43] Engineering National Academies of Sciences and Medicine, *Preventing Cognitive Decline and Dementia: A Way Forward* (National Academies Press, 2017).

[44] David C. Mohr, Heleen Riper, and Stephen M. Schueller, "A Solution-Focused Research Approach to Achieve an Implementable Revolution in Digital Mental Health," *JAMA Psychiatry* 75, no. 2 (2018): 113–114.

dynamics, are certainly promising.[45] Yet pervasive tracking of one's emotional state is at least intrusive and may affect the legitimate interest of any individual to keep control over information about his or her mood. Mood and mental health can now be digitally tracked through sensors that capture anything from breathing patterns, to galvanic skin response, from the tone of our voice, to sleep patterns, facial expressions, our where-abouts, and social media traces.[46] The possibility of being constantly monitorable as to our emotional states and mental health is certainly problematic from an ethical view-point as it sets the conditions for a form of granular psychological surveillance that is at odds with the values of pluralistic liberal societies. Even if these tools are employed in the context of a therapeutic relationship, their excessive use undermines a patient's capacity to remain autonomous and to maintain a sense of self-determination vis-à-vis his or her doctor.

AI IN PUBLIC HEALTH

Uses of algorithms in public health research and practice can have significant impact on population health.[47] Health is affected by several social parameters (e.g., income, educa-tion, dietary habits, environmental factors, community context) that are not confined in the healthcare systems. Understanding specific effects and interactions between health and various social conditions can lead to the development of more effective and efficient public health programs. Examples from AI-enabled multilevel modeling using socio-markers have already demonstrated such potential.[48] A particular area of AI application in public health is disease surveillance. Surveillance systems monitor disease incidence, outbreaks, and health behaviors. Typically these systems are state-funded and state-operated. Their purpose is to monitor the health of populations and subsequently to support decision-making for allocation of resources and types of interventions neces-sary to improve health. As a data-driven activity, surveillance can benefit substantially from algorithmic uses. Algorithms can sort through variables that are relevant for spe-cific health outcomes, they can recognize patterns and signals at a much faster pace, and they can be used to forecast epidemics and to model their trajectories. Such algorithms have been used to mine not only standard health data collected for surveillance by state institutions but also real-world data through social media. This seemingly unconventional

[45] Bokai Cao et al., "DeepMood: Modeling Mobile Phone Typing Dynamics for Mood Detection" (Proceedings of the 23rd ACM SIGKDD International Conference on Knowledge Discovery and Data Mining, ACM, 2017), 747–755.

[46] Paddy M. Barrett et al., "Digitising the Mind," *The Lancet* 389, no. 10082 (2017): 1877.

[47] Arash Shaban-Nejad, Martin Michalowski, and David L. Buckeridge, "Health Intelligence: How Artificial Intelligence Transforms Population and Personalized Health," *NPJ Digital Medicine* 1, no. 1 (October 2, 2018): 53.

[48] Eun Kyong Shin et al., "Sociomarkers and Biomarkers: Predictive Modeling in Identifying Pediatric Asthma Patients at Risk of Hospital Revisits," *NPJ Digital Medicine* 1, no. 1 (October 2, 2018): 50.

approach suffered an early blow when Google Flu Trend algorithms failed to show their promised predictive power.[49] Since then, however, AI-enabled analysis of social media data has produced several successful examples, including better prediction of epidemics[50] and detection of food poisoning cases.[51] The broader field of digital epidemiology is a rapidly evolving field focused on epidemiological models based on content posted online by social network users.[52] Forms of AI like natural language processing obviously play a crucial role for the further development of this field. Ethical challenges in this domain revolve mainly around consent. Many commentators have stressed that the terms of use for social media fall short of complying with the rigorous requirements for informed consent in the domain of health-related research.[53]

AI combined with mobile health applications also offers a new avenue for delivering public health intervention to populations. Of relevance here are expectations for health promotion to reach populations that are marginalized by targeting them with tailored interventions.[54] An area of contest in public health ethics has been the ethical legitimacy of nudging personal behavior for health-related purposes. AI will make this issue even more significant. Continuous surveillance, tailored nudging, and paternalistic interventions can generate an Orwellian form of individual control and constrained personal freedoms.[55] States and corporations with access to tools that can monitor and alter health-related behaviors can exercise significant power over large numbers of people to further their specific interests. While in a democratic and accountable state such policies can be vetted, be transparent, and revised as necessary, that is not necessarily the case everywhere nor is it the case when such behavioral manipulation occurs in arenas that are controlled entirely by institutions without public accountability.

There is significant enthusiasm for the use of AI in global health with funding agencies and international organizations investing already in public health activities in low- and middle-income countries. The World Health Organization has recently committed to promote AI to achieve universal health coverage, and many governments have been interested in taking stock of digital technologies to improve healthcare systems as they stated in a 2018 resolution on digital health that was adopted by the 71st World Health

[49] Declan Butler, "When Google Got Flu Wrong," *Nature News* 494, no. 7436 (2013): 155.

[50] Mohammed Ali Al-Garadi et al., "Using Online Social Networks to Track a Pandemic: A Systematic Review," *Journal of Biomedical Informatics* 62 (August 1, 2016): 1–11.

[51] Jenine K. Harris et al., "Using Twitter to Identify and Respond to Food Poisoning: The Food Safety STL Project," *Journal of Public Health Management and Practice: JPHMP* 23, no. 6 (December 2017): 577–580.

[52] Marcel Salathé et al., "Digital Epidemiology," *PLOS Computational Biology* 8, no. 7 (2012): e1002616, https://doi.org/10.1371/journal.pcbi.1002616; Antoine Flahault et al., "Precision Global Health in the Digital Age," *Swiss Medical Weekly* 147 (April 19, 2017): w14423, https://doi.org/smw.2017.14423.

[53] Jeffrey P. Kahn, Effy Vayena, and Anna C. Mastroianni, "Opinion: Learning as We Go: Lessons from the Publication of Facebook's Social-Computing Research," *Proceedings of the National Academy of Sciences* 111, no. 38 (September 23, 2014): 13677–13679.

[54] Brian Wahl et al., "Artificial Intelligence (AI) and Global Health: How Can AI Contribute to Health in Resource-Poor Settings?," *BMJ Global Health* 3, no. 4 (2018): e000798.

[55] Sarah Nettleton and Robin Bunton, "Sociological Critiques of Health Promotion," in *The Sociology of Health Promotion*, ed. Sarah Nettleton, Robin Bunton, and Roger Burrows (Routledge, 1995) 41–58.

Assembly.[56] This commitment increases the likelihood of AI entering rapidly the domain of health, adding urgency to the need of identifying and addressing the ethical tensions that AI generates.[57] The most pertinent are those related to the potential exacerbation of health disparities through biases that are perpetuated or reinforced by AI-enabled interventions. We discussed the problem of misrepresentation of certain populations in health-related data sets above. Several methods are currently under development to compensate for bias, but at the time the problem remains and requires attention.[58] Underserved populations present certain negative health outcomes due to well-known social deficits. Algorithms that produce decisions based on health outcomes alone, without factoring in their social causes, can result in significant harm and increased health inequalities. For example, if poor or less-educated people have performed worse after certain health interventions (due to poor access to care, working schedules, etc.), an algorithm can determine that people with these characteristics will always perform worse and recommend that they are not offered the intervention in the first place. This will exacerbate disparity in access to care and attainment of good health outcomes. More importantly, it will make such disparity less visible because the decision will bear the authoritative objectivity often attributed to numbers and that is typically expected from automated decision-making tools.

ADDRESSING THE ETHICAL CHALLENGES

The novelty represented by AI, and machine learning in particular, might be on the verge of pushing medical research, patient care, and public health into as yet uncharted ethical territories. The impact of AI in these three domains is particularly challenging to anticipate, and it is hard to predict whether expected benefits will offset emerging risks. In this scenario neither a precautionary approach nor a wait-and-see attitude is compatible with the widely accepted need to ensure ethically sustainable, socially robust, and responsible innovation in this domain. A precautionary approach implies erring on the side of containing possible risks when evidence about how a given phenomenon will evolve is scarce and the stakes are high in terms of potential harms.[59] As far as the use of AI in medicine is concerned, a precautionary approach would likely result in disproportionate constraints that might undermine the development of promising technologies. On the other hand, a more permissive "wait-and-see" approach, while being more

---

[56] See http://apps.who.int/gb/ebwha/pdf_files/WHA71/A71_R7-en.pdf (accessed April 4, 2019).

[57] Effy Vayena and Lawrence Madoff, "Navigating the Ethics of Big Data in Public Health," in *The Oxford Handbook of Public Health Ethics*, ed. A. C. Mastroianni, J. P. Kahn, and N. E. Kass (Oxford University Press, 2019): 354–367.

[58] Robert Challen et al., "Artificial Intelligence, Bias and Clinical Safety," *BMJ Quality & Safety* 28, no. 3 (March 1, 2019): 231.

[59] Elizabeth Charlotte Fisher, Judith S, Jones, and René von Schomberg, *Implementing the Precautionary Principle: Perspectives and Prospects* (Edward Elgar, 2006).

favorable to the development and rapid uptake of AI-driven solutions, would necessarily have to rely on existing ethical safeguards. But such safeguards, as we have seen, fall short of covering the rapidly expanding catalog of ethical issues that AI poses in the domain of biomedicine. The collection, use, and reuse of increasingly large amounts of personal data, as we have seen, calls into question the adequacy of key components of the existing regulatory toolkit, such as evidence standards, ethics review, and informed consent.[60]

What is needed to ensure responsible AI innovation is a governance approach that coevolves with the field itself, incorporating new governance actors and experimenting with new oversight mechanisms to cope with ethical challenges as they arise from practice. Such a governance model should primarily drive attention to the ethically controversial aspects of AI-driven innovation in biomedicine in order to ensure that emerging risks do not pass unnoticed. A second aim of an ideal governance frame would by that of channeling innovation toward socially beneficial outcomes. Finally, good governance should promote public trust in and accountability of the innovation process. These objectives demand a specific *systemic* approach to governing a complex phenomenon whose outcomes are still largely unpredictable.

In the last two decades, scholarship on governance of controversial areas of science and innovation has given substantial consideration to so-called adaptive governance as a model to cope with uncertainty in public policy.[61] Adaptive governance centers around constant monitoring of both the phenomenon at stake and the policy measures deployed to control it. In practical terms, this model invites oversight and regulation to take stock of evidence as it becomes available and promoting social learning among a variety of different governance stakeholders.[62] Drawing on the broad frame of adaptive governance, we have proposed a governance model for data-driven innovation in biomedicine called "systemic oversight."[63] Systemic oversight is specifically designed to address what gives rise to ethical issues in the use of big data and AI in biomedicine, that is, as we have seen, novel data sources, novel data uses, increased capacity to draw connections between disparate data points, and uncertainty about downstream effects of such increased classificatory powers. The systemic oversight approach is based on six principles offering guidance as to the desirable features of oversight structures and processes in the domain of data-intense biomedicine: adaptivity, flexibility, inclusiveness, reflexivity, responsiveness, and monitoring (the first letters of the principles form the acronym AFIRRM).

---

[60] Effy Vayena et al., "Digital Health: Meeting the Ethical and Policy Challenges," *Swiss Medical Weekly* 148 (2018): w14571.

[61] Carl Folke et al., "Adaptive Governance of Social-Ecological Systems," *Annual Review of Environment and Resources* 30, no. 1 (2005): 441–473.

[62] Brian Chaffin, Hannah Gosnell, and Barbara A. Cosens, "A Decade of Adaptive Governance Scholarship: Synthesis and Future Directions," *Ecology and Society* 19, no. 3 (2014): 56.

[63] Vayena and Blasimme, "Health Research with Big Data"; Blasimme and Vayena, "Towards Systemic Oversight in Digital Health."

Adaptivity refers to the capacity of governance bodies and mechanisms to guarantee appropriate forms of oversight for new data sources and new data analytics that get incorporated in research, patient care, or public health activities. *Flexibility* is the capacity to treat different data types based both on their source *and* on their actual use, and it is premised on the consideration that data acquire specific ethical meaning in different contexts of use. *Inclusiveness* stresses the need to include all affected parties in deliberations and decision-making practices about the use of data and algorithms in specific ambits. This component refers in particular to communities and actors that are historically marginalized, vulnerable, or otherwise excluded from the circuits of power, such as minorities and patient constituencies. *Reflexivity* prescribes careful scrutiny and assessment of emerging risks in the short run as well as in the long run in terms of the downstream effects of big data and AI on interests, rights, and values, for example, in terms of fair access to healthcare services, discrimination, stigmatization, medicalization, overdiagnosis, and so on.

We saw earlier that AI is a powerful generator of health-relevant information and thus exposes research participants, patients, and data subjects in general to unwanted leaks of personal data and information. *Responsiveness* refers therefore to the need for adequate mechanisms to mitigate the effects of unauthorized access to personal health-related information. Finally, *monitoring* expresses the need to predispose regular scrutiny of data-related activities and their effects on health-related practices in order to anticipate the emergence on new vulnerabilities and undesirable outcomes.

The implementation of the AFIRRM frame will require consideration for the well-characterized obstacles to adaptive governance in other policy domains. Particular attention needs to be paid to the composition of oversight bodies. The demands of inclusiveness, for example, can only be appropriately fulfilled if diverse stakeholders share at least a common understanding of the intended advantages and potential risks of using AI in biomedicine. It is possible, for instance, that automating hospital services through AI-driven triage systems caters to the financial interests of hospitals (by rationalizing resource allocation), while failing to meet the expectations of severely ill patients in terms of access to care. As a consequence, the inclusion of patients' perspectives into decisions about the adoption of such systems both requires and fosters the existence of shared visions about fairness in access to health services. Along similar lines, oversight mechanisms on the use and effects of AI in clinical practice must escape purely technical considerations about the safety and efficacy of automated clinical decisions. Downstream effects on the patient-doctor relationship or on the right of patients to decide whether they are open or not to highly automated decisions need to be considered. To this aim, new review processes for clinical validation as well as novel communication and consent requirements will have to be established. The same applies in the research domain when researchers interested in using large amounts of phenotypic data need to negotiate the terms of use with data subjects, some of which may have value-laden views about the ethical legitimacy of certain types of research.

With the advent of AI, the agenda of academic disciplines like clinical research ethics, medical ethics, and public health ethics is rapidly adapting to incorporate new issues and new controversies. Given its theoretical and thematic specificity, one may characterize this area as a separate subarea of study in applied ethics and call it "digital bioethics." Whether and how this scholarship will inform the emergence of new oversight tools remains to be seen. In the meantime, practical proposals, criteria, and best practices about the governance of AI-driven innovation in biomedicine are just starting to emerge. The U.K. National Institute for Clinical Excellence (NICE), the body advising the U.K. National Health Service (NHS) on matters related to health technology assessment, has just released guidance on clinical validation of digital health technologies (DHTs).[64] This guidance establishes evidence standards (grouped in four evidence tiers) according to the function that a given DHT is intended to perform. Such standards are going to be applied to DHTs harboring an AI component as well as to stand-alone AI software. In February 2019 the NHS released an updated version of its Code of Conduct for Data-driven Health and Care Technologies.[65] The principles proposed by this code include understanding users' needs, clearly defining the expected outcomes and benefits, lawful data processing, transparency, and evidence of safety and effectiveness (based on the NICE criteria). The NHS frame has been criticized for its lack of attention to the risk that AI in the healthcare space may widen social inequalities.[66] Still in the United Kingdom, the Wellcome Trust—a major funder of biomedical research in the country— has recently proposed a model called "dynamic oversight" for emerging science and technologies that partially resembles our own systemic oversight approach and the AFIRRM principles.[67]

In the United States, the American Medical Association released its policy on AI in 2018.[68] This document highlights the transformative potential of AI in the clinical domain and recommends that clinically validated AI should be aligned to best clinical practices, be transparent, be reproducible, be immune to data biases, and protect patients' privacy as well as the integrity of their personal information. In the United States, the FDA is the gatekeeper of AI-driven health innovation because it has statutory oversight power on medical devices and software as a medical device. In Europe, instead, the new 2017 Regulation on Medical Devices[69] relies on third parties (called notified bodies) issuing conformity certificates for medical devices. The FDA is piloting a precertification program to identify "manufacturers who have demonstrated a robust culture of quality and organizational excellence, and who are committed to monitoring

[64] See https://www.nice.org.uk/Media/Default/About/what-we-do/our-programmes/evidence-standards-framework/digital-evidence-standards-framework.pdf (accessed April 4, 2019).

[65] See https://www.gov.uk/government/publications/code-of-conduct-for-data-driven-health-and-care-technology/initial-code-of-conduct-for-data-driven-health-and-care-technology (accessed April 4, 2019).

[66] Melanie Smallman, "Policies Designed for Drugs Won't Work for AI," Nature 567, no. 7746 (2019): 7.

[67] See https://wellcome.ac.uk/sites/default/files/blueprint-for-dynamic-oversight.pdf (accessed April 4, 2019).

[68] See https://www.ama-assn.org/system/files/2019–01/augmented-intelligence-policy-report.pdf (accessed April 4, 2019).

[69] See https://eur-lex.europa.eu/legal-content/EN/TXT/PDF/?uri=CELEX:32017R0745 (accessed April 4, 2019).

real-world performance of their products once they reach the U.S. market."[70] In April 2019, the FDA also released a proposed regulatory framework for AI and machine learning medical software addressing the specific issue of algorithms that keep on training themselves based on new data acquired during clinical use.[71]

CONCLUSIONS

The current proliferation of guidelines and codes of conduct demonstrates the need for ethical and technical points of reference for this rapidly evolving field. Considering the broad scope of potential applications for research, clinical use, and public health, it is likely that some specific uses of AI will not be covered by existing oversight mechanisms. But reliance on existing regulatory tools alone will likely fail to ensure adequate levels of public trust and accountability. For this reason, we have advanced the systemic oversight/AFIRRM approach as a governance blueprint. Looking at the nature of ethical issues illustrated in this chapter in light of the AFIRRM principles, it seems at least advisable that certain measures be implemented in the short term. In the research domain, ethical review committees will have to incorporate reflexive assessment of the scientific and social merits of AI-driven research and, to this aim will likely have to open their ranks to new professional figures such as social scientists. Research funders, on the other hand, can require monitoring and responsiveness mechanisms to be part of research plans and could set up multidisciplinary committees to periodically assess data from such activities in order to adjust their funding policies in the future. When AI-driven research amounts to large-scale projects claiming data from entire communities or populations, adequate forms of inclusion must be experimented with in order to ensure social learning across different epistemic communities—including lay publics and nonacademic actors.

In the domain of patient care, clinical validation is a crucial issue. Ad hoc evidence standards are a necessary condition for responsible clinical innovation, but they are not sufficient to cover the breath of potential ethical issues we saw in this area. Hospitals could equip themselves with "clinical AI oversight bodies" charged with the task of advising clinical administrators regarding the adoption of a given AI technology and monitoring its effects on patient journeys and patients' engagement throughout the continuum of care. Moreover, consent requirements will need to be adapted to the presence of highly automated data-processing, for instance, in the domain of diagnostics.

In the public health sphere, the new level of granularity enabled by AI in disease surveillance and health promotion will have to be negotiated at the level of targeted communities or it will result in a sense of disempowerment and, as a consequence, in a lack of public trust. The acceptable limits of data collection and algorithmic analysis, in other

---

[70] See https://www.fda.gov/MedicalDevices/DigitalHealth/UCM567265 (accessed April 4, 2019).
[71] See https://www.regulations.gov/document?D=FDA-2019-N-1185–0001 (accessed April 4, 2019).

words, will have to result from community-wide inclusive deliberation, especially as to who is collecting and processing data and for which exact purposes.

These are just a few examples of initiatives that, if adopted, will contribute to the development AI into a socially robust technology. It is clear that we are at the very beginning of a foreseen transformation. Should this transformation occur, its real effects may be different from those that we are able to anticipate now. This level of uncertainty, however, shall not deter societal stakeholders—including scientific and clinical institutions—from experimenting with governance arrangements aimed at reaping the benefits of AI for human knowledge and health, while at the same time paying sufficient attention to emerging ethical challenges.

BIBLIOGRAPHY

Char, Danton S., Nigam H. Shah, and David Magnus. "Implementing Machine Learning in Health Care—Addressing Ethical Challenges." *New England Journal of Medicine* 378, no. 11 (March 15, 2018): 981–983.

He, Jianxing, Sally L. Baxter, Jie Xu, Jiming Xu, Xingtao Zhou, and Kang Zhang. "The Practical Implementation of Artificial Intelligence Technologies in Medicine." *Nature Medicine* 25, no. 1 (January 2019): 30.

Price, W. Nicholson II. "Black-Box Medicine." *Harvard Journal of Law & Technology* 28 (2015 2014): 419.

Smallman, Melanie. "Policies Designed for Drugs Won't Work for AI." *Nature* 567, no. 7746 (2019): 7.

Topol, Eric J. "High-Performance Medicine: The Convergence of Human and Artificial Intelligence." *Nature Medicine* 25, no. 1 (2019): 44.

Vayena, Effy and Alessandro Blasimme. "Health Research with Big Data: Time for Systemic Oversight." *Journal of Law, Medicine & Ethics* 46, no. 1 (2018): 119–129.

Vayena, Effy, Alessandro Blasimme, and I. Glenn Cohen. "Machine Learning in Medicine: Addressing Ethical Challenges." *PLOS Medicine* 15, no. 11 (2018): e1002689.

Yu, Kun-Hsing, Andrew L. Beam, and Isaac S. Kohane. "Artificial Intelligence in Healthcare." *Nature Biomedical Engineering* 2, no. 10 (October 1, 2018): 719–731.

CHAPTER 38

....

ETHICS OF AI IN LAW

Basic Questions

....

HARRY SURDEN

INTRODUCTION

....

THE use of artificial intelligence (AI) technology in the administration and practice of law raises basic ethical issues. This chapter surveys some of the most important ethical topics involving the use of AI within the legal system itself (but not its use within society more broadly), from the vantage point of the United States.

ETHICS, AI, AND LAW

....

Ethical issues surrounding AI use in law often share a common theme. As AI becomes increasingly integrated within the legal system, how can society ensure that core legal values are preserved? This reflects the idea that most democracies consider certain values to be central to how their legal systems operate. Among the most important of these legal values are: equal treatment under the law; public, unbiased, and independent adjudication of legal disputes; justification and explanation for legal outcomes; legal results arising from law, principle, and facts rather than social status or power; outcomes premised upon reasonable and socially justifiable grounds; the ability to appeal decisions and seek independent review; procedural fairness and due process; fairness in design and application of the law; public promulgation of laws; transparency in legal substance and process; adequate access to justice for all; integrity and honesty in creation and application of law; and judicial, legislative, and administrative efficiency.[1] The use of AI in

---

[1] Christopher B. Gray ed., *The Philosophy of Law: An Encyclopedia, Garland Reference Library of the Humanities*, vol. 1743 (New York: Garland, 1999).

law may diminish or enhance how these values are actually expressed within the legal system or alter their balance relative to one another. Many ethical topics thus examine how such central values might unintentionally (or intentionally) change with increased use of AI in the legal system.

For example, some scholars worry that the use of AI technology in the judicial system may make legal decisions more biased against certain social groups and undermine notions of equal treatment.[2] Others are concerned that automation might subtly elevate values such as efficiency at the expense of other core values such as due process.[3] Still others query whether the use of AI in law may shift power dynamics among members of society, elevating those who have the knowledge of, or access to, AI technology to the detriment of those who do not.[4] At a broader level, these questions are important because they implicate the basic ordering of society. The use of AI within law has the potential to subtly alter political, social, or legal power among societal groups and diminish (or enhance) the operation of fundamental institutional protections. At a narrower level, these topics are important because the legitimacy of legal systems depend, to some extent, on the reality and the perception that core legal values, such as equal treatment under the law, are actually reflected in how the system operates. Thus, to the extent that use of AI erodes (or is perceived as eroding) central legal norms, this could undermine the legitimacy of the legal system itself.

It is important, however, to establish a balanced view of the ethical issues raised by the use of AI within law. First, many examinations of AI use primarily come from a negative perspective, critiquing the ways in which AI might make the legal system less fair or just. To be clear, these critical assessments are both important and valid, and indeed, this chapter too will spend significant time identifying similar ethical concerns. However, it is important to observe that the use of AI in the law can also potentially strengthen desired values. Careful uses of AI may actually reduce bias, expose existing injustices, or increase access to the legal system and overall efficiency.[5] To the extent that AI is used to enhance values such as fairness, equality, or access to justice, the legal system, and society more broadly, may benefit. While it is important not to exaggerate the potential benefits of AI in law, it is also essential to acknowledge them alongside the critiques, as these positive points often go underemphasized in the scholarly literature.

Second, many ethical issues raised by the use of AI in the law are not truly new, but rather exist already, in one form or another, in the current legal structure. If true, why have these ethical issues come to be associated with the introduction of AI technology? One reason is that applying AI technology to the law often brings to the forefront latent issues that were previously only implicit. For example, some judges and police have

---

[2] Solon Barocas and Andrew Selbst, "Big Data's Disparate Impact," *California Law Review* 104, no. 3 (June 1, 2016): 671.

[3] Deirdre Mulligan and Bamberger, Kenneth, "Saving Governance-by-Design," *California Law Review* 106 (2018): 697.

[4] Danielle Keats Citron, "Technological Due Process," *Washington University Law Review* 85 (2008): 1249; Frank Pasquale, *The Black Box Society: The Secret Algorithms That Control Money and Information* (Cambridge, MA: Harvard University Press, 2015).

[5] Harry Surden, "Machine Learning and Law," *Washington Law Review* 89 (2014): 87.

always had undesirable biases, but it often only until data is systematically analyzed by AI systems that such biases become apparent. Similarly, the language of current laws and the design of institutional processes may implicitly weight some values (e.g., efficiency) over others (e.g., due process). However, the application of AI often results in such implicit patterns being reduced to explicit, mathematical form, where it can often be inspected.[6] Thus, if we apply AI algorithms to past judicial or police data, and examine the result, we may see exposed in the results biases or value weightings that lurked undiscovered prior to application of the technology. Similarly, in other cases, the computational efficiency of AI technology can magnify existing but subtle weightings or structural imbalances. Thus, while the use of AI can certainly introduce *new* biases, in other cases, the technology is merely exposing or magnifying existing biases or preferences in the system.

Third, it is important not to exaggerate the relative impact that AI will have on the law compared to other societal influences. For one, it is hard to predict to what degree AI technology will be incorporated into the legal system broadly. Second, there are many societal factors that combine to influence how core legal values are (or are not) actually expressed in the legal system. These factors include institutional design, political power, money, social power, existing institutional structures, tradition, and the use of non-AI-based technologies such as the internet. We do not know how significant an influence AI will be on the legal system relative to these other important aspects. While we should certainly pay close attention to the impact AI is having on law, and the ethical questions its use raises, we must also be careful not to overfocus on AI simply because it is relatively new and perhaps more exotic than these more familiar, traditional factors. In many cases, the comparative impact on the legal system of altering a traditional factor, such as institutional design, may substantially outweigh adjustments in the use of AI. Where relevant, this chapter will make these broader points.

That said, because the use of AI technology within law is relatively new, the ethical issues raised do merit close scrutiny. The impact that AI can have on law, legal institutions, actors, and their decisions, in some contexts, may be substantial but also hard to detect. Thus, this chapter's central theme is to closely examine the way in which AI technology may alter the legal system and its structures as the effect of technological change on legal substance, values, actors, and institutions can often be subtle.

WHAT IS ARTIFICIAL INTELLIGENCE?

Before examining the ethical questions raised by the use of artificial intelligence in law, it is important to first establish what "artificial intelligence" means. There is no universally

---

[6] Harry Surden, "Values Embedded in Legal Artificial Intelligence," SSRN Scholarly Paper (Rochester, NY: Social Science Research Network, March 13, 2017), https://papers.ssrn.com/abstract=2932333.

agreed-upon definition of "artificial intelligence," but one useful working description is, "the use of technology to automate tasks that, when done by human, require intelligence." For instance, outside of law, AI technology has been used to automate tasks such as playing chess and driving cars. These are considered "artificial intelligence" tasks, rather than automation tasks generally, because when humans engage in these activities, they activate higher-order brain functions such as reasoning, judgment, decision-making, vision, the use of abstractions, and other cognitive activities that are associated with human intelligence. Thus, when engineers take a task that requires higher-order cognitive abilities when a human performs it, and they automate it using technology, it is common to refer to that as an application of artificial intelligence.

This same definition works reasonably well when AI is used in the legal domain. In law, there are many tasks, such as the prediction of legal outcomes and legal analysis of factual situations, that when performed by judges or lawyers, engage various aspects of human cognition. If we use technology to fully or partially automate these legal tasks, it is common to consider this a use of "artificial intelligence" within law.

A different but equally useful way to think about "artificial intelligence" is in terms of the underlying technology that enables it. At a high level, artificial intelligence is usually treated as a subdiscipline of computer science, as much of the research and technology emerged from this domain. However, AI is truly an interdisciplinary enterprise, involving ideas, researchers, and research beyond computer science from fields such as statistics, mathematics, economics, neuroscience, psychology, logic, and philosophy, just to name a few.

At a lower level, the term "artificial intelligence" refers to a particular suite of technologies and approaches that have arisen from AI researchers and which have successfully been used to automate various activities involving human intelligence. From this research, two broad categories of AI technological approaches have emerged. The first group of AI technologies is broadly known as "machine learning," and the second category is referred to as "knowledge representation and rules-based AI". Let's briefly look at each broad group in turn, because each AI approach is used within the administration and practice of law to varying degrees.

Roughly speaking, machine learning refers to a category of AI approaches in which algorithms automatically learn patterns from large amounts of data. These learned patterns can then be harnessed to automate tasks such as driving a car, predicting credit card fraud, or recognizing handwriting. "Machine learning" itself is not one technique, but rather, refers to a variety of approaches that bear a family resemblance to one another. Among these approaches are "neural-networks/deep learning," "logistic regression," and "Bayesian inference." Their common trait is the ability discern useful patterns from data that can often be used to make automated decisions about new, never-before-seen data in new situations. Often machine learning techniques are applied to problems involving prediction and estimating probabilities.[7]

---

[7] Ajay Agrawal, Joshua Gans, and Avi Goldfarb, *Prediction Machines: The Simple Economics of Artificial Intelligence* (Boston: Harvard Business Review Press, 2018).

Importantly, machine learning AI algorithms require data in order to function. For example, machine learning algorithms that are able to predict the probability that a given credit card transaction is fraud can only do so because they have previously analyzed a data set of past fraudulent and nonfraudulent credit card transactions in which they have detected patterns associated with fraudulent activity. So the applicability of machine learning to a problem goes hand in hand with the availability of data, and where relevant data is unavailable or limited, machine learning approaches generally cannot be applied. Notably, however, machine learning is part art and part science, so significant human judgment goes into selecting and applying the data and algorithms to real-world problems. Overall, machine learning is the dominant mode of artificial intelligence today, and when most people informally speak of "AI," they are usually referring to a machine learning approach. In the context of the law, as will be discussed, machine learning is having a significant impact on prediction, the automated examination of legal documents, and the analysis of legal contexts.

The second major approach to AI, known as "knowledge representation and rules-based AI," also plays an important, albeit lesser, role in law today. Generally speaking, "knowledge representation" involves modeling some aspect of the world in a structured form that a computer can process and reason about. A good example of such a knowledge representation, rules-based system in law involves tax-compliance software. Such a system models the underlying logic and meaning of the U.S. personal income tax code, so that U.S. taxpayers can use it to comply with tax laws and compute tax liability. To create such a system, engineers, in conjunction with attorneys and accountants, might examine the U.S. personal income tax laws and aim to translate the underlying logic of these legal provisions into a set of computer rules that accurately reflect the underlying meaning.

In general, developing a knowledge-representation system involves modeling some real-world process or activity using formal computer rules that accurately reflect the underlying logic, structure, and knowledge-relationships underlying the activity. Such knowledge-based AI systems are sometimes referred to as "expert systems" because the computer rules of such systems reflect knowledge gleaned from domain experts such as lawyers. Although knowledge representation approaches to AI are not as dominant as machine learning today in law, they still represent a significant aspect of legal AI.

It is worth clarifying a final point. When laypeople hear the term "artificial intelligence," they often imagine that today's AI involves "machines that think." However, this is not the case. Today, the term "artificial intelligence" is a bit of a misnomer because current AI technology does not exhibit the advanced cognitive abilities that we normally associate with human intelligence. Rather, as explained previously, most AI approaches involve automated approximations—learning computer-based patterns, rules, or heuristics that can sometimes be used to produce "intelligent results without intelligence" in certain, limited settings.

Unfortunately, the media and corporate advertising often give the misimpression that today's AI technology does involve computers that can think, reason, or engage in arbitrary, novel conversations on original topics at levels that match or exceed human ability. That vision of AI—sometimes known as "Strong AI" or "artificial general intelligence" (AGI)—has long been a goal of artificial intelligence research, but at the moment, it remains merely aspirational. As of the writing of this chapter, it is this author's opinion that there is little to no evidence that such strong AI technology will be coming any time soon in the five-to-ten-year time frame.

The reason that it is important to clarify the current limitations of AI is that it is important to ground discussions about ethics, AI, and law within the *actual* capabilities of AI technology. Occasionally such analysis becomes distracted or confused by speculation about future technological developments concerning AI, which may or may not occur. Because such speculation about potential future developments that is uniformed by actual evidence rarely leads to productive analysis, this chapter will remain firmly grounded in evidence of the current and near-term (five years out) state of AI technology.

USE OF ARTIFICIAL INTELLIGENCE IN LAW

This part will examine some representative examples of the way AI is being used within the legal system and ethical questions that these uses raise. It is helpful to conceptually divide the users of AI within law into three groups: the administrators of law (e.g., judges, legislators, police), the practitioners of law (e.g., attorneys), and the users of law (e.g., ordinary citizens and businesses—those who comply with the law). This conceptual division is useful, because each group plays a different role in the legal system, and each uses AI within law in different ways.

AI Use by Administrators of Law

The term "administrators of law" is meant to cover the use of AI by government officials broadly and to distinguish from the use of AI by lawyers and ordinary citizens and businesses. Administrators of law in this context include government officials ranging from judges, legislators, regulatory officials to the police. Such government officials play a unique role in the legal system. They have the ability to officially interpret and apply the law and have the power of the state and its sanctions behind them. The use of AI by legal administrators has a different valence than the other groups since they have the most potential to impact societal balances. Because of this, this chapter will spend the majority of the focus on this group.

AI in Criminal Sentencing and Bail Determinations

One prominent example of AI use within law comes from the criminal context. Judges must make important decisions about the criminal defendants who come before them, including whether to release them on bail before trial, or what sentence to impose if convicted. An important factor in both decisions is the likelihood that a defendant will commit a crime if released. In the bail context, if a judge believes that a defendant is likely to commit a crime if released, she may deny bail, and in the sentencing context, a judge may impose a more severe sentence on a defendant seen as likely to reoffend.

Traditionally, judges have made such assessments without significant reliance on technology, incorporating a range of information, including witness testimony about the defendant and the crime, the defendant's past criminal history, the severity of the crime, and the judge's intuition and overall impressionistic assessments. Recently, however, some judges have also begun to rely upon information produced by machine learning algorithms, which include automated indications of risk. Such software is often referred to as "criminal risk-assessment" or "risk-determination software," and purports to predict the probability that a particular defendant will commit another crime if released, given information about that defendant.

It is helpful to have a general, high-level understanding as to how such AI prediction software is created in order to understand some of the ethical issues raised.[8] The central idea behind such machine learning–based risk assessment software is that it uses data about past criminal defendants and their history of reoffending to predict the probability that a new defendant will reoffend. Today, such criminal risk-assessment software is usually created by private, third-party companies that license or sell it to the government for use in the legal system.[9] To do this, data scientists from these companies, possibly with help from experts from the law and criminal domains, apply a variety of machine learning algorithms to the historical data to see if the AI system can automatically identify patterns associated with increased likelihood of reoffending.

Since the core of all such machine learning systems is data, the vendor creating the software will have to locate a source of data that is relevant to predicting criminal risk. Typical sources might include historical government data about past criminal defendants who have already come through the justice system. Such data is usually combined with other information about the defendants from private corporate sources such as credit score agencies and other data-collection agencies.[10] When put together, a data set might contain historical information about tens of thousands (or more) of defendants who have previously passed through the system. For each defendant, there might be hundreds of pieces of information about that defendant (also known as "variables," "features," or "factors"), such as the type of crime the defendant committed, her educational level, address, employment history, credit score, criminal history, family circumstances, and demographic information, along with information about whether that defendant ended up reoffending once she was released.

The goal in creating such a system is to use machine learning to try to identify in the historical data which of these hundreds of potentially predictive factors seem to be the

---

[8] In reality, the risk-prediction software and process for creating and using it is much more complex than the simple example given here and includes many more predictive variables than this illustration.

[9] Jeff Larson and Julia Angwin, "Machine Bias," *ProPublica* (May 23, 2016), https://www.propublica.org/article/machine-bias-risk-assessments-in-criminal-sentencing.

[10] Electronic Privacy Information Center, "EPIC—Algorithms in the Criminal Justice System," https://epic.org/algorithmic-transparency/crim-justice/ (accessed July 9, 2019).

most indicative of the likelihood that a defendant will commit a crime upon release. For instance (and oversimplifying greatly), imagine that the algorithm examines thousands of past defendants and their individual data points, and determines that two features are predictive of future offenses: (1) defendants who had a previous encounter with the justice system and who committed crimes shortly after release were extremely likely to do so again in the future (i.e., this data point is a strong predictor, which will get a high "weighting"), and (2) defendants who are unemployed were slightly more likely to reoffend (i.e., a weak predictor, which will get a low weighting). These are examples of two features (or factors) that might be used by an AI system to predict the future chance of offending for new defendant.

Having identified such predictive indicators, the AI algorithm outputs them into an "AI model," which is essentially a compact, computer representation of the pattern that was discovered. Such an AI model has a series of "weightings" about factors that tend to be predictive of reoffending and can be used to make a prediction on a new, never-before-seen defendant, based upon information about that person's background and circumstances. For example, imagine that that there are two new defendants before a judge, and the judge wants to use the risk-assessment software to predict the chances of either reoffending. Suppose that the court collects data on each defendant and determines that the first one was unemployed and had previously committed a crime upon release from bail, and the other had not previously committed a crime but was also unemployed. We have two, potentially predictive, data points on each defendant, which we can input into the AI software, which will apply its previously discovered model weightings to their particular data to make predictions about these new defendants. After analyzing the data for each defendant, the AI model might predict a high probability of reoffending for the first defendant (because the AI model weights having previously reoffended together with being unemployed as highly predictive), and a lower, but slightly above average probability for the second (because the AI model weights being unemployed as only slightly predictive). Such software will typically output a report with an overall risk-score for each defendant (e.g., risk rating on a scale from 1 to 10) to assist the judge in her decision. Based on these scores, a typical judge might decide to deny the first defendant bail but grant it to the second. The scores are merely recommendations, and, in principle, a judge is free to disregard them.

Importantly, creating such an AI predictive model requires a great deal of judgment and subjective choices on the part of the data scientists.[11] First, there are judgments about what data sets to use. Some data sets may be more reliable than others. There are also judgments about what data from the data sets to include or exclude when examining the data for predictive patterns. There are also judgments about which machine learning algorithms to use. There are many different machine learning algorithms, and each type of algorithm uses a different set of mathematical techniques to try to determine the "best" and "most-predictive" factors. However, because they often work very

---

[11] Joshua A. Kroll et al., "Accountable Algorithms," *University of Pennsylvania Law Review* 165 (2017): 633.

differently different algorithms can come up with different answers even on the same data. There are also judgments about how to validate and measure whether the model is working "well" or accurately or fairly. Finally, scientists often create multiple possible predictive models, and there are judgments about which, among many AI models to choose. Thus, data scientists have to use a combination of professional judgment, guessing, intuition, and domain knowledge to pick the best combination of machine learning algorithm and data points to analyze and use.

Ethical Issues and Government Officials Using AI in Decision-Making Process

As discussed earlier, a central theme of ethical inquiries is to what extent core legal values will be impacted by increased use of AI in law. The criminal risk-assessment example is instructive because it illustrates many of the most common issues that arise when government administrators use AI systems while making official decisions. The points raised will thus translate to other scenarios involving AI-aided government determinations.

Ethical Issue: Equal Treatment under the Law

Equal treatment for all under the law, regardless of status, is a core value in most legal systems. This norm posits that legal decisions should be based upon the law and the facts, but not upon a party's socioeconomic, political, racial, ethic, gender background, or a variety of other individual characteristics that are illegal or inappropriate to consider. Defendants in the same circumstances should be treated the same under the law regardless of status. The use of AI systems by judges (or other legal officials) to make decisions has raised concerns about this equality norm. Some scholars have worried that recommendations made by AI systems may disproportionately harm or benefit certain social groups at the expense of others.[12]

Unequal treatment from AI-based decisions can occur for a few reasons. Sometimes this happens when there are existing structural inequalities in society and these inequalities become reflected in the data used by AI systems. For example, let's imagine that the risk-prediction system discussed earlier was based partly upon historical police arrest data. In that example, the AI algorithm discovered a feature that was predictive of reoffense: a defendant's history of having reoffended after a past encounter with the justice system was highly indicative of a future offense upon release.

However, let's imagine that the police arrest behavior, upon which the data was based, was itself biased. This would result in subtle, potentially unjust skews in the data. For instance, suppose that individuals of all socioeconomic groups commit minor offenses (like driving without a seat belt) at the same rate. Suppose further that police tend to

[12] Solon Barocas and Andrew Selbst, "Big Data's Disparate Impact," *California Law Review* 104, no. 3 (June 1, 2016): 671, https://doi.org/10.15779/Z38BG31.

patrol and look for offenses more frequently in low-income areas and tend to stop (and arrest) lower-income individuals, while ignoring higher-income individuals, when observing this same offense in both groups. Such disparity in police treatment would create a misleading bias in the data. Offenses by lower-income individuals are being disproportionately recorded in the police data set and will appear in the data to occur at a higher rate, while offenses by higher-income individuals are being omitted from the data because they are not being recorded due to police discretion or patrol decisions.

Because AI algorithms are good at detecting patterns, an AI algorithm that examines this biased data will likely find these skews and subtly incorporate them into the AI predictive model. That model will mathematically indicate that low-income individuals are more likely to reoffend than high-income individuals, not due to true differences in offense rates but rather due to police stop, arrest, patrol, and data-recording behavior. If that AI model is then used to predict risk of reoffending for a new defendant, using upon information associated with her socioeconomic status, such as credit score, it might unjustifiably recommend that low-income defendants not receive bail while recommending that similarly situated high-income defendants be released on bail.

This illustrates an important point: machine learning models depend upon data, and existing societal or structural biases may be subtly embedded in data sets. When AI systems use data sets that are skewed in various ways, these same biases will then be reflected in the machine learning models in ways that are extremely hard to detect but which may offer disparate treatment to various societal groups based upon inappropriate categories. Worse yet, if widespread, such AI systems may not only encode existing structural or institutional biases but may inadvertently reinforce and strengthen those biases by making automated decisions that further put certain groups at a disadvantage (i.e., denying bail to low-income defendants at a disproportionately lower rate than merited).

There are other biases that can subtly creep into AI predictive models that can be hard to detect. The creators of AI systems have many subjective design decisions to make about how the system is created and operates. In the AI context, some of the choices include what data sets to use, what data to exclude or include, what AI algorithms to use or AI models to select, what information to emphasize or de-emphasize. All of these subtle choices might result in more or less favorable treatment to various social groups.

The designers of such systems, therefore, have a great deal of power. At any given point, the designers might make a series of subtle design decisions that might result in favorable or unfavorable treatment for different groups when applied broadly in society. Some design biases might be largely unintentional, such as when software engineers make a choice based upon a personal judgment without realizing that such a choice happens to benefit people like themselves. Others worry that unethical creators of such systems may intentionally make subtle design choices that deliberately benefit certain groups at the expense of others.[13] In that case, the use of such AI systems in government decision-making broadly may subtly shift social and political power dynamics by

---

[13] Kroll et al., "Accountable Algorithms," 633.

providing more favorable automated decisions for certain groups over others. Thus, one group of ethical questions surround the question: how can we ensure that the predictions created by AI predictive models, and relied upon by government officials, are facilitating the legal values of equal treatment under the law without regard for status?

However, in making such assessment of the fairness of AI-aided decision-making, one must always compare it to the baseline: what legal processes existed before the technology was introduced, and what biases are in the current system? Prior to the introduction of AI-aided technology, bail and sentencing decisions were made by judges based upon evidence, and also upon a judge's personal beliefs, discretion, intuition, and experience. Judges, like all humans, are subject to a variety of conscious and unconscious biases.[14] In all likelihood, many judge-based decisions were themselves biased in undesirable ways. In the same way that AI systems are subject to software design choices that can result in disparate treatment, so too are legal institutions and processes subject to decision—decisions that can significantly help or hinder various societal groups. For instance, the legal system contains a myriad of structural design choices, from what hours to keep courts open (i.e., weekday hours may benefit people with higher status jobs and more job flexibility), to the sophistication of language to use on court documents (i.e., complex language may disproportionately advantage highly educated individuals), to what information to emphasize on documents (i.e., information placed toward the back of a multipage document may go overlooked), to what language to translate official documents into (i.e., English-only documents may disadvantage non-English speakers). These and many other nontechnical but structural design choices in the legal system, made by those who have the power to make such decisions, have always had the potential to benefit certain societal groups over others. Although the introduction of AI systems does raise some novel issues of how software design can affect legal and social outcomes, similar subtle issues of preferential legal design have always existed in the legal system.[15]

This leads to an important point—just because we observe that AI legal models are explicitly and undesirably biased, does not mean that the biases they exhibit are *necessarily worse* than those in current legal structures, which too contain their own biases. Indeed, some have suggested that AI systems could actually foster more equal treatment under the law compared to the existing legal processes. In some cases, applying AI models to legal data can enhance the value of equal treatment by exposing unknown but existing biases in the current system that may have been overlooked. Machine learning systems are good at identifying patterns, and some of these patterns might reflect existing structural injustices that can be brought to the fore to be corrected once observed. Others suggest that data-based AI systems can add more consistency to bail, sentencing,

[14] Daniel Kahneman, *Thinking, Fast and Slow* (New York: Farrar, Straus and Giroux, 2013); Michael Brownstein, "Implicit Bias," in *The Stanford Encyclopedia of Philosophy*, ed. Edward N. Zalta (Stanford University, 2017), https://plato.stanford.edu/archives/spr2017/entries/implicit-bias/.

[15] Jon Kleinberg, Sendhil Mullainathan, and Manish Raghavan, "Inherent Trade-Offs in the Fair Determination of Risk Scores," in *8th Innovations in Theoretical Computer Science Conference (ITCS 2017)*, ed. C. H. Papadimitriou (Schloss Dagstuhl—Leibniz-Zentrum fuer Informatik, 2017), https://doi.org/10.4230/lipics.itcs.2017.43.

and other legal decisions as compared to the current system, involving thousands of different human judges, all with different backgrounds, experiences, and conscious and unconscious biases, applying considerable discretion and subjectivity.

While there is some merit to this point of view—as human decision makers are certainly not unbiased—one must take this point of view with a critical eye for several reasons. Much of this depends upon careful implementation of such systems and the recognition of their limitations. For one, as just discussed, the automated decisions of AI systems and other automated computer decisions often provide the illusion of mechanical neutrality. In some cases, people have a tendency to unjustifiably treat automated outcomes as unbiased and authoritative as compared to human-based decisions. However, as just discussed, bias can creep into automated systems, and we might be concerned that society improperly ignores the possibility of undesirable mechanical biases and unduly treats those decisions as somehow more objectively correct or precise than they truly are.

Finally, if the concern is truly implementing more equal treatment in the legal system, focus on the nuances of AI decision-assistance systems may be misplaced. As discussed earlier, there are many other factors that may more substantially affect how equally or fairly various groups are treated by the legal system, such as institutional design, funding, or political choices. If more equal treatment is truly a societal goal, it is likely that changing these other factors could have a much stronger overall impact than tweaking the details of AI systems. For instance, to actually achieve more equal outcomes for disadvantaged groups, time and effort might be better spent providing more funding for public defenders or making institutional design changes to legal systems or processes that are more friendly to these groups.

The point, of course, is not that we should ignore the details of AI legal systems that might lead to structural biases—of course we need to pay close attention to such nuances, lest those systems be poorly implemented. Rather, there is a danger that commentators spend undue amounts of time worrying about tweaks in AI legal systems—a topic that is relatively novel and exotic, spending efforts in finding marginal improvements in those technological systems—while ignoring other, more mundane interventions that might have a much substantial overall impact on improving core legal values.

Transparency and Explanation

Another set of concerns about the use of AI in law surrounds public transparency in legal adjudication. In theory, the predictions rendered by many AI systems should be transparent. Most AI systems are deterministic systems, which means that the outputs that they produce are entirely based upon the input data that goes in and the software and AI model that is used.[16] In other words, the same exact inputs applied to the same

---

[16] Andrew D. Selbst and Solon Barocas, "The Intuitive Appeal of Explainable Machines," *Fordham Law Review* 87 (March 2, 2018): 1085.

AI model in such a system should produce the same outputs, and this process can be completely recorded and audited. Thus, in principle, if we want to query why an AI system came to a particular prediction about a particular defendant, we should be able to determine exactly what happened by examining the input information about the defendant that went in (e.g., was the defendant unemployed), the AI model itself (what factors it considers and how much it weights it), and how the AI model treated that information (e.g., it took into account unemployment, but weighted it lightly with some numeric), and be able to reconstruct the computational process that led to the results.

In practice, however, such transparency of AI predictions is not so easy to reconstruct. For one, as discussed earlier, today many criminal risk-prediction systems are created by nongovernmental, private companies. These companies often do not make their AI models, or the underlying data or software necessary for reconstructing the decision, accessible to the public. Rather, these vendors often keep confidential the software code, the AI model and how it weights various factors, the data upon which the model was created, and the variables that the model considers in making its automated output. Often, they will use law itself—trade secret law or nondisclosure agreements—along with technical obfuscation, to keep the details of the AI models and automated decision-making process secret. Thus, even though in principle one might be able to computationally interrogate a criminal risk-assessment system to reconstruct why it came to the decision that it did, in practice, access to the necessary data, software, and details, is generally not possible.

Similarly, in most legal systems, it is a core value that the substantive criteria upon which legal decisions are made should be publicly promulgated to provide notice. To the extent that the details of such AI algorithms are kept secret, it is difficult to know upon what basis substantive decisions—such as defendant release decisions—were made and some argue that this undermines core legal values of public promulgation and notice. Thus, if transparency and notice are core values of legal decision-making, one might query how transparent automated decisions are whose details and substantive criteria are shielded by confidentially and secrecy. This also can impact the ability to appeal such decisions—another core legal value.

Even if the details of the AI systems were accessible, in some cases we still may not have full transparency as to the decision-making process for technical reasons. As mentioned, there are many different machine learning techniques. Some techniques, such as regression or decision trees, produce answers that are very easy to understand and inspect. By contrast, some other machine learning approaches, particularly neural-network and deep learning approaches, produce AI models that, while highly accurate, can be difficult, if not impossible, for humans to understand. This is known as the "interpretability problem," and it refers to the fact that these techniques often encode their patterns in extremely complex, mathematical models that are readily processable by computers but that are not interpretable to humans in meaningful terms, even to the programmers who created them. In other words, if an AI risk-assessment system is created using one of these less interpretable techniques, even if we were to inspect the input data and how it was applied by the AI model, we might not be fully able to understand why the algorithm came to the predictive decision that it did, in a way that is meaningful. Thus, to the extent that government-aided AI decisions are made using machine learning techniques that are relatively less interpretable, we may be concerned that the value of transparency in decision-making is diminished.

A related issue to transparency is the role of explanation. A core requirement in many legal systems is that judges, or other legal officials explain important legal decisions that affect people's lives or substantive rights. Officials often must explicitly justify them in writing using socially and legally acceptable reasons.[17] Some have worried that the increased use of AI in legal decision-making might diminish the ability to explain decisions in a meaningful way. If a judge follows the recommendation of an AI system, the output of such a system can often be traced computationally as a series of mathematical calculations and can produce a detailed audit of the data and computer steps that led to the decision, and even a statistical justification for why the decision was probabilistically accurate, but such an computational exposition does not amount to a socially acceptable justification or satisfactory explanation for a human defendant.[18] It may be little consolation to a disappointed defendant that "the system analyzed and mathematically decided that your rights should be denied." The legitimacy of legal adjudication depends, to some extent, on the performative and humanistic aspects of legal decisions—the ways in which parties come away from the courts *feeling* like they have had their opportunity to be heard and have been treated fairly and in a socially acceptable and justifiable way, quite apart from the underlying objective merits of the case. Thus, to the extent that explanation and justification is a core value of a legal system, some critics are concerned that the increased use of AI-based decision-making might undervalue the necessary humanistic and performative components of legal adjudication.

However, in other ways, the use of AI systems may enhance transparency. Once again, it is always important to compare the critiques of AI to the status quo and problems with existing processes. Although some AI systems may be difficult to inspect technologically, the human mind is not an observable system either. We cannot inspect the inner workings of a judge's brain to determine why she arrived at the decision she did. While judges often are required to publicly articulate reasons for reaching a particular decision, there is no way to verify that the decision was actually reached for the stated reasons. By contrast, when one uses an AI system, there is at least the possibility, if an interpretable machine learning technique is used, that the decision-making process can be completely reconstructed. Thus, in some regards, increased use of AI, provided it is carefully implemented, can enhance transparency compared to current legal processes.

---

[17] Margot E. Kaminski, "The Right to Explanation, Explained," SSRN Scholarly Paper (Rochester, NY: Social Science Research Network, June 15, 2018), https://papers.ssrn.com/abstract=3196985.

[18] Tim Miller, "Explanation in Artificial Intelligence: Insights from the Social Sciences," *ArXiv:1706.07269 [Cs]*, June 22, 2017, http://arxiv.org/abs/1706.07269.

ACCURACY

There is a strong value in legal systems coming accurate legal decisions. Accuracy is another way in which AI predictive systems provide improvements over the pretechnical status quo. Today, judges are tasked with making a variety of predictive decisions about parties, such as the probability of reoffending. But there is no reason to believe that judges are particularly well equipped for making accurate predictions along these lines.[19] Much research shows that humans reason poorly when it comes to probability due to various cognitive biases.[20] In other contexts outside of law, computer-aided predictions routinely outperform human predictions.[21] Thus, it may be the case that a carefully constructed, carefully implemented AI system may be more accurate in predicting actual risk of reoffending than human judges acting on intuition and experience.

However, in other cases, judge-made decision-making may be more accurate. AI systems can only make decisions based upon what has been encoded in data and what information the system creators have designed it to consider. Those limitations might exclude many relevant, but difficult to encode, pieces of information from the automated analysis, such as witness testimony, that could be highly predictive in certain cases. By contrast, judges can take into account a wide range of holistic and testimonial evidence in making a decision, much of which will be unavailable to the computerized algorithm when it cannot be easily captured in data. It is possible that, given this wider set of data points, judges can make more accurate decisions in certain contexts than the limited machines. Only empirical research will show whose predictions are more accurate. However, to the extent AI systems turn out to be more accurate overall, the ethical question in this sense may be whether AI systems should be more frequently used for such predictive tasks in order to result in fairer treatment for defendants.

SHIFTING OF ACCOUNTABILITY
IN DECISION-MAKING

Another set of ethical topics concerns accountability in official decision-making. In the current (nontechnologically enhanced) system, judges (or juries) make all of the crucial decisions concerning criminal defendants. There are, therefore, identifiable points of accountability—when a decision occurs, we know which official actor or body—judge or jury—made the decision. In the context of AI-aided decision-making, there may be a

---

[19] Jon Kleinberg et al., "Human Decisions and Machine Predictions," Working Paper (National Bureau of Economic Research, February 2017).

[20] Kahneman, *Thinking, Fast and Slow*.

[21] Agrawal, Gans, and Goldfarb, *Prediction Machines*.

subtle shift in this accountability. In principle, the outputs of predictive AI systems, like risk-assessment software, is merely a recommendation, that a judge is supposed to incorporate holistically along with all of the other evidence in order to make a considered judgment. However, there is the possibility that judges (or juries) using such systems will begin to habitually defer to the automated recommendations made by the system and adopt them reflexively.

If an AI-based system produces an automated risk assessment that has the aura of mathematical precision and objectivity, there are reasons to suspect that judges might opt to routinely adopt the automated recommendations by default even if they nominally retain the final discretion to come to a different conclusion. For example, such systems often provide scores of defendant risk of reoffending to the judge on some numerical scale, such as 1 (least risk) to 10 (maximum risk). Imagine that a system produces a relatively high risk-score for a given defendant—say 7 out of a maximum 10. It is hard to imagine a judge overriding such a high numeric indication, even if she would have come to the opposite result when holistically assessing the weight of the evidence and in the absence of an automated, numeric result. Indeed, judges have incentives not to override automated recommendations. Imagine that a judge was to release a defendant despite a high automated risk score, and that defendant were then to go to on commit a crime on release. The judge could be subject to backlash and criticism, given that there is now a seemingly precise prediction score in the record that the judge chose to override. The safer route for the judge is to simply adopt the automated recommendation, as she can always point to that numerical risk-score as a justification for her decision.

Such a scenario is potentially ethically problematic for several reasons. First, despite the apparent certainty of a numerical score such as "6 out of 10," such scores suffer from the problem of false precision. Such predictions—even automated predictions—are full of uncertainty and wide margins of error, and it is not at all clear what probability of risk a score such as "6"—separate from its context—is aiming to convey. Thus, judges may be likely to err on the side of caution in the face of such seemingly precisely, relatively high numeric scores.

More potentially problematic is the subtle shifting of accountability for substantive decisions away from the judge and toward the system. Currently, our system is constructed so that human judges are called upon to make judgments upon other humans. If judges begin routinely adopting, by the default, the recommendation of the system, this results in subtle shift of responsibility and accountability away from the judge and toward the AI recommendation systems and their creators. To the extent there is a value of accountability in having the locus of a decision located in a publicly appointed or elected judge who has made a considered evaluation of the evidence, such default adoption of automated recommendations may be problematic.

Another related issue is the shift of accountability from the public sector to the private sector. If indeed judges begin to routinely adopt automated recommendations without much additional consideration, the locus of the decision essentially shifts to the organization that designed and implemented the AI system—these days, often private companies. In that sense, the balance of legal judgments might essentially shift from the public sphere to the private sphere, subject to the design decisions of private corporations. One important value in many legal systems is public and independent adjudication of legal disputes, and, thus one potential ethical point of concern in legal decision-making partially or fully based upon AI systems is the shift in decision-making away from public officials and toward privately developed systems.

ETHICAL CONCERNS OF AI USE
BY PRACTITIONERS OF LAW

While most of the major ethical concerns in the use of AI in the legal system are raised in the context of administrators of law (such as judges), there are some parallel issues raised by the use of AI by practitioners of law—lawyers. This chapter will conclude by briefly highlighting a few of these issues.

One set of ethical issues concerns the increasing power of such AI systems. Today lawyers are called upon to make numerous types of predictions during the course of work, such as predicting the outcome of legal issues, or predicting which documents will be privileged or important or relevant to litigation or business matters. Traditionally, lawyers have produced such predictions using a combination of legal analysis, judgment, experience, and other professional analytical skills. In the past several years, some lawyers have begun to use AI systems in a number of settings that were traditionally in the purview of legal judgment, including automated document analysis, automated discovery, and in legal case outcome prediction.

For the sake of argument, imagine that in the near future, the predictions of case outcomes made by lawyers using AI systems begin to vastly outperform the predictions made by traditional lawyers using only their professional skills.[22] This future scenario raises several issues. For one, if the best and most accurate predictions are made by lawyers using AI systems, will the ethical or professional standards shift such that lawyers are obligated to use such systems rather than their using unassisted professional judgment as they have traditionally done? Additionally, such a system risks shifting power dynamics in law. Lawyers (and their clients) who have access to the best AI-based predictive tools might have increasingly significant advantages over less resourced lawyers and clients who do not. While it is true today that lawyers and clients who have more resources can often obtain better outcomes than less resourced clients despite the relative merits of their positions, it is possible that AI-based tools could exacerbate this divide. Thus, to the extent that access to justice and adjudication of legal outcomes based upon the merits are central values of the legal system, then the increased use of AI-based systems by lawyers may undermine these norms.

[22] Daniel Martin Katz, "Quantitative Legal Prediction—or—How I Learned to Stop Worrying and Start Preparing for the Data-Driven Future of the Legal Services Industry," *Emory Law Journal* 62 (2013): 909.

CONCLUSION

This chapter has surveyed some of the major ethical issues surrounding increasing the use of artificial intelligence systems within the legal system. The central ethical challenge is to identify the way in which the use of AI may be shifting core legal values and to ensure that these crucial values are preserved in the technological transition. A more positive view also identifies the ways in which AI technology can not only preserve central values but can also foster and enhance these values to the betterment of the legal system and society overall.

BIBLIOGRAPHY

Agrawal, Ajay, Joshua Gans, and Avi Goldfarb. *Prediction Machines: The Simple Economics of Artificial Intelligence*. Boston: Harvard Business Review Press, 2018.

Angwin, Julia and Jeff Larson. "Machine Bias." *ProPublica* (May 23, 2016). https://www.propublica.org/article/machine-bias-risk-assessments-in-criminal-sentencing.

Barocas, Solon and Andrew Selbst. "Big Data's Disparate Impact." *California Law Review* 104, no. 3 (June 1, 2016): 671. https://doi.org/10.15779/Z38BG31.

Calo, Ryan. "Artificial Intelligence Policy: A Primer and Roadmap." *UC Davis Law Review* 51 (2018): 37.

Citron, Danielle Keats. "Technological Due Process." *Washington University Law Review* 85 (2008): 1249.

Kaminski, Margot E. "The Right to Explanation, Explained." SSRN Scholarly Paper. Rochester, NY: Social Science Research Network, June 15, 2018. https://papers.ssrn.com/abstract=3196985.

Kleinberg, Jon, Sendhil Mullainathan, and Manish Raghavan. "Inherent Trade-Offs in the Fair Determination of Risk Scores." In *8th Innovations in Theoretical Computer Science Conference (ITCS 2017)*, edited by C. H. Papadimitriou. Dagstuhl: Schloss Dagstuhl—Leibniz-Zentrum fuer Informatik, 2017. https://doi.org/10.4230/lipics.itcs.2017.43.

Kroll, Joshua A. et al. "Accountable Algorithms." *University of Pennsylvania Law Review* 165 (2017): 633.

Miller, Tim. "Explanation in Artificial Intelligence: Insights from the Social Sciences." *ArXiv:1706.07269 [Cs]*, June 22, 2017. http://arxiv.org/abs/1706.07269.

Mulligan, Deirdre and Kenneth Bamberger. "Saving Governance-by-Design." *California Law Review* 106 (2018): 697.

Pasquale, Frank. *The Black Box Society: The Secret Algorithms That Control Money and Information*. Cambridge, MA: Harvard University Press, 2015.

Selbst, Andrew D. and Solon Barocas. "The Intuitive Appeal of Explainable Machines." *Fordham Law Review* 87 (March 2, 2018): 1085.

Surden, Harry. "Artificial Intelligence and Law: An Overview." *Georgia State University Law Review* 35 (2019).

CHAPTER 39

....

BEYOND BIAS

"Ethical AI" in Criminal Law

....

CHELSEA BARABAS

AI AS A DISCOURSE OF REFORM
....

THE term "artificial intelligence" (AI) has come and gone from popular parlance a number of times since the 1950s and has been used in reference to a wide range of computational methods.[1] Rather than a specific methodological regimen, AI is best understood as a sociotechnical concept, comprised of a set of logics and technocratic practices that encode a particular way of understanding the world in a given context.[2] In the context of the U.S. penal system, the term "AI" has been repeatedly invoked as part of a contested discourse of reform, the most recent incarnation in a long lineage of state efforts to use statistics to assert legitimacy during times of significant social change and upheaval.[3] Crime statistics have long served as the foundation for intense ideological struggles over how to understand the role of the carceral state in managing criminal behavior.

There is no precise way of distinguishing "artificial intelligence" from other data-driven decision-making regimes in criminal law. Mainstream and academic discourse on AI in the U.S. penal system encompasses a hodgepodge of computational techniques, ranging

[1] Pamela McCorduck, *Machines Who Think: A Personal Inquiry into the History and Prospects of Artificial Intelligence* (AK Peters/CRC Press, 2009).

[2] Madeleine Clare Elish and Danah Boyd, "Situating Methods in the Magic of Big Data and AI," *Communication Monographs* 85, no. 1 (2018): 57–80.

[3] Michel Foucault, *Power/Knowledge: Selected Interviews and Other Writings, 1972–1977* (Pantheon, 1980); Naomi Murakawa, *The First Civil Right: How Liberals Built Prison America* (Oxford University Press, 2014); Khalil Gibran Muhammad, *The Condemnation of Blackness* (Harvard University Press, 2011); Tony Platt, "'Street' Crime—A View from the Left," *Social Justice: A Journal of Crime, Conflict and World Order*, no. 9 (1978): 26.

from decades-old actuarial practices to machine learning algorithms that were not possible before the era of "big data."[4] Broadly speaking, these technologies are a mixture of new and old statistical methods that measure the strength of associations between a set of data points and an outcome of interest. These techniques are correlational at their core—their outputs typically come in the form of probabilistic distributions which are read as forecasts or predictions of future events. In criminal law, the data used to build these statistical models are usually administrative information collected by local police departments and administrations of the court, which are then interpreted using probabilistic computational methods.[5]

Contemporary debates regarding AI in criminal law are occurring at a time when there is increased demand within law enforcement agencies for an "upgrade" in popular discourse regarding the legitimacy of the carceral state.[6] Over the last three decades, rates of incarceration in the United States have skyrocketed. The United States incarcerates the largest number of people in the world, at a rate that is four times greater than the world average.[7] These statistics are driven by a gross overrepresentation of minority groups in prison—black and Latinx inmates make up 72 percent of the federal prison population and the majority of the state prison populations.[8] A wide range of scholarship has documented the unprecedented scale and impact of discriminatory police practices[9] and mass incarceration,[10] emphasizing that these developments are neither natural, nor sustainable.

In response to these challenges to the legitimacy of the carceral state, an authoritative discourse of reform has emerged, one which conceives of bias and inefficiency as the main issues to tackle under the rubric of "evidence-based reform." At the center of these efforts has been a call for the development and adoption of data-driven technologies that ostensibly support more fair and efficient policing and courtroom practices, using regression and machine learning algorithms. In this context, decades-old actuarial tools

[4] Sarah Brayne, "Big Data Surveillance: The Case of Policing," *American Sociological Review* 82, no. 5 (2017): 977–1008.

[5] Andrew Guthrie Ferguson, *The Rise of Big Data Policing: Surveillance, Race, and the Future of Law Enforcement* (NYU Press, 2017).

[6] Ruha Benjamin, "Catching Our Breath: Critical Race STS and the Carceral Imagination," *Engaging Science, Technology, and Society* 2 (2016): 145–156.

[7] Christopher Hartney, "US Rates of Incarceration: A Global Perspective" (National Council on Crime and Delinquency, November 2006), https://www.nccdglobal.org/sites/default/files/publication_pdf/factsheet-us-incarceration.pdf.

[8] Kelly Lytle Hernández, Khalil Gibran Muhammad, and Heather Ann Thompson, "Introduction: Constructing the Carceral State," *Journal of American History* 102, no. 1 (2015): 18–24.

[9] Michael W. Sances and Hye Young You, "Who Pays for Government? Descriptive Representation and Exploitative Revenue Sources," *Journal of Politics* 79, no. 3 (2017): 1090–1094.

[10] Sharon Dolovich, "Exclusion and Control in the Carceral State," *Berkeley Journal of Criminal Law* 16 (2011): 259; Craig Haney, "The Psychological Impact of Incarceration: Implications for Post-Prison Adjustment," *Prisoners Once Removed: The Impact of Incarceration and Reentry on Children, Families, and Communities* 33 (2003): 66.

are rebranded as "AI" and expanded data collection is framed as a pragmatic and politically neutral way forward amid increased social upheaval.[11]

The term "AI" is often used in reference to the development of machine learning algorithms that are "trained" to recognize patterns and trends in large data sets. Interest in these algorithms is fueled in part by the growing appetite and availability of data within law enforcement agencies.[12] As the state collects increasingly large amounts of data, there has been a commensurate growth in the interest of large technology companies, such as IBM, Palantir, and Amazon, to partner with government agencies in order to hone the state's data analytics capacities. Such public-private partnerships are often framed as "win-win" collaborations, ones which enable the expansion of state crime control capabilities while simultaneously giving private tech companies a competitive advantage in the race to develop sophisticated analytics platforms. These partnerships have given rise to a slew of new technologies branded as "artificial intelligence," which are sold to police departments and administrations of the court across the country. As a brand, AI is often invoked as a means of creating superhuman capabilities within law enforcement—AI is a machine that can ingest and impartially learn from the data fumes of human experience without ever growing tired.[13] In an effort to gain access to large government datasets, industry has embraced law enforcement as its target customer, building tools which support and reproduce the operational logics of the carceral state.

The Pursuit of "Fair, Accountable, and Transparent" Algorithms

In response to a growing number of studies which measure the disparate impact of criminal justice practices on racial minorities,[14] a number of leaders from across the political spectrum have called for the adoption of scientific tools that could increase the accuracy and efficiency of criminal justice operations by checking the implicit bias of officials. In this context, the hope is that regression and machine learning algorithms

[11] For example, in response to growing concerns over police brutality, FBI Director James Comey argued that "the first step to understanding what is really going on is to gather more and better data related to those we arrest, those we confront, for breaking the law and jeopardizing public safety and those who confront us. Data seems a dry and boring word, but without it we cannot understand our world and make it better." *James Comey—Address on Race and Law Enforcement*, Georgetown University Speech on Race and Law Enforcement (Washington, DC, 2015), https://www.americanrhetoric.com/speeches/jamescomeygeorgetownraceandlaw.htm.

[12] Sarah Brayne, "Surveillance and System Avoidance: Criminal Justice Contact and Institutional Attachment," *American Sociological Review* 79, no. 3 (2014): 367–391.

[13] Christopher Rigano, "Using Artificial Intelligence to Address Criminal Justice Needs," *NIJ Journal* no. 280, (October 8, 2018), https://www.nij.gov:443/journals/280/Pages/using-artificial-intelligence-to-address-criminal-justice-needs.aspx.

[14] Michelle Alexander, *The New Jim Crow: Mass Incarceration in the Age of Colorblindness* (The New Press, 2012); Bruce Western, *Punishment and Inequality in America* (Russell Sage Foundation, 2006).

can be used to course correct the cognitive pitfalls and implicit biases of key decision makers in the system by presenting evidence-based claims about the likelihood of future events.

By framing the issue of disparate impact in this way, academics and government officials effectively circumscribe the issue of racial disparity in terms of individually held beliefs and preferences, rather than as the byproduct of widespread organizational practices and cultural norms.[15] As Hoffmann points out, technology firms have also embraced unconscious bias as a social challenge which they can effectively overcome with the help of data-driven technology. Implicit bias is understood as a phenomenon which "is somehow apart from us yet can infect our decision-making…as opposed to something that is variously, but systematically cultivated and maintained."[16] In this uncritical framing of the problem, historical crime data are characterized as objective facts, a neutral "view from nowhere"[17] that stands in stark contrast to the flawed, fickle, and opaque subjectivity of human decision makers.

For example, this discourse is driving the rapid proliferation of pretrial risk assessments across the United States, where they are sold as a means of overriding judges' intuitive decision-making processes, through which they may "erroneously, and unwittingly, introduce bias through acquired stereotypes"[18] or succumb to well-known cognitive pitfalls, such as "availability bias."[19] Proponents of pretrial risk assessment point to a growing literature in behavioral science to illustrate the common cognitive fallacies of legal decision makers in order to make the case for why actuarial tools could support more objective and accurate decisions.[20]

In this context, contentious social issues, such as massive increases in pretrial detention rates, are reframed as data processing challenges, in which key decision makers (judges, police officers, etc.) would benefit from tools that help them to distinguish "signal from noise" when making time-sensitive decisions about potentially dangerous individuals.[21] Risk-assessment instruments purportedly home in on the most predictive

[15] Murakawa, *The First Civil Right: How Liberals Built Prison America*; Anna Lauren Hoffmann, "Where Fairness Fails: On Data, Algorithms, and the Limits of Antidiscrimination Discourse," *Information, Communication, and Society* 22, no. 7 (2019): 900–915.

[16] Hoffmann, "Where Fairness Fails: On Data, Algorithms, and the Limits of Antidiscrimination Discourse," 10.

[17] Donna Haraway, "Situated Knowledges: The Science Question in Feminism and the Privilege of Partial Perspective," *Feminist Studies* 14, no. 3 (1988): 575–599.

[18] Matthew DeMichele et al., "The Intuitive-Override Model: Nudging Judges toward Pretrial Risk Assessment Instruments," 2018, 9.

[19] Cass R. Sunstein, "Algorithms, Correcting Biases," *Social Research*, 2018.

[20] Sharad Goel et al., "The Accuracy, Equity, and Jurisprudence of Criminal Risk Assessment," *Equity, and Jurisprudence of Criminal Risk Assessment (December 26, 2018)*, 2018; Chris Guthrie, Jeffrey J. Rachlinski, and Andrew J. Wistrich, "Blinking on the Bench: How Judges Decide Cases," *Cornell Law Review* 93 (2007): 1; Jon Kleinberg et al., "Algorithmic Fairness," in *AEA Papers and Proceedings*, vol. 108, (AEA, 2018), 22–27; Richard Berk et al., "Fairness in Criminal Justice Risk Assessments: The State of the Art," *Sociological Methods & Research* (2018), https://doi.org/10.1177/0049124118782533.

[21] DeMichele et al., "The Intuitive-Override Model: Nudging Judges toward Pretrial Risk Assessment Instruments"; Goel et al., "The Accuracy, Equity, and Jurisprudence of Criminal Risk Assessment"; Kleinberg et al., "Algorithmic Fairness"; Sunstein, "Algorithms, Correcting Biases."

factors of an outcome of interest, helping to minimize the occurrence of "false positives and false negatives" in decisions over time. This is particularly important in contexts where risk management is framed in terms of high-stakes, life-and-death situations where there is little room for error.[22] As a result, predictive accuracy is often held up as a key selling point of these tools. In fact, accuracy has become a fetishized measure of a tool's worth—in cases of life and death, it doesn't matter *why* a prediction is accurate, so long as it is.[23]

Skeptics of algorithmic tools in criminal law have also centered accuracy and bias in their criticisms. There are a growing number of researchers who investigate the ways that protected class attributes, such as race and gender, mediate the accuracy of outputs produced by algorithmic tools, including risk assessment, predictive policing, and facial recognition software.[24] A number of high-profile studies have argued that, not only are algorithmic tools in criminal law not very accurate, but the burden of that inaccuracy is disproportionately borne by historically marginalized groups, who are often subject to higher false positive rates.[25] This discrepancy in accuracy is usually talked about in terms of bias—critics argue that algorithmic tools run the risk of reproducing or amplifying preexisting biases in the system.

These concerns have given rise to an influential community of researchers from both academia and industry who have formed a new regulatory science[26] under the rubric of "fair, accountable, and transparent algorithms" (FAT algorithms). In this research

---

[22] DeMichele et al., "The Intuitive-Override Model: Nudging Judges toward Pretrial Risk Assessment Instruments"; Goel et al., "The Accuracy, Equity, and Jurisprudence of Criminal Risk Assessment"; Sunstein, "Algorithms, Correcting Biases." For example, in spite of the fact that less than 8 percent of pretrial defendants are arrested for a violent crime while awaiting trial, the fear of rape or murder is repeatedly mentioned in the academic literature, which presents the risk of being assaulted, raped, or killed as an important issue to consider alongside the well documented harms of detention. These scholars repeatedly bring up these very rare crimes as a point of contrast to the well-documented harms of pretrial incarceration. The fear of violent crime was repeatedly invoked in interviews I had with judges, as well as in the mainstream press when covering the issue of pretrial release.

[23] For example, in a 2013 talk, a prominent statistician and criminologist argued, "I'm not trying to explain criminal behavior, I'm trying to forecast it. If shoe size or sunspots predicts that a person's gonna commit a homicide I want to use that information, even if I have no idea why it works." Richard Berk, *Forecasting Criminal Behavior and Crime Victimization*, Chicago Ideas, 2013, https://www.youtube.com/watch?v=rolFHPegLVQ&t=105s.

[24] Julia Angwin et al., "Machine Bias," *ProPublica* (May 23, 2016), https://www.propublica.org/article/machine-bias-risk-assessments-in-criminal-sentencing; Joy Buolamwini and Timnit Gebru, "Gender Shades: Intersectional Accuracy Disparities in Commercial Gender Classification," *Proceedings of Machine Learning Research* 81 (2018); Kristian Lum and James Johndrow, "A Statistical Framework for Fair Predictive Algorithms," *ArXiv:1610.08077 [Cs, Stat]*, October 25, 2016, http://arxiv.org/abs/1610.08077.

[25] Angwin et al., "Machine Bias"; Buolamwini and Gebru, "Gender Shades: Intersectional Accuracy Disparities in Commercial Gender Classification"; Jacob Snow, "Amazon's Face Recognition Falsely Matched 28 Members of Congress with Mugshots," *American Civil Liberties Union* (blog) (July 26, 2018), https://www.aclu.org/blog/privacy-technology/surveillance-technologies/amazons-face-recognition-falsely-matched-28.

[26] Sheila Jasanoff, *The Fifth Branch: Science Advisers as Policymakers* (Cambridge, MA: Harvard University Press, 1994).

community, criminal law applications have served as some of the most prominent thought exercises, used for illustrating the trade-offs of different technical choices in the design and implementation of algorithmic tools. These efforts have coalesced around two general approaches to what has been widely branded as "algorithmic fairness": (1) the development of formal fairness criteria and accuracy measures that illustrate the trade-offs of different algorithmic interventions, and (2) the development of "best practices" and managerialist standards for maintaining a baseline of accuracy, transparency, and validity in algorithmic systems. In the following sections, I outline these two approaches in greater detail before ultimately arguing that technocratic conceptions of bias and accuracy are not adequate conceptual anchors for this discussion, since they fail to interrogate the deeper normative, theoretical, and methodological premises of these predictive systems in the context of criminal law.

Formalized Fairness Criteria

The initial focus of the FAT algorithm community has been to map mathematical formalisms onto complex legal concepts such as discrimination, disparate impact, equal opportunity, and affirmative action.[27] In doing so, researchers claim that the goal is to create a foundation for more robust debates about the social desirability of algorithmic tools by providing "conceptual precision" in the form of mathematical formalisms regarding a tool's fairness.[28]

A number of researchers have pointed out that some fairness criteria are mutually incompatible,[29] which has given rise to deeper questions about what criteria of fairness should be met, across what groups.[30] These limitations have been framed in terms of trade-offs, which must be debated and resolved on a case-by-case basis. Formalizing these trade-offs is widely considered to be a pragmatic approach to criminal justice reform. For example, a prominent criminologist recently co-wrote a paper with a number of computer scientists, arguing that "one cannot expect any...tool to reverse centuries of racial injustice or gender inequality" in the criminal justice system.[31]

[27] Kleinberg et al., "Algorithmic Fairness"; Solon Barocas and A.D. Selbst, "Big Data's Disparate Impact," *California Law Review* 104 (2016); Moritz Hardt, Eric Price, and Nati Srebro, "Equality of Opportunity in Supervised Learning," *Advances in Neural Information Processing Systems*, 2016, 3315–3323; Cynthia Dwork et al., "Fairness through Awareness" (Proceedings of the 3rd Innovations in Theoretical Computer Science Conference, ACM, 2012), 214–226.

[28] Berk et al., "Fairness in Criminal Justice Risk Assessments: The State of the Art"; Richard Berk, *Machine Learning Risk Assessments in Criminal Justice Settings* (Springer, 2019).

[29] Berk et al., "Fairness in Criminal Justice Risk Assessments: The State of the Art"; Alexandra Chouldechova, "Fair Prediction with Disparate Impact: A Study of Bias in Recidivism Prediction Instruments," *Big Data* 5, no. 2 (2017): 153–163; Kleinberg et al., "Algorithmic Fairness."

[30] For example, it is theoretically impossible to design a classifier that simultaneously satisfies false positive parity and "predictive value parity," or equal calibration across protected classes. Chouldechova, "Fair Prediction with Disparate Impact: A Study of Bias in Recidivism Prediction Instruments."

[31] Berk et al., "Fairness in Criminal Justice Risk Assessments: The State of the Art."

Instead, they argued, the job of technical researchers is to delineate the trade-offs of different decisions in quantifiable terms, so that they can be transparently adjusted to reflect the preferences and values of different communities. The hope is that formalized definitions of fairness will increase the transparency of various trade-offs and bolster a more inclusive public discourse regarding the social desirability of these tools.[32]

In the context of criminal law, "equity," "fairness," and "accuracy" are defined as mathematical formalisms which are pitted against one another as competing values that can never be fully resolved unless there is a fundamental change in "base rates" of criminal activity across groups.[33] These researchers argue that differences in false positive rates across racial populations have more to do with real differences in the prevalence of criminal activity across those groups than with bias in the algorithm.[34] In these arguments, "unequal base rates" of criminal activity are uncritically characterized as an endemic issue across protected groups, rather than as a byproduct of discriminatory policing and courtroom practices.[35] As a result, a number of scholars have warned that attempts to balance false positive and false negative rates in risk assessments could result in higher rates of victimization in communities of color, because it would result in less accurate risk classifications. In these arguments, the risk of violent crime, such as murder, is frequently invoked. As Berk argues, "by far the leading cause of death among young African-American males is homicide. The most likely perpetrators of those homicides are other young African-American males. There are legitimate concerns about fair risk assessments for accused perpetrators, but no such concerns about the consequences of fair risk assessments for their possible victims. Is that fair?"[36]

Berk's assertion is based on a false binary distinction between "victims" and "perpetrators" of violent crime, in spite of a growing body of literature which has established a significant overlap across victim and offender populations—yesterday's victim is likely to become tomorrow's perpetrator, and vice versa.[37] Moreover, Berk uses statistics about the violent death of African Americans as a justification for racial profiling and preemp-

[32] Kleinberg et al., "Algorithmic Fairness."

[33] Berk, *Machine Learning Risk Assessments in Criminal Justice Settings*; Chouldechova, "Fair Prediction with Disparate Impact: A Study of Bias in Recidivism Prediction Instruments"; Sam Corbett-Davies and Sharad Goel, "The Measure and Mismeasure of Fairness: A Critical Review of Fair Machine Learning," *ArXiv Preprint ArXiv:1808.00023*, 2018; Goel et al., "The Accuracy, Equity, and Jurisprudence of Criminal Risk Assessment"; Kleinberg et al., "Algorithmic Fairness."

[34] Berk, *Machine Learning Risk Assessments in Criminal Justice Settings*; Corbett-Davies and Goel, "The Measure and Mismeasure of Fairness: A Critical Review of Fair Machine Learning"; Goel et al., "The Accuracy, Equity, and Jurisprudence of Criminal Risk Assessment."

[35] Richard Berk, *Using ML in Criminal Justice Risk Assessments—The Frontiers of Machine Learning*, 2017 Raymond and Beverly Sackler Forum, https://www.youtube.com/watch?v=gdEPPRhNu34; Anthony W. Flores, Kristin Bechtel, and Christopher T. Lowenkamp, "False Positives, False Negatives, and False Analyses: A Rejoinder to 'Machine Bias: There's Software Used across the Country to Predict Future Criminals. And It's Biased against Blacks,'" *Federal Probation* 80 (2016): 38–46.

[36] Berk, *Machine Learning Risk Assessments in Criminal Justice Settings*, 125.

[37] Wesley G. Jennings, Alex R. Piquero, and Jennifer M. Reingle, "On the Overlap between Victimization and Offending: A Review of the Literature," *Aggression and Violent Behavior* 17, no. 1 (2012): 16–26.

tive policing in African American communities. Khalil Muhammad calls this rhetorical strategy the "violence card," whereby proponents of crime-forecasting tools present statistics that, on their face, seem to speak for themselves. According to these people, Muhammad argues, "by knowing that this is what Black people do to each other, we need not have further conversation about any responsibility that lies outside the Black community" for their treatment.[38] Muhammad argues that this tactic is based on a very long tradition of respectability politics in U.S. carceral discourse, whereby harsh, pre-emptive policing practices in communities of color are understood solely in terms of deficiencies within those communities, as people who are seemingly incapable of treating even themselves with civility.[39] As a result, "accurate" risk assessments, and the detention-oriented risk management strategies that so often accompany them, are posited as interventions that serve the best interests of these communities, even if it means subjecting them to higher rates of false positive misidentification.

Managerialist "Best Practices"

In light of the tensions that arise given "unequal base rates" of criminal activity, many researchers in the FAT community have made a "don't let the perfect be the enemy of the good" appeal, arguing that a tool's social value is best understood in comparative terms—do algorithmic decision-making aids produce more accurate predictions than a human decision maker would make on their own?[40] These researchers characterize criticisms of algorithmic bias as impractical and perfectionist, arguing that current statistical practices, while not perfectly accurate, provide a pragmatic means of improving the overall accuracy and transparency of high-stakes decisions in criminal law.[41]

To bolster these claims, these scholars point to literature from the behavioral sciences in order to argue that, by and large, algorithms outperform human decision makers in accurately predicting outcomes like recidivism.[42] Others have tried to empirically test this "human versus machine" formulation with historical crime data. However, these

[38] Khalil Gibran Muhammad, *How Numbers Lie: Intersectional Violence and the Quantification of Race*, Radcliffe Institute for Advanced Study, 2016, 32:22, https://www.youtube.com/watch?v=broZYTGuW9M&t=2713s.

[39] What these statistics eschew is the fact that the vast majority of individuals who are arrested as a result of policies like "stop and frisk" are arrested for nonviolent, petty offenses, such as riding a bicycle on the sidewalk, public intoxication, loitering, etc. These offenses have nothing to do with increasing the safety of African American communities. Khalil Gibran Muhammad, *The Condemnation of Blackness—Khalil Gibran Muhammad Book Talk*, John Jay Research (New York, 2015), 12:30, https://www.youtube.com/watch?v=STKb-ai6874&t=392s.

[40] Berk et al., "Fairness in Criminal Justice Risk Assessments: The State of the Art"; Goel et al., "The Accuracy, Equity, and Jurisprudence of Criminal Risk Assessment"; Sunstein, "Algorithms, Correcting Biases"; Jared Sylvester and Edward Raff, "What About Applied Fairness?," *ArXiv Preprint ArXiv:1806.05250*, 2018.

[41] Berk, *Machine Learning Risk Assessments in Criminal Justice Settings*, 116.

[42] DeMichele et al., "The Intuitive-Override Model: Nudging Judges toward Pretrial Risk Assessment Instruments"; Goel et al., "The Accuracy, Equity, and Jurisprudence of Criminal Risk Assessment"; Sunstein, "Algorithms, Correcting Biases."

studies have proven challenging to do in most criminal justice scenarios, because counterfactual data are not available for measuring the comparative accuracy of different decisions (i.e., we do not know if an incarcerated person would have gone on to commit another crime had they been released). This challenge has not stopped researchers from taking elaborate measures to impute missing data in order to make bold claims about whether or not an algorithmic prediction is more accurate than a human forecast.[43] These researchers posit that algorithms have the potential to serve as a force for equity, if only appropriate safeguards could be put into place to minimize overall bias and maximize accuracy of their predictions.

To this end, some have sought to address issues of bias and accuracy in criminal justice algorithms by reformulating them in terms of narrower technical issues such as "sample bias," which can be addressed by regularly revalidating predictive models with data from local jurisdictions.[44] Scholars have pointed out that such practices are crucial for understanding the impact of changing conditions and specific policy interventions in the criminal justice system over time.[45] To this end, there is a growing body of literature within both academia and industry which aims to outline such standards and best practices for the ethical implementation of predictive algorithms.[46]

Generally speaking, these frameworks aim to minimize specific types of bias (sample bias, label bias, etc.) procedurally, through semi-regular validations of predictive models, in order to maximize their purported accuracy and minimize well-established forms of statistical bias. While these procedures are an important first step toward addressing a specific subset of issues regarding a tool's validity and generalizability, they are insufficient for addressing deeper issues regarding the way claims are constructed based on the available data. In the following section, I argue bias and accuracy are inadequate conceptual anchors for discussing the social implications of these tools, since they fail to interrogate the deeper theoretical and methodological premises of these data-intensive, algorithmically mediated systems.

THE LIMITS OF "FAT" ALGORITHMS

All of the previous arguments regarding accuracy and objectivity are built on a shared epistemological assumption that arrest, conviction, and incarceration data are best

[43] Kleinberg et al., "Algorithmic Fairness."

[44] Goel et al., "The Accuracy, Equity, and Jurisprudence of Criminal Risk Assessment"; Jon Kleinberg et al., "Discrimination in the Age of Algorithms" (SSRN 3329669, February 5, 2019).

[45] D.G. Robinson and J.L. Koepke, "Danger Ahead: Risk Assessment and the Future of Bail Reform," *Washington Law Review* 93 (2018); Megan Stevenson, "Assessing Risk Assessment in Action," *Minnesota Law Review* 103, no. 303 (2018).

[46] Arnold Foundation, "Arnold Ventures Statement of Principles on Pretrial Justice," https://www.arnoldventures.org/work/pretrial-justice/ (accessed April 2, 2019); Christopher Bavitz et al., "Assessing the Assessments: Lessons from Early State Experiences in the Procurement and Implementation of Risk Assessment Tools," *Berkman Klein Center Research Publication*, no. 2018–8 (2018); Berk, *Machine Learning Risk Assessments in Criminal Justice Settings*.

interpreted as information about individual and population-level criminal activity, rather than as data that primarily reflect law enforcement activity and the deeper historical disparities in how the police and court officials treat different groups and pursue various types of crime.[47] Numerous researchers have pointed out the fundamental measurement errors that occur when people uncritically characterize criminal justice data solely in terms of an individual's proclivity toward crime.[48] Scholars have long argued that not only are crime statistics partial and biased but their incompleteness is delineated clearly along power lines.[49] Arrest statistics are best understood as measurements of law enforcement practices, which tend to focus on "street crimes" carried out in low-income communities of color while neglecting other illegal activities that are carried out in more affluent and white contexts.[50] Similarly, conviction and incarceration data primarily reflect the decision-making habits of relevant actors, such as judges, prosecutors, and probation officers, rather than a defendant's criminal proclivities or guilt.[51]

In light of these criticisms, scholars have called for the systematic recharacterization of arrest, conviction, and incarceration data, as data that can inform important conversations regarding the disparate impact of specific policing and courtroom practices. As Ochigame argues, such a recharacterization would precipitate a fundamental shift in the attribution of agency and responsibility made in claims based on this data, away from the "antisocial behavior" of "risky individuals" and toward a carceral system that surveils, arrests, prosecutes, and incarcerates people in disparate ways.[52] Ultimately, these scholars argue that arrest, conviction, and incarceration data are not accurate measures of crime and that crime is not synonymous with danger or potential harm to the community.

Yet mainstream characterizations of police and court data continue to fuel deeply problematic conflations between concepts like arrest and dangerousness.[53] For example, Kleinberg et al. conflate arrest statistics with criminal activity in order to impute data about the probability of a defendant recidivating while awaiting trial.[54] These

[47] Delbert S. Elliott, "Lies, Damn Lies, and Arrest Statistics," Center for the Study and Prevention of Violence, 1995.
[48] Sharon Dolovich, "Exclusion and Control in the Carceral State," *Berkeley Journal of Criminal Law* 16 (2011): 259; David A. Harris, "The Reality of Racial Disparity in Criminal Justice: The Significance of Data Collection," *Law & Contemporary Problems* 66 (2003): 71; Rodrigo Ochigame, "The Illusion of Algorithmic Fairness" (March 25, 2019); Seth J. Prins and Adam Reich, "Can We Avoid Reductionism in Risk Reduction?," *Theoretical Criminology* 22, no. 2 (2018): 258–278.
[49] Platt, "'Street' Crime—A View from the Left"; Michelle Brown and Judah Schept, "New Abolition, Criminology and a Critical Carceral Studies," *Punishment & Society* 19, no. 4 (2017): 440–462.
[50] Laura Nader, "Crime as a Category—Domestic and Globalized," in *Crime's Power* (Springer, 2003), 55–76; Platt, "'Street' Crime—A View from the Left."
[51] Harris, "The Reality of Racial Disparity in Criminal Justice: The Significance of Data Collection."
[52] Ochigame, "The Illusion of Algorithmic Fairness."
[53] Lauryn P. Gouldin, "Distangling Flight Risk from Dangerousness," *Brigham Young University Law Review* (2016): 837; Paula Maurutto and Kelly Hannah-Moffat, "Assembling Risk and the Restructuring of Penal Control," *British Journal of Criminology* 46, no. 3 (2006): 438–454; Ochigame, "The Illusion of Algorithmic Fairness."
[54] Kleinberg et al., "Algorithmic Fairness."

calculations are then used to bolster an argument regarding whether or not pretrial risk assessments are more accurate than judges at predicting future crime. What this conversation eschews is the fact that pretrial detention is not constitutionally permissible, except in cases where the judge finds clear and convincing evidence that the defendant poses a significant flight risk or danger to the community. As Robinson and Koepke point out, the concept of "dangerousness" is ill defined in the courts and has led to a significant expansion in the use of pretrial detention,[55] in spite of the persistently low incidence of rearrest for violent crime.[56]

Given the extremely low rates of pretrial arrest for violent crime, it has proven quite challenging to develop actuarial risk assessments which can meaningfully differentiate the pretrial population according to their risk of such events. For example, on the Public Safety Assessment, the average difference in failure rates between defendants who are categorized as "low" and "high" risk for violent crime is less than six percentage points.[57] However, two layers of abstraction—a six-point ordinal scale and a "violence flag"—mask these meager relative differences across risk categories, making it challenging for practitioners to really reckon with the question of risk, or even relative risk, in probabilistic terms.[58]

Moreover, a number of pretrial risk assessments provide a risk score for "new criminal activity," which estimates the likelihood that a defendant will be rearrested for any

[55] Robinson and Koepke, "Danger Ahead: Risk Assessment and the Future of Bail Reform."
[56] Illinois Circuit Court of Cook County, "Model Bond Court Initiative," 2018, http://www. cookcountycourt.org/HOME/ModelBondCourtInitiative.aspx; Stevenson, "Assessing Risk Assessment in Action"; Pretrial Services Agency for D.C., "Release Rates for Pretrial Defendants within Washington, D.C., 2017; Pretrial Services Agency for D.C., "Performance Measures," https://www.psa. gov/?q=data/performance_measures (last visited May 11, 2018); Court Services and Offender Supervision Agency for the District of Columbia, FY 2016 Agency Financial Report, 27 (Nov. 15, 2016). In many jurisdictions, such as Kentucky, Washington, DC, and Cook County, the rate of arrest for violent crime during pretrial has been reported to be as low as less than 1 or 2 percent. For tools which specifically aim to measure rearrest for a violent offense, such as the PSA and COMPAS, the vast majority of defendants (about 92 percent) are predicted to not be arrested for a violent offense while awaiting trial. Sandra G. Mayson, "Dangerous Defendants," Yale Law Journal 127 (2017): 514.
[57] "PSA Results: For Reference When Making a Release Conditions Matrix" (template, n.d.), https:// psapretrial.org.
[58] If the PSA were optimized for predictive accuracy, then it would simply classify all defendants as "low risk," since the vast majority of defendants (over 91 percent) will not be arrested for a violent offense while awaiting trial. Yet, rather than optimize for accuracy, developers of the PSA have opted to create a binary categorization scheme which flags defendants who rate between 4 and 6 on an ordinal scale as "high risk," in spite of the fact that more than 92 percent of all these defendants will not go on to be arrested for such crimes. This inevitably generates a higher number of "false positives" (people who are "flagged" for danger but do not go on to commit a violent crime) in the outputs. This reality is masked by descriptions which characterize defendants who are flagged for danger as "three times more likely to be arrested for a violent crime." Billie Grobe, "Plenary 1: Guiding Pretrial Release w/PSA" September 2017). While this statement is technically true, such a framing masks the disturbing fact that the average difference in arrest rates between high- and low-risk defendants on tools like the PSA is less than six percentage points. "PSA Results: For Reference When Making a Release Conditions Matrix."

offense while awaiting trial.[59] This general recidivism score is sometimes provided as an additional point of consideration to decision makers, in spite of the fact that the Supreme Court and state high courts have not recognized the likelihood of nonviolent rearrest as a constitutionally permissible reason for detaining someone prior to their trial. In fact, to date the Supreme Court has only approved pretrial detention when someone is accused of "a serious crime [and] presents a demonstrable danger to the community."[60]

Yet, it is not uncommon for tools to actively conflate the likelihood of rearrest with dangerousness. For example, the Colorado Pretrial Assessment Tool defines a risk to "public safety" as any "new criminal filing," including for traffic stops and municipal offenses.[61] Still other tools, such as the Nevada Pretrial Risk Assessment, merge flight and dangerousness into one aggregate risk score, which poses an additional set of challenges.[62] Developers of these assessments often define their outcomes in terms of general recidivism in order to produce stronger associations between the inputs and outcome variables in their statistical models. This results in a significant expansion in the number of defendants who are rated as "moderate" or "high" risk for pretrial failure, and fuels a widespread conflation of general rearrest with dangerousness.

The conflation of generalized risk of arrest with dangerousness has serious implications for how police and judges interact with justice-involved individuals. In the case of pretrial risk assessment, it can lead to unwarranted detention of people who have not been convicted of a crime, which has serious ripple effects in terms of housing and employment instability, the disruption of social support structures, and the increased likelihood of conviction.[63] Proponents of risk assessment often make perfunctory acknowledgements of these issues regarding unwarranted pretrial detention, but then go on to place them beside other concerns regarding community safety, citing murder, rape, and assault as serious issues to weigh against the harms of widespread pretrial incarceration.[64]

Ironically, these associations are likely to fuel the very logical fallacies that these scholars purport to mitigate when developing these tools. By placing a widespread

---

[59] For example, pretrial risk assessments from Florida, Virginia, Ohio, Indiana, and the federal courts all purport to evaluate public safety risks. Yet, they define their outcome as arrest for any new crime, not just violent offenses. Mayson, "Dangerous Defendants," 514.

[60] United States v. Salerno, 481 U.S. 739, 750 (1987).

[61] Timothy Schnake, "'Model' Bail Laws: Re-drawing the Line Between Pretrial Release and Detention" (Center for Legal and Evidence-Based Practices, April 18, 2017), 109.

[62] Scholars have warned that combining flight and dangerousness into one score can lead to an overestimation of both types of risk and make it challenging to identify effective risk mitigating interventions. Gouldin, "Distangling Flight Risk from Dangerousness."

[63] Will Dobbie, Jacob Goldin, and Crystal S. Yang, "The Effects of Pretrial Detention on Conviction, Future Crime, and Employment: Evidence from Randomly Assigned Judges," *American Economic Review* 108, no. 2 (2018): 201–240; Arpit Gupta, Christopher Hansman, and Ethan Frenchman, "The Heavy Costs of High Bail: Evidence from Judge Randomization," *Journal of Legal Studies* 45, no. 2 (2016): 471–505; Paul Heaton, Sandra Mayson, and Megan Stevenson, "The Downstream Consequences of Misdemeanor Pretrial Detention," *Stanford Law Review* 69 (2017): 711. Dobbie, Goldin, and Yang, "The Effects of Pretrial Detention on Conviction, Future Crime, and Employment: Evidence from Randomly Assigned Judges."

[64] Berk, *Machine Learning Risk Assessments in Criminal Justice Settings*; Kleinberg et al., "Discrimination in the Age of Algorithms"; Sunstein, "Algorithms, Correcting Biases."

practice like pretrial detention beside the very rare occurrence of arrest for violent crime, scholars like Sunstein fuel an "availability bias," whereby the perception of violent crime is heightened due to the frequency with which it is invoked in mainstream and academic discourse regarding pretrial release.[65] This conflation may reflect widespread beliefs held by justice practitioners, who associate the number of prior arrests with a proclivity toward violence.[66] Rather than challenging this assumption, academic articles, industry white papers, and official government documents tend to reinforce this conflation by using general rearrest data as a proxy for danger, or by providing risk scores for "new criminal activity" alongside more modest estimates of risk of violence.

The "fundamental misattribution of agency"[67] in justice data and persistent conflation of rearrest with "danger" renders moot conversations regarding the accuracy of pretrial risk assessment forecasts, because the data used to measure accuracy is simply not representative of the outcome of interest. Some researchers recognize the limits of the available data but insist on making claims of crime prediction by framing the problem as a question of "sample bias" or "label bias." In an effort to make these tools more accurate and valid, these authors provide some quick technical fixes for addressing these narrow conceptualizations of bias.[68] Such efforts only reinforce the false association between arrest history and dangerousness and further conceal the fundamental misattribution of agency.[69]

This insistence on misleading framings of police and court data is fueled by the crucial rhetorical role they play in justifying punitive decisions. More representative framings of the data would produce less powerful claims, or they would give rise to research questions that directly challenge the practices and logics of the carceral state. The political economy of algorithmic systems rests largely on the fundamental misattribution of agency to make authoritative claims about an individual's criminal proclivities, which fuel and legitimize decisions to punish.[70] In this way, predictive algorithms that are based on these widespread mischaracterizations of the data underpin the moral economy that justifies the exclusion and repression of marginalized populations through the construction of "risky" or "deviant" profiles.[71]

[65] For example, Sunstein argues: "If defendants are incarcerated, the long-term consequences can be very severe. Their lives can be ruined. But if defendants are released, they might flee the jurisdiction or commit crimes. People might be assaulted, raped, or killed." This kind of side-by-side comparison of detention versus murder makes the prospect of unwarranted detention seem rather minor in comparison to the risk of lost life. Sunstein, "Algorithms, Correcting Biases," 2.

[66] This theme has come up repeatedly in interviews I have done with judges and other pretrial justice officials over the last two years.

[67] Ochigame, "The Illusion of Algorithmic Fairness."

[68] Berk, Machine Learning Risk Assessments in Criminal Justice Settings; Goel et al., "The Accuracy, Equity, and Jurisprudence of Criminal Risk Assessment."

[69] Ochigame, "The Illusion of Algorithmic Fairness."

[70] Harris, "The Reality of Racial Disparity in Criminal Justice: The Significance of Data Collection"; Muhammad, The Condemnation of Blackness; Ochigame, "The Illusion of Algorithmic Fairness."

[71] Dolovich, "Exclusion and Control in the Carceral State"; Harris, "The Reality of Racial Disparity in Criminal Justice: The Significance of Data Collection"; Michael J. Lynch, "The Power of Oppression: Understanding the History of Criminology as a Science of Oppression," Critical Criminology 9, no. 1–2 (2000): 144–152.

Critical criminologists have long argued that these interpretations of crime data are performative enactments of power structures, ones which fundamentally shape the discourse, methods, and epistemological assumptions of criminology and law enforcement practices.[72] Yet positivist subfields of the discipline continue to build predictive models to forecast "dangerousness," "new criminal activity," and "recidivism" based on this data. This issue has been a recurring tension within the field of criminology since the turn of the nineteenth century, when the meaning of arrest and incarceration statistics from the 1890 census were debated by early scholars of crime.[73] In the 1920s and 30s, actuarial methods of forecasting criminal behavior relied heavily on incorrect framings of arrest, conviction, and incarceration in order to make fallacious claims about crime prediction.[74] In the wake of the civil rights movement of the 1960s, critical criminologists argued that drastic increases in official crime statistics were more a byproduct of administrative changes in how crimes were reported than a result of real spikes in crime.[75] They pointed to alternative sources of crime data in order to resist the conflation of racial unrest with criminality in the late 1960s.[76]

More recently, David Harris cites numerous examples in which law enforcement officials have used arrest and incarceration statistics to justify racial profiling in the 1990s.[77] Officials pointed to statistics that reflect the overrepresentation of African Americans and Latinx in jails in order to justify racial profiling. They argued that their officers stopped and searched a disproportionate number of minorities, not because of racial animus but because, quite simply, the data showed that "that's where the criminals are."[78] These officials used arrest and incarceration data as a substitute for crime rate and, in doing so, laid the foundation for the state's own recursive logic, whereby it used internally generated numbers about arrest and incarceration as a justification for continuing the very practices that fueled those numbers.

Discourse regarding "fair, accountable, and transparent" AI is the most recent incarnation of this historical struggle over the interpretation of justice data. To date, the lion's share of research in this area has uncritically embraced the epistemological assumptions of mainstream criminology. In doing so, they continue a long tradition of centering reforms in the "sciences of oppression" which seek to profile and surveil marginalized

[72] Brown and Schept, "New Abolition, Criminology and a Critical Carceral Studies"; Platt, "'Street' Crime—A View from the Left."

[73] Muhammad, *The Condemnation of Blackness*.

[74] Bernard E. Harcourt, *Against Prediction: Profiling, Policing, and Punishing in an Actuarial Age* (University of Chicago Press, 2008).

[75] Vesla M. Weaver, "Frontlash: Race and the Development of Punitive Crime Policy," *Studies in American Political Development* 21, no. 2 (2007): 230–265.

[76] Platt, "'Street' Crime—A View from the Left."

[77] Harris, "The Reality of Racial Disparity in Criminal Justice: The Significance of Data Collection."

[78] *Id.* at 79. What these officials conveniently overlook were data which revealed that the "false positive" rate was much higher for African American males, meaning that the number of times that they searched that population and found nothing was much higher than other racial groups. Harris, "The Reality of Racial Disparity in Criminal Justice: The Significance of Data Collection"; Emma Pierson et al., "A Large-Scale Analysis of Racial Disparities in Police Stops across the United States," *ArXiv Preprint ArXiv:1706.05678*, 2017.

communities.[79] This scholarship not only provides a mechanism for the confinement and control of the "dangerous classes" but also creates the very processes through which these populations are turned into deviants to be controlled and feared.

In summary, attempts to render these tools more accurate by addressing narrow notions of "bias" simply miss the deeper methodological and epistemological issues regarding the fairness of these tools. As Hoffmann argues, we must grapple with the ways data-intensive, algorithmically mediated systems reinforce certain discursive frames over others—only then can we begin to unpack the ways such systems shape and constrain our ability to collectively pursue particular visions of justice.[80] Efforts to increase the accuracy of predictive systems run the risk of circumscribing these deeper ideological and epistemological struggles within a narrow technocratic debate about how to make these tools more valid, accurate, and fair.

THE WAY FORWARD: CHALLENGING FUNDAMENTAL ASSUMPTIONS

In the current political moment, the conversation regarding FAT algorithms has proven highly influential in shaping state and federal legislative efforts for reform. In the case of pretrial risk assessment, a number of states have passed legislation which acknowledges the risk of bias in risk-assessment tools. They call for the establishment of oversight committees and standards to ensure that specific types of bias are minimized, through semi-regular validation using updated data from local jurisdictions.[81] These efforts are very much aligned with the narrow formulation of "bias" embraced by many in the FAT community, eschewing deeper concerns regarding the epistemological soundness of these tools.

Yet, a growing number of thinkers are calling AI applications into question on more fundamental grounds. For example, in response to high-profile efforts to increase the representation of African Americans in data sets for facial recognition software (for the sake of increasing the software's accuracy),[82] Nabil Hassein argues:

> The reality for the foreseeable future is that the people who control and deploy facial recognition technology at any consequential scale will predominantly be our oppressors. Why should we desire our faces to be legible for efficient automated processing by

[79] Arnold Foundation, "Arnold Ventures Statement of Principles on Pretrial Justice."

[80] Hoffmann, "Where Fairness Fails: On Data, Algorithms, and the Limits of Antidiscrimination Discourse."

[81] Sarah Desmarais and Evan Lowder, "Pretrial Risk Assessment Tools: A Primer for Judges, Prosecutors, and Defense Attorneys" (MacArthur Foundation Safety and Justice Challenge, February 2019).

[82] Buolamwini and Gebru, "Gender Shades: Intersectional Accuracy Disparities in Commercial Gender Classification."

systems of their design?... The struggle for liberation is not a struggle for diversity and inclusion—it is a struggle for decolonization, reparations, and self-determination.[83]

In contrast to mainstream reform efforts, Hassein recontextualizes the issue of artificial intelligence within a structural critique of the carceral state as a fundamentally punitive system of social control. In doing so, he rejects attempts to improve the accuracy of technologies that are designed to make this system more accurate and efficient. Hassein then proposes a different set of values on which to base a counterimaginary about the future of the carceral state, one which centers the pursuit of agency and healing within historically marginalized communities.

It is important to note that this approach does not reject wholesale the use of data and technology in the carceral state, but rather requires a radical reformulation of the key concepts and assumptions which undergird the adoption of new technologies as a means of reform in this context—shifting away from measuring criminal proclivities and toward understanding processes of criminalization, from supporting law and order to increasing community safety and self-determination, and from surveillance of risky populations to accountability of state officials.

Shifting these fundamental assumptions is very important, as they inform (1) what questions are worth asking, (2) what data constitute relevant and authoritative evidence, and (3) the epistemological assumptions used to make claims based on the available evidence. In order to truly address the ethical stakes of artificial intelligence, we must embrace a radically different "sociotechnical imaginary" in order to redefine "not only what is attainable through science and technology, but also of how life ought, or ought not, be lived."[84] This requires a fundamental shift in who and what we conceive of as the object of analysis in data-driven regimes of reform. Rather than using data to profile and manage "risky populations," we should build systems to scrutinize the impacts of key policies and decision-making practices, as well as build more robust systems of accountability for the authority figures who drive outcomes.

Such an understanding of the role and function of the carceral state provides us with the critical framework we need in order to fundamentally reformulate the questions we ask, the way we characterize existing data, and how we identify and fill gaps in existing data regimes of the carceral state. The igniting of a critical sociotechnical imaginary is especially important in the current political moment, when the term "artificial intelligence" has been deployed as a means of justifying and depoliticizing the expansion of state and private surveillance amidst a growing crisis of legitimacy for the U.S. prison industrial complex. Under the authoritative rubric of "evidence-based reform" and "artificial intelligence," law enforcement officials have reframed contentious social issues in terms of technocratic shortcomings or issues of information access and interpretation.

[83] Nabil Hassein, "Against Black Inclusion in Facial Recognition," *Digital Talking Drum* (blog) (August 15, 2017), https://digitaltalkingdrum.com/2017/08/15/against-black-inclusion-in-facial-recognition/.

[84] Sheila Jasanoff and Sang-Hyun Kim, *Dreamscapes of Modernity: Sociotechnical Imaginaries and the Fabrication of Power* (University of Chicago Press, 2015), 4.

Efforts to increase the accuracy of predictive and evaluative systems run the risk of circumscribing deeper ideological and epistemological struggles within a narrow technocratic debate about how to make these processes more valid, accurate, and fair.

The key question is whether predictive tools reflect and reinforce punitive practices that drive disparate outcomes, and how data regimes interact with the penal ideology to naturalize these practices. Conversations regarding the ethical stakes of AI in criminal law must interrogate the default logics and assumptions of the carceral state, in order to address the foundational violence of law enforcement and courtroom practices. Only then can we hope to reimagine the use of data and technology to explore and substantiate a political vision that centers the creation of lasting alternatives to punishment and imprisonment, by increasing community safety and centering values of self-determination and healing in marginalized communities.

BIBLIOGRAPHY

Benjamin, Ruha. "Catching Our Breath: Critical Race STS and the Carceral Imagination." *Engaging Science, Technology, and Society* 2 (2016): 145–156.

Brown, Michelle, and Judah Schept. "New Abolition, Criminology and a Critical Carceral Studies." *Punishment & Society* 19, no. 4 (2017): 440–462.

Corbett-Davies, Sam, Emma Pierson, Avi Feller, Sharad Goel, and Aziz Huq. "Algorithmic Decision Making and the Cost of Fairness." In *Proceedings of the 23rd ACM SIGKDD International Conference on Knowledge Discovery and Data Mining*, 797–806. ACM, 2017.

Elliott, Delbert S. "Lies, Damn Lies, and Arrest Statistics." Center for the Study and Prevention of Violence, 1995.

Ferguson, Andrew Guthrie. "Policing Predictive Policing." *Washington University Law Review* 94 (2016): 1109.

Harcourt, Bernard E. *Against Prediction: Profiling, Policing, and Punishing in an Actuarial Age.* University of Chicago Press, 2008.

Kleinberg, Jon, Jens Ludwig, Sendhil Mullainathan, and Ashesh Rambachan. "Algorithmic Fairness." In *AEA Papers and Proceedings*, vol. 108, 22–27. AEA, 2018.

Muhammad, Khalil Gibran. *The Condemnation of Blackness.* Harvard University Press, 2011.

Ochigame, Rodrigo. "The Illusion of Algorithmic Fairness." Cambridge, MA: March 25, 2019.

Stevenson, Megan. "Assessing Risk Assessment in Action." *Minnesota Law Review* 103 (2018): 303.

CHAPTER 40

··

"FAIR NOTICE" IN
THE AGE OF AI

··

KIEL BRENNAN-MARQUEZ

INTRODUCTION

··

"FAIR NOTICE" is paramount to the rule of law. The maxim has ancient roots: people ought to know, in advance, what the law demands of them.[1] If not, something fundamental has gone awry. Much as the organization of state power may exhibit certain functional characteristics of a legal system, it is no longer, in an important sense, *lawful*.[2]

Stated so formally, it is hard to imagine the ideal inspiring too much pushback. More elusive are its practical implications. Cases dealing with "fair notice" problems—vagueness challenges, for instance—are often long on rhetoric but short on conceptual clarity.

---

[1] Lon L. Fuller, *The Morality of Law* (New Haven: Yale University Press, 1964), 34–37 (expounding this point through the memorable example of King Rex); Shon Hopwood, "Clarity in Criminal Law," *American Criminal Law Review* 54 (2017): 715–718 (tracing the history of the "fair notice" principle).

[2] What makes fair notice central to the rule of law is an interesting question, which I largely leave to one side here. My analysis is aimed simply to enrich the concept of fair notice, on the *assumption* that it is a concept worth taking seriously and trying to vindicate. In passing, however, I will note that commentary on fair notice writ large—why we care about notice in the first place—seems to focus almost entirely on instrumental arguments; notice is primarily valuable, perhaps exclusively valuable, for facilitating private ordering. See Scott Shapiro, *Legality* (New York: Belknap Press, 2011) (arguing that law both is a "plan," metaphorically speaking, and by extension enables citizens living under the law to make plans); Robert Ellickson, *Order Without Law* (Cambridge: Harvard University Press, 1991) (cataloging and extoling the virtues of legal predictability, insofar as it allows for private ordering); Friedrich Hayek, *The Road to Serfdom* (Chicago: University of Chicago Press, 1944). Though one can certainly, of course, imagine nonconsequentialist arguments in favor of notice. Perhaps it tells us something about the state of thinking about due process and legality today—or the state of thinking more generally—that nonconsequentialist arguments, centered on dignity, say, have not been more carefully developed.

In spite of, or perhaps because of, their hallowedness, notice principles have persisted for many centuries with little elaboration.

This is unfortunate—for many reasons, but especially because, going forward, "fair notice" will be among the key concepts for regulating the scope and role of AI in the legal system. AI, like its junior sibling, machine learning, unleashes a historically novel possibility: decision-making tools that are at once (1) powerfully accurate, and (2) inscrutable to their human stewards and subjects.[3] To determine when the use of AI-based (or AI-assisted) decision-making tools are consistent with the requirements of "fair notice," we need a sharper account of the principle's contours.

Hence the present chapter. In it, I develop a tripartite model of "fair notice," inspired by the problems—and opportunities—of AI. Specifically, I argue that lack of "fair notice" is used interchangeably to describe three distinct (if often overlapping) properties:

1. Notice of inputs
2. Notice of outputs
3. Notice of input-output functionality

Disentangling these forms of notice, and deciding which matter in which contexts (and for what reasons), will be crucial to the proper governance of AI. Particularly with respect to input-output functionality, there is persistent ambiguity about what *mode* of notice is relevant. For people to be "on notice" about how an input-output function works, is understanding of the function itself necessary? Must the function be transparent and explainable? Or is it sufficient, at least under some circumstances, for people to have a *heuristical understanding* of the function—that is, a pragmatic conception, imperfect but stable, of which inputs tend to lead to which outputs?

Boiled down, the upshot of this chapter is that the answer to the last question is "yes." In fact, there may be times when heuristical understanding is superior to actual understanding of an input-output function; or better put, when the reason we demand actual understanding is to *cultivate* heuristical understanding, because the latter is what ultimately matters to affected parties in practice. When this happens, a significant governance implication follows: we do not independently care about—and could, in principle, dispense with—actual understanding of input-output functionality, as long as heuristical understanding can be developed by other means.

The chapter has three parts. First, I craft the tripartite model of notice, weaving between doctrine (drawn from U.S. constitutional law) and normative theory, and connecting both to burgeoning questions of AI governance. Second, I distinguish more finely between two variants of notice of input-output functionality—actual and

---

[3] See Solon Barocas and Andrew Selbst, "The Intuitive Appeal of Explainable Machines," *Fordham Law Review* 87 (2018); Kiel Brennan-Marquez, "'Plausible Cause': Explanatory Standards in the Age of Powerful Machines," *Vanderbilt Law Review* 70 (2017): 1295. For general background on the link between explainability and accountability, Frank Pasquale, "A Rule of Persons, Not Machines: The Limits of Legal Automation," *George Washington Law Review* 87 (2019); Jonathan Manes, "Secret Law," *Georgetown Law Journal* 106 (2018).

heuristical—and explore the reasons we might care about one rather than the other. Third, I close by offering some remarks about the implications of these various categories for AI, in both the immediate and longer-term future.

A Tripartite Model of "Fair Notice"

If we imagine legal rules as input-output functions—such that any given rule can be described as an infinitely complex bundle of input-sets, each sufficient to trigger an output in the form of adverse treatment—then "fair notice" can describe three different things.

First, it can describe *notice of inputs*. By asking whether one had "fair notice" of the law, we might be asking if they knew or should have known which input-sets occasion adverse treatment. This is the most straightforward type of notice. If one genuinely does not know what conduct occasions adverse treatment, the rule of law has tripped out the gate.[4]

Second, it can describe *notice of outputs*. By asking whether one had "fair notice" of the law, we might be asking if they knew or should have known what consequences might be occasioned by an input-set. Here, the relevant question is not: "Will Conduct X occasion adverse treatment?" Rather, it is: "What kind of adverse treatment—or how *severe* of adverse treatment—does Conduct X occasion?"

Third, it can describe *notice of input-output functionality*. By asking whether one had "fair notice" of the law, we might be asking if they understood or should have understood the process by which a given input-set maps to specific adverse treatment. Why did Conduct X result—or why was it likely to result—in Consequence Y? Of the three, this is the strongest form of notice, because when satisfied, it entails notice on the first two dimensions as well.

Notice of Inputs

We begin at the beginning. What conduct—which input-sets—occasion adverse treatment? Commentators as diverse as Blackstone and Kafka have trained their attention on this question.[5] What is more, many canonical notice rules strive to ensure that ordinary people can move through the world with at least the rough beginnings of an answer. For example, concern about notice of inputs has long been understood to animate the rule of lenity, as a canon of construction in both criminal and immigration proceedings. If a statute is genuinely ambiguous between two (or more) readings, ties go, so to speak, to the defendant. Otherwise, one could be subject to adverse treatment on the basis of

---

[4] See Kiel Brennan-Marquez, "Extremely Broad Laws," *Arizona Law Review* 61 (2019) (discussing the notice problem—in the "notice of inputs" sense—in greater detail).

[5] See William Blackstone, *Commentaries* 1 (1765); Franz Kafka, *The Trial* (1925).

conduct—or in the language here, input-sets—that a reasonable person could have regarded as entirely lawful.[6]

The same is true of vagueness challenges. Vague statutes are problematic, the U.S. Supreme Court has made clear, for enshrining "unascertainable standards" that leave "[people] of common intelligence [to] guess at [the law's] meaning."[7] Part of the problem, of course, is arbitrary enforcement: the danger that application of unascertainable standards may come to "depend," for example, "[on] whether or not a policeman is annoyed."[8] But this is just the iceberg's tip. Even setting practical concerns about enforcement to one side, it is simply *unfair* for "ordinary people [not to] understand what conduct is prohibited."[9] It violates "notions of fair play,"[10] because it leaves people at the mercy of an enforcement system that, even while managing to avoid egregious miscarriages of justice, defies comprehension.

So, too, with the Supreme Court's ex post facto jurisprudence, which also strives to ensure that people are not punished for conduct they could not have known, at the time, was off limits. This "basic principle of fairness," the Supreme Court has made clear, reaches back to the common law.[11] Ordinary people have a right to insist that government, rather than legislating "vindictive[ly]" and retroactively, "abide by the rules of law it establishes [in advance]."[12] As Madison once summarized the point: ex post facto lawmaking is "contrary to the first principles of the social compact."[13] People must be "warn[ed] of applicable laws."[14]

Furthermore, concern regarding notice of inputs is not limited to the adverse treatment of ordinary people. It also reaches the adverse treatment of state officials. The Supreme Court has crafted numerous doctrines—qualified immunity, most prominently—to shield officials from liability at t_2 for decisions that a reasonable actor could have thought lawful at t_1.[15] In fact, the Supreme Court has even gone so far as to excuse police officers who *do not know the law* for performing stops and arrests pursuant to a

---

[6] See, e.g., United States v. Santos, 553 U.S. 507 (2008) (discussing the rule of lenity in the criminal context); INS v. St. Cyr, 533 U.S. 289, 320 (2001) (ditto in the immigration context).

[7] Coates v. City of Cincinnati, 402 U.S. 611, 614 (1971) (quoting Connally v. General Const. Co., 269 U.S. 385, 391 (1926)).

[8] 402 U.S. at 614.

[9] Kolender v. Lawson, 461 U.S. 352, 357 (1983). See also Johnson v. United States, 135 S. Ct. 2551 (2015) (striking down the so-called residual clause of the Armed Career Criminal Act—which provided for harsher sentences for convictions involving "conduct that presents a serious potential risk of physical injury to another"—on the ground that its open-ended standard "denies fair notice to defendants and invites arbitrary enforcement by judges").

[10] Connally v. General Const. Co., 269 U.S. 385, 391 (1926).

[11] Peugh v. United States, 569 U.S. 530, 544 (2013) (holding that sentencing based on guidelines promulgated after the offense of conviction occurred violates the Ex Post Facto Clause).

[12] See Carmell v. Texas, 529 U.S. 513, 533 (2000) (holding that a conviction obtained pursuant to a rule of evidence that changed after the conduct in question—but before the trial itself—constituted ex post facto punishment).

[13] *The Federalist No. 44.*   [14] *Peugh*, 569 U.S. at 544.

[15] For the Supreme Court's most recent comprehensive statement of the qualified immunity doctrine, see District of Columbia v. Wesby, 583 U.S. __ (2018).

legal error, so long as the error is reasonable; the rationale, in essence, is that it would be unfair to hold officers accountable for mistakes of law of which a reasonable person, reading the relevant statute in good faith, would not have been on notice.[16]

* * *

AI-related examples of input-opacity are legion. It would hardly be an exaggeration to say that notice of inputs is *the* notice concern that has preoccupied scholars in the AI governance space to date.[17] And this, for a simple reason: as of this writing, the status quo is so impoverished with regard to notice of inputs—since most information technology is developed in the private sector, most information-collection practices (which are ultimately responsible for populating AI-related inputs) are poorly understood—the proverbial fruit hangs remarkably low. This is not to deprecate the importance of notice regarding inputs. The latter is certainly important: often a necessary condition of meaningful understanding of how decision-making works.[18] The point is simply that for all its benefits, notice of inputs is the beginning, not the end, of the conversation about AI governance.

Notice of Outputs

It ought to come as little surprise, then, that notice of inputs is not the end of the line for due process doctrine. Courts also worry, with good reason, about notice of *outputs*. Even if there can be little doubt that a person was (or ought to have been) on notice that Conduct X would occasion adverse treatment, they are also entitled to an understanding, ex ante, of the type—and severity—of such treatment.

A recent illustration of this principle is *Marinello v. United States*, which centered on 26 USC § 7212(a), the so-called "Omnibus Clause" of the Internal Revenue Code. Sec. 7212(a) criminalizes the act of "corruptly or by force or threat of force ... obstruct[ing] or imped[ing], or endeavor[ing] to obstruct or impede, the due administration of [taxes]."[19]

---

[16] See Heien v. North Carolina, 574 U.S. __ (2015).

[17] See Frank Pasquale, *The Black Box Society* (Cambridge: Harvard University Press, 2015); Danielle Citron, "Technological Due Process," *Washington University Law Review* 85 (2008): 1256–1257 (exploring for input-notice with respect to algorithmic tools); Kate Crawford and Jason Schulz, "Big Data and Due Process: Toward A Framework to Redress Predictive Privacy Harms," *Boston College Law Review* 55 (2014): 119 (explaining that "[f]or Big Data to deliver the answers we seek, it must be accurate and include all appropriate inputs equally to overcome any signal problems"—and pointing to the problems that can result when inputs are unclear).

[18] See, e.g., Barocas and Selbst, "The Intuitive Appeal of Explainable Machines," 1118 (describing what happens when "faceless bureaucrac[ies] [] make[] consequential decisions" about which affected parties "have ... no understanding," and over which they exercise "no input"). See also David Luban, Alan Strudler, and David Wasserman, "Moral Responsibility in the Age of Bureaucracy," *Michigan Law Review* 90 (1992): 2355 (arguing that one of the central purposes of law is securing "what we might call the *moral intelligibility* of our lives," and expounding how the "horror of the bureaucratic process" is not so much "officials' mechanical adherence to duty" as "individual[s'] ignorance" of what is permitted, prohibited, and required of them as citizens).

[19] See 26 USC § 7212(a).

The dispute was over which kinds of "obstruction" or "impediment" qualify as predicate acts under the Omnibus Clause. How far, at the level of actus reus, does the clause reach? According to the government, the answer was simple: the clause reaches all noncompliance with tax rules. And its legal argument was equally simple: "impediment" means "a thing that impedes," and there is no doubt that deliberate acts of noncompliance *impede* the overall administration of taxes.

The Supreme Court disagreed. Holding for petitioner, Justice Breyer argued that the IRS's construction of "impediment," despite tracking the word's definition, simply encompassed too many low-level infractions. "Interpreted broadly," Breyer reasoned, "the provision could apply to a person who pays a babysitter $41 per week in cash without withholding taxes, leaves a large cash tip in a restaurant, fails to keep donation receipts from every charity to which he or she contributes, or fails to provide every record to an accountant."[20] And this would violate the "fair warning" principle—the identical twin of fair notice—that has long "led [the] Court...to exercise interpretive restraint."[21]

Crucially, however, the reason the government's construction flouted the "fair warning" principle was not that minor wrongdoing—such as paying a babysitter without withholdings—is permissible. It plainly violates the tax code. Nor was the problem that a reasonable person could not be expected to be *aware* of the relevant law. Ignorance does not ordinarily excuse violations,[22] but more to the point, Justice Breyer explicitly acknowledged the possibility that someone who pays a babysitter without withholdings (or the equivalent) "may believe that, in doing so, he is running the risk of having violated an IRS rule."[23] The problem is that no one, having committed such a minor offense, "would believe he [could] fac[e] a potential felony prosecution for tax obstruction."[24] In other words, the problem was the penalty's *severity*; or more exactly, the mismatch between the penalty's severity and the conduct's relative harmlessness.

The issue in *Marinello*—by the opinion's own terms—is notice of outputs, not notice of inputs. The idea is not that people will fail to appreciate that paying a babysitter under the table (or the equivalent) is prohibited. The idea is that even assuming the prohibition is clear and well known, there is still a gap between the statute's clear language and reasonable expectations about the statute will actually be enforced. In other words, the whole point of *Marinello* is that someone who fails to withhold from payments to a babysitter—even if he knows that doing so is wrong; indeed, even if he knows that doing so technically falls within the scope of 26 USC § 7212(a)—would never imagine being held criminally liable, down the line, for felony tax obstruction. And it is *that* variable, not the formal reach of tax law, that drove the "fair notice" analysis.

---

[20] *Id*. For background on the babysitter example, in particular, see 26 C.F.R. § 31.3102–1(a)(2017); IRS Publication 926, at 5–6 (2018).

[21] Marinello v. United States, 138 S. Ct. 1101, 1108 (2018).

[22] See, e.g., Edwin Meese and Paul Larkin Jr., "Reconsidering the Mistake of Law Defense," *Journal of Criminal Law and Criminology* 102 (2012) (discussing this proposition at length).

[23] 138 S. Ct. at 1108.   [24] *Id*.

Cases like *Marinello*, in which the Supreme Court explicitly acknowledges a mismatch between input-sets and outputs—conduct and penalty—are somewhat rare, given the long-standing prohibition on "proportionality" analysis in U.S. constitutional law. But they are hardly unheard of,[25] and more importantly, the *idea* that law should give people notice of likely penalties is intuitive to the point of self-evident. It would clearly be insufficient for the legal order to hand us a laundry list of proscriptions without any hint of which conduct was more or less vile, more or less prone to harsh consequences.[26] This hypothetical is somewhat unrelatable, of course, because in the real world we can typically rely on a rough correlation between the *malum in se* and the *malum prohibitum*. But such a legal order is hardly *unimaginable*—and lack of notice about particular outcomes offers a glimpse, however fleeting, of its nightmare.

* * *

In the AI context, problems regarding notice of outputs can take a variety of forms. For one thing, there can be proportionality mismatches along the lines of *Marinello*—input-sets can produce outputs that seem, in an intuitive sense, too extreme. For another thing, there can be "resilience" issues: that is, circumstances in which marginal changes to an input-set result in drastic changes to the relevant output, depriving people of a meaningful

---

[25] Another recent example is Maslenjak v. United States, 137 S. Ct. 1918 (2017). There, the government argued that any "false statement" made during the naturalization process, no matter how innocuous, and regardless of how many years (or decades) have elapsed since the statement occurred, is a sufficient basis to revoke someone's citizenship. The Supreme Court made short work of this position, explicitly identifying breadth as one of its infirmities. See Tr. Oral Arg. at 27–30, Maslenjak v. United States, 137 S. Ct. 1918 (No. 16–309) ("ROBERTS: I looked at the naturalization form, [and] there is a question. It's number 22. 'Have you ever ... committed, assisted in committing, or attempted to commit a crime or offense for which you were not arrested?' Some time ago, outside of the statute of limitations, I drove 60 miles an hour in a 55 mph zone [but] I was not arrested. Now, you say that if I answer [question 22] no, 20 years after I was naturalized as a citizen, you can knock at my door and say, guess what, you're not an American citizen after all. COUNSEL: Well— ROBERTS: Is that right? COUNSEL: Well, I would say two things. First, that is how the government would interpret that [question], that it would require you to disclose those sorts of offenses. ROBERTS: Oh, come on. You're saying that on this form, you expect everyone to list every time in which they drove over the speed limit ... [or] we can take away your citizenship"). See also Mellouli v. Lynch, 135 S. Ct. 1983 (2015) and Moncrieffe v. Holder, 133 S. Ct. 1678 (2013), both of which raised the question of whether extremely minor conduct reflected in state-level convictions can trigger deportation—in *Mellouli*, the conduct was possessing a sock ("drug paraphernalia"), whereas in Moncrieffe, it was possessing 1.3 grams of marijuana for social use (the equivalent of two or three small cigarettes). In both cases, the Supreme Court held the conduct insufficient to occasion such a severe penalty; and while it did not use the language of "fair notice," the cases can certainly understood to operate in that register.

[26] Another example along these lines is the Supreme Court's punitive damages jurisprudence, where a defendant may well be on notice that the conduct in question is forbidden—that is why the conduct formed the basis of liability—but they are surely *not* on notice about the possible consequences (since punitive damages could be anywhere from 1x to 100x the actual damage). See, e.g., State Farm Mut. Auto Ins. v. Campbell, 538 U.S. 408, 423 (2003) ("A defendant should be punished for the conduct that harmed the plaintiff, not for being an unsavory individual or business. Due process does not permit courts, in the calculation of punitive damages, to adjudicate the merits of other parties' hypothetical claims against a defendant under the guise of the reprehensibility analysis.").

understanding of the consequences their conduct is likely to bring about.[27] And of course these two problems (and perhaps others as well) can operate in tandem.

Notice of Input-Output Functionality

The third conception of "fair notice" is that people should be aware, not only of which input-sets occasion adverse treatment and of what sort of adverse treatment it is likely to be, but also of the process by which Conduct X maps to Consequence Y.

On this front, examples from doctrine are more elusive, since the Supreme Court rarely, if ever, articulates fair notice in terms of the relationship between conduct and legal consequences (let alone in the language of "input-output functionality"). But light shines through the cracks. Numerous areas of criminal procedure, for example, take root in the principle that we should understand how, or why, particular input-sets lead to particular legal consequences.

Take the Fourth Amendment's particularized suspicion standard. The requirement that police develop probable cause before performing (certain kinds of) searches and seizures is not only about notice of inputs and outputs—if you do X, Y, or Z, you are more likely to be stopped, searched, arrested. It is *also* about giving people insight into the process by which X, Y, and Z might be taken to justify stops, searches, and arrests. Namely, X, Y, and Z might be taken to justify stops, searches, and arrests because they are likely to seem to a reasonable observer like indicia of wrongdoing; they are likely, in context, to give rise to a plausible inference of criminality.[28] In this sense, the particularized suspicion standard conveys to ordinary people not only which input-sets are conducive to adverse treatment, but *why* they are: the inferential mechanisms by which state officials—here, police officers—will link inputs to outputs.

The point comes through most crisply, perhaps, when courts navigate the boundary between investigative searches, which require particularized suspicion, and "administrative searches," which do not. In *Delaware v. Prouse*, for example, the Supreme Court considered whether police may perform suspicionless traffic stops to verify—essentially as a spot check—drivers' licenses and vehicular registrations.[29] The state defended the program on the theory that its core purpose was administrative; the idea was to encourage compliance with licensing and registration laws, not to investigate criminal activity.[30] The Supreme Court disagreed, holding that suspicionless vehicle stops, even if pursued for administrative reasons, seemed too much like garden-variety police work: they "interfere with freedom of movement, are inconvenient, and consume time."[31]

---

[27] See Alex Stein, *Foundations of Evidence Law* 48 (Oxford: Oxford University Press, 2005) (unpacking the idea of epistemic "resiliency," as a measure of output-change relative to input-change). See also Marjorie A. McDiarmid, "Lawyer Decision Making: The Problem of Prediction," *Wisconsin Law Review* 1992 (1992): 1878–1880 (diagnosing lack of resilience as the issue highlighted by L. Jonathan Cohen's famous "gatecrasher" hypothetical).

[28] For background on this gloss of the Fourth Amendment, see Brennan-Marquez, *Plausible Cause.*

[29] 440 U.S. 648, 650 (1979).   [30] *Id.* at 658–659.   [31] *Id.* at 657.

More fundamentally, blessing suspicionless vehicle stops would cast a pall of uncertainty over driving at all times,[32] a fact that distinguishes suspicionless stops from, say, road-blocks and sobriety checkpoints, which are contained to particular areas and times.[33]

Prouse is a canonical holding, and rightly so. Its second rationale—that suspicionless stops to spot-check licenses and registration would cast a shadow over all driving—highlights the importance of input-output functionality. The government's position, in essence, was that being subject to suspicionless searches is a condition of driving: by deciding to drive (in Delaware), you would knowingly assume the risk of having to endure suspicionless searches, just as you knowingly take on all sorts of other burdens related to driving, such as buying insurance.

This argument hardly sounds crazy, indeed it may even sound plausible, if we focus solely on notice of inputs and outputs. The problem is that simply being told that driving (input) might occasion a stop (output) is not enough. We also want to know when and why stops are likely to occur. Which is to say, it matters *how* the input of "driving" maps to the output of "stop." Without that understanding, there is no functional difference—literally, the functions are indistinguishable—between good faith decisions, arbitrary decisions, biased decisions, pretextual decisions, and the like.

INPUT-OUTPUT FUNCTIONALITY: ACTUAL NOTICE, HEURISTICAL NOTICE, OR BOTH?

Yet a case like *Prouse*, even as it identifies the need for notice of input-output functionality, does not establish what *sort* of notice is required. In particular, it does not tell us whether the key variable is (1) which input-sets actually yield which outputs or, rather, (2) which input-sets correspond to which outputs, regardless of the underlying causal mechanisms. I refer to the former as "actual notice," and the latter as "heuristical notice."

This ambiguity is not surprising; for the answer, ultimately, is not static. It depends on the normative goal that motivates the call for notice. If the goal is to equip potential affected parties (like drivers) with an understanding of how their actions are likely to invite versus avoid certain outcomes (like entanglement with law enforcement)—a goal that might take many forms and stem from different founts, but I describe in umbrella terms as "navigability"—heuristical notice of input-output functionality may be sufficient.

---

[32] *Id.* (describing this concern in terms of the "substantial anxiety" that a suspicionless license-check regime would create for drivers).

[33] See Illinois v. Lidster, 540 U.S. 419, 425 (2004) (holding that suspicionless stops at "information-seeking" checkpoints are okay); Mich. Dep't of State Police v. Sitz, 496 U.S. 444 (1990) (likewise for sobriety checkpoints). See also *Prouse*, 440 U.S. 648, 657 (emphasizing the predictable elements of the logistics of traffic checkpoints: "the motorist can see that other vehicles are being stopped, he can see visible signs of the officers' authority, and he is much less likely to be frightened or annoyed by the intrusion").

In fact, it may even be superior to actual notice, insofar as the latter, despite disclosing more information, fails to enhance navigability by nonexperts on the ground.

If, on the other hand, the normative goal is something beyond navigability—if the point is, say, to affirm the dignity of affected parties, not just to help them understand how to avoid certain outcomes—heuristical notice may fall short in most, or even all, cases. The same is true, moreover, if the point is to constrain decision-making along certain high-salience dimensions. If, for example, the reason we care about looking "under the hood" is that certain input-output functions are forbidden (e.g., because they marshal variables like race or gender in unfair ways), then of course heuristical notice is no substitute for actual notice, for heuristical notice—the observation that certain inputs correspond to certain outputs—is what *prompts* normative concern, not what alleviates it.

Complicating matters further, demands for greater insight about input-output functionality can easily, in practice, be framed in terms of actual notice even when the true linchpin is heuristical notice—making it difficult to reason backward from the types of notice people *say* they care about. Credit scores, for example, have long been an area of notorious opacity, inspiring commentators to agitate in favor of greater transparency.[34] But it is not always clear—in fact it is frequently unclear—why, in this realm, opacity is so troubling. If opacity is troubling on navigability grounds, that is, because people affected by the credit system ought to have some control over their scores, then heuristical notice may be sufficient. In fact, as noted earlier, it may be preferable to actual notice, depending on the level of technicality at which the latter operates.[35] In many cases, surely, it will be more useful for an ordinary person to hear, "Adjustments to variables [X and Y] maximize your odds of an improved credit score," instead of receiving comprehensive, equation-laden "notice" of the scoring algorithm. Of course, if the problem with credit-scoring opacity goes beyond, or simply runs orthogonal to, navigability, heuristical understanding is unlikely to suffice. The idea is not to pick sides here. Rather, it is to appreciate how a demand for actual notice could either be (1) misguided entirely, or (2) instrumental to heuristical notice, though articulated in (misleadingly) noninstrumental terms—and that either of these errors could occur without parties on the front lines of policy debates being aware of them.

This last point is especially important, given the rhetorical appeal of actual notice of input-output functionality. The aspiration of actual notice—understanding how the world actually operates—is a natural call to arms. Its absence inspires outrage. Its possibility represents an easy focal point for mobilization. But those dynamics notwithstanding, it is not always clear that actual notice is what matters. In fact, it is not clear that even absent those dynamics (or at least, bracketing them for argument's sake), we can take demands for actual notice entirely seriously, given the confusion that surrounds fair notice in general.

---

[34] See Danielle Citron and Frank Pasquale, "The Scored Society: Due Process for Automated Predictions," *Washington Law Review* 89 (2014).

[35] See Barocas and Selbst, "The Intuitive Appeal of Explainable Machines" (describing this feature of heuristical understanding in terms of "intuitiveness").

Practically speaking, there are two risks here. The first is that demands for actual notice will fall short politically, and consequently, to quote the old maxim, the perfect will prove an enemy of the good. Which is to say, if heuristical notice is what matters, but actual notice is what becomes the rallying cry, there is danger that we will end up with neither—no actual notice of input-output functionality, because it represents too heavy a lift, and no heuristical notice, either, because heuristical notice was not emphasized in the first instance.

The second risk, in some sense the graver risk, is that actual understanding—even assuming it proves a tenable ideal in practice—will not *deliver* heuristical understanding. After all, it is possible to understand input-output functionality in a literal sense (i.e., to be privy to a complete mapping of which input-sets conduce to which outputs) without having a "ready at hand," navigable understanding of how the function operates in practice.

On this last point, consider a simple, non-AI example. Mary wants know who is likely to be stopped by police in Central Park for violating an "anti-vagrancy" statute; in essence, she wishes to know what constitutes "vagrancy" in a functional, not merely formal, sense. To answer this question, would Mary be better served to (1) read the municipal anti-vagrancy statute, (2) attend a police training on enforcement priorities in parks (in which supervisors explain to officers what kinds of behavior to target when enforcing the municipal anti-vagrancy statute), or (3) observe the patterns of actual police conduct in the local park for a few weeks? The answer, of course, is that it depends on the kind of understanding that Mary is looking for. The statute itself is unlikely to be of much help. Of course, it is also unlikely to be entirely useless—at least on the assumption that municipal codes bear some relation to what police actually do. But there are also likely to be aspects of the relevant input-output functionality that elude formal codification, making it likely that either attending a training, or observing officers "in the wild," will be more promising methods for giving Mary an actual sense of how police conduct their business.

Yet what of the distinction between these two methods? Training is an access point to actual understanding, whereas the patterns observed in the park are an access point to heuristical understanding. Which one Mary should care about depends on what her goal is. If her goal (as would surely be the case for many ordinary people) is to better calibrate her behavior so as to avoid intrusion from the police, it is not clear which method is superior. It could be that sitting in on the police training would tell her more than the patterns in the park—since, after all, training will pull back the curtain on departmental priorities—but it could also be that observing the police over a sustained period of time, and paying scrupulous attention to which variables correspond to intrusion in practice, will tell her more.[36]

---

[36] Possibilities along these lines abound. To take one particularly obvious (and sadly not uncommon example), suppose that in reality vagrancy stops occur much more frequently based on the race of the target. This pattern is unlikely, presumably, to surface in the training, though it may well surface in observational patterns.

What this hypothetical underscores is that the relationship between actual and heuristical understanding is often in flux, making it all the more important to be precise about ultimate goals. If the goal is to make a decision-making system as navigable as possible for ordinary people, then heuristical understanding ought to have priority. This hardly means that actual understanding is irrelevant—it may serve other functions and, as importantly, may operate in the service of heuristical understanding—but it does help to keep the goal in focus.

As it relates to AI, the ambiguity between actual and heuristical understanding is, if anything, even more severe. There are absolute limits, at least given existing technology, on the capacity of AI systems, in principle, to convey an actual understanding of their operation. Which means, put bluntly, that if actual understanding is the aspiration (or necessity), then AI-based systems may simply be disallowable—at least for the time being. If, on the other hand, the goal is heuristical understanding, as I suspect it is in many cases, then AI-based systems are not verboten; they simply require observation. As with any aspect of the natural world that we do not immediately understand by analogy or cognitive extrapolation, we may need to test AI-based systems to best figure out how they behave, and how affected parties might best respond.

But this is hardly cause for pessimism or alarm. On the contrary, experimentalism has long been the operative mechanism of heuristical knowledge, which makes for good news and bad news at once. At some level, they are the same news: namely, in many settings we do not care about actual understanding—making the so-called "black box" problem, in many guises, overstated—but we *do* care about heuristical understanding. Which means, acclimation matters. We need time to adjust to AI-based decisions, or really, to any decision-making system that has not yet been ingrained. But then again, of course we do: humans work in a different register and on a different timeframe than machines. It is little surprise that we would need, and that fair notice principles would *necessitate*, time to get our bearings.

SOME CONCLUDING THOUGHTS ABOUT AI

In closing, I want to offer a few thoughts about the how the tripartite model of notice applies to AI, in both the immediate future and longer term. Much as existing debate on AI governance has mobilized around the "notice of inputs" problem, this will soon—perhaps quite soon—cease to be the focal point of policy discussion. In short order, we will find ourselves in a world where notice of inputs, though important, is plainly insufficient to render AI systems accountable. We will soon come to embrace the reality that grasping how AI systems *work*, above and beyond having access to the data that propels them, is what ultimately matters.

Nevertheless, it remains an open question whether, when it comes to notice of input-output functionality, AI calls out for actual understanding, heuristical understanding, or both. In contexts where the goal is navigability, the answer may be that, in principle at least, heuristical understanding is sufficient; which raises the natural next question of how heuristical understanding will best be achieved. In contrast to an example like Mary wishing to know how an anti-vagrancy statute operates, many of us (at least at present) lack the capability—in terms of resources, skills, tools, and expertise—to observe the operation of AI-systems "in the wild." Such capability can certainly be developed; indeed, it may come to pass naturally. But it is worth considering what it will require.

In particular, there are two issues that may limit our capability to develop heuristical understanding of AI-driven systems. The first is the "intuitiveness" problem. The second—and at some level, the mirror image—is the "stationarity" problem.

The "intuitiveness" problem is that AI outputs can be insusceptible of meaningful human interpretation. Which is to say, a human observer can be aware that an input-set leads to a particular output—can even have tested that outcome scientifically and assured herself that she understands, heuristically, "how the system works" in this particular context—but still have no idea *why*.[37] Of course, this ignorance may prove ephemeral. Learning more about the world, observing more instances of the AI system's operations, or simply thinking more about the problem, may illuminate the underlying causal dynamics. Yet the *possibility* of nonintuitiveness, even in the face of robust heuristical knowledge, persists—representing an important bound on heuristical understanding.[38]

The "stationarity" problem, by contrast, is not about the way human modeling lags behind static patterns in reality. It is about the way that static human modeling, even when temporarily right, is outpaced by changes in reality: the internally dynamic tendency of data, and thus, of data-driven systems. The reason nonstationary systems prove difficult to navigate is not that their operation is opaque to human understanding. Rather, it is that human understanding quickly becomes obsolete.[39]

In short, AI-based systems can defy intuitive modeling, even if we have ample time to observe them—and even when intuitive modeling is possible, it can easily be drained of value as the AI-based system adapts. These are both, of course, issues with non-AI-based systems as well. When Mary tries to discern enforcement patterns in the park, it is always possible that she will (1) observe patterns that resist an everyday causal narrative, and/or (2) observe patterns at t_1 that—maybe even because of Mary's observations!—

---

[37] See James Grimmelmann and Daniel Westreich, "Incomprehensible Discrimination," *California Law Review Online* 7 (2016) (explaining the intuitiveness problem and exploring various statistical solutions to it in practice).

[38] To be clear, an intuitive conception of causality is neither necessary nor sufficient to capture *actual* causality; even putting aside the deep philosophical issues that attend to causality in general, it is clear that people can embrace "narratives" of causality that are deeply flawed, while still delivering (mistaken) heuristical understanding, and it is likewise possible for a theory of causality—say, one discovered by an AI system—that is *actually correct* but nevertheless deeply unintuitive given one's current understanding of the world. On these dynamics, see Barocas and Selbst, "The Intuitive Appeal of Explainable Machines," 1096–1098.

[39] See Motoaki Kawanabe and Masashi Sugiyama, *Machine Learning in Non-Stationary Environments* (Cambridge: MIT University Press, 2012).

will no longer hold at t$_2$. But in Mary's case, at least, there will likely be outward indicators as her understanding wears thin. She will observe patterns or facts that do not jibe with her existing causal theory. And she will reevaluate and experiment; she will craft a new heuristical account. This operation, however, demands a sense of context, which is just what AI-systems—at least given current technology—lack.[40] Going forward, one thing we will need determine is how much this "sense" has been responsible, ultimately, for safeguarding our heuristical understanding of the systems of power that shape our lives—and whether (and how) the sense might be replicated in the fast-approaching world of AI. In this answer, I suspect, lies our fate.

BIBLIOGRAPHY

Barocas, Solon and Andrew Selbst. "The Intuitive Appeal of Explainable Machines." *Fordham Law Review* 87 (2018).

Brennan-Marquez, Kiel. "'Plausible Cause': Explanatory Standards in the Age of Powerful Machines." *Vanderbilt Law Review* 70 (2017).

Brennan-Marquez, Kiel. "Extremely Broad Laws." *Arizona Law Review* 61 (2019).

Citron, Danielle. "Technological Due Process." *Washington University Law Review* 85 (2008).

Citron, Danielle and Frank Pasquale. "The Scored Society: Due Process for Automated Predictions." *Washington Law Review* 89 (2014).

Crawford, Kate and Jason Schulz. "Big Data and Due Process: Toward a Framework to Redress Predictive Privacy Harms." *Boston College Law Review* 55 (2014).

Grimmelmann, James and Daniel Westreich. "Incomprehensible Discrimination." *California Law Review Online* 7 (2016).

Manes, Jonathan. "Secret Law." *Georgetown Law Journal* 106 (2018).

Pasquale, Frank. *The Black Box Society*. Cambridge: Harvard University Press, 2015.

Pasquale, Frank. "A Rule of Persons, Not Machines: The Limits of Legal Automation." *George Washington Law Review* 87 (2019).

---

[40] See Hubert Dreyfus, *What Computers Still Can't Do: A Critique of Artificial Reason* (Cambridge: MIT University Press, 1992).

CHAPTER 41

....

AI AND MIGRATION MANAGEMENT

....

PETRA MOLNAR

INTRODUCTION: HIGH-RISK EXPERIMENTS WITH NEW TECHNOLOGIES IN MIGRATION

....

EXPERIMENTS with new technologies in migration management are increasing. An unprecedented number of people are on the move due to conflict, instability, environmental factors, and economic reasons. Receiving countries have to contend with the influx of large populations, straining resources and challenging border enforcement and national security. As a result, many states and international organizations involved in migration management are exploring technological experiments to manage migration. From big data predictions about population movements in the Mediterranean, to Canada's use of automated decision-making in immigration and refugee applications, to artificial intelligence (AI) lie detectors deployed at European borders, states and international organizations such as the UN High Commissioner for Refugees (UNHCR) are keen to explore the use of new technologies, yet often fail to take into account profound human rights ramifications and real impacts on human lives.

The introduction of new technologies effect both the processes and outcomes associated with decisions that would otherwise be made by administrative tribunals, immigration officers, border agents, legal analysts, and other officials responsible for the administration of immigration and refugee systems, border enforcement, and refugee response management. Technological implementations often come with the promise of increased fairness and efficiency. However, technological implementation exposes existing power relations in society. Technology is not inherently democratic and human rights impacts are particularly important to consider in humanitarian and forced migration contexts. Ethics do not go far enough—what is needed is a focus on rights, responsibilities, and enforcement mechanisms. An international human rights law framework is particularly useful for codifying and recognizing potential harms, because technology and its development are inherently global and transnational. The development and use of new technologies in migration management are largely unregulated. More oversight and accountability mechanisms will safeguard fundamental rights such as freedom from discrimination, privacy rights, and procedural justice safeguards such as the right to a fair decision maker and the rights of appeal.

TECHNOLOGIES ON THE MARGINS:
HOW IS AI MAKING DECISIONS?

AI, machine learning, automated decision systems, and predictive analytics are a series of overlapping terms and refer to a class of technologies that assist or replace the judgment of human decision makers. These systems process information in the form of input data using an algorithm to generate an output. In the migration context, training data can be body of case law, a collection of photographs, or a database of statistics, some or all of which have been precategorized or labeled based on the designer's criteria. These technologies can be used in various ways to augment or even replace a human decision maker in various facets of migration management.

Technology is developing at a rapid pace, and states are engaged in an international race for AI leadership, a "new gold rush."[1] This influx of interest and investment has made AI and machine learning attractive and well-funded research areas for the public and private sectors alike. Yet all of this rush to innovation occurs without robust global governance mechanisms. In this climate of global innovation, experimental new technologies are injected in the management of migration, whether in border spaces, refugee camps, or administrative decision-making. In response to complex issues like the global migration of millions, states and organizations are eager to see new technologies as a quick solution to what are otherwise tremendously complex and often intractable policy issues.

However, algorithms have been widely criticizes for being so-called black boxes.[2] This is because an algorithm's source code, its training data, or other inputs may be proprietary, and can be shielded from public scrutiny on the bases of intellectual property legislation or as confidential business assets. Moreover, when algorithms are used in immigration and refugee matters and form a nexus with issues of national security, both

---

[1] A. Shull, "In the Global Race for AI, How Do We Ensure We're Creating a Better World?," *Centre for International Governance Innovation* (February 15, 2019), https://www.cigionline.org/articles/global-race-ai-how-do-we-ensure-were-creating-better-world.

[2] See F. Pasquale, *The Black Box Society: The Secret Algorithms That Control Money and Information* (Cambridge: Harvard University Press, 2015); A. Burt, B. Leong, S. Shirrell, and G.X. Wang, "Beyond Explainability: A Practical Guide to Managing Risk in Machine Learning Models," *Future of Privacy Forum* (June 2018), https://fpf.org/wp-content/uploads/2018/06/Beyond-Explainability.pdf.

input data and source code may also be classified.[3] However, without being able to scrutinize input data to understand how the algorithm starts to make decisions, iterate, and improve upon itself in unpredictable or unintelligible ways, their logic becomes less and less intuitive to human oversight. The speed with which new technologies are being developed and introduced into various aspect of public and private life is quite extraordinary, particularly given the limited safeguards and discussions around regulation. Given the already problematic track record on discrimination on grounds of race[4] and gender,[5] and other human rights and civil liberties infringements, introducing new technologies into the opaque and discretionary space of migration management risks unintended consequences with profound impacts on human lives with few mechanisms of redress and oversight.[6]

Immigration, Iris-Scanning, and iBorderCtrl: New Technologies of Migration Management

Immigration and refugee decision-making sits at an uncomfortable legal nexus: the impact on the rights and interests of individuals is often very significant, even where the degree of deference is high and the procedural safeguards are weak. There is also a serious lack of clarity surrounding how courts will interpret administrative law principles like natural justice, procedural fairness, and standard of review where an automated decision system is concerned.

Four major areas of concern that are emerging in the technological experimentation in migration management are data collection, biometrics and informed consent, criminalization and surveillance, and automated decision-making.

Data-Driven Humanitarianism

Automated decision-making technologies require vast amount of data on which to learn.[7] States and international organizations are increasingly experimenting with

[3] Petra Molnar and Lex Gill, "Bots at the Gate: A Human Rights Analysis of Automated Decision Making in Canada's Immigration and Refugee System" (2018), https://ihrp.law.utoronto.ca/sites/default/files/media/IHRP-Automated-Systems-Report-Web.pdf.

[4] See A. Shapiro, "Reform Predictive Policing," *Nature* (January 25, 2017), https://www.nature.com/news/reform-predictive-policing-1.21338.

[5] See, for example, T. Simonite, "Machines Taught by Photos to Learn a Sexist View of Women," *Wired* (August 21, 2017), archived at https://perma.cc/8KUQ-LPJC.

[6] Molnar and Gill, "Bots at the Gate," 13.

[7] J. M. Balkin, "Free Speech in the Algorithmic Society: Big Data, Private Governance, and New School Speech Regulation," *University of California Davis Law Review* 51 (2018): 1149.

using so-called big data to predict population flows during and after conflict to deliver humanitarian aid and services based on these predictions.[8] Big data analytics require extremely large sets, which are analyzed for patterns and associations to make determinations about the likelihood of future human behavior. Multiple organs of the United Nations have begun relying on big data analytics to inform their policies. For example, the International Organization for Migration's Displacement Tracking Matrix[9] monitors populations on the move to better predict the needs of displaced people. The data sets which are used to make predictions can include mobile phone call records and geotagging, as well as analyses of social media activity. Data analytics are also used to predict likely successful outcomes of resettled refugees based on preexisting community links in the United States.[10] There is also the rise in the use of biometrics, or the "automated recognition of individuals based on their biological and behavioral characteristics," in migration management. Biometrics[11] can include fingerprint data, retinal scans, and facial recognition, as well as less well-known methods such as the recognition of a person's vein and blood vessel patterns, ear shape, and gait, among others. The United Nations has been relying on populating its data sets with biometrics, collecting bio-data on more than eight million people,[12] most of them fleeing conflict or needing humanitarian assistance.

However, data collection is not an apolitical exercise, particularly when powerful Global North actors such as states or international organizations collect information on vulnerable populations with no regulated methods of oversights and accountability. The increasingly fervent collection of data on migrant populations has been criticized for its potential to result in significant privacy breaches and human rights concerns.[13] For example, in the case of collecting biometric data on Rohingya refugees in Myanmar, the so-called datafication of refugee responses can result in oppressive governments easily

---

[8] O. De Backer, "Big Data and International Migration," United Nations Global Pulse: Pulse Lab Diaries (June 16, 2014), https://www.unglobalpulse.org/big-data-migration. The United Nations Development Programme (UNDP) is testing an online tool to be used by country offices in aggregating and visualizing the data they have been collecting in order to facilitate tracking and analyzing risks in their local contexts. The Crisis Risk Dashboard, UNDP (2018), http://www.europe.undp.org/content/geneva/en/home/partnerships/the-global-risk-platform.html.

[9] International Organization for Migration, "Displacement Tracking Matrix," https://www.globaldtm.info/ (accessed March 17, 2019).

[10] A. Shashkevich, "Stanford Scholars Develop New Algorithm to Help Resettle Refugees and Improve Their Integration," Stanford News (January 18, 2018), https://news.stanford.edu/2018/01/18/algorithm-improves-integration-refugees/.

[11] Biometrics Institute, "What Is Biometrics" (2019), https://www.biometricsinstitute.org/what-is-biometrics/ (accessed March 17, 2019).

[12] These enormous data sets are notoriously hard to track and can also include the retrofitting of old data with newly collected biometrics. See, for example, statements publicly made by UNHCR officials at the 2018 Humanitarian Congress in Berlin, Germany, http://humanitarian-congress-berlin.org/2018/ (accessed March 17, 2019).

[13] J. Crisp, "Beware the Notion That Better Data Lead to Better Outcomes for Refugees and Migrants," Chatham House (March 9, 2018), https://www.chathamhouse.org/expert/comment/beware-notion-better-data-lead-better-outcomes-refugees-and-migrants.

identifying groups and removing them from encampments.[14] China has also been collecting facial recognition and location tracking on its Muslim minority Uighur populations in a so-called "Muslim-tracking database."[15]

This data collection on marginalized groups is deeply historical and often openly justified by the group in power as necessary.[16] For example, Nazi Germany strategically collected vast amounts of data on Jewish communities to facilitate the Holocaust, including various registration schemes for food and slave labor of Jews, largely in partnership with the International Business Machines Corporation, known today as the ubiquitous IBM.[17] Various other genocides also relied on systematic tracking of groups, such as the Tutsi registries based on ethnicity identity cards, which facilitated the magnitude of the genocide in 1994.[18] Post 9/11, the United States also experimented with various modes of data collection on suspicious populations through the U.S. Department of Homeland Security's National Security Entry-Exit Registration System, which collected photographs, biometrics, and even first-person interview data from over 84,000 flagged individuals coming from mostly Arab states. While the registration of new individuals with this program ceased in 2011, the collected data remains within the purview of the U.S. government, with a state official publicly stating that the underlying regulatory framework remains in place, in the event that special registration is "needed again."[19] Not long after, the Trump administration echoed these sentiments with its plans to create a so-called "Muslim Registry," upheld by the U.S. Supreme Court,[20] or through its plans for an "Extreme Vetting Initiative," discussed in greater detail later in this chapter. All of these efforts highlight a common goal of tracking particular groups under the guise that more data is always better. Even global efforts such as the 2018 *Global Compact for Safe, Orderly and Regular Migration* foreground the preoccupation with collecting data, listing data collection as the first of its twenty-three objectives.[21]

---

[14] E. Thomas, "Tagged, Tracked and in Danger: How the Rohingya Got Caught in the UN's Risky Biometric Database," *Wired* (March 12, 2018), https://www.wired.co.uk/article/united-nations-refugees-biometric-database-rohingya-myanmar-bangladesh.

[15] C. Cimpanu, "Chinese Company Leaves Muslim-tracking Facial Recognition Database Exposed Online," *ZDNet* (February 14, 2019), https://www.zdnet.com/google-amp/article/chinese-company-leaves-muslim-tracking-facial-recognition-database-exposed-online/?__twitter_impression=true.

[16] R. Baretto, "Emerging Algorithms, Borders, and Belonging," *Humanity in Action* (2016), https://www.humanityinaction.org/knowledgebase/779-emerging-algorithms-borders-and-belonging (accessed March 18, 2019).

[17] E. Black, *IBM and the Holocaust: The Strategic Alliance between Nazi Germany and America's Most Powerful Corporation* (New York, NY: Dialog Press, 2012).

[18] Z. Rahman, "Dangerous Data: The Role of Data Collection in Genocides," *Engine Room* (2016), https://www.theengineroom.org/dangerous-data-the-role-of-data-collection-in-genocides/.

[19] Arab American Institute, "National Security Entry-Exit Registration System (NSEERS)" (2016), http://www.aaiusa.org/nseers (accessed March 18, 2019).

[20] Trump v. Hawaii, No. 17–965, 585 U.S.

[21] United Nations General Assembly, "Intergovernmental Conference to Adopt the Global Compact for Safe, Orderly and Regular Migration," A/CONF.231/3. Signed 19 December 2018.

In an increasingly anti-immigrant global landscape, criticisms have also surfaced that migration data has also been misinterpreted and misrepresented for political ends,[22] for example, to affect the distribution of aid dollars and resources. Inaccurate data can also be used to stoke fear and xenophobia, as seen in the characterization[23] of the group of migrants attempting to claim asylum at the U.S.–Mexico border. Societal fear is then used as justification for increasingly hard-line responses that contravene international law and present profound concerns around basic civil liberties and human rights.

Biometrics and Consent

Collection of vast amounts of data on particular groups also presents issues around data sharing and access.[24] While exchanging data on humanitarian crises or biometric identification is often presented as a way to increase efficiency and interagency and interstate cooperation, benefits from the collection do not accrue equally. Data collection and the use of new technologies, particularly in spaces with clear power differentials, raise issues of informed consent and the ability to opt out. For example, when people in Jordanian refugee camps have their irises scanned in order to receive their weekly food rations in an experimental new program, are they able to meaningfully say no? Or do they have to live with any discomfort they experience in having their biometric data collected if they want to feed their families that week? In contexts like these, efficiency seems to trump human dignity. In an investigation inside the Azraq refugee camp,[25] most refugees interviewed were uncomfortable with such technological experiments but felt that they could not refuse if they wanted to eat. Consent cannot be truly informed and freely given if it is given under coercion, even if the coercive circumstances masquerade as efficiency and promise improved service delivery. Moreover, individuals who choose not to participate in activities such as the use of biometric digital devices or social media— whether due to privacy concerns or simply as a matter of preference—may also be subject to prejudicial inferences about their credibility and trustworthiness simply for "opting out."[26]

Further, it is unclear where all this collected biometric data is going and whether affected groups have access to their own data. In the Jordanian iris-scanning pilot project,

[22] Nature Editorial Team, "Data on Movements of Refugees and Migrants Are Flawed," *Nature* (March 1, 2017), https://www.nature.com/news/data-on-movements-of-refugees-and-migrants-are-flawed-1.21568 (accessed March 1, 2019).

[23] S. Silverman, "The Bogus Demonization of the 'Migrant Caravan,'" *The Conversation* (December 10, 2018), https://theconversation.com/the-bogus-demonization-of-the-migrant-caravan-107562.

[24] D. Lyon, "Biometrics, Identification, and Surveillance," *Bioethics* 22(9) (2008): 499–508.

[25] B. Staton, "Eye Spy: Biometric Aid System Trials in Jordan," *IRIN* (May 18, 2016), http://www.irinnews.org/analysis/2016/05/18/eye-spy-biometric-aid-system-trials-jordan.

[26] J. Vertesi, "My Experiment Opting Out of Big Data Made Me Look Like a Criminal," *Time* (May 1, 2014), http://time.com/83200/privacy-internet-big-data-opt-out/.

the UNHCR expressly reserved the right to collect and share data to third parties,[27] including the private sector, without clear safeguards and significant privacy concerns. The United Nations' World Food Programme (WFP) was also recently criticized for partnering with data-mining company Palantir Technologies for a US$45 million contract and sharing 92 million aid recipients' data. Palantir has been heavily criticized for providing the technology that supports the detention and deportation programs run by the U.S. Immigration and Customs Enforcement (ICE) and the Department of Homeland Security.[28] It is not yet clear what data-sharing accountability mechanism will be in place during the WFP-Palantir partnership or whether data subjects will be able to opt out. Similarly in the criminal justice context, a recent investigation in the United States also revealed that voice prints, or the "unique, digitized vocal signatures that enable authorities to conduct voice recognition analysis on calls,"[29] are being collected from people in pretrial custody in Texas. This collection, developed by Securus Technologies, a prison telecommunications firm, is particularly problematic, given the legal norm that people in pretrial custody are to be presumed innocent. In the immigration context, voice recognition is now routinely used in Canadian immigration detention as an alternative to incarceration,[30] yet it is unclear whether this data is collected or shared with other government agencies or the private sector. While a fulsome discussion of the human rights ramification of this particular technology is beyond the scope of this chapter, it should be noted that such data sharing for people in administrative detention with fewer procedural safeguards than in the criminal justice context will likely breach various domestic and internationally protected rights.[31]

[27] The UNHRC also contracts its data management to the international firm Accenture. See, for example, UNHCR's Accenture contract at https://www.sciencedirect.com/science/article/pii/S0969476515301004 and https://www.accenture.com/t20161026T063323Z__w__/us-en/_acnmedia/Accenture/Conversion-Assets/DotCom/Documents/Global/PDF/Dualpub_15/Accenture-Unhcr-Innovative-Identity-Management-System.pdf.

[28] K. Hao, "Amazon Is the Invisible Backbone behind ICE's Immigration Crackdown," MIT Technology Review (October 22, 2018), https://www.technologyreview.com/s/612335/amazon-is-the-invisible-backbone-behind-ices-immigration-crackdown/. See also K. Conger, "Amazon Workers Demand Jeff Bezos Cancel Face Recognition Contracts with Law Enforcement," Gizmodo (June 21, 2018), https://gizmodo.com/amazon-workers-demand-jeff-bezos-cancel-face-recognitio-1827037509. A lawsuit has also recently been launched by the New York Civil Liberties Union: https://www.theverge.com/2018/12/12/18138243/nyclu-lawsuit-ice-immigration-risk-assessment-tool.

[29] G. Joseph and D. Nathan, "Prison Tech Company Is Questioned for Retaining 'Voice Prints' of People Presumed Innocent," The Appeal (February 12, 2019), https://theappeal.org/jails-across-the-u-s-are-extracting-the-voice-prints-of-people-presumed-innocent/.

[30] M. Blanchfield, "Canada to Use Voice Recognition, Monitoring Technology to Keep Migrants out of Detention," Global News (July 24, 2018), https://globalnews.ca/news/4350419/canada-migrant-detention-policy/, and S. Mayhew, "Canada Turns to Biometric Voiceprint Tech to Monitor Refugee Claimants," Biometric Update.Com (July 26, 2018), https://www.biometricupdate.com/201807/canada-turns-to-biometric-voiceprint-tech-to-monitor-refugee-claimants.

[31] See also P. Molnar, "Algorithms the New Jailers? The Use of New Technologies in Immigration Detention and Their Human Rights Implications," Special Issue—Refuge Journal (Fall 2019).

Criminalization and Securitization

Autonomous technologies are also increasingly used in monitoring and securing border spaces. For example, FRONTEX, the European Border and Coast Guard Agency, has been testing various unpiloted military-grade drones in the Mediterranean for the surveillance and interdiction of migrants' vessels hoping to reach European shores to facilitate asylum applications.[32] The ROBORDER project aims to create a "fully-functional autonomous border surveillance system with unmanned mobile robots including aerial, water surface, underwater and ground vehicles."[33] Various drone-related projects are also being explored in Morocco and other countries that serve as jumping-off points for the frontiers of so-called Fortress Europe. The United Nations is also experimenting with drones in various humanitarian spaces to better deliver aid, such as its drone corridor in Malawi.[34] The usage of military, or quasi-military, autonomous technology bolsters the nexus between immigration, national security, and the increasing push toward the criminalization of migration. Globally, states, particularly those on the frontiers of large numbers of migrant arrivals, have been using various ways to preempt and deter those seeking to legally apply for asylum.[35] This normative shift toward criminalization of migration works to justify increasingly hard-line and intrusive technologies such as drones and various border-enforcement mechanisms like remote sensors and integrated fixed-towers with infrared cameras to mitigate the "threat environment" at the border.[36] These technologies can have drastic results. While so-called "smart-border"[37] technologies have been called a more "humane" alternative to the Trump administration's calls for a physical wall, studies have documented that policies of prevention through deterrence using new surveillance technologies along the U.S.-Mexico border have actually increased migrant deaths and pushed migration routes toward more dangerous terrains through the Arizona desert.[38] Chambers et al. have found that migrant

[32] R. Csernatoni, "Constructing the EU's High-Tech Borders: FRONTEX and Dual-Use Drones for Border Management," *European Security* 27(2) (2018): 175–200.
[33] European Union, "Aims and Objectives," EU Horizons 2020 Research Project (2019), https://roborder.eu/the-project/aims-objectives/ (accessed April 14, 2019).
[34] UN Secretary General, "Secretary-General's Strategy on New Technologies," (2018), available at http://www.un.org/en/newtechnologies/images/pdf/SGs-Strategy-on-New-Technologies.pdf.
[35] See generally I. Atak and J. Simeon, *The Criminalization of Migration: Context and Consequences* (McGill-Queen's University Press, 2018).
[36] Ibid.
[37] Similar technologies are also deployed at various sited throughout the European Union. See, for example, European Commission, "Technical Study on Smart Borders" (2014), available at https://ec.europa.eu/home-affairs/sites/homeaffairs/files/what-we-do/policies/borders-and-visas/smart borders/docs/smart_borders_executive_summary_en.pdf. Canada's official position goes as far as to say that one of its main strategies is to "push our borders out" using prescreening, information-sharing, and enforcement cooperation to mitigate risk as far away from our borders as possible. See Government of Canada, "Customs and Border Management: Border Management in Canada," (January 29, 2018), https://www.canadainternational.gc.ca/eu-ue/policies-politiques/border-douanes.aspx?lang=eng.
[38] G.A. Boyce, S. Chambers, and S. Launius, "Democrats' 'Smart Border' Technology Is Not a 'Humane' Alternative to Trump's Wall," *The Hill* (February 11, 2019), https://thehill.com/opinion/

deaths have more than tripled since these new technologies have been introduced,[39] creating what anthropologist De León has called the "land of open graves,"[40] echoing the rising numbers of deaths in the Mediterranean. The use of these technologies by border enforcement is only likely to increase in the "militarized technological regime"[41] of border spaces, without appropriate public consultation, accountability frameworks, and oversights mechanisms.

Individual Automated Decision-Making in Immigration and Refugee Decisions

To deal with multiple complex migration crises, states are also experimenting with automating various facets of decision-making. For example, since at least 2014, Canada has been using some form of automated decision-making in its immigration and refugee system.[42] A 2018 University of Toronto report examined the human rights risks of using AI to replace or augment immigration decisions and argued that these processes create a laboratory for high-risk experiments within an already highly discretionary and opaque system.[43] The ramifications of using automated decision-making in the immigration and refugee space are far-reaching. Hundreds of thousands of people enter Canada every year through a variety of applications for temporary and permanent status.[44] Many come from wartorn countries and are seeking protection from violence and persecution. The Canadian government has confirmed that currently this type of technology is confined only to augmenting human decision-making and reserved for certain immigration applications only.[45] Transparency and oversight over future development on new technologies is needed.

In other jurisdictions, these experiments with automation are already in full force. For example, in the wake of the Trump administration's executive orders enforcing

immigration/429454-democrats-smart-border-technology-is-not-a-humane-alternative-to-trumps, and S. Chambers, G. Boyce, S. Launius, and A. Dinsmore, "Mortality, Surveillance and the Tertiary 'Funnel Effect' on the U.S.-Mexico Border: A Geospatial Modeling of the Geography of Deterrence," *Journal of Borderlands Studies* (2019), https://www.tandfonline.com/doi/abs/10.1080/08865655.2019.157 0861?journalCode=rjbs.

[39] Ibid.

[40] J. De Leon, *The Land of Open Graves Living and Dying on the Migrant Trail* (University of California Press, 2015).

[41] Csernatoni, "Constructing the EU's High-Tech Borders."

[42] K. Keung, "Canadian Immigration Applications Could Soon Be Assessed by Computers," *Toronto Star* (January 5, 2017), https://www.thestar.com/news/immigration/2017/01/05/immigration-applications-could-soon-be-assessed-by-computers.html.

[43] Molnar and Gill, "Bots at the Gate."

[44] Government of Canada, 2019 Annual Report to Parliament on Immigration, available at https://www.canada.ca/en/immigration-refugees-citizenship/corporate/publications-manuals/annual-report-parliament-immigration-2019.html.

[45] For example, temporary visa applications from India and China only. Conversations with Immigration, Refugees, and Citizenship Canada with the author.

increasingly hardline measures to stem immigration, a Vice Media investigation revealed that ICE has been amending its bail-determination algorithm at the U.S.-Mexico border to justify detention of migrants in every single case.[46] In 2017, ICE also unveiled its "Extreme Vetting Initiative," a process of automated assessments of immigrants to determine the probability that an applicant would be a "positively contributing member of society" and to national interests and to predict whether they intend to commit criminal or terrorist acts after entering the country.[47] Other countries such as Australia and New Zealand are also experimenting with using automated facial recognition technology based on biometrics to identify so-called future "troublemakers" which civil society organizations are fighting against on grounds of discrimination and racial profiling.[48] As discussed previously, instances of bias in automated decision-making and facial recognition type technology are widely documented.[49] When algorithms rely on biased data, they produce biased results.

These biases could have far-reaching results if they are embedded in the emerging technologies being used experimentally in migration. For example, in airports in Hungary, Latvia, and Greece, a new pilot project by a company called iBorderCtrl has introduced AI-powered lie detectors at border checkpoints.[50] Passengers' faces will be monitored for signs of lying, and if the system becomes more "skeptical" through a series of increasingly complicated questions, the person will be selected for further screening by a human officer. However, it is unclear how this system will be able to handle cultural differences in communication or account for trauma and its effects on memory, such as when dealing with a traumatized refugee claimant.[51] Refugee and immigration claims are filled with nuance and complexity, qualities that may be lost on automated technologies, leading to serious breaches of internationally and domestically protected human rights in the form of bias, discrimination, privacy breaches, and due process and

[46] D. Oberhaus, "ICE Modified Its 'Risk Assessment' Software So It Automatically Recommends Detention," *VICE* (June 26, 2018), https://motherboard.vice.com/en_us/article/evk3kw/ ice-modified-its-risk-assessment-software-so-it-automatically-recommends-detention.

[47] A. Glaser, "ICE Wants to Use Predictive Policing Technology for Its 'Extreme Vetting' Program," *Slate* (August 8, 2017), http://www.slate.com/blogs/future_tense/2017/08/08/ice_wants_to_use_ predictive_policing_tech_for_extreme_vetting.html, and K. Weill, "Algorithm May Decide Who Is a 'Contributing Member of Society,' Civil Rights Groups Warn," *The Daily Beast* (November 19, 2017), https://www.thedailybeast.com/algorithm-may-decide-who-is-a-contributing-member-of-society- civil-rights-groups-warn.

[48] L. Tan, "Immigration NZ's Data Profiling 'Illegal' Critics Say," *New Zealand Herald* (April 5, 2018), https://www.nzherald.co.nz/nz/news/article.cfm?c_id=1&objectid=12026585.

[49] See, for example, J. Vincent, "Gender and Racial Bias Found in Amazon's Facial Recognition Technology (Again)," *The Verge* (January 25, 2019), https://www.theverge.com/2019/1/25/18197137/ amazon-rekognition-facial-recognition-bias-race-gender.

[50] R. Picheta, *supra* n. 11. With Hungary and Greece being some of the crucial entry points for refugee claimants into mainland Europe, it is perhaps no accident that these locations were chosen as the site of experimentation.

[51] These issues also of course exist with human decision makers, and there are increasingly cogent critiques about officers misunderstanding how the psychological effects of repeated trauma can impacts person's ability to testify and appear "truthful." See, for example, the work of H. Evans Cameron, *Refugee Law's Fact-Finding Crisis: Truth, Risk, and the Wrong Mistake* (Cambridge University Press, 2018).

procedural fairness issues, among others. For example, as will be discussed in greater detail in the following, it is not yet clear how the right to a fair and impartial decision maker and the right to appeal a decision will be upheld during the use of automated decision-making systems. There is also the increasing proliferation of automated border gates, which stream travelers based on facial recognition present at most major airports in the European Union, which have also been criticized for potentially inculcating faulty facial recognition and discrimination based on euro-normative tropes and problematic "social sorting."[52]

Private sector products designed to support individuals interfacing with the immigration and refugee system also create new privacy risks. For example, Visabot is a Facebook Messenger-based AI application designed to help users apply for visas and green cards and to schedule appointments with the U.S. Citizenship and Immigration Service. Visabot has also launched a service to specifically assist young immigrants[53] who qualify for the DACA (Deferred Action for Childhood Arrivals) program. Although this program is designed to help at-risk migrants and potential immigrants, it comes with a significant privacy and security trade-off—Facebook, and other companies like it, operates within business models that primarily rely on the aggregation, analysis, and resale of their users' private information to third parties such as advertisers.

Unfortunately, government surveillance, policing, immigration enforcement, and border security programs can incentivize and reward industry for developing rights-infringing technologies.[54] Among them is Amazon's "Rekognition" surveillance and facial recognition system, which is being marketed explicitly for use by law enforcement. Using deep learning techniques, Rekognition is able to identify, track, and analyze individuals in real time, recognize up to one hundred people in a single image, and analyze collected information against mass databases of faces. This "person-tracking" service will allow the government to identify, investigate, and monitor "people of interest," including in crowded group photos and in public places such as airports.

The technology has already been criticized by the American Civil Liberties Union, which has demanded that Amazon stop allowing governments to use the technology, citing "profound civil liberties and civil rights concerns."[55] Amazon shareholders have also criticized the company's sale of the technology, citing long-standing issues of bias in

---

[52] There is also the increasing proliferation of automated border gates which stream travelers based on facial recognition present at most major airports in the European Union, which have also been criticized for potentially inculcating faulty facial recognition and discrimination based on euro-normative tropes and problematic "social sorting." See R. Barreto, "Emerging Algorithms, Borders, and Belonging," *Humanity in Action* (2016), https://www.humanityinaction.org/knowledgebase/779-emerging-algorithms-borders-and-belonging.

[53] K. Johnson, "Visabot Helps You Cut Green-Card Red Tape," *Venture Beat* (July 11, 2017), https://venturebeat.com/2017/07/11/visabot-helps-you-cut-green-card-red-tape/.

[54] N. Duarte, "ICE Finds Out It Can't Automate Immigration Vetting. Now What?," *CDT Blog* (May 22, 2018), https://cdt.org/blog/ice-cant-automate-immigration-vetting/.

[55] M. Cagle and N. Ozen, "Amazon Teams Up with Law Enforcement to Deploy Dangerous New Face Recognition Technology," *American Civil Liberties Union North California* (May 22, 2018), https://www.aclunc.org/blog/amazon-teams-law-enforcement-deploy-dangerous-new-face-recognition-technology.

facial recognition software, the threat of false positives, and the risk that markets for the technology would expand to include authoritarian regimes abroad—all of which may impact the company's stock valuation and increase financial risk. Amazon's own work-force has led this call and demanded that Amazon cut its ties[56] with the controversial data analytics firm called Palantir Technologies. Palantir is responsible for providing the technology that supports the detention and deportation programs run by the ICE and the Department of Homeland Security, which Amazon workers have decried as an "immoral U.S. policy"[57] and part of the United States' increasingly hard-line treatment of refugees and immigrants.

Nevertheless, there are also some encouraging developments. For example, an auto-matic robotic life raft called EMILY (Emergency Integrated Lifesaving Lanyard) has been deployed in the waters around the Greek islands to assist with rescuing refugees.[58] The UNHCR has been experimenting with a bot examining xenophobia and racism against refugees online[59] to help with advocacy strategies. Various AI techniques have also been used to try to predict the likely success of resettlement and integration in the United States using historical data.[60] New digital verification technologies have also made analyzing data coming from conflict zones more reliable, which can be beneficial for refugees requiring evidence to bolster their claims for protection.[61] Machine learn-ing has also been deployed in Mexico to assist with determining likely locations of mass graves.[62] A whole sector has also proliferated around creating various apps to assist refu-gees with accessing social services such as healthcare, banking, and language acquisi-tion, including various initiatives such as Techfugees, which foster entrepreneurship among refugee communities and whose tagline is "empowering the displaced through technology."[63]

However, piecemeal interventions under the guise of empowerment fail to consider that the issues around emerging technologies in the management of migration are not

[56] K. Conger, "Amazon Workers Demand Jeff Bezos Cancel Face Recognition Contracts with Law Enforcement," *Gizmodo* (June 21, 2018), https://gizmodo.com/amazon-workers-demand-jeff-bezos-cancel-face-recognitio-1827037509.
[57] Ibid.
[58] J. Franz, "It's a Buoy, It's a Life Raft, It's Emily—The Robotic Craft That's Saving Refugees off the Coast of Greece," *PRI* (May 1, 2017), https://www.pri.org/stories/2017-05-01/it-s-buoy-it-s-life-raft-it-s-emily-robotic-craft-s-saving-refugees-coast-greece.
[59] R. Moreno, "Teaching a 'Robot' to Detect Xenophobia Online," United Nations High Commissioner for Refugees (2017), http://www.unhcr.org/innovation/teaching-robot-detect-xenophobia-online/.
[60] Oxford University, "Using AI to Improve Refugee Integration," (October 2, 2018), http://www.ox.ac.uk/news/2018-10-02-using-ai-improve-refugee-integration.
[61] See, for example, Amnesty International's Digital Verification Project: https://www.amnesty.org/en/latest/news/2017/11/amnesty-international-and-trulymedia-join-forces-in-fight-against-fake-news/.
[62] J. Porup, "Hunting for Mexico's Mass Graves with Machine Learning," *Ars Technica* (April 17, 2017), https://arstechnica.com/information-technology/2017/04/hunting-for-mexicos-mass-graves-with-machine-learning/.
[63] Techfugees, "Techfugees: Empowering the Displaced with Technology" (2019), https://techfugees.com/ (accessed March 18, 2019).

about the inherent use of technology but rather about how it is used and by who. The monopolies of knowledge, which are being created function to consolidate power and authority over technological development, with states and private actors setting the stage for what is possible.[64] The unequal distribution of benefits from technological development privileges the private sector as the primary actor in charge of development, with states and governments wishing to control the flows of migrant populations benefiting from these technological experiments. Governments are the primary agents that benefit from data collection,[65] and affected groups are relegated to the margins. It is therefore not surprising that the regulatory and legal space around the use of these technologies remains murky and underdeveloped, full of discretionary decision-making, privatized development, and uncertain legal ramifications.

INTERNATIONAL HUMAN RIGHTS LAW AND MIGRATION MANAGEMENT TECHNOLOGIES

A number of internationally protected rights are already engaged in the increasingly widespread use of new technologies that manage migration. However, currently, there is no integrated regulatory global governance framework for the use of automated technologies and no specific regulations in the context of migration management. Much of the global conversation centers on ethics without clear enforceability mechanisms.

An international human rights law framework is useful for codifying and recognizing potential harms, because technology and its development are inherently global and translational. Under IHRL, states must commit to preventing violations from occurring, establish monitoring and oversight, and provide remedy and redress for rights violations to hold violators accountable.[66] This also includes the obligations of a state to protect individuals from harms perpetrated by third parties, including private entities.[67] However, states are willing to experiment with these new unregulated technologies in the space of migration precisely because it is a discretionary space of opaque decision-making. Moreover, much of migration management is also enacted by international organizations such as the UNHCR and various other bodies. As nonstate actors operating

---

[64] For a discussion on algorithms and their impacts on human imagination, see E. Finn, *What Algorithms Want: Imagination in the Age of Computing* (MIT Press, 2017).

[65] R. Okediji, "Does Intellectual Property Need Human Rights?," 51 *NYU Journal of International Law & Politics* 1 (2018).

[66] UN Human Rights Committee, "General Comment No. 31: The Nature of the Legal Obligation Imposed on States Parties to the Covenant," (May 26, 2004), UN Doc. CCPR/C/21/Rev.1/Add. 13, paras. 3–8.

[67] UN Human Rights Council, "Report of The Special Representative of The Secretary-General on The Issue of Human Rights and Transnational Corporations and Other Business Enterprises, John Ruggie, on Guiding Principles on Business and Human Rights: Implementing the United Nations 'Protect, Respect and Remedy' Framework" (March 21, 2011), UN Doc. A/HRC/17/31, Principles 1–10.

under various legal and quasi-legal authorities and regulations globally, international organizations are "arenas for acting out power relationships"[68] without being beholden to the responsibilities that states have to protect human rights.

Life and Liberty

The far-reaching impact of new technologies on the lives and security of persons affected should not be underestimated. The right to life and liberty is one of the most fundamental internationally protected rights and highly relevant to migration and refugee contexts. Multiple technological experiments already impinge on the right to life and liberty. The most stark example is the denial of liberty when migrants are placed in administrative detention at the U.S.-Mexico border. Immigration detention is already an opaque and discretionary phenomenon,[69] and the justification of increased incarceration on the basis of algorithms that have been tampered with shows just how far the state is willing to justify incursions on basic human rights under the guise of national security and border enforcement. In cases where an individual faces the psychological threat of deportation to a country where they face a substantial risk of torture (and the threat of that torture itself), the "security of the person" interest is also engaged.[70] Errors, miscalibrations, and deficiencies in training data can result in rights-infringing outcomes.

Equality Rights and Freedom from Discrimination

Given the problematic track record that automated technologies have on race and gender, it is very plausible that similar issues will, or have already, occurred in migration. For example, proxies for discrimination, such as country of origin, can be used to make problematic inferences leading to discriminatory outcomes. Algorithms are vulnerable to the same decision-making concerns that plague human decision makers: transparency, accountability, discrimination, bias, and error.[71] The opaque nature of immigration and refugee decision-making creates an environment ripe for algorithmic discrimination. Decisions in this system—from whether a refugee's life story is "truthful" to whether a

---

[68] T. Evans and P. Wilson, "Regime Theory and the English School of International Relations: A Comparison," 21 *Millennium: Journal of International Studies* (1992): 329, 330.

[69] S. Silverman and P. Molnar, "Everyday Injustices: Barriers to Access to Justice for Immigration Detainees in Canada," *Refugee Survey Quarterly* 35(1) (2016): 109–127.

[70] See, for example, Canadian Supreme Court jurisprudence such as *Suresh v. Canada (Minister of Citizenship and Immigration)*, 2002 SCC 1.

[71] Z. Tufekci, "Algorithmic Harms beyond Facebook and Google: Emergent Challenges of Computational Agency," *Colorado Technology Law Journal* (2017): 216–217, http://ctlj.colorado.edu/wp-content/uploads/2015/08/Tufekci-final.pdf.

prospective immigrant's marriage is "genuine"—are highly discretionary and often hinge on assessment of a person's credibility.[72] To the extent that these technologies will be used to assess "red flags," "risk," and "fraud," they also raise definitional issues, as it remains unclear what the parameters of these markers will be. For example, in the experimental use of AI lie detectors at EU airports, it is unclear what will constitute truthfulness and how differences in cross-cultural communication will be dealt with in order to ensure that problematic inferences are not encoded and reinforced into the system. The complexity of human migration is not easily reducible to an algorithm.

Privacy Rights

Privacy is not only a consumer or property interest: it is a human right, rooted in foundational democratic principles of dignity and autonomy.[73] The differential impacts of privacy infringements must be considered when analyzing the experiences of migrants. For example, if collected information is shared with repressive governments from whom refugees are fleeing, the ramifications can be life-threatening. Or, if automated decision-making systems designed to predict a person's sexual orientation are infiltrated by states targeting the LGBTQ community, discrimination and threats to life and liberty will likely occur. A facial recognition algorithm developed at Stanford University already purports to discern a person's sexual orientation from photos.[74] This use of technology has particular ramifications in the refugee and immigration context, where asylum applications based on sexual orientation grounds often rely on having to prove one's persecution based on outdated tropes around nonheteronormative behavior.[75] Furthermore, any data collected using such technologies could be shared with, or intercepted by, repressive governments if the person claiming asylum is unsuccessful and is returned to their country of origin.[76] It is the power of pattern recognition to extract personal details from available data that is concerning, particularly given the current proliferation of surveillance technologies already in use by authoritarian regimes.[77]

---

[72] See V. Satzewich, *Points of Entry: How Canada's Immigration Officers Decide Who Gets In* (UBC Press, 2015); and V. Satzewich, "Canadian Visa Officers and the Social Construction of 'Real' Spousal Relationships," *Canadian Review of Sociology* 51 (2014): 1, https://doi.org/10.1111/cars.12031.

[73] See L. Austin, "We Must Not Treat Data Like a Natural Resource," *Globe and Mail* (July 9, 2018), https://www.theglobeandmail.com/opinion/article-we-must-not-treat-data-like-a-natural-resource/.

[74] H. Murphy, "Why Stanford Researchers Tried to Create a 'Gaydar' Machine," *New York Times* (October 9, 2017), https://www.nytimes.com/2017/10/09/science/stanford-sexual-orientation-study.html.

[75] S. Reehag, "Patrolling the Borders of Sexual Orientation: Bisexual Refugee Claims in Canada," *McGill Law Journal* 53 (2008): 59.

[76] See Molnar and Gill, "Bots at the Gate."

[77] Privacy International, Submission of evidence to the House of Lords Select Committee on Artificial Intelligence, London, UK, September 6, 2017.

Principles of Natural Justice and Fair Process

Any discussion of pertinent human rights in migration must also include an analysis of administrative legal frameworks and principles of natural justice that are inherent in much of migration management. For example, in immigration and refugee decision-making, procedural fairness dictates that the person affected by administrative processes has a right to be heard, the right to a fair, impartial, and independent decision maker, the right to reasons (also known as the right to an explanation), and the right to appeal an unfavorable decision. However, it is unclear how administrative law will handle the augmentation or even replacement of human decision makers by algorithms. For example, while these technologies are often presented as tools to be used by human decision makers, the line between machine-made and human-made decision-making is not often clear. Given the persistence of automation bias or the predisposition toward considering automated decisions as more accurate and fair, it remains unclear what rubric human decision makers will use determine how much weight to place on the algorithmic predictions, as opposed to any other information available to them, including their own judgment and intuition.

Furthermore, when a person wishes to challenge an algorithmic decision, what will the appropriate standard of review look like? Inappropriate deference given to algorithmic decision-making has been widely documented.[78] It is unclear how tribunals and courts will assign reasonableness to automated decision-making, what standards of review will be used, and what mechanisms of redress will look like.

Technology is far from neutral. It reflects norms, values, and power in society. The development of technology occurs in specific spaces that are not open to everyone and its benefits do not accrue equally. Decision-making around implementation (and experimentation) occurs without consultation or even sometimes without consent of the affected groups. The growing role of the private sector in the governance of new technologies highlights the movement away from state responsibility to create governance structures in accordance with domestic and international principles under guise of proprietary technology, private interests, and discretion. However, the private sector already has an independent responsibility to ensure that technologies do not violate international human rights.[79] Technologists, developers, and engineers responsible for building this technology also have special ethical obligations[80] to ensure that their work does not facilitate human rights violations. There are also emerging conversations around

---

[78] See M. Koliska and N. Diakopoulos, "Disclose, Decode and Demystify: An Empirical Guide to Algorithmic Transparency," in *The Routledge Handbook of Developments in Digital Journalism Studies*, ed. Scott Eldridge II and B. Franklin (Routledge, 2018); see also M. Wilson, "Algorithms (and the) Everyday," *Information, Communication & Society* 20(1) (2017): 137, 141, 143–144, 147.

[79] United Nations Human Rights Office of the High Commissioner, "Guiding Principles on Businesses and Human Rights: 135 Implementing the United Nations 'Protect, Respect and Remedy' Framework" (2011), 13–16, http://www.ohchr.org/Documents/Publications/GuidingPrinciplesBusinessHR_EN.pdf.

[80] K.E. Martin, "Ethical Implications and Accountability of Algorithms," *Journal of Business Ethics* (2018), https://www.researchgate.net/publication/324896361.

taxation implications and the need to require global governance around the proprietary reliance on public data.[81]

The tension between private and public regulation also highlights an overall lack of institutional capacity to effectively regulate technology and a disjuncture between those who develop migration-related technology in the private sector, and those in the public sector who deploy it on specific populations. The so-called AI divide, or the gap between those who are able to design AI and those who do not, is broadening and highlights problematic power dynamics in participation and agency when it comes to the rollout of new technologies. Most often, the viewpoints of those most affected are excluded from the discussion, particularly around areas of no-go zones or ethically fraught usages. Overall, there is a lack of contextual analysis when thinking through the impact of new technologies resulting in great ethical, social, and political harm.

CONCLUSIONS: ACCOUNTABILITY AND OVERSIGHT MECHANISMS ARE URGENTLY NEEDED

Currently, no global regulatory framework exists to oversee the use of new technologies in the management of migration. Much of technological development occurs in so-called "black boxes," where intellectual property laws and proprietary considerations shield the public from access to data sets or full understanding of how the technology operates. States and the private sector are able to develop and test technologies without meaningful participation of affected populations. While conversations around the ethics of data and technology are taking place, ethics do not go far enough. What is necessary is analyzing how rights and freedoms are impacted and setting up meaningful regulatory frameworks of accountability.

While broad global strategies and regional mechanisms are being explored, we need a sharper focus on oversight mechanisms. Private sector actors already have an independent responsibility to ensure that the technologies they develop do not violate international human rights. Technologists, developers, and engineers responsible for building this technology also have special ethical obligations to ensure that their work does not facilitate human rights violations. Unfortunately, government surveillance, immigrations enforcement, and border security programs can incentivize and reward industry for developing rights-infringing technologies. Emerging technologies raise complex legal and ethical issues for businesses and engineers alike. Going forward, companies

[81] R. Medhora, "AI & Global Governance: Three Paths towards a Global Governance of Artificial Intelligence," *United Nations University Centre for Policy Research* (October 28, 2018), https://cpr.unu.edu/ai-global-governance-three-paths-towards-a-global-governance-of-artificial-intelligence.html.

engaged in the sale of new technology cannot turn a blind eye to how it will ultimately be used, or to its potential threat to human rights.

States and international organizations must also commit to creating and enforcing accountability and oversight mechanisms. The *Bots at the Gate Report* on Canada's use of automated decision-making in immigration and refugee applications highlights several recommendations that are also applicable globally: (1) commit to transparency and report publicly what technology is being developed and used; (2) adopt binding directives and laws that comply with internationally protected human rights obligations; (3) establish an independent body to oversee and review all use of automated technologies in migration management; and (4) foster conversations between policymakers, academics, technologists, and the civil society on the risks and promises of using new technologies.

These emerging conversations should also address the affected communities' lack of involvement in technological development. Rather than developing more apps and technology "for" or "about" refugees and migrants and collecting vast amounts of data, people with the lived experience of migration should be at the center of discussions around when and how emerging technologies should be integrated into refugee camps, border security, or refugee hearings, if at all.

BIBLIOGRAPHY

Austin, L. "We Must Not Treat Data Like a Natural Resource." *Globe and Mail* (July 9, 2018). https://www.theglobeandmail.com/opinion/article-we-must-not-treat-data-like-a-natural-resource/.

Benvenisti, E. "EJIL Foreword: Upholding Democracy amid the Challenges of New Technology: What Role for the Law of Global Governance?" Global Trust Working Paper, January 2018.

Chambers, S., G. Boyce, S. Launius, and A. Dinsmore, "Mortality, Surveillance and the Tertiary 'Funnel Effect' on the U.S.-Mexico Border: A Geospatial Modeling of the Geography of Deterrence." *Journal of Borderlands Studies* (2019). https://www.tandfonline.com/doi/abs/10.1080/08865655.2019.1570861?journalCode=rjbs.

Carens, J. *The Ethics of Immigration*. Oxford University Press, 2013.

Crisp, J. "Beware the Notion That Better Data Lead to Better Outcomes for Refugees and Migrants." *Chatham House* (March 9, 2018). https://www.chathamhouse.org/expert/comment/beware-notion-better-data-lead-better-outcomes-refugees-and-migrants.

Csernatoni, R. "Constructing the EU's High-Tech Borders: FRONTEX and Dual-Use Drones for Border Management." *European Security* 27(2) (2018): 175–200.

Farraj, A. "Refugees and the Biometric Future: The Impact of Biometrics on Refugees and Asylum Seekers." *Columbia Human Rights Law Review* 42 (2011): 891–941.

Johns, F. "Data, Detection, and the Redistribution of the Sensible in International Law." *American Journal of International Law* 111(1) (2017).

Magnet, S. *When Biometrics Fail: Gender, Race, and the Technology of Identity*. (Durham: Duke University Press, 2011).

McGregor, L., D. Murray, and V. Ng. "International Human Rights as a Framework for Algorithmic Accountability." *International and Comparative Law Quarterly* 68(2) (2019): 309–343.

Molnar, P. and Lex Gill, "Bots at the Gate: A Human Rights Analysis of Automated Decision Makin in Canada's Immigration and Refugee System" (2018). https://ihrp.law.utoronto.ca/sites/default/files/media/IHRP-Automated-Systems-Report-Web.pdf.

Noble, U.S. *Algorithms of Oppression: How Search Engines Reinforce Racism* (NYU Press, 2018).

Staton, B. "Eye Spy: Biometric Aid System Trials in Jordan." *IRIN* (May 18, 2016). http://www.irinnews.org/analysis/2016/05/18/eye-spy-biometric-aid-system-trials-jordan.

Zuboff, Shoshana. *The Age of Surveillance Capitalism: The Fight for a Human Future at the New Frontier of Power*. Profile Books, 2019.

CHAPTER 42

···

ROBOT TEACHING, PEDAGOGY, AND POLICY

···

ELANA ZEIDE

OVERVIEW

···

TODAY, many people discuss the problematic aspects of artificial intelligence (AI) opacity, the notorious "black box."[1] As other scholars have discussed, a lack of transparency poses problems for ensuring the accuracy, fairness, and contestability of individual determinations and group outcomes.[2] Algorithmic opacity makes it difficult for individuals and institutional actors to understand the basis for decisions and to evaluate their accuracy. This opacity is particularly troubling when institutions use machine learning to make high-stakes decisions about individuals, such as whether they receive a loan, qualify for a job, or get parole.[3] Academic and media scrutiny of the use of algorithmic tools that predict suspects' risk of recidivism, for example, has revealed that they are often inaccurate or perpetute existing bias unintentionally.[4] Scholars and lawsuits

---

[1] See Joshua A. Kroll, Solon Barocas, Edward W. Felten, Joel R. Reidenberg, David G. Robinson, and Harlan Yu, "Accountable Algorithms," *University of Pennsylvania Law Review* 165 (2016): 633; Danielle Keats Citron and Frank A. Pasquale, "The Scored Society: Due Process for Automated Predictions," *Washington Law Review* 89, no. 1 (2014): 89; Kate Crawford and Jason Schultz, "Big Data and Due Process: Toward a Framework to Redress Predictive Privacy Harms," *Boston College Law Review* 55, no. 1 (2014): 93; Pauline T. Kim, "Data-Driven Discrimination at Work," *William & Mary Law Review* 2017 (June 27, 2016); Mireille Hildebrandt, "The Dawn of a Critical Transparency Right for the Profiling Era," *Digital Enlightenment Yearbook 2012*, 41–56.

[2] Algorithmic Accountability; see, e.g., Nicholas Diakopoulos et al., "Principles for Accountable Algorithms and a Social Impact Statement for Algorithms," *FATML* (blog) (April 25, 2019), http://www.fatml.org/resources/principles-for-accountable-algorithms.

[3] See Citron and Pasquale, "The Scored Society," 89; Kim, "Data-Driven Discrimination at Work," 857; Rebecca Wexler, "Life, Liberty, and Trade Secrets: Intellectual Property in the Criminal Justice System," *Stanford Law Review* 70 (2018): 1343–1430.

[4] See Julia Angwin, Surya Mattu, Jeff Larson, and Lauren Kirchner, "Machine Bias: There's Software Used across the Country to Predict Future Criminals. And It's Biased against Blacks,"

object to public reliance on algorithmic tools outcomes, which shielded oversight by trade secret claims.[5] Critics call for regulations that require more transparency about data sources, algorithmic models, and group outcomes.[6]

This chapter highlights another important aspect of public reliance on privately developed AI tools: their displacement of professional authority, institutional account-ability, and public policymaking in education. It considers the example of AI instruc-tional platforms, often called "personalized learning systems." Today's technologies do give schools the ability to outsource the whole bundle of tasks we think of as "teaching." In doing so, the software must also define the relevant subject matter, metrics, and learning objectives—decisions traditionally made through the highly democratic governance of public school policymaking. Instructional software, however, is rarely subject to the same careful consideration and community scrutiny applied to face-to-face teaching.[7] This neglect cannot continue. AI instructional platforms not only require more trans-parency, but public accountability to avoid de facto delegation of the pedagogical and policy choices that shape America's education system.

Personalized Learning Systems

Since the Industrial Revolution, many have proposed or predicted that "teaching machines" that would automate part of the instruction process. AI pioneer Marvin Minsky articu-lated a vision of computer-controlled education that still resonates today:

> [W]e could try to build a personalized teaching machine that would adapt itself to someone's particular circumstances, difficulties, and needs. . . . It would help you by telling you what to read, stepping you through solutions, and teaching you about the subject in other ways it found to be effective for you. Textbooks then could be replaced by systems that know how to explain ideas to you in particular, because they would know your background, your skills, and how you best learn.[8]

ProPublica (blog) (May 23, 2016), https://www.propublica.org/article/machine-bias-risk-assessments-in-criminal-sentencing.

[5] See Wexler, "Life, Liberty, and Trade Secrets," 1343–1430; State v. Loomis, 881 NW 2d 749 (Wis., 2016).

[6] See Lauren Kirchner, "New York City Moves to Create Accountability for Algorithms," *Ars Technica* (December 19, 2017); Margot E. Kaminski, "Binary Governance: Lessons from the GDPR's Approach to Algorithmic Accountability," *Southern California Law Review* 92, no. 6 (2019); Citron and Pasquale, "The Scored Society," 89; Crawford and Schultz, "Big Data and Due Process," 93; Kim, "Data-Driven Discrimination at Work"; Hildebrandt, "The Dawn of a Critical Transparency Right for the Profiling Era," 41–56; Danielle Keats Citron, "Technological Due Process," *Washington University Law Review* 85 (2007): 1249.

[7] See infra, "Policy through Procurement."

[8] Marvin L. Minsky, Push Singh, and Aaron Sloman, "The St. Thomas Common Sense Symposium: Designing Architectures for Human-Level Intelligence," *AI Magazine* 25, no. 2 (2004): 113–125, 122.

Today's education technology still chases Minsky's dream as schools increasingly turn to technology to automate teaching. For the most part, however, machine teachers are not embodied humanoid robots but software driven by artificial intelligence. These "personalized learning systems" mimic dynamic human teaching—that is, communicating information, assessing student comprehension, and choosing the most appropriate feedback or another educational experience in response.[9] They collect data about learners' every interaction with digital platforms: when they log on, how much of a video they watch, even the passages they highlight. They use machine learning in real time to track students' progress, infer their competency, and choose the educational experience to provide next—which might be instructional materials, practice exercises and test questions, and struck feedback such as hints and encouragement.[10] The software uses historical data about how students with similar profiles fared to determine the choice most likely to lead to student success.

Automated instruction is easiest to apply to rule-based subject matter such as math, computer science, and languages. However, personalized learning systems can also employ natural language processing, speech recognition, and semantic analysis to assess learning in text-based subjects such as English composition. They can make noncognitive inferences about students' emotional states, such as motivation, and metacognitive skills such as collaborative problem-solving.[11] In sum, some of these personalized learning systems may perform many of the functions we expect from human teachers in the classroom, tracking learners' progress in real time and adapting instruction accordingly. Robotic teachers have now become reality, although they go by less threatening terms such as "personalized learning systems," "virtual teaching assistants," "smart" classrooms, and "intelligent tutors."[12]

Potential Benefits

Automated instructional systems offer several benefits.[13] Proponents—including prominent philanthropists and the U.S. Department of Education—present automated,

---

[9] Rose Luckin, "Towards Artificial Intelligence-Based Assessment Systems," *Nature Human Behaviour* 1, no. 3 (March 1, 2017): 0028, at 2., https://doi.org/10.1038/s41562-016-0028.

[10] EdSurge, *Decoding Adaptive* (London: Pearson, 2016), https://d3e7x39d4i7wbe.cloudfront.net/static_assets/PearsonDecodingAdaptiveWeb2.pdf.

[11] Luckin, "Towards Artificial Intelligence-Based Assessment Systems," at 2.

[12] Benjamin Herold, "What Does Personalized Learning Mean? Whatever People Want It To?," *Education Week* (November 7, 2018), https://www.edweek.org/ew/articles/2018/11/07/what-does-personalized-learning-mean-whatever-people.html; Office of Education Technology, U.S. Department of Education, "What Is Personalized Learning?," *Personalizing the Learning Experience: Insights from Future Ready Schools* (blog) (January 18, 2017), https://medium.com/personalizing-the-learning-experience-insights/what-is-personalized-learning-bc874799b6f.

[13] See, e.g., EdSurge, *Decoding Adaptive*, Rose Luckin, Wayne Holmes, Mark Griffiths, and Laurie B. Forcier, "Intelligence Unleashed: An Argument for AI in Education," (London: Pearson, 2016), http://discovery.ucl.ac.uk/1475756/1/PearsonIntelligenceUnleashedFINAL.pdf; Nazeema Alli, Rahim Rajan, and Greg Ratliff, "How Personalized Learning Unlocks Student Success," *Educause* (blog) (March 2016), https://er.educause.edu/~/media/files/articles/2016/3/erm1621.pdf; "How Personalized

adapative education software as a way for schools to move past the one-size-fits-all factory model of education.[14] Reformers and vendors promise that big data–driven education will improve individual student performance and engagement.[15] They promote personalized learning systems as a way to improve the quality of education in underserved and overcrowded classrooms and reduce disparities in educational achievement.

Inside the classroom, adaptive software may improve instruction by measuring student process more precisely and automatically incorporating the latest learning science insights. Personalized learning supporters predict that automated tools will free up time for teachers to turn their attention to an individual student, or to work with a small group on a different topic.[16] For example, automated assessment tools can greatly reduce the amount of time teachers must devote to grading.[17] As I discuss later, these systems can track student learning with extraordinary granularity. These platforms can also automatically incorporate the latest learning science and pedagogical research. For example, many personalized learning systems present concepts at spaced intervals to improve recall and retention.[18]

These systems also expand the scope of instruction at minimal cost. Once developed, online courses can reach an unlimited number of students without consuming physical resources or requiring further investment in additional teachers.[19] Learners can access instruction or take tests anytime, anywhere, on any mobile platform, "on demand."[20]

Possible Perils

Proponents highlight that algorithmic decision-making will be more consistent than humans when evaluating student performace.[21] However, while machine assessment

Learning Can Help Close the Attainment Gap," *Acrobatiq* (blog) (November 6, 2017), http://acrobatiq. com/how-personalized-learning-can-help-close-the-attainment-gap/.

[14] Andrew Calkins and Kelly Young, "From Industrial Models and 'Factory Schools' to What, Exactly?," *EdSurge* (March 3, 2016), https://www.edsurge.com/news/2016-03-03-from-industrial-models-and-factory-schools-to-what-exactly (last visited March 6, 2016).

[15] Audrey Watters, "Pearson and Knewton: Big Data and the Promise of Personalized Learning Hack Education" (2011), http://hackeducation.com/2011/11/01/pearson-and-knewton-big-data-and-the-promise-of-personalized-learning (last visited July 10, 2016); Tom Vander Ark, "The Future of Learning: Personalized Adaptive and Competency-Based DreamBox Learning," (2013), https://www. dreambox.com/white-papers/the-future-of-learning.

[16] Vander Ark, "The Future of Learning."

[17] Hubert.ai, "AI In Education—Automatic Essay Scoring," *Hubert.ai* (blog) (March 14, 2017), https://medium.com/hubert-ai/ai-in-education-automatic-essay-scoring-6eb38bb2e70 (last visited December 13, 2017).

[18] Hubert.ai. "AI in Education—Spaced Interval Learning," *Hubert.ai* (blog) (February 21, 2017), https://medium.com/hubert-ai/ai-in-education-spaced-interval-learning-b7ff1826d825.

[19] See, e.g., Jack M. Balkin and Julia Sonnevend, "The Digital Transformation of Education" (April 4, 2016), http://papers.ssrn.com/abstract=2759022.

[20] B. Hirsch, and J.W.P. Ng, "Education Beyond the Cloud: Anytime-Anywhere Learning in a Smart Campus Environment," in *2011 International Conference for Internet Technology and Secured Transactions (ICITST)*, 718–723 (IEEE, 2011).

[21] Viktor Mayer-Schönberger and Kenneth Cukier, *Learning with Big Data* (Houghton Mifflin Harcourt 2014).

may offer consistency, that is not the same as objectivity. Algorithmic analysis and machine learning can lead to biased assessments for many reasons. It may stem from inadvertent design decisions, incomplete datasets, or patterns that reflect existing inequities and historical discrimination.[22]

Further, computerized consistency reduces teachers' classroom autonomy. Big data sorts individuals into populations based on probabilities. This inevitably creates situations where students' instruction, evaluation, and credentials do not correspond to the specifics on the ground. This cuts against the highly contextualized decision-making characteristic of physical classroom settings. It goes against the long-standing endeavor to treat students equally regardless of their group affiliations—espoused by big data–oriented reformers as well as their critics.

Finally, these systems are sufficiently novel that there is minimal evidence that they are in fact effective or result in more equitable results.[23] At this stage, it is impossible to predict and difficult to detect what their impact will be and what unintended consequences may occur.[24]

COMPARING HUMAN AND ROBOT TEACHING

School adoption of education technology (edtech) often raises concerns about whether machines will replace, or dramatically reduce the importance of, human

[22] Wendy Nelson Espeland and Mitchell L. Stevens, "Commensuration as a Social Process," *Annual Review of Sociology* 24 (1998): 313–343; Neil Selwyn, Distrusting *Educational Technology: Critical Questions for Changing Times* (Routledge 2014).

[23] Audrey Watters, "The Overselling of Education Technology," *EdSurge* (March 16, 2016), https://www.edsurge.com/news/2016-03-16-the-overselling-of-education-technology; Audrey Watters, "Trend to Watch: (The Failure of) Ed-Tech Platforms," *Hack Education* (April 30, 2016), http://2016trends.hackeducation.com/2016/04/30/platforms.

[24] Beth Hawkins, "Does Personalized Learning Work? The Research Is Too Scant, Too New and Too Nuanced to Give a Clear Yes or No—At Least for Now," *The 74 Million* (blog) (March 25, 2019), https://www.the74million.org/article/does-personalized-learning-work-the-research-is-too-scant-too-new-and-too-nuanced-to-give-a-clear-yes-or-no-at-least-for-now/; Benjamin Herold and Andrew R. Molnar, "Are Companies Overselling Personalized Learning?," *Education Week* (November 7, 2018), https://www.edweek.org/ew/articles/2018/11/07/are-companies-overselling-personalized-learning.html; Benjamin Herold, "Personalized Learning: Modest Gains, Big Challenges, RAND Study Finds," *Ed Week* (blog) (July 11, 2017), http://blogs.edweek.org/edweek/DigitalEducation/2017/07/personalized_learning_research_implementation_RAND.html; John F. Pane, Elizabeth D. Steiner, Matthew D. Baird, Laura S. Hamilton, and Joseph D. Pane, *Informing Progress: Insights on Personalized Learning Implementation and Effects*, (Santa Monica, CA: RAND Corporation, 2017), https://www.rand.org/pubs/research_reports/RR2042.html; Ryan S. Baker, "Stupid Tutoring Systems, Intelligent Humans," *International Journal of Artificial Intelligence in Education* 26, no. 2 (June 2016): 600–614, https://doi.org/10.1007/s40593-016-0105-0; see, e.g., Benjamin Herold, " 'Teach to One' Personalized-Learning Model Has No Effect on Students' Math Scores, Federal Evaluation Finds—Digital Education—Education Week," *Ed Week* (blog) (February 21, 2019), https://blogs.edweek.org/edweek/DigitalEducation/2019/02/teach_to_one_personalized_learning_no_effect.html.

teachers.[25] Schools outsourcing instruction, assessment, and credentialing functions to companies end up outsourcing more fundamental decisions to them as well. The following section compares the mechanics of most personalized learning systems to the tasks performed by teachers when differentiating instruction in physical classrooms. It first gives a background account of teachers' primary tasks in differentiating instruction. It then explains how the machine-learning models in personalized learning systems seek to mimic the differentiation process in order to provide adaptive instruction.

Personalized learning systems build upon the ideal of one-to-one tutors who constantly evaluate student progress and tailor feedback or further instruction accordingly. This not-so-simple endeavor involves several different tasks, including communicating information, assessing learning, and evaluating pedagogical options. It also presumes that teachers can draw on their knowledge of the subject matter and its structure, a repertoire of instructional techniques to convey that information, and prior teaching experience to inform their pedagogical choices. Lastly, it assumes a larger structure that chooses learning materials, defines the curricula, and sets standards for performance and attainment. As described in the next section, this is traditionally the purview of administrators, school boards, state and federal education agencies, and the communities they serve.

Human Teaching

Teachers do more than deliver instructional content; ideally, they engage in dynamic communication with their pupils and adjust their approach in response to students' immediate needs. Teachers provide differentiated instruction by: (1) observing student performance; (2) assessing progress; and (3) informing and evaluating their real-time pedagogical decisions about the response most likely to promote student success. Differentiated teaching involves communicating complex concepts in way that is timely and effective given a myriad of contextual considerations. Automated teaching software, as discussed later, creates machine-learning models to perform these tasks.

Teaching, in its current conceptualization, involves dynamic communication between instructors and pupils.[26] Traditionally, teachers personalize learning informally as part

---

[25] Derek Briton, "Big Data and Learning Analytics: The 'New' Teaching Machine," in *The Precarious Future of Education*, ed. Jan Jagodinski (Springer, 2017); Bill Ferster, *Teaching Machines: Learning from the Intersection of Education and Technology* (Johns Hopkins University Press, 2014); Audrey Watters, "The History of "Personalization" and Teaching Machines," *Hack Education* (July 2, 2014), http://hackeducation.com/2014/07/02/personalization-teaching-machines; Gay L. Bisanz and Joanne Striley, "From Teaching Machines to Intelligent Tutoring Systems: New Insights into Automated Instruction," *PsycCRITIQUES* 39, no. 12 (1994): 1093–1095.

[26] See, e.g., Larry Cuban, "Will Teaching and Learning Become Automated? (Part 3)," *Larry Cuban on School Reform and Classroom Practice* (blog) (January 21, 2015), https://larrycuban.wordpress.com/2015/01/21/will-teaching-and-learning-become-automated-part-3/; Sarah D. Sparks, "Differentiated Instruction: A Primer," *Education Week* (January 28, 2015), https://www.edweek.org/ew/articles/2015/01/28/differentiated-instruction-a-primer.html; Lisa S. Goldstein, "Kindergarten Teachers

of the interactions in physical learning environments. They do so by observing students, assessing their proficiency, and adjusting their instruction. Broadly speaking, teachers do all of the following: collect information about students in real time; analyze this data to evaluate student progress and shortcomings regarding the skills, concepts, or knowledge of the subject at hand; consider various teaching options such as different pacing or content; choose the activity most likely to support student learning and progress; and act to implement those choices.

Teachers also observe students in class and their performance on assignments and tests. They will see puzzled looks on students' faces, observe that the majority of the class raises their hand eagerly about certain topics, and hear the confidence in a student's voice. Based on this information, they evaluate each student's real-time progress and problems. For example, if a student learning multiplication says that $10 \times 2 = 5$, the teacher may guess that the student is confusing multiplication and division and emphasize the difference between the two, even though she had planned to move to the next topic.

Teachers ultimately determine whether students have demonstrated enough proficiency to pass the class and give grades intended to reflect student performance and attainment. In most classrooms, teachers also periodically administer tests to measure student mastery with scores to incorporate into official grades. Traditionally, this summative assessment involves a separate set of information collected explicitly for summative and evaluative purposes on formal tests or assignments. The educational institution then uses this summative assessment to determine when to award students credits, when to move them on to the next grade level, and whether to place them in honors or basic classes. Standardized tests are also common means of summative assessment created by states or testing services (such as the college board's SAT). In short, teaching involves more than the act of adapting instruction; it requires consideration of pedagogical and institutional infrastructure.[27]

Robot Teaching

This subsection analyzes the components of an automated instructional system to illustrate the scope and significance of the choices made by technology developers. Automated personalized learning systems rely on data models in place of human or institutional decision-making processes and formal assessment. The data models they

Making 'Street-Level' Education Policy in the Wake of No Child Left Behind," *Early Education and Development* 19, no. 3 (May 30, 2008): 448–478.

[27] See Richard Edwards, "Software and the Hidden Curriculum in Digital Education," *Pedagogy, Culture & Society* 23, no. 2 (April 3, 2015): 265–279; Ben Williamson, "The Hidden Architecture of Higher Education: Building a Big Data Infrastructure for the 'Smarter University,'" *International Journal of Educational Technology in Higher Education* 15, no. 1 (December 2018): 12, https://doi.org/10.1186/s41239-018-0094-1; Paul Prinsloo, "Fleeing from Frankenstein's Monster and Meeting Kafka on the Way: Algorithmic Decision-Making in Higher Education," *E-Learning and Digital Media* 14, no. 3 (May 2017): 138–163.

create define digital curricula, textbooks, lesson plans, syllabi, and education standards. Learner models continuously evaluate student progress and proficiency. They serve the same functions as pop quizzes, exams, and grades. They also predict student potential, like standardized tests, and create credentials that can be used in place of grades and transcripts.

"Smart" education platforms assess learner progress without requiring separate tests. They instead embed assessment by using information about students' interactions with the digital platform and the actual answers they submit. A system, for example, might extrapolate learner progress using information about how much students have read on e-books and whether they selected an incorrect answer before submitting the correct one. Like teachers, pedagogical models in data-driven systems use real-time profile updates as input to calculate the content, pace, or activity most likely to promote pre-defined goals.

Take the example of the personalized learning system "AIAssess." It automatically differentiates instruction using machine-learning models to offer the most suitable math and science instruction based on students' real-time progress.[28] AIAssess provides educational content that is typically associated with textbooks and classroom activities. They are divided into discrete, modular experiences that assess and develop conceptual knowledge. These include tasks of increasing difficulty, as well as related hints and tips.

AIAssess maps the relevant subject matter, which might be algebraic concepts. A "knowledge component" includes fine-grained information about the steps involved in reaching a correct answer and receiving related feedback. Like classroom teachers, the system evaluates students' progress in real time to determine what to show students next, assessing student mastery and metacognition based on the steps they complete, hints they use, and difficulty of each question. The results are stored in a constantly updated learner profile, which, like a grade book, tracks students' progress and documents their performance.

AIAssess visualizes its inferences about students' performance on particular tasks, a set of tasks, and all complete tasks on a data dashboard.[29] It displays diagnostic conclusions to teachers on digital dashboard tools analyze this data into charts or categories.[30] A platform may, for example, organize data to show a "skill meter" that visually graphs learners' mastery of monitored skills.[31] However, students, teachers,

---

[28] Luckin, "Towards Artificial Intelligence-Based Assessment Systems," at 2.   [29] *Id.* at 1–2.

[30] Andrew S. Gibbons, "Review of Interactive Instruction and Feedback," *Educational Technology Research and Development* 41, no. 4 (1993): 104–108. Dan Kohen-Vacs et al., "Evaluation of Enhanced Educational Experiences Using Interactive Videos and Web Technologies: Pedagogical and Architectural Considerations," *Smart Learning Environment* 3 (2016).

[31] Albert T. Corbett and John R. Anderson, "Student Modeling and Mastery Learning in a Computer-Based Programming Tutor," in *Intelligent Tutoring Systems: Second International Conference, ITS '92*, ed. Claude Frasson, Gilles Gauthier, and Gordon I. McCalla (Springer, 1992), 413–420.

and parents cannot peer into the specific automated assessments and adaptations that shape each student's education trajectory and determine what they have learned.[32]

Obscured Transparency and Attenuated Accountability

This lack of transparency hinders student/parent agency and educator oversight. As with the use of AI human profiling and prediction in other contexts, some degree of legibility and "explainability" is a prerequisite to ensuring accurate and fair decisions about individuals and systemic legitimacy.[33] Students' and parents' rights to access and challenge personally identifiable student information in school records has been a core component of student privacy policy for forty-five years.[34] Teachers and administrators need a sufficient understanding of a software's inner working to be able to exercise their professional judgment about its use. Information about outcomes, especially with respect to minority and underserved populations, is similarly crucial for schools, school boards, and the stakeholders they serve to enable informed decisions about various machine teaching options. But even in the rare cases where schools can customize some aspects of personalized learning systems, those choices are typically not subject to public input or scrutiny, as I discuss in the following section.

CONTRASTING DEMOCRATIC AND
CODIFIED POLICYMAKING

Much of the conversation about personalized learning systems focuses on the parts that mimic teachers' in-class teaching while neglecting the rest of the information infrastructure that is just as significant in shaping education. Automated instruction requires considerable information to construct the necessary pedagogical infrastructure including: "(1) the curriculum, subject area and learning activities that each student is completing; (2) the details of the steps each student takes as they complete these activities; and (3) what counts as success within each of these activities and within each of the steps towards the completion of each activity."[35] Each of these components involves choices

---

[32] Sigrid Hartong, "Between Assessments, Digital Technologies and Big Data: The Growing Influence of 'Hidden' Data Mediators in Education," *European Educational Research Journal* 15(523) (2016).

[33] See, e.g., Citrom and Pasquale, "The Scored Society."

[34] Family Educational Rights and Privacy Act (FERPA), 20 U.S.C. § 1232g (2014); Elana Zeide, "Student Privacy Principles for the Age of Big Data: Moving Beyond FERPA and FIPPs," *Drexel Law Review* 8, no. 2 (Spring 2016): 339.

[35] Luckin, "Towards Artificial Intelligence-Based Assessment Systems," at 2.

about epistemology, pedagogy, and policy, all decisions traditionally made by educators, policymakers, and the communities they serve—decisions now being made by code created by private companies.

Democratic Pedagogy and Policy

Choices about education content, pedagogical approaches, and learning objectives have typically been subject to considerable public input, debate, and scrutiny. American public education is a highly democratic enterprise.[36] Schooling has long been seen as crucial to individual and collective success. That understanding is reflected in the public funding of schools and states' mandatory attendance requirements. Education's importance also surfaces in hotly contested public debates about what content students should learn, how best to teach them, and what school standards will measure success. Many of these decisions occur at the local or state level, with school boards having considerable impact on district policies.[37] This decentralized governance accommodates the highly heterogeneous nature of student bodies and communities across the country. It facilitates direct stakeholder input and accountability, with parents offering their opinions at school board meetings.

Local teachers, schools, and policymakers can take the unique circumstances of each class, school, and community into account. They are in close proximity and are readily accessible to the students, parents, and stakeholders they serve. They adapt to local needs and values. As part of the participatory and democratic process that has characterized public schooling in America for over a century, they receive and respond to student, parent, and other stakeholder input and will be held accountable for decisions that determine both individual student trajectories and the school and district-level choices that shape education policy.

America's K–12 education governance is highly decentralized. It has been "rooted in local policy, local management, and local financial control, that is deeply embedded in our historic national political culture."[38] While legislatures set broad education policies, most of the details come under the control of education agencies, particularly at the local level.[39] Local boards define policy for public school districts. Each state determines most of its own curricula, textbooks, and education standards, despite the recent increase in federal influence on academic substance and standards.

---

[36] Amy Gutmann, *Democratic Education* (Princeton University Press, 1987).
[37] *Id.*
[38] Michael W. Kirst, "The Political and Policy Dynamics of K–12 Education Reform from 1965 to 2010: Implications for Changing Postsecondary Education," in *Research Priorities for Broad-Access Higher Education* (Stanford CEPA 2010), at 1.
[39] See Patrick McGuinn and Paul Manna, "Education Governance in America: Who Leads When Everyone Is in Charge?," in *Education Governance for the Twenty-First Century: Overcoming the Structural Barriers to School Reform* ed. Paul Manna & Patrick McGuinn (Brookings Institution Press, 2013), at 9–10.

Within schools, teachers traditionally enjoy considerable autonomy over lesson plans, pedagogical choices, classroom instruction, and student evaluation, which can be adjusted on the fly for context and circumstances.

America's public education system operates through local control for both pragmatic and philosophical reasons.[40] Educational theorists and historians see this participation as a crucial component of America's education system.[41] This can lead to better tailored instructional choices, more informed student assessment, and academic policies aligned with community values. Such discretion can also, of course, leave room for biased or inconsistent decisions with respect to individual students and particular demographics. However, educational autonomy with community accountability has been at the core of the American education system since the Progressive movement.[42]

The highly public and participatory nature of these pedagogical and policy choices stands in stark contrast to the black boxes and invisible infrastructures of personalized learning systems. For example, textbook choices have often been a battleground for communities with different worldviews. They involve debates about whether to cover intelligent design or evolution or cover climate change.[43] The mechanisms for selecting textbooks are formal, complex, and contested.[44] Florida allows any citizen to weigh in on textbook choice.[45] Texas' Education Agency engages in a multiyear process to select textbooks.[46] Publishers submit textbooks that are reviewed by a panel, including community members such as university professors, public school teachers, parents, and businesses and industry representatives. The Education Agency holds a hearing open for public comments, posts submitted comments online, and convenes a second hearing for additional comments before ultimately putting the submissions to a vote.[47]

[40] Janet S. Hansen and Marguerite Roza, "Decentralized Decisionmaking for Schools: New Promise for an Old Idea?," *RAND Corporation*, 2005 at 2–3; Michael W. Kirst, "The Political And Policy Dynamics of K–12 Education Reform," at 1.

[41] Gutmann, Democratic Education.

[42] Michael W. Kirst, "The Political And Policy Dynamics of K–12 Education Reform," at 1.

[43] See, e.g., Gail Collins, "How Texas Inflicts Bad Textbooks on Us," *The New York Review of Books* (June 21, 2012); Theresa Harrington, "After Hours of Testimony, California State Board Rejects Two History Textbooks, Approves 10 Others," *EdSource* (Nov. 16, 2017), https://edsource.org/2017/after-hours-of-testimony-state-board-rejects-two-history-textbooks-approves-10-others/590118.

[44] Vincent Scudella, "State Textbook Adoption," Education Commission of the States (Sept. 2013) https://www.ecs.org/clearinghouse/01/09/23/10923.pdf; see also "Textbook Review in Public Schools," *Findlaw* (blog) (July 13, 2018), https://education.findlaw.com/curriculum-standards-school-funding/textbook-review-in-public-schools.html.

[45] "In Florida, a New Law Is Hitting Textbooks," *Science Friday* (blog), (July 13, 2018). https://www.sciencefriday.com/segments/in-florida-a-new-law-is-hitting-textbooks/.

[46] Dylan Baddour, "Explained: How Texas Picks Its Textbooks," *Houston Chronicle* (Sept. 15, 2016), https://www.houstonchronicle.com/local/explainer/article/Explained-how-Texas-picks-its-textbooks-9225732.php.

[47] *Id.*

Codified Pedagogy and Policy

Pedagogy through Personalization

The complex governance structures around adopting textbooks pose a sharp contrast to the unilateral and obscured policymaking that occurs with personalized learning systems without sufficient mechanisms for transparency and oversight. As discussed earlier, personalized learning systems perform many of these functions based on choices embedded in platform design and data processing. In doing so, personalized learning systems provide not only the educational content (such as a textbook or lecture) but also the scope of subject matter (such as curricula) and learning pathways through the material (such as syllabi and lesson plans). Analytics conduct formative assessment to inform instructional choices, just as teachers do in physical classrooms through observation and informal tools such as pop quizzes. Similar to standardized tests and exams, it performs the summative assessments that document when students have mastered the material. The outputs of feed into a learner profile that functions like a detailed grade book and can be used as a transcript.

Policy through Procurement

Schools outsourcing functions to private vendors is nothing new. However, until recently, much of this outsourcing related to ancillary services that supported schools' core education functions. Most third-party software performed organizational and institutional processes, not academic ones. With automated instructional tools, however, educators can delegate the entire instructional process, including the pedagogical and policy decisions that shape school curricula, metrics, and standards. Communities should be free to do so if desired. However, this displacement of authority and accountability should happen with the same consideration and scrutiny applied to textbook and standardized test selection.

Today, however, K–12 school districts evaluate and acquire education technology products haphazardly.[48] Schools rarely conduct formal needs assessments.[49] Educators and students play a limited role in edtech procurement.[50] Curriculum directors and technology and information officers make many of the dispositive decisions impacting school technology choice.[51] School treatment of education software—even learning

[48] See Natasha Singer, "Privacy Pitfalls as Education Apps Spread Haphazardly," *New York Times* (March 11, 2015), http://www.nytimes.com/2015/03/12/technology/learning-apps-outstrip-school-oversight-and-student-privacy-is-among-the-risks.html.

[49] Digital Promise, *Improving Ed-Tech Purchasing: Identifying the Key Obstacles and Potential Solutions for the Discovery and Acquisition of K–12 Personalized Learning Tools* (Nov. 13, 2014), at 10, available at https://digitalpromise.org/2014/11/13/improving-ed-tech-purchasing; Jennifer R. Morrison, Steven M. Ross, and Alan C.K. Cheung, "From the Market to the Classroom: How Ed-Tech Products Are Procured by School Districts Interacting with Vendors," *Educational Technology Research and Development* 67, no. 2 (April 1, 2019): 389–421, https://doi.org/10.1007/s11423-019-09649-4.

[50] Digital Promise, *Improving Ed-Tech Purchasing*, at 10; Morrison, Ross, and Cheung, "From the Market to the Classroom."

[51] Digital Promise, *Improving Ed-Tech Purchasing*, at 10; Morrison, Ross, and Cheung, "From the Market to the Classroom."

platforms—as simply another piece of technology is reflected in the fact that the funding districts use to purchase these systems from a supplemental budget, not the primary one for curricular and instructional needs.[52]

Procurement decisions often depend on anecdotal evidence from small pilots, marketing materials, or peer references.[53] Technology vendors rarely share rigorous proof of edtech efficacy or conduct formal ongoing oversight to ensure positive and equal outcomes. Because schools and policymakers do not demand more transparency and proof, "companies perceive little incentive to produce rigorous evidence."[54] After procurement, few schools have the resources to train teachers and administrators about AI-driven systems' strengths and weaknesses.[55]

Teaching Transparency and Public Accountability

Schools and education policymakers should not wait for public outcry but take a more proactive approach. The examples of democratic education decision-making noted earlier demonstrate that communities are more than willing to devote time, attention, and resources to oversee pedagogical and policy choices. The way forward requires algorithmic decisions to be explainable and accountable as they replace the judgment of publicly answerable actors. This involves not just transparency about individual determinations but also a more deliberate and public conversation about the impact of outsourcing public decision-making to private entities.

Parents, teachers, and students need to understand the parameters used to assess and promote learning. Administrators need to be able to tell when their technological tools are working for their specific student population. Policymakers and parents want to know that their school pedagogy and subject matter matches community values. Each of these stakeholders has minimal ability to evaluate these elements in adaptive learning tools due to the inscrutability of algorithmic calculations and the invisibility of the pedagogical and policy decisions embedded in the invisible information infrastructure.

This displacement of continuing human elements reduces teachers' autonomy, administrator authority, and policymakers' accountability. Without tools for greater transparency, decisions embedded in code shut students, parents, and educators out of this loop.[56] Instead of more readily available classroom teachers or on-site administrators, corporate entities handle these important decisions. There is no obvious authority to petition for an explanation or redress. Further, the students, parents, and teachers who manage to obtain information about underlying decision-making may still not be able to make sense of the complex algorithms and probabilistic decisions driving personalized learning.

[52] Digital Promise, *Improving Ed-Tech Purchasing*, at 20.
[53] Digital Promise, *Improving Ed-Tech Purchasing*, at 8; Morrison, Ross, and Cheung, "From the Market to the Classroom."
[54] Digital Promise, *Improving Ed-Tech Purchasing*, at 8.   [55] *Id.* at 20.
[56] Hartong, "Between Assessments, Digital Technologies and Big Data."

The responsibility for reform rests on schools and policymakers as much as technology developers. These stakeholders can act by adopting more rigorous and documented procedures for edtech procurement, implementation, and evaluation; requiring vendors to offer sufficient access to underlying data and information about outcomes; and cultivating data literacy among all stakeholders. The procurement process should impose transparency requirements aimed at teachers and local policymakers as much as student and parents. Ideally, schools and school boards, for example, would conduct formal instructional needs assessments to clarify implementation goals. At the very least, requests for information should require vendors to supply adequate proof of efficacy. Procurement should mandate sufficient mechanisms for transparency about individual decisions and access to outcomes for relevant populations and protected classes to enable ongoing review. Further, school administrators should make their choices with respect to significant pedagogical and policy choices public, with open platforms for commentary and participation similar to those already in place for traditional educational material and institutional standards.

CONCLUSION

With personalized learning software, students and parents cannot observe, let alone challenge, the many decisions that shape academic outcomes and subsequent life trajectories. Teacher and school officials cannot assess the accuracy, efficacy, and fairness of individual determinations or group outcomes. Private companies, rather than community members and public servants, set pedagogy and policy in practice. If schools are to remain relevant to the educational process itself, as opposed to just its packaging and context, educators and their stakeholders must be more proactive in demanding information from technology providers and setting internal protocols to ensure effective and consistent implementation. Those who choose to outsource instructional functions should do so with sufficient transparency mechanisms in place to ensure professional oversight guided by well-informed debate.

AI-driven software now includes components that make choices previously vested in teachers, school administrators, and education agencies. Personalized learning systems are an extreme example of the displacement of professional expertise and policymaking by machines. Without protocols for transparency these systems may undermine the important trust in these institutions—not only in their efficacy but also in their ultimate fairness. This transparency is not just important for algorithmic and school accountability, but also for students' ability to exercise agency over their own education.

Educators, stakeholders, and policymakers must at least examine the assumptions embedded in computer code. Software developers and vendors must create technical systems and resources to facilitate transparency, with respect to individual and design decisions. Education professionals and policymakers must, at the same time, cultivate sufficient technical and data literacy to be able to understand the strengths, limitations, and implications of AI-driven teaching tools. Schools adopting new teaching tools must also implement accompanying oversight and governance structures to match. Important pedagogical and policy decisions should never be inadvertent and invisible; they should be explicit and accountable to professionals and public leaders working in collaboration with their communities.

BIBLIOGRAPHY

EdSurge. *Decoding Adaptive*. London: Pearson, 2016. https://d3e7x39d4i7wbe.cloudfront.net/static_assets/PearsonDecodingAdaptiveWeb2.pdf.

Edwards, Richard. "Software and the Hidden Curriculum in Digital Education." *Pedagogy, Culture & Society* 23, no. 2 (April 3, 2015): 265–279. https://doi.org/10.1080/14681366.2014.977809.

Herold, Benjamin. "What Does Personalized Learning Mean? Whatever People Want It To." *Education Week* (November 7, 2018). https://www.edweek.org/ew/articles/2018/11/07/what-does-personalized-learning-mean-whatever-people.html.

Molnar, Michele and Benjamin Herold. "Are Companies Overselling Personalized Learning?" *Education Week* (November 7, 2018). https://www.edweek.org/ew/articles/2018/11/07/are-companies-overselling-personalized-learning.html.

Murphy, Robert F. "Artificial Intelligence Applications to Support K–12 Teacher and Teaching: A Review of Promising Applications, Challenges, and Risks." Santa Monica, CA: RAND Corporation, 2019. https://www.rand.org/pubs/perspectives/PE315.html.

Office of Education Technology, U.S. Department of Education. "What Is Personalized Learning?" *Personalizing the Learning Experience: Insights from Future Ready Schools* (blog) (January 18, 2017). https://medium.com/personalizing-the-learning-experience-insights/what-is-personalized-learning-bc874799b6f.

Selwyn, Neil. *Is Technology Good for Education?* Cambridge, MA: Polity, 2016.

Watters, Audrey. "The Histories of Personalized Learning." *Hackeducation* (blog) (June 9, 2017). http://hackeducation.com/2017/06/09/personalization.

Williamson, Ben. "The Hidden Architecture of Higher Education: Building a Big Data Infrastructure for the 'Smarter University.'" *International Journal of Educational Technology in Higher Education* 15, no. 1 (December 2018): 12. https://doi.org/10.1186/s41239-018-0094-1.

Zeide, Elana. "The Structural Consequences of Big Data-Driven Education." *Big Data* 5, no. 2 (June 1, 2017): 164–172. https://doi.org/10.1089/big.2016.0061.

CHAPTER 43

ALGORITHMS AND THE SOCIAL ORGANIZATION OF WORK

IFEOMA AJUNWA AND RACHEL SCHLUND

THE SOCIAL ORGANIZATION OF WORK

MUCH organizational theorizing has been conducted on the role of brokers and institutional intermediaries in connecting disparate groups within organizations[1] or in occluding lacunae in the network of corporate entities.[2] More recently, scholarly attention has shifted to the role of technology as an intermediary, mediating both access to work and the experience of work.[3] As Shoshana Zuboff observed, the introduction of new technology "wields the power of the slow-moving hand at the turning rim of a kaleidoscope." Zuboff argues that technology can never be introduced without an effect—rather any new technology must be parsed for both its affordances and foreclosures.[4]

Harry Braverman's seminal analysis of technology, Taylorist management, and the labor process demonstrated how managerial control is exerted through technology, and as Michael Burawoy noted in his ethnography, the most visible control technology in a

[1] David Obstfeld, "Social Networks, the Tertius Iungens Orientation, and Involvement in Innovation," *Administrative Science Quarterly* 50, no. 1 (2005): 100–130.

[2] Ronald S. Burt, *Structural Holes: The Social Structure of Competition* (Cambridge, MA: Harvard University Press, 1992).

[3] Hyman Louis, *Temp: How American Work, American Business, and the American Dream Became Temporary* (New York: Viking, 2018); Ifeoma Ajunwa and Daniel Greene, "Platforms at Work: Automated Hiring Platforms and Other New Intermediaries in the Organization of Work," *Research in the Sociology of Work* 33, no. 1 (forthcoming 2019): 1–53.

[4] Shoshana Zuboff, *In the Age of the Smart Machine: The Future of Work and Power* (New York: Basic Books, 1988).

factory was the assembly line.[5] The line coerced workers to keep pace or risk penalties both monetary and social. The proliferation of automated algorithms in the workplace raises questions as to how they might be used in the service of control and coercion. As some scholars have argued, machine learning algorithms have "prompted a data-centric reorganization of the workplace" and a *quantification* of the worker in a manner and to a degree, previously unseen in history.[6] This chapter considers ethical issues implicated by three algorithmic-driven work technologies: (1) automated hiring platforms, (2) wearable workplace technologies, and (3) customer relationship management.

Automated Hiring Platforms

Automated hiring platforms (AHPs) are "digital intermediaries that invite submission of data from one party through pre-set interfaces and structured protocols, process that data via proprietary algorithms, and deliver the sorted data to a second party."[7] The use of AHPs involves every stage of the hiring process, from the initial sourcing of candidates to the eventual selection of candidates from the applicant pool. This section describes how AHPs assist companies through each stage of the hiring process—sourcing, screening, interviewing, and selecting.[8]

During the initial sourcing stage of the hiring process, companies use AHPs to source or find attractive candidates using targeted advertising or matching technology.[9] Targeted advertising involves the use of machine learning algorithms to build predictive models based on data from job seekers and their online activity to automatically generate a pool of jobseekers with predetermined, sought-out characteristics that companies can use to target or exclude job seekers from viewing advertisements.[10] In the case of matching technologies, companies typically use personalized job boards to automatically generate a list of potential job candidates who match the characteristics the company is looking for in a job candidate.[11]

---

[5] Harry Braverman, *Labor and Monopoly Capital: The Degradation of Work in the Twentieth Century*, 25th anniversary ed. (New York: Monthly Review Press, 1998); Michael Burawoy, "Between the Labor Process and the State: The Changing Face of Factory Regimes under Advanced Capitalism," *American Sociological Review* 48, no. 5 (1983): 587–605.

[6] Ifeoma Ajunwa, "Algorithms at Work: Productivity Monitoring Platforms and Wearable Technology as the New Data-Centric Research Agenda for Employment and Labor Law," *St. Louis Law Journal* 63, no. 1 (forthcoming 2019).

[7] Ajunwa and Greene, "Platforms at Work: Automated Hiring Platforms and Other New Intermediaries in the Organization of Work."

[8] Miranda Bogen and Aaron Rieke, "Help Wanted: An Examination of Hiring Algorithms, Equity, and Bias" (Washington, D.C.: Upturn, 2018).

[9] *Id.*

[10] Pauline Kim and Sharion Scott, "Discrimination in Online Employment Recruiting," *St. Louis University Law Journal* 63, no. 1 (2018): 1–29.

[11] Sirui Yao and Bert Huang, "Beyond Parity: Fairness Objectives for Collaborative Filtering," in *31st Conference on Neural Information Processing Systems* (NIPS 2017), 1–10.

Following the initial sourcing stage of the hiring process, companies typically use AHPs to screen candidates—assessing candidates' potential to excel in the job position using predictive models.[12] For example, companies may embed behavioral or personality assessments within AHPs to predict how likely a job candidate is to work well with others or steal from the company.[13] Companies can also use AHPs to automatically review job candidates resumes to predict how closely a given resume matches a company's minimum or desired qualifications.[14] During the screening stage, AHPs typically cull the bottom 20 percent or so of the applicant pool before transmitting the remaining applicant pool to the interview stage of the hiring process.[15]

AHPs aid during the interviewing stage of the hiring process by creating interview guides for hiring managers based on areas of concern indicated by the assessments used in the screening process.[16] AHPs may also make use of video interviews—job applicants' interviews are recorded and their responses, vocal tone, and facial expressions are analyzed using machine learning algorithms, which compare current job applicants' responses to past interview responses from the company's top employees.[17]

During the final step in the hiring process, the selection phase, employers use AHPs in making the final hiring decision by automating background checks and helping to negotiate job offer terms. Automated background checks typically assess if a job applicant has a criminal history and is authorized to work.[18] Recently, some AHP vendors also offer social media background checks—a job applicant's social media and online history is deployed to predict how likely the job candidate will engage in toxic workplace behavior such as bullying, sexual harassment, or drug use.[19]

Employers can also use AHPs to help negotiate job offer terms. For example, some AHPs can use companies' data regarding previous job offers and acceptances to create predictive models to assess how likely a given job candidate will accept a given job offer.[20] Further, the predictive models can provide companies with potential ways in which to increase the likelihood a given job applicant will accept a given job offer such as by increasing salary, bonus, and other benefits.[21]

[12] Bogen and Rieke, "Help Wanted: An Examination of Hiring Algorithms, Equity, and Bias."
[13] Ajunwa and Greene, "Platforms at Work: Automated Hiring Platforms and Other New Intermediaries in the Organization of Work."
[14] Mariotti and Robinson, "Society for Human Resource Management 2017 Talent Acquisition Benchmarking Report," (SHRM, 2017).
[15] Ajunwa and Greene, "Platforms at Work: Automated Hiring Platforms and Other New Intermediaries in the Organization of Work."
[16] Id.
[17] Josh Bersin, "Talent Trends HR Technology Disruptions for 2018: Productivity, Design, and Intelligence Reign" (Deloitte University Press, 2017).
[18] Bogen and Rieke, "Help Wanted: An Examination of Hiring Algorithms, Equity, and Bias."
[19] Nathan J. Ebnet, "It Can Do More Than Protect Your Credit Score: Regulating Social Media Pre-employment Screening with the Fair Credit Reporting Act," *Minnesota Law Review* 97, no. 1 (2012): 306–336.
[20] Bogen and Rieke, "Help Wanted: An Examination of Hiring Algorithms, Equity, and Bias."
[21] Nagaraj Nadendla, "Introducing the Oracle Recruiting Cloud," filmed 2017 at OpenWorld 2017, San Francisco, CA, video, 26:18, https://video.oracle.com/detail/videos/most-recent/video/5701490825001/openworld-2017:-introducing-the-oracle-recruiting-cloud.

Current State of Use

The use of AHPS is on the rise. According to the Society for Human Resource Management, in 2016 approximately 22 percent of organizations used automated screening to review job applicants' resumes. A survey conducted by Deloitte University Press in 2017 revealed approximately 56 percent of companies surveyed were in the process of redesigning their human resources (HR) programs to utilized digital and mobile AHPs. Further, 51 percent of companies surveyed in 2017 were in the process of redesigning their companies to use digital business models. Additionally, 33 percent of the HR teams included in the survey were using artificial intelligence (AI) to implement HR solutions. The survey included data from 10,447 companies across the world, including Western Europe (25 percent), Latin and South America (17 percent), Asia (15 percent), North America (14 percent), Africa (10 percent), Central and Eastern Europe (8 percent), Nordic countries (7 percent), Oceania (3 percent), and the Middle East (2 percent). The companies surveyed were also from a variety of industries, including professional services (16 percent), financial services (13 percent), consumer business (13 percent), technology, media, and telecommunications (12 percent), manufacturing (11 percent), energy and resources (7 percent), life sciences and health care (6 percent), real estate (1 percent), and other (12 percent).[22] Thus, the use of AHPs is worldwide and spans a variety of industries.

Criticisms and Pitfalls

Coercive and Hierarchical

By design, AHPs resemble hierarchical and coercive structures aimed to maximize profit—clearly diverging from public and democratic social relations.[23] AHPs are coercive as they necessitate that workers consent to the information asymmetries and command structures embedded in the design of AHPs in order to gain employment, which one must attain to afford basic needs such as housing and food.[24] One can view the coercive and hierarchical nature of AHP design as the descendant of technologies of control that have dictated the social organization of work since the rise of scientific management in the nineteenth century.[25] Although the technologies of the nineteenth century, such as the assembly line and stopwatch monitoring, illustrates overt forms of technical control,

[22] Jeff Schwartz et al., "Rewriting the Rules for the Digital Age 2017 Deloitte Global Human Capital Trends" (Deloitte University Press, 2017).
[23] Ajunwa and Greene, "Platforms at Work: Automated Hiring Platforms and Other New Intermediaries in the Organization of Work."
[24] E. Anderson, *Private Government: How Employers Rule Our Lives (and Why We Don't Talk about It)* (Princeton, NJ: Princeton University Press, 2017).
[25] Burawoy, "Between the Labor Process and the State: The Changing Face of Factory Regimes under Advanced Capitalism."

AHPs, although less overt, also exert technical control by coercing job applicants' consent to hierarchical information asymmetries.

Information Asymmetry

The use of AHPs results in steep information asymmetries between job applicants and employers since job applicants must provide volumes of personal information to attain employment. However, employers do not reciprocate the information and insight they attain about job applicants—employers do not share the information they attain about job applicants with the job applicants, and the job applicants do not receive additional information about employers.[26]

Privacy Concerns

Coercing consent from job applicants to take part in personality assessments and to reveal identifying information that is used to gather additional information on applicants from third-party vendors renders an enormous amount of personal information. This information is stored, analyzed, and shared among industry partners, in ways unknown to the job candidate.[27] The collection, distribution, and storage of job applicant's personal information create numerous privacy concerns regarding the security and confidentiality of sensitive employee data.

Encoding of Bias

AHP designers claim that automating the hiring process will reduce hiring bias. The promise of reduced hiring bias derives from the belief that automated hiring systems are blind to protected characteristics such as gender, age, ethnicity, and sexual orientation.[28] However, the AHP is not an autonomous agent. The predictive models used to select employees from applicant pools are built from training data selected by the company. Training data is typically derived from the company's current high-sales employees' data, which is then used to detect patterns in the data to build predictive models to select similar job applicants—a process sometimes referred to as "cloning your best people."[29] The process of "cloning your best people" can result in encoding human bias. The idea being that "systematically biased data produces systemically biased analyses, regardless of the quality of those analyses."[30] For example, if women and racial minorities were underrepresented in a company's demographics, then

[26] Ajunwa and Greene, "Platforms at Work: Automated Hiring Platforms and Other New Intermediaries in the Organization of Work."

[27] Id.

[28] J. Meredith, "AI Identifying Steady Workers: E-Recruiting Firm Offering Tool to Determine How Long Job Seeker Will Stay Around," *Chicago Tribune* (July 16, 2001), http://articles.chicagotribune.com/2001-07-16/business/0107160013_1_unicru-neural-networks- employee.

[29] A. Overholt, "True or False: You're Hiring the Right People," *Fast Company* (February 2002), https://www.fastcompany.com/44463/true-or-false-youre-hiring-right-people.

[30] Ajunwa and Greene, "Platforms at Work: Automated Hiring Platforms and Other New Intermediaries in the Organization of Work."

training data would create a predictive model that would similarly undervalue applicants from those underrepresented groups.[31]

Discrimination

The encoding of human bias in predictive models used by AHPs can lead to discriminatory hiring practices. During the initial sourcing stage of the hiring process, the use of targeted advertising can result in discrimination when employers use protected characteristics such as ethnicity, gender, and age to target advertisements. Targeted advertising can also result in discrimination when employers use variables that are correlated with protected characteristics to target job advertisements, such as zip code.[32] During the screening stage of the hiring process, discrimination can result from using biased training data to predict minimum qualifications.[33] Furthermore, behavioral and personality assessments used in the screening process have been demonstrated to discriminate against people of color.[34] During the interview stage of the hiring process, the use of video interviews to analyze job applicants responses, vocal tone, and facial expressions can lead to discriminatory outcomes for people with regional and nonnative accents, speech impediments, visible disabilities, and darker skin tones due to the design flaws in speech recognition and facial analysis software.[35] During the selection phase of the hiring process, the use of social media background checks can reveal information about job applicants that employers are not legally permitted to use to inform hiring decisions, such as ethnicity, sexuality, disability, or pregnancy status.

WEARABLE WORKPLACE TECHNOLOGIES

Wearable technologies designed for the workplace—wearable workplace technologies—exist in a variety of forms that vary in terms of design and use, from wristbands used to track employee location and productivity to exoskeletons used to assist employees performing strenuous labor.[36] Examples of wearable workplace technologies include

[31] Ajunwa, "Algorithms at Work: Productivity Monitoring Platforms and Wearable Technology as the New Data-Centric Research Agenda for Employment and Labor Law."

[32] Kim and Scott, "Discrimination in Online Employment Recruiting."

[33] Ajunwa and Greene, "Platforms at Work: Automated Hiring Platforms and Other New Intermediaries in the Organization of Work."

[34] Craig Haney, "Employment Tests and Employment Discrimination: A Dissenting Psychological Opinion," *Industrial Relations Law Journal* 5, no. 1 (1982): 1–86.

[35] Rachael Tatman, "Gender and Dialect Bias in YouTube's Automatic Captions," in *Proceedings of the First ACL Workshop on Ethics in Natural Language Processing* (ACL, 2017), 53–59; Joy Buolamwini and Timnit Gebru, "Gender Shades: Intersectional Accuracy Disparities in Commercial Gender Classification," *Proceedings of the 1st Conference on Fairness, Accountability and Transparency, PMLR* 81, no. 1 (2018): 77–91.

[36] Timothy L. Fort, Anjanette H. Raymond, and Scott J. Shackelford. "The Angel on Your Shoulder: Prompting Employees to Do the Right Thing through the Use of Wearables," *Northwestern Journal of Technology and Intellectual Property* 14, no. 2 (2016): 139–170; Dov Greenbaum, "Ethical, Legal and Social Concerns Relating to Exoskeletons," *ACM SIGCAS Computers and Society* 45, no. 3 (2016): 234–239.

smart glasses, wrist- and finger-worn wearables, smart caps and helmets, and exoskeletons—among many others.[37]

Wearable workplace technologies in the form of smart glasses exist in a variety of designs, including see-through smart glasses with enhanced visual aid, smart glasses equipped with a thermographic camera, artificial reality glasses, and smart glasses with a monocular view.[38] See-through smart glasses with enhanced visual aid essentially consist of glasses with the properties of a static computer—allowing employees to consult manuals or guides, transcript notes, or look up records. A variety of industries use see-through smart glasses with enhanced visual aid, such as construction, manufacturing, field service, and healthcare, among others.[39] Smart glasses equipped with a thermographic camera are typically used in construction and manufacturing to assess machine fatigue by monitoring surface temperature and temperature distribution to predict when a machine will overheat. Artificial reality (AR) smart glasses project virtual information onto an employee's physical surroundings, allowing the employee to distinguish between virtual information and physical information. To illustrate, factory employees who fix machines can use AR glasses to project visual markers and schematics to guide their work.[40] Smart glasses with a monocular view afford employees a wider viewing angle of their surroundings and can produce high-resolution images. Many industries have implemented smart glasses with a monocular view, including telemedicine, remote assistance, and warehousing.[41]

Wrist- and finger-worn wearable workplace technologies also come in a variety of designs and provide different affordances. Examples of finger-worn workplace wearables include rings equipped with scanners and Bluetooth technology that allow employees to scan inventory and communicate hands-free.[42] Examples of wrist-worn workplace wearables include bracelets and bands equipped with GPS to track employee location, biosensors to record and analyze employee biometric data such as heart rate, accelerometers that track employee movement and activity, and wearable computer interfaces.[43]

[37] Ajunwa, "Algorithms at Work: Productivity Monitoring Platforms and Wearable Technology as the New Data-Centric Research Agenda for Employment and Labor Law"; Frost & Sullivan, "Wearable Technologies for Industrial Applications: Smart Glasses, Wrist-Worn Devices, HUDs Improve Productivity and Efficiency in Industrial Sector" (Frost & Sullivan, June 30, 2017); Greenbaum, "Ethical, Legal and Social Concerns Relating to Exoskeletons."

[38] Frost & Sullivan, "Wearable Technologies for Industrial Applications"; J.P. Gownder, "The Technology-Augmented Employee: How Emerging Technologies Like Artificial Intelligence Are Reshaping the Future of Work" (Forrester, 2018), https://www.forrester.com/report/ The+TechnologyAugmented+Employee/-/E-RES125811; Ajunwa, "Algorithms at Work: Productivity Monitoring Platforms and Wearable Technology as the New Data-Centric Research Agenda for Employment and Labor Law."

[39] Frost & Sullivan, "Wearable Technologies for Industrial Applications."

[40] J.P. Gownder, "The Technology-Augmented Employee: How Emerging Technologies Like Artificial Intelligence Are Reshaping The Future of Work."

[41] Frost & Sullivan, "Wearable Technologies for Industrial Applications."

[42] Id.; Fort, Raymond, and Scott, "The Angel on Your Shoulder: Prompting Employees to do the Right Thing through the Use of Wearables."

[43] Frost & Sullivan, "Wearable Technologies for Industrial Applications"; Ajunwa, "Algorithms at Work: Productivity Monitoring Platforms and Wearable Technology as the New Data-Centric Research

Wrist-worn workplace wearables are used across a variety of industries, with global market revenue projected to reach US$70 billion by 2020.[44]

Smart caps and helmets designed for the workplace can be equipped with augmented reality, Bluetooth technology, voice recognition, and even sensors to detect brain activity.[45] For example, smart caps and helmets equipped with augmented reality can be used to project blueprints and instructions for employees performing tasks such as welding and construction.[46] Further, smart caps and helmets equipped with sensors to detect brain activity can be used to measure an employee's level of fatigue or alertness.[47] A variety of industries have adopted smart caps and helmets such as fieldwork, transportation, construction, manufacturing, and product design.[48]

Wearable workplace technology in the form of exoskeletons are essentially wearable robotics that are typically designed to assist employees performing arduous tasks by increasing their strength and agility.[49] For example, exoskeletons used in construction and manufacturing can assist employees in lifting heavy tools.[50] Some exoskeletons are even equipped with technology that allows employers to monitor their employees' location, mood, and physical health.[51] A variety of industries have implemented exoskeletons such as construction, manufacturing, and geriatric care.[52]

Current State of Use

Wearable workplace technology has proliferated in the workplace. A report by Frost & Sullivan revealed that between January 2013 and December 2015 approximately 2,955 patents were registered in the United States for wearable technology designed for

Agenda for Employment and Labor Law"; Fort, Raymond, and Shackelford. "The Angel on Your Shoulder: Prompting Employees to do the Right Thing through the Use of Wearables."

[44] Frost & Sullivan, "Wearable Technologies for Industrial Applications."

[45] Id.; Karen Turner, "Are Performance-Monitoring Wearables an Affront to Workers' Rights?," Chicago Tribune (August 7, 2016), https://www.chicagotribune.com/bluesky/technology/ct-wearables-workers-rights-wp-bsi-20,160,807-story.html; Ben Coxworth, "SmartCap Monitors Workers' Fatigue Levels by Reading Their Brain Waves," New Atlas (January 13, 2012), https://newatlas.com/smartcap-measures-fatigue-brain-waves/21271/.

[46] Ajunwa, "Algorithms at Work"; Frost & Sullivan, "Wearable Technologies for Industrial Applications"; Turner, "Are Performance-Monitoring Wearables an Affront to Workers' Rights?"

[47] Ajunwa, "Algorithms at Work: Productivity Monitoring Platforms and Wearable Technology as the New Data-Centric Research Agenda for Employment and Labor Law"; Ben Coxworth, "SmartCap Monitors Workers' Fatigue Levels by Reading Their Brain Waves."

[48] Frost & Sullivan, "Wearable Technologies for Industrial Applications."

[49] Greenbaum, "Ethical, Legal and Social Concerns Relating to Exoskeletons."

[50] Ajunwa, "Algorithms at Work: Productivity Monitoring Platforms and Wearable Technology as the New Data-Centric Research Agenda for Employment and Labor Law"; Greenbaum, "Ethical, Legal and Social Concerns Relating to Exoskeletons."

[51] Ana Viseu, "Simulation and Augmentation: Issues of Wearable Computers," Ethics and Information Technology 5, no 1 (2003): 17–26.

[52] Greenbaum, "Ethical, Legal and Social Concerns Relating to Exoskeletons."

the workplace—illustrating the flourishing development of wearable workplace technologies.[53] Further, the majority of the 2,955 patents registered in the United States for wearable workplace technologies between January 2013 and December 2015 consisted of patents for wrist- and finger-worn wearables, such as wristwatches, ring scanners, and wrist bands—indicating wrist- and finger-worn wearables designed for the workplace remain a significant trend.[54]

The implementation of wearable workplace technologies is also on the rise. A survey conducted by Forrester in 2016 revealed 23 percent of information workers use wearable work technologies, demonstrating a 63 percent increase from 2015.[55] Further, an additional survey conducted by Forrester revealed that 62 percent of telecommunications organization executives described the implementation of wearable workplace technologies is a priority for their organization, which has grown from 52 percent in 2014.[56]

Adoption of wearable technology in corporate wellness programs is also increasing. A survey conducted by WorldatWork revealed that in 2016 approximately 27 percent of the organizations surveyed used wearable technology to encourage employee health and wellness.[57] A report by Gartner revealed that in 2017 an estimated 60 percent of corporate wellness programs include the use of wearable technology.[58] This trend is only predicted to increase—Gartner estimates that by 2021, 90 percent of wellness programs will include wearable technology.[59]

Criticisms and Pitfalls

Privacy Concerns

The increased use of wearable workplace technologies presents numerous privacy concerns regarding employee data. Wearable technologies collect volumes of sensitive, personal data from employees, creating issues regarding the collection, use, and distribution of employee data by employers.[60] Further, wearable workplace technologies

[53] Frost & Sullivan, "Wearable Technologies for Industrial Applications."   [54] Id.

[55] Boris Evelson and Michael Facemire, *Enterprise Business Intelligence: Now Always at Hand on Your Smartwatch* (Forrester, 2016), https://www.forrester.com/report/Enterprise+Business+Intelligence+Now+Always+At+Hand+On+Your+Smartwatch/-/E-RES129410.

[56] J.P. Gownder, "Deliver Digital Operational Excellence and Digital Customer Experience Innovation with Wearables" (Forrester, 2017), https://www.forrester.com/report/Deliver+Digital+Operational+Excellence+And+Digital+Customer+Experience+Innovation+With+Wearables/-/E-RES103381.

[57] WorldatWork, "Inventory of Total Rewards Programs & Practices" (WorldatWork, 2017), https://www.worldatwork.org/docs/research-and-surveys/survey-report-inventory-of-total-rewards-programs-and-practices.pdf.

[58] Christy Pettey, "Wearables Hold the Key to Connected Health Monitoring" (Gartner, 2018), https://www.gartner.com/smarterwithgartner/wearables-hold-the-key-to-connected-health-monitoring/.

[59] Id.

[60] Ifeoma Ajunwa, Kate Crawford, and Joel Ford, "Health Meets Big Data: An Ethical Framework for Health Information Collection by Corporate Wellness Programs," *Journal of Law, Medicine, and Ethics* 44, no.1 (2016): 474–480.

typically afford employers the ability to observe and track their employees' location and physiological activity—a practice that may violate the National Labor Relations Act.[61] Moreover, wearable workplace technologies collect large amounts of sensitive employee data, which remains stored on companies' servers—leaving sensitive employee data vulnerable to hacking by third parties.[62]

Discrimination

Wearable workplace technologies also present concerns regarding discrimination. Since wearables collect employee health data, such technologies could potentially reveal medical information that could be used to discriminate against employees. For example, the use of wearable technologies could facilitate discrimination against employees who have a medical condition or disability that prevents them from reaching productivity standards.[63] Additionally, wearables used in corporate wellness programs collect employee data outside of the workplace such as activity levels, weight, heart rate, and sleep quality.[64] The collection and use of employee data regarding health and lifestyle outside of the workplace present further discrimination concerns as this data could be used to determine employee benefits and compensation.[65]

Employee Safety and Compensation

Wearable workplace technologies can improve worker performance, but this can lead to reductions in workers' compensation for injuries. For example, wearable workplace technology designed to assist workers in arduous tasks may allow injured workers to return to work sooner than they would have without the wearable technologies assistance, reducing paid leave for workplace injuries.[66] Further, the use of data collected by wearable workplace technology could be used to deny employee compensation claims.[67] For example, if an employee causes an accident that leads to injury at work, an employer could use biometric data collected by wearable workplace technology to determine if the employee was sleep-deprived, shifting the blame onto the employee.[68]

[61] Ajunwa, "Algorithms at Work: Productivity Monitoring Platforms and Wearable Technology as the New Data-Centric Research Agenda for Employment and Labor Law"; U.S.C, "National Labor Relations Act," 29 § 157 (2012).

[62] Frost & Sullivan, "Wearable Technologies for Industrial Applications."

[63] Ajunwa, "Algorithms at Work: Productivity Monitoring Platforms and Wearable Technology as the New Data-Centric Research Agenda for Employment and Labor Law."

[64] Helen Nissenbaum and Heather Patterson, "Biosensing in Context: Health Privacy in a Connected World," in Quantified Biosensing Technologies in Everyday Life, ed. Dawn Nafus (Cambridge, MA: MIT Press, 2016), 79–100.

[65] Alexander H. Tran, "The Internet of Things and Potential Remedies in Privacy Tort Law," Columbia Journal of Law and Social Problems 50, no. 2 (2017): 263–298.

[66] Greenbaum, "Ethical, Legal and Social Concerns Relating to Exoskeletons."

[67] Ajunwa, "Algorithms at Work: Productivity Monitoring Platforms and Wearable Technology as the New Data-Centric Research Agenda for Employment and Labor Law"; Antigone Peyton, "A Litigator's Guide to the Internet of Things," Richmond Journal of Law & Technology 22, no. 3 (2016): 1–20.

[68] Ajunwa, "Algorithms at Work: Productivity Monitoring Platforms and Wearable Technology as the New Data-Centric Research Agenda for Employment and Labor Law."

Wearable workplace technologies also present concerns regarding employee safety. For example, wearable workplace technologies such as see-through smart glasses with enhanced visual aid or virtual reality glasses can cause distractions, which could lead to injury.[69] Furthermore, poorly designed exoskeletons could potentially damage muscles, tendons, and nerves.[70] Injuries caused by wearable workplace technologies could lead to employee lawsuits against employers.[71]

Inaccurate Predictions

Data collected by wearable workplace technologies are not always accurate. For example, employees can "game" wearable workplace technology design flaws to skew the results of the data.[72] The use of wearable workplace technology is also a form of surveillance, which could make some individuals nervous, thus skewing the accuracy of the data collected.[73]

CUSTOMER RELATIONSHIP MANAGEMENT

Customer relationship management (CRM) is an approach to managing current and potential customer interaction and experience with a company using technology.[74] CRM practices typically involve the use of customer data to develop customer insight to build customer relationships.[75] Customer data is collected from a wide range of resources: a company's website, telephone, email, live chat, advertising, social media, industry partners, and other third parties.[76] The primary purpose of CRM is to improve

[69] Jeremy P. Brummond and Patrick J. Thorton, "The Legal Side of Jobsite Technology," *Construction Today* (June 22, 2016), http://www.construction-today.com/sections/columns/2752-the-legal-side-of-jobsite-technology.

[70] Garry Mathiason et al., "The Transformation of the Workplace through Robotics, Artificial Intelligence, and Automation: Employment and Labor Law Issues, Solutions, and the Legislative and Regulatory Response" (Littler, 2016), https://www.littler.com/publication-press/publication/transformation-workplace-through-robotics-artificial-intelligence-and.

[71] Ajunwa, "Algorithms at Work: Productivity Monitoring Platforms and Wearable Technology as the New Data-Centric Research Agenda for Employment and Labor Law."

[72] Ifeoma Ajunwa; Kate Crawford, "When the Fitbit Is an Expert Witness," *The Atlantic* (November 19, 2014), https://www.theatlantic.com/technology/archive/2014/11/when-fitbit-is-the-expert-witness/382936/.

[73] Oliva Solon, "Wearable Technology Creeps into the Workplace," *Sydney Morning Herald* (August 7, 2015), https://www.smh.com.au/business/workplace/wearable-technology-creeps-into-the-workplace-20,150,807-gitzuh.html.

[74] Pennie Frow et al., "Customer Management and CRM: Addressing the Dark Side," *Journal of Services Marketing* 25, no. 2 (2011): 79–89.

[75] William Boulding et al., "A Customer Relationship Management Roadmap: What Is Known, Potential Pitfalls, and Where to Go," *Journal of Marketing* 69, no. 4 (2005): 155–166.

[76] Musfiq Mannan Choudhury and Paul Harrigan, "CRM to Social CRM: The Integration of New Technologies into Customer Relationship Management," *Journal of Strategic Marketing* 22, no. 2 (2014): 149–176; Satish Jayachandran et al., "The Role of Relational Information Processes and Technology Use in Customer Relationship Management," *Journal of Marketing* 69, no. 4 (2005): 177–192.

a company's relationships with customers—increasing customer value—to attract potential customers, retain current customers, and increase sales growth—increasing company value.[77]

The definition of CRM implementation and use remains debated in academic literature.[78] Pennie Frow and Adrian Payne conceptualize CRM implementation and use as five integrated processes: (1) strategy development, (2) value creation, (3) multichannel integration and consumer experience, (4) information management, and (5) performance assessment. The strategy development process involves assessing a firm's business strategy to develop a customer strategy that creates a base for implementing CRM. The value-creation process involves utilizing a firm's business and associated customer strategy to determine what value the firm can offer customers, what value customers can offer the firm, and how to integrate the exchange of both customer and company value. The multichannel integration and customer experience process involves deciding what channels (e.g., ways in which a firm interacts with customers) to use and integrate to improve customer experience. The information management process involves the collection, analysis, and use of customer data to develop customer insight to inform marketing practices. Finally, the performance assessment process involves evaluating the implementation and use of CRM to ensure it is achieving the intended results outlined by a firm's business strategy.[79]

Michael Fayerman provides an alternative conceptualization, describing the implementation and use of CRM as consisting of three components—operational, analytical, and collaborative. Operational CRM involves the integration and automation of sales, marketing, and customer support. The analytical component of CRM involves the collection, analysis, and utilization of customer data to develop customer insight to inform marketing strategy and practice. Finally, collaborative CRM involves creating partnerships with third parties to share customer data across organizations, which firms can then use to enhance customer experience through customization.[80]

Current State of Use

Customer relationship management is widely used by organizations, a trend that is only increasing. According to a survey conducted by Forrester in 2018, approximately 50 percent of small and medium-size organizations, defined as organizations with twenty to ninety employees, surveyed use CRM software, and 19 percent planned to implement CRM in

---

[77] Jayachandran et al., "The Role of Relational Information Processes and Technology Use in Customer Relationship Management"; William Boulding et al., "A Customer Relationship Management Roadmap: What Is Known, Potential Pitfalls, and Where to Go."

[78] Id.

[79] Adrian Payne and Pennie Frow, "A Strategic Framework for Customer Relationship Management," *Journal of Marketing* 69, no. 4 (2005): 167–176.

[80] Michael Fayerman, "Customer Relationship Management," *New Directions for Institutional Research* 113, no.1 (2002): 57–68.

2019.[81] Further, an estimated 65 percent of large organizations, defined as organizations with one thousand or more employees, surveyed use CRM software, and 18 percent planned to implement CRM in 2019.[82] Additionally, organizations are increasingly implementing the use of social media into their CRM strategy. For example, a survey conducted by the Aberdeen Group in 2012 revealed that 86 percent of organizations use social media to advertise to consumers.[83] Additionally, A survey conducted by MIT Sloan Management Review revealed that in 2013, approximately 65 percent of organizations used social media to develop insight into market shifts.[84]

Criticisms and Pitfalls

Differential Treatment of Customers

CRM claims sales and profits will increase by focusing on enhancing company-customer relationships; however, the practice of CRM leads to differential treatment of customers, focusing on enhancing certain company-customer relationships at the expense of others.[85] The idea being that favoritism of the most profitable customers will lead to increased profits.[86] However, in practice favoring certain customers at the expense of others leads to inequality and may not increase profits.

Favoritism results in an unequal distribution of outcomes—the favored group of customers receive explicit targeting and promotions, while the group of customers that are not favored do not receive explicit targeting and promotions. The unequal distribution of outcomes caused by favoritism may lead to perceptions of unfairness, which may cause favored customers to feel guilty or uneasy about their advantaged position, while customers who are not favored may feel angered or outraged about their disadvantaged position.[87] Essentially, the use of CRM to favor certain groups of customers at the expense of others leads to perceptions of unfairness, which can damage a company's reputation, leading some customers to disengage with the company and spread negative

---

[81] Kate Leggett, "The Five CRM Trends In 2019 That Will Shape Engagement, Relationships, And Revenue" (Forrester, 2019), https://www.forrester.com/report/The+Five+CRM+Trends+In+2019+That+Will+Shape+Engagement+Relationships+And+Revenue/-/E-RES148555.

[82] Id.

[83] Sumair Dutta, "Social Media and Customer Service: From Listening to Engagement" (Aberdeen Group, 2012), http://www.oracle.com/us/products/applications/aberdeen-social-customer-svc-1902160.pdf.

[84] David Kiron et al., "Social Business: Shifting Out of First Gear," MIT Sloan Management Review 55, no. 1 (2013): 1–32.

[85] Boulding et al., "A Customer Relationship Management Roadmap: What Is Known, Potential Pitfalls, and Where to Go."

[86] Bang Nguyen, Sooyeon Nikki Lee-Wingate, and Lyndon Simkin, "The Customer Relationship Management Paradox: Five Steps to Create a Fairer Organization," Social Business 4, no. 3 (2014): 207–230; Bang Nguyen and Lyndon Simkin, "The Dark Side of CRM: Advantaged and Disadvantaged Customers," Journal of Consumer Marketing 30, no. 1 (2013): 17–30.

[87] Monroe Xia and J. Cox, "The Price Is Unfair! A Conceptual Framework of Price Fairness Perceptions," Journal of Marketing 68, no. 1 (2004): 1–15.

information about the company.[88] In effect, such targeted promotions could also be seen as a form of digital redlining that disadvantages lower income customers, a population that has large overlaps with racial minorities.[89]

Exploiting Customer Relationships

A premise of CRM is "dual creation of value" for the company and the customer through information reciprocity.[90] The idea being that customers give companies their information which companies reciprocate by providing an enhanced shopping and buying experience.[91] Essentially companies attain customer information so that they can customize and enhance the customer's shopping and buying experience, which increases the likelihood the customer will continue to purchase from the company—creating both value for the customer (i.e., enhancing their shopping and buying experience) and the company (i.e., customer retention and increased profits). However, in practice, customer information is not reciprocated and leads to information asymmetry between the customer and the company because the customer is not always aware of when and how their data is being collected and used by the company.[92] The information asymmetry between the customer and the company may cause the customer to distrust the company with their information.[93] The Facebook–Cambridge Analytica data scandal presents an illustrative case.[94] In 2018, it was revealed that Facebook permitted the data analytics firm Cambridge Analytica to collect information on millions of Facebook users in order to target political campaign ads to those users.[95]

Information Misuse and Privacy Concerns

An essential component of CRM entails the collection and storage of consumer data. Consumers are typically unaware of when and how their data is collected and used by

[88] Nguyen and Simkin, "The Dark Side of CRM: Advantaged and Disadvantaged Customers"; Jennifer Lyn Cox, "Can Differential Prices Be Fair?," *Journal of Product & Brand Management* 10, no. 5 (2001): 264–275; F.M. Feinberg, A. Krishna, and Z.J. Zhang, "Do We Care What Others Get? A Behaviourist Approach to Targeted Promotions," *Journal of Marketing Research* 39, no. 3 (2002): 277–291.

[89] Margaret Hu, "Algorithmic Jim Crow," *Fordham Law Review* 86, no. 2 (2017): 633–696; Cathy O'Neil, "No Safe Zone: Getting Insurance," in *Weapons of Math Destruction: How Big Data Increases Inequality and Threatens Democracy* (New York, NY: Crow, 2016), 161–178.

[90] Satish Jayachandran et al., "The Role of Relational Information Processes and Technology Use in Customer Relationship Management"; William Boulding et al., "A Customer Relationship Management Roadmap: What Is Known, Potential Pitfalls, and Where to Go."

[91] Jayachandran et al., "The Role of Relational Information Processes and Technology Use in Customer Relationship Management."

[92] Pennie Frow et al., "Customer Management and CRM: Addressing the Dark Side."

[93] William Boulding et al., "A Customer Relationship Management Roadmap: What Is Known, Potential Pitfalls, and Where to Go."

[94] Carole Cadwalladr and Emma Grahm-Harrison, "Revealed: 50 Million Facebook Profiles Harvested for Cambridge Analytica in Major Data Breach," *The Guardian* (March 17, 2018), https://www.theguardian.com/news/2018/mar/17/cambridge-analytica-facebook-influence-us-election.

[95] *Id.*

companies, which creates numerous privacy concerns. Furthermore, companies will sell customer data to other firms without the customers' knowledge or permission, exacerbating privacy concerns.[96]

Dishonesty

CRM practices may sometimes entail misleading and confusing customers by hiding relevant information, which may cause customers to make buying decisions at their disadvantage. For example, companies can use CRM to generate complex pricing schemas that make it difficult for customers to compare pricing from other service providers. Additionally, companies can use CRM to generate continuous price and rate changes so that customers do not have time to compare pricing alternatives from other service providers accurately. Further, CRM performance measurement systems and employee reward structures can encourage dishonest company behavior, such as overcharging and upselling customers.[97]

Discrimination

Collecting and analyzing consumer data to generate consumer insight to inform marketing practices, such as targeted advertising, constitutes an essential component of CRM.[98] Companies collect and analyze consumer data to predict who their most profitable customers are and then target advertisements and promotions to those customers and other customers who share similar characteristics.[99] This practice of targeted advertising using predictive analytics leads to certain groups of customers to receive targeted advertising and promotions, while excluding other groups of customers, known as "digital redlining."[100] Digital redlining can lead to discrimination when companies exclude certain groups of customers based on protected characteristics, such as ethnicity,[101]

[96] Pennie Frow et al., "Customer Management and CRM: Addressing the Dark Side"; Joseph Turow, Lauren Feldman, and Kimberly Meltzer, "Open to Exploitation: America's Shoppers Online and Offline" (Philadelphia: Anneberg Public Policy Center of the University of Pennsylvania, 2005); Detlev Zwick and Nikhilesh Dholakia, "Whose Identity Is It Anyway? Consumer Representation in the Age of Database Marketing," *Journal of Macromarketing* 24, no. 1 (June 2004): 31–43; Lilian Edwards and Michael Veale, "Slave to the Algorithm? Why a 'Right to an Explanation' Is Probably Not the Remedy You Are Looking For," *Duke Law & Technology Review* 16, no. 1 (2017): 18–84; Ifeoma Ajunwa, "Workplace Wellness Programs Could be Putting Your Health Data at Risk," *Harvard Business Review* (January 19, 2017), https://hbr.org/2017/01/workplace-wellness-programs-could-be-putting-your-health-data-at-risk.

[97] Pennie Frow et al., "Customer Management and CRM: Addressing the Dark Side."

[98] *Id.*; Anthony Danna and Oscar H. Gandy, "All That Glitters Is Not Gold: Digging Beneath the Surface of Data Mining," *Journal of Business Ethics* 40, no. 1 (2002): 373–386.

[99] *Id.*

[100] Margaret Hu, "Algorithmic Jim Crow"; Cathy O'Neil, "No Safe Zone: Getting Insurance"; Marcia Stepanek, "Weblining: Companies Are Using Your Personal Data to Limit Your Choices—and Force You to Pay More for Products," *Bloomberg Business Week* (April 3, 2000), https://www.bloomberg.com/news/articles/2000-04-02/weblining.

[101] Elliot Zaret and Brock N. Meeks, "Kozmo's Digital Dividing Lines," *MSNBC* (April 11, 2000), https://web.archive.org/web/20001217050000/http://www.msnbc.com/news/373212.asp?cp1=1; Latanya

religion,[102] pregnancy status,[103] and gender[104] or proxies for protected characteristics.[105] For example, a ProPublica investigation revealed that companies were excluding customers by ethnic group from viewing targeted advertisements on Facebook using "ethnic affinity groups," a feature on Facebook that used online customer behavior to determine customer ethnicity—a proxy for the protected characteristic of ethnicity.[106]

FUTURE DIRECTIONS FOR RESEARCH

There has been recent empirical research investigating bias on online hiring platforms and also on CRM.

Customer Relationship Management

Hannak et al. investigated the effect of race and gender on online freelance marketplaces.[107] Specifically, Hannak and colleagues examined if perceived gender and race influence worker evaluations by customers, if the language of worker evaluations by customers differed for workers of different perceived genders and races, and if workers' perceived gender and race significantly associate with their search result rankings in online freelance marketplaces.[108] Overall, the findings demonstrate support for the effect of race and gender or bias in online freelance marketplaces. Hannak and colleagues hypothesized that biased customer evaluations of workers might indirectly cause the biased ranking of workers. In other words, since customer evaluations of workers revealed bias as a function of perceived race and gender, and worker rankings also revealed bias as a function of perceived race and gender, biased customer evaluations of workers might also cause biased rankings of workers.

Sweeney, "Discrimination in Online Ad Delivery," *Communications of the ACM* (May 2013); Julia Angwin and Terry Parris Jr., "Facebook Lets Advertisers Exclude Users by Race," *ProPublica* (October 28, 2016), https://www.propublica.org/article/facebook-lets-advertisers-exclude-users-by-race.

[102] Samuel Gibbs, "Google Alters Search Autocomplete to Remove 'Are Jews Evil' Suggestion," *The Guardian* (December 5, 2016), https://www.theguardian.com/technology/2016/dec/05/google-alters-search-autocomplete-remove-are-jews-evil-suggestion.

[103] Kashmir Hill, "How Target Figured Out a Teen Girl Was Pregnant Before Her Father Did," *Forbes* (February 16, 2012), https://www.forbes.com/sites/kashmirhill/2012/02/16/how-target-figured-out-a-teen-girl-was-pregnant-before-her-father-did/.

[104] Amit Datta, Michael Carl Tschantz, and Anupam Datta, "Automated Experiments on Ad Privacy Settings: A Tale of Opacity, Choice and Discrimination," *Proceedings of the 15th Privacy Enhancing Technologies Symposium* (2015): 92–112.

[105] Angwin and Parris Jr., "Facebook Lets Advertisers Exclude Users by Race."   [106] *Id.*

[107] A. Hannák, C. Wagner, D. Garcia, A. Mislove, M. Strohmaier, and C. Wilson, "Bias in Online Freelance Marketplaces: Evidence from Taskrabbit and Fiverr," *Proceedings of the 2017 ACM Conference on Computer Supported Cooperative Work and Social Computing* (2017): 1914–1933.

[108] *Id.*

Hannak and colleagues argue that online freelance marketplace designers should actively seek to mitigate the biases present in online freelance marketplaces. Hannak and colleagues present several examples, including, limiting the number of customer evaluations of workers that can be viewed, limiting customers' ability to pick workers by having the process automated, and adjusting individual workers' ratings when they are a product of systematic biased evaluation by customers.

Furthermore, Hannak and colleagues call for future research to investigate the impact of working conditions on the propensity for women and people of color to leave the freelance workforce. The researchers also call for future research to investigate the causal mechanisms behind the effect of biased customer evaluations of workers on hiring decisions.[109]

Automated Hiring and Recruitment

Chen and co-authors conducted an audit study of three resume search engines. Notably, they conducted experimental studies to investigate if the resume search engines directly used inferred gender to rank job seekers' posted resumes.[110] The findings support the existence of indirect gender discrimination at both the individual and group level for resume search engine rankings—presenting several key implications. Chen and colleagues argue for the adoption of ranking algorithms that account for indirect discrimination by making ranking algorithms "group fair by design." In other words, hiring websites that use ranking algorithms should ensure their ranking algorithms rank both male and female job candidates at a rate proportional to the distribution of the population. Furthermore, Chen and colleagues call for future research to investigate other hiring websites and how actual hirers or recruiters use resume search engines.[111]

BIBLIOGRAPHY

Ajunwa, Ifeoma. "The Paradox of Intervention as Anti-Bias Intervention," *Cardozo Law Review*, no. 41 (forthcoming, 2020).

Ajunwa, Ifeoma. "Age Discrimination by Platforms." *Berkeley Journal of Employment & Labor Law* 40, no. 63 (forthcoming, 2019).

Ajunwa, Ifeoma. "Algorithms at Work: Productivity Monitoring Platforms and Wearable Technology as the New Data-Centric Research Agenda for Employment and Labor Law." *St. Louis Law Journal* 63, no. 1 (forthcoming, 2019).

Ajunwa, Ifeoma, and Daniel Greene. "Platforms at Work: Automated Hiring Platforms and Other New Intermediaries in the Organization of Work." *Research in the Sociology of Work* 33, no. 1 (forthcoming, 2019): 1–53.

[109] *Id.*

[110] L. Chen, A. Hannak, R. Ma, and C. Wilson, "Investigating the Impact of Gender on Rank in Resume Search Engines," *Proceedings of the 2018 CHI Conference on Human Factors in Computing Systems* (2018).

[111] *Id.*

Boulding, William, Richard Staelin, Michael Ehret, and Wesley J. Johnston. "A Customer Relationship Management Roadmap: What Is Known, Potential Pitfalls, and Where to Go." *Journal of Marketing* 69, no. 4 (2005): 155–166.

Greenbaum, Joan M. *Windows on the Workplace: Technology, Jobs, and the Organization of Office Work.* 2d ed. New York: Monthly Review Press, 2004.

Nissenbaum, Helen and Heather Patterson. "Biosensing in Context: Health Privacy in a Connected World." In *Quantified Biosensing Technologies in Everyday Life*, edited by Dawn Nafus, 79–100. Cambridge, MA: MIT Press, 2016.

Pasquale, Frank. *The Black Box Society: The Secret Algorithms That Control Money and Information.* Cambridge, MA: Harvard University Press, 2015.

Srnicek, Nick. *Platform Capitalism.* Cambridge, UK: Polity Press, 2017.

Zuboff, Shoshana. *In the Age of the Smart Machine: The Future of Work and Power.* New York: Basic Books, 1988.

CHAPTER 44

SMART CITY ETHICS

How "Smart" Challenges Democratic Governance

ELLEN P. GOODMAN

INTRODUCTION

ARTIFICIAL intelligence is coming *to* the city. AI is coming *for* the city. Whether it is "to" or "for" depends on how cities deploy big data analytics in their sometimes halting, sometimes hurtling embrace of the Internet of Things and "smart city" agendas. Will they do it in ways that give control over city functions and citizen information to private companies and impenetrable algorithms, or will there be public control and accountability? Will the winner-take-all market logic of big tech turn the city into another platform for the exploitation of personal data and micro-targeted services, or will cities adopt policies that distribute power, protect public authority, and make space for alternative visions?

The term "smart cities" describes the growing role of data analytics and sensors in urban life.[1] The projects may be relatively modest and directed to a particular urban feature, like efficiently timed traffic lights. Or they may involve the wholesale construction of a new city oriented from the start around the collection and flow of data.[2] These are technologies that the city itself deploys, from the mundane storm-water sensor to the controversial facial recognition. Or they may be owned and managed by a private company,

---

[1] Anthony Townsend, *Smart Cities: Big Data, Civic Hackers, and the Quest for a New Utopia* (New York: W.W. Norton, 2013); Rob Kitchin, "The Real-Time City? Big Data and Smart Urbanism," *GeoJournal* 1(79) (2014).

[2] Caspar Herzberg, *Smart Cities, Digital Nations* (Petaluma, CA: Roundtree Press, 2018) (Cisco's efforts to create smart cities in Asia); Orit Halpern et al., "Test-bed Urbanism," *Public Culture*, 25(2) (2013): 272–306, 300 ("Never before in history have cities been subjected in such scale to the technocratic visions and trials of a few anonymized global companies.").

like on-demand mobility. In many cases, ostensibly public applications will actually be public-private hybrids where cities work with private vendors to design and implement management systems for smart mobility, smart sanitation, or other urban functions. The common feature of what Rob Kitchin calls "data-driven urbanism" is reliance on a "deluge of real-time, fine-grained, contextual and actionable data . . . [to] enable city systems to be managed in real time."[3]

Some integrations of information technologies into urban governance happen in contexts not typically associated with the "smart city" moniker because they do not involve instrumentation of physical space with sensors. Cities may use data analytics, frequently outsourced to private tech companies, to allocate resources such as school assignments, social welfare services and policing, thereby creating systems of algorithmic governance.[4] Just like more place-based data analytics, these applications intermediate between citizens and services, using data collection and analytics to deliver promised efficiencies and performance.

In their relation to smart technologies, cities sit abreast two different interests. One is to protect the public against private exploitation of data in the city. Another is to regulate and serve, using the data capabilities developed and operated in large part by private entities. Most of the critical energy around smart cities has focused on the first interest. There is a growing literature making the case for public intervention to limit private data accumulation and "surveillance capitalism."[5] One possible intervention is city control of or access to privately collected data. Public empowerment in this way, through data, may produce cities with augmented surveillance abilities that can use real-time monitoring for state regulatory control. For example, Los Angeles wanted to protect against excessive private exploitation of public rights of way with ride-sharing scooters and other mobile applications. To safeguard its public authority, it required all ride-sharing vehicles to share their trip origins and destinations with the city through an application programming interface (API).[6] While cabining private power, this intervention enhanced the city's surveillance powers. Concerns about power exercised through technology—whether this power is sufficiently transparent, constrained, and subject to democratic control—arise with respect to both public and private exercises. This chapter will focus on concerns related to private power, bracketing the other set of concerns related to state power.

As a chapter on smart city ethics, there are the preliminaries of scope and definition to consider. In theory, the ethics of a smart city would entail the whole range of ethical obligations of urban governance, including employment, housing, sustainability, and so

---

[3] Rob Kitchin, "The Ethics of Smart Cities and Urban Science," *Philosophical Transactions of the Royal Society A: Mathematical, Physical and Engineering Sciences* 374, no. 2083 (2016).

[4] Cathy O'Neil, *Weapons of Math Destruction: How Big Data Increases Inequality and Threatens Democracy* (New York: Crown, 2016).

[5] Shoshanna Zuboff, *The Age of Surveillance Capitalism: The Fight for a Human Future at the New Frontier of Power* (New York: Public Affairs, 2019).

[6] City of Los Angeles, Dockless On-Demand Personal Mobility Conditional Permit Rules and Guidelines—October 1, 2018, https://ladot.lacity.org/sites/g/files/wph266/f/LADOTDocklessCP.pdf.

on. One could simply attach to the use of data analytics in urban governance the normative goals of equity, inclusivity, economic opportunity, and sustainability. To be meaningful, discussion of smart city ethics as a special set of considerations requires a narrower focus on the distinctive technological affordances of data flows. Then there is the general question of what makes a set of normative goals "ethics" as opposed to "policies." The difference may be a matter of time—ethics are policy prescriptions in nascent form—or a matter of compulsion—ethics are aspirational policy prescriptions that for prudential or political reasons are best left to self-regulation rather than enforced through law. This chapter identifies normative concerns addressable through a variety of modalities and at various levels of government.

What follows is, first, a brief review of the smart city "problem" for democratic governance as it has emerged from an interdisciplinary literature of geography, law, urban studies, and other fields. The next part surveys the early ethical frameworks that seek to shape smart city deployments. The final part distills from the smart city discourse and practice a set of three normative concerns: privatization, platformization, and domination.

The Smart City Problem

Smart city projects are both branding efforts to attract capital and management strategies to improve urban operation. On the branding front, cities like Kansas City in the United States fight in the winner-take-all economy to advertise themselves as "the first true Smart City in the world."[7] London's smart city plan is a "roadmap to transform London into the smartest city in the world."[8] India's Smart Cities Mission to develop one hundred smart cities aims to produce "global" cities attractive to global capital.[9] On the management front, smart city proponents in city halls seek greater efficiency through technology, most often through data collection and analytics.[10] As Anthony Townsend puts it, "a smart city pursues the goals of effective services and efficient city systems through real-time monitoring and control."[11] Adam Greenfield identifies the smart city

[7] Kansas City, Request for Proposals, "Comprehensive Smart City Partnership with Kansas City Missouri," RFP NO. EV2556 (2018), http://kcmo.gov/wp-content/uploads/2018/06/RFP-ComprehensiveSmartCityPartnershipwithKCMO-Final.pdf (seeking "a firm to provide a fully integrated suite of sensors, networks, and data and analytics platforms").

[8] Greater London Authority, *Smarter London Together* (2018), https://www.london.gov.uk/sites/default/files/smarter_london_together_v1.66_-_published.pdf.

[9] Evgeny Morozov and Francesca Bria, *Rethinking the Smart City: Democratizing Urban Technology* (New York: Rosa Luxemburg Stiftung, 2018).

[10] Anthony Townsend, "Green Gadgets? The Smart-Cities Movement and Urban Environmental Policy," in *Remaking the Urban Social Contract: Health, Energy, and the Environment*, ed. Michael A. Pagano, 62–87 (Champaign: University of Illinois Press, 2016); Margarita Angelidou, "The Role of Smart City Characteristics in the Plans of Fifteen Cities," *Journal of Urban Technology* 24(4) (2017): 3–28.

[11] Robert Goodspeed, "Smart Cities: Moving beyond Urban Cybernetics to Tackle Wicked Problems," *Cambridge Journal of Regions, Economy and Society* 8(1) (2015): 79–92, 83 (critiquing the smart city discourse as an application of urban cybernetics).

as "a place where the instrumentation of the urban fabric, and of all the people moving through the city, is driven by the desire to achieve a more efficient use of space, energy and other resources."[12]

Smart city rhetoric and managerial goals often intersect with some version of sustainability discourse. The idealized smart city is instrumented with environmental sensors and resource management apps to reduce carbon emissions and increase carbon absorption. Cisco, one of the dominant corporations in the smart city market, made an early and splashy entry into the smart city development field around 2010 with its design of Songdo, South Korea. This city "was to be a prototype for sustainable urban life, an example of how a city could reduce its carbon footprint and resource usage in a world with ever-increasing population and climate-related problems."[13] As climate change events threaten cities of all sizes with floods, drought, fire, and sudden temperature swings, city managers struggle to adapt without the necessary budgets to harden or repair infrastructure. One of the selling points of smart city technologies is that they can improve climate mitigation strategies and make cities more "resilient" through data collection. It is thus through the smart city narrative that the "two discourses of financial austerity and sustainable environments intersect."[14]

What generates the purported benefits of smart city interventions is the flow of data.[15] It is thought that more data, generated by the surveillance of things and people, will produce a more effective allocation of resources. Cities can prioritize services such as the replacement of water pipes according to need.[16] They can provide for dynamic parking at the curb and congestion pricing on the roads. By combining topographical data with motor vehicle data, cities can better predict who needs help in a hurricane and crowdsource real-time information in emergencies. Where smart city implementations like the smart grid, school truancy data, or trash disposal touch most directly on resident decisions, there is an expectation that data can "nudge" users toward better choices.[17] Notwithstanding the extensive criticism and public objections lobbed at predictive policing and sentencing, the hope is that in criminal justice too, data-driven decision-making will yield a more efficient and just deployment of government power. In all these applications, the data-generated actions may be unfair or of suspect motivation.

---

[12] Adam Greenfield, *Radical Technologies: The Design of Everyday Life* (New York: Verso, 2018) ("If the ambition beneath the instrumentation of the body is nominal self-mastery, and that of the home convenience, the ambition at the heart of the smart city is nothing other than control.").

[13] Herzberg, *Smart Cities.*

[14] Chris Muellerleile and Susan L. Robertson, "Digital Weberianism: Bureaucracy, Information, and the Techno-rationality of Neoliberal Capitalism," *Indiana Journal of Global Legal Studies* 25, no. 1 (2018): 187–216.

[15] Rob Kitchin, "The Real-Time City?"

[16] Brandon A. Brooks and Alexis Schrubbe, "The Need for a Digitally Inclusive Smart City Governance Framework," *UMKC Law Review* 85 (2017): 943, 945–946 (discussing use of water sensors in Flint, Michigan, to detect when pipes carrying lead-polluted water need replacing).

[17] Karen Yeung, "'Hypernudge': Big Data as a Mode of Regulation by Design," *Information, Communication & Society* 20(1) (2017): 118–136.

There is no doubt of the motives in authoritarian-leaning regimes. Data flows are explicitly part of a system of population control. Smart city systems are able to ingest, analyze, and even act autonomously on integrated data from the digital and physical realm, facilitating control of the movement and activities of city residents.[18]

Just how the flow of data comes to deliver on smart city promises (and lead to smart city problems) is often mapped out in layers that resemble the Internet's design. At bottom is the infrastructure or hardware. For IBM, these are the "sensors, actuators, programmable logic controllers, and distributed intelligent sensors."[19] The middle layer is where data flows interconnect and integrate so that the data is rendered visible to city managers through some kind of control center or API. This has also been called the "digital layer."[20] The top layer is intelligence where the data flows are subject to computational power and analytics that produce performance dashboards, predictions, or even automated actions.[21]

Critiques of smart city projects have focused principally on the loss of personal liberty through surveillance[22] and the loss of public control, as a small number of technology companies come to manage, own, or obtain preferential access to essential digital infrastructure throughout a city.[23] These are connected to larger critiques of information platforms and the neoliberal privileging of the urban private.[24] Technological architectures that aggregate power in platforms and extract value from personal data, when instantiated in public space and physical infrastructure, intensify the dangers of data extraction that Shoshanna Zuboff calls "surveillance capitalism."[25] These have to do with loss of individual freedom entailed by constant evaluation and prediction. When private tech is embedded in the public realm, there is another danger that the transfer of the common wealth to private corporations will accelerate.[26] The section below entitled "Challenges to Democratic Governance," will further explore these concerns in connection with particular smart city projects and ethical frames.

[18] Kent E. Calder, *Singapore: Smart City, Smart State* (Washington, D.C.: Brookings, 2016).
[19] Michael Kehoe et al., "A Foundation for Understanding IBM Smarter Cities," *IBM Redguides for Business Leaders* 11 (2011).
[20] Ellen P. Goodman and Julia Powles, "Google's Urbanism," *Fordham Law Review* (forthcoming 2019).
[21] Shannon Mattern, "Mission Control: A History of the Urban Dashboard," *Places Journal* (2015).
[22] Janine S. Hiller and Jordan M. Blanke, "Smart Cities, Big Data, and the Resilience of Privacy," *Hastings Law Journal* 68 (2017): 309–354, 316; Kelsey Finch and Omer Tene, "Welcome to the Metropticon: Protecting Privacy in a Hyperconnected Town," *Fordham Urban Law Journal* 41 (2014): 1581; Maryiam Saifuddin and Chad Marlow, *How to Stop "Smart Cities" from Becoming "Surveillance Cities"* (Washington, D.C.: Sunlight Foundation 2018).
[23] Adam Greenfield, *Against the Smart City* (2013); Jathan Sadowski and Frank Pasquale, "The Spectrum of Control: A Social Theory of the Smart City," *First Monday* 20, no. 7 (2015): 71.
[24] Richard C. Schragger, "The Political Economy of City Power," *Fordham Urban Law Journal* 44 (2017): 98 ("The belief that cities are limited in their policy choices because real power resides in labor and capital markets is almost canonical.").
[25] Zuboff, *The Age of Surveillance Capitalism*.
[26] Jathan Sadowski and Roy Bendor, "Selling Smartness: Corporate Narratives and the Smart City as a Sociotechnical Imaginary," *Science, Technology, & Human Values* (2018): 1–24.

Added to these specific critiques is a more generalized skepticism of the technological determinism that propels smart city projects. The framing for public governance is often not whether to have certain surveillance technologies, but how to manage the data that smart city projects mine. Open to contestation is generally not *whether* to use the city as a sandbox for product development, but rather *how* to allocate intellectual property rights and manage deployment. This determinism Ben Green says is like looking at the world through "tech goggles."[27] It is not a new phenomenon, but is part of a tradition of urban utopianism that puts city planning beyond politics. Smart city implementations—especially at the infrastructure layer—can make technological determinism a reality by building in capacity iteratively. For example, when a streetlight upgrade to LEDs in a city includes modules for future surveillance technology, the city is already part way toward implementation of technology that the public neither considered nor approved. This scenario recapitulates private sector patterns. When Google shipped Nest thermostats containing inoperative microphones to millions of consumers, it became much more likely that these devices would be used in the future to record in the home. The prospect of future connectivity may be hidden or present as a product feature that becomes a surveillance reality without deliberation or consent. Technological creep of this kind may be efficient while also subversive.

One of the challenges for policymakers is that the ethical issues posed by tech in the city cross so many siloed domains and reach far into the future. The officials responsible for permitting public rights of way for infrastructure layer hardware, for example, are suddenly confronted with data privacy issues prevalent in the digital or intelligence layers. Add to this the possibility that the sort of tech used in the infrastructure layer (e.g., 5G wireless transmitters) comes to specify the configuration of city functions and data-sharing protocols, and the challenges of managing smart city risk are daunting.

In an attempt to mitigate these risks, scholars, policymakers, and citizen stakeholders are developing frameworks to address the smart city norms. The next section surveys a representative sample.

ETHICAL CODES IN THE FIELD

Privacy is the most well-developed area in the interdisciplinary scholarship of law, information science, geography, and urbanism. Rob Kitchin has proposed that data subjects "have full details of what data are being generated, what additional data are being inferred from them, *and* to have shared control and benefit in how all data relating to them are subsequently used."[28] Lilian Edwards has applied EU law to make similar

---

[27] Ben Green, *The Smart Enough City* (Cambridge: MIT Press, 2019).

[28] Rob Kitchin, "The Ethics of Smart Cities and Urban Science" (defining universe of ethical issues to include "privacy, datafication, dataveillance and geosurveillance, and data uses such as social sorting and anticipatory governance.").

proposals.[29] These and other proposals are designed to safeguard individual autonomy, drawing on human rights frameworks and connecting to more general prescriptions for AI ethics.[30] Another stream of scholarship deals with cybersecurity and calls for requirements to secure smart city connected devices against hacking and cyberattack.[31] These privacy and security data governance critiques coalesce in attempts to fashion comprehensive data policies for cities that go beyond whatever national privacy law conventions apply.

Civil society actors are moving to create functioning ethical codes for smart cities with different emphases. The Basque Declaration is a sustainability focused roadmap acclaimed by hundreds of European towns and cities.[32] It commits its adherents, among other things, to

- Select "smart technologies that . . . serve the interest of the citizens and the public good."
- Employ public procurement to enable "decentralised local solutions."
- Address "the digital divide in our local societies and provide the appropriate infrastructure and support needed for all groups to have equal access to information and digital services."
- Support "open data standards and take care that collected public data will not be controlled by private actors."

The Sharing Cities Declaration is a statement of agreement of a group of larger cities, including Athens, Barcelona, New York, Seoul, and Sao Paolo, on principles regarding the platform economy.[33] The statement privileges certain models for ride-sharing, co-housing, jobs provision, and other platform-mediated services in the city. The models favored are collaborative and open, provide for fair working conditions, prevent discrimination, support health and safety, promote environmental sustainability, protect citizens' digital rights and data sovereignty, protect city sovereignty and regulatory compliance, promote development of local economic ecosystems, preserve public spaces, and promote affordable housing. There is a separate statement on digital rights espousing "rights of privacy, security, information self-determination and neutrality,

[29] Lillian Edwards, "Privacy, Security and Data Protection in Smart Cities: A Critical EU Law Perspective," *European Data Protection Law Review* 2(1) (2016): 28–58.

[30] Luciano Floridi et al., "AI4People—An Ethical Framework for a Good AI Society: Opportunities, Risks, Principles, and Recommendations," *Minds and Machines* 28(4) (2018): 689–707.

[31] Scott R. Peppet, "Regulating the Internet of Things: First Steps toward Managing Discrimination, Privacy, Security & Consent," *Texas Law Review* 93(85) (2014); Fritz Allhoff and Adam Henschke, "The Internet of Things: Foundational Ethical Issues," *Internet of Things* 1–2, (2018): 55–66 (identifying informed consent, privacy, trust, information security, and physical safety as principal ethical issues).

[32] "The Basque Declaration: New Pathways for European Cities and Towns to Create Productive, Sustainable and Resilient Cities for a Livable and Inclusive Europe," Eighth European Conference on Sustainable Cities and Towns (2016).

[33] "Common Declaration of Principles and Commitments for Sharing Cities" (2018), http://www.share.barcelona/declaration/ (forty-two larger cities agree on principles regarding platform economy).

giving citizens a choice about what happens to their digital identity, who uses their data online, and for which purposes." There is also a requirement that platforms "enable algorithmic accountability and the portability of users' data, digital identity and reputations" and that cities can access "relevant data from firms operating in their territories" (including transportation, labor, and "all potential public interest information").[34] Another international consortium is the Cities for Digital Rights group, which has produced a very high-level declaration of city support for digital rights, including "open and ethical digital service standards."[35]

Dozens of U.S. cities have signed onto an Internet of Things set of best practices drafted by the city of New York.[36] This code focuses on data management and infrastructure. With respect to privacy and transparency, it prescribes that data be collected, transmitted, processed, and used only for legitimate purposes and that it should be anonymized by default and made accessible to maximize public benefit. There should be transparency about where sensors have been deployed and by whom, with clear expectations about maintaining the security of infrastructure and data flows.

Synthesizing the academic, city, and civil society proposals, Francesca Bria, formerly of the city of Barcelona, has advocated (and to various degrees implemented) an alternative democratically controlled vision of the smart city.[37] The basic thrust of this vision is that cities must take control of their digital futures and exercise "technological sovereignty." Such sovereignty entails promoting alternative data ownership regimes, alternative digital infrastructures, and alternative models of service provision, all with a view towards resisting private enclosure through data. Specifically, this version of smart city ethics would insist on a "data commons" so that private corporations, bound to share data into the commons, lack incentive to over-collect data for proprietary use. The data commons could also be used to foster collaborative alternatives to private ride sharing, housing, and other platforms.

There are many more policy and technological prescriptions the above survey might include; it is a partial picture of a quickly emerging set of reactions to an even faster moving deployment of technologies. The frameworks are kaleidoscopic, reflecting the breadth of smart city implementations. Nevertheless, it is possible to distill from these frameworks three central normative concerns that all relate to the maintenance of democratic governance. These are addressed in the following.

CHALLENGES TO DEMOCRATIC GOVERNANCE

Focusing on private power exercised through data flows, this section identifies three normative concerns running through the ethics-focused smart city literature and

---

[34] Theo Bass, Emma Sutherland, and Tom Symons, *Reclaiming the Smart City: Personal Data, Trust and the New Commons* (Nesta, 2018), https://media.nesta.org.uk/documents/DECODE-2018_report-smart-cities.pdf.

[35] https://citiesfordigitalrights.org/.   [36] https://iot.cityofnewyork.us/.

[37] Morozov and Bria, *Rethinking the Smart City*, 27–54.

stakeholder response to the technologies: the *privatization* of public functions and assets, the data-based *platformization* of services, and the threat of *domination* that concentrated technologies pose to individuals, public entities, and competitive markets.

Privatization

Public partnerships with technology companies may end up privatizing what are fundamentally public planning, regulatory, and enforcement functions, along with ownership of public assets. The smart city movement started in the C-suites of major telecommunications and technology companies like Cisco, IBM, and Microsoft as a set of products marketed to city managers with serious urban problems and considerable resource constraints.[38] Cities subject to financial austerity have been susceptible to promises of greater operating efficiency and private financing, and dependent on vendors for the development and implementation of technological change. The late twentieth-century neoliberal faith in markets and private capital shrunk the public capacity to solve problems.[39] In this environment, it was natural for cities to welcome private-public partnerships to finance smart city deployments while also using these partnerships to signal that the city was innovative and "open for business."

The role of the private venture in these smart city partnerships varies in kind and degree. The Amsterdam Smart City "innovation platform," for example, involves companies as well as educational institutions, and nonprofits, in smart energy and mobility pilots.[40] It is largely experimental and distributes participation among many partners, using mostly open data. In other cases, a vendor operates by itself to fulfill some public service that has been outsourced to the private sector. This is the role Uber plays, for example, in its partnership with the city of Columbus in the United States to fill in public transit gaps. Vendors are often engaged in some kind of data-sharing agreement with the city. In Dallas, for example, Ericsson is aggregating and analyzing traffic data to manage traffic in real time. The early smart city visions proffered by Cisco and IBM put a single company at the center of an integrated smart city nervous system, like IBM's Intelligent Operations Center, where data generated by diverse urban functions run through the company's control.[41] Newer approaches are evolving toward participation by multiple companies, with no single company serving as the city's brain.[42]

These partnerships or vendor relationships tend to vest significant power in private technology companies by virtue of the companies' control over data. It is to these dangers

[38] Evgeny Morozov, *To Save Everything, Click Here: The Folly of Technological Solutionism* (New York: Public Affairs, 2014).

[39] Jason Hackworth, *The Neoliberal City: Governance, Ideology, and Development in American Urbanism* (Ithaca, NY: Cornell University Press, 2007).

[40] Margarita Angelidou, "Four European Smart City Strategies," *International Journal of Social Science Studies* 4 (2016): 18.

[41] Donald McNeill, "IBM and the Visual Formation of Smart Cities," in *Smart Urbanism: Utopian Vision or False Dawn?*, ed. Simon Marvin et al. (London: Routledge, 2016), 34–51.

[42] McKinsey Global Institute, *Smart Cities: Digital Solutions for a More Livable Future* (2018).

that the Basque Declaration's and Barcelona's principle of open data and the Sharing Cities Declaration's principle of data access seem to be addressed. The notion is that if the underlying data is a shared resource, the ability to make use of the data and benefit from it will be widely dispersed. Whatever its merits, an open data policy will not solve the problem of concentrated power. Dominant companies like Alphabet have a huge advantage in data and data analytics. They can leverage insights gained from predictive models that will probably never be opened to scrutiny because of trade secret protection. Access to data may be less important from a competition perspective than access to other resources, including data analytics. Even where access to data is the key to market entry, having the wherewithal to clean and utilize massive amounts of data may itself be a scarce asset concentrated in big tech companies. It will thus require more than open data policies to ensure that private data power does not overwhelm the public interest in distributed benefits.

This sort of private data power can vest companies with quasi-public planning functions over transportation, development, and investment. In Toronto, Google affiliate Sidewalk Labs joined Waterfront Toronto, a public authority responsible for waterfront development in the city, as a "thinking partner" to co-create a Master Innovation and Development Plan.[43] In doing so, the public entity delegated much of the initial public engagement, data gathering, and priority setting to the company. The private entity in this case is not merely a consultant, but a partner that has planning responsibilities along with downstream opportunities for land development and technology contracts. One advocacy group described this arrangement as "governance through mercenaries." Instead of debating policies in public and making government responsible for them, the "mercenary just gets the job done, and gets paid. There is no vote, no debate, no statute, no regulation, no accountability."[44]

Vendors that deploy smart city applications can also become responsible at a later stage for regulatory functions.[45] Consider an algorithm that directs the police to target particular neighborhoods or residents for interventions. The vendors who control the algorithms are exercising a form of regulatory power through the policy choices—such as how to assess crime risks and which to prioritize—their programs implement.[46] Another example of delegated regulatory control is in the building context. A common smart city aspiration is to maximize flexible use of streets, structures, and other physical assets to increase efficiency. An outcome-based zoning code is a tool to achieve flexibility by setting usage limits (e.g., on occupancy levels) for a building, but otherwise permitting mixed use. This sort of code can make general-purpose buildings adaptable for

---

[43] Goodman and Powles, "Google's Urbanism."

[44] Canadian Civil Liberties Association, "Governing by Mercenary," (January 29, 2019), https://ccla. org/governing-by-mercenary/ (criticizing Sidewalk Labs control over Waterfront Toronto planning).

[45] Mireille Hildebrandt, "Algorithmic Regulation and the Rule of Law," *Philosophical Transactions of the Royal Society, A* 376: 20170355 (2018).

[46] Rebecca Wexler, "Life, Liberty, and Trade Secrets: Intellectual Property in the Criminal Justice System," *Stanford Law Review* 70 (2018): 1343–1429; Robert Brauneis and Ellen P. Goodman, "Algorithmic Transparency for the Smart City," *Yale Journal of Law & Technology* 20 (2018): 103–175.

residential or business use, or both at once. To the extent that a private vendor designs the code, collects the data, controls the analytics required to assess compliance, it has taken charge of the basic regulatory function of zoning.

Using the same example, it is not hard to imagine private enforcement as well. When use of a building exceeds the allowable limits of an outcome-based code, enforcement can take the form of fines or denial of access. Code violations, where enforcement is deputized to a private entity, can overlap with private contract violations, where private rights of action are adjudicated by algorithm. Suppose, for example, there is a landlord-tenant dispute about property use. Landlords can exploit real-time "smart" rental housing adjudication by locking tenants out upon a perceived breach of contract.[47] Unless there is due and public process, the vendor of the code or the smart contract is effectively the law enforcer. This has been the case with one of the first smart city applications: red-light cameras. One policy strategy to confront this challenge is simply to ban the technology, as the states of New Jersey and Ohio have done, concluding that they must not delegate the public police power to vendors whose interest is in collecting fees for red-light traffic violations. Another strategy is to cabin the functions of the private data company. In the case of the red-light cameras, another jurisdiction allowed the vendor only to make preliminary determinations that are ultimately subjected to official review.[48]

In addition to regulation and enforcement, smart cities can entail a privatization of public assets. Data is the best example. Cities collect data about residents, the environment, and physical objects within their jurisdiction. With access to this data, companies may be able to extract value without making any return to the public on the value taken. New York City tried to address this in its contract with another Google affiliate, Intersection, for the company to provide Wi-Fi kiosks on city streets in return for being allowed to advertise to residents based on their data.[49] The city negotiated to receive a share of the advertising revenue, thereby staking a claim to the monetary value of resident data. The city has deployed this revenue-share model with Microsoft, its partner in developing the Domain Awareness System. This is a network of sensors, databases, hardware, and software that puts "information, real-time analysis, and intelligence directly in the hands of [police] officers."[50] In return for the city's contribution of data to the system, it receives a cut of the revenue when Microsoft sells the system to other cities.

There is a tension between the values of privacy and return on investment. As soon as a city obtains a revenue share for the exploitation of citizen data, it has incentives as a market participant to exploit that data, while at the same time, in its role as regulator, it has incentives to safeguard resident data-privacy interests. The dual role of the city as

[47] Alfred Ng, "Your Landlord Turns Your Apartment into a Smart Home. Now What?," *CNET* (March 7, 2019).

[48] Jimenez v. State of Florida, SC16-1976 (2018).

[49] Ava Kofman, "Are New York's Free LinkNYC Internet Kiosks Tracking Your Movements?," *The Intercept* (September 8, 2018); G.R. Halegoua and J. Lingel, "Lit Up and Left Dark: Failures of Imagination in Urban Broadband Networks," *New Media & Society* 20 (2018): 4634–4652.

[50] New York Police Department, "Developing the NYPD's Information Technology" (2015).

venture partner and citizen protector is at the root of the second set of normative concerns discussed in the following.

Platformization

The "city as platform" is a key concept in smart city discourse and raises concerns about what kinds of social arrangements the platform privileges.[51] Having recognized the value of public data—data that the city already collects or that it may collect in future— cities are inviting service providers to innovate "on top" of the data. "Open data platforms" whereby cities make available public data are becoming relatively common and are recommended in the codes discussed earlier. In this model, networked nodes circulate data stored in the cloud. Governmental and private entities operationalize the data, run through algorithmic processes, to personalize services (e.g., housing or employment), nudge residents toward certain behaviors (e.g., conservation or voting), and construct differential opportunities (e.g., in education or commerce). The city as platform model in effect converts public and private services—treating them the same—to applications at the "edge" of a network, again along the lines of the internet.[52]

A principal concern here is with platform values. Platforms mine the data trails of human activity, ever more minutely observed. Curated data flows then propel users toward particular techno-social arrangements, depending on what the platform wants to optimize.[53] That might be engagement, as with Facebook, or the value of office real estate, as with the once high-flying WeWork co-working platform. What are the social, political, and economic arrangements that the city as platform tries to optimize?

Commercial platform technologies in the city like Uber and Airbnb have provided significant consumer value at the same time that they have produced negative externalities in the forms of congestion, increased housing costs, unregulated consumer risk, and unfair labor practices. Information platforms have proved that market segmentation and personalization can satisfy consumers while also, and through the same means, degrading social solidarity and well-being. Subjecting relationships to market rationality can open up and create new markets for the benefit of buyers and sellers. But it can also displace nonmarket relationships and produce externalized social costs not borne by buyers and sellers. These characteristics of platform markets raise normative questions for smart city extensions of the platform model.

---

[51] Sarah Barns, *Platform Urbanism: Negotiating Platform Ecosystems in Connected Cities*, (Singapore: Palgrave Macmillan, 2020).

[52] David Bollier, *The City as Platform: How Digital Networks Are Changing Urban Life and Governance* (Washington, D.C.: Aspen Institute, 2016); Stephen Goldsmith and Neil Kleiman, *A New City O/S: The Power of Open, Collaborative, and Distributed Governance* (Washington, D.C.: Brookings Institution Press 2017); Tim O'Reilly, "Government as a Platform," *Innovations: Technology, Governance, Globalization* 6, no. 1 (2011): 13–40.

[53] Tarleton Gillespie, "The Politics of 'Platforms,'" *New Media & Society* 12, no. 3 (2010): 347–364.

Efficiency is a principal value of digital platforms. Smart city implementations inflect urban governance with "instrumental rationality," insisting on the most efficient solution to public needs, as measured precisely through quantification and data.[54] The city as platform is also the city as "marketplace," with the products and services traded being quintessentially public goods like utilities, education, participation, or healthcare. In smart city imaginaries such as those designed for Toronto or Sangdo, users can order city amenities like park space and parking places through a portal or app, much as they would a car or food delivery. This may make efficient use of public resources and produce consumer value. But as civic exchanges are personalized, there is a risk to the collective and, indeed, a sense of the collective. The networked architecture of the distributed internet where individuals interact with a platform connecting them to service providers disintermediates civic institutions and political organizations. The networked nodes connect individuals to services through flows of data. It is not obvious where institutions like schools, libraries, political parties, or community organizations fit into this model. Market rationality can interrupt forms of civic life that have not yet or cannot be reduced to measurable data and served via app.[55] Values other than efficiency, like equity or sociability, may be driven out of the exchange. It is in part to address these concerns that the Sharing Cities Declaration tries to privilege cooperative structures that provide some of the benefits of platform exchanges without commodification.

As long as the prevailing platform models rely on mining behavioral data for profit, there will be problems of "privacy" better denoted as blows to liberty. It is for this reason that the ethical codes cited earlier all include data privacy protections. In the context of smart cities, these protections are of limited utility. Existing notice and choice regimes cannot scale to the ubiquitous instrumentation of place. Privacy-by-design solutions that rely on de-identification are vulnerable to the ease of re-identification and to the exploitation of inferences that can be derived even from anonymized data.[56] The data from mobile phones alone provide granular records of a life, even if de-identified.[57] Notice and choice as norms to protect privacy in smart cities will simply not work for data gathering that happens outside zones of choice. It is not feasible to opt out of, or to refuse to opt in to, systems of data collection embedded in the public

---

[54] Shannon Mattern, "Methodolatry and the Art of Measure: The New Wave of Urban Data Science," *Places* (2013); Evgeny Morozov, *To Save Everything, Click Here,* 5 (critiquing "solutionism" in urbanism); Orit Halpern et al., "Test Bed Urbanism," *Public Culture* 25(2) (2013): 274.

[55] Benjamin De La Peña, "Embracing the Autocatalytic City," *CityLab* (2013) (criticizing the model of the city as a machine to be tuned rather than a "stochastic chain of choices add[ing] up to an emergent whole.").

[56] Sandra Wachter and Brent Mittelstadt, "A Right to Reasonable Inferences: Re-Thinking Data Protection Law in the Age of Big Data and AI," *Columbia Business Law Review* (2018); Sandra Wachter, "Data Protection in the Age of Big Data," *Nature Electronics* 2 (6–7) (2019) ("The potential risks to data subjects do not end at the time data is collected and, therefore, data protection laws fail to guard against the potential harms of inferential analytics.").

[57] Jennifer Valentino-DeVries et al., "Your Apps Know Where You Were Last Night, and They're Not Keeping It Secret," *New York Times* (December 10, 2018).

realm, in the workplace, in shared or rental housing, or in utilities. The inadequacy of current data privacy regimes especially for captive residents argues for consideration of data collection and sharing bans. City bans on facial recognition technology may be harbingers of this move. Other possible approaches include enforceable duties of care imposed on all entities that touch data as well as data trusts that subject all public realm data to independent control.

Equity is a final concern raised by platformization. One of the promises of smart city projects is that they can improve governance and governmental responsiveness. E-government initiatives, which give residents more voice in urban governance and more access to government processes, were adopted early and continue to feature in vendor marketing. In surveys, cities have reported that having a more responsive government is one of their foremost smart city goals.[58] Whether a more responsive "city as platform" is also a more equitable city depends in part on the data inputs. From where does the data derive? How was the data corpus constructed? Measurement is political.[59] Not everyone and everything is counted, and some counts are inaccurate. How is the data used to train relevant artificial intelligence? What narratives are drawn from the models and data correlations? Determinations made throughout this process shape how resources and rights are allocated. For example, a park that is rarely used because of safety concerns might show up in the data as a park no one wants. That there exists unserved demand for the park and need for fundamental change to improve safety may not show up in the data.

To the extent that smart city data analytics do not "see" all residents with the same precision or interest, that is a feature of the longstanding "digital divide" problem. Data divides add to and reinforce the traditional "digital divide" problem, which has in the past referred to inequities in the distribution of digital connectivity and hardware. Those older problems, as well, have new salience in the smart city context, as the danger of exclusion and digital disadvantage grows when more and more basic functions are rendered exclusively through a digital platform. The Basque Declaration makes explicit the connection between digital inequality and smart city ethics by mandating attention to digital divide issues.

The potential for increased economic domination that platformization can create is just one form of domination—the subject of the next section.

Domination

The ethical norm of autonomy, and correspondingly nondomination, runs through everything discussed thus far. A city mediated by apps, portals, and authentication protocols makes its residents dependent on technologies they cannot interrogate or

[58]   United States Conference of Mayors, Cities of the 21st Century 6 (2016) (better governance is one of top three objectives for mayors).
[59]   McNeill, "IBM and the Visual Formation of Smart Cities."

meaningfully resist. Public officials reliant on vendors and private partners for basic operations may be similarly dependent. Information asymmetries and network effects can confer extraordinary and durable power on those entities that take control of data most effectively. In all these ways, smart city implementation poses risks of domination at the individual and systemic levels, and calls for strategies to distribute power in the interests of freedom.

Technical insecurity exposes smart city residents to the risk of domination by malfunction. Networked technology is buggy and brittle, susceptible to viruses, hacks, data breaches, and power failures. As smart city systems become more complex and interrelated, the risks of catastrophic failure grow. For example, "cloud-computing outages could turn smart cities into zombies" if power or connectivity outages undermine the biometric authentication used to "determine our rights and privileges as we move through the city—granting physical access to buildings and rooms, personalizing environments, and enabling digital services and content."[60] A smart city installation in South Korea, for example, provides real-time information on the water supply. The sensors and software systems are owned by private companies that supply the data to the city. When a sensor fails, the city has to shut down the system or coordinate among the companies to resolve the problem.[61]

Another form of systemic domination is market control. Because digital markets tend toward concentration, companies like IBM, Google, and Uber that take positions in smart city deployment may well end up dominating the market opportunities. Where city contracts are concerned, competitive procurement policies can mitigate this threat. However, these policies usually have a loophole for special-purpose vendors—an exemption frequently exploited in the technology area where dominant companies have unique data-gathering and analytics capabilities. This was the case in the state of Illinois, for example, where the smart city company Replica (another Google affiliate) benefited from a "sole-source" contract for transport analytics. Replica merges private data from mobile phones and social media with data from the public realm, like license-plate readers and bike-shares to show in real time "the total number of people on a highway or local street network, what mode they're using…, and their trip purpose."[62] Once they gain a preferred position, big data companies can then further entrench themselves in city functions. Data dominance leads recursively to even more data power, especially if the company plays the platform role of mediating between residents and services. As Bria and Morozov have observed: "Many smart city projects are conceived as proprietary urban operating systems; this leads to market domination by just a handful of corporate actors and intensifies pervasive targeting of consumers through sensor technologies and surveillance mechanism."[63]

[60] Anthony Townsend, "Smart Cities: Buggy and Brittle," *Places Journal* (October 2013).

[61] Sawyer Clever et al., "Ethical Analyses of Smart City Applications," *Urban Science* 2, no. 4 (2018): 96.

[62] Ava Kofman, "Google's Sidewalk Labs Plans to Package and Sell Location Data on Millions of Cellphones," *Intercept* (January 28, 2019).

[63] Morozov and Bria, *Rethinking the Smart City*, 39.

In the urban operating system, public officials and front-line workers may be as dependent on the platform as any other user. They may access data through an API (perhaps privately operated) and be fed instructions based on upstream algorithmic processing. In order to understand the algorithmic rules or recommendations they are tasked with implementing, humans need to know a lot about how and why the system produced the outputs it did.[64] Consider, for example, algorithmic prediction deployed in the family services context. A social worker may be presented with two cases flagged for intervention, but one has a higher risk score. That worker cannot exercise professional judgment in prioritizing those cases without knowing how the scores were developed, how much distance there is between them, and other relevant features. Absent this understanding, social workers and police, teachers and inspectors, can all become deskilled and ever more reliant on the directions of a machine they do not understand and fear second-guessing.[65]

More materially, cities can become dependent on systems that lock them into proprietary data and software. A criminal justice data vendor, Palantir, enticed city police departments to use its data analytics product at very low cost or for free. Once the cities were dependent on the company to access the data, Palantir made it difficult for them to go elsewhere or develop the same capabilities in-house.[66] The cities became data vassals to the companies with data power. It is this concern that is addressed by the Basque Declaration's privileging of procurement using "decentralised local solutions," presumably to neutralize the power of large concentrated companies. The Sharing Cities Declaration's emphasis on city "sovereignty" addresses some of the same concerns. As for smart city security, the Internet of Things best practices seek to harden the networked infrastructure. Ultimately, no cybersecurity best practice will rescue citizens and systems from failure. The challenge is to build in redundancy to reduce dependencies, whether that means technical workarounds, alternative business models, or a public workforce that remains in the decisional loop.

CONCLUSION

Smart city deployments raise normative concerns for the health of democratic governance and individual freedom. Especially when they are spearheaded by private companies or with public-private partnerships, there are risks that data collection and data analytics will concentrate power in unaccountable entities. These entities will then be able to

---

[64] Michael Ananny and Kate Crawford, "Seeing without Knowing: Limitations of the Transparency Ideal and Its Application to Algorithmic Accountability," *New Media & Society* 20 (2018): 973–989.

[65] John Danaher, "The Threat of Algocracy: Reality, Resistance and Accommodation," *Philosophy & Technology* 29 (2016): 245 (raising concerns about deference to algorithmic output by human decision makers who cannot understand how the algorithms work).

[66] Mark Harris, "How Peter Thiel's Secretive Data Company Pushed into Policing," *Wired* (August 9, 2017).

shape resident experiences and opportunities without their consent or possibly even their knowledge. The specific form of these threats fall into the categories of privatization, platformization, and domination. Policy responses are required to preserve public authority over algorithmic governance and public assets, to make space for forms of service provision off the platform, and to distribute power over urban governance.

BIBLIOGRAPHY

Edwards, L. "Privacy, Security and Data Protection in Smart Cities: A Critical EU Law Perspective." *European Data Protection Law Review* 2(1) (2016): 28–58.

Halpern, O. et al., "Test Bed Urbanism." *Public Culture* 25(2) (2013): 274.

Kitchin, R., "The Real-Time City? Big Data and Smart Urbanism." *GeoJournal* 79(1) (2014).

Marvin, S., A. Luque-Ayala, and C. McFarlane, eds. *Smart Urbanism: Utopian Vision or False Dawn?* London: Routledge, 2016.

Morozov, E. and F. Bria. *Rethinking the Smart City: Democratizing Urban Technology.* New York: Rosa Luxemburg Stiftung, 2018.

Townsend, A., *Smart Cities: Big Data, Civic Hackers, and the Quest for a New Utopia.* New York: W.W. Norton, 2013.

Yeung, K. "'Hypernudge': Big Data as a Mode of Regulation by Design." *Information, Communication & Society* 20(1) (2017): 118–136.

INDEX

Note: Figures are indicated by an *f* following the page number.

INDEX   871